China-
708
964-7374

TAKE BACK the NIGHT

Social Psychology

Social Psychology

SHARON S. BREHM

State University of New York
at Binghamton

SAUL M. KASSIN

Williams College

HOUGHTON MIFFLIN COMPANY BOSTON TORONTO

Geneva, Illinois Palo Alto Princeton, New Jersey

Sponsoring Editor: Rebecca J. Dudley
Senior Associate Editor: Jane Knetzger
Senior Project Editor: Carol Newman
Production/Design Coordinator: Jennifer Waddell
Senior Manufacturing Coordinator: Priscilla Bailey
Marketing Manager: Pamela Shaffer

Interior design: Janet Theurer
Cover design: Diana Coe
Cover image: Devera Ehrenberg, Boston, MA

Credits

p. 93: Figure 3.3 From L. Ross, T. M. Amabile, and J. L. Steinmetz, "Social roles, social control, and biases in social perception processes," *Journal of Personality and Social Psychology, 35* (1977): 485–494. Copyright © 1977 by the American Psychological Association. Reprinted by permission; ***p. 150:*** *Figure 4.7* Figure adapted from *The Psychology of Rumor* by Gordon W. Allport and Leo J. Postman copyright © 1947 and renewed 1975 by Holt, Rinehart and Winston, Inc., reproduced by permission of the publisher; ***p. 215:*** *Table 6.5* From P. Shaver, C. Hazan and D. Bradshaw, "Love as attachment: The integration of three behavioral systems" in R. J. Sternberg and M. L. Barnes (Eds.), *The Psychology of Love*. Copyright © 1988 by Yale University Press. Reprinted by permission; ***p. 254:*** *Figure 7.3* From C. D. Batson, *The Altruism Question*. Copyright © 1991 by Lawrence Erlbaum Associates, Inc. Reprinted by permission; ***p. 317:*** *Figure 8.9* Adapted with the permission of the Free Press, a Division of Simon & Schuster Inc. from *The Question of Pornography: Research Findings and Policy Implications* by Edward Donnerstein, Daniel Linz, and Steven Penrod. Copyright © 1987 by The Free Press; ***p. 334:*** *Figure 9.2 "A Classic Case of Suggestibility"* from *The Psychology of Social Norms* by Muzafer Sherif. Copyright 1936 by Harper & Brothers, renewed 1964 by Muzafer Sherif. Reprinted by permission of HarperCollins Publishers, Inc.; ***p. 359:*** *Figure 9.6* "Factors that Influence Obedience" from *Obedience to Authority* by Stanley Milgram. Copyright © 1974 by Stanley Milgram. Reprinted by permission of HarperCollins Publishers, Inc.; ***pp. 357–358:***, *Tables 9.3 and 9.4* Excerpts from *Obedience to Authority* by Stanley Milgram. Copyright © 1974 by Stanley Milgram. Reprinted by permission of HarperCollins Publishers, Inc.; ***p. 470:*** *(bottom): Figure 12.3* From G. R. Loftus and E. F. Lostus, *Human Memory: The Processing of Information*. Copyright © 1976 by Lawrence Erlbaum Associates, Inc. Reprinted by permission of the author and publisher; ***p. 519:*** *Figure 13.7* From S. Schachter, R. Ouellette, B. Whittle, and W. Gerin, "Effects of trend and of profit or loss on the tendency to sell stock," *Basic and Applied Psychology, 8* (1987): 259–71. Copyright © 1987 by Lawrence Erlbaum Associates, Inc. Reprinted by permission; ***p. 530:*** *Figure 14.2* From A. Baum and S. Valins, *Architecture and Social Behavior: Psychological Studies of Social Density*. Copyright © 1977 by Lawrence Erlbaum Associates, Inc. Reprinted by permission.

(credits continue on p. C–1.)

Printed in the U.S.A.

Library of Congress Catalog Card Number: 95-76931

ISBN: 0-395-73630-7

1 2 3 4 5 6 7 8 9-DW-99 98 97 96 95

To the indelible memory of
Edward E. Jones
whose work enriched social psychology
and whose presence
inspired us all

Education—whether its object be children or adults, individuals or an entire people, or even oneself—consists in creating motives.

Simone Weil

Brief Contents

Contents

Preface

Revising a textbook is like planning a large public ceremony. There are lots of people involved. It's exciting as well as nerve wracking. And there's so much to do, one hardly knows where to begin. Most important, both endeavors seek to communicate effectively with a large and diverse audience. Amidst the hurly-burly of preparation and the hoopla of presentation, a memorable public ceremony—be it a graduation, a wedding, an inauguration, or an anniversary celebration—stays true to the meaning of the event. So, too, should a textbook be firmly grounded in its essential purpose: to be a good teacher.

Good teachers connect with their students—speaking their language while teaching them a new one; motivating them to think, to reconsider, and to seek out new knowledge. Good teachers are dynamic, interactive, and challenging. Our primary goal for the Third Edition of *Social Psychology* has been to make it an even better teacher than it has been before. We hope that our readers will find that we've succeeded.

CONTRIBUTIONS TO EFFECTIVE LEARNING

In preparing the Third Edition, we carefully examined every aspect of the book in terms of its contribution to effective learning. The results of this process can be seen in the content, organization, and presentation of this new edition, as well as in the new ancillary materials that accompany it.

The Content of the Text

Ultimately, of course, the content of any textbook reflects the field of study that it covers. But content is more than Joe Friday's "the facts, ma'am, just the facts." A good teacher uses specific material to develop students' more general skills. Consider, for example, the eight areas that Thomas McGovern and his colleagues (1991) identified as fundamental aspects of an undergraduate education in psychology:

- Knowledge base
- History of psychology
- Research methods and statistical skills
- Thinking skills
- Language skills
- Information gathering and synthesis skills
- Interpersonal skills
- Ethics and values

Student learning in each of these basic areas is enhanced by the content included in this text.

Comprehensive, Up-to-Date Scholarship The bedrock of all teaching is knowledge. If one's own understanding is inadequate or in error, transmitting that information to others is not helpful and can be harmful. For a textbook to qualify as a standard work that lays the foundation of a student's *knowledge base*, its content must be comprehensive and up-to-date.

Like its predecessors, the Third Edition offers a broad, balanced perspective on social psychology. You will read detailed descriptions of classic studies from *the history of social psychology*, as well as reports of the latest research findings from over 700 new references. Here are a few examples of topics that are new to this edition or receive expanded coverage:

- Improving the accuracy of self-reports (Chapter 1)
- The role of values in science (Chapter 1)
- Autobiographical memory (Chapter 2)
- Multicultural perspectives on the self (Chapter 2)
- Self-fulfilling prophecies (Chapter 3)
- Cross-cultural research on the fundamental attribution error (Chapter 3)
- Implicit and explicit stereotypes (Chapter 4)
- Social identity theory (Chapter 4)
- The sociobiology of mate selection (Chapter 5)
- Mere exposure (Chapter 5)
- Same-sex friendships (Chapter 6)
- Gender differences in sexual attitudes, roles, and perceptions (Chapter 6)
- Group selection as an evolutionary basis for helping (Chapter 7)
- Helping in cities (Chapter 7)
- Gender differences in aggression (Chapter 8)
- Sexual aggression among college students (Chapter 8)
- Cultural influences on conformity (Chapter 9)
- Awareness of norms (Chapter 9)
- Physiological measures of attitudes (Chapter 10)
- Emotional appeals in persuasion (Chapter 10)
- Effects of electronic communication (Chapter 11)
- Cross-cultural communication during negotiations (Chapter 11)
- Interrogations and confessions (Chapter 12)
- Suggestibility effects in children's eyewitness testimony (Chapter 12)
- The use of integrity tests in the workplace (Chapter 13)
- Affirmative action (Chapter 13)
- Physiological reactivity and immune functioning (Chapter 14)
- Prevention programs to reduce high-risk sexual behaviors (Chapter 14)

You will also notice that we discuss a wide array of theoretical perspectives, making every effort to be impartial in our evaluations and attempting to provide students with enough background in *research methods* to permit them to reach some conclusions of their own. The Third Edition continues our well-established commitment to excellence in scholarship.

Emphasizing Connections with Contemporary Events To cover the world of social psychology is one thing. But to cover the real world is quite another. Yet, we try to do both. Why? As it turns out, making the connection between contemporary events and the principles of social psychology is a remarkably effective way to improve students' learning. Both teachers and students have told us how much they value this feature of our book.

References to current events make the text more accessible to students; they see something they recognize immediately. Moreover, trying to understand contemporary issues in social psychological terms motivates students to apply their critical *thinking skills*. They learn social psychology more quickly and more thoroughly. And their interest in a specific issue or event can serve as the basis for course assignments that emphasize oral or written *language skills*, or strengthen *information gathering and synthesis skills* by requiring some form of research.

Because we are convinced that this approach provides unique pedagogical benefits, we have used it more frequently and more systematically in the Third Edition. We invite you to flip open this text to any page and start reading. Very soon, you'll come across a written description, a figure, a table, a photo, or a cartoon that refers to people, places, events, and issues that are prominent in contemporary culture.

Some of what you'll see includes AIDS; the conflicts in Bosnia and Rwanda; the O. J. Simpson trial; *Schindler's List*; the major league baseball strike; the Whitewater scandal; the Oklahoma City bombing; President Clinton; the kidnapping of Polly Klaas; peacemaking efforts in Israel and Northern Ireland; entertainment figures like Johnny Carson and Michael Jackson; the Susan Smith case; former president Jimmy Carter's negotiation efforts in North Korea and Haiti; *The Bridges of Madison County*; the election of Nelson Mandela; the Tailhook scandal and coverup; the 1994 World Cup soccer games; Speaker of the House, Newt Gingrich; the destruction of the Branch Davidian compound at Waco; the 1994 Northridge, California earthquake; sports figures like Magic Johnson, Michael Jordan, and Nancy Kerrigan; and the cast of *Seinfeld*.

Extensive Coverage of Diversity It has been said that, "social science can only be a truly *social* science when it recognizes that individual lives are not only lived in a social context, but are created in it" (Lewontin, 1995, p. 69). To fully grasp the power of social forces, one must compare diverse social contexts.

In this textbook, we seek to understand the social psychological differences associated with gender, race, ethnicity, sexual orientation, nationality, and culture—as well as the similarities that extend across various social groups. Our coverage of diversity is not an add-on; it is fully incorporated in the main body of the text. It is also extensive. For example, at last count, this edition describes research conducted in thirty-five countries. Multicultural perspectives are particularly emphasized in Chapter 2 on the Social Self, Chapter 4 on Perceiving Groups, Chapter 6 on Intimate Relationships, and Chapter 9 on Conformity. The study of the social psychological aspects of human diversity can help students become more informed and more thoughtful about *interpersonal relations* as well as about *ethics and values*.

The Organization of the Content

Of all the challenges faced by teachers and textbooks, perhaps the greatest is to put information together in a way that is both accurate and understandable. A strong organizational framework plays a crucial role in meeting this challenge. There is nothing worse for a student than having to wade through a "laundry list" of endless studies whose connection with each other remains a profound mystery. In contrast, a strong structure keeps the student on track and facilitates the development of conceptual understanding.

But the tail should not wag the dog. Since organizational structure is a means to an end, not an end in itself, we believe that it should be kept simple and relatively unobtrusive. In this edition, as in the previous ones, we start with an internal focus on *Social Perception* (Part I), move outward to *Social Interaction* (Part II) and *Social Influence* (Part III), and conclude with *Applying Social Psychology* (Part IV). Many teachers and students find this a smooth and sensible progression that is easy to follow.

Some teachers, however, prefer to reshuffle the deck to develop a chapter order that better fits their specific needs. There is no problem in doing this. Each chapter stands on its own and does not assume that other chapters have already been read. Equally important, each chapter has its own strong organizational structure designed to fit the relevant theory and research. In essence, each chapter tells a conceptual story. This story comes complete with:

- A narrative preview and chapter outline
- Key terms highlighted in the text, defined in the margin, listed at the end of the chapter, and reprinted in an alphabetized glossary at the end of the book. Both the list and the glossary provide page numbers for easy location of the term.
- A bulleted review summarizing major points at the end of each chapter.

The Presentation of Material

Even when the content is superb and the organization is sound, teachers and textbooks have not crossed the finish line. There is still presentation. A mumbler can destroy the world's best (on paper) lecture. A highly accurate, beautifully organized textbook can lose its readers in an impenetrable thicket of jargon and ten-line-long sentences. Like organizational structure, presentation is a means to an end; it cannot substitute for scholarship and conceptual clarity. At its best, however, presentation can enhance learning.

For the Third Edition, we've made a number of what we believe will be helpful changes in presentation and format. We've worked on our writing, trying to make it less dense and more crisp. We've enhanced the illustration program—adding figure drawings, verbal examples, and post-its highlighting major findings. We've increased the number of photos and cartoons, emphasizing key points in the text. And we've packaged it all in a new trim size, creating a livelier look on the page. These changes are designed to make the Third Edition more inviting, more accessible, and more enjoyable for students.

A Reader and Other Ancillaries

In conversations with teachers and students about our text as well as in the written comments of reviewers, two suggestions were at the top of most people's lists: Give us some original research articles, they said, and strengthen the ancillaries. We did. The reader, *Readings in Social Psychology: The Art and Science of Research,* comes shrink-wrapped free with the book and contains sixteen original articles, each with a brief introduction and questions to stimulate students' critical thinking about issues at the heart of "doing" social psychology. These articles represent some of the most creative and accessible research, both classic and contemporary, of topical interest to students.

The other ancillaries, available separately, have been completely revised and considerably expanded. They are now absolutely first-rate, and we believe they will receive an enthusiastic response from both teachers and students.

Each chapter of the *Study Guide* facilitates student learning through the use of a chapter outline, learning objectives, a review of key terms and concepts, multiple-choice questions with explanations for why the correct answer is the best choice, and a new set of practice essay questions with sample answers.

The *Test Bank* features an extensive set of improved multiple-choice questions and new essay questions with sample answers. The objective questions are keyed to learning objective and text page and noted as involving either mastery or application of facts and concepts. The computerized test bank for IBM or Macintosh computers contains all of the questions in the test bank in an easy-to-use, menu-driven format that allows for customization to each instructor's needs.

The *Instructor's Resource Manual* includes learning objectives, lecture outlines, discussion topics, classroom exercises, handouts, and audiovisual resource suggestions. The completely revised classroom exercises feature a new "What if This Bombs?" section that offers tips for making the most of every activity.

An extensive set of *overhead transparencies* includes images from within and outside the text's illustration program that were chosen with the help of several instructors to ensure pedagogical effectiveness.

A wide variety of *videos and films* are available through your Houghton Mifflin sales representative.

ACKNOWLEDGMENTS

Textbooks are a team effort. As always, we are grateful to Houghton Mifflin Company for its commitment to quality as the first priority. We also want to express our appreciation to all those individuals whose considerable talents and countless hours of hard work are visible on every page of this book: Becky Dudley, Sponsoring Editor; Jane Knetzger, Senior Associate Editor; Carol Newman, Senior Project Editor; Charlotte Miller, Art Editor; and Ann Schroeder, Photo Editor.

And then there are our colleagues who reviewed various drafts of the Third Edition. None of them can be blamed for our shortcomings. Each and every one of them helped to make this a better book. We thank them for their comments and suggestions.

Julie A. Allison, *Pittsburgh State University*
Anthony Ambrosio, *Wichita State University*
Dan Batson, *University of Kansas*
Leonard Berkowitz, *University of Wisconsin*
Ellen Berscheid, *University of Minnesota*
Monica Biernat, *University of Kansas*
Jonathon D. Brown, *University of Washington*
Peter Carnevale, *University of Illinois at Urbana-Champaign*
Dorothee Dietrich, *Hamline University*
David Dunning, *Cornell University*
Nancy Dye, *Humboldt State University*
Alan Feingold, *Yale University*
Solomon M. Fulero, *Sinclair Community College*
James Hamilton, *University of Alabama*
Vicki S. Helgeson, *Carnegie Mellon University*

Susan S. Hendrick, *Texas Tech University*
James L. Hilton, *University of Michigan*
Theresa Tyler Holt, *Middlesex County College*
Thomas T. Jackson, *Fort Hays State University*
D. Brett King, *University of Colorado at Boulder*
Fredrick Koenig, *Tulane University*
David A. Kopplin, *Baylor University*
M. B. Kroon, *Free University of Amsterdam*
Marianne LaFrance, *Boston College*
Herbert L. Leff, *University of Vermont*
Michael Leippe, *Adelphi University*
Kenneth E. Leonard, *Research Institute on Addictions*
Stephen J. Lepore, *Carnegie Mellon University*
Barbara McCaffrey, *Stark Technical College*
Kim Mooney, *St. Lawrence University*
Rupert W. Nacoste, *North Carolina State University*
Leonard Newman, *University of Illinois at Chicago*
Karen O'Quin, *Buffalo State College*
Paul B. Paulus, *University of Texas at Arlington*
Gary Poole, *Simon Fraser University*
John W. Reich, *Arizona State University*
Bruce Rind, *Temple University*
Richard M. Ryckman, *University of Maine*
James A. Shepperd, *University of Florida*
Richard C. Sherman, *Miami University*
Steve Slane, *Cleveland State University*
Charles Stangor, *University of Maryland*
David L. Wolske, *College of the Southwest*

Finally, we are especially grateful to Steven Fein and Steven Spencer for putting together an excellent reader and creating a set of exciting, top-of-the-line ancillaries. Their work has added a whole new dimension to this text.

Sharon S. Brehm

Saul M. Kassin

About the Authors

Sharon S. Brehm is Professor of Psychology and Dean of Harpur College of Arts and Sciences at the State University of New York at Binghamton. Born and raised in Roanoke, Virginia, she received her B.A. from Duke University, her M.A. from Harvard University, and returned to Duke for her Ph.D. She completed an internship in clinical psychology at the University of Washington Medical Center in Seattle. From 1975 to 1990, she was on the faculty at the University of Kansas. Brehm has been a Fulbright Senior Research Scholar in Paris and a visiting professor in Germany and Italy. Her books include *The Application of Social Psychology to Clinical Practice,* a recognized classic in the field, and *Intimate Relationships,* a popular textbook now in its second edition. She serves as a consultant on a wide range of issues in higher education.

Saul M. Kassin is Professor of Psychology at Williams College, Williamstown, Massachusetts. Born and raised in New York City, he graduated with a B.S. from Brooklyn College. After receiving his Ph.D. in personality and social psychology from the University of Connecticut, he spent one year at the University of Kansas and two years at Purdue University. In 1984, he was awarded a U.S. Supreme Court Judicial Fellowship, and in 1985, he received a postdoctoral fellowship in the Psychology-Law Program at Stanford University. Kassin is the author of the textbook *Psychology*, and has coauthored or edited six scholarly books, including *The American Jury on Trial: Psychological Perspectives* and *Confessions in the Courtroom.* His research interests are in social perception and its applications to evidence, trial procedure, and jury decision-making.

Social Psychology

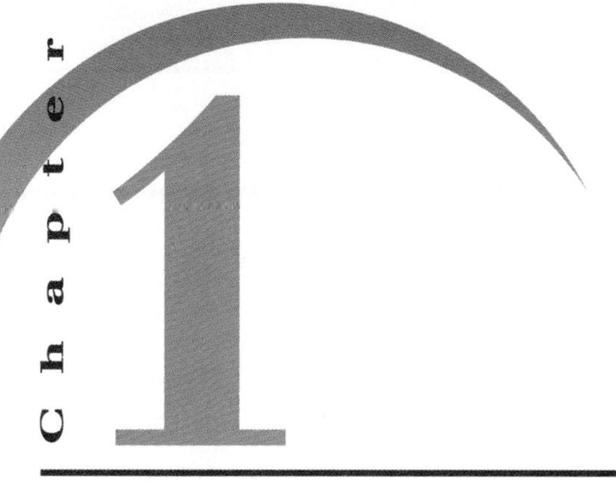

Chapter 1 Introduction to Social Psychology

PREVIEW

This chapter introduces you to the study of social psychology. We begin by *getting to know it,* considering the definition and history of the field. Next, we provide *an overview of research methods in social psychology:* how social psychologists come up with and test ideas. In the concluding section, we turn to important questions about *ethics and values in social psychology.*

OUTLINE

Think about your experiences over the past few weeks. What was your happiest moment? What was your saddest one? What made you feel secure? What put you on edge? It's a safe bet that at least one, and probably more, of your answers to these questions describes an interaction you had with another person. For the overwhelming majority of human beings, life is a series of social events.

We don't just fall passively into social interactions; we actively seek them. People go home for the holidays; play the dating game; make friends; give parties; build networks; pledge an enduring commitment; decide to have children. And there's more. Much of our leisure time is devoted to observing others, real or fictional. We watch people on TV, in the movies, and on stage. We survey the passing scene from a park bench or sidewalk café. We take photographs, make videos, and read about the "rich-and-famous" as well as the "down-and-out." People-watching is our most popular spectator sport.

For those of us fascinated by our own social interactions and by the behavior of others, social psychology is a dream come true. Scientific rather than anecdotal, systematic rather than haphazard, social psychology enlarges our understanding of individuals and their social world. Just consider a small sample of the questions you'll explore in this textbook:

PART I Social Perception

Chapter 2 The Social Self

- What do you think about yourself? How do you feel about yourself?

Chapter 3 Perceiving Persons

- Why is it that your first impressions of other people often stick like glue regardless of what happens afterwards?

Chapter 4 Perceiving Groups

- Why is it so difficult to overcome stereotypes and prejudices about social groups to which you don't belong?

PART II Social Interaction

Chapter 5 Interpersonal Attraction

- Why are you attracted to some people but not at all interested in others?

Chapter 6 Intimate Relationships

- What is love?

Chapter 7 Helping Others

- Why do we help others? Is it for their benefit or for our own?

Chapter 8 Aggression

- Does watching violence on TV increase aggressive behavior in real life?

PART III Social Influence

Chapter 9 Conformity

- Why do so many of us conform in the clothes we wear and the opinions we express?

Chapter 10 Attitudes

- What persuasive techniques are used by politicians to win votes and advertisers to sell products?

Chapter 11 Group Processes

- Why do groups of highly intelligent individuals sometimes make remarkably bad decisions?

PART IV Applying Social Psychology

Chapter 12 Law

- Are juries influenced by the media hype of pretrial publicity?

Chapter 13 Business

- Can a person be an effective leader in some situations but not in others?

Chapter 14 Health

- How do people cope with stress?

Social psychology covers a lot of ground, addressing issues of great significance in people's lives.

The value of social psychology's perspective on human behavior is widely recognized. Courses in social psychology are often required for undergraduate majors in business, education, and journalism as well as in psychology and sociology. Although most advanced graduates with a Ph.D. in social psychology

People-watching at a sidewalk cafe is a pleasant way to spend a sunny afternoon. Social psychology is a scientific version of this popular pastime, enlarging our understanding of individuals and their social world.

hold faculty appointments in colleges or universities, they also work in medical centers, law firms, business organizations, and government agencies. Constantly expanding their horizons, social psychologists seek new knowledge and new opportunities to apply what they have learned.

The purpose of this chapter is to provide you with a broad overview of the field. By the time you finish it, you should be ready and (we hope) eager for what lies ahead.

SOCIAL PSYCHOLOGY: GETTING TO KNOW IT

We begin by defining the new territory you're about to enter. Then we map out the history of the development of social psychology, from its origins to contemporary trends and issues.

What Is Social Psychology?

social psychology The scientific study of the way individuals think, feel, desire, and act in social situations.

Social psychology is the scientific study of the way individuals think, feel, desire, and act in social situations. Let's look at each part of this definition.

The Scientific Study There are many approaches to understanding how people think, feel, desire, and act. We can learn about human behavior from novels, films, history, philosophy—to name just a few possibilities. What makes social psychology different from these artistic and humanistic endeavors is that social psychology is a science. It applies the *scientific method* of systematic observation, description, and measurement to the study of the human condition.

Of the Way Individuals Think, Feel, Desire, and Act In addition to social psychology, many other disciplines employ scientific techniques to study human behavior: for example, anthropology, communication studies, economics, political science, and sociology. All of these disciplines, including social psychology, are called *social sciences*.

The social sciences differ in terms of which aspects of behavior they examine. Some concentrate on relatively limited, specific content areas. Economists, for instance, conduct research on economic issues and political scientists on political ones. Social psychology opts for a broader view, studying many different behaviors that occur in many different settings. Research on attitudes (see Chapter 10) offers a good illustration. By investigating a variety of specific attitudes (including, but not limited to, those about economics and politics), social psychologists attempt to establish general principles of attitude formation and change that will apply in a variety of situations. This search for general principles is characteristic of social psychology's approach to a diverse array of human behaviors.

The level of analysis also sets social psychology apart from some other social sciences. Sociology, for instance, classifies people in terms of their nationality, race, socioeconomic class, and other *group factors*. In contrast, social psychology typically focuses on the *individual*. Even when social psychologists study groups of people, they usually emphasize the behavior of the individual in the group context.

Research methods provide another distinction. Far more than other social sciences, social psychology uses experiments to investigate human behavior. Later in this chapter, we describe the basic features of an experiment. In sum, social psychology is characterized by a broad perspective, a focus on the individual, and the frequent use of an experimental methodology.

In Social Situations But how can we separate the subdiscipline of social psychology from the larger field of psychology? As a whole, the discipline of psychology is an immense, sprawling enterprise, the 800-pound gorilla of the social sciences. There is considerable debate about how it should be defined and, indeed, whether it even can be defined (Bower, 1993; Koch, 1993). Nevertheless, much of psychology emphasizes the scientific method, takes a broad perspective with a focus on the individual, and employs experimental techniques. So what makes social psychology unique?

The obvious answer is found in the name, *social* psychology, which indicates a particular concern with behavior in *social* situations. For over a decade, however, questions have been raised about just how "social" social psychology is (Carlson, 1984; Kenrick, 1986). In fact, the "socialness" of social psychology varies. Attempting to establish general principles of human behavior, social psychologists sometimes examine nonsocial factors that affect our thoughts, emotions, motives, and actions.

A study on information processing and close relationships makes the point (Fletcher et al., 1994). How do people process information that bears on their beliefs about the importance of intimacy and passion in close relationships? It depends on the strength of those beliefs. In this research, individuals who strongly believed that intimacy and passion were essential for a good relationship processed belief-relevant information equally quickly when this was the only task they had ("no load") or when they were simultaneously trying to remember a string of numbers ("memory load"). In contrast, those with weak beliefs processed belief-relevant information much more slowly when they also had to struggle with the digit-memorization task (see Figure 1.1). There is nothing social

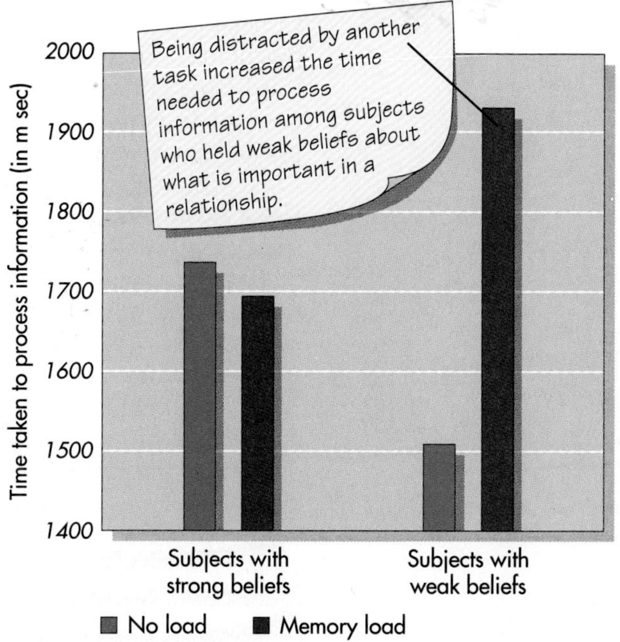

Figure 1.1 **Beliefs and Information.** In this research, subjects were classified according to whether they had strong or weak beliefs about the importance of intimacy and passion in close relationships. Those with strong beliefs processed belief-relevant information equally quickly when there was ("memory load") or was not ("no load") a competing task. However, those with weak beliefs took much more time to process this information when there were other demands on their attention. (Adapted from Fletcher et al., 1994.)

about memorizing digits. But the finding itself has clear implications for social interactions: Among strong believers, beliefs about what is important in a relationship are consistently related to the way these individuals perceive and evaluate information about relationships; among weak believers, the association is more variable, depending on other demands for their attention. Although not everything social psychologists study is itself a social phenomenon, whatever they examine is relevant to social behavior.

From Past to Present

Social psychology has a rich and complex heritage. Here, we sketch just a few highlights, but even this brief review vividly illustrates the strength of the research traditions that bind the field together (Berscheid, 1992). To explore the history of social psychology is to take a trip "back to the future." Questions and concerns originating in the past influence today's endeavors and set the stage for tomorrow's insights.

The Gathering Forces: 1880–1935 Like most such honors, the title of "founder of social psychology" has many potential recipients and not everyone agrees on who should prevail (Farr, 1991). But if you write a textbook, you have to make the call, and ours is to declare a tie between the American psychologist Norman Triplett and the French agricultural engineer Max Ringelmann.

Triplett published the first research article in social psychology at the end of the nineteenth century (1897–1898); Ringelmann's research was conducted in the 1880s but wasn't published until 1913. The issues addressed by these two early researchers continue to be of vital interest: Will an individual's performance be enhanced by the presence of others? Or will individual performance decline in a group setting? Chapter 11 on Group Processes looks at the answers provided by current research.

Despite their pride of place in the history of social psychology, neither Triplett nor Ringelmann actually established social psychology as a distinct field of study. Credit for this creation goes to the writers of the first three textbooks in social psychology: English psychologist William McDougall (1908) and Americans Edward Ross (1908) and Floyd Allport (1924). These authors announced the arrival of a new approach to the social aspects of human behavior. Social psychology was born.

Great Advances: 1936–1945 In its infancy, social psychology was nurtured by some extraordinarily creative individuals. One of them was Muzafer Sherif. Born in Turkey and educated both there and in the United States, Sherif was a gifted researcher who had an acute awareness of how behavior is affected by the social environment. In 1936, he published a ground-breaking study of social influence. As described in more detail in Chapter 9 on Conformity, participants in this research observed a visual illusion—a dot of light that was actually stationary but appeared to move. Watching alone, participants differed considerably in their individual estimates of the light's movement. When they watched together in groups, however, their estimates of the light's movement converged. The light itself never budged, but opinions moved toward a common perception.

Sherif's research was crucial for the development of social psychology because it demonstrated that it is possible to study the complex human behavior of social influence in a rigorous, scientific manner. This innovation, startling at the time,

Will the performance of individuals, such as the members of this sailing crew, improve or decline when they work as a group? The two founders of social psychology, American psychologist Norman Triplett and French agricultural engineer Max Ringelmann, sought answers to this question. Chapter 11 on Group Processes brings you up-to-date on the latest research in this area.

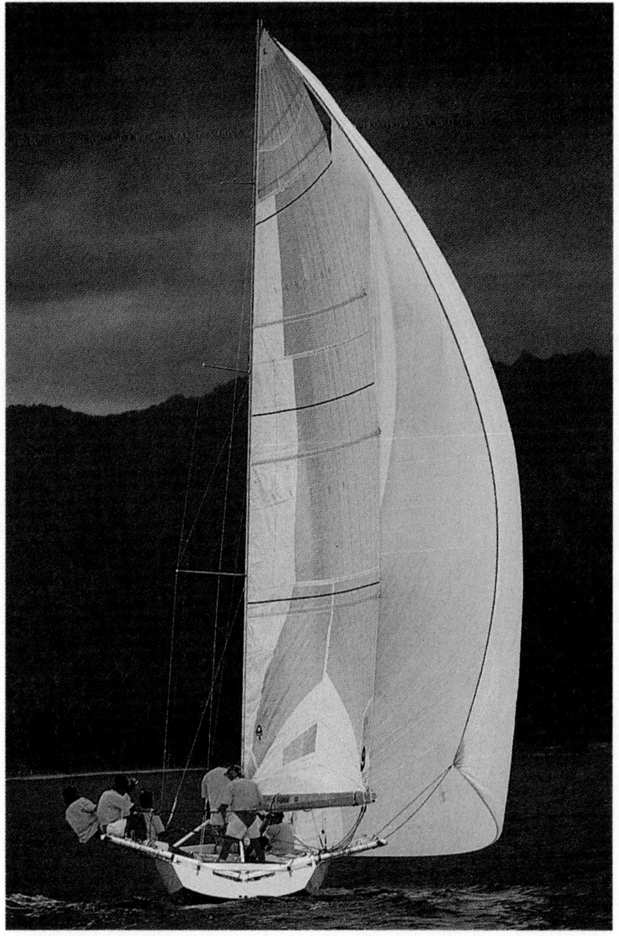

laid the foundation for what was to become one of the major topics in social psychology. Research and theory on social influence are discussed throughout this text, particularly in Part III on Social Influence.

Another great contributor to social psychology, Kurt Lewin, was a bold and creative theorist whose concepts have had lasting effects on the field (Bargal et al., 1992). For example, his concept of the *life space* established the fundamental principle in social psychology that what we do depends to a large extent on how we perceive and interpret the world around us. Different people can see the same situation differently, and their behavior will vary accordingly.

But, having fled the Nazi onslaught in Germany, Lewin knew only too well that human beings are not immune from forces and events that were unimaginable before they struck. It's not surprising, then, that in his *field theory,* Lewin (1935) proposed that *behavior* is a function of the *interaction* between the *person* and the *environment:* $B = f(PE)$. This conviction, that both internal and external factors affect behavior, helped create a unified view that was distinct from the other major psychological paradigms during Lewin's lifetime: psychoanalysis, with its emphasis on internal motives and fantasies; and behaviorism, with its focus on external rewards and punishments.

interactionist perspective An emphasis on how both an individual's personality and environmental characteristics influence behavior.

Lewin's position was an early version of what today is known as the **interactionist perspective** (Blass, 1984). This approach combines personality psychology

Built on the legacy of Kurt Lewin, one of the leading figures in the development of the field, applied social psychology contributes to the solution of social problems. Throughout this text, we describe the application of social psychological principles to societal concerns such as classroom interaction (see Chapter 4 on Perceiving Groups) and environmental conservation (see Chapter [illegible] on Group Processes).

(which usually stresses internal, psychological differences among *individuals*) with social psychology (which often examines differences among external *situations*). The marriage, or at least serious dating, between these two branches of psychology has produced an important area of research and theory (Kihlstrom, 1987; Snyder & Ickes, 1985). In this book, we examine the impact of both individual and situational differences, alone and together.

Yet another aspect of Lewin's enormous influence was his persistent interest in the application of social psychology. Through his research on practical issues, such as how to promote more economical and nutritious eating habits (Lewin, 1947), he showed how social psychology could enlarge our understanding of social problems and contribute to their solution. Built on Lewin's legacy, applied social psychology flourishes today in areas such as advertising, business, education, environmental protection, health, law, politics, public policy, religion, and sports. Throughout this text, we draw on the findings of applied social psychology to illustrate the implications of social psychological principles for our daily lives. In Part IV, three prominent areas of applied social psychology are discussed in detail: law, business, and health.

The Classical Period: 1946–1960 After World War II, American psychology shared in the nation's general prosperity. Government funding for research increased, helping social psychology to establish a stronger sense of its own identity. Major contributors generated systematic programs of research in topic areas that are still of great significance. Table 1.1 lists some of the people and topics involved in what could be called social psychology's golden age.

Confidence and Crisis: 1961–1975 With its foundation firmly in place, social psychology entered a period of expansion and enthusiasm. The sheer range of its investigations was staggering. Social psychologists considered how people thought (Kelley, 1967) and felt (Schachter, 1964) about themselves and others. They studied interactions in groups (Moscovici & Zavalloni, 1969) and social

Table 1.1 Major Contributors to Social Psychology During the Classical Period (1946–1960)

Contributor	Topic Area	Discussed in This Text
Gordon Allport	Prejudice and stereotyping	Perceiving Groups (Chap. 4)
Solomon Asch	Conformity Person perception	Conformity (Chap. 9) Perceiving Persons (Chap. 3)
Leon Festinger	Cognitive dissonance Social comparison	Attitudes (Chap. 10) The Social Self (Chap. 2)
Fritz Heider	Attribution theory Balance theory	Perceiving Persons (Chap. 3) Interpersonal Attraction (Chap. 5)
Carl Hovland	Attitudes and persuasion	Attitudes (Chap. 10)
John Thibaut and Harold Kelley	Social exchange	Intimate Relationships (Chap. 6)

These individuals developed systematic programs of research in topic areas that continue to be of great significance in social psychology.

problems such as why people fail to help others in distress (Latané & Darley, 1970). They examined aggression (Bandura, 1973), physical attractiveness (Berscheid & Walster, 1974b), and stress (Glass & Singer, 1972). All of these topics are discussed in this text. For the field as a whole, it was a time of great productivity.

Ironically, it was also a time of crisis and heated debate. Many of the strong disagreements during this period can be understood as a reaction to the dominant research method of the day: the laboratory experiment. Those social psychologists who questioned this type of research maintained that certain practices were unethical (Kelman, 1967), that experimenters' expectations influenced their subjects' behavior (Orne, 1962; Rosenthal, 1966), and that the theories being tested in the laboratory were historically and culturally limited (Gergen, 1973). Those who favored laboratory experimentation contended that their procedures were ethical, their results valid, and their theoretical principles widely applicable (McGuire, 1967). For a while, social psychology seemed split in two.

An Era of Pluralism: 1976 to the Present Fortunately, both sides won. As we will see later in this chapter, more rigorous ethical standards for research were instituted, more stringent procedures to guard against bias were adopted, and more attention was paid to possible cross-cultural differences in behavior. But the baby was not thrown out with the bath water. Laboratory experiments continued. They did, however, get some company, as a single-minded attachment to one research method evolved into a broader acceptance of many methods. The logic behind a pluralistic approach is compelling (Houts et al., 1986):

- Since different topics require different kinds of investigations, a range of research techniques is needed.
- Since no research method is perfect, a *multimethod* investigation of a topic increases our confidence that the results obtained do not simply reflect the peculiar characteristics of any one approach.

The various research methods used by today's social psychologists are described in the next section of this chapter.

Pluralism in social psychology extends far beyond its methods. There are also important variations in what aspects of human behavior are emphasized. People think, feel, desire, and act. But how do you slice the pie? One approach, which we might call "hot," focuses on *emotion* and *motivation* as determinants of our thoughts and actions (Zajonc, 1984). Another, which we could call "cold," places the emphasis on *cognition,* holding that people's thoughts affect how they feel, what they want, and what they do (Lazarus, 1984). Of course, some social psychologists prefer to put both slices on their plate or to divide up the behavioral whole into entirely different pieces. Nevertheless, the contrast between the "hot" and "cold" perspectives reflects some very real differences in how to conceptualize human behavior.

In this text, we describe both points of view. For instance, the theory of cognitive dissonance (Festinger, 1957), discussed in Chapter 10 on Attitudes, is one of the most influential theories ever developed in social psychology. Dissonance theory is, in our terms, very "hot": When what we do conflicts with what we believe, we *feel* uncomfortable and we are *motivated* to reduce this discomfort, often by changing our attitudes and opinions.

Even though dissonance is a classic example of a "hot" drive-reduction model (when hungry, eat; when dissonant, strive for consistency), it is—as the name indicates—strongly cognitive as well. Dissonance and consonance exist in the mind of the individual. In this sense, dissonance theory served as at least one parent to what became known as **social cognition,** the study of how we perceive, remember, and interpret information about ourselves and others.

social cognition The study of how people perceive, remember, and interpret information about themselves and others.

Social cognition is social psychology's contribution to the "cognitive revolution" of the 1980s (Friman et al., 1993). Suddenly, or so it seemed, researchers from a wide array of disciplines—including psychology, philosophy, computer science, and the burgeoning interdisciplinary field of neuroscience—discovered a common interest in cognitive processes and the effects of cognition on behavior. Today, social cognition is one of the most creative and exciting areas in social psychology. Theory and research in social cognition are discussed throughout this text, particularly in Part I on Social Perception.

Another source of pluralism in contemporary social psychology is found in the increasing effort to develop an international and multicultural perspective. Although, as we have seen, individuals from many countries helped establish the field, social psychology achieved its greatest professional recognition in the United States and Canada. It is estimated that today some 75 to 90 percent of social psychologists live in North America (Smith & Bond, 1993; Triandis, 1994). And, consistent with the concerns raised earlier by Gergen (1973), social psychology has been called "culture-bound" (Berry et al., 1992) and "largely monocultural" (Moghaddam et al., 1993).

This aspect of social psychology is rapidly changing, with profound consequences for our view of human behavior:

- The greater emphasis by British and European social psychologists on the meaning and impact of group membership has vastly increased the "socialness" of social psychology (Moreland et al., 1994). Major contributions described later in this book include social identity theory (Tajfel, 1982; Turner, 1987) and minority influence (Moscovici, 1980; Mugny, 1982).
- Cross-cultural research has revealed important distinctions between collectivist cultures (more typical in Africa, Asia, and Latin America) and individualistic ones (more typical in North America and Europe). Chapter 2 on the Social Self examines current theory and research in this area.

These are but two examples of the cross-cultural interactions and comparisons that are taking place today. In this text, we describe research conducted in Argentina, Australia, Brazil, China, Colombia, Denmark, Finland, France, Ger-

Cross-cultural research helps us break out of our culture-bound perspective. Even some of the most basic human behaviors differ across cultures. Take, for example, eating. As this photo of the largest Chinese restaurant in Thailand illustrates, people in collectivist cultures, which emphasize interdependence and group goals, often eat in large groups (Triandis, 1994). People in individualistic cultures, which emphasize independence and personal goals, usually prefer eating under less crowded conditions.

many, Great Britain, Hong Kong, Hungary, India, Indonesia, Ireland, Israel, Italy, Japan, Korea, Mexico, the Netherlands, New Zealand, Nigeria, Norway, Papua New Guinea, Poland, Russia, South Africa, Spain, Sweden, Taiwan, Venezuela, and the former Yugoslavia as well as Canada and the United States. As our knowledge expands, we should be able to see much more clearly both the behavioral differences among cultures and the similarities we all share.

We have now defined the field and traced its development across more than a century. But the portrait is still incomplete. People do social psychology. How do they do it? In the next section, we look at social psychology in action.

AN OVERVIEW OF RESEARCH METHODS IN SOCIAL PSYCHOLOGY

The research process involves coming up with ideas, testing those ideas, and interpreting the meaning of the results obtained. Understanding this process is crucial for your study of social psychology. Subsequent chapters in this book emphasize *what* social psychologists have found in their research. Here, we examine *how* they go about finding something.

Hypotheses and Theories

It all begins with an idea, a vision of what might be. Like everyone else, social psychologists get ideas about human behavior from events in their own lives, informal observations of others, books they read, and what they see on TV. In addition, social psychologists are stimulated by each other's work. A new idea often takes shape in response to those already proposed, enlarging an existing viewpoint or offering a radically different alternative.

hypothesis A testable prediction about the conditions under which an event will occur.

Initial ideas may be so vague that they amount to little more than a hunch or an educated guess. Some vanish with the break of day. But others can be shaped into a **hypothesis:** an explicit, testable prediction about the conditions under

Table 1.2 Thinking About Behavior: Common Sense Versus Science

Issue	Common Sense	Scientific Thinking
Accepted sources and expressions of truth and knowledge	Authority. Intuition. Television and other media. Superstition. What experience has taught me. What everybody knows. What only stands to reason. Dictionary definition.	Evidence. Observation. Correlational studies. Experimental results. Data, polls, surveys, and statistics. Deductions from formal theory.
Accepted interpretations of behavior	Free will. "The unvarnished truth." Simple explanation. "Tell it like it is." Explanation by naming. Exceptions prove the rule.	Determinism. Complex causality. "More research is needed." Explanation by theory. Exceptions disprove the rule.
Nature of mental states	Tangible realities. Factual entities.	Inferences from behavior. Abstract concepts.
Quantitative vs. qualitative outlook	Qualitative: Some human traits and aspects of experience cannot be measured.	Quantitative: If it exists at all, it exists in some amount and it can be measured.

Like everyone else, social psychologists use common sense in getting ideas about human behavior. However, these initial ideas are then subjected to the discipline of the scientific method, which allows the social psychologist to formulate precise hypotheses, conduct research, and build theories. Some of the differences between common-sense ideas and scientific thinking are summarized in this table. (Based on Kimble, 1994.)

which an event will occur. Formulating a hypothesis is the first step toward planning and conducting research. It allows us to move from the realm of common sense to the rigors of the scientific method. Some of the differences between common-sense ideas and scientific thinking are described in Table 1.2.

theory An organized set of principles used to explain observed phenomena.

As hypotheses proliferate and data accumulate, the next step in the research process is to propose a **theory:** an organized set of principles used to explain observed phenomena. Theories are usually evaluated in terms of three criteria: simplicity, comprehensiveness, and generativity. All else being equal, the best theories are elegant and precise; encompass all of the relevant information; and lead to new hypotheses, further research, and better understanding.

In social psychology, there are many theories. Social psychologists do not attempt the all-encompassing grand theory, such as those of Freud or Piaget, which you may have studied in introductory psychology. Instead, they rely on more precise "minitheories" that address limited and specific aspects of the way people behave, make explicit predictions about behavior, and allow meaningful empirical investigation.

Most social psychological theories are highly generative. They stimulate systematic programs of research by the theory's advocates. They may also provoke sharp criticism by the theory's opponents. Beginning students of social psychology are often surprised by the lack of consensus in the field. In part, such disagreement reflects the fact that social psychology is a very young science. At this stage in its development, premature closure is a worse sin than contradiction or even confusion. But debate is an essential feature of even the most mature science. It is the fate of *all* scientific theories to be criticized and, eventually, surpassed: "The currency of science is not truth, but doubt" (Overbye, 1993).

basic research Research whose goal is to increase the understanding of human behavior, often by testing hypotheses based on a theory.

applied research Research whose goals are to enlarge the understanding of naturally occurring events and to find solutions to practical problems.

Basic and Applied Research Is testing a theory the purpose of research in social psychology? For some researchers, yes. **Basic research** seeks to increase our understanding of human behavior and is often designed to test a specific hypothesis from a specific theory. **Applied research** has a different purpose: to make use of social psychology's theories or methods to enlarge our understanding of naturally occurring events and to contribute to the solution of social problems (Cook et al., 1985; Rodin, 1985).

Despite their differences, basic and applied research are closely connected in social psychology. Some researchers switch back and forth between the two: today basic, tomorrow applied. Some studies test a theory *and* examine a real-world phenomenon simultaneously. As a pioneer in both approaches, Kurt Lewin (1951) set the tone when he cautioned basic researchers not to be disdainful or fearful of the complexities of social problems and urged applied researchers to remember that "there is nothing so practical as a good theory."

Correlations: Looking for Associations

correlation An association between two variables. A correlation is positive when both variables increase or decrease together. It is negative when as one variable increases, the other decreases.

Whenever a social psychologist has a good idea, basic or applied, the question "How do we test it?" is sure to follow. One of the most popular answers is: with a correlation. A **correlation** is an association between two factors that vary in quantity. When a correlation is *positive,* as one variable increases, so does the other; as one decreases, so does the other. When a correlation is *negative,* the two variables go in opposite directions: one up, the other down. And when there is *no correlation,* there is no relationship at all. These three types of patterns are illustrated in Figure 1.2.

Mathematically, correlations are computed in terms of the *correlation coefficient,* which ranges from +1.0 to −1.0. A perfect positive correlation has a correlation coefficient of +1.0; a perfect negative correlation has a correlation

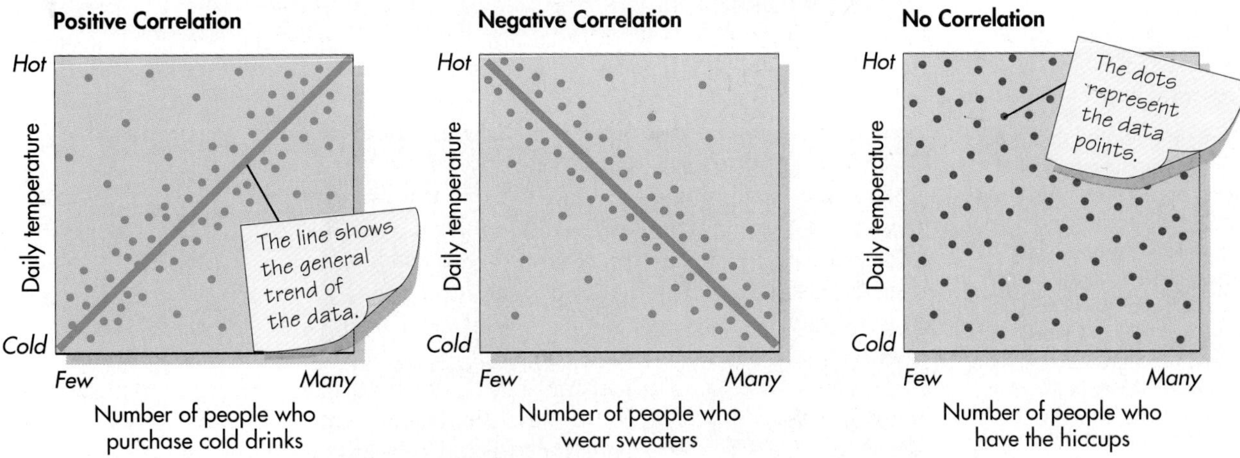

Figure 1.2 **Correlations: Positive, Negative, and None.** Correlations reveal a systematic association between two variables. Positive correlations indicate that variables are in sync: Increases in one variable are associated with increases in the other, decreases with decreases. Negative correlations indicate that variables go in opposite directions: Increases in one variable are associated with decreases in the other. When two variables are not systematically associated, there is no correlation.

coefficient of −1.0; and the total absence of any correlation has a correlation coefficient of 0. Since most correlations are not perfect, one way or the other, most correlation coefficients have more moderate values such as +.39 or −.67.

Typically, correlations are obtained by comparing the scores of different individuals on the factors of interest. Consider the notion that "birds of a feather flock together." If the proverb holds for people as well as for our feathered friends, we would expect that similarity and interpersonal attraction would have a positive correlation. And they do. As discussed in Chapter 5 on Interpersonal Attraction, similarity on various dimensions is associated with liking and with establishing a relationship:

- College students living in the same dormitory like those with similar attitudes more than they like those with dissimilar attitudes (Newcomb, 1961).
- Couples who are dating, cohabiting, engaged, or married are more similar in their level of physical attractiveness than are randomly paired couples who have no relationship with each other (Feingold, 1988).

Correlations can also be computed for a single individual over a number of repeated measurements. In his study of emotional experience, Seymour Epstein (1983) examined both types of correlations: *between* (different individuals) and *within* (a single individual). Participants in this research rated their feelings on each of twenty-eight days. Comparing different individuals, the totals for sadness and anger were positively correlated, with a correlation coefficient of +.51. People who reported more sad feelings than did others reported more anger as well. This finding suggests that people differ on the general tendency to experience negative emotions. But what about each individual, each day at a time? Here sadness and anger were uncorrelated. For a specific individual, being sad neither increased nor decreased the likelihood of being angry. Thus, between individuals, sadness and anger were associated; but within individuals, sadness and anger were independent. Together these two types of correlations give us a more complete picture of emotional experience than does either one alone.

Correlations obtained at a single point in time are called *concurrent*. Those obtained at different times from the same individuals are called *prospective*. Prospective studies are especially useful in determining whether certain behaviors

Being in a relationship is correlated with having similar levels of physical attractiveness. But a correlation cannot identify the cause of this association. Chapter 5 on Interpersonal Attraction discusses both correlational and experimental research on the role of similarity in the attraction process.

at a young age are associated with certain behaviors at an older age. For example, correlations between early viewing of TV violence and later aggressive behavior are described in Chapter 8 on Aggression.

Correlational research has many advantages. It can study the associations of naturally occurring variables that cannot be manipulated or induced—such as gender, race, ethnicity, and age. It can examine phenomena that would be difficult or unethical to create for research purposes. For instance, it would be difficult to create love, but would it be unethical? It would certainly be unethical to create sexual abuse. Correlational research also offers a great deal of freedom in where variables are measured. Participants can be brought into a laboratory specially constructed for research purposes, or they can be approached in a real-world setting (often called "the field") such as a shopping mall or airport.

Despite these advantages, however, correlational research has one, very serious disadvantage. And here it is in bright, bold letters:

Correlation Is Not Causation.

In other words, a correlation cannot demonstrate a cause-and-effect relationship. Instead of revealing a specific causal pathway, a correlation contains within it three possible causal effects: A could cause B; B could cause A; or a third variable C could cause both A and B.

Take, for example, Stephen Carter's (1994) illustration of the pitfalls of mistaking an association for a causal effect: "the charming but statistically naive point somebody came up with years ago: television viewership and lung cancer were both increasing, so one must cause the other" (p. 64). This seems a ridiculous conclusion (which is why Carter cites it), but how could such a correlation ever have occurred? Let's review the possibilities.

1. Did TV sets emit some cancer-causing agent? There's no evidence of such an effect.
2. Did lung cancer cause TV viewing? It seems quite implausible.
3. Could some third variable have caused both TV viewing and lung cancer? Perhaps greater economic prosperity gave more people the funds to buy both TVs and cigarettes. It sounds reasonable, but we cannot know for sure. Third variables are the bane of correlational research: So many of them could be involved in any specific association that we can never be confident we've tracked them all down.

By subjecting a correlation to this kind of systematic analysis, we can develop new hypotheses to guide future research. And by gathering large sets of correlations and using complicated statistical techniques to crunch the data, we can develop highly accurate predictions of future events. Astronomy, after all, is a purely correlational science. But still, correlation is not causation. Remember it.

Experiments: Looking for Cause and Effect

experiment A form of research that can demonstrate causal relationships because (1) the experimenter has control over the events that occur and (2) subjects are randomly assigned to conditions.

If we want to examine cause-and-effect relationships, we will need to conduct an **experiment.** Experiments in social psychology range from the very simple to the almost incredibly elaborate. All of them, however, share two essential characteristics.

1. The researcher has *control* over the experimental procedures: manipulating the variables of interest while ensuring uniformity elsewhere. All those who participate as subjects in the research are treated in exactly the same manner—except for the specific differences the experimenter wants to create. By exercising

"Well, you don't look like an experimental psychologist to me."

control, the researcher attempts to ensure that differences obtained after the experimental manipulation are produced only by that manipulation and are not affected by other events in the experiment.

2. Subjects are *randomly assigned* to the different manipulations (called "conditions") included in the experiment. If there are two conditions, who goes where may be determined by simply flipping a coin. If there are many conditions, a computer program may be used. However it's done, random assignment means that subjects are *not* assigned to a condition on the basis of their personal or behavioral characteristics. By randomly assigning subjects to experimental conditions, the experimenter attempts to ensure a level playing field. On the average, the subjects assigned to one condition are no different from the subjects assigned to another condition. Differences that appear between conditions after an experimental manipulation can therefore be attributed to the impact of that manipulation and not to any pre-existing differences between subjects.

Because of experimenter control and random assignment of subjects, an experiment is a powerful technique for examining cause and effect. Both characteristics serve the same goal: to eliminate the influence on subjects' behavior of any factors other than the experimental manipulation. By ruling out alternative explanations for research results, we become more confident that we understand just what has, in fact, caused a certain behavior to occur.

Speaking the Language of Research To illustrate some of the terms used to describe experimental procedures, consider an experiment by Kenneth Leonard (1989) on the effects of alcohol on aggression. The subjects were male undergraduates who had agreed to participate in a study on "the influence of alcohol on perceptual-motor skills." Only subjects who indicated that they drank alcohol were included. When each subject arrived at the research laboratory, he was randomly assigned to receive either no drink of any kind or a combination of vodka and ginger ale designed to produce the level of blood alcohol concentration legally defined as intoxication.

Each subject was then informed that he would be competing against another subject on an experimental task and that the loser on each trial would receive an electric shock administered by the winner. Actually, there was no other subject; tape-recorded messages and programmed responses during the task were used to simulate the opponent's behavior. At the beginning of the first trial, half of the subjects (randomly assigned within the alcohol and no-alcohol conditions) were led to believe that their opponent intended to administer the most severe shock available; the other half were led to believe that the opponent intended to use only the mildest possible shock. After the first trial was over, however, all subjects learned that their opponent had set the minimum shock level. They then prepared for the second trial.

independent variables The factors manipulated in an experiment to see if they affect the dependent variables.

dependent variables The factors measured in an experiment to see if they are affected by the independent variables.

In an experiment, researchers manipulate **independent variables** and examine the effect of these manipulations on the **dependent variables.** There were two independent variables in Leonard's study of alcohol and aggression:

1. Whether the subject drank alcohol: alcohol versus no alcohol
2. The opponent's intentions: aggressive cue versus nonaggressive cue

The outcome being studied—the dependent variable—was the level of shock that subjects selected before each trial to be administered to the opponent in the event that the subject was the winner on that trial. Thus, the results in this experiment consist of the level of shock selected before each trial by subjects in each of the four conditions outlined in Figure 1.3.

Results obtained in an experiment are examined by means of statistical analyses that allow the researcher to determine how likely it is that the results could have occurred by chance. The standard convention is that if a result could have occurred by chance only 5 or fewer times in 100 possible outcomes, then the result is *statistically significant* and should be taken seriously. But significant results are not absolutely certain. In essence, statistical significance is an attractive betting proposition. The odds are quite good (at least 95 out of 100) that the effects obtained in the study were due to the experimental manipulation of the independent variable. But there is still the possibility (as high as 5 out of 100) that the findings were merely a chance occurrence.

The results of Leonard's study of alcohol and aggression are depicted in Figure 1.4. As you can see, these findings differed on each of the two trials. On the first trial, subjects who believed the opponent had aggressive intentions selected higher levels of shock than did those who believed the opponent had nonaggressive intentions. This result, in which the levels of a single independent variable produce differences in the dependent variable, is called a *main effect.* The other possible main effect in this experiment was not significant: There was no difference in the

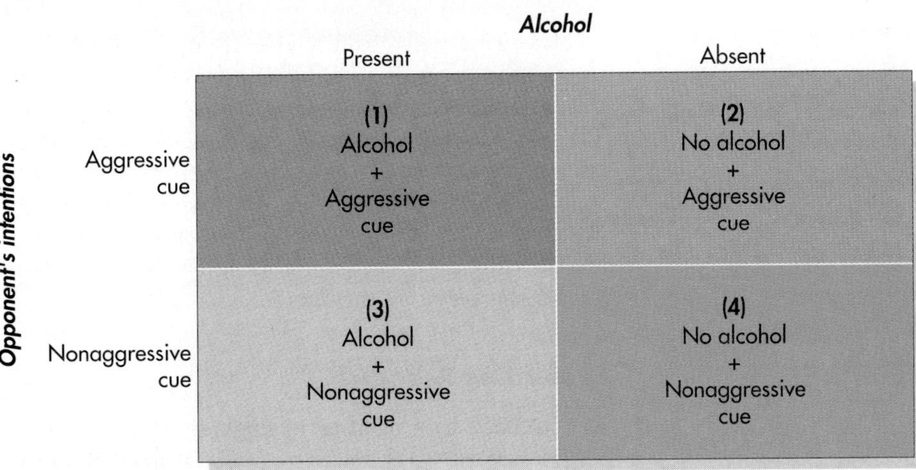

Figure 1.3 **Alcohol and Aggression: The Conditions.** Subjects in Leonard's research on alcohol and aggression either drank alcohol or did not. Then they learned that their opponent's intentions were either aggressive or nonaggressive. Combining these two independent variables creates the four conditions displayed here. (Based on Leonard, 1989.)

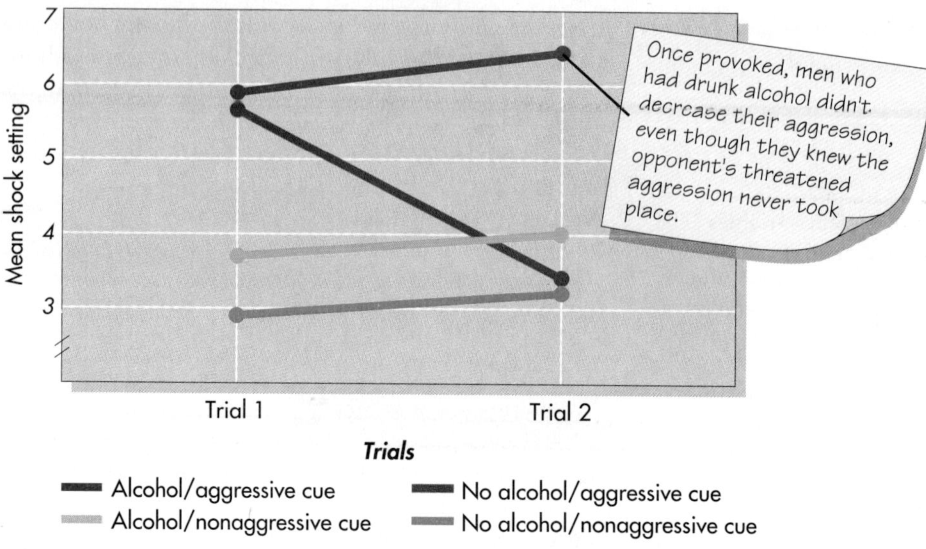

Figure 1.4 **Alcohol and Aggression: The Results.** On the first trial, only one independent variable produced a difference: Subjects who anticipated an aggressive opponent were more aggressive than those who anticipated a nonaggressive opponent. Before the second trial, all subjects learned that the opponent had behaved nonaggressively. On that trial, there was an interaction between the two independent variables: Only those subjects who had consumed alcohol *and* had initially expected the opponent to be aggressive were highly aggressive in their own behavior. (Adapted from Leonard, 1989.)

level of shock selected before the first trial between subjects who had drunk alcohol and those who had not had anything to drink.

On the second trial, however, both independent variables affected the dependent variable. Subjects who initially believed that the opponent had aggressive intentions *and* who had consumed alcohol were more aggressive than subjects in any of the other three conditions. Having taken a few stiff shots of vodka, they kept right on with their aggressive behavior, even though they knew that the opponent had not selected a severe shock. In contrast, subjects in the aggressive-cue condition who had not consumed alcohol were able to adjust their response to the opponent's unexpectedly peaceful behavior. Statistically, this kind of joint effect of two independent variables is called an *interaction*.

Now for a word to the wise. If you look back to Figure 1.1, you'll see another interaction between two independent variables. In this case, however, only one of the variables (competing task: "no load" versus "memory load") was manipulated. The other variable (relationship beliefs: strong believers versus weak ones) was a subject characteristic that existed before the research took place. It was not manipulated and subjects were not assigned randomly to the belief conditions. In other words, this may look like an experiment, but it isn't. It's a correlation. To tell the difference between correlational and experimental research, you need to keep a sharp eye on the details.

Evaluating Research

Researchers, too, need to be eagle-eyed, especially when they are planning their projects. It's always better to detect a problem early on, when improvements can be made before the data are collected. This section describes how to evaluate the quality and meaning of research endeavors. Although we will highlight experimental procedures, much of what we have to say applies to correlational studies as well.

internal validity The degree to which there can be reasonable certainty that the independent variables in an experiment caused the effects obtained on the dependent variables.

Internal Validity: Having Confidence in the Results When an experiment is properly conducted, its results are said to have **internal validity:** There is reasonable certainty that the independent variable did, in fact, cause the effects obtained on the dependent variable (Cook & Campbell, 1979). As noted earlier, both experimenter control and random assignment seek to rule out alternative explanations of the research results, thereby strengthening their internal validity.

Experiments also include *control groups* for this purpose. Typically, a control group consists of subjects who experience all of the experimental procedures except the experimental manipulations. In Leonard's study on alcohol and aggression, subjects who didn't drink alcohol and didn't hear their supposed opponent express aggressive intentions (condition #4 in Figure 1.3) served as a control group. As a sort of "dry run," the control group provides a base line against which to compare what happens when the independent variables are activated. However, the internal validity of Leonard's research is weakened by the fact that no-alcohol subjects *knew* they weren't drinking alcohol. Perhaps subjects' beliefs about whether they had consumed alcohol, rather than the actual impact of alcohol, affected their behavior. A stronger design would have compared subjects who all thought they were consuming alcohol, but only some of whom really did so.

Outside the laboratory, creating control groups in field experiments that examine real-life events raises many practical and ethical problems (Cook & Shadish, 1994). For example, research on new medical treatments for deadly diseases, such as AIDS, faces a terrible dilemma. Individuals randomly assigned to the control group receive the standard treatment, but they are excluded for the duration of the study from what could turn out to be a life-saving new intervention. Yet without such a comparison, it is extremely difficult to determine which new treatments are effective and which ones are useless. Although AIDS activists used to oppose including control groups in treatment research, they have recently become more supportive of this approach (Gorman, 1994).

Personal biases in Experiment

In assessing internal validity, researchers need to consider their own role as well. Unwittingly, they can sometimes sabotage their own research. Here's how:

- Before they conduct a study, experimenters usually make an explicit prediction, or at least have a strong expectation, about the effect of an independent variable.
- If they know what conditions subjects have been assigned to, they may, without realizing it, treat subjects in one condition differently from the way they treat subjects in another condition.
- Since the experimenter's behavior can affect the subject's behavior, the results could then be produced by the experimenter's actions rather than by the independent variable.

experimenter expectancy effects The effects produced when an experimenter's expectations about the results of an experiment affect his or her behavior toward a subject and thereby influence the subject's responses.

The best way to protect an experiment from the influence of experimenters' expectations—called **experimenter expectancy effects** (Rosenthal, 1976)—is to keep them uninformed about assignments to conditions. If experimenters do not know the condition to which a subject has been assigned, they cannot treat subjects in different conditions differently.

Leonard's study of alcohol and aggression was conducted by a single experimenter who was aware of subjects' experimental assignments. Since the experimenter did sometimes interact directly with the subject, experimenter expectancy effects, though unlikely, could have affected the results. In an effort to reduce the opportunity for such effects to occur, the interaction between the experimenter and each subject was minimized by the use of tape-recorded instructions at various points in the experiment.

external validity The degree to which there can be reasonable confidence that the same results would be obtained for other people and in other situations.

External Validity: Generalizing the Results In addition to guarding internal validity, researchers are concerned about **external validity**, the extent to which the results obtained under one set of circumstances would also occur in a different set of circumstances (Berkowitz & Donnerstein, 1982). When an experiment has external validity, its findings can be assumed to generalize to other people and to other situations. As we will see, both the subjects who participate and the setting in which the experiment takes place have an impact on external validity.

representative sample A sample that reflects the characteristics of the population of interest.

Because social psychologists often seek to establish universal principles of human behavior, their ideal sample of subjects should be representative of all human beings all over the world. Such an all-inclusive **representative sample** has never been seen and probably never will be. Representative samples of more limited populations do exist. For example, samples representative of all registered voters in the United States are often used in surveys examining political preferences and opinions. Using sophisticated sampling methods, such surveys can provide a reasonably accurate snapshot of this population during a specific period of time (Fowler, 1993).

convenience sample A sample selected because subjects are readily available to the researcher.

But social psychologists rarely study representative samples. Usually, they rely on a **convenience sample** drawn from a population that is readily available to the researcher, which accounts for why so much of social psychological research is conducted on college students. The common practice of using convenience samples in social psychological research poses a crucial question: Is it possible to

A representative sample includes individuals who possess the characteristics of the population that is being studied. Suppose we're interested in the people who attended this football game. A representative sample drawn from this population would be much smaller in number (making it possible for us to interview them), but have a similar composition in terms of basic demographic factors such as gender, race, ethnicity, age, and occupation.

establish universal principles of human behavior with research on nonrepresentative samples?

Those who favor the use of convenience samples point to some very real practical issues. Representative samples are fine for surveys requiring short answers to a short list of questions. But what about complex, time-consuming experiments like Leonard's? The expense of bringing subjects from a large geographic area into his lab would be staggering. And various extraneous variables (travel fatigue, disruptions in one's regular routine) could distort the results. Advocates of convenience samples also contend that there is no contradiction between universal principles and particular subjects. Indeed, the more basic the principle, the less it matters who participates in the research.

However, the drawbacks to convenience samples are clear. Strictly speaking, the results of Leonard's research can be generalized only to young adult males who currently drink alcohol, attend a specific university, and are willing to participate in a psychology experiment in order to earn some money. Presumably, Leonard wants to generalize his results much more broadly, but our confidence in the external validity of any study that uses a convenience sample is necessarily reduced. Reacting against the prevalence of convenience samples in social psychology, David Sears (1986) offered a spirited argument for the many advantages of including subjects from a variety of backgrounds and life experiences. Have social psychologists taken Sears's advice to heart? Partly. As noted earlier in this chapter, social psychological research is now conducted in many countries, ensuring the participation of subjects from different societies.

But what about research on racial and ethnic minorities living in the United States? Here, the record is much less encouraging. To determine the percentage of research articles on African Americans that appeared in six leading journals published by the American Psychological Association during 1970 to 1989, Sandra Graham (1992) selected articles that met two criteria: (1) African Americans were included as subjects, *and* (2) African Americans were the population of interest or the results were analyzed by race.

The findings from this analysis are displayed in Table 1.3. In all the journals surveyed, the percentage of articles on African Americans declined from the earliest time period (1970–1974) to the most recent one (1985–1989). The *Journal of Personality and Social Psychology,* the only social psychology journal in the study, consistently had the lowest percentage among the six journals. Graham's research provides only a partial view of the bigger picture: Other minority groups were not studied, nor were other psychology journals. Even so, these data establish an important goal for all of psychology and, especially, for the branch of psychology that has a strong tradition of research on such topics as stereotypes, prejudice, social norms, and intergroup conflict. To become a better science, social psychology must become more inclusive.

External validity is also affected by the place where research is conducted. Since field research occurs in real-life natural settings rather than in the artificial arrangements of a laboratory, aren't its results more generalizable to actual behavior? The answer depends on where you stand on the issue of mundane versus experimental realism (Aronson & Carlsmith, 1968). **Mundane realism** refers to the extent to which the research setting resembles the real-world setting of interest. Theodore Newcomb's (1961) research, in which he set up an entire college dormitory in order to study interpersonal attraction, is a striking example of mundane realism. Advocates of mundane realism contend that if research procedures are more realistic, research findings are more likely to reveal what really goes on.

mundane realism The degree to which the experimental situation resembles places and events that exist in the real world.

Table 1.3 Percentage of Research Articles on African Americans

Journal	1970–1974	1985–1989	Total: 1970–1989
Journal of Counseling Psychology	5.8%	5.3%	4.7%
Journal of Educational Psychology	8.1%	3.7%	6.1%
Journal of Applied Psychology	5.3%	2.3%	4.3%
Developmental Psychology	8.0%	2.6%	4.6%
Journal of Consulting and Clinical Psychology	3.1%	2.0%	3.1%
Journal of Personality and Social Psychology	3.1%	.3%	1.6%

As you can see, the percentage of research articles on African Americans included in these journals published by the American Psychological Association declined from the earliest period surveyed (1970–1974) to the most recent one (1985–1989). Across the entire period (1970–1989), the only social psychological journal examined (the *Journal of Personality and Social Psychology*) had the lowest percentage of such articles. These findings indicate that social psychology needs to become more inclusive in the subjects that it studies. (Adapted from Graham, 1992.)

experimental realism The degree to which experimental procedures are involving to subjects and lead them to behave naturally and spontaneously.

In contrast, **experimental realism** refers to the degree to which the experimental setting and procedures are real and involving *to the subject,* regardless of whether they resemble real life or not. Leonard's research on alcohol and aggression was a far cry from the bars and sporting events where this volatile mixture often occurs. But extensive research conducted with similar procedures indicates that this experimental scenario is highly involving for subjects. If their experiences are real to them, say those who favor experimental realism, subjects' behavior in the lab will be as natural and spontaneous as it would be in the real world.

deception Research methods that provide false information to subjects.

Like many researchers who strive to create a highly involving experience for subjects, Leonard had to rely on **deception,** providing subjects with false information about experimental procedures. In Leonard's study, the supposed opponent didn't actually exist. Sometimes, however, social psychologists employ *confederates,* who act as though they are subjects in the experiment but are really working for the experimenter. Deception not only strengthens experimental realism, it also allows the experimenter to manufacture situations in the laboratory that would be difficult to observe in a natural setting; to study potentially harmful behaviors, such as aggression, in a regulated, safe manner; and to assess people's spontaneous reactions rather than socially acceptable presentations. But the use of deception creates some serious ethical concerns, which we examine later in this chapter.

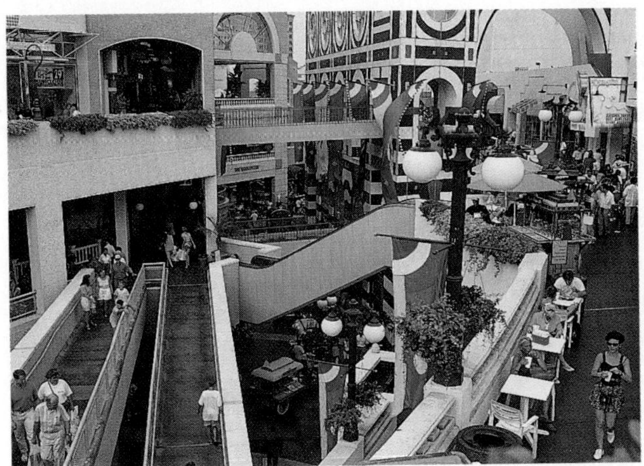

Mundane realism, the degree to which the research setting resembles the real world, is maximized in field research. For example, we could study actual littering behavior in the shopping mall pictured above. But experimental realism, the degree to which procedures are real and involving to the subject, can be very high in laboratory research. The participants in the mock trial seen in the photo on the right take their roles very seriously.

Measure for Measure

Having designed a study and checked it over for internal and external validity, the researcher must now select the measures to be used. In this section, we consider two types of measures: self-reports and observations. Then we describe how findings from different studies can be combined.

Self-Reports: Going Straight to the Source Collecting *self-reports*—in which subjects disclose their thoughts, feelings, desires, and actions—is a widely used measurement technique in sound psychology. One popular self-report measure, the Rosenberg Self-Esteem Scale, is presented in Table 1.4.

Self-reports give the researcher direct access to an individual's beliefs and perceptions. But self-reports are not always accurate and can be misleading. For example, the desire to look good to ourselves and others can influence how we respond. As Shakespeare put it in the play from which we took the title of this section, "It oft falls out, to have what we would have, we speak not what we mean." According to research on the "bogus pipeline," subjects who are led to believe that their responses will be verified by an infallible lie-detector report facts more accurately and endorse socially *un*acceptable opinions more frequently than those not told about such a device (Aguinis et al., 1993; Roese & Jamieson, 1993). The bogus pipeline is, in fact, bogus; no such infallible device exists. But belief in its powers enhances truth-telling.

Self-reports are also affected by the way in which questions are asked. Differences in wording can sometimes produce very different responses. Here are a few examples:

1. *The structure of the question* In a Roper poll, adult Americans were asked, "Does it seem possible or does it seem impossible to you that the Nazi extermination of the Jews never happened?" One in three respondents indicated it was possible that the Holocaust never occurred. However, when Katherine Moschandreas (1993) posed a more direct question—"Do you believe that the Holocaust happened?"—only one in ten of her sample expressed doubt or disbelief.

2. *The political correctness of the topic.* In a telephone poll of adult Americans conducted by *Time* magazine, 53 percent said that the government is spending too much money "on welfare." But only 23 percent said the government is spending too much money "on assistance to the poor."

Table 1.4 The Rosenberg Self-Esteem Scale

Indicate whether you *strongly agree, agree, disagree,* or *strongly disagree* with each of these statements.

1. I feel that I'm a person of worth, at least on an equal plane with others.
2. On the whole, I am satisfied with myself.
3. I wish I could have more respect for myself.
4. I certainly feel useless at times.
5. At times I think I am no good at all.
6. I feel that I have a number of good qualities.
7. All in all, I am inclined to feel that I am a failure.
8. I am able to do things as well as most other people.
9. I feel that I do not have much to be proud of.
10. I take a positive attitude toward myself.

To score responses on this scale, score items 1, 2, 6, 8, and 10 in a positive direction (*strongly agree* = 4, etc.), and items 3, 4, 5, 7, and 9 in a reversed direction (*strongly agree* = 1, etc.). The highest possible score is 40; the lowest possible is 10. Higher scores indicate higher self-esteem.

Self-reports are a widely used measurement technique in social psychology. The Rosenberg Self-Esteem Scale measures an individual's perception of his or her self-worth. (Rosenberg, 1965)

3. *The available response alternatives.* When German adults were asked how many hours a day they watched TV, only 16.2 percent said they watched more than 2.5 hours per day when "more than 2.5 hours" was the *maximum* possible response. But when "up to 2.5 hours" was the *minimum* response alternative, 37.5 percent reported they watched TV for more than 2.5 hours (Schwarz et al., 1985). These results are displayed in Table 1.5.

Sensitive to possible inaccuracies in self-reports, psychologists have developed ways to reduce the time that elapses between an actual experience and the person's report of it. Fresher, it is assumed, is better. Three variations on this theme have been identified (Wheeler & Miyake, 1992):

1. *Interval-contingent.* Respondents report their experiences at regular intervals, usually once a day. They may report events since the last report, or how they feel at the moment, or both. Though less intrusive than the two other methods discussed below, interval-contingent reporting can be disruptive and unpleasant for some subjects (Affleck et al., 1994).

2. *Signal-contingent.* Respondents report their experiences as soon as possible after being signaled to do so, usually by means of a radio-controlled beeper or a preprogrammed wrist terminal (Marco & Suls, 1993). This approach, called the experience sampling method (Larsen & Csikszentmihalyi, 1983), permits the collection of reports several times daily and minimizes the problems of relying on memories of what happened. The major drawbacks to using the experience sampling method include its intrusive interruption of normal activities and the possi-

Table 1.5 How Many Hours of TV Did They Watch?

Maximum = "More than 2.5 hours"	Percentage	
Up to 0.5 hour	7.4	
0.5 to 1 hour	17.7	
1 hour to 1.5 hours	26.5	
1.5 hours to 2 hours	14.7	
2 hours to 2.5 hours	17.7	
More than 2.5 hours	**16.2**	
Minimum = "Up to 2.5 hours"	**Percentage**	
Up to 2.5 hours	62.5	
2.5 hours to 3 hours	23.4	
3 hours to 3.5 hours	7.8	
3.5 hours to 4 hours	4.7	37.5
4 hours to 4.5 hours	1.6	
More than 4.5 hours	0	

Depending on which scale was presented to them, only a small number (16.2 percent) or a much larger one (37.5 percent) of the German adults in this survey said they watched more than 2.5 hours of TV each day. Changing the response alternatives given to respondents can change their self-reports. (Adapted from Schwarz et al., 1985.)

bility that it may miss thoughts or events that are very important but occur only rarely.

3. *Event-contingent.* Respondents report on a designated set of events as soon as possible after such events have occurred. For example, the Rochester Interaction Record (RIR) is an event-contingent, self-report questionnaire used by subjects to record every social interaction lasting ten minutes or more that occurs during the course of the study, usually a week or two (Nezlek, 1993; Reis & Wheeler, 1991). The RIR includes measures of quantitative variables (such as length of the interaction and the number of other people present) as well as qualitative variables (such as intimacy, satisfaction, and social influence). Event-contingent methods are less intrusive than beeper prompts and obtain more immediate information than do interval-contingent approaches.

Whatever their differences, most self-report methods require subjects to provide specific answers to specific questions. In contrast, *narrative studies* collect lengthy responses on a general topic. Narrative materials can be generated by subjects at the researcher's request or taken from other sources (such as diaries, letters, speeches, press conferences, and books). These accounts are then analyzed in terms of a coding scheme developed by the researcher. Although narrative studies are conducted on a wide range of topics, they are perhaps most common in research on political behavior (Tetlock et al., 1994) and close relationships (Baumeister & Wotman, 1992; Harvey et al., 1992).

Mark Twain wrote this love letter to Olivia Langdon, his future wife, on May 12,1869. Narrative studies code such material in terms of categories relevant to the psychological process being researched.

Out of the depths of my happy heart wells a great tide of love & prayer for this priceless treasure that is confided to my life-long keeping.

You cannot see its intangible waves as they flow toward you, darling,

But in these lines you will hear, as it were, the distant beating of its surf.

Observations: Looking On However they are obtained, self-reports are not the only available window on human behavior. Researchers can also observe people's actions (Weick, 1985). Sometimes these observations are very simple, as when a researcher notes which of two items a person selects. At other times, however, the observations are more elaborate and (like the coding of narrative accounts) require that interrater reliability be established. **Interrater reliability** refers to the level of agreement among multiple observers of the same behavior. Only when different observers agree can the data be trusted. For example, in the Dyadic Interaction Paradigm developed by William Ickes and his colleagues (1990), the interaction between two strangers meeting for the first time is videotaped. Two independent observers then work from the videotapes to assess such behaviors as

interrater reliability The degree to which different observers agree on their observations.

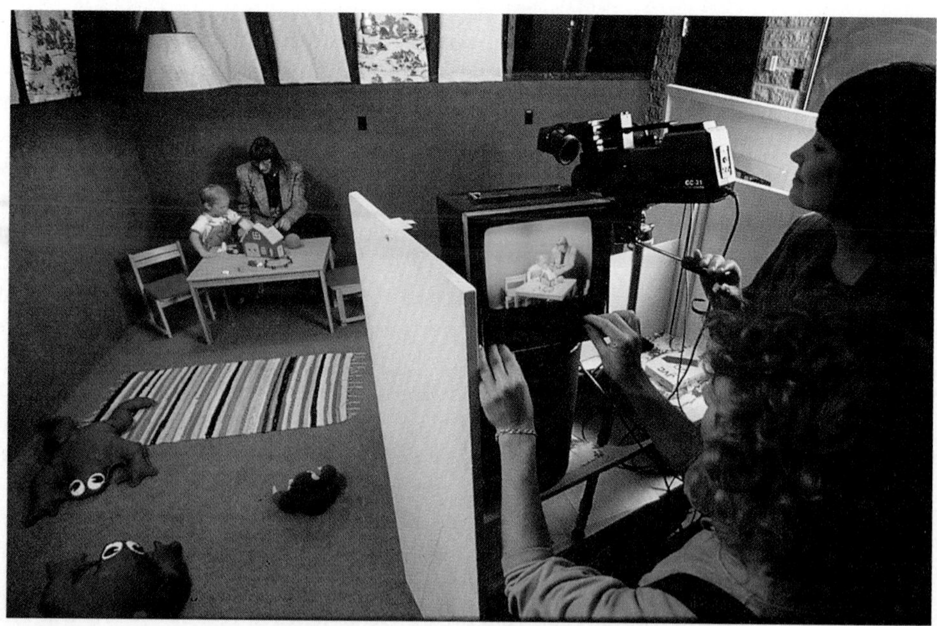

Observational methods provide a useful alternative to self-reports. For example, studies of young children, whose verbal skills are limited, often rely on observations.

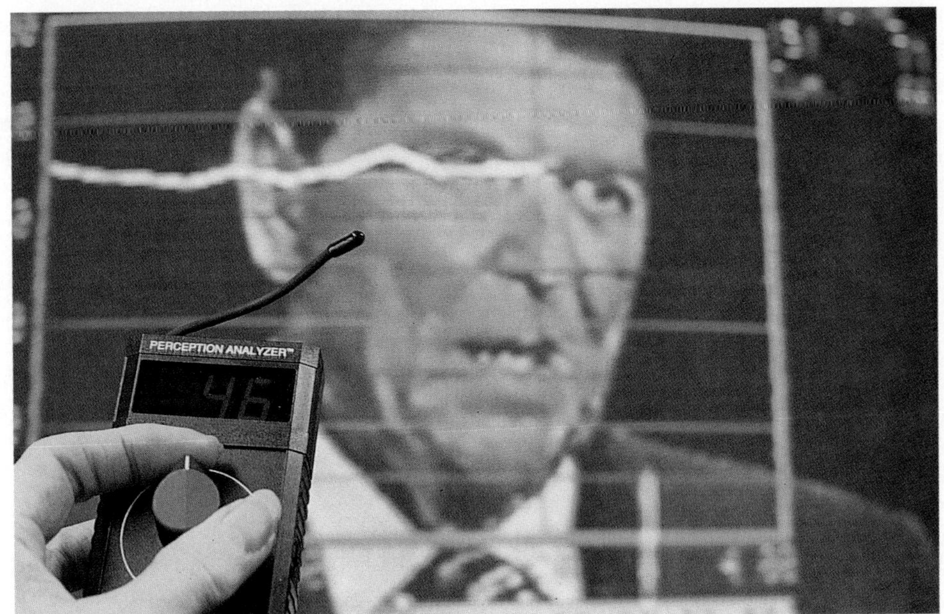

Computerized video technology, such as this Perception Analyzer™, allows researchers to track subjects' moment-by-moment reactions to events on the screen (in this case a presidential debate). It can also simultaneously display the average ratings of groups of subjects in a graph superimposed over the video. This technology can help researchers study the dynamics of social influence.

interpersonal distance, body posture, looking at each other, and smiling. The extent to which the two observers agree on each behavior determines the degree of interrater reliability.

Machines, too, can do the watching. Physiological responses are tracked by various kinds of equipment, the most well known of which is the electrocardiogram, which measures heart rate (Blascovich & Kelsey, 1990; Cacioppo & Tassinary, 1990). The speed of a response to a stimulus (called *response latency*) is recorded by a computer (Fazio, 1990). Indeed, throughout social psychology, much of what used to be done by human voice or hand—instructions given, materials presented, measures taken—is now computerized.

The advantage of observational methods is that they avoid our sometimes faulty recollections and distorted interpretations of our own behavior. Actions can speak louder than words. But if individuals know they are being observed, observational methods are as vulnerable as self-reports to people's desire to present themselves in a favorable light.

Archival research is another method of tracing the patterns of human behavior. In archival research, records of previous behavior (such as sports statistics, divorce decrees, and crime rates) are studied, not ongoing actions. For instance, one way to examine whether individuals in established relationships tend to have similar levels of physical attractiveness is to inspect wedding pictures published in the newspaper. Archival records such as these are *unobtrusive measures* that do not produce the self-protective maneuvers sometimes engaged in by individuals who know they are being studied (Webb et al., 1981).

Literature Review: Putting It All Together Like all sciences, social psychology depends on cumulative knowledge. Each study makes a contribution, but no single finding can close a case. Results obtained in different studies must be summarized and, if possible, integrated. The kind of summary found in textbooks like this one is known as a *narrative review:* The authors read the relevant literature and use their own best judgment about how to put it all together.

In the past, narrative reviews also attempted to declare winners and losers by adding up the "hits" (confirmations) and "misses" (disconfirmations) among studies testing a specific hypothesis. Narrative reviews are no longer used for this purpose. Instead, psychologists apply a set of statistical procedures called *meta-analysis* to combine the quantitative results from multiple studies (Rosenthal, 1991). Compared with a narrative review, meta-analysis provides a more reliable and precise conclusion about whether there is adequate support for a hypothesis (Miller & Cooper, 1991; Schmidt, 1992). In addition, meta-analysis examines possible reasons why the size of an effect varies among different studies. Many of the literature reviews cited in this text are based on meta-analyses.

ETHICS AND VALUES IN SOCIAL PSYCHOLOGY

Regardless of where research is conducted (in the lab or in the field), what kind of method is used (correlational or experimental), or what kind of measures are employed (self-reports or observations), ethical issues must always be considered. Researchers in all fields have a moral and legal responsibility to abide by ethical principles. In social psychology, the use of deception caused particular concern (Baumrind, 1985; Kelman, 1967), and several studies provoked fierce debate about whether they went beyond the bounds of ethical acceptability. Each of these studies addressed a disturbing topic:

- Would people obey orders to harm an innocent person?
- Would people assigned to a role that permitted brutal behavior toward others begin to act brutally?
- Could some flimsy reference to "authority" and a promise of "immunity" induce people to break the law?

No one, then or now, disputes the importance of these questions. What has been debated, however, is whether the significance of the research topic justified exposing subjects to possibly harmful psychological consequences. Table 1.6 summarizes each of these studies and the debate about their ethicality. Under today's provisions for the protection of human subjects, probably none of these studies could be conducted in its original form. In the following sections, we describe current policies and procedures as well as continuing concerns.

Institutional Review Boards: The Ethical Watchdogs

In 1974, the agency then called the United States Department of Health, Education, and Welfare established regulations for the protection of human subjects. These regulations created institutional review boards (IRBs) at all institutions seeking federal funding for research involving human subjects (McCarthy, 1981). Charged with the responsibility for reviewing research proposals to ensure that the welfare of subjects was adequately protected, IRBs were to be the "watchdogs" of research.

Although researchers have become accustomed to submitting their proposals to IRBs, questions persist about the appropriate role of these boards. For example, should IRBs act as censors? Few, if any, researchers or board members would endorse such a practice. But an experiment by Stephen Ceci and his colleagues (1985) found that university IRBs were more likely to approve politically neutral

Table 1.6 Some Controversial Studies in Social Psychology

	Milgram's Research on Obedience (Milgram, 1963, 1974)	**Zimbardo's Prison Simulation (Zimbardo et al., 1973)**	**The "Ubiquitous Watergate" Study (West et al., 1975)**
Description	Subjects were instructed to continue delivering electric shocks to a protesting individual as part of a supposed learning study (see Chap. 9).	Under very realistic circumstances, undergraduates were assigned to play the role of a prisoner or a prison guard (see Chap. 12).	Experimenters approached people in a public place and asked them to engage in illegal activities. Some were informed that these activities were sanctioned by authorities, who would protect them from prosecution.
Topic	How far will people go when they are told to obey?	How much influence do social roles exert on behavior?	Will people agree to break the law when told that they will not be held responsible for their actions?
Implications	Can this research help us understand how terrible events, such as the Holocaust of the Jews in World War II, take place in human society?	Can this research help us understand how people in certain societal roles can behave brutally toward others?	Can this research help us understand how people can be induced to break the law when they believe they can get away with it?
Potential Harm	Anxiety experienced during the study as subjects confronted difficult decisions and unusual circumstances; guilt and lowered self-esteem after the study for those who behaved in ways that were discrepant with their moral principles and views of themselves; anger at the researchers for having caused their anxiety and undesirable behavior.		
Sources for Further Reading	Initial critique by Baumrind (1964); initial reply by Milgram (1964); summary by Miller (1986).	Critique by Savin (1973a, 1973b); reply by Zimbardo (1973).	Commentary by Cook (1975).

Several controversial studies provoked concern about research ethics in social psychology. The three studies described here addressed issues crucial to society but created debate about whether the importance of the topics justified exposing subjects to the possibility of being harmed by research procedures.

proposals than socially sensitive ones having implications for societal groups or policies. Socially sensitive topics often raise serious ethical questions that require careful scrutiny by investigators and IRBs (Sieber & Stanley, 1988). Properly conducted, however, socially sensitive research can offer vital information needed to address major societal issues (Melton et al., 1988; Scarr, 1988).

Another question about the role of IRBs asks whether they should review the scientific merits of research proposals in addition to their ethical quality. It appears that at least some IRBs have expanded their responsibilities in this way

(Rosnow et al., 1993), a development on which researchers hold very different opinions.

Robert Rosenthal (1994) believes that IRBs should evaluate scientific merit. Poor-quality research, he says, wastes time and money that could be spent in more productive endeavors, and the ill-founded conclusions of such research could be damaging to society. Since ethics and scientific merit are inextricably intertwined, IRBs should consider both. Not so, responds David Sears (1994), "Not everything is a moral or ethical issue" (p. 237). Judgments of scientific competence are, and should be, separate from judgments of ethical quality. A scientifically superb study can be an ethical disaster, and vice versa. Besides, Sears contends, IRBs do not have the time, expertise, or information necessary to make an informed evaluation of scientific merit. With the voices of two such highly regarded psychologists raised loud and clear, we can expect this controversy to continue.

Informed Consent: Do You (Really) Want to Participate?

Besides submitting their research to government-mandated IRBs, researchers must also abide by their profession's code of ethics. The American Psychological Association's (APA) statement of ethics, *Ethical Principles of Psychologists* (1992), considers a wide range of ethical issues, including those related to research procedures and practices. The APA code stipulates that researchers are obligated to guard the rights and welfare of all those who participate in their studies.

informed consent An individual's deliberate, voluntary decision to participate in research, based on the researcher's description of what will be required during such participation.

One such obligation is to obtain **informed consent.** Individuals must be asked whether they wish to participate in the research project and must be given enough information to make an informed decision. Deceiving research participants about "significant aspects that would affect their willingness to participate, such as physical risks, discomfort, or unpleasant emotional experiences" is explicitly not permitted, although withholding less vital information is presumably allowed. The APA code also recognizes that research "involving only anonymous questionnaires, naturalistic observations, or certain kinds of archival research" may not require informed consent.

In principle, informed consent is absolutely essential for the protection of human subjects. Only if you know what you would be getting into can you decide whether you want to get involved. In practice, however, it can be difficult to ensure that consent is, in fact, informed. In the wake of concerns that patients participating in psychiatric research may have been inadequately informed, the head of one research center said he had distributed an "eight-page, single-spaced" consent form to the university's Human Subjects Protection Committee (Willwerth, 1994). The more information, the better--right? Not necessarily. A study by Traci Mann (1994) found that, at least for some subjects and some research procedures, a shorter, less detailed informed consent form was understood better than a longer, more detailed one. To make the practice of obtaining informed consent as effective as the principle says it should be, we will need more research on how best to communicate this information.

Debriefing: Telling All

Have you ever participated in psychological research? If so, what was your reaction to this experience? Have you ever been deceived about the hypothesis or procedures of a study in which you were a subject? If so, how did you feel about it? Most research on subjects' reactions indicates that they have positive attitudes about their participation, even when they were deceived about some aspects of a study (Christensen, 1988). Indeed, deceived subjects sometimes have expressed *more* favorable opinions than those who have not been deceived (Smith & Richardson, 1983). In a more recent survey, however, the two groups did not differ in their attitudes toward research or in their perceptions of the trustworthiness of others (Sharpe et al., 1992).

These findings are reassuring, but they do not remove the obligation of researchers to use deception only when nondeceptive alternatives are not feasible. In addition, whenever deception has been used there is a special urgency to the requirement that, once the data have been collected, researchers fully inform their subjects about the nature of the research in which they have participated. This process of disclosure is called **debriefing**. During a debriefing, the researcher goes over all procedures, explaining exactly what happened and why. Deceptions are revealed, the purpose of the research is discussed, and the researcher makes every effort to help the subject feel good about having participated. A skillful debriefing takes time and requires close attention to the individual subject (Aronson et al., 1985; Mills, 1976; Ross et al., 1975).

debriefing A disclosure, made to subjects after research procedures are completed, in which the researcher explains the purpose of the research, attempts to resolve any negative feelings, and emphasizes the scientific contribution made by subjects' participation.

But does it work? Does debriefing *dehoax* the subject, clearing up deceptions and getting the facts straight? Does debriefing *desensitize* the subject, removing any and all distress caused by experimental procedures? From his review of research on debriefing, David Holmes (1976a, 1976b) concluded that if done with "care, effort, and vigilance," debriefing can be effective in both getting the facts

Social psychology experiments don't reach this level of deception, nor are subjects likely to be so startled by the debriefing! But whenever subjects are deceived about research procedures or purposes, it is especially important to provide a full and thorough debriefing.

straight and removing distress. Not everyone agrees. Some question the success of debriefing in establishing the true facts (Greenberg & Folger, 1988). And college students are concerned that subjects may be reluctant to express feelings of embarrassment during debriefing and, therefore, continue to feel uncomfortable afterwards (Fisher & Fyrberg, 1994). Since both the facts and the feelings are important, researchers must always seek ways to improve the effectiveness of the debriefing process.

Values and Science: Points of View

Ethical principles are based on moral values, which set standards for and impose limits on the conduct of research just as they do on personal behavior. When the potential benefits of research for humankind are high and the potential costs are ethically acceptable, there is a moral imperative to try to carry out the research. But when the human costs are too high in terms of the suffering of participants, the moral imperative is to refrain.

Ethical issues are an appropriate focus for moral values in science, but do values affect science in other ways as well? As we have seen, Rosenthal and Sears disagree about whether incompetent science is, by definition, also ethically flawed and, by implication, morally wrong. More typically, however, the debate about the relationship between science and values concentrates on scientific objectivity. Consider this statement by Senator Orrin Hatch: "We in Congress look to social science to provide us unbiased and objective information" (1982, p. 1036). Is this possible for social psychology or any other social science? Is it desirable?

If what the senator has in mind is a *totally* unbiased, value-free science, the odds for meeting this goal are not good. For example, when Timothy Wilson and his colleagues (1993) found that scientists evaluated studies on important topics more favorably than methodologically identical studies on unimportant topics, they concluded, "Our infatuation with the importance of the topic of a study can make us overlook its imperfections" (p. 325).

In his presidential address to the National Council on Family Relations, Brent Miller (1993) cited his own increasing awareness of the role of values: "In the early 1980s I considered adolescent pregnancy as an area of research that I could approach as an objective social scientist. Since then I have come to realize how naive I was and that even the definitions of the problems, let alone their potential solutions, are absolutely riddled with values—those deeply held beliefs about right and wrong" (p. 12).

And, after describing how investigators have emphasized individual rather than societal factors in substance abuse, Keith Humphreys and Julian Rappaport (1993) commented that, "Researchers are just doing what they often unwittingly do—perpetuating the status quo by being uncritical about the problems that are handed to them by powerful others" (p. 897). David Kipnis (1994) made a similar point in his explanation for why social psychologists conduct so much research on social influence: "For the most part, research applications that validate the existing social order are [financially] supported" (p. 169).

Infatuated by important topics, wrestling with beliefs about right and wrong, under the thumb of those who control funding for research—this all seems a long way from "unbiased and objective." Such a long way that perhaps the search for objectivity is only a self-serving illusion. Perhaps the more forthright approach is to adopt a psychology of political advocacy: "championing causes that one believes good for the culture; . . . condemning movements or policies that seem inimical to human welfare" (Gergen, 1994, p. 415).

But there is another view. From this perspective, science can never be completely unbiased and objective because it is a human enterprise. Scientists choose what to study and how to study it; their choices are affected by personal values as well as by professional rewards. To acknowledge these influences, however, is not to embrace them. Quite the contrary. Such influences are precisely why the scientific method is so important.

As Stanley Parkinson (1994) puts it, "Scientists are not necessarily more objective than other people; rather, they use methods that have been developed to minimize self-deception" (p. 137). Objectivity in science, says Stephen Jay Gould (1994), "is the willingness (even the eagerness in truly honorable practitioners) to abandon a favored notion when testable evidence disconfirms key expectations . . . " (p. 26). By scrutinizing their own behavior and adopting the rigors of the scientific method, scientists attempt to free themselves of their preconceptions and, thereby, to see reality more clearly, even if never perfectly.

You've read what others have said about values and science. But what do you think about all this? How *do* values influence science? How *should* values affect scientific inquiry?

Your introduction to the field of social psychology is now complete. You have gone step by step through a definition of social psychology, a review of its history and research methods, and a consideration of ethics and values. As you study the material presented in the coming chapters, the two of us who wrote this book invite you to share our enthusiasm. You can look forward to information that overturns common-sense assumptions, to lively debate and heated controversy, and to a better understanding of yourself and other people. Welcome to the world according to social psychology. We hope you enjoy it!

REVIEW

SOCIAL PSYCHOLOGY: GETTING TO KNOW IT

What Is Social Psychology?

- Social psychology is the scientific study of the way individuals think, feel, desire, and act in social situations.
- Like all sciences, social psychology relies on the systematic approach of the scientific method.
- Distinctive characteristics of social psychology include a broad perspective, a focus on the individual, and the frequent use of experiments.
- Seeking to formulate general principles of social behavior, social psychologists examine the effects of nonsocial as well as social factors.

From Past to Present

- Early research by Triplett and Ringelmann established an enduring topic in social psychology: how the presence of others affects an individual's performance.
- Sherif's work laid the foundation for later studies of social influence, and the legacy of Kurt Lewin is still evident throughout much of social psychology.
- After World War II, social psychology prospered and major contributors developed systematic programs of research.
- In the 1960s and early 1970s, there was intense concern about the ethics of research procedures, the validity of research results, and the generalization of conclusions based on research.

- Today's social psychology is pluralistic in its research methods, its views of human behavior, and its increasing efforts to develop an international and multicultural perspective.

AN OVERVIEW OF RESEARCH METHODS IN SOCIAL PSYCHOLOGY

Hypotheses and Theories

- A theory brings many hypotheses together and creates new ones.
- Theories in social psychology are specific rather than comprehensive and generate research by both supporters and opponents.
- The goal of basic research is to increase understanding of human behavior.
- The goal of applied research is to increase understanding of real-world events and contribute to the solution of social problems.

Correlations: Looking for Associations

- A correlation indicates a positive or negative association between two variables.
- A correlation cannot demonstrate causation.

Experiments: Looking for Cause and Effect

- Experiments require (1) control by the experimenter over events in the experiment and (2) random assignment of subjects to conditions.
- An experiment examines the effects of the independent variables on the dependent variables.
- Results that are statistically significant could have occurred by chance only 5 or fewer times out of 100.
- In a main effect, the levels of a single independent variable produce differences in the dependent variable. In an interaction, two (or more) independent variables jointly affect the dependent variable.

Evaluating Research

- Internal and external validity address the nature of research results.
- Experimental findings have internal validity to the extent that changes in the dependent variable can be attributed to the independent variable.
- Control groups strengthen internal validity; experimenter expectancy effects weaken it.
- Research results have external validity to the extent that they can be generalized to other people and other situations.
- A representative sample strengthens external validity; a convenience sample weakens it.
- Mundane and experimental realism refer to the nature of research procedures: The more realistic the procedures (real-world setting or highly involving lab study), the greater the external validity.
- Deception is sometimes used to increase experimental realism.

Measure for Measure

- Self-reports are the most popular measure of human behavior.
- Self-reports can be distorted by efforts to make a good impression and differences in the wording of a question can produce different responses.
- To increase accuracy, some approaches emphasize the need to collect self-reports as soon as possible after the actual experience.
- Narrative studies analyze the content of lengthy responses on a general topic.
- Observations can be made by human observers, collected by machines, or derived from existing archival records.
- Meta-analysis is used to integrate the quantitative results of different studies.

ETHICS AND VALUES IN SOCIAL PSYCHOLOGY

- Ethical issues are particularly important in social psychology because of the use of deception in some research.
- The publication of several controversial studies increased attention to ethical concerns.

Institutional Review Boards: The Ethical Watchdogs

- Established by the federal government, IRBs are responsible for reviewing research proposals to ensure that the welfare of subjects is adequately protected.
- Research indicates that IRBs may apply different standards to socially sensitive research than to politically neutral projects.
- The question of whether IRBs should review scientific merit as well as ethical quality elicits intense debate.

Informed Consent: Do You (Really) Want to Participate?

- The American Psychological Association's code of ethics requires psychologists to secure informed consent from research subjects.

- More research is needed to determine what kind of consent form will be most informative.

Debriefing: Telling All

- Most subjects have positive attitudes about their participation in research, even if they were deceived about some aspects of the study.
- Whenever deception has been used, a full debriefing is essential: disclosing all the facts and making sure the subject does not experience any distress.

Values and Science: Points of View

- By means of ethical principles, moral values set standards for and impose limits on the conduct of research.
- There are various views of the relation between values and science. What's your position?

KEY TERMS

social psychology, p. 6
interactionist perspective, p. 9
social cognition, p. 12
hypothesis, p. 13
theory, p. 14
basic research, p. 15
applied research, p. 15
correlation, p. 15
experiment, p. 17
independent variables, p. 19
dependent variables, p. 19
internal validity, p. 21
experimenter expectancy effects, p. 21
external validity, p. 22
representative sample, p. 22
convenience sample, p. 22
mundane realism, p. 23
experimental realism, p. 24
deception, p. 24
interrater reliability, p. 28
informed consent, p. 32
debriefing, p. 33

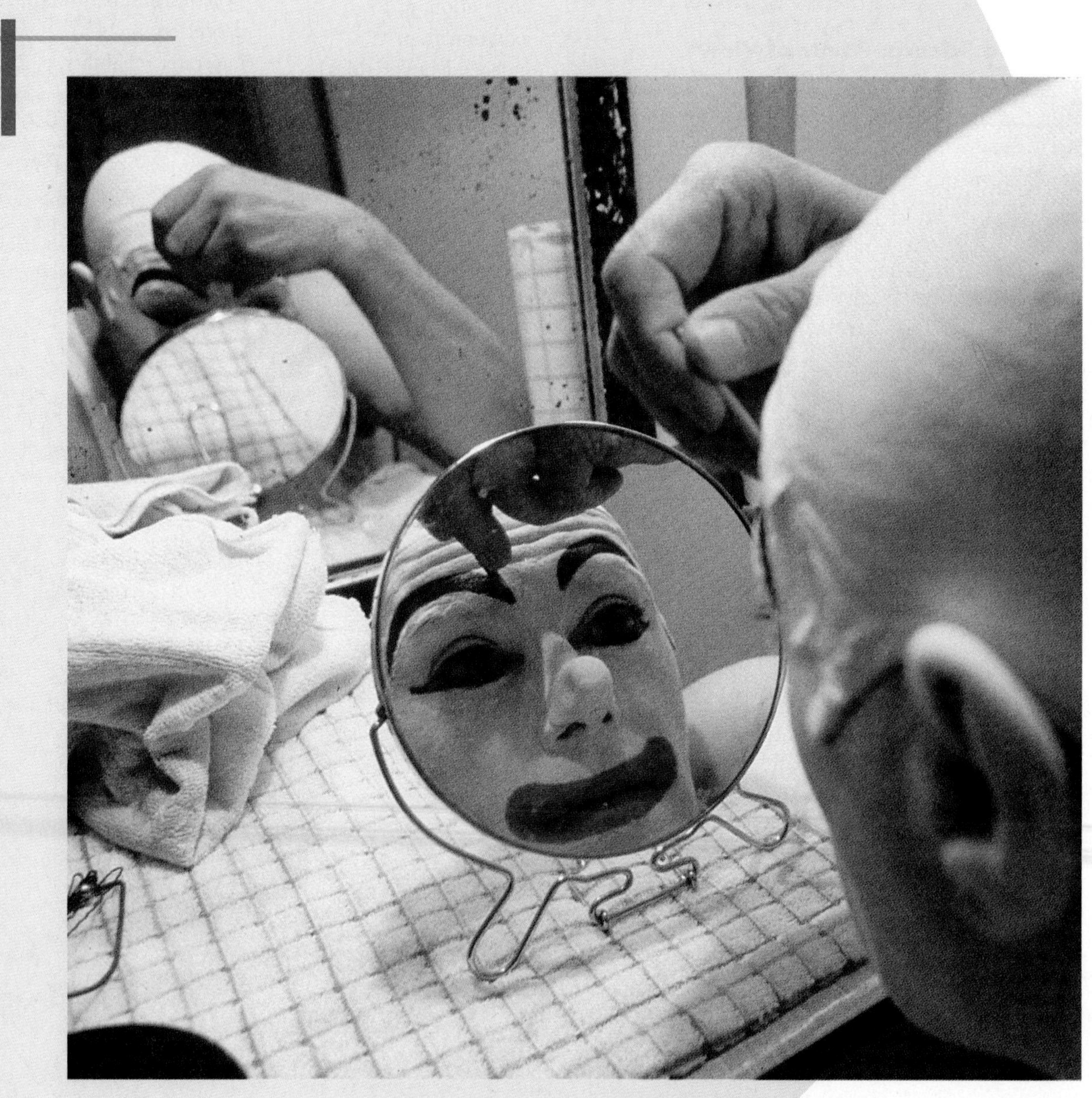

Chapter 2

The Social Self

PREVIEW

This chapter examines three interrelated aspects of the "social self." First, it considers the *self-concept* and the question of how people come to understand their own actions, emotions, and motivations. Second, it considers *self-esteem,* the affective component, and the question of how people evaluate themselves and defend against threats to their self-esteem. Third, it considers *self-presentation,* a behavioral manifestation of the self, and the question of how people present themselves to others. As we will see, the self is complex and multifaceted.

OUTLINE

Can you imagine living a meaningful or coherent life without a clear sense of who you are? In *The Man Who Mistook His Wife for a Hat,* neurologist Oliver Sacks (1985) described such a person—a patient named William Thompson. According to Sacks, Thompson suffered from an organic brain disorder that impairs a person's memory of recent events. Unable to recall anything for more than a few seconds, Thompson was always disoriented and lacked a sense of inner continuity. The effect on his behavior was startling. Trying to grasp a constantly vanishing identity, Thompson would construct one tale after another to account for who he was, where he was, and what he was doing. From one moment to the next, he would improvise new identities—a grocery store clerk, minister, or medical patient, to name just a few. In social settings, Thompson's behavior was especially intriguing. As Sacks (1985) observed,

> The presence of others, other people, excite and rattle him, force him into an endless, frenzied, social chatter, a veritable delirium of identity-making and -seeking; the presence of plants, a quiet garden, the nonhuman order, making no social demands upon him, allow this identity-delirium to relax, to subside. (p. 110)

Thompson's plight is unusual, but it highlights two important points—one about the private "inner" self, the other about the "outer" self we show to others. First, the capacity for self-reflection is necessary for people to feel as if they understand their own motives and emotions and the causes of their behavior. Unable to ponder his own actions, Thompson appeared vacant and without feeling—"de-souled," as Sacks put it. Second, the self is heavily influenced by social factors. Thompson himself seemed compelled to put on a face for others and to improvise characters for the company he kept. We all do, to some extent. We may not create a kaleidoscope of multiple identities as Thompson did, but the way we manage ourselves is influenced by the people around us.

This chapter examines the ABCs of the self: *affect, behavior,* and *cognition.* First, we ask a cognitive question: How do people come to know themselves, develop a self-concept, and maintain a stable sense of identity? Second, we explore an affective, or emotional, question: How do people evaluate themselves, enhance their self-images, and defend against threats to their self-esteem? Third, we confront a behavioral question: How do people present themselves to others and regulate their actions according to interpersonal demands? As we'll see, the self is a topic that in recent years has attracted unprecedented interest among social psychologists (Banaji & Prentice, 1994).

THE SELF-CONCEPT

Have you ever been at a noisy gathering and yet managed to hear someone at the other end of the room mention your name? If so, then you experienced the "cocktail party effect"—the ability to pick a personally relevant stimulus out of a complex environment (Moray, 1959; Wood & Cowan, 1995). To cognitive psychologists, this phenomenon shows that people are selective in their attention. To the social psychologist, it also shows that the self is an important object of our own attention.

Beginnings of the Self-Concept

When you stand in front of a mirror, what do you see? If you were a dog, a cat, or some other animal, you would not realize that the image you see is you, your own reflection. Except for human beings, only great apes—chimpanzees, gorillas, and orangutans—seem capable of self-recognition. How can we know what non-humans think about mirrors? In a series of studies, Gordon Gallup (1977) placed different species of animals in a room with a large mirror. At first, they greeted their images by vocalizing, gesturing, and making other social responses. After several days, the great apes—but not the other animals—began to use the mirror to pick food out of their teeth, groom themselves, blow bubbles, and make faces for their own entertainment. From all appearances, they recognized themselves.

In other studies, Gallup anesthetized the animals, painted an odorless red dye on their brows, and returned them to the mirror. Upon seeing the red spot, only the apes reached for their brows—proof that they perceived the image as their own. By using the same red dye test, developmental psychologists have found that most human infants begin to recognize themselves in the mirror between eighteen and twenty-four months of age (Lewis & Brooks-Gunn, 1979). Many researchers believe that self-recognition among great apes and humans is the first clear expression of the concept "me" (Povinelli et al., 1994).

self-concept The sum total of an individual's beliefs about his or her own personal attributes.

The ability to see yourself as a distinct entity is a necessary first step in the evolution and development of a **self-concept**, the sum total of beliefs you have about yourself. The second step involves social factors. Many years ago, sociologist Charles Horton Cooley (1902) used the term *looking-glass self* to suggest that other people serve as a mirror in which we see ourselves. Expanding on this idea, George Herbert Mead (1934) added that we often come to know ourselves by imagining what significant others think of us and then incorporating these perceptions into our self-concept. It is interesting that when Gallup tested his apes, those that had been raised in isolation—without exposure to peers—could not recognize themselves in the mirror. Only after such exposure did they begin

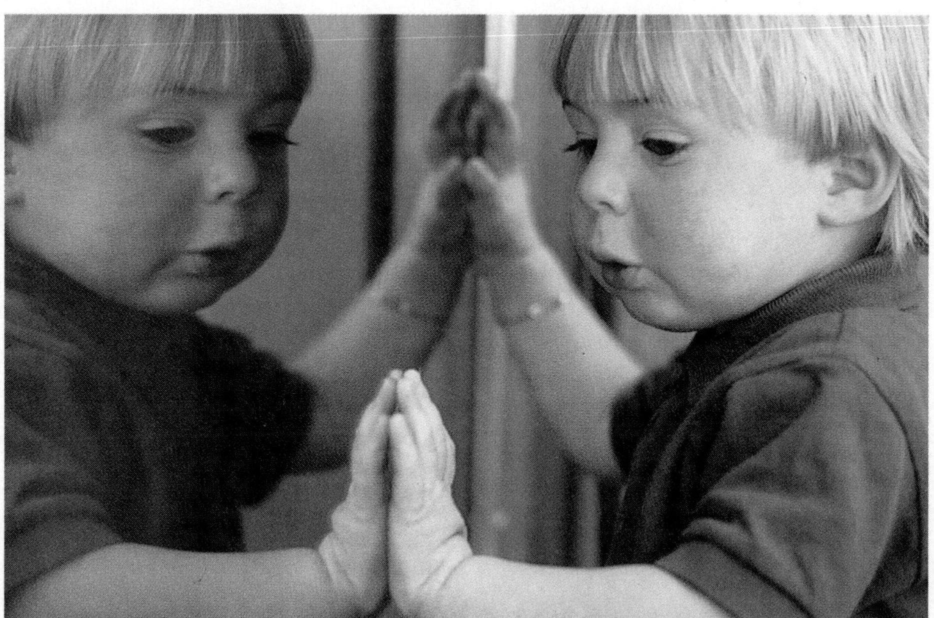

Infants begin to recognize themselves in the mirror between 18 and 24 months of age.

to show signs of self-recognition. Among human beings, our self-concepts match our *perceptions* of what others think of us, as Cooley and Mead would have predicted. But there's a hitch: what we think of ourselves often does not match what specific others *actually* think of us (Felson, 1989; Shrauger & Schoeneman, 1979; Kenny & DePaulo, 1993).

In recent years, social psychologists have broken new ground in their efforts to understand the social self. The key question is, Where do our self-concepts come from? In the coming pages, four sources are considered: introspection, perceptions of our own behavior, influences of other people, and autobiographical memory.

Introspection

Let's start at the beginning: How do people achieve insight into their own beliefs, attitudes, emotions, and motivations? Common sense makes this question seem ludicrous. After all, don't you know what you think because *you* think it? And don't you know how you feel because *you* feel it? Look through popular books on how to achieve self-insight, and you'll find both answers to be yes. Whether the prescribed technique is meditation, psychotherapy, religion, dream analysis, or hypnosis, the advice is basically the same: self-knowledge is derived from introspection, a looking inward at one's own thoughts and feelings.

If these how-to books are correct, it stands to reason that no one can know you as well as you know yourself. Indeed, for others to know you at all, they would need information about your inner states, not just about your behavior. Do you agree? Susan Andersen and Lee Ross (1984) interviewed college students and asked them to discuss various personal topics: relationships with family and friends, career goals, important decisions and conflicts, and past experiences. Before the interview, subjects were instructed to focus on their thoughts and feelings, their overt behavior, or a mixture of both. Afterward, subjects who had described their thoughts and feelings rated the interviews as more informative of themselves than did those who had focused only on their behavior. Independent observers—strangers to the speakers themselves—felt the same way.

People assume that to truly know someone you must have access to private, subjective experiences. But is this really the case? Although people place a good deal of faith in introspection, some social psychologists are not sure that this faith is justified. Several years ago, Richard Nisbett and Timothy Wilson (1977) found that research subjects often cannot accurately explain the causes or correlates of their own behavior. This observation has forced researchers to confront a thorny question: Does introspection improve the *accuracy* of self-knowledge?

Wilson (1985) says no. In fact, he contends that introspection can sometimes impair self-knowledge. In a series of studies, he found that the attitudes subjects reported having about different objects corresponded closely to their behavior toward those objects. The more subjects said they enjoyed a task, the more time they spent on it; the more attractive they found a scenic landscape, the more pleasure they revealed in their facial expressions; the happier they said they were with a current dating partner, the longer the relationship ultimately lasted. But after subjects had been told to analyze the reasons for how they felt, reported attitudes no longer corresponded to behavior.

Too much introspection can also impair various types of judgments. In one study, Wilson and Jonathan Schooler (1991) had subjects taste and rate five brands of strawberry jam. Those who were asked to list the reasons for their taste preferences agreed less with *Consumer Reports* experts than did those who made their ratings without analysis. In another study, Wilson and Suzanne LaFleur (1995) had college students make predictions about their relationship with a fellow student in the upcoming semester—predictions were later verified. Subjects who were told to write down the reasons before making the predictions were ultimately less accurate than those who made predictions without explicit analysis. Apparently, it is possible to think *too* much, only to get confused.

So, is introspection futile? Not necessarily. As Murray Millar and Abraham Tesser (1989) point out, people can reflect on their own behavior by listing either *reasons* or *feelings*. Whether this reflection provides valuable self-insight depends on whether the behavior in question is caused more by cognitive or affective factors, thoughts, or feelings. For behaviors that are cognitively driven, such as making investment decisions, listing reasons may well increase the accuracy of self-knowledge. But for behaviors that are affectively determined, such as romantic relationships, it may not. To determine why you like a certain puzzle, enjoy a work of art, or love another person, focusing on your feelings is more helpful than making a list of reasons.

The usefulness of introspection may also depend on the amount of time people have and the cognitive resources available for self-reflection. Gregory Hixon and William Swann (1993) asked people to rate themselves on various attributes (intelligence, athletic ability, physical attractiveness, social skills, and musical and artistic talent). Some subjects had to think simultaneously about another task, while others were free to concentrate only on the self-ratings. Each subject's responses were later compared to a friend's ratings of that subject on the same attributes. The result: The self-friend ratings were more highly correlated when subjects focused on the task than when they could not. According to Hixon and Swann, introspection can increase self-insight—provided we have enough time and cognitive resources.

Perceptions of Our Own Behavior

self-perception theory The theory that when internal cues are difficult to interpret, people gain self-insight by observing their own behavior.

Regardless of what we can learn from introspection, Daryl Bem (1972) believes people can learn about themselves the same way outside observers do—by watching their own behavior. Bem's **self-perception theory** is simple yet profound. To the extent that internal states are weak or difficult to interpret, people infer what they think or how they feel by observing their own behavior and the situation in which it takes place. Think about it. Have you ever listened to yourself argue with someone, only to realize with amazement how angry you were? Or have you ever devoured a sandwich in record time, only then to conclude that you must have been incredibly hungry? In each case, you made an inference about yourself by watching your own actions.

There are limits to self-perception, of course. According to Bem, people do not infer their own internal states from behavior that occurred in the presence of compelling situational pressures such as reward or punishment. If you argued or wolfed down a sandwich because you were paid to do so, you probably would *not* assume that you were angry or hungry. In other words, people learn about themselves through self-perception only when the situation alone seems insufficient to have caused their behavior.

A good deal of research supports self-perception theory. When people are gently coaxed into doing something, and when they are not otherwise certain about how they feel, they come to view themselves in ways that are consistent with the

As suggested by self-perception theory, we sometimes infer how we feel by observing our own behavior.

Drawing by Frascino; © 1991 The New Yorker Magazine, Inc.

"I don't sing because I am happy. I am happy because I sing."

behavior (Chaiken & Baldwin, 1981; Fazio, 1987; Schlenker & Trudeau, 1990). Thus, subjects induced to describe themselves in flattering terms scored higher on a later test of self-esteem than did those who were led to describe themselves more modestly (Jones et al., 1981; Rhodewalt & Agustsdottir, 1986). Similarly, subjects who were maneuvered by leading questions into describing themselves as introverted or extroverted came to define themselves as such later on, unless they were certain of this aspect of their personality (Fazio et al., 1981; Swann & Ely, 1984). British author E. M. Forster anticipated the theory well when he asked, "How can I tell what I think 'til I see what I say?"

Self-Perceptions of Emotion Draw the corners of your mouth back and up and tense your eye muscles. Okay, relax. Now raise your eyebrows, open your eyes wide, and let your mouth drop open slightly. Relax. Now pull your brows down and together and clench your teeth. Relax. If you followed these directions, you would have appeared to others to be feeling first happy, then fearful, and finally angry. The question is, How would you have appeared to yourself?

facial feedback hypothesis The hypothesis that changes in facial expression can lead to corresponding changes in emotion.

Social psychologists who study emotion have asked precisely that question. Viewed within the framework of self-perception theory, the **facial feedback hypothesis** states that changes in facial expression can lead to corresponding changes in the subjective experience of emotion. To test this hypothesis, James Laird (1974) told subjects that they were taking part in an experiment on activity of the facial muscles. After attaching electrodes to subjects' faces, he showed them a series of cartoons. Before each one, the subjects were instructed to contract certain facial muscles in ways that created either a smile or a frown. As

Laird predicted, subjects rated what they saw as funnier, and reported feeling happier, when they were smiling than when they were frowning. In follow-up research, subjects were similarly induced through posed expressions to experience fear, anger, sadness, and disgust (Duclos et al., 1989).

But why? With 80 muscles in the human face that can create over 7,000 expressions, can we actually vary our own emotions by contracting certain muscles and wearing different expressions? Research suggests that we can, though it is not clear what the results mean. Laird argues that facial expressions affect emotion through a process of self-perception: "If I'm smiling, I must be happy." Other researchers maintain that facial movements spark emotion by producing physiological changes in the brain (Izard, 1990). For example, Robert Zajonc (1993) argues that smiling causes facial muscles to increase the flow of air-cooled blood to the brain, a process that produces a pleasant state by lowering brain temperature. Conversely, frowning decreases blood flow, producing an unpleasant state by raising temperature. According to this analysis, people need not infer how they feel. Rather, facial expressions evoke physiological changes that produce an emotional experience.

To demonstrate, Zajonc and his colleagues (1989) asked subjects to repeat certain vowels twenty times each, including the sounds "ah," "e," "u," and the German vowel "ü." In the meantime, temperature changes in the forehead were measured and subjects reported on how they felt. As shown in Figure 2.1, "ah" and "e" (sounds that cause people to mimic smiling) lowered forehead temperature and elevated mood, whereas "u" and "ü" (sounds that cause us to mimic frowning) increased temperature and dampened mood. Apparently, movement of the facial muscles can influence emotion even when people are not aware that they are wearing a particular facial expression. This research teaches a useful lesson: It's possible to alter how you feel by putting on the right face.

As predicted by self-perception theory, other expressive behaviors such as body posture can also provide us with sensory feedback and influence the way

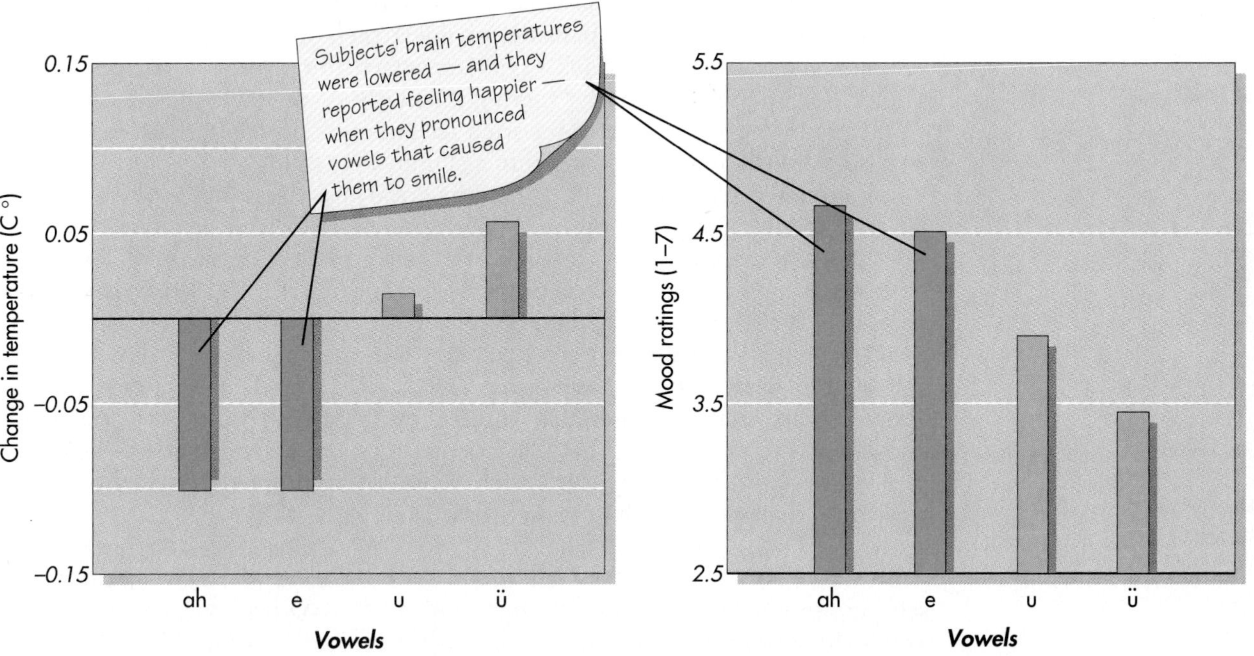

Figure 2.1 Facial Feedback and Emotion. Subjects were asked to repeat different vowel sounds. As shown, "ah" and "e"—sounds that cause us to mimic smiling—lowered brain temperature (left) and elevated mood (right). In contrast, "u" and "ü"—vowels that cause us to mimic frowning—raised brain temperature (left) and dampened mood (right). (Zajonc et al., 1989.)

In a scene from *Once Bitten,* actor Jim Carrey had a terrified look on his face. How did he really feel at the time? Supporting the facial feedback hypothesis, many actors claim that they come to experience the emotions they express.

we feel. When people feel proud, they stand erect with their shoulders raised, chest expanded, and head held high (*expansion*). When dejected, however, people slump over with their shoulders drooping and head bowed (*contraction*). Clearly, your emotional state is revealed in the way you carry yourself. But is it also possible that the way you carry yourself affects your emotional state? Can people lift their spirits by expansion, or lower their spirits by contraction? Yes. Sabine Stepper and Fritz Strack (1993) arranged for subjects to sit in either a slumped or upright position by varying the height of the table they had to write on. Those forced to sit upright reported feeling more pride after succeeding at a task than did those who were put into a slumped position.

Emotional states can even be evoked by vocal cues. Research shows that people tend to speak quickly and raise their voice when fearful or anxious, but to slow down and lower the voice when sad or depressed. Can the way you speak influence the way you feel? Aron Siegman and Stephen Boyle (1993) had subjects talk about experiences that had made them anxious or sad. For some events, subjects spoke at a normal rate; for others, they were instructed to speak either fast-and-loud or slow-and-soft. The result: Speech style amplified emotions. Talking about anxiety-related events made subjects more anxious when they spoke fast and loud, whereas talking about sad events made them feel sadder when they spoke slow and soft. Apparently, our emotions can be influenced by sensory feedback from the voice as well as from the face and body.

Self-Perceptions of Motivation Without quite realizing it, Mark Twain was a self-perception theorist. In *The Adventures of Tom Sawyer,* written in the late 1800s, he quipped, "There are wealthy gentlemen in England who drive four-horse passenger coaches twenty or thirty miles on a daily line, in the summer, because the privilege costs them considerable money; but if they were offered wages for the service that would turn it into work then they would resign."

Twain's hypothesis—that reward for an enjoyable activity undermines interest in that activity—seems to contradict intuition and a good deal of psychological research. After all, aren't we all motivated by reward, as declared by B. F. Skinner and other behaviorists? The answer depends on how "motivation" is defined.

As a keen observer of human behavior, Twain anticipated a key distinction between intrinsic and extrinsic motivation. *Intrinsic motivation* originates in factors within a person. People are said to be intrinsically motivated when they engage in an activity for its own sake, out of sheer enjoyment, without expecting tangible payoff for their efforts. Eating a fine meal, listening to music, spending time with friends, and working on a hobby are among the activities you might find intrinsically motivating. In contrast, *extrinsic motivation* originates in factors outside the person. People are said to be extrinsically motivated when they engage in an activity as a means to an end—to win money, grades, or recognition; to fulfill obligations; or to avoid punishment. As the behaviorists have said, people do strive for reward. The question is, What then happens to the intrinsic motivation once that reward is no longer available?

From the standpoint of self-perception theory, Twain's hypothesis makes sense. When someone is rewarded for listening to music, or playing games, or eating tasty food, his or her behavior becomes *over*justified, or *over*rewarded, and can be attributed to extrinsic as well as intrinsic motives. For self-perceivers, such **overjustification** can be dangerous: observing that their efforts have paid off, people begin to wonder if the activity was ever worth pursuing in its own right. This problem has been observed in numerous experiments (Deci & Ryan, 1985; Lepper & Greene, 1978; Pittman & Heller, 1987).

overjustification The tendency for intrinsic motivation to diminish for activities that have become associated with reward or other extrinsic factors.

Mark Lepper and his colleagues (1973), for example, gave preschool children an opportunity to play with colorful felt-tipped markers—an opportunity most could not resist. By observing how much time the children spent on the activity, the researchers were able to measure their intrinsic motivation. Two weeks later, the children were divided into three groups, all about equal in terms of initial levels of intrinsic motivation. In one, the children were simply asked to draw some pictures with the markers. In the second, they were told that if they used the markers they would receive a "Good Player Award," a certificate with a gold star and a red ribbon. In the third group, the children were not offered a reward for drawing pictures, but then—like those in the second group—they received a reward when they were done.

About a week later, the teachers placed the markers and paper on a table in the classroom while the experimenters observed through a one-way mirror. Since no rewards were available on this occasion, the amount of free time the children spent playing with the markers reflected their intrinsic motivation. As predicted, those children who had expected and received a reward for their efforts were no longer as interested in the markers as they had been. Subjects who had not received a reward were not adversely affected, nor were those who had unexpectedly received the reward. Having played with the markers without the promise of reward, these children remained intrinsically motivated (see Figure 2.2).

The paradox that reward undermines rather than enhances intrinsic motivation has been observed in many settings with both children and adults. Deadlines, competition, evaluation, and other extrinsic factors can also have this detrimental effect (Enzle & Anderson, 1993). Accept money for a hobby or

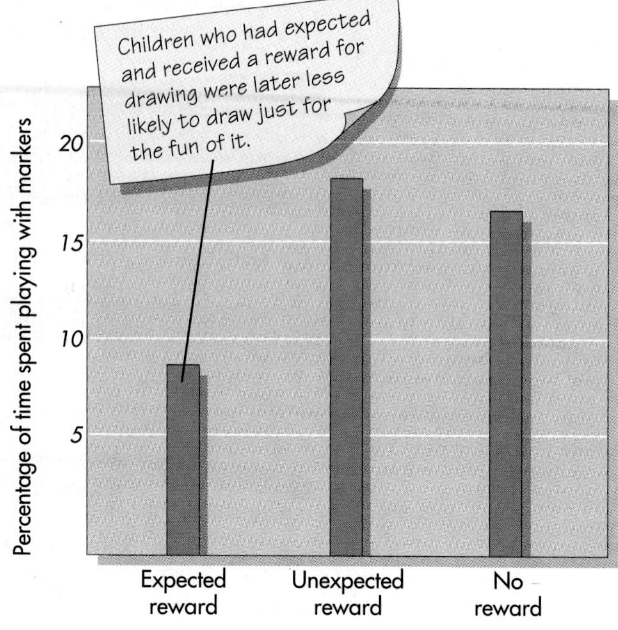

Figure 2.2 Paradoxical Effects of Reward on Intrinsic Motivation. In this study, an expected reward undermined children's intrinsic motivation to play with felt-tipped markers. Children who received an unexpected reward or no reward did not lose interest. (Lepper et al., 1973.)

leisure activity and, before you know it, what used to be "play" comes to feel like "work."

The overjustification effect can have serious implications for the ways in which parents socialize their children, classroom teachers use reward to improve study habits, and business managers structure incentive programs to increase worker productivity. So are we to conclude that reward and other extrinsic factors should always be avoided? No, it depends on how the reward is perceived—and by whom. If a reward is presented in the form of verbal praise, or as a special "bonus" for superior performance, then it can actually *enhance* intrinsic motivation by providing positive feedback about one's competence (Harackiewicz, 1979; Rosenfield et al., 1980; Cameron & Pierce, 1994).

Individual differences in motivational orientation toward work must also be considered. For intrinsically oriented people who say that "What matters most to me is enjoying what I do" and that "I seldom think about salary and promotions," reward may well be unnecessary—and perhaps detrimental (Amabile et al., 1994). Yet for those who tend to be focused on the achievement of specific goals, such extrinsic inducements as reward, game scores, and competition can have a positive effect on intrinsic motivation (Harackiewicz & Elliot, 1993; Elliot & Harackiewicz, 1994).

Influences of Other People

As we noted earlier, Cooley's (1902) theory of the looking-glass self emphasized that other people help us define ourselves. In this section, we will see the importance of this proposition.

Social Comparison Theory Suppose a stranger were to ask, "Who are you?" If you had only five minutes to answer, would you mention your ethnic or religious background? What about your hometown? Would you describe your talents and your interests or your likes and dislikes? Faced with this question, people tend to describe themselves in ways that set them apart from others in their immediate local environment (McGuire & McGuire, 1988). Among children, boys are more likely to cite their gender when they grow up in families that are predominantly female, and girls do the same when they live in homes that are predominantly male (McGuire et al., 1979). On the college campus, "nontraditional" older students are more likely to mention their age than are traditional younger students (Kite, 1992). Regardless of whether the unique attribute is gender, age, height, or eye color, the pattern is basically the same—and the implication is intriguing: change someone's social surroundings, and you can change that person's spontaneous self-description.

social comparison theory The theory that people evaluate their own abilities and opinions by comparing themselves to others.

This reliance on distinguishing features in self-description indicates that the self is a social construct and that we define ourselves in part by making comparisons with others. Indeed, that is what Leon Festinger (1954) proposed in his **social comparison theory.** Festinger argued that when people are uncertain about their abilities or opinions—that is, when objective information is not available—they evaluate themselves by drawing comparisons with similar others. The theory seems reasonable enough, but is it valid? Over the years, social psychologists have put social comparison theory to the test, focusing on two key questions: (1) *When* do we turn to others for comparative information? (2) Of all the people who inhabit the Earth, *to whom* do we choose to compare ourselves? (Suls & Wills, 1991; Wood, 1989).

As Festinger had proposed, the answer to the "when" question appears to be that people engage in social comparison in states of uncertainty, when more objective means of self-evaluation are not available. The answer to the "to whom" question, however, is that when we evaluate our own taste in music, or value on the job market, or athletic ability, we look toward others who are similar in relevant ways (Goethals & Darley, 1977; C. T. Miller, 1984; Wheeler et al., 1982). If you're curious about your flair for writing, for example, you're more likely to compare yourself to other college students than to high school students or best-selling authors. There are exceptions to this rule, of course. Later in the chapter, we will see that people often cope with personal inadequacies by focusing on others who are *less* able or *less* fortunate than themselves.

Two-Factor Theory People seek social comparison information to evaluate their abilities and opinions. But do we also use others to determine something as personal and subjective as our own *emotions?* In experiments on affiliation, Stanley Schachter (1959) found that when subjects were frightened into thinking they would receive painful electric shocks, most sought the company of others who were in the same predicament. Nervous and uncertain about how they should be feeling, subjects wanted to affiliate with similar others, presumably for the purpose of comparison. Yet when they were not fearful, and expected only mild shocks, or when the "others" were not participants in the same experiment, subjects preferred to be alone. As Schachter put it, "Misery doesn't just love any kind of company; it loves only miserable company" (p. 24).

Intrigued by the possibilities, Schachter and his research team took the next step. Could it be, they wondered, that when people are uncertain of how they feel, their emotions are actually determined by the reactions of others around them? In answer to this question, the researchers proposed that two factors are necessary to feel a specific emotion. First, the person must experience physiological arousal—a racing heart, perspiration, rapid breathing, a tightening of the stomach. Second, the person must make a *cognitive interpretation* that explains

two-factor theory of emotion The theory that the experience of emotion is based on two factors: physiological arousal and a cognitive interpretation of that arousal.

the source of that arousal. And that is where the people around us come in: their reactions help us to interpret our own arousal.

To test this provocative **two-factor theory of emotion,** Schachter and Jerome Singer (1962) injected male subjects with epinephrine, a drug that produces physiological arousal. Although one group was forewarned about the actual side effects, a second group was not. In a third group, subjects were injected with a harmless placebo. Before the drug (which was described as a vitamin supplement) actually took effect, subjects were left alone with a male confederate introduced as another subject who had received the same injection. For some subjects, the confederate behaved in a euphoric manner. For twenty minutes, he bounced around happily, doodling on scratch paper, sinking jump shots into the waste basket, flying paper airplanes across the room, and playing with a Hula-Hoop. For other subjects, the confederate displayed anger, ridiculing a questionnaire they were filling out, and, in a fit of rage, ripping it up and hurling it into the waste basket.

Think for a moment about these various situations. Subjects in the *drug-informed* group begin to feel their hearts pound, their hands shake, and their faces flush. Having been told to expect these symptoms, however, they need not search for an explanation. Subjects in the *placebo* group do not become aroused in the first place, so they have no symptoms to explain. But now consider the plight of the subjects in the *drug-uninformed* group, who suddenly become aroused without knowing why. Trying to identify the sensations, these subjects, according to the theory, should take their cues from someone else in the same predicament—namely, the confederate.

In general, the experimental results supported Schachter and Singer's line of reasoning. Drug-uninformed subjects reported feeling relatively happy or angry depending on the confederate's performance. In many instances, they even exhibited similar kinds of behavior. One subject, for example, "threw open the window and, laughing, hurled paper basketballs at passersby." In the drug-informed and placebo groups, however, subjects were, as expected, less influenced by these social cues.

Schachter and Singer's two-factor theory has attracted a good deal of controversy, as some experiments have corroborated their findings but others have not. Overall, however, one limited but important conclusion can safely be drawn: when people are unclear about their own emotional states, they sometimes interpret how they feel by watching others (Reisenzein, 1983). The "sometimes" part of the conclusion is important. For others to influence your emotion, your level of physiological arousal cannot be too intense, or else it will be experienced as aversive—regardless of the situation (Maslach, 1979; Zimbardo et al., 1993). Also, research shows that other people must be present as a possible explanation for arousal *before* its onset. Indeed, once people are aroused, they turn for an explanation to events that preceded the change in their physiological state (Schachter & Singer, 1979; Sinclair et al., 1994).

In subsequent chapters, we will see that the two-factor theory of emotion has far-reaching implications for passionate love and other affective experiences.

Autobiographical Memory

Philosopher James Mill once said, "The phenomenon of the Self and that of Memory are merely two sides of the same fact." If the story of patient William Thompson at the start of this chapter is any indication, Mill was right. Without autobiographical memories—recollections of the sequences of events that have touched your life (Rubin, 1986; Conway, 1990)—you would have no self-concept. Think about it. Who would you be if you could not remember your parents or childhood playmates, the places you lived, the schools you attended, the books you read, and the experiences you had? Clearly, memories shape the self-concept. In this section, we'll see that the self-concept shapes our memories as well (Greenwald & Pratkanis, 1984; Ross, 1989; Baumeister & Newman, 1994).

When people are prompted to recall their own experiences, they typically report more events from the recent than from the distant past, and they often have difficulty dating these events. There are, however, two exceptions to these rules. One is that people in general retrieve a large number of personal memories from their late adolescence and early adulthood. This "reminiscence peak" may reflect the fact that these are formative and busy years in one's life (Fitzgerald, 1988). Second, although people often cannot attach correct dates to past events, they make better estimates when using personal or historical landmarks such as "after my grandfather died" or "the year the Rangers won the Stanley Cup" (Friedman, 1993).

Obviously, not all experiences leave the same impression. Indeed, some events are so vivid that they seem to occupy a special place in memory. Ask people who are old enough to remember November 22, 1963, and they probably can tell you exactly what was happening, where they were, and with whom, the moment they heard the news that John F. Kennedy had been shot. For events of great personal or societal impact, people seem to have "flashbulb memories"—memories that are as vivid as a snapshot (Brown & Kulik, 1977). So, is information linked to highly emotional events permanently stored? No. Research shows that such memories may not be more accurate than normal (McCloskey et al., 1988), although people gain more and more confidence in these recollections (Weaver,

Although adults recall more experiences from the recent than distant past, we retain many memories from late adolescence and early adulthood. These formative years are best captured by high-school yearbook photos—such as those of actors Sharon Stone and Tom Hanks.

1993). Accurate or not, flashbulb memories "feel" special and serve as prominent landmarks in the biographies we write about ourselves.

In contrast, there is a period of life that seems entirely lost to us. Reflect on your earliest memory. It probably was not the sight of the doctor's hands in the delivery room, or the first time you waved, or even the first step you took as a toddler. An intriguing aspect of autobiographical memory is that most people cannot recall anything that happened before the age of three or four, a phenomenon known as "childhood amnesia" (Dudycha & Dudycha, 1941). Are such early memories impossible? It's hard to say. Some researchers have observed adults who report on certain critical events from the age of two—such as moving, the birth of a sibling, or the death of a family member (Usher & Neisser, 1993). But other researchers caution that these reports may not be memories at all but, rather, educated guesses or stories derived from parents, photographs, and other sources (Loftus, 1993).

By linking the present to the past and providing us with a sense of inner continuity, autobiographical memory is a vital part of one's identity. As we'll see, the self guides our recollections in three important ways: through the self-reference effect, the egocentric bias, and the hindsight bias.

self-reference effect The finding that information is recalled better when it is relevant to the self than when it is not.

The **self-reference effect** refers to the fact that people are more likely to remember a word, concept, or event if they think about it in relation to the self than in other contexts. In one study, subjects sat at a computer and looked at forty trait adjectives (for example, *shy, friendly, ambitious*). On some trials, subjects were told to consider whether the words were self-descriptive; on others, they were to judge the word's length, sound, or meaning. When later tested, subjects remembered more words that they had considered in relation to themselves than for other purposes (Rogers et al., 1977). Apparently, the self is like a mnemonic device: by viewing new information as personally *relevant,* we consider that information more fully and organize it around common themes. The self-reference effect is thus greater when the words to be recalled accurately describe the subject than when they do not (Bellezza, 1992). The net result is an improvement in memory (Greenwald & Banaji, 1989; Klein & Loftus, 1988; Conway & Dewhurst, 1995).

egocentric bias Bias toward perceiving and recalling oneself as a central actor in past events.

Self-relevance can also distort our recollections of the past. According to Anthony Greenwald (1980), autobiographical memory is colored by the **egocentric bias**, as people tend to overemphasize their own role in past events. As Greenwald put it, "The past is remembered as if it were a drama in which the self was the leading player" (p. 604). To illustrate egocentricity at its best (or worst), let's turn the clock back to a momentous event in American history: the Senate Watergate hearings of 1973. The witness was John Dean, former counsel to President Richard Nixon. Dean had submitted a 245-page statement in which he recounted word for word the details of many conversations. Dean's memory seemed so impressive that he was called "the human tape recorder." Then in an ironic twist of fate, Nixon had taped the meetings that Dean recalled. Was Dean accurate? A comparison of his testimony with the actual tapes revealed that although he correctly remembered the gist of his White House meetings, he consistently exaggerated his own role and his own importance in the events. Ulric Neisser (1981), who analyzed Dean's testimony, wondered, "Are we all like this? Is everyone's memory constructed, staged, self-centered?" The answer is yes—there is a bit of John Dean in all of us. Thus, when college basketball players from opposing teams were asked to describe a turning point in the games they played against each other, 80 percent of them referred to plays initiated by their own team (Ross & Sicoly, 1979).

hindsight bias The tendency, once an event has occurred, to overestimate one's ability to have foreseen the outcome.

Another feature of autobiographical memory is the **hindsight bias,** our tendency to think after an event that we knew beforehand what would happen. Historians are sometimes criticized for making the past seem inevitable in hindsight. Apparently, we all do. After learning a new fact or the outcome of some event—whether it's a drop in the stock market, the outcome of a trial, an earthquake, or the winner of the last Super Bowl—people tend to say, "I knew it all along" (Fischhoff, 1975; Hawkins & Hastie, 1990; Wood, 1978).

When it comes to the self, the implications of 20/20 hindsight are intriguing. Do people revise their fading personal histories in light of current information? Michael Ross and his colleagues (1981) addressed this question by changing subjects' attitudes on an issue and then asking those subjects to report on their past behaviors. In one experiment, for example, subjects listened to a medical expert argue convincingly for or against the wisdom of brushing teeth after every meal. Later, supposedly as part of a different experiment, those who had heard the favorable argument reported that they brushed their teeth more often in the previous two weeks than did those who had heard the unfavorable argument. Having adopted new attitudes, subjects "updated" their recall of past behaviors. Other research as well has shown that people will often recall their own past behavior in ways that cast themselves in a positive light (Goethals & Reckman, 1973; Klein & Kunda, 1993).

Contemplating the social ramifications of these findings, Ross (1989) suggested that our revisionist tendencies could account for the tendency of successive generations of parents to bemoan how today's children are not as responsible as those who grew up in the good old days. According to Ross, adults do not compare the younger generation to what they themselves were like at a comparable age. Instead, adults forgetfully assume that they used to be as they are in the present. By comparison, the next generation is bound to appear deficient. After studying adult development, psychiatrist George Vaillant (1977) drew a similar conclusion: "It is all too common for caterpillars to become butterflies and then to maintain that in their youth they had been little butterflies. Maturation makes liars of us all" (p. 197).

Self-Schemas

Thus far we have seen that people learn about themselves through introspection, by observing their own behavior, by comparing themselves to others, and by organizing their personal memories around existing beliefs about the self. But what, specifically, does the self-concept consist of, and how does it affect our views of the world?

self-schemas Beliefs people hold about themselves that guide the processing of self-relevant information.

According to Hazel Markus (1977), the cognitive molecules of the self-concept are called **self-schemas:** beliefs about oneself that guide the processing of self-relevant information. Self-schemas are to an individual's total self-concept what hypotheses are to a theory, what books are to a library. You can think of yourself as masculine or feminine, independent or dependent, liberal or conservative, introverted or extroverted. Indeed, any specific attribute may have relevance to the self-concept for some people but not for others. The self-schema for body weight is a good example. People who regard themselves as extremely overweight or underweight, or for whom body image is a conspicuous aspect of their self-concept, are considered *schematic* with respect to weight. In contrast, those who do not regard their own weight as extreme or as an important part of their lives are *aschematic* on that attribute (Markus et al., 1987).

Self-schemas are important because they lead us to interpret and recall our life experiences according to personally relevant themes. For body-weight schematics, a wide range of otherwise mundane events—a trip to the supermarket, new clothing, dinner at a restaurant, a day at the beach, or a friend's eating habits—may trigger self-relevant thoughts. When processing information, people (1) make rapid judgments about themselves on matters that are relevant to self-schemas, (2) are quick to notice, recall, or reconstruct past events that fit their own self-schemas, and (3) reject information that is inconsistent with their self-schemas (Kihlstrom & Cantor, 1984). People often view others through the lens of their self-schemas as well. Body-weight schematics, for example, always seem to notice whenever someone *else* eats too much or gains another pound.

Consisting of many self-schemas, the self is multifaceted. In fact, people think not only about their current selves but about *possible selves* as well—what they might become, would like to become, and are afraid of becoming in the future. Thus, when college students were asked to rate themselves on a list of attributes, there were marked differences between current views of the self and possible selves. Most imagined possibilities were in a positive direction, as most students believed it possible for them to become good parents, happy, physically fit, rich, well respected, secure, and successful (Markus & Nurius, 1986). Conceptions of possible selves provide people with an imaginary blueprint for future goals and plans (Ruvolo & Markus, 1992).

Multicultural Perspectives

In America, "the squeaky wheel gets the grease." In Japan, "the nail that stands out gets pounded down." In America, parents tell their children to be independent, self-reliant, and assertive, a "cut above the rest." In Japan, children are raised to fit into their community. These differences illustrate two contrasting cultural orientations: one values *individualism,* and the other values *collectivism* (Triandis, 1994).

In what cultures are these differing views the most extreme? In a worldwide study of 116,000 employees of IBM, Geert Hofstede (1980) found that the most fiercely independent people were from the United States, Australia, Great Britain, Canada, and the Netherlands, in that order. In contrast, the most interdependent people were from Venezuela, Colombia, Pakistan, Peru, and Taiwan.

Individualism and collectivism are so deeply ingrained in a culture that they mold our very self-conceptions and identities. According to Hazel Markus and

Reflecting an *interdependent* view of the self, children in Japan are taught to fit in to the community. Reflecting a more *independent* view of the self, children in the United States are encouraged to express their individuality.

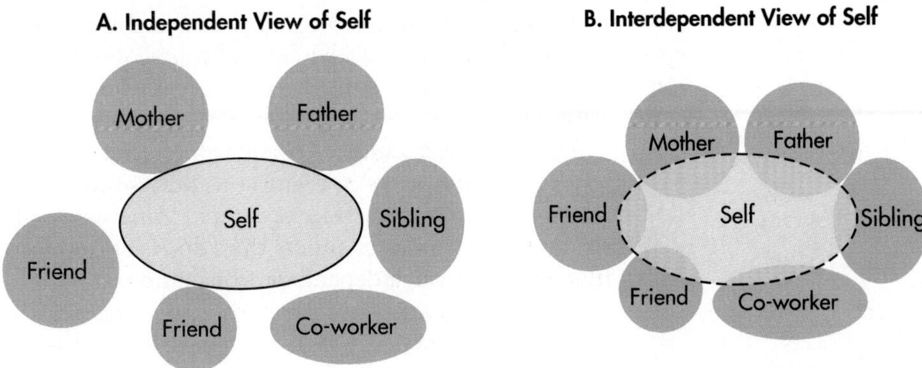

Figure 2.3 **Cultural Conceptions of Self.** As depicted here, different cultures foster different conceptions of the self. Many westerners have an *independent* view of the self as an entity that is distinct, autonomous, and self-contained. Yet many Asians, Africans, and Latin Americans hold an *interdependent* view of the self that encompasses others in a larger social network. (Markus & Kitayama, 1991.)

Shinobu Kitayama (1991), most North Americans and Europeans have an *independent* view of the self as an entity that is distinct, autonomous, self-contained, and endowed with unique dispositions. Yet in much of Asia, Africa, and Latin America, people hold an *interdependent* view of the self as part of a larger social network that includes one's family, co-workers, and others to whom we are socially connected. People with an independent view say that "the only person you can count on is yourself" and "I enjoy being unique and different from others." In contrast, those with an interdependent view are more likely to agree that "I'm partly to blame if one of my family members or coworkers fails" and "My happiness depends on the happiness of those around me" (Triandis, 1989; Oyserman, 1993; Singelis, 1994). These contrasting orientations toward the self are illustrated in Figure 2.3.

Research shows that there is a link between cultural orientation and conceptions of the self. David Trafimow and his colleagues (1991) had North American and Chinese college students complete twenty sentences beginning with "I am. . . . " As shown in Figure 2.4, the Americans were more likely to fill in the blank with trait descriptions ("I am shy"), whereas the Chinese were more likely

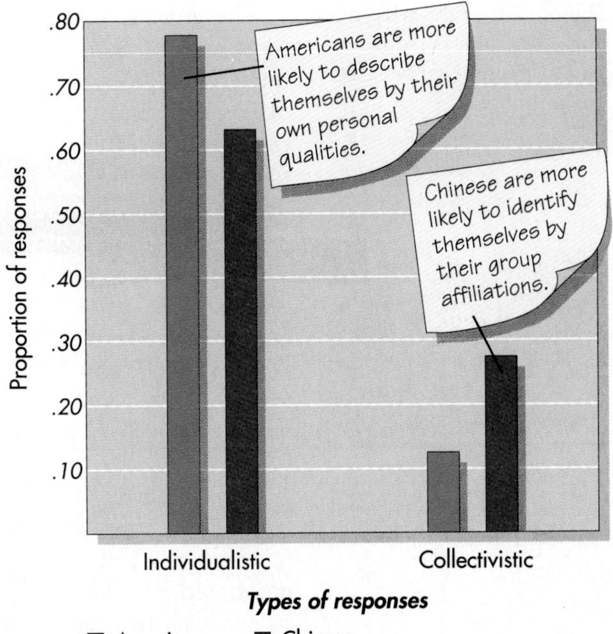

Figure 2.4 **Cultural Orientations and Conceptions of Self.** University students with an American or Chinese background completed twenty "I am . . ." sentences. As shown, the Americans more often filled in the blank with statements concerning a personal quality (left), while Chinese subjects were more likely to cite affiliations with a demographic or social group (right). These results support the notion that there are different cultural orientations toward the self. (Trafimow et al., 1991.)

to identify themselves by group affiliations ("I am a college student"). It's no wonder that in China, the family name comes *before* one's personal name. Similar differences are found between Australian and Malaysian subjects (Bochner, 1994).

How do these cultural orientations influence the way we perceive, evaluate, and present ourselves in relation to others? Markus and Kitayama (1991) report on two interesting differences. First, American college students perceive themselves as less similar to others than do Asian Indian students, reinforcing the idea that people with independent conceptions of the self believe they are unique. Second, Americans are more likely to express jealousy, pride, and other "ego-focused" emotions that affirm the self as an autonomous entity, whereas non-westerners are more likely to experience "other-focused" emotions that promote social harmony. In Japan, for example, people often report feelings of *oime* ("indebtedness to someone"), *fureai* ("connection with someone"), and *shitashimi* ("familiarity to someone").

As researchers examine cultural influences on conceptions of the self, many questions remain. Can the differences trigger conflict between cultures? What about individual variations within a culture? Research conducted in North America indicates that men are more likely to derive a positive self-image by fulfilling the goals of independence and autonomy, while women define themselves somewhat more by their social connections (Josephs et al., 1992). Is this gender difference universal? Can it trigger conflict and misunderstanding between men and women? Perhaps researchers will have answers to these questions in the years to come.

SELF-ESTEEM

How do you feel about yourself? Are you generally satisfied with your appearance, personality, abilities, and friendships? Are you optimistic about your future? When it comes to the self, people are hardly cool, objective, dispassionate observers. Rather, we are judgmental, emotional, and highly self-protective of our **self-esteem**—an affectively charged component of the self.

self-esteem An affective component of the self, consisting of a person's positive and negative self-evaluations.

The word *esteem* comes from the Latin *aestimare,* which means "to estimate or appraise." Self-esteem thus refers to our positive and negative evaluations of ourselves (Coopersmith, 1967). Some individuals have a higher self-esteem than others do—and this attribute can have a profound influence on the way they think and feel about themselves. It is important to keep in mind, however, that although some people have a higher self-esteem than others, a feeling of self-worth is not a single trait etched permanently in stone but, rather, a state of mind that varies in response to success, failure, changes in fortune, social interactions, and other experiences (Heatherton & Polivy, 1991). Research suggests that people who have an unstable, fluctuating self-esteem react more strongly to positive and negative life events than do people whose sense of self-worth is stable and secure (Kernis & Waschull, 1995). Also, since the self-concept consists of numerous self-schemas, some parts of the self are judged more favorably, or more clearly, than other parts of the self (Fleming & Courtney, 1984; Pelham & Swann, 1989).

Self-esteem is linked in important ways to how people approach their daily lives. Those who feel good about themselves tend to be happy, healthy, successful, and productive. They tend to persist longer at difficult tasks, sleep better at night, and have fewer ulcers. They are also more accepting of others and less likely to conform to peer pressure. In contrast, people with low self-esteem are more anxious, depressed, pessimistic about the future, and prone to failure (Brown, 1991).

As shown in Figure 2.5, part of the problem is that people who lack self-esteem bring to new tasks a self-defeating attitude that traps them in a vicious cycle. Expecting to fail, and fearing the worst, they become anxious, exert less effort, and "tune out" on important challenges. Then, when they do fail, people with low self-esteem blame themselves and end up feeling even more incompetent (Brockner, 1983). People with a low self-esteem do experience happiness and pride when they succeed. But their feelings of self-worth plummet after failure (Brown & Dutton, in press).

A good deal of research shows that people are motivated to keep up a positive self-image because self-esteem helps to protect us from our deeply rooted fear of death and other anxieties (Solomon et al., 1991; Greenberg et al., 1992). As if that weren't bad enough, people low in self-esteem may also be prone to illness. Recent research suggests that making people aware of their negative self-evaluations can have adverse effects on the activity of certain white blood cells in the immune system—the body's capacity to ward off disease (Strauman et al., 1993).

Self-Discrepancies

self-discrepancy theory The theory linking the perception of discrepancies between a person's self-concept and various self-guides to specific, negative emotional states.

What determines how people feel about themselves? According to the **self-discrepancy theory** of E. Tory Higgins (1989), your self-esteem is defined by the match between how you see yourself and how you want to see yourself. As a demonstration, try the following exercise. On a blank sheet of paper, write down ten traits that describe the kind of person you think you *actually* are (smart? easygoing? sexy? excitable?). Next, list ten traits that describe the kind of person

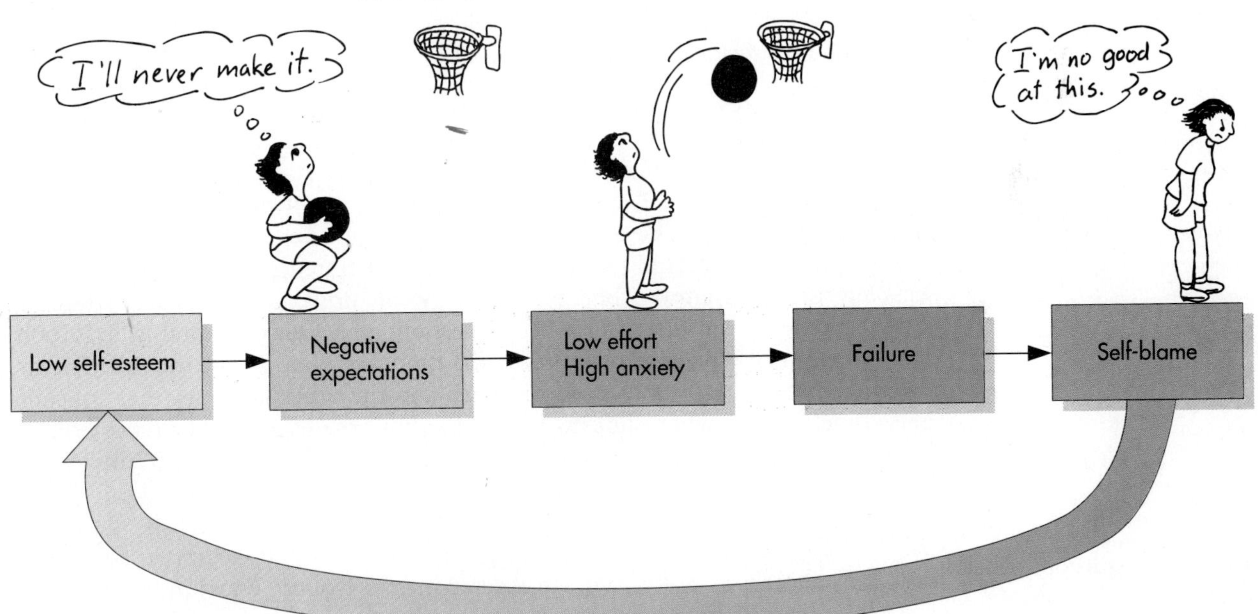

Figure 2.5 **The Vicious Cycle of Low Self-Esteem.** Low self-esteem triggers a self-defeating cycle in which negative expectations impair performance and, in turn, reinforce low self-esteem.

you think you *ought* to be, characteristics that would enable you to meet your sense of duty, obligation, and responsibility. Then make a list of traits that describe an *ideal* of what you would like to be, an ideal that embodies your hopes, wishes, and dreams. If you follow these instructions, you should have three lists—your actual self, your ought self, and your ideal self.

Research shows that these trait lists can be used to predict your self-esteem and emotional well-being. The first list is your self-concept. The others represent your personal standards or "self-guides." To the extent that you fall short of meeting these standards, you will have a lowered self-esteem, negative emotion, and in extreme cases a serious affective disorder. The specific consequence depends on which of the self-guides you fail to achieve. If there's a discrepancy between your actual and ought selves, you will feel guilty, ashamed, and resentful. You might even suffer from excessive fears and anxiety-related disorders. If the discrepancy is between your actual and ideal selves, you will feel disappointed, frustrated, sad, and unfulfilled. In extreme cases, you might become depressed (Higgins et al., 1986; Scott & O'Hara, 1993; Strauman, 1992).

Every one of us must live with some degree of discrepancy between our self-concept and our self-guides. Nobody is perfect. Yet we do not all suffer from the symptoms of anxiety-related disorders and depression. Why? According to Higgins (1989), the consequences of self-discrepancy depend on two factors. The first is simply the *amount* of discrepancy: the more of it there is, the more intense is the emotional discomfort. The second factor is *accessibility:* the more aware of a discrepancy you are, then, again, the more intense is the discomfort. The second factor raises an important question: Assuming everyone has self-discrepancies to cope with, what influences their accessibility? What is it that makes you self-conscious about *your* personal shortcomings? For an answer, we turn to self-awareness theory.

Self-Awareness

If you carefully review your daily routine—classes, work, chores at home, leisure activities, social interactions, and meals—you will probably be surprised at how little time you actually spend thinking about yourself. An interesting study makes the point. More than 100 people, ranging in age from nineteen to sixty-three, were equipped with an electronic beeper that sounded every two hours or so between 7:30 A.M. and 10:30 P.M. for a week. Each time the beeper went off, subjects interrupted whatever they were doing, wrote down what they were thinking at that moment, and filled out a brief questionnaire. Out of a total of 4,700 observations, only 8 percent of all recorded thoughts were about the self. For the most part, attention was focused on work and the other activities that consume one's time. In fact, when subjects did think about themselves, they reported feeling relatively unhappy and wished they were doing something else (Csikszentmihalyi & Figurski, 1982).

self-awareness theory The theory that self-focused attention leads people to notice self-discrepancies, thereby motivating either an escape from self-awareness or a change in behavior.

Self-Focusing Situations Is self-reflection unpleasant? If so, is it because it makes us acutely aware of our self-discrepancies? Robert Wicklund and his colleagues believe that the answer is yes (Duval & Wicklund, 1972; Wicklund, 1975; Wicklund & Frey, 1980). According to their **self-awareness theory,** people are not usually self-focused, but certain situations predictably force us to turn inward and become the objects of our own attention. When we talk about ourselves, glance into a mirror, stand before an audience or camera, watch ourselves on videotape, or occupy a conspicuous position within a group, we enter a state of self-awareness that leads us naturally to compare our behavior to internal standards. This comparison often results in a negative discrepancy and a temporary reduction in self-esteem as we discover that we fall short of our ideal and ought selves. Thus, when people are placed in front of a mirror, they often experience a negative mood state (Hass & Eisenstadt, 1990). In fact, the more self-absorbed people are in general, the more likely they are to suffer from alcoholism, depression, anxiety, and other clinical disorders (Ingram, 1990).

Is there a solution? Self-awareness theory suggests that there are two ways to cope with such discomfort: (1) "shape up" by behaving in ways that reduce our self-discrepancies, or (2) "ship out" by withdrawing from self-awareness. According to Charles Carver and Michael Scheier (1981), the solution chosen depends on whether people think they can successfully reduce their self-discrepancy—and whether they're pleased with the progress they make once they try (Duval et al., 1992). If so, they tend to match their behavior to personal or societal standards; if not, they tune out, seek distractions, and turn attention away from the self. This process is depicted in Figure 2.6.

In general, research supports these predictions (Gibbons, 1990). When people are self-focused, they are more likely to behave in ways that are consistent either with their own personal values or with socially accepted ideals. In an interesting field study, for example, Halloween trick-or-treaters—children wearing costumes, masks, and painted faces—were greeted at a researcher's door and left alone to help themselves from a bowl of candy. Although the children were asked

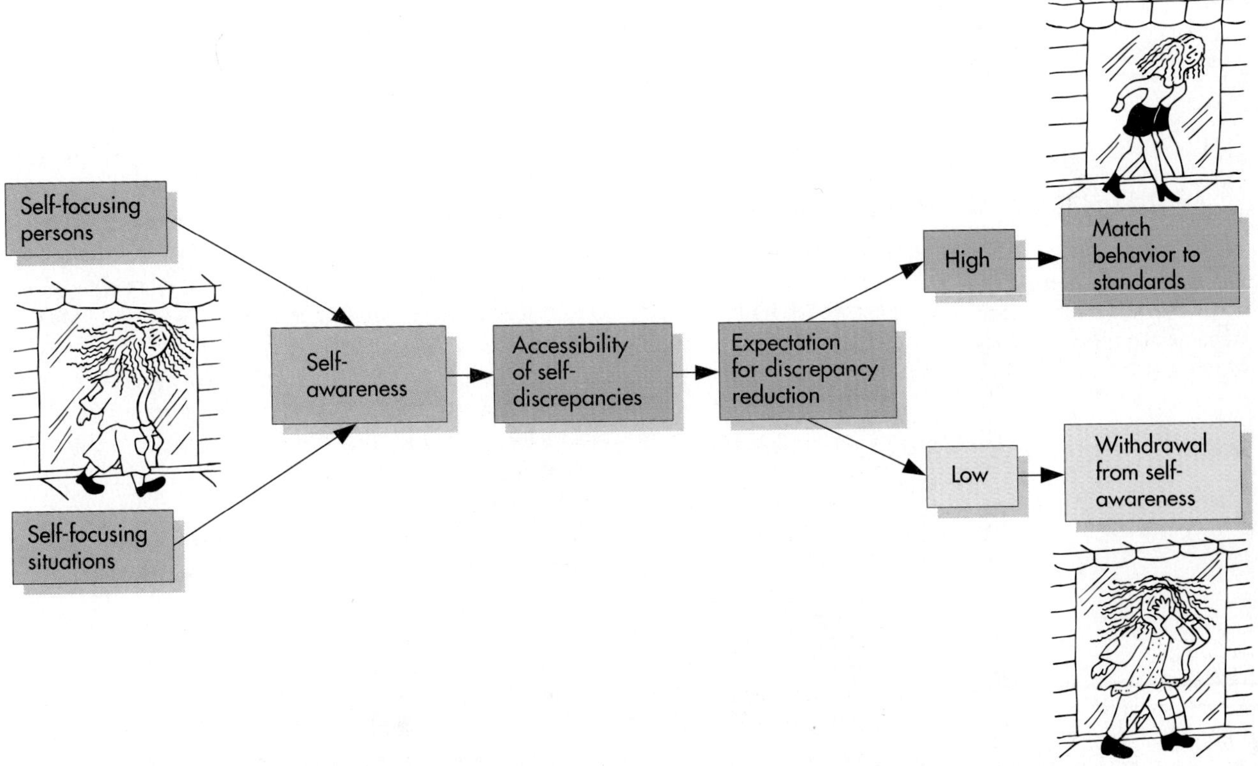

Figure 2.6 **The Causes and Effects of Self-Awareness.** Self-awareness pressures people to reduce self-discrepancies by matching their behavior to personal or societal standards, or by withdrawing from self-awareness.

not to take more than one piece, 34 percent violated the request. When a full-length mirror was placed right behind the candy bowl, however, the number of violators dropped to only 12 percent. Apparently, the mirror forced the children to become self-focused, leading them to behave in a way that was consistent with public standards of desirable conduct (Beaman et al., 1979).

The specific standard that serves as a self-guide may also depend on which significant others in one's life come to mind at a given moment. In a study of "private audiences," Mark Baldwin and John Holmes (1987) asked one group of female college students to visualize campus friends and another group to think about their parents. Minutes later, ostensibly as part of another experiment, they read a sexually permissive article and rated how much they enjoyed it. Half of the subjects were seated in front of a mirror for this task and half were not. Results supported self-awareness theory: subjects who were self-focused by the mirror behaved in ways that would please their private audience. As if they were being observed, these subjects reported liking the sexual article more after thinking about their friends than after thinking about their parents.

When self-discrepancy reduction seems unlikely, individuals take a second route: escape from self-awareness. However, this coping strategy has some disturbing implications. One concerns the use of alcohol. According to Jay Hull, people often drown their sorrows in a bottle as a way to escape from the negative implications of self-awareness. To test this hypothesis, Hull and Richard Young (1983) administered what was supposed to be an IQ test to male subjects and gave false feedback suggesting that they had either succeeded or failed. Supposedly as part of a separate study, subjects were then asked to taste and evaluate different wines. As they did so, experimenters kept track of how much they drank during a fifteen-minute tasting period. As predicted, subjects who were prone to self-awareness drank more wine after failure than after success, presumably to escape the blow to their self-esteem. Among subjects not prone to self-awareness, there was no difference in alcohol consumption. Similar results were obtained in a study of men hospitalized for alcoholism and released. After three months, those who were both self-conscious and under stress were the most likely

People often drown their sorrows in a bottle to escape from the negative implications of self-awareness.

Drawing by Cline; © 1991 The New Yorker Magazine, Inc.

"More wine! Less truth!"

to relapse into heavy drinking (Hull et al., 1986). Indeed, many people expect alcohol to grant mental relief from their problems (Leigh & Stacy, 1993).

Claude Steele and Robert Josephs (1990) believe that alcoholic intoxication provides more than just a means of tuning out on the self. By causing people to lose touch with reality and shed their inhibitions, it also evokes a state of "drunken self-inflation." In one study, for example, subjects rated their actual and ideal selves on various traits—some important to self-esteem, others not important. After drinking either an 80-proof vodka cocktail or a harmless placebo, subjects re-rated themselves on the same traits. As measured by the perceived discrepancy between actual and ideal selves, subjects who were drinking expressed inflated views of themselves on traits they considered important (Banaji & Steele, 1989).

According to Roy Baumeister (1991), drug abuse, masochism, binge eating, and spiritual ecstasy may also serve escapist functions. Suicide may be the ultimate form of escape. In advancing this provocative notion, Baumeister argues that people contemplate suicide when they (1) realize they're falling short of personal standards, (2) accept the blame for failure, (3) focus too much attention on the self, (4) experience negative affect, such as depression, (5) think in rigid short-sighted terms to cope mentally with the anguish, and thus (6) shed the inhibitions that would normally prevent them from harming themselves. This theory cannot be tested directly, but Baumeister presents various suicide statistics compatible with his theory. Consistent with the hypothesis that suicide victims are highly self-focused is a finding that suicide notes—compared to the notes written by people who face death by illness—contain more first-person pronouns (*I* and *me*). In short, says Baumeister, suicide is a desperate act of last resort whose main purpose is "oblivion"—a complete loss of self-awareness.

private self-consciousness A personality characteristic of individuals who are introspective, often attending to their own inner states.

public self-consciousness A personality characteristic of individuals who focus on themselves as social objects, as seen by others.

Self-Focusing Persons Just as *situations* evoke self-awareness, certain *individuals* are characteristically more self-focused than others. Research has revealed an important distinction between **private self-consciousness**—the tendency to introspect on our *inner* thoughts and feelings—and **public self-consciousness**—the tendency to focus on our *outer* public image (Fenigstein et al., 1975; Buss, 1980). Table 2.1 presents a sample of items used to measure these traits.

Research shows that private and public self-consciousness are distinct traits. People who score high on a test of *private* self-consciousness tend to fill in incomplete sentences with first-person pronouns, are quick to make self-descriptive statements, and are acutely aware of changes in their internal bodily states (Mueller, 1982; Scheier et al., 1979). In contrast, those who score high on a test of *public* self-consciousness are sensitive to the way they are viewed from an outsider's perspective. Thus, when people were asked to draw a capital letter *E* on their foreheads, 43 percent of those with high levels of public self-consciousness, compared to only 6 percent of those with low levels, oriented the *E* so that it was backward from their own standpoint but correct for an outside observer (Hass, 1984). People who are high in public self-consciousness are also particularly sensitive to the ways in which others share their opinions (Fenigstein & Abrams, 1993).

The distinction between private and public self-awareness has implications for the ways in which we reduce self-discrepancies. According to Higgins (1989), people are motivated to meet either their own standards or the standards held for them by significant others. Perhaps self-awareness theorists who draw the public-private distinction can tell us which of these discrepancies is likely to cause trouble at a particular time for a particular individual. When you're privately self-conscious, you listen to an inner voice and try to reduce discrepancies rela-

Table 2.1 How Self-Conscious Are You?

Items That Measure Private Self-Consciousness

- I'm always trying to figure myself out.
- I'm constantly examining my motives.
- I'm often the subject of my fantasies.
- I'm alert to changes in my mood.
- I'm aware of the way my mind works when I work on a problem.

Items That Measure Public Self-Consciousness

- I'm concerned about what other people think of me.
- I'm self-conscious about the way I look.
- I'm concerned about the way I present myself.
- I usually worry about making a good impression.
- One of the last things I do before leaving my house is look in the mirror.

These sample items appear in the Self-Consciousness Scale. How would you describe yourself on both the public and the private aspects of self-consciousness? (Fenigstein et al., 1975.)

tive to your own personal standards; when you're publicly self-conscious, however, you try to match your behavior to socially accepted norms. As illustrated in Figure 2.7, there may be "two sides of the self: one for you and one for me" (Scheier & Carver, 1983, p. 123).

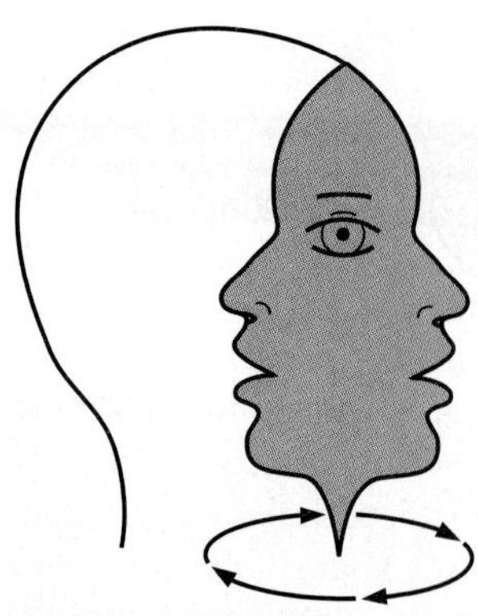

Figure 2.7 **Revolving Images of Self.** According to self-awareness theory, people try to meet either their own standards or standards held for them by others—depending, perhaps, on whether they are in a state of private or public self-consciousness. As Scheier and Carver (1983, p. 123) put it, there are "two sides of the self: one for you and one for me." (C. R. Snyder et al., 1983.)

Self-Enhancement

We have seen that self-awareness can create discomfort and lower self-esteem by focusing attention on discrepancies. People often avoid focusing on themselves, but such avoidance is not always possible. How, then, does the average person cope with his or her faults, inadequacies, and uncertain future?

Let's begin with a stark fact about human behavior. Most often, most people think highly of themselves. Time and again, research has shown that subjects view positive traits as more descriptive of themselves than negative traits. Compared to others, people view themselves as better, overestimate their contribution to a team effort, exaggerate their control over life events, predict that they have a brighter future, and seek more information about their strengths than about their weaknesses (Taylor, 1989). People also evaluate their own personality traits as being more desirable than traits that are not self-descriptive (Dunning et al., 1991). Illustrating the "mere ownership effect," people even rate the letters in their name more favorably than the other letters of the alphabet (Hoorens & Nuttin, 1993) and judge various consumer products that they own to be better than comparable products that they do not own (Beggan, 1992).

It's not that we consciously and deliberately flatter ourselves. The response is more like a reflex. Indeed, when subjects are busy or distracted as they make self-ratings, their judgments are quicker and even more favorable (Paulhus et al., 1989; Hixon & Swann, 1993). We can't all be perfect, nor can we all be better than average. So what supports this common illusion?

In the 1982 movie *The Big Chill*, the following dialogue suggests at least one answer:

SAM: Why is it what you just said strikes me as a massive rationalization?

MICHAEL: Don't knock rationalization. Where would we be without it? I don't know anyone who could get through the day without two or three juicy rationalizations. They're more important than sex.

SAM: Ah, come on. Nothing's more important than sex.

MICHAEL: Oh yeah? You ever gone a week without a rationalization?

In this section, we examine four methods used to rationalize or otherwise enhance self-esteem: self-serving cognitions, self-handicapping, basking in the glory of others, and downward social comparisons.

Self-Serving Cognitions How well did you do on the Scholastic Aptitude Test (SAT)? James Shepperd (1993) recently questioned college students about their performance on this infamous test and uncovered two interesting patterns. First, subjects overestimated their actual test scores by an average of 17 points. This inflationary distortion was most pronounced among those with relatively low scores, and it persisted somewhat even when subjects knew that the experimenter would check their academic files. Second, a majority of subjects whose SAT scores were low described their scores as inaccurate and the test in general as invalid. In fact, the test scores for the group as a whole were predictive of their grade point averages.

When students receive exam grades, those who do well take credit for their success; those who do poorly complain about the instructor and the test questions. When researchers have articles accepted for publication, they credit the quality of their work; when articles are rejected, they blame the editor and reviewers. When gamblers win a bet, they view themselves as skillful; when they lose, they moan and groan about fluke events that transformed near victory into defeat. When professional athletes win, they fill the sports pages with self-congratulatory quotes; when they lose, they gripe about the officials. Whether people are high or low in self-esteem, explain their outcomes publicly or in pri-

In casinos, racetracks, and lotteries, people lose billions of dollars a year in gambling. This self-defeating behavior persists in part because people exaggerate their control over random events and then make excuses for their losses.

vate, and try to be honest or to make a good impression, there is bias: People take credit for success and distance themselves from failure (Schlenker et al., 1990).

People are also unrealistically optimistic. Students who were asked to predict their own future compared to that of the average person believed they would graduate higher in their class, get a better job, have a happier marriage, and give birth to a gifted child. They also believed they were less likely to get fired or divorced, have a drinking problem, become depressed, or suffer from a heart attack (Weinstein, 1980). There are numerous other examples as well. In polls taken between 1952 and 1980, American voters—regardless of whether they supported the ultimate winner or loser—expected their candidate to prevail by a 4-to-1 ratio (Granberg & Brent, 1983). Similarly, sports fans often let their team preferences interfere with the bets they place, even when they are trying to be "objective" (Babad & Katz, 1991).

Obviously, the future is not always bright, so what supports this unwavering optimism? Ziva Kunda (1987) finds that people bolster their rosy outlook by holding elaborate theories that link their own personal attributes to desirable outcomes. In one study, for example, subjects who had been involved in a serious high school relationship believed that such an experience promotes a stable marriage. Yet those who were not romantically involved believed that a *lack* of experience promotes a happy-ever-after ending. It is no wonder that Kunda's subjects estimated that there was only a 20 percent chance that their own marriages would end in divorce—despite knowing that the divorce rate is 50 percent.

Self-Handicapping "My dog ate my homework. I had a flat tire. I was up all night. My alarm didn't go off. My computer crashed. I had a headache." On occasion, all of us have made excuses for past performance. Sometimes we come up with excuses in anticipation of a future performance as well. Particularly when people are afraid that they might fail in an important situation, they use illness, shyness, anxiety, pain, trauma, and other disclaimers (Snyder & Higgins, 1988). Why? By admitting to a limited physical or mental weakness, we can shield ourselves from what could be the most painful attribution of all—a lack of ability.

Making verbal excuses is one way to cope with the threatening implications of failure. Under certain conditions, this strategy is taken one step further: People actually *sabotage* their own performance. It seems paradoxical, but people may purposely set themselves up for failure in order to protect their self-esteem (Higgins et al., 1990).

self-handicapping Behaviors designed to sabotage one's own performance in order to provide a subsequent excuse for failure.

First described by Stephen Berglas and Edward Jones (1978), **self-handicapping** refers to actions people take to handicap their own performance in order to build an excuse for anticipated failure. To demonstrate, Berglas and Jones recruited college students for an experiment supposedly involving the effects of drugs on intellectual performance. All subjects worked on a twenty-item test of analogies and were told that they had done well, after which they expected to work on a second, similar test. For one group, the problems were relatively easy, leading subjects to expect more success; for a second group, the problems were insoluble, leaving subjects confused about their initial success and worried about possible failure. Before taking the second test, subjects were given a choice of two drugs: Actavil, which was supposed to improve performance, or Pandocrin, which was supposed to impair it.

Although no drugs were actually administered, most subjects who were confident about the upcoming test selected the Actavil; in contrast, male subjects—but not the females—who feared the outcome of the second test chose the Pandocrin.

By handicapping themselves, these men set up a convenient excuse for failure—an excuse, we should add, that may have been intended more for the experimenter's benefit than for that of the subjects themselves. Indeed, a follow-up study showed that although self-handicapping occurs when the experimenter witnesses the subjects' drug choice, it is reduced when the experimenter is not present while that choice is being made (Kolditz & Arkin, 1982).

People differ in the extent to which they use self-handicapping as a defense (Rhodewalt, 1990), and there are different ways to do so. For example, men often handicap themselves by taking drugs (Higgins & Harris, 1988), neglecting to practice (Hirt et al., 1991), and giving a performance enhancer to their rival (Shepperd & Arkin, 1991). Women instead tend to report stress and physical symptoms (Hirt et al., 1991; Smith et al., 1983). People even differ in their reasons for self-handicapping. After all, the strategy offers two distinct benefits: a defensive excuse in case you fail (it's not your fault) and enhanced credit if you succeed (you must be amazing).

Which of those two benefits do we seek most? According to Dianne Tice (1991), it depends on our motivation. People who are low in self-esteem need to protect their fragile self-image by avoiding failure at all costs. Those high in self-esteem seek to enhance their image through bold, against-the-odds success. To test this hypothesis, Tice asked subjects varying in self-esteem to work on a task that measures nonverbal intelligence. Half were told that the task identifies people who are intellectually deficient, thus highlighting the motive to avoid failure. The others were told that the task identifies people who are extraordinarily gifted, highlighting the motive for success. All subjects were allowed to practice as long as they wished. As predicted, low-self-esteem subjects practiced less when they tried to protect themselves from possible failure, and high-self-esteem subjects practiced less in order to boost themselves by success. (These strategies were used only when the task was important to the self-concept.) Other researchers have also observed this difference (Rhodewalt et al., 1991; Wood et al., 1994). For people lacking self-esteem, self-handicapping offers a face-saving defense against failure. For those high in self-esteem, it is used to enhance the self through success (see Figure 2.8).

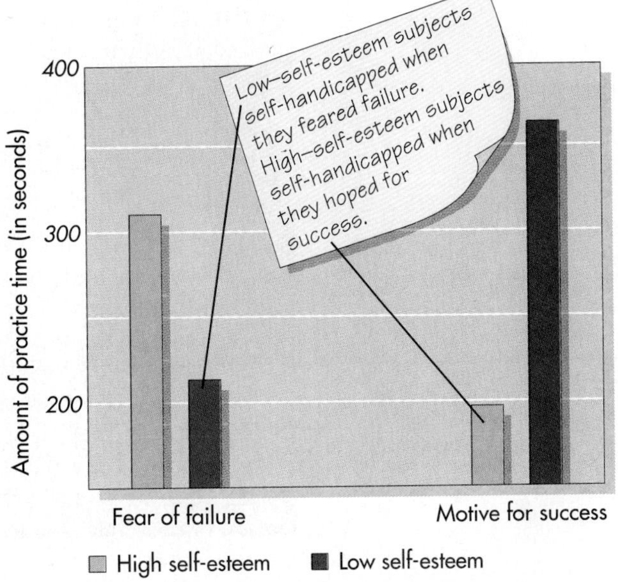

Figure 2.8 Self-Handicapping: To Protect or Enhance Self-Esteem? Subjects worked on a task that supposedly measured intelligence. When success was prominent, high–self-esteem subjects practiced less. When the fear of failure was prominent, low–self-esteem subjects practiced less. This pattern suggests that self-handicapping is a face-saving defense against failure for people low in self-esteem and an opportunity for enhancement through success for those high in self-esteem. (Tice, 1991.)

Whatever the goal, self-handicapping seems an ingenious strategy: by stacking the odds against us, the self is insulated from failure and enhanced by success. Unfortunately, this strategy is not without considerable cost. Sure, it may ease the pressure to succeed, but sabotaging ourselves—by not studying or practicing, by drinking too much or taking drugs, or by faking an illness—also increases the likelihood of failure. Sometimes we just have to take risks in order to forge ahead in life.

bask in reflected glory (BIRG) Increasing self-esteem by associating with others who are successful.

Basking in the Glory of Others To some extent, your self-esteem is influenced by individuals and groups with whom you identify. According to Robert Cialdini and his colleagues (1976), people often **bask in reflected glory (BIRG)** by showing off their connections to successful others. Cialdini's team first observed BIRGing on the university campuses of Arizona State, Louisiana State, Notre Dame, Michigan, Pittsburgh, Ohio State, and Southern California. On the Monday mornings after a football game, they counted the number of school sweat shirts worn on campus and found that more of them were worn if the team had won its game on the previous Saturday. In fact, the larger the margin of victory, the more school shirts were counted.

To evaluate the effects of self-esteem on BIRGing, Cialdini gave students a general-knowledge test and rigged the results so half would succeed and half would fail. The students were then asked to describe in their own words the outcome of a recent football game. In these descriptions, students who thought they had just failed a test were more likely than those who thought they had succeeded to share in their team's victory by exclaiming that "*we* won" and to distance themselves from defeat by lamenting how "*they* lost." In another study, subjects coming off a recent failure were quick to point out that they had the same birth date as someone known to be successful—thus BIRGing by a merely coincidental association (Cialdini & De Nicholas, 1989).

Sports fans bask in the reflected glory of their teams—and experience a boost in their self-esteem after "we win."

If self-esteem is influenced by our links to others, how do we cope with friends, family members, teammates, and co-workers of low status? Again, consider sports fans, an interesting breed. As loudly as they cheer in victory, they often turn and jeer their teams in defeat. This behavior seems fickle, but it is consistent with the notion that people derive part of their self-esteem from associations with others. In one study, subjects took part in a problem-solving team that succeeded, failed, or received no feedback about its performance. Subjects were later offered a chance to take home a team badge. In the success and no-feedback groups, 68 and 50 percent, respectively, took badges; in the failure group, only 9 percent did (Snyder et al., 1986). In a second study, students who were committed to a career in psychology but insecure about it were quick to reject a fellow student who was an embarrassment to their major (Wagner et al., 1990). It appears that the tendency to bask in reflected glory is matched by an equally powerful tendency to CORF—that is, to "cut off reflected failure." In fact, one study revealed that avid sports fans temporarily lose faith in their own mental and social abilities after their favorite team suffers defeat (Hirt et al., 1992).

Downward Social Comparisons Earlier we discussed Festinger's (1954) theory that people evaluate themselves through social comparison with similar others. But let's contemplate the implications. If the people around us achieve *more* than we do, what does that do to our self-esteem? Perhaps the many adults who shy away from class reunions to avoid having to compare themselves with former classmates are acting out an answer to that question.

downward social comparisons Defensive tendency to compare ourselves to others who are worse off than we are.

Festinger fully realized that people don't always seek objective information and that social comparisons are sometimes made in self-defense. When a person's self-esteem is at stake, he or she may benefit from making **downward social comparisons**—comparisons with others who are inferior, less successful, less happy, or less fortunate (Hakmiller, 1966; Wills, 1981; Wood, 1989). When people who are low in self-esteem suffer a setback, downward comparisons have an uplifting effect on their mood and outlook for the future (Aspinwall & Taylor, 1993; Gibbons & McCoy, 1991).

To preserve their own self-esteem, people dissociate from others who fail.

Drawing by Leo Cullum; © 1992 The New Yorker Magazine, Inc.

"Your mother and I have seen your report card, and we've decided to distance ourselves from you."

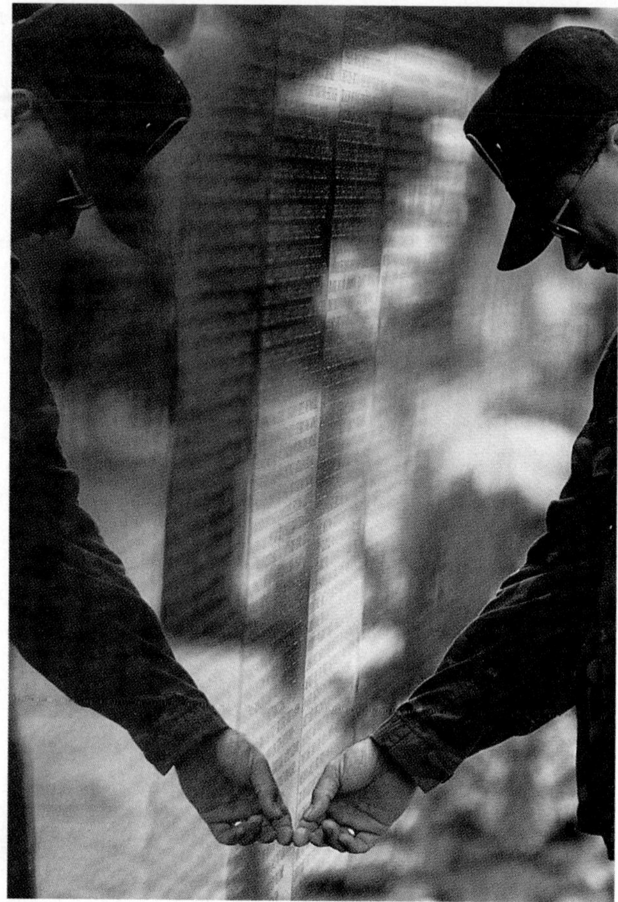

When Vietnam veterans returned in defeat more than twenty years ago, they were neglected, even scorned by the American public. It seems that the tendency to bask in reflected glory is matched by an equally powerful need to cut off reflected failure.

The benefits of downward comparison can be seen in the classroom. Educators used to be puzzled by the finding that disadvantaged elementary school children often score higher on measures of academic self-esteem than do children from affluent, academically minded schools. The reason: Students feel better about themselves when surrounded by classmates who are lower rather than higher in their levels of achievement. Apparently, it's better to be a big fish in a small pond than a small fish in a big pond (Marsh & Parker, 1984).

There are also striking implications for health-related issues. When victimized by tragic life events—a crime, an accident, a disease, or the death of a loved one—people often cope in two ways: they affiliate with others who are adjusting well, role models who offer hope and guidance, but they compare themselves to others who are worse off, a form of downward social comparison (Taylor & Lobel, 1989). Clearly, it helps to know that life could be worse, which is why most cancer patients compare themselves to others who are *not* adjusting well (Wood et al., 1985) and believe they are in better shape than their peers (Taylor et al., 1986).

Interviews with breast cancer patients tell the story. One woman who had only a lump removed wondered "how awful it must be for women who have had a full mastectomy." An older woman who had a mastectomy said: "The people I really feel sorry for are these young gals. To lose a breast when you're so young must be awful." Yet a young mastectomy patient derived comfort from the fact that "if I hadn't been married, this thing would have really gotten to me" (Taylor, 1989, p. 171). As these quotes poignantly reveal, there's always someone to whom we can favorably compare ourselves for the sake of coping. In the words of a terminally ill patient who appeared on the CBS documentary *A Time to Die,* "It's not the worst thing that could happen."

Unfortunately, it's not always possible to defend the self via downward comparison. Think about it. When a sibling, spouse, or close friend has more success than you do, what happens to your self-esteem? Abraham Tesser (1988) predicts two possible reactions. On the one hand, you might feel proud of your close association with this successful other, as in the process of basking in reflected glory. If you've ever bragged about the achievements of a loved one as if they were your own, you know fully well how "reflection" can bolster self-esteem. On the other hand, you may feel overshadowed by the success of this other person and experience social comparison jealousy—a mixture of emotions that include envy, resentment, and a drop in self-esteem.

According to Tesser, the key to whether one feels the pleasure of reflection or the pain of jealousy is the self-relevance of the other person's success. When close

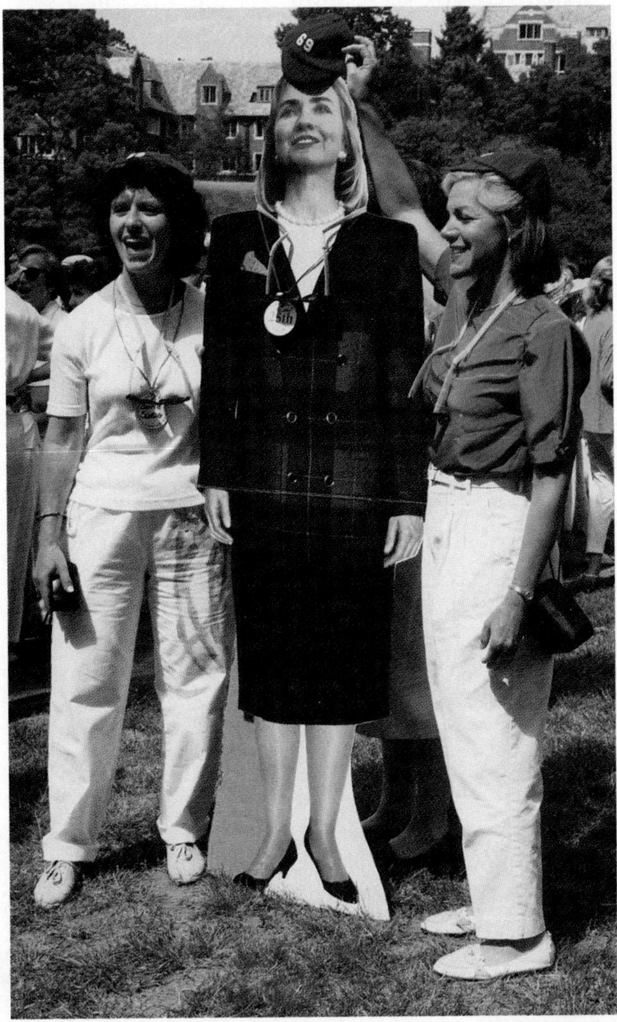

At their 25th reunion, these Wellesley College graduates, Class of '69, stand alongside a lifesize figure of Hillary Clinton, their most famous classmate. For these women, the association is a source of pride.

friends surpass us in ways that are vital to our self-concept, we get jealous and distance ourselves from them in order to keep up our own self-esteem. When intimate others surpass us in ways that are not important to our self-concept, however, we take pride in their triumphs through a process of reflection (Tesser & Collins, 1988; Tesser et al., 1989). Applying this model to family dynamics, Tesser (1980) found that college students were most likely to report friction with their brothers or sisters when the two were close in age and when there was a disparity in their levels of ability.

Realities, Illusions, and Mental Health

> I refuse to be intimidated by reality anymore. . . . Reality is the leading cause of stress amongst those in touch with it. . . . Now, since I put reality on a back burner, my days are jam-packed and fun-filled. (Lily Tomlin as Trudy, the Bag Lady)

Psychologists used to maintain that an accurate perception of reality is vital to mental health. More and more, however, this view is being challenged by research on the mechanisms of self-defense. Consistently, people delude themselves and others with biased cognitions, self-handicapping, BIRGing, and downward comparison. Are these strategies and illusions a sign of health and well-being, or are they symptoms of a disorder?

When Shelley Taylor and Jonathon Brown (1988) reviewed all the relevant research, they found that individuals who are depressed or low in self-esteem actually have more realistic views of themselves than do most others who are better adjusted. Their self-appraisals are more likely to match appraisals of them made by neutral observers; they make fewer self-serving attributions to account for success and failure; they are less likely to exaggerate their control over uncontrollable events; and they make more balanced predictions about their future. They are also more likely to compare themselves to similar others rather than to make downward social comparisons (Wheeler & Miyake, 1992; Swallow & Kuiper, 1993). Based on these results, Taylor and Brown (1988) reached the provocative conclusion that positive illusions promote happiness, the desire to care for others, and the ability to engage in productive work—hallmark attributes of mental health: "These illusions help make each individual's world a warmer and more active and beneficent place in which to live" (p. 205).

Taylor and Brown are not alone in their conclusion. Many psychologists now believe that the mechanisms of "self-deception" are adaptive not only for the lives of individuals but for the evolution of the human species (Lockard & Paulhus, 1988). On the other hand, Randall Colvin and Jack Block (1994) argue that it is premature to draw any radical conclusions from existing research—that even if positive illusions temporarily elevate one's mood and self-esteem, their long-term effects are unclear. Indeed, Baumeister and Scher (1988) warn that illusions can give rise to chronic patterns of self-defeating behavior. People may escape from self-awareness through drug abuse and suicide, self-handicap themselves into underachievement and failure, deny health-related problems until it's too late, and rely on the illusion of control to protect them from the tender mercies of the gambling casino. Studies also show that people who blame others for their own misfortunes are worse off emotionally than those who do not externalize the blame (Tennen & Affleck, 1990).

Reality or illusion: Which is more adaptive? Are *you* better off overestimating your abilities or the control you can exert over events in your life? Are you better off as the eternal optimist or the hard-nosed realist? This thorny debate is likely to continue for years to come (Colvin & Block, 1994; Taylor & Brown, 1994).

SELF-PRESENTATION

The human quest for self-knowledge and self-esteem tells us about the inner self. The portrait is not complete, however, until we paint in the outer layer, the behavioral expression of the social self. Most people are concerned, at least to some extent, about the image they present to others. The fashion industry, cosmetic counters, diet centers, and the endless search for miracle drugs that grow hair, remove hair, whiten teeth, freshen breath, and smooth out wrinkles, all exploit our preoccupation with physical appearance. Similarly, people are concerned about the impressions they convey through their public *behavior*. What, as they say, will the neighbors think?

In *As You Like It,* William Shakespeare wrote, "All the world's a stage, / And all the men and women merely players." This insight was first put into social science terms by sociologist Erving Goffman (1959), who argued that life is like a theater and that each of us acts out certain *lines,* as if from a script. Most important, said Goffman, is that each of us assumes a certain *face,* or social identity, that others help us to maintain. Inspired by Goffman's theory, social psychologists study **self-presentation:** the process by which we try to shape what others think of us, and what we think of ourselves (Leary & Kowalski, 1990; Schlenker & Weigold, 1992; Tedeschi, 1981).

self-presentation Strategies people use to shape what others think of them.

An act of self-presentation may take many different forms. It may be conscious or unconscious, accurate or misleading, and intended for an external audience or for ourselves. In this section, we look at the varied goals of self-presentation and the ways in which people try to achieve these goals.

The Two Faces of Self-Presentation

There are basically two types of self-presentation, each serving a different motive. *Strategic self-presentation* consists of our efforts to shape others' impressions in specific ways in order to gain influence, power, sympathy, or approval.

Out of need for self-presentation, people worry about their physical appearance.

Drawing by Mankoff; © 1994 The New Yorker Magazine, Inc.

"I think I'll pass—I'm having a really bad-nose day."

Motivated to make a good impression, this job applicant observes his own behavior in preparation for an upcoming interview.

Prominent examples of strategic self-presentation are everywhere: in personal ads, in political campaign promises, in defendants' appeals to the jury. The specific goals include the desire to be seen as likable, competent, moral, dangerous, or helpless. Whatever the goal, people try to control their self-presentations in part through the use of nonverbal behaviors (DePaulo, 1992). For example, women sometimes eat less in front of men in order to appear appropriately feminine (Mori et al., 1987; Pliner & Chaiken, 1990).

The specific identities that people try to present vary from one person and situation to another (Leary & Kowalski, 1990). There are, however, two strategic self-presentation goals that are particularly common. The first is *ingratiation,* a term used to describe acts that are motivated by the desire to "get along" and be *liked.* The second goal is *self-promotion,* a term used to describe acts that are motivated by a desire to "get ahead" and be *respected* for one's competence (Arkin, 1981; Jones & Pittman, 1982). These goals are so basic to social behavior that they develop at an early stage. When driven by a desire to be selected as a partner for a competitive game, even second-grade children talk themselves up (Aloise-Young, 1993).

On the surface, it seems easy to achieve these goals. When people want to be liked, they put their best foot forward, smile a lot, nod their heads, express agreement, and, if necessary, resort to favors, compliments, and apple-polishing flattery. When people want to be admired for their competence, they try to impress others by talking about themselves and immodestly showing off their knowledge, status, and exploits. In both cases, there are tradeoffs. As the term *brown-nosing* all too graphically suggests, ingratiation tactics need to be subtle or else they will backfire (Jones, 1964). Similarly, people who constantly trumpet their own achievements are seen as self-absorbed and boastful—and are disliked as a result (Godfrey et al., 1986).

Self-presentation may give rise to other problems as well. In a provocative article entitled "Self-presentation can be hazardous to your health," Mark Leary and his colleagues (1994) reviewed evidence suggesting that the need to project a

Ingratiation is a strategy often used to curry favor.

Drawing by Richter; © 1992 The New Yorker Magazine, Inc.

"Great-looking tie!"

favorable public image can lure us into unsafe patterns of behavior. For example, self-presentation concerns can increase the risk of AIDS (when men are too embarrassed to buy condoms and talk openly with their sex partners), skin cancer (when people bake under the sun to get an attractive tan), eating disorders (when women overdiet, or use amphetamines, laxatives, and forced vomiting to stay thin), drug abuse (when teenagers smoke, drink, and use drugs to impress their peers), and accidental injury (when young men drive recklessly to appear brave and fearless to others).

The second main self-presentation motive is *self-verification:* the desire to have others perceive us as we genuinely perceive ourselves. According to William Swann (1987), people are highly motivated to verify their existing self-concept in the eyes of others. Swann and his colleagues have gathered lots of evidence for this hypothesis—and have found, for example, that people selectively elicit, recall, and accept personality feedback that confirms their self-conceptions. In fact, people sometimes bend over backward to correct others whose impressions are positive but mistaken. In one study, subjects interacted with a confederate who later said that they seemed dominant or submissive. When the comment was consistent with the subject's self-concept, it was accepted. When it was inconsistent, however, subjects went out of their way to prove the confederate wrong: those who perceived themselves as dominant but were labeled submissive later behaved more assertively than usual; those who viewed themselves as submissive but were labeled dominant subsequently became even more docile (Swann & Hill, 1982).

Self-verification seems desirable, but wait—when people have a negative self-concept, do they want others to share that impression? Nobody is perfect, and everyone has some faults. But do we really want to verify these faults? Do those of us who feel painfully shy, socially awkward, or insecure about an ability want others to see these weaknesses? Or would we rather present ourselves as bold, graceful, and competent? What happens when the desire for self-verification clashes with the need for self-enhancement?

Seeking to answer this question, Swann and his colleagues (1992b) asked subjects to fill out a self-concept questionnaire and then to choose an interaction

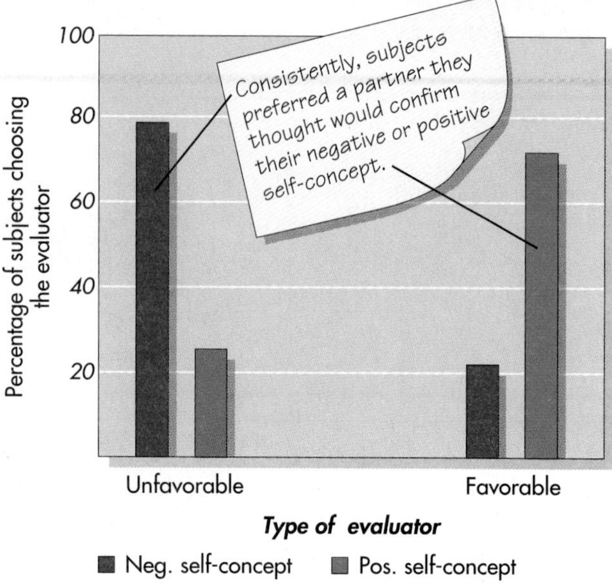

Figure 2.9 **What's More Important: Self-Verification or Self-Enhancement?** Subjects filled out a self-concept scale and were then asked to choose an interaction partner from two subjects—one who had evaluated them favorably, the other unfavorably. As shown, subjects with a positive self-concept wanted a partner who saw them favorably (right), but those with a negative self-concept preferred someone who saw them unfavorably (left). In this situation, the desire for self-verification overpowered the need for self-enhancement. (Swann et al., 1992b.)

partner from two other subjects—one who supposedly had evaluated them favorably, the other unfavorably. The result? Although subjects with a positive self-concept wanted someone who viewed them in a positive light, 78 percent of those with a negative self-concept preferred an evaluator who confirmed their admitted shortcomings (see Figure 2.9).

If people seek self-verification from laboratory partners, it stands to reason that they would want the same from their close relationships. In a study of married couples, husbands and wives separately answered questions about their self-concept, spouse, and commitment to the marriage. As predicted, people who had a positive self-concept expressed more commitment to partners who appraised them favorably, while those with a negative self-concept felt more committed to partners who appraised them *un*favorably (Swann et al., 1992a).

Regarding important aspects of the self-concept, research shows that people would rather reflect on and learn more about their own positive qualities than their negative ones (Sedikides, 1993). Still, however, it appears that the desire for self-verification is powerful—and can even, at times, overwhelm the need for self-enhancement. We all want to make a good impression, but we also want others in our lives to have an *accurate* impression, one that is compatible with our own self-concept.

High and Low Self-Monitoring

Although self-presentation is a way of life for all of us, it differs considerably among individuals. Some people are generally more conscious of their public image than others. Also, some people are more likely to engage in strategic self-presentation, while others seem to prefer self-verification. According to Mark Snyder (1987), these differences are related to a personality trait called **self-monitoring:** the tendency to regulate one's own behavior to meet the demands of social situations.

self-monitoring The tendency to change behavior in response to the self-presentation concerns of the situation.

Individuals who are high in self-monitoring appear to have a repertoire of selves from which to draw. Sensitive to strategic self-presentation concerns, they

Table 2.2 Self-Monitoring Scale

1. I find it hard to imitate the behavior of other people.
2. At parties and social gatherings, I do not attempt to do or say things that others will like.
3. I can only argue for ideas which I already believe.
4. I can make impromptu speeches even on topics about which I have almost no information.
5. I guess I put on a show to impress or entertain others.
6. I would probably make a good actor.
7. In a group of people I am rarely the center of attention.
8. In different situations and with different people, I often act like very different persons.
9. I am not particularly good at making other people like me.
10. I'm not always the person I appear to be.
11. I would not change my opinions (or the way I do things) in order to please someone or win their favor.
12. I have considered being an entertainer.
13. I have never been good at games like charades or improvisational acting.
14. I have trouble changing my behavior to suit different people and different situations.
15. At a party I let others keep the jokes and stories going.
16. I feel a bit awkward in company and do not show up quite as well as I should.
17. I can look anyone in the eye and tell a lie with a straight face (if for a right end).
18. I may deceive people by being friendly when I really dislike them.

Are you a high or low self-monitor? For each statement, answer *True* or *False*. When you are done, give yourself one point if you answered *T* to items 4, 5, 6, 8, 10, 12, 17, and 18. Then give yourself one point if you answered *F* to items 1, 2, 3, 7, 9, 11, 13, 14, 15, and 16. Count your total number of points. This total represents your Self-Monitoring Score. Among North American college students, the average score is about 10 or 11. (Snyder & Gangestad, 1986.)

are poised, ready, and able to modify their behavior as they move from one situation to another. As measured by the Self-Monitoring Scale (Snyder, 1974; Snyder & Gangestad, 1986), they are likely to agree with such statements as "I would probably make a good actor" and "In different situations and with different people, I often act like very different persons." In contrast, low self-monitors are self-verifiers by nature, appearing less concerned about the propriety of their behavior. Like character actors always cast into the same role, they express themselves in a consistent manner from one situation to the next, exhibiting what they regard as their true and honest self. On the Self-Monitoring Scale, low self-monitors say that "I can only argue for ideas which I already believe" and "I have never been good at games like charades or improvisational acting" (see Table 2.2).

Social psychologists disagree on (1) whether the Self-Monitoring Scale measures one global trait or a combination of two or more specific traits (Briggs &

Cheek, 1988; Lennox, 1988) and on (2) whether high and low self-monitors represent two discrete types of people or points along a continuum (Gangestad & Snyder, 1991; Miller & Thayer, 1989). Either way, the test scores can be used to predict important social behaviors. Concerned with a public image, high self-monitors—not only adults but children as well (Graziano et al., 1987)—go out of their way to learn about others with whom they might interact and about the rules for appropriate action. Then, once they have the situation sized up, they modify their behavior (Danheiser & Graziano, 1982; Shaffer et al., 1982). If a situation calls for conformity, high self-monitors conform; if the same situation calls for autonomy, they refuse to conform. In contrast, low self-monitors maintain a relatively consistent posture across situations (Snyder & Monson, 1975).

In the coming chapters, we will see that because so much of our behavior is influenced by social norms, self-monitoring is relevant to many aspects of social psychology. This fact may also have interesting developmental implications. A survey of eighteen- to seventy-three-year-olds revealed that self-monitoring scores tend to drop with age—presumably because people become more settled and secure about their personal identities as they get older (Reifman et al., 1989). For now, however, ponder this question: Is it better to be a high or low self-monitor? Is one orientation inherently more adaptive than the other?

The existing research does not enable us to make this kind of value judgment. Consider high self-monitors. Quite accurately, they regard themselves as *pragmatic,* flexible, and adaptive and as able to cope with the diversity of life's roles. But wait—they could also be described as fickle, or as phony opportunists, more concerned with appearances than with reality and willing to change colors like a chameleon just to fit in. Now think about low self-monitors. They describe themselves as *principled* and forthright; they are without pretense, always speaking their mind so others know where they stand. Of course, they could also be viewed as stubborn, insensitive to their surroundings, and unwilling to compromise just to get along. Concerning the relative value of these two orientations, then, it is safe to conclude that neither high nor low self-monitoring is necessarily undesirable—unless carried to the extreme. Goffman (1955) made the same point many years ago, when he wrote:

> Too little perceptiveness, too little *savoir faire,* too little pride and considerateness, and the person ceases to be someone who can be trusted to take a hint about himself or give a hint that will save others embarrassment. . . . Too much *savoir faire* or too much considerateness and he becomes someone who is too socialized, who leaves others with the feeling that they do not know how they really stand with him, nor what they should do to make an effective long-term adjustment. (p. 227)

EPILOGUE: THE MULTIFACETED SELF

Throughout history, writers, poets, philosophers, and personality theorists have portrayed the self as an enduring aspect of the human personality, as an invisible "inner core" that is stable over time and slow to change. The struggle to "find yourself" and "be true to yourself" is based on this portrait. In recent years, however, social psychologists have discovered that at least part of the self is malleable—molded by life experiences and varying from one situation to the next. From this perspective, the self has many different faces.

When you look into the mirror, what do *you* see—one self or many? Do you see a person whose self-concept is enduring or one whose identity seems to change from time to time? Do you see a person whose strengths and weaknesses are evaluated with an objective eye or one who is insulated from unpleasant truths by mechanisms of self-defense? Do you see a person who has an inner, hidden self that is different from the face shown to others?

Based on the material presented in this chapter, the answer to such questions seems always to be the same: the self has all these characteristics. More than a hundred years ago, William James (1890) said that the self is not simple but complex and multifaceted. Based on current theories and research, we can now appreciate just how right James was. Sure, there's an aspect of the self-concept that seems accessible only through introspection and that is stable over time. But there's also an aspect that changes with the company we keep and the information we get from other people.

When it comes to self-esteem, there are times when we are self-focused enough to become acutely aware of our shortcomings. Yet there are also times when we guard ourselves through self-serving cognitions, self-handicapping, BIRGing, and downward comparisons. Then there is the matter of self-presentation. It's clear that each of us has a private self consisting of our inner thoughts and feelings, memories, and self-schemas. But it is equally clear that we also have an outer self, portrayed by the roles we play and the masks we wear in public. As you read through the pages of this text, you will see that these cognitive, affective, and behavioral components of the self are not separate and distinct but interrelated. They are also of great significance for the rest of social psychology.

REVIEW

THE SELF-CONCEPT

- The self-concept is the sum total of a person's beliefs about his or her own attributes. It is the cognitive component of the self.

Beginnings of the Self-Concept

- Recognizing oneself as a distinct entity is the first step in the development of a self-concept.
- Human beings and apes are the only animals to recognize their mirror-image reflections as their own.
- As Cooley's "looking-glass self" suggests, social factors are a necessary second step.

Introspection

- People believe that introspection is a key to knowing the true self.
- But research shows that introspection sometimes diminishes the accuracy of self-reports.

Perceptions of Our Own Behavior

- Bem's self-perception theory states that when internal states are difficult to interpret, we infer our inner states by observing our own behavior and the surrounding situation.
- Based on self-perception theory, the facial feedback hypothesis states that facial expressions can produce, not just reflect, an emotion state (smiling can cause people to feel happy).
- But it's unclear whether the emotion occurs via self-perception or because facial expressions trigger physiological changes that produce the emotional response.
- Based on self-perception theory, the overjustification effect is that people sometimes lose interest in activities for which they were previously rewarded.

Influences of Other People

- According to social comparison theory, people who are uncertain of their own opinions and abilities often

evaluate themselves via comparisons with similar others.
- Schachter and Singer proposed that the experience of emotion is based on two factors: physiological arousal and a cognitive label for that arousal.
- Under certain conditions, people interpret their own arousal by watching others in the same situation.

Autobiographical Memory

- Memory of one's life events is critical to the self-concept.
- There are three ways in which the self guides our recollections.
- First is the self-reference effect—that people are more likely to remember something if it relates to the self than if encountered in other contexts.
- Second is that autobiographical memory is shaped by an egocentric bias, as people overemphasize their own roles in past events.
- Third, the hindsight bias leads people to revise their personal histories in light of new information about themselves.

Self-Schemas

- A self-schema is a specific belief about oneself that guides the processing of information.
- On matters relevant to self-schemas, people make rapid judgments about themselves and are quick to recall past actions or predict future actions.

Multicultural Perspectives

- Cultures foster different conceptions of self.
- Many Europeans and North Americans hold an independent view of themselves as autonomous.
- People in many other cultures hold an interdependent view of the self that encompasses their social connections.
- These cultural differences influence the way we perceive, feel about, and present ourselves in relation to others.

SELF-ESTEEM

- Self-esteem is a person's positive and negative evaluations of self.
- People with low self-esteem can get caught in a vicious cycle of self-defeating behavior.

Self-Discrepancies

- According to self-discrepancy theory, large discrepancies between one's actual self and self-guides produce a lowered self-esteem and affective disorders.
- Discrepancies between the actual and ideal selves are related to feelings of disappointment and depression.
- Discrepancies between the actual and the ought selves are related to shame, guilt, and anxiety.
- The emotional effects depend on the amount of discrepancy and whether it is accessible to awareness.

Self-Awareness

- In general, people spend little time thinking about themselves.
- But certain situations (mirrors, cameras, audiences) increase self-focus. And certain people are generally more self-conscious than others.
- Self-awareness forces us to notice self-discrepancies and can produce a temporary reduction in self-esteem.
- To cope, we adjust our behavior to meet standards or we withdraw from the self-focusing situation.
- Heavy drinking and suicide can be viewed as ways of escaping from self-awareness.

Self-Enhancement

- Most people think highly of themselves and protect their self-esteem. There are four ways this can be achieved.
- One is through self-serving cognitions such as taking credit for success but denying the blame for failure.
- Second, people make excuses and even self-handicap (for example, through drug use or reduced effort) in order to excuse anticipated failure.
- Third, people often bask in reflected glory, boosting self-esteem from associations with successful others.
- Fourth, people compare themselves to others who are less happy, less successful, or less fortunate.
- When others surpass us in ways important to our self-concept, we become jealous and distance ourselves from them. When surpassed in ways that are not self-relevant, we feel pride and seek closeness.

Realities, Illusions, and Mental Health

- Recent research suggests that certain positive illusions may foster mental health.
- An alternative view is that in the long run such illusions promote self-defeating behavior patterns.

SELF-PRESENTATION

- Self-presentation is the process by which we try to shape what others think of us and even what we think of ourselves.

The Two Faces of Self-Presentation

- There are basically two motives for self-presentation.
- The first is strategic, consisting of efforts to shape others' impressions in order to be liked or respected.
- The second motive is self-verification, by which we try to get others to perceive us as we genuinely perceive ourselves.

High and Low Self-Monitoring

- Individuals differ in the tendency to regulate their behavior to meet the demands of social situations.
- High self-monitors modify their behavior, as appropriate, from one situation to the next.
- Low self-monitors express themselves in a more consistent manner, exhibiting at all times what they regard as their true self.

EPILOGUE: THE MULTIFACETED SELF

- As this chapter has shown, the self is not simple but complex and multifaceted.

KEY TERMS

KVET

Chapter 3

Perceiving Persons

PREVIEW

This chapter examines how people come to know, or think they know, other persons. First, we introduce the *elements of social perception*—those aspects of persons, situations, and behavior that guide initial observations. Next, we examine how people make explanations, or *attributions,* for the behavior of others and how they form integrated *impressions* based on initial perceptions and attributions. We then consider *confirmation biases,* the subtle ways in which initial impressions lead people to distort later information, setting in motion a self-fulfilling prophecy.

OUTLINE

When major-league baseball players went on strike on August 8, 1994, making it the first season in ninety years to close without a World Series, angry fans disagreed on who was to blame: Were the players being greedy, or were the owners at fault? When President Clinton was mired in the so-called Whitewater scandal, voters and news analysts were suspicious: Had Bill and Hillary broken the law in past financial dealings, or were the allegations motivated by partisan politics? When South Carolina mother Susan Smith confessed to the drowning murder of her two young sons in November 1994, everyone wondered: Is she evil or just plain crazy? When Michael Jackson announced his marriage to Lisa Marie Presley, people were skeptical: Were Jackson and Presley in love, or was the singer just trying to clean up his tarnished image? And when couples divorce after years of marriage, friends and relatives often ask: Whose fault was it?

Whatever the topic—sports, business, politics, crime, law, or personal events at home—we are all active and interested participants in **social perception**, the processes by which people come to understand one another. This chapter is divided into four sections. First we look at the "raw data" of social perception—persons, situations, and behavior. Second, we examine how people explain and analyze behavior. Third, we consider how people integrate their observations into a coherent impression of other persons. Fourth, we discuss some of the subtle ways in which our impressions create a distorted picture of reality, often setting in motion a self-fulfilling prophecy. As you read this chapter, you will notice that the various processes are considered from a perceiver's vantage point. Keep in mind, however, that in the events of life, you are both a *perceiver* and a *target* of others' perceptions.

social perception A general term for the processes by which people come to understand one another.

OBSERVATION: THE ELEMENTS OF SOCIAL PERCEPTION

As our opening examples suggest, understanding others may be difficult, but it's a vital part of everyday life. How do we do it? What kinds of evidence do we use? One cannot actually "see" someone's greed, or political motives, or mental state, any more than a detective can see a crime that was already committed. So, like a detective who tries to reconstruct events by turning up witnesses, fingerprints, blood samples, and other evidence, the social perceiver comes to know others by relying on indirect clues—the elements of social perception. These clues arise from three sources: persons, situations, and behavior.

Persons: Judging a Book by Its Cover

Have you ever had the experience of meeting someone for the first time and immediately forming an impression based only on a quick "snapshot" of information? As children, we were told not to judge a book by its cover, that things are not always what they seem, that appearances are deceptive, and that all that glitters is not gold. As adults, however, we can't seem to help ourselves.

The 1994 baseball strike and the marriage of Michael Jackson and Lisa Marie Presley were two events that led people to ask "why"—thus triggering the processes of social perception.

In 500 B.C., the mathematician Pythagoras looked into the eyes of prospective students to determine if they were gifted. At about the same time, Hippocrates—the founder of modern medicine—used facial features to make diagnoses of life and death. In the nineteenth century, Viennese physician Franz Gall introduced a carnival-like science called "phrenology" and claimed to assess people's character by the shape of their skull. And in 1954, psychologist William Sheldon mistakenly concluded from flawed studies of adult men that there is a strong link between physique and personality.

People may not measure each other by bumps on the head, as phrenologists used to do, but first impressions are influenced in subtle ways by a person's height, weight, skin color, hair color, eyeglasses, and other aspects of appearance (Alley, 1988; Bull & Rumsey, 1988; Herman et al., 1986). As social perceivers, we are even influenced by a person's name. For example, Robert Young and his colleagues (1993) found that fictional characters with "older generation" names such as Harry, Walter, Dorothy, and Edith are judged less popular and less intelligent than those with "younger generation" names such as Kevin, Michael, Lisa, and Michelle.

The human face in particular attracts more than its share of attention. For example, Diane Berry and Leslie Zebrowitz-McArthur (1986) have found that adults who have baby-faced features—large round eyes, high eyebrows, round cheeks, a large forehead, smooth skin, and a rounded chin—are seen as warm, kind, naive, weak, honest, and submissive. In contrast, adults with mature fea-

We often make snap judgments about others based on just a tiny sample of information.

"You're not at all like your answering machine."

In 1989, Richard Singleton was arrested and charged with the shooting murder of a seventeen-year-old boy in Sacramento. When his baby-faced picture appeared in the newspapers, people were shocked.

tures—small eyes, low brows and a small forehead, wrinkled skin, and an angular chin—are seen as stronger, more dominant, and less naive. Thus, in small claims court, judges are more likely to favor baby-faced defendants accused of intentional wrongdoing, but they tend to rule against baby-faced defendants accused of negligence (Zebrowitz & McDonald, 1991). And in the workplace, baby-faced job applicants are more likely to be recommended for employment as daycare teachers, whereas mature-faced adults are considered to be better suited for work as bankers (Zebrowitz et al., 1991).

What accounts for these findings? And why, in general, are people so quick to judge others by appearances? There are three possible explanations. One is that human beings are genetically programmed to respond gently to infantile features so that real babies are treated with tender loving care. Another possibility is that we simply learn to associate infantile features with helplessness and then generalize this expectation to baby-faced adults. Third, maybe there is an actual link between appearance and behavior—a possibility suggested by the fact that subjects exposed only to photos or brief videotapes of strangers formed impressions that correlated with the self-descriptions of these same strangers (Berry, 1990; Kenny et al., 1992). Whatever the explanation, the perceived link between appearance and behavior may account for the shock that we sometimes experience when our expectations are disconfirmed (see above photo).

Situations: The Scripts of Life

In addition to our beliefs about persons, each of us has preset notions about certain types of situations—scripts that enable us to anticipate the goals, behaviors, and outcomes likely to occur in a particular setting (Abelson, 1981; Read, 1987). Based on past experience, people can easily imagine the sequences of events likely to unfold in a typical greeting or at the shopping mall or dinner table. The more experience you have in a given situation, the more detail your scripts should contain. As described in Roger Axtell's (1993) best-seller, *Do's and Taboos Around the World,* many scripts are culture-specific. As a dinner guest in Bolivia, you should clean your plate to prove that you enjoyed the meal. Eat in an Indian home, however, and you'll see that native guests leave some food on the plate to show the host that they had enough to eat.

In a study of the American "first date" script, John Pryor and Thomas Merluzzi (1985) asked college students to list the sequence of events that take place in this situation. From these lists, a picture of a typical first date emerged. Sixteen steps were identified, including: (1) male arrives; (2) female greets male at door; (3) female introduces date to parents or roommate; (4) male and female discuss plans and make small talk; (5) they go to a movie; (6) they get something to eat or drink; (7) male takes female home; (8) if interested, he remarks about a future date; (9) they kiss; (10) they say good night. Sound familiar? Additional research shows that dating is a clearly scripted event about which men and women show high levels of agreement (Rose & Frieze, 1993). Pryor and Merluzzi then randomized their list of events and asked subjects to arrange them into the appropriate order. They found that subjects with extensive dating experience were able to organize the statements more quickly than those who had less dating experience. For people who are familiar with a script, the events fall into place like the pieces of a puzzle.

A knowledge of social settings provides an important context for understanding other people's verbal and nonverbal behavior. For example, this knowledge leads us to expect someone to be polite during a job interview, playful at a picnic, and rowdy at a keg party. Scripts influence social perceptions in two ways. First, we sometimes see what we expect to see in a particular situation. In one study, subjects looked at photographs of human faces that had ambiguous expressions. When subjects were told that the person in the photo was being threatened by a vicious dog, they saw the expression as fearful; when told that the person had just won money, subjects interpreted the *same* expression as a sign of happiness (Trope, 1986). Second, people use what they know about social situations to ex-

In Spain, people are always late for appointments—except when attending a bullfight, a situation whose "script" calls for punctuality.

plain the causes of human behavior. As described later in this chapter, an action seems to offer more information about a person when it departs from the norm than when it is common. In other words, you would learn more about someone who is rowdy during a job interview or polite at a keg party than if it were the other way around.

Behavioral Evidence

An essential first step in social perception is to recognize what someone is doing at a given moment. Identifying actions from movement is surprisingly easy. Even when actors dressed in black move about in a dark room with point lights attached only to the joints of their body, people easily recognize such complex acts as walking, running, jumping, exercising, and falling (Johansson et al., 1980).

More interesting, perhaps, is that people derive *meaning* from their observations by dividing the continuous stream of human behavior into discrete units. By having subjects observe someone on videotape and press a button whenever they detect a meaningful action, Darren Newtson and his colleagues (1987) have found that some perceivers break the behavior stream into a large number of fine units, whereas others break it into a small number of gross units. While watching a baseball game, for example, you might press the button after each pitch, after each batter, after every inning, or only after runs are scored.

The manner in which people divide a stream of behavior can influence perceptions in important ways. Subjects who are told to break an event into fine units rather than gross units attend more closely, detect more meaningful actions, and remember more details about the actor's behavior than do gross-unit subjects (Lassiter et al., 1988). Fine-unit subjects become more familiar with the actor they've observed, so they also come to view that actor in more positive terms (Lassiter, 1988). As we will see in Chapter 5, familiarity often heightens attraction.

The Silent Language of Nonverbal Behavior Behavioral cues are used not only to identify someone's actions but also to determine his or her inner states. Sometimes, people tell us how they feel. At other times, however, they do not tell us, they are themselves not sure, or they actively try to conceal their intentions and true feelings. For these reasons, we often tune in to a silent language, the language of **nonverbal behavior.**

nonverbal behavior Behavior that reveals a person's feelings without words—through facial expressions, body language, and vocal cues.

What kinds of nonverbal cues do people use to judge how someone is feeling? In *The Expression of the Emotions in Man and Animals,* Charles Darwin (1872) proposed that the *face* expresses emotion in ways that are innate and understood by people all over the world. Contemporary research supports this notion. Numerous studies have shown that when presented with photographs similar to those on page 87, people can reliably identify at least six "primary" emotions: happiness, fear, sadness, anger, surprise, and disgust. In one study, subjects from ten different countries—Estonia, Germany, Greece, Hong Kong, Italy, Japan, Scotland, Sumatra, Turkey, and the United States—exhibited high levels of agreement in their recognition of these emotions (Ekman et al., 1987). Although questions have been raised about this research (Russell, 1994), it seems that from one end of the world to the other, a smile is a smile, and a frown is a frown, and everyone knows what they mean—even when the expressions are "put on" by actors and not genuinely felt (Gosselin et al., 1995).

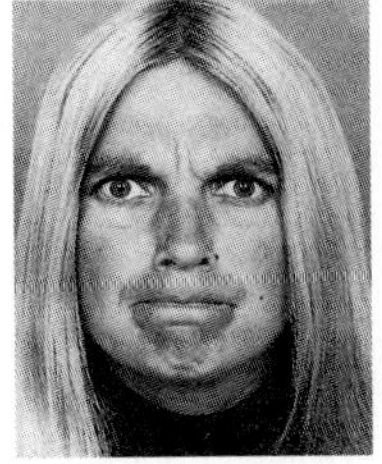
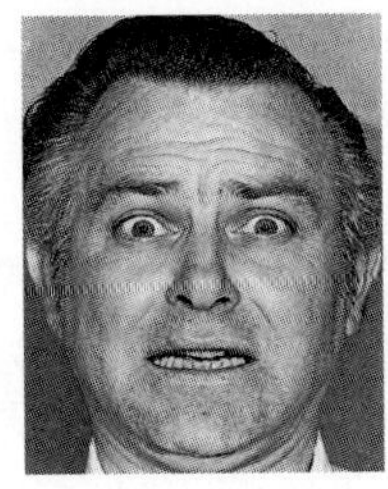
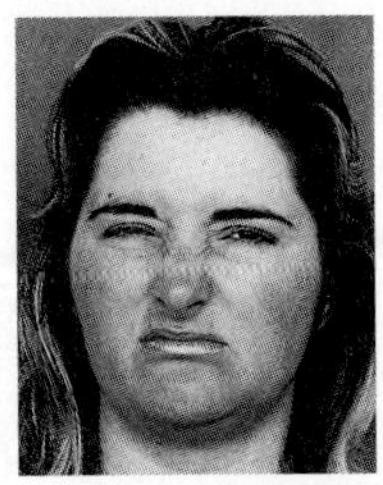
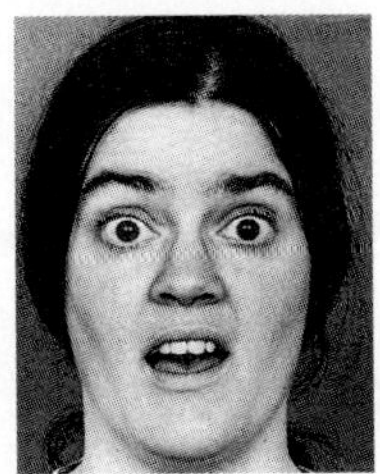

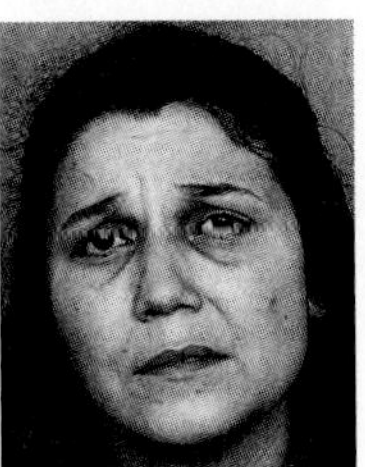

Can you tell how these individuals are feeling? If you are like most people, regardless of your culture, you will have little trouble recognizing the emotions portrayed. (Copyright Paul Ekman 1975.)

Darwin believed that the ability to recognize emotion in others has survival value for all members of a species. This hypothesis suggests that some emotions are more important to identify than others. Thus, it may be more adaptive to know when someone else is angry (and hence prone to lash out in violence) than to know when someone is happy, a nonthreatening emotion. So, are people more sensitive to signs of anger than to those of happiness? In a series of experiments, Christine and Ranald Hansen (1988) asked subjects to find discrepant facial expressions in photographs of crowds consisting of happy, neutral, or angry faces. In some pictures, all individuals wore the same expression; in others, there was a single discrepant expression. As Darwin would have predicted, subjects exhibited the "face-in-the-crowd effect": they were quicker to spot discrepant angry faces than they were to locate discrepant faces that were happy or neutral. Indeed, Joel Aronoff and his colleagues (1992) believe that anger is universally recognized by fixed geometric patterns on the face. As shown in Figure 3.1, anger can be "seen" in triangular eyes that point toward the nose and other hard, downward lines in the forehead, cheeks, mouth, and chin. Such patterns are common in the threatening ceremonial masks of many cultures.

Other nonverbal cues can also influence social perception, enabling us to make quick and often accurate judgments of others (Ambady & Rosenthal, 1993). For example, social perceivers are often fluent readers of *body language*—

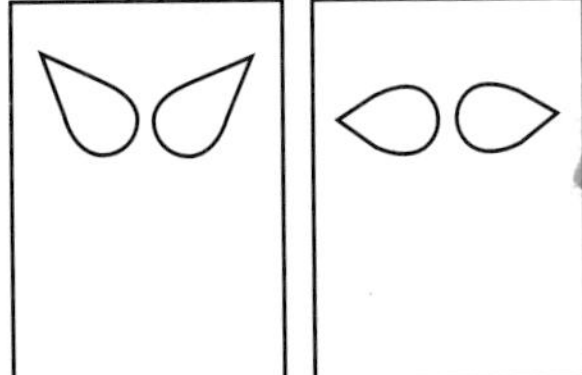
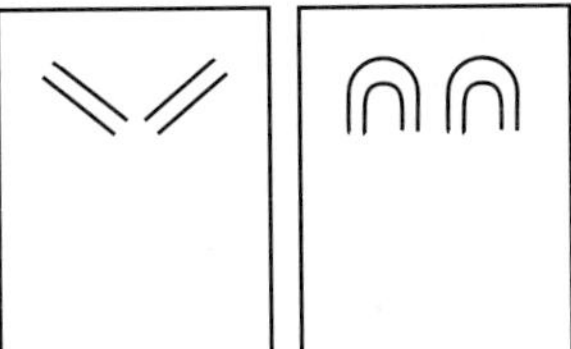
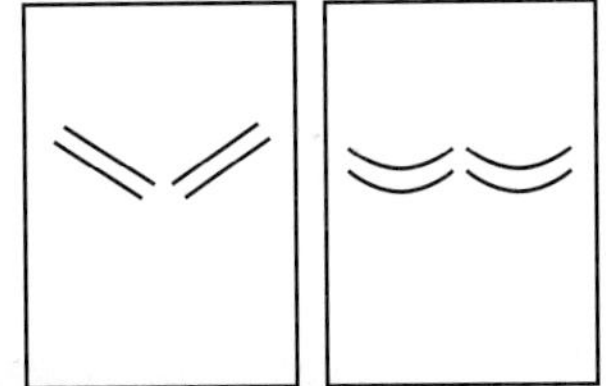
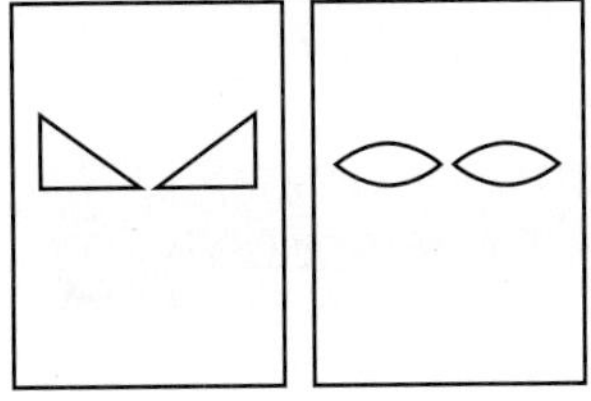

Figure 3.1 **The Face of Anger.** Anger is universally recognized by the geometric patterns in the face—specifically, by hard, downward, and pointed lines. In the examples shown in the drawings, the left form of each pair seems angrier than the one on the right (Aronoff et al., 1988). The same effect can be seen in the protective masks worn by National Hockey League goalies and in the ceremonial masks from Africa and Bali.

the ways people stand, sit, walk, and express themselves through various gestures. Thus, men and women who have a youthful walking style—who sway their hips, bend their knees, pick up their feet, and swing their arms in a bouncy rhythm—are seen to be happier and more powerful than those who walk slowly, take shorter steps, and stiffly drag their feet (Montepare & McArthur, 1988).

Eye contact, or *gaze,* is also a common form of nonverbal communication. Eyes have been called the "windows of the soul." In many cultures, people tend to assume that someone who avoids eye contact is evasive, cold, fearful, shy, or indifferent; that frequent gazing signals intimacy, sincerity, self-confidence, and respect; and that the person who stares is tense, angry, and unfriendly. Typically, however, eye contact is interpreted in light of a pre-existing relationship. If a relationship is friendly, frequent eye contact elicits a positive impression. If a relationship is not friendly, eye contact is seen in negative terms. It has been said that if two people lock eyes for more than a few seconds, they are either going to make love or kill each other (Kleinke, 1986; Patterson, 1983).

Another powerful, primitive form of nonverbal behavior is *touch*—the congratulatory high-five, the sympathetic pat on the back, the joking elbow in the ribs, and the loving embrace being just a few familiar examples. Physical touching has long been regarded as an expression of friendship, nurturance, sexual interest, and the like. However, it may also serve other functions. Several years ago, Nancy Henley (1977) observed that men, older persons, and those of high socioeconomic status were more likely to touch women, younger persons, and individuals of lower status than the other way around. Henley's interpretation: Touching is an expression not only of intimacy but of dominance and control.

Researchers are particularly intrigued by the sex differences that Henley had observed. In one study, Brenda Major and others (1990) watched people in city streets, parks, shopping malls, beaches, airports, and other public settings. The result: Men were more likely to touch women than women were to touch men. A difference did not exist, however, among children or in places where friends ritually greet or say good-by to each other. In another study, Judith Hall and Ellen Veccia (1990) observed 4,500 pairs and found in mixed-sex interactions that although men were more likely than women to initiate contact with the hand, the overall sex differences were more complicated. For example, men were more likely to put their arms around women, whereas women were more likely to link arms with men.

Distinguishing Truth from Deception Social perception is tricky because people sometimes try to hide or stretch the truth about themselves. Poker players bluff to win, witnesses lie to protect themselves, and politicians make campaign promises they don't intend to keep. On occasion, everyone tells something less than "the truth, the whole truth, and nothing but the truth." We make excuses, present ourselves in a particular light, or pretend in order to be polite. Can social perceivers tell the difference? Can *you* tell when someone is lying?

Sigmund Freud, the founder of psychoanalysis, once said that "no mortal can keep a secret. If his lips are silent, he chatters with his fingertips; betrayal oozes out of him at every pore" (1905, p. 94). Paul Ekman and Wallace Friesen (1974) revised Freud's observation by pointing out that some pores "ooze" more than others. Specifically, Ekman and Friesen proposed that some channels of communication are difficult for deceivers to control, while others are relatively easy. To test this hypothesis, they showed a series of films—some pleasant, others disgusting—to a group of female nurses. While watching, subjects were instructed either to report their honest impressions of these films or to conceal their true feelings. Through the use of hidden cameras, the subjects were videotaped. Others acting as observers then viewed the tapes and judged whether subjects had been truthful or deceptive. The results showed that the level of judgment accuracy was influenced by which types of nonverbal cues the observers were exposed to. Observers who watched tapes that focused on the body were better at detecting deception than were those who saw tapes focused on the face. The face can communicate emotion, but, unlike nervous movements of the hands and feet, it is relatively easy for deceivers to control.

This study was the first of many. In other studies as well, one group of subjects made truthful or deceptive statements while another group read the transcripts, listened to audiotapes or watched videotapes, and then tried to evaluate the statements. This research shows that people frequently make mistakes in their judgments of truth and deception, too often accepting what is said at face value and giving speakers the benefit of the doubt. Even people who regularly make these kinds of judgments for a living—detectives, judges, psychiatrists, and polygraphers (who administer lie-detector tests) for the CIA, FBI, and military—are prone to error (Ekman & O'Sullivan, 1991; see Table 3.1).

What seems to be the problem? After reviewing more than thirty studies, Miron Zuckerman and his colleagues (1981) concluded that there is a *mismatch* between the behaviors actually associated with deception and those used by perceivers to detect deception. Specifically, there are four channels of communication that give relevant information: words, the face, the body, and the voice. When people have a reason to lie, *words* alone cannot be trusted. The *face* is also controllable. We tend to think that people do not smile when they lie, but it is common for deceivers to mask their real feelings with false smiles that do not stretch up to the eye muscles (Ekman et al., 1990). Indeed, psychophysiological research confirms that there are two types of smiles—one more genuine than the other (Ekman & Davidson, 1993; Frank et al., 1993). The *body* is somewhat more revealing than the face, as deception is often accompanied by fidgety movements of the hands and feet and by restless shifts in posture. Finally, the *voice* is the leakiest, most revealing cue. When people lie, especially when they are highly motivated to do so, their voice rises in pitch and the number of speech hesitations increases.

In light of these findings, it appears that perceivers tune in to the wrong channels of communication. Too easily seduced by the silver tongue and the smiling

Lie-detection experts with experience at making judgments of truth and deception were shown brief videotapes of ten women telling the truth or lying about their feelings. Considering that there was a fifty-fifty chance of guessing correctly, the accuracy rates were remarkably low. Only a sample of U.S. Secret Service agents posted a better-than-chance performance. (Ekman & O'Sullivan, 1991.)

Table 3.1 Can the "Experts" Catch a Liar?

Observer Groups	Accuracy Rates
College students	52.82
CIA, FBI, and military	55.67
Police investigators	55.79
Trial judges	56.73
Psychiatrists	57.61
U.S. Secret Service agents	64.12

face, we often fail to notice the restless body and quivering voice. Ironically, subjects become more accurate in their judgments of truth and deception when they are too busy to attend closely to what a speaker says (Gilbert & Krull, 1988), when they're instructed to pay more attention to the telltale body or voice than to the face (DePaulo et al., 1982), and when they are not themselves anxious about social interaction (DePaulo & Tang, 1994).

Every now and then, the targets of social perception face an awkward communication dilemma. Being observed by more than one audience, they sometimes find it necessary to send mixed messages—one truthful, the other deceptive. You may recall that American pilots captured during the 1991 Persian Gulf War were videotaped as they confessed to war crimes and denounced U.S. policy. Forced to make these statements, these pilots had to convince their captors that their performance would be believed yet at the same time communicate to viewers back home that they were being coerced. A similar dilemma confronts teenagers who confide in a close friend within earshot of a parent, or politicians who address audiences consisting of opposing special-interest groups. Can people tell the truth to one audience while concealing it from another? What strategies are used? As perceivers, are we sensitive to "hidden" messages?

Referring to this predicament as the *multiple audience problem*, John Fleming (1994) and others are seeking answers to these questions. In one study, Fleming and John Darley (1991) asked high school students to make videotapes in which they communicate the location of a secret meeting to an audience of peers while concealing it from an audience of parents and other adults. As it turned out, the students were able to achieve their objectives, inasmuch as peers who saw the videotapes were more likely than adult observers to guess the correct location of the meeting. The students were able to send their covert message by using private hand signals and slang expressions known only by their teenaged peers.

ATTRIBUTION: FROM ELEMENTS TO DISPOSITIONS

To interact effectively with others, we find it useful to know how they feel and when they can be trusted. But to understand people well enough to predict their future behavior, we must also identify their *dispositions*—stable characteristics such as personality traits, attitudes, and abilities. Since we cannot actually see dispositions, we infer them from what a person says and does. In this section, we look at the processes that lead us to make these inferences.

The Logic of Attribution

Do you ever think about the influence you have on other people? What about the roles of heredity, childhood experiences, and social forces? Do you wonder why some people succeed while others fail? Individuals differ in the extent to which they seek to explain the events of human behavior—and in the degree of confidence they have in their own ability to do so (Weary & Edwards, 1994). Among college students, for example, psychology majors are more curious about such matters than are natural-science majors (Fletcher et al., 1986). Although there are differences among us, people in general ask "why?" when faced with important events that are negative or unexpected (Hastie, 1984; Weiner, 1985).

To make sense of our social world, we try to understand the causes of our own

attribution theory A group of theories that describe how people explain the causes of behavior.

personal attribution Attribution to internal characteristics of an actor, such as ability, personality, mood, or effort.

situational attribution Attribution to factors external to an actor, such as the task, other people, or luck.

correspondent inference theory The theory that we make inferences about a person when his or her actions are freely chosen, unexpected, and result in a small number of desirable effects.

and other people's behavior. But what kinds of explanations do we make, and how do we go about making them? In a classic book entitled *The Psychology of Interpersonal Relations*, Fritz Heider (1958) took the first step toward answering these questions. To Heider, we are all scientists of a sort. Motivated to understand others well enough to manage our social environment, we observe, analyze, and explain their behavior. The explanations we come up with are called *attributions*, and the theory that describes the process is called **attribution theory.** The questions posed at the beginning of this chapter—regarding the baseball strike, the Whitewater scandal, the South Carolina woman who murdered her two children, the marriage of Michael Jackson and Lisa Marie Presley, and couples that divorce—are questions of attribution.

Although people come up with different kinds of explanations for the events of human behavior, Heider found it useful to group these explanations into two categories: personal and situational. When baseball players go on strike, angry fans can blame the players for being greedy (a **personal attribution**), or they can find fault with the player agents, owners, or outside societal and economic forces (a **situational attribution**). When competitors or lovers clash, we blame one party, or both parties, or the circumstances. The task for the attribution theorist is to determine not the *true* causes of these events but our *perceptions* of the causes. For now, two major attribution theories are described.

Jones's Correspondent Inference Theory According to Edward Jones and Keith Davis (1965), each of us tries to understand others by observing and analyzing their behavior. Jones and Davis's **correspondent inference theory** predicts that people try to infer from an action whether the action itself corresponds to an enduring personal characteristic of the actor. Is the person who commits an act of aggression a beast? Is the person who donates money to charity an altruist? To answer these kinds of questions, people make inferences on the basis of three factors.

The first factor is a person's degree of *choice*. Behavior that is freely chosen is more informative about a person than behavior that is coerced. In one study, subjects read a speech, presumably written by a college student, that either favored or opposed Fidel Castro, the communist leader of Cuba. Some subjects were told that the student had freely chosen this position, and others were told that the student was assigned the position by a professor. When asked to determine the student's true attitude, subjects were more likely to assume a correspondence between his or her essay (behavior) and attitude (disposition) when the student had a choice than when he or she was assigned to the role (Jones & Harris, 1967; see Figure 3.2). Keep this study in mind. It supports correspondent inference theory, but, as we will see later, it also demonstrates one of the most tenacious biases of social perception.

The second factor that leads people to make dispositional inferences is the *expectedness* of behavior. As previously noted, an action tells us more about a person when it departs from the norm than when it is typical, part of a social role, or otherwise expected under the circumstances (Jones et al., 1961). Thus, people think they know more about a student who wears three-piece suits to class or a citizen who openly refuses to pay taxes than about a student who wears blue jeans to class or a citizen who files tax returns on April 15.

Third, people consider the intended *effects* or consequences of someone's behavior. Acts that produce many desirable outcomes do not reveal a person's specific motives as clearly as acts that produce only a single desirable outcome

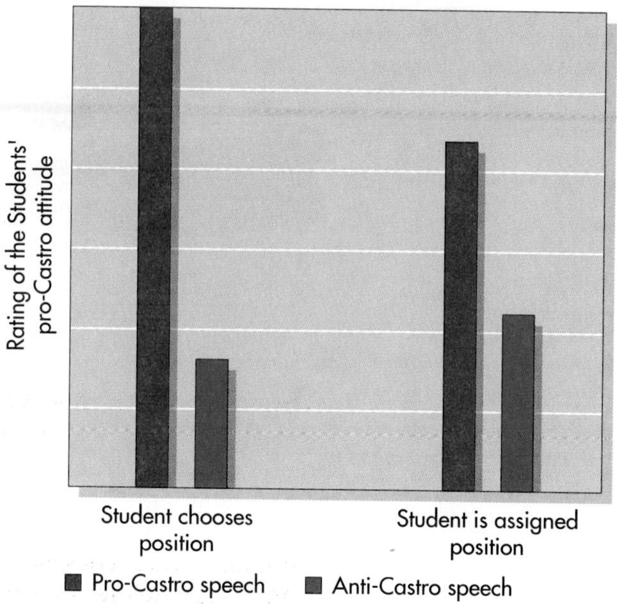

Figure 3.2 **What Does This Speechwriter Really Believe?** As predicted by correspondent inference theory, subjects who read a student's speech (behavior) were more likely to assume that it reflected the student's true attitude (disposition) when the position taken was freely chosen (left) rather than assigned (right). But also note the evidence for the fundamental attribution error. Even subjects who thought the student had been assigned a position inferred the student's attitude from the speech. (Jones & Harris, 1967.)

(Newtson, 1974). For example, you are likely to be uncertain about exactly why a person stays on a job that is enjoyable, high paying, and in an attractive location—three desirable outcomes, each sufficient to explain the behavior. In contrast, you may feel more certain about why a person stays on a job that is tedious and low paying but is in an attractive location—only one desirable outcome.

Kelley's Covariation Theory Correspondent inference theory seeks to describe how perceivers try to discern an individual's personal characteristics from a slice of behavioral evidence. However, behavior can be attributed not only to personal factors but to situational factors as well. How is this distinction made? In Chapter 1, we noted that the causes of human behavior can be derived only by conducting *experiments*. That is, one has to make more than a single observation and compare behavior in two or more settings in which everything stays the same except for the independent variables. Like Heider, Harold Kelley (1967) believes that people are much like scientists in this regard. They may not observe others in a laboratory, but they too make comparisons and think in terms of "experiments." According to Kelley, people make attributions by using the **covariation principle:** In order for something to be the cause of a behavior, it must be present when the behavior occurs and absent when it does not. Three kinds of covariation information are particularly useful: consensus, distinctiveness, and consistency.

covariation principle A principle of attribution theory that people attribute behavior to factors that are present when a behavior occurs and absent when it does not.

To illustrate these concepts, imagine you are standing on a street corner one hot, steamy evening minding your own business, when all of a sudden a stranger comes out of an air-conditioned movie theater and blurts out, "Great flick!" Looking up, you don't recognize the movie title, so you wonder what to make of this "recommendation." Was the behavior (the rave review) caused by something about the person (the stranger), the stimulus (the film), or the circumstances (say, the air-conditioned theater)? Possibly interested in spending a night at the movies, how would you proceed to explain what happened? What kinds of information would you want to obtain?

Thinking like a scientist, you might seek out *consensus information* to see how different persons react to the same exact stimulus. In other words, how do other moviegoers feel about this film? If others also rave about it, the stranger's behavior is high in consensus and is attributed to the stimulus. If others are critical of the same film, the behavior is low in consensus and is attributed to the person.

Still thinking like a scientist, you might also want to have *distinctiveness information* to see how the same person reacts to different stimuli. In other words, how does this moviegoer react to other films? If the stranger is critical of other films, the target behavior is high in distinctiveness and is attributed to the stimulus. If the stranger raves about everything, however, then the behavior is low in distinctiveness and is attributed to the person.

Finally, you might seek *consistency information* to see what happens to the behavior at another time when the person and the stimulus both remain the same. How does this moviegoer feel about this film on other occasions? If the stranger raves about the film on video as well as in the theater, the behavior is high in consistency. If the stranger does not always enjoy the film, the behavior is low in consistency. According to Kelley, behavior that is consistent is attributed to the stimulus when consensus and distinctiveness are also high, and to the person when they are low. In contrast, behavior that is low in consistency is attributed to transient circumstances, such as the temperature of the movie theater.

Kelley's theory and the predictions it makes are represented in Figure 3.3. Does this model describe the kinds of information *you* seek when you try to determine what causes people to behave as they do? Yes, research shows that subjects who are instructed to make attributions for various events do, in general, follow the logic of covariation (Cheng & Novick, 1990; Fosterling, 1992; Hewstone & Jaspars, 1987; McArthur, 1972).

Attribution Biases

When the theories of attribution were first proposed, they were represented by such complicated flow charts, cubes, formulas, and diagrams that many social psychologists began to wonder: Do people really analyze behavior in the way that one might expect of computers? Do we have the time, the motivation, or the cognitive capacity for such elaborate and mindful processes? The answer is sometimes yes, sometimes no. As social perceivers, we are limited in our ability to

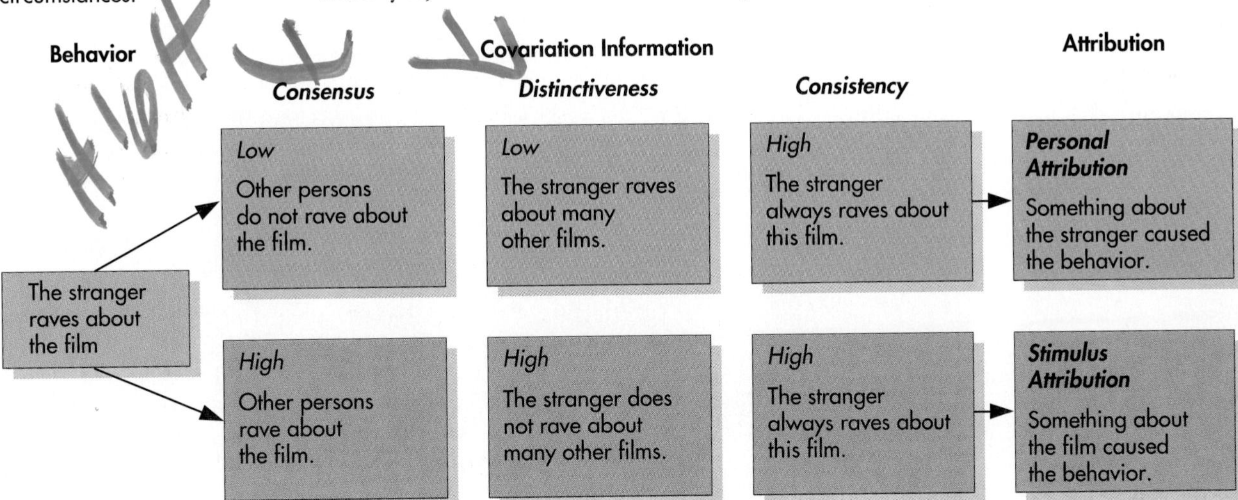

Figure 3.3 Kelley's Covariation Theory. For behaviors that are high in consistency, people make personal attributions when there is low consensus and distinctiveness (top row) and stimulus attributions when there is high consensus and distinctiveness (bottom row). Behaviors that are low in consistency (not shown) are attributed to passing circumstances.

process all relevant information, or we may lack the kinds of training needed to employ fully the principles of attribution theory. More important, we often don't make an effort to think carefully about our attributions. With so much to explain and not enough time in the day, people take mental short cuts, cross their fingers, hope for the best, and get on with life. The problem is that with speed comes bias and perhaps even a loss of accuracy. In this section, we examine some of the short cuts and their consequences—the biases of attribution.

Cognitive Heuristics Attribution theory assumes that people base their social judgments on an objective reading of behavioral facts and figures. For example, it is assumed that to draw firm conclusions about an individual, we compare his or her behavior to social *norms*. Actions that are atypical, or low in consensus, are attributed to the person; those that are typical, or high in consensus, are attributed to the situation. The theory is quite logical, even intuitive. Yet researchers find that the average person, unlike the scientist, often fails to make adequate use of normative information (Borgida & Brekke, 1981; Kassin, 1979). Why? According to Daniel Kahneman, Amos Tversky, and others, the problem can be traced to the use of **cognitive heuristics**, information-processing "rules of thumb" that enable us to make judgments that are quick—but often in error (Kahneman et al., 1982; Gilovich, 1991; Nisbett & Ross, 1980).

cognitive heuristics Information-processing short cuts that enable us to make judgments that are quick but often in error.

Many cognitive heuristics lead people to make judgments that defy logic (see Table 3.2). One that has particularly troublesome effects on attribution is the

Table 3.2 Cognitive Heuristics

Heuristics	Examples
Representativeness A tendency to assume, despite odds to the contrary, that someone belongs to a certain group if he or she resembles or "represents" a typical member.	When people read about a conservative man who enjoys math puzzles and has no interest in politics, they guess that he's an engineer rather than a lawyer—even if randomly selected from a group of seventy lawyers and thirty engineers (Kahneman & Tversky, 1973).
Availability The tendency to estimate the likelihood of an event based on the ease with which instances of it are "available" in memory.	The more often a country is in the news, the more people say they know about it—and the higher are their estimates of its population (Brown & Siegler, 1992).
Framing The tendency to be influenced by the way an issue is presented, or "framed."	People are more likely to recommend a new medical treatment if it is said to have a 50 percent "success rate" rather than a 50 percent "failure rate" (Levin et al., 1988).
Anchoring The tendency for numerical estimates to be biased by an initial starting point, or "anchor."	People asked if the odds of nuclear war were more or less than 1 percent later estimated a likelihood of 11 percent. Those initially asked if the odds were more or less than 90 percent gave estimates of 26 percent (Plous, 1989).
Simulation The tendency to predict and explain an event outcome based on how easy it is to imagine alternative scripts or "simulations" of it.	When people hear that a passenger was killed in an airline crash, they find it more tragic if they learn that he had just switched from another flight ("if only . . .") than if he had been scheduled for weeks (Miller et al., 1990).

availability heuristic, a tendency to estimate the likelihood of an event by how easily instances of it come to mind. To demonstrate this phenomenon, Tversky and Kahneman (1973) asked subjects: Which is more common, words that start with the letter *r* or words that contain *r* as the third letter? In actuality, the English language has many more words with *r* as the third letter than as the first. Yet most subjects guessed that more words begin with *r*. The reason? It's easier to bring to mind words in which *r* appears first rather than third. Clearly, our estimates of likelihood are heavily influenced by events that are readily available in memory (MacLeod & Campbell, 1992).

false-consensus effect The tendency to overestimate the consensus of our own opinions, attributes, and behaviors.

The availability heuristic can lead us astray in two ways. First, it gives rise to the **false-consensus effect,** a tendency for people to overestimate the extent to which others share their opinions, attributes, and behaviors (Ross et al., 1977b; Marks & Miller, 1987). This bias is pervasive. Whether people are asked to predict how others feel about defense spending, abortion, Campbell's soup, certain types of music, or appropriate behavior, they consistently exaggerate the percentage of others who behave similarly or share their views.

To illustrate the point, Joachim Krueger and Russell Clement (1994) asked subjects to indicate whether they agree or disagree with a series of statements taken from a well-known personality test. Later, subjects were asked to estimate the percentage of people in general who would agree with these same statements. As shown in Table 3.3, subjects' beliefs about other people were biased by their own responses. In part, this false consensus bias is a by-product of the availability heuristic. Since we tend to associate with others who are like us in important ways, we are more likely to see and later recall instances of similar rather than dissimilar behavior (Deutsch, 1989). Interestingly, people do *not* exhibit this bias when asked to estimate the behavior of people from groups other than their own (Mullen et al., 1992).

base-rate fallacy The finding that people are relatively insensitive to consensus information presented in the form of numerical base rates.

A second consequence of the availability heuristic is that social perceptions are influenced more by one vivid life story than by hard statistical facts. Have you ever wondered why so many people buy lottery tickets despite the astonishingly low odds, or why so many travelers are afraid to fly even though they are more likely to perish in a car accident? These behaviors are symptomatic of the **base-rate fallacy**—the fact that people are relatively insensitive to numerical base

Table 3.3 The False-Consensus Effect

Statements	Agree	Disagree
I sweat very easily on cool days.	44.54	29.26
I enjoy reading love stories.	53.49	47.12
I would like to be a singer.	56.50	39.71
I think most people would lie to get ahead.	66.12	48.36
I am a very sociable person.	65.16	59.17

In this study, subjects who agreed or disagreed with forty statements estimated the percentage of other people who would agree with the same statements. As shown in this sample of items, subjects' estimates of population consensus were biased by their own views. (Krueger & Clement, 1994.)

In casinos all over the world, bells, flashing lights, blaring sirens, and coins jingling into metal trays make it seem as if everyone is winning. Falling prey to the base-rate fallacy, gamblers are influenced more by these vivid events than by the objective odds.

rates, or probabilities, and are influenced instead by graphic, dramatic events such as the sight of a million-dollar lottery winner celebrating on TV or a gross photograph of bodies being pulled from the wreckage of a plane crash. The base-rate fallacy can thus lead to misperceptions of risk. Indeed, people overestimate the number of those who die in shootings, fires, floods, hurricanes, terrorist bombings, and accidents—and underestimate the death toll caused by strokes, heart attacks, diabetes, and other mundane events (Slovic et al., 1982). With stories of drug dealing so prominent in the news, it is no wonder that many Americans think that drug abuse is on the rise when, in fact, it is not (Eisenman, 1993).

Every day, we are besieged by both types of information: we read the unemployment rate, and we watch personal interviews with frustrated job seekers; we read the casualty figures of war, and we witness the agony of a parent who has lost a child in combat. Logically, statistics that summarize the experiences of many people are more informative than a single and perhaps atypical case, but perceivers march to a different drummer. As long as a personal anecdote is seen as relevant (Schwarz et al., 1991b) and the source as credible (Hinsz et al., 1988), it seems that one good image is worth a thousand numbers.

The Fundamental Attribution Error By the time you finish reading this textbook, you will know the cardinal lesson of social psychology: people are profoundly influenced by the *situational* context of behavior. This point is not as obvious as it may seem. For instance, parents are often surprised to hear that their mischievous child, the family monster, is a perfect angel in the classroom. And students are often surprised to observe that their favorite professor, so eloquent in the lecture hall, may stumble over words in less formal gatherings. These reactions are symptomatic of a well-documented aspect of social perception. When people explain the behavior of others, they tend to overestimate the role of personal factors and overlook the impact of situations. Because this bias is so pervasive, and sometimes so misleading, it has been called the **fundamental attribution error** (Ross, 1977).

fundamental attribution error The tendency to focus on the role of personal causes and underestimate the impact of situations on other people's behavior.

Evidence of the fundamental attribution error was first reported in the Jones and Harris (1967) study described earlier, in which subjects read an essay presumably written by a student. In that study, subjects were more likely to infer the student's true attitude when the position taken was freely chosen than when they thought that the student had been assigned to it. But look again at Figure 3.2, and you'll notice that even when subjects thought the student had no choice but to assert a position, they still used the speech to infer his or her attitude. This finding has been repeated many times. Whether the essay topic is nuclear power, abortion, drug laws, or the death penalty, the results are essentially the same (Jones, 1990).

People fall prey to the fundamental attribution error even when they are fully aware of the situation's impact on behavior. In one experiment, the subjects themselves were assigned to take a position, whereupon they swapped essays and rated each other. Remarkably, they still jumped to conclusions about each other's attitudes (Miller et al., 1981). In another experiment, subjects inferred attitudes from a speech even when they were the ones who had assigned the position to be taken (Gilbert & Jones, 1986).

A fascinating study by Lee Ross and his colleagues (1977) demonstrates the fundamental attribution error in a more familiar setting, the TV quiz show. By a flip of the coin, subjects were randomly assigned to play the role of either the questioner or contestant in a quiz game, while spectators looked on. In front of the contestant and spectators, the experimenter instructed the questioner to write ten challenging questions from his or her own store of general knowledge. If you

Kramer, Elaine, Jerry, and George play distinctive roles on the TV show, *Seinfeld*. But what are these individuals really like? Illustrating the fundamental attribution error, viewers often assume that actors in real life are like the characters they play on TV.

are a trivia buff, you can imagine how esoteric these questions can be: Who was the first governor of Idaho? What team won the NHL Stanley Cup in 1968? It is no wonder that contestants correctly answered only about 40 percent of the questions asked. When the game was over, all participants rated the questioner's and contestant's general knowledge on a scale of 0 to 100.

Picture the events that transpired. The questioners appeared more knowledgeable than the contestants. After all, they knew all the answers. But a moment's reflection should remind us that the situation put the questioner at a distinct advantage (there were no differences between the two groups on an objective test of general knowledge). Did subjects take the questioner's advantage into account, or did they assume that the questioners actually had greater knowledge? The results were startling. Spectators rated the questioners as above average in their general knowledge and the contestants as below average. The contestants even rated themselves as inferior to their partners. Like the spectators, they too were fooled by the loaded situation (see Figure 3.4).

What's going on here? Why do social perceivers consistently make assumptions about persons and fail to appreciate the impact of situations? According to Daniel Gilbert and Patrick Malone (1995), the problem stems in part from *how* we make attributions. Attribution theorists used to assume that people survey all the evidence and then decide on a personal or situational attribution. Instead, it now appears that social perception is a two-step process: first we identify the behavior and make a quick personal attribution; then we correct or adjust that inference to account for situational influences. The first step is simple and automatic, like a reflex; the second requires attention, thought, and effort (see Figure 3.5).

Several research findings support this hypothesis. First, without realizing it, people often form quick impressions of others based on a brief sample of behavior (Lupfer et al., 1990; Newman & Uleman, 1989; Moskowitz, 1993). Second,

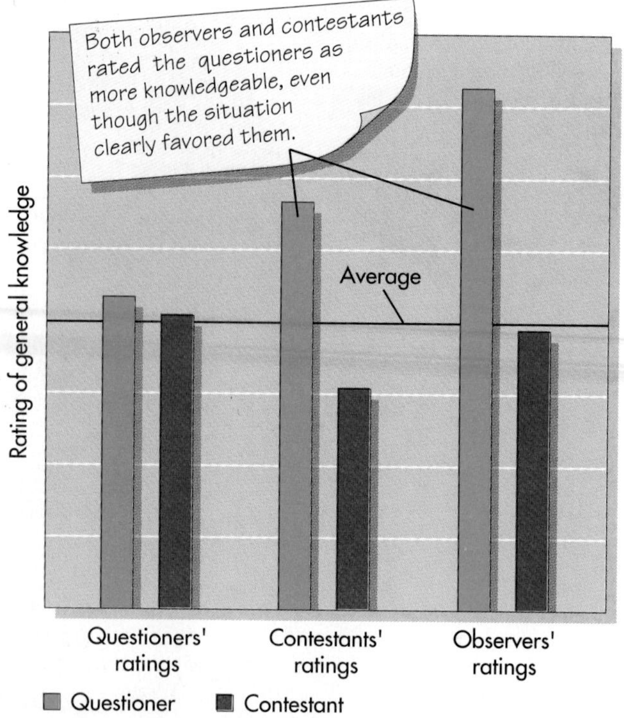

Figure 3.4 Fundamental Attribution Error and the TV Quiz Show. Even though the simulated quiz show situation placed questioners in an obvious position of advantage over contestants, observers rated the questioners as more knowledgeable (right). Questioners did not overrate their general knowledge (left), but contestants, like the observers, rated themselves as inferior (middle). These results illustrate the fundamental attribution error. (Ross et al., 1977.)

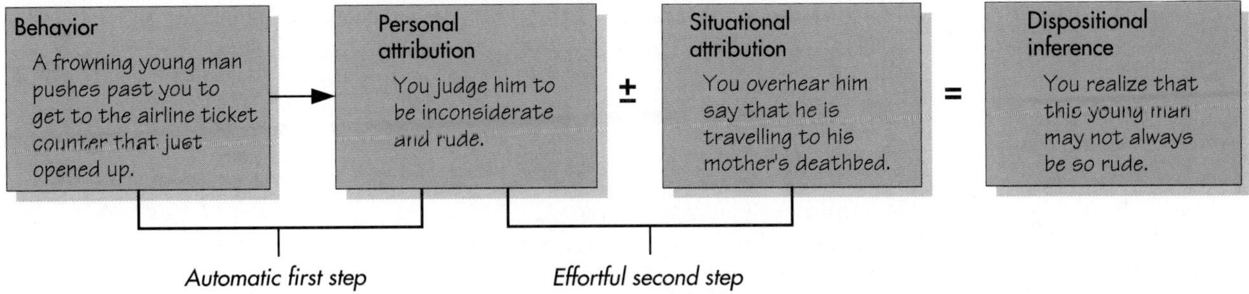
Behavior
A frowning young man pushes past you to get to the airline ticket counter that just opened up.
Personal attribution
You judge him to be inconsiderate and rude.
±
Situational attribution
You overhear him say that he is travelling to his mother's deathbed.
=
Dispositional inference
You realize that this young man may not always be so rude.
Automatic first step
Effortful second step

Figure 3.5 Two-Step Model of the Attribution Process. Traditional attribution theories assumed that people analyze behavior by searching for a personal or situational cause. The two-step model suggests that people make personal attributions *automatically* and then must consciously adjust that inference in order to account for situational factors.

perceivers are *more* likely to commit the fundamental attribution error when they are cognitively busy, or distracted, as they observe the target person (Gilbert & Osborne, 1989; Gilbert et al., 1992). Third, people are *less* likely to commit the fundamental attribution error when they take time before making their judgments (Burger, 1991), when they are highly motivated to make a careful judgment (Webster, 1993; Webster & Kruglanski, 1994), and when they are suspicious that the target has ulterior motives for his or her behavior (Fein et al., 1990; Hilton et al., 1993). This last point is important. In a series of experiments, Steven Fein, James Hilton, and Dale Miller found that suspicion—a state of mind that leads us to think critically about others—eliminates the problem.

Since the two-step model predicts that personal attributions are automatic but that later adjustment for situational factors requires conscious thought, it makes sense to suggest that when attention is divided, when the attribution is made hastily, or when perceivers are lacking in motivation, the second step suffers more than the first. As Gilbert and his colleagues (1988) put it, "The first step is a snap, but the second one's a doozy" (p. 738).

Why is the first step such a snap, and why does it seem so natural for people to assume a link between acts and personal dispositions? There are two possible explanations. The first is based on Heider's (1958) insight that people see dispositions in behavior because of a perceptual bias, something like an optical illusion. When you listen to a speech or watch a quiz show, the actor is the conspicuous *figure* of your attention; the situation fades into the *background* ("out of sight, out of mind," as they say). According to Heider, people attribute events to factors that are perceptually conspicuous, or *salient*. To test this hypothesis, Shelley Taylor and Susan Fiske (1975) varied the seating arrangements of subjects who watched as two actors had a carefully staged conversation. In each session, the subjects were seated so that they faced actor A, actor B, or both. When later questioned about their observations, they rated the actor they faced as the more dominant member of the pair, the one who set the tone and direction.

A second explanation is that perhaps culture teaches us to commit the fundamental attribution error. As we saw in Chapter 2, westerners believe that individuals are autonomous, motivated by internal forces, and responsible for their own actions. Yet many nonwestern "collectivist" cultures take a more holistic view that emphasizes the relationship between individuals and their social roles. To test the hypothesis that differing cultural worldviews are related to attributions, Joan Miller (1984) asked American subjects and Asian Indian subjects of varying ages to describe the causes of positive and negative behaviors they had observed in their lives. Among young children, there were no cultural differences. With increasing age, however, the American subjects made more personal attributions, while the Indian subjects made more situational attributions (see Figure 3.6). In

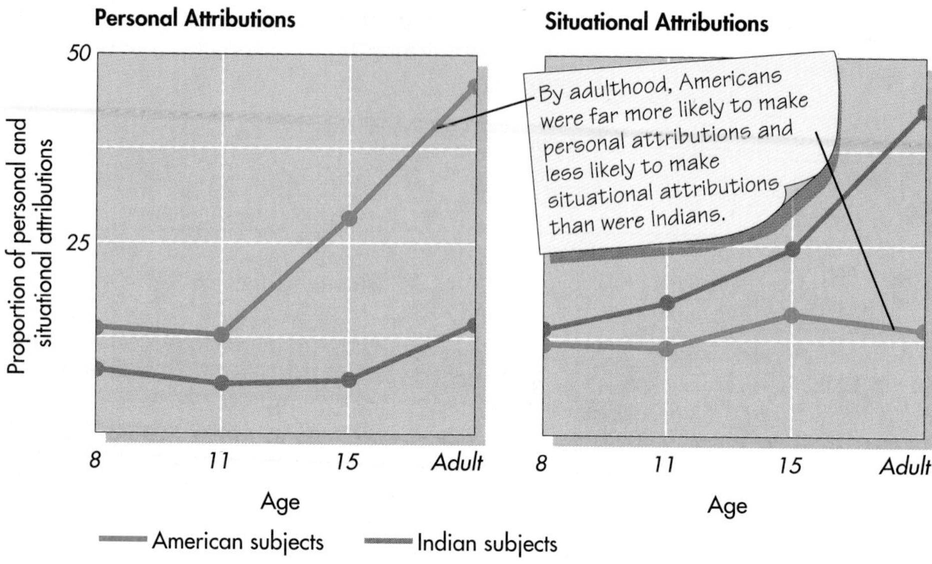

Figure 3.6 **Fundamental Attribution Error: A Western Bias?** American and Asian Indian subjects of varying ages described the causes of negative actions they had observed. Among young children, there were no cultural differences. With increasing age, however, Americans made more personal attributions and Indian subjects made more situational attributions. Explanations for positive behaviors followed a similar pattern. This finding suggests that the fundamental attribution error is a western phenomenon. (Miller, 1984.)

another study, Michael Morris and Kaiping Peng (1994) compared students from the United States and China. They found no cultural differences in the perception of *physical* events; but for social behaviors, the American subjects made attributions that were more personal and less situational. It is important to recognize that individuals within a given culture also differ in their individualist versus collectivist orientations—differences that are related to the attributions they make (Newman, 1993). As a general rule, however, it appears that the fundamental attribution error is largely a western phenomenon.

The Actor-Observer Effect People may commit the fundamental attribution error when they explain the behavior of others, but do we exhibit the same bias in explaining our own behavior? Think about it. Are you shy or outgoing, or does your behavior depend on the situation? Are you calm or intense, quiet or talkative, lenient or firm? Or, again, does your behavior in these regards depend on the situation? Now pick a friend and answer the same questions about his or her behavior. Do you notice a difference? Chances are, you do. Research shows that people are more likely to say "It depends on the situation" to describe themselves than to describe others. When Lewis Goldberg (1978) administered 2,800 English trait words to fourteen groups, each containing 100 subjects, he found that 85 percent checked off more traits for others than for themselves.

actor-observer effect The tendency to attribute our own behavior to situational causes and the behavior of others to personal factors.

The tendency to make personal attributions for the behavior of others and situational attributions for ourselves is called the **actor-observer effect** and has been widely demonstrated (Jones & Nisbett, 1972; Watson, 1982). In one study, 60 prison inmates and their counselors were asked to explain why the inmates had committed their offenses. The counselors cited enduring personal characteristics; the prisoners referred to transient situational factors (Saulnier & Perlman, 1981). In another study, an analysis of "Dear Abby" letters appearing in the newspaper revealed that people seeking advice explained the behavior of others in more dispositional terms than they used to explain their own actions (Schoeneman & Rubanowitz, 1985).

There are two bases for the difference between actors and observers. First, people have more privileged *information* about themselves than about others—enough to know that their behavior changes from one situation to the next (Prentice, 1990; White & Younger, 1988). Second, observers focus *attention* on the actor whose behavior they try to explain, but actors must attend to the situation that guides their behavior. Absorbed in a conversation, you gaze at your partner; playing tennis, you keep your eye on the ball; taking an exam, you concentrate on the questions. The result is that actors find it easier to make judgments about situations, and observers find it easier to make judgments about persons (Bassili & Racine, 1990). Thus, when actors and observers review the actor's behavior on videotape from each other's visual perspective, the effect is reversed (Storms, 1973).

Motivational Biases As we saw in Chapter 2, people tend to make favorable, self-serving, one-sided attributions for their own behavior. Research conducted on students, teachers, parents, workers, athletes, and others shows that we take more credit for success than for failure. Similarly, people seek more information about their strengths than about their weaknesses, overestimate their contribution to group efforts, exaggerate their control, and predict a rosy future. The false-consensus effect described earlier also has a self-serving side to it. Research suggests that we overestimate the extent to which others think, feel, and behave as we do, in part to reassure ourselves that our own ways are correct, normal, and appropriate (Sherman et al., 1984; Alicke & Largo, 1995).

Additional motives can influence our attributions for the behavior of others. For example, William Klein and Ziva Kunda (1992) showed subjects the performance on a practice quiz of another subject, a male target, who was later expected to become either their partner or their opponent in a competition. In all cases, the target had answered the practice questions correctly. The reason for his success? Hoping he was not too competent, subjects who thought that the target was to be their opponent perceived him as less able than those who thought he was their prospective partner. To justify their wishful thinking, the subjects reasoned that the task was easy and that luck was a contributing factor.

At times, personal defensive motives lead us to blame others for their misfortunes. Consider the following classic experiment. Subjects thought they were taking part in an emotion-perception study. One subject, actually a confederate, was selected randomly to take a memory test while the others looked on. Each time the confederate made a mistake, she was jolted by a painful electric shock (actually, there was no shock; what subjects saw was a staged videotape). Since subjects knew that only the luck of the draw had kept them off the "hot seat," you might think they would react with sympathy and compassion. Not so. In fact, the subjects belittled the hapless confederate (Lerner & Simmons, 1966).

belief in a just world The belief that individuals get what they deserve in life, an orientation that leads people to disparage victims.

Melvin Lerner (1980) argues that the tendency to be critical of victims stems from our deep-seated **belief in a just world.** According to Lerner, people need to view the world as a just place in which we "get what we deserve" and "deserve

Attributions of blame are often biased by self-serving motivations.

"And see that you place the blame where it will do the most good."

what we get"—a world where hard work and clean living always pay off and where laziness and a sinful lifestyle are punished. To believe otherwise is to concede that we, too, are vulnerable to the cruel twists and turns of fate. So how do people defend themselves from this realization? If people cannot help or compensate the victims of misfortune, they turn on them. Thus, it is often assumed that poor people are lazy, that crime victims are careless, that battered wives provoke their abusive husbands, and that gay men with AIDS lack moral integrity. As you might expect, cross-national comparisons reveal that people in poorer countries are less likely than those in more affluent countries to believe in a just world (Furnham, 1993).

The tendency to disparage victims may seem to be just another symptom of the fundamental attribution error: too much focus on the person and not enough on the situation. But the conditions that trigger this tendency suggest there is more to it. Studies of *defensive attribution* show that accident victims are held more responsible for their fate when the consequences of the accident are severe rather than mild (Walster, 1966), when the victim is in a situation similar to the perceiver's (Shaver, 1970), and when the perceiver is emotionally aroused by the event (Thornton et al., 1986) or generally anxious about threats to the self (Thornton, 1992). In other words, the more threatened we feel by an apparent injustice, the greater the need to protect ourselves from the implication that *it* could happen to *us*. One way to defend against just-world violations is to distance ourselves psychologically from victims through disparagement. Fortunately, people do not resort to derogation when they can restore justice by helping the victim (Lerner & Simmons, 1966) or when they are prompted to take the victim's perspective (Aderman et al., 1974).

INTEGRATION: FROM DISPOSITIONS TO IMPRESSIONS

When behavior is attributed to situational factors, we do not generally make inferences about the actor. However, personal attributions often lead us to infer

Some people openly disparage gay men with AIDS and blame them for their fate. This reaction may stem from the need to believe that the world is just, and that tragedy strikes only those who are sinful or careless—not us.

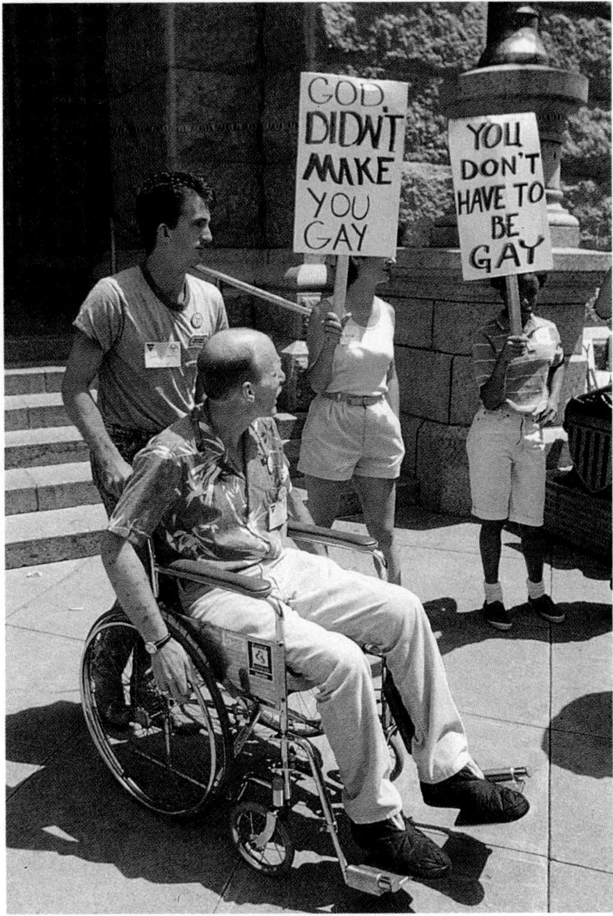

that the actor has a certain trait, or disposition—that the leader of a failing business is incompetent or that a former enemy who extends the olive branch is peaceful. Human beings are not one-dimensional, however, and one trait does not a person make. To have a complete picture of someone, social perceivers must assemble the various bits and pieces into a unified impression.

Information Integration: The Arithmetic

impression formation The process of integrating information about a person to form a coherent impression.

Once personal attributions are made, how are they combined into a single coherent picture of a person? How do we approach the process of **impression formation**? Do we simply add up all of a person's traits and calculate a mental average, or do we combine the information in more complicated ways? Anyone who has written or received letters of recommendation will appreciate the practical implications. Suppose you're told that an applicant is friendly and intelligent, two highly favorable qualities. Would you be more or less impressed if you then learned that this applicant was also prudent and even-tempered, two moderately favorable qualities? If you are more impressed, then you are intuitively following a *summation* model of impression formation: the more positive traits there are, the better. If you are less impressed, then you are using an *averaging* model: the higher the average value of all the various traits, the better.

To quantify the formation of impressions, Norman Anderson (1968) had subjects rate the desirability of 555 traits on a 7-point scale. By calculating the average ratings, he obtained a *scale value* for each trait (*sincere* had the highest scale value; *liar* had the lowest). In an earlier study, Anderson (1965) used similar values and compared the summation and averaging models. Specifically, he asked a group of subjects to rate how much they liked a person described by two traits with extremely high scale values (*H, H*). A second group received a list of four traits, including two that were high and two that were moderately high in their scale values (*H, H, M+, M+*). In a third group, subjects received two extremely low, negative traits (*L, L*). In a fourth group, they received four traits, including two that were low and two that were moderately low (*L, L, M−, M−*). What effect did the moderate traits have on impressions? As predicted by an averaging model, the moderate traits diluted from rather than added to the impact of the highly positive and negative traits. The practical implication for those who write letters of recommendation is clear. Applicants are better off if their letters include only the most glowing comments and omit favorable remarks that are somewhat more guarded in nature.

After extensive amounts of research, it now appears that although people combine traits by averaging, the process is somewhat more complicated. Consistent with Anderson's (1981) **information integration theory,** impressions formed of others are based on an integration of (1) personal dispositions of the perceiver and (2) a *weighted* average, not a simple average, of the target person's characteristics (Kashima & Kerekes, 1994). Let's look more closely at these two sets of factors.

information integration theory The theory that impressions are based on (1) perceiver dispositions and (2) a weighted average of a target person's traits.

Deviations from the Arithmetic

Like other aspects of our social perceptions, impression formation does not follow the rules of cold logic. Weighted averaging may describe the way most people combine different traits, but the whole process begins with a warm-blooded human perceiver, not a computer. Thus, certain deviations from the "arithmetic" are inevitable.

Perceiver Characteristics To begin with, perceivers differ in the kinds of impressions they form of others. Some people seem to measure everyone with an intellectual yardstick; others look for physical beauty, a friendly smile, a sense of humor, or a firm handshake. Whatever the attribute, each of us is more likely to notice and recall certain traits rather than others (Higgins et al., 1982; Bargh et al., 1988). Thus, when subjects are asked to describe a group of target persons, there's often more overlap between the various descriptions provided *by* the same *perceiver* than there is between descriptions provided *for* the same *target* (Dornbusch et al., 1965; Park, 1986).

Which characteristics we tend to notice in others may also change from time to time, depending on recent experiences. Have you ever noticed that once a novel word slips into conversation, it gets repeated over and over again? If so, you have observed **priming,** the tendency for frequently or recently used concepts to come to mind easily and to influence the interpretation of new information.

priming The tendency for recently used words or ideas to come to mind easily and influence the interpretation of new information.

The effect of priming on impressions was first demonstrated by E. Tory Higgins and his colleagues (1977). Subjects were presented with a list of trait words, ostensibly as part of a memory experiment. In fact, the task was designed as a priming device to plant certain ideas in their minds. Some subjects read words that evoked a positive image: *brave, independent, adventurous.* Others read words that evoked a more negative image: *reckless, foolish, careless*. Later, in what they thought was an unrelated experiment, subjects read about a man who climbed mountains, drove in a demolition derby, and crossed the Atlantic in a sailboat. As predicted, subjects' impressions were shaped by the trait words they had earlier memorized. Those exposed to positive words later formed more flattering impressions of the character than those exposed to negative words. All subjects read the same description, yet they formed different impressions depending on what was already on their mind. Priming works best when the prime words are presented so rapidly that subjects are not aware of the exposure (Bargh & Pietromonaco, 1982)—and is effective unless subjects are highly motivated to make judgments of others that are accurate and objective (Martin et al., 1990; Sedikides, 1990; Thompson et al., 1994).

Just as recent experiences prime people to view others in a certain light, *mood* can also influence the impressions we form of others (Forgas, 1995). For example, Joseph Forgas and Gordon Bower (1987) told subjects that they had performed very well or poorly on a test of social adjustment. As expected, this feedback altered the subjects' moods; it also affected their outlook on others. When presented with behavioral information about various characters, subjects spent more time attending to positive facts and formed more favorable impressions when they were happy than when they were sad. Follow-up research shows that the biasing effects of mood are particularly pronounced when we form impressions of others who are atypical, requiring more thought and effort in order to be understood (Forgas, 1992).

In short, the combined effect of individual differences, recent experiences, and fluctuating mood point to an important conclusion: that, to some extent, impression formation is in the eyes of the beholder.

Target Characteristics Just as all perceivers are not created equal, all traits are not created equal either. In recent years, personality researchers have discovered that individuals can reliably be distinguished from one another along five broad traits, or "factors": extroversion, emotional stability, openness to experience, agreeableness, and conscientiousness (Goldberg, 1993; Digman, 1990; McCrae & John, 1992). Are some of these factors easier to judge than others? Yes. Based on their review of thirty-two studies, David Kenny and his colleagues (1994) found that social perceivers are most likely to agree in their judgments of a target's extroversion—that is, in the extent to which he or she is sociable, friendly, fun-loving, outgoing, and adventurous. It seems that this characteristic is relatively easy to spot. Indeed, different perceivers often agree on it even when rating a target person whom they are seeing for the first time.

The valence of a trait—whether it is considered socially desirable or undesirable—also determines its impact on our final impressions. Specifically, research shows that people exhibit a *trait negativity bias,* the tendency for negative information to weigh more heavily than positive information (Coovert & Reeder, 1990; Skowronski & Carlston, 1989). This means that we are likely to form more extreme impressions of a person who is said to be untrustworthy than of one who is said to be honest. We tend to view others favorably, so we are quick to take notice and pay careful attention when this expectation is violated (Pratto & John, 1991). One bad trait may be enough to destroy a person's reputation—regardless of other qualities. Research on American political campaigns confirms the point: public opinion is shaped more by a candidate's "negatives" than by positive information (Lau, 1985; Klein, 1991).

Extroversion is a trait that is easy for us to detect in others. Compared to people who are introverted, extroverts are more outgoing, impulsive, adventurous, and sensation-seeking.

The impact of trait information on our impressions of others depends not only on characteristics of the perceiver and target but on context as well. Two contextual factors are particularly important in this regard: (1) implicit theories of personality, and (2) the order in which we receive information about one trait relative to other traits.

Implicit Personality Theories When O. J. Simpson was charged with brutally murdering his ex-wife Nicole and her friend, everyone was shocked. Simpson was a national hero—athletic, attractive, charming, intelligent, and successful. Once the premier running back in the National Football League, Simpson went on to become a sports broadcaster, Hollywood actor, and proud father of three children.

It is easy to understand why people reacted to the charges with such disbelief. Simpson just didn't seem like *the kind of person* who would commit a cold-blooded murder. That reaction is based on an **implicit personality theory**—a network of assumptions about the relationships among various types of people, traits, and behaviors. Knowing that someone has one trait leads us to infer the presence of other traits as well (Bruner & Tagiuri, 1954; Schneider, 1973; Sedikides & Anderson, 1994). For example, you might assume that a person who is unpredictable is also dangerous or that someone who talks slowly is also slow-witted. You might also assume that certain traits are linked to certain behaviors (Reeder & Brewer, 1979; Reeder, 1993)—that a beloved sports hero like O. J. Simpson, for example, could not possibly stab his ex-wife to death.

implicit personality theory A network of assumptions people make about the relationships among traits and behaviors.

Solomon Asch (1946) was the first to discover that the presence of one trait often implies the presence of others as well. Asch told one group of subjects that an individual was "intelligent, skillful, industrious, warm, determined, practical and cautious." Another group read an identical list of traits, except that the word *warm* was replaced by *cold*. Although only one term was changed, the two groups formed different impressions. Subjects inferred that the warm person was also happier and more generous, good-natured, and humorous than the cold per-

central traits Traits that exert a powerful influence on overall impressions.

son. When two other words were varied (*polite* and *blunt*), however, the differences were less pronounced. Asch concluded that *warm* and *cold* are **central traits,** meaning that they suggest the presence of certain other traits and exert a powerful influence on final impressions. The impact of central traits is not limited to studies using trait lists, either. When college students in different classes were led to believe that a guest lecturer was a warm or cold person, their impressions after the lecture were consistent with these beliefs, even though he gave the same lecture to everyone (Kelley, 1950; Widmeyer & Loy, 1988).

primacy effect The tendency for information presented early in a sequence to have more impact on impressions than information presented later.

The Primacy Effect The order in which a trait is discovered also influences its impact on social perception. It is often said that first impressions are critical, and social psychologists are quick to agree. Studies show that information has greater impact when presented early in a sequence rather than late—a phenomenon known as the **primacy effect.**

In another of Asch's (1946) experiments, one group of subjects learned that a person was "intelligent, industrious, impulsive, critical, stubborn, and envious." A second group received exactly the same list but in reverse order. Rationally speaking, the two groups should have felt the same way about the person. But instead, subjects who heard the first list—in which the more positive traits came first—formed more favorable impressions than did those who heard the second list. Similar findings were obtained among subjects who watched a videotape of a woman taking an SAT-like test. In all cases, she correctly answered fifteen out of thirty multiple-choice questions. But subjects who observed a pattern of initial success followed by failure perceived the woman as more intelligent than did those who observed the opposite pattern of failure followed by success (Jones et al., 1968). Although there are exceptions, people tend to be more heavily influenced by the "early returns."

Why is the primacy effect so powerful? There are two major reasons. The first is that once perceivers think they have formed an accurate impression, they become less attentive to subsequent contradictory information. Thus, when subjects read a series of statements about a person, the amount of time they spent reading declined steadily as they proceeded through the list (Belmore, 1987). Does this mean we are doomed to a life of primacy? Not necessarily. Unstimulated, attention may wane. But if perceivers are sufficiently motivated to avoid tuning out, primacy is diminished (Anderson & Hubert, 1963; Benassi, 1982; Kruglanski & Freund, 1983; Webster & Kruglanski, 1994).

More unsettling is the second reason for primacy, known as the *change-of-meaning hypothesis*. Once people form an impression, they later interpret inconsistent information in light of that impression. Asch's research shows just how malleable the meaning of a trait can be. When people are told that a kind person is *calm,* they assume that he or she is gentle, peaceful, and serene. When a cruel person is said to be *calm,* however, the same word is interpreted to mean cool, shrewd, and calculating. There are many examples to illustrate the point. Based on your first impression, the word *proud* can mean self-respecting or conceited, *critical* can mean astute or picky, and *impulsive* can mean spontaneous or reckless.

It is remarkable just how creative we can be in our efforts to transform a bundle of contradictions into a coherent, integrated impression. For example, the person who is said to be "good" but is also "a thief" can be viewed as a character like Robin Hood (Burnstein & Schul, 1982). Or that person can be seen to have changed over time (Silka, 1989). Asch and Henri Zukier (1984) presented subjects with inconsistent trait pairs and found that they used different strategies to reconcile the conflicts. For example, a brilliant-foolish person may be "very bright on abstract matters, but silly about day-to-day practical tasks," a sociable-lonely person has "many superficial ties but is unable to form deep relations," and a cheerful-gloomy person may simply be someone who is "moody."

CONFIRMATION BIASES: FROM IMPRESSIONS TO REALITY

> "Please your majesty," said the knave, "I didn't write it and they can't prove I did; there's no name signed at the end." "If you didn't sign it," said the King, "that only makes the matter worse. You must have meant some mischief, or else you'd have signed your name like an honest man."

This exchange, taken from Lewis Carroll's *Alice's Adventures in Wonderland,* illustrates the power of existing impressions. It is striking but often true: once people make up their minds about something—even if they have incomplete information—they become more and more unlikely to change their minds when confronted with evidence. Political leaders thus refuse to withdraw their support for government programs that don't work and scientists stubbornly defend their theories in the face of conflicting research data. These instances are easy to explain. Politicians and scientists have a personal investment in their opinions, for pride, funding, and reputation may be at stake. But what about people who more innocently fail to revise their opinions, often to their own detriment? What about the baseball manager who clings to strategies that are ineffective or the trial lawyer who repeatedly selects juries according to false stereotypes? Why are they often so slow to face the facts? As we will see, people are subject to various **confirmation biases**—the tendency to *interpret, seek,* and *create* information in ways that verify existing beliefs.

confirmation bias The tendency to seek, interpret, and create information that verifies existing beliefs.

Perseverance of Beliefs

Imagine you are looking at a slide that is completely out of focus. Gradually, it becomes focused enough so that the image is less blurry. At this point, the experimenter wants to know if you can recognize the picture. The response you're likely to make is interesting. Subjects have more trouble making an identification if they watch the gradual focusing procedure than if they simply view the final, blurry image. In the mechanics of the perceptual process, people apparently form early impressions that interfere with their subsequent ability to "see straight" once presented with improved evidence (Bruner & Potter, 1964). As we will see in this section, social perception is subject to the same kind of interference—yet another reason why first impressions often stick like glue even after we are forced to confront information that discredits our existing beliefs.

Consider what happens when you're led to expect something that does not materialize. In one study, John Darley and Paget Gross (1983) asked subjects to evaluate the academic potential of a nine-year-old girl named Hannah. One group was led to believe that Hannah came from an affluent community in which both parents were well-educated professionals (high expectations). A second group thought that she was from a run-down urban neighborhood and that both parents were uneducated blue-collar workers (low expectations). As shown

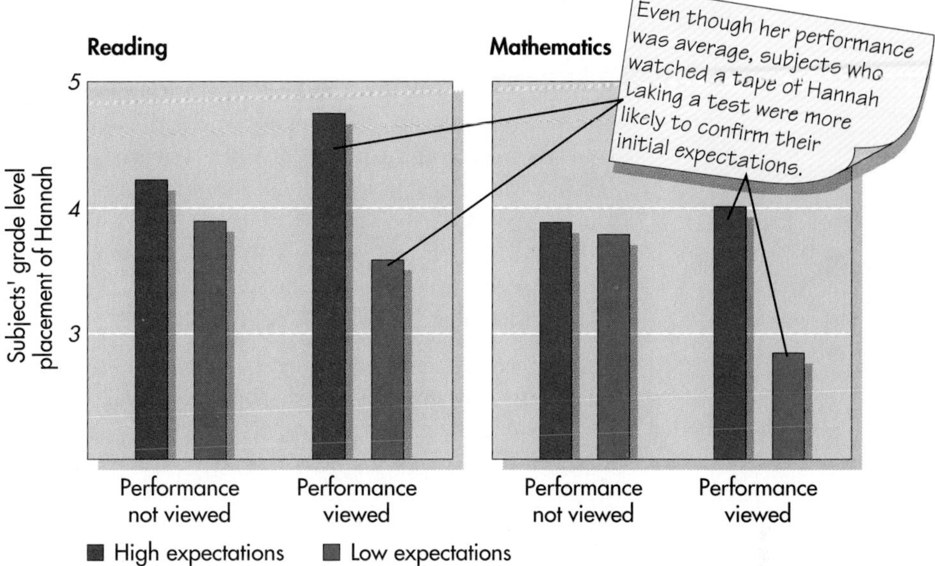

Figure 3.7 **Mixed Evidence: Does It Extinguish or Fuel First Impressions?** Subjects evaluated the potential of a schoolgirl. Without seeing her test performance, those with high expectations rated her slightly higher than did those with low expectations. Among subjects who watched a tape of the girl taking a test, the expectations effect was even greater.

in Figure 3.7, subjects in the first group were slightly more optimistic in their ratings of Hannah's potential than were those in the second group. In each of these groups, however, half the subjects watched a videotape of Hannah taking an achievement test. Her performance on the tape seemed average. She correctly answered some difficult questions but missed others that were relatively easy. Look again at Figure 3.7 and you'll see that even though all subjects saw the same tape, Hannah now received much lower ratings of ability from subjects who thought she was poor and higher ratings from those who thought she was affluent. Apparently, presenting an identical body of mixed evidence did not extinguish the biasing effects of beliefs—it *fueled* these effects. Similar results have been found in other research as well (Plous, 1991).

Events that are ambiguous enough to support contrasting interpretations are like inkblots: we see in them what we want or expect to see. So, what about information that plainly disconfirms our beliefs? What then happens to our first impressions? Craig Anderson and his colleagues (1980) addressed this question by supplying subjects with false information. After the subjects had time to think about the information, they were told that it was untrue. In one experiment, half the subjects read case studies suggesting that people who take risks make better firefighters than do those who are cautious. The others read cases suggesting the opposite conclusion. Next, subjects were asked to come up with a theory for the suggested correlation. The possibilities are easy to imagine: "He who hesitates is lost" supports risk-taking, whereas "You have to look before you leap" supports caution. Finally, subjects were led to believe that the session was over and were told that the information they received was false, manufactured for the sake of the experiment. Subjects, however, did not abandon their firefighter theories. Instead they exhibited **belief perseverance,** sticking to initial beliefs even after they were discredited. Apparently, it's easier to get people to build a theory than to convince them to tear it down. Indeed, even social psychologists are slow to change their pet theories in light of inconsistent research data (Greenwald et al., 1986).

belief perseverance The tendency to maintain beliefs even after they have been discredited.

Why do beliefs often outlive the evidence on which they are supposed to be based? The problem is that when people conjure up explanations that make sense, those explanations take on a life of their own. In fact, once people form an opinion, that opinion is strengthened by merely *thinking* about the topic—even without articulating the reasons for it (Tesser, 1978). And therein lies the solution. By asking subjects to consider why an *alternative* theory might be true, belief perseverance can be reduced or eliminated (Anderson & Sechler, 1986).

Confirmatory Hypothesis Testing

Social perceivers are not passive recipients of information. Like detectives, we ask questions and actively search for clues. But do we seek information objectively, or are we inclined to confirm the suspicions we already hold? Mark Snyder and William Swann (1978) addressed this question by having pairs of subjects who were strangers to one another take part in an interview. In each pair, one subject was to interview the other. But first that subject was falsely led to believe that his or her partner was either introverted or extroverted (actually, the subjects were assigned on a random basis to these conditions) and was then told to select questions from a prepared list. Those who thought they were talking to an introvert chose mostly introvert-oriented questions ("Have you ever felt left out of some social group?"), while those who thought they were talking to an extrovert asked extrovert-oriented questions ("How do you liven up a party?"). Expecting a certain kind of person, subjects unwittingly sought evidence that confirmed their expectations. By asking loaded questions, in fact, the interviewers actually gathered support for their beliefs. Thus, neutral observers who later listened to the tapes were also left with the mistaken impression that the interviewees really were as introverted and extroverted as the interviewers had assumed.

This last part of the study is powerful but, in hindsight, not all that surprising. Imagine yourself on the receiving end of an interview. Asked about what you do to liven up parties, you would probably talk about organizing group games, playing dance music, and telling jokes. On the other hand, if you were asked about difficult social situations, you might talk about being nervous before oral presentations or about what it feels like to be the new kid on the block. In other words, simply by going along with the questions that are asked, you supply evidence confirming the interviewer's beliefs. Thus, perceivers set in motion a vicious cycle: thinking someone has a certain trait, they engage in a one-sided search for information and, in doing so, they create a reality that ultimately supports their beliefs (Zuckerman et al., 1995).

Are people so blinded by their existing beliefs that they cannot manage an objective search for evidence? It depends. In the task devised by Snyder and Swann, people conduct a biased, confirmatory search for information. Even professional counselors trained in psychotherapy select questions designed to confirm their own hypotheses (Haverkamp, 1993). Thankfully, however, different circumstances produce less biasing results. When subjects are not certain of their beliefs and are concerned about the accuracy of their impressions (Kruglanski & Mayseless, 1988), when they are allowed to prepare their own interviews (Trope et al., 1984), or when the available nonconfirmatory questions are better than the confirmatory questions (Skov & Sherman, 1986), then people pursue a more balanced search for information.

The Self-fulfilling Prophecy

In 1948, sociologist Robert Merton told a story about Cartwright Millingville, president of the Last National Bank during the Depression. Although the bank was solvent, a rumor began to spread that it was floundering. Within hours, hundreds of depositors were lined up to withdraw their savings before no money was left to withdraw. The rumor was false, but the bank eventually failed. Using stories such as this, Merton proposed what seemed like an outrageous hypothesis: that a perceiver's expectation can actually lead to its own fulfillment, a **self-fulfilling prophecy.**

self-fulfilling prophecy The process by which one's expectations about a person eventually lead that person to behave in ways that confirm those expectations.

Merton's hypothesis lay dormant within psychology until Robert Rosenthal and Lenore Jacobson (1968) published the results of a study entitled *Pygmalion in the Classroom*. Noticing that teachers had higher expectations for better students, they wondered if teacher expectations *influenced* student performance rather than the other way around. To address the question, they told teachers in a San Francisco elementary school that certain pupils were on the verge of an intellectual growth spurt. The results of an IQ test were cited but, in fact, the pupils were randomly selected. Then eight months later, when real tests were administered, the "late bloomers"—but not children assigned to a control group—improved their IQ scores by as much as 30 points. They were also evaluated more favorably by their classroom teachers.

When the Pygmalion study was first published, it was greeted with chagrin. If positive teacher expectations can increase student performance, can negative expectations have the opposite effect? And what about the social implications? Could it be that affluent children are destined for success and that disadvantaged children are doomed to failure because educators hold different expectations for them? Many researchers were critical of the study and skeptical about the generality of the results.

Unfortunately, these findings cannot be swept under the proverbial rug. Teachers form expectations early in the school year—based, perhaps, on a student's background or reputation, physical appearance, initial performance, and standardized-test scores. Teachers then alter their behavior toward the student accordingly. If expectations are high rather than low, students receive more attention, emotional support, challenging homework, and praise. To some extent, teacher expectations are predictive of academic performance because teachers are often accurate in their initial assessments of ability (Jussim, 1989). Still, it's important to recognize that teacher expectations—even when they were totally fabricated by researchers—significantly *influenced* student performance in 36 percent of 400 experiments designed to test the hypothesis (Rosenthal, 1985).

This phenomenon is at work in noneducational settings too, including business organizations and the military. For example, in a study of twenty-nine platoons that consisted of a thousand men in the Israeli Defense Forces, Dov Eden (1990) led some platoon leaders to expect that the group of trainees they were about to receive had great potential (in fact, these groups were of average ability). After ten weeks, the trainees who were assigned to the high-expectation platoons obtained higher scores than the others on written exams and on the ability to operate a weapon.

When expectations lead us to alter the behavior of others, the prophecy we fulfill is called self-fulfilling prophecy. But how does it work? How do social perceivers transform their expectations of others into reality? Research indicates that the phenomenon occurs as a three-step process (see Figure 3.8). First, a per-

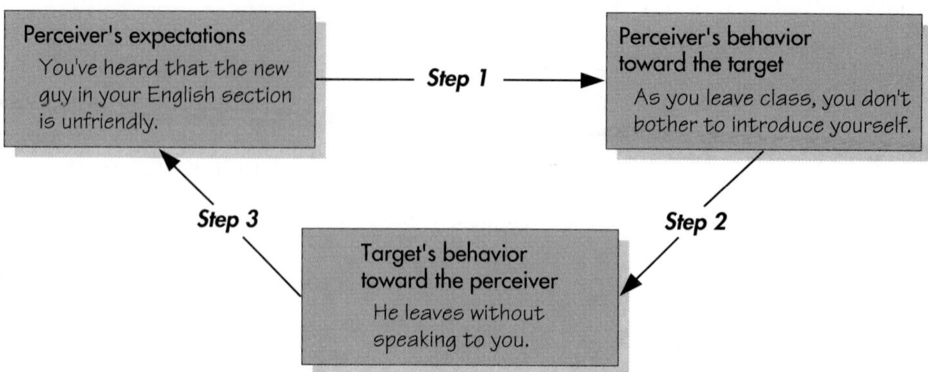

Figure 3.8 The Self-fulfilling Prophecy as a Three-Step Process. How do people transform expectations into reality? (1) A perceiver has expectations of a target person. (2) The perceiver then behaves in a manner consistent with those expectations. (3) The target unwittingly adjusts his or her behavior according to the perceiver's actions.

ceiver forms an impression of a target person—an impression that may be based on interactions with the target or on other information. Second, the perceiver behaves in a manner that is consistent with that first impression. Third, the target person unwittingly adjusts his or her behavior to the perceiver's actions. The net result: behavioral confirmation of the perceiver's first impression. Both inside and outside the classroom, the self-fulfilling prophecy is a powerful phenomenon (Cooper & Good, 1983; Darley & Fazio, 1980; Harris & Rosenthal, 1985; Harris et al., 1994).

But now let's straighten out this picture of human nature. It would be a sad commentary on human nature if each of us was so easily molded by others' perceptions into appearing brilliant or stupid, introverted or extroverted, competitive or cooperative, warm or cold. The effects are well established, but there are limits (Jussim, 1991). Indeed, by viewing the self-fulfilling prophecy as a three-step process, it is possible to identify the links in the chain that can be broken to prevent the vicious cycle.

Consider the first step, the link between one's expectations and behavior toward the target person. In the typical study, perceivers try to get to know the target on only a casual basis and are not necessarily driven to form an accurate impression. But when perceivers are highly motivated to seek the truth (as when they are considering the target as a possible teammate or opponent), they start to probe for an accurate assessment and, in so doing, often fail to confirm expectations (Darley et al., 1988; Hilton & Darley, 1991).

The link between expectations and behavior depends in other ways as well on a perceiver's interaction goals and motivations (Snyder, 1992). In one study, John Copeland (1994) put either the perceiver or the target into a position of relative power. In all cases, the perceiver interacted with a target who was said to be introverted or extroverted. In half the pairs, the perceiver was given the power to accept or reject the target as a teammate for a money-winning game. In the other half, it was the target who was empowered to choose a teammate. The two subjects interacted, the interaction was recorded, and then neutral observers listened to the tapes and rated the target person. So, did perceivers cause the targets to behave as introverted or extroverted, depending upon initial expectations? Yes and no. Illustrating what Copeland called "prophecies of power," Figure 3.9 shows that high-power perceivers triggered the self-fulfilling prophecy, as in past research, but that low-power perceivers did not. In the low-power situation, the perceivers spent less time getting to know the target person and more time trying to be liked. Other researchers have similarly found that perceivers do not confirm

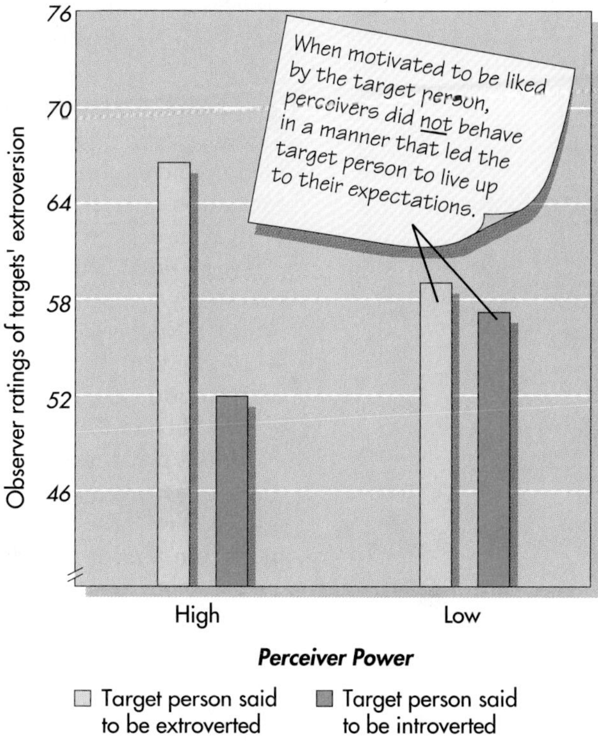

Figure 3.9 Prophecies of Power. In this study, perceivers interacted with a target person said to be introverted or extroverted. In half the pairs, the perceiver was in a position of power; in the other half, the target had power. Did perceivers cause targets to behave according to expectations? As shown, only high-power perceivers produced the self-fulfilling prophecy. In contrast, apparently, low-power perceivers spent less time trying to know the target person and more time trying to be liked. (Copeland, 1994.)

expectations when they're primarily motivated to self-present and get along (Neuberg et al., 1993; Snyder & Haugen, 1994).

Now consider the second step, the link between a perceiver's behavior and the target's response. In much of the past research, as in much of life, target persons are not aware of others' false impressions. Thus, it is unlikely that Rosenthal and Jacobson's (1968) "late bloomers" knew of their teachers' high expectations or that Snyder and Swann's (1978) "introverts" and "extroverts" knew of their interviewers' misconceptions. But what if they had known? How would *you* react if you found yourself cast in a certain light? When it happened to subjects in one experiment, they managed to overcome the effect by behaving in ways that forced the perceivers to abandon their expectations (Hilton & Darley, 1985).

As you may recall from the discussion of self-verification in Chapter 2, this result is most likely to occur when perceiver expectations clash with a target person's self-concept. Thus, when targets who viewed themselves as extroverted were interviewed by perceivers who believed they were introverted (and vice versa), what changed as a result of the interaction were the perceivers' beliefs—not the targets' behavior (Swann & Ely, 1984). Social perception is a two-way street (McNulty & Swann, 1994). It's important to recognize that the persons we judge have their own prophecies to fulfill.

SOCIAL PERCEPTION: THE BOTTOM LINE

Trying to understand people—whether they are professional athletes, political leaders, criminal defendants, entertainers, or loved ones closer to home—is no easy task. As you reflect on the material in this chapter, you will notice that there are two radically different views of social perception. One suggests that the process is quick and relatively automatic. Without much thought, effort, or awareness, people make rapid-fire snap judgments about others based on physical appearance, preconceptions, or just a hint of behavioral evidence. According to the second view, however, the process is relatively mindful. People observe others carefully and reserve judgment until their analysis of the target person, behavior, and situation is complete. As suggested by theories of attribution and information integration, the process is eminently logical.

In light of recent research, it is now safe to conclude that both accounts of social perception are correct. Sometimes our judgments are made instantly; at other times they are based on a more painstaking analysis of behavior (Brewer, 1988; Fiske & Neuberg, 1990; Fiske, 1993). Either way, we often steer our interactions with others along a path that is narrowed by first impressions, a process that can set in motion a self-fulfilling prophecy. The various aspects of social perception, as described in this chapter, are summarized in Figure 3.10.

At this point, we must confront an important question: How *accurate* are people's impressions of each other? For years, this question has proved provocative but hard to answer (Cronbach, 1955; Kenny, 1994). Granted, people often depart from the ideals of logic and exhibit bias in their social perceptions. In this chapter alone, we have seen that perceivers tend to rely on cognitive heuristics without regard for numerical base rates; overlook situational influences on behavior; disparage victims whose misfortunes threaten their sense of justice; form premature first impressions primed by recent experiences and fluctuating moods; and interpret, seek, and create evidence in ways that support these impressions.

To make matters worse, we often have little awareness of our limitations, leading us to feel *overconfident* in our judgments. In a series of studies, David Dunning and his colleagues (1990) asked college students to predict how a target person would react in different situations. Some subjects made predictions about a fellow student whom they had just met and interviewed, and others made predictions about their roommates. In both cases, subjects reported their confidence in each prediction, and accuracy was determined by the responses of the target persons themselves. The results were clear: regardless of whether they judged a stranger or a roommate, subjects consistently overestimated the accuracy of their predictions. People even overestimate their ability to predict their own behavior. When ninety-eight first-year students made 3,800 self-predictions about the upcoming academic year—predictions that were later verified ("Will you decide on a major?" "Will you call your parents more than twice a month?" "Will you

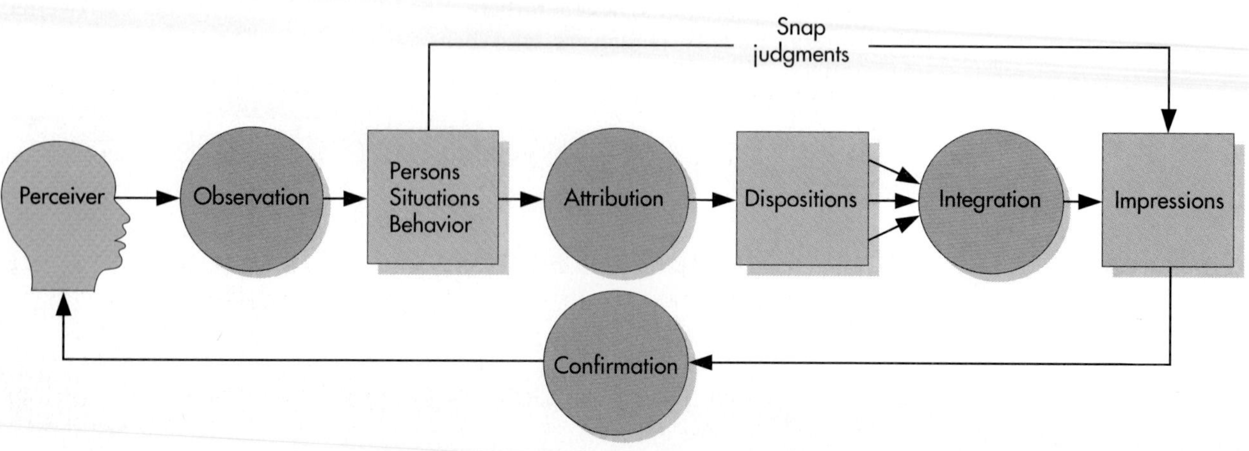

Figure 3.10 **The Processes of Social Perception.** Summarizing Chapter 3, this diagram depicts the processes of social perception. As shown, it begins with the observation of persons, situations, and behavior. Sometimes, we make snap judgments from these cues. At other times, we form impressions only after making attributions and integrating these attributions. Either way, our impressions are subject to confirmation biases and the risk of a self-fulfilling prophecy.

have a steady boyfriend/girlfriend?")—they estimated that they would be accurate 82 percent of the time. As it turned out, their accuracy rate was only 68 percent (Vallone et al., 1990).

Standing back from the material presented in this chapter, you may find the list of shortcomings, punctuated by the problem of overconfidence, to be long and depressing. So, how can this list be reconciled with the triumphs of civilization? Or to put it another way, "If we're so dumb, how come we made it to the moon?" (Nisbett & Ross, 1980, p. 249). Part of the answer stems from the realization that *bias*—that is, a deviation from the rules of logic—does not necessarily result in *error*—defined as real-life judgments that are incorrect (Funder, 1987). The fundamental attribution "error" is a good example: we may make personal attributions to the neglect of situations, but sometimes behavior really *is* caused by personal factors (Funder, 1982; Harvey et al., 1981).

It is true that people fall prey to the biases identified by social psychologists and probably even to some biases that have not yet been noticed. It is also true that we often get fooled by con artists, misjudge our partners in marriage, and hire the wrong job applicants. As Thomas Gilovich (1991) points out, more Americans believe in ESP than in evolution, and there are twenty times more astrologers than astronomers. The problem is, these biases can have harmful consequences—giving rise, as we'll see in Chapter 4, to stereotypes, prejudice, and discrimination. Yet despite our imperfections, there are four reasons to be guardedly optimistic about our competence as social perceivers:

1. The more experience people have with each other, the more accurate they are. For example, although subjects exhibit a limited ability to assess the personality of strangers they meet in the laboratory, they are generally better at judging their friends and acquaintances (Colvin & Funder, 1991; Malloy & Albright, 1990; Paunonen, 1989).
2. Although people are not good at making global judgments of others (that is, at knowing what people are like across a range of settings), we can make more circumscribed predictions of how others will behave in our own presence. You may misjudge the personality of a roommate or co-worker, but to the extent that you can predict your roommate's actions at home or your co-worker's actions on the job, the mistakes may not matter (Swann, 1984).
3. Social perception skills can be enhanced in people who are taught the rules of probability and logic (Nisbett et al., 1987). For example, graduate students in psychology—because they take courses in statistics—tend to improve in their ability to reason about everyday social events (Lehman et al., 1988).
4. People can form more accurate impressions of others when motivated by a concern for accuracy and open-mindedness than by a need for immediacy, confirmation, and closure (Kruglanski, 1989; Webster & Kruglanski, 1994). Many studies described in this chapter have shown that people exhibit less bias when there is an incentive for accuracy within the experiment (Kunda, 1990; Neuberg, 1989) or when they make judgments that have adaptive significance (Baron, 1988).

In sum, research on the accuracy of social perceptions offers a valuable lesson: to the extent that we observe others with whom we have had time to interact, make judgments that are reasonably specific, have some knowledge of the rules of logic, and are sufficiently motivated to form an accurate impression, the problems can be minimized. Indeed, being aware of the biases described in this chapter may well be a necessary first step toward a better understanding of others.

REVIEW

OBSERVATION: THE ELEMENTS OF SOCIAL PERCEPTION

- To understand others, social perceivers rely on indirect clues—the elements of social perception.

Persons: Judging a Book by Its Cover

- People often make snap judgments of others based on physical appearances (for example, adults with baby-faced features are seen as having childlike qualities).

Situations: The Scripts of Life

- People have preconceptions or "scripts" about certain types of situations. These scripts guide our interpretations of behavior.

Behavioral Evidence

- People derive meaning from behavior by dividing it into discrete, meaningful units.
- Nonverbal behaviors are often used to determine how others are feeling.
- From facial expressions, people all over the world can identify the emotions of happiness, fear, sadness, surprise, anger, and disgust.
- Body language, gaze, and touch are also important forms of nonverbal communication.
- People use nonverbal cues to detect deception but are typically not accurate in making these judgments because they pay too much attention to the face and neglect cues that are more revealing.

ATTRIBUTION: FROM ELEMENTS TO DISPOSITIONS

- Attribution is the process by which we explain people's behavior.

The Logic of Attribution

- People begin to understand others by making personal or situational attributions for their behavior.
- Correspondent inference theory states that people learn about others from behavior when it is freely chosen, unexpected, and results in a small number of desirable outcomes.
- From multiple behaviors, we base our attributions on three kinds of covariation information: consensus, distinctiveness, and consistency.

Attribution Biases

- People depart from the logic of attribution theory in several ways.
- First, we use cognitive heuristics—rules of thumb that enable us to make judgments that are quick but often in error.
- Second, we tend to commit the fundamental attribution error, overestimating the role of personal factors and underestimating the impact of situations.
- Third, the actor-observer effect reveals that although people tend to make personal attributions for others, they attribute their own behavior to situational factors.
- Fourth, we often make biased attributions for the behavior of others. Needing to believe in a just world, for example, people criticize victims and hold them responsible for their fate.

INTEGRATION: FROM DISPOSITIONS TO IMPRESSIONS

Information Integration: The Arithmetic

- The impressions we form are based on an averaging of a person's traits, not on a summation.
- According to information integration theory, impressions are based on perceiver predispositions and a weighted average of individual traits.

Deviations from the Arithmetic

- Perceivers differ in their sensitivity to certain traits and in the impressions they form.
- Differences stem from characteristics of the perceiver, the target, implicit personality theories, and the primacy effect.

CONFIRMATION BIASES: FROM IMPRESSIONS TO REALITY

- Once an impression is formed, people become less likely to change their minds when confronted with nonsupportive evidence.
- People tend to interpret, seek, and create information in ways that confirm existing beliefs.

Perseverance of Beliefs

- First impressions may survive even in the face of inconsistent information.
- Ambiguous evidence is interpreted in ways that bolster first impressions.
- The effect of evidence that is later discredited perseveres because people formulate theories to support their initial beliefs.

Confirmatory Hypothesis Testing

- Once perceivers have beliefs about someone, they seek further information in ways that confirm those beliefs.

The Self-fulfilling Prophecy

- As shown by the effects of teacher expectancies on student achievement, first impressions set in motion a self-fulfilling prophecy.
- This is the product of a three-step process: (1) a perceiver forms an expectation of a target, (2) the perceiver behaves accordingly, and (3) the target adjusts to the perceiver's actions.
- This self-fulfilling prophecy effect is powerful but limited.
- When perceivers are motivated to seek the truth or to get along with the target, they do not produce the self-fulfilling prophecy.
- When targets know of the perceivers' expectations and believe them to be false, they actively seek to disconfirm.

SOCIAL PERCEPTION: THE BOTTOM LINE

- Sometimes people make snap judgments; at other times they evaluate others by analyzing their behavior.
- Research suggests that our judgments are biased and that we are overconfident.
- Still, there are reasons to be optimistic about our competence as social perceivers.

KEY TERMS

social perception, p. 82
nonverbal behavior, p. 86
attribution theory, p. 91
personal attribution, p. 91
situational attribution, p. 91
correspondent inference theory, p. 91
covariation principle, p. 92
cognitive heuristics, p. 94
false-consensus effect, p. 95
base-rate fallacy, p. 95
fundamental attribution error, p. 96
actor-observer effect, p. 100
belief in a just world, p. 101
impression formation, p. 103
information integration theory, p. 104
priming, p. 104
implicit personality theory, p. 106
central traits, p. 107
primacy effect, p. 107
confirmation bias, p. 108
belief perseverance, p. 109
self-fulfilling prophecy, p. 111

Chapter 4

Perceiving Groups

PREVIEW

This chapter considers how people think, feel, and behave toward members of social groups. We begin by examining *stereotypes,* beliefs about groups that influence our judgments of individuals. Next, we examine *prejudice,* negative feelings toward others based on their group membership. To illustrate these problems, we then focus on *sexism,* a form of discrimination based on gender, and *racism,* a form of discrimination based on a person's skin color or ethnic heritage. The possible ways to reduce discrimination are also discussed.

OUTLINE

Ann Hopkins was hoping to become a partner in one of the largest accounting firms in the country. Her record was impeccable. In just a few years, Hopkins had single-handedly brought in more than $25 million in contracts, tops among her peers. Yet she was denied a partnership even though several less productive men were promoted. According to Hopkins, it was because she was a woman. As in most disputes, however, there are two sides to the story. The firm claimed that Hopkins was abrasive, overbearing, and hard to work with. Some partners complained that she used profanity and was insensitive to co-workers. One member of the firm was even said to have quit because he could not tolerate working with her.

Was Ann Hopkins rejected because of her personality, her gender, or a combination of the two? Hopkins took the case to court and claimed she was described by partners as a "macho" woman who needed to take a course at "charm school." One partner advised her to "wear make-up, have my hair styled, and wear jewelry." What do these comments prove? To address this question, Hopkins sought expert testimony from social psychologist Susan Fiske. Citing the research presented in this chapter, Fiske concluded that Hopkins was a likely victim of sex discrimination. The trial judge agreed, and by a 6 to 3 vote so did the U.S. Supreme Court (Fiske et al., 1991).

Sex discrimination claims raise difficult questions about biases in social perception. Equally troubling questions are raised by claims of racial discrimination,

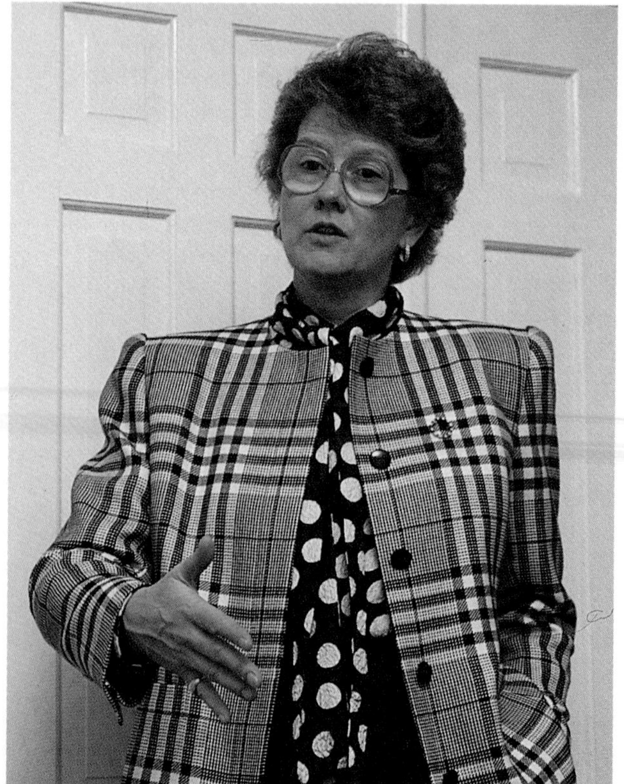

Despite an exceptional record of productivity, Ann Hopkins was denied partnership in a large accounting firm. Was it because she was a woman perceived to be too much like a man?

The 1991 beating of black motorist Rodney King by four white police officers was captured on videotape. Was this incident an act of racism?

as in the 1991 beating of black motorist Rodney King by white Los Angeles police officers. The incident took place one night after police cars chased King, who was speeding, stopped his car, and cornered him on the street. After King resisted arrest, one officer fired a 50,000-volt "stun gun" at his chest, knocking him to the ground. Three others then kicked and clubbed him repeatedly with their nightsticks. King suffered a fractured skull, a crushed cheekbone, burn marks on his chest, a broken ankle, and various internal injuries (Lacayo, 1991; Prud'Homme, 1991).

To many concerned citizens, this horrifying incident was an act of pure racism, like an old-fashioned lynching. What's worse, they say, this case received attention only because a bystander happened to record the beating with his home video camera. That videotape later became the centerpiece of a police brutality trial against the four officers. It seemed like an open-and-shut case. But then on April 29, 1992, a California jury returned a verdict that sent shock waves across the country: not guilty. Was the beating racially motivated? Would King have been similarly treated if he were white? How can we ever know for sure when behavior stems from prejudice?

discrimination Any behavior directed against persons because of their membership in a particular group.

The term **discrimination** is used to describe *behaviors* directed against persons because of their membership in a particular group. It would be nice to think of discrimination as a sin of the past. Unfortunately, recent incidents suggest that it still exists and that its victims are avoided, excluded, rejected, belittled, and attacked because of the groups to which they belong. What do we mean by "group"? Actually, there are many kinds of groups—such as families, political parties, nations, states, religions, and ethnic subcultures. For the purposes of this chapter, a **group** is defined as two or more people perceived as having at least one of the following characteristics: (1) direct interactions with each other; (2) joint membership in a social category based on sex, race, or other attributes; (3) a shared, common fate.

group Two or more persons perceived as related because of their interactions, membership in the same social category, or common fate.

Figure 4.1 **Perceiving Groups: Three Reactions.** There are two paths to discrimination: one based on stereotypes, the other on prejudice. Note also that there are other mutual links among these variables. Discriminatory practices may support stereotypes and prejudice; stereotypes may cause people to become prejudiced; and prejudiced people may use stereotypes to justify their feelings.

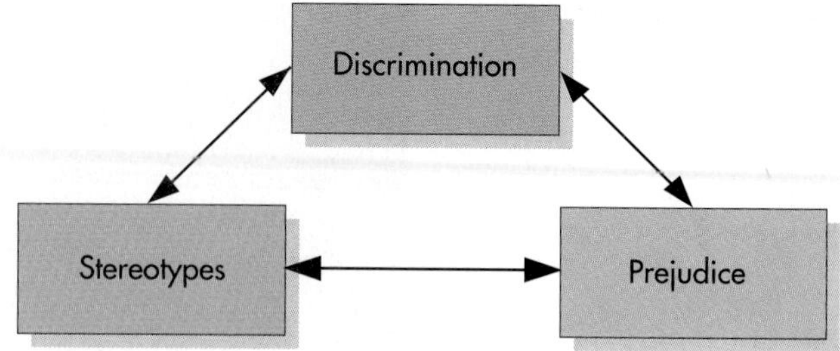

This chapter is divided into four parts. First, we consider the causes and effects of *stereotypes*—beliefs that people have about individuals based on their membership in a social group. Second, we examine *prejudice,* which consists of negative feelings about others because of their connection to a social group. To put these problems in concrete terms, we then focus on *sexism* and *racism,* two historically common forms of discrimination. For the most part, stereotypes and prejudice are discussed separately. Note, however, that our beliefs and feelings influence each other, that both give rise to discrimination, and that discriminatory behavior, in turn, fuels stereotypes and prejudices (see Figure 4.1).

STEREOTYPES

stereotypes Beliefs that associate groups of people with certain traits.

A **stereotype** is a belief that associates a whole group of people with certain traits. When you stop to think about it, the list of well-known stereotypes seems endless. Consider some examples: The Japanese are sneaky, athletes are brainless, librarians are quiet, Italians are emotional, Jews are materialistic, accountants are dull, Californians are laid back, and used-car salesmen can't be trusted as far as you can throw them. Now, be honest: How many of these images ring a familiar bell? In this section, we raise three questions: (1) How do stereotypes form? (2) How do they influence our perceptions of individuals? (3) What keeps them alive when so often they prove to be wrong?

How Stereotypes Form: Cognitive Foundations

The origins of stereotypes can be traced to a number of different sources (Allport, 1954). From a historical perspective, stereotypes spring from past events. Thus, it can be argued that slavery in America gave rise to the portrayal of Blacks as inferior, just as the sneak attack on Pearl Harbor in World War II fostered a belief that the Japanese cannot be trusted. From a political perspective, stereotypes are viewed as a means by which groups in power come to rationalize war, religious intolerance, and economic oppression. And from a sociocultural perspective, it has been argued that real differences between social groups contribute to the birth of perceived differences. Each of these perspectives has something unique to offer. Social psychologists, however, pose a different question: Regardless of how stereotypes are born within a culture, how do they grow and operate in the minds of individuals?

The formation of stereotypes involves two related processes. The first is *categorization.* As perceivers, we routinely sort single objects into groups rather than

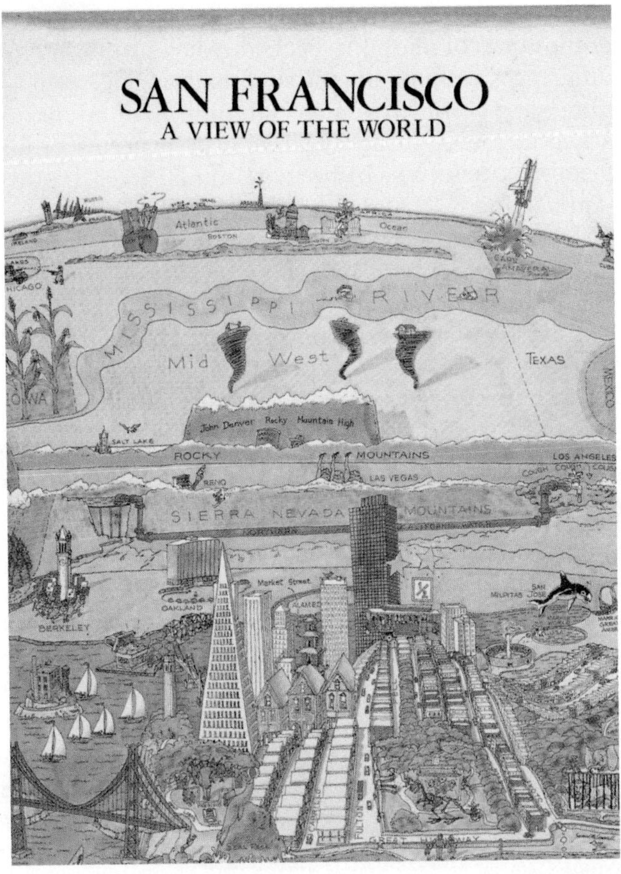

Stereotypes can spring from the outgroup homogeneity effect, the tendency to assume that "they" are all alike.

think of each as unique. Biologists classify animals into families; archaeologists divide time into eras; geographers split the Earth into regions. Likewise, people sort each other on the basis of gender, race, and other common attributes—in a process called **social categorization.** In some ways, social categorization is natural and adaptive. By grouping people the way we group foods, animals, and other objects, we form impressions quickly and use past experience to guide new interactions. There is, however, a serious drawback. Like lumping apples and oranges together because both are fruit, categorizing people leads us to overestimate the differences *between* groups and to underestimate the differences *within* groups (Wilder, 1986; Stangor & Lange, 1994).

social categorization The classification of persons into groups on the basis of common attributes.

The second process that promotes stereotyping follows directly from the first. Although grouping humans is much like grouping objects, there is a key difference. When it comes to *social* categorization, perceivers themselves are members or nonmembers of the categories they employ. Groups that you identify with—your country, religion, political party, or even the hometown sports team—are called *ingroups,* whereas groups other than your own are called *outgroups.* This tendency to carve the world into "us" and "them" has important consequences.

One consequence is a phenomenon known as the **outgroup homogeneity effect,** a pervasive tendency for social perceivers to assume that a greater similarity exists among members of outgroups than among members of ingroups. In other words, there may be fine and subtle differences between "us," but "they" are all alike (Linville & Jones, 1980). There are three types of evidence for this bias. First, when people are asked to estimate how many group members share a cer-

outgroup homogeneity effect The tendency to assume that there is greater similarity among members of outgroups than of ingroups.

tain stereotyped characteristic, percentage estimates are higher in ratings of outgroups than of ingroups. Second, when people are asked to estimate the range of differences within a population, that range is seen as narrower when the population being considered is an outgroup than an ingroup. Third, when people are asked to rate a group of individuals in terms of how alike they are, outgroup members are seen as being more similar to each other than are ingroup members (Park & Judd, 1990; Ostrom & Sedikides, 1992).

Research shows that these effects are common. Indeed, there are many real-life examples. Americans who arrive from China, Korea, Taiwan, and Vietnam see themselves as different, but to the western eye they are all Asian. Business majors like to talk about engineering types, engineers talk about business types, liberals lump together all conservatives, teenagers lump together all old people, and as the natives of New York City proclaim their cultural and ethnic diversity, outsiders talk of the typical New Yorker.

As a result of the outgroup homogeneity effect, people are quick to generalize from a single individual to a whole group. In a study that illustrates this point, students from Rutgers and Princeton—rival universities in the state of New Jersey—watched a videotape of a subject in a decision-making study. After being told that the study was held at either Rutgers or Princeton, subjects saw the target person make a series of choices (for example, between classical and rock music). When later asked to predict the percentage of other subjects who made the same choices, students assumed that there was greater similarity between the target person and other subjects at the rival university than at their own (Quattrone & Jones, 1980).

There are two reasons for the tendency to perceive outgroups as homogeneous. First, we often do not notice subtle differences among outgroups because we have little personal contact with them. Think about your family, or your favorite sports team, and specific individuals come to mind. Think about an unfamiliar outgroup, however, and you are likely to think in abstract terms about the group as a whole. Indeed, research shows that the more familiar people are with an outgroup, the less likely they are to perceive it as homogeneous (Linville et al., 1989). A second problem is that people often do not encounter a representative sample of outgroup members. The Princetonian who sees only those Rutgers students who cruise into town for a Saturday football game, screaming at the top of their lungs, sees only the most avid rival fans—hardly a diverse lot (Quattrone, 1986).

How Stereotypes Distort Perceptions of Individuals

Social categorization and the outgroup homogeneity effect help to explain how beliefs about *groups* develop. Now, let's consider how these beliefs influence the perception of *individuals*. Remember Ann Hopkins, the productive but abrasive accountant? In her court case, Hopkins claimed that her aggressive manner proved offensive only because it clashed with traditional conceptions of women. Is her claim justified? Is the same tough-mindedness more acceptable in a man?

contrast effect A tendency to perceive stimuli that differ from expectations as being even more different than they really are.

As a general rule, judgments of a stimulus are influenced by the discrepancy between that stimulus and one's expectations. When a stimulus differs only slightly from expectations, the difference is barely noticed, if at all. When a stimulus varies considerably from expectations, however, the perceived difference is magnified as the result of a **contrast effect**. To illustrate, imagine that you've been presented with three buckets of water—one cold, one hot, and the third at room temperature. After placing your right hand into the cold water and your left hand into the hot water, you place both hands simultaneously into the third bucket. You can probably predict the odd result: even though both hands are in the same water, your right hand now feels warm and your left hand feels cool. The temperature you feel depends on the sensation that preceded it.

Like this influence on physical sensations, contrast effects can also affect *social* perceptions. In a study by Melvin Manis and his colleagues (1988), subjects read sentences ostensibly written by mental patients at two hospitals and were led to believe that one group of patients was seriously disturbed but the other was not. Subjects then evaluated new sentences that depicted a *moderate* level of psychopathology. The results paralleled the water-temperature test. When the material was supposedly written by disturbed patients, the sentences seemed normal. When the same sentences were thought to emanate from the more normal group, however, they seemed relatively disturbed. These results support Ann Hopkins's analysis of the workplace. As we'll see, gender stereotypes lead people to expect warm, gentle women and assertive, forceful men. Since those who break the mold are subject to contrast effects, it is conceivable that Ann Hopkins seemed tougher and more abrasive than a man would under the same circumstances. Similarly, a gentle man would seem more passive and weak than a woman would in the same situation.

How Stereotypes Survive: Self-Perpetuating Mechanisms

As generalized beliefs, stereotypes offer us quick and convenient summaries of social groups. As *over*generalized beliefs, however, they cause us to overlook the diversity within categories and form mistaken impressions of specific individuals. In general, it is difficult to determine the accuracy of a stereotype (Judd & Park, 1993). Still, researchers have focused on the question, Why do stereotypes endure?

illusory correlation An overestimate of the association between variables that are only slightly or not at all correlated.

Illusory Correlations One answer can be found in the **illusory correlation:** a tendency for people to overestimate the link between variables that are only slightly or not at all correlated. Illusory correlation was first discovered by Loren Chapman (1967), who presented subjects with lists of paired words such as *lion-tiger, lion-eggs, bacon-tiger,* and *bacon-eggs*. Subjects then estimated how often each word was paired with every other word. Two biases were found. First, even though all words were paired an equal number of times, subjects overestimated the number of times conspicuous items were paired—for example, words that were longer than the others on the list (*blossoms-notebook*). Second, subjects overestimated the frequency of word pairs that were meaningfully associated in their own minds (*lion-tiger, bacon-eggs*).

Is it possible that these same two biases lead people to perceive false support for existing stereotypes? David Hamilton and his colleagues believed so. In one study, Hamilton and Robert Gifford (1976) tested the hypothesis that distinctive persons and actions—those that capture attention simply because they are novel or deviant—produce illusory correlations. Subjects read a series of sentences, each describing a desirable or an undesirable behavior on the part of someone who belonged to one of two groups, A or B. Overall, two-thirds of the behaviors were desirable ("visited a sick friend in the hospital") rather than undesirable ("was late to work"), and two-thirds involved members of hypothetical group A (the majority) rather than group B (the minority). The ratio of desirable to undesirable acts was the same for the two groups, so objectively subjects should not have formed an impression more favorable toward either group. But they did. As shown in Figure 4.2, subjects overestimated the number of times that the two relatively infrequent variables—undesirable acts and group B members—were paired together. With respect to stereotyping, the implications are clear: Unless otherwise motivated, people overestimate the joint occurrence of distinct variables such as minority groups and deviant acts (Schaller, 1991). Further research shows that such pairings attract attention, leading us to inflate in memory the number of such instances that had been observed (McConnell et al., 1994).

Next, Hamilton and Terrence Rose (1980) reasoned that stereotypes would lead people to expect real groups and traits to fit together like bacon and eggs. In their study, subjects read twenty-four sentences, each linking someone from a familiar occupation (*doctor, accountant, salesman, stewardess, librarian,* and *waitress*) to a trait (*wealthy, perfectionist, thoughtful, timid, enthusiastic, talkative, productive, serious, attractive, comforting, busy,* and *loud*). Each occupation was paired equally often with each trait. Yet subjects later overestimated the number of times they had read about timid accountants, wealthy doctors, talkative salesmen, attractive stewardesses, serious librarians, and loud waitresses. Jaded by preconceived notions, subjects saw correlations that were expected but did not exist.

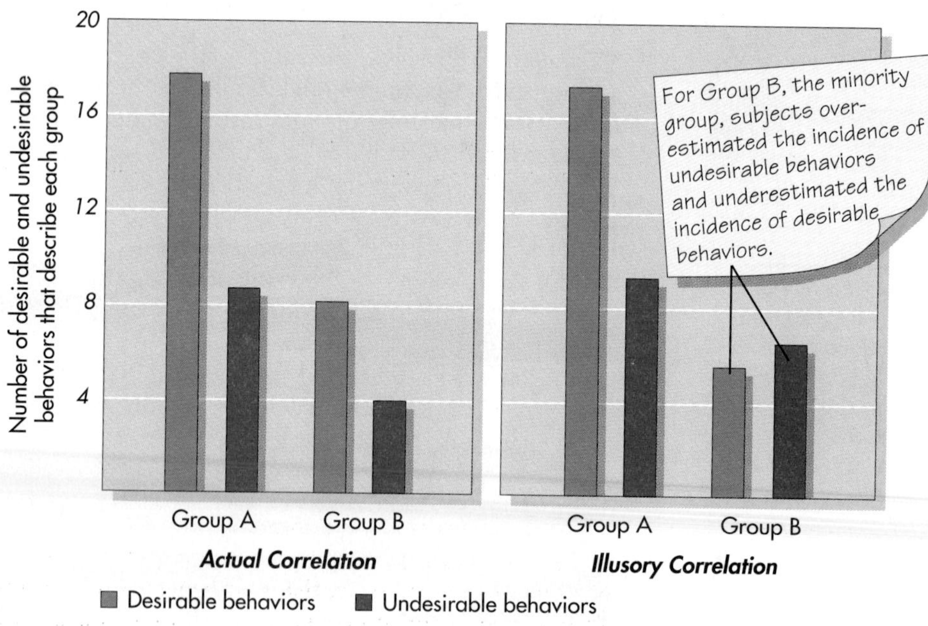

Figure 4.2 The Illusory Correlation. Subjects read sentences, each pairing a person from group A or group B with either a desirable or an undesirable behavior. Notice the actual correlation on the left side: Two-thirds of the persons were from group A, two-thirds of the behaviors were desirable, and the ratio of desirable to undesirable behaviors was exactly the same for the two groups. The illusory correlation on the right side, however, shows that subjects overestimated how often the two infrequent variables (group B members and undesirable acts) appeared together. (Hamilton & Gifford, 1976.)

Research on illusory correlations helps to explain the formation and stubborn persistence of stereotypes. First, members of minority groups—precisely because they are distinctive in the population—are under the spotlight, so everything they do gets blown out of numerical proportion. Second, pre-existing stereotypes may be sustained by false support. The person who thinks politicians are dishonest will overestimate the number of corruption scandals that occur in government compared to other settings. Likewise, someone who believes that the mentally ill are dangerous will overestimate the number of murders committed by deranged psychiatric patients compared to those by other violent criminals. Once a stereotype is in place, we are quick to notice the supporting evidence.

Subcategorizations Have you ever noticed that people often manage to hold negative views about a social group even when they like individual members of that group? One of the unnerving paradoxes of social perception is that stereotypes stubbornly survive one disconfirmation after the next. The question is, Why?

Social psychologists used to view stereotypes as broad, sweeping categories—Blacks, Whites, young people, old people, men, women, and so on. We now know, however, that many stereotypes consist of more limited, specific *subcategories*. Research on conceptions of different groups illustrates the point. When subjects were asked to sort pictures of elderly persons into piles and then rate the pictures on various traits, three subcategories emerged: grandmotherly types, distinguished elder statesmen, and inactive senior citizens (Brewer et al., 1981). Similarly, people readily distinguish among black athletes, urban ghetto Blacks, and middle-class Blacks (Devine & Baker, 1991). Conceptions of men and women are also highly differentiated. Common female subtypes include career woman, chick, feminist, and housewife; males are cast into such subtypes as career man, intellectual, jock, playboy, and punk (Eckes, 1994).

Subcategories seem less objectionable than general stereotypes because they are more precise. But now consider the implications. Confronted with Ann Hopkins, or with any woman who is not overly warm and nurturant, people can either develop a more diversified image of females or toss the mismatch into a special subtype—say, "career women." To the extent that people create this subcategory, their existing image of women-in-general will remain relatively intact. Similarly, to the extent that white Americans dismiss their amiable black neighbors as atypical "middle-class Blacks," unflattering images of Blacks-in-general may also resist change. This problem was depicted in the 1989 movie *Do the Right Thing*, in which a white bigot is asked to reconcile his racist views with the fact that Magic Johnson was his favorite basketball player and Eddie Murphy his favorite actor. "Let me explain myself," he replied. "They're black, but they're not really black. . . . It's different."

Donna Desforges and her colleagues (1991) note that exposure to a member of a group may force a revision of beliefs about the group as a whole by means of a three-step chain of events. First, through social categorization, we initially *expect* the individual to fit a stereotypical mold. Second, after exposure or personal contact, we *adjust* our impressions of that individual, making his or her social categories less relevant. Third, confronted with a mismatch between our stereotype and observations, we *generalize* from the individual to the group as a whole. This last step is the key.

Does disconfirming evidence about individual members lead people to revise their beliefs, or are groups destined to remain trapped in the shadow of their stereotypes? According to Renée Weber and Jennifer Crocker (1983), there are certain conditions under which generalization takes place. These investigators reasoned that target persons who disconfirm a stereotype *can* force a revision of that stereotype if they are otherwise viewed as representative members of the group. To test this hypothesis, Weber and Crocker had subjects read about corporate lawyers who did not fit the usual image (they wore ill-fitting clothes and could not analyze problems or draw logical conclusions). For some subjects, the sample lawyers came from the demographic group typically expected (white, married, and rich). For others, the lawyers were atypical (black, single, and poor). Later, when subjects were asked to report on their beliefs about corporate lawyers in general, atypical members were dismissed as flukes, leaving the overall stereotype relatively untarnished. When typical members disconfirmed the stereotype, however, subjects revised their beliefs about the group as a whole.

These results suggest a general rule. Whether people judge human beings or inanimate objects, their beliefs about a whole category change more after exposure to cases viewed as *typical,* rather than as atypical, of the stereotyped group (Johnston & Hewstone, 1992; Rothbart & Lewis, 1988). For members of stereotyped groups, this phenomenon creates a difficult dilemma. To overcome the negative expectations, they should try to present themselves as *atypical* members of the group, as exceptions to the rule. Yet to foster a change in the stereotype, these same people should want to appear *typical,* inviting perceivers to generalize to the group as a whole. This conflict of interest explains why one of this book's authors reacted with mixed feelings the day a friend said, "You're pretty normal for a psychologist!"

Confirmation Biases In Chapter 3, we saw that first impressions are often slow to change because people process information in ways that tend to verify their existing beliefs. According to William von Hippel and his colleagues (1995), similar biases are at work in the stubborn maintenance of stereotypes.

One problem is that people given an opportunity to learn more about a person or stereotyped group seek information that is likely to confirm the stereotype. To demonstrate, Lucy Johnston and Neil Macrae (1994) offered subjects a chance to ask questions about "physics students"—a group considered to be interested in new technology. Among the questions they could ask, some were consistent with the stereotype ("Would you like to see more courses devoted to developments in technology?"); others were inconsistent ("Do you think that students should get involved in political issues?") or irrelevant ("Where do you plan to go on holiday this year?"). The result: Subjects preferred stereotype-consistent questions over those designed to explore other aspects of the group. Apparently, stereotypes shape the information we seek—and find—about others.

Stereotypes are also maintained by subtleties of the language we use. Anne Maass and her colleagues (1995) have suggested that people are more likely to use personal, trait-like terms to describe behavior when it is consistent with a stereotype than when it is inconsistent. In a study conducted in Italy, these researchers asked subjects to select descriptions of events that involved characters said to be from the northern or southern part of the country (these groups are seen as different, with southern Italians believed to be more hospitable and northerners more industrious). Each event depicted a stereotypic behavior. In one episode, for example, a young couple brings a woman into a bedroom, and one of them says, "Don't worry, you can stay with us for these two months. Just feel at home." How did subjects label this transaction? Given a choice of labels that ranged from purely descriptive ("Has prepared a room for a friend") to interpretive and trait-like ("Is hospitable"), subjects selected more interpretive language for acts that were consistent with the stereotype. When the generous couple was from northern Italy, they were merely preparing a room. Yet when that same couple was from the south, they were being hospitable—a description that serves to maintain the regional stereotype.

Stereotyping: A Necessary Evil?

If we assume that stereotypes are born of the human tendency to categorize objects, it's easy to justify the result as an innocent by-product of the way we think. In other words, "Don't blame me, it can't be helped." Is it reasonable to draw this conclusion? Is stereotyping an inevitable, if not necessary, evil? There are two points of view.

Stereotypes as Implicit and Automatic According to Anthony Greenwald and Mahzarin Banaji (1995), stereotypes are often activated without our awareness and operate at an unconscious or "implicit" level. It just happens. The following experiments illustrate the point:

1. As subjects worked on a computer, words such as *poor, slavery, Harlem,* and *jazz* flashed across the screen so rapidly that subjects were not even aware of the exposure. Yet moments later, in an unrelated task, these subjects were more likely to judge a male target person as aggressive—consistent with a negative stereotype of Blacks (Devine, 1989).
2. Subjects were instructed to complete word fragments such as *ri_e* and *poli_e*. When the items were presented on tape by an Asian woman, subjects who were also distracted by another task created words that are stereotypic of Asians, words such as *rice* and *polite* (Gilbert & Hixon, 1991).
3. Subjects worked at unscrambling sentences, some of which portrayed acts of aggression ("cuts off other drivers") or dependence ("won't go alone"). Later, ostensibly as part of a different experiment, they read about Donald or Donna, a male or female target person. Consistent with popular images of men and women, subjects exposed to the aggression phrases judged Donald as more aggressive, while those who had worked on dependence phrases judged Donna as more dependent (Banaji et al., 1993).

Clearly, stereotypes can be activated without our awareness and influence our judgments of others. This conclusion makes you wonder if the process is somehow adaptive. Does stereotyping benefit perceivers in any way? Neil Macrae and his colleagues (1994) recently tested the hypothesis that by simplifying the way we form impressions of others, stereotypes free up cognitive resources that can be used in other activities. In this study, subjects simultaneously worked on two tasks: (1) they made judgments of target persons based on trait lists printed on a computer screen, and (2) they tried to monitor a tape-recorded passage on an unfamiliar topic (the economy and geography of Indonesia). In the first task, some subjects but not others received stereotype labels along with the trait lists (for example, a person described as creative, sensitive, and temperamental was also said to be an "artist").

How well were subjects able to perform at the two tasks? There were two key results. First, subjects given the stereotype labels later recalled more of the stereotypic traits on the lists (for example, "artist" subjects were more likely to recall that the person was creative, temperamental, and sensitive). Second, subjects given the stereotype labels also scored higher in a multiple-choice test of the prose-monitoring task. This last result suggests that stereotypes function as "energy-saving devices." To the extent that you judge others you meet by falling back on old preconceptions, you have more cognitive resources available for other activities.

Stereotypes as Explicit and Controlled Is stereotyping necessary and inevitable? To be sure, some degree of social categorization is automatic and so, probably, is the formation of stereotypes. But none of us needs to be trapped into evaluating specific persons in terms of social categories. Research shows that three factors enable us to overcome stereotypes and judge others on a more individualized basis (Fiske & Neuberg, 1990).

The first factor is the amount of *personal information* we have about someone. Once such information is available, stereotypes and other preconceptions lose relevance and impact. Thus, when subjects read about a man or woman who consistently reacted to difficult situations by behaving assertively or passively, their impressions of that person were influenced more by his or her actions than by gender (Locksley et al., 1980). In fact, people will often set aside their stereotypes even when the personal information they have is not clearly relevant to the judgment they have to make (Hilton & Fein, 1989).

The second factor is a perceiver's cognitive *ability* to focus on an individual member of a stereotyped group. Research shows that people are most likely to form an impression that is based on existing stereotypes when they're busy (Gilbert & Hixon, 1991) or pressed for time (Pratto & Bargh, 1991)—and unable to think carefully about the unique attributes of a single person. In an intriguing test of this ability hypothesis, Galen Bodenhausen (1990) classified subjects by their circadian arousal patterns, or biological rhythms, into two types: "morning people" (who describe themselves as most alert early in the morning) and "night people" (who say they peak much later, in the evening). By random assignment, subjects took part in an experiment in human judgment that was scheduled at either 9 A.M. or 8 P.M. The result? Morning people were more likely to use stereotypes when tested at night; night owls were more likely to do so early in the morning. Other research shows that people are also more likely to use stereotypes when they are under the influence of alcohol than when they are sober (von Hippel et al., 1995). When we are tired, or drunk, and lack the mental energy to individualize their judgments, we fall back on simple-minded rules of thumb.

The third factor is *motivation.* When social perceivers are highly motivated to form an accurate impression of someone (say, if they're in an interdependent relationship or if they need to compete against the person), they often manage to set aside their pre-existing beliefs (Neuberg, 1989; Ruscher & Fiske, 1990). In one study, subjects expected to interact with a former mental patient who had supposedly been treated for schizophrenia. Ordinarily, people would prejudge this individual according to their beliefs about mental illness. But when subjects were told that they would be working with the person to earn money based on their joint performance, they paid more attention to the patient's personal characteristics (Neuberg & Fiske, 1987). Sufficiently motivated, people can make individualized judgments of others—provided they are not otherwise distracted (Pendry & Macrae, 1994).

To summarize, research shows that we *can* stop ourselves from making hasty, stereotypic judgments when we have personalized information and are able and willing to use that information. But how easy is it, really, to inhibit the tendency to categorize and stereotype? Research in other contexts suggests that sometimes the harder you try to suppress an unwanted thought, the less likely you are to succeed. Try *not* to think about a white bear for the next thirty seconds, and that image will pop to mind with remarkable frequency. Try not to worry about how long it's taking you to fall asleep, and you'll stay awake. Try not to think about an itch, or the chocolate cheesecake in the fridge . . . well, you get the idea (Wegner, 1994).

Knowing how difficult it is to suppress unwanted thoughts, Macrae and his colleagues (1994) presented subjects with a color photograph of a male skinhead and asked them to write a paragraph describing the person. Half the subjects were warned that social perceptions are often biased by stereotypes—and that they should try to avoid this bias. After completing the task, all subjects were given a second skinhead photograph to evaluate, this time without a special instruction. So, was the warning effective? Consistent with the notion that people can control the use of stereotypes, analyses of the descriptions revealed that the warning initially reduced stereotyping. The effect, however, was short-lived. In fact, the same subjects who managed to control themselves in the first task later used *more* stereotypes in the second task. This post-suppression "rebound" suggests that it may be hard for us to keep from using stereotypes on a consistent, long-term basis (see Figure 4.3).

PREJUDICE

Stereotypes may form and endure as a result of the way we categorize people and distinguish between ingroups and outgroups. This cognitive perspective—in which stereotypes are considered a by-product of the way human beings think—suggests that if people could be prevented from viewing each other in categorical terms, or were enlightened by accurate information, discrimination throughout the world would be eliminated. But would it, really? Is the way we *think* about groups all that matters? If you look back at Figure 4.1, you'll see that there is another potent factor to consider: how people *feel* about the social groups they encounter. In this section, we trace a second path to discrimination, one based on our motivations and emotions.

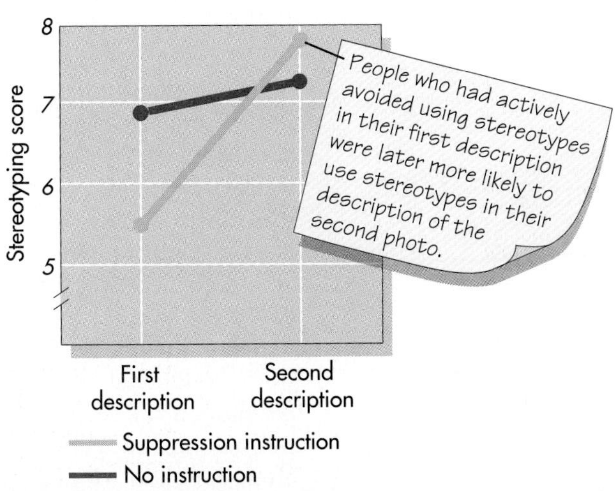

Figure 4.3 Stereotypes on the Rebound. Subjects were shown a picture of a skinhead and asked to write a description. Some were instructed to avoid the use of stereotypes; others were not. Later, all subjects evaluated a second skinhead, this time without instruction. As shown, instructed subjects suppressed the use of stereotypes in the first task, thus demonstrating an ability to control themselves (left). But the same subjects were later more likely to use stereotypes in the second task—evidence of a post-suppression "rebound" effect (right). This result suggests that it's hard to inhibit the use of stereotypes on a long-term basis. (Data from Macrae et al., 1994.)

prejudice Negative feelings toward persons based on their membership in certain groups.

Prejudice—a term used to describe our negative feelings toward persons based on their membership in a group—is one of the most tenacious social problems of modern times. In Germany, neo-Nazis terrorize Turkish immigrants. In the Middle East, Israelis and Palestinians fight what seems to be an eternal battle. And in what used to be the Soviet Union, raging ethnic conflicts are too numerous to mention.

The streets of America are also witness to bigotry. On the Long Island Railroad, Colin Ferguson expressed his "black rage" by shooting white commuters. On the campus of a large university, members of a fraternity painted their faces black and held a mock slave auction. In other incidents, swastikas were spray-painted on synagogue doors, and rocks and bottles were thrown at gays in a parade. Stories like these bring to life an important point: People's attitudes—toward Whites, Blacks, Jews, homosexuals, and other groups—are often fueled by anxiety, frustration, and other emotions (Stangor et al., 1991; Stephan et al., 1994).

It's worth noting that perceptions of prejudice are influenced not only by objective actions but by social context as well. For example, Miriam Rodin and her colleagues (1990) suggested that discrimination is most likely to prompt charges of prejudice when it singles out members of historically victimized groups. In a series of studies, subjects read about an incident in which a group was excluded, derogated, or unequally treated. In each case, the race, gender, age, or sexual preference of the actor and target was varied. The result: Subjects saw more prejudice in acts that discriminated against Blacks, women, old people, and homosexuals than in acts that had targeted Whites, men, young people, and heterosexuals. This asymmetry is pervasive—and accounts for why all-white student associations and all-male groups often provoke charges of racism and sexism while black student unions and women's groups do not. Apparently, people understand that discrimination by historically victimized groups may be motivated by the need for self-protection or solidarity, not necessarily by prejudice.

Robbers Cave: Setting the Stage

Clearly, some people are more prejudiced than others. The problem is so widespread, however, that it seems nobody is immune. Social psychologists have thus sought to identify the situational factors that give rise to prejudice. This section describes a classic study of intergroup conflict, a study that set the stage for theories focusing on the role of social situations.

We begin our analysis in an unlikely place: Robbers Cave State Park, Oklahoma. In the summer of 1954, a small group of eleven-year-old boys—all white, healthy, middle-class youngsters, all strangers to one another—arrived at a 200-acre camp located in a densely wooded area of the park. The boys spent the first week or so hiking, swimming, boating, and camping out. After a while, they gave themselves a group name and printed it on their caps and T-shirts. At first, the boys thought they were the only ones at the camp. Soon, however, they discovered that there was a second group and that tournaments had been arranged between the two groups.

What these boys didn't know was that they were subjects in an elaborate study conducted by Muzafer Sherif and his colleagues (1961). Parents had given permission for their sons to take part in an experiment for a study of competitiveness and cooperation. The two groups were brought in separately, and only after each had formed its own culture was the other's presence revealed. Now, the "Rattlers" and the "Eagles" were ready to meet. They did so under tense circumstances, competing against each other in football, a treasure hunt, tug-of-war, and other events. The winning team of each event was awarded points, and the tournament winner was promised a trophy, medals, and other prizes. Almost overnight the groups turned into hostile antagonists, and their rivalry escalated into a full-scale war. Group flags were burned, cabins were ransacked, and a food fight that resembled a riot exploded in the mess hall. Keep in mind that the subjects in this study were well-adjusted boys, not street-gang members. Yet as Sherif (1966) noted, a naive observer would have thought the boys were "wicked, disturbed, and vicious" (p. 85).

Creating a monster through competition was easy. Restoring the peace, however, was not. First the experimenters tried saying nice things to the Rattlers about the Eagles and vice versa, but the propaganda campaign did not work. Then the two groups were brought together under noncompetitive circumstances, but that didn't help either. What did eventually work was the introduction of **superordinate goals**, mutual goals that could be achieved only through cooperation between the groups. For example, the experimenters arranged for the camp truck to break down, and both groups were needed to pull it up a steep hill. This strategy worked like a charm. By the end of camp, the two groups were so friendly that they insisted on traveling home on the same bus. In just three weeks, the Rattlers and Eagles experienced the kinds of changes that often take generations to unfold: They formed close-knit groups, went to war, and made peace.

superordinate goals Shared goals that can be achieved only through cooperation among individuals or groups.

Realistic Conflict Theory

The events of Robbers Cave mimicked the kinds of conflict that plague people all over the world (Taylor & Moghaddam, 1994). The simplest explanation for this conflict is *competition*. Assign strangers to groups, throw the groups into contention, stir the pot, and soon there's conflict. This recipe is not limited to boys at summer camp, either. Intense animosity was also aroused, for example, among a thousand corporate executives who were placed in competing groups as part of a management training program (Blake & Mouton, 1984).

The view that direct competition for valuable but limited resources breeds hostility between groups is called **realistic conflict theory** (Levine & Campbell, 1972). As a simple matter of economics, one group may fare better in the struggle for land, jobs, or power than another group. The loser becomes frustrated and resentful, the winner feels threatened and protective—and before long, conflict heats to a rapid boil. Chances are, a good deal of prejudice in the world is driven by the realities of competition (Olzak & Nagel, 1986; Taylor & Moghaddam, 1994).

realistic conflict theory The theory that hostility between groups is caused by direct competition for limited resources.

If realistic conflict theory is correct, however, then prejudice is likely to be found only among people who fear that the quality of their lives is being threatened by an outgroup. Not so. White Americans who are not affected by desegregated schools and low-income housing are just as prejudiced against Blacks as those who are personally touched by these policies (Kinder & Sears, 1981; Sears & Kinder, 1985). Could it be that realistic conflict is *un*related to prejudice? As more and more white Americans complain bitterly about affirmative action policies that give preference to minorities, it seems that competition does fuel prejudice. It has been suggested, for example, that a good deal of racial tension springs from resentment among those who feel that affirmative action gains are achieved at their expense (D'Souza, 1991).

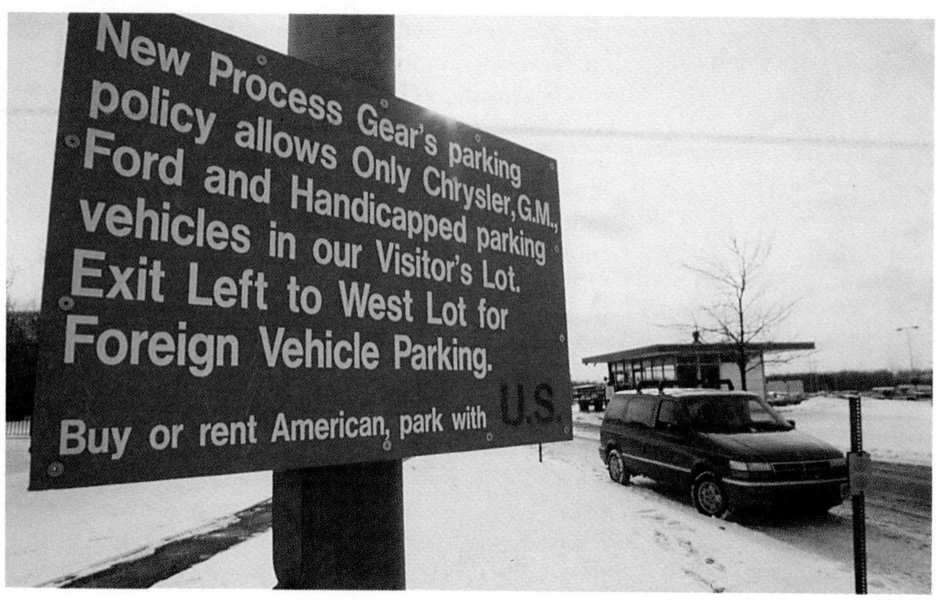

Increased global economic competition triggers hostilities between countries.

relative deprivation Feelings of discontent aroused by the belief that one fares poorly compared to others.

To reconcile matters, we must make an important distinction. Simply put, people become resentful not because of what they lack per se but because of their **relative deprivation**—the belief that they fare poorly compared to others (Crosby, 1976; Olson et al., 1986). What matters to the proverbial Smiths is not the size of their house per se but whether it is larger than the Jones's house next door. There are two different sources of discontent: *egoistic* deprivation, a concern for one's own self-interest, and *fraternal* deprivation, a concern for the interest of one's *group* (Runciman, 1966). This distinction is crucial to the theory that competition breeds prejudice. In the United States, antiblack feelings are related not to personal gains or losses but to the fear that Whites as a group are falling behind (Bobo, 1988). The same result—that we resent those who threaten the ingroup—can account for the negative feelings of black Americans for white Americans (Abeles, 1976), French Canadians for their English-speaking neighbors (Guimond & Dubé-Simard, 1983), and Muslims for the Hindus in India (Tripathi & Srivastava, 1981).

Why are people so sensitive about the status and integrity of their ingroups relative to rival outgroups, even when personal interests are not at stake? Could it be that personal interests really *are* at stake, that our protectiveness of ingroups is nourished by a concern for the self? If so, could that explain why people all over the world believe that their own nation, culture, language, and religion are better and more deserving than others?

Social Identity Theory

These questions were first raised in a study of high school boys in Bristol, England, conducted by Henri Tajfel and his colleagues (1971). The boys were shown a series of dotted slides and their task was to estimate the number of dots on each. The slides were presented in rapid-fire succession, so the dots could not be counted. Later, the experimenter told subjects that some people are chronic "overestimators" and that others are "underestimators." As part of a second, entirely separate task, subjects were supposedly divided for the sake of convenience into groups of overestimators and underestimators (in fact, they were divided randomly). Knowing who was in their group, subjects were told to allocate points to each other, points that could be cashed in for money.

This procedure was designed to create *minimal groups*—persons categorized on the basis of trivial, minimally important similarities. Tajfel's overestimators and underestimators were not long-term rivals, did not have a history of antagonism, were not frustrated, did not compete for a limited resource, and were not even acquainted with each other. Still, subjects consistently allocated more points to members of their own group than to those of the other group. This pattern of discrimination, called **ingroup favoritism,** has been found in studies performed in many countries. Even in groups that are constructed by the flip of a coin, subjects favor others with whom they are aligned (Messick & Mackie, 1989). They also make more favorable, "ethnocentric" attributions for the successes and failures of fellow ingroup members than for those of others (Weber, 1994).

ingroup favoritism The tendency to discriminate in favor of ingroups over outgroups.

The preference for ingroups is so powerful that its effects can be measured by the language we use. According to Charles Perdue and his colleagues (1990), "ingroup" pronouns such as *we, us,* and *ours* trigger positive emotions, while "outgroup" pronouns such as *they, them,* and *theirs* elicit negative emotions. These investigators presented subjects with numerous pairs of letter strings on a computer—each pair containing both a pronoun and a nonsense syllable ("we-xeh," "they-yof"). Their task was to decide as fast as possible which letter string in each pair was a real word. They didn't realize it, but one nonsense syllable was always paired with ingroup pronouns, another with outgroup pronouns. Afterward, subjects were asked for their reactions to each of the nonsense syllables. The result: Items previously paired with ingroup words were considered more pleasant than those paired with outgroup words. The ingroup-outgroup distinction has such emotional meaning for people that it can bias their views of an unfamiliar string of letters . . . or person.

To explain ingroup favoritism, Tajfel (1982) and John Turner (1987) proposed **social identity theory.** According to this theory, each of us strives to enhance our self-esteem, which has two components: a *personal* identity and various collective or *social* identities that are based on the groups to which we belong. In other words, people can boost their self-esteem through their own personal achievements or through affiliation with successful groups. What's nice about the need

social identity theory The theory that people favor ingroups over outgroups in order to enhance their self-esteem.

At the World Cup Soccer games of 1994, patriotic sports fans basked in the glory of their team's success. The American fans shown here enjoyed the first World Cup victory by a U.S. team in forty-four years.

for social identity is that it leads us to derive pride from our connections with others. What's sad, however, is that we often feel the need to belittle "them" in order to feel secure about "us." Religious fervor, racial and ethnic conceit, and patriotism may all fulfill this darker side of our social identity. The theory is summarized in Figure 4.4.

Social identity theory makes two basic predictions: (1) threats to one's self-esteem heighten the need for ingroup favoritism, and (2) expressions of ingroup favoritism enhance one's self-esteem. Research generally supports these predictions (Hogg & Abrams, 1990; Turner et al., 1994). In one study, Steven Fein and Steven Spencer (1993) gave subjects positive or negative feedback about their performance on a test of social and verbal skills—feedback that temporarily raised or lowered their self-esteem. These subjects then took part in what was supposed to be a second experiment in which they evaluated a job applicant. All subjects received a photograph of a young woman, her resumé, and a videotape of a job interview. In half the cases, the woman was named Maria D'Agostino and depicted as Italian; in the other half, she was Julie Goldberg and depicted as Jewish (on the campus where the study was held, a negative stereotype of the "Jewish American Princess" was specifically evoked by upper-middle-class Jewish women from New York).

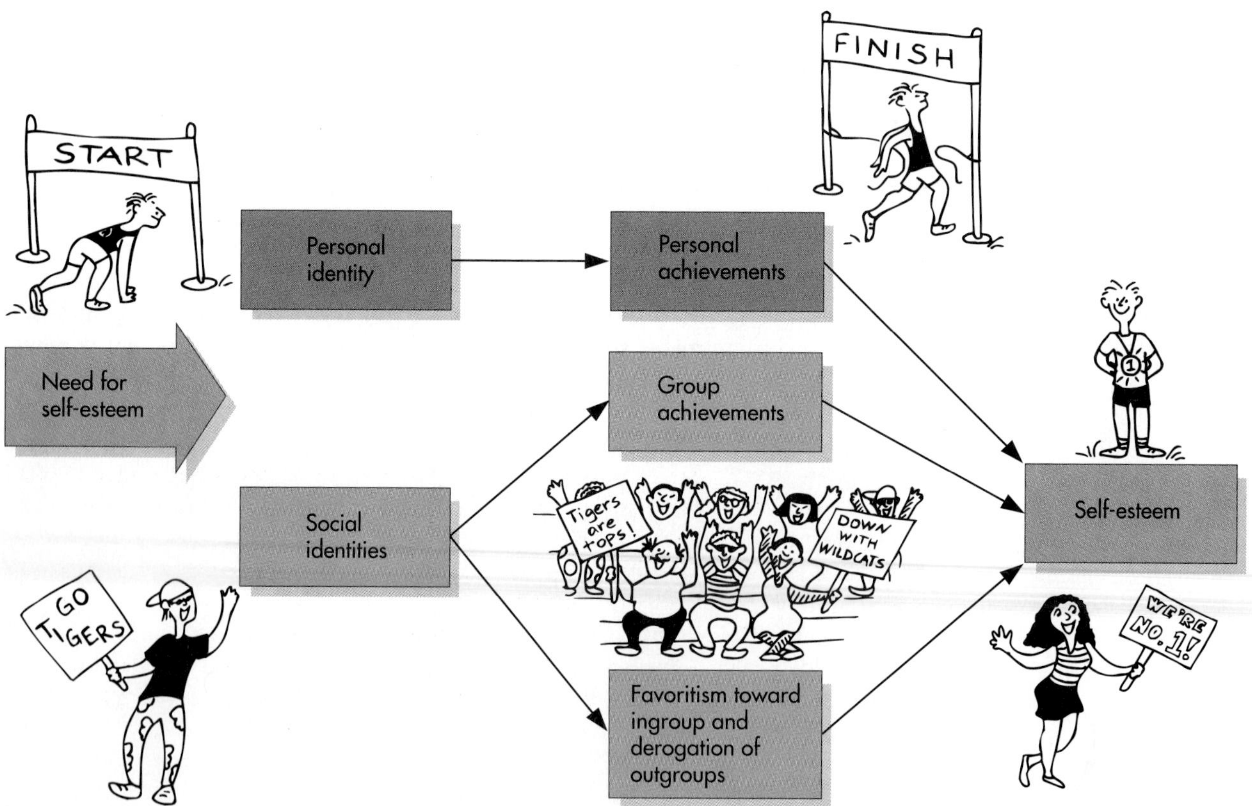

Figure 4.4 Social Identity Theory. Tajfel and Turner claim that people strive to enhance self-esteem, which has two components: a personal identity and various social identities that derive from the groups to which we belong. Thus, people may boost their self-esteem by viewing their ingroups more favorably than outgroups.

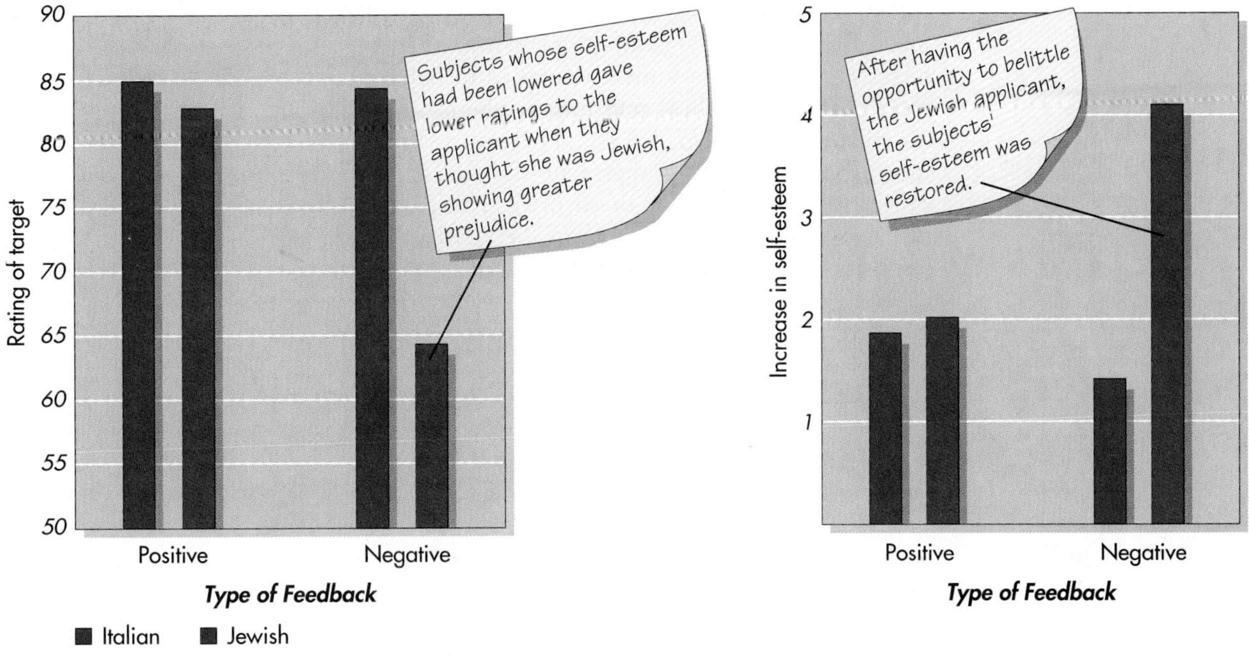

Figure 4.5 **Self-Esteem and Social Identity.** Subjects received positive or negative feedback and then evaluated a female job applicant believed to be Italian or Jewish. There were two key results: (1) subjects whose self-esteem had been lowered by negative feedback evaluated the woman more negatively when she was Jewish rather than Italian (left); and (2) negative feedback subjects given the opportunity to belittle the Jewish woman showed a post-experiment increase in self-esteem (right). (Fein & Spencer, 1993.)

As predicted by social identity theory, there were two important results (see Figure 4.5). First, among subjects whose self-esteem had been lowered by negative feedback, Julie Goldberg was rated more negatively than Maria D'Agostino—even though their pictures and credentials were the same. Second, negative feedback subjects given an opportunity to belittle the Jewish woman later exhibited a post-experiment increase in self-esteem. A blow to one's self-image evokes prejudice—and the expression of prejudice helps to restore that image. Other researchers have also found support for this theory (Branscombe & Wann, 1994).

What precise conditions arouse social identity motives? According to Marilyn Brewer (1991), one important consideration is the relative size of one's ingroup. Noting that people want to belong to groups that are small enough for them to feel unique, Brewer points out that ingroup loyalty—and outgroup prejudice—are more intense for groups that are in the minority than for members of large and inclusive majorities. Indeed, when Brewer (1993) told subjects they were in the majority or minority in their dot-estimation performance, she found greater ingroup favoritism among those believing that their group was in the minority.

A second important factor is a person's status relative to others in the ingroup. Jeffrey Noel and his colleagues (1995) theorized that people are most motivated to derogate outsiders when their ingroup status is marginal and when they are in the presence of fellow ingroup members. To test this hypothesis, these investigators recruited active (fully accepted) and pledge (under initiation) members of fraternities and sororities to take part in a study. Subjects were asked to rate members of their own campus group and of rival groups on various positive and negative traits. Some subjects were led to believe that they would publicly share their ratings with fellow ingroup members, and others were told that their evaluations would be kept private. The result: Ratings of outgroup members were most negative among pledges who thought that their responses would be seen by others in their fraternity or sorority. This finding suggests that people publicly derogate outsiders in part to win the favor of fellow ingroup members. It is important to note, however, that individuals differ in the extent to which their total self-esteem is influenced by ingroups—and in the extent to which they view others in ways that are consistent with social identity theory (Crocker & Luhtanen, 1990; Kowalski & Wolfe, 1994).

Social identity theory poses another interesting question: If self-esteem is influenced by the status of our ingroups relative to outgroups, how do people cope with ingroups of low status or with weak ingroup members? How do *you* cope with associations you find embarrassing? The theory predicts two possible reactions: risk a loss of self-esteem, or distance yourself from those in question. So which is it? To examine the question, José Marques (1990) and his colleagues conducted studies in which subjects had to evaluate ingroup and outgroup members who behaved in positive or negative ways. In one study, subjects listened to two taped speeches, one of high quality and one of low quality. One was made by a fellow law student, the other by a philosophy student. The researchers varied which of the two made the better speech. As it turned out, subjects overrated the ingroup speaker who performed well but underrated the ingroup speaker who performed poorly. To preserve the integrity of the ingroup, people may be excessively harsh in their treatment of less able fellow members—at least when the ingroup is important to their social identities (Branscombe et al., 1993).

So far, we have seen that stereotypes are enduring images of social groups that lead people to overlook diversity within outgroups and rush to judgment about specific individuals. We have also seen that prejudice can stem from competition for resources or the need to favor ingroups in the service of self-esteem. We now put these problems into concrete terms by focusing on sexism and racism, two common forms of discrimination.

SEXISM

When a baby is born, the first words uttered ring loud and clear: "It's a boy (girl)!" Immediately, the newborn receives a gender-appropriate name and is showered with gender-appropriate gifts. Over the next few years, the typical boy is supplied with toy trucks, baseballs, hammers, guns, and chemistry sets; the typical girl is furnished with dolls, stuffed animals, toy make-up kits, sewing machines, and tea sets. As they enter school, the boy is expected to earn money by delivering newspapers and to enjoy math and computers; the girl is expected to babysit and to enjoy crafts, music, and social activities. These distinctions then persist in college, as male students major in economics and the sciences, and female students thrive in the arts, languages, and humanities. In the work force, men become doctors, construction workers, auto mechanics, airplane pilots, investment bankers, and engineers. In contrast, women become secretaries, schoolteachers, nurses, flight attendants, bank tellers, and housewives. Back on the home front, the life cycle begins again when a man and woman have their first baby and discover that "It's a girl (boy)!"

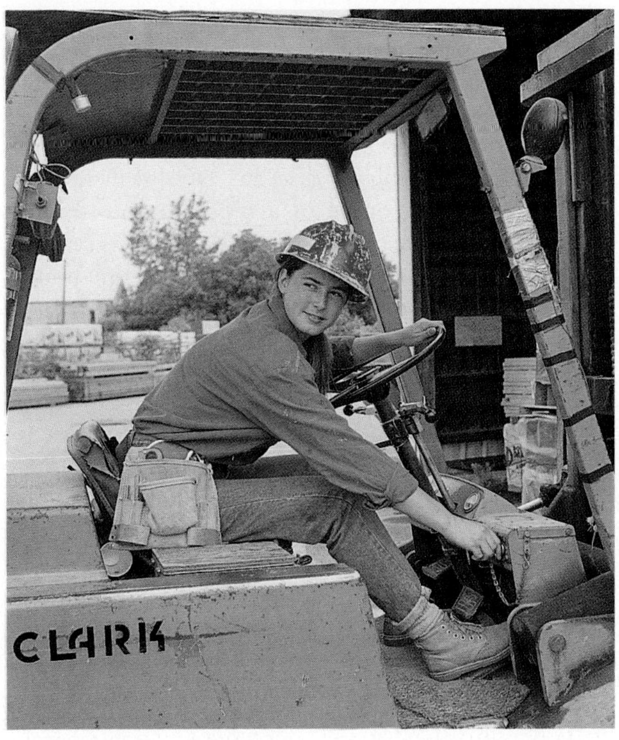

Sex differences in occupations are sometimes so striking that we're quick to notice those who break the mold.

Gender Stereotypes: Blue for Boys, Pink for Girls

sexism Discrimination based on a person's gender.

The traditional pinks and blues are not as distinct today as they used to be. Many gender barriers of the past have broken down and the colors have somewhat blended together. Nevertheless, **sexism**—discrimination based on a person's gender—still exists. Indeed, it begins with the fact that sex is the most conspicuous social category we use to identify ourselves and others (Stangor et al., 1992; Zarate & Smith, 1990).

Whenever people are asked to describe the typical man and woman, males are said to be more adventurous, assertive, aggressive, independent, and task-oriented; females are thought to be more sensitive, gentle, dependent, emotional, and people-oriented. These images are so universal that they were reported by 2,800 college students from thirty different countries of North and South America, Europe, Africa, Asia, and Australia (Williams & Best, 1982). The images are also salient to young children—who identify themselves and others as boys or girls by three years of age, form gender-stereotypic beliefs about toys and other objects soon after that, and then use their simplified stereotypes in judging others (Biernat, 1991; Martin et al., 1990). Even infants can tell the difference. In one study, nine-month-olds who were shown pictures of all-male or all-female faces spent less and less time looking—until a face of the opposite sex appeared. This result tells us what the infants themselves could not: that they distinguish between men and women (Leinbach & Fagot, 1993).

Beliefs about males and females are so deeply ingrained that they influence the behavior of adults literally the moment a baby is born. In a fascinating study, the first-time parents of fifteen girls and fifteen boys were interviewed within twenty-four hours of the baby's birth. There were no differences between the male and female newborns in height, weight, or other aspects of physical appearance. Yet the parents of girls rated their babies as softer, smaller, and more finely featured. The fathers of boys saw their sons as stronger, larger, more alert, and better coordinated (Rubin et al., 1974). Could it be there really were differences that only the parents were able to discern? Doubtful. In another study, men and women were shown a videotape of a nine-month-old baby. Half were told they were watching a boy, the other half a girl. All subjects saw the same tape, yet their perceptions were biased by gender beliefs. At one point, for example, the baby burst into tears over a jack-in-the-box. How did the subjects interpret this reaction? *He* was *angry,* and *she* was *frightened* (Condry & Condry, 1976).

People all over the world make sharp distinctions between boys and girls, men and women. The issue is not *whether* these stereotypes exist but (1) when do they influence our social perceptions, (2) are they accurate, and, if not, (3) why do they endure? Let's begin with the first question: When do gender stereotypes bias our perceptions of men and women?

What Activates Gender Stereotypes?

According to Kay Deaux and Brenda Major (1987), three types of factors determine whether gender stereotypes will be activated: the perceiver, the target, and the situation. To begin with, some *perceivers* are more gender-focused than others. Sandra Bem (1981) refers to people who have masculine or feminine gender-role orientations as "gender schematics" and claims that they are prone to divide the world into masculine and feminine terms. In contrast, people who are balanced in their orientations are "gender *a*schematic" perceivers for whom sex is not a dominant social category. Studies show that individuals differ in the extent to which gender influences their social judgments. In one experiment, subjects listened to a group discussion and then tried to recall who said what. Those who were gender schematic were more likely to confuse the different members of the opposite sex. For these subjects, "they" all looked and sounded alike—a symptom of the outgroup homogeneity effect (Frable & Bem, 1985; Carpenter, 1993). In general, gender schematics are more likely to pay attention to the sex of a job applicant, to assume that someone referred to by the generic "he" is male not fe-

To gender-schematic perceivers, even food may be categorized as masculine or feminine.

male, and to form negative impressions of those who violate cultural norms for acceptable male and female behavior (Frable, 1989).

Characteristics of the *target person* can also activate gender stereotypes. People who are highly masculine or feminine in their physical appearance elicit the perception that they are masculine or feminine in other ways as well (Deaux & Lewis, 1984). Even a simple title can activate the stereotype. In a study by Kenneth Dion (1987), subjects read about a woman who used a particular title. When she used the title *Ms.* rather than *Miss* or *Mrs.,* she was assumed to be more assertive, achievement oriented, and dynamic, but also cold, unpopular, and unlikely to have a happy marriage. These beliefs are triggered not by the *Ms.* title itself but by women who state a preference for that title (Dion & Cota, 1991).

Certain kinds of clothing also bring our attention to gender. Consider an incident that took place just a few years ago. Brenda Taylor, a Florida attorney, was fired because she dressed for work in designer blouses, tight-fitting skirts, and ornate jewelry. Her supervisor complained that her appearance in court "created the impression that she was a bimbo interested only in meeting men" (Associated Press, 1988). Did Taylor's attire undermine her credibility? Studies show that clothing can have this effect. When business administrators viewed videotaped interviews of female applicants for a management position, they gave the women more positive recommendations when they were dressed in a "masculine" navy suit than when they wore a softer, more "feminine" light-colored dress (Forsythe, 1990).

Finally, certain *situations* are more likely than others to make gender salient. Deaux and Major (1987) point out that a nursery school, an auto mechanic's shop, and a singles bar are the kinds of settings that naturally prompt us to make

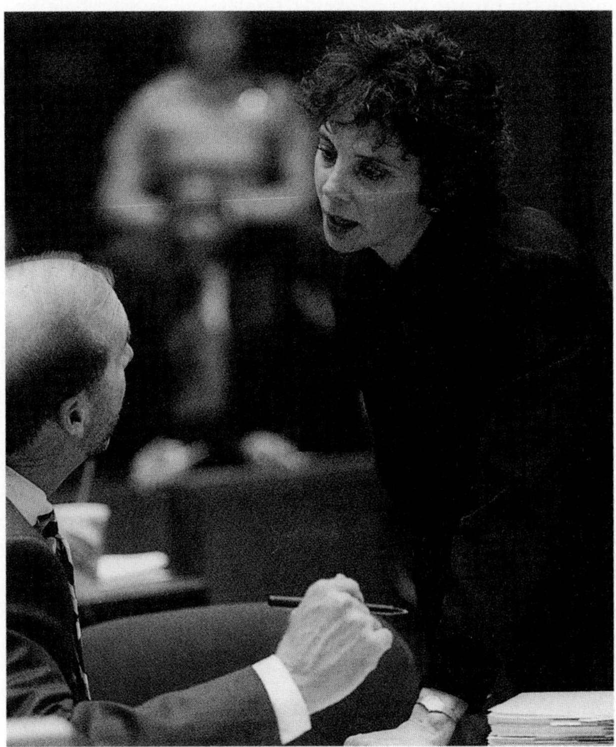

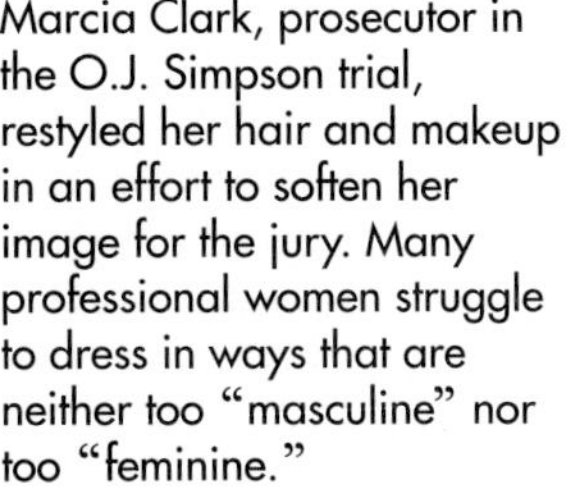

Marcia Clark, prosecutor in the O.J. Simpson trial, restyled her hair and makeup in an effort to soften her image for the jury. Many professional women struggle to dress in ways that are neither too "masculine" nor too "feminine."

gender distinctions. Especially important is a person's prominence relative to others in the situation. Picture a man in an all-female group or a woman in an all-male group. Research shows that they draw an abundance of attention, which makes them self-conscious and impairs their performance on cognitive tasks (Lord & Saenz, 1985; Saenz, 1994). Tokens are also likely to be viewed in gender-stereotypic terms: The token male is seen as more masculine ("father figure, leader, or macho type"), and the token female as more feminine ("motherly type, a bitch, or the group secretary"), than when the same individuals are judged in balanced, mixed-sex groups (Fiske et al., 1991). Again, we're reminded of Ann Hopkins and others who have minority status in an organization. In the limelight, whatever they do is noticed and scrutinized—and blown out of proportion.

Are Gender Stereotypes Accurate?

Gender stereotypes are so widespread that one wonders if they are accurate. Based on years of research, two conclusions can be drawn. First, people's beliefs about the differences between men and women contain a kernel of truth (Maccoby & Jacklin, 1974; Eagly & Wood, 1991; Feingold, 1994; Swim, 1994). Second, at least some of these beliefs may oversimplify and exaggerate that truth (Spence et al., 1985; Tavris, 1992). Yes, most men are somewhat more aggressive, competitive, assertive, and task-focused than most women. And yes, most women are more sensitive, cooperative, nurturant, and people-focused than most men. But our stereotypes about men and women may be stronger and more numerous than the differences themselves.

A study by Carol Lynn Martin (1987) provides support for this last point. Subjects were presented with a list of thirty traits that were stereotypically masculine, feminine, or neutral. They were asked to circle those traits that accurately described themselves. Then a separate group of subjects received the same list and estimated the percentages of men and women in general for whom each trait was an accurate description. By comparing the percentages of male and female subjects who *actually* found the traits self-descriptive with the *estimated* percentages, Martin found that expectations exceeded reality: In actuality, the "masculine" traits were just slightly more self-descriptive of men, and the "feminine" traits, of women; yet the estimated differences were more substantial. Like the cartoonist who draws caricatures, we tend to stretch, expand, and enlarge the ways in which men and women differ.

Why Do Gender Stereotypes Endure?

If men and women are more similar than people think, why do exaggerated perceptions of difference endure? Earlier in this chapter, we described two reasons why stereotypes, like cats, have nine lives. The same mechanisms apply to perceptions of gender. Expecting male-female differences, people tend (1) to perceive illusory correlations, overestimating the percentage of masculine men and feminine women, and (2) to dismiss individuals who don't match the gender stereotype as exceptions to the rule or representatives of a subcategory. Additional explanations have also been proposed to explain why gender stereotypes in particular are so stubborn.

Cultural Institutions In some ways, male-female distinctions are fostered by cultural institutions. Studies show that children's "Dick and Jane" readers, TV

"That was a fine report, Barbara. But since the sexes speak different languages, I probably didn't understand a word of it."

Depicting gender stereotypes, cartoonists play up the popular notion that men and women have little in common.

shows, cartoons, and magazines tend to overportray male and female characters in traditional roles. Gone are the days when women were depicted merely as housewives who frantically cooked, polished, and ironed everything in sight. Still, some gender stereotyping persists—for example, in TV commercials (Lovdal, 1989), children's books (Purcell & Stewart, 1990), and recently produced rock music videos, as presented on MTV (Hansen, 1989).

More to the point is the fact that media depictions can influence viewers. In a series of studies, Florence Geis and her colleagues created two sets of TV commercials (Geis et al., 1984; Jennings et al., 1980). In one set, male and female characters were portrayed in stereotypic fashion: a woman served her working man his dinner or behaved in a coy, alluring manner. In the other, the roles were reversed, with the man playing the domestic seductive role. Female college students watched one of the two sets. Those who saw the stereotypical ads later expressed lower self-confidence, less independence, and fewer career aspirations in experimental tasks than did those who viewed counter-stereotypical ads. Whether or not consumers purchase the products explicitly advertised on television, they do seem to buy the implicit messages about gender—messages that may set in motion a self-fulfilling prophecy (Geis, 1993).

Media images of men and women also differ in other subtle ways. In any visual representation of a person—such as a photograph, drawing, or painting—you can measure the relative prominence of the face by calculating the percentage of the vertical dimension occupied by the model's head. When Dane Archer and his colleagues (1983) inspected 1,750 photographs from *Time, Newsweek,* and other magazines, they found what they called "face-ism," a bias toward greater facial prominence in pictures of men than of women. This phenomenon is so prevalent that it appeared in analyses of 3,500 photographs from different countries, classic portraits painted in the seventeenth century, and the amateur drawings of college students.

Why is the face more prominent in pictures of men than of women? One possible interpretation is that face-ism reflects historical conceptions of the sexes. The face and head symbolize the mind and *intellect*—which are traditionally associated with men. With respect to women, more importance is attached to the heart, emotions, or perhaps just the body. Indeed, when people evaluate models from photographs, those pictured with high facial prominence are seen as smarter and more assertive, active, and ambitious—regardless of their gender (Schwarz & Kurz, 1989). Another interpretation is that facial prominence signals power and *dominance*. Consistent with this hypothesis, Miron Zuckerman and Suzanne Kieffer (1994) examined magazine photos, portraits, and postage stamps, and uncovered a bias toward greater facial prominence in pictures of Whites than of Blacks. They also found that people pictured with high facial prominence were seen as more dominant—regardless of their race. Whatever the explanation, it's clear that stereotypes can be perpetuated by the subtleties of the human portrait.

Social Roles Theory There is another reason for the durability of gender stereotypes. Imagine a secretary typing a letter for a corporate vice president. Now, admit it: Didn't you visualize a *female* secretary working for a *male* executive?

social roles theory The theory that small gender differences are magnified in perception by the contrasting social roles occupied by men and women.

Alice Eagly's (1987) **social roles theory** states that although the perception of sex differences may be based on actual differences, it is magnified by the unequal social roles occupied by men and women. The process involves three steps. First, through a combination of biological and social factors, a division of labor between the sexes has emerged over time—at home and in the work setting. Men are more likely to work in construction or business; women are more likely to care for children and take lower-status jobs. Second, since people behave in ways that fit the roles they play, men are more likely than women to wield physical, social, and economic power. Third, these behavioral differences provide a continuing basis for social perception, leading us to perceive men as dominant "by nature" and women as domestic "by nature," when in fact the differences reflect the roles they play. In short, sex stereotypes are shaped by—and often confused with—the unequal distribution of men and women into different social roles (see Figure 4.6).

If Eagly's theory is correct, then perceived differences between men and women are based on real behavioral differences mistakenly assumed to arise from gender rather than social roles. To test this hypothesis, Eagly and Valerie Steffen (1984) asked subjects for their impressions of fictitious men or women who had a full-time job or worked as a homemaker. Individuals employed outside the home were viewed in relatively masculine terms—regardless of their sex. In contrast, those who worked inside the home were seen in relatively feminine terms—again, regardless of whether they were male or female. Social roles, not

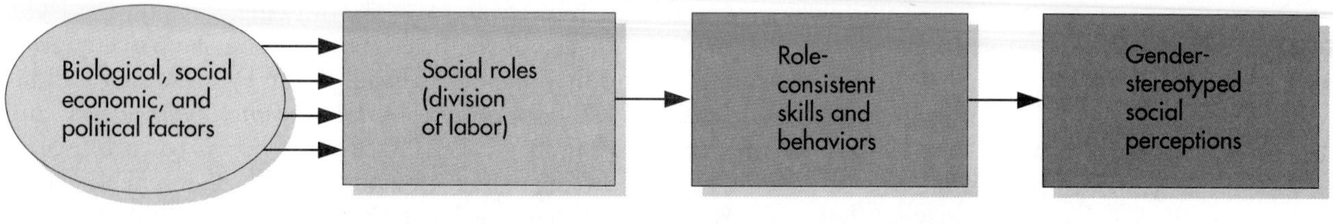

Biological, social economic, and political factors → Social roles (division of labor) → Role-consistent skills and behaviors → Gender-stereotyped social perceptions

Figure 4.6 Eagly's Social Roles Theory of Gender Stereotypes. According to social roles theory, stereotypes of men as dominant and women as subordinate persist because men occupy higher-status positions in society. This division of labor, a product of many factors, leads men and women to behave in ways that fit their social roles. But rather than attribute the differences to these roles, people attribute the differences to gender.

gender, gave rise to stereotypic perceptions. When the roles are reversed, the gender stereotypes disappear (Eagly & Wood, 1982).

Carrying the theory one step further, Eagly and Mary Kite (1987) raised an intriguing possibility. If our perceptions of foreign nations are influenced by news images, and if newsworthy events are dominated by men in prominent positions, then our stereotypes of nations should be based primarily on our images of the *men* in those nations. Think about it. When Iraqi soldiers stormed into Kuwait in 1990, Iraqis were regarded as impassioned, belligerent people. But did the image apply to the inconspicuous Iraqi women, many of whom cover their faces in public? Eagly and Kite asked subjects for their impressions of the men and women of fourteen nationalities. As predicted, the stereotypical Cuban, Egyptian, or Chinese person closely matched perceptions of the men in the corresponding countries but not those of the women.

Sex Discrimination: A Double Standard?

It could be argued that variety is the spice of life and that there's nothing inherently wrong with gender stereotypes as long as men and women are portrayed as different but equal. But are masculine and feminine attributes equally valued? Are men and women judged by the same standard, or is there—as Ann Hopkins maintained—a "double standard"? (See Table 4.1.)

Many years ago, Philip Goldberg (1968) asked students at a small women's college to evaluate the content and writing style of some articles. When the material was supposedly written by John McKay rather than Joan McKay, it received higher ratings, a result that led Goldberg to wonder if even women were prejudiced against women. Certain other studies showed that people often devalue the performance of women who take on tasks usually reserved for men (Lott, 1985) and attribute their achievements to luck rather than ability (Deaux & Emswiller, 1974; Nieva & Gutek, 1981). It now appears, however, that the devaluation of

Table 4.1 How to Tell a Businessman from a Businesswoman

A businessman is aggressive; a businesswoman is pushy.
He loses his temper because he's so involved in his job; she's a bitch.
He follows through; she doesn't know when to quit.
He is a man of the world; she's been around.
If he drinks it's because of job pressure; she's a lush.
He's never afraid to say what he thinks; she's always shooting off her mouth.
He's close-mouthed; she's secretive.
He's a stern taskmaster; she's hard to work for.
He climbed the ladder of success; she slept her way to the top.

Are men and women judged by a double standard? This table is exaggerated for effect, but it makes you wonder about evaluations in the classroom and on the job. (Doyle, 1983.)

Recent labor statistics reveal that men and women occupy very different positions in the work force. (Data from U.S. Bureau of the Census, 1994.)

Table 4.2 Sex Differences in Occupation

Occupation	% Men	% Women
Airline pilot	96	4
Auto mechanic	99	1
Bartender	47	53
Child-care worker	3	97
Computer programmer	66	34
Dentist	90	10
Dental assistant	1	99
Lawyer, judge	77	23
Physician	78	22
Registered nurse	6	94
Real estate sales	49	51
Secretary	1	99
Teacher, elementary	14	86
Teacher, college	57	43
Telephone operator	13	87
Telephone repairer	88	12

women is not common. More than a hundred studies modeled after Goldberg's indicate that people are *not* generally biased by gender in the evaluation of performance (Swim et al., 1989; Top, 1991).

In other ways, however, sex discrimination still exists. Look at Table 4.2, and you'll notice some striking sex differences in occupational choice, even today in the 1990s. Think about it. How many female airline pilots have you met lately? What about male secretaries? Sex discrimination during the early school years paves the way for diverging career paths in adulthood. Then, when equally qualified men and women compete for a job, gender considerations enter in once again.

A study by Peter Glick and his colleagues (1988) illustrates this point. These investigators sent a fictitious resumé to 212 business professionals. In all cases, the applicant was a recent college graduate named either Ken or Kate Norris. In one version of the resumé, Ken or Kate was said to have worked in a sporting goods store and on a grounds crew and had led the varsity basketball team (a masculine profile). In a second version, Ken or Kate worked in a jewelry store, taught aerobics, and was captain of a cheerleading squad (a feminine profile). After reading the resumés, subjects indicated whether they would interview the applicant for three jobs—sales manager for a machinery company (a masculine job), dental receptionist (a feminine job), and administrative bank assistant (a gender-neutral job). The result? Although the applicant's background influenced hiring decisions, men were still favored for the so-called masculine job and women were favored for the so-called feminine job. Indeed, when Glick (1991) assessed people's perceptions of different occupations, he found that some were

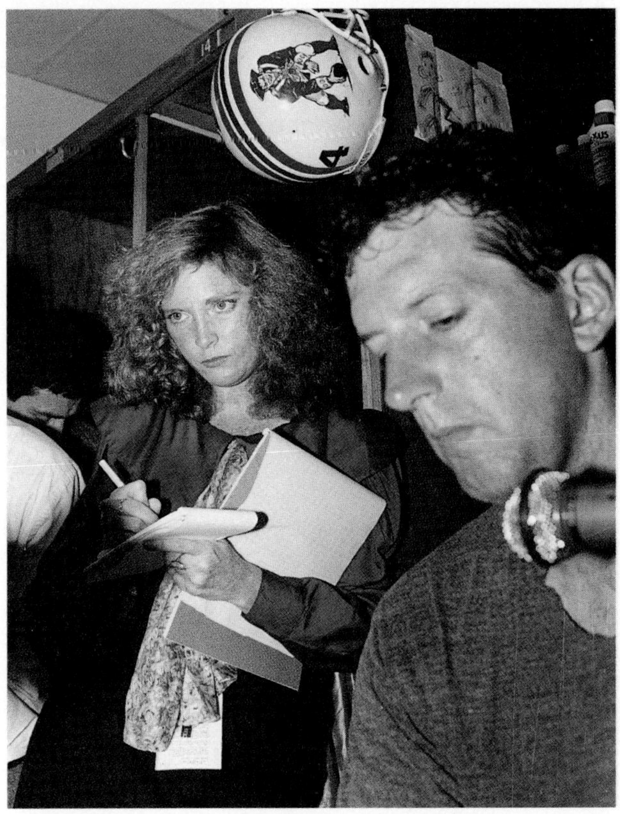

Sex discrimination can take many forms. Lisa Olson, pictured here, was a sports reporter for the *Boston Herald.* According to Olson, one Sunday afternoon in 1990, several New England Patriots football players exposed themselves and made lewd remarks while Olson was in the locker room trying to conduct a postgame interview.

clearly identified as men's jobs and others as women's jobs. It seems that once an occupation is typecast as male or female, it's difficult to write a new gender-free script.

RACISM

In October 1994, South Carolina mother Susan Smith tearfully told the police that her two young boys, seated in the family car, had been abducted at gunpoint by a young black man wearing a knit cap. She helped a police artist draw a sketch of the menacing suspect, a sketch that was displayed throughout the county. Two weeks later, Smith confessed that she had driven the car off a concrete boat ramp and watched it sink into a cold dark lake. It was she, not a black man, who murdered the children (Lacayo, 1994). Had Smith tried to exploit racial prejudice, or was her claim merely born of a sick and troubled mind? And what about racism in general, how common is it?

Modern Racism: The Disease

In a classic study of ethnic stereotypes, Daniel Katz and Kenneth Braly (1933) found that white college students viewed the average white American as smart, industrious, and ambitious. Yet they saw the average African American as superstitious, ignorant, lazy, and happy-go-lucky. In follow-up surveys conducted in 1951, 1967, and 1982, these negative images of blacks had largely faded (Dovidio & Gaertner, 1986).

This police artist sketch depicts Susan Smith's false claim that a black man had abducted her children.

Or had they? According to public opinion polls, racial prejudice in the United States has dropped sharply since World War II. In 1942, most Whites felt that Blacks of equivalent income should live in separate neighborhoods and that black children should attend separate schools. Challenged by the civil rights movement, these views became less popular. Soon, very few Americans would openly express such racist sentiments (Schuman et al., 1985). The question is, can the polls be trusted, or has racism simply gone underground?

People tend to associate anti-Black prejudice with images of old-fashioned racism characterized by slavery, lynch mobs, the Ku Klux Klan, the segregation of public facilities, the claim that African Americans are inferior—and, more recently, the beating of Rodney King. This overt form of bigotry may have declined, but it appears to have been replaced by **modern racism**—a subtle form of prejudice that surfaces in less direct ways whenever it is safe, socially acceptable, or easy to rationalize. In short, the overt symptoms of racism may have changed, but the underlying disease remains (Gaertner & Dovidio, 1986; Katz et al., 1986; McConahay, 1986).

modern racism A form of prejudice that surfaces in subtle ways when it is safe, socially acceptable, and easy to rationalize.

According to theories of modern racism, many people are racially ambivalent. They want to see themselves as fair, but they still harbor feelings of anxiety and discomfort in the presence of other racial groups (Hass et al., 1992). There is a good deal of evidence for this ambivalence. For example, many white Americans pay lip service to the *principles* of racial equality, but in *practice* they oppose mixed marriages, black political candidates, and racially symbolic policies (Sears & Allen, 1984).

If people who are prejudiced will not admit it, how do we know that racism still exists? Several methods have been used (Crosby et al., 1980). One is the *bogus pipeline,* a phony lie-detector test in which subjects are attached with electrodes to a machine that supposedly records their true feelings. Since people don't want to get caught lying, this method elicits more honest answers to sensi-

The burning cross stands as a terrifying symbol of the Ku Klux Klan and its old-fashioned racism. Incidents like this may be less common today than in the past, but more subtle forms of modern racism persist.

tive questions. For example, white college students rated Blacks in more negative terms when the bogus pipeline was used than when it was not (Sigall & Page, 1971).

Modern racism can also be detected without asking direct questions. Samuel Gaertner, John Dovidio, and others have found that *reaction time*—the speed it takes to answer a question—can be used to uncover hidden prejudices. In one study, white subjects read word pairs and pressed a button whenever they thought the words fit together. In each case, the word *Blacks* or *Whites* was paired with either a positive trait (clean, smart, etc.) or a negative trait (stupid, lazy, etc.). The results were revealing. Subjects did not openly associate Blacks with negative terms or Whites with positive terms, and they were equally quick to reject the negative terms in both cases. However, subjects were *quicker* to respond to positive words when paired with the word *Whites* than with *Blacks*. Since it takes less time to react to stimuli that fit existing attitudes, this finding suggests that subjects were unconsciously more predisposed to associate positive traits with Whites than with Blacks (Dovidio et al., 1986; Gaertner & McLaughlin, 1983).

This result may seem subtle, but it suggests that racial prejudice is so deeply ingrained in our culture that negative stereotypes are as difficult to break as a bad habit (Devine, 1989). In fact, many Whites who consider themselves nonprejudiced admit that they sometimes do not react toward Blacks as they should—an insight that causes them to feel embarrassed, guilty, and ashamed of themselves (Devine et al., 1991). Indeed, similar emotions are aroused in nonprejudiced people who imagine themselves reacting negatively toward homosexuals (Monteith et al., 1993).

Cognitive Symptoms No matter how well hidden they are, negative stereotypes bias social perceptions. In a classic demonstration, Gordon Allport and Leo Postman (1947) showed subjects a picture of a subway train filled with passengers. In the picture were a black man dressed in a suit and a white man holding a razor (see Figure 4.7). One subject viewed the scene briefly and then described it to a second subject who had not seen it. The second subject communicated the description to a third subject and so on, through six rounds of communication. The result: In more than half the sessions, the final subject's report indicated that the black man, not the white man, held the razor. Some subjects even reported that he had waved it in a threatening manner. As Allport and Postman explained, "The distortion may occur even in subjects who have no anti-Negro bias. It is an unthinking cultural stereotype that the Negro is hot tempered and addicted to the use of razors and weapons" (p. 63).

The way people *interpret* events is also influenced by race, even today. In one study, white subjects watched on a TV screen a staged interaction involving two men (Duncan, 1976). A discussion developed into a heated argument, and one man seemed to shove the other. When the protagonist was white and the victim black, only 17 percent of the subjects saw the shove as an act of violence. Most said it was just "horseplay." Yet when the protagonist was black and the victim white, "violence" interpretations rose to 75 percent. A similar result was obtained in a study of sixth-grade children (Sagar & Schofield, 1980) as well as among first-graders—but, interestingly, only when these children were tested by white, not black, experimenters (Lawrence, 1991).

Behavioral Symptoms In modern racism, prejudice against minorities surfaces only when it is safe, socially acceptable, and easy to rationalize. Three studies illustrate this point.

Figure 4.7 **How Racial Stereotypes Distort Social Perceptions.** After briefly viewing this picture, one subject described it to a second subject, who described it to a third, and so on. After six rounds of communication, the final report often placed the razor blade held by the white man into the black man's hand. This study illustrates how racial stereotypes can distort social perception. (Adapted from Allport & Postman, 1947.)

In a study of aggression, Ronald Rogers and Steven Prentice-Dunn (1981) had white subjects administer electric shocks to another subject, supposedly as part of a biofeedback experiment. All the subjects were instructed to deliver the same number of shocks, but they could adjust the intensity as they saw fit. In fact, no shocks were received, and the second subject was really a black or white confederate trained to treat the subject in either a friendly or an insulting manner. As shown in Figure 4.8, the results fit the portrait of modern racism. Subjects chose to deliver *less* intense shocks to the friendly confederate when he was black than when he was white—a pattern of *reverse discrimination* indicating that subjects bent over backward to appear nonracist. In response to the insulting confederate, however, subjects delivered *more* intense shocks if he was black than if he was white—a pattern of *modern racism* in which people act upon their hostile feelings whenever doing so can be rationalized in nonracial terms.

Another study revealed that modern racism is also evident when people refuse to help others of another race. In this case, white female subjects participated in work groups in which either a black or white confederate needed assistance to complete the task. When subjects were led to believe that the confederate had tried hard, or when the request was made by a third party, most subjects were willing to offer help. But when subjects were led to believe that the confederate had not worked hard and there was no pressure of a third-party request, they refused to help the black confederate more often than they refused to help the white one. Once again, as soon as circumstances allowed subjects to excuse a negative response, they discriminated on the basis of race (Frey & Gaertner, 1986).

In a third study, sixty-two trained therapists watched a staged interaction between another therapist and a female client. The "client" was either black or white and behaved in a manner that was either normal or depressed. So, how was the woman perceived? In the normal condition, evaluations were favorable and unaffected by race. In the depressed condition, however, subjects evaluated the client more negatively when she was black than when she was white. Apparently, the client's psychological disorder provided enough cover for latent prejudices to surface (Jenkins-Hall & Sacco, 1991).

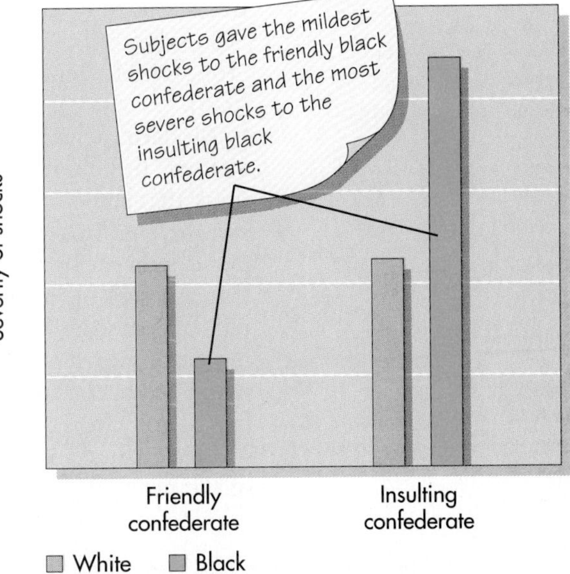
Subjects gave the mildest shocks to the friendly black confederate and the most severe shocks to the insulting black confederate.
Severity of shocks
Friendly confederate
Insulting confederate
White
Black

Figure 4.8 **Interracial Aggression in the Laboratory.** In a study of aggression, subjects delivered the mildest shocks to a friendly black confederate and the most intense shocks to an insulting black confederate. This pattern suggests that people go out of their way to appear nonprejudiced (left) but then act on hostile feelings when they have a socially acceptable excuse (right). (Rogers & Prentice-Dunn, 1981.)

A troubling aspect of modern racism is that although it adversely affects its victims, it can be invisible to its perpetrators. In the context of a job interview, for example, Carl Word and his colleagues (1974) found that when white subjects questioned an applicant who was black as opposed to white, they sat farther away, made more speech errors, and held shorter interviews—a cool interpersonal style that caused the interviewees to behave in a more nervous and awkward manner. For black men and women on the job market, the implications are sobering. And there's more. Thomas Pettigrew and Joanne Martin (1987) note that when minorities enter the workplace, they confront three biases: (1) negative racial stereotypes lead employers and co-workers to hold low expectations that are hard to overcome; (2) in organizations with few minorities, those who are hired draw more than their share of attention, leading perceivers to exaggerate both the positive and the negative; and (3) it is often believed that minorities are hired as "tokens," a belief that raises even more doubts about their competence. Together, these biases subject minority employees to what Pettigrew and Martin call "triple jeopardy."

The Victim's Plight In a book entitled *Race,* Studs Terkel (1992) interviewed ordinary Americans, both black and white, about what he calls "the American obsession." Terkel tells penetrating real-life stories that reveal the depth and scope of the problem. In some cases, he observes old-fashioned prejudice. In other cases, however, the prejudice is more subtle—as when Terkel's friend's wife, who is white, drove through a black neighborhood in Chicago: "The people at the corners were all gesticulating at her. She was very frightened, turned up the windows, and drove determinedly. She discovered after several blocks, she was going the wrong way on a one-way street and they were trying to help her. Her assumption was they were blacks and were out to get her" (p. 3).

Another instance involved Terkel himself. He boarded a bus one morning and deposited his fare, only to have the driver, a black man, say he was a dime short. Terkel was sure he had paid the right amount, but he reached into his pocket and pulled out another dime. "Oh, I understood the man," he thought. "I know the history of his people's bondage. It was his turn—a show of power, if only in a small way. If that's how it is, that's how it is." Then a few moments later: "As I was about to disembark, I saw a dime on the floor. My dime. I held it up to him. 'You were right.' He was too busy driving to respond. I waved: 'Take it easy.' 'You, too,' he replied. I've a hunch he'd been through something like this before" (p. 6).

Modern racism may seem invisible, but it can be painful and humiliating to its victims. Terkel interviewed a young black woman who said, "It infuriates me to think that some little white woman would get on the elevator with my father and assume, just by the color of his skin, that he's going to harm her, and clutch her purse tighter. To think that my father, who's worked hard all his life, put us through school, loves us, took care of us—to think that she would clutch her purse because he's there. The thought of it makes me so angry" (p. 7). Similarly, a professor talked about the time a black professional he knows, a college graduate who lived in the suburbs, visited a nearby country club. "Someone handed him a bag of golf clubs," he said. "They thought he was a caddy" (p. 96).

In the United States, Blacks and Whites openly disagree about the magnitude of the problem. Surveys show that most white Americans believe that racial discrimination is on the decline in housing, education, and employment, but most

For victims of prejudice, it can be difficult to interpret even the positive evaluations of others.

"I like you, Jim, not because you're black but because you have excellent qualifications."

black Americans maintain that the problem still exists (Sigelman & Welch, 1991). There are even marked differences of opinion among highly paid athletes. Just a few years ago, *Sports Illustrated* surveyed 300 athletes who played in the NFL, NBA, and Major League Baseball. The results were striking: 63 percent of black respondents, compared to 2 percent of their white teammates, believed that Blacks in their sport were victims of discrimination—in salaries, fan support, treatment by coaches, management opportunities, and commercial endorsements (Johnson, 1991).

According to Jennifer Crocker and Brenda Major (1989), victims of discrimination sometimes cope by attributing life's outcomes to prejudice—a strategy that has both benefits and drawbacks. In a study by Crocker and her colleagues (1991), black subjects described themselves on a questionnaire, supposedly to be evaluated by an unknown white student who sat in an adjacent room. Subjects were told that they were either liked or disliked by this student; then they took a self-esteem test. As shown in Figure 4.9, self-esteem scores predictably rose after positive feedback and declined after negative feedback. But when subjects thought the evaluating student had seen them through a one-way mirror, negative feedback did *not* lower their self-esteem. In this situation, subjects coped by blaming the unfavorable evaluations on prejudice. However, there was a drawback: one-way mirror subjects who received positive feedback showed a *decrease* in self-esteem. The reason? Instead of internalizing the credit for success, these subjects attributed the praise to patronizing, reverse discrimination.

Racism is a chronic social disease that is transmitted from one generation to the next and afflicts millions. It distorts perceptions and behavior and harms its victims, who, in turn, misperceive others in an effort to protect themselves. Can the problem be treated?

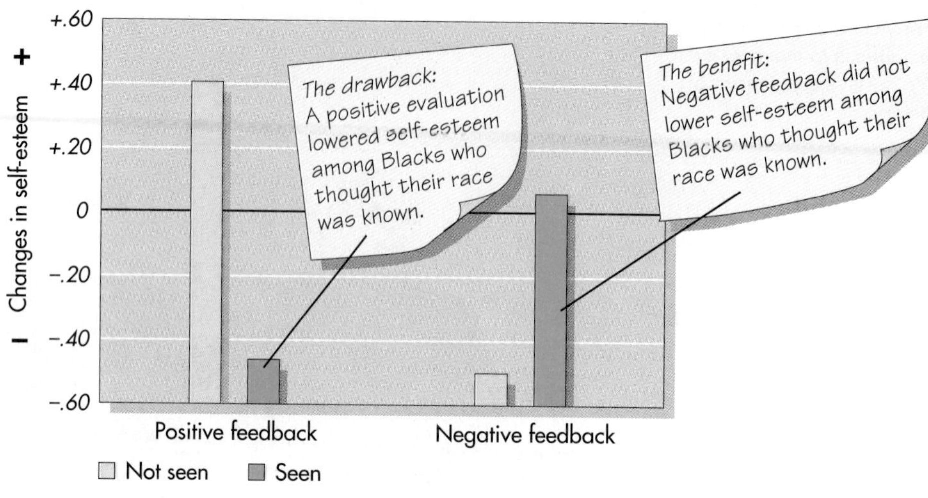

Figure 4.9 **Attributions to Prejudice: Benefits and Drawbacks.** Black subjects received a positive or negative evaluation from a white student in a nearby room. They thought the white student had or had not seen them through a one-way mirror. In the unseen condition, self-esteem increased after positive feedback and decreased after negative feedback. For subjects who thought the evaluator saw them, negative feedback did not lower self-esteem (the benefit), but positive feedback did (the drawback). Thinking the evaluator knew they were black, subjects attributed the feedback to racial factors; thus, they denied themselves both the blame for failure and the credit for success. (Data from Crocker et al., 1991.)

Intergroup Contact: The Cure?

> See that man over there?
> Yes.
> Well, I hate him.
> But you don't know him.
> That's why I hate him.
> (Allport, 1954, p. 253)

Modern racism is difficult to overcome because it lurks like a wolf in sheep's clothing and manifests itself in indirect ways. Is there a solution? Can stereotypes and prejudice be wiped out by a mass media blitz designed to inform people that their expectations and fears are unfounded? Social psychologists used to think that such efforts at persuasive communication would work, but they do not. There is, however, reason for hope.

School Desegregation: The Great Experiment In the historic 1954 case of *Brown v. Board of Education of Topeka,* the U.S. Supreme Court ruled that racially separate schools were inherently unequal, in violation of the Constitution. In part, the decision was informed by empirical evidence supplied by thirty-two eminent social scientists on the harmful effects of segregation on the self-esteem and academic achievement of black students as well as on race relations (Allport et al., 1953). The Supreme Court's decision propelled the nation into a large-scale social experiment. One question remained: What would be the effect?

Trying to combat racism, artist Mark Heckman put this billboard up on a highway near Chicago. His objective was to give white Americans a taste of discrimination. Did it work? It's hard to tell. After a day, vandals painted swastikas and the letters KKK on the poster. After two days, it was taken down in response to a flurry of protest calls.

At the time, the *Brown* decision was controversial. Many Americans opposed school desegregation, arguing that morality cannot be legislated and that forcing interracial contact would only escalate the conflict. Meanwhile, others advanced the **contact hypothesis,** which states that under certain conditions, direct contact between members of rival groups will reduce stereotyping, prejudice, and discrimination (Allport, 1954; Amir, 1969; Stephan, 1985).

contact hypothesis The theory that direct contact between hostile groups will reduce prejudice under certain conditions.

Despite the Court's ruling, desegregation proceeded slowly. There were stalling tactics, lawsuits, and vocal opposition to busing. Many schools remained untouched until the early 1970s. Then, as the dust began to settle, research brought the grave realization that little had changed, that contact between black and white schoolchildren was not working. Walter Stephan (1986) reviewed studies conducted during and after desegregation and found that although 13 percent reported a decrease in prejudice among Whites, 34 percent reported no change and 53 percent reported an *increase.* These findings forced social psychologists to challenge the wisdom of their testimony to the Supreme Court and to reexamine the contact hypothesis that had guided that advice in the first place (Cook, 1984; Gerard, 1983; Miller & Brewer, 1984).

The Contact Hypothesis: A Re-examination Is the original contact hypothesis wrong? No. Although desegregation did not immediately produce the desired changes, the conditions necessary for successful intergroup contact did not exist in the public schools. Nobody ever said that deeply rooted prejudices can be erased just by throwing groups together. According to the contact hypothesis, four conditions must exist for contact to succeed.

First, the two groups should be of *equal status,* at least in the contact situation. Blacks and Whites had interacted long before 1954, but too often in situations where Blacks worked at a clear disadvantage in lower-status jobs or in outright servitude. If anything, such unequal-status contacts only perpetuated existing negative stereotypes. You may recall Eagly's (1987) theory that gender stereotypes are sustained by the different social roles played by men and women. The same logic applies to the perception of Blacks and Whites. Desegregation situations that did promote equal-status contact—as in the army and public housing projects—have been successful (Pettigrew, 1969). When the public schools were desegregated, however, white children were coming from more affluent families, were better prepared, and were academically more advanced than their black peers (Cohen, 1984).

Second, successful contact requires *personal interactions* between individuals. When people are divided into social categories, as we have seen, ingroups tend to assume that outgroup members are all alike. Through intimate, one-on-one interactions, these categories should break down and outgroup members should be perceived in more individualized terms (Brewer & Miller, 1984; Wilder, 1986). In schools, however, interracial contact among individual children is uncommon. The school is not a melting pot. After the bus arrives, students gravitate toward members of their own race in the playground, the cafeteria, and the classroom. What's more, the problem is compounded when students are "tracked" based on grades, a policy that further separates advantaged white students from disadvantaged black students. In short, *desegregation* does not ensure *integration* (Epstein, 1985; Schofield, 1982).

The third condition for successful contact is that the opposing groups engage in *cooperative activities* to achieve superordinate goals. In the Robbers Cave study described earlier, this strategy transformed bitter enemies into allies. Yet the typical classroom is filled with competition, the wrong ingredient. Picture the scene. The teacher stands in front of the class and asks a question. Many children wave their hands, each straining to catch the teacher's eye. Then, as soon as one student is called on, the others groan in frustration. In the competition for the teacher's approval, they are losers—hardly a scenario fit for positive intergroup contact (Aronson, 1988).

Why is the introduction of superordinate goals important? One possibility is that cooperation breaks down the psychological barrier between groups, leading members to re-categorize the two groups into one and reducing ingroup favoritism (Bettencourt et al., 1992). To test this hypothesis, Gaertner and his colleagues (1990) brought six subjects into the laboratory and divided them into two three-person groups. Each group took a name, wore color-coded ID tags, and worked on a decision-making task. Next, the two groups were brought together and either listened to others discussing a problem (a neutral interaction) or joined forces to solve the problem themselves (a cooperative encounter). The re-categorization hypothesis was supported in two ways. First, despite initial allegiances, 58 percent of the subjects in the cooperative condition said they felt like one large group rather than two separate groups, an increase compared to only 28 percent in the neutral condition. Second, when subjects rated each other, those in the cooperative condition did not show the usual ingroup favoritism bias. Rather than derogate former outgroup members, they saw them as more likable, honest, and similar to themselves. Thanks to cooperation, "they" became part of "us" (see Figure 4.10).

Finally, intergroup contact can work only if it is supported by *social norms.* When it comes to racial attitudes and behavior, people are profoundly influenced by what others say and do. In one study, subjects expressed more prejudice after they overheard a confederate utter a racial slur (Greenberg & Pyszczynski, 1985). In a second study, college students being interviewed about a racial incident on campus conveyed more racist sentiment after they heard a fellow student do the same (Blanchard et al., 1991). And in a third study, subjects were more likely to rate an outgroup member as "typical" when they were with fellow ingroup members, presumably a partisan audience, than when they were alone

Figure 4.10 **Intergroup Cooperation: Re-categorizing "Them" as Part of "Us."** After working in separate three-person groups, six subjects were assembled for a neutral or cooperative interaction. Then they reported their impressions of each other. In the neutral condition, subjects rated former ingroup members more favorably than outgroup members (left). In the cooperative condition, however, evaluations of the outgroup were more favorable (right). (Data from Gaertner et al., 1990.)

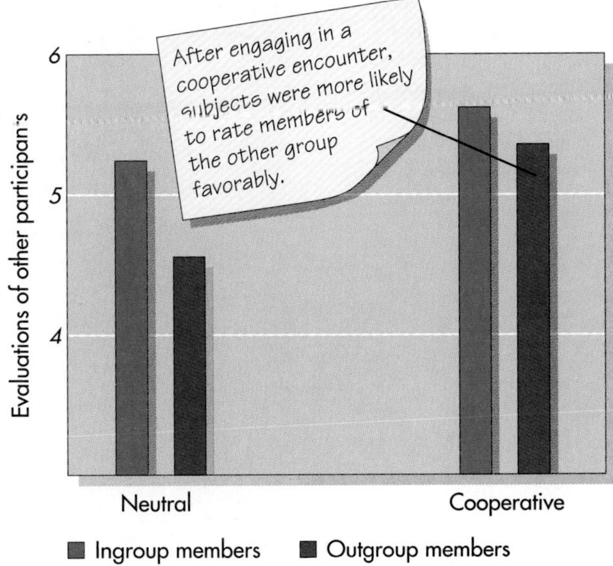

(Wilder & Shapiro, 1991). Norms have a powerful impact on us. Yet in the case of school desegregation, the social climate was not supportive. Many principals, teachers, and local officials objected, and many parents boycotted busing. The four necessary conditions of the contact hypothesis are summarized in Table 4.3.

Although many problems have plagued school desegregation efforts, research shows that prejudice *can* be reduced in situations that satisfy the chief requirements of the contact hypothesis (Cook, 1985). Perhaps the most successful demonstration of this point took place on the baseball diamond. On April 15, 1947, Jackie Robinson played first base for the Brooklyn Dodgers—and became the first black man to break the color barrier in American sports. In a story told by Anthony Pratkanis and Marlene Turner (1994), Robinson's opportunity came through Dodger owner Branch Rickey, who felt that integrating baseball was

Table 4.3 The Contact Hypothesis: Necessary Conditions

1. ***Equal status*** The contact should occur in circumstances that place the two groups in an equal status.
2. ***Personal interaction*** The contact should involve one-on-one interactions among individual members of the two groups.
3. ***Cooperative activities*** Members of the two groups should join together in an effort to achieve superordinate goals.
4. ***Social norms*** The social norms, defined in part by relevant authorities, should favor intergroup contact.

Four conditions are deemed necessary for intergroup contact to serve as a treatment for racism. However, many desegregated schools have failed to create a setting that meets these conditions.

Jackie Robinson and Branch Rickey discuss Robinson's contract with the Brooklyn Dodgers. The deal had great historical significance. The two men also went on to become good friends.

both moral and good for the game. Rickey knew all about the contact hypothesis and was assured by a social scientist friend that a team could furnish the conditions needed for it to work: equal status among teammates, personal interactions, dedication to a common goal, and a positive climate from the owner, managers, and coaches. The rest is history. Rickey signed Robinson and created the situation necessary for success. Baseball was integrated. In 1947 Jackie Robinson was named Rookie of the Year, and in 1962 he was elected into the Hall of Fame. At his induction ceremony, Robinson asked three people to stand beside him: his mother, his wife, and his friend, Branch Rickey.

jigsaw classroom A cooperative learning method used to reduce racial prejudice through interaction in group efforts.

The Jigsaw Classroom Working in the classroom, Elliot Aronson and his colleagues (1978) developed a cooperative learning method called the **jigsaw classroom.** In newly desegregated public schools in Texas and California, they assigned fifth-graders to small racially and academically mixed groups. The material to be learned within each group was divided into subtopics, much the way a jigsaw puzzle is broken into pieces. Each student was responsible for learning one piece of the puzzle, after which all members took turns teaching their material to one another. In this system, everyone—regardless of race, ability, or self-confidence—needs everyone else if the group as a whole is to succeed.

The method produced impressive results. Compared to children in traditional classes, those in jigsaw classrooms grew to like each other more, liked school more, were less prejudiced, and had higher self-esteem. What's more, academic test scores improved for the minority students and remained the same for white students. Much like an interracial sports team, the jigsaw classroom offers a promising way to create a truly integrated educational experience. It also provides a model of how to use interpersonal contact to promote greater tolerance of diversity.

Outlook: Toward a Colorblind Society? Consistent with the contact hypothesis, interracial contact can break new ground in the fight against racism. But what, specifically, should be the goal? Should the differences between groups be ignored or acknowledged? One view is that we should strive to become *colorblind,* a state of mind in which race and ethnic heritage have no bearing on the way people are treated. In a colorblind society, healthy race relations occur when categories are dissolved and individuals are perceived on a strictly personal basis (Brewer & Miller, 1984; Wilder, 1986). But is this goal possible, or even desirable?

One implication of social identity theory is that social categories should *not* be erased, because people derive pride and self-esteem from ingroup connections (Hewstone & Brown, 1986). In other words, racial and ethnic diversity should be celebrated, not ignored. The same argument is made from another perspective. Based on a study of an integrated school, Janet Schofield (1986) observed that in an effort to treat all students equally, teachers bent over backward to create an environment in which race was never discussed. The problem with this strategy is that because modern racism surfaces when it can be rationalized in socially acceptable terms, a supposed *lack* of racial awareness provides too comfortable a setting for discrimination.

PROBLEMS AND PROSPECTS

The sex discrimination case of Ann Hopkins and the beating of Rodney King invite us to think carefully about stereotypes and prejudice: about their origins, their effects, and possible solutions. Now let's review what we know and can expect from the future.

Stereotypes are beliefs that ultimately lead us to overlook the diversity within groups and jump to conclusions about specific persons. Once formed, stereotypes are hard to erase. Indeed, even if individual perceivers are not biased, stereotypes are often preserved by the forces of culture and can be slow to change. The problems stemming from prejudice and intergroup conflict are equally daunting. Negative feelings toward outgroups arise from competition for limited resources and from the need to favor ingroups over outgroups in order to boost self-esteem. Modern racism is a particularly acute problem, one that is poised and ready to strike at the first provocation.

Sexism and racism are similar in some respects, but different in others. Both women and racial minorities occupy low-status social roles, and both are known victims of discrimination. But sexism rests heavily on caricatures of men and women, whereas racism is further inflamed by negative emotions toward racial outgroups. In addition, research shows that people believe sex differences are more likely than race differences to be biologically rooted (Martin & Parker, 1995).

It is interesting that despite the differences, there may be a single solution to both problems: change behavior, and hearts and minds should follow. Hire men for "feminine" jobs and women for "masculine" jobs, and gender stereotypes may well begin to fade. Likewise, bring Whites, Blacks, and other minorities together as close, cooperative equals, and racial prejudice may also diminish. It's not reasonable to expect these changes overnight, and we may even have to conclude that at least some degree of discrimination is inevitable among human beings. But there is much room, and much hope, for improvement.

REVIEW

- Discrimination is influenced by both beliefs and feelings about social groups.

STEREOTYPES

- The incidents involving Ann Hopkins and Rodney King illustrate the problems in sexism and racism, respectively.
- Stereotypes are beliefs that associate groups of people with certain types of characteristics.

How Stereotypes Form: Cognitive Foundations

- The formation of stereotypes begins with the tendency for people to group themselves and others into social categories.
- Social categorization spawns the outgroup homogeneity effect, a tendency to assume that there is more similarity among members of outgroups than ingroups.
- This bias leads us to generalize from individuals to whole groups and vice versa.

How Stereotypes Distort Perceptions of Individuals

- Behaviors that differ markedly from stereotypic expectations are judged to be even more discrepant than they really are, as the result of a contrast effect.

How Stereotypes Survive: Self-Perpetuating Mechanisms

- People perceive illusory correlations between groups and traits that are distinctive—and when the correlations fit prior notions.
- Group members who do not fit the mold are often subcategorized, leaving the overall stereotype intact. They force a revision of beliefs only when they are otherwise typical members of the group.
- People tend to seek and interpret events in ways that confirm existing stereotypes.

Stereotyping: A Necessary Evil?

- Stereotypes are often activated without our awareness and operate at an unconscious or "implicit" level.
- By simplifying the way we form impressions, stereotypes free up cognitive resources for use in other activities.
- Perceivers can ignore stereotypes and form more individualized impressions of others when they have personal information—and the ability and motivation to use that information.
- But research also suggests that it may be hard for people to suppress the use of stereotypes on a consistent, long-term basis.

PREJUDICE

- Prejudice refers to negative feelings toward persons based on their membership in certain groups.

Robbers Cave: Setting the Stage

- In the Robbers Cave study, boys from rival groups were brought together through tasks that required intergroup cooperation.

Realistic Conflict Theory

- Realistic conflict theory maintains that direct competition for resources gives rise to prejudice.
- Prejudice is aroused by perceived threats to an important ingroup.

Social Identity Theory

- Subjects categorized into arbitrary minimal groups discriminate in favor of the ingroup.
- Social identity theory maintains that self-esteem is influenced by the fate of social groups with which we identify.
- Research shows that threats to the self cause ingroup favoritism, which in turn increases self-esteem.
- Ingroup favoritism is more intense for people in small minority groups and among those who need to elevate their ingroup status.
- People also distance themselves from ingroups, or from individual members, that fail.

SEXISM

- Sexism is a form of discrimination based on a person's gender.

Gender Stereotypes: Blue for Boys, Pink for Girls

- Across the world, men are described as assertive, independent, and task-oriented; women as sensitive, dependent, and people-oriented.
- Gender stereotypes are so deeply ingrained that they bias perceptions of baby boys and girls.

What Activates Gender Stereotypes?

- Gender stereotypes bias the social judgments of some perceivers more than others. They also influence perceptions of target persons who are highly masculine or feminine in appearance, or who are viewed in situations that heighten the salience of gender.

Are Gender Stereotypes Accurate?

- Although there are differences between men and women, stereotypes are often stronger than the actual differences.

Why Do Gender Stereotypes Endure?

- Cultural institutions foster gender distinctions in portrayals of males and females.
- Perceived differences between men and women are magnified by the contrasting social roles they occupy.

Sex Discrimination: A Double Standard?

- There are some striking sex differences in occupational choices.
- Men and women are judged more favorably when they apply for jobs that are consistent with gender stereotypes.

RACISM

- Racism is a form of discrimination based on a person's skin color or ethnic heritage.

Modern Racism: The Disease

- Over the years, surveys have recorded a decline in negative views of black Americans.
- Researchers have uncovered a more subtle, modern racism that surfaces in less direct ways when people can rationalize racist behavior.
- Cognitively, people recall and interpret ambiguous actions in negative terms when the individual being perceived is black.
- Behaviorally, white subjects are more aggressive, less helpful, and more unflattering to black confederates when such actions are safe, socially acceptable, and easy to rationalize.
- Victims of discrimination often cope by attributing their outcomes to prejudice—a strategy that has both benefits and drawbacks for their self-esteem.

Intergroup Contact: The Cure?

- Following the 1954 ruling in *Brown v. Board of Education,* the U.S. Supreme Court ordered public schools to desegregate.
- According to the contact hypothesis, desegregation should reduce prejudice.
- Desegregation did not cure the problem, but it was also the case that the key conditions of intergroup contact—equal status, personal interactions, the need to achieve a common goal, and social norms—did not exist.
- As in the jigsaw classroom, positive changes can occur when the conditions necessary for intergroup contact do exist.

PROBLEMS AND PROSPECTS

- Despite the differences between sexism and racism, one solution may serve both problems: change behavior, and hearts and minds will follow.

KEY TERMS

discrimination, p. 121
group, p. 121
stereotype, p. 122
social categorization, p. 123
outgroup homogeneity effect, p. 123
contrast effect, p. 124
illusory correlation, p. 125
prejudice, p. 132
superordinate goals, p. 133
realistic conflict theory, p. 133
relative deprivation, p. 134
ingroup favoritism, p. 135
social identity theory, p. 135
sexism, p. 139
social roles theory, p. 144
modern racism, p. 148
contact hypothesis, p. 155
jigsaw classroom, p. 158

Chapter 5

Interpersonal Attraction

PREVIEW

This chapter examines how people become attracted to each other. First, we describe *the role of rewards* in the attraction process. Then we consider four factors that influence whether social encounters will be rewarding: *characteristics of the individual* who is attracted, *characteristics of others* who are perceived as attractive, *the fit between people* attracted to each other, and *situational influences* on social interactions.

OUTLINE

No one ever expected that Robert Waller's *The Bridges of Madison County* would become a runaway best-seller. The story was too short; its author, a former professor of management, too obscure; its plot, too trite. And yet this novel of the four-day summer romance between Robert Kincaid, world-traveling photographer, and Francesca Johnson, midwestern housewife, quickly rose to the top of the charts. Readers snatched it from the racks in urban bookstores, suburban malls, airports, and supermarkets; it was also immensely popular on college campuses. *The Bridges of Madison County* struck a deep, responsive chord in millions of people, but no one seemed quite sure why.

Perhaps, though, the novel's success isn't really so surprising. At its heart, this is a story that celebrates the unpredictability of interpersonal attraction. Who would have thought that two such different individuals could be so attracted to each other? As Robert says in one of his letters to Francesca, "We could have flashed by one another like two pieces of cosmic dust" (p. 141). Instead, they collided—and therein lies the book's appeal. People are fascinated by the possibility that an unlikely, unexpected, intense attraction might be right around the corner.

All of us, at some time or another, have been startled by our reaction to someone we've just met. Why do we like some people so much so quickly—and yet *dis*like others so much so swiftly? Attraction often seems strange and unaccountable, a kind of wild card in the deck of human behavior.

This chapter unravels some of the mysteries of first encounters. The theories and research findings described here will help us better understand the process of attraction. But there is no danger of ending up with some dull, routine formula. Attraction is like looking through a kaleidoscope: Even when we recognize the shifting, sliding pieces, we can still be surprised by the pattern that emerges.

THE ROLE OF REWARDS

Interpersonal attraction is based on rewarding experiences with another human being (Lott & Lott, 1974). Such experiences create a positive emotional response, which strengthens our desire to be with that individual (Clore & Byrne, 1974). But what kinds of rewards do we receive from others?

Some people provide us with *direct rewards,* showering us with attention, support, understanding, and other rewarding behaviors. We also respond to rewarding personal characteristics such as beauty, intelligence, and a good sense of humor. And then there are external rewards to be considered. Some people give us access to valuable commodities (such as money, status, or information) that we could not have secured on our own. The more direct rewards (behaviors, personal characteristics, valuable commodities) we receive, the more attracted we are to the person who provides them.

But what about just being with an individual under enjoyable circumstances? Suppose you meet someone at a victory celebration for your favorite basketball team. Are you more likely to be attracted at that time and place than you would be if you met the same person on another, less euphoric occasion? *Rewards by as-*

Attending a pep rally together could start a close friendship or spark a romance. Just as rewarding experiences produced by an individual increase attraction, so do rewarding experiences associated with someone strengthen the desire to be with that person.

sociation are a clear possibility. We can become attracted to people we happen to associate with a positive, rewarding experience—even though they are not responsible for that experience.

balance theory The theory that people desire consistency in their thoughts, feelings, and social relationships.

reciprocity A quid-pro-quo mutual exchange—for example, liking those who like us.

Fritz Heider's (1958) **balance theory** points to another type of reward we can obtain from others: the pleasure of consistency. Balanced relationships, says the theory, are rewarding; imbalanced ones are distressing. Between two people, balance is created by **reciprocity**: a mutual, quid-pro-quo exchange between what we give and what we receive. We are attracted to those we believe are attracted to us (Curtis & Miller, 1986). In groups of three or more individuals, a balanced social constellation requires liking someone whose relationships with others parallel our own. Usually, we like those who are friends of our friends and enemies of our enemies (Aronson & Cope, 1968). But if you've ever had a good friend who was also a friend of someone you detested, you know full well the awkwardness and discomfort of *un*balanced relationships. We don't expect our friends and enemies to get along (Chapdelaine et al., 1994).

Acknowledging the role of rewards is a necessary first step in describing when and how attraction occurs. But there is more to come. Not all rewards are equal or equally likely. In the following pages, we examine four factors that influence whether initial encounters will be rewarding: our own needs, the other person's characteristics, the fit between us, and the situational context. Although we consider each of these factors one by one, the relationship among them is dynamic and interactive. Characteristics of an individual, for example, can modify the effect of the situation—and vice versa.

You should also note that most research on attraction (and on intimate relationships, the topic of Chapter 6) has focused on heterosexuals. We do not know how well these specific findings apply to homosexual relationships and this uncertainty limits our understanding. Nevertheless, the basic processes described in this and the next chapter appear to influence the lives of a great many individuals and couples, regardless of their sexual orientation (Kurdek, 1992).

CHARACTERISTICS OF THE INDIVIDUAL

Do some people make friends under almost any circumstances? Do some people respond enthusiastically to almost anyone's opening lines? In other words, are some people more likely than others to become attracted? To answer this question, we take a look at four kinds of personal characteristics that contribute to a person's readiness to approach other people: self-esteem, social motives, social difficulties, and interpersonal expectations.

Self-Esteem: Confidence Versus Desire

The notion that self-esteem, a person's evaluation of his or her own worth, affects attraction to others has long been a source of contention. Sigmund Freud (1922), the founder of psychoanalysis, and Theodore Reik (1944), who developed his own school of psychotherapy, both traced interpersonal attraction back to dissatisfaction with oneself. Other prominent psychotherapists, such as Karen Horney (1939) and Harry Stack Sullivan (1947), disagreed. They believed that genuine and spontaneous attraction to others requires feeling secure and confident about oneself. So which is it? Does attraction flow from weakness or from strength?

At first, the role of dissatisfaction seemed to win out. In a 1965 study by Elaine Walster (now Hatfield), female subjects received bogus feedback rigged by the experimenter. Those whose self-esteem was lowered by being told that they had a poor personality liked a friendly male confederate more than did subjects whose self-esteem was bolstered by positive feedback about their personality. Subsequent research, however, failed to confirm these initial results, finding no evidence of a direct relationship between self-esteem and attraction to others (Sprecher & Hatfield, 1982). Does self-esteem, then, have no effect on how eagerly people will respond to the kindness of strangers? Were Freud, Reik, Horney, and Sullivan all wrong?

Actually, they were all right, but none of them realized that high and low self-esteem have different effects on different aspects of the attraction process (Dion & Dion, 1988). High self-esteem allows people to pursue potential social rewards despite the risk of failure. But since their desire for these rewards is less, they may be less motivated to approach those to whom they are attracted. In contrast, people low in self-esteem feel a greater desire for positive regard from others and may be especially grateful when they receive it. However, their concerns about appearing foolish or being rejected can stifle their initiative and prevent them from acting. In other words, those with a *weak* desire for social rewards feel self-assured in going after them, while those who have a *strong* desire lack the confidence necessary for pursuit. Confidence and desire cancel each other out, and self-esteem ends up having little overall effect on attraction. In the following sections, we turn to some social motives and social difficulties that have a more direct connection with our social inclinations.

Social Motives: Affiliation and Intimacy

Building on the pioneering work of Henry Murray (1938) and David McClelland (1951), Dan McAdams (1982) distinguished between two social motives that prompt people to seek out social contact:

- *The need for affiliation (Naff):* The desire to establish and maintain many rewarding interpersonal relationships

Individuals high in the need for affiliation find social activities enjoyable. Those high in the need for intimacy seek close, confiding relationships.

- *The need for intimacy (Nint):* The preference for warm, close, communicative relationships

The need for affiliation inspires active, controlling social behavior with an emphasis on the breadth and quantity of social contacts. Compared to people whose Naff is weak, individuals with a strong Naff communicate more with other people, find social activities more enjoyable, and react more positively to the company of others (McClelland, 1985). In contrast, the need for intimacy gives rise to more passive, less controlling social behavior, with an emphasis on the depth and quality of social relations (McAdams, 1988). Compared to those whose Nint is relatively low, individuals with a strong Nint are more trusting and confiding in their relationships and experience a greater sense of well-being (McAdams & Bryant, 1987; McAdams et al., 1984).

In the long run, the need for intimacy may be the better predictor of an individual's overall psychosocial adjustment. Consider the results of a prospective study that examined the relationship between the social motives of a group of male college graduates at age thirty and their well-being some seventeen years later (McAdams & Vaillant, 1982). The strength of these men's need for affiliation as young adults did *not* predict their middle-aged adjustment, measured by such factors as job enjoyment and marital satisfaction. But their youthful need for intimacy did foretell their future. Those who had been high in Nint were better adjusted than those whose Nint had been low. As time goes by, attraction based on the quality of relationships may yield greater benefits than attraction based on the quantity of social rewards.

Social Difficulties: Anxiety and Loneliness

Naff and Nint are positive social motives; they stimulate people to seek the rewards of social interactions. But as we have seen, there can also be a troubling side of attraction: wanting to approach someone but being afraid to do so. It's a common, sometimes painful, experience. Here, we examine two social difficulties that deprive people of the rewarding social interactions they desire.

social anxiety A feeling of discomfort in the presence of others, often accompanied by the social awkwardness and inhibition characteristic of shyness.

Social Anxiety: The Fear of Failure **Social anxiety** is the emotion we experience when we are uncomfortable in the presence of others (Leary, 1983). It is often accompanied by *shyness*—social awkwardness, inhibition, and a tendency to avoid social interaction (Bruch et al., 1989; Zimbardo, 1977). People suffering from social anxiety find it hard to make small talk before class, call someone on the phone for a date, enter a room full of strangers, or meet people at parties.

Social anxiety comes in two varieties. The *state* of social anxiety is a momentary experience that flares up at a certain time or in a certain place, and then passes. The *trait* of social anxiety is more enduring: a characteristic of certain individuals that persists over time and across situations. For those chronically afflicted, their anxiety locks them into increasingly unpleasant social interactions (DePaulo et al., 1990; Jones & Carpenter, 1986; Meleshko & Alden, 1993). Such individuals tend to reject other people, perhaps because they fear being rejected themselves. They are withdrawn and ineffective in social interactions, perhaps because they perceive negative reactions even where there are none (Pozo et al., 1991). In fact, however, other people often do react negatively to interactions with socially anxious individuals. Each of these behaviors strengthens the others, as illustrated in Figure 5.1. Caught in a trap, the person can't get out.

Interactions with the opposite sex may be particularly likely to spring this trap. Two studies on shyness make the point. In one, shy women were less likely than nonshy women to ask a man for assistance on a task; shy and nonshy men didn't differ in their willingness to ask a woman for help (DePaulo et al., 1989). In another, subjects were unexpectedly left alone in a waiting room with an opposite-sex confederate. Compared with nonshy men, shy men felt uncomfortable and self-conscious, and their behavior was awkward and inhibited; shy and nonshy women didn't differ (Garcia et al., 1991). Thus, shy men and women find different types of interactions with the opposite sex to be problematic. Shy women withdraw from encounters that require them to be assertive about their needs; shy men find informal, unstructured interactions especially disturbing.

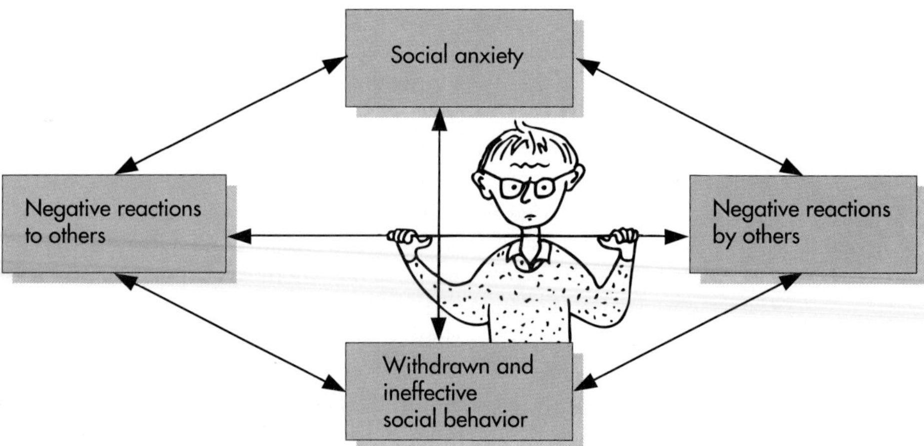

Figure 5.1 Social Anxiety: An Interpersonal Trap. Individuals who are socially anxious often experience unsatisfying social interactions. Social anxiety is associated with negative reactions to others, withdrawn and ineffective social behavior, and negative reactions by others. These components can interact and trap the person into an ever-worsening state of social anxiety and dissatisfaction. People who are lonely or depressed experience similar social difficulties.

"Hope you don't mind, Charlene—I've always been more comfortable with a script in front of me."

Feelings of social discomfort can arise from a number of sources (Leary, 1987). They can be a learned reaction to unpleasant encounters, as social problems in the past contribute to social anxiety about the future. In addition, social anxiety has a significant cognitive component. Socially anxious individuals often believe that they lack the skills necessary for social success (Maddux et al., 1988). Even if the person actually has such skills, the belief that they are lacking affects feelings and behavior in social situations. When an individual wants to impress others but is convinced that the chances for success are low, social anxiety shoots up like a weed in the gap between desire and confidence (Schlenker & Leary, 1982).

If thoughts and beliefs can increase social anxiety, then perhaps they can also reduce it. Consider, for example, speaking in public. For some people, it's easy. For others, it's pure agony. Those who have suffered from speech anxiety know the symptoms only too well: pulse racing, palms sweaty, throat dry, breathing labored, body sometimes shivering or shaking. Can the belief about what caused this nervousness influence how nervous a person feels? It seems so. When James Olson (1988) led subjects to believe they were hearing a "subliminal noise" that would make them feel tense and anxious, these individuals were able to give a smoother, more fluent speech than were subjects who had been told that the noise would not have any side effects. At first glance, this result is puzzling: Those who thought the noise would make them anxious performed calmly. What's going on?

misattribution An inaccurate explanation that shifts the cause for arousal from the true source to another one.

Olson's approach to speech anxiety was based on the attribution theories described in Chapter 3. The technique he used, called **misattribution,** switches the explanation for the physiological symptoms of arousal from the true source (such as a person's own anxiety) to a different source (such as noise). This switch helps the individual avoid the cycle of ever-escalating arousal produced by anxiety-provoking explanations: "I'm so anxious; I know I'm just going to fall apart when they call on me." Instead, the subjects in Olson's experiment who were told that the noise would make them tense and anxious could say to themselves, "What, me anxious about having to give a speech? No way. It's just this noise that has me a little rattled."

Under certain conditions, misattribution can improve performance and the ability to cope. However, there are limits to its effectiveness (Olson & Ross, 1988; Reisenzein, 1983). One of the most important is the level of arousal. For a misattribution to take hold, the true cause of arousal must be uncertain so that the person can accept a calming alternative. But when arousal is intense, people usually know why they feel it and won't believe another explanation (Conger et al., 1976; Nisbett & Schachter, 1966). For this reason, efforts to misattribute the source of severe cases of anxiety are unlikely to have much effect.

The misattribution treatment of social anxiety attempts to *remove* anxiety-producing explanations for a person's emotional state. Robert Montgomery and Frances Haemmerlie (1986, 1987) took a different tack. They developed a procedure to *provide* anxiety-reducing explanations for the person's social outcomes. This procedure, the *biased interaction technique,* has been used primarily with individuals suffering from "dating anxiety"—social anxiety about interacting with potential romantic partners. Let's see how it works.

Participants in this research were heterosexual male and female undergraduates who reported high levels of dating anxiety. Unknown to them, the experimenters had enlisted opposite-sex confederates who were instructed to act in a friendly fashion with the subjects. Over the course of several days, each subject engaged in two successful social encounters with each of five different confederates.

This scripted set of actions confronted subjects with a positive outcome for which all unfavorable attributions were blocked. Could they attribute their social success to something peculiar about a particular interaction partner? No, they met a number of people and were successful with all of them. Could they conclude that they just happened to encounter some people who were temporarily in an extra-friendly mood? No, their success was consistent over time. The only plausible explanation was that they succeeded because of their own attractive behavior and characteristics. This attribution was expected to increase self-confidence and reduce anxiety.

It did. After their social successes, subjects experienced less dating anxiety and their actual dating increased. You might wonder, however, what happened when subjects were debriefed and informed that their successful encounters were rigged by the experimenters. According to Montgomery and Haemmerlie (1987), they didn't care! "What seemed of most interest was the fact that they had enjoyed the interactions and felt good about having done well in them" (p. 142).

Despite this reluctance to look a gift horse in the mouth, the biased interaction technique isn't likely to be applied on a widespread basis. It takes a lot of personnel, and therapists and counselors don't like to dupe their clients, even for a noble purpose. Fortunately, though, the general principle behind the biased interaction technique doesn't require elaborate stage management. The critical ingredient is for people to take credit for a success by attributing the cause to their own efforts and characteristics (Brehm & Smith, 1986). Usually, such attributions do not have to be engineered and manufactured. But they can and should be encouraged.

Loneliness: The Feeling of Isolation Of all social difficulties, loneliness is probably the most common. Loneliness can occur during any time of transition or disruption: during the first year at college, after a romantic breakup, on a new job, when loved ones move far away. **Loneliness** is a feeling of deprivation about one's existing social relations. But what makes people feel deprived? According

loneliness A feeling of deprivation about existing social relations.

to some researchers, loneliness is produced by a discrepancy between what we actually have and what we want (Perlman & Peplau, 1981). From this perspective, even if we have a jam-packed social calendar, we will still feel lonely if we want more social activity. Recent research, however, indicates that regardless of what they consider to be an ideal or typical level of social activity, individuals who have more social contact are less lonely (Archibald et al., 1995).

According to Robert Weiss (1973), there are two types of loneliness. In *social isolation,* a person feels deprived of a network of friends or relatives; in *emotional isolation,* a person feels deprived of a single, intense relationship. These two kinds of loneliness share a common emotional core, and there is some debate about how clearly they can be distinguished (Russell et al., 1984; Vaux, 1988a). Either one could be momentary (state loneliness) or a long-lasting characteristic of the individual (trait loneliness).

Contrary to the stereotype of the lonely old person, the loneliest people in American society are adolescents and young adults (Peplau et al., 1982; Rubenstein & Shaver, 1982). In fact, loneliness declines with age, at least up to the point where age-related difficulties such as poor health may interfere with social activities (Schultz & Moore, 1984). Regardless of age, however, the loss of a close relationship increases loneliness. Widowed, divorced, and separated individuals are lonelier than those who are married or have never been married (Perlman & Peplau, 1981). As for gender, the evidence is mixed and no firm conclusion can yet be drawn about the extent to which men and women differ in their experience of loneliness (Tornstam, 1992).

Loneliness often strikes at the same time as social anxiety and depression (Jones & Carpenter, 1986). Like social anxiety, loneliness and depression are characterized by the debilitating pattern of social interaction illustrated in Figure 5.1. Compared with people who are not lonely, those who are hold more negative opinions about others (Wittenberg & Reis, 1986). Lonely people also lack social skills in their interactions with others and are less socially responsive

Loneliness is especially common among adolescents and young adults. Realizing that many of their peers are lonely, too, may help individuals avoid blaming themselves for being lonely.

(Jones et al., 1982; Solano & Koester, 1989). And, at least under some circumstances, they are negatively evaluated by others (Lau & Gruen, 1992; Rotenberg & Kmill, 1992). Depressed individuals exhibit the same general pattern: rejection of others, awkward or inadequate social skills, and negative evaluations from others (Rook et al., 1994; Segrin & Dillard, 1992). Just as the socially anxious are pessimistic about others' responses to them, so are depressed individuals, who sometimes perceive more negative reactions than actually exist (Pietromonaco et al., 1992).

In addition, those suffering from social anxiety, loneliness, or depression are socially cautious (Pietromonaco & Rook, 1987; Vaux, 1988b). They tend to avoid interpersonal situations that pose the risk of rejection. Although this caution may reduce social failures, it also cuts down on opportunities for social success. People who perceive greater risk in interacting with others have less rewarding social encounters (Nezlek & Pilkington, 1994). As the saying goes, "Nothing ventured, nothing gained." Overall, there is a strong resemblance among social anxiety, loneliness, and depression (Anderson & Harvey, 1988). Each one involves personal distress and social dissatisfaction. Chapter 14 on Health examines the causes and consequences of depression in more detail.

We have seen how a favorable attribution for social success can build confidence among people with dating anxiety. Causal attributions also appear to have important effects on loneliness. When Carolyn Cutrona (1982) examined the duration of loneliness among first-year college students, she found that it lasted longer among those who initially blamed aspects of themselves—their shyness, personality, fear of rejection, or lack of social skills—for their lonely feelings.

This kind of self-blame relies on an *internal, stable attribution* for loneliness. Internal attributions locate the cause of a condition or event in the person rather than external circumstances; stable attributions focus on enduring causes rather than temporary, changeable ones. Blaming themselves by making an internal, stable attribution for loneliness may discourage people from trying to meet others and make friends (Peplau et al., 1979). In contrast, explanations based on attributions that are external, unstable, or both offer the possibility that things can be changed for the better (see Figure 5.2). With a more hopeful attitude, the lonely person can take a few more social risks and gain more opportunities for social satisfaction. Hope lets us dare to be attracted.

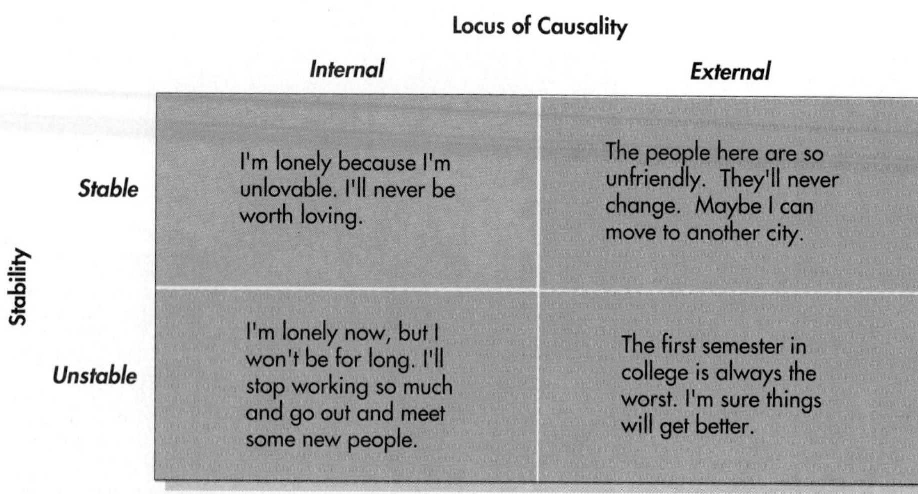
Locus of Causality
Internal
External
Stability
Stable
I'm lonely because I'm unlovable. I'll never be worth loving.
The people here are so unfriendly. They'll never change. Maybe I can move to another city.
Unstable
I'm lonely now, but I won't be for long. I'll stop working so much and go out and meet some new people.
The first semester in college is always the worst. I'm sure things will get better.

Figure 5.2 Causal Attributions for Loneliness. The explanations that people give for why they are lonely may influence how long they stay lonely. An internal, stable attribution is associated with prolonged loneliness. (Based on Shaver & Rubenstein, 1980.)

Expectations and Reality

People's expectations and beliefs can come true by setting in motion a *self-fulfilling prophecy* (see Chapter 3). For example, when a teacher has high expectations for a student, the student performs better; when an interviewer thinks an interviewee is extroverted, the interviewee behaves accordingly. A classic study by Mark Snyder and his colleagues (1977) demonstrates that the power of self-fulfilling prophecies also makes its mark on initial encounters.

Subjects in this experiment were pairs of unacquainted male and female subjects who had no opportunity to see each other before they were assigned to separate rooms. All subjects were given some background information about each other, and the men also received a photograph of their supposed partner. In fact, the photographs had been prepared before the experiment began and were of women who never participated in the study. Half of the male subjects received a photo of a physically attractive woman; the other half received one of a physically unattractive woman. After reading the information and seeing the photograph, the men rated their impressions of their female partner. All subjects then engaged in a brief conversation over headphones. Independent judges later rated the tapes of these interactions; some listened only to what the men said, others listened only to the women.

When Snyder and his colleagues examined male subjects' initial impressions, they found that those who expected to interact with a physically attractive woman also expected her to have more socially desirable personality characteristics. Furthermore, analysis of conversational behavior indicated that men who believed their partner was attractive were themselves more sociable and outgoing. But how did the female subjects behave? Compared to women interacting with men who received unattractive photographs, those thought to be attractive were warmer, more confident, and more animated. By means of their own behavior, men who expected an attractive partner created one.

The effects of expectations on attraction are not limited to audio-only conversations between men and women. Research by Monica Harris and her colleagues (1992) found that elementary school boys, too, are susceptible. Those led to believe that another boy they were about to meet had a serious behavior problem were less friendly and talked less often during the interaction than those who were not given any information about the other boy's behavior. In turn, the boys who had been labeled as having a behavior problem took less personal credit for a good performance on a cooperative task and said their partners were meaner. At any age, expectations are powerful. Sometimes, the characteristics of others that affect attraction reside, at least initially, in us.

CHARACTERISTICS OF OTHERS

Although our own needs and expectations influence attraction, the other person isn't just a blank screen on which we project whatever picture we want to see. That person's actual characteristics also affect our response. Some aspects of an individual are not apparent until after we get to know that person reasonably well, but one feature shows up right away: physical appearance. In this section, we examine the effects of physical appearance on interpersonal attraction. We then discuss how an individual's evaluation *of* others can influence that person's attractiveness *to* others. Is it better to be a "liker" or to play hard to get? We'll soon see.

Physical Attractiveness

Beauty is only skin deep, but it is still a force to be reckoned with. Good looks confer a distinct social advantage: People are attracted to and react more favorably toward individuals who are physically attractive (Hatfield & Sprecher, 1986). This preferential response to good-looking individuals is particularly strong for *perceptions* of another's appearance. If we perceive someone to be highly physically attractive, we're more attracted to that person than to someone we perceive as less attractive. Replace our own perceptions with judges' ratings and good looks still prevail, though the effect is weaker. There is a bias for beauty. But why?

What Creates the Bias for Beauty? Four possibilities have been highlighted. First, aesthetic appeal affects our response. People, as much as objects, are more rewarding to be with when we find their appearance pleasing. However, what makes a person's looks appealing is not well understood. Some researchers believe that people respond favorably to characteristics that satisfy various interpersonal motives. For example, perhaps smiling increases perceived attractiveness because those who smile are viewed as more likely to meet the perceiver's need for a friendly social interaction (Reis et al., 1990).

Then again, aesthetic appeal could simply be a matter of averages. According to research conducted by Judith Langlois and Lori Roggman (1990), a composite of many faces is the most attractive. When undergraduate subjects rated pictures of other undergraduates, they gave more positive ratings to computer-generated

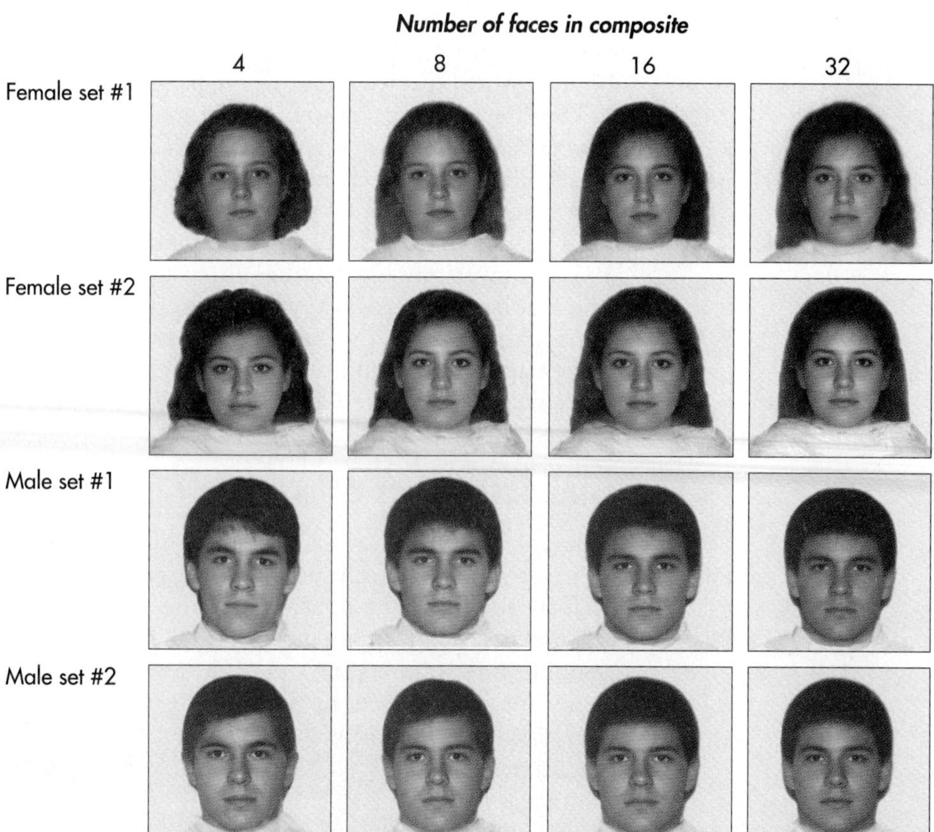

Figure 5.3 Is Average Better? Using computer-generated composites similar to those displayed here, Langlois and Roggman (1990) found that 16- and 32-face composites were rated as more attractive than the individual faces on which they were based.

composites averaged across sixteen and thirty-two faces than to the individual pictures used in the composites. Ratings of composites based on fewer faces did not differ from those given to individual pictures. Some computer composites similar to those used in this study are displayed in Figure 5.3.

Langlois and her colleagues (1994) maintain that average faces are more attractive because, by definition, they are more prototypically facelike and, thus, seem more familiar to us. They set the norm from which more unusual faces differ. But is this norm constant across time and place? Would the face that launched a thousand ships off to the Trojan War get more than a passing glance today? Perhaps so. Judgments of facial attractiveness are often consistent among raters of varying ages and different ethnic backgrounds (Langlois & Roggman, 1990). Ironically, even researchers who contest the notion that averageness is attractive provide evidence of cross-cultural consistency, finding that men and women from Scotland and Japan make similar evaluations of computer-generated faces of Japanese women (Perrett et al., 1994).

Facial attractiveness appears to be relatively consistent across different cultures. Those who are regarded as good-looking in one culture are also judged to be attractive by people from a different culture. The individuals pictured here are from Egypt, Venezuela, Kenya, and Japan.

Still, one wonders. The accepted standard of bodily attractiveness for females has changed a great deal from the ample proportions considered ideal in the past to the thin, athletic form currently in vogue (Lamb et al., 1993). The mass-media standard for hair color among white women in America has also shifted across time. Although the majority of women pictured in magazines published from 1950 to 1989 were brunettes, redheads were featured more often in the 1950s than subsequently and blondes appeared more often in the 1970s than in earlier decades (Rich & Cash, 1993).

As for faces, take a look at two other computer-generated composites displayed below. One combines the features of the famous beauties of the 1950s; the other is based on the faces considered beautiful in the 1980s. If you find the latter more attractive than the former, your reaction suggests that the standard of facial attractiveness is subject to change. And once the standard changes, perhaps the rest of us hurry to catch up. Or maybe, as the writer Harold Brodkey suggests, it goes the other way around: "We have come to resemble one another, and our celebrated figures have moved along with us in the trend" (p. 31).

Despite the importance of aesthetic appeal, it's doubtful that the bias for beauty is solely a matter of sheer viewing pleasure. A second possible reason for this bias is that people overgeneralize from appearance, assuming that those who are attractive on the outside also have the inner goodness of attractive personal characteristics. This assumption is called the **what-is-beautiful-is-good stereotype** (Dion et al., 1972) and includes a number of personal characteristics (Eagly et al., 1991). Physically attractive individuals are seen as more socially competent than those who are less attractive. In addition, they are regarded as more intellectually competent, better adjusted, and more self-assertive. However, physical attractiveness has little effect on judgments of integrity or of concern for others. And, on one characteristic, what is beautiful is perceived as bad: Physically attractive individuals are viewed as more vain than those who are less attractive.

what-is-beautiful-is-good stereotype The belief that physically attractive individuals also possess desirable personality characteristics.

The beautiful-is-good stereotype seems to operate with amazing speed (Locher et al., 1993). Told to make judgments about college graduates applying for a job, undergraduates viewed each of a set of head-and-shoulders slides for just 100 milliseconds. As the photographs whizzed by, subjects rated the more attractive individuals as better suited for the job and more likely to be cooperative at work.

The computer-generated composite on the left combines the beautiful faces of the 1950s: Bette Davis, Audrey Hepburn, Grace Kelly, Sophia Loren, and Marilyn Monroe. The one on the right combines the beauties of the 1980s: Jane Fonda, Jacqueline Bisset, Diane Keaton, Brooke Shields, and Meryl Streep. Which one do you find more attractive? (Burson et al., 1986.)

There are two ways in which this fast-acting stereotype could influence attraction. First, believing that someone is good as well as beautiful doubles the pleasure of being with that person. The reward of being in the presence of personal superiority is added to that of being in the presence of a pleasing appearance. Second, the what-is-beautiful-is-good stereotype could produce a self-fulfilling prophecy (Langlois, 1986). Believing that beauty is associated with desirable traits, people may be especially friendly and supportive in their behavior toward a physically attractive person, who in turn may respond by developing the expected characteristics. For example, the strongest stereotype held about good-looking individuals is that they are socially competent. Is this fact or fiction? Could the social encouragement and positive expectations they experience help them develop good social skills?

In fact, physical attractiveness (as rated by judges) is associated with higher levels of social skills (Feingold, 1992b). These skills offer the third possible explanation for why beautiful people elicit more positive responses from others. Interactions with the socially adept are usually more rewarding than those with the socially inept.

The fourth possible basis for the social bias in favor of physically attractive people focuses on the social profit that may come from associating with good-looking people. Are we hoping that the glitter will rub off? If so, then *assimilation* should be the rule. Usually it is. When people are observed together, those of average attractiveness are judged as more attractive when they are with someone who is very good-looking. They are judged as less attractive in the presence of someone who is relatively unattractive. Assimilation occurs with same-sex pairs, both male and female (Geiselman et al., 1984). Among opposite-sex pairs, men benefit from being paired with a highly attractive woman (Sigall & Landy, 1973). However, evaluations of women are not affected by the looks of a male partner (Bar-Tal & Saxe, 1976).

Now, think about another kind of association. People aren't always observed together. Sometimes we see one and then another. How do these sequential comparisons play out? Here, *contrast* is the rule. The perceived attractiveness of an average person loses from comparison with someone who is very good-looking, but gains from comparison with a less attractive individual (Wedell et al., 1987).

The most commonly accepted explanation for these findings follows the reward-emotion-attraction pathway we mentioned earlier in this chapter. When people are observed together, the rewarding presence of a beautiful person should lift our mood and increase our attraction to everything and everyone nearby. During sequential observations, the switch from the beautiful to the average should lower our mood and decrease our attraction. It sounds reasonable.

But wait a minute, how do most of us feel about our *own* physical attractiveness when we observe someone else who is a perfect 10? Although there may be some exceptions (Brown et al., 1992), exposure to attractive *same-sex* others usually decreases our own perceived attractiveness (Thornton & Moore, 1993). And we don't feel good about it. In research by Douglas Kenrick and his colleagues (1993), subjects who viewed facial photographs of highly attractive same-sex individuals experienced a less positive mood than did those who viewed average faces. Viewing highly attractive opposite-sex individuals created a more positive mood (see Figure 5.4). Regardless of their mood, subjects who looked at highly attractive photos gave lower attractiveness ratings to subsequent photos of average faces. These results suggest that the effect of emotional response on perceived attractiveness may be less powerful than had been supposed. Even when we too are suffering from comparison, we still inflict it on others.

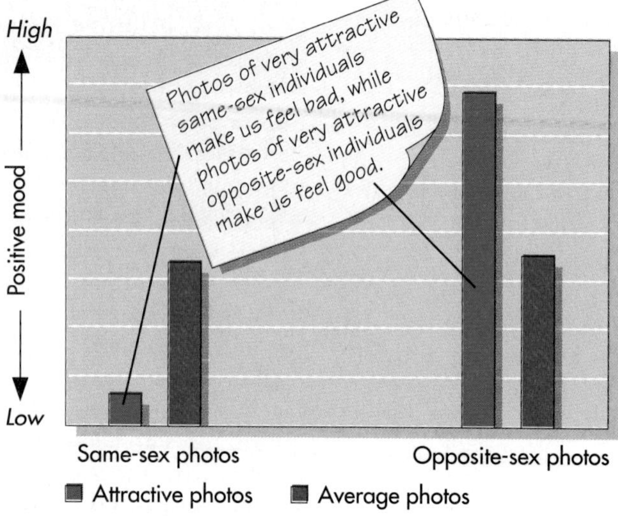

Figure 5.4 How Do We Feel When We See a Perfect 10? When subjects viewed facial photos of same-sex individuals, those who saw highly attractive people felt worse than those who saw average people. However, when viewing photos of opposite-sex individuals, those who saw highly attractive people felt better. Nevertheless, seeing highly attractive photos first consistently produced lower attractiveness ratings for subsequent average photos. (Data from Kenrick et al., 1993.)

We have now examined four possible causes of the social bias in favor of physically attractive individuals:

- The joy of seeing them
- The beautiful-is-good stereotype
- Their better social skills
- The desire to benefit from associating with them

Although none of these factors completely accounts for the bias, they may all make some contribution. But what are the consequences of beauty's advantage? Is being beautiful always beneficial, or is there a price to pay?

The Gains and Losses of Beauty No doubt about it, extremely good-looking people have a significant social edge. They are less lonely, less socially anxious (especially about interactions with the opposite sex), more popular, more sexually experienced, and, as we noted earlier, more socially skilled (Feingold, 1992b). The social rewards for physical attractiveness appear to get off to an early start. Mothers of highly attractive newborns engage in more affectionate interactions with their babies than do mothers of less attractive infants (Langlois et al., 1995).

Given such benefits, one would expect that the beautiful would also have a significant psychological advantage. But they don't. Physical attractiveness (as rated by judges) has little if any association with self-esteem, mental health, personality traits, or intelligence (Feingold, 1992b). One possible reason why beauty doesn't affect psychological well-being is that *actual* physical attractiveness, as evaluated by others, may have less impact than *self-perceived* physical attractiveness. People who view themselves as physically attractive do report higher self-esteem and better mental health than those who believe they are unattractive (Feingold, 1992b). But judges' ratings of physical attractiveness are only modestly correlated with self-perceived attractiveness. When real beauties do not see themselves as beautiful, their appearance may not be psychologically valuable.

Even self-perceived attractiveness may have its drawbacks. People don't just accept social rewards without question; they interpret the meaning of such positive encounters. Do those who think they are attractive trust praise from others? Or do they discount it? To examine this issue, Brenda Major and her colleagues (1984) studied the reactions of men and women who saw themselves as either very attractive physically or quite unattractive. Each subject wrote an essay and

Individuals who are judged by others as extremely attractive, but who do not see themselves this way, are unlikely to benefit psychologically from being beautiful.

"I remember when the first boy liked me, I couldn't believe it."
—Michelle Pfeiffer, movie star

"I grew up the ugliest, scariest, beastliest creature you ever saw."
—Karen Alexander, model

"That I'm found attractive is bizarre to me."
—Uma Thurman, movie star

was told it would be judged by another subject of the opposite sex, who was described as interested in potential dating relationships. Half of the subjects were informed that this person would be watching them through a one-way mirror while they wrote the essay; the other half were led to believe that their evaluator could not see them. Actually, there was no evaluator, and all subjects received an identical, highly positive evaluation of their work. Subjects were then asked why their essay had been so favorably reviewed.

As expected, subjects' willingness to attribute their positive evaluations to the quality of their work was affected by both their physical attractiveness and whether they thought they were observed (see Figure 5.5). Unattractive subjects felt better about the quality of their work after getting a glowing evaluation from someone who could see them. But attractive subjects felt less confident about their work when the favorable evaluation came from someone who could see them. For the physically attractive, being seen can mean disbelieving.

Figure 5.5 **When Being Seen Leads to Disbelief.** Subjects who believed they were physically unattractive were more likely to cite the quality of their work as the reason for receiving a positive evaluation when they thought they were seen by the evaluator. However, subjects who believed they were attractive were less likely to credit the quality of their work when they thought they were seen. (Data from Major et al., 1984.)

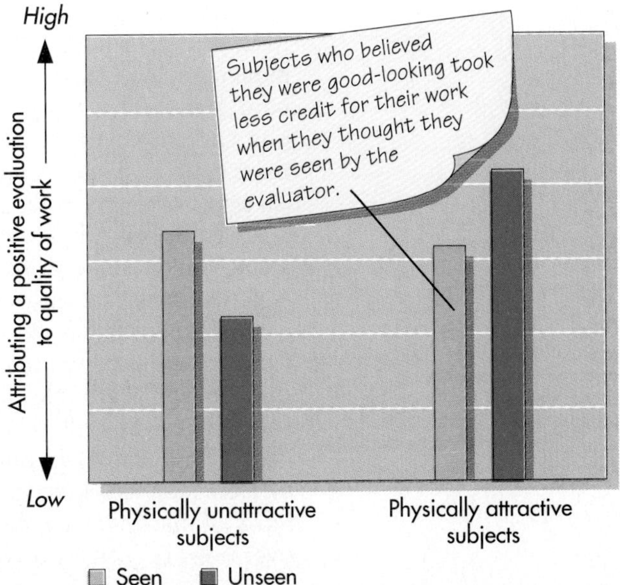

Physically attractive individuals may also fail to benefit from the social bias for beauty because of pressures they experience to maintain their appearance. In contemporary American society, such pressures are particularly strong in regard to the body. Although both facial and bodily appearance contribute to perceived attractiveness, an unattractive body appears to be a greater liability than an unattractive face (Alicke et al., 1986). Such a "body bias" can produce a healthy emphasis on nutrition and exercise. But it can sometimes lead to distinctly unhealthy consequences. For example, men may pop steroids in order to build up impressive muscles. Among women, the desire for a beautiful body often takes a different form.

Women are more likely than men to suffer from what Janet Polivy and her colleagues (1986) call the "modern mania for slenderness." This zeal for thinness is promoted by the mass media. Roseanne aside, popular female characters in TV shows are more likely than popular male characters to be exceedingly thin; women's magazines stress the need to maintain a slender body more than do men's magazines (Silverstein et al., 1986b).

How do women react to this barrage of extremely slender female images? When Eric Stice and Heather Shaw (1994) showed magazine photographs to female undergraduates, those who saw ultra-thin female models became more unhappy, experienced more intense feelings of shame and guilt, and expressed greater body dissatisfaction than those who viewed average-weight models. Compared to men, women are more critical and worry more about their appearance (Pliner et al., 1990), although this gender difference may be reversed between gay males and lesbians (Gettelman & Thompson, 1993).

In the extreme, an obsession with thinness can contribute to serious disorders such as *bulimia* (food binges that alternate with purging by means of vomiting, laxatives, excessive exercise, or fasting) and *anorexia nervosa* (self-imposed starvation, which can be fatal). Both bulimia and anorexia nervosa are far more common among women (Striegel-Moore et al., 1986). However, some men—such as athletes required to meet strict weight limits—also run a high risk for eating disorders (DePalma et al., 1993).

As noted earlier in this chapter, the thin standard of body attractiveness is a modern invention. When Brett Silverstein and his colleagues (1986a) examined the "curvaceousness" of models appearing in two popular women's magazines from 1901 through 1981, they found two periods during which the bodies of these models were particularly streamlined: the 1920s and the 1970s. Interestingly, both eras were also characterized by greater opportunities for women in education and employment. This correlation cannot prove causation, but it does raise some provocative questions. When liberation is in, must curves be out? Is a boyish appearance the price of admission into "a man's world"?

Overall, being beautiful appears to be a mixed blessing. There are some real gains, but there seem to be some serious losses as well. This tradeoff between benefits and costs raises the question of long-term effects. In the long run, are beautiful people happier? To answer this question, Ellen Berscheid and her colleagues (1972) compared the physical attractiveness of college students (based on their college yearbook pictures) with their adjustment when they reached middle age. There was little relationship between youthful appearance and later happiness. Those who had been especially good-looking during college were more likely to have married, but physical attractiveness in college failed to predict later reports of marital satisfaction and contentment with life. This study suggests that, over time, beauty is *not* destiny.

Liking "Likers" Versus Pursuing the Hard-to-Get

Research on physical attractiveness demonstrates that appearance can influence attraction. But behavior is also important, as indicated by the following imaginary exchange in a newspaper advice column:

> Dear Eddy,
>
> I've just read in my social psychology textbook that people like people who are good-looking. Did I really need a textbook to tell me that? I've known it all my life. The problem is that I'm not good-looking. So what can I do? How can I get people to like me? (Surgery is out of the question.)
>
> Yours truly,
>
> Desperately Seeking Social Survival

Suppose Eddy wrote back:

> Dear Desperate,
>
> You'll be glad to know that things aren't as bad as you think. There's an easy way to get people to like you—without surgery. Just like them. In fact, like everyone and everything. People like to be liked, and they like likers.
>
> Best wishes,
>
> Eddy

Eddy's advice to Desperate is certainly worth considering. As noted in our discussion of balance theory, people like those who like them. They also like those who express positive emotions (Sommers, 1984) and positive opinions (Lynn & Bates, 1985), as well as those who like themselves (Swann et al., 1992c). Likers are in demand. But Eddy's advice has to be taken with a few grains of social psychological salt.

First, likers aren't liked by everyone. Research on self-verification (see Chapter 2) shows that individuals who think badly of themselves often prefer someone who evaluates them unfavorably. Dating relationships, however, appear to be relatively immune from the need for self-verification. Regardless of their self-view, individuals reported more intimacy in their relationship when they were evaluated more positively by their partner (Swann et al., 1994). Among these dating couples, likers prevailed.

But likers may be penalized for their upbeat response to life. Others may take their praise for granted and find them less rewarding to be with than people whose compliments have to be earned (Aronson & Linder, 1965). And likers can be at a disadvantage when it comes to judgments of intellectual ability, being seen as nice but a bit dim (Amabile, 1983a).

Moreover, even though most people like likers, they may be inclined to pursue the hard-to-get, who are more selective in their social choices. It's a familiar script. What would novels and movies, TV shows and musicals do without it? Would the Phantom of the Opera have been so madly in love with Christine if she had loved him in return? In social psychology, however, the **hard-to-get effect** turned out to be harder to get than was originally anticipated (Walster et al., 1973).

hard-to-get effect The tendency to prefer people who are highly selective in their social choices over those who are more readily available.

The problem, say Rex Wright and Richard Contrada (1986), is that being hard to get *decreases* our attraction when the other person is fully committed to someone else or has absolutely no interest in us. These turndowns are usually turnoffs. But when such concerns are eliminated, a moderately selective individual is consistently preferred over a nonselective person. On the other hand, since extremely selective people can be perceived as conceited and arrogant, they are typically viewed as less attractive than the moderately selective. On the whole, it appears that Desperate should temper Eddy's advice with a little moderation.

THE FIT BETWEEN US

We have now examined how our own characteristics and those of others influence attraction. But what about the way we go together? In attraction, the fit between two people may have a greater effect than their specific, individual characteristics in isolation. As we will see in this section, some joint arrangements appear to work better than others.

Complementarity: Is It a Good Fit?

Proverbial wisdom says that "opposites attract," a phenomenon known as complementarity. For example, aren't people who need to dominate others attracted to those who need to be submissive? Apparently not. Complementarity in needs and personality does not seem to affect attraction (O'Leary & Smith, 1991). On this point, proverbial wisdom seems to have missed the boat.

Resource Exchange: Your Asset for Mine

Another way differences can fit together involves the resources that people possess. The traditional resource exchange in heterosexual relationships pairs the beauty of women with the wealth of men (Elder, 1969). Such an arrangement sounds out-of-date in a time of more equal opportunity, but is it? Research on the "dating marketplace" has tracked the rise and fall of various interpersonal commodities by asking individuals what they value in a potential mate and by examining their own advertisements, such as personals ads published in newspapers and magazines.

Judging from the results of most of these studies, men and women continue to make a deal (Feingold, 1990, 1992a; Sprecher et al., 1994; Willis & Carlson, 1993). Men value and seek physical attractiveness in a mate more than do women, although this gender difference is stronger when people estimate the importance of physical appearance than when they actually interact with someone. Women value and seek socioeconomic status in a mate more than do men. In the words of one investigator, the search for a heterosexual mate seems to feature "men as success objects and women as sex objects" (Davis, 1990).

These preferences are not restricted to the United States. David Buss (1989) found the same basic pattern among respondents from thirty-three different countries (including Australia, Brazil, China, Nigeria, and Poland, as well as North America and Western Europe). Men in most countries rated "good looks" in a mate as more important than did women; women rated "good financial prospect" and "ambition and industriousness" as more important than did men. In all the countries included in this study, men preferred to be older than their spouses, while women preferred to be younger.

sociobiology The application of the principles of evolutionary biology to the understanding of social behavior.

But having found a pattern, the more difficult—and interesting—task is to explain it. Why are these gender differences in mate preferences so widespread? From the perspective of **sociobiology,** which applies the principles of evolutionary biology to the understanding of social behavior, this particular heterosexual fit is a product of natural selection (Buss, 1994; Kenrick, 1994). Since reproductive success is crucial for the survival of a species, natural selection should have favored the mating behaviors that promote the conception, birth, and survival of offspring. If so, the genes underlying these behaviors could have become part of our evolutionary heritage.

Sociobiologists believe that optimal mating behaviors differ dramatically between men and women (Buss & Schmitt, 1993; Trivers, 1972). Men, they say, best ensure their reproductive success by inseminating many different women, selected for their reproductive capacity. From many seeds, at least one oak should grow. Men therefore rely on easily observable external cues such as (attractive) physical appearance that can serve as a rough guide to (young) age and (good) health. Women, however, grow only one oak at a time. Their parental investment in each child is necessarily greater, and their reproductive success is said to be best enhanced by careful selection of a mate who can provide the resources necessary for the well-being of mother and child. Thus, conclude the sociobiologists, what men and women want in a mate differs and these differences are determined, at least in part, by evolved psychological tendencies that are universal and genetically transmitted.

Not surprisingly, the sociobiological analysis of mate selection is controversial. How do you separate the effects of evolution from the effects of culture? In addressing this concern, researchers have begun to focus on more subtle aspects of the attraction process. Consider, for example, the following findings, all of which are consistent with the sociobiological account:

- Men are more attracted to women with a low waist-to-hip ratio (in which the waist is smaller than the hips) than to those with a high ratio (Singh, 1993). Among women, a low waist-to-hip ratio is reliably associated with reproductive capacity and good health.
- Women's judgments of physical attractiveness are more influenced than men's judgments by information (especially negative information) received from same-sex peers (Graziano et al., 1993). Thus, compared with men, women's evaluations of external cues of attractiveness are less certain and more flexible.

Married four times with each wife younger than the one before, Johnny Carson seems a perfect example of the sociobiological perspective on mate selection. There's just one problem. His current wife, pictured here, was in her mid-thirties when they married. If Carson's multiple attractions are based on evolutionary pressures to maximize reproductive success, why doesn't he prefer those even younger women who are at the peak of their reproductive capacity?

- Men have lower standards than do women for potential short-term mates, as would be expected for a sexual strategy seeking to maximize number of partners (Buss & Schmitt, 1993; Kenrick et al., 1993).
- Women's anticipation of a larger income of their own does *not* reduce their preference for men with good financial prospects (Wiederman & Allgeier, 1992).
- Men's preference for a younger mate becomes stronger as they age, serving to maintain their access to women who can bear children (Kenrick & Keefe, 1992).

Have the sociobiologists proved their case? Probably not. Just because certain behaviors are common does not necessarily imply that they are universal evolutionary products built into our genes. As R. C. Lewontin and his colleagues (1984) have noted, "This argument confuses the observation with the explanation. If its circularity is not evident, one might consider the claim that, since 99 percent of Finns are Lutherans, they must have a gene for it" (p. 255).

Furthermore, there is considerable debate about what David Buss (1994) called "an acid test for the evolutionary basis of sex differences in the desires for a mate" (p. 60). Does the sociobiological account, with its emphasis on reproductive advantage, adequately describe the mate-selection preferences of homosexuals, who cannot reproduce with the same-sex partners they prefer? Emphasizing that both homosexual and heterosexual men place more value on youth and attractiveness than do homosexual and heterosexual women, Buss believes that sociobiology passes the test.

However, most research on mate-selection preferences suggests that a lower grade might be in order. Although differences between men and women regardless of their sexual orientation are frequently obtained, differences between same-sex individuals who differ in sexual orientation also occur (Bailey et al., 1994; Deaux & Hanna, 1984; Gonzales & Meyers, 1993; Jankowiak et al., 1992). In short, preferences for a romantic partner are often influenced by *both* gender and sexual orientation, an outcome not predicted by sociobiology.

Equally problematic for the sociobiological perspective is the evidence for cultural influences on heterosexual mate-selection preferences. For example, men's desire for a younger mate was greater in the past than it is now and is currently greater in traditional societies than in more modern ones (Glenn, 1989; Kenrick & Keefe, 1992). Significant historical shifts in the age of the men that women marry have also been documented (Atkinson & Glass, 1985). The difficulty in untangling the effects of culture from those of evolution ensures that the application of evolutionary theory to human behavior will continue to provoke debate and controversy (*Psychological Inquiry*, 1995).

Similarity: Liking Those Just Like Us

One of the problems with proverbial wisdom is that it contradicts itself. The same folklore that brought us "opposites attract" tells us that "birds of a feather flock together." But this time, proverbial wisdom is on a better track. According to most research, similarity plays a powerful role in interpersonal attraction. Among women, their belief that a stranger of the opposite sex is similar to them consistently has a stronger effect on attraction than their view of the stranger's physical attractiveness (Feingold, 1991). Among men, the relative importance of similarity and physical attractiveness varies across different situations. This section considers several types of similarity and concludes with a discussion of possible reasons for its role in the attraction process.

"I like walks in the rain, old barns, and Edna St. Vincent Millay. Does that ring any bells?"

Similarity I: Demographics, Personality, and Mood It is a striking phenomenon: On a wide range of demographic characteristics (such as age, education, race, religion, and socioeconomic status), those who go together (friends, dates, spouses) resemble each other (Warren, 1966). These correlations, however, cannot prove a causal relationship between similarity and attraction. Though still correlational, a more compelling case would be made if we could measure people's demographic characteristics *before* they met, and then see if those who are similar like each other more than do those who are dissimilar. This is exactly what Theodore Newcomb (1961) did in one of the most elaborate studies ever conducted in social psychology. Setting up an entire college dormitory for his research, Newcomb found that those residents who were similar in pre-existing demographic characteristics (such as age, college major, and urban versus rural background) liked each other more than did those who were dissimilar.

But demographic similarity does not seem to have as strong an effect on attraction as it once did. In our increasingly multicultural society, people of different races, religions, and ethnicity are more likely to marry than ever before (Smolowe, 1993). The number of interracial marriages in the United States has more than tripled over the past two decades. Interfaith and interethnic marriages have also increased: 52 percent of Jews, 65 percent of Japanese Americans, and 70 percent of American Indians now marry individuals from other religious and ethnic backgrounds. The children of mixed couples are creating categories never dreamed of by the census takers: for example, Japanese-Filipino-German-Irish-Buddhist-Catholic American, or American Indian-Black-White-Hungarian-French-Catholic-Jewish American. What kinds of similarity will individuals of such diverse backgrounds find attractive?

Though weaker than its correlation with demographic factors, attraction is also associated with similarity in personality (Boyden et al., 1984; Caspi & Harbener, 1990). In addition, attraction and mood similarity have at least a passing acquaintance. In one study, for example, previously unacquainted undergraduates with similar moods (both feeling depressed; neither feeling depressed) were more satisfied with a half-hour interaction than were pairs whose moods differed (Locke & Horowitz, 1990). Perhaps people in similar moods, even bad ones, ex-

In the United States today, individuals from different racial, ethnic, and religious backgrounds are more likely to marry than ever before.

perience a rewarding sense of being *simpático*. However, such rewards may be short-lived. Similarity in depressed mood is *not* associated with greater satisfaction among marital couples (McLeod & Eckberg, 1993). If one or both spouses are depressed, marital quality is reduced.

Similarity II: Physical Attractiveness Have you ever noticed how people react to couples in which one partner is gorgeous and the other quite plain? Disconcerted by an apparent "mismatch," observers are startled and their comments are sometimes cruel. People expect couples to be similar in physical attractiveness. When these expectations are disconfirmed, judgments about the couple and the individuals involved become more unstable, susceptible to transient influences such as the perceiver's own mood (Forgas, 1993).

matching hypothesis The proposition that people are attracted to and form relationships with those who are similar to them in particular characteristics, such as physical attractiveness.

Social psychologists, too, expected that the **matching hypothesis**—the proposition that people would prefer similar others—would apply to physical attractiveness. But the trouble they ran into offers a good illustration of how results obtained in the laboratory may not always agree with those found in the real world. In the laboratory, some studies confirmed the hypothesis (Berscheid et al., 1971), but others didn't (Walster et al., 1966). Research outside the laboratory produced a much more consistent picture (Feingold, 1988). Repeatedly, there was evidence of a match in physical attractiveness among dating, engaged, cohabiting, and married couples.

In addition, similarity in level of physical attractiveness is associated with progress in the relationship. Clients of a professional dating service were more likely to begin and continue dating when they were similar in physical attractiveness (Folkes, 1982). Dating couples who were similarly attractive were more likely than dissimilar couples to grow closer and more in love over time (Murstein, 1972). Married couples, however, are an exception. Research has usually *not* found an association between similarity in physical attractiveness and marital satisfaction (White, 1980), though a *decline* in similarity may contribute to marital problems (Margolin & White, 1987).

A study of college roommates conducted by Linda Carli and her colleagues (1991) indicates that a physical mismatch may be especially disturbing to the more attractive individual. In this research, highly attractive individuals expressed concern about the disadvantages of being associated with someone less physically attractive ("My roommate interferes with my social life"). Less attractive individuals were envious but also well aware of the social advantages of rooming with a very attractive person ("My roommate helps me to meet other people"). Accordingly, only the more attractive individuals preferred similar to dissimilar roommates.

At this point, we need to step back and reconsider that sharp discrepancy between the results obtained in the laboratory and those found among actual couples. Why is similarity in physical attractiveness so weak in creating attraction in the laboratory and yet so strongly associated with real-world attachments? The exact reasons for this difference are not known, but two possible explanations are often mentioned (Aron, 1988).

First, since the real-world findings are correlational, various causal possibilities could be involved. Could being attracted to someone produce similarity in physical attractiveness? People who like each other may influence each other on such appearance-related actions as exercise, alcohol consumption, and choice of clothing and hairstyle. Or could the effect be more subtle? It has been suggested that people who spend time together grow to look alike because they unconsciously mimic each other's facial expressions, thereby cutting the same wrinkles in the same places (Zajonc et al., 1987). It is unlikely, however, that attraction or togetherness causes similarity. There does *not* appear to be a strong convergence over long-term relationships in appearance, health, personality, or lifestyle (Hinsz, 1989; Tambs & Moum, 1992).

But what about the lure of fantasy choices? Subjects in the lab may simply have taken advantage of the artificial setting and selected the most attractive alternative rather than opting for the more realistic choice they would make in their daily lives. This possibility highlights the need to be careful about generalizing from laboratory results to real-life behavior. Making the wrong decision is

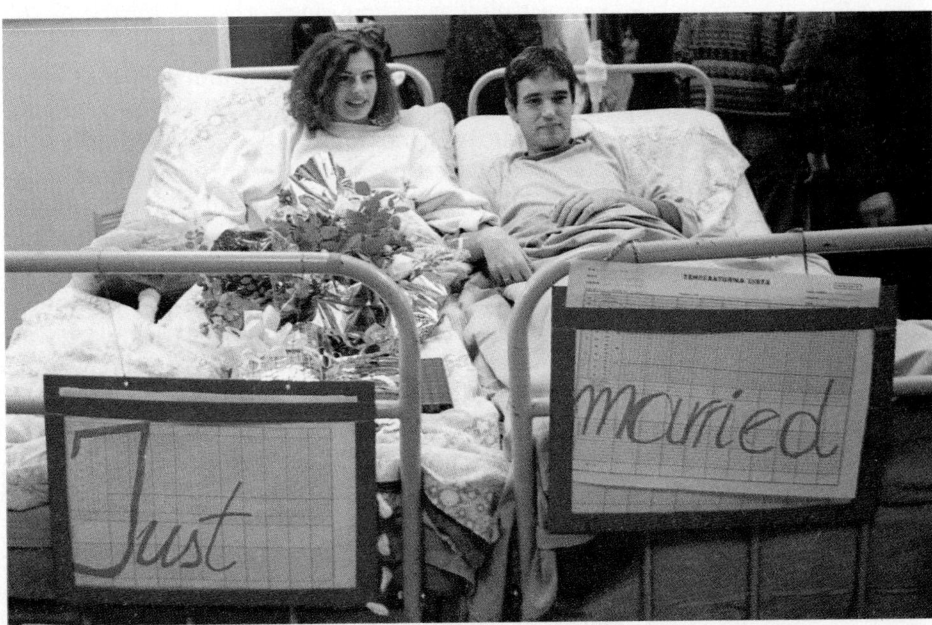

Having suffered similar tragedies, this Bosnian couple who both lost legs during a Serbian attack helped each other keep hope alive.

"I think who got to look like whom is less important than our still being together after twenty-five years."

much less costly when you're under a scientific microscope than when you're out there making real choices in the real world.

Similarity III: Attitudes The final type of similarity we will discuss is attitudinal, sharing similar opinions, beliefs, and values. There are two kinds of attitudinal similarity. *Perceived similarity* refers to the belief that someone shares your attitudes, although this may not be true. In *actual similarity,* there is an objective match between people's attitudes. Spouses, for instance, often have similar attitudes about appropriate behaviors for men and women (Huston & Geis, 1993).

The effects of these two kinds of attitudinal similarity differ in how they come about. Again, Newcomb's (1961) experimental dormitory provides a unique setting for understanding the process of attraction. When Newcomb traced attraction across the school year, he found that perceived similarity in attitudes was associated immediately and continuously with liking among the college students in his dorm. Since this association occurred before students knew each other's true attitudes, attraction was the active ingredient. When we are attracted to people, we believe they share our attitudes (Marks & Miller, 1982). In turn, perceived attitudinal similarity enhances liking even further.

But what about the effects of actual attitude similarity on attraction? Here, the time course is much slower, as people have to get to know each other in order to find out about each other's attitudes. In Newcomb's research, the strength of the association between actual attitudinal similarity and liking increased gradually throughout the school year. Actual attitudinal similarity can also be manipulated experimentally. Subjects presented with an attitude survey supposedly filled out by another subject (but in fact rigged by the experimenter) like people with similar attitudes more than those with dissimilar ones (Byrne, 1971).

The role of attitudinal similarity in attraction is sometimes underestimated (McCaul et al., 1995). For example, college students and state legislators believe that voters prefer politicians who consistently maintain their views, even if these positions differ from those of the voter. But when undergraduate subjects were exposed to scenarios in which consistency and similarity were varied, only similarity

Drawing by H. Martin; © 1994 The New Yorker Magazine, Inc.

"Excuse me, may I see your invitation?"

influenced subjects' evaluations. Politicians whose views agreed with subjects' attitudes were regarded more favorably than politicians with dissimilar views.

According to Milton Rosenbaum (1986), however, social psychologists have overestimated the role of attitudinal similarity in attraction. Instead of similarity creating attraction, he maintains that attitudinal *dis*similarity produces interpersonal repulsion—the desire to avoid someone. Similarity, he says, is expected and often not even noticed, but dissimilarity is surprising and grabs our attention. The belief that dissimilarity is more powerful than similarity is not restricted to a focus on attitudes. Indeed, David Lykken and Auke Tellegen (1993) argue that when it comes to mate selection, *all* forms of interpersonal similarity are irrelevant. Like Rosenbaum, they endorse what we might call the radical repulsion position: After the individual discards the 50 percent of the population who are least similar, an "inherently random" process takes over.

Donn Byrne and his colleagues contend that the anti-similarity forces have greatly underestimated the effects of attitudinal similarity (Byrne et al., 1986; Smeaton et al., 1989). In rebuttal, they propose a two-step model that puts similarity back into the picture (see Figure 5.6). First, people avoid associating with those who are dissimilar. On this step, everyone agrees. But then, according to the pro-similarity camp, people distinguish among those still remaining and are attracted to those who are most similar. On this step, the debate continues.

Figure 5.6 A Two-Stage Model of the Attraction Process. Proposed by Donn Byrne and his colleagues (1986), the two-stage model of attraction holds that we first avoid dissimilar others and then approach similar others.

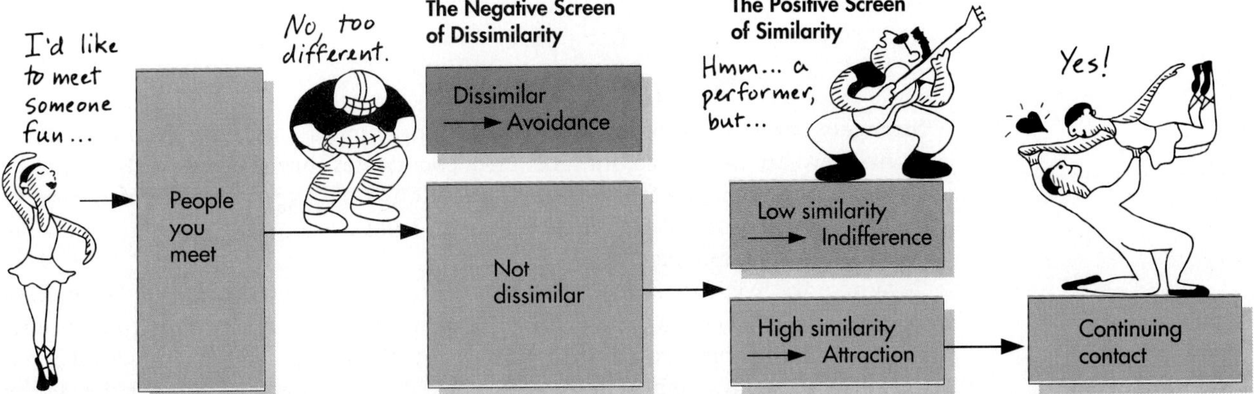

Why Is Similarity Attractive (or Dissimilarity Not)? Regardless of whether you favor similarity, repulsion, or both as influences on attraction, there's still a need for an explanation for how they work. The reason usually offered is that similarity increases self-confidence by reassuring us that others are just like us and agree with us, while dissimilarity decreases attraction because it poses a threat to self-evaluation and our understanding of the world around us (Byrne & Clore, 1970).

But not everyone would subscribe to this account. For example, perhaps we like similar others and dislike dissimilar others because of *anticipatory reciprocity* (Aronson & Worchel, 1966). Meeting people who agree with our beliefs and opinions, we anticipate that they will like us and, therefore, like them in (anticipated) return. In the same way, the anticipation of being disliked leads us to dislike dissimilar people. When people's expectations about whether the other person would like them were compared with perceived similarity of the other person's attitudes, expectations had the stronger effect on attraction (Condon & Crano, 1988).

Other analyses focus more specifically on the similarity side of the equation. Perhaps the pursuit of similarity actually reflects a search for someone who will live up to our ideals. Usually, our ideals are quite close to the way we see ourselves—only better. In an elaborate series of studies, meeting ideal standards had a greater effect on attraction than did similarity (Wetzel & Insko, 1982). Researchers have also suggested that the match between partners on physical attractiveness occurs automatically in the interpersonal "marketplace," as people seek the *very* best but have to settle for what's available (Kalick & Hamilton, 1986, 1988). The fact that people end up with partners of similar attractiveness would, then, be an accidental by-product of supply and demand rather than a deliberately sought outcome.

So how much fine tuning do we exercise over our social choices? Is the process inherently random after some point? Do we settle when we have to? These issues, along with the debate over whether similarity or dissimilarity should get the lion's share of the credit, need much more research before they can be resolved. What we know now raises many interesting questions for future study.

SITUATIONAL INFLUENCES

Our portrait of the attraction process is nearly complete. We have gathered up the individual pieces and carefully considered the way they fit together. But what do they fit into? Attraction doesn't occur in a void. It happens in a specific situation. In this section, we consider situational influences that help determine whether individuals experience a close encounter or a near miss.

Proximity: Being There

Strangely enough, we often overlook the single most important factor in attraction. There are, of course, long-distance encounters through personals ads, video dating services, and electronic communications such as e-mail, on-line networks, and bulletin boards (Ahuvia & Adelman, 1992). Still, most people meet when they're in the same place at the same time.

Where we live, for example, can determine what friends we make. When Leon Festinger and his colleagues studied friendship patterns in married-student housing, they found that people were more likely to become friends with residents of nearby apartments than with those who lived farther away (Festinger, 1951; Fes-

Physical proximity is usually required for attraction to develop. But today's communication technology has produced many alternative ways of being there. This American man met the Russian woman who became his wife through a video dating service.

tinger et al., 1950). Moreover, proximity appears to influence dating behavior: Students tend to date those living in the same type of housing (off-campus apartments, dormitories, or fraternity and sorority houses) in which they reside (Whitbeck & Hoyt, 1994).

The effects of proximity are not, however, always positive. You don't always love the one you're with. Neighbors can be the best of friends, or the worst of enemies. An investigation of a condominium complex in California found that while residents established most of their friendships with people who lived in the same housing cluster, most of the people they *dis*liked lived there as well (Ebbesen et al., 1976). Proximity provides the opportunity for social interactions, but it doesn't determine their quality.

personal space The physical distance people prefer to maintain between themselves and others.

Personal Space: Very Close Encounters Another spatial factor that can affect interpersonal attraction is **personal space,** the distance you prefer between yourself and others. There are many influences—individual, situational, and cultural—on these spatial comfort zones (Hall, 1966; Hayduk, 1983). But personal space typically contracts when we're attracted to and comfortable with someone—and expands when we're not.

Sometimes the personal space we prefer is an indicator of fears and prejudices. In one study, female undergraduates who expected to interview an AIDS patient arranged the chairs for the interview farther apart than did those expecting to interview a homosexual, a cancer patient, or another student (Mooney et al., 1992). Subjects' attitudes toward homosexuality and AIDS did not predict the social distance they preferred, and it's doubtful that those who expected to interview the AIDS patient were consciously aware of their actions. People with AIDS, however, are acutely aware that reluctance to come close to them has a number of damaging consequences, including social isolation and inadequate medical care.

Like other forms of territory, personal space can be intruded upon. When someone violates our personal space by coming closer than we expect or desire, our reactions to that individual intensify. People we like, we like more when they get close; people we don't like, we like even less up close (Storms & Thomas, 1977). Violations of personal space increase arousal, which magnifies the delights of a positive reaction or the discomfort of a negative one (Knowles, 1980).

Familiarity: Once Is Not Enough

As every real estate agent knows, location plays a crucial role in the attraction process. But so does *familiarity*, the actual frequency of contact. Folk wisdom takes a dim view of familiarity, which it says "breeds contempt." Not necessarily. In most cases, familiarity breeds liking. According to Robert Zajonc (1968), **mere exposure**—simple repeated contact with something or someone—is sufficient to increase attraction.

mere exposure The phenomenon whereby the more often people are exposed to a stimulus, the more positively they evaluate that stimulus.

To examine Zajonc's proposition, imagine yourself in the following situation. You're enrolled in a psychology class that meets in Doonesbury Hall. Three times a week, you trudge over to class, shaking the cobwebs out of your head and trying your best to be alert. The lecture hall holds 200 students. You come in the door and look down the tiered seats to the front where your instructor stands. During the semester, you're vaguely aware of another student who sits at the front of the class, but you never talk with her and you probably wouldn't recognize her if you saw her somewhere else. At the end of the term, you attend a special session where you are shown photographs of four women and asked some questions about them. Only then do you learn that you have participated in research on the mere exposure effect.

Now view these events from the perspective of the researchers, Richard Moreland and Scott Beach (1992). These investigators selected four women, all of whom looked like typical college students, to be confederates in this study. One of the confederates had a very easy job; she had her picture taken. The other three were also photographed and, in addition, attended the psychology class, each for a different number of classes: five, ten, or fifteen (out of the forty total for the term). Under these conditions, did the frequency of mere exposure affect attractiveness? Yes. In the questionnaires completed after photographs of all four women were viewed, ratings on various traits (such as popularity, attractiveness, honesty, and intelligence) and beliefs about liking the person, enjoying spending time with her, and wanting to work with her on a mutual project lined up like ducks in a row. The more classes a woman attended, the more attractive she was perceived to be.

Overall, the lessons of this research are clear. If you want to be liked, hang around. But are some kinds of hanging better than others? It seems so. Consider this surprising finding: Frequency of exposure has a stronger effect on liking when the stimulus is *not* recognizable (Bornstein & D'Agostino, 1992). Subjects shown stimuli for 5 milliseconds expressed greater liking for those they had seen more frequently, even though they could not distinguish previously seen stimuli from those they had never seen before. Exposure frequency also increased liking for stimuli displayed for 500 milliseconds (ample time for recognition), but this effect was weaker.

Does this mean that *you* must be unrecognizable in order to maximize your chances of benefiting from the mere exposure effect? We're happy to report that the answer is no. The key factor is probably not recognition of the stimulus but, rather, awareness of the relationship between exposure and liking (Bargh, 1992). If the stimulus cannot be recognized, such awareness cannot occur. But if the stimulus can be recognized, the mere exposure effect is apt to be stronger when it doesn't occur to perceivers that they like what they know. Which brings us back to the classroom experiment described earlier. Students in this class had only a vague awareness that some of the female confederates were more familiar than others. They were concentrating on other things (on the lecture, one hopes), and the confederates didn't draw attention to themselves. Thus, for attraction to flourish, *unobtrusive* mere exposure seems the best approach. Be there, always be there, but stay cool.

Powerful as it is, mere exposure isn't foolproof. Boredom limits its effects (Bornstein, 1989)—and so does hostility. If you strongly dislike someone or something to begin with, repeated exposure can increase your unfavorable opinions (Perlman & Oskamp, 1971). For example, research on student exchange programs revealed that for many students, the stresses and strains of adjusting to a foreign culture create negative attitudes toward the host country (Stroebe et al., 1988). The longer the students who participated in this study stayed in a foreign country, the more negative their attitudes became. Perhaps an even longer period of adjustment would create a more favorable view of the host country. Nevertheless, it does appear that, despite everyone's good intentions, familiarity can sometimes breed contempt.

Affiliation, Attributions, and Overcoming Obstacles

Earlier in this chapter, we described various characteristics and behaviors of individuals that affect attraction. Among them were the need for affiliation, the role of attributions, and the increase in attraction toward someone who is selectively hard to get. In this section, we examine the situational parallels of each of these individual factors.

Stressful Situations: Is Togetherness Useful? In his systematic study of the origins of situationally induced affiliation (see Chapter 2), Stanley Schachter (1959) compared individuals anticipating a physically painful event with people anticipating a more neutral experience. He found that those expecting to receive electric shocks were more likely to want to wait with others (specifically, others in the same predicament). In contrast, when Irving Sarnoff and Philip Zimbardo (1961) placed their subjects in the awkward predicament of expecting to engage in the embarrassing behavior of sucking on large nipples and pacifiers, the desire to wait with others fell off drastically. It's puzzling. Why do those in fearful misery love company, while those in embarrassed misery seek solitude?

According to Yacov Rofé (1984), there is a simple answer: utility. Rofé proposes that stress will increase the desire to affiliate only when being with other people is perceived to be useful in reducing the negative impact of the stressful situation. And the utility of affiliation depends, in part, on the type of stress. Schachter's subjects had good reason to believe that affiliation would be useful. They would have the opportunity to compare their emotional reactions with those of others to help judge whether they really needed to be fearful. For subjects in the study by Sarnoff and Zimbardo, however, affiliation had little to offer. Embarrassment is a form of social anxiety, and being with others is more likely to increase this type of stress than to reduce it.

Personal characteristics also influence affiliation in stressful circumstances. Some individuals—females and those who are first-born in their family—are more likely than others to affiliate. Perhaps their life experiences (such as social approval for dependent behavior and strong doses of parental attention) have led them to believe that other people can help them adjust to stress. Furthermore, the

Table 5.1 Affiliation Under Stress

Circumstances That Affect Utility	Factors That Increase Affiliation Under Stress	Factors That Decrease Affiliation Under Stress
Type of Stress	• Manageable fear	• Unmanageable fear • Embarrassment
Characteristics of the Person Experiencing the Stress	• First-born • Female	• Later-born • Male
Characteristics of the Potential Affiliate	• Similar to the person experiencing stress • Able to handle the stressful situation	• Dissimilar to the person experiencing stress • Unable to handle the stressful situation

According to Rofé (1984), stress increases the desire to affiliate with others only when the person under stress believes that the presence of others will reduce that stress. The perception of others' utility for stress reduction is influenced by the three major circumstances described here.

characteristics of others contribute to whether we draw closer to them in a stressful situation. For example, we ask more questions of and exchange more glances with those who can help us cope than with those who can't offer any assistance (Kulik et al., 1994). Table 5.1 summarizes the circumstances in which affiliation under stress is most and least likely to occur.

attribute ambiguity Circumstances in which the causes of behavior are unclear.

Attribute Ambiguity: Undercover Operations Movies and TV shows often feature the sometimes comic anxiety that erupts when calling a potential date for the first time. The nervous caller hopes that attraction is mutual but fears rejection. This risky business is much less threatening under the cover of **attribute ambiguity,** circumstances in which the exact causes of a person's behavior are hard to pinpoint (Snyder & Wicklund, 1981).

A study by William Bernstein and his colleagues (1983) investigated the effects of attribute ambiguity on people's willingness to approach an attractive member of the opposite sex. Each of the male college students who participated in this research walked into an experimental room arranged as illustrated in Figure 5.7. Directly in front of the door was a partition dividing the far end of the room into two cubicles. Each cubicle was furnished with two chairs and a table with a video monitor on it. An attractive young woman was seated in one of the cubicles watching the monitor.

With the scene set, the plot could unfold. Each subject was told that the woman was another research subject (she was actually a confederate) and that she had been given the same information he was about to receive. Half of the subjects were then informed that a different movie would play on each monitor. The other half were told that because of a broken VCR the same movie had to be played on both monitors. At this point, the subject was allowed to choose where he wanted to sit.

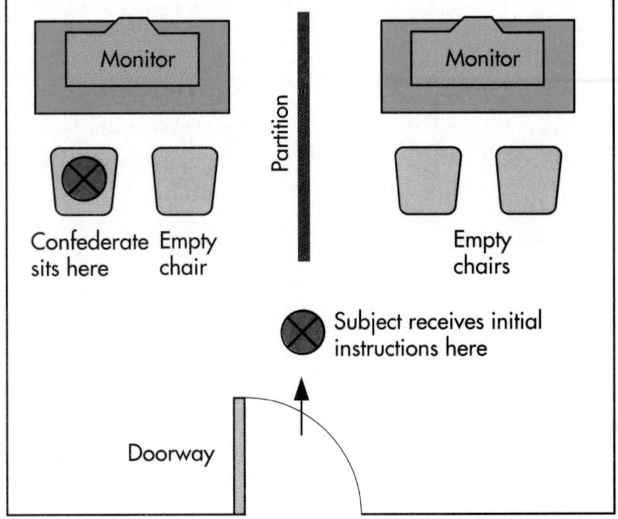

Figure 5.7 Watching a Film With or Without You. When male subjects entered the room in a study on attribute ambiguity, they encountered two cubicles, each containing a TV monitor. In one, there was also an attractive female confederate. Some subjects were told that the two monitors would play different movies; others were told that the same film would play on both monitors. Only in the different-movie condition could subjects use their desire to see a particular film as a good excuse to sit next to the attractive woman.

It's easy to imagine the subjects' thoughts. Most of those in the same-movie condition probably wanted to enjoy the company of an attractive woman while watching the film, but they faced a difficult dilemma. Since *he* knows that *she* knows that both monitors will show exactly the same material, what excuse does he have? Subjects in the different-movie condition had a much easier time of it. They could always say (and perhaps even believe) that they just happened to like the movie playing on her monitor better than the other one. With excuse in hand, the guys were free to move in. And they did. Among subjects in the different-movie condition, a whopping 75 percent joined the young woman in her cubicle, compared with a meager 25 percent in the same-movie condition. In an ambiguous situation, there's more room to maneuver.

psychological reactance The theory that people react against threats to specific behavioral freedoms by perceiving a threatened freedom as more attractive and trying to re-establish it.

Psychological Reactance: Barriers to Romance As we saw earlier, opposites don't attract. But what about opposition to one's choices or desires? The theory of **psychological reactance** focuses on the role of opposition as a motivational force. According to this theory, individuals possess a set of specific behavioral freedoms—actions, thoughts, and feelings in which they feel free to engage (Brehm & Brehm, 1981). When a freedom is threatened, the person reacts by perceiving that behavior as more attractive and becoming motivated to re-establish it.

Sometimes reactance reduces interpersonal attraction (Wright et al., 1992). For example, have you ever played the matchmaker by insisting that your unattached, single friends just *have* to get together? Be forewarned: This tactic can backfire. Motivated to preserve the freedom to make their own romantic choices, your friends may become *less* attracted to each other than they would have been without your encouragement.

Reactance can also increase interpersonal attraction. The hard-to-get effect described earlier in this chapter could be produced by the potential dating partner's selectivity acting as a threat to the freedom to date that person. Or consider what happens when people are about to lose their chance to get a date for the evening. Is Mickey Gilley's oldie-but-goldie still true? Do "the girls all get prettier at closing time"? In some bars in Texas (Pennebaker et al., 1979) and the Midwest (Gladue & Delaney, 1990) they did—and so did the boys. Members of the opposite sex were seen as more physically attractive as the night wore on. Or what about Romeo and Juliet? In one study, unmarried couples who reported increasing parental interference in their relationship said their love was getting stronger (Driscoll et al., 1972). From the perspective of reactance theory, barriers just make us want to jump higher.

We should, however, be careful not to overestimate the influence of reactance in interpersonal attraction. As indicated, the hard-to-get effect has proved surprisingly elusive. Moreover, the lack of a strong correlation between attractiveness ratings and bar patrons' stated desire to meet the opposite sex raises doubts about the reactance theory explanation of the closing-time effect (Gladue & Delaney, 1990). And, finally, the Romeo-and-Juliet effect is an exception to the general rule. Usually, the more *support* we have from friends and family, the more loving, satisfied, and committed our romantic attachments will be (Sprecher & Felmlee, 1992). In the next chapter, we take a look at some other factors that influence the quality of intimate relationships.

REVIEW

THE ROLE OF REWARDS

- Attraction is based on rewarding experiences with an individual.
- Rewarding interpersonal experiences produce a positive emotional response, which increases our desire to be with that person.
- An individual can be rewarding directly or by association.
- Balanced relationships, such as liking those who like us, are also rewarding.

CHARACTERISTICS OF THE INDIVIDUAL

Self-Esteem: Confidence Versus Desire

- Individuals high in self-esteem have a relatively weak desire for social rewards, but feel self-assured in pursuing them.
- Those low in self-esteem have a relatively strong desire for social rewards, but lack the confidence necessary for pursuit.
- Because confidence and desire tend to cancel each other out, self-esteem ends up having little overall effect on attraction.

Social Motives: Affiliation and Intimacy

- The need for affiliation produces active, controlling social behavior with an emphasis on the quantity of social contacts.
- The need for intimacy produces more passive, less controlling social behavior with an emphasis on the quality of social interactions.

Social Difficulties: Anxiety and Loneliness

- Social anxiety and loneliness are both associated with unrewarding social interactions.
- Misattribution, switching the explanation for arousal from the true source to a different one, can reduce anxiety and improve performance.
- Taking credit for social successes reduces anxiety and encourages more active social behavior.
- Loneliness lasts longer when people attribute it to their own personal characteristics.

Expectations and Reality

- By means of a self-fulfilling prophecy, how attractive we expect others to be can determine how attractive they actually become.

CHARACTERISTICS OF OTHERS

Physical Attractiveness

- People respond more favorably to physically attractive individuals.
- Possible reasons for this bias for beauty include aesthetic appeal, the what-is-beautiful-is-good stereotype, more skillful social behavior by physically attractive individuals, and the desire to increase one's own perceived attractiveness through association with attractive others.
- Greater psychological well-being is experienced by people who judge themselves to be attractive, but not by those viewed as attractive by others.
- People who believe themselves to be attractive often discount the praise they receive for nonsocial endeavors.
- The ultra-thin ideal promoted by the media increases body dissatisfaction among women.
- In the long run, physical attractiveness does not predict happiness.

Liking "Likers" Versus Pursuing the Hard-to-Get

- People are usually attracted to likers.
- But indiscriminate likers can be taken for granted and seen as unintelligent.
- Those who are moderately hard-to-get are usually preferred over those who are nonselective or extremely selective.

THE FIT BETWEEN US

Complementarity: Is It a Good Fit?

- Complementarity in needs or personality does *not* affect attraction.

Resource Exchange: Your Asset for Mine

- Just as men regard youth and physical attractiveness as particularly important in an opposite-sex mate, so do women regard economic success.
- Sociobiology views these differential preferences as the genetically based products of natural selection, but cultural influences are also apparent.
- Mate-selection preferences are often influenced by both gender and sexual orientation.

Similarity: Liking Those Just Like Us

- Five types of similarity are associated with greater attraction: demographic, personality, mood, physical attractiveness, and attitudinal.
- It has been argued that instead of similarity producing attraction, *dis*similarity produces repulsion.
- Alternatively, people may react first to dissimilarity and later to similarity.
- Various reasons have been proposed to explain why similarity increases (or dissimilarity decreases) attractiveness.

SITUATIONAL INFLUENCES

Proximity: Being There

- Proximity sets the stage for social interactions but does not determine their quality.
- Personal space preferences can be a subtle indicator of fears and prejudices.
- Violations of our personal space intensify our reactions to others.

Familiarity: Once Is Not Enough

- More frequent contact with someone usually produces greater attraction, especially if the perceiver is not aware of this connection between exposure and liking.
- But repeated contact with someone who is strongly disliked can increase hostility.

Affiliation, Attributions, and Overcoming Obstacles

- The desire to affiliate with others will increase in stressful situations when being with others is perceived to be useful in reducing stress.
- An ambiguous situation allows people to reduce the personal risk of rejection in approaching those to whom they are attracted.
- Situational barriers making it harder to be with someone can sometimes increase attraction.

KEY TERMS

balance theory, p. 165
reciprocity, p. 165
social anxiety, p. 168
misattribution, p. 169
loneliness, p. 170
what-is-beautiful-is-good stereotype, p. 176
hard-to-get effect, p. 181
sociobiology, p. 183
matching hypothesis, p. 186
personal space, p. 191
mere exposure, p. 192
attribute ambiguity, p. 194
psychological reactance, p. 195

Rollerblade
Rollerblade

Chapter

6 Intimate Relationships

PREVIEW

This chapter begins by *defining intimate relationships.* Two ways to get *from attraction to love* are considered in detail: *building a relationship* through the gradual accumulation of rewards versus experiencing different *types of relationships.* Next, *relationship issues* of sexuality, jealousy, and social power are discussed, followed by an analysis of *conflict in relationships.* The concluding section describes some important factors involved in *coping after a relationship ends.*

OUTLINE

The British royal family is known for many things, but—surely to their dismay—their intimate relationships have always captured the public's attention. Henry VIII still holds the record among reigning monarchs: six marriages, at considerable cost to most of the women involved ("divorced, beheaded, died; divorced, beheaded, survived"). His daughter, Elizabeth I, drove her advisors to distraction by her on-again, off-again attitude toward the politically advantageous marriages they were promoting—but to no avail: Elizabeth, the Virgin Queen, stayed single. Centuries later, Edward VIII gave up the throne to marry the woman he loved. And in our own time, the storybook wedding of Prince Charles and Princess Diana deteriorated into a tabloid frenzy of well-publicized marital discord, ending in their formal separation.

The topsy-turvy world of attachment and dissolution is not limited to royalty. When researchers asked 300 American college students to weigh the importance of having a satisfying and enduring relationship with a romantic partner against the importance of other life goals (such as getting a good education, having a successful career, and making a contribution to a better society), 73 percent said they would sacrifice a majority of their other life goals rather than give up a satisfying relationship (Hammersla & Frease-McMahan, 1990). And yet these students live in a society in which 50 to 60 percent of first marriages taking place today are expected to end in divorce (Spanier, 1992).

The discrepancy between the endurance most people want and the disruption many will have is particularly dramatic in the United States, which has the dubious distinction of owning the world's highest divorce rate (Phillips, 1988). In Japan, for example, the rate is much lower (Cornell, 1989). And even in the United States, there is considerable variation among the states (see Figure 6.1). Nevertheless, divorce is increasingly a major player on the global stage and we can expect concerns about relationships to intensify worldwide during the twenty-first century.

There is, of course, no magic formula for creating a satisfying relationship. But bringing to bear your own beliefs, values, and personal experiences on the information presented in this chapter can be a useful endeavor. In order to strengthen our relationships, we must first improve our understanding.

The story of a royal marriage from beginning to end.

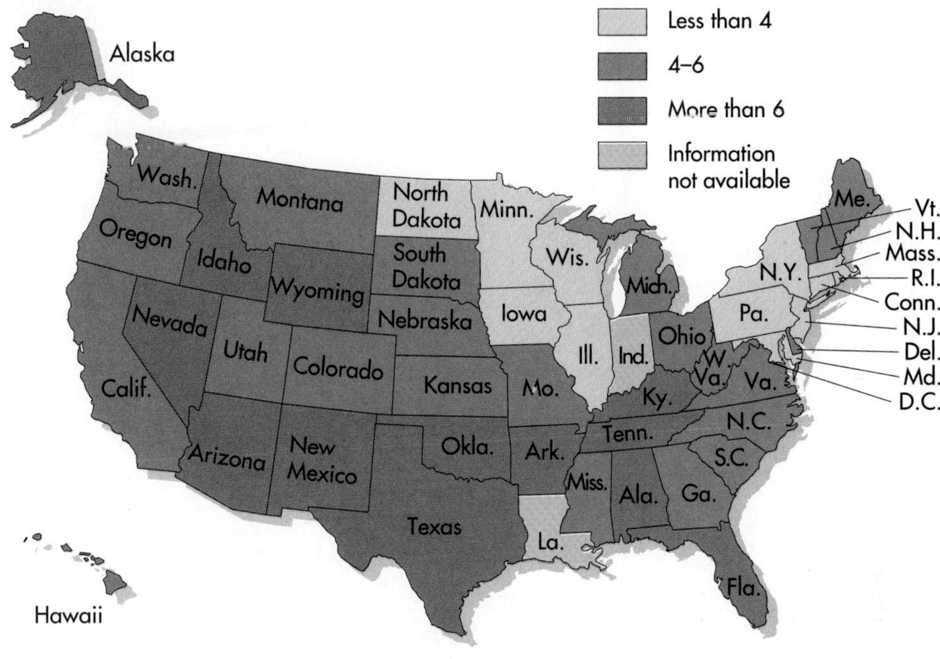

Figure 6.1 Divorce American Style. The United States has the world's highest divorce rate. But, as you can see, the rate (per 1,000 population) varies among the states. (National Center for Health Statistics, 1993.)

DEFINING INTIMATE RELATIONSHIPS

intimate relationships Close relationships between two adults involving at least one of the following: emotional attachment, fulfillment of psychological needs, and interdependence.

Although there are many significant relationships in people's lives, social psychology has concentrated on adult relationships between friends, dating partners, lovers, and spouses (Berscheid, 1994; Brehm, 1992; Hatfield & Rapson, 1993; Hendrick & Hendrick, 1992a). These **intimate relationships** often involve three basic components:

- Emotional attachment, feelings of affection and love
- Fulfillment of psychological needs, such as sharing feelings and gaining reassurance (Weiss, 1969)
- Interdependence between the individuals, each of whom has a meaningful and enduring influence on the other (Berscheid & Peplau, 1983)

But not all intimate relationships include all three of these components. A summer's romance, for example, is emotionally intense, but in the fall people resume their independent lives. An "empty shell" marriage revolves around the spouses' coordinated daily activities, but emotional attachment is weak and psychological needs go unmet. Whatever the combination of love, need fulfillment, and interdependence, intimate relationships also vary in other characteristics. Some are sexual; some are not. Sexual orientation differs: heterosexual or homosexual. Some partners make a strong commitment to a long-lasting relationship; others merely drop by for a brief stay. Feelings about the relationship run the gamut from joyful to painful, from loving to hateful—with emotional intensity ranging all the way from mild to megawatt.

Intimate relationships come in all shapes and sizes. It is still possible, however, to sort out some of the basic factors that affect their development, quality, and endurance. We start by tracing the road that runs from attraction to love.

Drawing by Maslin; © 1994 The New Yorker Magazine.

FROM ATTRACTION TO LOVE

Psychologically speaking, there's quite a distance from the attractive initial encounters described in Chapter 5 to the intimate relationships discussed here. How do we get from one to the other? Three basic forms of locomotion have received the most attention: (1) in stages, (2) step by step, and (3) by leaps and bounds.

stage theories Theories reflecting the view that relationships develop through a specific set of stages in a specific order.

Stage theories of relationship development propose that relationships go through a specific set of stages in a specific order. For example, the *stimulus-value-role (SVR) theory* says there are three: the stimulus stage in which attraction is based on external attributes such as physical appearance, the value stage in which attachment is based on similarity of values and beliefs, and the role stage in which commitment is based on successful performance of relationship roles such as husband and wife (Murstein, 1986, 1987). All three factors are supposed to have some influence throughout a relationship, but each one is said to be first and foremost during only one stage (see Figure 6.2).

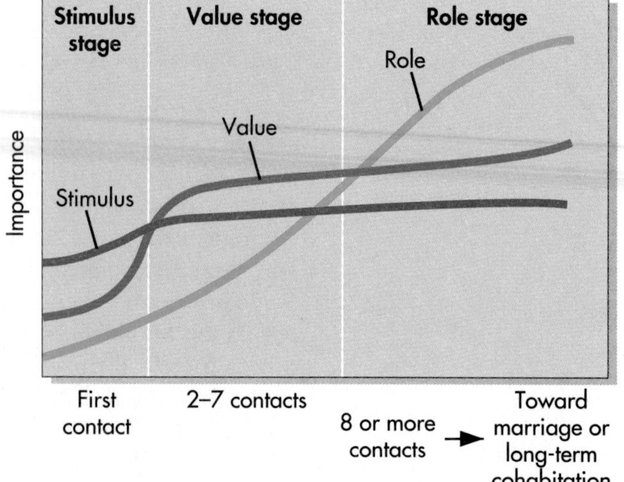

Figure 6.2 **Stages of Courtship.** According to Murstein's stimulus-value-role theory, each stage in a relationship is characterized by one dominant factor. The theory maintains that these stages occur in a fixed sequence: stimulus first, then value, and then role. (Murstein, 1987.)

In evaluating a stage theory, the critical issue is *sequence*. Does the value stage always precede the role stage? Or might a couple work out roles before exploring whether their values are compatible? Most investigators believe that it is highly unlikely that intimate relationships evolve through a fixed sequence of stages (Leigh et al., 1987; Stephen, 1987). The difficulty in coming up with a standard sequence is illustrated by a series of studies on newlywed couples (Surra & Huston, 1987). Subjects' retrospective reports of how their relationship developed indicated that progress toward marriage took a number of different paths. Significant shifts in relationship development did not occur in the same order for every couple, nor did every couple go through the same shifts. One size did not fit all.

If intimate relationships don't all follow the same script, what does account for how they change? Every relationship has some sort of developmental history: the ups, the downs, the stalls, the accelerations. What pushes a relationship up, pulls it down, or keeps it steady? For an answer, we could go back to the attraction hat and pull out the same rabbit: rewards. Love, we might say, is just like attraction, only more so. Both depend on experiencing positive emotions in the presence of another person, but love requires more rewarding experiences than does attraction. Step by step, as rewards pile up, love develops. Or, step by step, as rewards diminish, love erodes. Quantity counts.

But some would disagree. It's easy to see the objection. Just think about your own relationships. Are your feelings toward someone you love simply a more intense version of your feelings toward someone you like? Is the love of a close friend the same as the love of a romantic partner? If not, you can appreciate the argument that there are qualitative differences between various kinds of affection. According to this perspective, there's a difference in kind rather than simply a difference in degree: A great leap is required to take us from liking to loving, and love itself comes in different forms.

Both of these versions of how we get from attraction to love have something to offer (Sternberg, 1987). Progress on the road from attraction to love depends on the quantity of fuel in the tank *and* on the kind of engine providing the power. The next section takes a closer look at the quantitative, cost-accounting approach to building a relationship. Differences between various types of relationships are considered later in the chapter.

BUILDING A RELATIONSHIP

Social exchange is the most popular framework for analyzing the development of a relationship. After describing the basic principles of social exchange, we examine a specific model called equity theory. Then we focus on self-disclosure, a particularly intimate social exchange.

Social Exchange: The Intimate Marketplace

social exchange A perspective that views people as motivated to maximize benefits and minimize costs in their relationships with others.

Social exchange theory is an economic model of human behavior. This perspective assumes that just as a person's behavior in the marketplace is motivated by the desire to maximize profits and minimize losses, these same motives determine behavior in social relationships (Homans, 1961; Thibaut & Kelley, 1959). Social exchange provides a general perspective for analyzing all kinds of relationships—with a boss or a teacher as well as with a friend or a lover.

The fundamental premise of social exchange theory is quite simple: Relationships that provide more rewards and fewer costs will be more satisfying and endure longer. Between intimates, rewards include companionship, love, consolation in times of distress, and sexual gratification if the relationship is a sexual one. But there are also costs: working to maintain the relationship, making compromises to keep the peace, suffering in times of conflict, and giving up other opportunities in order to continue the present arrangement.

The development of an intimate relationship is clearly associated with the overall level of rewards. Dating couples who initially have many rewarding interactions are less likely to break up than those who start out with relatively few rewards (Lloyd et al., 1984). Dating couples who experience greater increases in rewards as their relationship continues are more likely to stay together than are those who experience only small increases or suffer declines (Berg & McQuinn, 1986).

But what about costs? Early in a relationship—during the "honeymoon" period—costs may be relatively unimportant (Hays, 1985). Honeymoons can't last forever, though. In her study of dating couples, Caryl Rusbult (1983) found that costs first entered into the equation at about three months. Before that, costs were not related to satisfaction; after that, reports of increasing costs were accompanied by diminished satisfaction with the relationship. In established relationships, both rewards and costs weigh in. Married couples (Margolin & Wampold, 1981) and cohabiting gay and lesbian couples (Kurdek, 1991a) who perceive rewards to be high and costs low are more satisfied with their relationships.

comparison level (CL) The average, general outcome an individual expects in a relationship.

Rewards and costs do not occur in a psychological vacuum. People bring to their relationships certain expectations about the balance sheet to which they are entitled. John Thibaut and Harold Kelley (1959) coined the term **comparison level (CL)** to refer to this average, expected outcome in relationships. A person with a high CL expects to have rewarding relationships; someone with a low CL expects to have unrewarding relationships. Relationships that meet or exceed an individual's expectations are more satisfying than those that fall below expectations (Michaels et al., 1984). Even a bad relationship can look pretty good to someone who has a low CL.

comparison level for alternatives (CLalt) The average, general outcome an individual expects from alternative relationships or lifestyles.

Another kind of expectation, about alternatives to the relationship, creates a context for commitment—the intention to continue the present relationship. Here, too, Thibaut and Kelley (1959) coined a term—**comparison level for alternatives (CLalt).** This refers to people's expectations about what they would receive in an alternative relationship or lifestyle. If the rewards available in such alternatives are believed to be high, a person will be less committed to staying in the present relationship (Drigotas & Rusbult, 1992). But when people perceive few acceptable alternatives (a low CLalt), they tend to remain—even in an unsatisfying relationship that fails to meet their general expectations (CL). Not only do alternatives influence commitment; commitment also influences alternatives. Committed individuals are less interested in alternative partners, viewing them as relatively unattractive (Johnson & Rusbult, 1989; Simpson et al., 1990).

investment Resources put into a relationship that cannot be retrieved if that relationship ends.

The final element in the basic model of social exchange is investment. An **investment** is something an individual puts into a relationship that he or she cannot recover if that relationship ends (Kelley, 1983). If you don't like the way a relationship is working out, you can pack your clothes, grab your stereo, and take your cat. But what about the time and effort you put into trying to make it last, and those romantic alternatives and career opportunities you gave up? Investments increase commitment (Rusbult & Buunk, 1993). Because of those things we can't take with us, we're more likely to stay.

The social exchange framework of rewards, costs, CL, CLalt, and investments is diagrammed in Figure 6.3. The strength of its components varies depending on the circumstances, but the overall model is an effective predictor of commitment to a relationship. In turn, commitment is the best predictor of the endurance of premarital relationships (Cate & Lloyd, 1992), is greater for engaged or married partners than for those who are dating (Stanley & Markman, 1992), and is associated with returning to an abusive relationship (Rusbult & Martz, 1995).

equity theory The theory that people are most satisfied with a relationship when the ratio between benefits and contributions is similar for both partners.

Equity: A Balanced Arrangement **Equity theory** is a specific version of how social exchange operates in interpersonal interactions (Messick & Cook, 1983; Walster et al., 1978a). According to this theory, people are most satisfied with a relationship when the ratio between what they get out of a relationship (benefits) and what they put into the relationship (contributions) is similar for both partners. Thus, the basic equity formula is

$$\frac{\text{Your Benefits}}{\text{Your Contributions}} = \frac{\text{Your Partner's Benefits}}{\text{Your Partner's Contributions}}$$

Equity is different from equality. From the viewpoint of equity theory, it's the balance that counts. If one partner obtains more benefits from the relationship

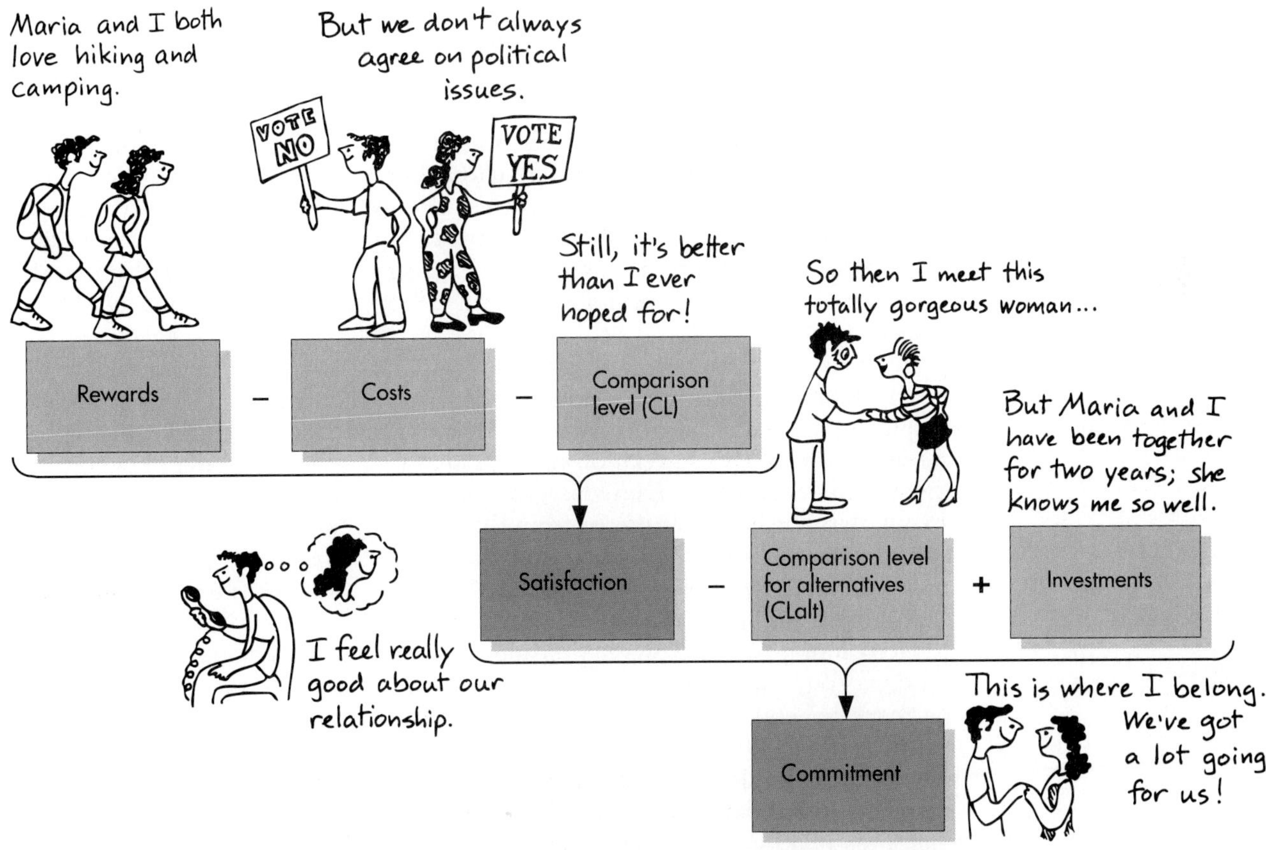

Figure 6.3 Relational Building Blocks. The building blocks of social exchange are rewards, costs, comparison level, comparison level for alternatives, and investments. These factors are strongly associated with the satisfaction and commitment partners experience in their relationship.

The overbenefited can be quite satisfied with the arrangement.

"We had the usual exchange of gifts—she gave me this diamond collar, and I ate all my dinner."

but also makes a greater contribution, the relationship is still equitable. In an *in*equitable relationship, the balance is disturbed. One of the partners (called the *overbenefited*) receives more benefits than are deserved on the basis of contributions made, while the other partner (called the *underbenefited*) receives fewer benefits than deserved.

Both overbenefit and underbenefit are often unhappy states. Individuals who are underbenefited feel angry and resentful because they are giving more than their partner for the benefits they receive. The overbenefited feel guilty and uncomfortable because they are benefiting unfairly. Both kinds of inequity are associated with negative emotions among college-age dating couples (Walster et al., 1978b), married couples (Schafer & Keith, 1980), and the friendships of elderly widows (Rook, 1987).

In terms of satisfaction with a relationship, however, being underbenefited is usually more unpleasant than being overbenefited (Hatfield et al., 1982). For example, a national survey of married women with at least one child found that those who thought their relationship was unfair perceived a greater likelihood of divorce than did those who thought the relationship was fair (Katzev et al., 1994). But women who suffered from the inequity ("unfair to me") perceived divorce as more likely than those who benefited from the inequity ("unfair to him"). Typically, people prefer to receive too much rather than too little—even if they feel bad about it.

Determining whether a relationship is equitable is a complicated cognitive process. You have to tally up your own benefits and contributions, compute your partner's benefits and contributions, and compare the two. Rodney Cate and Sally Lloyd (1988) have their doubts about whether people go to all this trouble when much simpler calculations might suffice. In a series of studies, these researchers found that the absolute level of rewarding outcomes was a better predictor of relationship satisfaction and endurance than was either equality of rewards or equity (Cate et al., 1988). The more good things people said they received from the relationship, the better they felt about it.

Differences in the context of a relationship may be one reason why equity theory has an uneven track record in predicting relationship satisfaction. Consider, for example, variations in the family life cycle. Among Australian subjects, both equity and a high level of rewards were associated with greater marital satisfaction for married individuals who were childless or had all of their children at home (Feeney et al., 1994). However, only the level of rewards predicted marital satisfaction for parents whose children had begun to leave home, while only equity was associated with marital satisfaction for parents whose children had all left home.

The importance of equity may also differ between men and women. In a study of Dutch adults, perceived inequity of their marriage or cohabiting relationship was not correlated with men's desire for an extramarital affair or the actual number of extramarital affairs they reported (Prins et al., 1993). However, compared with women who perceived their current relationship as equitable, those who felt underbenefited or overbenefited reported more desire for an affair and a greater number of them (Figure 6.4). Surprisingly, underbenefited women were *not* more interested in extramarital liaisons than were those who were overbenefited. In fact, the trend was in the opposite direction! Perhaps sometimes there can be too much of a good thing.

Equity theory maintains that equity causes satisfaction, but research on actual relationships is by necessity correlational. Could it go the other way? Are satisfied partners less likely than the dissatisfied to count their blessings or the lack of them? It seems plausible, but so far the evidence at hand supports the original recipe. A one-year prospective study of Dutch couples found that perceived equity predicted relationship satisfaction better than satisfaction predicted equity (VanYperen & Buunk, 1990). Again, these results were stronger for women than for men, providing yet another indication of a possible gender difference—at least in Holland—in the impact of equity on intimate relationships.

Self-Disclosure: Growing Closer

self-disclosure Revelations about the self that a person makes to other people.

Think for a moment about your most embarrassing experience, your most cherished ambitions, and your sex life. Would you bare your soul on these private matters to a stranger? To a casual acquaintance? To a friend or a lover? The willingness to reveal intimate facts and feelings, called **self-disclosure,** plays a major role in intimate relationships (Derlega et al., 1993).

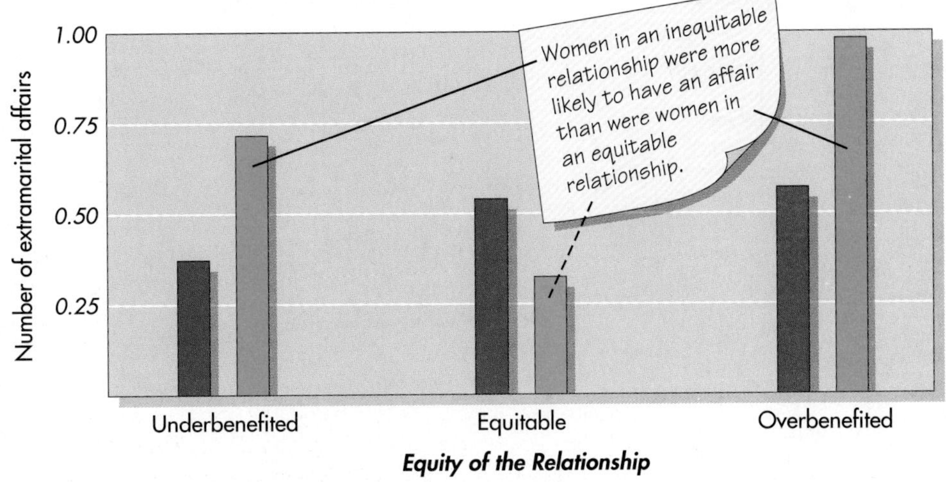

Figure 6.4 **Equity and Affairs.** In a study conducted in the Netherlands, men's perception of the equity of their current relationship was not significantly associated with the number of extramarital affairs they reported. Among women, however, those who believed they were underbenefited or overbenefited reported more affairs than those who viewed their current relationship as equitable. (Adapted from Prins et al., 1993.)

theory of social penetration A theory about the development of close relationships that emphasizes the gradual increase in the breadth and depth of exchanges between partners.

According to Irving Altman and Dalmas Taylor (1973), self-disclosure is a basic social exchange that occurs as relationships develop. Their **theory of social penetration** holds that relationships progress from superficial exchanges to more intimate ones. At first, people give relatively little of themselves to another person and receive relatively little in return. When initial encounters are rewarding, however, exchanges become *broader,* involving more areas of their lives, and *deeper,* involving more important and sensitive areas. As depicted in Figure 6.5, social interaction grows from a narrow, shallow sliver to a wider, more penetrating wedge.

A variety of activities, such as sharing possessions and engaging in physical expressions of affection, may be involved in the social penetration process, but self-disclosure has been the best documented. In their research, Altman and Taylor found that the longer people interacted with one another, the more topics they were willing to discuss and the more personally revealing they became. However, the length of a relationship is by no means a perfect predictor of the level of self-disclosure. In addition to the steady march of progress depicted by Altman and Taylor, three other pathways have been identified (Derlega et al., 1993): (1) too much, too soon (a fast start followed by quick decline); (2) locking in (a fast start followed by a plateau); and (3) maxing out (a steady rise followed by a plateau or slow decline).

Whatever path it follows, more extensive and intimate self-disclosure is associated with greater emotional involvement in dating relationships (Rubin et al., 1980) and greater satisfaction in marriage (Hansen & Schuldt, 1984). As Nancy Collins and Lynn Miller (1994) indicate, there are multiple connections between self-disclosure and relationship quality:

- We disclose to those we like.
- We like those who disclose to us.
- We like those to whom we have disclosed.

Specific patterns of self-disclosure vary according to the state of the relationship. During an initial encounter between strangers, *self-disclosure reciprocity* is the rule. It is polite to match the level of self-disclosure offered by new acquaintances, disclosing more if they do so and drawing back if their self-disclosure de-

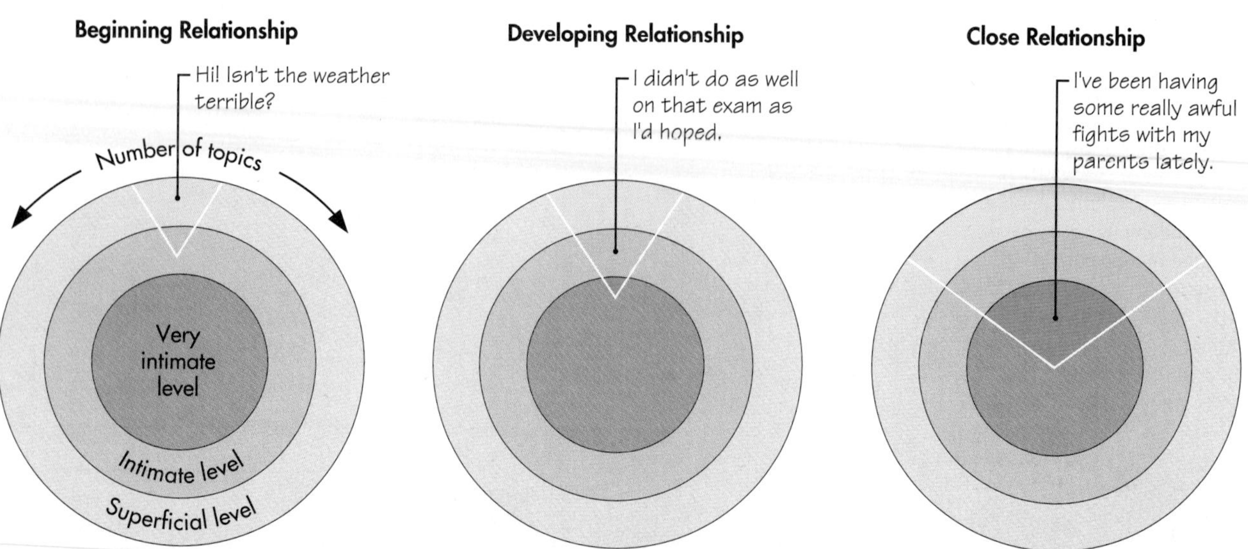

Figure 6.5 From a Sliver to a Wedge. According to the theory of social penetration, as a relationship becomes closer, partners increase the breadth of their exchanges (covering a wider range of topics) and also the depth (revealing more intimate information).

clines (Cunningham et al., 1986). Once a relationship is well established, however, strict reciprocity occurs much less frequently (Altman, 1973; Derlega et al., 1976).

Among couples whose relationship is in trouble, two different patterns of self-disclosure have been noted. For some, both breadth and depth decrease as partners withdraw from their relationship (Baxter, 1987). For others, breadth of self-disclosure contracts as satisfaction declines, but depth of self-disclosure increases—as the distressed partners bombard each other with cruel and angry statements (Tolstedt & Stokes, 1984). In this case, the social *de*penetration process resembles neither the sliver of a superficial relationship nor the wedge of a satisfying intimate relationship—but, rather, a long, thin dagger of discontent.

Individual Differences in Self-Disclosure Of all the possible individual differences that could affect self-disclosure, gender has received by far the most attention. Do men and women differ in their willingness to share their private, intimate thoughts with others? To find out, Kathryn Dindia and Mike Allen (1992) conducted an extensive meta-analysis of 205 studies involving 23,702 subjects. Their conclusion was "yes . . . but." Yes, there is a gender difference: Women disclose more than men. But the overall difference is small and varies with the gender of the recipient. As you can see in Table 6.1, women's disclosures to women are much greater than men's disclosures to women or to men; women's disclosures to men are somewhat greater than men's disclosures to women but the same as men's disclosures to men.

Unfortunately, the meta-analysis by Dindia and Allen has one very serious limitation. Because there were not enough studies on diverse populations to meet statistical requirements, only data from North American white subjects were analyzed. Most researchers, however, believe that there are significant cultural differences in self-disclosure (Cozby, 1973; Hill & Stul, 1987). Consider, for example, a study that compared the everyday social behavior of American students with that of Chinese students in Hong Kong (Wheeler et al., 1989). Total disclosure (self and other combined) was higher among the Chinese than among the Americans. In opposite-sex interactions, no gender differences were found. In same-sex interactions, however, American women reported more disclosure than did American men, while Chinese women and men did not differ. Clearly, more research on individuals from different cultures, races, and ethnic backgrounds is required for a better understanding of self-disclosure.

Among North American Whites, women usually engage in more self-disclosure than do men. This gender difference is maximized when women disclose to other women (the top two rows of the table) and reduced when women disclose to men (the bottom two rows of the table). (Data from Dindia & Allen, 1992.)

Table 6.1 Gender Differences in Self-Disclosure

Recipient of Disclosure	Discloser		
	Female		Male
Female	♀ → ♀	›	♂ → ♀
Same Sex	♀ → ♀	›	♂ → ♂
Opposite Sex	♀ → ♂	›	♂ → ♀
Male	♀ → ♂	=	♂ → ♂

Same-Sex Friendships: His and Hers Among North American Whites, the greater self-disclosure to same-sex recipients by women suggests that their same-sex friendships would be more intimate than men's. That seems to be the case. Women's friendships tend to be based on emotional sharing; men's, on engaging in common activities (Hays, 1988; Sherrod, 1989). Paul Wright (1982) captured the essence of this difference in his terms "face-to-face" versus "side-by-side."

More recently, Wright has expressed concern that gender differences in same-sex friendships not be exaggerated out of all proportion (Duck & Wright, 1993; Wright, 1988). Women, too, engage in common activities with their female friends. Men, too, share their feelings with their male friends. The gender difference occurs on the average; it is not absolute. Both men and women also evaluate their same-sex friendships favorably, but, on the average, women evaluate them more favorably. This gender difference has been documented among adolescents as well as adults, and in New Zealand and Hong Kong as well as in the United States (Aukett et al., 1988; Wheeler et al., 1989; Wright & Keple, 1981).

These gender differences in same-sex friendships are characteristic of heterosexuals. Research by Peter Nardi and Drury Sherrod (1994) on same-sex friendships among homosexuals paints a very different picture. In this study, gay men and lesbians did *not* differ on self-disclosure, common activities, or satisfaction with their friendships. Why are homosexual same-sex friendships more similar than heterosexual ones? We don't know—yet. But once again we can see the value of conducting research on diverse populations. If we want to avoid tunnel vision, we need to use a wide-angle lens.

Women's friendships tend to be "face-to-face", based on self-disclosure and emotional sharing. Men's friendships tend to be "side-by-side," based on engaging in common activities.

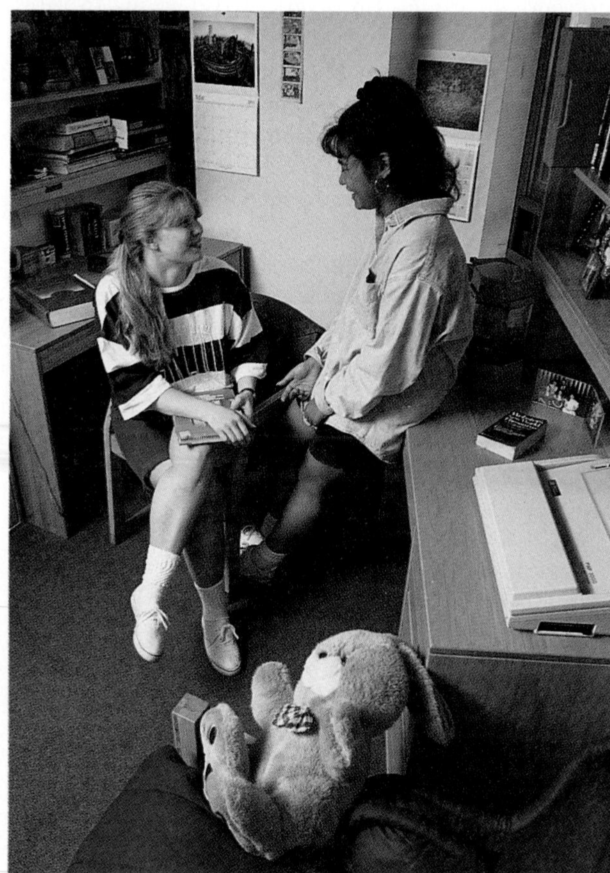

TYPES OF RELATIONSHIPS

Social exchange models emphasize quantity: the more (rewards, equity, and self-disclosure), the better (satisfaction, endurance, and intimacy). In this section, we focus on theories that emphasize qualitative differences in types of relationships. From this perspective, changes in the amount of positive experiences in one type don't necessarily create another type. It's like eating ice cream: No matter how much Wavy Gravy you consume, you still won't end up with Chunky Monkey.

Liking Versus Loving: The Great Divide?

Take a look at the six questions listed in Table 6.2 and, on a scale from 1 ("not at all") to 10 ("totally"), answer them based on your feelings toward a *friend.* Next, answer the same questions based on your feelings toward a current or past *romantic partner.* Then follow the scoring procedure described at the bottom of the table.

When Zick Rubin (1973) asked a large number of college students to respond to items similar to those in Table 6.2, they gave high ratings to their friends on items like those listed under A and high ratings to their romantic partners on items like those listed under B. On the basis of their responses, Rubin developed a Liking Scale and a Loving Scale to measure these two types of relationships. Do your answers coincide with this distinction? Do you like your friends (high scores in section A) and love your romantic partners (high scores in section B)?

Some items from the two scales used by Rubin to distinguish between liking and loving. (Based on Rubin, 1973.)

Table 6.2 Liking and Loving

Answer each of the following questions on a scale from 1 = *not at all* to 10 = *totally.* Answer them first with a good friend in mind, and then while thinking of a romantic partner.

	Friend	Partner
1. This person is one of the most likable people I know.		
2. I feel I can confide in this person about virtually anything.		
3. This person is the sort of person I would like to be.		
4. I would forgive this person for practically anything.		
5. I have great confidence in this person's good judgment.		
6. I would do almost anything for this person.		
A. Sum of your responses to questions 1 + 3 + 5 =		
B. Sum of your responses to questions 2 + 4 + 6 =		
Which is greater: A or B?		

Rubin's approach treats liking and loving as two distinct and, to some extent, mutually exclusive reactions to an intimate relationship. There is some question, however, about just how sharp the difference is. For example, Kenneth and Karen Dion (1976) gave Rubin's two scales to casual daters, people dating each other exclusively, engaged couples, and married couples. Although casual daters reported more liking than loving, liking and loving did not differ among those in more committed relationships. Perhaps one reason for the overlap between these two scales is that Rubin's version of love is pretty tame. Later in this chapter, we describe a much more intense type of loving that differs more clearly from liking.

Exchange Versus Communal Relationships Margaret Clark and her colleagues offer another comparison between types of relationships. According to Clark, people operate on the strict cost-accounting of social exchange only in **exchange relationships.** Here, people prefer immediate quid-pro-quo, tit-for-tat repayment for benefits given to each other. They want costs to be quickly offset by compensation, leaving the overall balance at zero. In contrast, people in **communal relationships** respond to each other's needs over the course of the relationship, without regard to whether they have given or received a benefit.

exchange relationships Relationships in which the participants expect and desire strict reciprocity in their interactions.

communal relationships Relationships in which the participants expect and desire mutual responsiveness to each other's needs.

Exchange relationships are most often found between strangers and casual acquaintances, but some important long-term arrangements (for example, between business partners) may also fall into this category (Clark & Mills, 1993). Although one can have a weak communal relationship with a stranger, strong communal relationships are usually limited to significant others such as close friends, romantic partners, and family members. As summarized in Table 6.3, people behave quite differently depending on whether they are involved in (or want to obtain) an exchange or communal relationship. In an exchange relationship, we keep the books on who gets what; in a communal relationship, we stay responsive to the other person's well-being.

The difference between communal and exchange relationships appears to reflect a fundamental variation in human interaction. Based on his fieldwork in West Africa, Alan Fiske (1992) claims that there are four cross-culturally valid models of social relations. Of these, communal sharing and equality matching parallel communal and exchange relationships, respectively. (Fiske's other two models are based on dominance and equity.) Although the communal-versus-exchange distinction has been criticized as overly broad, it is also viewed as reflecting a basic dichotomy in social interaction (Haslam & Fiske, 1992).

One of the most interesting issues raised by Clark's work concerns the underlying principle that sustains behavior in communal relationships (Batson, 1993). Are communal relationships free of any social exchange considerations whatsoever; do those involved give without any desire to receive? Or do partners in a communal relationship rely on an extended and more subtle version of social exchange, assuming that benefits will balance out in the long run?

Responding to such questions, Clark and her colleague Judson Mills (1993) make two major points. First, they declare that it doesn't matter why people adopt a communal norm. But once, for whatever reason, the norm is adopted, the motivation to respond to the other's needs automatically ensues. Second, they offer a very narrow definition of a benefit as "something that one person chooses to give to another which is of use to the person receiving it" and note that "many satisfactions or rewards that derive from relationships . . . are not benefits" (p. 687).

Let's think about what all this means. Imagine a person, Chris, who loves to be loved. In order to be loved, Chris goes out looking for a relationship and finds

Table 6.3 Exchange and Communal Relationships

Situation	Exchange Relationships	Communal Relationships
We help the other person.	Our mood may become less positive. Our self-evaluation does not change. We like the other person who pays us back immediately.	Our mood becomes more positive, as does our self-evaluation. Our liking for the person who pays us back immediately may decrease.
The other person does us a favor.	We don't like the person who does not ask for immediate repayment.	We like the person who does not ask for immediate repayment.
We are working with the other person on a joint task.	We want to make sure that our contribution can be distinguished from the other person's contribution.	We don't make any clear distinction between the work of the other person and our own work.
The other person may need some help.	We keep track of the other person's needs only when we expect that person to have an opportunity in the near future to take care of our needs.	We keep track of the other person's needs even when that person will not have an opportunity in the near future to take care of our needs.

Exchange relationships require strict cost-accounting; communal relationships are based on responsiveness to each other's needs. The research summarized here indicates how people behave differently in these two types of relationships. (Based on Clark, 1984; Clark & Mills, 1979; Clark et al., 1989; Clark et al., 1986; Clark & Waddell, 1985; Williamson & Clark, 1989, 1992.)

one with Sandy. Chris is scrupulous about observing the communal norm: Every need Sandy has is met, with enthusiasm. Not surprisingly, Sandy adores Chris, who is happy to be loved. They are never so crude as to exchange useful items (except maybe on holidays). Is this a communal relationship? Is this an exchange relationship? Is this a good relationship? Would you want one like it? Later, in Chapter 7 on Helping Others, we'll consider in more detail various possible motives for responding to the needs of others.

How Do I Love Thee? Counting the Ways

Both Rubin and Clark see a vital difference between a relationship that is *not* love (liking, exchange relationships) and one that *is* (loving, communal relationships). But love itself is not always the same. The poet Elizabeth Barrett Browning asked, "How do I love thee?" and then went on to "count the ways"—of which there are many. When subjects in one study (Fehr & Russell, 1991) were asked to list all the types of love they could come up with, they produced 216 items! In this section, we examine varieties of loving experiences as they have been defined and counted by social psychologists.

companionate love A secure, trusting, stable partnership.

passionate love Romantic love characterized by high arousal, intense attraction, and fear of rejection.

The most common approach divides love into two types (Hatfield, 1988). **Companionate love** is a secure, trusting, stable partnership—similar in many ways to what Rubin called liking. **Passionate love** is a state of high arousal: Being loved by the partner is ecstasy; being rejected is agony. If you examine the Passionate Love Scale in Table 6.4, you can see that it describes a much more

Table 6.4 The Passionate Love Scale

Answer each of the following items in terms of this scale:

1	2	3	4	5	6	7	8	9
Not at all true				Moderately true				Definitely true

1. I would feel deep despair if _____ left me.
2. Sometimes I feel I can't control my thoughts; they are obsessively on _____ .
3. I feel happy when I am doing something to make _____ happy.
4. I would rather be with _____ than anyone else.
5. I'd get jealous if I thought _____ were falling in love with someone else.
6. I yearn to know all about _____ .
7. I want _____ —physically, emotionally, mentally.
8. I have an endless appetite for affection from _____ .
9. For me, _____ is the perfect romantic partner.
10. I sense my body responding when _____ touches me.
11. _____ always seems to be on my mind.
12. I want _____ to know me—my thoughts, my fears, and my hopes.
13. I eagerly look for signs indicating _____ 's desire for me.
14. I possess a powerful attraction for _____ .
15. I get extremely depressed when things don't go right in my relationship with _____ .

This questionnaire asks you to describe how you feel when you are passionately in love. Think of the person whom you love most passionately *right now*. If you are not in love right now, think of someone you loved before. Enter that person's name in the blank line in each question, and respond according to how you felt at the time your feelings were most intense. Higher scores on this scale indicate greater passionate love. (Based on Hatfield & Rapson, 1987.)

intense state of affairs than does Rubin's Loving Scale. The contrast between companionate and passionate love runs throughout several more elaborate classifications.

attachment style The way a person typically interacts with significant others.

In their perspective on love, Phillip Shaver and Cindy Hazan (1993) propose that just as children display different kinds of attachment to their parents (Ainsworth et al., 1978), so do adults exhibit a specific **attachment style** in their romantic relationships. There is continuing debate about the number and measurement of adult attachment styles (Collins & Read, 1990; Griffin & Bartholomew, 1994; Simpson, 1990), but most research asks subjects to choose among or rate the three types listed in Table 6.5.

As you would expect, people who indicate that a secure style of attachment best depicts their experiences and feelings report more satisfying romantic relationships than do those who select either of the two insecure styles: avoidant or anxious/ambivalent (Hazan & Shaver, 1987). Secure subjects describe highly positive interactions, characterized by happiness, friendship, and trust. Avoidant

Table 6.5 Attachment Styles

Which of the following best describes your feelings? Don't look at the labels provided in the caption until *after* you've made your selection.

A. I find it relatively easy to get close to others and am comfortable depending on them and having them depend on me. I don't often worry about being abandoned or about someone getting close to me.

B. I am somewhat uncomfortable being close to others; I find it difficult to trust them completely, difficult to allow myself to depend on them. I am nervous when anyone gets too close, and often, love partners want me to be more intimate than I feel comfortable being.

C. I find that others are reluctant to get as close as I would like. I often worry that my partner doesn't really love me or won't want to stay with me. I want to merge completely with another person, and this desire sometimes scares people away.

The way we typically interact with significant others is called an attachment style. The first type of attachment style is called "secure," the second "avoidant," and the third "anxious/ambivalent." (Shaver et al., 1988.)

subjects indicate a fear of closeness. And anxious/ambivalent subjects report a love life full of emotional extremes, obsessive preoccupation, sexual attraction, desire for union with the partner, and love at first sight. Thus, there are striking parallels between the secure attachment style and companionate love, as well as between the anxious/ambivalent style and passionate love.

Looking back, adults with different attachment styles report different childhood experiences. In research conducted in Australia and the United States, secure subjects described positive family relationships, while avoidant subjects spoke of difficulties with their mother and anxious/ambivalent subjects mentioned difficulties with their father (Feeney & Noller, 1990; Hazan & Shaver, 1987). Insecure attachment styles are also associated with problems in adjustment. For example, among Israeli students surveyed after the 1991 Gulf War, insecure individuals living in an area targeted by Iraqi Scud missiles reported greater psychological distress than did secure individuals (Mikulincer et al., 1993). Among U.S. undergraduate women, an insecure attachment style is correlated with depression (Carnelley et al., 1994).

But what are the long-term consequences of attachment styles? Does the style you endorse today foretell your relational outcomes tomorrow? To some extent, yes. The relationships of secure individuals are likely to endure. However, the long-term relationship status of insecure individuals has turned out to be surprisingly hard to predict. An avoidant style is sometimes associated with the breakup of a relationship (Kirkpatrick & Hazan, 1994), but sometimes with remaining with the original partner (Kirkpatrick & Davis, 1994). Similarly, an anxious-ambivalent style is sometimes associated with breaking up (Shaver & Brennan, 1992), but sometimes, especially among women, with staying together (Kirkpatrick & Davis, 1994; Kirkpatrick & Hazen, 1994).

The stability of attachment styles has also been investigated. Most research indicates that they are moderately to highly consistent over time (Keelan et al.,

1994; Scharfe & Bartholomew, 1994). For instance, Lee Kirkpatrick and Cindy Hazan (1994) found that 70 percent of their subjects selected the same attachment style four years after their initial response. But this also means, of course, that attachment style changed for almost one-third of their subjects. With some exceptions (Scharfe & Bartholomew, 1994), there is increasing evidence that changes in attachment style are associated with relationship experiences (Feeney et al., 1994; Hazan et al., 1991; Kirkpatrick & Hazan, 1994; Kojetin, 1993). Unexpected outcomes appear to have the greatest impact (Shaver & Hazan, 1993). After a romantic disaster, secure individuals may become insecure; after a romantic success, insecure individuals may become secure.

What, then, is an attachment style? Is it an enduring characteristic of the person—representations of and expectations about close relationships formed by childhood experiences with significant others? Or does it reflect the quality of recent experiences in relationships? More likely than either of these extremes is a mixture of both. Attachment style, it seems, consists of what we bring to a relationship and what we find when we get there.

We turn now to two other ways of classifying different types of love. John Lee (1988) identifies six styles of loving, most with distinctly unmemorable names: storge, eros, ludus, mania, agape, and pragma (think SELMAP). As you can see in Table 6.6, these styles differ in commitment, intensity, expected reciprocity, and desired characteristics. Typically, men obtain higher scores on ludus than do women; women score higher on storge, mania, and pragma (Hendrick & Hendrick, 1995b).

Love styles appear to be strongly influenced by social factors. Sharing a common social environment is a better predictor of love-style similarity than is degree of genetic closeness (Waller & Shaver, 1994). Furthermore, love styles vary across cultures. For instance, American students report higher levels of storge, friendship-like romantic relationships, than do French students (Murstein et al., 1991). Among students from three different countries, those from the United States had the highest scores on storge and eros; those from Russia on ludus, mania, and agape; and Japanese students reported especially low levels of eros and agape (Sprecher et al., 1994).

Research conducted in the United States suggests that storge is similar to companionate love; mania, to passionate love (Hendrick & Hendrick, 1992). Eros seems to partake of the best of both: a passionate yet secure style of loving.

Robert Sternberg's (1986) triangular theory of love focuses on three components in the experience of love:

Intimacy: The emotional component, which involves feelings of closeness

Passion: The motivational component, which reflects romantic, sexual attraction

Commitment: The cognitive component, which includes the decisions people make about being in love and the degree of their commitment to the partner

Of these, commitment is the strongest and most consistent predictor of relationship satisfaction and endurance (Acker & Davis, 1992; Whitley, 1993). If, as some research indicates (Acker & Davis, 1992), intimacy is not a separate component, then the triangle collapses—leaving only passion and commitment, which strongly resemble the two types of love we started with: passionate and companionate.

In light of all these different ways to divide up love, how many types are there? It's hard to tell. Efforts to integrate these various schemes and come up with one

Table 6.6 Styles of Loving

Storge	The Storgic lover prefers slowly developing attachments that lead to lasting commitment.
Eros	The Erotic lover is eager for an intense relationship with intimacy and strong physical attraction.
Ludus	The Ludic lover is playful in love and likes to play the field.
Mania	The Manic lover is demanding and possessive toward the beloved, and has a feeling of being "out of control."
Agape	The Agapic lover is altruistic, loving without concern for receiving anything in return.
Pragma	The Pragmatic lover searches for a person with the proper vital statistics: job, age, religion, etc.

According to Lee, storge, eros, and ludus are the three primary "colors" of love, from which all other types are derived. Mania, agape, and pragma are three of the major secondary types. (Based on Lee, 1977, 1988.)

set of categories have produced inconsistent results (Hendrick & Hendrick, 1989; Levy & Davis, 1988). Currently, there is considerable interest in the tripartite division of adult attachment styles. But the contrast between companionate and passionate love still appears to be the most fundamental distinction among those who are willing to be attached. Let's look at these two types more closely.

Passionate Love: The Thrill of It Because of its intensity, passionate love is the stuff of great drama. But were we not so accustomed to it, in fictional accounts and perhaps in our own lives, we might regard it as a very odd creature. Recall those social exchange theories described earlier that picture satisfaction and commitment as increasing with rewarding experiences and decreasing with accelerating costs. But in passionate love, costs don't seem to put out the fire. Indeed, the more difficulties the passionate lover encounters, the more in love he or she may become (Hindy et al., 1989). How can unpleasant, even painful experiences increase love?

According to Elaine Hatfield (formerly Walster) and Ellen Berscheid, the answer lies in arousal. Drawing on Schachter's (1964) two-factor theory of emotion, described in Chapter 2, they propose that passionate love consists of (1) diffuse physiological arousal and (2) the belief that this arousal is caused by a reaction to the beloved (Berscheid & Walster, 1974a; Walster, 1971).

excitation transfer The process whereby arousal caused by one stimulus is added to arousal from a second stimulus and the combined arousal is attributed to the second stimulus.

Often the connection between arousal and love is obvious. In the presence of the romantic partner of our dreams, we feel a sudden surge of sexual desire. We know we are aroused and we know why. But the two-factor analysis of passionate love goes beyond the obvious. As described in Chapter 5, arousal can be *mis*attributed. Passionate attraction should increase, say Hatfield and Berscheid, whenever people mistakenly attribute their feelings of arousal to their partner rather than to the true source of their arousal. Dolf Zillmann (1978, 1984) calls the process **excitation transfer.** Arousal caused by one stimulus is transferred and

Is the infatuated lover in this cartoon a victim of excitation transfer? He thinks that what he likes about New York is Claudia. But perhaps the arousal produced by being in the Big Apple fuels his attraction and he only likes Claudia because they're in New York.

Drawing by Weber; © 1984 The New Yorker Magazine, Inc.

"The thing I like about New York, Claudia, is you."

added to arousal elicited by a second stimulus. The combined arousal is then perceived as caused only by the second stimulus.

The possibility that unpleasant arousal, such as fear, might be mislabeled as sexual attraction was first put to the test on two bridges located in a scenic tourist spot (Dutton & Aron, 1974). One of the bridges, the Capilano Canyon Suspension Bridge in North Vancouver, British Columbia, is a nightmare for anyone the least bit afraid of heights: a 450-foot-long, 5-foot-wide passageway that twists in the wind 230 feet above a rocky gorge. Nearby, the other bridge used in the study is more stable and closer to the ground.

Whenever an unaccompanied young man walked across one of these bridges, he was met by a male or female research assistant. The research assistant asked him to participate in a brief experiment in which he answered a few questions. Before parting, the research assistant mentioned that if the subject wanted more information about the study, he could give the assistant a call at home. You can probably guess who was most likely to pick up the phone: subjects met by a female research assistant on the suspension bridge. Fear had sparked attraction.

Or maybe not. Perhaps it's just comforting to be with someone when we're feeling distressed. To rule out the possibility that it's relief rather than arousal that fuels attraction, Gregory White and his colleagues (1981) had to create arousal without distress. How? A little exercise can do it. Male subjects ran in place for either two minutes or fifteen seconds. Then they watched a videotape of a woman they expected to meet later in the study. The woman, an experimental confederate, had been made up to look either physically attractive or unattractive. After watching the video, subjects rated the woman's attractiveness. Those who had exercised for two minutes rated the physically attractive woman as more attractive and the unattractive woman as less attractive than did those who had exercised for fifteen seconds. Without any distress that needed comforting, exercise-produced arousal intensified subjects' initial emotional reaction, positive or negative, to a member of the opposite sex.

The implications of this research are mind-boggling. Is passionate love totally at the mercy of airplanes, bridges, exercise, and other happenstances? Fortunately for our peace of mind, the answer is no. Misattribution and excitation transfer have their limits. One limit is imposed by the passage of time. After the stimulus is gone, arousal declines over time, leaving nothing to be transferred (Zillmann et al., 1974).

Another limit may be set by attributional clarity (White & Kight, 1984). If excitation transfer depends on *mis*attribution, knowing the real reason for our initial arousal will short-circuit the process. Some researchers, however, doubt that misattribution is necessary for one source of arousal to fuel another (Mauro, 1992). Instead, a simple process of response facilitation could suffice (Allen et al., 1989). Whenever arousal is present, no matter what its source or the degree to which we are aware of that source, our response will be energized. Think about it. When you know you're out of breath and your heart's beating fast because of your workout in the gym, could you still be more inclined to fall in love?

Whatever its moment-by-moment determinants, passionate love appears to be a widespread, perhaps even universal human phenomenon. In their review of anthropological research on 166 cultures, William Jankowiak and Edward Fischer (1992) detected at least some indications of passionate love in 147 of them. Not all societies, however, have the same beliefs about passionate attachments. For example, young adults in the United States and Italy have a more favorable view of passionate love, seeing it as a distinct positive emotion, than do young adults in China, who view it as sometimes positive but also as a distinct negative emotion—"sad love" (Shaver et al., 1992).

Cultural variation is also found in opinions about the proper relationship between love and long-term commitment. Here's the question: If a man or woman had all the other qualities you desired, would you marry this person if you were *not* in love? Among students surveyed in the United States and Japan, over 80 percent said they would *not* marry someone with whom they were not in love (Sprecher et al., 1994). Only 64 percent of Russian students, however, were convinced that love and marriage should go together. In this same study, romantic attitudes (including beliefs that love will overcome any obstacle, that there's only one true love for each individual, and that love strikes at first sight) followed a somewhat different cross-cultural pattern: Russian and American students were more romantic than Japanese students.

But even in the United States, home of a remarkably strong and consistent prolove ideology, there are some doubts. Does passionate love last, or is it just a passing fancy? Although more research is needed before we can reach a firm conclusion, the available evidence suggests that, on average, passionate love diminishes over time (Acker & Davis, 1992). The decrease, however, is relatively small (Tucker & Aron, 1993). Taken in the context of the typical decline in satisfaction that occurs in long-term relationships (Vaillant & Vaillant, 1993), passionate love may be a more robust human connection than we might have expected.

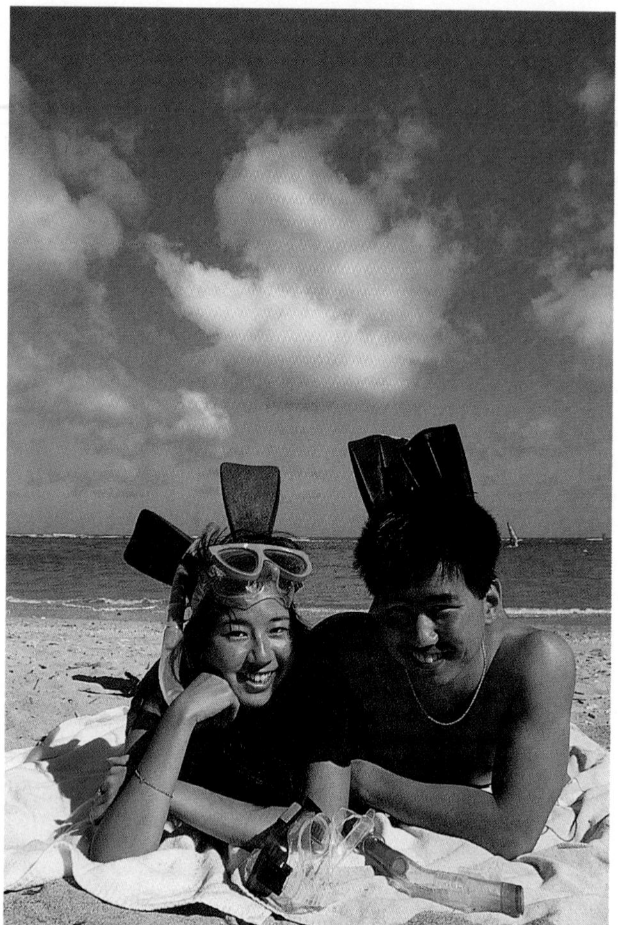

Friendship-based love is associated with relationship satisfaction among young people as well as the middle-aged.

Companionate Love: The Trust in It With all its intense arousal, passionate love is a sexualized, if not necessarily sexual, love. In contrast, companionate love has a broader scope, existing between friends as well as lovers. Companionate love rests on a foundation of trust, caring, honesty, respect, and friendship. These companionate features play a central role in people's conception of love (Fehr, 1993). Passionate, romantic features are also included in the concept, but are viewed as more peripheral.

Companionate love is often thought of as a middle-aged phenomenon. But, at least in the United States, this is not the case. As we saw earlier, American college students report higher levels of storge, the love style most closely resembling friendship, than do students in France, Russia, or Japan. Moreover, in personal accounts of romantic relationships written by U.S. students and coded for love style, storge appeared much more frequently than either the positive passion of eros or the anxious passion of mania (Hendrick & Hendrick, 1993). Indeed, the importance of friendship-based love extends across the life span, being associated with relationship satisfaction for both college students and middle-aged married adults (Grote & Frieze, 1994). Like the sturdy, steady tortoise in Aesop's fable, companionate love may seem outpaced by the far flashier eruption of passionate love, but it can still manage to cross the finish line well ahead.

RELATIONSHIP ISSUES

In an intimate relationship, partners' feelings for each other are closely intertwined with the way they deal with basic issues in the relationship. A trusting, generous love helps them cope better with these issues, just as sensitive and sensible coping increases trust and affection. Relationship issues thus offer an opportunity to strengthen a relationship. But they also pose the danger of angry, unresolved disagreements. Here we consider three of the most intimate, and potentially explosive, issues that couples face: sex, jealousy, and power.

Sexuality

Never before in human history have sexual choices been as difficult and complex as in the 1990s. On the one hand, we live in a sex-saturated culture. Each year, on TV alone, U.S. teenagers see nearly 14,000 sexual encounters (Cole et al., 1993). And rates of sexual activity among these teens are high, with the vast majority having sexual intercourse before the age of nineteen (see Figure 6.6). On the other hand, the potential negative consequences of sex are unmistakable: unwanted pregnancy, various nonfatal sexually transmitted diseases, and AIDS. What's a person to do? The answer, we suggest, is to be informed—get the facts and know your options. This section is part of that educational process.

Sex and Satisfaction For some reason, talking about sex often turns into talking about food. So here are some culinary metaphors for you to think about. Is having sex like adding butter to a sauce—does it make a crucial difference in satisfaction with the relationship? Or is sex more like the raisin on a cake? When the relationship as a whole is good, sex can top it off. But if the cake is a flop, no little raisin is going to rescue it.

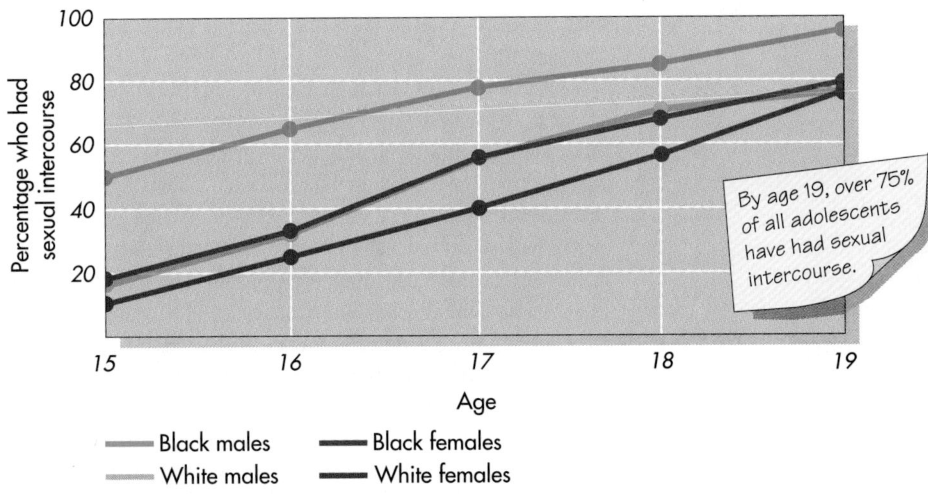

Figure 6.6 **Rates of Sexual Intercourse Among Adolescents.** The percentage of adolescents who have had sexual intercourse increases sharply from age 15 to age 19. At each age, the highest percentage is found among black males, but the rate of increase across age is similar for all groups. (Miller, 1993; data from Moore et al., 1992.)

To see which recipe is more accurate, we can compare relationships that last with those that don't. It does appear that dating relationships with sex continue longer than those without. In one study, college students who were having sex with their dating partner were more likely three months later to still be dating the same person than were those who were not having sex at the time they were first contacted (Simpson, 1987). But wait a minute. This is a correlation, which doesn't specify cause and effect. Perhaps having a closer relationship to start with increased the likelihood of having sex *and* of enduring longer. As it turns out, even when satisfaction with the relationship was taken into account, sexually active relationships endured longer.

Three months, of course, is a very short period. To examine more lasting effects, we can compare married couples who lived together before marriage with those who did not cohabit. Both sorts of couples may have engaged in premarital sex, but on the average those who cohabited before marriage should have had more of it. If more sex means a better relationship, then cohabitation should be a plus. It isn't. It's a minus. The marriages of couples who cohabited before marriage are less satisfying and less likely to endure than are the marriages of those who did not cohabit (DeMaris & Rao, 1992; Hall & Zhao, 1995).

Explanations for this association differ, but reduced commitment to the relationship appears to be a crucial ingredient (Booth & Johnson, 1988; Thomson & Colella, 1992). For example, increased risk for marital instability is much greater for serial cohabitors, who lived with more than one person prior to marriage, than for single-instance cohabitors, who only lived with their future spouse (DeMaris & MacDonald, 1993; Sweet & Bumpass, 1992). Moreover, the association between cohabitation and problems in marriage may be a thing of the past (Schoen, 1992). When cohabitation was rare, perhaps uncommitted individuals were especially likely to engage in it. But now, when cohabitation is much more common in North America and Western Europe, a broad range of people participate, and, among recent marriages, cohabitation seems not to have any effect on marital success. In any event, there is no indication that the greater access to regular sexual activity available to cohabitors has long-term benefits for their relationship.

Rather than viewing sex as the prime mover in determining the quality and endurance of a relationship, we might be better advised to regard it as a part of the larger relational whole. Typically, sexual satisfaction is correlated with overall satisfaction in the relationship for both heterosexual and homosexual couples (Henderson-King & Veroff, 1994; Kurdek, 1991c; Sprecher & McKinney, 1993). In turn, sexual and relationship satisfaction are associated with good communication about sexual desires and preferences (Cupach & Comstock, 1990). Talking about sex, however, appears to be easier for homosexual couples than for heterosexual couples (Masters & Johnson, 1979). We now examine some gender differences in attitudes, roles, and perceptions that might confuse the sexual signals that heterosexual men and women send and receive.

Seeing Sex Differently What do men and women want? When downtown pedestrians and college students were asked to select ten private wishes from a list of forty, much of what they wanted was much the same (Ehrlichman & Eichenstein, 1992). But there was one striking difference. Men strongly favored the wish "to have sex with anyone I choose." A comprehensive review of twenty-one measures of sexual attitudes and behavior obtained a similar gender differ-

Table 6.7 The Sociosexual Orientation Inventory

For the questions dealing with behavior, write your answers in the blank spaces provided. For the questions dealing with thoughts and attitudes, circle the appropriate number on the scales provided.

1. With how many different partners have you had sex (sexual intercourse) within the past year?

   ____

2. With how many different partners do you foresee yourself having sex during the next five years? (Please give a *specific, realistic* estimate.)

   ____

3. With how many different partners have you had sex on *one and only one* occasion?

   ____

4. How often do you fantasize about having sex with someone other than your current dating partner? (Circle one).
   1. never
   2. once every two or three months
   3. once a month
   4. once every two weeks
   5. once a week
   6. a few times each week
   7. nearly every day
   8. at least once a day

5. Sex without love is OK

   1 2 3 4 5 6 7 8 9

   I strongly disagree — I strongly agree

6. I can imagine myself being comfortable and enjoying "casual" sex with different partners.

   1 2 3 4 5 6 7 8 9

   I strongly disagree — I strongly agree

7. I would have to be closely attached to someone (both emotionally and psychologically) before I could feel comfortable and fully enjoy having sex with him or her.

   1 2 3 4 5 6 7 8 9

   I strongly disagree — I strongly agree

Scoring: Reverse the values in Item 7 so that 1 = 9, 2 = 8, etc. Items then receive the following weights:

Item 1 × 5 = ________
Item 2 × 1 = ________
Item 3 × 5 = ________
Item 4 × 4 = ________
(Total of items 5, 6, & 7) × 2 = ________
Total = ________

The Sociosexual Orientation Inventory measures an individual's willingness to engage in uncommitted sexual interactions. The average score for men is about 68; for women, around 39. (Based on Simpson & Gangestad, 1991.)

ence: Men were more likely than women to have a positive attitude toward casual sex (Oliver & Hyde, 1993). Men also reported having had more numerous sexual partners, a finding that has appeared in surveys in Great Britain, France, and Finland as well as the United States (Laumann et al., 1994). One widely used measure of actual and potential engagement in uncommitted sex, the Sociosexual Orientation Inventory (SOI), is displayed in Table 6.7. As expected, men score higher than women on the SOI (Simpson & Gangestad, 1991).

In Chapter 5 we described the sociobiological explanation for men's more permissive sexual attitudes and more unrestricted sexual behavior. From this perspective, men's wider-ranging sexual interest is the product of evolutionary pressures to ensure reproductive success (Buss, 1994; Kenrick, 1994). But note, there is considerable variability *within* the sexes (Simpson & Gangestad, 1992). Some men score lower than some women on the SOI. And those with higher SOI scores, men *and* women, display the preference for physically attractive mates that sociobiologists regard as part of the male sexual strategy. Whatever influence evolution had on human sexual attitudes and behavior, it did not create an impassable divide between men and women.

In heterosexual interactions, men and women also differ in the sexual roles they play. Asked by Suzanna Rose and Irene Hanson Frieze (1993) to write the script for a first date, college students gave men a more proactive part (pick up date, make out, kiss goodnight) and women a more reactive one (wait for date, accept/reject date's moves). This division of sexual labor has been summarized in the phrase "men as go-getters and women as gate-keepers" (Zillmann & Weaver, 1989, p. 95). Although the gate-keeper role appears relatively passive, it is actually quite influential: On any *joint* activity, the more restrictive partner will call the shots. Accordingly, women's SOI scores (but not men's) predict how early a couple has sex (Simpson & Gangestad, 1991) and wives' sexual attitudes (more than husbands') predict the sexual satisfaction and adjustment of both partners (Smith et al., 1993).

Perhaps because of the roles they play, men and women tend to have different perceptions of others' sexual inclinations. Men seem to live in a more sexualized world, perceiving more interest in sexual activities than do women (Muehlenhard, 1988). This worldview is often a general one: Men see greater sexual intent in other men as well as in women (Abbey, 1982; Bostwick & DeLucia, 1992). Gender differences in sexual perceptions are influenced by the perceiver's characteristics, being especially likely among those high in social anxiety (Kowalski, 1993b) and those who hold more conservative, traditional attitudes toward women (Kowalski, 1993a). The behavior of the other person also affects sexual perceptions. Compared with women, men perceive a woman as having a *greater* desire for sex when her behavior is less explicitly sexual (Kowalski, 1992).

Given these differences in sexual attitudes, roles, and perceptions, it's not surprising that heterosexual men and women encounter difficulties in communicating about sex with each other. When Antioch College tried to improve heterosexual communication by requiring students to obtain explicit verbal consent for each aspect of sexual intimacy, some thought this a wonderful idea; others found it ridiculous. But whether we agree with Antioch's approach or not, we should all share its concerns. Miscommunication between the sexes about sex can damage a relationship; it can also contribute to the potential for sexual coercion and assault. We examine the troubling topic of intimate violence in Chapter 8 on Aggression.

The AIDS Crisis When historians look back on sexuality across the ages, they can see an immense array of patterns and trends and changes. But one sharp dividing line towers over all the rest: pre-AIDS and post-AIDS. Because of AIDS, sex today is different from what it used to be.

AIDS (acquired immune deficiency syndrome) is one of the deadliest human diseases ever known. By 1995, more than 441,000 cases had been reported in the United States, and AIDS had become the leading killer of Americans aged 25 to 44. Current estimates by the Public Health Service indicate that about 1 to 1.5 million Americans are infected with HIV, the human immunodeficiency virus that causes AIDS. Worldwide, the number of HIV-infected individuals is thought to exceed 17 million, with the most rapid spread of AIDS now occurring in Asia. Some basic facts about AIDS are summarized in Table 6.8.

To date, there have been two major waves in the AIDS epidemic. The victims of the first wave were gay men, who still account for slightly over 50 percent of

Table 6.8 Some Facts About AIDS

1. *Can you get AIDS from casual contact?* Apparently not. There is no documented case of the transmission of AIDS from casual contact, even among families of people with AIDS.

2. *Are dental and medical personnel at greater risk for HIV infection?* Yes. Because HIV can be transmitted through direct contact between an open sore and blood, dental and medical personnel must take special precautions to protect themselves. More than forty healthcare workers have been infected on the job. In contrast, Kimberly Bergalis's dentist is the only professional healthcare worker specifically linked to infections among his patients, and his role in their infection is disputed by some scientists.

3. *If a person thinks that he or she might be infected, should this person get tested?* Absolutely. It is important to know whether you are infected in order not to infect others. In addition, those who are infected should discuss possible treatments with their physicians. Although the effectiveness of AZT (the primary medication used against AIDS) in delaying the onset of AIDS has been questioned, taking AZT during pregnancy reduces by two-thirds the risk of infecting the unborn child.

4. *Can a person be infected with HIV and still test negative?* Yes. There is a "window" of at least a few weeks between becoming infected and producing enough antibodies to be detected by a test for HIV.

5. *Are all babies who test positive for HIV at birth actually infected with HIV?* No. Since the usual test for HIV cannot distinguish between maternal antibodies and the baby's own antibodies, a number of babies who aren't infected test positive. Among babies born to HIV-infected mothers, about 25 percent are actually infected. For adults as well as babies, more than one test is always required to establish a diagnosis.

6. *Do all persons infected with HIV develop AIDS?* Initially, scientists believed that everyone infected with HIV would eventually develop AIDS. But recent studies of people who are healthy despite having been HIV-infected for up to 17 years have raised a more hopeful possibility. It is now estimated that some 5 percent of those infected are long-term survivors who may have beaten the virus entirely. The effort to determine how these individuals are able to hold HIV in check is one of the most active areas of current AIDS research.

7. *Is AIDS always fatal?* To date, it appears that AIDS is always fatal. But as new treatments become available, it is possible that AIDS will become a chronic disease, like diabetes or high blood pressure, that can be managed.

In coping with the AIDS epidemic, it is essential to have accurate information. Here are some of the basic facts, as best we know them in the light of current research.

new cases (Elmer-Dewitt, 1991). Most of these individuals, however, were infected many years ago. The incidence of new HIV infections among gay men has declined dramatically, although there is concern that younger men may not have adopted safe-sex practices as thoroughly as have older individuals (Gardner & Wilcox, 1993). The victims of the second wave are intravenous-drug users, and the spread of HIV infection among this population is increasing rapidly.

No large "third wave" of heterosexually transmitted AIDS has yet appeared in the United States, but there is every reason to be concerned. Seventy-five percent of HIV infections worldwide are estimated to result from heterosexual intercourse. And in 1992, for the first time, more American women were infected through sex than through drug use. Although men still constitute the vast majority of new cases, women are twelve times more likely than men to be infected during heterosexual intercourse (Ickovics & Rodin, 1992), and the 1994 increase in AIDS was six times greater among women than in the population as a whole.

The only guaranteed, foolproof method of avoiding a sexually transmitted disease is abstinence. For individuals who are sexually active, the use of latex condoms is the principal safe-sex method for reducing the risk of infection. Condom use appears to be increasing in the United States, but a recent report from the

The AIDS quilt honors the lives of those who have died from one of the deadliest diseases in human history.

Centers for Disease Control and Prevention found that almost half of the sexually active high school students who were surveyed said they did not use a condom the last time they had sex. To a large extent, the AIDS crisis is a behavior-change crisis. In Chapter 14 on Health, we consider a number of factors that can help people help themselves by practicing healthy behaviors.

Jealousy

Jealousy has a long, tragic history. The Song of Solomon says it's "cruel as the grave." Shakespeare called it "the green-eyed monster." And in the highly publicized 1995 trial of O. J. Simpson, prosecutor Christopher Darden claimed that Simpson had killed his ex-wife Nicole "for a reason almost as old as mankind itself. He killed her out of jealousy. He killed her because he couldn't have her."

jealousy The reaction to a perceived threat to a relationship.

Jealousy is created by a perceived threat to a relationship. But the threat doesn't have to actually exist, nor even the relationship itself. All celebrities know the dangers of becoming the target of a stranger's obsessive fantasies. According to Gregory White, *primary appraisal* of the threat is the first of four major phases in the experience of jealousy (White, 1981a; White & Mullen, 1989). Some individuals are more likely to perceive a threat than others. For instance, you have to be old enough. When children were confronted with a "social triangle" in which their mother ignored them and attended to another child, only a few children as young as 8.4 months were judged to have displayed a jealous response (Masciuch & Kienapple, 1993). By 1.5 years of age, however, most children reacted jealously.

Feelings about the relationship can also affect primary appraisal. Individuals who feel inadequate and inequitably treated in their relationship are more often jealous than those who are more confident and believe they are fairly treated (White, 1981a, 1981b). Since short-term relationships (like dating) provide less security than long-term relationships (like marriage), people with chronic doubts about their own self-worth may be especially prone to jealousy in the early stages of a relationship (Melamed, 1991). In addition, those who are highly dependent on a relationship are more likely to experience jealousy (Buunk, 1991).

But the strongest, and potentially most destructive, feelings of jealousy appear to arise from a specific kind of threat: to sexual exclusivity (Mathes, 1992). In heterosexual relationships, sexual infidelity is more disturbing to men than to women (Buss et al., 1992), especially in more traditional societies (Betzig, 1989; Buss & Schmitt, 1993). Research by Bram Buunk and Ralph Hupka (1987) also documented some cross-cultural differences in the sorts of behaviors that elicit sexual jealousy. Relative to responses from other national groups, kissing elicited high levels of sexual jealousy from Hungarians; dancing and sexual relations, from those in the former Soviet Union; flirting, from those in what used to be Yugoslavia; and sexual fantasies, from the Dutch. Subjects from Ireland, Mexico, and the United States reported relatively lower levels of sexual jealousy in response to these behaviors.

During the next phase of the jealousy experience, *secondary appraisal,* people try to understand the situation better and begin to think of ways to cope with it. Although some people are able to think clearly at this point, some may leap to irrational conclusions: "I bet *everyone* knows she's cheating on me"; "I'll *never* be happy without him." The third aspect of jealousy is the individual's *emotional reaction.* Jealousy can produce a large and varied range of emotional reactions. These feelings are usually negative (Sharpsteen, 1993), but positive reactions (such as excitement, love, feeling alive) sometimes occur (Pines & Aronson, 1983). The distrust, anxiety, and anger of jealousy—when you fear the loss of what you have—differ from the feelings of inferiority, longing, and resentment produced by envy—when you want what someone else has (Parrott & Smith, 1993).

Finally, the person's perceptions, thoughts, and feelings will influence how that person attempts to *cope with jealousy.* Coping also varies tremendously, from constructive actions to destructive rampages, and can be influenced by personal characteristics. For example, an anxious/ambivalent attachment style (see p. 214) is associated with a reluctance to seek social support when jealous, and depression is associated with self-blame for the incident (Radecki-Bush et al., 1993).

As Jeff Bryson (1991) discovered, there are numerous cross-cultural differences in coping with jealousy. Subjects in this research were university students in the United States and four European countries (France, Germany, Italy, and the Netherlands). Asked about their feelings and actions when they were jealous, subjects' responses were scored in terms of nine different coping factors. Table 6.9 lists these factors and indicates which national groups scored very high or very low on each one. Bryson's own (tongue-in-cheek) summary of the results is worth quoting:

> It appears that, when jealous, the French get mad, the Dutch get sad, the Germans would rather not fight about it, the Italians don't want to talk about it, and the Americans are concerned about what their friends think! (p. 191)

In addition to these cross-cultural patterns, there were some notable gender differences in the responses of U.S. students. As you can see from Table 6.9, American men said that when they were jealous, they became aggressive and were interested in other people. American women said they attempted to feign

Table 6.9 Coping with Jealousy in Five Countries

Coping Responses (with sample item from each factor)	National Groups with Highest Scores	National Groups with Lowest Scores
Reaction to Betrayal ("Feel betrayed")	France	Netherlands
Emotional Devastation ("Feel less able to cope with other aspects of my life")	Netherlands	United States (men only)
Aggression ("Threaten the other person")	France United States (men only)	Germany United States (women only)
Impression Management ("Try to make my partner think I don't care")	United States (women only)	All four European countries
Reactive Retribution ("Flirt or go out with other people")	United States (men only)	Netherlands
Relationship Improvement ("Become more sexually active with my partner")	United States France	Italy
Monitoring ("Question my partner about his/her activities")	Netherlands United States	Italy
Intropunitiveness ("Feel guilty about being jealous")	France United States	Italy
Social Support Seeking ("Talk to close friends about my feelings")	United States (women only) Netherlands	Italy

University students from the United States and four European countries responded to a questionnaire asking them how they react when jealous. Their answers indicated clear cultural differences in coping with jealousy, but strong gender differences appeared only among American students. (Data from Bryson, 1991.)

indifference and wanted to talk to friends about their feelings. Only the Americans in this study showed such strong gender differences.

Jealousy creates pain and suffering in people's lives, and it can be fatal. No doubt, most of us want to be able to cope constructively with it. But how? Some strategies for better coping that have been suggested include reducing irrational beliefs, enhancing self-esteem, improving communication skills, and increasing equity in the relationship (White & Mullen, 1989). According to Peter Salovey and Judith Rodin (1988), a sense of independence and self-worth may be the crucial ingredient. Those who can avoid the pitfalls of endless recrimination and forge ahead with their own lives should have a much better chance of escaping the destructive effects of the green-eyed monster.

Social Power

Even though we sometimes don't like to admit it, power is a basic aspect of social life. It can be seized, lost, or given up. It can be used for good, evil, or trivial purposes. But it is there to be reckoned with in all relationships—between friends as well as lovers, among co-workers as well as family members. This section describes some of the characteristics of social power as it operates in intimate relationships.

Power and Resources Typically, social power is defined as the ability to influence others and to resist their influence on us (Huston, 1983). But Eric Dépret and Susan Fiske (1993) take a different view. They argue that social power is the ability to control what happens to another individual. Although having power over other people's outcomes is usually associated with having influence over their attitudes and behavior, Dépret and Fiske maintain that it's outcome-control, rather than social influence, that lies at the heart of social power.

Among the various ways to analyze social power, the social exchange perspective described earlier in this chapter is the most widely adopted. According to this view, power is based on the control of valuable resources (Blood & Wolfe, 1960). If a person has control over something you want, that person has power over you.

Different types of power are based on having different types of resources (French & Raven, 1959; Frost & Stahelski, 1988). For example, our friends have *referent power* over us because we identify with them and want them to like us. Employers have *reward power* because they control promotions and raises; they also have *coercive power* because they can fire an employee. Regardless of the type of power, two factors affect the amount of power that resources provide.

First, resource-based power requires that a resource be valued. If someone controls a resource that you don't care about, that person has no power over you. Although people differ considerably in how much they value various resources, some basic resources—such as money, love, and prestige—are valued by most (Foa & Foa, 1980). The value of the relationship itself can also affect the power that intimate partners have over each other. In general, if the relationship is more important to one partner than to the other, the one who values the relationship less has more power (Caldwell & Peplau, 1984; Sprecher, 1985). As the *principle of least interest* bluntly states: "That person is able to dictate the conditions of association whose interest in the continuation of the affair is least" (Waller & Hill, 1951, p. 191).

Second, alternatives affect resource-based power. When a resource you value is controlled by a large number of people, then no single person has ultimate power over you. In a relationship, those who have attentive admirers waiting in the wings (a sky-high CLalt) will have more power than those who have no other offers (a low CLalt).

sex ratio The number of men per 100 women in a given population. When men outnumber women, the sex ratio is high; when women outnumber men, the sex ratio is low.

Consider, for example, the **sex ratio** in a society: the number of men per 100 women (Guttentag & Secord, 1983; Secord, 1983). A high ratio, over 100, means that there are more men than women; a low ratio, under 100, means fewer men than women. In order to determine sex ratios for marriage, researchers compare unmarried women over eighteen with slightly older unmarried men. An age difference is built into the comparison because, on average, women marry older men, a difference of 2.5 years in the United States.

Sex ratios have varied dramatically over the past generation. Throughout the post–World War II baby boom (1945–1960), more babies were born each year than in the preceding year: more in 1949 than in 1948; more in 1955 than in 1954. Thus, when these boomers reached adulthood, there were *more* marriage-eligible women than slightly older, marriage-eligible men. The balance of power favored men. But what happened when the baby boom was over? After 1960, the birthrate declined; fewer babies were born each year than in the one before. And when these individuals reached adulthood, there were *fewer* marriage-eligible women than slightly older, marriage-eligible men. Thus, in the mid-1980s, low sex ratios gave way to high ones, which are expected to prevail through at least the year 2000 (Pedersen, 1991). The balance of power now favors women.

Presumably, sex ratios affect behavior in a subtle and indirect fashion. People don't check out the census data to calculate their social power before going on a date. But through experience and observation, most of us have a general sense of what relational alternatives are available. Sex ratios that deviate greatly from parity are likely to be noticed and to influence the feelings and choices of individual men and women.

Sex ratios may be particularly important for African Americans (Bulcroft & Bulcroft, 1993; South, 1993). High rates of mortality and incarceration among black men in the United States have created unusually low sex ratios. This is a disturbing phenomenon because higher sex ratios among African Americans are associated with more stable families: more husband-wife families, more children living in husband-wife families, and higher percentages of marital births (Fossett & Kiecolt, 1993). Stable family structures require available partners.

The Process of Power Resources create the basis of power, but power is expressed through behavior. Sometimes the process of power takes place in conversations. How we talk to another person can reflect, and reinforce, the power balance between us. For example, men are more likely to dominate discussions of neutral topics as well as traditionally masculine topics, while women are conversationally dominant only on traditionally feminine subjects (Brown et al., 1990). Men also tend to interrupt women more than vice versa (West & Zimmerman, 1983), and interruptions have been interpreted as an indicator of greater social power (Kollock et al., 1985). But interruptions can have a different function, reflecting engagement and spontaneity: Friends interrupt each other more than do casual acquaintances (Planalp & Benson, 1992) and young girls interrupt each other more than do young boys (McCloskey & Coleman, 1992). An adequate understanding of the meaning of an interruption requires careful consideration of the circumstances in which it occurs.

The same can be said for touch. In her influential book *Body Politics,* Nancy Henley (1977) maintained that men touch women more often than women touch men because the use of touch is an expression of higher status and greater social power. Subsequent research confirmed Henley's observation that intentional touches with the hand are greater from male to female than from female to male (Hall & Veccia, 1990; Major et al., 1990). But the meaning of this phenomenon remains uncertain. Touch can be intrusive and demeaning, used to impose dominance over the person being touched. Alternatively, it can function as a gesture of solidarity, indicating warmth and concern. For example, touching each other in public may serve as a signal that a couple is making the transition from a superficial relationship to a closer one. Couples who are seriously dating engage in more public touching than do either casual daters or married couples (Guerrero & Andersen, 1991).

"Let's go someplace where I can talk."

Possible gender differences in the ways that people get their way, called power strategies, have also been examined. The stereotype is that women employ indirect power strategies such as manipulating, hinting, pleading, and withdrawing, while men adopt more direct strategies such as asking, persuading, and bargaining. Actually, the relationship between power strategies and gender turns out to be considerably more complex (Aida & Falbo, 1991). And there is some evidence that when men and women are equally successful in their careers and confident about themselves, both prefer direct strategies (Steil & Weltman, 1992). However, even if men and women don't always behave in accordance with their stereotypical style, the stereotypes themselves are widely believed (Gruber & White, 1986).

The Outcome of Power No matter how people try to get their way, in the end someone does. And the outcome of power can affect people's satisfaction with their relationship. Research conducted by Steven Beach and Abraham Tesser (1993) found that marital satisfaction was higher when couples allocated decision-making power such that each person exercised more power on decisions that mattered to that individual.

But power plays don't always occur on a level playing field. Typically, men are expected to be more dominant than women. To judge for yourself whether this expectation still holds, check out your local media. Research on TV commercials, magazine advertisements, and stories in teen magazines indicates that the stereotypes of the dominant male and the dependent female are presented to the public on a daily basis (Furnham & Bitar, 1993; Hawkins & Aber, 1993; Peirce, 1993). But how do these expectations and stereotypes affect our relationships?

For women, the interpersonal consequences of dominant behavior are often negative. Both women and men report less satisfaction with female-dominated relationships than with those that are either egalitarian or male dominated. This negative view of female dominance is found in the United States (Gray-Little & Burks, 1983) and in more traditional societies such as India (Shukla & Kapoor, 1990). Among individuals involved in a dating relationship, greater perceptions of the woman's power relative to the man's were associated with a greater breakup rate (Felmlee, 1994).

Women who interrupt men are also judged unfavorably (LaFrance, 1992). One study even found that female interruptions were correlated with the endurance of a relationship (Filsinger & Thoma, 1988). In this research, the verbal interactions of thirty-one dating couples were observed in the laboratory; whether or not the woman interrupted the man served as a measure of female dominance. Five years later, when twenty-one couples completed a questionnaire describing the status of their relationship, an astonishing 80 percent of the couples in which the woman had interrupted the man had broken up!

For men, the consequences of dominant behavior are not as clear. Sometimes, dominant men are rated as more sexually attractive and desirable as a date than are nondominant men (Sadalla et al., 1987), but not always (Rainville & Gallagher, 1990). Sometimes dominant men are disliked (Sadalla et al., 1987), but not always (Carli, 1990). Perhaps it depends on the kind of dominance on display. According to Lauri Jensen-Campbell and her colleagues (1995), dominance always involves active engagement with the environment, but the quality of the dominant person's interaction with others can vary. In other words, there are nice dominants and nasty ones. Which type do women like? Female subjects in this research consistently preferred an agreeable man more than a disagreeable one. But in some circumstances, they were also more attracted to a dominant man than to a nondominant one. Typically, the combination was unbeatable: The most attractive men were both agreeable and dominant. "Do nice guys really finish last?" Jensen-Campbell and her colleagues asked. The answer, it seems, is that some nice guys (the dominant ones) come in first.

CONFLICT IN RELATIONSHIPS

Disagreements about sex, jealousy, and power can create serious conflict in intimate relationships (Kurdek, 1994). Whatever the cause, virtually all couples experience some degree of conflict at some time during their relationship. The issue, then, is not whether conflict occurs, but how the couple responds to it. By developing a better understanding of intimate conflict, we should be able to manage it more constructively. The following lessons about conflict are well worth learning.

Problems in Communication: "You Just Don't Understand"

One of the major sources of conflict in an intimate relationship is the difficulty couples have in talking about their disagreements. When relationships break up, communication problems are cited as one of the most common causes by both heterosexual and homosexual couples (Kurdek, 1991b; Sprecher, 1994). But how does "bad communication" differ from "good communication"? Studies comparing happy and distressed couples have discovered two communication patterns that often occur in troubled relationships.

negative affect reciprocity The quid pro-quo exchange of behaviors expressing negative feelings.

The first pattern is called **negative affect reciprocity,** the quid-pro-quo, tit-for-tat exchange of expressions of negative feelings (Gottman & Levenson, 1988; Noller & Fitzpatrick, 1990). Among both distressed and happy couples, expressions of negative affect tend to elicit more in-kind responses than expressions of positive affect. But negative affect reciprocity, especially in nonverbal behavior, is greater among distressed couples than among happy ones. Distressed partners seem locked into a duel. Smiles pass by unnoticed, but every glare, every disgusted look, provokes a sharp response. The inability to terminate unpleasant nonverbal interactions has been found among distressed couples in Germany and Australia as well as in the United States (Halford et al., 1990). Although both men and women engage in negative affect reciprocity, one specific combination—*more* reciprocity of the man's negative affect by the woman and *less* reciprocity of the woman's negative affect by the man—seems to exert a particularly damaging effect on satisfaction in a long-term heterosexual relationship (Levenson & Gottman, 1985).

demand/withdraw interaction pattern When one partner is nagging, critical, and insistent about discussing relationship problems, while the other is withdrawn, silent, and defensive.

Unhappy relationships are also characterized by the **demand/withdraw interaction pattern** (Christensen & Heavey, 1993). This pattern has three components:

- *Initiation:* The demanding partner attempts to initiate discussion of relationship problems; the withdrawing partner tries to avoid discussion.
- *Interaction:* During discussion, the demanding partner nags and demands; the withdrawing partner is silent and withdrawn.
- *Criticism:* During discussion, the demanding partner criticizes; the withdrawing partner is defensive.

Unhappy couples are more likely than happy ones to engage in the demand/withdraw interaction pattern. Among married couples, wives are more often demanding and husbands withdrawing.

Although men and women can both be demanding or withdrawing, research on married couples indicates that wives are more often demanding and husbands withdrawing. This gender-based configuration is more strongly associated with wives' marital dissatisfaction than with husbands'.

Consider the gender differences we have just described: the negatively responsive woman, the unresponsive man; the demanding woman, the withdrawing man. Sound familiar? Both of these communication patterns seem related to gender differences in emotional experience and expressivity. Perhaps because of expectations about their appropriate social roles, women usually report more intense emotions and are more emotionally expressive (Grossman & Wood, 1993). She keeps saying "Warm up" while he keeps urging "Calm down." Couples caught in this bind may well find themselves echoing the title of Deborah Tannen's (1990) immensely popular book on gender differences in communication: "You just don't understand."

According to John Gottman (1994), there's nothing wrong with being either warm or calm. The problem, he says, lies in the discrepancy. Gottman maintains that healthy, stable relationships are most likely when both partners have similar styles of dealing with conflict. Conflict-avoiders can find common ground; highly volatile argue-over-everything types can sustain a passionate attachment; and validating, considerate partners can work through their problems.

Gottman's view is intuitively appealing, based on twenty years of his own research on intimate communication, and consistent with some work by others

"And do you, Deborah Tannen, think they know what they're talking about?"

(Fitzpatrick, 1988). Nevertheless, it may be somewhat oversimplified. Conflict avoidance, for instance, is often associated with relationship distress. In one study, couples who reported the most avoidance also reported the most disagreement and were the most at risk for separation or divorce (McGonagle et al., 1993). In another, couples who shared the belief that conflict should be avoided were more unhappy two years later than were those who believed that conflict should not be avoided (Crohan, 1992). Marital interaction patterns may also vary by race or ethnicity. For example, black newlyweds tend to be more disclosing and affectionate, *and* more withdrawing and unsupportive, than white newlyweds (Oggins et al., 1993).

Whatever one's style, there are two major approaches to reducing the negative effects of conflict. The first is so obvious that it is often overlooked: increase satisfaction with the relationship. According to Gottman and his colleague Robert Levenson (1992), marital stability requires "a fairly high balance of positive to negative behaviors" (p. 230). Thus, if there is a difficult conflict over one issue, partners can, and should, search for ways to be more rewarding to each other in other aspects of their relationship. As the balance of positives-to-negatives improves, so should overall satisfaction, which in turn can reduce conflict (Huston & Vangelisti, 1991; Noller et al., 1994).

The second approach to managing conflict constructively is to try to understand the partner's point of view. Being sensitive and understanding about what the partner thinks and how the partner feels enhances the quality of the relationship (Honeycutt et al., 1993; Long & Andrews, 1990) and reduces conflict (Stets, 1993). But what motivates individuals in the heat of a quarrel to make that effort to understand? Presumably, it helps if they believe that there is, in fact, a communication problem. For this reason, intimate relationships between people with different native languages may have a certain advantage. When difficulties arise in intercultural relationships, the partners are likely to assume that they need to work harder on communicating (Fontaine, 1990). But what if the cause of trouble in the relationship is perceived to lie elsewhere?

The Attributional Trap

As it turns out, identifying the cause of relationship problems is closely associated with the quality of that relationship (Bradbury & Fincham, 1990; Holtzworth-Munroe & Jacobson, 1987). Happy couples make *relationship-enhancing* causal attributions. Negative, undesirable behavior by the partner is brushed off—discounted as a reflection of situational influences ("A bad day"), deemed temporary in nature ("It'll pass"), and viewed as unlikely to extend to other areas of the relationship ("That's just a sore spot"). But positive, pleasant behavior by the partner is taken much more seriously: seen as characteristic of that person, stable across time, and likely to be repeated in other areas of the relationship. Satisfied partners minimize the bad (through external, unstable, and specific attributions) and maximize the good (through internal, stable, and global attributions).

Unhappy couples flip the attributional coin by making *distress-maintaining* causal attributions. While happy partners give each other the benefit of the doubt, distressed couples don't give an inch. For them, negative behaviors of the partner are characteristic of the person ("That's *so* typical"), long lasting ("It's always like this"), and extensive ("Everything turns out this way"). In contrast, positive behaviors get discounted as external, unstable, and specific. Sad to say, distressed partners maximize the bad and minimize the good. Figure 6.7 diagrams these attributional patterns.

These different interpretations of the partner's behavior would seem to make it hard for partners to change direction. Over time, the happy should get happier and the miserable more miserable. But do they? Do attributions for the partner's behavior *lead* to differences in satisfaction, or do they simply *reflect* how people already feel? Research by Frank Fincham and Thomas Bradbury (1993) indicates that a causal connection is possible. Individuals who initially made more distress-maintaining causal attributions reported less marital satisfaction a year later. On the other hand, as Fineham and Bradbury suggest, the relationship between attributions and satisfaction may be reciprocal, with each one influencing the other.

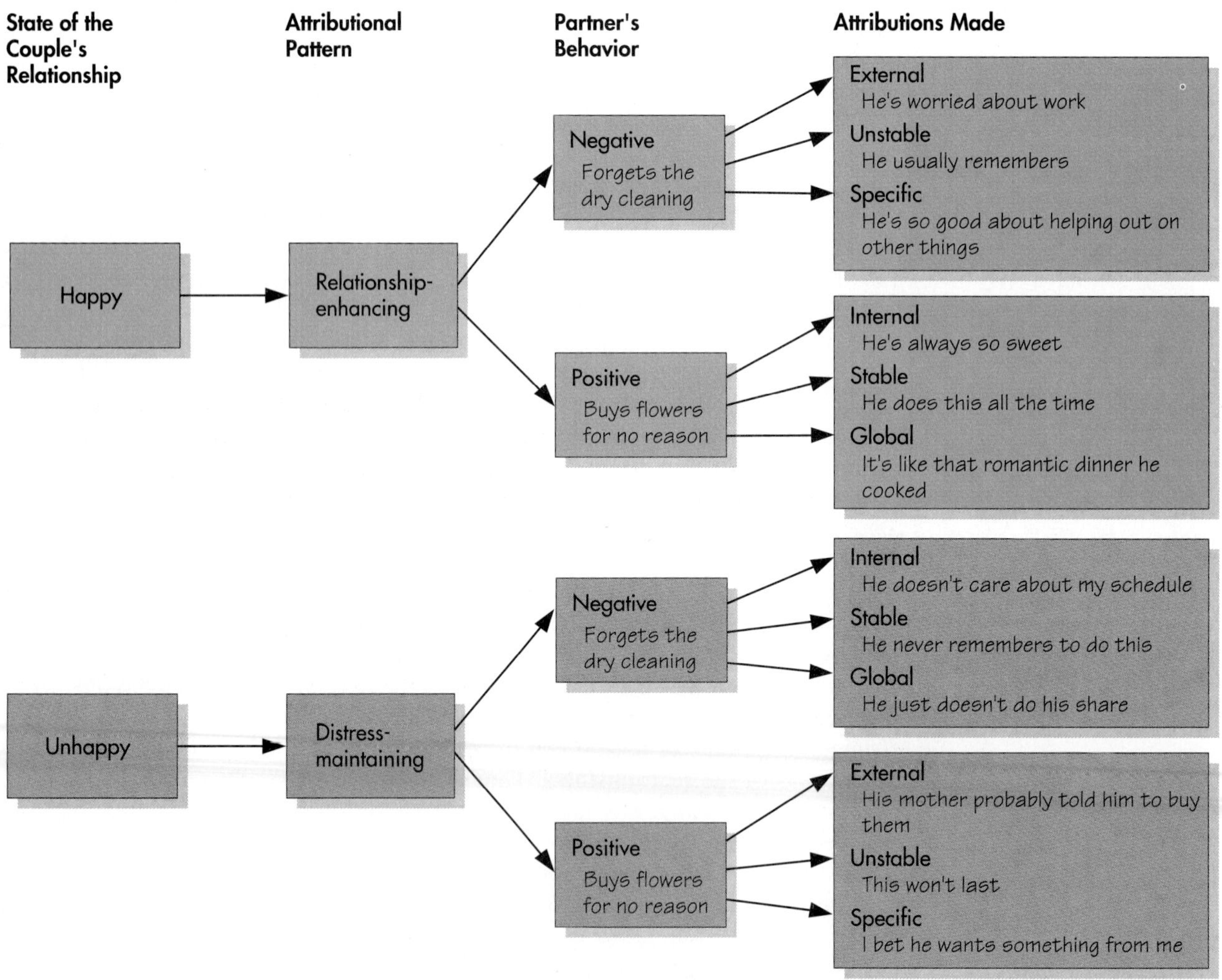

Figure 6.7 **Patterns of Attributions Made by Happy and Unhappy Couples.** The pattern of attributions made for a partner's behavior varies with the state of the relationship. Happy couples discount the negative and accent the positive; unhappy couples reverse the process.

Marital distress is also associated with certain kinds of responsibility attributions for negative events. Unhappy partners are more likely than happy ones to blame the partner, to believe the partner acted intentionally, and to view the partner as selfishly motivated (Bradbury & Fincham, 1992). The potential effects of both causal and responsibility attributions on relationship quality highlights an important conclusion: Trying to understand the other person's point of view during conflict is not sufficient. In addition, we must consider whether our own point of view is distorted and biased. Distress-maintaining attributions can sometimes be traps of our own making. If so, it's our job to dismantle them.

COPING AFTER A RELATIONSHIP ENDS

Conflict does not always lead to the dissolution of a relationship. Indeed, handled skillfully with genuine concern for the partner, conflict can strengthen an intimate attachment. When a relationship does end, the experience can be traumatic (Kitson & Morgan, 1990; Stroebe & Stroebe, 1986). But not everyone is devastated by such a loss. What makes the difference?

Interdependence and Expectations

Earlier in this chapter, we indicated that the interdependence of partners is a central characteristic of intimate relationships. In an interdependent relationship, partners' lives are intertwined. What each one does affects what the other one can do and wants to do (Berscheid & Peplau, 1983). Like a social glue, interdependence bonds partners together. The more interdependent partners are, the longer their relationship should last and the greater distress they should experience if it ends (Berscheid, 1983). The Relationship Closeness Inventory (RCI) measures three aspects of interdependence: frequency (amount of time spent together), diversity (variety of shared activities), and strength (degree of influence one partner has on the other). High scores on the RCI were associated with longer-lasting relationships in one study (Berscheid et al., 1989) and with more post-breakup distress in another (Simpson, 1987).

Expectations also play a major role in reactions to the loss of an intimate relationship. Coping is often more difficult for both heterosexual and homosexual individuals if the partner's desire for separation was not anticipated (Brehm, 1992; Kurdek, 1991b) or if the partner dies unexpectedly (Hansson et al., 1988). But research on the reactions of widows suggests that mere anticipation of the loss of a partner is not the key to improving adjustment (Remondet et al., 1987). Instead, anticipation will be helpful to the extent that it allows the individual to engage in coping behaviors before the loss has actually occurred. Those women who began to do things on their own and planned for the future before their husband's death experienced less emotional disruption afterward. By actively beginning to cope, people create positive expectations about being able to manage their own emotional distress, and these expectations are associated with better adjustment after the loss of a relationship (Mearns, 1991).

Closeness and Identity

Think about someone you care about. Now, answer a simple question: How close are the two of you? Because the answer is sometimes hard to put into words, Arthur Aron and his colleagues (1992) created a pictorial measure of relationship closeness, the Inclusion of Other in the Self (IOS) Scale (see Figure 6.8). When undergraduates were contacted three months after completing the IOS Scale, those who had indicated lower levels of closeness were more likely to have broken up with their romantic partner. Among individuals still involved, those with higher IOS scores anticipated more distress if they were to experience a breakup. The research conducted by Aron and his colleagues indicates that there are two major aspects of interpersonal closeness: feeling close and behaving close. Measures of interdependence, like the Relationship Closeness Inventory described earlier, appear to focus primarily on close behavior. The IOS Scale, however, assesses both aspects and thus may be especially useful in predicting the endurance of a relationship and the difficulty of coping after it has ended.

Just as closeness to another affects our reactions to a relationship, so can the configuration of various aspects of ourselves. For some individuals, their relationships with others are crucial to their own identity. For other individuals, their relationships are just one part of their lives, relatively separate from other identities (as a student, employee, athlete, and so on). Research on undergraduates who had experienced the end of a significant romantic relationship a few weeks earlier found that those for whom relationships played a more central role in their self-definition were more upset by the breakup (Smith & Cohen, 1993).

A Delicate Balance

An ironic theme runs throughout much of the research on coping. We are, to put it mildly, darned if we do and darned if we don't. Those factors that contribute to the endurance of a relationship (interdependence, the expectation of staying together, closeness, and the importance of relationships to one's own identity) turn out to be the same factors that intensify distress and make coping more difficult after a relationship ends. How do you balance making the psychological investment necessary for a lasting relationship against holding back enough for self-protection?

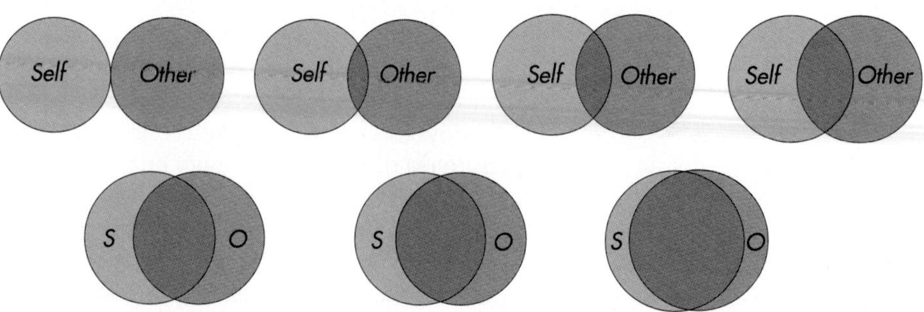

Figure 6.8 **How Close Is Your Relationship?** The Inclusion of Other in the Self (IOS) Scale is a one-item, pictorial measure of relationship closeness. Choosing a picture with less overlap between the circles indicates less closeness; choosing one with more overlap indicates more closeness. (Aron et al., 1992.)

In the United States and other Western countries, various demographic markers indicate how problematic traditional forms of commitment have become: a high divorce rate, more single-parent families, more cohabiting couples, and more never-married individuals. But the desire for enduring intimate relationships has not disappeared. Quite the contrary. Gays and lesbians seek legal recognition of same-sex marriages. Some 75 percent of divorced individuals remarry (Spanier, 1992). Stepfamilies forge a new sense of what it means to "be family" (Ganong & Coleman, 1994). It seems that we are in the midst of a great and compelling search, as millions of men and women try to find ways to love responsibly, to commit wholeheartedly, and, if necessary, to create a new life with dignity. Our hope for the future rests on what all of us discover.

REVIEW

DEFINING INTIMATE RELATIONSHIPS

- Adult intimate relationships include at least one of three components: emotional attachment, fulfillment of psychological needs, and interdependence.

FROM ATTRACTION TO LOVE

- Although stage theories propose that intimate relationships go through a specific sequence of stages, evidence for a fixed sequence is weak.
- Two other views of relationship development emphasize either the step-by-step accumulation of rewards or the sharp distinction between different types of relationships.

BUILDING A RELATIONSHIP

Social Exchange: The Intimate Marketplace

- According to social exchange theory, people seek to maximize gains and minimize costs in relationships.
- Higher rewards, lower costs, and an outcome that meets or exceeds a person's comparison level (CL) are associated with greater satisfaction.
- Lower expectations about alternatives to the relationship (CLalt) and greater investments in the relationship are associated with greater commitment.
- Equity theory holds that satisfaction will be greatest when the ratio between benefits and contributions is similar for both partners.
- Both the overbenefited and the underbenefited experience negative emotions, but the underbenefited are usually less satisfied.
- The importance of equity may vary across the family life cycle and may be greater for women than for men.

Self-Disclosure: Growing Closer

- As predicted by the theory of social penetration, self-disclosure between partners often becomes broader and deeper over time. Other patterns of self-disclosure have also been identified.
- Self-disclosure is closely connected to relationship quality and varies as a function of the state of the relationship.
- Among North American Whites, women usually self-disclose more than men do. Research on more diverse populations is needed to determine the extent of this gender difference.
- Among heterosexuals, women's friendships are based more on emotional sharing, men's on engaging in common activities. But the same-sex friendships of gay men and lesbians are quite similar.

TYPES OF RELATIONSHIPS

Liking Versus Loving: The Great Divide?

- Liking and loving are distinct kinds of intimate relationships, but not all couples distinguish between the two.

- People in exchange relationships prefer immediate reciprocity; people in communal relationships are responsive to each other's needs.

How Do I Love Thee? Counting the Ways

- The most common approach to distinguishing among different types of love divides love into two categories: passionate and companionate.
- Three attachment styles have also been identified. Those with secure styles report having more satisfying relationships than do those with insecure styles (anxious/ambivalent and avoidant).
- Love can be divided into six love styles and a triangle of three components.
- By means of excitation transfer, arousal caused by a love-irrelevant experience is added to arousal elicited by the beloved, thereby increasing passionate attraction.
- In the United States, companionate love is associated with relationship satisfaction for both college students and middle-aged married adults.

RELATIONSHIP ISSUES

Sexuality

- The greater access to regular sexual activity enjoyed by cohabiting couples does not increase their chances of marital success.
- In comparison with women, men are more permissive than women in their sexual attitudes and behavior, more often proactive in sexual situations, and more likely to perceive others to be interested in sex.
- Although new cases of HIV infection have dramatically declined among gay men in the United States, they are increasing among intravenous-drug users and heterosexuals, especially women.

Jealousy

- Jealousy is created by a perceived threat to a relationship.
- The strongest feelings of jealousy are produced by a threat to sexual exclusivity.
- Jealous individuals can develop irrational beliefs about their situation; emotional reactions involved in jealousy are mostly, but not entirely, negative.
- There are cross-cultural differences in coping with jealousy and, at least in the United States, some striking gender differences.

Social Power

- Social power can be defined in terms of influencing others' behaviors or controlling their outcomes.
- The partner who values a relationship least has the most power, and people who have more relational alternatives have more power in their relationships.
- In the United States, sex ratios have gone from low (more women than men) to high (more men than women) in a generation. Among African Americans, however, sex ratios remain low and may be a destabilizing influence on families.
- The meaning of behaviors such as interruptions and touch, which can sometimes express and reinforce power, varies in different situations.
- For women, the relationship consequences of dominant behavior are often negative; for men, dominance combined with agreeableness is preferred by women.

CONFLICT IN RELATIONSHIPS

Problems in Communication: "You Just Don't Understand"

- Compared with happy couples, those who are unhappy in their relationship engage more often in negative affect reciprocity and the demand/withdraw interaction pattern.
- During conflict, women are more likely to be negatively responsive and demanding; men are more likely to be unresponsive and withdrawn.
- Partners can reduce the negative effects of conflict by increasing rewarding behaviors in other areas of the relationship and by making an effort to understand each other's point of view.

The Attributional Trap

- Happy couples make relationship-enhancing causal attributions, while unhappy ones make distress-maintaining ones.
- Unhappy couples are also more likely to attribute responsibility for negative events to the partner.

COPING AFTER A RELATIONSHIP ENDS

Interdependence and Expectations

- Interdependent partners have longer-lasting relationships and experience more distress if the relationship ends.
- An unexpected loss creates more distress than one that has been anticipated.

Closeness and Identity

- Closeness in a relationship involves both feelings and behavior. Those who perceive greater closeness have longer lasting relationships.
- Individuals for whom relationships play a central role in their self-definition are more likely to be upset by the end of a relationship.

A Delicate Balance

- The challenge of our time is to find ways to love responsibly, to commit wholeheartedly, and, if necessary, to make a new life with dignity.

KEY TERMS

intimate relationships, p. 201
stage theories, p. 202
social exchange, p. 203
comparison level (CL), p. 204
comparison level for alternatives (CLalt), p. 204
investment, p. 204
equity theory, p. 205
self-disclosure, p. 207
theory of social penetration, p. 208
exchange relationships, p. 212
communal relationships, p. 212
companionate love, p. 213
passionate love, p. 213
attachment style, p. 214
excitation transfer, p. 217
jealousy, p. 226
sex ratio, p. 229
negative affect reciprocity, p. 233
demand/withdraw interaction pattern, p. 233

Helping Others

PREVIEW

This chapter describes the social psychology of giving and receiving help. First, we examine *personal, interpersonal, and situational influences* that affect whether a potential helper will provide assistance to a person in need. Then, people's *reactions to receiving help* are considered. In the concluding section, we discuss *the helping connection,* the role of social ties in promoting helpfulness to others.

OUTLINE

Once you've read the book or seen the movie, it's hard to forget *Schindler's List.* At first glance, Oskar Schindler was the classic shady operator: selling pots and pans on the black market; bribing officers in the German Army to award contracts to his company; cheating on his wife; partying with Amon Goeth, the sadistic killer in charge of the local forced-labor camp. Schindler didn't seem the type to look after anyone other than himself. And yet from 1939 to 1945, against incredible odds, in constant danger of being found out, this most unlikely hero rescued over 4,000 Jewish men, women, and children from Hitler's "final solution."

Schindler's List is the story of heroism on a grand scale. But it also raises some troubling questions. If Oskar was such an ordinary human being, flawed in so many ways, why weren't there more like him? Why was his heroic helping such an exception to the general rule of active complicity or passive compliance with a murderous regime? In other words, why did Oskar help when so many others didn't? There is no simple answer. The determinants of helping behavior are complex and multifaceted (Schroeder et al., 1995). Even so, helping another person always involves three basic components: the individual who helps, the one who receives help, and the situation in which help occurs.

In this chapter, we examine these components one by one. *Why* do people help? *Whom* do they help? *When* do they help? We then explore the other side of helping: how people react to the help they receive. The concluding section concentrates on a major, recurring theme—social connection—that underlies much of the theory and research on helping. By the end of this chapter, will you have *the* explanation for Oskar Schindler's courageous commitment to saving lives? No. But you should have a broader, more compelling grasp of those factors that influence helping—both Schindler's and your own.

Oskar Schindler (second from left) loved to party. His drinking buddies in the German military and the Nazi Party would never have guessed that Schindler was using his contacts with them to help Jews survive.

PERSONAL INFLUENCES: WHY DO PEOPLE HELP?

Although few individuals reach the heights of heroic helping, virtually everyone helps somebody sometime. People give their friends a ride on a bad-car day; donate money, food, and clothing for disaster relief; baby-sit for a relative; work as a volunteer for charitable activities; pick up the mail for a neighbor who's out of town. The list of everyday acts of kindness is endless. But why do people help? Let's look at some genetic, emotional, and motivational factors that may have an impact.

Genetic Factors in Helping

We begin with evolution. As described in Chapter 5, *sociobiology* is the application of the principles of evolutionary biology to the understanding of social behavior. After discussing some sociobiological theories of helping, we examine whether an innate tendency to help might be stronger for some individuals than for others.

The "Selfish Gene" From the perspective of sociobiology, human social behavior should be analyzed in terms of its contribution to reproductive success: the conception, birth, and survival of offspring. If a specific social behavior enhances reproductive success, the genetic underpinnings of that behavior are more likely to be passed on to subsequent generations and could eventually become part of the common inheritance of the species.

Of course, in order to reproduce, the individual must survive long enough to do so. Being helped *by* others should increase the chances of survival. But what about being helpful *to* others? Since helping others can be costly in terms of time and effort, and is sometimes dangerous to the helper, being helpful would seem to decrease one's chances of survival. Shouldn't any genetically based propensities for helping have dropped out of the gene pool long ago?

Maybe not. There is an alternative to individual survival. You can also preserve your genes by promoting the survival of those who share your genetic make-up, even if you perish in the effort to help them. By means of this indirect route to genetic survival, the tendency to help blood relatives, called **kinship selection,** could become an innate characteristic (Hamilton, 1964). From the outside, helping a relative looks self-sacrificing. On the inside, however, the "selfish gene" plots its immortality (Dawkins, 1989).

kinship selection Preferential helping of blood relatives, so that genes held in common will survive.

Since kinship selection serves the function of genetic survival, preferential helping of blood relatives should be stronger when the biological stakes are higher. This appears to be the case. Kinship has a greater effect on the intention to help in life-and-death situations than in more ordinary circumstances (Burnstein et al., 1994). Furthermore, intentions to help kin in life-threatening situations are influenced by reproductive-related factors. For example, people say they would help youthful relatives more than either infants or older adults, and healthy relatives more than those in poor health.

The Reciprocal Partnership At best, however, kinship selection provides only a partial explanation for helping. Relatives are not always helpful to each other. And even though relatives may get preferential treatment, most people help out nonkin as well. What's the reproductive advantage of helping someone who isn't related to you? The most common sociobiological answer is *reciprocity* (Krebs, 1987). If Chris helps Sandy and Sandy helps Chris, both Chris and Sandy increase their chances of survival and reproductive success. So long as everyone abides by this golden rule, everyone benefits.

Unfortunately, however, some people cheat—taking help from others but not providing it in return. Once cheating enters the picture, the possible evolutionary path of helping becomes a great deal more complicated (Cosmides & Tooby, 1992). Moreover, the notion of reciprocity as a human universal has great difficulty explaining its immense variation. Within a society, individuals differ in their beliefs about reciprocity and in their reciprocity-relevant behaviors (Cotterell et al., 1992).

The nature and understanding of reciprocity also vary across cultures (Moghaddam et al., 1993). In one study, for instance, most of the Hindu Indian college students who participated viewed reciprocity as a moral obligation, while most of the American college students regarded it as a personal choice (Miller & Bersoff, 1994). Compared to someone who helped spontaneously, an individual who engaged in reciprocal helping was perceived as equally helpful by Indian students, but as a less helpful person by American students. As we will see later in this chapter, people often do reciprocate the help they receive, but reciprocity is not so simple a social transaction as it might at first appear.

The Cooperative Group Kinship selection and reciprocal helping reflect the sociobiological emphasis on the gene as the actual unit of natural selection (only genes are transmitted across generations) and on the individual as the functional unit of selection (genes don't exist apart from organisms). But what about

On college campuses, students often make a deal: If you help me move my stuff, I'll help you move yours. According to sociobiologists, the human tendency to engage in reciprocal helping could be a genetically transmitted product of evolution.

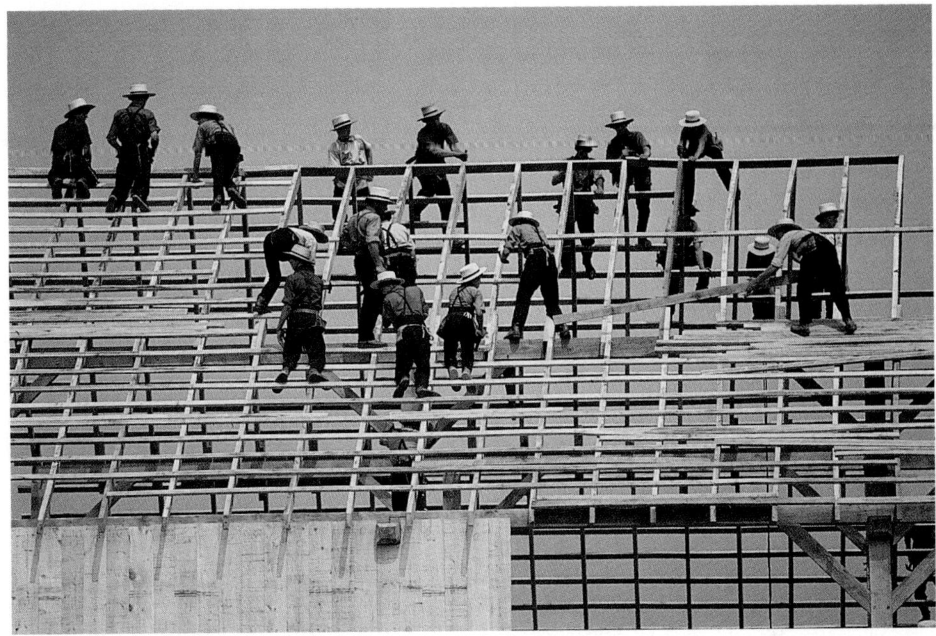

Among the Amish, cooperation within the group is an essential feature of their way of life. Some evolutionary theorists believe that helping other members of one's social group is an innate tendency among all human beings.

groups? Some evolutionary theorists believe that natural selection operates across the full biological hierarchy: from genes, to organisms, to groups, to species (Gould, 1992).

According to David Wilson and Elliott Sober (1994), group selection plays a major role in evolution: Human beings increase their reproductive success by protecting their own self-interest vis-à-vis other individuals *and* by protecting their group's interest vis-à-vis other groups. Kinship selection is a form of group selection that occurs only in groups of genetic relatives. But the kind of group selection proposed by Wilson and Sober can also operate in groups of unrelated individuals, producing helping behavior based on a social connection rather than a blood relationship. Thus, say Wilson and Sober, cooperation and helpfulness among members of a social group (especially when the group faces an external threat) could be an innate, universal tendency.

Personality Up to this point, we have considered whether helping could be a genetically transmitted product of evolution. But perhaps helping runs in families rather than through the whole human race. According to J. Philippe Rushton and his colleagues (1984), some individuals have a stronger genetically based propensity to help than do others. Rushton has examined a wide range of actions and feelings in his research on helping, including helpful behavior to people who are not blood relatives, spontaneous helping not based on anticipated reciprocity, and positive social emotions such as kindness and sympathy.

The self-reported characteristics of twins offer some support for Rushton's argument. Genetically identical (monozygotic) twins are more similar in the helpful behavioral tendencies and helping-related emotions they report than are fraternal (dizygotic) twins, who share only a portion of their genetic make-up (Davis et al., 1994; Matthews et al., 1981; Rushton et al., 1986). Taken at face value, these findings indicate that helpfulness is an inherited trait, especially pronounced in some families and some individuals. But there is room for doubt. Twin studies using self-report questionnaires provide relatively weak evidence of heritability (Plomin & Fulker, 1987).

Rushton (1981), however, believes that the evidence for the heritability of helpfulness points to a genetic basis for what he calls the *altruistic personality.* A person with such a personality is said to engage in many different kinds of helpful behaviors across a wide range of situations, even when there are no external rewards to be gained by the helper. But, so far, the altruistic personality has been hard to find, and the relationship between personality and helping seems much more complex. George Knight and his colleagues (1994) have suggested, for example, that an interacting "conglomerate" of numerous dispositional traits influences prosocial behavior and that the traits included in such a conglomerate differ depending on the situation. In any event, no single characteristic, or set of characteristics, associated with being helpful in all places at all times has yet been identified. Personality is relatively constant, but helping is often remarkably varied.

Emotional Factors in Helping

Perhaps because of this variability, many researchers have focused on the role of emotion in helping behavior. Emotions are notoriously changeable, swayed by internal processes (such as memories, desires, and expectations) as well as by external events. Does how we feel affect how we respond to a person in need? Let's see.

Good Mood: A Spirit of Generosity Sunshine in Minneapolis gives us a good clue. Over the course of a year, pedestrians in this city were stopped and asked to participate in a survey of social opinions. When Michael Cunningham (1979) tabulated their responses according to the weather conditions, he discovered that people answered more questions on sunny days than on cloudy ones. Moving his investigation indoors, Cunningham found that sunshine is truly golden: The more the sun was shining, the more generous were the tips left by restaurant customers. Sunshine and helping seem to go together, but what's the connection?

Probably it's the mood we're in, as a sunny day cheers us up and a cloudy day damps us down. In fact, helping is increased by all kinds of pleasant, mood-lifting experiences: being successful on a task (Isen, 1970), reading pleasant positive statements (Aderman, 1972), being offered a cookie (Isen & Levin, 1972), imagining a Hawaiian vacation (Rosenhan et al., 1981), and listening to a comedy routine by Steve Martin (Wilson, 1981). On the job, being in a good mood seems to be the major determinant of a wide range of behaviors (such as helping co-workers, making constructive suggestions, and spreading good will) that improve workplace quality and increase organizational effectiveness (George & Brief, 1992). When we're happy, we're helpful—a state of affairs known as the **good mood effect.**

good mood effect The effect whereby a good mood increases helping behavior.

Despite strong evidence of the effect itself, it's not clear how it occurs (Carlson et al., 1988). One possibility, called the *mood maintenance hypothesis,* is that happy people are motivated to keep their good mood going. For example, individuals in a happy mood have a strong preference for viewing videotapes they expect to make them happy rather than those they expect to be agreeable or interesting (Wegener & Petty, 1994). So do people expect that helping others will make them happy? Among readers of *Better Homes and Gardens,* the answer is a resounding yes. Those who responded to a questionnaire in the magazine ex-

Being in a good mood increases helping, and helping others makes us feel good. Both this teenage volunteer and the elderly woman she visits are enjoying their interaction.

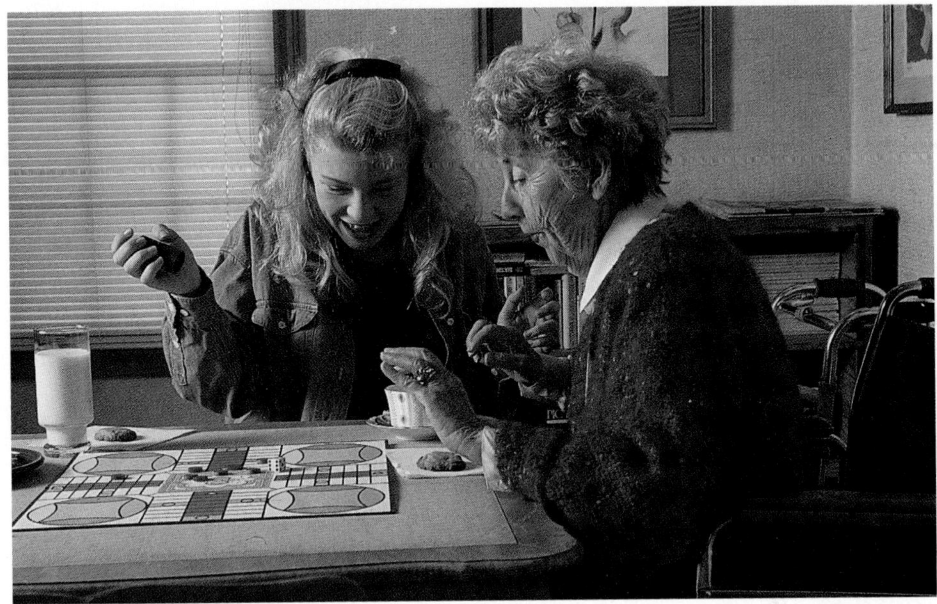

tolled the self-benefits of helping, saying it gave them a "helper's high" (Luks, 1988). And it does. Helping others, particularly those with whom we desire a closer relationship, makes us feel good (Williamson & Clark, 1992).

Alternatively, people in a good mood may be more helpful because they have more happy thoughts. Various kinds of positive thoughts can influence helping. When we feel good, we are more aware of the rewards of helping and expect helping to be a more pleasant experience (Isen et al., 1978). A good mood also increases positive thoughts about other people (Forgas & Bower, 1987), and the more we like someone the more we should be willing to help that person. Or, perhaps, good moods increase helping by means of positive thoughts about the rewarding nature of social activities (Cunningham et al., 1990). There is ample evidence that individuals who are usually in a good mood engage in more social activities (Watson et al., 1992). Figure 7.1 illustrates these various paths from feeling good to doing good.

Whatever its exact cause, the good mood effect has two striking features. First, it doesn't last very long. Typically, the increase in helping produced by a good mood is of short duration (Isen et al., 1976). Second, it kicks in quite early in life. The good mood effect occurs among people of all ages, and even young children help more when they feel happy and cheerful (Moore et al., 1973).

Negative Emotions: Do They Help? Since a good mood increases helping, does a bad mood decrease it? Not necessarily. Under some circumstances, negative feelings can elicit positive behavior toward others (Carlson & Miller, 1987). Here, we examine three ways this could occur: feeling guilty after a transgression, becoming self-aware, and seeking relief from sadness.

guilt Feelings of discomfort or distress produced by people's belief that they have violated their own personal standards or the fear that others will perceive such violations.

For judges and lawyers, guilt is the consequence of a behavior: A guilty person is one who has broken the law. Psychologically, **guilt** is broader and fuzzier. We feel guilty when we believe that we have violated our own personal standards or fear that others may perceive such a violation. But feelings of guilt do not necessarily stem from actual behavior. People who lead blameless lives can sometimes

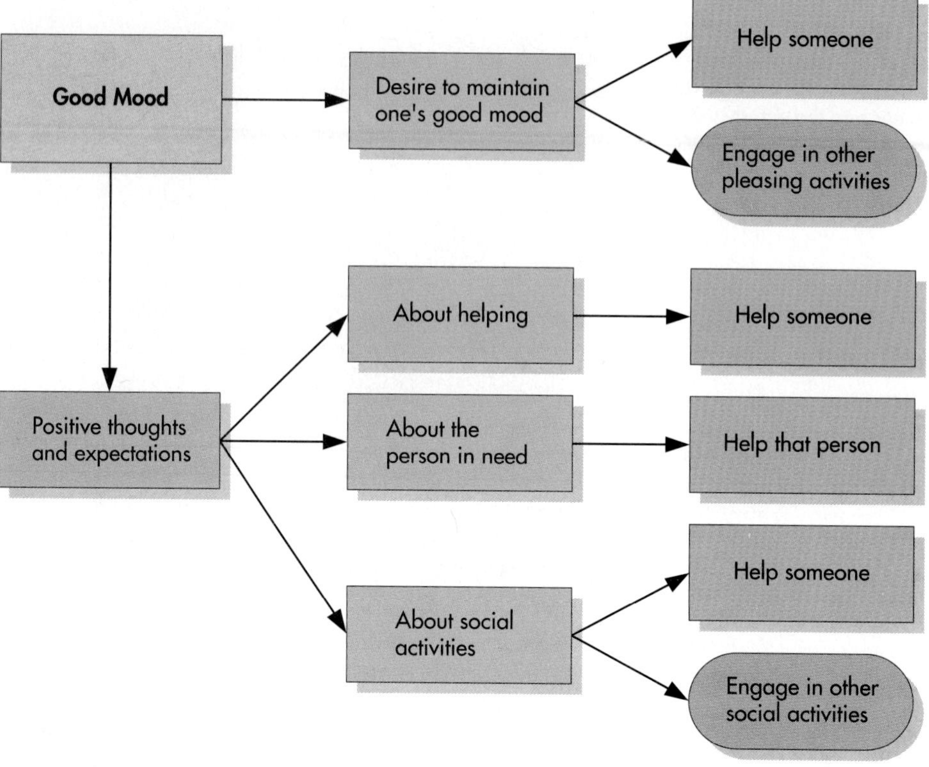

Figure 7.1 **Effects of a Good Mood on Helping: Alternative Paths.** How does a good mood increase helping? One possibility is that the desire to maintain a good mood leads to helping because helping makes people (continue to) feel good. Alternatively, positive thoughts generated by being in a good mood may lead people to help in order to obtain the rewards they expect from being helpful. You should note that a good mood can also energize actions other than helping.

feel terribly guilty, while those who wreak havoc wherever they go may never suffer the least little twinge.

We usually assume that the same person who triggers our guilt receives our help. Have you ever felt guilty about getting too worked up during a trivial disagreement with a friend? Did you gratefully seize the next available opportunity to help that individual? In such cases, being helpful restores an existing relationship that we value. But the impact of guilt on helping can be much more widespread.

Imagine yourself in the following situation. A stranger approaches you on the street and asks you to use his camera to take his picture for a school project. You get ready, aim, and . . . nothing. The camera doesn't work. Looking concerned, the stranger says the camera is rather delicate, asks you if you touched any of the dials, and informs you that it will have to be fixed. You continue on your way down the street. As you pass a young woman, she drops a file folder containing some papers. Now, here's the question: Are you more likely to help the woman pick up her papers because you think you broke the other person's camera?

Probably. In an experiment that used this setup, 80 percent of subjects who were led to believe that they had broken the man's camera helped the woman pick up her papers; only 40 percent of subjects who had no broken-camera experience stopped to help (Cunningham et al., 1980). Thus, subjects who unintentionally harmed one individual were more helpful to the next person. According to Roy Baumeister and his colleagues (1994), such spillover effects provide an especially vivid demonstration of the interpersonal nature of guilt and its function of enhancing, maintaining, and repairing relationships. Feeling guilty, they contend, motivates us to strengthen whatever social relations are at hand.

Self-awareness is closely related to guilt feelings. As described in Chapter 2, focusing on the self increases our sensitivity to discrepancies between our values and our actions (Wicklund, 1975). Since such discrepancies are unpleasant, self-aware individuals are strongly motivated to live up to their own internal standards. You can become more aware of yourself in various ways—such as seeing yourself in a mirror or store window, reading your name in the newspaper, or hearing your name called out in class.

The effects of self-focus on helping depend on whether you pay more attention to yourself or to your values (Gibbons & Wicklund, 1982). Thinking about our own needs takes our mind off the needs of others. But when the value of helping is particularly important for an individual or particularly conspicuous in a specific situation, then self-awareness increases helping because the individual wants to behave in accordance with this personal standard. For example, becoming self-aware during the Christmas season, when values of love and charity are prominent in many people's minds, should increase helping behavior—but not among those worried about getting all their Christmas shopping done in time!

The influence of self-awareness on helping is also affected by people's feelings. When people are in a good mood, anxious self-concerns are reduced (Berkowitz, 1987). With fewer self-concerns to distract from the desire to live up to helpful standards, the self-aware individual in a good mood should be more willing to lend a hand.

But what about a bad mood? Here, the key is whether people accept responsibility for their feelings (Rogers et al., 1982). If the responsibility is placed elsewhere, negative feelings neither enhance self-awareness nor increase helping. However, assuming the responsibility for our own distress allows us to respond to the plight of others. When an individual takes personal responsibility for a bad mood, self-awareness is intensified and—as long as the value of helping is important—helpful behaviors multiply. These relationships among mood, self-awareness, and helping are depicted in Figure 7.2.

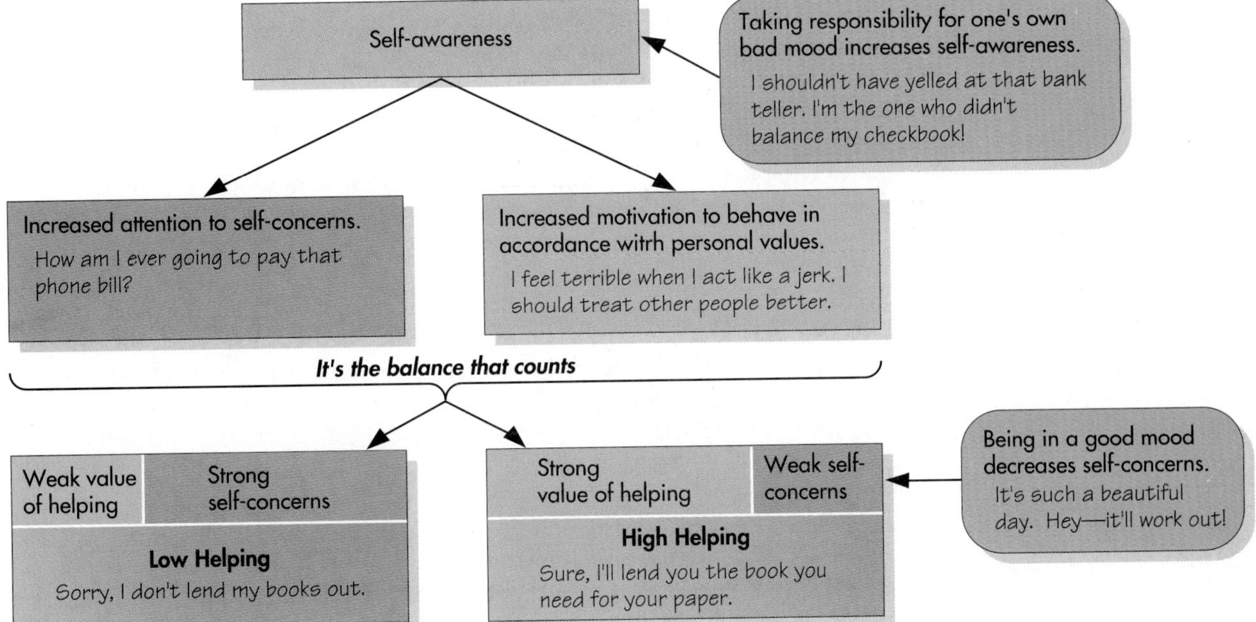

Figure 7.2 Self-Awareness and Helping: A Delicate Balance. The effect of self-awareness on helping depends on the balance between the value of helping and self-concerns. Increased self-awareness will increase helping when the value of helping is strong and self-concerns are weak. As you can see, taking responsibility for one's own negative mood increases self-awareness, while being in a good mood decreases self-concerns.

negative state relief model The proposition that people help others in order to counteract their own feelings of sadness.

Guilt and self-awareness can promote helpful behavior because people want to avoid feeling bad about failing to do the right thing. In their **negative state relief model,** Robert Cialdini and his colleagues stress that people also want to avoid feeling sad (Cialdini et al., 1973; Manucia et al., 1984). As noted earlier, people know that helping makes them feel good. So, if helping can serve as a mood maintenance strategy, could it also serve as a mood repair technique? Yes, says Cialdini. When you're suffering from the blues or the blahs, you will help in order to feel better.

It seems reasonable, but the evidence is mixed—leading to a vigorous debate on the pros (Cialdini & Fultz, 1990) and cons (Miller & Carlson, 1990) of the negative state relief model. Recent research offers an even split, for and against the key assumption that sadness elicits a desire for positive experiences. In one study, greater expectations of feeling sad were correlated with a stronger preference for listening to a pleasant radio broadcast (Fultz & Nielsen, 1993). In another, however, subjects in a sad mood did *not* differ from those in a neutral mood in their preference for watching a happy videotape and were *less* likely than those in a happy mood to prefer the happy video (Wegener & Petty, 1994). At this point, the negative state relief model is down, but certainly not out—and more research is needed before making the final call.

Looking back over this section, you might begin to notice an interesting pattern. Each possible emotional effect on helping that we've described is tied, one way or another, to self-interest. People in a good mood help in order to maintain their happiness or because they have greater expectations of a happy outcome. People in a bad mood help in order to feel less guilty, more consistent with their values, or less sad. It seems that the reason we help others is to help ourselves. But wait. There is another point of view.

Motivational Factors in Helping

egoistic Motivated by the desire to increase one's own welfare.

Although most psychological theories assume an **egoistic,** self-interested bottom line, not everyone is content with this account of the motives for human behavior. Consider, for example, the many college students who participate in volunteer activities: tutoring refugees and disadvantaged youngsters, serving meals at a food kitchen, signing up potential bone marrow donors, working in community service agencies—the list goes on and on (Sanoff & Leight, 1994). Are they all just looking out for number one?

altruistic Motivated by the desire to increase another's welfare.

Daniel Batson (1991) thinks not. He believes that some helpful actions are **altruistic,** motivated by the desire to increase another's welfare. Batson's definition of altruism differs from others' use of the term. On the one hand, he is less inclusive than Rushton, whose notion of an altruistic personality implies that all helpful actions in the absence of a clear external reward are altruistic. On the other hand, he is more inclusive than those who restrict altruism to helpful actions requiring personal sacrifice by the helper. For Batson, it's the nature of the helper's motive that counts. Regardless of whether you win the gold or lose your shirt, so long as your primary motive is to help the other person, your behavior is altruistic.

Empathy and Altruism Batson's model of altruism is based on his view of the consequences of empathy, which has long been viewed as a basic factor in promoting positive behavior toward others (Eisenberg & Miller, 1987). Although its definition has been much debated, most researchers regard empathy as a multidi-

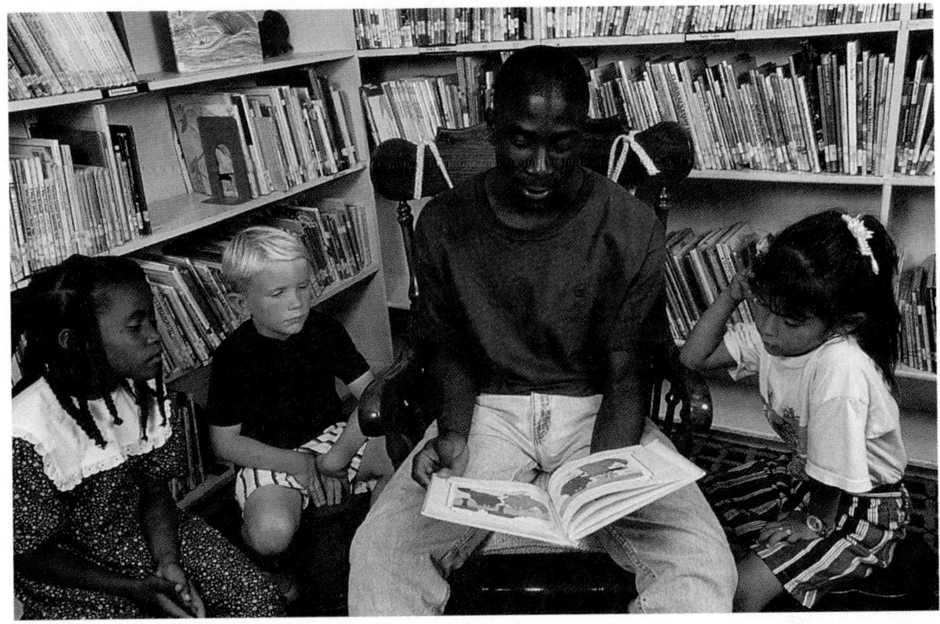

This college student reading to children at a local library is just one of many thousands of students who participate in volunteer activities. Why do they take the time and make the effort to help others? Is their motivation egoistic or altruistic?

mensional phenomenon with both cognitive and emotional components (Davis, 1994; Eisenberg et al., 1994). The major cognitive component of empathy is *perspective-taking,* using the power of imagination to try to see the world through someone else's eyes. There are two basic emotional components. One is *personal distress:* self-oriented reactions to a person in need—such as being alarmed, troubled, or upset. In contrast, *empathic concern* involves other-oriented feelings such as sympathy, compassion, and tenderness.

According to Batson, perspective-taking is the first step toward altruism. Perceiving someone in need and imagining how that person feels create other-oriented feelings of empathic concern, which in turn produce the altruistic motive to reduce the other person's distress. However, if the perspective of the needy person is *not* adopted, the perceiver experiences self-oriented feelings of personal distress, which elicit the egoistic motive to reduce one's own distress. The basic features of Batson's **empathy-altruism hypothesis** are outlined in Figure 7.3, which appears on the next page.

empathy-altruism hypothesis The proposition that empathic concern for a person in need produces an altruistic motive for helping.

But now comes the hard part. As outside observers, how can we tell the difference between egoistic and altruistic motives? In both cases, the person helps, but for different reasons. Confronted with this puzzle, Batson came up with an elegant solution. It depends, he says, on how easy it is to escape from a helping situation. When empathic concern is low, people can satisfy their motive to reduce their own distress through helping the person in need *or* through escaping from the scene of the victim's suffering. Out of sight, out of mind—so long, personal distress. But when empathic concern is high, people have no such choice. Only by helping the victim can the motive to reduce the victim's distress be satisfied. This logic lets us separate the sheep from the goats. When a person's motive is egoistic, helping should decline if it's easy for the individual to escape from the situation. When a person's motive is altruistic, however, help will be given regardless of the ease of escape.

To see how this works, put yourself in the position of a subject in an experiment conducted by Batson and his colleagues (1981). Arriving at the research

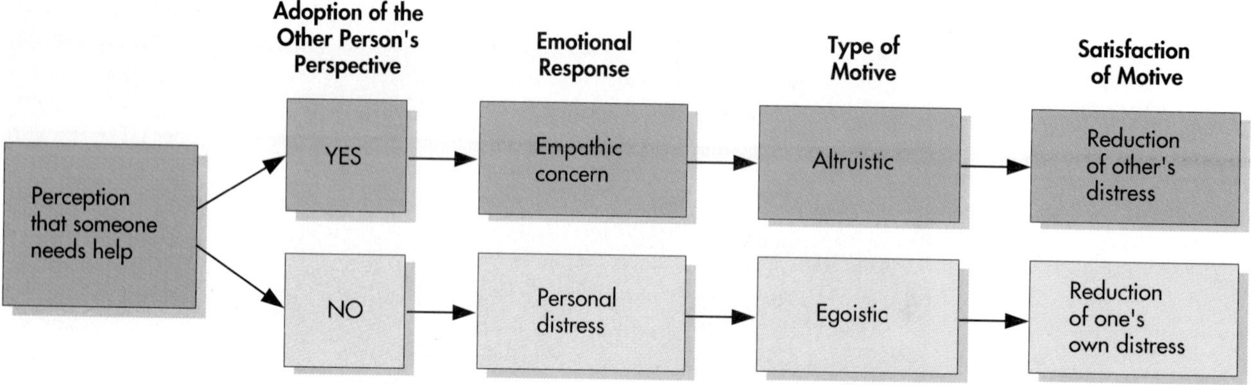

Figure 7.3 **The Empathy-Altruism Hypothesis.** According to the empathy-altruism hypothesis, taking the perspective of a person in need creates feelings of empathic concern, which produce the altruistic motive to reduce the other person's distress. When people do *not* take the other's perspective, they experience feelings of personal distress, which produce the egoistic motive to reduce their own discomfort. (Based on Batson, 1991.)

laboratory, you're told that although another subject, Elaine, is a few minutes late, you should go ahead and read an information sheet. The material you're given informs you that the upcoming study will investigate task performance under unpleasant conditions. One of the participants will perform a task while receiving random electric shocks; the other will observe. Drawing lots to determine assignments, you're relieved at your good fortune: You'll be the observer while Elaine performs the task.

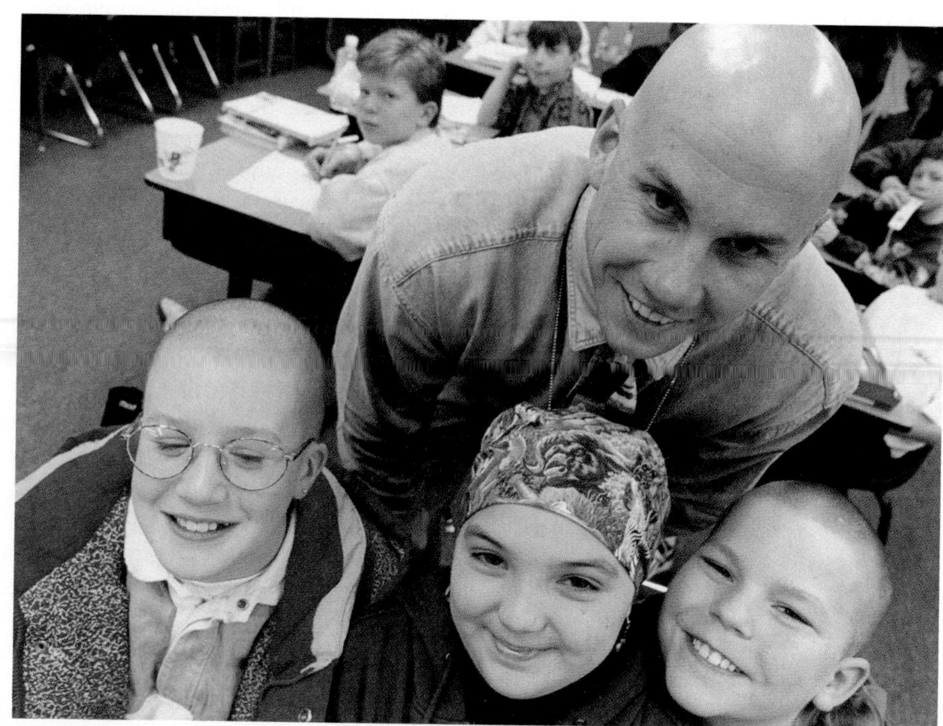

According to the empathy-altruism hypothesis, taking the perspective of someone in need is the first step toward altruism. When Sarah DeCristoforo returned to school after receiving chemotherapy for leukemia, her teacher and two friends actually put themselves in her place in one highly visible respect—they shaved their heads. Here, Sarah, wearing a scarf, is surrounded by her supporters.

You are then escorted to the observation room. Over closed-circuit TV, you see that Elaine has arrived and is hooked up to some scary-looking equipment. After receiving a number of shocks, she appears quite uncomfortable. Asking for a glass of water, she tells the experimenter about a frightening childhood experience when she was thrown from a horse against an electric fence. For Elaine, the shocks she is now receiving are very unpleasant, but she says she wants to go on. The experimenter hesitates; perhaps Elaine should stop at this point. And then the experimenter has a bright idea. Would *you* be willing to trade places?

Actually, Elaine was a trained confederate and never got shocked. But the experimental procedures created a compelling dilemma for subjects. Would they suffer for someone else? The answer rests on the combinations of empathic concern and difficulty of escape manipulated in the experiment. Since similarity increases empathic thoughts and feelings (Houston, 1990), half of the subjects were told that Elaine's personal values and interests were very similar to their own. The other half were told they were quite different. To create an easy-escape condition, half the subjects were informed that they could leave after witnessing two of the ten trials during which Elaine would receive random shocks. Those in the difficult-escape condition were required to witness all ten trials. The experimenter's invitation to trade places came at the end of two trials, letting easy-escape subjects off the hook but keeping difficult-escape subjects still dangling.

So, who agreed to trade places with Elaine? As you can see in Figure 7.4, the vast majority of high-empathic-concern subjects helped out, regardless of the ease or difficulty of escape. Most low-empathic-concern subjects also helped when they knew they would have to continue to watch Elaine suffer unless they took her place. But when they believed they could leave right away, most of the low-empathic-concern subjects did not come to Elaine's rescue. Just as the empathy-altruism hypothesis predicted, when the escape hatch was wide open, subjects with little empathic concern took the easy way out. Those with high empathic concern stayed to help.

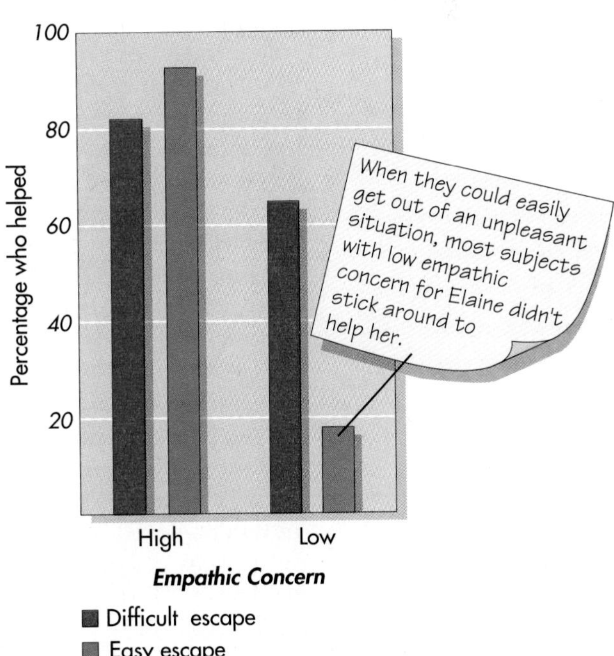

Figure 7.4 **When Empathy Helps.** These results supported the predictions made by the empathy-altruism hypothesis. When empathic concern was high, most people helped regardless of whether escape was easy or difficult. But among subjects with low levels of empathic concern, fewer people helped when escape was easy than when it was difficult. (Based on Batson et al., 1981.)

Egoistic Alternatives Can we conclude, then, that altruism really does exist? Batson and his colleagues believe so. Others are not so sure and offer egoistic alternatives. The ensuing debate between these different perspectives has been as intense as a championship match at Wimbledon.

The first egoistic contender is empathy-specific punishment for not helping. Perhaps people learn from experience that an empathic response *should* increase helping. If so, they could anticipate feeling guilty whenever they respond empathically but fail to help the person in need. They might then help in order to avoid guilt. This explanation, however, does not seem to hold. Neither external sources of guilt feelings (such as social disapproval for not helping) nor internal sources (when the decision of whether to help is completely private) can account for the helpful inclinations produced by empathic concern (Batson et al., 1988; Fultz et al., 1986).

Second, there are potential empathy-specific rewards for helping. Negative state relief, described earlier in this chapter, could be one. Perhaps empathic concern for a person in need increases feelings of sadness, which in turn increase the need for mood enhancement. During a flurry of volleys back and forth across the net, evidence was secured in favor of the negative-state-relief explanation (Cialdini et al., 1987; Schaller & Cialdini, 1988) and against it (Batson et al., 1989). But the empathy-altruism hypothesis gained an important advantage when its position was supported by a team of investigators without any previous commitment to either side (Schroeder et al., 1988).

Another egoistic alternative involving empathy-specific rewards emphasizes positive well-being rather than negative relief. Kyle Smith and his colleagues (1989) maintain that empathic concern enhances the helper's sensitivity to the good feelings experienced by the person receiving help. There's only one hitch. You can't share the recipient's joy unless you know the person was actually helped. If there's no way for you to find out whether your efforts were successful, empathic concern should *not* increase helping.

In a test of this proposition, subjects watched a videotape of an interview with a young woman who said she was having difficulty coping with the stresses and strains of her first year in college. Half of the subjects were told that if they provided suggestions and advice to help this person, they would see another videotaped interview with her later in the semester, during which she would report how their advice had affected her adjustment to college. The other subjects were told that, regardless of whether they offered advice, they would not have any further contact with the person they had seen in the videotape. On the basis of their self-reported responses to the video, subjects were categorized as high versus low in relative empathy (empathic concern minus personal distress).

Empathic joy seemed to win the match. Subjects high in relative empathy who expected to be able to find out about the effectiveness of their helpful behavior were more likely to offer advice to the stressed-out college student than were subjects in the other three conditions (see Figure 7.5). Contrary to the empathy-altruism hypothesis, empathy did not increase helpfulness among subjects who did not expect feedback.

But team Batson came right back. If individuals help in order to secure the delights of empathic joy, they should be eager to hear about successful outcomes and uninterested in failures. In fact, however, this preference for "the good news only, please" is characteristic of individuals *low* in empathic concern (Batson et al., 1991). Those high in empathic concern want to know the outcome of their efforts regardless of whether successful helping is likely or improbable. They ap-

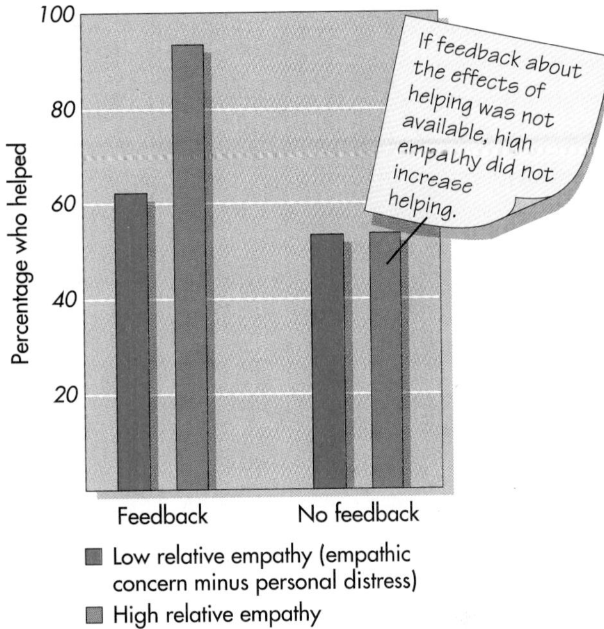

Figure 7.5 Joyful Helping and the Need to Know. These results supported the predictions made by the empathic joy hypothesis. Among subjects who believed they could obtain feedback about the effects of their helpful behavior, more of those high in relative empathy helped than did those low in relative empathy. But when feedback was not available, high relative empathy did *not* increase helping. (Based on K. D. Smith et al., 1989.)

pear genuinely interested in the other's well-being—which, of course, is exactly what the empathy-altruism hypothesis contends.

Is Altruism Limited? Despite the egoistic alternatives that continue to be proposed, the evidence for the empathy-altruism hypothesis is quite strong. Nevertheless, it has its limits. One limitation is set by the existence of multiple motives for helping. Batson has never claimed that *all* helping is altruistically motivated. No doubt, many helpful acts are best explained in terms of the processes we consider elsewhere in this chapter. And any single helpful action can be the result of a mixture of egoistic and altruistic motives. Mark Snyder (1993) suggests, for example, that the most effective way to increase helping is to encourage people to recognize and feel comfortable with the convergence of self-oriented and other-oriented concerns.

Another limit is created by the fact that motives do not guarantee behavior. Empathic concern does not always increase helping, as shown by studies in which the needy individual is disliked by the potential helper (Otten et al., 1991), the person needs help on a problem that differs from the problem that initially aroused empathic concern (Dovidio et al., 1990), or the potential helper expects to have to endure significant suffering in order to help (Batson et al., 1983). Are these failures of the empathy-altruism hypothesis? Or do they reflect limits on altruism itself? In Batson's view, such findings indicate that altruism does not exist in a cost-free psychological universe. When egoistic costs are greater than the altruistic motive can bear, the other-oriented impulse cannot prevail. Perhaps in order to avoid such internal conflicts, people who anticipate being asked for high-cost assistance often avoid empathy-inducing experiences (Shaw et al., 1994).

A possible third limitation cuts even closer to the fundamental nature of altruism. Distinguishing between egoistic and altruistic motives requires the assumption that there is a clear divide between the self and the other. What if there isn't? What if, as Daniel Wegner (1980, p. 133) suggests, empathy reflects "a basic confusion between ourselves and others"? What if, as Arthur Aron and his colleagues (1991, 1992) propose, those in close relationships incorporate the other into the self? If you feel someone else's needs as deeply as you feel your own, then there should be no difference between an egoistic motive and an altruistic one. Is there a level of love, compassion, and caring that lies beyond altruism? Think about it.

INTERPERSONAL INFLUENCES: WHOM DO PEOPLE HELP?

However influential they might be, personal factors alone do not a helper make. The characteristics of the person in need are important as well. Are some people more likely than others to receive help? Are some helpers particularly responsive to certain kinds of individuals who need assistance? Here, we explore some of the interpersonal aspects of helping.

Perceived Characteristics of the Person in Need

Although there are potentially many characteristics of a person in need that might affect whether that individual is helped, researchers have paid special attention to personal attractiveness and the responsibility for needing assistance.

It Helps to Be Attractive In Chapter 5, we described the social advantages enjoyed by physically attractive individuals. The bias for beauty also affects helping, as Peter Benson and his colleagues (1976) observed in a large metropolitan airport. Darting into a phone booth to make a call, each of 604 travelers discovered some materials supposedly left behind accidently by the previous caller (but actually planted by the experimenters): a completed graduate school application form, a photograph of the applicant, and a stamped, addressed envelope. In some packets, the photo depicted a physically attractive individual; in others, the person was relatively unattractive. What was a busy traveler to do? When the researchers checked their mail, they found that people were more likely to send in the materials of good-looking applicants than those of the less attractive applicants.

Physical appearance, of course, is only one aspect of attractiveness. Friendly individuals also receive a more generous response (Lynn & Mynier, 1993). And, sometimes, the charisma of one person can determine how much help other people receive. On Thursday November 7, 1991, Earvin "Magic" Johnson Jr. announced to a stunned public that he had contracted HIV, the virus that causes AIDS. By coincidence, Louis Penner and Barbara Fritzsche (1993) had just completed a study in which college undergraduates were given the opportunity to assist a graduate student who was described as having AIDS. These investigators decided to repeat their study three more times after Magic's announcement. As you can see in Figure 7.6, the amount of time subjects were willing to volunteer increased after the announcement, but then declined back to the pre-announcement baseline. It appears that for a while, the immense attractiveness of Magic Johnson spread like a protective cloak over others who were HIV-positive and increased the help they received. Unfortunately, once the shock wore off, so did the help.

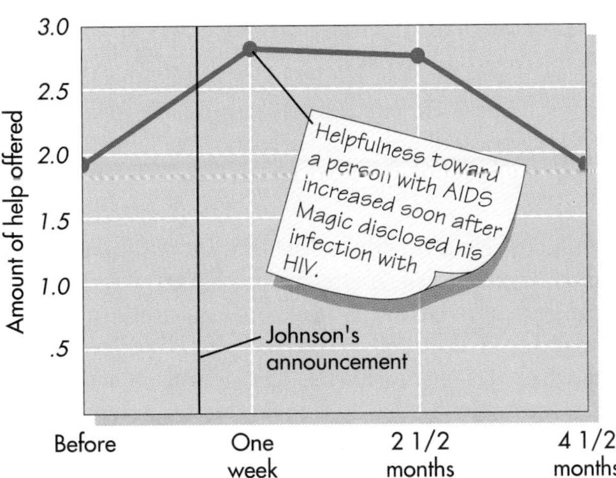

Figure 7.6 **Magic's Influence on Helping Others.** Soon after basketball superstar Magic Johnson announced that he was infected with HIV, there was an increase in the amount of time volunteered by college undergraduates to assist a graduate student who had AIDS. However, four and one-half months after the announcement, the amount of time volunteered returned to the pre-announcement level. (Penner & Fritzsche, 1993.)

It Hurts to Be Responsible At some time or another, most students have had the experience of being asked to lend their class notes to a classmate. Has this ever happened to you? If so, you can compare your reactions to those of the subjects in a study conducted by Richard Barnes and his colleagues (1979). In this research, students received a call from an experimental confederate posing as another student, who asked to borrow their class notes to prepare for an upcoming exam. The reason for this request varied. To some subjects, the caller said, "I just don't seem to have the ability to take good notes. I really try to take good notes, but sometimes I just can't do it." Other students were told that "I just don't seem to have the motivation to take good notes. I really can take good notes, but sometimes I just don't try." You probably won't be surprised to learn that the caller received much more help from those who were informed he had tried yet failed than from those who were told he hadn't tried at all.

Bluntly stating that you didn't even try to help yourself may seem like an obvious way to ensure that others won't help you out. But even when the circumstances are more complex and the causes more subtle, people's beliefs about the needy individual's responsibility influence helping. The attribution-affect-action theory (or triple A, for short) sets out the steps (Schmidt & Weiner, 1988; Weiner, 1993). When people attribute a person's need for assistance to factors beyond the individual's control, they do not hold that person responsible, feel sympathy and pity for the person's plight, and are likely to help. However, when people perceive a person's difficulties as caused by controllable factors, they hold the person responsible, feel angry or irritated, and are less likely to help.

Ultimately, attributions of responsibility reside in the mind of the perceiver. And perceivers differ in the attributions they make for the same need for assistance. Political conservatives, for instance, are more likely to attribute personal responsibility than are political liberals. Are, then, conservatives less helpful? Not necessarily. When asked to allocate educational resources to an alcoholic, conservatives were less generous than liberals (Skitka & Tetlock, 1993). But when the person in need was described as having successfully quit drinking and regularly attending Alcoholics Anonymous meetings, conservatives allocated *more* resources than did liberals. If you're seeking help from a conservative, it's a good idea to dwell on all those obstacles you've overcome.

The Fit Between Giver and Receiver

The impact of political ideology on helping illustrates a general point. Some potential helpers are particularly responsive to some kinds of potential recipients. In this section, we look at a variety of ways in which helping depends on the fit between a giver and a receiver.

Similarity: Helping Those Just Like Us Similarity may be the closest fit of all. All kinds of similarity—from dress to attitudes to nationality—increase our willingness to help (Dovidio, 1984). Indeed, similarity seems to be the common denominator for a number of psychological processes that affect helping. Similarity increases attraction (Byrne, 1971), and, as we have seen, perceived attractiveness increases helping. Likewise, similarity increases empathy (Houston, 1990), and, as we have seen, empathic concern increases helping.

The influence of similarity could even be a form of kinship selection. If similarity in appearance reflects the degree of genetic overlap (or, at least, if people think it does), then sociobiologists would expect people to help similar-looking relatives more than dissimilar ones (Segal, 1993). We might also help similar, though biologically unrelated individuals because we overgeneralize the assumption that what looks alike must genetically be alike (Krebs, 1987).

The strong, multiply determined effect of similarity on helping suggests that members of the same race would help each other more than members of different races. However, research on black-white helping in the United States indicates that the effects of racial similarity are highly variable. For instance, Faye Crosby and her colleagues (1980) found a same-race helping bias in 44 percent of the studies they reviewed. Sometimes Whites were more biased, sometimes Blacks. In the remaining studies, there was either no discrimination or reverse discrimination in which people helped those of a different race *more* than they helped members of their own race.

There's no simple way to iron out all these inconsistencies, but we should examine some of the issues they raise. First, although helping can be a compassionate response to another, it can also be seen as a sign of superiority over the person who needs help (Rosen et al., 1986). Thus, cross-racial helping isn't always a sign of egalitarian attitudes. Second, public displays of racial prejudice risk social disapproval, and prejudiced individuals may bend over backward, in public at least, to avoid revealing their attitudes. As discussed in Chapter 4, however, modern racism relies on more subtle forms of discrimination. For example, if people are provided with an excuse *not* to help, racial discrimination in helping is more likely (Frey & Gaertner, 1986). And then there are those little signs of consideration—picking up something a person has dropped, bringing someone a cup of coffee—that may be withheld from those whose presence is resented (Dovidio & Gaertner, 1981, 1983). For newcomers on the job or in the neighborhood, these little things can mean a lot, making them feel welcomed—or shut out.

Closeness: A Little Help for Our Friends As we would expect, people are usually more helpful toward those they know and care about than toward strangers or superficial acquaintances (Clark et al., 1987; Schoenrade et al., 1986). But there may be an exception to this general rule: What if a person's ego is threatened? According to the *self-evaluation maintenance model* (Tesser, 1988), there are two very different responses to knowledge of a superior performance by a significant other. If the achievement occurs in an area *not* relevant to our own ego, we can indulge in the delight of BIRGing, basking in reflected glory. If the area is relevant to our own ego, however, we may experience envy and resentment.

To apply this perspective to helping behavior, suppose you have just finished working on a task and are told that you performed "a little below average." Then two other people take their turns at the same task; one of them is a stranger and the other a close friend. You are asked to give some clues to each individual. The available clues differ in their level of difficulty. Some are easy and will boost the person's performance; others are so difficult that they will interfere with a good performance. Will you give your friend easier, more helpful clues than you give to the stranger?

As the self-evaluation maintenance model would predict, it depends on the task. When subjects found themselves in the situation we've just described, those who believed that the task was a trivial game helped their friend more than they helped the stranger (Tesser & Smith, 1980). But when the task was important and relevant to their own self-esteem, subjects were slightly *less* helpful to their friend than to the stranger (see Figure 7.7). In a conflict between our own ego and the welfare of a friend, the need to protect our self-esteem can sometimes overcome our helpful inclinations.

Gender and Helping Here's a quick, one-question quiz: Who helps more, men or women? Before you answer, consider the following situations.

A. Two strangers pass on the street. Suddenly, one of them needs help that might be dangerous to give. Other people are watching. The person in need is female.

B. Two individuals have a close relationship. Every so often one of them needs assistance that takes time and energy to provide but is not physically dangerous. No one else is around to notice whether help is given. The person who needs help is either male or female.

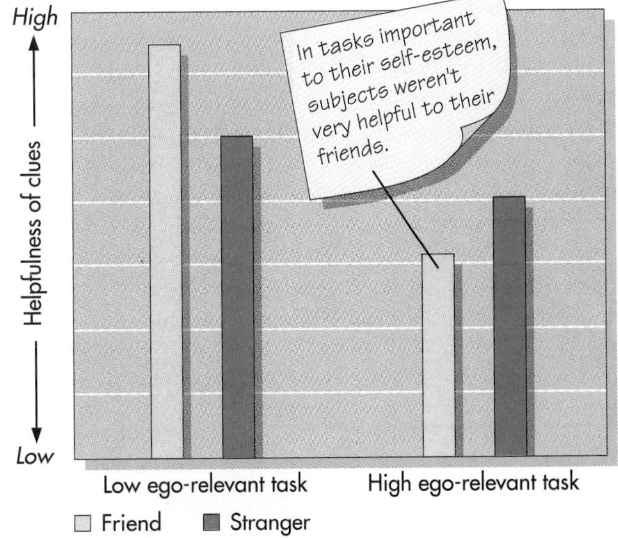

Figure 7.7 Not Giving Much Help to Our Friends. People usually help their friends more than they help strangers, but not always. In this study, subjects who thought they had performed poorly on a task gave clues on the same task to a friend and a stranger. When the task was not important for subjects' self-esteem, they gave more helpful clues to their friend than to the stranger. When the task was highly ego-relevant, they gave slightly less helpful clues to their friend than to the stranger. (Data from Tesser & Smith, 1980.)

Is your answer the same for both situations? It shouldn't be. Situation A is a classic male-helper scenario. Here, the helper is a "knight in shining armor"—physically brave and chivalrous, rescuing a lady in distress. Because social psychologists have tended to focus on these kinds of emergency situations, their research has found that, on the average, men are more helpful than women and women receive more help than do men (Eagly & Crowley, 1986).

Situation B is the classic female-helper scenario. Every day, millions of women—mothers, sisters, wives, and female friends—provide TLC for their loved ones (Kessler et al., 1985). Though it lacks the high drama of an emergency intervention, this type of helping, called "social support," plays a crucial role in the quality of our lives. In Chapter 14, we describe the effects of social support on physical and psychological health.

Helping in a Just World We've seen three ways in which the fit between givers and receivers increases helping: similarity, closeness (which may be disrupted by a threat to one's self-esteem), and the relationship between gender and the type of help the person needs. Here's a fourth and final example. As you may recall from Chapter 3, the *belief in a just world* rests on the assumption that people get what they deserve: that good people will secure life's blessings and only bad people will suffer (Lerner, 1980).

Presumably this belief is so compelling, despite its obvious inaccuracy, because it has such a comforting implication: If *we* are good, *we* will be rewarded. Although believing in a just world may be common, there are marked individual differences in the strength of this belief (Rubin & Peplau, 1975). By definition, a strong believer in a just world is relatively unsympathetic to victims of misfortune.

But will a strong just-worlder refuse to help? Let's see. In a study conducted just before the Christmas holidays, college students were given a chance to donate their research-participation earnings to needy families (Miller, 1977). Some

Awareness of the suffering of innocents undermines the self-comforting belief in a just world where people get what they deserve.

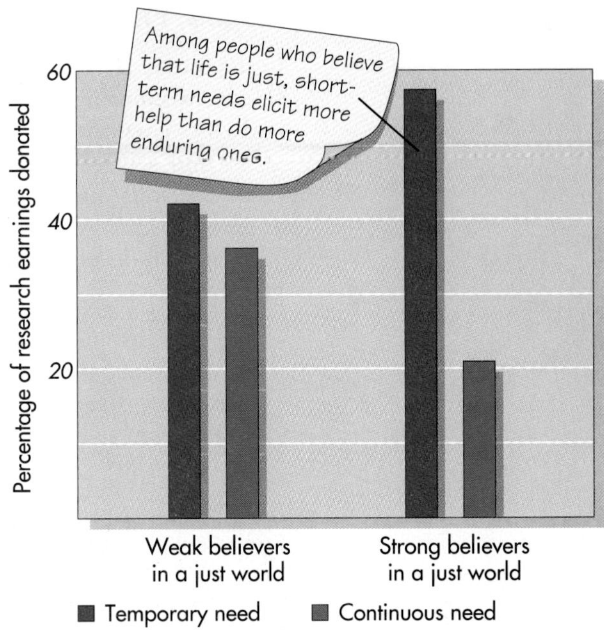

Figure 7.8 **Belief in a Just World and Duration of Need.** On the basis of questionnaire responses, subjects were divided into weak and strong believers in a just world. Asked to donate money to needy families, weak believers gave similar amounts regardless of the duration of need. Strong believers, however, gave more to temporarily needy families than to those whose need was longer lasting. (Data from Miller, 1977.)

subjects were told that the department of psychology was raising money for families who needed help at Christmas time. Others were informed that the psychology department's fund-raising activities for needy families were a year-long effort; no mention was made of the special needs of families at Christmas. Subjects whose belief in a just world was relatively weak donated at similar, moderate levels for both Christmas-specific or year-long neediness. In contrast, strong just-worlders made a sharp distinction. Temporary need over Christmas produced considerable generosity, but continuous need was met with Scrooge-like stinginess (see Figure 7.8).

Whenever injustice can be easily and quickly rectified, believers in a just world are more willing to help (Bierhoff et al., 1991). By aiding someone who needs just a little help to set things right, the just-world believer confirms that, yes indeed, things work out and life is fair. But what about suffering that is widespread and enduring? Here, the help provided by any one individual is but a drop in a very large bucket, and the strong believer is less likely to contribute. Enduring needs for help pose a threat to the belief in a just world because they convey an unwanted message: Things don't always work out and life isn't always fair. It takes courage and dedication to get past that message and continue helping. Oskar Schindler knew the world he lived in was not just, but he didn't let that stop him.

SITUATIONAL INFLUENCES: WHEN DO PEOPLE HELP?

If helping is to occur, there has to be a giver and a receiver. There also has to be a context, a frame. Every potential helping opportunity takes place in a specific situation that can affect the outcome. In this section, we examine the impact of a wide range of situational factors on helping.

Models, Norms, and Rewards

In the movie *It Could Happen to You,* Nicolas Cage and Bridget Fonda play two wacky, wonderful, remarkably helpful individuals trying to do good in the big bad city. They feel out of place, "like freaks." For a while, it appears that the greed and self-interest of others will do them in. But then what went around comes back around. Their helpfulness inspires others to imitate them, and Cage and Fonda are saved from misfortune.

Helpful models are not confined to romantic comedies. Here are some real-life possibilities:

- You see someone at the side of the highway struggling to change a flat tire.
- You approach a table where volunteers are collecting money for famine-relief efforts.
- You hear the announcement of a blood-donation drive.

Now, think about your own behavior. Would you be more likely to help—change the tire, contribute money, donate blood—if you observed someone else help first? Probably. Observing helpful models usually does increase helping (Bryan & Test, 1967; Macaulay, 1970; Sarason et al., 1991).

Why do models of helping expand the help that's available? Three reasons stand out. First, they provide an example of behavior for us to imitate directly. Second, when they are rewarded for their helpful behavior, models teach us that helping is valuable, which strengthens our own inclination to be helpful. Third, the behavior of models informs us about the standards of conduct in our society. In the next section, we focus on some help-relevant societal standards.

social norms General rules of conduct reflecting standards of social approval and disapproval.

Social Norms: A Helpful Standard General rules of conduct established by society are called **social norms.** These norms embody standards of socially approved and disapproved behavior. They are learned from what people say and from what they do (Rice & Grusec, 1975). Today, the mass media convey a great deal of information about normative expectations, and TV is an especially powerful influence (Hearold, 1986; Oskamp, 1988).

Two sets of social norms bear directly on helping. The first consists of norms based on fairness. The *norm of reciprocity* establishes quid-pro-quo transactions as a socially approved standard: People who give to you should be paid back (Schopler, 1970). Accordingly, people usually help those who have helped them, especially when the initial assistance was given voluntarily (Gross & Latané, 1974).

This bumper sticker promotes a social norm of helpfulness to others.

Today, I will commit one random act of senseless KINDNESS... Will You?

© 1993 THE KINDNESS CRUSADE
(805) 395-4612

Equity, described in Chapter 6 on Intimate Relationships, is the basis of another norm calling for fairness in our treatment of others (Walster et al., 1978a). The *norm of equity* prescribes that people who are overbenefited (receiving more benefits than earned) should help those who are underbenefited (receiving fewer benefits than earned). Such help restores an equitable balance.

norm of social responsibility A moral standard emphasizing that people should help those who need assistance.

norm of justice A moral standard emphasizing that people should help those who deserve assistance.

Other help-relevant social norms go beyond an immediate sense of fairness to a larger sense of what is right. The **norm of social responsibility** dictates that people should help those who *need* assistance (Berkowitz, 1972). This norm creates a sense of duty and obligation, to which people respond by giving more help to those in greater need of it (Bornstein, 1994). The **norm of justice,** however, requires people to help because others *deserve* their assistance (Lerner & Meindl, 1981). This norm creates a standard of what is morally correct.

Although these last two norms often coincide and can be hard to tell apart, they differ in terms of the principles they express. The norm of social responsibility is person based, calling on us to be responsive to people's needs regardless of how these needs came about. In contrast, the norm of justice is rule based, calling on us to meet the needs of those who merit our assistance. Some would argue that justice is the higher moral standard (Kohlberg, 1981). Others believe that social responsibility has the stronger claim on moral superiority (Gilligan, 1982).

The social norms of reciprocity, equity, social responsibility, and justice can have powerful effects. Yet sometimes they fail to produce the helpful behavior they prescribe. Why? Perhaps altruism interferes. The motive to help one specific individual for whom we feel empathic concern may disrupt more evenhanded assistance based on general principles of fairness and morality (Batson et al., 1995). But this generality poses its own problems. So social norms are so general, so abstract, that it is not clear when they apply. People differ considerably in what they regard as unfair or immoral and in the remedies they propose in different situations.

One reason they differ is that the meaning of a social norm is influenced by the society in which we live. As illustrated in Figure 7.9, children and adults in the United States are less likely than children and adults in India to believe that people have an obligation to provide assistance to children, friends, or strangers whose need for help is not extreme (J. G. Miller et al., 1990). It appears that the Hindu Indians who participated in this study regard social responsibilities as an absolute moral obligation, while Americans apply the norm of social responsibility more selectively.

personal norms An individual's feelings of moral obligation to provide help to specific others in specific situations.

Personal Norms and Parental Effects Because social norms are so general and leave so much room for interpretation, Shalom Schwartz (1977) doubts their usefulness for understanding when helping will occur. Instead, Schwartz believes that we should focus on **personal norms:** an individual's feelings of moral obligation to provide help to *specific* others in *specific* situations (Schwartz & Howard, 1982). Heroic helpers, like Oskar Schindler who tried so hard to save everyone on his list, may have especially strong personal norms (Meindl & Lerner, 1983). Those who risk their lives to help others often deviate radically from the norms of their society, yet their behavior is not random or unprincipled. It conforms to their own personal standards. But how do these individualized norms develop?

Parental behavior may make an important contribution. In one study, for example, empathic concern for others at age thirty-one was greater for those subjects whose family life at age five was characterized by higher scores on four factors: father's involvement in child care; mother's tolerance of the child's de-

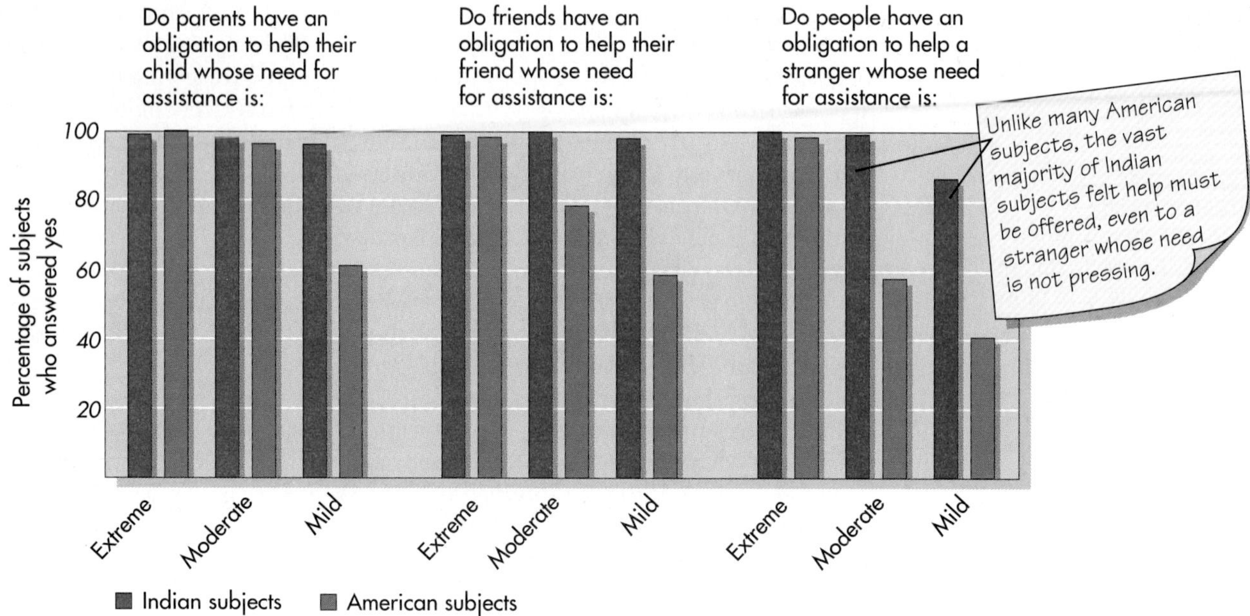

Figure 7.9 **The Norm of Social Responsibility in India and the United States.** These results compare the proportion of children and adults in India with the proportion of children and adults in the United States who said that people in different social situations have an obligation to help. As you can see, most Indian subjects perceived this obligation to exist regardless of the extent of need. In contrast, American subjects indicated that the obligation to help was reduced when the need for assistance was less extreme, especially when the person in need was a stranger. (Data from J. G. Miller et al., 1990.)

pendent behavior, her inhibition of the child's aggression, and her satisfaction with the maternal role (Koestner et al., 1990). The child's own behavior seemed to have little long-term significance, although more disobedience in the home was associated with lower levels of empathic concern in adulthood.

Heroic helpers themselves also emphasize parental influence. Oskar had a troubled relationship with his father, but he respected his father's opinions. And Hans Schindler regarded Hitler with contempt. Other individuals who helped Jews escape from the Nazis describe an intense identification with at least one parent who was a model of high moral standards (London, 1970; Oliner & Oliner, 1988). Committed civil rights activists, interviewed in the mid-1960s, reported a similar pattern of strong parental identification (Rosenhan, 1970). The good that parents do can live after them.

The Role of Rewards Based on crucial beliefs and values, personal norms are a significant part of the self-concept. In turn, one's self-concept affects helping: Labeling someone as a helpful person increases that individual's helpful behavior (Kraut, 1973; Strenta & DeJong, 1981). Indeed, because individuals with high self-esteem compensate for failure by increasing their positive view of themselves as kind, considerate, and sensitive, they help more after failure than after success (Brown & Smart, 1991).

External rewards, however, reduce self-perceptions of being a helpful person (Batson et al., 1978), suggesting that helping might be vulnerable to the overjustification effect. As indicated in Chapter 2, people rewarded for engaging in an intrinsically enjoyable activity subsequently engage less in that activity if rewards are not provided (Deci & Ryan, 1985). Although there are a number of possible explanations for the overjustification effect, it could be a matter of self-perception. Once people have expected and received a material reward for participating in an activity, they may come to perceive that the reward, not their own enjoyment, is what motivates them. Without the reward, there's no urge to act.

Research by Richard Fabes and his colleagues (1989) confirms that helping too can be overjustified. In this study, elementary school children who had previously been rewarded for helping "poor, sick children in the hospital" were less likely to continue to help in the absence of rewards for doing so. Even children who had simply seen another child rewarded for helping were less helpful in the later, free-choice situation. But note, this decline in helping occurred only among children whose mothers reported a favorable attitude toward using rewards to influence their children's behavior (see Figure 7.10). Perhaps the extensive use of rewards in child-rearing weakens children's sense of their own internal motivation, making them more susceptible to overjustification.

But what about those internal motivational pressures: the self-administered pats on the back for being helpful, the guilt pangs for failing to help? These too can affect our self-perceptions. When college students thought about why they helped others in circumstances where no external rewards were expected, their perceptions of their own *selfish* motives for helping were *increased* (Batson et al., 1987). Presumably these individuals were reminded of internal, self-interested rewards and punishments related to helping, leading them to feel less altruistic.

Now let's take the next step. If *external* rewards can decrease subsequent helping, will self-perceived *internal* rewards also reduce helpful inclinations? Maybe yes; maybe no. On the one hand, volunteers at a crisis center who emphasized altruistic reasons for helping were more likely to complete their nine-month term of service than were those who placed more importance on egoistic reasons for

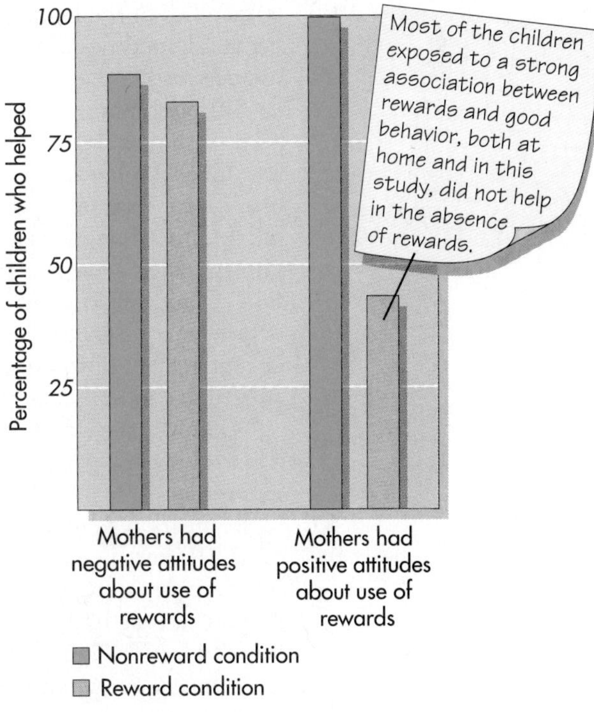

Figure 7.10 **Overjustification at a Young Age.** Among children whose mothers had negative attitudes toward the use of rewards to influence their children's behavior, associating helping with a reward did not influence helping behavior. In contrast, for children whose mothers had positive attitudes toward the use of rewards, associating helping with an external reward decreased the proportion who helped. (Based on Fabes et al., 1989.)

helping (Clary & Orenstein, 1991). On the other hand, AIDS volunteers who initially endorsed self-oriented motives, such as gaining understanding and developing personal skills, remained active volunteers for a longer period of time than did those who had initially emphasized other-oriented motives, such as humanitarian values and community concern (Omoto & Snyder, 1995).

The difference between the findings of these two studies may lie in the costs of helping. Working at a crisis center requires hard work and dedication, but the stresses and strains of helping persons with AIDS (PWAs) can be enormous. It has been said that "the good, and perhaps romanticized, intentions related to humanitarian concern simply may not be strong enough to sustain volunteers faced with the tough realities and personal costs of working with PWAs" (Snyder, 1993, p. 258). When helping demands more of us, does self-interest keep us going?

The Place Where We Live

We have seen how models, norms, parents, and rewards can influence helping behavior. But what about where we live? Does that make a difference in whether we will help someone in need? Over thirty years ago, these questions took on a special urgency because of what happened to Kitty Genovese. Returning home from work at 3 A.M. on the morning of March 13, 1964, the twenty-eight-year-old Genovese was stalked, stabbed, and raped just thirty-five yards from her own apartment building. Thirty-eight of her neighbors witnessed her ordeal. Lights went on, windows went up, but no one intervened. Finally, after a half hour of terror, one man called the police, but Genovese was dead.

The murder of Kitty Genovese shocked the nation. Were her neighbors to blame? It seemed unlikely that all thirty-eight of them could have been moral monsters. Attention shifted next to the place where the crime occurred: Queens, New York. Then, as now, the New York City metropolitan area, like other large cities in the United States, had a high rate of homicides. In the midst of the hectic, sometimes frantic pace of a big city, are pleas for help doomed to go unanswered?

Although place of residence does not seem to affect how much those in close relationships help each other (Franck, 1980; Korte, 1980), a large city does have a number of characteristics that might reduce help to strangers. Stanley Milgram (1970), for example, proposed that cities produce *stimulus overload* among their inhabitants. Bombarded by sights and sounds, city residents may wear a coat of unresponsive armor to protect themselves from being overwhelmed by stimulation. Claude Fischer (1976) noted that the residents of large urban areas are a heterogeneous group—composed of diverse nationalities, races, and ethnic backgrounds. Such diversity could diminish the sense of similarity with others, reduce empathic concern, and result in less helping.

Whatever the exact causes, people are less likely to help in urban areas than in rural ones (Steblay, 1987). A study of fifty-five Australian communities, ranging in population from 999 to over 3 million, found that spontaneous, informal help to strangers was greater where the population was smaller (Amato, 1983). Recently, Robert Levine and his colleagues (1994) examined six kinds of helping in thirty-six U.S. cities, with populations ranging from 350,000 to over 2 million. As you can see in Table 7.1, Rochester, New York, wins the title of "Most Helpful City." Although greater population was associated with less helping, density (population per square mile) was a more powerful predictor. High-density conditions are often quite stressful (Paulus, 1988). Helping in these U.S. cities was also

Table 7.1 Helping in the U.S.A.

	Dropped pen		**Hurt leg**		**Change**		**Blind person**		**Lost letter**		**United Way**	
	Percent who returned a pen dropped by a researcher walking past.		Percent who helped researcher with a leg brace pick up dropped magazines.		Percent who checked for change when asked for change by researcher.		Percent who told researcher in dark glasses, carrying white cane, when light turned green.		Percent of lost stamped, addressed letters mailed by finder.		Annual per capita contribution to United Way.	
Overall Rank												
1. Rochester, NY	50%	18th	63%	16th	50%	19th	92%	3d	83%	12th	$37.18	1st
2. Houston	71	3	68	12	73	2	80	13	77	20	17.34	19
3. Nashville	60	8	83	2	60	6	88	4	73	24	20.56	9
4. Memphis	71	4	76	6	54	15	82	12	80	17	18.09	16
5. Knoxville, TN	54	13	46	29	71	3	93	2	90	6	16.85	20
6. Louisville, KY	71	2	43	32	79	1	73	18	80	17	18.79	15
7. St. Louis	50	18	65	15	63	5	83	10	83	12	22.88	5
8. Detroit	67	5	58	22	67	4	60	24	93	3	17.40	18
9. East Lansing, MI	54	14	58	22	58	9	86	7	93	3	16.57	22
10. Chatta-nooga, TN	39	27	92	1	54	15	56	28	83	12	33.70	2
11. Indian-apolis	44	25	48	28	60	7	83	10	93	3	23.35	4
12. Columbus, OH	42	26	46	30	50	19	85	7	87	7	33.06	3
13. Canton, OH	46	22	71	10	58	8	67	20	87	7	20.10	12
14. Kansas City, MO	33	31	69	11	54	13	100	1	73	24	22.41	6
15. Worcester, MA	63	8	56	25	50	19	57	26	91	5	18.83	14
16. Santa Barbara, CA	59	9	59	20	56	11	75	16	80	17	11.92	26
17. Dallas	50	18	60	19	42	25	88	4	73	24	20.85	8
18. San Jose, CA	44	23	71	18	56	11	60	24	84	9	16.66	21
19. San Diego	56	12	75	7	35	32	50	32	100	1	11.35	28
20. Springfield, MA	75	1	57	24	38	31	50	32	72	27	20.19	11
21. Atlanta	49	21	67	13	44	23	75	16	63	31	19.55	13
22. Bakersfield, CA	57	11	63	17	50	19	88	4	57	35	4.84	35
23. Buffalo	28	34	44	31	54	13	80	13	73	24	17.62	17
24. San Francisco	67	5	29	34	39	29	56	28	84	9	14.09	24
25. Youngstown, OH	29	53	63	17	51	17	56	28	80	17	11.37	27

When six types of helping were studied in thirty-six U.S. cities, Rochester, New York, received the best marks. This research found that higher density (population per square mile) and higher cost-of-living were strongly associated with less helping. The twenty-five highest-ranking cities are listed here. (Adapted from the Boston Globe, 1994; based on data from Levine et al., 1994.)

associated with the cost of living: The higher the costs, the less help was provided, suggesting that feeling strapped can interfere with being helpful.

The Unhelpful Crowd

It appears, then, that Kitty Genovese was at a serious disadvantage in needing spontaneous emergency help in a densely populated, high-cost-of-living urban environment from people she didn't know well. Even so, Bibb Latané and John Darley (1970) were not convinced that the stresses and strains of city life fully explained why she didn't get the help she needed. To test an alternative explanation, these two researchers set out to see if they could produce unresponsive bystanders under laboratory conditions. Let's take a close look at one of their studies.

When a subject arrived, he or she was taken to one of a series of small rooms located along a corridor. Speaking over an intercom, the experimenter explained that he wanted subjects to discuss personal problems often faced by college students. Subjects were told that to protect confidentiality the group discussion would take place over the intercom system and the experimenter would not be listening. Participants were required to speak one at a time, taking turns. Some subjects were assigned to talk with one other person; others joined larger groups of three or six people.

Although one participant did mention in passing that he suffered from a seizure disorder that was sometimes triggered by study pressures, the opening moments of the conversation were uneventful. But soon an unexpected problem developed. When the time came for this person to speak again, he stuttered badly, had a hard time speaking clearly, and sounded as if he were in very serious trouble:

> I could really-er-use some help so if somebody would-er-give me a little h-help-uh-er-er-er-er c-could somebody-er-er-help-er-uh-uh-uh [choking sounds]. . . . I'm gonna die-er-er-I'm . . . gonna die-er-help-er-er-seizure-er [chokes, then quiet].

Confronted with this situation, what would *you* do? Would you interrupt the experiment, dash out of your cubicle, and try to find the experimenter? Or would you sit there—concerned, but unsure about how to react?

As it turns out, subjects' responses to this emergency were strongly influenced by the size of their group. Actually, all subjects were participating alone, but tape-recorded material led them to believe that others were present. All the subjects who thought that only they knew about the emergency left the room quickly to try to get help. In the larger groups, however, subjects were less likely and slower to intervene. Thirty-eight percent of the subjects in the six-person groups never left the room at all! This research led Latané and Darley to a chilling conclusion: The more bystanders there are, the *less* likely the victim will be helped. In the **bystander effect,** the presence of others inhibits helping.

bystander effect The effect whereby the presence of others inhibits helping.

Before the pioneering work of Latané and Darley, most people would have assumed just the opposite. Isn't there safety in numbers? Don't we feel more secure rushing in to help when others are around to lend their support? Latané and Darley overturned this common-sense assumption and provided a careful, step-by-step analysis of the decision-making process involved in emergency interventions. In the following sections, we examine each of five steps toward helping: noticing something unusual, interpreting it as an emergency, taking responsibility for getting help, deciding how to help, and providing assistance. We also consider the reasons why people sometimes fail to take one of these steps and, therefore, do not help.

Noticing The first step toward being a helpful bystander is to notice that someone needs help or, at least, that something out of the ordinary is happening. Subjects in the seizure study could not help but notice the emergency. In many situations, however, the problem isn't always perceived. The presence of others can be distracting and divert attention away from indications of a victim's plight. As noted earlier, people may also fail to notice that someone needs help when they are caught up in their own self-concerns.

The parable of the Good Samaritan, from the Gospel of Luke, provides a telling example. On the road from Jerusalem to Jericho, three people—a priest, a Levite, and a Samaritan—pass a man lying half-dead by the roadside. The only one who helps is the Samaritan, a social and religious outcast in Jewish society of that time. The moral of the tale is that people with low status are sometimes more virtuous than those enjoying high status and prestige. Why? Perhaps in part because high-status individuals tend to be busy people, preoccupied with their own concerns and rushing around to important engagements. Such characteristics may prevent them from noticing a victim in need of assistance.

In their research, John Darley and Daniel Batson (1973) brought this ancient story to life. They asked seminary students to think about what they wanted to say in an upcoming talk. Half of them were told that the talk was to be based on the parable of the Good Samaritan; the other half expected to discuss the jobs that seminary students like best. All subjects were then instructed to walk over to a nearby building where the speech would be recorded. At this point, subjects were told that they were running ahead of schedule, that they were right on time,

The first step toward providing help in an emergency is to notice that someone needs assistance. Sometimes, however, people recognize a victim's plight, but deliberately choose to look away.

or that they were already a few minutes behind schedule. On the way to the other building, all subjects passed a research confederate slumped in a doorway, coughing and groaning. Which of these future ministers stopped to lend a helping hand?

Surprisingly, the topic of the upcoming speech had little effect on helping. The pressure of time, however, made a real difference. Of those who thought they were ahead of schedule, 63 percent offered help—compared with 45 percent of those who believed they were on time and only 10 percent of those who had been told they were late. In describing the events that took place in their study, Darley and Batson noted that "on several occasions a seminary student going to give his talk on the parable of the Good Samaritan literally stepped over the victim as he hurried on his way!"

Interpreting Noticing the victim is a necessary first step toward helping, but it is not enough. People must interpret the meaning of what they notice. Cries of pain can be mistaken for shrieks of laughter; heart-attack victims can appear to be drunk. So observers wonder: Does that person really need help? In general, the more ambiguous the situation, the less likely it is that bystanders will intervene (Clark & Word, 1972).

Interpretations of the relationship between a victim and an attacker also affect whether help will be provided. Consider, for example, how people react when they see a woman attacked by a man. Research by Lance Shotland and Margaret Straw (1976) indicates that most observers of such an incident will believe that the attacker and victim have a close relationship with each other as dates, lovers, or spouses—even when no information about their relationship is actually available. This inference can have very serious implications since, as Shotland and Straw documented, intervening in domestic violence is perceived to be more dangerous to the helper and less desired by the victim than is intervening in an attack by a stranger. Given such beliefs, the response to a scene staged by Shotland and Straw was predictable: More than three times as many observers tried to stop an assault by a stranger than attempted to intervene in an assault by a husband.

It's not only women who are in danger if they are perceived as having a close relationship with their attacker: Children also suffer. The 1993 murder of two-year-old James Bulger by two ten-year-old boys was the British equivalent of the Kitty Genovese slaying. James was dragged, kicking and screaming, for two and a half miles from a shopping mall to the railroad track where he was battered to death. Sixty-one people admitted that they had seen the boys. Most did nothing. One asked a few questions but didn't intervene. The reason? As one witness put it, he thought the boys were "older brothers taking a little one home." When people think "family," they think "it's OK, it's safe." But sometimes it isn't.

Perhaps the most powerful information available during an emergency is the behavior of other people. Startled by a sudden, unexpected, possibly dangerous event, a person looks quickly to see what others are doing. Others do likewise. As everyone looks at everyone else for clues about how to behave, the entire group is paralyzed by indecision. When this happens, the person needing help is a victim of **pluralistic ignorance.** In this state of ignorance, each individual believes that his or her own thoughts and feelings are different from those of other people, even though everyone's behavior is the same. Each bystander thinks that other people aren't acting because somehow they know there isn't an emergency. Actually, everyone is confused and hesitant; but, imputing wisdom to others, each observer concludes that help is not required.

pluralistic ignorance The state in which people mistakenly believe that their own thoughts and feelings are different from those of others, even though everyone's behavior is the same.

This videotape recorded the abduction of two-year-old James Bulger, as he was led away from the shopping mall by the two ten year-olds (one holding James' hand, the other walking in front of them) who later murdered him. At least sixty-one people noticed the boys. No one intervened.

Pluralistic ignorance is not restricted to emergency situations (Miller & McFarland, 1987; Prentice & Miller, 1993). Have you ever sat through a class feeling totally at sea? You want to ask a question, but you're too embarrassed. No one else is saying anything, so you assume they all find the material a snap. Finally, you dare to ask a question. And, suddenly, hands shoot up in the air all over the classroom. No one understood the material, yet everyone assumed that everyone else was breezing along. Pluralistic ignorance in the classroom interferes with learning. In an emergency situation, it can lead to disaster—unless someone breaks out of the pack and dares to help. Then others are likely to follow.

Taking Responsibility Noticing a victim and recognizing an emergency are crucial steps, but by themselves they won't ensure that a bystander will come to the rescue. The issue of responsibility remains. When help is needed, who is responsible for providing it? If a person knows that others are around, it's all too easy to place the responsibility on *them*. People often fail to help because of the **diffusion of responsibility,** the belief that others will or should intervene. Presumably, each of those thirty-eight people who watched and listened to Kitty Genovese's murder thought someone else would do something to stop the attack.

diffusion of responsibility The belief that others will or should take the responsibility for providing assistance to a person in need.

But remember those helpful subjects in the seizure study who thought that they alone heard the other person's cry for help? Diffusion of responsibility cannot occur if an individual believes that only he or she is aware of the victim's need. When more than two people are involved, the odds that diffusion of responsibility will occur depend on the social configuration. Personal responsibility diminishes most when there are few victims and many potential helpers, as in the 1-to-38 ratio involved in the Genovese murder. As the number of victims increases, or the number of potential helpers decreases, help is more likely to occur (Wegner & Schaefer, 1978).

Diffusion of responsibility usually takes place under conditions of anonymity. Bystanders who do not know the victim personally are more likely to see others as responsible for providing help. Accordingly, if the psychological distance between a bystander and the victim is reduced, there will be less diffusion of responsibility and more help. In one study, the mere *anticipation* of meeting someone, who then needed help before the meeting actually took place, was sufficient to eliminate diffusion of responsibility (Gottlieb & Carver, 1980).

Reducing the psychological distance among bystanders can also counteract the diffusion of responsibility. Established groups in which members know each other are usually more helpful than groups of strangers (Rutkowski et al., 1983). And sometimes the emergency itself can create a sense of unity. During the 1992 riots in Los Angeles, four people (a dating couple and two unrelated individuals) saw live TV coverage of the beating of truck driver Reginald Denny. None of them had ever met Denny, but they rushed to the scene and, once there, skillfully coordinated an almost impossible rescue mission. As one of them said, "At that moment we all clicked at the same time. We knew we had a task to do."

In addition, the diffusion of responsibility can be defeated by a person's role. A group leader, even if only recently assigned to that position, is more likely than other group members to act in an emergency (Baumeister et al., 1988). And some occupational roles increase the likelihood of intervention. Registered nurses, for example, do not diffuse responsibility when confronted by a possible physical injury (Cramer et al., 1988). Even when there's no direct relationship between one's occupation and the type of assistance that's needed, job requirements can still influence helping behavior. On Sunday, March 27, 1994, Jack Santos, a YMCA security guard, ran across two highways, passed a dozen passive observers, and put out the fire from the burning clothes of Jack Ordner, who had been thrown from his gasoline tanker when it overturned and burst into flames. Santos was neither a professional firefighter nor a medical specialist, but he was used to taking charge during an emergency.

Deciding How to Help Having assumed the responsibility to help, the person must now decide how to help. Bystanders are more likely to offer *direct* help when they feel competent to perform the actions required. For instance, individu-

Seeing the beating of Reginald Denny as it was carried live on TV, these four people rushed to the scene and rescued him.

Soon after the 1995 Oklahoma City bombing, a police officer found one-year-old Baylee Almon in the rubble and handed her over to a firefighter. As trained professionals with specific assignments, emergency workers were not hindered by the diffusion of responsibility and knew exactly what kind of direct intervention they could provide. They saved many lives, but not Baylee's, who died minutes after this picture was taken.

als who have received Red Cross training in first-aid techniques are more likely to provide direct assistance to a bleeding victim than are those without training (Shotland & Heinold, 1985). Communities—such as King County, Washington—that have a first-class emergency medical system and a large number of individuals trained in cardiopulmonary resuscitation (CPR) have greatly increased the survival rate of heart-attack victims.

But people who do not possess the skills that would make them feel competent to intervene directly do have an option available. They can decide to help *indirectly* by calling for assistance from others (Penner et al., 1973). In many situations, indirect helping is by far the wiser course of action. Physical injuries are best treated by medical personnel; dangerous situations such as domestic violence are best handled by police officers; and that friendly looking individual standing by the side of a stalled car on a lonely road is best picked up by the highway patrol. Even those trained in CPR are now advised to call 911 before starting CPR on an adult victim. Calling others in to help is safe, simple, and effective. A prompt phone call can be a lifeline.

Providing Help The final step in the intervention process is to take action. Here, too, the presence of others can have an impact. Latané and Darley point out that people sometimes feel too socially awkward and embarrassed to act helpfully in a public setting. When observers do not act in an emergency because they fear making a bad impression on other observers, they are under the influence of **audience inhibition.** Worrying about how others will view us will not, however, always reduce helping. When people think they will be scorned by others for failing to help, the presence of an audience increases their helpful actions (Schwartz & Gottlieb, 1980).

audience inhibition A person's reluctance to help for fear of making a bad impression on observers.

Letting concerns about social approval affect emergency helping seems inappropriate. It makes a potential helper sound like a cold, calculating sort of person. But according to Jane Piliavin and her colleagues (1981), potential helpers do take potential rewards and costs into account when deciding whether to respond to an emergency. The **arousal:cost-reward model** of helping stipulates that both emotional and cognitive factors determine whether bystanders to an emergency will intervene. Emotionally, bystanders experience the shock and alarm of personal distress; this unpleasant state of arousal motivates them to do something to reduce it. What they do, however, depends on the "bystander calculus," their computation of the costs and rewards associated with helping. When potential rewards (to self and victim) outweigh potential costs (to self and victim), bystanders will help (Dovidio et al., 1991). But raise those costs and lower those rewards, and victims stand a good chance of having to do without.

arousal:cost-reward model The proposition that people react to emergency situations by acting in the most cost-effective way to reduce the arousal of shock and alarm.

Being Helped: One Versus Many As you can see in Figure 7.11, providing help in an emergency is a challenging process. At each step along the way, there are barriers and diversions that can prevent a potential helper from becoming an actual one. Most of these obstacles are social in nature, demonstrating Latané and Darley's point that individuals are less likely to intervene in an emergency when others are present than when they are alone with the victim.

But what about the probability that the victim will be helped? Won't a greater number of potential helpers compensate for each person's hesitation? Isn't there, after all, safety in numbers? Not in emergencies. Although the difference is relatively small, victims are more likely to receive help if the full weight of their plight rests on the shoulders of only one bystander (Latané & Nida, 1981).

REACTIONS TO RECEIVING HELP

Thus far, we've described those factors that influence whether helping will occur. Now, we turn to what happens *after* it takes place. The last time someone helped you, how did you feel? Grateful, relieved, comforted—anything else? Embarrassed, obligated, inferior? Receiving help is often a positive experience, but sometimes it has drawbacks for the recipient. There are costs in providing help, and there can be costs in receiving it.

Help That Supports Versus Help That Threatens

The most extensive examination of reactions to receiving help has been conducted by Jeffrey Fisher and Arie Nadler (Fisher et al., 1982; Nadler & Fisher, 1986). According to their **threat-to-self-esteem model**, receiving help is experienced as *self-supportive* when the recipient feels appreciated and cared for, but as *self-threatening* when the recipient feels inferior and overly dependent. If recipients feel supported by the help they receive, they respond positively: feeling good, accepting the help, and being grateful to the donor. If, however, recipients feel threatened, they have a negative emotional reaction and evaluate both the help and the helper unfavorably.

threat-to-self-esteem model The theory that reactions to receiving assistance depend on whether help is perceived as supportive or threatening.

There are three conditions under which receiving help is most likely to be perceived as threatening. First, individuals with high self-esteem tend to react more negatively to receiving help than do those with low self-esteem. Presumably, people who regard themselves as highly competent are especially sensitive to the implication that they are unable to take care of themselves. Second, being helped by

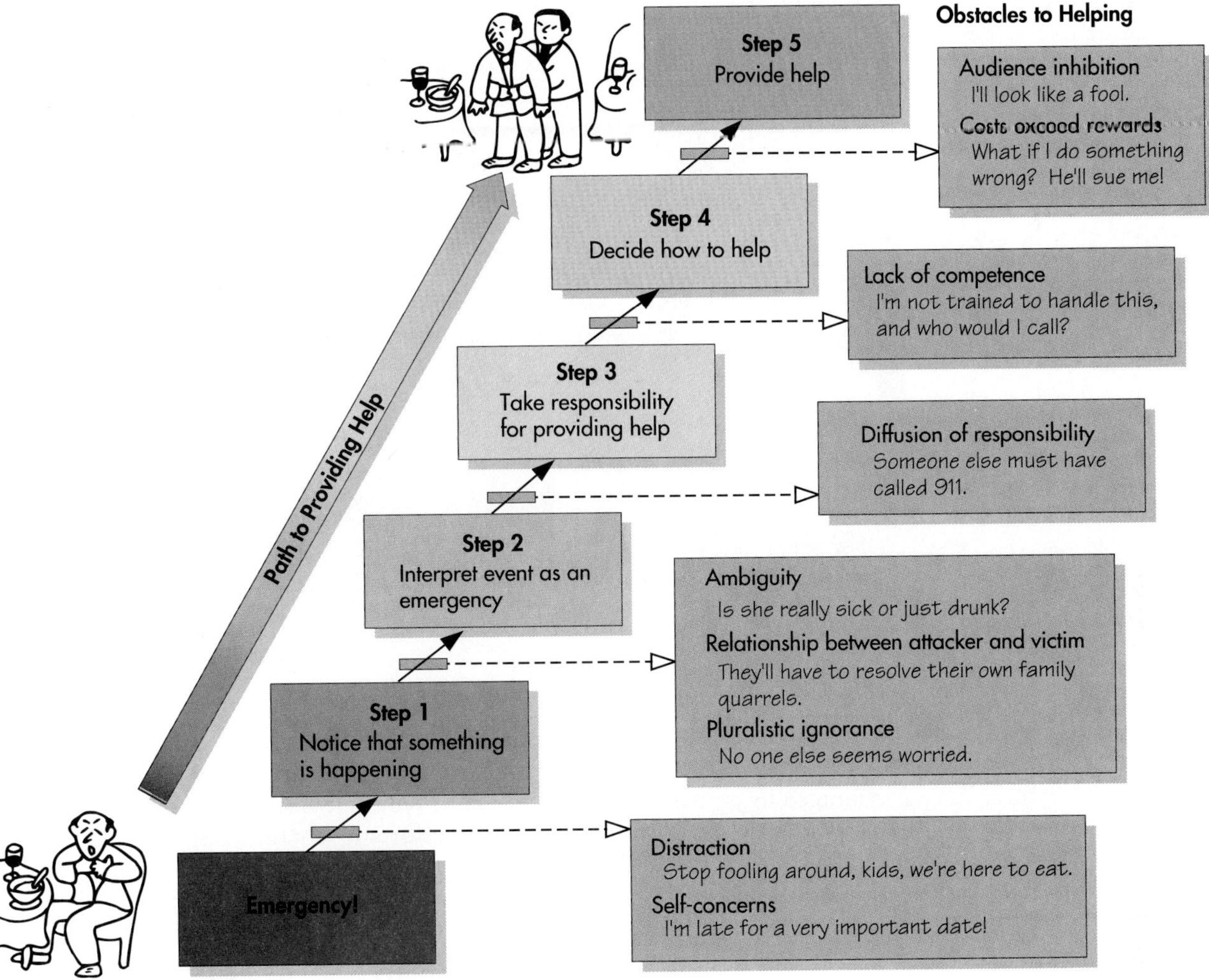
Obstacles to Helping
Step 5
Provide help
Audience inhibition
I'll look like a fool.
Costs exceed rewards
What if I do something wrong? He'll sue me!
Step 4
Decide how to help
Lack of competence
I'm not trained to handle this, and who would I call?
Step 3
Take responsibility for providing help
Diffusion of responsibility
Someone else must have called 911.
Path to Providing Help
Step 2
Interpret event as an emergency
Ambiguity
Is she really sick or just drunk?
Relationship between attacker and victim
They'll have to resolve their own family quarrels.
Pluralistic ignorance
No one else seems worried.
Step 1
Notice that something is happening
Emergency!
Distraction
Stop fooling around, kids, we're here to eat.
Self-concerns
I'm late for a very important date!

Figure 7.11 The Five Steps to Helping in an Emergency. On the basis of their analysis of the decision-making process in emergency interventions, Latané and Darley (1970) outlined five steps that lead to providing assistance. But there are obstacles that can interfere and, if a step is missed, the victim won't be helped.

a similar other highlights the contrast between the recipient's need for assistance and the generosity of the provider. Alike in other ways, this one difference may imply that the recipient is inferior. The third condition under which receiving help is often experienced as threatening involves the type of relationship the recipient has with the provider and the area in which help has been received. As would be expected from Tesser's self-evaluation maintenance model (see page 260), receiving help from a significant other on an ego-relevant task is threatening to an individual's self-esteem.

Usually, however, help from those who are close to us will be seen as supportive. High self-esteem does not appear to prompt negative reactions to assistance by a sibling (Searcy & Eisenberg, 1992). And the negative effects of similarity probably do not apply to close relationships, in which similarity is expected and desired (Wills, 1992). Even ego-relevant help may elicit positive, rather than negative, reactions from partners in an interdependent relationship (Clark, 1983a; Cook & Pelfrey, 1985). In such relationships, feelings of inferiority are less likely to arise, as each person sometimes helps, sometimes receives. Mutuality makes receiving help less threatening. So does a very young age. Since dependency is more acceptable for children than for adolescents and adults, children less often react negatively to being helped (Shell & Eisenberg, 1992).

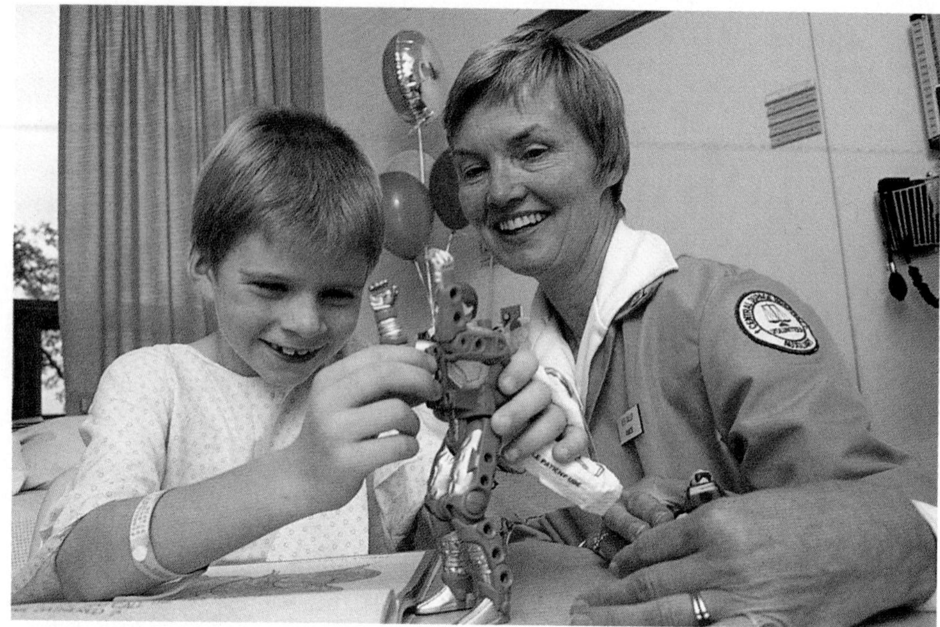

Since dependency is more acceptable for children than for older individuals, children are less likely to perceive help as threatening. As pictured here, they usually react positively to those who helped them out.

Seeking Help from Others

The threat-to-self-esteem model, summarized in Figure 7.12, also describes when recipients are most likely to seek subsequent help from others. Help-seeking is encouraged by a positive reaction to the help initially received. When the reaction to help is negative, however, subsequent efforts to obtain assistance will depend on the individual's *perceived control* over future events. An individual who has experienced threatening help and is pessimistic about the likelihood of future control feels helplessly dependent on the kindness of others (Coates et al., 1983). Help will again be sought, but at a high price to self-esteem. In general, highly dependent individuals seek help more than do those who are not as dependent (Bornstein et al., 1993).

An individual who has experienced threatening help but is optimistic about the likelihood of future control reacts differently. This person avoids seeking help from others and relies instead on self-help efforts. Because receiving help threatened self-esteem in the past, self-reliance is preferred in the future. Indeed, any factor that increases a person's tendency to regard help-seeking as an indication of personal inferiority should decrease that person's willingness to seek help (Rosen, 1983). For example, since people usually feel less secure in superficial relationships than in close attachments, it's often harder to seek help from strangers than from significant others (Clark, 1983b).

Gender also influences the willingness to seek help. Remember that time you and a member of the opposite sex got lost while driving in unfamiliar territory? Who wanted to stop early on and ask for directions? Who kept insisting that help wasn't necessary until you almost ran out of gas? For relatively minor problems at least, men ask for help less frequently than do women (McMullen & Gross, 1983). Less socially acceptable for men, help-seeking is more threatening to their self-esteem (Wills & DePaulo, 1991).

There is a great irony about refusing to seek help in order to protect self-esteem. If your own success depends on obtaining information and assistance

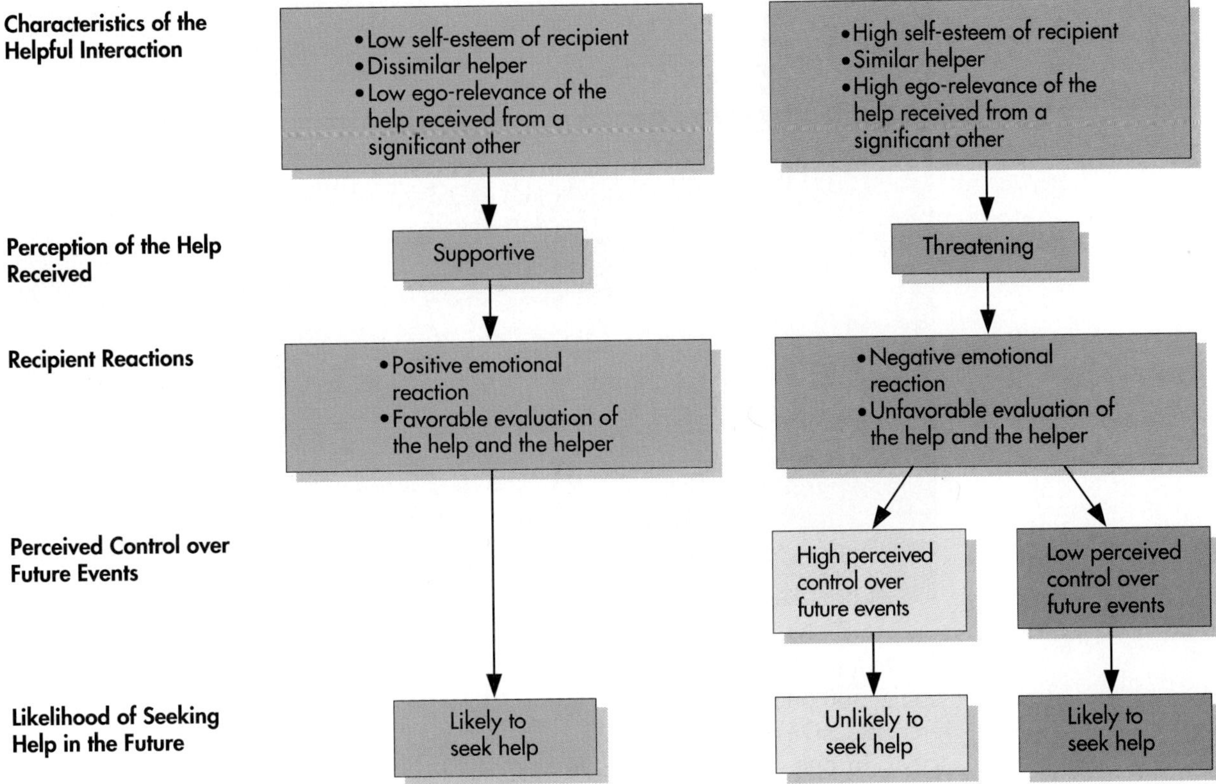

Figure 7.12 **The Threat-to-Self-Esteem Model of Recipient Reactions to Aid.** This model describes how people react when they receive help from others. Help perceived as supportive leads to positive responses; help perceived as threatening creates negative reactions. The threat-to-self-esteem model also describes the circumstances under which people will seek help in the future.

from others, then not seeking help *increases* the likelihood of failure and damage to self-esteem. The cure for this self-destructive paradox is to recognize "the utility of humility" (Weiss & Knight, 1980). Research on city-dwelling and kibbutz-residing Israelis indicates that such recognition is most likely when success is most important (Nadler, 1986). City residents valued individual achievement more than group accomplishment. Kibbutz residents, however, valued group accomplishment more than individual achievement. So when did people ask for help? When task performance was to be judged on the basis of individual scores, city dwellers sought more help than did those who lived on kibbutzim. But when task performance was to be judged on the basis of the average score of all group members, kibbutz residents sought more help than did city dwellers. If success really matters, people can swallow their pride and ask others to help them out.

THE HELPING CONNECTION

As we have seen, helping is a social transaction between a specific giver and receiver interacting in a specific situation. Sometimes help is given; sometimes it isn't. Sometimes help is sought; sometimes it isn't. There is no single, simple formula for determining when there will be help and when there won't be. But there is a consistent theme that appears repeatedly in this chapter: a sense of connection.

The importance of a sense of connection is vividly demonstrated by a cross-cultural comparison. First, consider one of the great social tragedies of our time: homelessness. Nobody knows for sure how many people are homeless today in

Homelessness may be a symptom of a profound loss of social connection in American society.

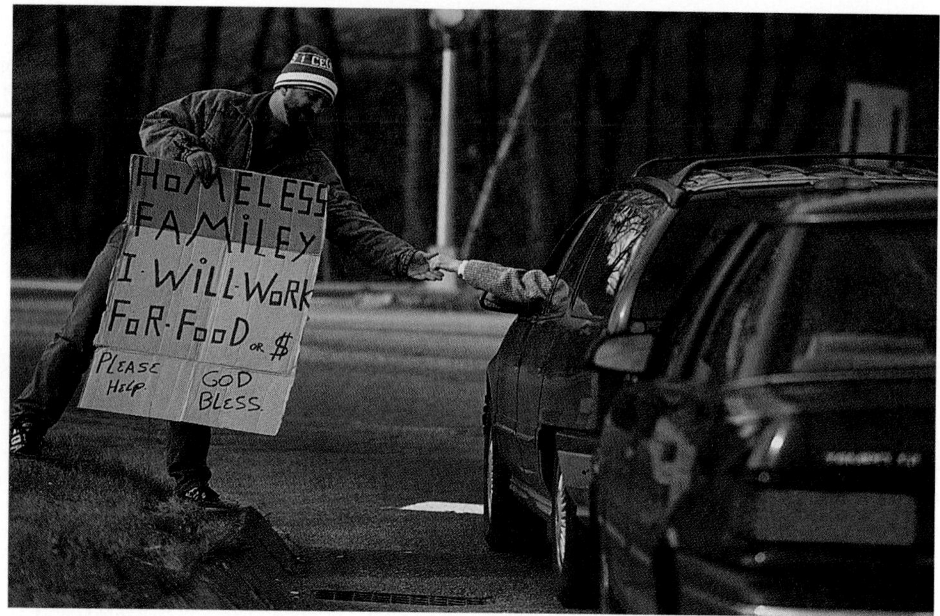

the United States. However, most surveys estimate that on any specific night some 300,000 to 400,000 men, women, and children are without a home (Jencks, 1994). "Enough," says Peter Rossi (1990), "to populate a medium-sized city." In one of the richest countries on earth, people sleep on the street, carry their belongings in grocery carts, and rummage through piles of garbage to find food.

Now, compare American homelessness with an anthropologist's account of life among the Moose (pronounced "MOH-say") in West Africa:

> Moose welcome anyone who wishes to join the community and move into the village. New arrivals have only to say where they wish to build their homes, and the user of the land in question gives it up for the newcomer's residence. I experienced this myself when I moved into the village and arranged to build huts and a living compound for my family: No one expected any compensation, and indeed, we were gradually assimilated into the family of our hosts. . . . Water is even scarcer than land. . . . Each of the two years that I lived there, the well ran dry and villagers had to walk miles to get water for themselves and their stock from other villages, carrying it home on their heads. Each of these other villages shared their water until their wells were nearly dry, without expecting any reciprocation for the water. Even in these circumstances, any stranger who comes into the village may ask for a drink, and any visitor is offered water. (Fiske, 1991, pp. 190–191)

Among some of the poorest people on earth, no one goes without shelter, or remains thirsty as long as anyone has water to drink.

How can we account for the extraordinary difference between American homelessness and Moose hospitality? Homelessness is, of course, a complex phenomenon affected by many specific economic and political factors. But it may also be a symptom of a profound loss of social connection in American society (Wuthnow, 1991). Among the Moose, no such loss has occurred. Their sense of being intimately connected to others binds them to those who live in their village and to strangers who arrive in their midst.

The relationship between helping and interpersonal connection runs like a bright red thread through much of the research on helping. For example:

- Sociobiology emphasizes the genetic connection of kinship selection, the two-person connection of reciprocity, and the collective connection of group cooperation.
- People in a good mood engage in more social activities, including helping.
- One of the major functions of guilt is to enhance, maintain, and repair relationships.
- Two kinds of connections lie at the heart of the empathy-altruism hypothesis: the cognitive connection of perspective-taking and the emotional connection of empathic concern.
- Perceived similarity increases helping.
- In an emergency, bystanders who know the victim or know each other are more likely to intervene.
- In a close relationship, it's easier to give and more comfortable to receive.

Taken as a whole, these theories and research findings suggest that helping requires the recognition of individual human beings with whom we can have a meaningful connection. Which brings us back to Oskar Schindler. He didn't know most of the people he rescued. He didn't share their religion or their nationality. But he felt a deep, personal sense of connection with them as individuals. Each of their lives mattered to him. And so, on their behalf, he wheeled and dealed, charmed and conned, spent his money and devised his schemes. There was nothing remarkable about Oskar before the war or afterward. For six long years though, during some of the most horrible events in human history, he fulfilled his responsibility to help. It's doubtful that Oskar Schindler ever read the words that the English poet John Donne wrote almost 400 years ago. But he would have understood them.

> No man is an island, entire of itself. Every man is a piece of the continent, a part of the main. If a clod be washed away by the sea, Europe is the less, as well as if a promontory were, as well as if a manor of thy friends or of thine own were. Any man's death diminishes me, because I am involved in mankind. And therefore never send to know for whom the bell tolls; it tolls for thee.

REVIEW

PERSONAL INFLUENCES: WHY DO PEOPLE HELP?

Genetic Factors in Helping

- Sociobiologists have proposed three ways in which helping could become an innate, universal behavioral tendency: kinship selection, in which people protect their own genes by helping close relatives; reciprocal helping, in which those who give also receive; and group selection, in which members of a social group help each other survive.
- Some research suggests that individual differences in helping may be inherited, creating a genetic basis for an altruistic personality. However, no one personality characteristic, or set of characteristics, is associated with helping in all situations.

Emotional Factors in Helping

- A good mood increases helpfulness.
- Perhaps people in a good mood help in order to maintain their positive mood. Or they may help because they have more positive thoughts and expectations about helpful behavior, the person in need, or social activities in general.

- Three ways in which negative moods could increase helping have also been examined: feeling guilty after a transgression, becoming self-aware, and seeking relief from sadness.
- From all of these perspectives, helping is viewed as essentially egoistic—motivated by a desire to benefit oneself.

Motivational Factors in Helping

- According to the empathy-altruism hypothesis, taking the perspective of a person perceived to be in need creates the other-oriented emotion of empathic concern, which in turn produces the altruistic motive to reduce the other's distress.
- Not taking the other's perspective creates the self-oriented emotion of personal distress, which produces the egoistic motive to reduce one's own distress.
- When people are altruistically motivated, they will help even when escaping from the helping situation is easy.
- Alternatives to the empathy-altruism hypothesis include empathy-specific punishments for not helping and empathy-specific rewards for helping such as negative state relief and empathic joy.

INTERPERSONAL INFLUENCES: WHOM DO PEOPLE HELP?

Perceived Characteristics of the Person in Need

- Attractive individuals are more likely to receive help than are those who are less attractive.
- People are more willing to help when they attribute a person's need for assistance to events under the person's control rather than to uncontrollable causes. Some individuals are more likely than others to make attributions of personal responsibility.

The Fit Between Giver and Receiver

- In general, perceived similarity to a person in need increases willingness to help. But research on racial similarity has yielded inconsistent results.
- People usually help significant others more than a stranger, except when helping threatens their own ego.
- Men help female strangers in potentially dangerous situations more than women do; women help friends and relations in everyday situations more than men do.
- Individuals who have a strong belief in a just world are more willing to provide assistance when a need is temporary than when it is continuous.

SITUATIONAL INFLUENCES: WHEN DO PEOPLE HELP?

Models, Norms, and Rewards

- Observing a helpful model increases helping.
- Social norms that promote helping are based on a sense of fairness or on standards about what is right.
- Personal norms are individualized and specific standards of conduct, perhaps derived from parental models.
- A person's self-concept influences helping behavior; those who perceive themselves as helpful individuals are usually more helpful.
- External rewards for helping diminish self-perceptions of being a helpful individual and decrease helpful behavior when rewards are no longer available.
- Awareness of internal rewards also diminishes self-perceptions of being a helpful individual. But it is not clear how such awareness affects actual helping.

The Place Where We Live

- Residents of densely populated urban areas are less likely to provide spontaneous, informal help to strangers than are residents of smaller or less densely populated communities.

The Unhelpful Crowd

- Research on the bystander effect, in which the presence of others inhibits helping in an emergency, indicates why the five steps necessary for helping to occur may not be taken.
- The distractions of others and our own self-concerns may impair our ability to notice that someone needs help.
- Under ambiguous circumstances, some interpretations—such as the belief that an attacker and a victim have a close relationship or the mistaken inferences drawn from pluralistic ignorance—reduce bystander intervention.
- In the diffusion of responsibility, people fail to take responsibility because they assume that others will.
- Bystanders are less likely to offer direct aid when they do not feel competent to do so. They can, however, call for assistance from others.

- Even if people want to help, they tend not to do so if they fear that behaving in a helpful fashion will make them look foolish or conclude that there are other, less costly ways to reduce their shock and alarm.
- Overall, victims are more likely to be helped if there is only one bystander present at an emergency.

REACTIONS TO RECEIVING HELP

Help That Supports Versus Help That Threatens

- The threat-to-self-esteem model distinguishes between help perceived as supportive, which produces positive reactions, and help perceived as threatening, which creates negative reactions.
- Help is most likely to be perceived as threatening by a recipient with high self-esteem who receives help from a similar provider or from a significant other on an ego-relevant task.
- In close, interdependent relationships, receiving help is usually a positive experience.

Seeking Help from Others

- Receiving supportive help encourages the recipient to seek assistance again when needed.
- Individuals who receive threatening help will seek further help if they are pessimistic about their ability to control future events but not if they anticipate being in control.
- People are usually more willing to seek help from a person they are close to than from a stranger.
- Women seek help more often than do men. A greater desire for success increases willingness to seek the help necessary to succeed.

THE HELPING CONNECTION

- The large number of homeless individuals and families in the United States may reflect, at least in part, a loss of social connection in American society.
- Consistent with theory and research in this chapter, helping seems to require the recognition of individuals with whom we can have a meaningful connection.

KEY TERMS

kinship selection, p.245
good mood effect, p.248
guilt, p.249
negative state relief model, p.252
egoistic, p.252
altruistic, p.252
empathy-altruism, p.253 hypothesis
social norms, p.264
norm of social responsibility, p.265
norm of justice, p.265
personal norms, p.265
bystander effect, p.270
pluralistic ignorance, p.272
diffusion of responsibility, p.273
audience inhibition, p.275
arousal:cost-reward model, p.276
threat-to-self-esteem model, p.276

MPDC
1319
MPDC
621
MPDC
373
MPDC
451
MPDC
746
MPDC
223
MPDC
798
MPDC
75

Chapter 8

Aggression

PREVIEW

In this chapter, we examine a disturbing aspect of human behavior: aggression. First, we ask, *"What is aggression?"* and consider its definition. After describing possible *origins of aggression,* we explore a variety of *social and situational influences.* We next turn to *media effects* on aggression and then to the *intimate violence* that can occur in close relationships. Throughout the chapter, we emphasize ways to prevent or reduce aggressive actions.

OUTLINE

The rest of the world has always perceived the United States as an extraordinarily violent country. Now, the homefolks are beginning to share that view. Pick up a newspaper, turn on the radio or TV, leaf through a newsmagazine—the violence in America seems to pour out in a great, unending stream:

- During a slumber party in her home, twelve-year-old Polly Klaas was kidnapped and later murdered.
- In a gang-related shooting spree, eleven-year-old Robert Sandifer is alleged to have accidentally killed fourteen-year-old Shavon Dean, an innocent bystander. Three days later, Sandifer himself was found dead, killed execution-style by two bullets to the back of his head. Two members of Sandifer's own gang, sixteen-year-old Cragg Hardaway and fourteen-year-old Derrick Hardaway, were accused of his murder.
- Chanting racial slurs, a white mob beat Lu Nguyen, a Vietnamese-American student, to death.
- While buying a morning newspaper at a shopping mall, Christopher Wilson was abducted at gunpoint, driven to an isolated field, doused with gasoline, and set on fire—leaving him with burns over 40 percent of his body.
- Nicole Brown Simpson and Ronald Goldman were slashed to death outside her condominium; her ex-husband, O. J. Simpson, was tried for the murders.

As they survey the carnage around them, Americans are stunned and horrified. The dramatic escalation of violence committed by and against young people is particularly shocking (Children's Defense Fund, 1994; Commission on

A memorial to Polly Klaas, who was kidnapped from a slumber party in her home and later murdered.

Violence and Youth, 1993; Eron et al., 1994; Hammond & Yung, 1993). Here are some of the facts, and some of the figures are illustrated in Figure 8.1.

- Although the overall murder rate has declined since 1980, murders committed by individuals aged fourteen to twenty four have increased sharply.
- Murder is the leading cause of death among teenage and young adult African-American males and females, with particularly high levels among eighteen to twenty-four-year-olds.
- Murder is the third leading cause of death among children aged five to fourteen, exceeded only by accidents and cancer.

What's going on? How did it come to this? Unfortunately, there is no simple explanation for the presence of violence—in the United States or in any other so-

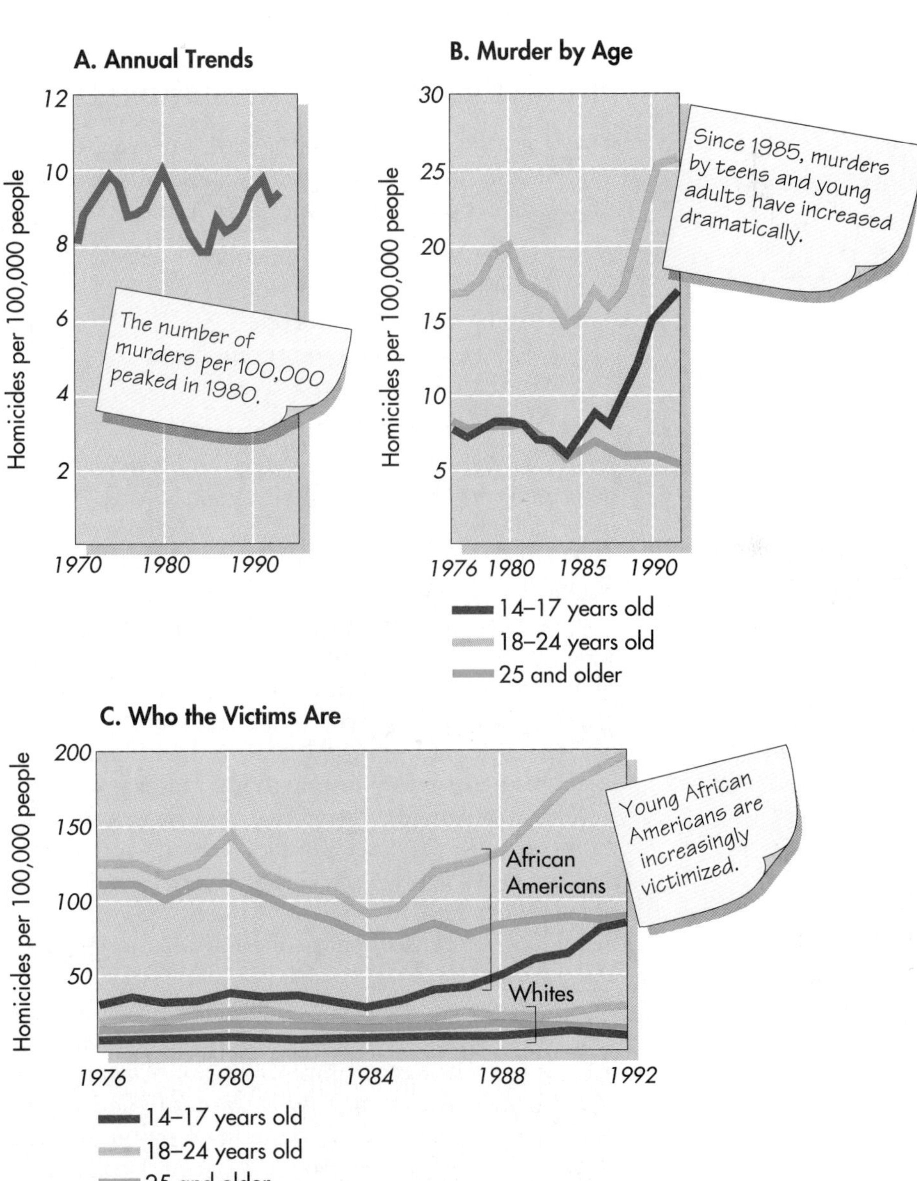

Figure 8.1 Murder American Style. Here are three grim snapshots taken of violence in the United States. Figure A depicts changes in the overall murder rate since 1970. Figure B shows age-related trends among murderers. Figure C classifies homicide victims by race and age. (Data from Newsweek, 1995)

ciety. Nor is there any obvious, easy way to reduce it. Social scientists, politicians, and concerned citizens continue to debate the merits of gun control, capital punishment, community policing, preventative programs, longer prison sentences, and media censorship.

Despite these complexities, however, the fundamental basis of violence is absolutely clear: the human capacity for aggression. In this chapter, we focus primarily on aggression by individuals, examining factors that increase it as well as those that decrease it. Aggression by groups, such as rampaging mobs or warring nations, will be discussed in Chapter 11 on Group Processes. Although it is often unsettling to think about aggression, the better we can understand this aspect of human behavior, the better equipped we will be to protect ourselves, our loved ones, and our society from its terrible consequences.

PINNING IT DOWN: WHAT IS AGGRESSION?

The word is a familiar one, part of our everyday vocabulary, but the concept of "aggression" can be surprisingly hard to pin down. Consider, for example, the following actions. Which ones do you think are aggressive?

- Accidentally injuring someone
- Shooting to kill but missing
- Hurling insults at someone
- Deliberately failing to prevent harm
- Murdering for money
- Striking out in a rage

Researchers, too, have engaged in classification exercises like this in order to determine the meaning of aggression. Not everyone agrees on every point, but most definitions share a number of common features (Baron & Richardson, 1994; Berkowitz, 1993). Putting them together, we can define **aggression** as behavior that is intended to injure another person.

aggression Behavior intended to injure another person.

This definition rules out the first example in our list. Accidentally injuring someone is *not* an aggressive act because there is no intent to harm. Similarly, actions that produce harm as an unintended by-product are not aggressive. The physician who administers a painful treatment does not act aggressively. The second example, however, is ruled in. Intentional efforts to injure that do not succeed *are* aggressive. Shooting to kill is an aggressive act, even if the bullet misses.

Of course, any definition that relies on an individual's intentions has a serious drawback. We can't see another person's intentions, so how do we know what they are? And whose view do we accept if people disagree about someone's intentions? When defined in terms of intent, aggression lies ultimately in the eye of the beholder. The consequences of a harmful act may be obvious to everyone, but its characterization as aggressive is a matter of subjective judgment.

Aggressive behaviors come in many forms. Words as well as deeds can be aggressive. Quarreling couples who intend their spiteful remarks to hurt are behaving aggressively. Even failure to act can be aggressive. If you know your boss is in a lousy mood and doesn't want to see anyone, but you deliberately decide not to warn a bouncy co-worker preparing to barge right in, that's aggression.

To distinguish them from less harmful behaviors, extreme acts of aggression are called *violence*. Some other terms in the language of aggression refer to emotions and attitudes. *Anger* consists of strong feelings of displeasure in response to a perceived injury; the exact nature of these feelings (for example, outrage, hate, or irritation) depends on the specific situation (Russell & Fehr, 1994). *Hostility* is a negative, antagonistic attitude toward another person or group. Anger and hostility are often closely connected to aggression, but not always. People can be angry at others and regard them with great hostility without ever trying to harm them. And aggression can occur without a trace of anger or hostility, as when a contract killer murders a perfect stranger in order to "make a killing" financially.

instrumental aggression Inflicting harm in order to obtain something of value.

The aggression of a hired gun is an example of **instrumental aggression.** Here, harm is the means to a desired end. At their first trial, which ended in hung juries, Lyle and Erik Menendez were accused by the prosecution of murdering their mother and father in order to obtain their parents' wealth. The brothers claimed they had killed to protect themselves from what they perceived to be an impending attack. Although the prescribed legal consequences for murder-for-money and self-defense are vastly different, both fit the terms of instrumental aggression. If it were easier to obtain the goal (money or self-protection) in some other way, aggression would not occur.

emotional aggression Inflicting harm for its own sake.

In **emotional aggression,** the means and the end coincide. Harm is inflicted for its own sake. Emotional aggression is often impulsive, carried out in the heat of the moment. The jealous lover strikes out in rage; fans of rival soccer teams go at each other with fists and clubs. Emotional aggression, however, can also be calm, cool, and calculating. Revenge, so the saying goes, is a dish best eaten cold.

The definitions we have discussed are the crucial first steps in the study of aggression. They provide the framework for the theories and research described in the following pages. But aggression raises moral questions that go beyond scientific findings. Is all aggression morally wrong? If not, what kinds of threats justify what kinds of aggression? To answer such questions, each of us needs to carefully consider our own principles and values. Where do *you* draw the line?

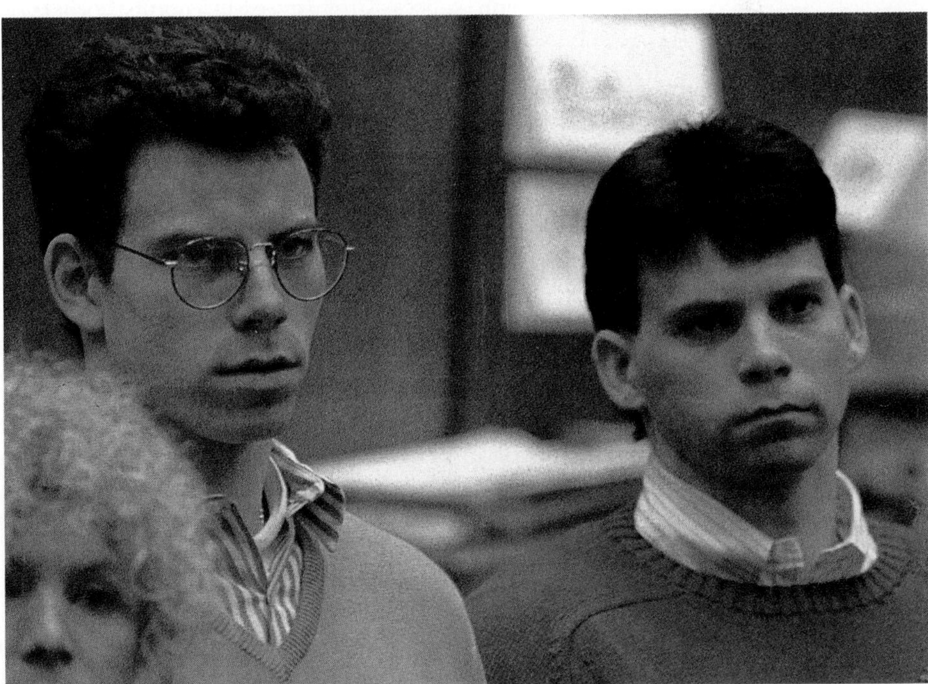

Erik and Lyle Menendez in court during their first trial for the murder of their parents.

ORIGINS OF AGGRESSION

Given the subject matter, it's not surprising that people have strong differences of opinion about the origins of aggression. Is aggression an innate characteristic of human beings, or is it learned through experience? This either/or way of phrasing the question is called the "nature-nurture debate." Let's look at both sides.

Is Aggression Innate?

Here, we examine four approaches to the issue of whether aggression is innate: instinct theories, sociobiology, behavior genetics, and gender differences.

Instinct Theories On November 11, 1918, a human catastrophe finally ended. Covered in mud, lungs blasted by gas, millions of soldiers had died to gain bits and pieces of contested territory. For an Austrian physician named Sigmund Freud, the slaughter on the battlefields of Europe during World War I marked a turning point. Rejecting his prewar version of psychoanalysis, Freud (1920) proposed a grim new concept: the *death instinct*—a profound, unconscious desire to escape the tensions of living by becoming still, inanimate, dead. This impulse toward self-destruction does not, according to Freud, exist unchallenged. There is also a life instinct, which motivates human beings to preserve and reproduce themselves. Paradoxically, Freud considered aggression toward others to be a momentary victory for the life instinct. In aggression, the force of the death instinct is deflected outward at others rather than aimed inward toward the original target of the self.

Like Freud, Konrad Lorenz (1966) regarded aggression as an innate, instinctual motivation. Unlike Freud, who believed that the life and death instincts are antagonistic, Lorenz saw the will to live and the will to aggress as entirely compatible. Based on his observations of animals in their natural habitat, Lorenz argued that aggression secures an advantage in the struggle to survive. The individual who successfully aggresses against others gains access to valuable resources such as food, territory, and desirable mates. Since only those who survive are able to reproduce, natural selection would produce an aggressive instinct in humans as well as in animals.

Despite the widespread attention that these theories received at the time they were formulated, they no longer have much influence on scientific research. The primary reason for their fall from favor is their reliance on circular reasoning. Why do people aggress? Because they have an aggressive instinct. How do we know that aggression is instinctive? Because people aggress. Case closed. But shut off from the exploration of testable alternatives, circular reasoning is a logical and scientific dead end.

Sociobiology There are clear similarities between Lorenz's instinct theory and sociobiology, the application of evolutionary biology to the development of social behavior. For example, sociobiologists Leda Cosmides and John Tooby share Lorenz's belief that human warfare originated in attempts to obtain valuable resources (Gibbons, 1993). These investigators, however, maintain that the earliest battles between men were fought over women rather than over food or land. To be well fed and have a safe territory can prolong life and indirectly enhance reproductive success—but having a mate is essential.

In contrast to Lorenz, however, sociobiology emphasizes genetic survival rather than survival of the individual. Since at least some of a person's genes can be transmitted through the reproductive success of blood relatives, evolution should have favored the *inhibition* of aggression against those who are genetically related to us. For example, according to Martin Daly and Margo Wilson (1988), birth parents are much less likely to abuse or murder their own offspring than stepparents are to harm stepchildren.

As noted in Chapters 5 and 7, sociobiology is a controversial approach to human social behavior. Perhaps the most fundamental problem faced by sociobiological accounts of aggression is historical and cultural diversity (Ruback & Weiner, 1995). Within any society, the amount of aggression varies across time. Between societies, as illustrated in Figure 8.2, there are large differences in the rate of violence. If aggression is innate and universal, how could people differ so much in when and where they display it? Faced with such variation, even some researchers who believe that aggression is an evolved characteristic have concluded that its occurrence is primarily determined by social factors (Lore & Schultz, 1993).

Behavior Genetics Sociobiology attempts the difficult task of tying together evolution, genetic transmission, and behavior. Behavior genetics settles for the complexities of connecting the last two. And here, variation is a blessing rather than a curse. To trace a line of genetic transmission (heritability), scientists exam-

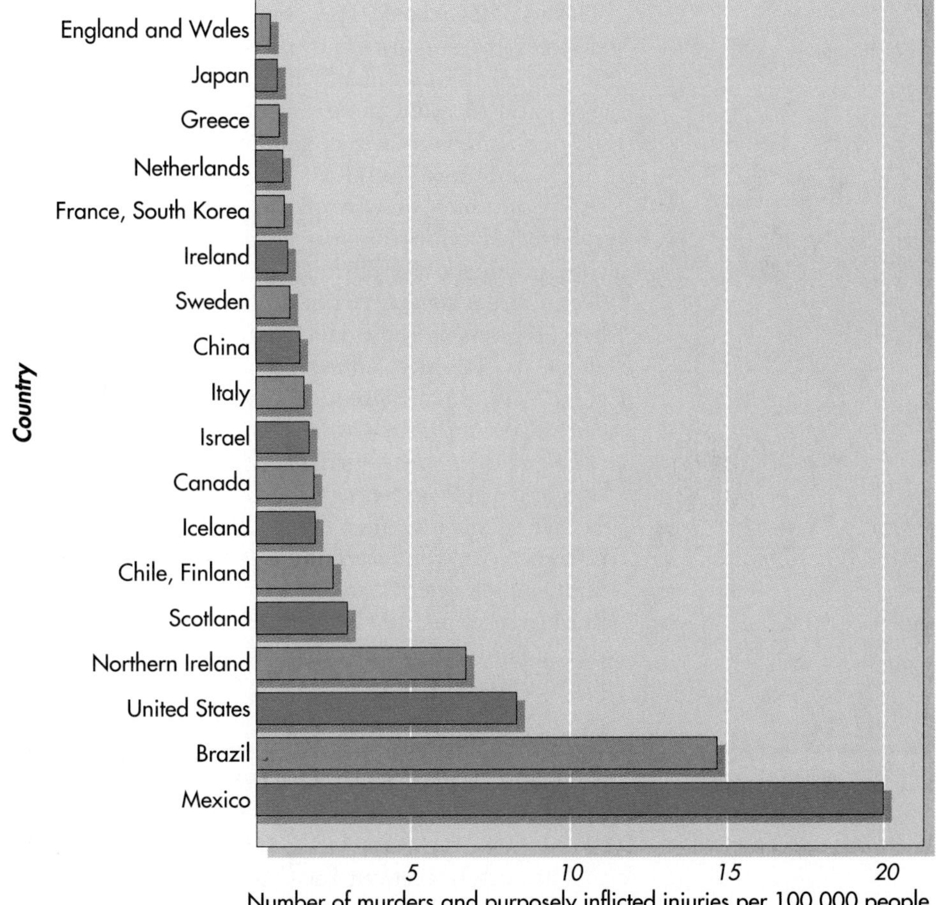

Figure 8.2 **Violence Around the World.** As you can see, the level of violence varies widely among different countries. These figures indicate the number of violent incidents per 100,000 people, as reported in the late 1980s. (Data from United Nations, 1989.)

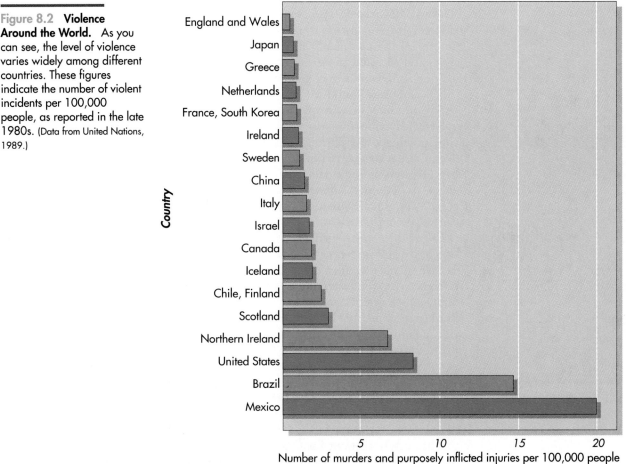

ine differences between individuals or groups. Two types of studies are typically employed in research on human subjects. In twin studies, monozygotic twins (who are identical in their genetic make-up) are compared with dizygotic twins (who share only part of their genes). On any inherited trait, the former will be more similar than the latter. Twin studies on aggression have produced mixed results and do not yield any clear judgment about the heritability of aggressive behavior (Plomin et al., 1990; Yoshikawa, 1994).

Adoptee studies are also used in behavior genetics research. On any inherited trait, adopted children will resemble their biological parents more than they resemble their adoptive parents. One of the most elaborate adoptee studies on aggression was conducted by Sarnoff Mednick and his colleagues (Mednick et al., 1987; Mednick & Kandel, 1988). These investigators analyzed the criminal records of Danish children adopted by nonkin between 1924 and 1947, along with the criminal records of the biological and adoptive parents. Although both male and female adoptees were included in this research, the low level of criminal convictions among women restricted most of the analyses to men. When type of crime was taken into account, it was found that the criminality of the biological parents predicted the percentage of sons convicted of *property* crimes, but not the percentage convicted of *violent* crimes. Since violent crimes would seem the better indicator of aggression, these findings do not provide strong support for the heritability of aggressive inclinations.

Gender Differences The greater number of criminal convictions among male adoptees in Denmark is not a fluke. It is typical for men to be convicted of crimes more often than women. Until quite recently, it was also typical for research on aggression to focus more on men than on women. But this is rapidly changing and our understanding of gender differences in aggression is growing both more precise and more complex.

Whether men or women are more aggressive is influenced by the type of aggressive behavior. In most societies, men are more *physically* aggressive than women (Björkqvist & Niemelä, 1992). There are, however, some exceptions. Over a recent ten-year period, women engaged in physical aggression more often than did men on the small Pacific island of Vanatinai, a province of Papua New Guinea (Lepowsky, 1994). In another island society—Margarita, Venezuela—women's physical aggressiveness appeared to be more prolonged and violent than men's (Cook, 1992).

The evidence for a gender difference in *verbal* aggression is decidedly mixed. Among college students in the United States, men report being more verbally aggressive than do women (Buss & Perry, 1992; Gladue, 1991). However, no such difference was found among a large, representative sample of American couples (Straus & Sweet, 1992), nor among eight to eighteen-year-olds in Finland (Björkqvist et al., 1992). A third type of aggression, called *indirect,* refers to the social manipulation of others in order to harm the target person: for example, spreading false stories, engaging in gossip and backbiting, and trying to get others to dislike the target. In research conducted in Finland and in Buenos Aires, Argentina, females appeared to engage in indirect aggression more often than did men (Björkqvist et al., 1992; Hines & Fry, 1994). Despite these variations across type of aggression, men and women, at least in the United States, do not seem to differ in their feelings of anger (Averill, 1982; Buss & Perry, 1992).

What might account for the typical gender difference in physical aggression? There are a number of possible explanations. One focuses on the relative balance

Men are more physically aggressive than women in most societies, but women, too, commit acts of physical violence. Here, a young woman is being brutally initiated into a gang by other female gang members.

of sex hormones, which is normally determined by the sex chromosomes that establish a person's biological sex. Although the male sex hormone is present in both sexes, males usually have higher levels of testosterone than do females. If testosterone affects aggressive behavior, then it could serve as the connection between biological sex and aggression. A number of studies have documented an association between testosterone and aggression. For example, prison inmates (both male and female) who had committed an unprovoked violent crime had higher testosterone levels than did those who had committed a nonviolent crime (Dabbs et al., 1987; Dabbs et al., 1988). Similarly, male college students with high levels of testosterone were more aggressive on an experimental task than were those with low levels (Berman et al., 1993).

Intriguing as they are, such correlational findings cannot prove that testosterone causes aggression. There are other alternatives. For example, some research suggests that it can go the other way, with aggression increasing testosterone levels (Baron & Richardson, 1994). Stress may also be involved: Higher levels of stress are associated with higher levels of testosterone (Thompson et al., 1990), and testosterone levels are better predictors of antisocial behavior for subjects low in socioeconomic status than for those with greater income and education (Dabbs & Morris, 1990; Dabbs et al., 1990). Perhaps people who are poor and badly educated are more vulnerable to the kinds of stressors that simultaneously elevate both testosterone and aggression.

Testosterone levels can be identified only by laboratory analysis. Another possible biological explanation for gender differences in physical aggression emphasizes a more visible characteristic. Most men have more bulk and more muscle than most women. If more women were built like Arnold Schwarzenegger, would they be more physically aggressive?

Whatever the effects of biological characteristics such as testosterone and physique, most researchers agree that social roles have a strong influence on physical aggression (Eagly & Steffen, 1986; Eagly & Wood, 1991). As described in Chapter 4, males and females are socialized to fill different roles in society. Aggression is a central aspect of gender-related role expectations, usually regarded as more socially acceptable for males than for females.

But not always. Mothers, for example, are often expected to discipline their children, thereby giving women greater latitude in aggressive behavior when fulfilling the maternal role. And private interactions may be less constrained by social norms than public behavior. Research by Jennifer Lightdale and Deborah Prentice (1994) suggests that when external social influences on aggression are reduced by making people feel anonymous, men and women are more likely to be equally aggressive. As we will see later in this chapter, women engage in relatively high rates of aggression in the home—toward their partners and their children. This consideration of social roles takes us from the "nature" side of the coin to the "nurture" side, to which we now turn.

Is Aggression Learned?

Regardless of the precise contribution of genetic and biological factors, the importance of experience is clear: Aggressive behavior is strongly affected by learning (Bandura, 1973; Patterson, 1986). Rewards obtained by aggression today increase its use tomorrow. Such rewards come in two flavors: *positive* reinforcement, when desired outcomes are obtained, and *negative* reinforcement, when undesirable outcomes are prevented or stopped. The child who gets a toy by hitting the toy's owner is likely to hit again. So, too, the child who can stop other children from teasing by shoving them away has learned the fateful lesson that aggression pays.

But what about punishment? Here, things get a bit more complex (Baron & Richardson, 1994; Berkowitz, 1993). On the one hand, punishment can decrease aggression when it

- immediately follows the aggressive behavior.
- is strong enough to deter the aggressor.
- is consistently applied and perceived as fair and legitimate by the aggressor.

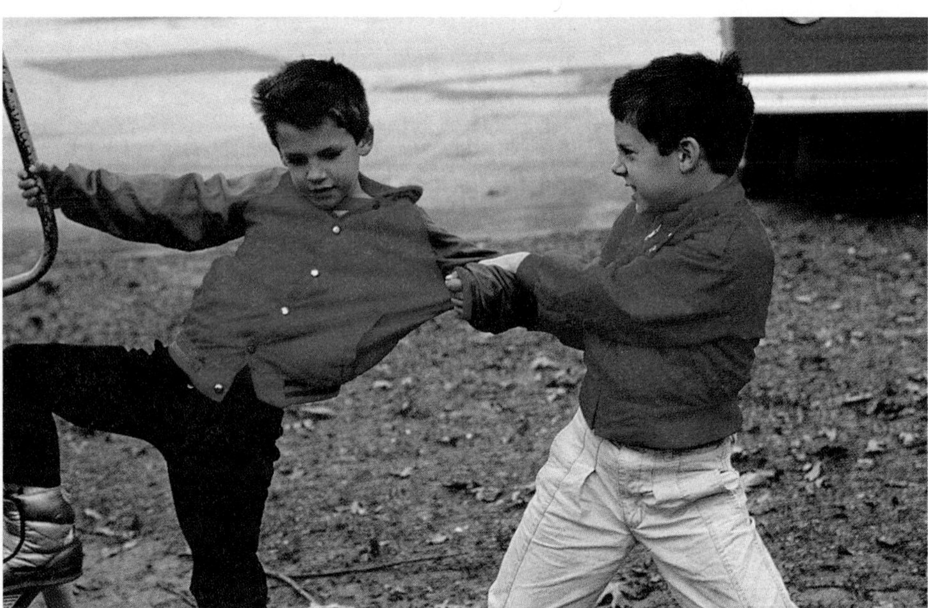

When children get what they want by being aggressive, their aggressive behavior increases.

On the other hand, such stringent conditions are seldom met. When courts are overburdened and prisons are overcrowded, as they are in the United States, the relationship between crime and punishment can seem more like a lottery than a rational system in which the punishment fits the crime (Smolowe, 1994).

There are some other problems with punishment. It's less likely to be effective when the instrumental aggressor doesn't see any other way to obtain the desired goal and when the emotional aggressor is extremely angry. Moreover, punishment perceived as unfair or arbitrary can provoke retaliation. Perhaps most troubling, however, is that punishment, especially when delivered in an angry or hostile manner, offers a model to imitate, aggressively. The children of parents who report using harsh physical punishment are more aggressive in school than children whose parents report relying on other kinds of responses to the child's misbehavior (Weiss et al., 1992).

social learning theory The proposition that behavior is learned through the observation of others as well as through the direct experience of rewards and punishments.

The power of models to modify behavior is a crucial tenet of Albert Bandura's (1977b) **social learning theory.** Social learning theory emphasizes that we learn from the example of others as well as from direct experience with rewards and punishments. Models influence the prosocial, helpful behavior described in Chapter 7. They also affect antisocial, aggressive behavior. In an early study, Bandura and his associates (1961) observed the behavior of mildly frustrated children. Those who had previously watched an adult throw around, punch, and kick an inflatable Bobo doll were more aggressive when they later played with the doll than were those who had watched a quiet, subdued adult. Subsequent research has amply demonstrated that a wide range of aggressive models can elicit a wide range of aggressive imitations (Bandura, 1983; Baron & Richardson, 1994; Berkowitz, 1993).

Models whose aggression succeeds in obtaining desired goals, without being punished for their behavior, are the most likely to increase aggression among observers. But even those who are punished can have an effect. Postwar increases in homicide rates have been documented not only in rewarded, victorious countries that watched their soldiers prevail, but also in punished, defeated nations that

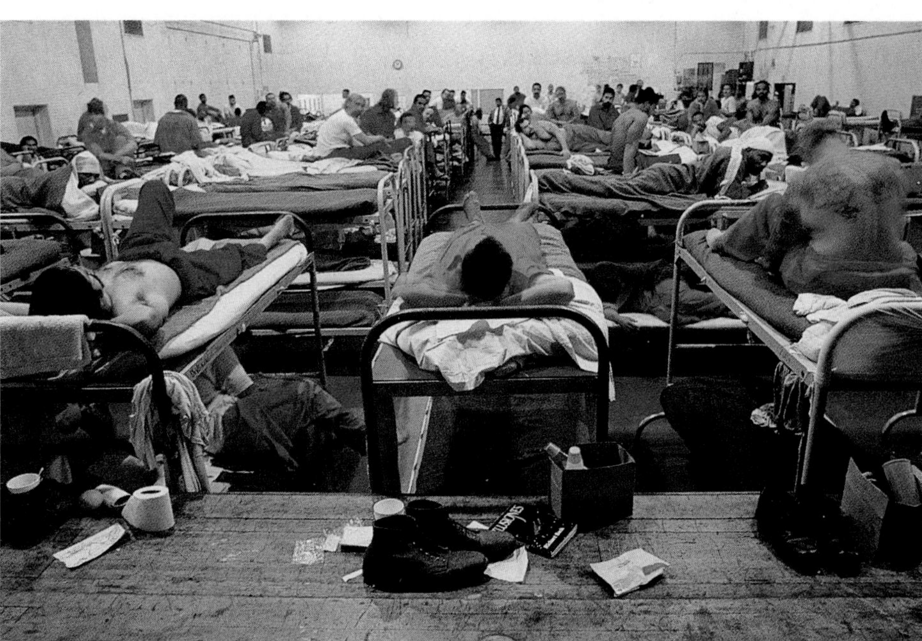

Because of overcrowded prisons, such as this converted gymnasium, many convicts are released before they have served their full sentence. Jail time becomes, in the words of a man charged with armed robbery, "a game or a joke." (Smolowe, 1994).

Young Palestinians imitate adult behavior by playing the "Intifada game."

saw their soldiers overwhelmed (Archer & Gartner, 1984). And for some, punishment seems to increase the influence of a model. Paul Hill, sentenced to death for murdering a physician and his bodyguard outside a Florida abortion clinic, said he didn't think of killing anyone himself until he saw Rachelle Shannon convicted for wounding a physician in Kansas: "I was encouraged and emboldened by her example."

Fortunately, changing the model can change the consequences: Nonaggressive models decrease aggressive behavior (Baron & Kepner, 1970; Donnerstein & Donnerstein, 1976). Observing a nonaggressive response to a provoking situation teaches a peaceful alternative and strengthens existing restraints against aggression. In addition, observing someone who is calm and reasonable may help an angry person settle down rather than strike out (Baron & Richardson, 1994). Aggression can spread like wildfire. But nonviolence, too, can be contagious.

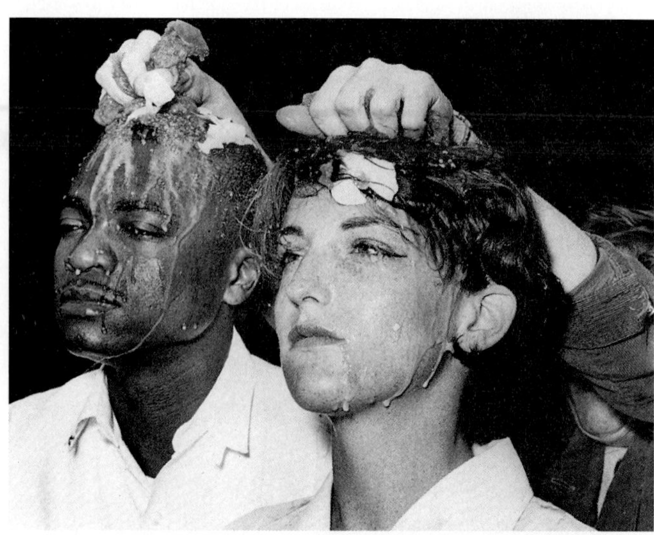

This photo, taken during the 1960's, shows civil rights demonstrators being trained to remain nonviolent despite the abusive and aggressive behavior they would encounter.

Nature Versus Nurture: The Terms of the Debate

Recently, the origins of aggression became not only a source of scientific disagreement but a political controversy as well (Johnson, 1993; Toufexis, 1993). Should the federal government sponsor a conference on genetics and crime? Should it fund research on early identification of the potential for aggressive actions and on programs to reduce this potential? Those who opposed these projects feared that innocent children might be stigmatized and their human rights abridged. Those who favored federal funding argued that it was essential to study possible early predictors in order to develop more effective ways to reduce violence. The scientific community was split; politicians lined up on different sides; and, in the end, the federal initiatives were shelved.

This incident highlights the bottom line, one might even say the battle line, in the debate about the determinants of aggression: Is aggression, to any significant extent, "born" through genetic inheritance or stable biological characteristics present at birth? However important it may be, this contentious issue should not obscure the considerable agreement that exists on other points. The effects of learning are not disputed; aggression is, at least to some extent, "made" by experience. Nor is there any doubt that in aggression, as in all human behavior, biology and environment interact. What *is* questioned is how much each contributes to the final product. In the next section, we explore various aspects of the social and physical environment that affect aggressive actions.

SOCIAL AND SITUATIONAL INFLUENCES ON AGGRESSION

Mark Twain's novel *The Prince and the Pauper* is a tale of two characters who exchange social roles with each other. The plot of an early Eddie Murphy film *Trading Places* hinges on a similar device. Both the novel and the film reflect an enduring fascination with the way behavior changes in response to a new environment. They also depict individuals thinking about the new places in which they find themselves. As we will see, both environmental circumstances and people's thoughts affect whether aggressive behavior will occur.

Frustration: Aggression as a Drive

In 1939, the year that World War II began, John Dollard and his colleagues published *Frustration and Aggression,* one of the most influential books on aggression ever written. This book sets forth two major propositions, which taken together are called the **frustration-aggression hypothesis:**

frustration-aggression hypothesis The idea that (1) frustration always elicits the motive to aggress and (2) all aggression is caused by frustration.

- Frustration produced by interrupting a person's progress toward an expected goal will always elicit the motive to aggress.
- All aggression is caused by frustration.

Dollard and his colleagues claimed that the motive to aggress is a psychological drive that resembles physiological drives like hunger. Just as food deprivation elicits a hunger drive, so, they said, does frustration elicit an aggressive drive. Just as the hunger drive prompts the search for food, so, they claimed, does the aggressive drive prompt the attempt to inflict injury. But hunger does not always result in eating. Sometimes there's no food to be found or there's a fear of punishment if one grabs a piece of another's feast. Similarly, argued Dollard and his colleagues, the drive to aggress can be blocked if the source of the frustration is not present or the potential aggressor fears punishment for attacking.

Such obstacles, however, were not viewed by Dollard and his colleagues as permanent barriers against aggression. Instead, they believed that the aggressive drive seeps out in the form of **displacement**, deflecting the inclination to aggress from the real target only to land on a substitute. After a bad day at work or at school, do you come home and yell at the first available target—be it man, woman, or beast?

displacement Aggressing against a substitute target because aggressive acts against the source of the frustration are inhibited by fear or lack of access.

If so, would yelling at an innocent bystander reduce your inclination to take revenge on the person who gave you a hard time? The efficacy of such substitute actions was warmly endorsed by Dollard and his colleagues in their notion of **catharsis.** Just as hunger can be satisfied by hamburgers as well as by caviar, so any aggressive act should reduce the motive to engage in any other aggressive behavior. Since the Dollard group defined aggression quite broadly—to include making hostile jokes, telling violent stories, cursing, and observing the aggression of others, real or fictional—they held out the hope that engaging in some relatively harmless pursuit could drain away energy from more violent tendencies.

catharsis The reduction of the motive to aggress that is said to result from any imagined, observed, or actual act of aggression.

Problems and Limitations Obviously, there is a connection between frustration and aggression. Break into a line of shoppers at the supermarket or interrupt a student cramming for an exam, and you can see it for yourself. But does frustration *always* produce the desire to aggress? Is *all* aggression the product of frustration?

Critics were quick to point out that the Dollard group had overstated their case. Early on, Neal Miller (1941), one of the originators of the hypothesis, acknowledged that frustration does not always produce aggressive inclinations. Subsequent research indicated that frustration is most likely to produce an aggressive response when people are thwarted from reaching an important goal to which they feel entitled (Blanchard & Blanchard, 1984; Worchel, 1974). The other absolute, that all aggression is caused by frustration, was soon overturned as well. In the following pages, we will consider many other causes of aggression.

The concept of displacement was also subjected to close scrutiny. In 1940, Carl Hovland and Robert Sears proposed that aggression by Whites against Blacks reflected the displacement of aggressive tendencies actually caused by economic frustration. Reviewing information on fourteen southern states from 1882 to 1930, these investigators found a strong negative correlation between economic indicators and the number of lynchings of African-American men. When the southern economy declined, more lynchings occurred. Subsequent studies have confirmed this correlation between economic distress and racial violence (Beck & Tolnay, 1990; Hepworth & West, 1988).

However, these findings do not prove the validity of the concept of displacement. The requirements for a convincing demonstration of displacement are stringent (Berkowitz, 1962), and, overall, the evidence for its role in channeling aggressive behavior is inconclusive (Zillmann, 1979). As we will see later in this chapter, other processes (such as level of arousal and an individual's thoughts) can account for why it's possible to be provoked by one person but aggress against someone else.

Perhaps because it seemed to offer a way to control aggression, the concept of catharsis received particular attention. Dollard and his colleagues described catharsis as a two-step sequence. First, aggression reduces the level of physiological arousal. Second, because arousal is reduced, people are less angry and less likely to aggress further. It sounds logical and lots of people believe it. It has been said, for example, that "spectator sports give John Q. Citizen a socially acceptable way to lower his steam pressure by allowing him to spin his wheels and toot his whistle" (Proctor & Eckerd, 1976, p. 83).

But, put to the test, catharsis has not lived up to its advertisement. Most researchers doubt that catharsis is the panacea that the Dollard group hoped it would be (Baron & Richardson, 1994; Berkowitz, 1993). Here's why:

- Imagined aggression or the observation of aggressive models is more likely to increase arousal and aggression than to reduce them.
- Actual aggression can lower arousal levels. However, if aggressive intent remains, "cold-blooded" aggression can still occur. Furthermore, if aggression-produced reduction of arousal feels good to the aggressor, this reward makes it more likely that aggression will occur again.
- Even relatively low levels of aggression can chip away at restraints against more violent behavior.

Since most aggressors do not seek to utterly destroy the individual they attack, aggressive behavior that reaches a limited goal may well reduce the likelihood of further aggression at that time. In the long run, however, successful aggression now sets the stage for more aggression later. In short, relying on catharsis is dangerous medicine—more likely to inflame aggression than to put it out.

A New Look Like Hamlet who felt he had suffered "the slings and arrows of outrageous fortune," the frustration-aggression hypothesis seemed torn and tattered after having to bear so much criticism and revision. But Leonard Berkowitz's (1989) reformulation put the hypothesis in a new perspective. According to Berkowitz, the main point about frustration is that it is an unpleasant experience that creates negative, uncomfortable feelings.

This approach makes sense of why some frustrations increase aggression while others don't. Whatever makes frustration more unpleasant—such as the loss of an important goal, an interruption that is unexpected, an interference perceived as arbitrary and unjustified—increases its tendency to produce aggression. Moreover, by defining frustration as only one of a large number of events that produce negative emotions and increase aggression, Berkowitz made a direct connection between the pioneering work of the Dollard group and more recent research.

Negative Affect: The Temperature's Rising

The key concept of negative affect opens all sorts of aggressive doors. In addition to frustrating experiences, a wide variety of noxious stimuli can create negative feelings and increase aggression: noise (Geen & McCown, 1984), crowding (Fisher et al., 1984), physical pain (Berkowitz & Heimer, 1989), bad odors (Rotton & Frey, 1985), and cigarette smoke (Zillmann et al., 1981). Reactions to one of the most common unpleasant conditions, hot weather, are especially intriguing. Many people assume that temperature and tempers rise together. Are they right?

Robert Baron would reply, "Yes, up to a point." From Baron's perspective, the effects of temperature and other unpleasant stimuli on aggression can best be understood in terms of the *negative affect escape model* (Baron, 1977; Baron &

Richardson, 1994). This model holds that as the intensity of noxious stimuli increases, so do negative affect and aggression—up to the point where nonaggressive responses such as escape or fatigue become dominant and aggression declines.

At first it seemed that the negative affect escape model could explain the violence that sometimes erupts during a long, hot summer (Baron & Ransberger, 1978). This research found that the number of urban riots that occurred in the United States from 1967 to 1971 initially increased as the temperature rose, peaking during those days when the temperature was around 81 to 85 degrees Fahrenheit. At still higher temperatures, the number of riots declined (see Figure 8.3A).

Subsequent research, however, has not found a turning point. Instead, it has documented a continuing increase. As the temperature goes up, so does the incidence of aggressive behaviors such as murder, rape, assault, and wife-battering (Anderson, 1989). How can we solve the puzzle created by these conflicting findings?

Here's a clue. If we plot the number of baseball games that take place in a season according to the temperature on the day they were played, the greatest number of games occurs during those days when the temperature is . . . what? You got it: in that same range of 81 to 85 degrees (Carlsmith & Anderson, 1979; see Figure 8.3B). But what's going on? Why would the outbreak of riots and the number of baseball games peak in the same temperature range?

Normal temperature variation solves the puzzle. Days with temperatures of 81 to 85 degrees are more frequent in the summer than are days with other temperatures. Thus, there is more opportunity for both baseball games and aggression to occur at these moderate temperatures. When temperature frequency is taken into

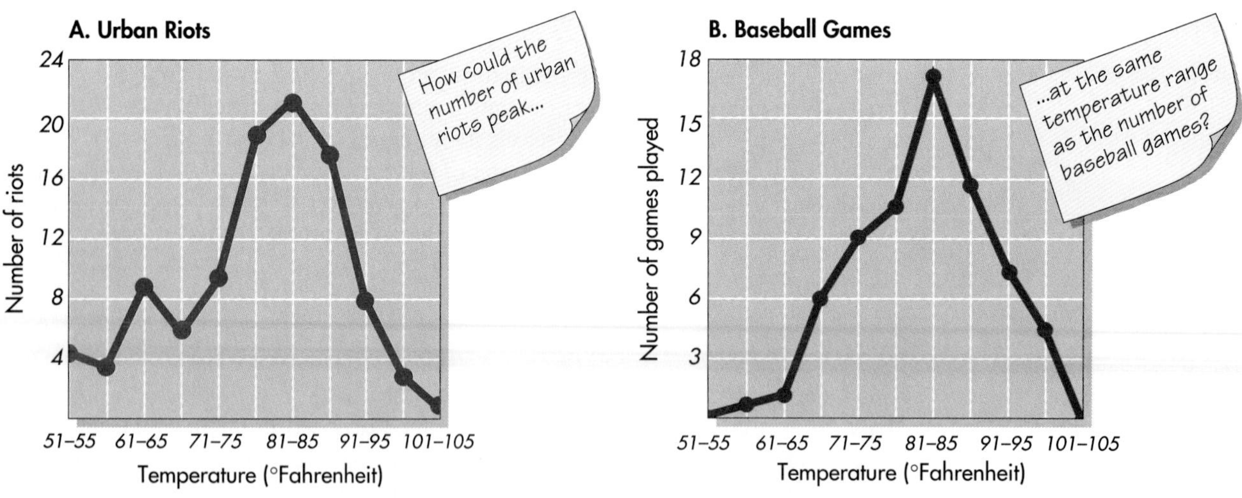

Figure 8.3 **Temperature, Riots, and Baseball.** Both of these figures display the relationship between temperature and a behavioral event: in Figure A, the number of urban riots; in Figure B, the number of baseball games. But baseball games, unlike riots, are scheduled in advance. How could they both peak at 81 to 85 degrees? The answer: This temperature range occurs more frequently during the summer, providing more opportunities for any behavior to occur. (Figure A: Baron & Ransberger, 1978; Figure B: Carlsmith & Anderson, 1979.)

account, there is no turning point. Aggressive behavior continues to increase as the temperature climbs. Of course, the increase in aggressive behavior as the temperature rises can't continue indefinitely. At some point, aggression must decline because people sicken and even die during extreme heat. So it's possible that carefully constructed research will be able to find a turning point even within the range of normal temperatures (Anderson & DeNeve, 1992; Bell, 1992). Still, across a variety of geographical locations and types of violence, more heat means more aggression.

Positive Affect: Reducing Retaliation

Like frustration and noxious stimuli, the unpleasant experience of provocation also increases aggression. When people are provoked by attack or insult, they often retaliate (Dengerink et al., 1978). Retaliation is particularly prevalent in cultures that place a high premium on protecting one's honor by responding aggressively to insults (Nisbett, 1993). For example, argument-related murders committed by white males occur at a much higher rate in the South and Southwest than in other regions in the United States. Regional differences in felony-related murders are much smaller or even reversed.

But why does provocation trigger retaliatory aggression? The answer would seem to be a familiar one: negative affect. If so, then creating positive emotional reactions should cancel out negative feelings and thereby reduce retaliatory aggression. It does. In one study, subjects were first provoked and angered by an experimental confederate (Baron & Ball, 1974). They were then shown funny cartoons or neutral pictures. Presented with an opportunity to retaliate by delivering electric shocks as part of a supposed learning experiment, those who had seen the cartoons delivered fewer shocks. Feeling good appears to be incompatible with anger and aggression. Feeling concerned about others has similar effects. An empathic response to another person reduces aggression against that individual (Miller & Eisenberg, 1988).

Arousal: "Wired" for Action

Research on negative and positive affect clearly indicates that the type of emotion influences aggression. The intensity of arousal is important as well. In Chapter 6,

Positive emotional responses are incompatible with anger and aggression.

"Well, darn, Ted, I just can't stay mad at you."

we described the process of *excitation transfer* in which the arousal created by one stimulus can intensify an individual's emotional response to another stimulus (Zillmann, 1979, 1984). For example, men who initially engaged in vigorous exercise were later more attracted to an attractive female than were those who had barely moved (White et al., 1981). Physical exercise is a highly arousing but emotionally neutral experience. Can it increase aggression as well as attraction?

For an answer, consider a study conducted by Dolf Zillmann and his colleagues (1972). Male subjects were either angered or not by an experimental confederate, and then either did or did not engage in strenuous physical exercise. Next, all subjects were given the opportunity to shock the confederate in the context of a supposed learning experiment. As the researchers had predicted, angered subjects who had exercised delivered shocks of greater intensity than did subjects who had not been angered or who had not exercised. The scope of excitation transfer is not limited to physical exercise. Noise, violent motion pictures, arousing music—all have been shown to increase aggression (Zillmann, 1983). Later in this chapter, we will describe the effects of another arousing stimulus—pornography—on the inclination to aggress.

Thus far, we have treated the type of emotion and the intensity of physiological arousal as separate territories. But they can be unified. Focusing primarily on retaliatory aggression, the **arousal-affect model** (Sapolsky, 1984; Zillmann & Bryant, 1984) provides a systematic integration that summarizes a number of the findings we've discussed (see Figure 8.4). Experiences that create negative emotions increase aggression; add high arousal and the combination could be lethal. Experiences that are emotionally neutral have little impact on aggression, *unless* they are highly arousing. Experiences that create positive emotions and low arousal decrease aggression. Now comes the hard part: experiences that produce positive emotions and high arousal. Will aggression decrease because a positive emotional experience is incompatible with unpleasant angry feelings? Or will aggression increase because there's a lot of arousal available for transfer? It's a tough call and could go either way—depending on the individual, the situation, and the thoughts that come to mind.

arousal-affect model The proposal that aggression is influenced by both the intensity of arousal and the type of emotion produced by a stimulus.

Type of Emotion	Intensity of Physiological Arousal: *Low*	Intensity of Physiological Arousal: *High*
Negative	Aggression increases	Aggression greatly increases
Neutral	No effect	Aggression increases
Positive	Aggression decreases	Aggression increases or Aggression decreases

Figure 8.4 The Arousal-Affect Model. According to this model, aggression is influenced by both the intensity of physiological arousal and the type of emotion produced by a stimulus.

Thought: Automatic and Considered

Step by step, we have been making our way toward a comprehensive theory of social and situational influences on aggression. We've examined three kinds of unpleasant experiences (frustration, noxious stimuli, and provocation) that create negative affect. We've considered how changes in negative affect (decreasing it by positive emotions, intensifying it by high arousal) produce corresponding changes in aggression. The next step is to add cognition. People don't just feel; they also think. What is the role of thought in aggressive behavior?

cognitive-neoassociation analysis The view that unpleasant experiences create negative affect, which in turn stimulates associations connected with anger and fear. Emotional and behavioral outcomes then depend, at least in part, on higher-order cognitive processing.

According to Leonard Berkowitz, it has a star part. His perspective, called the **cognitive-neoassociation analysis,** emphasizes how feelings and thoughts interact (Berkowitz, 1990, 1993). Negative affect, says Berkowitz, automatically stimulates various thoughts, memories, expressive motor reactions, and physiological responses associated with both of two basic reaction tendencies: fight and flight. These associations give rise to rudimentary emotional experiences of anger and fear. Situational cues can intensify or weaken such automatic associations.

Subsequently, higher-order cognitive processes come into play. People think about how they feel, make causal attributions for what led them to feel this way, and weigh the consequences of acting on their feelings. Event-related information is examined during these more deliberate considerations, which produce more clearly differentiated feelings of anger or fear. Higher-order cognitive processing can also suppress or enhance the action-tendencies associated with these feelings. Berkowitz's analysis is diagrammed in Figure 8.5. Let's take a closer look at two major components of this view of aggression: situational cues and cognitive mediators.

Situational Cues The deadliest aggression in the United States comes from the barrel of a gun.

- Guns are the second fastest rising cause of death, exceeded only by AIDS.
- Over 60 percent of murders are committed with guns.
- More people die from gunshots than from traffic accidents in California, Louisiana, Nevada, New York, Texas, Virginia, and the District of Columbia.
- Nearly half of all Americans have firearms in the home; those who keep guns are almost three times more likely to be killed at home as those who don't.
- In a national survey of students in the sixth through twelfth grades, 59 percent said they knew where to get a gun if they needed one, 15 percent said they'd carried a handgun in the past thirty days, and 11 percent said they'd been shot at.
- The number of gun-related murders committed by juvenile offenders aged ten to seventeen has more than doubled since 1976 (see Figure 8.6).

Faced with such gruesome statistics, the National Rifle Association (NRA) responds that guns should not be blamed. People, the NRA says, pull the trigger. Guns are the instrument, not the cause.

But are guns entirely neutral? Or does the presence of a weapon act as a situational cue that increases the likelihood of aggression? In a classic study designed to address these questions, male subjects who had been provoked by an experimental confederate delivered more shocks to him when a revolver and rifle were

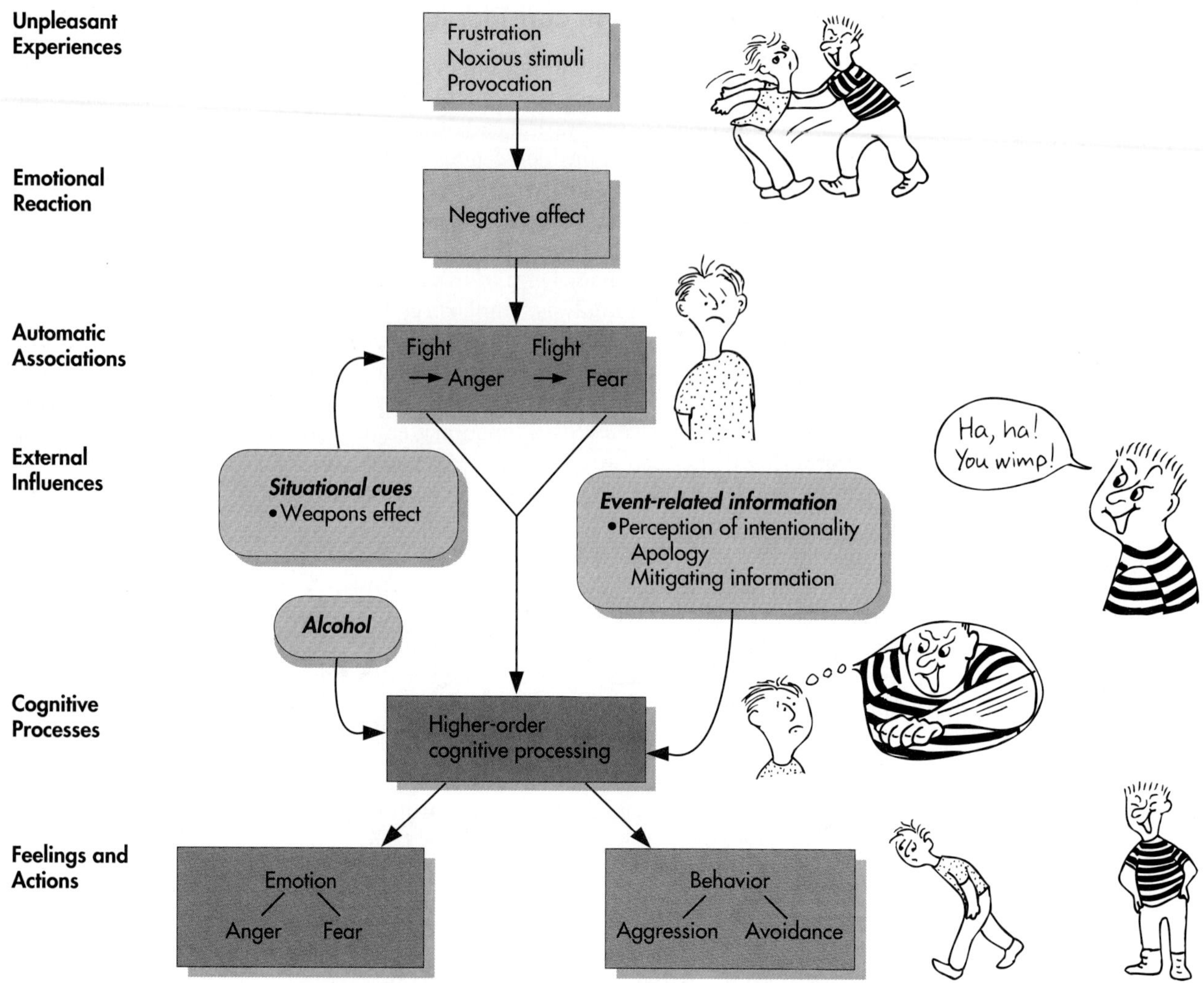

Figure 8.5 A Cognitive-Neoassociation Analysis. Berkowitz's model of aggression holds that unpleasant experiences create negative affect, which in turn stimulates automatic associations connected with fear and anger. External influences and higher-order processing then shape the feelings and actions that result.

present than when badminton racquets and shuttlecocks were scattered about (Berkowitz & LePage, 1967). This tendency for the presence of guns to increase aggression is called the **weapons effect.** As Berkowitz put it: "The finger pulls the trigger, but the trigger may also be pulling the finger" (1968, p. 22).

weapons effect The tendency of weapons to increase the likelihood of aggression by their mere presence.

In general, any object or external characteristic that is associated with (1) successful aggression or (2) the negative affect of pain or unpleasantness can serve as an aggression-enhancing situational cue (Berkowitz, 1993). Such cues can have very strong effects, increasing aggression among people who are in a neutral mood as well as among those who have been angered by provocation (Carlson et al., 1990).

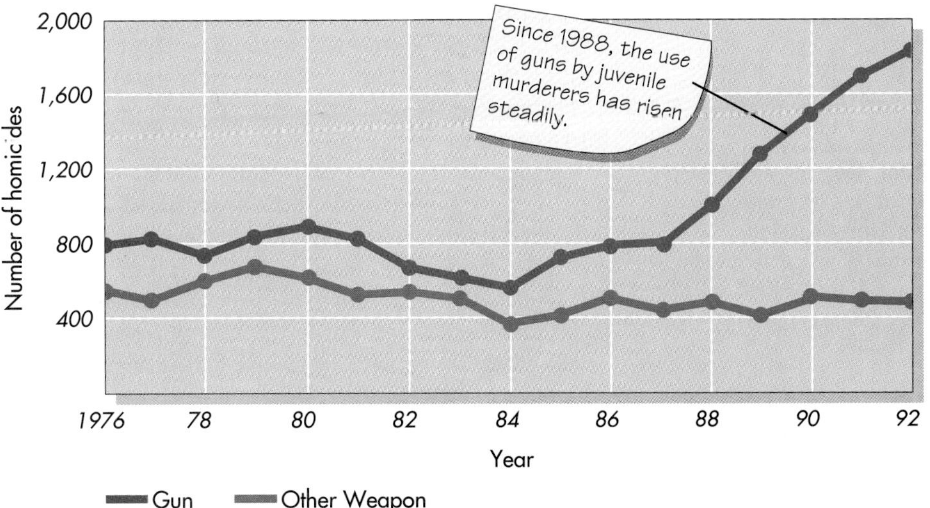

Figure 8.6 **Murder by Gun.** Among youthful offenders aged ten to seventeen, the number of gun-related homicides has increased dramatically. (Data from Newsweek, 1995)

Cognitive Control Situational cues affect a network of automatic associations. More complex, event-related information influences the deliberate, thoughtful consideration that we call higher-order cognitive processing. What if, for example, a person who has injured you claims that the action was unintentional? You have to think it over and decide whether you're convinced. If you are, the person may get a pass. Compared with harmful actions judged as intentional, those perceived as *un*intentional are less often perceived as hostile and less likely to elicit anger and aggression (Betancourt & Blair, 1992; Ferguson & Rule, 1983).

But even given the same information, not all perceivers come up with the same interpretation. Socially maladjusted children, who are chronically aggressive and

As handgun murders reach epidemic proportions in the United States, handgun ownership, especially among women, is also increasing.

rejected by their peers, see hostile intent where others don't (Crick & Dodge, 1994). Such perceptions then increase aggression and peer-rejection even further, locking these children into an ever-escalating vicious cycle.

Perhaps because it reduces the perception of intent, apologizing for having hurt someone reduces the victim's tendency to retaliate (Ohbuchi et al., 1989). **Mitigating information** indicating that an individual should not be held responsible for aggressive acts should also diminish perceived intent to harm. In criminal law, defendants are excused for aggression that is thought to result from insanity, coercion, ignorance, or self-defense. In our personal lives, too, we find room for forgiveness. The friend whose love affair just broke up, the co-worker whose job is in danger—we don't hold them fully responsible for their actions.

mitigating information Information about a person's situation indicating that he or she should not be held fully responsible for aggressive actions.

Whether we refrain from retaliating against them, however, may depend on when we learn about their stressful situation. In one study, subjects who were aware of mitigating information before being attacked by another person stayed calm and were unaggressive (Zillmann & Cantor, 1976). Those who learned about the other person's stressful situation only after being provoked experienced decreased physiological arousal but still retaliated. Sometimes mitigating information is "too little, too late."

Some conditions make it more difficult to engage in higher-order processing. High arousal, for example, impairs the cognitive control of aggression (Zillmann et al., 1975). So does alcohol. Implicated in the majority of violent crimes, suicides, and automobile fatalities, alcohol consumption increases aggressive behavior (Bushman & Cooper, 1990). Even among individuals who are usually *not* aggressive and who are *not* provoked, those who drink more, aggress more (Bailey & Taylor, 1991). Moreover, clean living in the past will not protect you. As illustrated in Figure 8.7, people who usually drink very little are *more* responsive to the aggression-enhancing effects of alcohol than are those who have more experience with alcohol (Laplace et al., 1994).

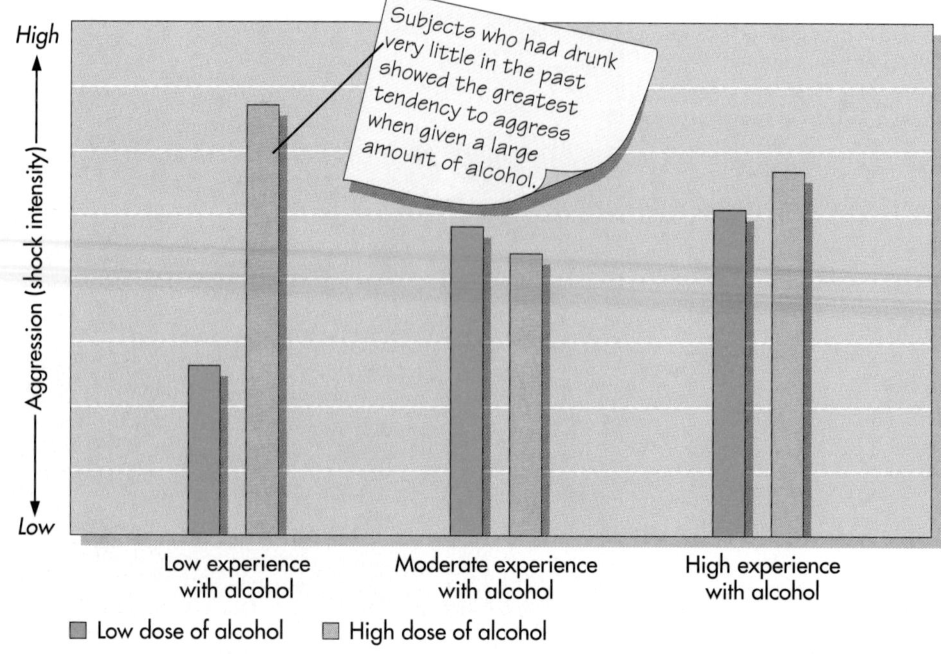

Figure 8.7 Drinking, History, and Aggression. In this study, male subjects were told they were competing on a reaction-time task with another subject. Half of them consumed a high dosage of alcohol; the other half consumed a low dosage. On the first trial, without any provocation by their opponent, the difference in aggressiveness between intoxicated and nonintoxicated subjects was greatest among those who had little previous experience with alcohol. (Data from Laplace, et al., 1994.)

But how does alcohol increase aggression? According to most investigators, drinking disrupts the way we process information (Steele & Josephs, 1990; Taylor & Leonard, 1983). Where there are multiple cues, as is the case in most interpersonal situations, intoxicated people respond to initial, salient information about the situation but often miss later, more subtle indicators. In a study described in detail in Chapter 1, subjects who were told that an opponent intended to aggress against them were aggressive in return, regardless of whether they had consumed alcohol (Leonard, 1989). Then they discovered that their opponent had not, in fact, carried out his intentions. Subjects who had not consumed alcohol quickly reduced their aggressive behavior. Intoxicated subjects, however, kept right on zapping their opponent. When drunks get going, they're hard to stop.

Multiple Causes, Multiple Cures

As we have seen, there are many events and conditions that influence aggression. Moreover, the impact of any given situation often involves a variety of psychological factors. Hot temperatures, for instance, affect arousal and cognitions as well as emotions (Anderson et al., 1995). Thus, we cannot hope for a single, simple cure. But multiple causes create the potential for multiple ways to reduce aggression. Based on the research we've reviewed in this chapter, here's a list of some possible steps that could be taken:

- Enlarge opportunities to achieve the goals valued by society (such as social approval, status, financial success) through nonviolent means.
- Reward nonaggressive behavior.
- Provide attractive models of peaceful behavior.
- Reduce all forms of aggression in our society, including physical punishment of children, capital punishment of criminals, and war.

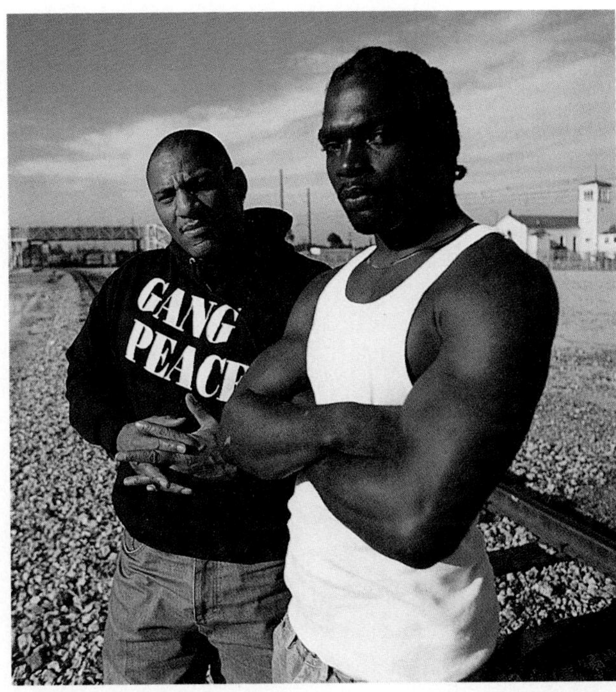

Each of us can do something to reduce aggression. Common Ground, an outreach organization in Los Angeles, helped bring about a truce between two warring gangs. Two of the members of Common Ground are pictured here.

- Reduce frustration by improving the quality of life in housing, health care, employment, and child care.
- Provide fans and air-conditioned shelters when it's hot.
- Reduce access to and display of weapons.
- Apologize when you've angered someone, and regard apologies as a sign of strength—not weakness. Encourage others to do likewise.
- Stop and think when you feel your temper rising. Control it instead of letting it control you.
- Discourage drinking and support efforts to provide treatment for alcohol abuse.

Personally, you may not agree that all of these actions are desirable—and you may prefer others that are not mentioned. That's your choice. What's important is to realize that each of us can do something to reduce aggression. There are many paths to take toward this common goal.

MEDIA EFFECTS: SCENES OF VIOLENCE

Having examined aggression under a microscope, looking at specific factors that can contribute to it, we now focus on a bigger picture. To gain a better understanding of the causes and consequences of aggressive behavior, we explore two types of mass media presentations in which the display of aggression may elicit more of it.

Depictions of Nonsexual Violence

Testifying before a U.S. Senate subcommittee, Leonard Eron had some startling figures to report. Assuming that a child watches two to four hours of TV a day, Eron estimated that by the end of elementary school "he or she would have seen

Although most of the research on displays of nonsexual violence has focused on TV and movies, there are many other sources of violent presentations, such as this violent video game, Mortal Kombat.

8,000 murders and more than 100,000 other acts of violence" (DeAngelis, 1993). Might all this murder and mayhem on the screen spill over into real life? The senators thought so, and faced with mounting political pressure, the major TV networks agreed to insert a warning label before high-violence prime-time shows: "Due to some violent content, parental discretion is advised."

But violence on TV is not limited to the major networks or to prime time. There is violence on cable, in cartoons, on news shows, and in commercials. And then there are all those other sources of violent portrayals: movies, newspapers, newsmagazines, video games, music videos, and song lyrics. Although most of the research on scenes of nonsexual violence has concentrated on TV and films, the findings point to some basic ways in which various kinds of violent depictions can increase the likelihood of aggressive behavior.

Immediate Effects Does life imitate art? Sometimes it seems that way. Charles Manson's murderous gang wrote the title of a Beatles' song, *Helter Skelter,* in blood at a multiple-murder site. (Actually, they misspelled it: "Healter Skelter.") A five-year-old who set a fire was said to have been imitating an incident on *Beavis and Butt-head.* Table 8.1 lists some other cases in which there was a close connection between real-life violence and the fictional kind.

No one can ever prove that a specific fictional depiction was the primary cause of a specific act of violence. There are always other possibilities. But, as indicated earlier, research under controlled conditions in the laboratory has amply documented that aggressive models, live or on film, increase aggressive behavior among children and adults (Geen & Thomas, 1986; Liebert & Sprafkin, 1988). Here, the causal effect is clear. With control, however, comes artificiality, and doubts have been expressed about whether what is found in the lab will also occur in the real world (Freedman, 1988b).

Field experiments in a real-world setting such as a school offer one way to address this issue. When Wendy Wood and her colleagues (1991) examined both laboratory and field experiments conducted with children and adolescents, they found that exposure to aggressive films increased aggressive behavior in the laboratory, the classroom, the lunchroom, the playground, and the athletic field. Al-

Although it's impossible to prove that any specific violent fiction caused a specific violent action, there have been some close connections. (*Time,* 1993.)

Table 8.1 Violent Fictions and Facts

Violent Fiction	Violent Fact
Murder in the Heartland, TV movie	Shooting death in Canada, 1993
MacGyver, TV series	Fatal homemade bomb in France, 1992
Stained Glass, heavy-metal album by Judas Priest	Shotgun suicide/maiming in Reno, Nevada, 1985
Taxi Driver, movie	John Hinckley's attempted assassination of Ronald Reagan, 1981
The Deer Hunter, movie (after its airing on TV)	Deadly games of Russian roulette, 1981
Kojak, TV series	Fatal shooting and robbery of elderly neighbor, 1977
Born Innocent, TV movie	Rape of a nine-year-old girl, 1974

though laboratory experiments produced somewhat stronger results than those conducted in natural environments, the aggression-inducing effects of filmed models occurred in both types of settings.

But what about the "real" real world—where no experiment is being conducted? Here, we must rely on correlational research, which cannot prove causation. Nevertheless, correlational findings are similar to those obtained in laboratory and field experiments. Drawing primarily on newspaper stories and TV coverage, David Phillips (1983, 1986) found an association between a wide variety of media reports and an equally wide variety of aggressive behaviors. For example, following the media blitzes surrounding heavyweight championship prizefights, homicides in the general population increased. Of particular interest is Phillips's repeated finding that mass media effects tend to peak a few days after the event was reported and then fade (Miller et al., 1991). This sequence suggests that the immediate impact of a violent model on aggressive behavior is short-lived.

Long-Term Effects There may, however, be longer-lasting consequences. Is viewing violence at an *early age* associated with more aggressive behavior at a *later age?* To answer this question, most of the relevant prospective research has concentrated on TV. The results of a twenty-two-year study, known as the Rip Van Winkle project, indicated that early exposure to TV violence was related to later aggression, but only among males (Eron & Huesmann, 1984; Eron et al., 1972; Lefkowitz et al., 1977). A more limited three-year study came to a very different conclusion: that early exposure to TV violence had no association with later aggressive behavior for either boys or girls (Milavsky et al., 1982).

In an extensive cross-cultural study, Rowell Huesmann and Leonard Eron (1986) collaborated with researchers around the world to examine the relationship between TV violence and aggression among children in five different coun-

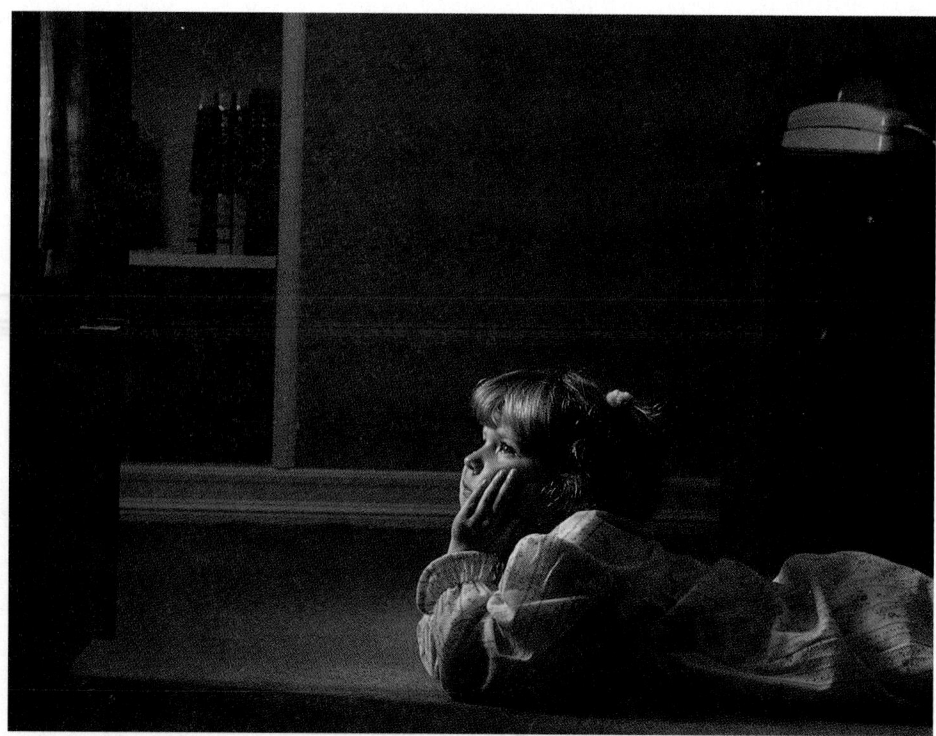

Prospective studies examine the same subjects over a period of time so that changes in behavior can be observed. A number of such studies have investigated whether viewing TV violence at an early age is associated with aggressive behavior at a later age.

tries: Australia, Finland, Israel, Poland, and the United States. Their findings highlighted the importance of three major factors.

One is gender. Contrary to previous indications that exposure to TV violence had a greater impact on boys than on girls, no consensus regarding the role of gender emerged from these studies. In Poland and among urban residents in Israel, early exposure to TV violence predicted later aggression for both boys and girls. In the United States, this relationship was obtained only for girls. It also appears that the relationship between watching violent TV shows and being aggressive may sometimes be a two-way street, with exposure to TV violence increasing aggressiveness and aggressive children seeking out violence on TV. Evidence suggesting such a bidirectional pattern was found for girls in the United States.

A third factor is identification with aggressive TV characters. Among boys in the United States and Finland, those who at a young age viewed a substantial amount of violent TV and identified with aggressive TV characters were most likely to become highly aggressive later in life. Taking all of these factors into account, researchers found evidence of a connection between early viewing of TV violence and later aggression for children in Finland, Poland, the United States, and urban areas in Israel. No such connection was established for Australian children or for those living on kibbutzim in Israel.

Though not entirely consistent in their findings, prospective studies raise the clear possibility that viewing violence now could lead to doing it later. But how? As noted earlier, immediate effects (such as direct imitation, automatic associations, and immediate disinhibition of constraints) are probably not long lasting. More enduring consequences may require more fundamental changes in values and attitudes.

habituation Adaptation to something familiar, so that both physiological and psychological responses are reduced.

Beyond Imitation One way in which values and attitudes could be changed by exposure to violent images is through the process of **habituation.** A novel stimulus gets our attention and, if it's sufficiently interesting or exciting, elicits physiological arousal. But when we get used to something, our reactions diminish.

Familiarity with violence reduces our physiological response to it and may make us more accepting of it.

Familiarity with violence reduces physiological arousal to new incidents of violence (Geen, 1981; Thomas, 1982). Desensitized to violence, we may become more accepting of it. It has been suggested, for example, that constantly replaying the videotapes of violent events, such as the beatings in Los Angeles of Rodney King and Reginald Denny, may make it more difficult for prosecutors to obtain a conviction. At least one reporter thought so: "Repeated viewing of the brutal videotape may have anesthetized the jury, so that it counted for less in their final judgment" (Lacayo, 1993, p. 47).

cultivation The process by which the mass media (particularly television) construct a version of social reality for the viewing public.

Another way that depictions of violence could change values and attitudes is through what George Gerbner and his colleagues (1980, 1986) call **cultivation.** Cultivation refers to the capacity of the mass media to construct a social reality that people perceive as true, even if it isn't. Consider, for example, fear. If the media paint a picture of a violent world, people may become more fearful, more distrustful, more likely to arm themselves, and more likely to behave aggressively in what they perceive as a threatening situation. A *Los Angeles Times* poll suggested that media hype may, indeed, add fuel to the fear of crime. Depending on how you measure it, violent crime (excluding murders) either decreased slightly (police reports) or increased 5.6 percent (interviews with a representative national sample) during 1993. Murders increased 3.2 percent. But the percentage of Americans who designated crime as the country's most important problem *doubled* from June 1993 to January 1994. Sixty-five percent of those surveyed said that news coverage was the most important influence on their attitudes, citing both nationally publicized cases (such as the Polly Klaas kidnapping) and locally reported violence.

Mass media cultivation may also affect the acceptability of aggressive behavior. In one study, male subjects given an aggressive interpretation of a film they had just watched were later more aggressive than those given a nonaggressive interpretation (Berkowitz & Alioto, 1973). Pictures, then, don't tell the whole story; media effects often depend on how the event we see is "pitched" or "framed." And what about the moral of the story? Isn't it better to see morally justified aggression in which the "bad guys" get their just desserts than morally unjustified aggression in which the "good guys" suffer? Not at all. Research on this issue reveals that subjects, especially angry ones, are usually more aggressive after watching justified aggression (Berkowitz, 1965). Seeing acceptable violence can make violence more acceptable.

What Can We Do About It? Based on their review of the relevant research, a task force on television and society, appointed by the American Psychological Association (APA), concluded that, "There is clear evidence that television violence can cause aggressive behavior and can cultivate values favoring the use of aggression to resolve conflicts" (Huston et al., 1992, p. 136). The Commission on Violence and Youth (1993), also appointed by APA, agreed and stated that "children's exposure to violence in the mass media, particularly at young ages, can have harmful lifelong consequences" (p. 33). However, both the task force and the Commission recognized that the media do not operate in a vacuum. People are influenced by their family, peers, social values, and opportunities for education and employment. Nor are all individuals the same; individual differences in personality may heat up or tone down the impact of aggressive displays (Bushman & Green, 1990). Nevertheless, what we see in media presentations of violence is not a pretty picture.

The question, then, is what can we do about it? Government censorship is one answer, but not a very popular one. Not only would the constitutional guarantee of freedom of speech be threatened, but the practical task of screening all possible sources of violent images (TV, movies, video games, print media, computer games, electronic networks—to list just the obvious ones) boggles the mind. Moreover, there's a psychological problem. Censorship can boomerang and make whatever is forbidden seem that much more desirable (Worchel, 1992).

Another alternative is to use public pressure to increase media self-censorship. Both the rating system used by the movie industry and the recently instituted TV advisory were created in response to concerns raised by the public and their political representatives. Of course, the most powerful kind of public pressure would be a commercial boycott. If violence did not sell, the media would not produce it. Unfortunately, however, violence continues to be a money-maker.

At this point, then, education may well be the most effective approach. For example, programs have been developed to curb children's undesirable reactions to TV (Eron, 1986, 1987; Singer & Singer, 1983). These programs recommend that parents select shows that provide compelling, vivid prosocial models for their children. An extensive review by Susan Hearold (1986) is encouraging in this regard. Her analysis indicated that prosocial TV programs produce stronger effects on behavior than do antisocial TV programs. Parents have also been advised to watch television with their children and to teach them how TV differs from real life, how imitating TV characters can produce undesirable outcomes, and how children might be harmed by watching TV (Huesmann et al., 1983). This kind of ongoing parental tutorial takes significant time and effort. But given the extent of media depictions of violence in our society, strengthening children's critical viewing skills is a wise investment.

Pornographic Materials

Just as citizens, scientists, and politicians have been concerned about the possibly harmful consequences of mass media presentations of nonsexual violence, they have also been troubled by mass media displays of sexual material. Such displays are highly visible and widely available. Books, magazines, and videos cater to a range of sexual interests, from the ordinary to the bizarre. Heavy metal and rap groups rely on obscenities to get their fans' attention. Dial-a-porn lines rake in millions for the phone company and a tidy profit for themselves. Sexually explicit subscription services and sexually oriented games bring sex into the computer age. Opposition to pornography is equally prominent. Parents, religious leaders, consumer groups, and feminist activists lobby legislators and go to court to obtain greater constraints on the availability of sexually explicit materials.

Attempts to ban specific works, such as James Joyce's novel *Ulysses* and Robert Mapplethorpe's photos, indicate that the definitions of such terms as *obscenity, erotica,* and *pornography* are often a matter of personal opinion. One person's smut is another person's masterpiece. Because of the weight of subjective judgment in such definitions, the term **pornography** is used here to refer to explicit sexual material, regardless of its moral or aesthetic qualities. It is crucial, however, to distinguish between nonviolent and violent pornography in discussing the relationship between pornographic displays and aggression.

pornography Explicit sexual material.

Nonviolent Pornography Earlier in this chapter, we described the arousal-affect model, which proposes that both the type of emotion and the intensity of arousal produced by a stimulus influence aggression (see page 302). The results of research on nonviolent pornography confirm the importance of these factors (Don-

Here, protestors demonstrate against a lounge where a teenage stripper was employed. As sexually explicit performances and images have become more widely available and highly visible in our society, so has opposition to pornography increased.

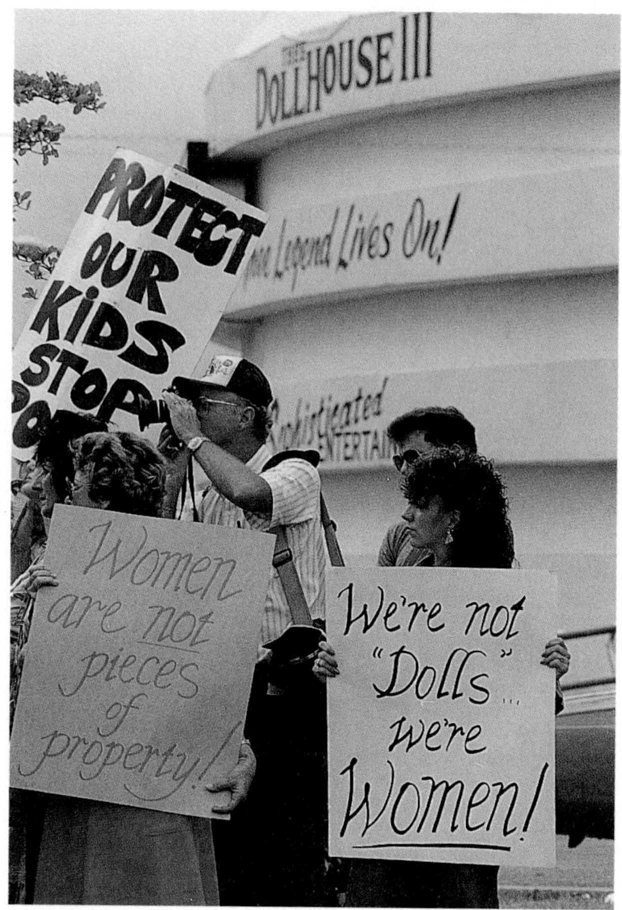

nerstein et al., 1987). For many people, viewing soft-focus attractive nudes elicits a pleasant emotional response and low levels of sexual arousal. Such materials usually reduce retaliatory aggression against a same-sex confederate. However, most people are shocked and disgusted by crude displays of sexual activities. Their emotional response is negative, and their arousal is heightened by alarm, sexual feelings, or both. These kinds of pornographic materials usually increase aggression toward a same-sex confederate.

But what about aggression toward the opposite sex? Since the vast majority of pornography is designed to appeal to heterosexual males, investigators have been especially interested in whether pornographic materials have a specific effect on men's aggression against women (Donnerstein, 1984). It does, but only when restraints against male-to-female aggression are reduced.

Reasoning that repeated opportunities to aggress could reduce such restraints, Edward Donnerstein and John Hallam (1978) gave male subjects two chances to retaliate against either a male or female confederate who had angered them. On the first opportunity to retaliate, subjects who had watched a sexually explicit "stag" film (arousing but nonviolent) were more aggressive than those who had not watched any film at all. This effect was similar for both confederates. Like many other arousing stimuli, nonviolent pornography can increase aggression against whatever target is available. On their second opportunity, however, subjects who had watched the pornographic film aggressed more against the female confederate than against the male confederate (see Figure 8.8). Other types of arousing material do *not* produce this gender-specific increase.

Much of the research on pornography exposes subjects to only one "dose" of pornography. What about viewing many pornographic images over an extended period of time? To investigate this issue, Dolf Zillmann and Jennings Bryant (1984) showed either eighteen or thirty-six pornographic films to male and female college students over the course of six weeks. These films were X-rated but nonviolent. Control subjects saw neutral films or no films at all. After the exposure period, all subjects returned to the laboratory for two follow-up sessions which assessed (1) physiological arousal in response to new, unfamiliar pornography, (2) aggressiveness toward a same-sex confederate, and (3) attitudes.

This research obtained a clear habituation effect: Repeated prior exposure to pornography diminished physiological arousal in response to new pornography, especially among those who had previously been exposed to the greater number of pornographic films. As arousal subsided, so did the power of pornography to intensify aroused behaviors. After seeing new pornography, subjects who had been exposed to a large number of pornographic films were *less* aggressive than control subjects in response to provocation by a same-sex confederate. That's the good news.

But now here's the bad news. In the second follow-up session, subjects read about a rape trial; they also expressed their opinion of the women's liberation movement. Those who had previously been exposed to a large number of pornographic films recommended a lighter sentence for the rapist and indicated less

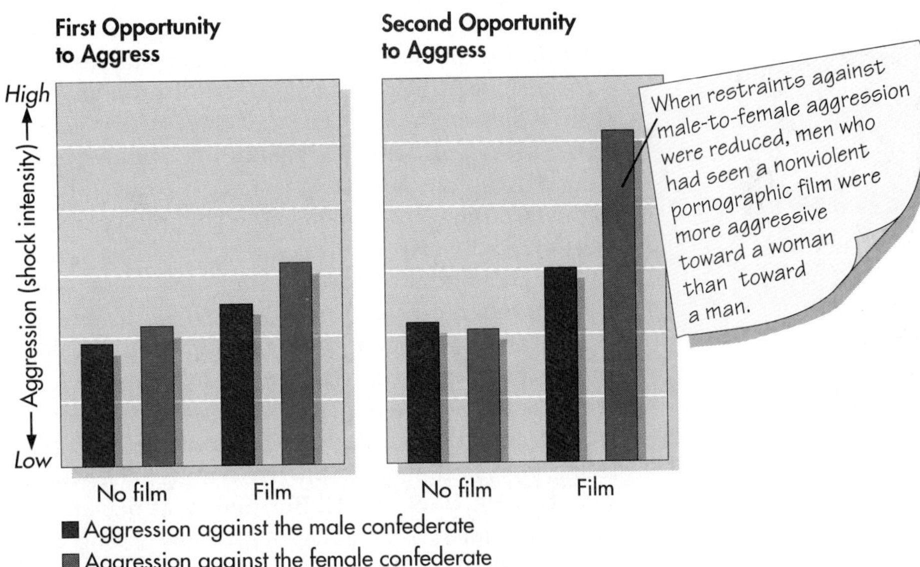

Figure 8.8 The Second Time Around. In this study, male subjects were given two chances to retaliate against a male or female confederate who had provoked them. On both occasions, those who had watched a nonviolent pornographic film aggressed more than did those who had not seen a film. Levels of aggression against the man and woman were similar on the first opportunity to retaliate. On the second opportunity, however, subjects who had watched the pornographic film aggressed significantly more against the woman than against the man. (Adapted from Donnerstein & Hallam, 1978.)

support for the women's liberation movement than did control subjects. The same results were obtained for both male and female subjects. When only the male subjects were asked to respond to a series of questions that measured callousness toward women, more negative attitudes toward women were expressed by those with prior exposure to a "heavy dose" of pornography. Once again, we see that habituation affects both arousal and attitudes. Prior exposure to massive amounts of pornography reduced arousal-based aggression, but increased the kind of insensitive attitudes that could promote acceptance of future aggression—by others or by ourselves.

Some nonviolent pornographic materials seem to specialize in trivializing rape and depersonalizing women as objects for sexual gratification (Zillmann & Weaver, 1989). James Check and Ted Guloien (1989) describe the content of this kind of dehumanizing pornography as "sexual interactions in which the woman [is] portrayed as hysterically responsive to male sexual demands, [is] verbally abused, dominated, and degraded, and in general [is] treated as a plaything with no human qualities other than her physical attributes" (p. 163). When Check and Guloien compared male subjects who did not see any pornography with those who viewed dehumanizing pornography, they found that exposure to pornography increased subjects' reports that they would force a woman to do something sexual against her will and would commit rape if they were assured of not getting caught.

Violent Pornography Adding violence to pornography greatly increases the possibility of harmful effects. Violent pornography is a triple threat: It brings together high arousal; negative emotional reactions such as shock, alarm, and disgust; and aggressive thoughts. In a meta-analysis of 217 studies on the relationship between TV violence and aggression, violent pornography had a stronger effect than any other type of program (Paik & Comstock, 1994). And there is substantial evidence that this effect is gender-specific (Donnerstein et al., 1987; Linz et al., 1987; Malamuth & Donnerstein, 1982). Male-to-male aggression is no greater after exposure to violent pornography than after exposure to highly arousing but nonviolent pornography. Male-to-female aggression, however, is markedly increased.

Like most experiences that intensify arousal (such as physical exercise), *non*violent pornography increases aggression only among subjects who have been provoked. But, like guns and alcohol, some violent pornography can increase aggression even in the absence of provocation. The prime ingredient in such materials is the portrayal of women as willing participants who "enjoy" their own victimization. In one study, violent pornography that emphasized the victim's suffering increased aggression only among men who had been provoked (Donnerstein & Berkowitz, 1981). But films that depicted female sexual response to acts of sexual violence increased aggression among both provoked and unprovoked male subjects (see Figure 8.9).

We might like to believe that violent pornographic images are rare, found only in the most extreme varieties of hard-core porn. Not true. In one survey of male college students, 36 percent reported having viewed materials during the past year that featured forced sexual acts against women; 25 percent said they had looked at materials depicting rape (Demaré et al., 1993). An examination of video pornography revealed that soft-core "adult" films available over the counter contained more sexually violent material than did hard-core films sold under the counter (Palys, 1986).

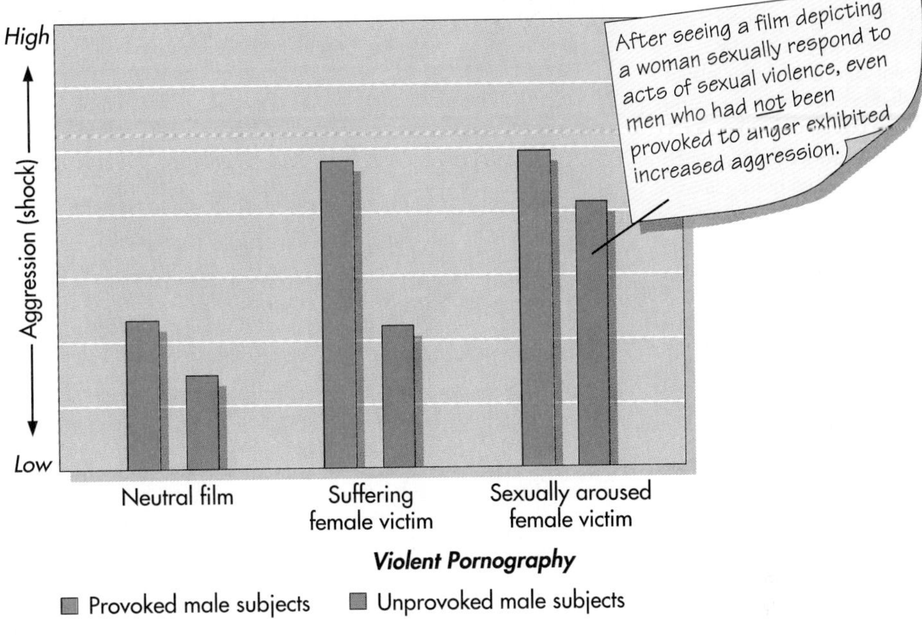

Figure 8.9 When Provocation Isn't Necessary. Arousing stimuli usually increase aggression only when someone is angry because of a previous provocation. Accordingly, violent pornography depicting a suffering female victim significantly increased aggression only among provoked male subjects in this study. As you can see, however, violent pornographic films depicting a sexually aroused female victim increased aggression even among unprovoked men. (Data from Donnerstein & Berkowitz, 1981. Figure adapted from Donnerstein et al., 1987.)

The impact of such "adult," R-rated, sexually violent material on sexually related attitudes and beliefs was investigated in a field study that arranged for 115 college students to attend movies at campus theaters (Malamuth & Check, 1981). Half of these students saw the commercially successful movies *Swept Away* and *The Getaway,* both of which depict women who become sexually aroused by a sexual assault and romantically attracted to their assailant. The other half watched feature-length movies without sexually aggressive content. Several days later, all subjects filled out a questionnaire in class along with the rest of their classmates. This questionnaire measured attitudes toward violence directed at women and beliefs about rape (see Table 8.2).

Compared with those who had not seen the movies depicting sexual assault, male subjects who had viewed these films reported greater acceptance of interpersonal violence against women and somewhat greater acceptance of rape myths. In contrast, women's acceptance of interpersonal violence against women and of rape myths tended to decline after viewing depictions of male-to-female sexual aggression. Figure 8.10 displays the findings for both men and women.

Some research examines the effects of combining violent pornography with negative attitudes toward women. For example, Neil Malamuth has developed what he calls the "rapist's profile." Men fit the profile if they have relatively high levels of sexual arousal in response to violent pornography and also express attitudes and opinions indicating acceptance of violence toward women. These indi-

Widely used in research on pornography, these two scales assess attitudes about violence toward women and beliefs about the nature of rape. A few items from each one are shown here. (Based on Burt, 1980.)

Table 8.2 Attitudes About Sex and Aggression

Acceptance of Interpersonal Violence (Toward Woman): AIV Scale

1. Being roughed up is sexually stimulating to many women.
2. Many times a woman will pretend she doesn't want to have intercourse because she doesn't want to seem loose, but she's really hoping the man will force her.
3. A man is never justified in hitting his wife.

Scoring: Persons scoring high in acceptance of violence toward woman agree with items 1 and 2 but disagree with item 3.

Rape Myth Acceptance: RMA Scale

1. If a woman engages in necking or petting and she lets things get out of hand, it is her own fault if her partner forces sex on her.
2. Any female can get raped.
3. Many women have an unconscious wish to be raped, and may then unconsciously set up a situation in which they are likely to be attacked.
4. In the majority of rapes, the victim is promiscuous or has a bad reputation.

Scoring: Persons scoring high in acceptance of rape myths agree with items 1, 3, and 4 but disagree with item 2.

viduals report more sexually coercive behavior in the past and more sexually aggressive intentions for the future (Malamuth, 1986; Malamuth et al., 1986). Among male college students given an opportunity to retaliate against a female confederate who had angered them, those who fit the rapist's profile were more aggressive (Malamuth, 1983).

In a variation on Malamuth's model, Dano Demaré and his colleagues (1993) examined the correlates of self-reported use of violent pornography and of nega-

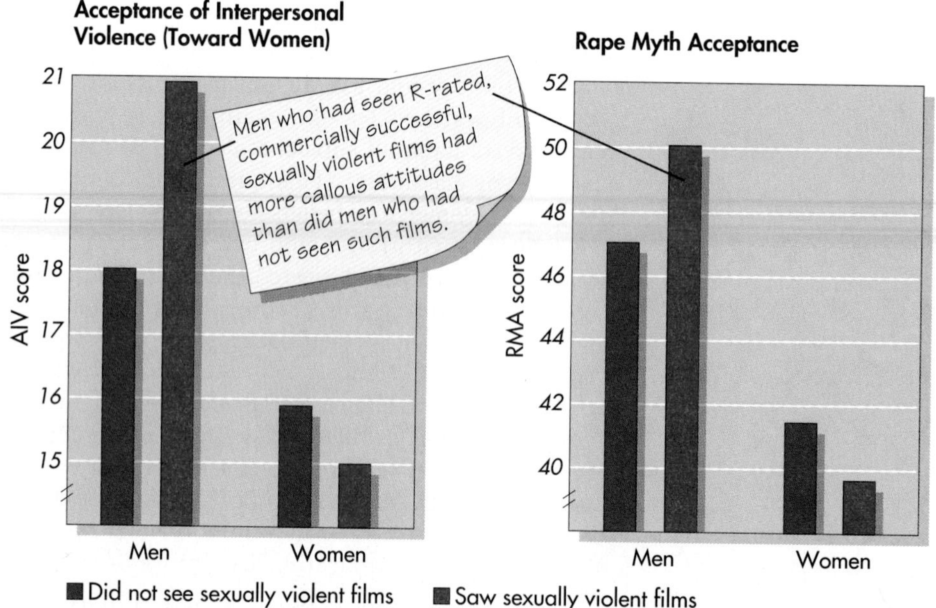

Figure 8.10 It Doesn't Have to Be X-rated. After watching R-rated sexually violent films, men reported greater acceptance of interpersonal violence toward women and somewhat greater acceptance of rape myths than did men who had not seen these films. In contrast, women's ratings on these two scales declined slightly after watching the sexually violent films. (Based on Malamuth & Check, 1981.)

tive attitudes toward women. As you can see in Figure 8.11, male college students who expressed more anti-women attitudes said that, assuming they would not get caught, they would be more likely to force sex with a woman and to rape her. Those who reported more frequent use of sexually violent pornography also expressed more sexually aggressive intentions and, in addition, more often said they had actually used coercion and force during sex. Comparisons of the predictive power of using violent pornography versus having negative attitudes toward women found that pornography had a stronger effect on overall sexual aggression, but that the best prediction was obtained when both pornography and attitudes were included in the equation.

Assessing the Possible Danger Does the availability of pornography, then, increase the possibility of sexual assault? The correlational evidence bearing on the relationship between pornography and sex crimes is difficult to interpret (Marshall, 1989). Studies of retrospective reports by rapists about their experiences with pornography have yielded conflicting results (Malamuth & Billings, 1986). Nor do cross-cultural comparisons point to any clear relationship. Extremely violent pornography is widely available in Japan, but the incidence of rape is very low. India, in contrast, bans explicit sex (and even kissing) from commercial films but has a high incidence of rape (Pratap, 1990).

In the laboratory, the developing chain of evidence has a number of missing links. Because of ethical constraints, only relatively low levels of *nonsexual* actual aggression have been studied. Although pornography, especially violent pornography, does increase nonsexual aggression in the laboratory, it is not certain that these findings generalize to actual behavior (Freedman, 1988a). Studies of *sexual* aggression measure attitudes and self-reports, which can reflect or in-

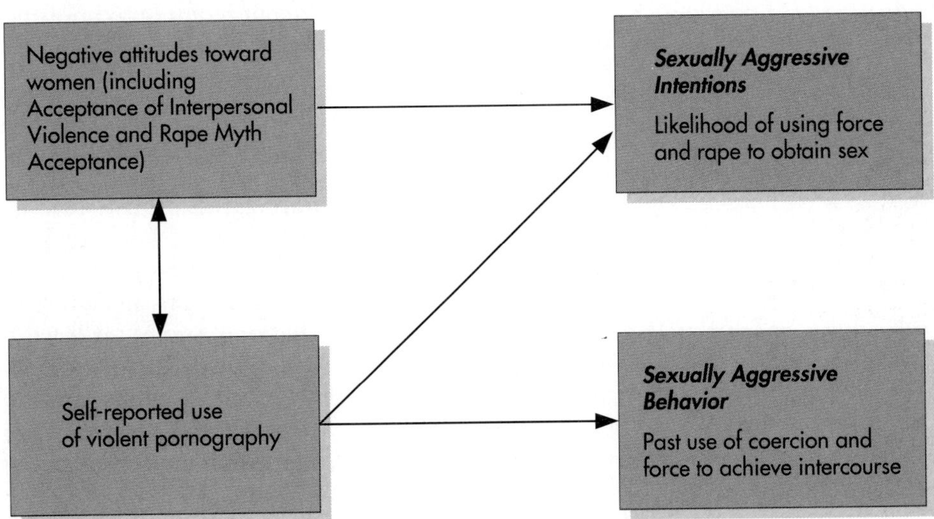

Figure 8.11 **Attitudes, Pornography, and Sexual Aggression.** Although the endorsement of negative attitudes toward women and the self-reported use of violent pornography are associated with each other, it is possible to examine their separate effects. Both are correlated with sexually aggressive intentions. But only pornography use is correlated with self-reported past behavior. Overall, the strongest prediction of sexually aggressive intentions and behavior is obtained when both attitudes and pornography use are taken into account. (Based on Demaré et al., 1993.)

fluence actual behavior but are not identical to it. Despite these limitations, however, existing research does indicate the clear possibility that pornography could contribute to sexual aggression against women.

What Can We Do About It? The question of what to do about the potentially harmful effects of pornography leads to the same options described for depictions of nonsexual violence. Should pornography be banned? Should consumers be educated? Banning pornography raises all of the political, practical, and psychological difficulties discussed earlier. In addition, banning explicit sexual material would not prevent dehumanizing portrayals of women as sex objects or titillating but fully clothed scenes of rape and sexual assault.

According to Daniel Linz and his colleagues, the real villains are violence, sexual or not, and the demeaning and degrading messages about women contained in pornographic depictions, violent or not (Linz & Donnerstein, 1992; Linz et al., 1992). Although these investigators think it would be possible to develop an informative rating system labeling both violence and sex in mass media materials, they are not optimistic about the media's willingness to do so. More promising, they say, are educational efforts to increase viewers' critical skills in evaluating media depictions of violence and sex.

A model for such efforts can be found in the debriefing provided to research subjects exposed to violent pornography (Donnerstein et al., 1987). This debriefing emphasizes that rape myths are inaccurate and that violent pornography is unrealistic. Among individuals presented with this information, there are long-term reductions in acceptance of rape myths. Sex-education programs that emphasize the desirability of being respectful and considerate toward one's sexual partner may also be beneficial. In one study, a sex-education program conducted before subjects were exposed to pornography reduced acceptance of rape myths and increased sympathy for rape victims (Intons-Peterson et al., 1989). Education and the public commitment required to implement it are important means of defense against sexual violence.

INTIMATE VIOLENCE: TRUST BETRAYED

All violence is shocking, but aggression between intimates is especially disturbing. We want to feel safe with those we know and love, and yet far too often that sense of security is destroyed by violence. Among the homicides committed in 1992, at least 47 percent of the victims knew their murderer (see Figure 8.12). According to a three-year national survey, at least 75 percent of rapes are committed by a person the victim knows (Kilpatrick et al., 1992). The victims of intimate violence are children as well as adults, and the assault that takes place is often sexual as well as physical. In this section, we examine three major types of intimate violence: sexual aggression among college students, physical aggression between partners, and child abuse.

Sexual Aggression Among College Students

Acquaintance rape (often called "date rape") is a serious problem among college students. In the United States, over 25 percent of 3,187 female students surveyed at 32 college campuses reported having experienced either an attempted or completed rape since age 14; over 50 percent of these assaults occurred during a date

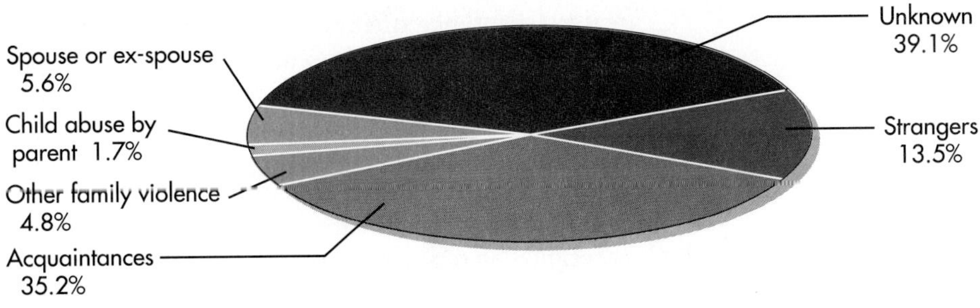

Figure 8.12 **Who Kills Whom?** Among 1992 homicides, at least 12 percent were committed by a spouse, ex-spouse, or other relative. The kinds of relationships between victims and murderers classified as acquaintances are not specified. But it is reasonable to assume that a significant proportion were romantic or sexual in nature. The unknown murderers were probably mostly strangers, but presumably some were known by their victims. (Data from Newsweek, 1995.)

(Koss et al., 1987; Warshaw, 1988). When all types of unwanted sexual interactions are included, a majority of college women and about a third of college men say they have experienced coercive sexual contact (Cate & Lloyd, 1992; Struckman-Johnson & Struckman-Johnson, 1994). Rates of sexual coercion among Canadian college students appear to be similar (DeKeseredy et al., 1993).

Although a number of factors are associated with sexual aggression among college students, four seem particularly important. First there is gender. Both men and women report that men are more likely to engage in coercive behavior—psychological as well as physical—in order to obtain sex (Poppen & Segal, 1988).

Another significant influence, alcohol consumption, is involved in a majority of sexually aggressive incidents between college students (Cate & Lloyd, 1992). Not only does actual consumption increase aggressive behavior, but the mere belief that one has consumed alcohol (even if one hasn't) heightens sexual arousal and sexual interest (Baron & Richardson, 1994). Furthermore, the cognitive effects of intoxication, in which salient cues are noticed but subtle ones are missed (see page 307), may disrupt interpersonal communication (Richardson & Hammock, 1991). As emphasized in Chapter 6, gender differences in sexual attitudes, roles, and perceptions can create serious communication problems in heterosexual relationships. Indeed, sexually aggressive men are particularly likely to misperceive women's sexually relevant communications (Malamuth & Brown, 1994). Adding alcohol to the mismatch could produce an explosive situation.

Prior sexual experience is also associated with coercive sexual behavior. In research conducted by F. Scott Christopher and his colleagues (1993a) on almost a thousand college students, both men and women who reported a greater number of previous sexual partners were more likely to indicate that they had used coercive and aggressive tactics in sexual interactions. Although the exact meaning of this correlation is unclear, it may reflect the consequences of a person's view of sexual relationships. In one study, for example, college men who described themselves as taking a manipulative, game-playing, uncommitted approach to relationships reported more sexually aggressive intentions (Sarwer et al., 1993).

Attitudes toward rape and toward women constitute the fourth major factor associated with coercive sexual behavior. Both men and women who express a greater acceptance of rape myths (see Table 8.2) report greater use of coercive and aggressive tactics of sexual influence (Christopher et al., 1993a). In a more detailed examination of the responses of male subjects, Christopher and his colleagues (1993b) found that attitudes like rape myth acceptance are also associated with hostility toward women, which has an indirect effect (through anger and negative relationship experiences) on these tactics (see Figure 8.13). In light of these findings, it is encouraging that rape awareness workshops appear to reduce acceptance of rape myths and increase sympathy for a female rape victim (Szymanski et al., 1993). Again, education has a crucial role to play in reducing sexual aggression.

Physical Aggression Between Partners

Where were you on Friday, June 17, 1994? If that seems an impossible question to answer, let's put it this way: Where were you during the slow-motion police chase of O. J. Simpson on the highways of southern California? As millions watched, it was sometimes hard to remember that this was real life, not fiction.

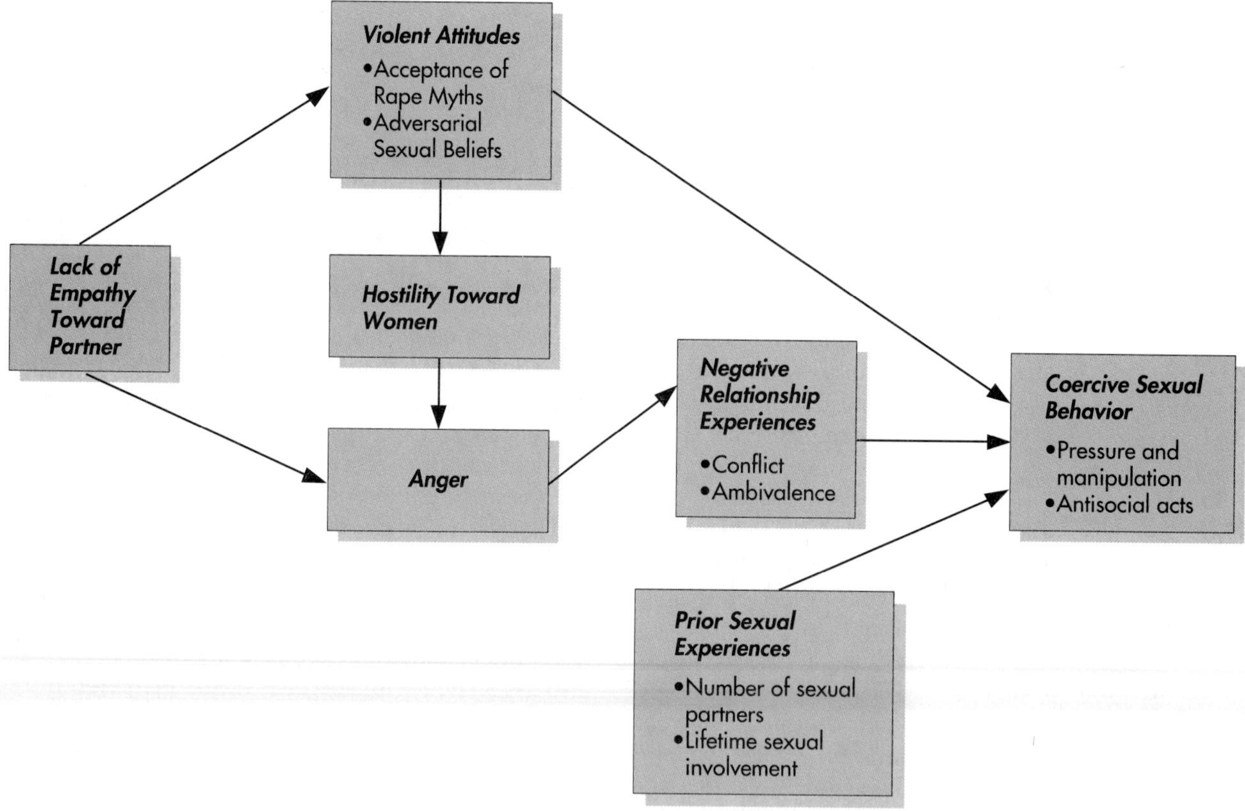

Figure 8.13 **Sexual Aggressiveness Among College Men.** The results of this study indicate that a number of psychological variables are involved in sexual aggression. Emotions (empathy, hostility, anger), experience (with sex and in relationships), and attitudes were all associated—directly or indirectly—with self-reported coercive sexual behavior by college men. (Based on Christopher et al., 1993b.)

The public image of O. J. Simpson and Nicole Brown Simpson was glamorous and harmonious. The private reality was quite different. In her safety deposit box, she kept photographs of what she looked like after he beat her.

As more information became available, it was equally hard to grasp that sports hero and TV commentator Simpson was a convicted wife-beater with a history of terrorizing his former wife. Regardless of the outcome of Simpson's trial for the murder of Nicole Brown Simpson and Ronald Goldman, this case, like no other before it, intensified public concern about domestic abuse.

In the United States, there is good reason for this concern (Biden, 1993; Gibbs, 1993; Koss et al., 1994):

- Domestic violence is the leading cause of injury for women aged fourteen to forty-four.
- At least one-third of female homicide victims are murdered by a husband or a boyfriend.
- In 1991, 1,320 women were murdered by a husband or boyfriend, and 624 men were murdered by a wife or girlfriend.

But partner abuse is not limited to the United States; it is a worldwide phenomenon (Hoffman et al., 1994; Holloway, 1994). Occurring throughout human history, it is not a new development. Only in recent years, however, has a concerted effort been made to document the extent of this often very private form of violence. According to two national surveys conducted in the United States in 1975 and 1985, spouse abuse stayed relatively constant during this period (Hampton et al., 1989; Straus & Gelles, 1986). But police reports of nonlethal assault doubled from 1980 to 1990, perhaps reflecting increasing awareness that, like violence between strangers, violence between intimates is a crime. This same awareness, along with tougher laws and a greater number of shelters for battered women, may account for the striking decrease in the rate of domestic murders of black women from 1976 to 1992; among white women, however, the rate remained essentially stable.

One of the most surprising results of the national surveys in 1975 and 1985 was the high level of wife-to-husband abuse, which in terms of severe violence (such as kicking, hitting, beating, threatening with a weapon, and using a weapon) was consistently higher than the level of husband-to-wife abuse. Prospective research on aggression during the first years of marriage also found higher rates of wife-to-husband abuse (O'Leary et al., 1989). These studies, however, did not examine the consequences of spouse abuse. Usually these outcomes are more damaging to women, who are more often killed, seriously injured, or sexually assaulted during domestic disputes than are men (Browne, 1993; Stets & Straus, 1990).

Similar findings have been obtained in studies of violence among unmarried couples. A greater proportion of women than men say they have been physically aggressive with a dating partner, but more women than men report having sustained an injury inflicted during a date (Sugarman & Hotaling, 1989). Different types of intimate relationships, however, have different levels of violence (Makepeace, 1989; Stets & Straus, 1989). The average level of physical violence is lowest among dating couples, intermediate among married couples, and highest among cohabiting couples. The exact causes for the association between cohabitation and physical abuse are not known, but it may result from the stresses and strains of living together without a strong commitment to the relationship (Stets, 1991).

Like most aggressive actions, violence between partners is multiply determined (Dutton et al., 1994; Gelles & Straus, 1988; Holtzworth-Munroe & Stuart, 1994; Williams, 1992; Yoshikawa, 1994). Among the factors associated with increased partner aggression are personal characteristics (such as age, attitudes toward violence, drug and alcohol abuse, and personality), socioeconomic status (which includes income and education), interpersonal conflict, stress, social isolation, and the experience of growing up in a violent family.

Child Abuse

Children who grow up in a violent family not only witness aggression; they often bear the brunt of it. Tragically, child abuse is not a rare occurrence. It is estimated that each year in the United States over a million children are physically abused (Gelles & Cornell, 1990) and over 150,000 are sexually abused (National Center on Child Abuse and Neglect, 1988). National survey data indicate that over 60 percent of rape victims are under eighteen (Kilpatrick et al., 1992). David Finkelhor and Jennifer Dziuba-Leatherman (1994) conclude that the available evidence "strongly suggests that children are more victimized than adults are" (p. 173).

Children are abused by strangers as well as by family members, but severe abuse, particularly of young children, is more often inflicted by parents and caretakers. Boys suffer more physical abuse than do girls, and mothers are more likely than fathers to physically abuse their children (Straus et al., 1980). In contrast, girls suffer more sexual abuse than do boys, and fathers are more likely than mothers to sexually abuse their children (Russell, 1984). There are conflicting findings, however, about whether men or women are more likely to murder their children. Although a 1994 study by the Justice Department found that more children were killed by mothers than by fathers, a 1995 report by the U.S. Advisory Board on Child Abuse and Neglect concluded that men—both fathers and boyfriends—were more often responsible for child homicides.

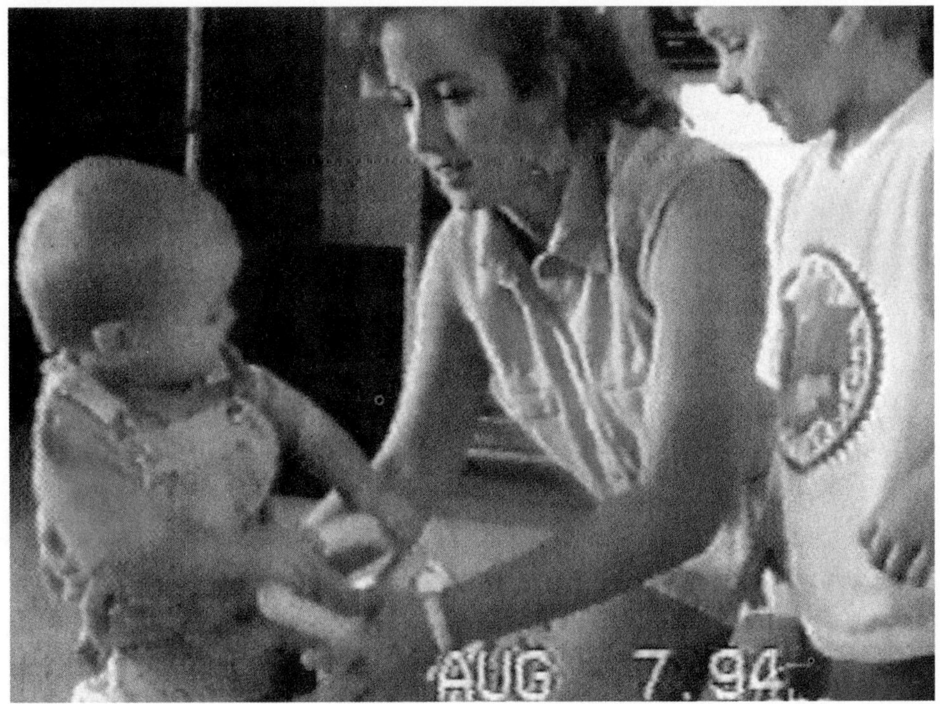

Susan Smith, shown here in a home video with her two boys, claimed at first that her sons had been kidnapped. But then she confessed to having drowned them and was convicted of two counts of murder. In 1988, when Smith was sixteen, her stepfather signed a court order acknowledging that he had sexually molested her.

Like partner aggression, child abuse is multiply determined (Belsky, 1993; Davies & Cummings, 1994; Wolfe, 1985). Among the factors associated with increased child abuse are personal characteristics of the abusing parent (such as personality and substance abuse) and of the child (younger children are more often abused by family members); the family's socioeconomic status; stressful experiences; social isolation; marital conflict; and the abusing parent's having been abused as a child.

cycle of family violence The transmission of domestic violence across generations.

The Cycle of Family Violence At this point, you should begin to see a pattern emerging: the connection between violence in childhood and violence as an adult. This connection is called the **cycle of family violence** (see Figure 8.14). Children who witness parental violence or who are themselves abused are more likely as adults to inflict abuse on intimate partners or, perhaps, to be a victim of intimate violence (Malinosky-Rummell & Hansen, 1993; Simons et al., 1993; Widom, 1989). They are also more likely to abuse their own children. In turn, their children are more likely to interact violently with each other (Patterson, 1984) and to aggress against their parents (Peek et al., 1985). This intergenerational transmission of domestic violence is by no means inevitable, however (Zigler et al., 1988). Most people who witness or experience abuse in their families of origin are not abusive or abused in their families of procreation (Emery, 1989). The cycle of family violence refers to an average tendency, not an absolute certainty.

Reducing Family Violence Family violence is a matter of grave societal concern and, since it is multiply determined, must be addressed by a variety of approaches (Berkowitz, 1993; Feindler & Becker, 1994; Gelles & Cornell, 1990; Koss et al., 1994). For example, reporting laws require certain individuals, such as physi-

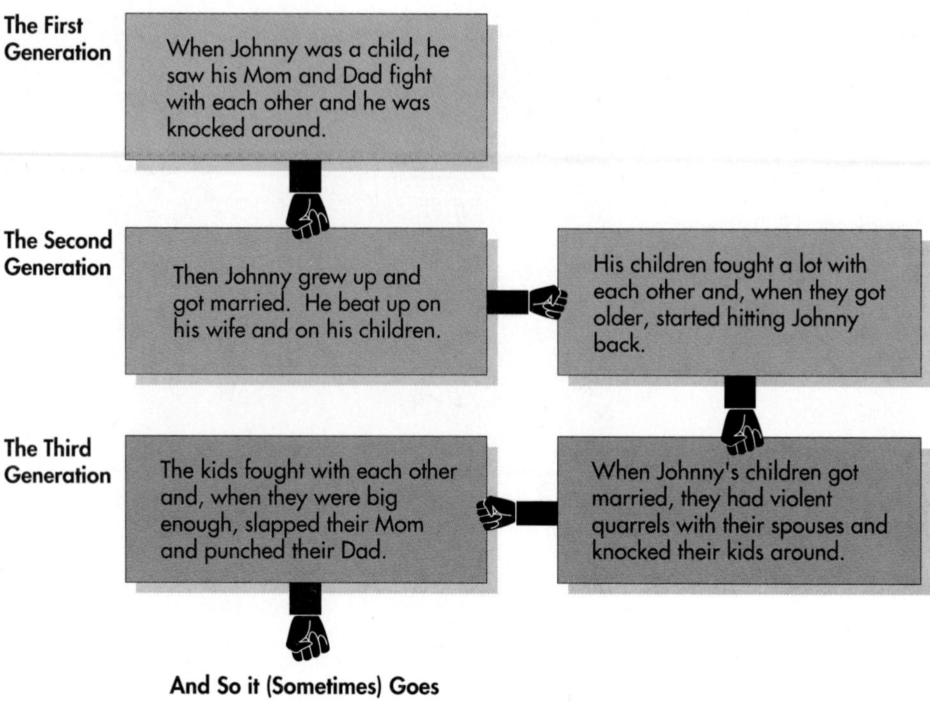

Figure 8.14 **The Cycle of Family Violence: A Sad Saga.** The cycle of family violence refers to the tendency for domestic violence in one generation to be transmitted to the next generation. This cycle is not, however, inevitable. Most people who witness or experience family violence as a child are not abusive or abused as adults.

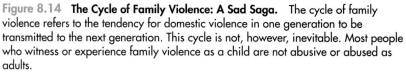

cians, to report suspected cases of child abuse, and some localities provide a toll-free number for calls from the general public. Since 1990, twenty-eight states have enacted "stalking laws" making it illegal to harass, threaten, or follow individuals; these sorts of behaviors are often the prelude to violence inflicted on a former spouse. Though controversial (Sherman, 1992), mandatory arrest policies for domestic assault have been enacted in twenty-five states. Shelters for battered women and their children provide protection and, often, various social services such as legal referrals, psychological counseling, and employment assistance. Families in which a child has been abused may be required by court order to participate in family therapy; if necessary, an abused child can be removed from the home. Either by court order or voluntarily, many abusing men and women participate in group therapy sessions. Some cities and states require that police, prosecutors, and judges receive special training to help them better understand the causes and consequences of domestic violence.

Specific programs that protect victims of abuse and reduce the likelihood of continued violence by abusers are vitally important. But family violence takes place in a larger context. According to Jay Belsky (1993), poverty is "undoubtedly the major risk for child abuse and neglect" (p. 428). Thus, protecting families from violence also requires providing family members with educational and employment opportunities. Furthermore, as noted throughout this chapter, attitudes have a strong influence on aggressive behavior. If society legitimizes and glorifies violence, all of us are at risk.

REVIEW

PINNING IT DOWN: WHAT IS AGGRESSION?

- Aggression is behavior intended to injure another person.
- Anger is an emotional response to perceived injury; hostility is an antagonistic attitude.
- Instrumental aggression occurs as a means to obtain a desired outcome.
- In emotional aggression, harm is inflicted for its own sake.

ORIGINS OF AGGRESSION

Is Aggression Innate?

- Both Freud and Lorenz regarded aggression as an innate instinct, but the circular reasoning of such instinct theories is unscientific.
- Sociobiology views aggression as a universal, innate characteristic favored by natural selection but limited by the need to protect the genes of one's relatives.
- Thus far, there is no conclusive evidence that individual differences in aggression are produced by genetic inheritance.
- In most (but not all) societies, men are more physically aggressive than women. This difference could be caused by biological factors, social roles, or both.

Is Aggression Learned?

- Aggression is increased by rewards.
- Aggression is decreased by punishment only under specific conditions that are often not met in the real world.
- Social learning theory emphasizes the influence of models on the behavior of observers.
- Models whose aggression succeeds in obtaining desired goals, without being punished, are the most likely to be imitated. But even punished models may encourage aggression by observers.
- Peaceful models can decrease aggressive responses by observers.

Nature Versus Nurture: The Terms of the Debate

- Everyone agrees that aggression is affected by learning and experience.
- No one disputes that in all human behavior, including aggression, biology and environment interact.
- The question is whether genetic inheritance or stable biological factors present at birth have a significant effect on aggressive behavior.

SOCIAL AND SITUATIONAL INFLUENCES ON AGGRESSION

Frustration: Aggression as a Drive

- The frustration-aggression hypothesis proposes that frustration will always produce the motive to aggress and that all aggression is caused by frustration.
- But, in fact, frustration produces many motives and aggression is caused by many factors.
- According to the frustration-aggression hypothesis, displacement will occur if aggression against the source of frustration is inhibited. Research has yet to offer convincing support for this notion.
- The frustration-aggression hypothesis holds that any aggressive action reduces the motive to engage in further aggression, a process called catharsis. In the long run, however, aggression now is likely to increase aggression later.
- Frustration is only one of a number of unpleasant experiences that produce negative affect and increase aggression.

Negative Affect: The Temperature's Rising

- Noxious stimuli are another source of negative affect.
- According to the negative affect escape model, increasing the intensity of noxious stimuli will increase aggressive responses up to a point, after which nonaggressive responses, such as escape or collapse, will predominate.
- Although the predicted turning point did appear in early research on the effects of hot weather, this finding resulted from the greater frequency of certain temperatures.
- Recent research indicates that aggression continues to increase as the temperature rises.

Positive Affect: Reducing Retaliation

- Being attacked or insulted by someone is another experience that produces negative affect, and retaliation to provocation is a major source of aggressive behavior.
- Positive emotional responses are incompatible with negative affect and reduce retaliatory aggression.

Arousal: "Wired" for Action

- Highly arousing stimuli, neutral as well as negative, increase retaliatory aggression.
- The arousal-affect model holds that both the type of emotion and the intensity of arousal influence aggression, which is greatest in response to experiences that combine negative affect and high arousal.

Thought: Automatic and Considered

- Berkowitz's cognitive-neoassociation analysis of aggression proposes that unpleasant experiences create negative affect, which, in turn, stimulates automatic associations connected with anger and fear. Behavioral and emotional outcomes then depend, at least in part, on higher-order cognitive processing.
- Situational cues, such as the presence of a gun, are presumed to influence automatic associations and can increase aggressive behavior even among individuals who have not been provoked.
- More deliberate thoughts that affect aggression include the perception of intent, which is reduced by mitigating information indicating that a person was not fully responsible for harmful acts.
- High arousal impairs the cognitive control of aggression, as does alcohol.

Multiple Causes, Multiple Cures

- Since aggression is determined by many factors, there is no one way to end it, but there are many ways to reduce it.

MEDIA EFFECTS: SCENES OF VIOLENCE

Depictions of Nonsexual Violence

- In laboratory and field experiments, exposure to aggressive models increases aggressive behavior among adults and children.
- Intense media coverage of violent events is correlated with subsequent increases in violent behavior.
- The results of prospective research indicate that the relationship between early viewing of TV violence and later aggression varies across cultures and is influenced by gender, the seeking out of violent shows by already aggressive children, and identification with aggressive TV characters.
- Since we habituate to familiar stimuli, repeated observations of violence reduces physiological arousal to new incidents but may make aggression more acceptable.
- Through cultivation of a social reality, the mass media can intensify fear of aggression and encourage aggressive behavior.
- Educational efforts may be more successful than censorship in reducing media-induced aggression.

Pornographic Materials

- Nonviolent pornography that is only mildly arousing reduces retaliatory aggression against someone of the same sex.
- When normative restraints against male-to-female aggression are reduced, nonviolent but highly arousing pornography specifically increases male-to-female aggression more than male-to-male aggression.
- Massive exposure to nonviolent pornography produces habituation, which reduces arousal-based aggression but increases callous attitudes that may lower restraints against future aggression.
- Exposure to dehumanizing nonviolent pornography increases sexually aggressive intentions.
- Violent pornography increases male-to-female aggression more than male-to-male aggression.
- When a female is portrayed as enjoying violent sex, even unprovoked men become more aggressive and become more accepting of violence against women.
- The combination of interest in violent pornography and negative attitudes toward women is a strong predictor of self-reported sexual aggression in the past and sexually aggressive intentions for the future.
- Education may be more effective than censorship in reducing sexual aggression.

INTIMATE VIOLENCE: TRUST BETRAYED

Sexual Aggression Among College Students

- Men are more likely than women to engage in sexually coercive behavior.
- Alcohol consumption is involved in a majority of sexually aggressive incidents.
- Greater prior sexual experience is associated with coercive sexual behavior by both men and women.

- Attitudes toward rape and toward women are associated with coercive sexual behavior.

Physical Aggression Between Partners

- National survey data indicate that spouse abuse remained relatively constant from 1975 to 1985.
- Some studies have found that women engage in more aggressive behavior against a partner than do men, but women are more likely to be killed, seriously injured, or sexually abused.
- The level of physical violence is highest among cohabiting couples.

Child Abuse

- Children are more likely to be victimized than adults.
- Mothers are more likely than fathers to physically abuse their children; fathers are more likely than mothers to sexually abuse their children.
- Children who witness parental violence or are themselves abused are more likely as adults to abuse their partners and their own children. But most people escape from this cycle of family violence.
- Protecting the victims of family violence and preventing its recurrence require a wide range of interventions.

KEY TERMS

aggression, p. 288
instrumental aggression, p. 289
emotional aggression, p. 289
social learning theory, p. 295
frustration-aggression hypothesis, p. 297
displacement, p. 298
catharsis, p. 298
arousal-affect model, p. 302
cognitive-neoassociation analysis, p. 303
weapons effect, p. 304
mitigating information, p. 306
habituation, p. 311
cultivation, p. 312
pornography, p. 313
cycle of family violence, p. 325

Chapter

9 Conformity

PREVIEW

This chapter examines three ways in which our behavior is influenced by others. First, we consider the reasons why people exhibit *conformity* to group norms. Second, we describe the kinds of strategies used to elicit *compliance* with direct requests. Third, we analyze the causes and effects of *obedience* to the commands of authority. The chapter concludes with a discussion of the *continuum of social influence*.

OUTLINE

Sports fans spread the "wave" around a stadium and chant "de-fense" in a spectacular show of unison. TV producers insert canned laughter into situation comedies as a way of increasing viewer responsiveness. Political candidates trumpet the inflated results of their own public opinion polls to attract new voters to the "winning side." And bartenders, waiters, waitresses, and musicians stuff dollar bills into tip jars at the start of an evening to encourage their customers to follow suit.

As these examples illustrate, people often imitate one another automatically and without conflict. Of course, you don't need to be a social psychologist to realize that we have an impact on each other's behavior. But how, and with what effect? When we use the term *social influence,* we refer to the ways in which people are affected by real and imagined pressures from others (Kiesler & Kiesler, 1969). The kinds of influences brought to bear on an individual come in different shapes and sizes. In this chapter, we consider three that vary in the degree of pressure exerted on a person—*conformity, compliance,* and *obedience.*

As depicted in Figure 9.1, conformity, compliance, and obedience are not distinct, qualitatively different "types" of influence. In all three cases, the influence

In sports stadiums, restaurants, and other settings, people often imitate each other automatically and without conflict.

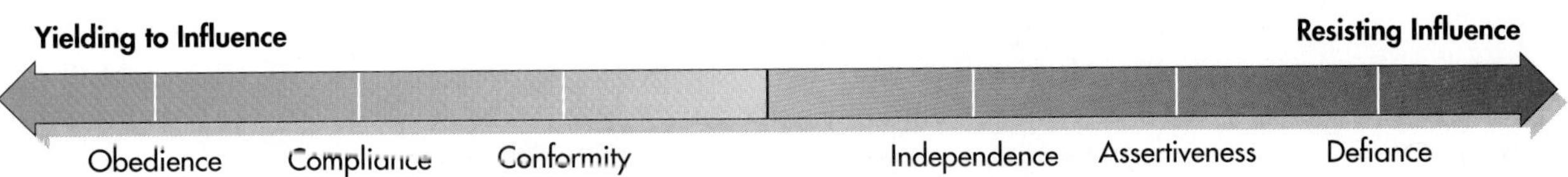

Figure 9.1 **Continuum of Social Influence.** Social influences vary in the degree of pressure they bring to bear on an individual. People may (1) *conform* to group norms or maintain their independence, (2) *comply* with requests or be assertive, and (3) *obey* or defy the commands of authority.

may emanate from a person, a group, or an institution. And in all instances, the behavior in question may be constructive (helping others), destructive (hurting others), or neutral. It is useful to note, however, that social influence varies, as points along a continuum, according to the degree of pressure exerted on the individual. It is also useful to note that we do not always succumb under pressure. People may conform or maintain their independence from others; they may comply with direct requests or react with assertiveness; they may obey the commands of authority or oppose powerful others in an act of defiance. In this chapter, we consider the factors that lead people to yield to or resist social influence.

CONFORMITY

It is hard to find behaviors that are *not* in some way affected by exposure to the actions of others. As social animals, we are vulnerable to a host of subtle, almost reflex-like influences. We often yawn when we see others yawning and laugh when we hear others laughing. To demonstrate the point, research confederates stopped on a busy street in New York City, looked up, and gawked at the sixth-floor window of a nearby building. Films shot from behind the window indicated that about 80 percent of passers-by stopped and gazed up when they saw these confederates (Milgram et al., 1969).

conformity The tendency to change our perceptions, opinions, or behavior in ways that are consistent with group norms.

When social psychologists talk of **conformity,** they refer to the tendency for people to change their perceptions, opinions, and behavior in ways that are consistent with group norms. With this definition in mind, would you call yourself a conformist or a nonconformist? Do you ever feel pressured to follow what others are doing? At first, you may want to deny the tendency to conform and, instead, declare your individuality. Think about it, though. When was the last time you appeared at a formal wedding dressed in blue jeans or remained seated during the national anthem at a sports event? People find it remarkably difficult to breach social norms. In an interesting illustration, social psychology research assistants were supposed to ask subway passengers to give up their seats—a conspicuous violation of the norm of acceptable conduct. As it turned out, however, many of the assistants could not carry out their assignment. In fact, some of those who tried it became so anxious that they pretended to be ill just to make their request appear justified (Milgram & Sabini, 1978).

With conformity being so widespread, it is interesting and ironic that research subjects (at least in North America) who are coaxed into conforming to a group norm will often not admit it. Instead, they reinterpret the task and rationalize their own behavior as a way to see themselves as independent (Buehler & Griffin,

1994). People understandably have mixed feelings about conformity. After all, some degree of conformity is essential if individuals are to coexist peacefully, as when people assume their rightful place in a waiting line. Yet at other times, conformity can have harmful consequences, as when people drink too heavily at parties or tell offensive ethnic jokes because others are doing the same. For the social psychologist, the goal is to understand the conditions in which people follow along and the reasons for that behavior.

The Early Classics

In 1936, Muzafer Sherif published a classic laboratory study of how norms develop in small groups. His method, also described in Chapter 1, was ingenious. Male students, who believed they were participating in a visual perception experiment, sat in a totally darkened room. Fifteen feet in front of them, a small dot of light appeared for two seconds, after which subjects were asked to estimate how far it had moved. This procedure was repeated several times. Although subjects didn't realize it, the dot of light always remained motionless. The movement they thought they saw was, in reality, an optical illusion known as the *autokinetic effect:* in darkness, a stationary point of light appears to move, sometimes erratically, in various directions.

At first, subjects sat alone and reported their judgments to the experimenter. After several trials, Sherif found that subjects settled in on their own stable perceptions of movement, with most estimates ranging from one to ten inches (although one subject gave an estimate of eighty feet!). During the next three days, subjects returned to participate in three-person groups. As before, lights were flashed and subjects, one by one, announced their estimates. As shown in Figure 9.2, initial estimates varied considerably, but subjects later converged on a common perception. Eventually, each group established its own set of norms.

Some fifteen years after Sherif's demonstration, Solomon Asch (1951) constructed a very different scenario for testing how people's beliefs affect each other. To appreciate what Asch did, imagine yourself in the following situation. You sign up for a psychology experiment, and when you arrive, you find six other subjects waiting around a table. Soon after you take an empty seat, the ex-

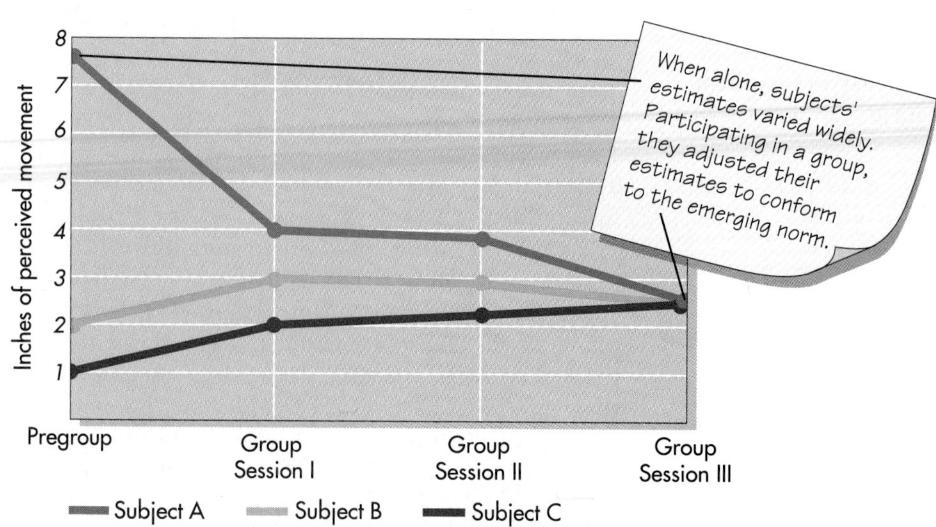

Figure 9.2 A Classic Case of Suggestibility. This graph taken from Sherif's study shows how three subjects' estimates of the apparent movement of light gradually converged. Before the subjects came together, their perceptions varied considerably. Once in groups, however, subjects conformed to the norm that had developed. (Sherif, 1936.)

Figure 9.3 Line Judgment Task Used in Asch's Conformity Studies. Which comparison line—A, B, or C—is the same in length as the standard line? What would you say if you found yourself in a unanimous majority that answered A or C? The subjects in Asch's experiments conformed to the majority about a third of the time. (Asch, 1955.)

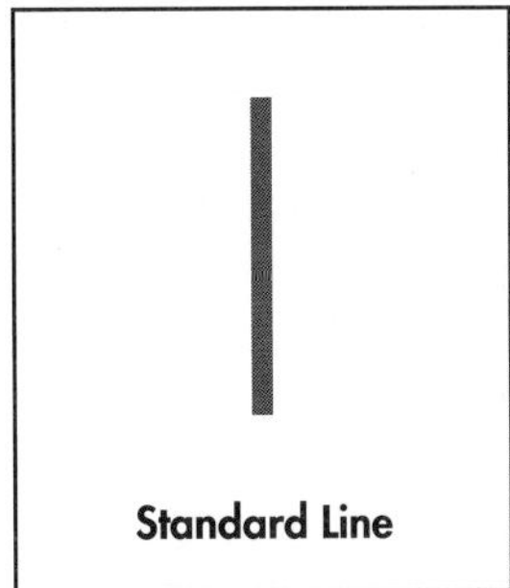

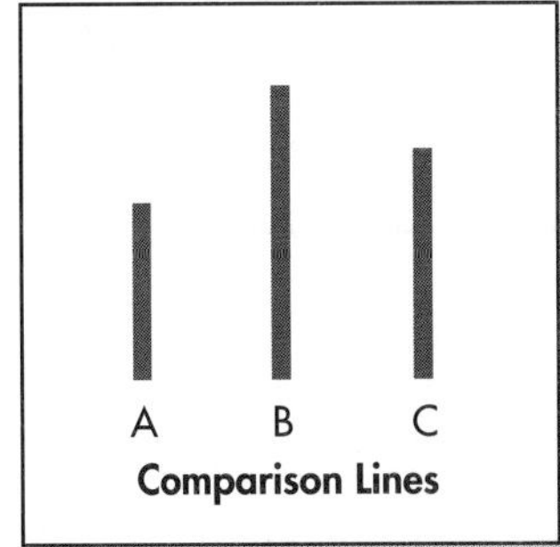

perimenter explains that he is interested in the ability to make visual discriminations. As an example, he asks you and the others to indicate which of three comparison lines is identical in length to a standard line.

That seems easy enough. The experimenter then says that after each set of lines is shown, you and the others should take turns announcing your judgments out loud in the order of your seating position. Beginning on his left, the experimenter asks the first person for his judgment. Seeing that you are in the next-to-last position, you patiently await your turn. The opening moments pass uneventfully. The discriminations are clear, and everyone agrees on the answers. On the third set of lines, however, the first subject selects what is quite clearly the wrong line. Huh? What happened? Did he suddenly lose his mind, his eyesight, or both? Before you have the chance to figure this one out, the next four subjects choose the same wrong line. Now what? Feeling as if you have entered the Twilight Zone, you wonder if you misunderstood the task. And you wonder what the others will think if you have the nerve to disagree. It's your turn now. You rub your eyes and take another look. What do you see? Better yet, what do you do?

Figure 9.3 gives an idea of the bind in which Asch's subjects found themselves—caught between the need to be right and the desire to be liked (Insko et al., 1982; Ross et al., 1976). As you may suspect by now, the other "subjects" were confederates—and had been trained to make incorrect judgments on twelve out of eighteen presentations. There seems little doubt that the real subjects knew the correct answers. In a control group, where they made judgments in isolation, they made almost no errors. Yet Asch's subjects went along with the incorrect

After two uneventful rounds in Asch's study, the subject (seated second from the right) faces a dilemma. The answer he had to give in the third test of visual discrimination differs from that of the first five confederates, who are all in agreement. Should he give his own answer, or conform to theirs?

majority about 37 percent of the time—far more often than most of us would ever predict. Not everyone conformed, of course. About 25 percent of the subjects refused to agree on any of the incorrect judgments. Yet 50 percent went along on at least half of the critical presentations. The remaining subjects conformed on an occasional basis. Similarly high levels of conformity were observed when Asch's study was repeated thirty years later (Larsen, 1990).

Looking at Sherif's and Asch's research, let's compare these classic studies of social influence. Obviously, both demonstrate that our perceptions can be heavily influenced by others. But how similar are they really? Did Sherif's and Asch's subjects exhibit the same kind of conformity, and for the same reasons, or is the resemblance in their behavior more apparent than real?

Right from the start, it was clear that these studies differed in some important ways. In Sherif's research, subjects were quite literally "in the dark," so they naturally turned to others for guidance. When physical reality is ambiguous and we are uncertain of our own judgments, as in the autokinetic situation, others can serve as a valuable source of information (Festinger, 1954). Yet Asch's subjects found themselves in a much more awkward position. Their task was relatively simple, and they could see with their own eyes what answers were correct. Still, they often followed the incorrect majority. In interviews, many of Asch's subjects reported afterward that they went along with the group even though they were not convinced by it. Those who did not conform said they felt "conspicuous" and "crazy," like a "misfit" (Asch, 1956, p. 31).

Why Do People Conform?

These two studies demonstrate that people conform for two very different reasons: informational and normative (Crutchfield, 1955; Deutsch & Gerard, 1955). Through **informational influence,** people conform because they want to be correct in their judgments and they assume that others who agree on something must be right. In Sherif's autokinetic task, as in other ambiguous situations, it is thus natural to assume that four eyes are better than two. **Normative influence,** however, leads people to conform because they fear the negative consequences of appearing deviant. Wanting to be accepted, we often avoid behaving in ways that make us stick out like a sore thumb. To be sure, people like to think of themselves as unique. But disagreement and conflict can be stressful. It's easy to see why. Research shows that individuals who stray from the group's norm are often disliked, rejected, ridiculed, and laughed at (Schachter, 1951; Levine, 1989)—especially when the group needs to reach a consensus (Kruglanski & Webster, 1991). The saying "To get along, go along" may seem distasteful, but it refers to a real fact of social life.

informational influence Influence that produces conformity when a person believes others are correct in their judgments.

normative influence Influence that produces conformity when a person fears the negative social consequences of appearing deviant.

Usually, informational and normative influences operate jointly (Insko et al., 1983). Even some of Asch's subjects admitted that they came to agree with their group's erroneous judgments. Still, the distinction between the two types of influence is important not just for understanding why people conform but because they produce different types of conformity: private and public (Allen, 1965; Kelman, 1961). Like beauty, conformity may be skin deep, or it may penetrate beneath the surface. **Private conformity,** also called true acceptance or conversion, describes those instances in which others cause us to change not only our overt behavior but our minds as well. To conform at this level is to be truly persuaded that others are correct. In contrast, **public conformity** (sometimes called compliance, a term that is used later in this chapter to describe a different form of influence) refers to a superficial change in behavior. People often respond to

private conformity The change of beliefs that occurs when a person privately accepts the position taken by others.

public conformity A superficial change in overt behavior, without a corresponding change of opinion, produced by real or imagined group pressure.

Table 9.1 Two Types of Conformity

Experimental Task	Primary Effect of Group	Depth of Conformity Produced
Sherif's Ambiguous Autokinetic Effect	Informational influence	Private acceptance
Asch's Simple Line Judgments	Normative influence	Public conformity

A comparison of Sherif's and Asch's studies suggests different kinds of conformity for different reasons. Sherif used an ambiguous task, so others provided a source of information and influenced the subjects' true opinions. Asch used a task that required simple judgments of a clear stimulus, so most subjects exhibited occasional public conformity in response to normative pressure but privately did not accept the group's judgments.

normative pressures by pretending to agree even when privately they do not. This often happens when we want to curry favor with others. The politician who tells constituents whatever they want to hear is a case in point.

How, you might be wondering, can social psychologists ever tell the difference between the private and the public conformist? After all, both exhibit the same change in their observable behavior. The difference is that compared to the individual who merely acquiesces in public, a person who is truly persuaded maintains that change even when others are out of the picture. When this distinction is applied to Sherif's and Asch's research, the results come out as expected. At the end of his study, Sherif (1936) retested subjects alone and found that their estimates continued to reflect the norm previously established in their group—even among subjects who were retested a full year after the experiment (Rohrer et al., 1954). In contrast, when Asch (1956) had subjects write down their answers privately, the level of conformity dropped sharply (Deutsch & Gerard, 1955; Mouton et al., 1956).

Table 9.1 summarizes the comparison of Sherif's and Asch's studies and the depths of social influence they demonstrate. Looking at this table, you can see that the difficulty of the task is crucial. When reality cannot easily be validated by physical evidence, as in the autokinetic situation, people turn to others for information and conform because they are truly persuaded by that information. When reality is clear, however, the cost of dissent becomes the major issue. As Asch found, it can be difficult to depart too much from others even when you know that they—not you—are wrong. So you play along. Privately, you don't change your mind. But you nod your head in agreement anyway.

Majority Influence

Realizing that people often succumb to peer pressure is only the first step in understanding the process of social influence. The next step is to identify the situational and personal factors that make us more or less likely to conform. We know that people tend to conform when the social pressure is intense and they are insecure about how to behave (Campbell & Fairey, 1989; Santee & Maslach,

1982). But what creates these feelings of pressure and insecurity? Here, we look at four factors: the size of the group, awareness of the norms, the presence of an ally, and the personal characteristics of the subject.

Group Size: The Power in Numbers Common sense would suggest that as the number of people in a majority increases, so should their impact. Actually, it is not that simple. Asch (1956) varied the size of groups, using one, two, three, four, eight, or fifteen confederates, and he found that conformity increased with group size—but only up to a point. Once there were three or four confederates, the amount of *additional* influence exerted by the rest was negligible. Other researchers have obtained similar results (Gerard et al., 1968).

Beyond the presence of three or four others, additions to a group are subject to the law of "diminishing returns" (Knowles, 1983; Mullen, 1983; Tanford & Penrod, 1984). As we will see later, Bibb Latané (1981) likens the influence of people on an individual to the way light bulbs illuminate a surface. When a second bulb is added to a room, the effect is dramatic. When the tenth bulb is added, however, its impact is barely felt, if at all. Economists say the same about the perception of money. An additional dollar seems greater to the person who has only three dollars than to the one who has three hundred.

Another possible explanation is that as more and more people express the same opinion, an individual is likely to suspect that they are acting either in "collusion" or as "spineless sheep." According to David Wilder (1977), what matters is not the actual number of others per se but one's perception of how many distinct others, thinking independently, there are. Indeed, Wilder found that subjects were more influenced by two groups of two than by one four-person group, and by two groups of three than by one six-person group. Conformity increased even further when subjects were exposed to three two-person groups. When faced with a majority opinion, we do more than just count the number of warm bodies—we try to assess the number of independent minds.

Awareness of the Norms The size of a majority may influence the amount of pressure that is felt, but social norms give rise to conformity only when we know and focus on those norms. This may sound like an obvious point, yet we often misperceive what is normative—particularly when others are too afraid or embarrassed to publicly present their true thoughts, feelings, and behaviors (Miller & McFarland, 1991; Miller & Prentice, 1994). One common example concerns perceptions of alcohol usage. In college-wide surveys, Deborah Prentice and Dale Miller (1993) found that most students overestimated how comfortable their peers were with the level of drinking on campus. What's more, those who overestimated how others felt about drinking at the start of the school year eventually conformed to this misperception in their own attitudes and behavior. The point is, we are influenced not by social norms per se but by our *perceptions* of the norms.

Knowing how others are behaving in a situation is necessary for conformity, but these norms are likely to influence us only when they are brought to our awareness, or "activated." This point is demonstrated in a series of studies on littering. In the first study, researchers had confederates pass out handbills to amusement park visitors and varied the amount of litter there was in a particular section of the park (an indication of how others behave in that setting). The result: The more litter there was, the more likely visitors were to toss their handbills to the ground (Cialdini et al., 1990).

A second study showed that passers-by were most influenced by the prior behavior of others in a situation where their attention was drawn to the existing norm. In this instance, subjects were observed in a parking garage that was either clean or cluttered with cigarette butts, candy wrappers, paper cups, and trash. In half of the cases, the norm that was already in place—clean or cluttered—was brought to their attention by a confederate who threw paper to the ground as he walked by. In the other half, the confederate passed by without incident. As subjects reached their cars, they found a "Please Drive Safely" handbill tucked under the windshield wiper. So, did they toss the paper to the ground or take it with them? The results showed that subjects were most likely to conform (in other words, to litter more when the garage was cluttered than when it was clean) when the confederate had littered—an act that drew attention to the existing norm. In short, social norms had to be "activated," or brought to mind, to influence behavior (Cialdini et al., 1991).

In a third study, which was set in a clean or cluttered outdoor parking lot, some subjects watched a confederate toss a fast-food restaurant bag to the ground, while others saw him bend over and pick a bag up—also an act that led subjects to take notice of the existing norm. So, did subjects litter? As shown in Figure 9.4, the second confederate had the greater influence. In this situation, littering was inhibited not only when the parking lot was clean but even when it

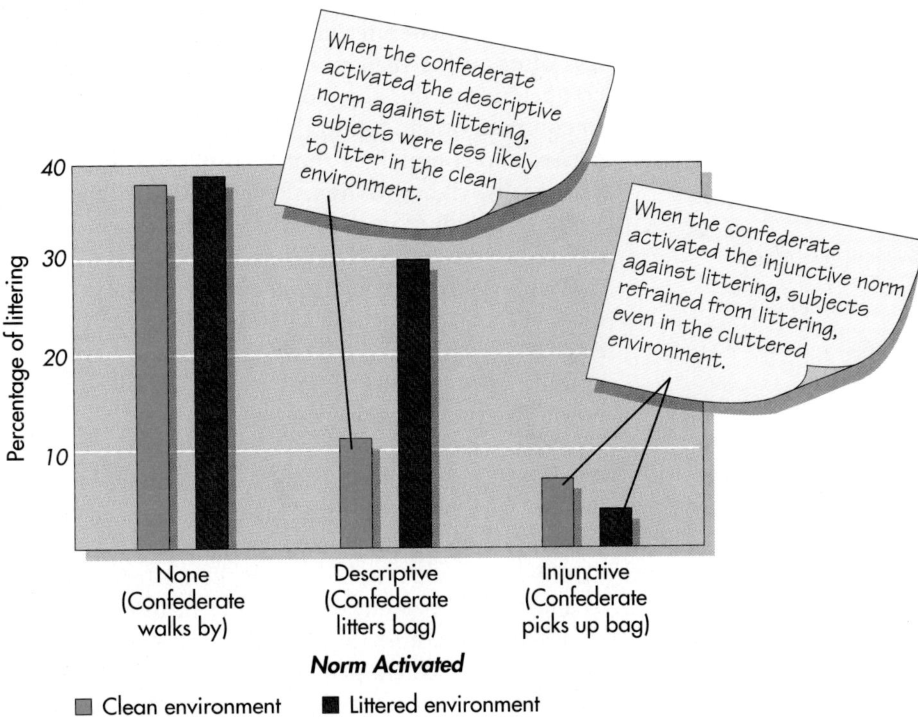

Figure 9.4 **The Power of Descriptive and Injunctive Norms.** In a clean or cluttered parking lot, some subjects saw a confederate toss a bag to the ground and others saw him pick a bag up—both acts that bring attention to the existing norm. Exposure to the first confederate inhibited littering in the clean setting, but exposure to the second was effective in the cluttered setting as well. Apparently, littering made subjects aware of the descriptive norms of how others *do* behave, whereas cleaning up made them aware of injunctive norms that specify how people *should* behave. (Reno et al., 1993.)

was cluttered. Apparently, the two situations activated different types of social norms. When the confederate littered, subjects were made aware of *descriptive norms* that simply informed them of how most others *do* behave. When the confederate went out of his way to pick up someone else's trash, however, subjects were exposed to *injunctive norms* that specify how people in general *should* behave. By linking behavior to signs of social approval and disapproval, injunctive norms have a powerful influence on us (Reno et al., 1993).

An Ally in Dissent: Getting By with a Little Help In Asch's (1951) initial experiment, subjects found themselves pitted against unanimous majorities. But what if they had an ally, a partner in dissent? Investigating this issue, Asch found that the presence of a single confederate who agreed with the subject reduced conformity by almost 80 percent. This finding, however, does not tell us why the presence of an ally was so effective. Was it because he or she *agreed* with the subject or because he or she *disagreed* with the majority? In other words, were the views of the subjects strengthened because a dissenting confederate offered validating *information* or because dissent per se reduced *normative* pressures?

A series of experiments explored these two possibilities. In one, Vernon Allen and John Levine (1969) led subjects to believe they were working together with four confederates. Three of these others consistently agreed on the wrong judgment. The fourth either followed the majority, agreed with the subject, or made a third, also incorrect judgment. This last variation was the most interesting: even when the confederate did not validate their own judgment, subjects conformed less often to the majority. In another study, Allen and Levine (1971) varied the competence of the ally. Some subjects received support from an average person. In contrast, others found themselves supported by someone who wore very thick glasses and complained that he could not see the visual displays. Not a very reassuring ally, right? Wrong. Even though subjects derived less comfort from this supporter than from one who seemed more competent at the task, his presence still reduced their level of conformity.

Two important conclusions follow from this research. First, it is substantially more difficult for people to stand alone for their convictions than to be part of even a tiny minority. Second, *any* dissent—whether it validates an individual's opinion or not—can break the spell cast by a unanimous majority and reduce the normative pressures to conform.

Age and Sex Differences We all know some people who conform more than others. Asch found individual differences in his research. Attempts to identify personality traits that breed conformity, however, have met with little success. Conformist traits may exist, but their effects on behavior vary from one situation to another. Consistent with the interactionist perspective described in Chapter 1, someone who conforms in one setting may behave autonomously in another setting (Marlowe & Gergen, 1969; Moscovici, 1985).

Although personality factors are hard to pin down, there are age differences in conformity. Parents know fully well, for example, that their adolescent sons and daughters are all too quick to turn to peers for guidance on how to dress, what music to listen to, and how to behave in ways that are "cool." Are junior and senior high school students more vulnerable to peer pressure than younger children and adults? The answer is yes, at least during the early stages of adolescence. Thomas Berndt (1979) asked students in grades 3, 6, 9, and 12 how they would react if their friends tried to get them to see a movie, help a new kid on the block, cheat on a test, soap windows on Halloween, or participate in other activities. As shown in Figure 9.5, conformity rose steadily, peaked in the ninth grade, and then declined. The tendency to conform is weak for actions that are immoral or illegal, but young adolescents are particularly at risk, as they want desperately to "fit in" (Brown et al., 1986; Gavin & Furman, 1989).

Are there also gender differences in conformity? Based on Asch's initial studies, social psychologists used to think that women, once considered the "weaker" sex, conform more than men. In light of more recent research, however, it appears that two additional factors have to be considered. First, sex differences depend on how comfortable subjects are with the experimental task. Frank Sistrunk and John McDavid (1971) had male and female subjects answer questions on stereotypically masculine, feminine, and gender-neutral topics. Along with each question, subjects were told the percentage of others who agreed or disagreed. Although females conformed to the contrived majority more on the masculine items, males conformed more on the feminine items (there were no sex differences on the neutral questions). This finding suggests that one's familiarity with the issue at hand, not gender, is what affects conformity. Ask about football or video war games, and women acquiesce more than men. Ask about family planning and fashion design, and the pattern is reversed (Eagly & Carli, 1981).

A second factor is the type of social pressure people face. As a general rule, sex differences are weak and unreliable. But there is an important exception: in face-to-face encounters, where people must openly disagree with each other, small differences do emerge. In fact, when subjects think they are being observed, women conform more and men conform less than they do in a more private situation (Eagly & Chravala, 1986; Eagly et al., 1981b). Why does being "in public" create such a divergence in behavior? Alice Eagly (1987) argues that in front of others, people worry about how they come across and feel pressured to behave in

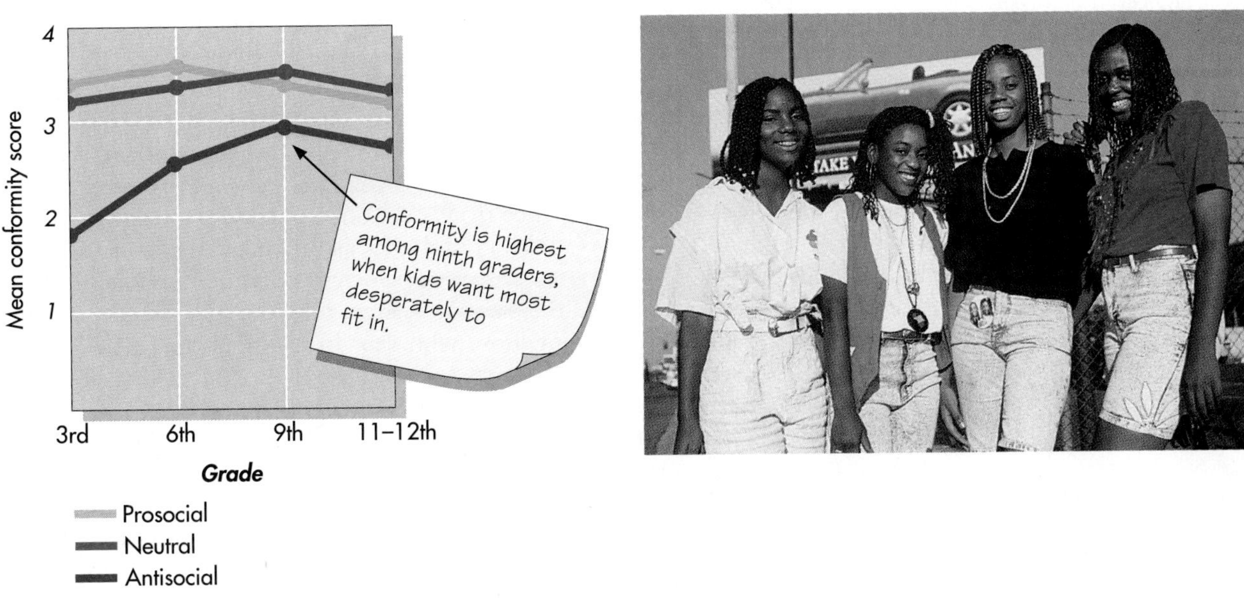

Figure 9.5 Conformity in Childhood and Adolescence. Students in grades 3, 6, 9, and 12 reported on how they would react if pressured by peers to participate in certain activities. As shown, conformity rose steadily, peaked in the ninth grade, and then declined. Particularly for young adolescents who want desperately to fit in—in the way they act, dress, and wear their hair—it's difficult to "just say no." (Berndt, 1979.)

ways that are "acceptable" within traditional gender-role constraints. At least in public, men make it a point to behave with fierce independence and autonomy, while women play a gentler, more docile role.

Cultural Influences Cultures vary in their implicit rules of conduct, or social norms. In Roger Axtell's (1993) best-seller, *Do's and Taboos Around the World,* world travelers are warned about some of these differences. Dine in an Indian home, for example, and you should leave food on the plate to show the host that the portions were generous and that you had enough to eat. Yet as a dinner guest in Bolivia, you show your appreciation by cleaning your plate—and in Saudi Arabia, you should stuff yourself. Shop in an outdoor market in Iraq, and you should expect to negotiate the price of everything you buy. Plan an appointment in Brazil, and the person you're scheduled to meet is likely to be late. Nothing personal. Even the way we space ourselves from each other is culturally determined. Americans, Canadians, Germans, British, and Northern Europeans keep a polite distance between themselves and others—and feel "crowded" by the touchier, nose-to-nose style of the French, Greeks, Arabs, Mexicans, and people of South America.

Just as cultures differ in their social norms, so too they differ in the extent to which people adhere to those norms. As we saw in Chapter 2, there are two different cultural orientations toward persons and their relationships to groups. Some cultures value **individualism**—and the virtues of independence, autonomy, and self-reliance, while others value **collectivism**—and the virtues of interdependence, cooperation, and social harmony. Under the banner of individualism, personal goals take priority over group allegiances. Yet in collectivistic cultures, the person is, first and foremost, a loyal member of a family, team, company, church, and state.

individualism A cultural orientation in which independence, autonomy, and self-reliance take priority over group allegiances.

collectivism A cultural orientation in which interdependence, cooperation, and social harmony take priority over personal goals.

What determines whether a culture becomes individualistic or collectivistic? Speculating on the origins of these orientations, Harry Triandis (1994) suggests that there are three key factors. The first is the *complexity* of a society. As people live in more complex industrialized societies (compared, for example, to a life of food-gathering among desert nomads) there are more groups to identify with, which means less loyalty to any one group and a greater focus on personal rather than collective goals. Second is the *affluence* of a society. As people begin to prosper, they gain financial independence from each other, a condition that promotes social independence as well as mobility and a focus on personal rather than collective goals. The third factor is *heterogeneity.* Societies that are homogeneous or "tight" (where members share the same language, religion, and social customs) tend to be rigid and intolerant of those who veer from the norm. Societies that are culturally diverse or "loose" (where two or more cultures coexist) are more permissive of dissent—thus allowing for more individual expression.

Research shows that autonomy and independence are most highly valued in the United States, Australia, Great Britain, Canada, and the Netherlands, in that order. In contrast, many cultures of Asia, Africa, and South America value interpersonal harmony and conformity—fitting in for the sake of the community (Hofstede, 1980). Among the Bantu of Zimbabwe, for example, an African tribe in which acts of nonconformity are severely punished, 51 percent of the subjects placed in an Asch-like situation conformed—more than the approximately 30 percent typical in the United States (Whittaker & Meade, 1967). In fact, John Berry (1979) compared subjects from seventeen cultures and found that conformity rates ranged from a low of 18 percent among Eskimo hunters of Bafin Island to a high of 60 percent among village-living Temne farmers of West Africa.

These photographs were taken of "average-income" families posing in front of their homes and material possessions. Representing the individualistic orientation common among affluent societies is the Skeen family of Pearland, Texas (top). Representing the collectivist orientation found in more impoverished societies is the Natoma family of Kouakourou, Mali (bottom).

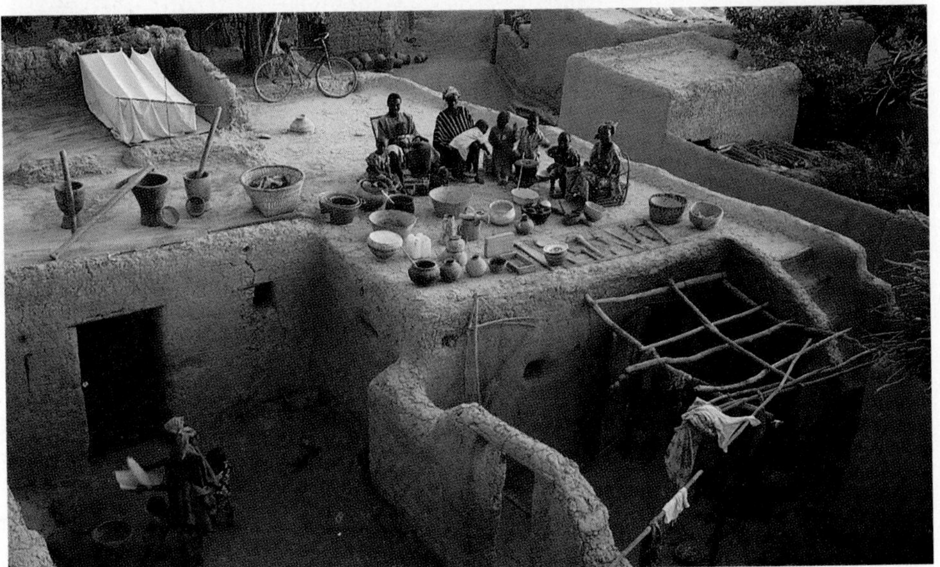

Minority Influence

It is not easy for individuals who express unpopular views to enlist support from others. Philosopher Bertrand Russell once said, "Conventional people are roused to frenzy by departure from convention, largely because they regard such departure as criticism of themselves." He may have been right. People who stand tall for their beliefs against the majority are generally seen as competent and honest, though they are also disliked (Bassili & Provencal, 1988; Levine, 1989).

Resisting pressure to conform and maintaining one's independence may be socially difficult, but it is not impossible. History's famous trend setters, heroes, villains, and creative minds are the living proof: Joan of Arc, Muhammad, Darwin, and Gandhi, to name just a few, were dissenters of their time who continue to capture the imagination. So are some of the people of everyday life who make waves and rock boats. In a book entitled *The Dissenters,* anthropologist

Langston Gwaltney (1986) recorded dialogues with "ordinary" nonconformists such as an Irish man who befriended Blacks in a racist community, a New England grandma who risked arrest to protest nuclear weapons, and a group of nuns who sued their church. Then there's human behavior in the laboratory. Social psychologists were so intrigued by Asch's initial finding that subjects conformed 37 percent of the time that textbooks like this one routinely refer to "Asch's conformity study." Yet the often-neglected flip side of the coin is that Asch's subjects refused to acquiesce 63 percent of the time—thus also indicating the power of independence (Friend et al., 1990).

Twelve Angry Men, a classic film starring Henry Fonda, provides a good illustration of how a lone dissenter cannot only resist the pressure to conform but can convince others to follow. Almost as soon as the deliberation-room door closes, the jury in this film takes a show-of-hands vote. The result is an eleven-to-one majority in favor of conviction, with Fonda the lone holdout. Through ninety minutes of heated deliberation, Fonda works relentlessly to plant a seed of doubt in the minds of his trigger-happy peers. In the end, the jury reaches a unanimous verdict: *not* guilty.

Sometimes art imitates life, sometimes it does not. In this instance, Henry Fonda's heroics are highly atypical. When it comes to jury decision making, we'll see in Chapter 12 that the majority almost always wins. Yet in juries, as in other small groups, there are occasional exceptions. Thanks to Serge Moscovici, Edwin Hollander, and others, we now know quite a bit about the characteristics of effective nonconformists and the strategies they use to act as agents of social change (Hollander, 1985; Maass & Clark, 1984; Moscovici, 1980; Mugny & Perez, 1991).

The Power of Style According to Moscovici, majorities are powerful by virtue of their sheer *numbers* and inherent power, while nonconformists derive power from the *style* of their behavior. It is not just what they say that matters, but how they say it. To exert influence, says Moscovici, those in the minority must be forceful, persistent, and unwavering in support of their views. Yet at the same time, they must appear flexible and open-minded. Confronted with a consistent yet evenhanded opposition, members of the majority will sit up, take notice, and rethink their own positions.

Why should a consistent behavioral style prove effective? One possible reason is that unwavering repetition draws more interest and attention than dissenters typically get from the mainstream, and this is a necessary first step to social influence. Another possibility is that consistency signals that the dissenter is not likely to yield, thus leading those in the majority to feel pressured to seek compromise. A third possible reason is that when people are confronted with someone with self-confidence and dedication who takes an unpopular stand and refuses to back down, they may assume that he or she has a point. Unless the dissenter is perceived to be biased, obstinate, or just plain crazy, this situation would lead those in the majority to re-examine their own views. Of course, it helps if members of the majority categorize those in the minority as "us" rather than "them." John Turner (1991) finds that dissenters have greater influence when they're similar to those in the majority instead of dissimilar in ways that are relevant.

Based on their meta-analysis of ninety-seven minority influence experiments, Wendy Wood and her colleagues (1994) concluded that there is strong support for the consistency hypothesis. In one study, for example, Moscovici and his colleagues (1969) turned Asch's procedure on its head by confronting real subjects with a *minority* of confederates who made incorrect judgments. In groups of six, subjects took part in what was supposed to be a study of color perception. They viewed a series of slides—all blue, but differing in intensity. For each slide, the subjects took turns naming the color. Although the task was simple, two confederates announced that the slides were green. When the confederates were *consistent*—that is, when both made incorrect green judgments for all slides—they had a surprising degree of influence. About a third of all subjects incorrectly reported seeing at least one green slide, and 8 percent of all responses were incorrect. Later research confirmed that the perception of consistency is a key factor.

Based on the fact that dissent often breeds hostility, Edwin Hollander (1958) recommends a different approach. Hollander warns that people who seek positions of leadership or challenge a group without first becoming accepted full-fledged members of that group run the risk of having their opinions fall on deaf ears. As an alternative to Moscovici's consistency strategy, Hollander says that to influence a majority, people should first conform in order to establish their credentials as competent insiders. By becoming members of the mainstream, they accumulate **idiosyncrasy credits**, or "brownie points." Then, as soon as enough good will has been collected within the group, a certain amount of deviance will be tolerated. Several studies have shown that this "first conform, then dissent" strategy, like the "consistent dissent" approach, is effective (Bray et al., 1982; Lortie-Lussier, 1987).

idiosyncrasy credits Interpersonal "credits" that a person earns by following group norms.

A Chip Off the Old Block? Regardless of which strategy is used, minority influence is a force to be reckoned with. But does it work just like the process of conformity, or is there something different about the way minorities and majorities effect change? There are two opposing viewpoints. Some theorists believe that a *single process* accounts for both directions of social influence—that minority influence is just like a "chip off the old block" (Latané & Wolf, 1981; Tanford & Penrod, 1984). Others have taken a *dual-process* approach (Moscovici, 1980; Nemeth, 1986). In this second view, majorities and minorities both exert influence, but in very different ways. Majorities, because they have power and control, elicit public conformity by bringing stressful normative pressures to bear on the individual. But minorities, because they are seen as seriously committed to their views, produce a deeper and more lasting private conformity, or *conversion*, by leading others to rethink their original positions.

To evaluate these competing single- and dual-process theories, researchers have compared the effects of majority and minority viewpoints on subjects who are otherwise neutral on an issue in dispute. At this point, the following conclusions can be drawn. On direct or public measures of conformity, majorities have the clear upper hand over minorities. On indirect private measures of conformity, however, minorities tend to exert a strong impact (Clark & Maass, 1990; Moscovici & Personnaz, 1991)—at least when their dissent is not on an issue of great personal relevance, a situation that leads subjects to resist influence (Trost et al., 1992). As Moscovici so cogently argued, we are all changed in a meaningful but subtle way by minority opinion. Because of social pressures, we may be too intimidated to admit it, but the impact is there (Wood et al., 1994).

According to Charlan Nemeth (1986), dissenters serve a valuable purpose. Sometimes their views are correct; at other times they are not. But simply through their willingness to remain independent, minorities can force other group members to think more carefully, more openly, and more creatively about a problem, thus enhancing the quality of a group's decisions. In one study, for example, subjects exposed to a minority viewpoint on how to solve anagram problems later found more novel solutions themselves (Nemeth & Kwan, 1987). In another study, those exposed to a consistent minority view on how to recall information later recalled more words from a list they were trying to memorize (Nemeth et al., 1990).

Earlier, we saw that people are more willing to express their opposition to incorrect majorities when a group lacks unanimity. But what about opposition to *unanimous* incorrect majorities? Can people muster enough courage to resist conformity pressure when they truly believe they are right? To examine this possibility, Nemeth and Cynthia Chiles (1988) placed subjects into color-perception groups in which a single confederate consistently or inconsistently dissented—by judging blue slides to be green all or some of the time—or voiced no dissent at all. Later, subjects participated in a new group in which all other members judged a series of red slides as orange—the Asch script all over again. The reaction? As with Asch's line judgments, the task was simple and straightforward. On their own, subjects were incorrect in fewer than 1 percent of the responses. And up against a unanimous group, subjects without prior exposure to dissent made conformity errors 70 percent of the time. But subjects who had witnessed dissent in an earlier experiment had the courage to step forward and oppose the incorrect majority. The more consistent the observed dissent, the more independent subjects later became.

COMPLIANCE

compliance Changes in behavior that are elicited by direct requests.

In conformity situations, people follow implicit group norms. But another common form of social influence occurs when people make direct *explicit* requests of us in the hope that we will comply. Situations calling for **compliance** take many forms. These include a friend's request for help, sheepishly prefaced by the question "Can you do me a favor?" They also include a salesperson's pitch for business, prefaced by the dangerous words "Have I got a deal for you!" Sometimes, the request itself is up front and direct; what you see is what you get. At other times, it is part of a subtle and more elaborate manipulation.

How do people get others to comply with self-serving requests? How do police interrogators get crime suspects to confess? How do TV evangelists draw millions of dollars in contributions for their ministries? How do *you* exert influence? Do you use threats, promises, deceit, politeness, or reason? Do you hint, coax, sulk, negotiate, throw tantrums, or pull rank whenever you can? The compliance strategies we use depend on how well we know a person, on our status in a relationship, and on our personality, culture, and the nature of the request (Bisanz & Rule, 1989; Buss et al., 1987; Holtgraves & Yang, 1992).

By observing the masters of influence—advertisers, fund raisers, politicians, and business leaders—social psychologists have learned a great deal about the subtle but effective strategies commonly used. What we see is that people often get others to comply with their requests by setting traps. Once caught in one of these traps, the unwary victim often finds it difficult to escape.

The Discourse of Making Requests

There is a memorable scene in the film *Beverly Hills Cop II* in which comedian Eddie Murphy, speaking at a rate far too fast for anyone to comprehend, manages to convince a team of builders to abandon work on a house that he wants to use for the weekend. This scene illustrates the rapid-fire sales pitch at its best. The other guys never had a chance. Murphy capitalized on the fact that fast talkers are assumed to be intelligent and well informed (Apple et al., 1979). He also benefited from the element of surprise. Caught off guard, people tend to capitulate quickly. For example, when New York City subway passengers were forewarned that someone might ask for their seat, only 28 percent of them said yes when later approached. When the request took passengers by surprise, however, the compliance rate doubled to 56 percent (Milgram & Sabini, 1978).

People can also be disarmed by the phrasing of a request. As illustrated by Eddie Murphy's masterful use of doubletalk, *how* you ask for something can be more important than *what* you ask for. Consider, for example, requests that sound reasonable but offer no real reason for compliance. Ellen Langer and her colleagues (1978) found that words alone can sometimes trick us into submission. In their research, an experimenter approached people who were using a library copying machine and asked to cut in. Three different versions of the same request were used. In one, subjects were simply asked, "Excuse me. I have five pages. May I use the Xerox machine?" In a second version, the request was justified by the added phrase "because I'm in a rush." As you would expect, more subjects stepped aside when the request was justified (94 percent) than when it was not (60 percent). A third version of the request, however, suggests that the reason offered had little to do with the increase in compliance. In this case, subjects heard the following: "Excuse me. I have five pages. May I use the Xerox machine because I have to make some copies?" If you read this request closely, you'll see that it really offered no reason at all. Yet 93 percent of the subjects in this condition complied! It was as if the appearance of reason, triggered by the word *because,* was all that was necessary. Indeed, Langer (1989) finds that the mind is often on "automatic pilot," as we respond *mindlessly* to words without fully processing the information they are supposed to convey. At least for requests that are relatively small, "sweet little nothings" may be enough to win compliance.

It is interesting that although the state of mindlessness can make us vulnerable to compliance, it can also have the opposite effect. For example, many city dwellers automatically, as in a reflex action, walk past panhandlers on the street looking for a handout. According to Michael Santos and his colleagues (1994), the way to increase compliance in situations like this one is to disrupt the mindless refusal response by making a request that is so unusual that it piques the target person's interest. To test the effect of this "pique technique," they hired a

Mindlessness makes people vulnerable to compliance

confederate to approach people on the street and make a request that was either typical ("Can you spare a quarter?") or strange ("Can you spare 37 cents?"). The result: Strange pleas elicited more comments and questions from those who were targeted—and produced a 60 percent increase in the number of people who gave money.

The Norm of Reciprocity

In earlier chapters we described a simple but powerful social norm. Known as the *norm of reciprocity,* it dictates that we treat others as they have treated us (Gouldner, 1960). On the negative side, this norm can be used to sanction retaliation against those who cause us harm: "An eye for an eye." On the positive side, it leads us to feel obligated to repay others for acts of kindness. Thus, when we receive gifts, invitations, and free samples, we usually go out of our way to return the favor.

The norm of reciprocity contributes to the predictability and fairness of social interaction. However, it can also be used to exploit us. Dennis Regan (1971) examined this possibility in the following study. Individual subjects were brought together with a confederate—who was trained to act in a likable or unlikable manner—for an experiment on "aesthetics." In one condition, the confederate did the subject an unsolicited favor. He left during a break and returned with two bottles of Coca-Cola, one for himself and the other for the subject. In a second condition, he returned from the break empty-handed. In a third condition, the subjects were treated to a Coke—but by the experimenter, not the confederate. The confederate then told subjects in all conditions that he was selling raffle tickets at 25 cents apiece and asked if they would be willing to buy any. On the average, subjects bought more raffle tickets when the confederate had earlier brought them a soft drink than when he had not. The norm of reciprocity was so strong that subjects returned the favor even when the confederate was not otherwise a likable character. In fact, subjects in this condition spent an average of 43 cents on raffle tickets. At a time when soft drinks cost less than a quarter, the confederate made a handsome quick profit on his investment! Clearly, the norm of reciprocity can be used to trap us into compliance.

Exploiting the norm of reciprocity, department store sales clerks offer customers free samples of perfume and other products.

Some people are more likely than others to exploit the norm of reciprocity in this manner. According to Martin Greenberg and David Westcott (1983), individuals who use reciprocity to elicit compliance are called "creditors" because they always try to keep others in their debt so they can cash in when necessary. On a questionnaire that measures *reciprocation ideology,* people are identified as creditors if they agree with such statements as "If someone does you a favor, it's good to repay that person with a greater favor." On the receiving end, some people more than others try not to accept favors that might later set them up for exploitation. On a scale that measures *reciprocation wariness,* people are said to be wary if they express the suspicion that, for example, "Asking for another's help gives them power over your life" (Eisenberger et al., 1987).

Setting Traps: Sequential Request Strategies

People who raise money or sell for a living know that it often takes more than a single plea to win over a potential donor or customer. Social psychologists share this knowledge and have studied several compliance techniques that are based on making two or more related requests. *Click!* The first request sets the trap. *Snap!* The second captures its prey. In a fascinating book entitled *Influence,* Robert Cialdini (1993) describes a number of sequential request methods in vivid detail. These methods are presented in the following pages.

The Foot in the Door Folk wisdom has it that one way to get a person to comply with a sizable request is to start small. First devised by traveling salespeople peddling vacuum cleaners, hair brushes, cosmetics, magazine subscriptions, and encyclopedias, the trick is to somehow get your "foot in the door." The expression need not be taken literally, of course. The point of the **foot-in-the-door technique** is to break the ice with a small initial request that the customer can't refuse. Once a first commitment is elicited, the chances are increased that another, larger request will succeed.

foot-in-the-door technique A two-step compliance technique in which an influencer prefaces the real request by first getting a person to comply with a much smaller request.

Jonathan Freedman and Scott Fraser (1966) tested the impact of this technique in a series of field experiments. In one, an experimenter pretending to be employed by a consumer organization telephoned a group of female homemakers in Palo Alto, California, and asked if they would be willing to answer some questions about household products. Those who consented were then asked a few innocuous questions and thanked for their assistance. Three days later, the experimenter called back and made a considerable, almost outrageous, request. He asked subjects if they would allow a handful of men into their home for two hours to rummage through their drawers and cupboards so they could take an inventory of household products.

The foot-in-the-door technique proved to be very effective. When subjects were confronted with only the very intrusive request, 22 percent consented. Yet among those surveyed earlier, the rate of agreement more than doubled, to 53 percent. This basic result has now been repeated over and over again. People are more likely to donate time, money, blood, the use of their home, and other resources once they have been induced to go along with a small initial request. Although the effect is often not as dramatic as that obtained by Freedman and Fraser, it does appear in a variety of circumstances (Beaman et al., 1983; Dillard, 1991).

The practical implications of the foot-in-the-door technique are obvious. But *why* does it work? Although several explanations have been suggested, the one that seems the most plausible is based on self-perception theory—that people infer their attitudes by observing their own behavior. This explanation suggests that a two-step process is activated (DeJong, 1979). First, by observing your behavior in the initial, small compliance situation, you adopt an image of yourself as the kind of person who is generally cooperative when approached with that kind of request. Second, having made that attribution, and being confronted with the more burdensome request, you seek to respond in ways that maintain this self-image. Thus, the foot-in-the-door technique should succeed only when you attribute an initial act of compliance to your own personal characteristics.

Research evidence generally supports this explanation. If the first request is too trivial or if subjects are paid for their first act of compliance, they won't view themselves as inherently cooperative. Under these conditions, the technique does *not* work (Seligman et al., 1976; Zuckerman et al., 1979). Likewise, the effect occurs only when people are motivated to be consistent with their self-image. If subjects are unhappy about what their initial behavior implies about them, if they are too young to appreciate the implications, or if they don't care about behaving in ways that are personally consistent, then again the technique does *not* work (Eisenberg et al., 1987; Kraut, 1973).

Knowing that a foot in the door increases compliance is both exciting and troubling—exciting for the owner of the foot, but troubling for the owner of the door. As Cialdini (1993) put it, "You can use small commitments to manipulate a person's self-image; you can use them to turn citizens into 'public servants,' prospects into 'customers,' prisoners into 'collaborators.' And once you've got a person's self-image where you want it, he or she should comply *naturally* with a whole range of requests that are consistent with this new self-view" (p. 64).

Low-Balling Another two-step trap, perhaps the most unscrupulous of all compliance techniques, is also based on the "start small" idea. Imagine yourself in the following situation. You're at a local automobile dealership and, after some negotiation, the salesperson offers a great price on the car of your choice. You cast aside other considerations, shake hands on the deal, and as the salesperson goes off to "write it up," you begin to feel the thrill of owning the car of your dreams. Absorbed in fantasy, you are interrupted by the sudden return of the salesperson. "I'm sorry," he says. "The manager would not approve the sale. We have to raise the price by another $450. Otherwise, we lose money. I'm afraid that's the best we can do." As the victim of an all-too-common trick known as **low-balling,** you are now faced with a difficult decision. On the one hand, you are really wild about the car. You've already enjoyed the pleasure of thinking it's yours; and the more you think about it, the better it looks. On the other hand, you don't want to pay more money, and you have an uneasy feeling in the pit of your stomach that you're being duped. What do you do?

low-balling A two-step compliance technique in which the influencer secures agreement with a request but then increases the size of that request by revealing hidden costs.

Salespeople who use this tactic are betting that you'll go ahead with the purchase despite the added cost. If the behavior of research subjects is any indication, they are often right. In one study, for example, experimenters phoned introductory psychology students and asked if they would be willing to participate in an experiment for extra credit. Some subjects were told up front that the session would begin at the uncivilized hour of 7 A.M. Knowing that, only 31 percent volunteered. But other subjects were low-balled. Only *after* they agreed to participate did the experimenter inform them of the 7 A.M. starting time. Would that be okay? Whether or not it was, the procedure achieved its objective—the sign-up rate increased to 56 percent (Cialdini et al., 1978).

Low-balling is an interesting technique. Surely, once the low ball has been thrown, most recipients suspect they were misled. Yet they go along. Why? The reason appears to be based on the psychology of commitment (Kiesler, 1971). Once people make a particular decision, they justify it to themselves by thinking of all its positive aspects. As they become increasingly committed to a course of action, they grow more resistant to changing their mind, even if the initial reasons for their action have been changed or withdrawn entirely. In the automobile dealership scenario, you might very well have decided to purchase the car because of the price. But then you would have thought about its sleek new appearance, the leather interior, the sun roof, and the sound quality on the CD player. By the time you learned that the price would be more than you bargained for, it was too late—you were already hooked.

Low-balling also produces another form of commitment. When people do not suspect duplicity, they feel a nagging sense of unfulfilled obligation to the person with whom they negotiated. Thus, even though the salesperson was unable to complete the original deal, you might feel obligated to buy anyway, having already agreed to make the purchase. This commitment to the other person may account for why low-balling works better when the second request is made by the same person than by someone else (Burger & Petty, 1981).

The Door in the Face Although shifting from an initial small request to a larger one can be effective, as in the foot-in-the-door and low-ball techniques, oddly enough the opposite is also true. In *Influence,* Cialdini (1993) describes the time he was approached by a Boy Scout and asked to buy two five-dollar tickets to an upcoming circus. Having better things to do with his time and money, he declined. Then the boy asked if he would be interested in buying chocolate bars at a dollar apiece. Even though he doesn't like chocolate, Cialdini—an expert on social influence—bought two of them! After a moment's reflection, he realized what had happened. Whether the Boy Scout planned it that way or not, Cialdini had fallen for what is known as the **door-in-the-face technique.**

door-in-the-face technique A two-step compliance technique in which an influencer prefaces the real request with one that is so large that it is rejected.

The technique is as simple as it sounds. An individual makes an initial request so large that it is sure to be rejected and then comes back with a second, more reasonable request. The assumption is that the second request will stand a better chance after the first one has been declined. Plagued by the sight of uneaten chocolate bars, Cialdini and his colleagues (1975) evaluated the effectiveness of the door-in-the-face technique. They stopped college students on campus and asked if they would volunteer to work without pay at a youth counseling program for juvenile delinquents. The commitment of time would be forbidding: roughly two hours a week for the next two years! Not surprisingly, everyone who was approached politely slammed the proverbial door in the experimenter's face. But then the experimenter followed up with a more modest proposal, asking subjects if they would be willing to take a group of delinquents on a two-hour trip to the zoo. The strategy worked like a charm. Only 17 percent of the students confronted with *only* the second request agreed. But of those who initially declined the first request, 50 percent said yes to the zoo trip. You should note that the door-in-the-face technique does not elicit only empty promises. Most subjects who comply subsequently do what they've agreed to do (Cialdini & Ascani, 1976).

Why is the door-in-the-face technique such an effective trap? One possibility involves the principle of *perceptual contrast:* after exposure to a very large request, the second request "looks smaller." Two dollars' worth of candy bars is not bad compared to ten dollars for circus tickets. Likewise, taking a group of kids to the zoo seems trivial compared to two years of volunteer work. As intuitively sensible as this explanation seems, Cialdini and his colleagues (1975) concluded that perceptual contrast is only partly responsible for the effect. When subjects heard the large request without actually having to reject it, their compliance rate increased only slightly (25 percent) relative to the 17 percent who complied after only the small request.

A second, more compelling explanation for the effect is that of *reciprocal concessions*. A close cousin of the reciprocity norm, this refers to the pressure to respond to changes in a bargaining position. When an individual backs down from a large request to a much smaller one, we view that move as a concession that should be matched by our own compliance. Thus, the door-in-the-face technique does not work if the second request is made by a different person (Cialdini et al., 1975). Nor does it work if the first request is *so* extreme that it comes across as an insincere "first offer" (Schwarzwald et al., 1979).

That's Not All, Folks! If the notion of reciprocal concessions is correct, then a subject shouldn't actually have to refuse the initial offer in order for the shift to a smaller request to work. Indeed, another familiar sales strategy manages to use concession without first eliciting refusal. In this strategy, a product is offered at a particular price, but then, before the buyer has a chance to respond, the seller adds, "And that's not all!" At that point, either the original price is reduced or a bonus is offered to sweeten the pot. The seller, of course, intends all along to make the so-called concession.

that's-not-all technique A two-step compliance technique in which the influencer begins with an inflated request, then decreases it's apparent size by offering a discount or bonus.

This ploy, known as the **that's-not-all technique,** seems awfully transparent, right? Surely, no one falls for it, right? Jerry Burger (1986) was not so sure. He predicted that people are more likely to make a purchase when a deal seems to have improved than when the same deal is offered right from the start. To test this hypothesis, Burger set up a booth at a campus fair and sold cupcakes. Some customers who approached the table were told that the cupcakes cost 75 cents each. Others were told that they cost a dollar, but then, before they could respond, the price was reduced to 75 cents. Rationally speaking, Burger's manipulation did not affect the ultimate price, so it should not have affected sales. But it did. When customers were led to believe that the final price was reduced, sales increased from 44 to 73 percent.

At this point, let's step back and look at the various compliance techniques described in this section. All of them are based on a two-step process that involves a shift from a request of one size to another. What differs is whether the small or large request comes first and how the transition between steps is made (see Table 9.2). Moreover, all these strategies work in subtle ways by manipulating the target person's self-image, commitment to the product, feelings of obligation to the seller, or perceptions of the real request. It is even possible to increase compliance by making a chain of requests that use a combination of techniques (Goldman, 1986) or by prefacing the request by asking "How are you feeling?"—a question that typically elicits a favorable first response from strangers (Howard, 1990a). When you consider the various traps, you have to wonder whether it's ever possible to escape.

Assertiveness: When People Say No

Robert Cialdini (1993) opened his book with a confession: "I can admit it freely now. All my life I've been a patsy." As a past victim of compliance traps, Cialdini

Table 9.2 Sequential Request Strategies

Request Shifts	Technique	Description
From Small to Large	Foot in the door	Begin with a very small request; secure agreement; then make a separate larger request.
	Low-balling	Secure agreement with a request, and then increase the size of that request by revealing hidden costs.
From Large to Small	Door in the face	Begin with a very large request that will be rejected; then follow that up with a more modest request.
	That's not all	Begin with a somewhat inflated request; then immediately decrease the apparent size of that request by offering a discount or bonus.

Various compliance techniques are based on a sequence of two related requests. *Click!* The first request sets the trap. *Snap!* The second captures the prey. Research has shown that the four sequential request strategies summarized in this table are all effective.

is not alone. Many people find it difficult to be assertive in interpersonal situations. Faced with an unreasonable request from a friend, spouse, or stranger, they become anxious at the mere thought of putting a foot down and refusing to comply. Indeed, there are times when it is uncomfortable for anyone to say no. However, just as we can maintain our autonomy in the face of conformity pressures, we can also refuse direct requests—even clever ones. The trap may be set, but you don't always have to get caught.

According to Cialdini, the ability to resist the pressures of compliance rests, first and foremost, on vigilance. If a stranger hands you a gift and then launches into a sales pitch, you should recognize the tactic for what it is and not feel indebted by the norm of reciprocity. And if you strike a deal with a salesperson who later reneges on the terms, you should be aware that you're being thrown a low ball. Indeed, that is exactly what happened to one of the authors of this book. After a full Saturday afternoon of careful negotiation at a local car dealer, Mr. and Mrs. Kassin finally came to terms on an acceptable price. Minutes later, the salesman returned with the news that the manager would not approve the deal. The cost of an air conditioner, which was to be included, would now have to be added on. Familiar with the research, Saul turned to his wife and exclaimed, "Carol, it's a trick; they're low-balling us!" Realizing what had happened, Carol was furious. She went straight to the manager and made such a scene in front of other customers that he backed down and honored the original deal.

What happened in this instance? Why did recognizing the attempted manipulation produce such anger and resistance? As this story illustrates, compliance techniques work smoothly only if they are hidden from view. The problem is not only that they are attempts to influence us but that they are based on deception.

Compliance techniques are powerful only if they are not transparent.

"Bernie's problem is his technique draws attention to itself."

Flattery, gifts, and other ploys often elicit compliance, but not if they are perceived as insincere (Jones, 1964) and not if the target has a high level of reciprocity wariness (Eisenberger et al., 1987). Likewise, the sequential request traps are powerful to the extent that they are subtle and cannot be seen for what they are (Schwarzwald et al., 1979). People don't like to be deceived. In fact, just feeling manipulated leads us to react with anger, psychological reactance, and stubborn noncompliance . . . unless the request is a command and the requester is a figure of authority.

OBEDIENCE

Allen Funt, the creator and producer of the original TV program *Candid Camera,* spends as much time observing human behavior in the real world as most psychologists do. When asked what he has learned from his people-watching, he replied, "The worst thing, and I see it over and over, is how easily people can be led by any kind of authority figure, or even the most minimal signs of authority." He went on to cite the time he put up a road sign that read "Delaware Closed Today." The reaction? "Motorists didn't question it. Instead they asked, 'Is Jersey open?'" (Zimbardo, 1985, p. 47).

Funt is right about the way people react to authority. Taught from birth that it's important to respect legitimate forms of leadership, people think twice before defying parents, teachers, employers, coaches, and government officials. In fact, children seem to understand at a young age that certain authority figures have power in some domains but not others (Laupa & Turiel, 1993). The problem is, the mere symbols of authority—titles, uniforms, badges, or the trappings of success, even without the necessary credentials—can sometimes turn ordinary people into docile servants. Leonard Bickman (1974) demonstrated this phenomenon in a series of studies in which a male research assistant stopped passers-by on the streets of Brooklyn and ordered them to do something unusual. Sometimes, he pointed to a paper bag on the ground and said, "Pick up this bag for me!" At other times, he pointed to an individual standing beside a parked car and said, "This fellow is over-parked at the meter but doesn't have any change. Give him a dime!" Would anyone really take this guy seriously? When he was dressed in street clothes, only a third of the subjects followed his orders. But when he wore a security guard's uniform, nearly nine out of every ten subjects obeyed! Even when the uniformed assistant turned the corner and walked away after issuing his com-

Taken to extreme, blind obedience can have devastating results. In World War II, Nazi officials killed millions, many said, "because I was just following orders."

mand, the vast majority of passers-by followed his orders. Clearly, uniforms signify the power of authority (Bushman, 1984, 1988). This must be what Allen Funt had in mind. Unfortunately, blind **obedience** is not always that funny.

obedience Behavior change produced by the commands of authority.

If people are willing to take inappropriate orders from a total stranger, how far will they go when it really matters? The pages of history lead us to believe the worst. In World War II, Nazi soldiers and officials participated in the slaughter of millions of Jews, as well as Poles, Russians, gypsies, and homosexuals. Yet, when they were tried for these crimes, the Nazi defense was always the same: "I was just following orders."

Surely, you must be thinking, those events were highly unusual. They say more about the Nazis as individuals—their prejudices, frustrations, and sick minds—than they do about obedience to authority. But two lines of evidence suggest otherwise. First, interviews with Nazi war criminals have failed to uncover signs of an inherently evil character. Indeed, many otherwise reputable physicians participated in the war crimes (Lifton, 1986). Adolf Eichmann, one of the most notorious of the Nazi war criminals, was described by his interrogator as "utterly ordinary" (Arendt, 1963; Von Lang & Sibyll, 1983). Second, the monstrous events of World War II do not stand alone in modern history. Today, crimes of obedience are committed routinely in the service of ruthless totalitarian regimes around the world (Kelman & Hamilton, 1989). On one extraordinary occasion, such obedience was carried to its limit. In 1978, 900 members of the People's Temple cult obeyed an order from the Reverend Jim Jones to kill themselves.

Milgram's Research: Forces of Destructive Obedience

During the time that Eichmann was being tried for his Nazi war crimes, Stanley Milgram (1963) began a dramatic series of experiments that culminated in his 1974 book, *Obedience to Authority.* For many years, the ethics of this research has been the focus of much debate. Those who say it was not ethical point to the potential psychological harm to which the subjects were exposed. In contrast, those who believe that Milgram's research met appropriate ethical standards emphasize the contribution it makes to our understanding of an important social problem. They conclude that, on balance, the extreme danger that destructive obedience poses for all humankind justified Milgram's unorthodox methods. Consider both sides of the debate, which were summarized in Chapter 1, and make your own judgment. Now, however, take a more personal look. Imagine yourself as one of the approximately 1,000 subjects who found themselves in the following situation.

The experience begins when you arrive at a Yale University laboratory and meet two men. One is the experimenter, a stern young man dressed in a gray lab coat and carrying a clipboard. The other is a middle-aged gentleman named Mr. Wallace, an accountant who is slightly overweight and average in appearance. You exchange introductions, and then the experimenter explains that you and your co-subject will take part in a study on the effects of punishment on learning. After lots have been drawn, it is determined that you will serve as the teacher and that Mr. Wallace will be the learner. So far so good.

Soon, however, the situation takes on a more ominous tone. You find out that your job is to test the learner's memory and administer electric shocks of increasing intensity whenever he makes a mistake. You are then escorted into another room where the experimenter straps Mr. Wallace into a chair, rolls up his sleeves, attaches electrodes to his arms, and applies "electrode paste" to prevent blisters and burns. As if that isn't bad enough, you overhear Mr. Wallace telling the experimenter that he has a heart problem. The experimenter responds by conceding that the shocks will be painful but reassures Mr. Wallace that they will not cause "permanent tissue damage." In the meantime, you can personally vouch for the painfulness of the shocks, because the experimenter stings you with one that is supposed to be mild. From there, the experimenter takes you back to the main room, where you are seated in front of a "shock generator," a machine with thirty switches that range from 15 volts, labeled "slight shock," to 450 volts, labeled "XXX."

Your role in this experiment is straightforward. First you read a list of word pairs to Mr. Wallace through a microphone. Then you test his memory with a series of multiple-choice questions. The learner answers each question by pressing one of four switches that light up signals on the shock generator. If his answer is correct, you move on to the next question. If it is incorrect, you announce the correct answer and shock him. When you press the appropriate shock switch, a red light flashes above it, relay switches click inside the machine, and you hear a

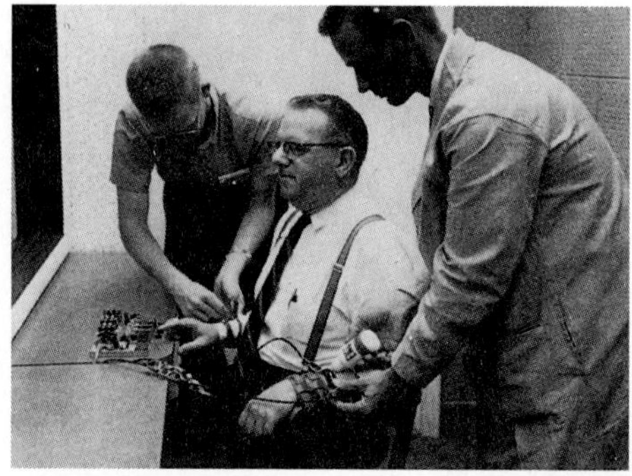

The shock generator used in Milgram's research is similar to the machine used in studies of aggression described in Chapter 8. The subjects in Milgram's study were instructed to administer shocks of increasing intensity to Mr. Wallace, the confederate being strapped into his chair.

loud buzzing sound go off in the learner's room. After each wrong answer, you are told, the intensity of the shock should be increased by 15 volts.

You aren't aware, of course, that the experiment is rigged and that Mr. Wallace—who is actually a confederate—is never really shocked. As far as you know, he gets zapped each time you press one of the switches. As the session proceeds, the learner makes more and more errors, leading you to work your way up the shock scale. As you reach 75, 90, and 105 volts, you hear the learner grunt in pain. At 120 volts, he begins to shout. If you're still in it at 150 volts, you hear the learner cry out, "Experimenter! That's all. Get me out of here. My heart's starting to bother me now. I refuse to go on!" Screams of agony and protest continue. At 300 volts, he says he absolutely refuses to continue. By the time you surpass 330 volts, the learner falls silent and fails to respond—not to be heard from again. Table 9.3 lists his responses in grim detail.

As subjects administered progressively more intense shocks, they heard the learner moan, groan, protest, and complain. All subjects heard the same programmed set of responses. Eventually, the learner fell silent and ceased to respond. (Milgram, 1974.)

Table 9.3 The Learner's Protests in the Milgram Experiment

75 volts	Ugh!
90 volts	Ugh!
105 volts	Ugh! *(louder)*
120 volts	Ugh! Hey this really hurts.
135 volts	Ugh!!
150 volts	Ugh!!! Experimenter! That's all. Get me out of here. I told you I had heart trouble. My heart's starting to bother me now. Get me out of here, please. My heart's starting to bother me. I refuse to go on. Let me out.
165 volts	Ugh! Let me out! *(shouting)*
180 volts	Ugh! I can't stand the pain. Let me out of here! *(shouting)*
195 volts	Ugh! Let me out of here. Let me out of here. My heart's bothering me. Let me out of here! You have no right to keep me here! Let me out! Let me out of here! Let me out! Let me out of here! My heart's bothering me. Let me out! Let me out!
210 volts	Ugh!! Experimenter! Get me out of here. I've had enough. I won't be in the experiment any more.
225 volts	Ugh!
240 volts	Ugh!
255 volts	Ugh! Get me out of here.
270 volts	*(Agonized scream.)* Let me out of here. Let me out of here. Let me out of here. Let me out. Do you hear? Let me out of here.
285 volts	*(Agonized scream.)*
300 volts	*(Agonized scream.)* I absolutely refuse to answer any more. Get me out of here. You can't hold me here. Get me out. Get me out of here.
315 volts	*(Intensely agonized scream.)* I told you I refuse to answer. I'm no longer part of this experiment.
330 volts	*(Intense and prolonged agonized scream.)* Let me out of here. Let me out of here. My heart's bothering me. Let me out, I tell you. *(Hysterically)* Let me out of here. Let me out of here. You have no right to hold me here. Let me out! Let me out! Let me out! Let me out of here! Let me out! Let me out!

Somewhere along the line, you probably turn to the experimenter for guidance. What should I do? Don't you think I should stop? Shouldn't we at least check on him? You might even confront the experimenter head-on and refuse to continue. Yet in answer to your inquiries, the experimenter—firm in his tone and seemingly unaffected by the learner's distress—prods you along as follows:

- Please continue (or please go on).
- The experiment requires that you continue.
- It is absolutely essential that you continue.
- You have no other choice, you *must* go on.

What do you do? In a situation that begins to feel more and more like a bad dream, do you follow your conscience or obey the experimenter?

Milgram described this procedure to psychiatrists, college students, and middle-class adults, and he asked them to predict how they would behave. On average, these groups estimated that they would call it quits at the 135-volt level. Not a single person thought he or she would go all the way to 450 volts. When asked to predict the percentage of *other* people who would deliver the maximum shock, those interviewed gave similar estimates. The psychiatrists estimated that only one out of a thousand subjects would exhibit that kind of extreme obedience. They were wrong. In Milgram's initial study involving forty men from the surrounding New Haven community, subjects exhibited an alarming degree of obedience, administering an average of twenty-seven out of thirty possible shocks. In fact, twenty-six of the forty subjects—*65 percent*—delivered the ultimate punishment of 450 volts. The complete results are shown in Table 9.4.

The Obedient Subject At first glance, it is easy to view these results as a lesson in the psychology of cruelty and conclude that Milgram's subjects were seriously disturbed (Bierbrauer, 1979; Safer, 1980). But research does not support such a simple explanation. To begin with, subjects in a control group who were not prodded along by an experimenter refused to continue early in the shock sequence. Moreover, Milgram found that virtually all experimental subjects, including those who administered severe shocks, were tormented by the experience. Many of them pleaded with the experimenter to let them stop. When he refused, they went on. But in the process, they trembled, stuttered, groaned, perspired, bit their lips, and dug their fingernails into their flesh. Some subjects

In Milgram's original experiment, subjects exhibited a troubling inclination to obey blindly. This table shows the number and percentage of male subjects who delivered shocks of varying maximum intensity in response to the experimenter's commands. (Milgram, 1974.)

Table 9.4 Milgram's Baseline Results

	Subjects Who Stopped at This Level	
Shock Level (Volts)	Number	Percent
300	5	12.5
315	4	10.0
330	2	5.0
345	1	2.5
360	1	2.5
375–435	1	2.5
450	26	65.0

burst into fits of nervous laughter. On one occasion, said Milgram, "we observed a [subject's] seizure so violently convulsive that it was necessary to call a halt to the experiment" (1963, p. 375).

Was Milgram's 65 percent baseline level of obedience attributable to his unique sample of male subjects? Not at all. Forty women who participated in a later study exhibited precisely the same level of obedience: 65 percent threw the 450-volt switch. Before you jump to the conclusion that something was amiss in New Haven, consider the fact that Milgram's basic finding has been obtained in several different countries and with children as well as college students and older adults (Shanab & Yahya, 1977, 1978). Obedience in the Milgram situation is so universal that it led one author to ask, "Are we all Nazis?" (Askenasy, 1978).

The answer, of course, is no. An individual's character can make a difference, and some people, depending on the situation, are clearly more obedient than others (Blass, 1991). In the aftermath of World War II, a group of social scientists, searching for the root causes of prejudice, sought to identify individuals with an *authoritarian personality* and developed a questionnaire known as the F-Scale to measure it (Adorno et al., 1950; Stone et al., 1993). What they found is that people who get high scores on the F-Scale (F stands for "Fascist") are rigid, dogmatic, sexually repressed, ethnocentric, intolerant of dissent, and punitive. They are submissive toward figures of authority but aggressive toward subordinates. Indeed, subjects with high F scores are also more willing than low scorers to administer high-intensity shocks in Milgram's obedience situation (Elms & Milgram, 1966).

Although personality characteristics may make a person vulnerable or resistant to destructive obedience, what seems to matter most is the situation in which people find themselves. By carefully varying particular aspects of his basic scenario, as shown in Figure 9.6, Milgram was able to identify factors that increase

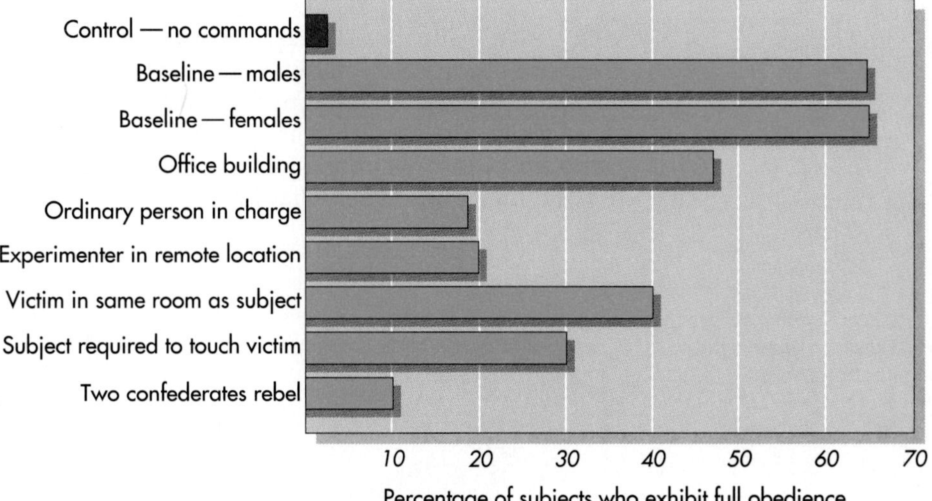

Figure 9.6 Factors That Influence Obedience. Milgram varied many factors in his research program. Without commands from an experimenter, fewer than 3 percent of the subjects exhibited full obedience. Yet in the standard baseline condition, 65 percent of male and female subjects followed the orders. To identify factors that might reduce this level, Milgram varied the location of the experiment, the status of the authority, the subject's proximity to the victim, and the presence of confederates who rebel. The effects of these variations are illustrated here. (Milgram, 1974.)

and decrease the 65 percent baseline rate of obedience. Three factors in particular are important: the authority figure, the proximity of the victim, and the experimental procedure (Miller, 1986).

The Authority What is most remarkable about Milgram's findings is that a lab-coated experimenter is *not* a powerful figure of authority. Unlike a military superior or employer, the psychology experimenter in Milgram's research could not ultimately enforce his commands. Still, his physical presence and his apparent legitimacy played major roles in drawing obedience. When Milgram diminished the experimenter's status by moving his lab from the distinguished surroundings of Yale University to a rundown urban office building in nearby Bridgeport, Connecticut, the rate of total obedience dropped to 48 percent. When the experimenter was replaced with an ordinary person, who was supposedly another subject, there was a dramatic reduction to 20 percent. Similarly, Milgram found that when the experimenter was in charge but issued his commands by telephone, only 21 percent of the subjects fully obeyed. (In fact, when the experimenter was not watching, many subjects feigned obedience by pressing the 15-volt switch.) One conclusion, then, is clear. At least in the Milgram setting, destructive obedience requires the physical presence of an authority figure.

If an experimenter can exert such control over research subjects, imagine the control wielded by truly powerful authority figures—present or not. An intriguing field study examined the extent to which hospital nurses would obey unreasonable orders from a doctor (Hofling et al., 1966). Using a fictitious name, a male physician called several female nurses on the phone and told them to administer a drug to a specific patient. His order violated hospital regulations: the drug was uncommon, the dosage was too large, and the effects could have been harmful. Yet out of the twenty-two nurses contacted, twenty-one of them had to be stopped as they prepared to obey the doctor's orders.

The Victim Situational characteristics of the victim are also important in destructive obedience. Milgram noted that Nazi war criminal Adolf Eichmann felt sick when he toured concentration camps but only had to shuffle papers from behind a desk to play his part in the Holocaust. Similarly, the B-29 pilot who dropped the atom bomb on Hiroshima in World War II said of his mission, "I had no thoughts, except what I'm supposed to do" (Miller, 1986, p. 228). These

People are often obedient in the presence of powerful figures of authority.

"Nice touch, Jenkins. I like a man who salutes."

events suggest that because Milgram's subjects were physically separated from the learner, they were able to distance themselves emotionally from the consequences of their actions.

To examine the effects of a victim's proximity on destructive obedience, the learner in one of Milgram's studies was seated in the same room as the subject. Under these conditions, only 40 percent fully obeyed. When subjects were required to physically grasp the victim's hand and force it onto a metal shock plate, full obedience dropped to 30 percent. These findings represent significant reductions from the 65 percent baseline. Still, three out of ten subjects were willing to use brute force in the name of obedience.

The Procedure Finally, there is the situation created by Milgram. A close look at the dilemma his subjects experienced reveals two particularly important aspects of the experimental procedure. First, subjects were led to feel relieved of any personal sense of *responsibility* for the victim's welfare. The experimenter said up front that he was accountable. So, when subjects are led to believe that *they* are responsible, their level of obedience drops considerably (Tilker, 1970). The ramifications of this finding are immense. In military and other organizations, individuals often occupy positions in the middle of a hierarchical chain of command. Eichmann was a middle-level bureaucrat who received orders from Hitler and transmitted them to others for implementation. Caught between individuals who make policy and those who carry it out, how personally responsible do those in the middle feel for their role in the chain of events? Wesley Kilham and Leon Mann (1974) examined this issue in an obedience study that cast subjects into one of two roles: the transmitter (who took orders from the experimenter and passed them on) and the executant (who actually delivered the shocks). As predicted, transmitters were more obedient (54 percent) than executants (28 percent).

The second feature of Milgram's scenario that promoted obedience is gradual escalation. Subjects began the session by delivering mild shocks and then, only gradually, escalated to voltage levels of high intensity. After all, what's another 15 volts compared to the current level? By the time subjects realized the frightening implications of what they're doing, it had become more difficult for them to escape (Gilbert, 1981). This sequence is like the foot-in-the-door technique. In Milgram's words, people become "integrated into a situation that carries its own momentum. The subject's problem . . . is how to become disengaged from a situation which is moving in an altogether ugly direction" (1965, p. 73). We should point out that obedience by momentum is not restricted to Milgram's research paradigm. As reported by Amnesty International, at least ninety countries today torture political dissidents. Those who are recruited for the dirty work are trained, in part, through an escalating series of commitments (Haritos-Fatouros, 1988).

Obedience to authority is a social issue of such importance that one wonders whether Milgram's results would be repeated today in a different but analogous situation. The answer is yes. In a series of experiments, Dutch social psychologists Wim Meeus and Quinten Raaijmakers (1986) constructed a moral dilemma much like Milgram's. Rather than commanding subjects to inflict physical pain, however, they engaged subjects in behavior intended to cause psychological harm. When subjects arrived at a university laboratory, they met a man—actually a confederate—who was there to take a test as part of a job interview. If the applicant passed the test, he would get the job; if he failed, he would not. Supposedly without the applicant's knowledge, the experimenter told subjects that he was interested in the ability to work under stress. The subject's task was to read various test questions to the applicant, over a microphone from a nearby room, and to programmatically harass the applicant by making an escalating series of negative remarks. As the applicant worked on the test, then, subjects made statements such as "If you continue like this, you will fail the test," and "This job is much too difficult for you. You are more suited for lower functions."

As the events proceeded, the applicant protested. He pleaded with the subject to stop making him nervous, then angrily refused to tolerate the abuse, eventually falling into a state of despair. Showing visible signs of tension, the applicant faltered in his test performance and failed to get the job. As in Milgram's research, the obedience question was straightforward: How many subjects would obey the experimenter's orders through the entire set of fifteen stress remarks, despite the apparent harm caused to a real-life applicant? In a control group that lacked a prodding experimenter, not a single subject persisted. But when the experimenter ordered subjects to go on, 92 percent of all subjects, male and female, exhibited complete obedience—even though they saw the task as unfair and distasteful. This result led the investigators to conclude that obedience is a compelling social phenomenon brought about by the docile manner in which people relate to figures of authority—"even in the Netherlands in the 1980's."

Defiance: When People Rebel

It is easy to despair in light of the impressive array of forces that compel people toward blind obedience. But there's good news. Just as social influence processes can breed a subservience to authority, they can also breed defiance and rebellion. As in the following study, the actions of a group are often much harder to control than the behavior of a single individual.

Pretending to be part of a marketing research firm, William Gamson and his colleagues (1982) recruited people to participate in a supposed discussion of "community standards." Scheduled in groups of nine, subjects were told that their discussions would be videotaped for a large oil company that was suing the manager of a local service station who had spoken out against higher gas prices. After receiving a summary of the case, most subjects sided with the station manager. But there was a hitch. The oil company wanted evidence to win its case, said the experimenter—posing as the discussion coordinator. He told each of the group members to get in front of the camera and express the company's viewpoint. Then he told them to sign an affidavit giving the company permission to edit the tapes for use in court.

You can see how the obedience scenario was supposed to unfold. Actually, only one of thirty-three groups even came close to following the script. In all the others, people became incensed by the coordinator's behavior and refused to continue. Some groups were so outraged that they planned to take action. One group even threatened to blow the whistle on the firm by calling local newspapers. Faced with one emotionally charged mutiny after another, the researchers had to discontinue the experiment.

Why did this study produce such active, often passionate revolt when Milgram's had revealed such utterly passive obedience? Could it reflect a difference between the 1960s, when Milgram's studies were conducted, and the 1980s? Although many college students believe that people would conform less today than in the past, there is no relationship between the year a study was conducted and the level of obedience it produced (Blass & Krackow, 1991). So what accounts for the contrasting results? One key difference is that Milgram's subjects were

People are more likely to protest the command of authority in groups than on their own. In August of 1991, crowds gathered in the streets of Moscow to resist an attempted coup by hard-line communists. Despite a history of passive obedience, the Russians shown in this picture jeered the troops and blocked their tanks. Finding safety and encouragement in numbers, their efforts prevailed.

alone, and Gamson's were in groups. As historian Michael Walzer notes, "Disobedience, when it is not criminally but morally, religiously, or politically motivated, is always a *collective* act" (cited in R. Brown, 1986, p. 17).

The earlier discussion of conformity indicated that the mere presence of one ally in an otherwise unanimous majority gives individuals the courage to dissent. Perhaps the same holds true for obedience. Notably, Milgram never had more than one subject present in the same session. But in one experiment, he did use two confederates who posed as co-teachers along with the real subject. In these sessions, one confederate refused to continue at 150 volts and the second at 210 volts. These disobedient models had a profound influence on subjects' willingness to defy the experimenter; in their presence only 10 percent of subjects delivered the maximum level of shock (see Figure 9.6).

We should add that groups are not a perfect safeguard against destructive obedience. Groups often trigger aggression, as we'll see in Chapter 11. For example, the followers of Jim Jones were together when they collectively followed his command to die. And lynch mobs are just that—groups, not individuals. Clearly, there is power in sheer numbers. That power can be destructive, or it can be used for constructive purposes. The presence and support of others often provides the extra ounce of courage that people need to resist orders they find offensive.

THE CONTINUUM OF SOCIAL INFLUENCE

As we have seen, social influence on behavior ranges from the implicit pressure of group norms, to the traps set by direct requests, to the powerful commands of authority. In each case, people choose whether to react with conformity or independence, compliance or assertiveness, obedience or defiance. At this point, let's step back and consider two important questions. First, although different kinds of pressure influence us for different reasons, is it possible to predict all the effects with a single, overarching principle? Second, what do theory and research on social influence say about human nature?

Social Impact Theory

social impact theory The theory that social influence depends on the strength, immediacy, and number of source persons relative to target persons.

In 1981, Bibb Latané proposed that a common bond among the different processes leads people toward or away from social influence. Specifically, Latané proposed **social impact theory,** which states that social influence of any kind (the total impact of others on a target person) is a function of their strength, immediacy, and number. According to Latané, social forces act on individuals in the same way that physical forces act on an object. Consider, for example, how overhead lights illuminate a surface. The total amount of light cast on a surface depends on the strength of the bulbs, their distance from the surface, and their number. As illustrated in the left portion of Figure 9.7, the same factors apply to social impact as well.

The *strength* of a source is determined by its status, ability, or relationship to a target. The stronger the source, the greater is the influence. When people view the other members of a group as competent, they are more likely to conform in their judgments. When it comes to compliance, sources enhance their strength by making targets feel obligated to reciprocate a small favor. And to elicit obedience, authority figures gain strength by wearing uniforms or flaunting their prestigious affiliations. *Immediacy* refers to a source's proximity in time and space to the target. The closer the source, the greater its impact. Milgram's research offers the best example. Levels of obedience were higher when the experimenter issued commands in person rather than from a remote location. When the victim suffered in close proximity to the subject, the victim acted as a contrary source of influence, and obedience levels dropped. Finally, the theory predicts that as the *number* of sources increases, so does their influence—at least up to a point. You may recall that as Asch (1956) increased the number of confederates from one to four, conformity rose. Further increases, however, had only a negligible additional effect.

According to social impact theory, an army officer will exert influence to the extent that he is strong (in a position of power), immediate (physically close), and numerous (backed by others in the institution) relative to his trainees.

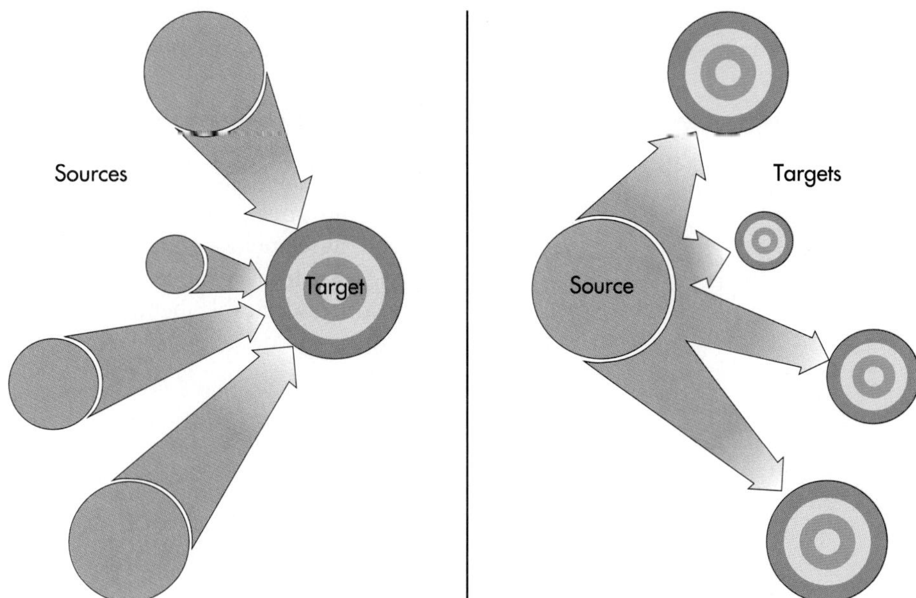

Figure 9.7 **Social Impact: Source Factors and Target Factors.** According to social impact theory, the total influence of other people on a target individual depends on three factors related to the source persons: their strength (size of source circles), immediacy (distance to the target), and number (number of source circles). Similarly, the total influence is diffused, or reduced, by the strength (size of target circles), immediacy (distance from source circle), and number of target persons. (Latané, 1981.)

Social impact theory also predicts that people sometimes resist social pressure. According to Latané, this resistance is most likely to occur when social impact is *divided* among many strong and distant *targets*, also as seen in the right part of Figure 9.7. There should be less impact on a target who is strong and far from the source than on one who is weak and close to the source; and there should be less impact on a target person who is accompanied by other targets than on one who stands alone. Thus, we have seen that conformity is reduced by the presence of an ally and that levels of obedience drop when subjects are in the presence of rebellious peers.

Social impact theory has been challenged and defended on various grounds (Jackson, 1986; Mullen, 1985; Sedikides & Jackson, 1990). On the one hand, it does not enable us to explain the processes that give rise to social influence or answer *why* questions. On the other hand, social impact theory is useful for predicting social influence—to determine *when* it will occur. Whether the topic is conformity, compliance, or obedience, social impact theory sets the stage for further research in years to come.

Perspectives on Human Nature

From the material presented in this chapter, what general conclusions might you draw about human nature? Granted, social influence is more likely to occur in some situations than in others. But are people generally malleable or unyielding? Is there a tilt toward accepting influence or toward putting up resistance?

There is no single, universal answer. As we saw earlier, some cultures value autonomy and independence, while others emphasize conformity to one's group. Even within a given culture, values may change over time. To demonstrate the point, ask yourself: If you were a parent, what traits would you like your child to develop? When this question was put to American mothers in 1924, they selected "obedience" and "loyalty," key characteristics of conformity. Yet when mothers were asked the same question fifty-four years later, they cited "independence" and "tolerance of others," key characteristics of autonomy. Similar trends were found in surveys conducted in West Germany, Italy, England, and Japan (Remley, 1988).

Is it possible that today's children—tomorrow's adults—will exhibit greater resistance to the various forms of social influence? If so, what effects will this trend have on society as a whole? Cast in a positive light, conformity, compliance, and obedience are good and necessary human responses. They promote group solidarity and agreement—qualities that keep groups from being torn apart by dissension. Cast in a negative light, a lack of independence, assertiveness, and defiance are undesirable behaviors that lend themselves to narrow-mindedness, cowardice, and destructive obedience—often with terrible costs. For each of us, and for society, the trick is to strike a balance.

REVIEW

- Conformity, compliance, and obedience are three kinds of social influence, varying in the degree of pressure brought to bear on an individual.

CONFORMITY

- Conformity is the tendency for people to change their behavior to be consistent with group norms.

The Early Classics

- Two classic experiments illustrate contrasting types of conformity.
- Sherif presented groups of subjects with an ambiguous task and found that their judgments gradually converged.
- Using a simpler line-judgment task, Asch had confederates make incorrect responses and found that subjects went along a third of the time.

Why Do People Conform?

- Sherif found that people exhibit private conformity, using others for information in an ambiguous situation.
- Asch's studies indicated that people conform in their public behavior to avoid appearing deviant.

Majority Influence

- As the size of an incorrect unanimous majority increases, so does conformity—up to a point.
- People conform to perceived social norms when these norms are brought to mind—particularly when they are injunctive rather than descriptive.
- The presence of one dissenter reduces conformity, even when he or she disagrees with the subject and lacks competence at the task.
- Young adolescents are particularly vulnerable to peer pressure.
- Women conform more than men on "masculine" tasks and in face-to-face settings, but not on gender-neutral tasks or in private settings.
- Conformity rates are higher in cultures that value collectivism than in those that value individualism.

Minority Influence

- Sometimes minorities resist pressures to conform and are able to influence majorities.
- In general, minority influence is greater when the source is an ingroup member.
- According to Moscovici, minorities exert influence by taking a consistent and unwavering position.
- Hollander claims that to exert influence, a person should first conform to the mainstream, and then dissent.
- Majority influence is greater on direct and public measures of conformity but minorities have an impact on private, indirect measures of conformity.
- People gain courage to resist conformity pressures after watching others do the same.

COMPLIANCE

- A common form of social influence occurs when we respond to direct requests.

The Discourse of Making Requests

- People are more likely to comply when taken by surprise and when the request *sounds* reasonable.

The Norm of Reciprocity

- We often comply when we feel indebted to a requester who has done us a favor.
- People differ in whether they use reciprocity for personal gain and in whether they are wary of falling prey to this strategy.

Setting Traps: Sequential Request Strategies

- Four compliance techniques are based on a two-step request: the first step sets a trap, and the second elicits compliance.
- Using the foot-in-the-door technique, a person prefaces a "real" request by getting someone to comply with a smaller request.
- In low-balling, one person gets another to agree to a request but then increases the size of that request by revealing hidden costs. Despite the increase, people often follow through on their agreement.
- With the door-in-the-face technique, the real request is preceded by a large one that is rejected. People then comply with the second request because it is seen as a concession to be reciprocated.
- The that's-not-all technique begins with a large request. Then the apparent size of the request is reduced by the offer of a discount or bonus.

Assertiveness: When People Say No

- Many people find it hard to be assertive. Doing so requires that we be vigilant and recognize the traps.

OBEDIENCE

- When the request is a command, and the requester is a figure of authority, the resulting influence is called obedience.

Milgram's Research: Forces of Destructive Obedience

- In Milgram's research, subjects were ordered by an experimenter to deliver increasingly painful shocks to a confederate.
- Sixty-five percent of the subjects obeyed completely but felt tormented by the experience.
- Obedience levels are influenced by various situational factors, including subjects' physical proximity to both the authority figure and the victim.
- Two aspects of Milgram's procedure also contributed to the high levels of obedience: (1) subjects did not feel personally responsible, and (2) the orders escalated gradually.
- In recent studies analogous to Milgram's, subjects exhibited high rates of obedience when told to inflict psychological harm on another person.

Defiance: When People Rebel

- Just as processes of social influence breed obedience, they can also support acts of defiance, as groups are more difficult to control than individuals.

THE CONTINUUM OF SOCIAL INFLUENCE

Social Impact Theory

- Social impact theory predicts that social influence depends on the strength, immediacy, and number of source persons who exert pressure relative to target persons who absorb that pressure.

Perspectives on Human Nature

- There is no single answer to the question of whether people are conformists or nonconformists.
- There are cross-cultural differences in social influence, and values change over time even within specific cultures.

KEY TERMS

conformity, p. 333
informational influence, p. 336
normative influence, p. 336
private conformity, p. 336
public conformity, p. 336
individualism, p. 342
collectivism, p. 342
idiosyncrasy credits, p. 345
compliance, p. 346
foot-in-the-door technique, p. 349
low-balling, p. 350
door-in-the-face technique, p. 351
that's-not-all technique, p. 352
obedience, p. 355
social impact theory, p. 364

NO on 104
Clinton Gore
JOBS NOT BOMBS
Reality
FIGHT AIDS NOT ITS VICTIMS
IF YOU THINK THE SYSTEM IS WORKING ASK SOMEONE WHO ISN'T
ARE YOU WILLING TO DIE FOR EXXON?
BOXER
United States Senate
PEACE ON EARTH BEGINS AT HOME
TRY IGNORANCE
Get That Warmonger Out Of the White House
FIGHT RACISM
NO NUKES
NATIONAL HEALTH CARE NOW
FREE THE BEACHES
Mike Dukakis
POVERTY IS VIOLENCE
BE ALL YOU CAN BE. WORK FOR PEACE.
Stop Diablo Canyon
SAVE THE RUSSIAN RIVER
Rooting for the future.
K-LITE 100 FM
GERTIE'S CRABS
TOO HIP
HANDGUN CONTROL
KCET
SI NO VOTAS NO TE QUEJES
BUILD HOMES NOT BOMBS

Chapter 10

Attitudes

OUTLINE

PREVIEW

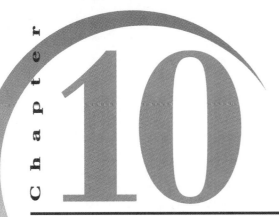

This chapter examines social influences on attitudes. We define *attitudes* and discuss how they are measured and when they are related to behavior. Then we consider two methods of changing attitudes. First, we look at source, message, and audience factors that elicit persuasion through the media of *communication*. Second, we consider theories and research showing that people often change their attitudes as a consequence of their own *actions*.

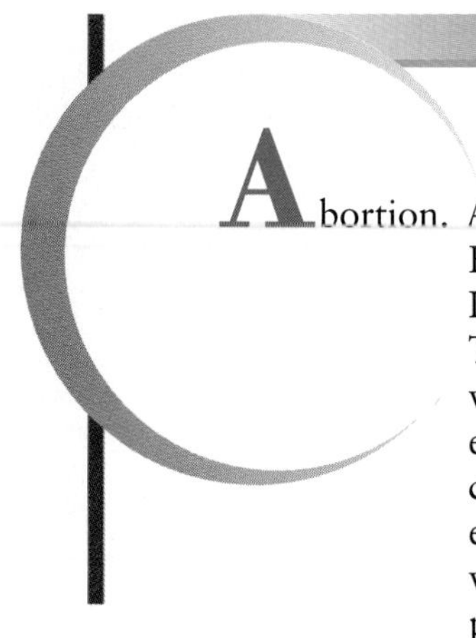

Abortion. Affirmative action. Bill Clinton. Condoms in high schools. The death penalty. Family values. Gays in the military. Newt Gingrich. Gun control. Health care. Immigration. Rush Limbaugh. Multiculturalism. School prayer. Social Security. Taxes. Welfare reform. Anyone who follows politics in the United States, or anywhere else for that matter, knows how passionately people feel about their leaders and the issues they represent. Attitudes and the mechanisms of attitude change, or persuasion, are a vital part of human social life. This chapter addresses three sets of questions: (1) What is an attitude, how can it be measured, and what is its link to behavior? (2) What kinds of persuasive communications lead people to change their attitudes? (3) Why do we often change our attitudes as a result of our own actions?

THE STUDY OF ATTITUDES

Do you favor or oppose a ban on assault weapons? Should smoking be banned in public places? Would you rather listen to rock music or jazz, drink Coke or Pepsi, work on an IBM computer or a Mac? As these questions suggest, each of us has positive and negative reactions to various persons, objects, and ideas. These reactions are called **attitudes.** If you think about the chapters you've read, you'll realize just how pervasive attitudes are. For example, self-esteem is an attitude that each of us has about ourselves, attraction is a positive attitude toward another person, and prejudice is a negative attitude about certain groups.

attitude A positive or negative reaction to a person, object, or idea.

In *The Psychology of Attitudes,* Alice Eagly and Shelly Chaiken (1993) noted that there are two schools of thought on how the term *attitude* should be defined. One is that an attitude is a combination of affective, behavioral, and cognitive reactions to an object (Breckler, 1984; Rajecki, 1982). According to this *tricomponent* approach, an attitude is (1) a positive or negative, or mixed, *affective* reaction consisting of our feelings about an object; (2) a *behavioral* predisposition, or tendency to act in a certain manner toward an object; and (3) a *cognitive* reaction, as our evaluation of an object is based on relevant beliefs, images, and memories (Judd et al., 1991).

Thoughts and feelings are not always related to each other, nor do they necessarily guide our behavior. Due to this lack of consistency, many social psychologists prefer to keep the three components separate and use the word *attitude* in primarily affective terms (Petty & Cacioppo, 1986; Pratkanis, 1989; Zanna & Rempel, 1988). In this *single-component* definition, an attitude is a positive or negative evaluation of an object, expressed at some level of intensity—nothing more, nothing less. *Like, dislike, love, hate, admire,* and *detest* are the kinds of words people use to describe their attitudes.

How Attitudes Are Measured

In 1928, Louis Thurstone published an article entitled "Attitudes Can Be Measured." What Thurstone failed to anticipate, however, is that measurement is a

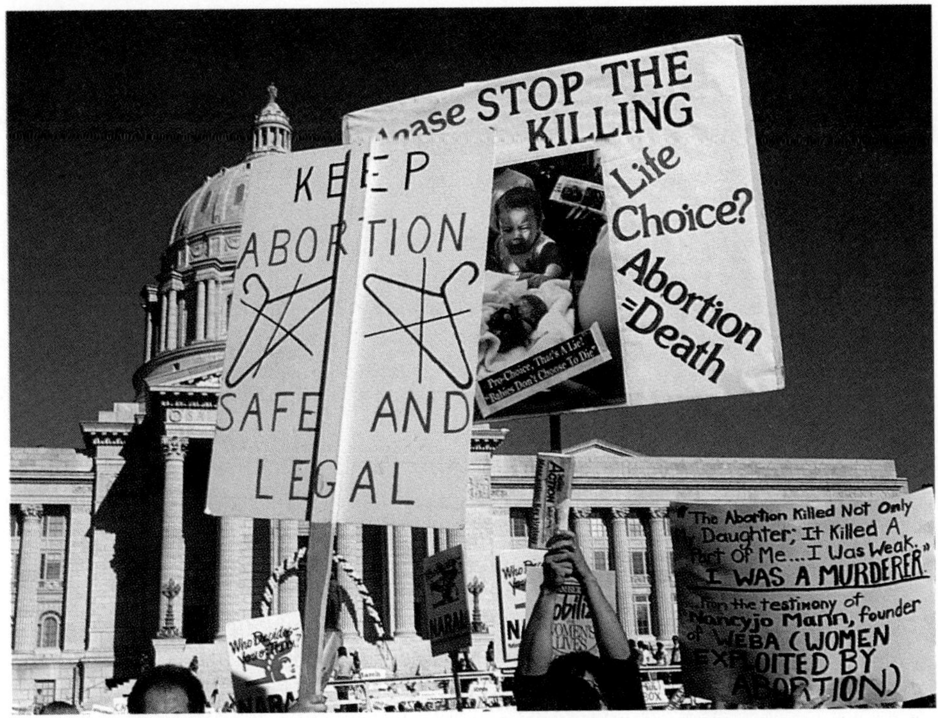

As seen in this confrontation between pro-choice and anti-abortion forces, people are often very passionate about their attitudes.

tricky business. Indeed, several years ago, one review of the research uncovered more than five hundred different methods of determining an individual's attitude (Fishbein & Ajzen, 1972).

Self-Report Measures The easiest way to assess a person's attitude about something is to ask. The method of *self-report* is direct and straightforward. But attitudes are sometimes too complex to be measured by a single question. As recognized by public opinion pollsters, one problem is that responses to a single question can be heavily influenced by wording, context, and other extraneous factors. For example, six hundred Americans were recently asked if the government was spending too much money on "assistance to the poor," and only 23 percent agreed. Yet when the same question was asked about "welfare," the agreement rate rose to 53 percent (*Time,* 1994). In another survey, respondents who were asked if "People should have the freedom to express their opinions publicly" were more likely to say yes if the preceding question was about the Catholic Church than if it was about the American Nazi Party (Ottati et al., 1989). Clearly, responses to attitude questions are influenced by the context in which they are asked (Tourangeau et al., 1991; Simmons et al., 1993).

Recognizing the problems with single-question measures, researchers commonly use multiple-item questionnaires known as *attitude scales* (Dawes & Smith, 1985; Robinson et al., 1991; Crites et al., 1994). Attitude scales come in different forms, perhaps the most popular being the *Likert Scale,* named after its inventor, Rensis Likert (1932). In this technique, subjects are presented with a list of statements about an attitude object and are asked to indicate on a multiple-point scale how strongly they agree or disagree with each statement. Each respondent's total attitude score is derived by summing his or her responses to all the items. However, whether attitudes are measured by one question or by a full-blown scale, the results should be interpreted with caution. All self-report measures assume that people express their true opinions. Sometimes this is a reasonable assumption to make, but often it is not. Wanting to make a good impression on others, people are reluctant to admit to their failures, weaknesses, unpopular opinions, and prejudices.

One approach to this problem is to increase the accuracy of self-report measures. To get respondents to answer attitude questions more truthfully, researchers sometimes use the *bogus pipeline,* an elaborate mechanical device that supposedly records our true feelings—like a lie-detector test. Not wanting to get caught in a lie, subjects tend to answer attitude questions with less social desirability bias when they think that deception would be detected by the bogus pipeline (Jones & Sigall, 1971; Roese & Jamieson, 1993).

Covert Measures A second approach to the self-report problem is to use indirect, covert measures of attitudes. One possibility in this regard is to use observable behavior—such as facial expressions, tone of voice, and body language. For example, Gary Wells and Richard Petty (1980) unobtrusively videotaped college students listening to a speech and noticed that when the speaker took a position that subjects agreed with (that tuition costs should be lowered), most made vertical head movements. But when the speaker took a contrary position (that tuition costs should be raised), head movements were in a horizontal direction. Without realizing it, subjects had signaled their attitudes by nodding and shaking their heads.

Although behavior provides clues, it is far from perfect as a measure of attitudes. Sometimes we nod our heads because we agree; at other times we nod to be polite. The problem is that people monitor their overt behavior just as they monitor self-reports. What about internal, physiological reactions that are difficult, if not impossible, to control? Does the body really betray how we feel? In the past, researchers tried to divine attitudes from involuntary physical reactions such as perspiration, heart rate, and pupil dilation. The results, however, were always the same: measures of arousal may well reveal the *intensity* of one's attitude toward an object but not whether that attitude is positive or negative. On the physiological record, love and hate look very much the same (Petty & Cacioppo, 1983).

facial electromyograph (EMG) An electronic instrument that records facial muscle activity associated with emotions and attitudes.

Although physiological arousal measures cannot distinguish between positive and negative attitudes, there are some exciting new alternatives. One is the **facial electromyograph (EMG).** As shown in Figure 10.1, different muscles in the face contract when we are happy than when we are sad. Some of the muscular changes cannot be seen with the naked eye, however, so the facial EMG is used. To determine whether the EMG can be used to measure the affect associated with attitudes, John Cacioppo and Richard Petty (1981) recorded facial muscle activity of subjects as they listened to an agreeable or disagreeable message. The agreeable message increased activity in the cheek muscles, the facial pattern characteristic of happiness. The disagreeable message sparked activity in the forehead and brow area, the facial patterns associated with sadness and distress. Outside observers who watched the subjects were unable to see these subtle changes. Apparently, muscles in the human face reveal smiles, frowns, and other reactions to attitude objects that otherwise are hidden from view (Cacioppo et al., 1986; Tassinary & Cacioppo, 1992).

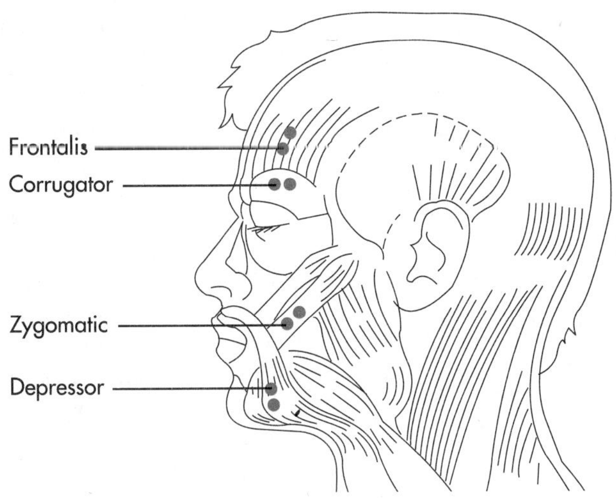

Figure 10.1 The Facial EMG: A Covert Measure of Attitudes. The facial EMG makes it possible to detect differences between positive and negative attitudes. Notice the major facial muscles and recording sites for electrodes. When people hear a message with which they agree rather than disagree, there is a relative increase in EMG activity in the depressor and zygomatic muscles but a relative decrease in the corrugator and frontalis muscles. These changes cannot be seen with the naked eye. (Cacioppo & Petty, 1981.)

Electrical activity in the brain may also assist in the measure of attitudes. In 1929, Hans Burger invented a machine that could detect, amplify, and record "waves" of electrical activity in the brain through electrodes pasted to the surface of the scalp. The instrument is called an *electroencephalograph,* or EEG, and the information it provides takes the form of line tracings called *brain waves.* Based on an earlier discovery—that certain patterns of electrical brain activity are triggered by exposure to stimuli that are novel or inconsistent—Cacioppo and his colleagues (1993) had subjects list ten items they liked and ten they did not like within various object categories (fruits, sports, movies, universities, etc.). Later, these subjects were brought into the laboratory, wired to an EEG, and presented with a list of category words that depicted the objects they liked and disliked. The result: The brain-wave pattern normally triggered by inconsistency increased more when a disliked stimulus appeared after a string of positive items, and when a liked stimulus was shown after a string of negative items, than when either stimulus evoked the same attitude as the items that preceded it. Although more research is needed, this discovery suggests that attitudes may be betrayed by electrical activity in the brain.

The Link Between Attitudes and Behavior

People take for granted the notion that attitudes influence behavior. It is natural to assume that voters' opinions of opposing candidates predict their selection on election day, that consumers' attitudes toward competing products influence the purchases they make, and that feelings of prejudice give rise to discrimination. As sensible as these assumptions seem, however, the link between attitudes and behavior is far from automatic.

Sociologist Richard LaPiere (1934) was the first to notice that attitudes and behavior don't always go hand in hand. In the 1930s, LaPiere took a young Chinese couple on a three-month, 10,000-mile automobile trip, visiting 250 restaurants, hotels, and campgrounds throughout the United States. Although prejudice against Asians was widespread at the time, the couple was refused service only once. Yet when LaPiere wrote back to the places they had visited and asked if they would accept Chinese patrons, more than 90 percent of those who returned an answer said they would not. Self-reported attitudes did not correspond with behavior.

This study was provocative but seriously flawed. LaPiere measured attitudes several months after his trip, and during that time the attitudes may have changed. He also did not know whether those who responded to his letter were the same people who had greeted the couple in person. It is even possible that the Chinese couple was served wherever they went only because they were accompanied by LaPiere himself.

Despite these problems, LaPiere's study was the first of many to find a lack of correspondence between attitudes and behavior. In 1969, Allan Wicker reviewed all the applicable research and concluded that attitudes are correlated with behavior only weakly, if at all. Sobered by Wicker's conclusion, researchers were puzzled: Could it be that voting does *not* follow from our political opinions, that consumer purchasing is *not* based on attitudes toward a product, or that discrimination is *not* related to underlying prejudice? Is the study of attitudes useless to those interested in human social behavior? No, not at all. During the next few years, researchers went on to identify the conditions under which attitudes and behavior are correlated. Stephen Kraus (1995) recently analyzed this research and concluded that "attitudes significantly and substantially predict future behavior" (p. 58). In fact, Kraus calculated that there would have to be 60,983 new studies reporting a zero correlation before this conclusion would have to be revised!

Attitudes in Context One important factor is the level of *correspondence,* or similarity, between attitude measures and behavior. Perhaps the reason that LaPiere (1934) did not find a correlation between self-reported prejudice and discrimination was that he had asked proprietors about Asians in general but then observed their actions toward only one couple. To predict a single act of discrimination, he should have measured people's more specific attitudes toward a young, well-dressed, attractive Chinese couple accompanied by an American professor.

Analyzing more than a hundred studies, Icek Ajzen and Martin Fishbein (1977) found that attitudes correlate with behavior only when attitude measures closely match the behavior in question. Illustrating the point, Andrew Davidson and James Jaccard (1979) tried to use attitudes to predict whether women would use birth control pills within the next two years. Attitudes were measured in a series of questions ranging from very general ("How do you feel about birth control?") to very specific ("How do you feel about using birth control pills during the next two years?"). The more specific the initial attitude question was, the better it predicted the behavior. Other researchers as well have replicated this finding (Kraus, 1995).

The link between our feelings and our actions should also be placed within a broader context. Attitudes are one determinant of social behavior, but there are other determinants as well. This limitation formed the basis for Fishbein's (1980) *theory of reasoned action,* which Ajzen (1991) then expanded into the **theory of planned behavior.** This theory states that attitudes influence behavior through a process of deliberate decision making—and that their impact is limited in four respects (see Figure 10.2).

theory of planned behavior The theory that attitudes toward a specific behavior combine with subjective norms and perceived control to influence a person's action.

First, as just described, behavior is influenced less by general attitudes than by attitudes toward a specific behavior. Second, behavior is influenced not only by

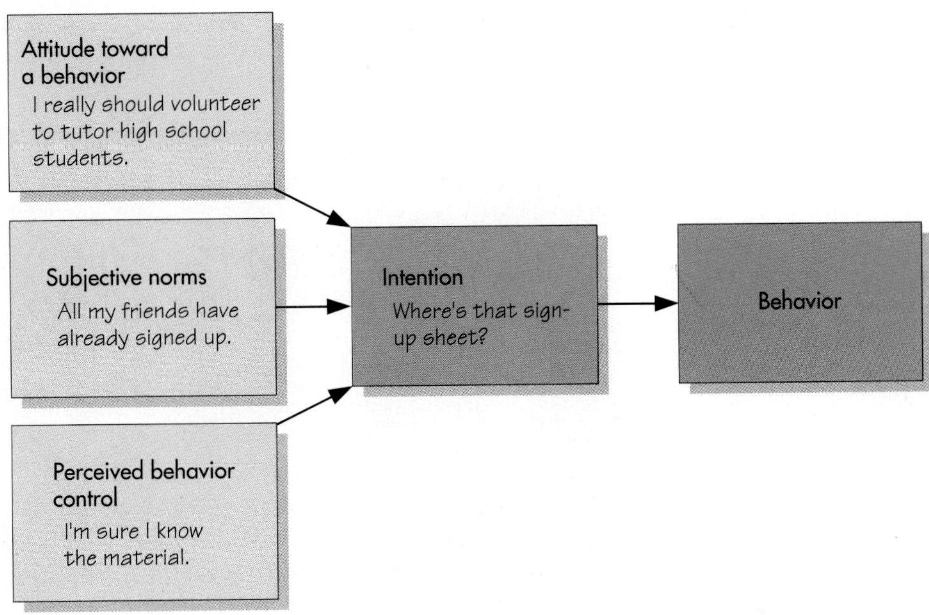
Attitude toward
a behavior
I really should volunteer
to tutor high school
students.
Subjective norms
All my friends have
already signed up.
Perceived behavior
control
I'm sure I know
the material.
Intention
Where's that sign-
up sheet?
Behavior

Figure 10.2 Theory of Planned Behavior. According to the theory of planned behavior, attitudes toward a specific behavior combine with subjective norms and perceived control to influence a person's intentions. These intentions, in turn, guide but do not completely determine behavior. This theory places the link between attitudes and behavior within a broader context. (Ajzen, 1991.)

attitudes but by *subjective norms*—beliefs about what others think we should do. As we saw in Chapter 9, social pressures toward conformity, compliance, and obedience often lead us to behave in ways that are at odds with our inner convictions. Third, attitudes give rise to behavior only when we perceive the behavior to be within our *control.* To the extent that people lack confidence in their ability to engage in some behavior, they are unlikely to form an intention to do so. Fourth, although attitudes (along with subjective norms and perceived control) contribute to an *intention* to behave in a particular manner, people often do not or cannot follow through on their intentions.

A good deal of research supports the theories of reasoned action and planned behavior (Ajzen & Madden, 1986; Fishbein & Stasson, 1990; Madden et al., 1992). Indeed, this general approach—one that places the link between attitudes and behavior within a broader context—has successfully been used to predict a wide range of behaviors such as losing weight, donating blood, using condoms, exercising, smoking, attending church, shoplifting, voting, choosing an occupation, and making moral and ethical decisions (Sheppard et al., 1988; Kurland, 1995).

Strength of the Attitude According to the theories of reasoned action and planned behavior, specific attitudes combine with social factors to produce behavior. Sometimes attitudes have a greater influence on behavior than do other factors; sometimes they have less. In large part, it depends on the importance or *strength* of the attitude. Each of us has some views that are nearer and dearer to the heart than others. Computer jocks often become attached to IBM, Apple, or other competing brands. Political activists have fiery passions for one political party over others. In each case, the attitude is held with confidence and is difficult to change (Schuman & Johnson, 1976; Petty & Krosnick, 1993).

Why are some attitudes stronger than others? One provocative hypothesis, as advanced by Abraham Tesser (1993), is that strong attitudes are rooted in our genetic make-up. Research shows that on some issues, identical twins have more

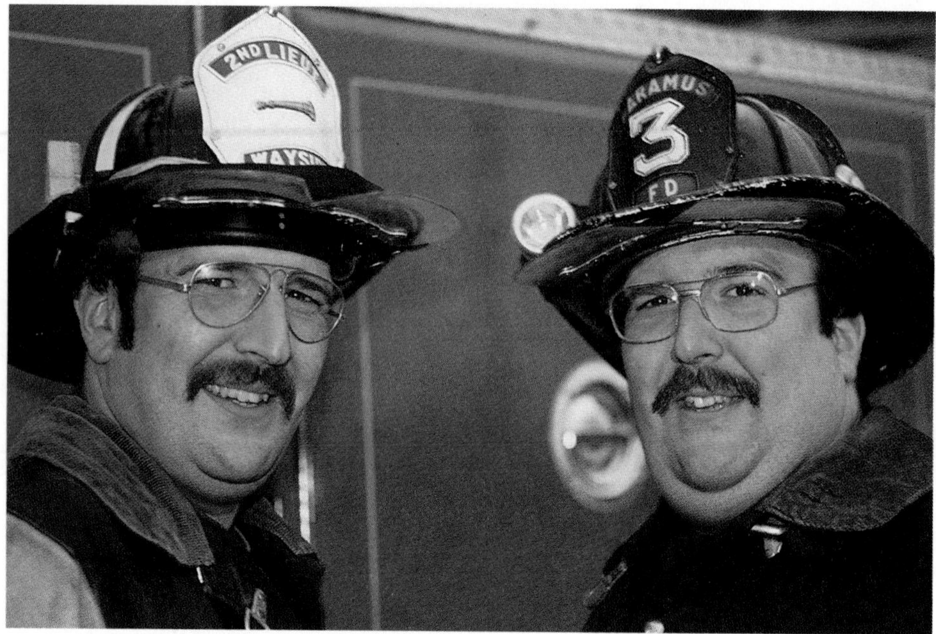

Chances are, these identical twins have more in common than being firefighters. Research suggests that people may be genetically predisposed to hold certain attitudes.

similar attitudes than do fraternal twins, and that twins raised apart are as similar to each other as are those raised in the same home. This evidence suggests that people are predisposed by nature to hold certain attitudes. Indeed, Tesser found that when asked about attitudes for which there seems to be a genetic link (such as attitudes toward sexual promiscuity, religion, and the death penalty), subjects were quicker to respond and less likely to alter their views in the direction of social norms. Tesser speculates that as a result of inborn physical, sensory, and cognitive abilities, temperament, and personality traits, individuals are biologically predisposed to hold certain strong attitudes.

Whether or not there is a genetic link, David Boninger and his colleagues (1995) have identified three psychological factors that consistently distinguish between our strongest and weakest attitudes. These investigators asked people to reflect on their views toward defense spending, gun control, the legalization of marijuana, abortion rights, and other issues. They found that those attitudes that people held the most passionately were on issues that (1) directly affected their own outcomes and self-interests; (2) related to deeply held philosophical, political, and religious values; and (3) were of concern to their close friends, family, and social ingroups.

Several factors indicate the strength of an attitude and its link to behavior. One is that people tend to behave in ways that are consistent with their attitudes when they are well informed. For example, college students were asked which of two candidates they preferred in an upcoming local election for mayor. Those who knew the campaign issues were later the most likely to actually vote for their favored candidate (Davidson et al., 1985). In another study, students were questioned about their views on various environmental issues and later were asked to take action—to sign petitions, participate in a recycling project, and so on. Again, the more informed the students were, the more consistent their environmental attitudes were with their behavior (Kallgren & Wood, 1986).

Second, the strength of an attitude is indicated not only by the amount of information on which it is based but also by how that information was acquired in the first place. Research shows that attitudes are more stable and more predictive of behavior when they are formed through direct personal experience than when they are based on indirect, secondhand information. In a series of experiments, for example, Russell Fazio and Mark Zanna (1981) introduced two groups of subjects to a set of puzzles. One group actually worked on sample puzzles; the other group merely watched someone else working on them. Subjects then reported their interest in the puzzles (attitude) and were given an opportunity to spend time on them (behavior). As it turned out, attitudes and behaviors were more consistent among subjects who had previously sampled the puzzles. Attitudes born of direct experience are especially resistant to change (Wu & Shaffer, 1987).

A third factor is that strong attitudes are highly *accessible* to awareness, which means they are quickly and easily brought to mind (Fazio, 1990). To return to our earlier examples, computer jocks think often about their computer preferences, and political activists think often about their party allegiances. It turns out that many attitudes—not just those we feel strongly about—are easily brought to mind by the mere sight or even mention of the attitude object (Bargh et al., 1992). Of course, situational factors can also bring an attitude into awareness. Attitudes thus correlate with behavior more when people become self-focused by staring into a mirror (Gibbons, 1978), when they overhear others discussing the issue (Borgida & Campbell, 1982), or when they are questioned repeatedly (Powell & Fazio, 1984). Interestingly, people are quick to assume a connection between attitude strength and accessibility. When researchers activated a particular attitude by having subjects express it over and over again, the subjects later came to perceive that attitude as personally more important (Roese & Olson, 1994).

To summarize, recent research on the link between attitudes and behavior leads to an important conclusion. Our feelings toward an object do not always determine our actions because other factors must be taken into account. However, when attitudes are strong and specific to a behavior, the effects are beyond dispute. Under these conditions, voting *is* influenced by political opinions, consumer purchasing *is* affected by product attitudes, and racial discrimination *is* rooted in feelings of prejudice. Attitudes are important determinants of behavior. The question now is, how can attitudes be changed?

PERSUASION BY COMMUNICATION

On a day-to-day basis, we are all involved in the process of changing attitudes. Advertisers flood consumers with images to sell new cars, soft drinks, laundry detergents, and sneakers. Likewise, politicians make speeches, pass out bumper stickers, and kiss babies to win votes. Attitude change is sought whenever parents socialize their children, scientists advance theories, religious groups seek converts, or trial lawyers argue cases to a jury. Some appeals work, others do not. Some are subtle, others are blatant. Some serve the public interest, while others serve personal interests. The point is, there is nothing inherently evil or virtuous about changing attitudes, a process known as **persuasion.** We do it all the time.

persuasion The process of changing attitudes.

If you wanted to change someone's attitude, you would probably try by making a persuasive *communication*. Appeals made in person and through the mass media rely on the spoken word, the written word, and the image that is worth a thousand words. What determines whether an appeal succeeds or fails? To understand why certain approaches are effective while others are not, we need to know *how* and *why* persuasive communications work. For that, we need a road map of the persuasion process.

Two Routes to Persuasion

It's a familiar scene in American politics: every four years, presidential candidates launch extensive campaigns for office. In a way, if you've seen one election, you've seen them all. The names and dates may change, but over and over again opposing candidates accuse each other of ducking the issues and turning the election into a flag-waving, slogan-chanting popularity contest. True or not, these accusations show that politicians are keenly aware that they can win votes through two completely different methods. They can stick to the issues, or they can base their appeals on other grounds.

To account for these alternative approaches, Richard Petty and John Cacioppo (1986) proposed a dual-process model of persuasion. This model assumes that we do not always process communications the same way. When people think critically about the contents of a message, they take a **central route to persuasion** and are influenced by the strength and quality of the arguments. When people do not think critically about the contents of a message but focus instead on other cues, they take a **peripheral route to persuasion.** As we'll see, the route taken depends on whether people are willing and able to scrutinize the information contained in the message itself.

central route to persuasion The process in which a person thinks carefully about a communication and is influenced by the strength of its arguments.

peripheral route to persuasion The process in which a person does not think carefully about a communication and is influenced instead by superficial cues.

The Central Route In the first systematic attempt to study persuasion, Carl Hovland and his colleagues (1949, 1953) started the Yale Communication and Attitude Change Program. They proposed that for a persuasive message to have influence, the receivers of that message must learn its contents and be motivated to accept it. According to this view, people can be persuaded only by arguments they attend to, comprehend, and retain in memory. Whether the message takes the form of a personal appeal, a newspaper editorial, a sermon, or a TV commercial, these basic requirements remain the same.

Several years later, William McGuire (1969) reiterated the information-processing steps necessary for persuasion and, like the Yale group before him, distinguished between the learning or *reception* of a message, a necessary first step, and its later *acceptance*. In fact, McGuire (1968) used this distinction to explain the surprising finding that a receiver's self-esteem and intelligence are unrelated to persuasion. In McGuire's scheme, these characteristics have opposite effects on reception and acceptance. People who are smart or high in self-esteem are better able to learn a message but are less likely to accept its call for a change in attitude. People who are less smart or low in self-esteem are more willing to accept the message but may have trouble learning its contents. Overall, then, neither group is generally more vulnerable to persuasion than the other—a prediction that is supported by a good deal of research (Rhodes & Wood, 1992).

For Anthony Greenwald (1968) and others, persuasion requires a third, intermediate step: **elaboration.** To illustrate, imagine you are offered a job and your prospective employer tries to convince you over lunch to accept. You listen closely, learn the terms of the offer, and understand what it means. But if it's an impor-

elaboration The process of thinking about and scrutinizing the arguments contained in a persuasive communication.

In presidential politics, candidates try to win votes by addressing the issues, as in a press conference (the central route), or through the use of banners, music, and other theatrics, as in a convention (the peripheral route).

tant interview, your head will spin with questions as you weigh the pros and cons and contemplate the implications: Would I have to move? Is there room for advancement? Am I better off staying where I am? Confronted with personally significant messages, we don't just listen for the sake of collecting information. We think about that information. Thus, the message is effective to the extent that it leads us to dwell on favorable rather than unfavorable thoughts.

These theories of attitude change all share the assumption that the recipients of persuasive appeals are attentive, active, critical, and thoughtful. This assumption is correct—some of the time. When it is, and when people consider a message carefully, their reaction depends on its contents. In these instances, messages have greater impact when they are easily learned than when they are difficult and when they stimulate favorable rather than unfavorable elaboration. Ultimately, strong arguments are persuasive and weak arguments are not. On the central route to persuasion, the process is eminently thoughtful, often logical.

The Peripheral Route "The receptive ability of the masses is very limited, their understanding small; on the other hand, they have a great power of forgetting." The author of this statement was Adolf Hitler (1933, p. 77). Believing that people are poor processors of information, Hitler relied heavily in his propaganda on the use of slogans, uniforms, marching bands, flags, and other symbols. For Hitler, "Meetings were not just occasions to make speeches, they were carefully planned theatrical productions in which settings, lighting, background music, and the timing of entrances were devised to maximize the emotional fervor of an audience" (Qualter, 1962, p. 112). Do these ploys work? Can the masses be handily manipulated into persuasion? As Hitler's method suggests, audiences are not always thoughtful. Sometimes people do not follow the central route to persuasion but instead take a short cut along the peripheral route. Rather than try to learn the message and think through the issues, they respond to superficial cues. Two kinds of peripheral cues are particularly compelling: heuristics and attributions.

On the peripheral route to persuasion, people often evaluate a communication by using simple-minded **heuristics**, or rules of thumb (Chaiken, 1987; Chaiken et al., 1989). If a communicator has a good reputation, speaks fluently, or writes well, we tend to assume that his or her message must be correct. Likewise, if a message contains a long litany of arguments or intimidating statistics, then again we assume that it must be correct. Rather than take the time to scrutinize all the

heuristic A rule of thumb used to evaluate a message superficially, without careful thinking about its content.

speaker's arguments, we take the easy way out, accepting the message according to heuristics.

Another way people evaluate persuasive messages without carefully considering the content is by making quick *attributions* about the speaker's motives (Eagly et al., 1981a). Confronted with speakers who appear to argue against their own interests, for example, we attribute what they say to the evidence, not to self-serving motives. The liberal who takes a conservative position on some policy and the advertiser who issues a warning on the dangers of the advertised product are both likely to turn more than a few heads. Other attribution rules are also used. Consider the use of consensus information. If an entire panel of speakers agrees on a topic, or if an audience cheers its approval, we assume that the evidence is valid.

Route Selection Thanks to Petty and Cacioppo's (1986) two-track distinction between the central and peripheral routes, we can better understand why the persuasion process seems so logical on some occasions, yet so illogical on others. Voters may select their candidate according to the issues or according to images. Juries may base their verdicts on evidence or on a defendant's appearance. And consumers may base their purchases on marketing reports or on product images. The process that is engaged depends on whether we have the *ability* and the *motivation* to take the central route or whether we rely on peripheral cues instead.

To understand the conditions that lead people to take one route or the other, it's helpful to view persuasive communication as the outcome of three factors: a *source* (who), a *message* (says what and in what context), and an *audience* (to whom). Each of these factors influences a receiver's approach to a persuasive communication. If a source speaks clearly, if the message is important, if there is a bright and captive audience that cares about the issue and has time to absorb the information, then that audience will be willing and able to take the effortful central route. But if the source speaks at a rate too fast to comprehend, if the message is trivial, or if the audience is distracted, pressed for time, or uninterested, then the less strenuous peripheral route is taken.

A key determinant in the selection of a route is one's level of personal involvement—that is, the extent to which a message has relevance for one's values and goals (Johnson & Eagly, 1989; Petty & Cacioppo, 1990). Certain techniques can be employed to increase involvement. For example, the use of rhetorical questions—a technique used in roughly 30 percent of all radio commercials (Howard, 1990b)—motivates people to think about and process a message more carefully (Burnkrant & Howard, 1984; Petty et al., 1981b). Certain source characteristics can also heighten levels of audience involvement. For example, research indicates that white Americans think more fully about persuasive arguments when the speaker is Black or Hispanic (White & Harkins, 1994).

Figure 10.3 presents a road map of persuasive communication. In the next three sections, we follow this map from the input factors, through the central or peripheral routes, to the end result: persuasion.

The Source

From the moment he announced that he was infected with the virus that causes AIDS, basketball star Magic Johnson became a powerful spokesman for health organizations seeking to educate the public. Why was Johnson, who is not a

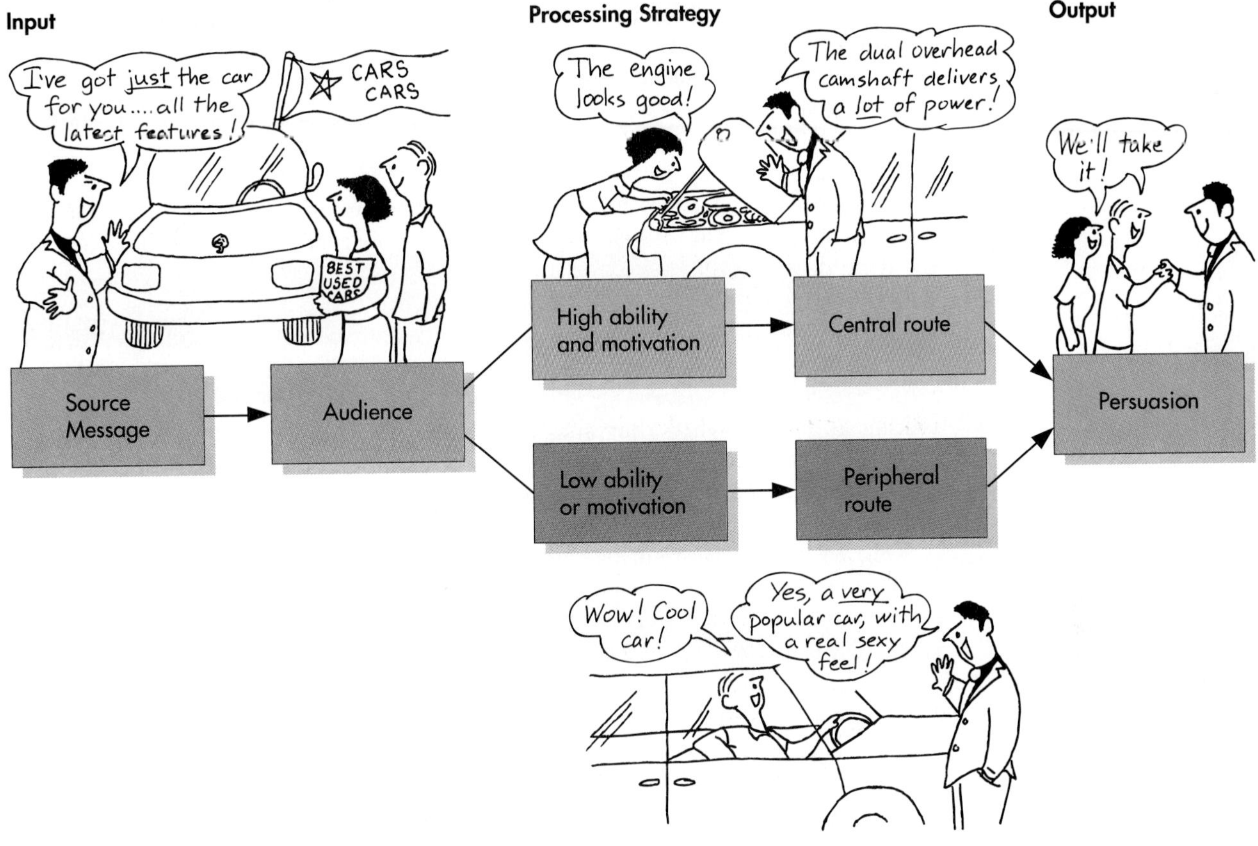

Figure 10.3 **Two Routes to Persuasion.** Based on characteristics of the source, message, and audience, recipients of a communication take either a central or a peripheral route to persuasion. On the central route, people are influenced by strong arguments and evidence. On the peripheral route, persuasion is based on heuristics and other superficial cues. This two-process model helps explain how persuasion can seem logical on some occasions and illogical on others.

medical expert, so effective in this role? In general, what makes some communicators more effective than others? There are two key characteristics: credibility and likability.

Credibility Imagine you are waiting in line in a supermarket, and you catch a glimpse of a swollen headline: "Doctors Report Cure for AIDS!" As your eye wanders across the front page, you discover that you are reading the *National Enquirer.* What would you think? Now imagine that you are reading through periodicals in a university library, and you come across a similar article—but this time it appears in the *New England Journal of Medicine.* Now what would you think?

Chances are, you would react with more excitement to the medical journal than to the supermarket tabloid—even though both sources report the same news. In a study conducted during the cold war era of the 1950s, subjects read a speech advocating the development of nuclear submarines. The speech elicited more agreement when it was attributed to an eminent American physicist than when the source was said to be the former Soviet newspaper *Pravda* (Hovland & Weiss, 1951). Likewise, when subjects read a speech favoring more lenient treatment of juvenile offenders, they changed their attitudes more when they thought the speaker was a judge rather than a convicted drug dealer (Kelman & Hovland, 1953).

Why are some sources more believable than others? Why were the medical journal, the physicist, and the judge more credible than the tabloid, *Pravda,* and the drug dealer? For communicators to be seen as credible, they must have two characteristics: competence and trustworthiness. *Competence* refers to a speaker's ability. People who are knowledgeable, smart, or well spoken, or who have impressive credentials, are persuasive by virtue of their expertise (Hass, 1981). Experts can have a disarming effect on us. We assume they know what they're talking about. So when they speak, we listen. And when they take a position, even one that is extreme, we yield. Unless an expert contradicts us on issues that are personally important (Heesacker et al., 1983), people tend to accept what he or she says without much scrutiny (Maddux & Rogers, 1980).

Still, we are confronted by plenty of experts in the world whose opinions do not sway us. The reason is that expertise is not enough. To be credible, communicators must also be *trustworthy*—that is, they must be willing to report what they know truthfully and without compromise. If a speaker can be bought off, has an ax to grind, or is simply telling an audience what it wants to hear, that speaker will be suspected of bias. Common sense arms us with a simple rule of caution: beware of those who have something to gain from successful persuasion. This rule sheds light on a classic problem with celebrity endorsements in advertising: The more products a celebrity endorses, the less trustworthy he or she appears to be to consumers (Tripp et al., 1994). The same rule also explains why speakers are judged as more credible when they present a balanced two-sided message in which they acknowledge and refute opposing arguments, than when their message is purely one-sided (Crowley & Hoyer, 1994).

The self-interest rule has other interesting implications. One is that people are impressed by others who take unpopular stands or argue against their own interests. When subjects read a political speech accusing a large company of polluting a local river, those who thought that the speechmaker was a pro-environment candidate addressing an environmentalist group perceived him to be biased. In contrast, subjects who thought he was a pro-business candidate addressing company supporters assumed he was sincere (Eagly et al., 1978). Trust is also established by speakers who are not purposely trying to change our views. For this reason, people are influenced more when they think they are accidentally overhearing a persuasive communication than when they receive a sales pitch intended for their ears (Walster & Festinger, 1962). That's why advertisers often use the "overheard communicator" trick in which the source tells a buddy about a new product that really works. Feeling as if they are eavesdropping on a personal conversation, viewers assume that what one friend says to another can be trusted.

Likability More than anything else, Magic Johnson's power as an AIDS spokesman is based on his popularity, his charm, his winning smile, and his "regular guy" image that people can identify with. Do these qualities enhance a communicator's effectiveness? As Dale Carnegie (1936) implied in the title of his classic best seller, *How to Win Friends and Influence People,* being liked and being persuasive go hand in hand. So what makes a communicator likable? As described in Chapter 5, two factors that enhance attraction are *similarity* and *physical attractiveness.*

A study by Diane Mackie and her colleagues (1990) illustrates the importance of similarity. Students at the University of California at Santa Barbara read a strong or a weak speech that argued against the continued use of the SATs. Half of the subjects were led to believe that the speech was written by a fellow UCSB student; the other half thought the author was a student from the University of New Hampshire. Very few subjects changed their attitudes after reading the weak arguments. Many who read the strong message did change their attitudes—but only when it was delivered by a fellow UCSB student.

The link between similarity and persuasiveness has implications for those who wish to exert influence. We're all similar to one another in some respects. We might agree with each other's politics, share a common friend, have similar tastes in food, or enjoy spending summers on the same beach. Aware of the social benefits of similarity, the astute communicator can use common bonds to enhance his or her impact on an audience. There are limits, however. Similarity increases persuasion most when the similarities seem relevant to the content of the communication (Berscheid, 1966).

When it comes to physical attractiveness, advertising practices suggest that beauty is also persuasive. After all, billboards, magazine ads, and TV commercials are filled with glamorous "supermodels"—tall, slender (for women), muscular (for men), with glowing complexions and radiant smiles. Sure, these models can turn heads, you may think; but can they change minds?

In a study that addressed this question, male and female college students approached others on campus and introduced themselves as members of an organization that was trying to get the university to stop serving meat during breakfast and lunch. In each case, they gave reasons for the position and then asked their subjects to sign a petition. The result: Attractive communicators were able to convince 41 percent of their subjects to sign the petition, whereas those who were less attractive succeeded only 32 percent of the time (Chaiken, 1979). Sometimes, a speaker's physical appearance matters more than the quality of his or her arguments and presentation (Kahle & Homer, 1985; Pallak, 1983).

The Sky's Not the Limit: When What You Say Is More Important Than Who You Are Thus far, it must seem as if the source of a persuasive message is more important than the message itself. Is this true? Advertisers have long debated the issue of celebrity endorsements. David Ogilvy (1985), a giant in advertising, says that celebrities are not effective because viewers know they've been bought and paid for. Ogilvy is not alone in his skepticism. Still, many advertisers scramble furiously to sign high-priced models, entertainers, and athletes. From Michael Jordan to Nancy Kerrigan, Jamie Lee Curtis, Shaquille O'Neal, Jerry Seinfeld, Cindy Crawford, and Candice Bergen, TV commercials regularly feature a parade of stars. The bigger the star, supposedly the more valuable the endorsement.

Compared to the contents of a message, does the source really make the difference that advertisers pay for? Are we so impressed by the expert and so drawn to the charming face that we embrace whatever they have to say? Are we so scornful of nonexperts and unattractive people that their presentations fall on deaf ears? In light of what is known about the central and peripheral routes to persuasion, the answer to these questions is, it depends.

First, a receiver's *involvement* plays an important role. When a message has personal relevance to your life, you pay attention to it and think critically about

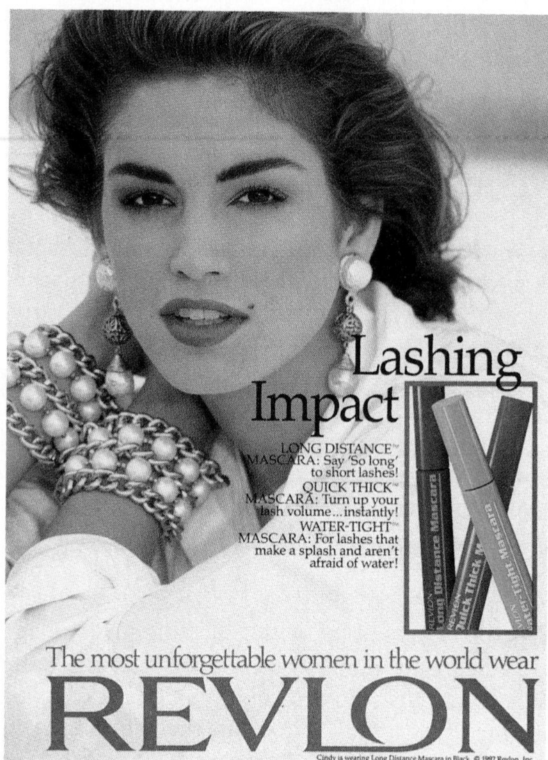

Advertisers are so convinced that beauty sells products that they hire glamorous supermodels like Cindy Crawford.

its arguments and implications. When a message does not have relevance, however, you may take the source at face value and spend very little time scrutinizing the information. For example, Richard Petty and his colleagues (1981a) had students listen to a speaker who proposed that seniors should be required to take comprehensive exams in order to graduate. Three aspects of the communication situation were varied. First, subjects were led to believe that the speaker was either an education professor at Princeton University or a high school student. Second, subjects heard either reasoned arguments based on hard evidence or a weak message based on anecdotes and personal opinion. And third, subjects were told either that the proposed exams might be used in the following year (uh oh, that means me!) or that they would not take effect for another ten years (who cares, I'll be long gone by then!).

As predicted, personal involvement determined the relative impact of source expertise and speech quality. Among subjects who would not be affected by the proposed change, attitudes were based largely on the speaker's credibility: The professor was persuasive, the high school student was not. Among subjects who thought that the proposed change would affect them directly, attitudes were based on the quality of the speaker's proposal: Strong arguments were persuasive, weak arguments were not. As depicted in Figure 10.4, people followed the source rather than the message under low levels of involvement, illustrating the peripheral route to persuasion. But message factors outweighed the source under high levels of involvement, when subjects cared enough to take the central route to persuasion. Likewise, the tilt toward likable communicators is reduced when receivers take the central route (Chaiken, 1980).

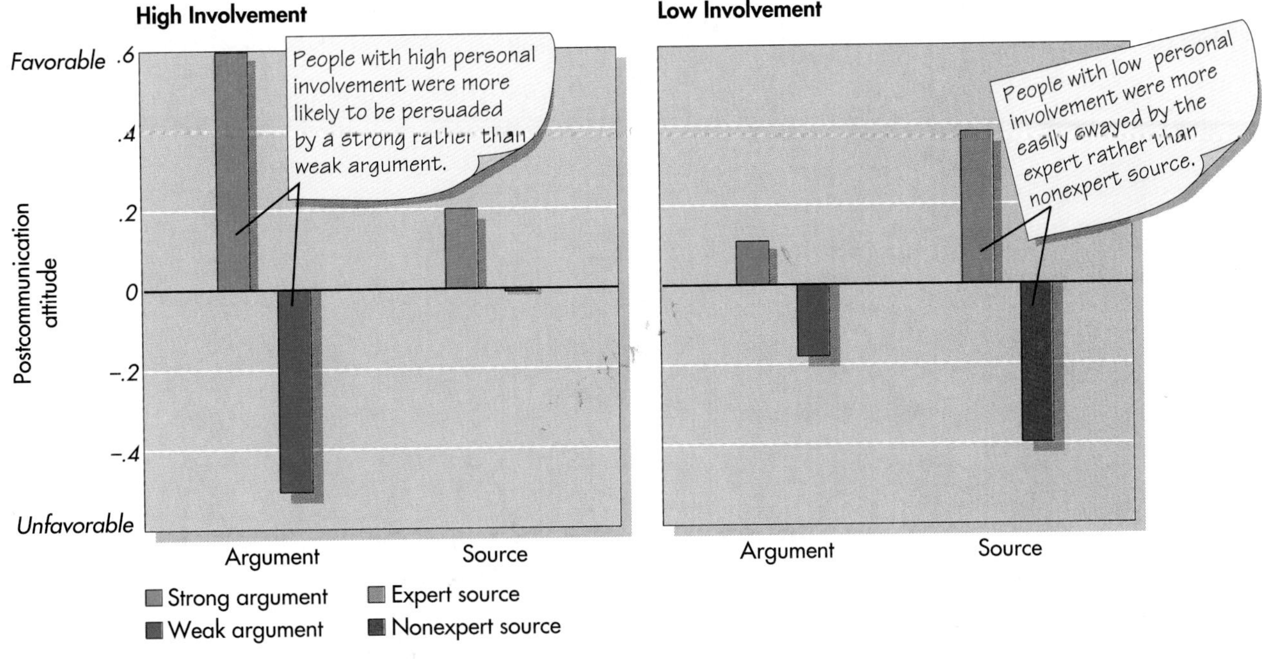

Figure 10.4 Source Versus Message: The Role of Audience Involvement. Subjects who were high or low in their personal involvement heard a strong or weak message from an expert or nonexpert. For high-involvement subjects (left), persuasion was based on the strength of arguments, not on source expertise. For low-involvement subjects (right), persuasion was based more on the source than on the arguments. Source characteristics have more impact on those who don't care enough to take the central route to persuasion. (Petty et al., 1981a.)

There is a second limit to source effects. It is often said that time heals all wounds. Well, it may also heal the effects of a bad reputation. Hovland and Weiss (1951) varied communicator credibility (for example, the physicist versus *Pravda)* and found that the change had a large and immediate effect on persuasion. But when they remeasured subjects' attitudes four weeks later, the effect had vanished. Over time, the attitude change produced by the credible source decreased and the change caused by the noncredible source increased. This latter finding—the delayed persuasive impact of a noncredible communicator—is called the **sleeper effect.**

sleeper effect A delayed increase in the persuasive impact of a noncredible source.

To explain this unforeseen result, the Hovland group proposed the *discounting cue hypothesis.* According to this hypothesis, people immediately discount what noncredible communicators say, but over time they dissociate what is said from who says it. In other words, people tend to remember the message but forget the source (Pratkanis et al., 1988). To examine the role of memory in this process, Herbert Kelman and Carl Hovland (1953) reminded a group of subjects of the source's identity before their attitudes were reassessed. If the sleeper effect was due to forgetting, they reasoned, then it could be eliminated through reinstatement of the link between the source and the message. As shown in Figure 10.5, they were right. When subjects' attitudes were measured after three weeks, those who were not reminded of the source showed the usual sleeper effect.

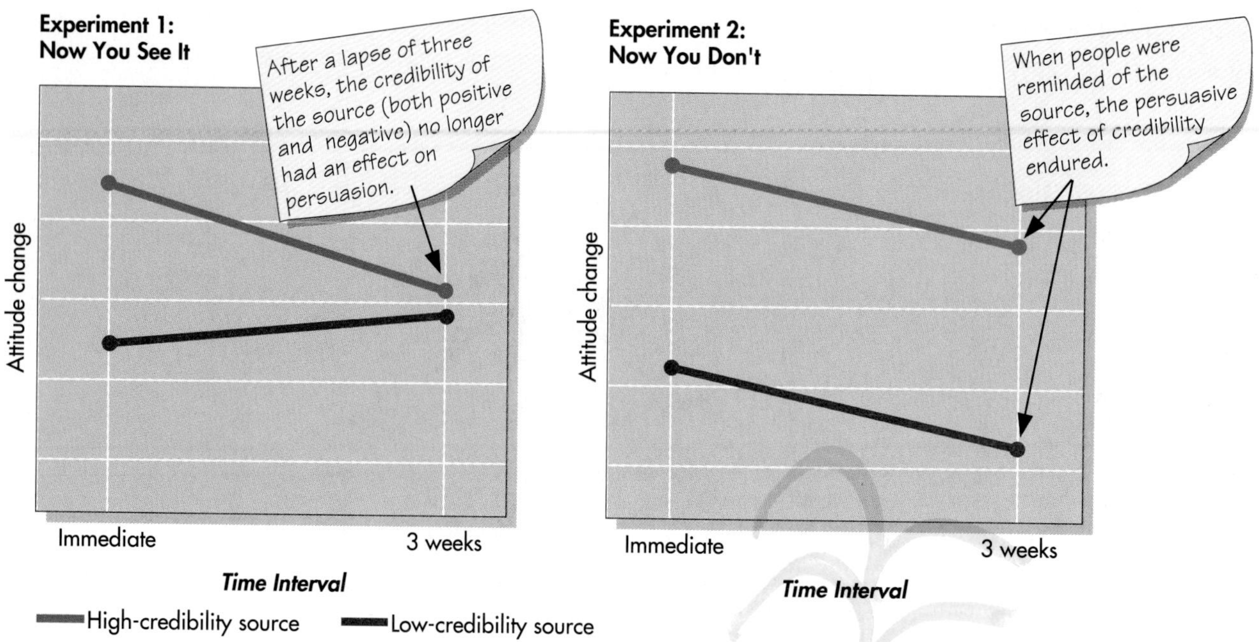

Figure 10.5 **The Sleeper Effect.** In Experiment 1, subjects changed their immediate attitudes more in response to a message from a high- than from a low-credibility source. When attitudes were remeasured after three weeks, the high-credibility source lost impact and the low-credibility source gained impact—the sleeper effect. In Experiment 2, the sleeper effect disappeared when subjects were reminded of the source. (Kelman & Hovland, 1953.)

Those who were reminded of the source did not. For these latter subjects, the effects of high and low credibility endured.

The sleeper effect generated a good deal of controversy (Cook et al., 1979; Greenwald et al., 1986). There was never a doubt that credible communicators lose some of their initial impact over time. But researchers had a harder time finding evidence for the delayed persuasion by a noncredible source. Exasperated by their own failures to obtain this result, Paulette Gillig and Anthony Greenwald (1974) thus wondered, "Is it time to lay the sleeper effect to rest?" The answer is no.

More recent research shows that the sleeper effect is reliable—provided that subjects don't learn who the source is until *after* they receive the original message (Greenwald et al., 1986; Gruder et al., 1978; Pratkanis et al., 1988). To appreciate the importance of timing, imagine you're flipping through a magazine and you come across what appears to be a review of a new CD. Before you begin reading, however, you notice in the fine print that this so-called review is really an advertisement. Aware that you can't trust what you read, you skim the ad and reject it. Now imagine the same situation, except that you read the entire ad before realizing what it is. Again, you reject it. But notice the difference. This time, you had read the message with an open mind. You may have rejected it later, but after a few weeks the information has a chance to sink in and influence your evaluation of the CD. This experience illustrates the sleeper effect.

Research on the sleeper effect shows that people often remember the message but forget the source.

Drawing by Ed Fisher; © 1976 The New Yorker Magazine, Inc.

"It is a superb vision of America, all right, but I can't remember which candidate projected it."

The Message

Obviously not all sources are created equal, as some are more credible or likable than others. On the peripheral route to persuasion, audiences are influenced heavily, maybe too heavily, by these and other source characteristics. But when people care about an issue, the strength of the message determines its success. On the central route to persuasion, what matters most is whether a scientist's theory is supported by the data or whether a manufacturer has a sound product. Keep in mind, however, that the target of a persuasive appeal comes to know a message only through the medium of communication: *what* a person has to say and *how* that person says it.

Informational Strategies Communicators often struggle over how to present an argument to maximize its impact. Should a message be long and crammed with facts or short and to the point? Is it better to present a partisan one-sided message or to take a more balanced two-sided approach? And how should the various arguments be ordered—from strongest to weakest, or the other way around? These are the kinds of questions that are studied by persuasive-communication researchers.

Often the most effective strategy to use depends on whether the audience is processing the message on the central or the peripheral route. Consider the length dilemma. When people process a message lazily, with their eyes and ears half-closed, they often fall back on a simple heuristic: The longer a message, the more valid it must be. In this case, length gives the appearance of factual support—regardless of the quality of the arguments (Petty & Cacioppo, 1984; Wood et al., 1985). Thus, as David Ogilvy (1985) concluded from his many years of advertising experience, "The more facts you tell, the more you sell" (p. 88).

When people process a communication carefully, however, length is a two-edged sword. If a message is long because it contains lots of supporting information, then longer does indeed mean better. The more supportive arguments you can offer, or the more sources you can find to speak on your behalf, the more persuasive will be your appeal (Harkins & Petty, 1981). But if the added arguments are weak, or if the new sources are redundant, an alert audience will not be tricked by length alone. When increasing length means diluting quality, an appeal might well *lose* impact (Harkins & Petty, 1987; Petty & Cacioppo, 1984).

When opposing sides try to persuade an audience, presentation order becomes a relevant factor as well. In the summer before the 1992 presidential election, as in most recent elections, the Democrats held their national convention a month or so before the Republicans held theirs. These events are watched on television by millions of voters. Do you think the order in which they are scheduled places one party at an advantage? If you believe that information presented first has more impact, you are predicting a *primacy effect* (advantage to the Democrats). If you believe that information presented last has the edge, you are predicting a *recency effect* (advantage to the Republicans).

There are good reasons for both predictions. On the one hand, first impressions are important. On the other hand, memory fades over time and people often recall only the last thing they heard before making a decision. Confronted with these contrasting predictions, Norman Miller and Donald Campbell (1959) searched for the "missing link" that would determine the relative effects of primacy and recency. They discovered that the missing link is *time*. In a jury simulation study, they had subjects (1) read a summary of the plaintiff's case, (2) read a summary of the defendant's case, and (3) make a decision. The researchers varied how much time separated the two messages and then how much time elapsed between the second message and the decisions. When subjects read the second message right after the first and then waited a whole week before reporting their opinion, a primacy effect prevailed, and the side that came first was favored. Both messages faded equally from memory, so only the greater impact of first impressions was left. Yet when subjects made a decision immediately after the second message but a full week after the first, there was a recency effect. The second argument was fresher in memory, thus favoring the side that went last. Using these results as a guideline, let's return to our original question: What is the impact on election day of how the national conventions are scheduled? Think for a moment about the placement and timing of these events. The answer appears in Figure 10.6.

Figure 10.6 Effects of Presentation Order and Timing on Persuasion. This study demonstrated the role of presentation order and the timing of opposing arguments on persuasion. As applied to our example, the Democratic and Republican conventions resemble the fourth row of this figure. From these results, it seems that the scheduling of such events is fair, promoting neither primacy nor recency.

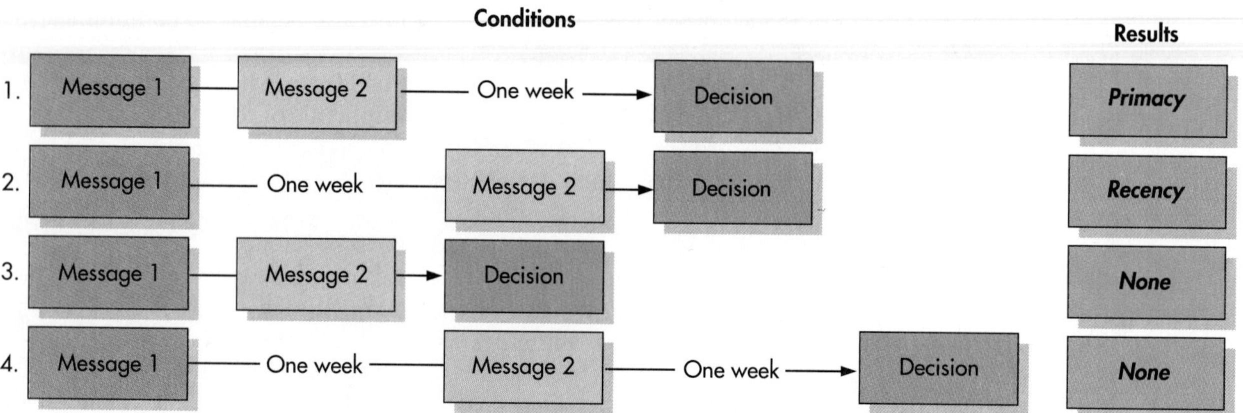

Message Discrepancy Persuasion is a process of changing attitudes. But just how much change should be sought? Before addressing an audience, all communicators confront a critical strategic question. How extreme a position should they take? How *discrepant* should a message be from the audience's position in order to have the greatest impact? Common sense suggests two opposite answers. One approach is to take an extreme position—the more change you advocate, the more you get. Another approach is to exercise caution—if you push for too much change, the audience will reject the message outright. Which approach seems more effective? Imagine trying to convert your conservative friends into political liberals, or the other way around. Would you stake out a radical position in the hope of moving them toward the center, or would you preach moderation so as not to be cast aside?

Research shows that communicators should adopt a compromise between the two approaches and advocate a position that is moderately discrepant from that of the audience. In other words, increasing discrepancy results in greater change—but only up to a point, beyond which it produces less change. This relationship between discrepancy and persuasion can be pictured as an upside-down *U*. But there is a complicating factor. Experts more than nonexperts can get away with taking an extreme position.

In a study by Stephen Bochner and Chester Insko (1966), subjects read an essay arguing that the average adult sleeps too much and should get either 8, 7, 6, 5, 4, 3, 2, 1, or 0 hours of sleep per night. For some subjects, the essay author was identified as a Nobel Prize–winning physiologist. For others, he was said to be a YMCA director. In both cases, attitude change increased with message discrepancy up to a point, then decreased. How extreme that point was, however, depended on the source. Figure 10.7 shows that when the YMCA director recommended as few as three hours of sleep, the amount of attitude change decreased. For the physiologist, however, that decrease was not evident until he recommended no sleep at all! Either way, additional research shows that commu-

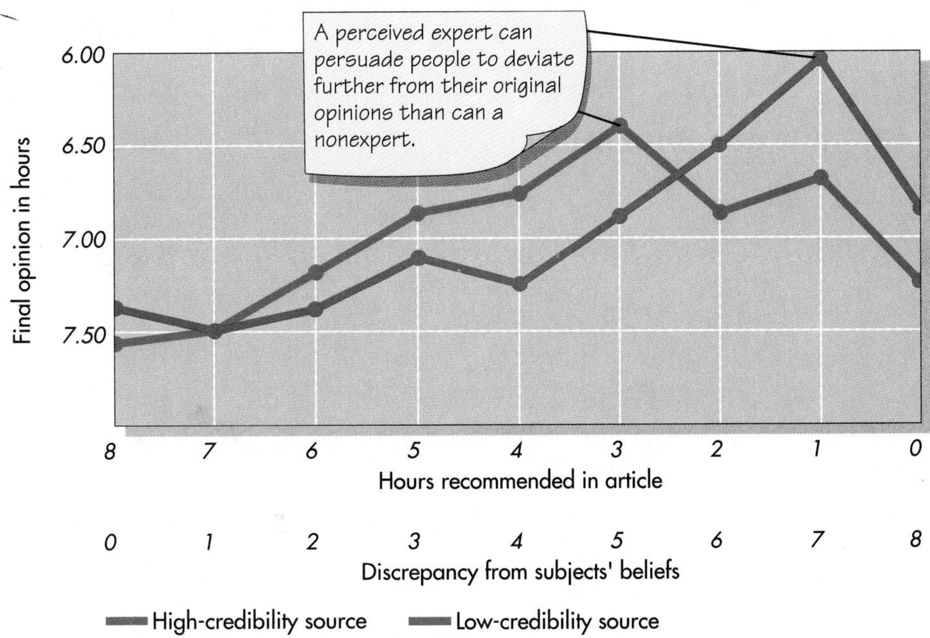

Figure 10.7 Message Discrepancy and Attitude Change. Subjects, believing that adults should get eight hours of sleep per night, read an essay that recommended varying amounts of less sleep. As shown, attitude change increased with message discrepancy up to a point, then decreased. Note that a high-credibility source was persuasive at higher levels of discrepancy than was a low-credibility source. (Bochner & Insko, 1966.)

nicators must always ensure that their arguments are based on premises that the audience finds acceptable, not offensive (Holtgraves & Bailey, 1991).

Fear Appeals Many trial lawyers say that to win cases, they have to appeal to jurors through the heart rather than the mind. Sure, evidence is important, they say. But what also matters is whether the jury views their client with anger, disgust, affection, sympathy, or sadness. Of course, very few messages are based entirely on rational argument or on emotion. And it's possible that the best approach to take depends on whether an attitude is based more on beliefs or on feelings about the object in question (Edwards, 1990; Millar & Millar, 1990). In this section, we look at the role of fear in the persuasion process.

It is a common technique to use fear, or scare tactics. During U.S. presidential campaigns, candidates will often use negative advertising to frighten people about the consequences of voting for their opponents. Certain religious cults use scare tactics to indoctrinate new members. So do public health organizations that graphically portray the victims of cigarette smoking, drugs, and unsafe sex. That is why magazine ads for condoms so often use fear appeals—the most extreme being "I enjoy sex but I don't want to die for it" (Struckman-Johnson et al., 1990). Even commercial advertisers try to frighten consumers into buying their products. After all, who would want to get caught with dandruff, bad breath, body odor, or a dirty collar?

Is fear effective? If so, is it better to arouse just a little nervousness or to trigger a full-blown anxiety attack? To answer these questions, social psychologists have

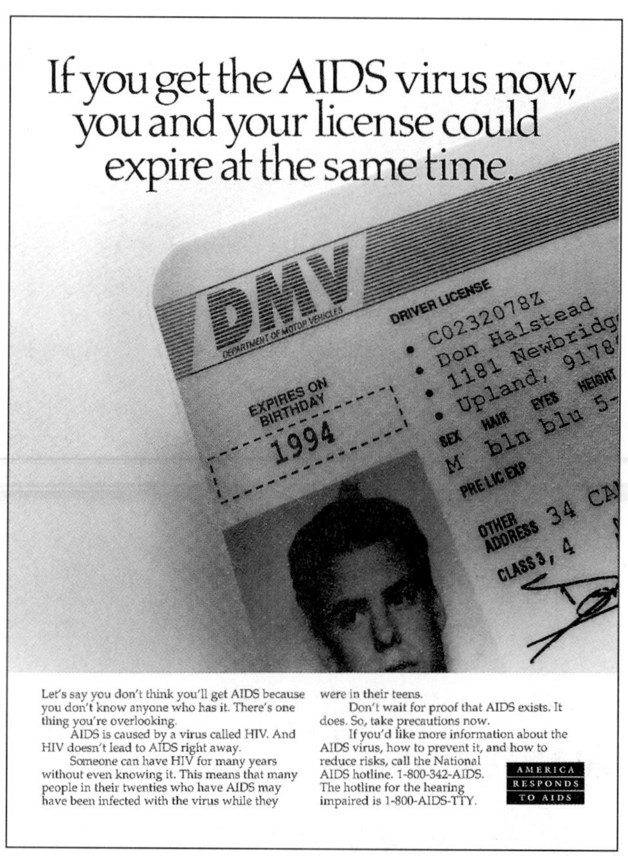

If you get the AIDS virus now, you and your license could expire at the same time.
DMV
DEPARTMENT OF MOTOR VEHICLES
DRIVER LICENSE
EXPIRES ON BIRTHDAY
1994
Let's say you don't think you'll get AIDS because you don't know anyone who has it. There's one thing you're overlooking.
AIDS is caused by a virus called HIV. And HIV doesn't lead to AIDS right away.
Someone can have HIV for many years without even knowing it. This means that many people in their twenties who have AIDS may have been infected with the virus while they were in their teens.
Don't wait for proof that AIDS exists. It does. So, take precautions now.
If you'd like more information about the AIDS virus, how to prevent it, and how to reduce risks, call the National AIDS hotline. 1-800-342-AIDS. The hotline for the hearing impaired is 1-800-AIDS-TTY.
AMERICA RESPONDS TO AIDS

It is common for public health organizations to use fear, or scare tactics, to change attitudes.

compared the effects of communications that vary in their fearfulness. In the first such study, Irving Janis and Seymour Feshbach (1953) found that high levels of fear arousal did not generate increased agreement with a communication. Since then, however, research has shown that high fear does motivate change—in part, by increasing our incentive to think carefully about the persuasive arguments contained in the message (Baron et al., 1994).

Fear arousal may increase the incentive to change, but ultimately its impact depends on the strength of the arguments—and on whether the message also contains reassuring advice on how to avoid the threatened danger (Leventhal, 1970; Rogers, 1983; Witte, 1992). This last point is important. Without specific instructions on how to cope, people may feel helpless, panic, and tune out. In one study, for example, subjects with a chronic fear of cancer were less likely than others to detect the logical errors in a message that called for regular cancer checkups (Jepson & Chaiken, 1990). When clear instructions are included, however, high dosages of fear are effective. Anti-smoking films that tell smokers how to quit lead to more negative attitudes about cigarettes when they show gory lung-cancer operations rather than charts filled with dry statistics (Leventhal et al., 1967). And driving-safety films are more effective when they show broken bones and bloody accident victims rather than controlled collisions involving plastic crash dummies (Rogers & Mewborn, 1976).

Positive Emotions Fear helps to induce persuasion, but so does positive emotion. In one study, subjects were more likely to agree with a series of controversial arguments when they snacked on peanuts and soda than when they did not eat (Janis et al., 1965). In another study, subjects liked a TV commercial more when it was embedded in a program that was upbeat rather than sad (Mathur & Chattopadhyay, 1991). Research shows that people are "soft touches" when they're in a good mood. Depending on the situation, food, drinks, a soft reclining chair, tender memories, a success experience, breathtaking scenery, and pleasant music can lull us into a positive emotional state—ripe for persuasion (Schwarz et al., 1991a).

According to Alice Isen (1984), people tend to view the world through rose-colored glasses when they are feeling good. Filled with high spirits, we become more sociable, more generous, and generally more positive in our opinions. We also make decisions more quickly and with relatively little thought. As a result, positive feelings activate the peripheral route to persuasion, allowing superficial cues to take on added importance (Worth & Mackie, 1987). What is it about feeling good that leads people to take short cuts rather than the more effortful central route to persuasion? There are at least two possible explanations. One is that people are *motivated* to savor the moment and protect their happy mood—not ruin it by concentrating on new information (Isen, 1984). The second is that a positive emotional state is distracting, causing the mind to wander and impairing one's *ability* to think quickly and concentrate on persuasive arguments (Mackie & Worth, 1989; Mackie et al., 1992). Either way, research shows that positive emotion facilitates persuasion under both high and low levels of audience involvement (Petty et al., 1993).

Subliminal Messages In 1957, Vance Packard published *The Hidden Persuaders,* an exposé of Madison Avenue. As the book climbed the best-seller list, it awakened in the public a fear of being manipulated by forces that could not be seen or heard. What had Packard uncovered? In the 1950s, amid growing fears of communism and the birth of rock 'n' roll, a number of advertisers were said to be using *subliminal advertising,* the presentation of commercial messages outside of conscious awareness. It all started in a drive-in movie theater in New Jersey, where the words "Drink Coke" and "Eat popcorn" were secretly flashed on the screen for a third of a millisecond. The audience never noticed the message, yet Coke sales were said to have increased 18 percent and popcorn sales 58 percent over a six-week period of intermissions (Brean, 1958).

This incident was followed by others. A Seattle radio station presented subaudible anti-TV messages during its programs ("TV is a bore"), department stores played music tapes over public address systems that contained subaudible antitheft statements ("If you steal, you'll get caught"), and advertisers embedded faint erotic images in visual ads to heighten the appeal of their products. Subliminal messages in rock music have also raised concern. In one case, the families of two young men who committed suicide blamed the British rock group Judas Priest for subliminal lyrics that promoted satanism and suicide on their *Stained Glass* album (National Law Journal, 1990). Clearly, people believe in the power of hidden persuaders.

Can subliminal advertising really influence us without awareness? At the time of the New Jersey movie theater scandal, research on the topic was so sketchy, and the public so enraged by the sinister implications, that the matter was dropped like a hot potato. But today there is renewed interest and new research developments. In what has become a multimillion dollar industry, companies sell self-help tapes that play soft music or nature sounds and also contain fleeting messages designed to help you relax, lose weight, stop smoking, make friends, raise self-esteem, and even improve your sex life.

Research shows that the impact of subliminal messages is limited. In Chapter 5, we saw that exposure to a stimulus—whether it's a foreign word, an object, or a face—increases our liking for that stimulus even if it cannot later be recognized. But what about subliminal messages to drink Coke, eat popcorn, or purchase a particular product? And what about the subliminal self-help tapes for which consumers pay $29.95? In 1982, Timothy Moore reviewed existing research and concluded that "what you see is what you get"—nothing, "complete scams." Moore was right. The original Coke-and-popcorn study was exposed as a publicity stunt, a hoax (Pratkanis, 1992).

Is there any other evidence to support this covert form of influence? No. In a controlled experiment, Anthony Greenwald and his colleagues (1991) had subjects listen for five weeks to a music tape that contained a hidden message designed either to improve memory or raise self-esteem. For half the subjects, the tapes were correctly labeled; for others, the labels were reversed. Subjects were tested both before and after the five-week period. They were also questioned afterward on their beliefs concerning the tapes. Did subjects think they were helped by the tapes? Did they actually improve? There were two key results. First, test scores on *objective* measures of memory and self-esteem were no higher after exposure to the tapes than before. Second, however, subjects *perceived* an improvement in their memory or self-esteem—depending on which label was on the tape, not on which message the tape actually contained. Other researchers have found that subliminal weight-loss tapes are similarly ineffective (Merikle & Skanes, 1992). Apparently, "What you expect is what you believe, but not necessarily what you get" (Pratkanis et al., 1994, p. 251).

The Audience

Although source and message factors are important, the astute communicator also takes his or her audience into account. Presentation strategies that succeed with some people may fail with others. Audiences on the central route to persuasion, for example, bear little resemblance to those found strolling along the peripheral route. In this section, we'll see that the impact of a message is influenced by two additional characteristics: the receiver's personality and his or her expectations.

Individual Differences: What Turns You On? Right from the start, social psychologists tried to identify types of people who were more or less vulnerable to persuasion. But it turns out that few individuals are *consistently* easy or difficult to persuade. As a result of this insight, the search for individual differences is now guided by an interactionist perspective. Assuming that each of us can be persuaded more in some settings than in others, researchers look for the right "match" between characteristics of the message and characteristics of an audience. Thus we ask, What kinds of messages turn *you* on?

Earlier we saw that people process information more carefully when they are highly involved. Involvement can be determined by the importance and self-relevance of a message. According to Cacioppo and Petty (1982), however, there are also individual differences in the extent to which people become involved and take the central route to persuasion. Specifically, they have found that individuals differ in the extent to which they enjoy and participate in effortful cognitive activities or, as they call it, the **need for cognition** (NC). People who are high rather than low in their need for cognition like to work on hard problems, search for clues, make fine distinctions, and analyze situations. These differences can be identified by items contained in the Need for Cognition Scale, some of which are shown in Table 10.1.

need for cognition (NC) A personality variable that distinguishes people on the basis of how much they enjoy effortful cognitive activities.

The need for cognition has interesting implications for changing attitudes. If people are prone to approach or avoid effortful cognitive activities, then the knowledgeable communicator could design messages unique to a particular audience. In theory, the high-NC audience should receive information-oriented ap-

Table 10.1 Need for Cognition Scale: Sample Items

1. I really enjoy a task that involves coming up with new solutions to problems.
2. Thinking is not my idea of fun.
3. The notion of thinking abstractly is appealing to me.
4. I like tasks that require little thought once I've learned them.
5. I usually end up deliberating about issues even when they do not affect me personally.
6. It's enough for me that something gets the job done; I don't care how or why it works.

Are you high or low in the need for cognition? These statements are taken from the NC Scale. If you agree with items 1, 3, and 5 and disagree with items 2, 4, and 6, you would probably be regarded as high in your NC. (Cacioppo & Petty, 1982.)

peals, and the low-NC audience should be treated to appeals that rely on the use of peripheral cues. The theory is fine, but does it work? Can a message be customized according to the information-processing style of its recipients? In a test of this hypothesis, subjects read an editorial that consisted of either a strong or a weak set of arguments. As predicted, the higher their NC scores were, the more the subjects thought about the material, the better they recalled it, and the more persuaded they were by the strength of its arguments (Cacioppo et al., 1983). In contrast, people who are low in the need for cognition are persuaded by cues found along the peripheral route—such as a speaker's reputation and physical appearance (Cacioppo & Petty, 1984), the reactions of others in the audience (Axsom et al., 1987), and a positive mood state (Petty et al., 1993).

Just as people high in the need for cognition crave information, other personality traits are associated with attraction to other kinds of messages. Consider individual differences in the trait of *self-monitoring*. As described in earlier chapters, high self-monitors regulate their behavior from one situation to another out of concern for public self-presentation. Low self-monitors are less image conscious and behave instead according to their own beliefs and preferences. In the context of persuasion, it is possible that high self-monitors are particularly responsive to messages that promise desirable social images. Whether the product is beer, soda, blue jeans, or a car, this technique is common in advertising, where often the image is the message.

To test the self-monitoring hypothesis, Mark Snyder and Kenneth DeBono (1985) showed image- or information-oriented magazine ads to high and low self-monitors. In an ad for Irish Mocha Mint coffee, for example, a man and woman were depicted as relaxing in a candlelit room over a cup of coffee. The image-oriented version promised to "Make a chilly night become a cozy evening," while the informational version offered "A delicious blend of three

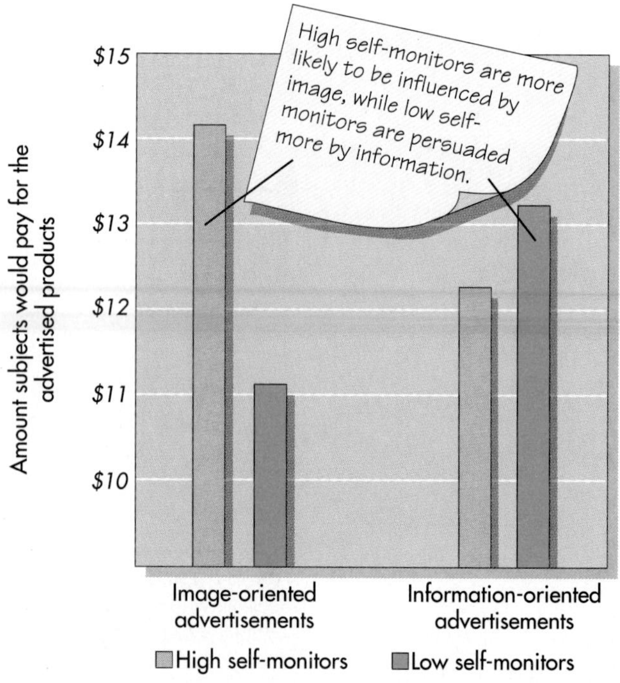

Figure 10.8 Informational and Image-Oriented Ads: The Role of Self-Monitoring. High and low self-monitors estimated how much they would pay for products presented in image-oriented or informational magazine ads. As shown, high image-oriented self-monitors preferred products depicted in image-oriented ads (left), while low self-monitors preferred those depicted in informational ads (right). (Adapted from Snyder & DeBono, 1985.)

great flavors—coffee, chocolate, and mint." As predicted, high self-monitors were willing to pay more for products after reading imagery ads, while low self-monitors were influenced more by the information-oriented appeals. As shown in Figure 10.8, this study suggests that a message may be persuasive to the extent that it meets the psychological needs of its audience (DeBono, 1987; DeBono & Packer, 1992).

Cultural factors also play an important role. In other chapters, we saw that cultures differ in the extent to which they value individualism versus collectivism. In light of these differences, Sang-Pil Han and Sharon Shavitt (1994) compared the contents of magazine advertisements in the United States, an individualistic country, and Korea, a country with a collectivistic orientation. They found that American ads focused more on personal benefits, individuality, competition, and self-improvement, while Korean ads focused more on the integrity, achievement, and well-being of one's family and other ingroups. Clearly, there are different ways to appeal to the people of these two cultures (see Table 10.2). In a second study, Han and Shavitt constructed two sets of ads for various products. One set portrayed individuals ("Treat yourself to a breath-freshening experience"), and the other set featured groups ("Share this breath-freshening experience"). Both sets were presented to American and Korean subjects. The result: Americans were persuaded more by individualistic ads, and Koreans preferred the collectivistic ads. To be persuasive, a message should appeal to the culturally shared values of its audience.

Forewarning: Ready or Not, Here I Come! Probably the toughest audience to persuade is the one that knows you're coming. When people are aware that someone is trying to change their attitude, they become motivated to resist. All

Table 10.2 Cultural Values in Advertising

Some Individualistic Ads

"She's got a style all her own"

"You, only better"

"How to protect the most personal part of the environment: Your skin"

"A leader among leaders"

"Make your way through the crowd"

Some Collectivistic Ads

"A more exhilarating way to provide for your family"

"We have a way of bringing people closer together"

"Celebrating a half-century of partnership"

"Our family agrees with this selection of home furnishings"

"Your business success: Harmonizing with Sunkyong"

The statements listed here were taken from the American and Korean ads analyzed by Han and Shavitt (1994, pp. 346–347). Note the differences between those classified as individualistic versus collectivistic.

they need is some time to collect their thoughts and come up with a good defense. Jonathan Freedman and David Sears (1965) discovered this when they told high school seniors to expect a speech on why teenagers should not be allowed to drive (an unpopular position, as you can imagine). The students were warned either two or ten minutes before the talk began or not at all. Those who were the victims of a sneak attack were the most likely to agree with the speaker's position. Those who had a full ten minutes' warning were the least likely to agree. Apparently, to be forewarned is to be forearmed. But why?

At least two processes are at work. To understand them, let's take a closer look at what forewarning does. Subjects in the Freedman and Sears (1965) study were put on notice in two ways: (1) They were informed of the position the speaker would take, and (2) they were told that the speaker intended to change their attitudes. Psychologically, these two aspects of forewarning have different effects.

inoculation hypothesis The idea that exposure to weak versions of a persuasive argument increases later resistance to that argument.

The first effect is cognitive. Knowing in advance what position a speaker will take enables us to come up with counterarguments and, as a result, to become more resistant to change. To explain this effect, William McGuire (1964) drew an analogy: Protecting a person's attitudes from persuasion, he said, is like inoculating the human body against disease. In medicine, injecting a small dose of infection into a patient stimulates the body to build up a resistance to it. According to this **inoculation hypothesis**, an attitude can be immunized the same way. As with flu shots and other vaccines, our defenses can be reinforced by exposure to weak doses of the other side's position before we actually encounter the full presentation. Studies of negative political advertising show that inoculation can be used to combat the kinds of attack messages that sometimes win elections (Pfau & Burgoon, 1988; Pfau et al., 1990). It has even been suggested that parents can protect children from advertising propaganda by exposing them to small doses of TV commercials, while critically discussing the claims that are made (Pratkanis & Aronson, 1992).

Simply knowing that someone will try to persuade us also elicits a motivational reaction, as we brace ourselves to resist the attempt—regardless of what position is taken. As a TV viewer, you have no doubt heard the phrase "And now, we pause for a message from our sponsor." What does this warning tell us? Not knowing yet who the sponsor is, even the grouchiest among us is in no position to object. Yet imagine how you would feel if an experimenter said to you, "In just a few minutes, you will hear a message prepared according to well-established principles of persuasion and designed to induce you to change your attitudes." If you are like the subjects who actually heard this forewarning, you may be tempted to reply, "Oh yeah? Try me!" Indeed, subjects rejected that message without counterargument and without much advance notice (Hass & Grady, 1975).

When people think that someone is trying to change their attitude or otherwise manipulate them, a red flag goes up. That red flag is called *reactance,* a concept introduced in Chapter 5. People want the freedom to think, feel, and act as they (not others) choose. When we sense that a specific freedom is threatened, we become motivated to maintain it. When we sense that a freedom is slipping away, we try to restore it. The net result is that when someone comes on too strong, we often exhibit a "boomerang effect," or *negative attitude change,* by moving in a direction opposite to the one advocated—even when the speaker's position is consistent with our own (Heller et al., 1973). Sometimes, the motive to protect a freedom can supersede our desire to hold a specific opinion.

Psychological reactance often triggers attitude change in a direction opposite to the one advocated—even when the speaker's position is consistent with one's own.

Drawing by Mort Gerberg; © 1994 The New Yorker Magazine, Inc.

"And just who the hell are you to tell me I'm entitled to my opinion?"

PERSUASION BY OUR OWN ACTIONS

Anyone who has ever acted on stage knows how easy it is to become so absorbed in a role that the experience seems real. Feigned laughter can make an actor feel happy, and crocodile tears can turn into sadness. Even in real life, the effect can be dramatic. In 1974, Patty Hearst—a sheltered college student from a wealthy family—was kidnapped. By the time she was arrested months later, she was a gun-toting revolutionary who called herself Tania. How could someone be so totally converted? In Hearst's own words, "I had thought I was humoring [my captors] by parroting their clichés and buzzwords without believing in them. . . . In trying to convince them I convinced myself."

Role Playing: All the World's a Stage

The Patty Hearst case illustrates the powerful effects of *role playing.* Of course, you don't have to be kidnapped or terrorized to know how it feels to be coaxed into behavior that is at odds with your inner convictions. People often engage in attitude-discrepant behavior as part of a job, for example, or to please others. As commonplace as this seems, it raises a rather profound question. When we play along, saying and doing things that are discrepant with our own attitudes, do we begin to change those attitudes as a result? How we feel can determine the way we act. Is it also possible that the way we act can determine how we feel?

According to Irving Janis (1968), attitude change persists more when it is inspired by our own behavior than when it stems from passive exposure to a persuasive communication. Janis conducted a study in which one group of subjects listened to a speech that challenged their positions on a topic and others were handed an outline and asked to give the speech themselves. As predicted, subjects changed their attitudes more after giving the speech than after listening to it (Janis & King, 1954). According to Janis, role playing works by forcing people to learn the message. That is why people remember arguments they come up with on their own better than they do arguments provided by others (Slamecka & Graff, 1978). In fact, attitude change is more enduring when people who read a

Waiters and waitresses must smile and be polite as part of their job. If "saying is believing," then such role-playing may actually trigger positive attitudes toward customers.

persuasive message merely *expect* that they will later have to communicate it to others (Boninger et al., 1990).

There's more to role playing than improved memory. The effects of enacting a role can be staggering—in part because it is so easy to confuse what we do, or what we say, with how we really feel. Think about the times you've dished out compliments you didn't mean, or smiled at someone you didn't like, or nodded your head in response to a statement you disagreed with. We often shade what we say to please a particular listener. What's fascinating is not the fact that we make adjustments to suit others but the powerful effects this role playing has on our own private attitudes. For example, subjects in one study read about a man and then described him to someone who supposedly liked or disliked him. As you might expect, subjects described the man in more positive terms when their listener was favorably disposed. In the process, however, they also convinced themselves. At least to some extent, "saying is believing" (Higgins & Rholes, 1978).

Consider the implications. We know that attitudes help determine behavior—as when people help others whom they like and hurt those whom they dislike. But research on role playing emphasizes the flip side of the coin—that behavior can determine attitudes. Perhaps we come to like people because we have helped them and blame those whom we have hurt. To change people's inner feelings, maybe we should begin by focusing on their behavior. Why do people experience changes of attitude in response to changes in their own behavior? One answer to this question is provided by the theory of cognitive dissonance.

Cognitive Dissonance Theory: The Classic Version

Many social psychologists believe that people are motivated by a desire for cognitive consistency—a state of mind in which one's beliefs, attitudes, and behaviors are all compatible with each other (Abelson et al., 1968). Cognitive consistency theories seem to presuppose that people are generally logical. Leon Festinger (1957), however, turned this assumption on its head. Struck by the irrationality of human behavior, Festinger proposed *cognitive dissonance theory,* which states that a powerful motive to maintain cognitive consistency can give rise to irrational and sometimes maladaptive behavior.

According to Festinger, we hold many cognitions about ourselves and the world around us. These cognitions include everything we know about our own beliefs, attitudes, and behavior. Although most of our cognitions coexist peacefully, at times they clash. Consider some examples. You say you're on a diet, yet you just dove head first into a chocolate mousse. Or you waited on line for hours to get into a rock concert, and then the music was disappointing. Or you baked for hours under the hot summer sun, even though you knew of the health risks. Each of these scenarios harbors inconsistency and conflict. You have already committed yourself to one course of action, yet you realize that what you did is inconsistent with your attitude.

cognitive dissonance An unpleasant psychological state often aroused when a person holds two conflicting cognitions.

Under certain specific conditions, discrepancies such as these can evoke an unpleasant state of tension known as **cognitive dissonance.** But discrepancy doesn't always produce dissonance. If you had to break a diet for a family Thanksgiving dinner, your indiscretion would not lead you to experience dissonance. Or if you mistakenly thought the mousse you ate was low in calories, only later to find out the truth, then, again, you would not experience much dissonance. As we'll see, what really hurts is knowing that you committed yourself to an attitude-discrepant behavior freely and with some knowledge of the consequences. When that happens, dissonance is aroused, and you become motivated to reduce it. There are many possible ways to do so, as shown in Table 10.3. Often the easiest is to change your attitude to bring it in line with your behavior.

Right from the start, cognitive dissonance theory captured the imagination. Festinger's basic proposition is simple, yet its implications are far-reaching. In this section, we examine three research areas that demonstrate the breadth of what dissonance theory has to say about attitude change.

Table 10.3 Ways to Reduce Dissonance

Techniques	Examples
Change your attitude.	"I don't really need to be on a diet."
Change your perception of the behavior.	"I hardly ate any chocolate mousse."
Add consonant cognitions.	"Chocolate mousse is very nutritious."
Minimize the importance of the conflict.	"I don't care if I'm overweight—life is short, mousse is great!"
Reduce perceived choice.	"I had no choice; the mousse was prepared for this special occasion."

"I need to be on a diet, yet I just dove head first into a chocolate mousse." If this were you, how would you reduce the dissonance aroused by the discrepancy between your attitude and behavior?

One way to reduce dissonance is to minimize the importance of the conflict.

"It's a crazy idea, but it just might work."

Justifying Attitude-Discrepant Behavior: When Doing Is Believing Imagine for a moment that you are a subject in the classic study by Leon Festinger and J. Merrill Carlsmith (1959). As soon as you arrive, you are greeted by an experimenter who says that he is interested in various measures of performance. Wondering what that means, you all too quickly find out. The experimenter hands you a wooden board containing forty-eight square pegs in square holes and asks you to turn each peg a quarter turn to the left, then a quarter turn back to the right, then back to the left, then back again to the right. The routine seems endless. After thirty minutes, the experimenter comes to your rescue. Or does he? Just when you think things are looking up, he hands you another board, another assignment. For the next half-hour, you are to take twelve spools of thread off the board, put them back, take them off, and put them back again. By now, you're just about ready to tear your hair out. As you think back over better times, even the first task begins to look good.

Finally, you're done. After one of the longest hours of your life, the experimenter lets you in on a secret: There's more to this experiment than meets the eye. You were in the control group. To test the effects of motivation on performance, other subjects are being told that the experiment will be fun and exciting. You don't realize it, but you are now being set up for the critical part of the study. Would you be willing to tell the next subject that the experiment is enjoyable? As you hem and haw, the experimenter offers to pay for your services. Some subjects are offered one dollar, others are offered twenty dollars. In either case you agree to help out. Before you know it, you find yourself in the waiting room trying to dupe an unsuspecting fellow student (who is really a confederate).

By means of this elaborate, staged presentation, subjects were goaded into an attitude-discrepant behavior, an action that was inconsistent with their private attitudes. They knew how dull the experiment really was, yet they raved about it. Did this conflict arouse cognitive dissonance? It depends on how much subjects were paid. Suppose you were one of the lucky ones offered twenty dollars for your assistance. By today's standards, that payment would be worth eighty dollars—surely a sufficient justification for telling a little white lie, right? Feeling well compensated, these subjects experienced little, if any, dissonance. But wait a minute. Suppose you were paid only one dollar. Surely your integrity is worth more than that, don't you think? In this instance, you have **insufficient justification** for going along—so you need a way to cope. According to Festinger (1957), unless you can deny your actions (which is not usually possible), you will feel

insufficient justification A condition in which people freely perform an attitude-discrepant behavior without receiving a large reward.

pressured to change your attitude about the task. If you can convince yourself that the experiment wasn't all bad, then saying it was interesting would be all right.

The results were just as Festinger and Carlsmith had predicted. When the experiment was presumably over, subjects were asked how they felt about the pegboard tasks. Control group subjects, who did not mislead a confederate, openly admitted that the tasks were boring. So did those in the twenty-dollar condition, who had ample justification for what they did. However, subjects who were paid only one dollar rated the experiment as somewhat enjoyable. Having engaged in an attitude-discrepant act without sufficient justification, these subjects reduced cognitive dissonance by changing their attitude. The results can be seen in Figure 10.9.

self-persuasion The processes by which people change their attitudes in response to their own actions.

Two aspects of this study are noteworthy. First, it demonstrated the phenomenon of **self-persuasion:** when people behave in ways that are discrepant with their attitudes, they sometimes go on to change those attitudes—without any exposure to a persuasive communication. To appreciate the powerful implications of this phenomenon, consider that in a recent study, Michael Leippe and Donna Eisenstadt (1994) found that white college students who were coaxed into writing an essay in favor of setting aside new scholarship funds only for black students later reported more favorable attitudes toward Blacks in general. The second major contribution of Festinger and Carlsmith's study is that its results contradicted the time-honored belief that big rewards produce great change. In fact, the more subjects were paid for their inconsistent behavior, the more justified they felt and the *less* likely they were to change their attitudes.

insufficient deterrence A condition in which people refrain from engaging in a desirable activity, even when only mild punishment is threatened.

Just as a small reward is insufficient justification for attitude-discrepant behavior, mild punishment is **insufficient deterrence** for attitude-discrepant *non*behavior. Think about it. What happens when people refrain from doing something they really want to do? Do they devalue the activity and convince themselves that they never really wanted to do it in the first place? In one study, children were prohibited from playing with an attractive toy by being threatened with a mild or severe punishment. All subjects refrained. As cognitive dissonance theory predicts, however, only those subjects faced with the mild punishment—an insufficient deterrent—later showed disdain for the forbidden toy. Those who

Figure 10.9 The Dissonance Classic. Subjects in a boring experiment (attitude) were asked to say that it was enjoyable (behavior) to a fellow student. One group was paid a dollar to lie; a second group was offered twenty dollars. In a third group that did not have to lie, subjects admitted that the task was boring. So did those paid twenty dollars—ample justification for what they did. Subjects paid only one dollar, however, rated the task as more enjoyable. Behaving in an attitude-discrepant manner without justification, the one-dollar subjects reduced dissonance by changing their attitude. (Festinger & Carlsmith, 1959.)

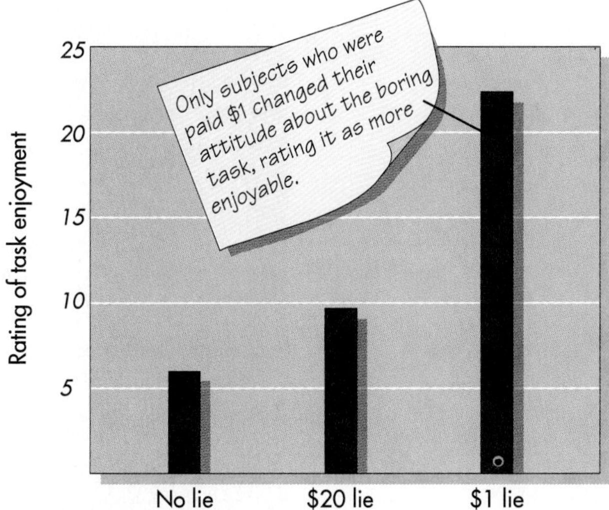

confronted the threat of severe punishment did not (Aronson & Carlsmith, 1963). Once again, cognitive dissonance theory turned common sense on its head: the less severe the threatened punishment, the more attitude change was produced.

Justifying Effort: Coming to Like What We Suffer For Have you ever spent tons of money or tried really hard to achieve something, only to discover later that it wasn't worth all the effort? This kind of inconsistency between effort and outcome can arouse cognitive dissonance and motivate a change of heart toward the unsatisfying outcome. The hypothesis is simple but profound: We alter our attitudes to justify our suffering.

In a classic test of this hypothesis, Eliot Aronson and Judson Mills (1959) invited female students to take part in a series of group discussions about sex. But there was a hitch. Because sex is a sensitive topic, subjects were told that they would have to pass an "embarrassment test" before joining the group. The test consisted of reading sexual material aloud in front of a male experimenter. One group of subjects experienced what amounted to a *severe* initiation in which they had to recite obscene words and lurid passages taken from paperback novels. A second group underwent a *mild* initiation in which they read a list of more ordinary words pertaining to sex. A third group was admitted to the discussions without an initiation test.

Moments later, all subjects were given earphones and permitted to listen in on the group they would soon be joining. Actually what they heard was a tape-recorded discussion about "secondary sex behavior in the lower animals." It was dreadfully boring. When it was over, subjects were asked to rate how much they liked the group members and their discussion. Keep in mind what dissonance theory predicts: The more time or money or effort you choose to invest in something, the more anxious you will feel if the outcome proves disappointing. One

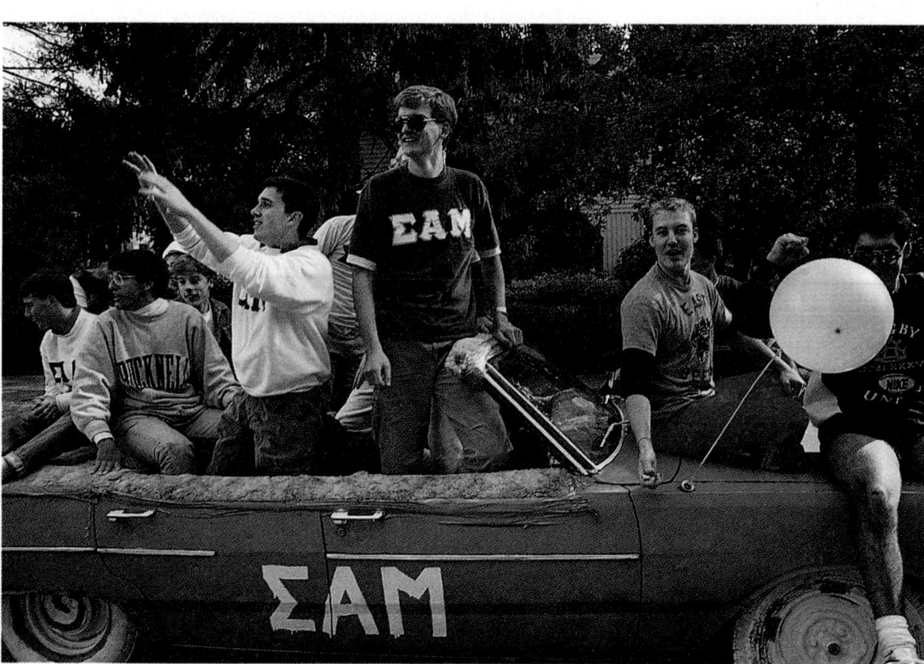

Initiation rites help to foster loyalty among members of college fraternities.

way to cope with this inconsistency is to alter your attitudes. That's exactly what happened. Subjects who endured a severe initiation rated the discussion group more favorably than did those who endured little or no initiation.

It's important to note that embarrassment is not the only kind of "effort" we feel the need to justify to ourselves. As a general rule, the more you pay for something—whether you pay in physical exertion, pain, time, or money—the more you will come to like it. This principle has provocative implications. For example, research suggests that the harder psychotherapy patients have to work at their own treatment, the more likely they are to feel better when that treatment is over (Axsom, 1989; Axsom & Cooper, 1985). Effort justification may also help to explain why college fraternities and sororities foster lifelong loyalties, or why 58 percent of Vietnam veterans, compared to only 29 percent of other Americans, say that "The U.S. was right to get involved in the Vietnam war" (Witteman, 1990). Even today, more than twenty years later, those who risked their lives in that war must justify the nightmare.

Justifying Difficult Decisions: When Good Choices Get Even Better Whenever we make difficult decisions—whether to marry, what school to attend, what job to accept—we experience dissonance. By definition, a decision is difficult when the alternative courses of action are about equally desirable. Marriage offers comfort and stability; staying single keeps a door open for new relationships. One job might pay more money; the other might involve more exciting work. Once people make tough decisions like these, they are at risk, as negative aspects of the chosen alternative and positive aspects of the unchosen alternative are at odds with their decision. According to dissonance theory, people try to rationalize whatever they decide by exaggerating the positive features of the chosen alternative and the negative features of the unchosen alternative.

In an early test of this hypothesis, Jack Brehm (1956) recruited female subjects to evaluate various consumer products, presumably as part of a marketing research project. After rating a toaster, a coffee pot, a radio, a stopwatch, and other products, subjects were told that they could take one home as a gift. In the high-dissonance condition, subjects were offered a difficult choice between two items they found equally attractive. In the low-dissonance group, they were offered an easier choice between a desirable and an undesirable item. After receiving their gift, subjects read a few research reports, then re-evaluated all the products. The results provided strong support for dissonance theory. In the low-dissonance group, subjects' post-decision ratings were about the same as their pre-decision ratings. But in the high-dissonance condition, subjects' ratings increased for the chosen item and decreased for the nonchosen item. Subjects torn between two equivalent alternatives coped by reassuring themselves that they had made the right choice.

This phenomenon appears in a wide range of settings. For example, Robert Knox and James Inskter (1968) took dissonance theory to the racetrack and found that bettors who had already placed two dollars on a horse were more optimistic about winning than were those who were still standing in line. Similarly, Dennis Regan and Martin Kilduff (1988) visited several polling stations on election day and found that voters were more likely to believe that their candidates would win when they were interviewed after submitting their ballots than before. Since bets and votes cannot be taken back, people who committed themselves to a decision were motivated to reduce post-decision dissonance. So they convinced themselves that the decision they made was right.

Cognitive Dissonance Theory: A New Look

Following in Festinger's bold footsteps, generations of social psychologists explored the implications of cognitive dissonance theory. Through systematic research, it became evident early on that Festinger's (1957) original theory was not to be the last word. People do change attitudes to justify attitude-discrepant behavior, effort, and difficult decisions. But for dissonance to be aroused, certain conditions must be present. As summarized by Joel Cooper and Russell Fazio's (1984) "New Look at Dissonance Theory," we now have a pretty good idea of what those conditions are, and why.

According to Cooper and Fazio, four steps are necessary for the arousal and reduction of dissonance. First, a person's attitude-discrepant behavior must produce unwanted *negative consequences.* Recall Festinger and Carlsmith's (1959) initial study. Not only did subjects say something they knew to be false, they also deceived a fellow student into taking part in a painfully boring experiment. Had these subjects lied without causing hardship, they would *not* have changed their attitudes to justify the action (Cooper et al., 1974). To borrow an expression from schoolyard basketball, "no harm, no foul." In fact, it appears that negative consequences arouse dissonance even when people's actions are consistent with their attitudes—as when college students who wrote against fee hikes were led to believe that their essays had backfired, leading a university committee to favor an increase (Scher & Cooper, 1989).

The second necessary step in the process is a feeling of *personal responsibility* for the unpleasant outcomes of behavior. Personal responsibility consists of two factors. The first is the freedom of *choice.* When people believe they had no choice but to act as they did, there is no dissonance and no attitude change (Linder et al., 1967). Had Festinger and Carlsmith coerced subjects into raving about the boring experiment, the subjects would not have felt the need to further justify what they did by changing their attitudes. But the experimental situation led subjects to think that their actions were voluntary and that the choice was theirs. Pressured without realizing it, subjects believed that they did not have to comply with the experimenter's request.

For people to feel personally responsible, they must also believe that the potential negative consequences of their actions were *foreseeable* at the time (Goethals et al., 1979). When the outcome could not have been anticipated, then there's no dissonance and no attitude change. Had Festinger and Carlsmith's subjects lied in private, only later to find out that their statements were tape-recorded for subsequent use, then, again, they would not have felt the need to further justify their behavior.

The third necessary step in the process is physiological *arousal.* Right from the start, Festinger viewed cognitive dissonance as a state of discomfort and tension that people seek to reduce—much like hunger, thirst, and other basic drives. Research has shown that this emphasis was well placed. In a study by Robert Croyle and Joel Cooper (1983), subjects wrote essays that supported or contradicted their own attitudes. Some subjects were ordered to do so, but others were led to believe that the choice was theirs. During the session, electrodes were attached to each subject's fingertips to record physiological arousal. As predicted by cognitive dissonance theory, those who freely wrote attitude-discrepant essays were the most aroused. Other researchers have found similar results (Elkin & Leippe, 1986). In fact, subjects who write attitude-discrepant essays in a "free-choice" situation report feeling high levels of discomfort—which subside once they change their attitudes (Elliot & Devine, 1994).

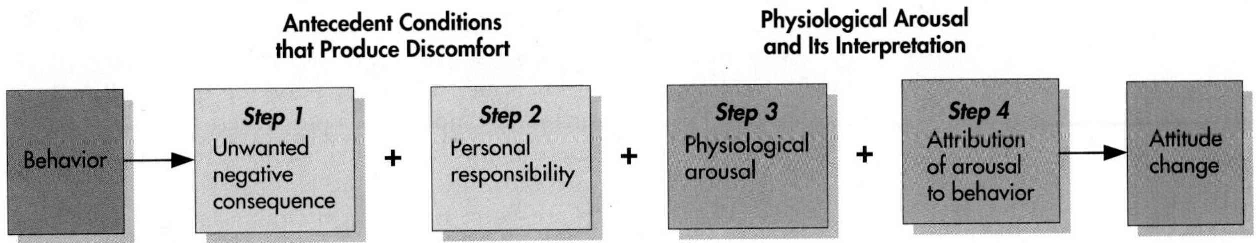

Figure 10.10 Necessary Conditions for the Arousal and Reduction of Dissonance. Research suggests that four steps are necessary for attitude change to result from the production and reduction of dissonance.

The fourth step in the dissonance process is closely related to the third. It isn't enough to feel generally aroused. The person must also make an *attribution* for that arousal to his or her own behavior. Suppose you just lied to a friend, or studied for an exam that was canceled, or made a tough decision that you might soon regret. Suppose further that even though you are upset, you believe your discomfort is caused by some external factor, not by your dissonance-producing behavior. Under these circumstances, will you exhibit attitude change as a symptom of cognitive dissonance? No, probably not. When subjects are led to attribute their dissonance-related arousal to a drug they have supposedly taken (Zanna & Cooper, 1974), to the anticipation of painful electric shocks (Pittman, 1975), or to a pair of prism goggles they had to wear (Losch & Cacioppo, 1990), attitude change does not occur. Figure 10.10 summarizes the four steps in the production and reduction of dissonance.

Alternative Routes to Self-Persuasion

It is important to distinguish between the empirical facts as uncovered by dissonance researchers and the theory that is used to explain them. The facts themselves are clear: under certain conditions, people who behave in attitude-discrepant ways go on to change their attitudes. Whether this phenomenon reflects a human need to reduce dissonance, however, is a matter of some controversy. Over the years, three other explanations have been proposed.

Self-Perception Theory Daryl Bem's (1965) *self-perception theory,* as described in Chapter 2, posed the first serious challenge to dissonance theory. Noting that people don't always have firsthand knowledge of their own attitudes, Bem proposed that we infer how we feel by observing ourselves and the circumstances of our own behavior. This sort of self-persuasion is not fueled by the need to reduce tension or justify our actions. Instead, it is a cool, calm, and rational process in which people interpret ambiguous feelings by observing their own behavior. But can Bem's theory replace dissonance theory as an explanation of self-persuasion?

Bem confronted this question head-on. What if neutral observers who are not motivated by the need to reduce dissonance were to read a step-by-step description of a dissonance study and predict the results? This approach to the problem was ingenious. Bem reasoned that observers can have the same behavioral information as the subjects themselves, but they don't experience the same personal conflict. If observers generate the same results as real subjects, it would show that dissonance arousal is not necessary for the resulting changes in attitudes.

To test his hypothesis, Bem (1967) described the Festinger and Carlsmith (1959) study to observers and had them guess subjects' attitudes. Some were told about the one-dollar condition, some about the twenty-dollar condition; others read about the control group procedure. The results closely paralleled the original study. As observers saw it, subjects who said the task was interesting for twenty dollars didn't mean it—they just went along for the money. But those who made the claim for only one dollar must have been sincere. Why else would they have gone along? As far as Bem was concerned, subjects themselves reason the same way. No conflict, no arousal—just inference by observation.

So should we conclude that self-perception, not dissonance, is what's necessary to bring about attitude change? That's a tough question. It's not easy to come up with a critical experiment to distinguish between these theories. Both predict the same results, but for different reasons. And both offer unique support for their own points of view. On the one hand, Bem's observer studies show that dissonance-like results *can* be obtained without arousal. On the other hand, the subjects of dissonance manipulations *do* experience arousal, which seems necessary for attitude change to take place. Can we say that one theory is right, and the other wrong?

Fazio and his colleagues (1977) concluded that both theories are right but apply to different situations. When people behave in ways that are strikingly at odds with their attitudes, they feel the unnerving effects of dissonance and change their attitudes to rationalize their actions. When people behave in ways that are not terribly discrepant with how they feel, however, they experience relatively little tension and form their attitudes as a matter of inference. In short, highly discrepant behavior produces attitude change through dissonance, whereas slightly discrepant behavior produces change through self-perception.

Impression-Management Theory Another alternative to a dissonance view of self-persuasion is based on *impression-management theory,* which says that what matters is not a motive to *be* consistent but a motive to *appear* consistent. Nobody wants to be called fickle or to be viewed as a hypocrite. So we calibrate our attitudes and behaviors only publicly—just to present ourselves to others in a particular light (Baumeister, 1982; Tedeschi et al., 1971). Or perhaps we are motivated not to appear consistent but by a desire to avoid being held responsible for the unpleasant consequences of our actions (Schlenker, 1982). Either way, this theory places the emphasis on our concern for self-presentation. According to this view, then, subjects in the Festinger and Carlsmith study simply did not want the experimenter to think they had sold out for a paltry sum of money.

If the impression-management approach is correct, then cognitive dissonance does not produce attitude change at all—only reported change. In other words, if subjects were to state their attitudes anonymously, or if they were to think that the experimenter could determine their true feelings through physiological measures, the dissonance-like effects should vanish. At times, the effects do vanish, but at other times they do not. In general, studies have shown that although self-persuasion can be motivated by impression management, it can also occur in situations that do not clearly arouse self-presentation concerns (Baumeister & Tice, 1984).

Self-Affirmation Theory A third competing explanation relates self-persuasion to the self. According to Elliot Aronson, acts that arouse dissonance do so because they threaten the self-concept (Aronson, 1969; Thibodeau & Aronson, 1992). This being the case, Festinger and Carlsmith's subjects were motivated to change their attitudes toward the boring task in order to repair damage to the self, not to resolve inconsistency.

Claude Steele (1988) takes the notion two steps further. First, dissonance-producing situations—engaging in attitude-discrepant behavior, exerting wasted effort, or making difficult decisions—set in motion a process of *self-affirmation* that is designed to revalidate the integrity of the self-concept. Second, this revalidation can be achieved in many ways, not just by resolving dissonance. Self-affirmation theory makes a unique prediction: If the active ingredient in dissonance situations is a threat to the self, then people who have an opportunity to affirm the self in other ways will not suffer from the effects of dissonance. Give Festinger and Carlsmith's one-dollar subjects a chance to donate money, help a victim in distress, or solve a problem, and their self-concepts should bounce back without further need to justify their actions.

Research supports this hypothesis. For example, Steele and his colleagues (1993) gave subjects positive or negative feedback about a personality test they had taken. Next, they had subjects rate ten popular music albums, and then offered them a choice of keeping either their fifth- or sixth-ranked album. Soon after making the decision, subjects were asked to rerate the albums. As predicted by dissonance theory, most subjects coped with the decision by inflating their ratings of the chosen album relative to the unchosen album. The key word, however, is *most.* Among positive-feedback subjects, ratings did not change. In a second study, subjects with high or low self-esteem participated in the same decision-making task. Half of the subjects first took a self-esteem test that focused attention on their high or low status; the other half did not. As shown in Figure 10.11, most subjects inflated their post-decision ratings of the chosen album relative to the unchosen album. However, those who had high self-esteem and were focused on that strength did not exhibit this effect. Apparently, getting a glowing personality report and focusing on one's positive self-image are self-affirming experiences—enough to overcome the need to reduce dissonance.

To summarize, dissonance theory maintains that people change their attitudes to justify attitude-discrepant behaviors, efforts, and decisions. Self-perception theory argues that the change occurs because people infer how they feel by observing their own behavior. Impression-management theory claims that the atti-

Figure 10.11 Overcoming Dissonance Through Self-Affirmation. Subjects high or low in self-esteem rated ten record albums, chose between the fifth- or sixth-ranked album, and then rerated the items. As shown, most subjects increased their ratings of the chosen album relative to the unchosen album. But when subjects first took a test that made them reflect on their self-esteem, highs did not exhibit the effect. It appears that focusing on a personal strength is a self-affirming experience—enough to overcome the need to reduce dissonance. (Steele et al., 1993.)

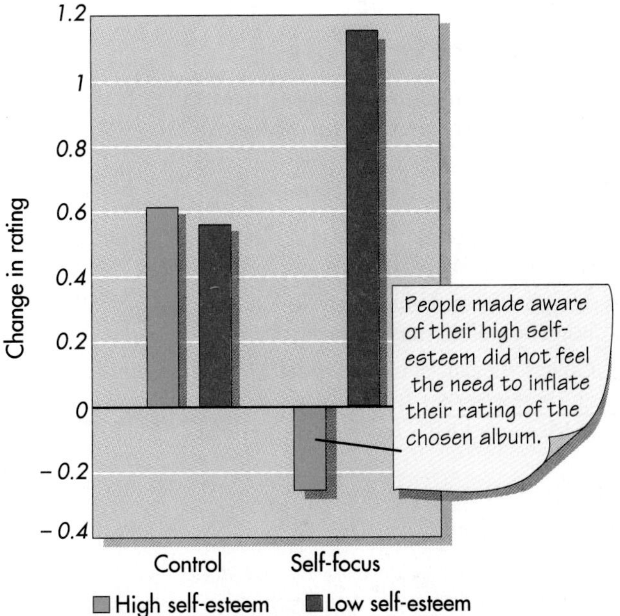

Figure 10.12 Theories of Self-Persuasion: Critical Comparisons. Here we compare the major theories of self-persuasion. Each alternative challenges a different aspect of dissonance theory. Self-perception theory assumes that attitude change is a matter of inference, not motivation. Impression-management theory maintains that the change is more apparent than real, reported for the sake of public self-presentation. Self-affirmation theory contends that the motivating force is a concern for the self and that attitude change will not occur when the self-concept is affirmed in other ways.

	Theories			
	Cognitive Dissonance	*Self-Perception*	*Impression Management*	*Self-Affirmation*
Is the attitude change motivated by a desire to reduce discomfort?	Yes	No	Yes	Yes
Does a person's private attitude really change?	Yes	Yes	No	Yes
Must the change be directly related to the attitude-discrepant behavior?	Yes	Yes	Yes	No

tude change is spurred by self-presentation concerns. And self-affirmation theory says that the change is motivated by threats to the self (see Figure 10.12).

Attitudes and attitude change are an important part of social life. In this chapter, we have seen that persuasion can be achieved in different ways. The most common approach is through communication from *others*. Faced with newspaper editorials, junk mail, books, TV commercials, and other messages, we take one of two routes to persuasion. On the central route, attitude change is based on the merits of the communication. On the peripheral route, it is based on superficial cues. A second, less obvious means of persuasion originates within *ourselves*. When people behave in ways that run afoul of their true convictions, they often go on to change their attitudes. Once again, there is not a single route to such change, but many: Dissonance, self-perception, impression management, and self-affirmation are among the possible avenues.

REVIEW

THE STUDY OF ATTITUDES

- An attitude is a combination of affective, behavioral, and cognitive reactions toward an object.

How Attitudes Are Measured

- The most common way to measure attitudes is through self-reports such as attitude scales.
- To get respondents to answer questions honestly, the bogus pipeline may be used.
- Covert measures may also be used. Such measures include nonverbal behavior, the facial electromyograph (EMG), and EEG brain-wave patterns.

The Link Between Attitudes and Behavior

- Attitudes do not necessarily correlate with behavior, but under certain conditions there is a correlation.
- Attitudes predict behavior best when they're specific rather than general and strong rather than weak.
- Attitudes compete with other influences on behavior.

PERSUASION BY COMMUNICATION

- The most common approach to changing attitudes is persuasive communication.

Two Routes to Persuasion

- When people think critically about a message, they take the central route to persuasion and are influenced by the strength of the arguments.
- When people do not think carefully about a message, they take the peripheral route to persuasion and are influenced instead by peripheral cues.

- The route taken depends on whether people have the ability and motivation to fully process the communication.

The Source

- Attitude change is greater for messages delivered by a source that is high rather than low in credibility (competence and trustworthiness).
- Attitude change is also greater when the source is high rather than low in likability (similarity and physical attractiveness).
- When an audience has a high level of personal involvement, source factors are less important than message quality.
- The sleeper effect shows that people often forget the source but not the message, so the effects of source credibility dissipate over time.

The Message

- On the peripheral route, lengthy messages are persuasive. On the central route, length works only if the added information does not dilute the message.
- Whether it is advantageous to present an argument first or second depends on how much time elapses—between the two arguments and between the second argument and the final decision.
- The more extreme the message, the greater the attitude change produced—but only up to a point.
- High-fear messages motivate attitude change when they contain strong arguments and instructions on how to avoid the threatened danger.
- Positive emotion also facilitates attitude change, as people are easier to persuade when they're in a good mood.
- Research shows that subliminal messages do not produce meaningful changes in attitudes.

The Audience

- People are not consistently hard or easy to persuade. Rather, different kinds of messages influence different kinds of people.
- People who are high in the need for cognition are persuaded more by the strength of an argument.
- People who are high in self-monitoring are influenced more by image-oriented appeals.
- To be persuasive, a message should also appeal to the cultural values of its audience.
- Forewarning increases resistance to persuasive communication. It inoculates the audience by providing the opportunity to generate counterarguments, and it arouses reactance.

PERSUASION BY OUR OWN ACTIONS

Role Playing: All the World's a Stage

- The way people act can influence how they feel, as behavior can determine attitudes.

Cognitive Dissonance Theory: The Classic Version

- Under certain conditions, inconsistency between attitudes and behavior produces an aversive state called cognitive dissonance.
- Motivated to reduce the tension, people will often change their attitudes to justify (1) attitude-discrepant behavior, (2) wasted effort, and (3) difficult decisions.

Cognitive Dissonance Theory: A New Look

- Four conditions must be met for dissonance to be aroused: (1) an act with unwanted consequences, (2) a feeling of personal responsibility, (3) arousal or discomfort, and (4) the attribution of arousal to the attitude-discrepant act.

Alternative Routes to Self-Persuasion

- Alternative explanations of dissonance-related attitude change have been proposed.
- Self-perception theory states that people logically infer their attitudes by observing their own behavior.
- Impression-management theory says that people are motivated only to appear consistent to others.
- According to self-affirmation theory, dissonance is triggered by threats to the self and can be reduced without a change of attitude through self-affirming behaviors.

KEY TERMS

attitude, p. 370
facial electromyograph (EMG), p. 372
theory of planned behavior, p. 374
persuasion, p. 377
central route to persuasion, p. 378
peripheral route to persuasion, p. 378
elaboration, p. 378
heuristic, p. 379
sleeper effect, p. 385
need for cognition (NC), p. 393
inoculation hypothesis, p. 396
cognitive dissonance, p. 399
insufficient justification, p. 400
self-persuasion, p. 401
insufficient deterrence, p. 401

Chapter 11

Group Processes

PREVIEW

This chapter describes social influence in a group context. First, we focus on *collective processes,* the effects of the presence of others on an individual's behavior. Then, we turn to *group processes* among individuals directly interacting with each other. In the final section on *cooperation, competition, and conflict,* we examine how groups intensify or reconcile their differences.

OUTLINE

Some of the best—and some of the worst—aspects of human behavior occur in groups. A loving family is one of the greatest gifts that life has to offer. But the rampages of mob violence create a whirlwind of death and destruction. In the hit musical *The Who's Tommy,* cast and crew work together in an extraordinary display of precision and coordination: People sing and dance; props fly on and off stage; the orchestra plays; the scenery shifts; lights flash; a battery of TV screens multiplies the live action. And, yet, off Broadway in the real world, long-lasting, seemingly intractable conflicts between groups produce the unspeakable horrors of Sarajevo and Rwanda.

To understand why groups are such a powerful force in people's lives, we need to adopt a form of double vision—looking at groups from the inside and from the outside. Internally, groups influence and are influenced by the behavior of their own members. Externally, groups interact with each other. Like an individual, groups move—toward a goal, toward violence, toward peace—in response to both internal impulses and external conditions. This chapter explores both of these perspectives.

COLLECTIVE PROCESSES: THE PRESENCE OF OTHERS

In one of her most memorable lines, the American writer Gertrude Stein insisted that a "rose is a rose is a rose." No such claim of uniformity has ever been made for groups. Groups vary tremendously in size, organization, and purpose. As noted in Chapter 4, a *group* is usually defined as a set of individuals having at least one of the following characteristics: (1) direct interactions with each other; (2) joint membership in a social category based on some enduring attribute such as sex, race, or ethnicity; and (3) a shared, common fate.

Working together in a group, people can create magnificent spectacles, such as this scene from the Broadway musical *The Who's Tommy.* Working against each other, groups can produce death and destruction, as shown in this photo of a crowded marketplace in Sarajevo demolished by a mortar bomb fired into the city by the Bosnian Serbs.

But there is another kind of group. Those in which people engage in a common activity but have little if any direct interaction with each other are called **collectives.** The audience watching *The Who's Tommy* is a collective; so is a mob. We begin our discussion of groups by examining collective processes.

collectives People engaged in common activities but with minimal direct interaction.

Social Facilitation: When Others Arouse Us

Social psychologists have long been fascinated by how the presence of others affects behavior. In Chapter 1, we declared a tie for the title of "founder of social psychology." One of the winners was Norman Triplett, whose article "The Dynamogenic Factors in Pacemaking and Competition" (1897–1898) is often cited as the earliest publication in social psychology.

Triplett began his research by studying the official bicycle records from the Racing Board of the League of American Wheelmen for the 1897 season. He noticed that cyclists who competed against others performed better than those who cycled alone against the clock. After dismissing various theories of the day (our favorite is "brain worry"), he proposed his own hypothesis: The presence of another rider releases the competitive instinct, which increases nervous energy and enhances performance. To test this proposition, Triplett got forty children to wind up fishing reels, alternating between performing alone and working parallel to each other. On the average, winding time was faster when the children worked side by side rather than alone.

But later research following in Triplett's footsteps was disappointing. Sometimes the presence of others (side by side or with an audience out front) enhanced performance; at other times performance declined. Stumped by such contradictory findings, it seemed that Triplett's promising lead had turned into a blind alley. But then Robert Zajonc (1965, 1980) offered an elegant solution: The presence of others increases arousal, which affects performance in different ways depending on the task at hand. Let's see how this works.

The Zajonc Solution

According to Zajonc, the road from presence to performance requires three steps.

1. The presence of others creates an increase in nonspecific *drive,* usually defined as diffuse arousal that energizes behavior. Although the notion of "drive" remains a convenient shorthand, the actual physiological effects of the presence of others are more complicated than was originally assumed (Blascovich, 1992; Cacioppo et al., 1990).
2. Increased drive enhances an individual's tendency to perform the *dominant response.* The dominant response is the reaction elicited most quickly and easily by a given stimulus. For example, if someone says "bacon," most people think "eggs."
3. The quality of a person's performance will vary according to the type of *task.* On an easy task (one that is simple or well learned), the dominant response is usually correct. But on a difficult task (one that is complex or unfamiliar), the dominant response is often incorrect.

Putting these three steps together (see Figure 11.1) yields the following scenarios. Suppose you are trying to memorize some easy associations like "bacon-eggs." Here, the presence of others will increase arousal, elicit the dominant response, and *enhance* your performance. But what if your task is more difficult?

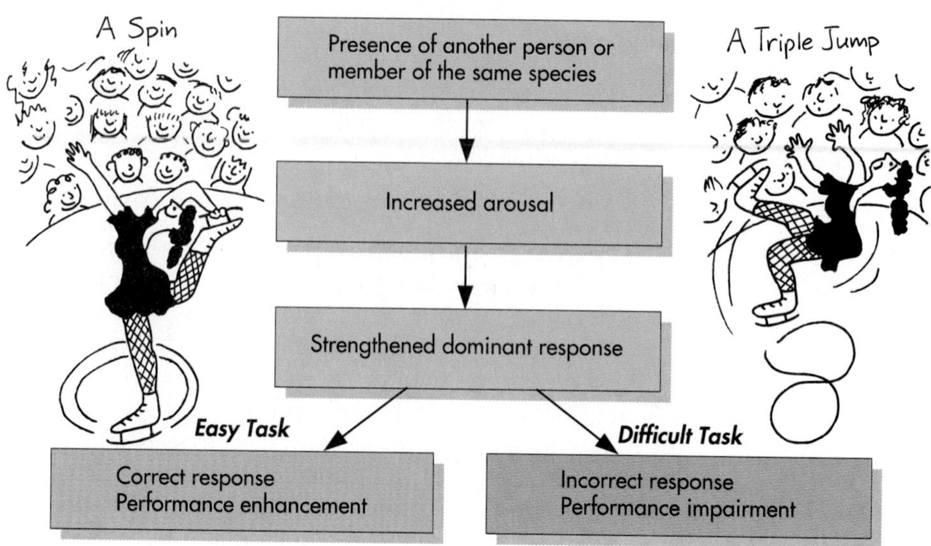

Figure 11.1 Social Facilitation: The Zajonc Solution. According to Zajonc, the presence of others increases arousal, which strengthens the dominant response to a stimulus. On an easy task, the dominant response is usually correct and thus the presence of others enhances performance. On a difficult task, the dominant response is often incorrect and thus the presence of others impairs performance.

If you are trying to learn some strange associations such as "bacon-algebra," the presence of others will increase arousal, elicit the dominant response, and *impair* your performance. You'll start to say "eggs," which will interfere with your remembering "algebra."

Taken as a package, these two effects of the presence of others—helping performance on easy tasks, but hurting performance on difficult tasks—are known as **social facilitation.** Unfortunately, this term has been a prime source of confusion for countless students before you. The trick is to remember that only easy tasks are facilitated. On difficult ones, social "facilitation" damages performance.

social facilitation The finding that the presence of others enhances performance on easy tasks but impairs performance on difficult tasks.

Zajonc says that social facilitation is universal—occurring not only in human activities but also among animals and even insects. Consider, for instance, cockroaches. How fast will they run? In a study by Zajonc and his colleagues (1969), participating insects were placed in a brightly lit start box connected to a darkened goal box. When the track was a simple one, with a straight runway between the start box and the goal box, cockroaches running in pairs ran more quickly toward the goal box than did those running alone. But in a more complex maze, with a right turn required to reach the goal box, solitary cockroaches outraced pairs.

Despite its predictive power, Zajonc's formulation has its critics. Two aspects of his theory have received particular attention. Zajonc maintains that social facilitation is uniquely *social.* But is it? Could nonsocial, inanimate objects have the same impact? Zajonc is also convinced that the **mere presence** of others is sufficient to affect performance. But some researchers have their doubts. Perhaps social facilitation effects will occur only when the others who are present have certain characteristics. These issues have produced various alternative explanations of social facilitation, and we turn now to two of the major variations on Zajonc's theme.

mere presence The theory that the mere presence of others is sufficient to produce social facilitation effects.

evaluation apprehension The theory that the presence of others will produce social facilitation effects only when those others are seen as potential evaluators.

Evaluation Apprehension

The first and most thoroughly researched alternative, **evaluation apprehension,** accepts the uniquely social character of social facilitation but rejects mere presence (Cottrell, 1968; Henchy & Glass, 1968). According to this perspective, performance will be enhanced or impaired only in the presence of others who are in a position to evaluate that performance. Usually, presence and potential evaluation go hand in hand. To pry them apart, researchers have come up with some rather unusual procedures. In one study, for example, subjects worked on a task alone, in the presence of two other supposed subjects (actually confederates), or in the presence of two blindfolded confederates supposedly preparing for a perception study (Cottrell et al., 1968). Compared with subjects working alone, those working in the presence of seeing confederates were more likely to come up with dominant responses. In the presence of the blindfolded confederates, however, dominant responses were no more frequent than among subjects working alone.

distraction-conflict theory The theory that the presence of others will produce social facilitation effects only when those others distract from the task and create attentional conflict.

Distraction Another approach to social facilitation, **distraction-conflict theory,** points out that being distracted while we're working on a task creates attentional conflict (Baron, 1986). We're torn between focusing on the task and inspecting the distracting stimulus. Conflicted about where to pay attention, our arousal increases. Distraction-conflict theory maintains that there's nothing uniquely social about "social" facilitation. People, of course, can be distracting, but so can crashing objects, blaring music, and glittering lights. Mere presence is also called into question. People are not always distracting; a familiar presence we take for granted should leave our performance untouched.

Table 11.1 compares the three theories of social facilitation we have described. Is one of them right and the others wrong? Probably not. Comprehensive reviews of the research evidence have drawn different conclusions about which theory has the best track record (Bond & Titus, 1983; Guerin, 1986). It seems likely that all three of the basic elements described by these theories (mere presence, evaluation, and attention) contribute to the impact others have on our own performance. And there's more to come.

Social Loafing: When Others Relax Us

The tasks employed in research on social facilitation produce individually *identifiable* results. What each person does is known. But on some tasks, efforts are *pooled* so that the specific performance of any one individual cannot be deter-

Table 11.1 Social Facilitation: Questions and Answers

	Answers		
Questions	Mere Presence	Evaluation Apprehension	Distraction-Conflict
Is it uniquely social?	Yes	Yes	No
Is mere presence sufficient?	Yes	No	No

For theories of social facilitation, the major issues in dispute are whether it is produced only by social stimuli and whether the mere presence of others is sufficient. As you can see, the three theories described in the text provide different answers to these questions.

mined. That other founder of social psychology, French agricultural engineer Max Ringelmann, investigated group performance on these kinds of collective endeavors. In research conducted during the 1880s, Ringelmann discovered that compared with what people produced on their own, individual output declined when they worked together on simple tasks like pulling a rope or pushing a cart (Kravitz & Martin, 1986; Ringelmann, 1913).

social loafing A group-produced reduction in individual output on easy tasks where contributions are pooled.

Nearly a hundred years later, Bibb Latané and his colleagues (1979) found that group-produced reductions in individual output, called **social loafing,** still flourish. When college students were told to cheer or clap as loudly as they could, the sound pressure generated by each individual decreased as the size of the group increased (see Figure 11.2). Social loafing is not restricted to simple motor tasks. Sharing responsibility with others reduces the amount of effort people put into cognitive tasks as well (Weldon & Gargano, 1988). When others are there to pick up the slack, people slack off.

But social loafing is not inevitable. According to a meta-analysis of seventy-eight studies conducted by Steven Karau and Kipling Williams (1993), social loafing declines or is eliminated entirely when

- people believe that their own performance can be evaluated by themselves or others.
- the task is important or meaningful to those performing it.
- co-workers are *not* expected to perform well, so to loaf is to risk failure on the task.
- people believe that their own efforts are necessary for a successful outcome.
- the group is valued by its members.
- the group is small.
- those working on the task are women rather than men.
- those working on the task are from eastern cultures (China, Japan, and Taiwan) rather than from western cultures (Canada and the United States).

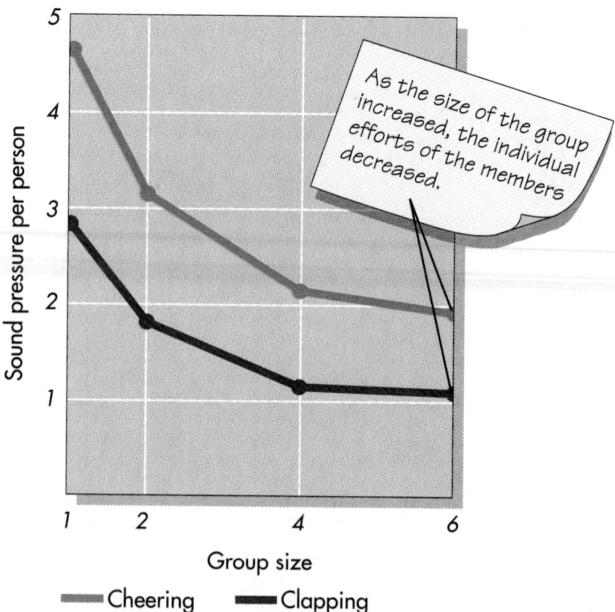

Figure 11.2 **Social Loafing: When Many Produce Less.** Social loafing is a group-produced reduction in individual output on simple tasks. In this study, college students were told to cheer or clap as loudly as they could. The sound pressure produced by each of them decreased as the size of the group increased. (Latané et al., 1979.)

Here, Chinese farmers cooperate on a task in which individual contributions cannot be identified. Social loafing on such tasks occurs less often in eastern cultures than in western ones.

Social loafing seems, then, to be an entirely rational response to a person's goals and values. The more important the task or, at least, their own contribution to it, the less people will loaf. And less loafing takes place when people care about the group or are usually more socially oriented. If you were an employer concerned about social loafing among your employees, these findings could suggest a number of remedies. What would you do?

Unifying the Paradigms You may have noticed that the perceived possibility of evaluation affects both social facilitation and social loafing. The recognition of this connection between the two research traditions has prompted some investigators to attempt a unified approach (Harkins & Szymanski, 1987; Sanna, 1992). Although the two models that have been proposed differ in some details, both highlight the close relationship between presence and evaluation:

- When individual contributions can be identified (social facilitation), the presence of others *increases* evaluation: Comparisons can be made.
- When individual contributions are pooled (social loafing), the presence of others *decreases* evaluation: Each person's performance is swallowed up in the group product.

Now, add task difficulty and four predictions pop out like bread from a toaster.

- When the presence of others increases evaluation of an individual's work: (1) Performance on easy tasks should be enhanced because we're more motivated. That's social facilitation, part one. (2) Performance on difficult tasks should be impaired because the pressure gets to us. That's social facilitation, part two.
- When the presence of others decreases evaluation of an individual's work: (3) Performance on easy tasks should be impaired because we're uninspired. That's social loafing. (4) Performance on difficult tasks should be enhanced because we're free from anxiety. There's no official name for this effect, but we're inclined to call it "social security."

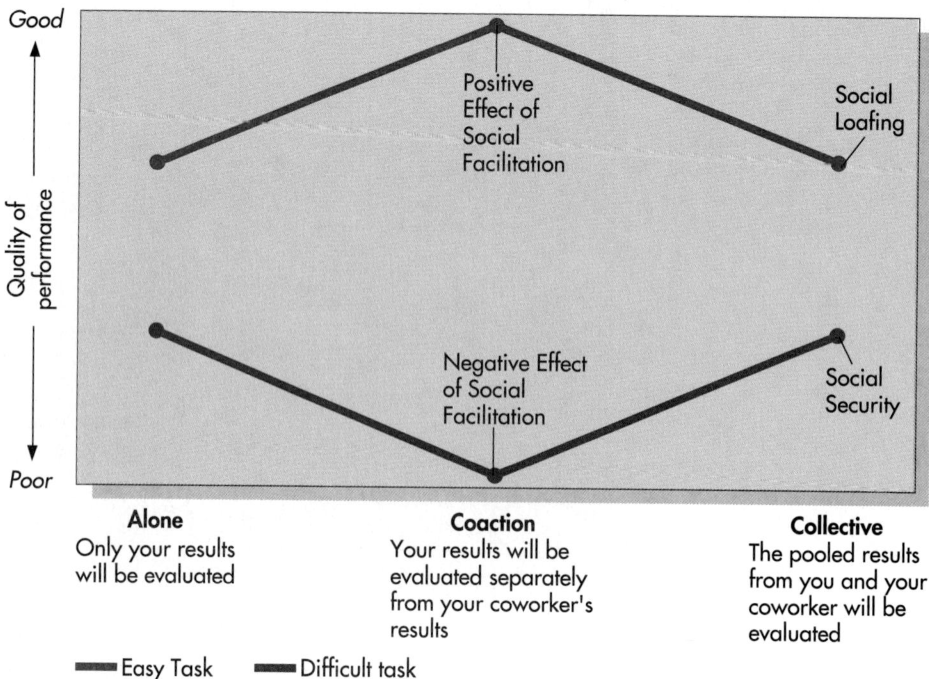

Figure 11.3 Unifying the Paradigms: Presence and Evaluation. The relationship between the presence of others and the potential for evaluation is the key to a unified paradigm of social facilitation and social loafing. When individual performance can be evaluated, the presence of others enhances performance on easy tasks, but impairs performance on difficult endeavors. When contributions are pooled across individuals, the pattern reverses, as performance declines on easy tasks but improves on difficult ones. (Adapted from Jackson & Williams, 1985; Sanna, 1992.)

These predictions have been confirmed in several studies using different methods and measures (Jackson & Williams, 1985; Sanna, 1992). The typical pattern of results is diagrammed in Figure 11.3. A unified view of social facilitation and social loafing has important practical implications for maximizing performance when individuals are working together. In team sports, for example, coaches would be well advised to evaluate each player's performance against a weak opponent, but to stress team spirit and overall group effort during a tough game. Unification is also historically satisfying: the two founders, Triplett and Ringelman, together at last.

Deindividuation: When People Lose Control

Some other pioneers in social psychology regarded the presence of others as considerably more profound, and more troubling. Based on their research in France, Gabriel Tarde (1890) and Gustave Le Bon (1895) thought of collective influence as virtually mesmerizing. They maintained that, under the sway of the crowd, people would turn into copycat automatons or, worse still, uncontrollable mobs.

The destructive capacity of collectives has left a bloody trail throughout human history: pogroms against Jews in Eastern Europe and Russia; lynchings of

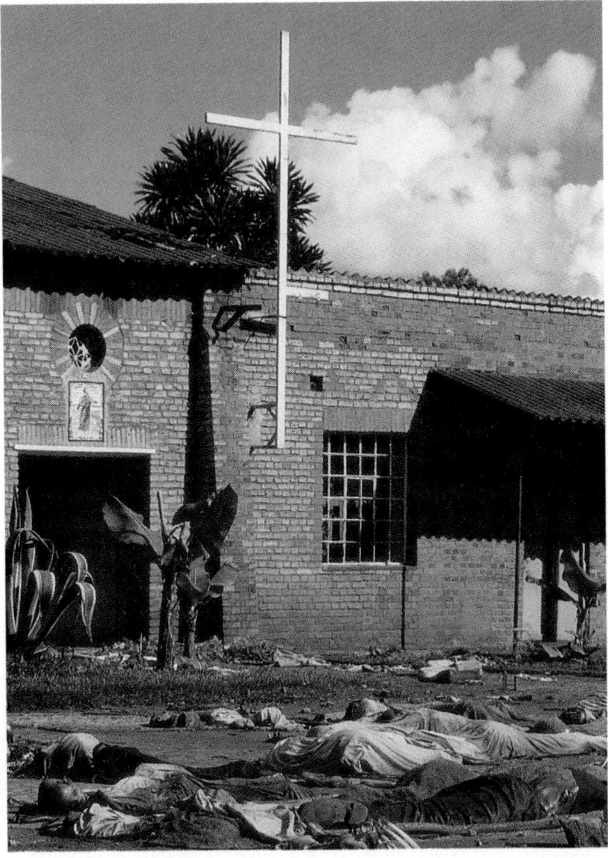

Death in Rwanda, where no sanctuary was sufficient to protect the Tutsi people from the violence of their Hutu neighbors.

African Americans in the United States; the indiscriminate murder and rape of the civilian population when the Japanese Army entered undefended Nanking, China, in 1937; neo-Nazi attacks against immigrant workers from Asia and Africa living in today's unified Germany; the slaughter of an estimated 500,000 Tutsi by the Hutu in Rwanda. What turns an unruly crowd into a violent mob?

No doubt many of the factors described in Chapter 8 often contribute to violence by groups as well as by individuals: imitation of aggressive models, intense frustration, high temperatures, alcohol consumption, and the presence of weapons that trigger aggressive thoughts and actions. But then there's **deindividuation,** the loss of a person's sense of individuality and the reduction of normal constraints against deviant behavior. Most investigators believe that deindividuation is a collective phenomenon that occurs only in the presence of others (Diener et al., 1976; Festinger et al., 1952).

deindividuation The loss of a person's sense of individuality and the reduction of normal constraints against deviant behavior.

Environmental Cues In order to understand deindividuation, we must examine the physical and social environment in which it takes place. According to Steven Prentice-Dunn and Ronald Rogers (1982, 1983), two types of environmental cues—accountability and attentional—increase deviant behavior (see Figure 11.4).

Accountability cues affect the individual's cost-reward calculations. When accountability is low, those who commit deviant acts are less likely to be caught and punished, and people may deliberately choose to engage in gratifying but

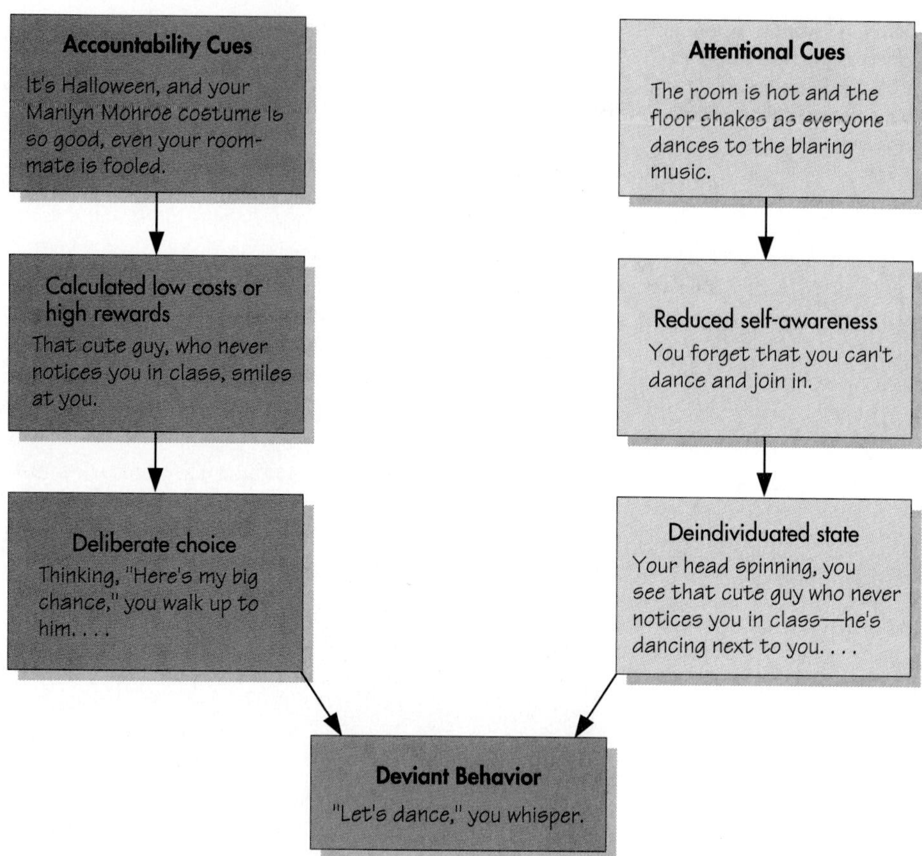

Figure 11.4 Environmental Cues and Deviant Behavior. Two different routes to deviant behavior have been identified. In one, accountability cues, such as anonymity, signal a reduction in the likelihood that a person can be held accountable for deviant actions. In the other, attentional cues, such as intense environmental stimulation, focus attention away from the self. Both pathways lead to the same destination: People behave in ways that differ from their ordinary conduct.

usually inhibited behaviors. Consider, for instance, features of the environment (such as being in a large crowd, or wearing masks or hoods) that create anonymity. What would you do if you could be totally anonymous, indeed invisible, for twenty-four hours? Among college students asked this question, their most frequent responses involved criminal acts; the single most common response was "rob a bank" (Dodd, 1985).

Research on actual behavior provides even more compelling evidence of the effects of anonymity. In the laboratory, anonymity is created by various devices: not mentioning subjects' names; telling them they will remain unidentified; and, sometimes, having them dress up in enveloping clothing, complete with hoods masking their faces from view. In contrast, control subjects are addressed by name, wear large name tags, and retain their regular clothing. Compared with controls, those who are anonymous are more aggressive (Zimbardo, 1970), especially when all subjects have been physiologically aroused without their awareness (Taylor et al., 1991). Gender differences may also be modified. In one study, men were more aggressive than women when individuals were identifiable. But protected by anonymity, men and women were equally aggressive (Lightdale & Prentice, 1994).

Attentional cues, the second type of environmental characteristic that increases deviant behavior, focus a person's attention away from the self. Prentice-Dunn and Rogers maintain that when a person's self-awareness declines, a change in consciousness takes place. In this "deindividuated state," the individual attends less to internal standards of conduct, reacts more to the immediate situation, and is less sensitive to long-term consequences of behavior (Diener, 1980). Behavior slips out from the bonds of cognitive control, and people act on impulse.

Have you ever been at a party with flashing strobe lights and music so loud that you could feel the room vibrate? If so, did it seem that you were somehow merging with the pulsating crowd and that your individual identity was slipping away? Intense stimulation from the environment is probably the most common attentional cue reducing self-awareness. In laboratory research, groups of subjects placed in a highly stimulating environment (loud rock music, jokes, puzzles, color video games) were more uninhibited, extreme, and aggressive in their actions (Diener, 1979; Prentice-Dunn & Rogers, 1980; Spivey & Prentice-Dunn, 1990).

Crowds and Identity In terms of personal responsibility, there is a vast difference between the effects of accountability and attentional cues. To engage in a forbidden action because you think you won't get caught is a deliberate decision. But to lose the ability to exercise self-control is a case of diminished capacity. Although the theoretical distinction is clear, the application to real life is more complicated. Being in a large crowd, for instance, can increase anonymity *and* decrease self-awareness. Perhaps because of this double impact, larger groups are associated with greater violence. Research by Brian Mullen (1986) on newspaper accounts of sixty lynchings of African Americans that occurred between 1899 and 1946 found that as the size of the mob increased relative to the number of victims, the brutality of the lynching intensified.

If crowds can be lethal, should individuals in the crowd be held legally responsible for their actions? At least in some cases, judges and juries seem to think not. In 1990, for instance, a South African judge cited deindividuation as a major reason for drastically reducing the sentences handed out to six members of an Xhosa-speaking mob that had burned to death an eighteen-year-old woman suspected of collaborating with the Zulu Inkatha police (Colman, 1991). The murder occurred during a time of enormous turbulence and violence in the township, including the killing of eleven Xhosa-speaking people by the Inkatha police less than two months earlier. A similar defense was offered in the trial of Damian Williams and Harry Watson for the beating of Reginald Denny. This assault took place during the 1992 Los Angeles riots, which erupted after four white police officers were acquitted on charges of beating Rodney King. Williams and Watson received relatively light sentences. After the trial, one juror said, "I see them just as two human beings. They just got caught up in the riot. I guess maybe they were in the wrong place at the wrong time." What do *you* think?

Despite the association between crowds and violence, the loss of personal identity does not always produce antisocial behavior. In a study by Robert Johnson and Leslie Downing (1979), female undergraduates donned a robe resembling either those worn by Ku Klux Klan members or a nurse's uniform. Half of the subjects were individually identified throughout the study; the others were not. All subjects were then given the opportunity to increase or decrease the intensity of electric shocks delivered to a supposed other subject (actually, an experimental confederate) who had previously behaved in an obnoxious manner. Subjects wearing the KKK costume increased shock levels in both the identified and anonymous conditions. However, among those in nurse's apparel, anony-

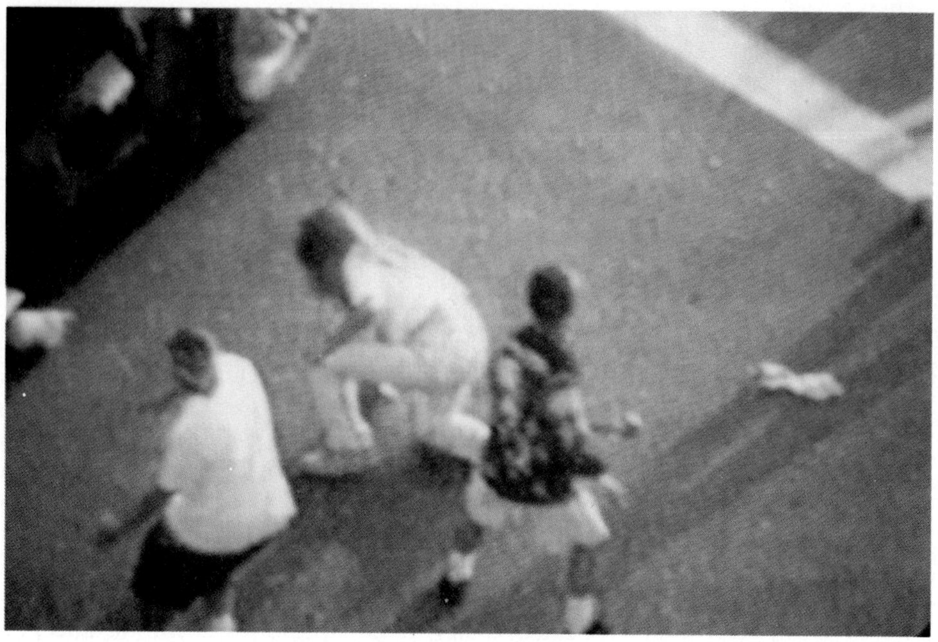

A deindividuation defense, such as that offered during the trial of Damian Williams and Harry Watson for the beating of truck-driver Reginald Denny during the 1992 Los Angeles riots, argues that individuals should not be held legally responsible for their actions during mob violence.

mous subjects *decreased* shock intensity at a rate four times greater than did identified subjects!

These findings (displayed in Figure 11.5) make a telling point: Sometimes becoming less accountable, or less self-aware, allows us to be *more* responsive to the needs of others. Whether deindividuation is for better or for worse seems to reflect the characteristics of the group (Reicher, 1984; Reicher & Levine, 1994). As personal identity and internal controls are submerged, social identity and so-

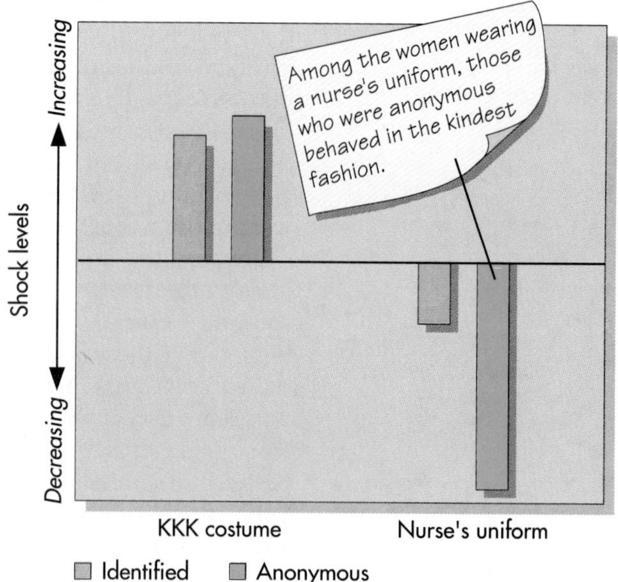

Figure 11.5 **Anonymous Goodness.** Regardless of whether they were individually identified or anonymous, female subjects wearing a KKK robe increased the intensity of shocks they administered to an experimental confederate. Among those wearing a nurse's uniform, however, anonymous subjects *decreased* shock intensity much more than did individually identified subjects. (Data from Johnson & Downing, 1979.)

cial standards emerge. If a group defines itself ("us") in terms of prejudice and hatred against another group ("them"), deindividuation can ignite an explosion of violence. But if a group defines itself in terms of concern for the welfare of others, deindividuation can spark an expansion of goodness. The consequences of losing your personal identity depend on what you lose it to.

GROUP PROCESSES: INTERACTING WITH OTHERS

Influential as they can be, collectives are only minimally social. People are in the same place at the same time working on a common task or reacting to the same event, but they don't engage in extensive interaction with each other. In this section, we examine social influence in groups where interaction among members is more direct and meaningful.

Joining a Group

Interactive groups come in all shapes and sizes: large and small, highly organized and quite informal, short term and long lasting. Sometimes group membership is involuntary. You didn't choose your family. But membership in most interactive groups is voluntary. You decide to join an existing group or get together with others to create a brand-new one. Why do people join groups? How do groups develop over time?

There are two distinct, but sometimes overlapping, reasons for joining groups (Hogg et al., 1993; Prentice et al., 1994). Some we join for their own sake. Perhaps a particular group gives us the social status we desire; perhaps it allows us to engage in activities we enjoy; perhaps it provides a way to fulfill religious or civic obligations we take seriously. In any event, being affiliated and identified with the group is important to us. Alternatively, we may join a group simply because we like the members and want to have the opportunity to interact with them. In this instance, the group itself doesn't matter all that much to us. Whatever their reason for joining, individuals preparing to do so are usually optimistic about the group. They expect more rewards than costs, believe that the anticipated rewards will be more positive than the anticipated costs will be negative, and think that rewards are more likely than costs to occur (Brinthaupt et al., 1991).

Once an individual has joined a group, a process of adjustment takes place. The individual assimilates into the group, making whatever changes are necessary to fit in. At the same time, the group accommodates to the newcomer, making whatever changes are necessary to include that individual. Not surprisingly, groups that need more members in order to function effectively go out of their way to accommodate newcomers (Cini et al., 1993).

Socialization of a new member into a group often relies heavily on the relationship between newcomers and established members (Moreland & Levine, 1989). Newcomers model their behavior on what the old-timers do; old-timers may hold explicit training sessions for newcomers. And, acting as mentors, old-timers develop close personal relationships with newcomers in order to help them be successful in the group. Having a mentor is useful to anyone joining a new group but may be especially helpful to those, such as women and people of color, who are joining groups from which they were previously excluded (Irons & Moore, 1985).

People join a group to obtain at least one of two basic social rewards: affiliation with the group itself and interaction with individual group members.

Roles, Norms, and Cohesiveness

Despite their variation in specific characteristics, all interactive groups can be described in terms of three essential components: roles, norms, and cohesiveness (Forsyth, 1990; Levine & Moreland, 1990). People's *roles* in a group, their set of expected behaviors, can be formal or informal. Formal roles are designated by titles: teacher or student in a class, vice president or account executive in a corporation. Informal roles are less obvious but still powerful. For example, Robert Bales (1958) proposed that regardless of people's titles, enduring groups give rise to two fundamental types of roles: an instrumental role to help the group achieve its tasks, and an expressive role to provide emotional support and maintain morale. The same person can fill both roles, but often they are assumed by different individuals.

Bales's view of group roles is patterned after the division of labor in the traditional family between the "breadwinner" father and the "caretaking" mother. Does this pattern still hold? Are males more likely to take an instrumental, task-oriented role and females an expressive, socially oriented role? Under some circumstances, yes. In mixed-sex groups working on tasks that allowed for both kinds of roles, males engaged in more task-oriented activity and females in more positive social behavior (Wood, 1987; Wood et al., 1985b).

But under other circumstances, no. When participants in a mixed-sex group were given feedback indicating either high or low competence, those who believed they were highly competent were more task oriented, while those who perceived themselves as lacking competence engaged more often in positive social behaviors (Wood & Karten, 1986). The same pattern of results was obtained for both men and women. Thus, among men and women who feel equally competent about task performance, the roles they adopt and the manner in which they behave are often quite similar (Dovidio et al., 1988a, 1988b).

Interactive groups also establish *norms,* rules of conduct for members. Like roles, norms may be either formal or informal. Fraternities and sororities, for example, usually have written rules for the behavior expected from their members. Informal norms are more subtle. What do I wear? Is it OK for me to call him? Who double-dates with whom? Who pays for this or that? Figuring out the unwritten rules of the group can be a time-consuming and, sometimes, anxiety-provoking endeavor.

The third characteristic of interactive groups, *cohesiveness,* refers to the forces exerted on a group that push its members closer together (Cartwright & Zander, 1960; Festinger, 1950). Such forces can be positive (rewards obtained within the group) or negative (costs involved in leaving the group). Various factors contribute to cohesiveness, including attraction to group members, commitment to the group task, and group pride (Cota et al., 1995; Festinger, 1950; Zaccaro & McCoy, 1988). Of these three, commitment to the task has the strongest effect on group performance: Those who are more committed perform better (Mullen & Copper, 1994). Outside forces, too, affect cohesiveness, which increases in response to an enemy's attack (Lanzetta, 1955).

As noted in Chapter 9, there are strong pressures toward behavioral and attitudinal conformity in highly cohesive groups: Members conform to prevailing group norms and reject those who deviate (Schachter, 1951; Wright et al., 1986). Whistle blowers who refuse to keep silent about unethical or incompetent practices often have to bear the full weight of the cohesive group deployed against them. In 1992, Paula Coughlin, a Navy lieutenant and helicopter pilot, informed the national news media about the infamous 1991 Tailhook convention at which

In highly cohesive groups, members conform to the prevailing group norm.

"This might not be ethical. Is that a problem for anybody?"

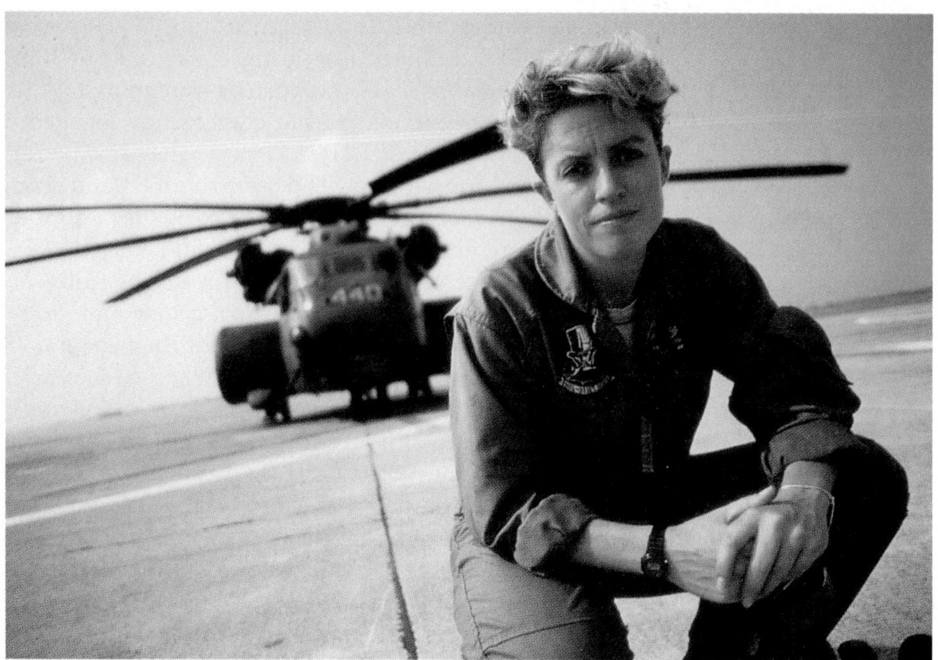

Paula Coughlin, former Navy lieutenant and helicopter pilot, who informed the public about the sexual misconduct of Navy and Marine aviators at the 1991 Tailhook convention.

83 women were molested by Navy and Marine aviators. Her revelations ended the stonewalling that had prevailed until then: The Secretary of the Navy resigned and 140 harassment cases were investigated. Yet none of these cases led to a court-martial. Isolated and discouraged, Coughlin resigned.

Coughlin's experience illustrates how difficult it is to confront a cohesive group. Since it's easier to speak up when you have allies, people are more likely to blow the whistle when there are more witnesses to the wrongdoing (Miceli et al., 1991). After Coughlin went public, other women joined her. But even when their charges are verified, whistle blowers are seldom welcomed back into the fold. The Tailhook saga, however, did not end with Coughlin's resignation. In 1994, a federal jury found that the Las Vegas Hilton, where the convention took place, had failed to provide adequate security and awarded Coughlin $6.7 million in damages.

Group Polarization: Gaining Conviction

Once a group has formed—with roles, norms, and some degree of cohesiveness—it begins to make decisions and take actions. The issues faced by groups range from the trivial ("Where do we party?") to the profound ("Should we make war—or peace?"). Whatever the issue, the attitudes of group members affect what they do. How does being in a group influence people's opinions?

The key to answering this question is to realize that most groups consist of individuals who hold roughly similar views. People are attracted to groups that share their attitudes, and those who disagree with the group usually leave by their own choice or are ejected by the others. But similar does not mean identical. Although the range of opinion is relatively restricted, there are still differences.

You might think that discussion of these differing points of view would result in some overall compromise as everyone moves toward the group average. It sounds reasonable. But it isn't what happens. Instead, individuals who start off with similar opinions end up with more extreme positions after group discussion. Conservatives become more conservative, liberals more liberal, radicals more radical, reactionaries more reactionary. Talking it over intensifies preexisting attitudes.

group polarization The exaggeration through group discussion of initial tendencies in the thinking of group members.

This effect is called **group polarization,** the exaggeration through group discussion of initial tendencies in the thinking of group members (Moscovici & Zavalloni, 1969; Myers & Lamm, 1976). It is more likely to occur on important issues (Kerr, 1992b). Consider, for example, racial prejudice. In one study, high school students responded to an initial questionnaire and were classified as high, medium, or low on racial prejudice (Myers & Bishop, 1970). Groups of like-minded students then met for a discussion of racial issues, with their individual attitudes on these issues assessed before and after their interaction. Group polarization was dramatic. Students low in prejudice to begin with were even *less* prejudiced after the group discussion; students moderate or high in prejudice became even *more* prejudiced.

What creates group polarization? Three processes are usually emphasized (Kaplan, 1987; Mackie, 1986):

1. According to *persuasive arguments theory*, the greater the number and persuasiveness of the arguments to which group members are exposed, the more extreme their attitudes become (Vinokur & Burnstein, 1974). Some arguments provide new information to those group members hearing them for the first time. Sometimes, however, what we hear from others validates our own reasoning. Group polarization intensifies when a participant makes an argument and then hears it repeated by others in the group (Brauer et al., 1995).

2. But group polarization is also created by simply discovering other people's opinions, even if no arguments are presented (Brown, 1965; Sanders & Baron, 1977). Here, *social comparison* is at work. As described in Chapter 2, individuals develop their view of social reality by comparing themselves with others (Festinger, 1954). The construction of social reality in like-minded groups is a two-step process. First, people discover more support for their own opinion than they had originally anticipated. Second, this discovery sets up a new, more extreme norm and motivates group members to go beyond that norm. If believing X is good, then believing triple X is even better. By adopting a more extreme attitudinal position, people can distinguish themselves in the group in a manner approved by the group (Lamm & Myers, 1978).

3. In addition, group polarization is influenced by a concept you may recall from Chapter 4: *social categorization,* the tendency for people to categorize themselves and others in terms of social groups (Turner & Oakes, 1989). The social categorization approach compares how individuals react to information from ingroups (to which they belong or want to belong) and outgroups (to which they don't belong and don't want to). Group polarization typically occurs only among ingroup members, while the opinions of outgroups are disregarded (Hogg et al., 1990; Mackie & Cooper, 1984).

In short, group polarization grows out of what takes place in a group discussion: Group members express their own views and hear arguments made and positions taken by other members of their own group. The impact of a group discussion on our subsequent attitudes depends on what we say, what we hear, and from whom we hear it.

Groupthink: Losing Perspective

The persuasion, social comparison, and social categorization processes involved in group polarization may set the stage for an even greater, and perhaps more dangerous, bias in group decision making. Take, for instance, three decisions made by American presidents and their advisers:

- Kennedy's approval of the Bay of Pigs invasion in Cuba
- Nixon's attempt to stonewall the Watergate scandal
- Reagan's agreement to trade arms for hostages with Iran

As we now know, these decisions were seriously flawed and resulted in disastrous military or political consequences. What went wrong?

groupthink A group decision-making style characterized by an excessive tendency among group members to seek concurrence.

According to Irving Janis (1982), the culprit is **groupthink,** an excessive tendency to seek concurrence among group members. Groupthink emerges when the need for agreement takes priority over the motivation to obtain accurate knowledge and make appropriate decisions. Janis believed that three characteristics contribute to the development of groupthink:

1. Since *highly cohesive groups* are more likely to reject members with deviant opinions, Janis thought they would be more susceptible to groupthink.
2. *Group structure* was also said to be important. Groups that are composed of people from similar backgrounds, isolated from other people, directed by a strong leader, and lacking in systematic procedures for making and reviewing decisions should be particularly likely to fall prey to groupthink.
3. Finally, Janis emphasized that *stressful situations* can provoke groupthink. Under stress, urgency can overrule accuracy, and the reassuring support of other group members becomes highly desirable.

Behavioral Symptoms In Janis's formulation, groupthink is a kind of social disease and infected groups display behavioral symptoms such as the following:

- *Overestimation of the group:* Members maintain an illusion of invulnerability and an exaggerated belief in the morality of the group's positions. Did Kennedy and his advisers sufficiently question the wisdom of the invasion plan they had inherited from the Eisenhower administration? Or did they think that, as the "best and brightest," they could surely pull off a little invasion?
- *Closed-mindedness:* Members rationalize the correctness of the group's actions and believe stereotypes about the characteristics of the targets of these actions. Did Nixon and his advisers ever think seriously about what was appropriate for political activities in a democracy? Or were they convinced that anything goes against "the enemy"?
- *Increased pressures toward uniformity:* The pressures to sustain group cohesiveness grow increasingly strong. Group members censor their own thoughts and act as "mindguards" to discourage deviant thoughts by other group members. People who refuse to conform are expelled from the group. Did Reagan and those who supported the exchange with Iran really listen to those who opposed it? Or were officials who wouldn't join the team and support the policy, such as Secretary of State George Shultz, cut out of the loop?

By preventing an open consideration of alternatives, the behavioral symptoms of groupthink can result in the defective decision making outlined in Figure 11.6.

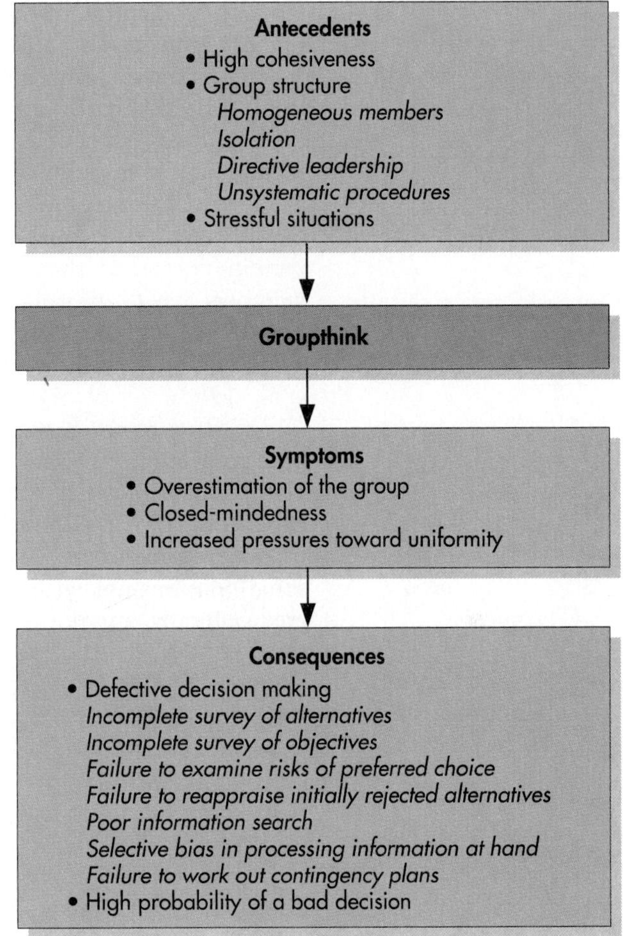

Figure 11.6 **Charting the Course of Groupthink.** Irving Janis depicted groupthink as a kind of social disease, complete with antecedents, symptoms, and long-term consequences. (Based on Janis, 1982.)

In turn, a defective decision-making process increases the likelihood that a group will make bad decisions.

To guard against groupthink, Janis urged groups to make an active effort to process information more carefully and accurately. He recommended that decision-making groups

- consult widely with outsiders.
- have leaders who explicitly encourage criticism.
- establish a strong norm of critical review of all decisions.

Convinced that groupthink posed a serious threat to the well-being of individuals, groups, and the society as a whole, Janis was hopeful that groups adopting this preventative approach would have a better chance of making wise choices and implementing effective actions.

Research on Groupthink Much of the research on groupthink has involved case studies and historical analyses, frequently focusing on the deliberations and actions of government and military officials (McCauley, 1989; Tetlock et al., 1992). But the potential range of groupthink goes much further. Groupthink tendencies have been identified in groups as diverse as a university board of trustees

(Hensley & Griffin, 1986) and autonomous work groups in a battery assembly plant (Manz & Sims, 1982).

If Janis's model is to be adequately tested, however, more rigorous experimental or correlational studies are essential. This research provides only mixed support, and the role of cohesiveness is especially controversial. Some evidence favors Janis's view that cohesiveness can damage information processing by a group. For instance, Tatsuya Kameda and Shinkichi Sugimori (1993) found that strong pressures toward cohesiveness produced poor decision making: Requiring unanimity rather than majority rule for a new decision decreased group members' use of information that conflicted with their initial decision. The combination of high cohesiveness and the threat of public knowledge of a bad decision has also been shown to reduce the quality of group decision making (Turner et al., 1992).

But other research suggests that cohesiveness may have little if any direct impact on groupthink (Flowers, 1977; Leana, 1985; Tetlock et al., 1992). It is even possible that cohesiveness *reduces* groupthink (Longley & Pruitt, 1980; McCauley, 1989). Deviant opinions may be easier to express and more likely to be taken seriously in a well-established group whose members have strong personal relationships with each other. In fact, when group performance is considered generally, and not restricted to groupthink alone, cohesiveness does increase the quality of the group's work—though the effect is relatively small (Mullen & Copper, 1994). Clearly, the relationship between cohesiveness and groupthink is more complex and variable than Janis initially assumed.

Some structural factors may be particularly important in setting the stage for groupthink. Groups perceived by their members as isolated from others perform more poorly than do groups perceived as more open to outsiders (Moorhead & Montanari, 1986). In addition, groups led by highly directive leaders who voice their preference for a specific course of action are more susceptible to groupthink (Flowers, 1977; Leana, 1985; Tetlock et al., 1992). However, Ramon Aldag and Sally Fuller (1993) caution against the oversimplified notion that directive leadership always impairs group performance. As described in Chapter 13, a vigorous, inspiring leader is often highly effective.

Under stressful conditions, individuals differ in their resistance to groupthink (Callaway et al., 1985). But there appears to be a general tendency for groups to close ranks and reject deviant opinions when coping with stressful events such as an impending deadline (Kruglanski & Webster, 1991). Nevertheless, situational stressors in and of themselves may not be sufficient to create groupthink (Tetlock et al., 1992).

At this point, the jury is still out on groupthink. Certainly, some groups make appallingly bad decisions. And such groups often seem to be characterized by strong internal bonds, directive leadership, and the stress of a perceived threat from outsiders. The self-destructive actions of the cults led by Jim Jones and David Koresh serve as a stark reminder that such ingredients can have deadly consequences. Despite the intuitive appeal of the groupthink model, however, there are many gaps and contradictions in the relevant research. The concept of groupthink makes a valuable contribution to our understanding of group process, but it's not the last word.

Group Performance

Group polarization and groupthink are examples of how groups can go wrong, ending up with attitudes that are too extreme and decisions that are seriously

Groupthink may have influenced the decisions made by David Koresh and the Branch Davidians to kill federal agents and set their own compound on fire rather than surrender to arrest.

flawed. But aren't two, or more, heads usually better than one? According to Ivan Steiner (1972), it depends on the type of task.

1. On an *additive* task, the group product is the *sum* of all the members' contributions. Donating to a charity is an additive task, so is making noise at a pep rally. As we have seen, people often indulge in social loafing during additive tasks. Even so, groups usually outperform a single individual. Each member's contribution may be less than it would be if that person worked alone, but the group total is still greater than what could be provided by one person.
2. On a *conjunctive* task, the group product is determined by the individual with the *poorest* performance. Mountain-climbing teams are engaged in such a task; the "weakest link" will determine their success or failure. Because of this vulnerability to the poor performance of any one group member, group performance on conjunctive tasks tends to be worse than the performance of a single, average individual.
3. On a *disjunctive* task, the group product is determined by the performance of the individual with the *best* performance. Trying to solve a problem or develop a strategy is a disjunctive task: What the group needs is a single successful idea regardless of the number of failures. In principle, groups have an edge on individuals in the performance of disjunctive tasks: The more people involved, the more likely it is that someone will make a breakthrough. In practice, however, group process can interfere with coming up with ideas and with getting them accepted.

brainstorming A technique that attempts to increase creative ideas by encouraging group members to speak freely without criticizing their own or others' contributions.

We turn now to some of the problems in coordination and communication that can reduce the effectiveness of group performance.

Brainstorming: Coming Up with Ideas During the 1950s, advertising executive Alex Osborn developed a technique called **brainstorming,** designed to enhance the productivity of problem-solving groups. The ground rules for brainstorming call for a free-wheeling, creative approach:

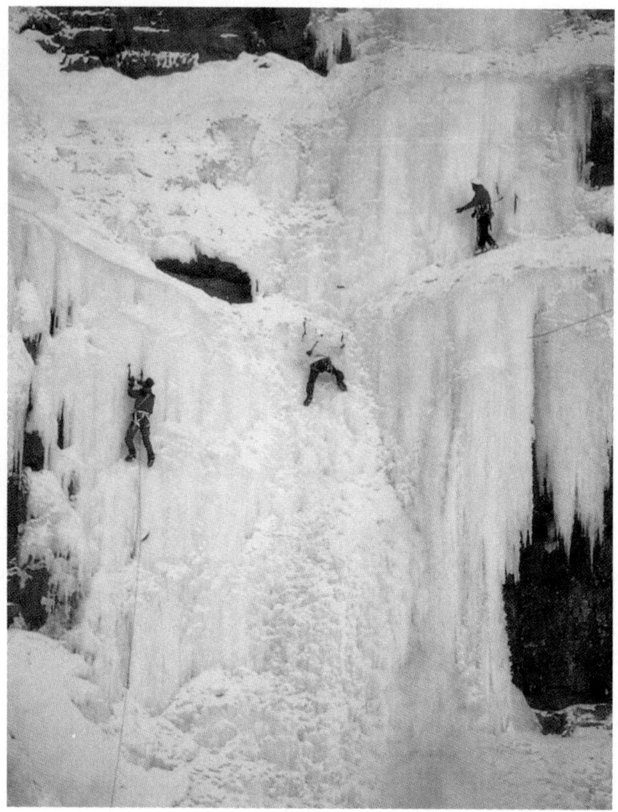

Just as the strength of a chain depends on its weakest link, the group product on a conjunctive task is determined by the individual with the poorest performance. In mountain climbing, for example, if one person slips or falls, the whole team is endangered.

- Express all ideas that come to mind, even if they sound crazy.
- The more ideas, the better.
- Don't worry whether the ideas are good or bad; they can be evaluated later.
- All ideas belong to the group, so members should feel free to build on each other's work.

Osborn (1953) claimed that by using these procedures, groups could generate more and better ideas than could individuals working alone. The gimmick caught on, and brainstorming was soon a popular exercise in business, government, and education. But when the research caught up with the hype, it turned out that Osborn's faith in group process was unfounded. In fact, "nominal groups" (several individuals working alone) produce a greater number of better ideas than do real groups in which members interact with each other (Paulus et al., 1995).

A number of possible explanations have been proposed for why brainstorming is ineffective (Mullen et al., 1991). One prime candidate is *production blocking* (Diehl & Stroebe, 1991; Stroebe & Diehl, 1991). Alone, people produce at their own pace without any distractions. In a group, they have to listen to what others are saying while they wait their turn to speak up. Distracted by listening to others, people forget some of their ideas. Another possibility is *performance matching* (Paulus & Dzindolet, 1993). Alone, people set their own standards. In a group, each person's standard can be influenced by the performance of the other participants, and an initially poor performance by group members can perpetuate itself as each individual matches the low standard that prevails. For example, the poor performance of socially anxious individuals in interactive groups appears to establish a low level of productivity that disrupts the performance of other group members who are not socially anxious (Camacho & Paulus, 1995).

Despite the research evidence, however, brainstorming is still a popular device in many organizations. Why are people so reluctant to give it up? One reason is that those who participate in brainstorming groups are enthusiastic supporters (Paulus et al., 1993; Stroebe et al., 1992). Interactive group members evaluate their own performance more favorably than do individuals in nominal groups. They also enjoy themselves more. And those who have *not* participated in an interactive group believe that such groups are highly productive. Both the experienced and the inexperienced cling to the illusion that brainstorming works.

In the computer age, their wishful thinking might come true. Electronic brainstorming combines the freedom of individuals working alone at a computer with the stimulation of receiving the ideas of others on the screen. In small groups, electronic brainstorming levels the playing field: Groups sharing their ideas perform as well as, but not better than, nominal groups (Gallupe et al., 1991). In larger groups, however, electronically interacting groups generate more ideas than do nominal groups (Dennis & Valacich, 1993). Brainstorming may have found its true home on the information superhighway.

Biased Sampling: Getting Ideas on the Table Brainstorming stresses the need for creativity. On some tasks, however, simply sharing information is crucial for good performance. Unfortunately, as Garold Stasser (1992) points out, not all the information available to individual members will necessarily be brought before the group. Instead, information that is shared among group members is more likely to enter the group discussion than information that is not common knowledge. Stasser calls this process *biased sampling*.

Biased sampling is an especially serious problem when there is a "hidden profile," in which the sum total of information held by all group members favors an alternative that individual members regard as inferior. In one study, for example, university students read descriptions of hypothetical candidates for student-body president before gathering in four-person groups to decide which candidate to endorse (Stasser & Titus, 1985). Actually, candidate A was by far the best, having eight positive and four negative characteristics. Candidate B had only four positive characteristics along with four negative ones. Among subjects given full information, 67 percent preferred candidate A.

But some subjects were not fully informed about all of the candidates' characteristics. And the partial information they received created a misleading impression. Information was distributed so that each partial-information subject was aware of two positives and four negatives for candidate A, and of four positives and one negative for candidate B. Not surprisingly, only 23 percent of these subjects favored candidate A.

The important issue, however, is whether group members who received partial information were able to share their knowledge and thereby detect candidate A's true but hidden profile. After discussing the candidates, 83 percent of the full-information groups endorsed candidate A. In contrast, only 18 percent of the partial-information groups selected what was, in fact, the best candidate. Unshared information did not become common knowledge, and, inadequately informed, these groups made a bad decision.

Sometimes, bad decisions have tragic consequences. The commission formed to investigate the loss of the space shuttle *Challenger,* in which all seven crew members were killed, concluded that inadequate sharing of information contributed to the disaster: "If the decision-makers had known all the facts, it is highly unlikely that they would have decided to launch" (*Report of the Presidential Commission,* 1986, p. 82).

Not everyone, though, agrees that failure to get the facts on the table was the major cause of the accident. In their analysis, Barbara Romzek and Melvin Dubnick (1987) cite the political pressures put on NASA to complete the launch of the space shuttle and the transfer of decision-making authority within NASA from expert professionals to administrators. These developments changed the grounds on which the launch decision was made and increased the likelihood that safety would *not* come first. Under some circumstances, group discussion has little impact on later decisions, serving primarily as a justification for individuals to act according to their prior judgments (Gigone & Hastie, 1993).

It's not easy to improve the thoroughness and meaningfulness of group discussions. Increasing the importance of the task does *not* change the greater attention paid to shared than to unshared information, nor does explicit training that highlights the need to attend to the full range of information (Larson et al., 1994). One factor that does make a difference, however, is whether participants view the task as having a correct solution or as being a subjective judgment. In one study, 65 percent of the groups seeking a solution discovered the hidden profile, compared with only 35 percent of the groups making a judgment (Stasser & Stewart, 1992). When groups believe there is a correct solution, they are more likely to find it.

Communication Networks: The Flow of Ideas Information processing within groups is strongly influenced by the group's *communication network,* which defines who can speak with whom. In a classic study, Harold Leavitt (1951) investigated the effects of four different types of communication networks, shown in Figure 11.7. Two of these networks (the wheel and the Y) are highly centralized; in each, group member C plays a key role in the flow of information. One net-

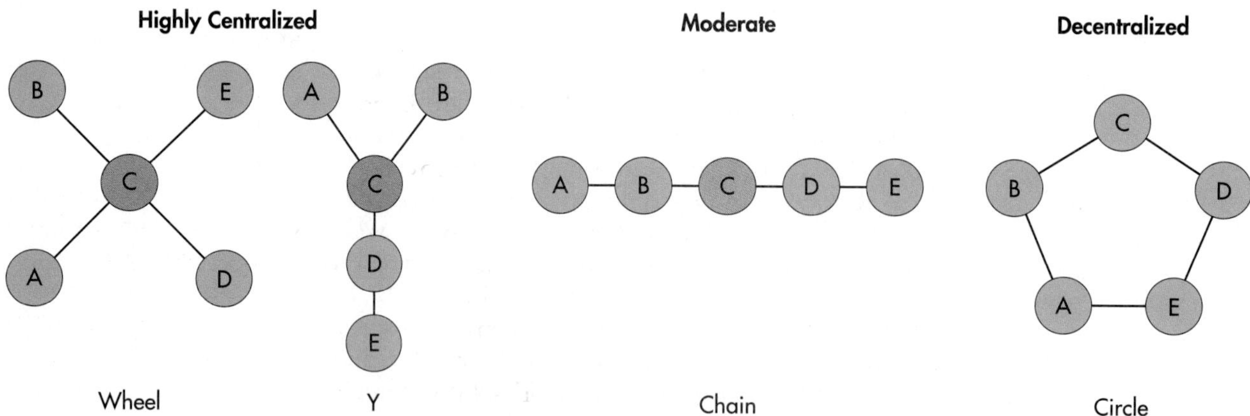

Figure 11.7 Centralized and Decentralized Communication Networks. In Leavitt's research, subjects participated in one of four communication networks. The wheel and the Y are highly centralized; in each, group member C plays the central role in the flow of information. The chain is less centralized; C has only a slightly more important role than other group members. The circle is decentralized; all members have an equal role in conveying information. (Based on Leavitt, 1951.)

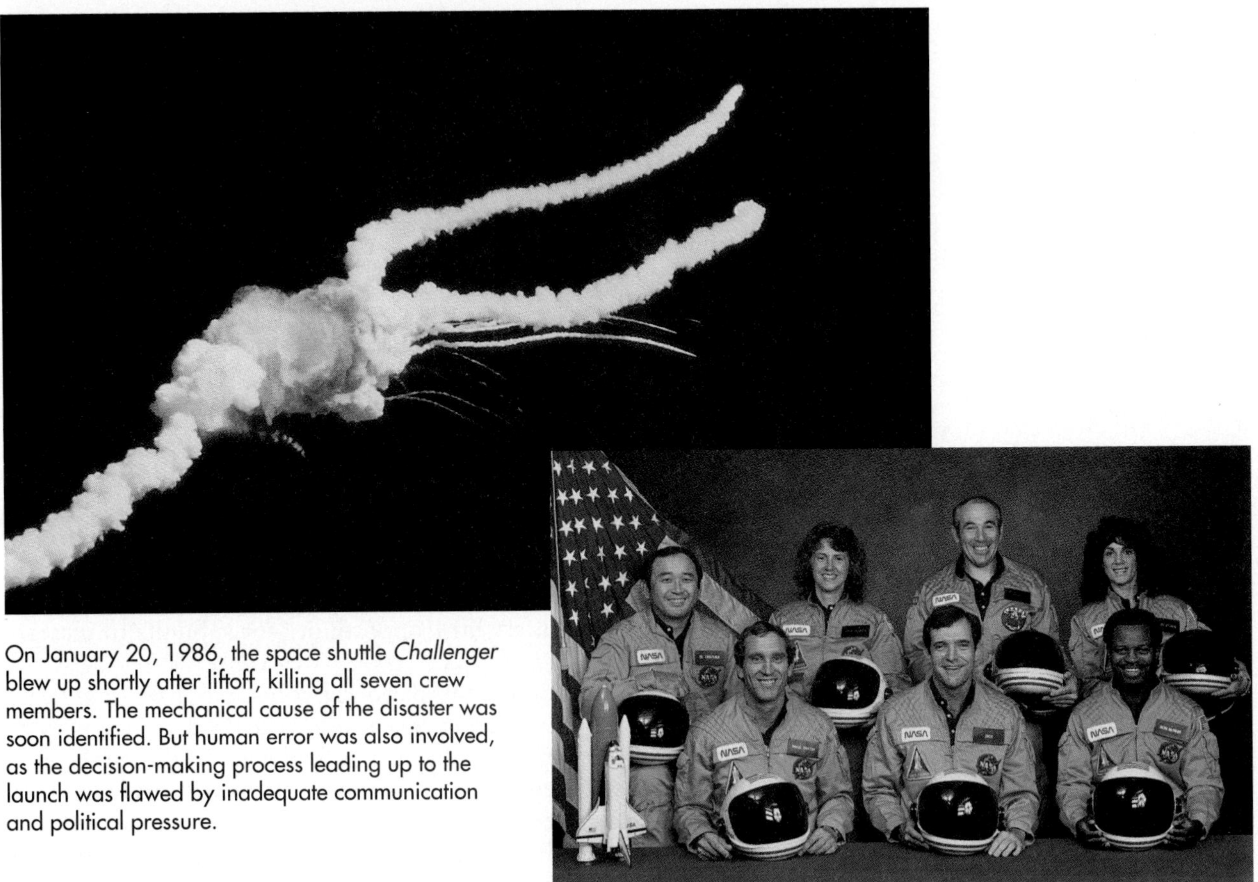

On January 20, 1986, the space shuttle *Challenger* blew up shortly after liftoff, killing all seven crew members. The mechanical cause of the disaster was soon identified. But human error was also involved, as the decision-making process leading up to the launch was flawed by inadequate communication and political pressure.

work (the chain) is less centralized; the importance of C's role is reduced. The fourth network (the circle) is *de*centralized; all members have an equal role in conveying information. Overall, subjects who participated in the two highly centralized communication networks (the wheel and the Y) were faster and more accurate in their performance than were those who participated in the other two networks.

But centralization does not always improve performance. In Leavitt's research, the task was relatively simple. When Marvin Shaw (1954) presented groups with a more difficult and complicated task, groups with a *less* centralized network (the chain) made fewer errors than did those with a highly centralized network (the wheel). Taken together, the research by Leavitt and Shaw identifies two dimensions involved in the effects of communication networks on performance: efficiency and information overload. Simple tasks benefit from the efficiency of centralized communication networks. However, when the group faces a more difficult situation, with a complex task or under stressful working conditions, individuals occupying crucial roles can be overwhelmed by information overload and perform poorly.

The *Challenger* disaster points out another drawback to highly centralized communication networks. Problems with the O-ring seals on the shuttle had been noted in February 1984, and a meeting to discuss the rings was scheduled for May 30. But then the two officials responsible for holding the meeting left

NASA. The meeting never took place, and the need for such a meeting was never communicated to those who took over the jobs of the key officials. It was, in the words of former deputy administrator Hans Mark, "a classic example of having something fall between the 'cracks'" (Romzek & Dubnick, 1987, p. 234). Centralized networks, which place heavy responsibility for communication on one person or just a few individuals, create the potential for very large cracks and fatal mistakes.

But communication can also go awry in decentralized networks. When the Soviets shot down Korean Airlines flight 007 in 1983, the United States initially claimed that the deliberate destruction of a commercial airplane had occurred. Even at the time, however, one U.S. military intelligence unit concluded that the Soviets had made a terrible mistake, confusing flight 007 with a military reconnaissance plane in the same area. According to journalist Seymour Hersh (1986), this information was not communicated to high-level policy makers in the most effective way. Why? Because the various intelligence units were locked into a competitive, noncooperative relationship. Research by Philip Bonacich and Sherry Schneider (1992) confirmed the general proposition they derived from this incident: Individuals occupying mid-level positions are much less communicative in a decentralized network (where they can augment their own power base) than in a highly centralized one (which offers little opportunity for subunits to increase their clout).

The potential for competition in decentralized networks may have significant implications for electronic communication. Because it usually does not provide any explicit information about users' social status, E-mail tends to flatten the hierarchy, reducing the differences in participation by high- and low-status individuals (Dubrovsky et al., 1991). More equal participation should provide better, more inclusive information. But it could also promote the formation of competitive subnetworks that withhold information for their own advantage. Research on electronic communication has only just begun (McGrath & Hollingshead, 1994), and we have much to learn about its effects on group behavior and performance.

COOPERATION, COMPETITION, AND CONFLICT: RESPONDING TO DIFFERENCES

The importance of group performance is crystal clear for some of the crucial issues confronting our world today. What determines whether people will act responsibly to protect the environment? What factors contribute to the escalation of conflict? Are there ways to reduce conflict once it has started? For answers to these questions, both individual characteristics and group processes must be considered. In Chapter 13, we examine the effectiveness of specific kinds of leadership in specific organizational circumstances. Here, we describe individual and group influences on cooperation, competition, and conflict. When there are differences between us, how do we respond?

Mixed Motives and Difficult Dilemmas

Imagine that you have to make a choice between cooperating with others on a project or competing against them to win first place. Each option has possible benefits along with potential costs. You feel torn between wanting to cooperate and wanting to compete, and these mixed motives create a difficult dilemma.

What do you do? This section takes a close look at how people resolve the tension between their cooperative and competitive inclinations.

The Prisoner's Dilemma Game We begin with a detective story. Two partners in crime are picked up by the police for questioning. Although the police believe they have committed a major offense, there is only enough evidence to convict them on a minor charge. In order to sustain a conviction for the more serious crime, the police will have to convince one of them to testify against the other. Separated during questioning, the criminals weigh their alternatives (see Figure 11.8). If neither confesses, they will both get a light sentence on the minor charge. If both confess and plead guilty, they will both receive a moderate sentence. But if one confesses and the other stays silent, the confessing criminal will secure immunity from prosecution while the silent criminal will pay the maximum penalty.

This story formed the basis for the research paradigm known as the *prisoner's dilemma game (PDG)*. In the two-person PDG, subjects are given a series of choices in which they have the option of cooperating or competing. If both individuals make the cooperative choice, they both obtain a moderate reward. If both make the competitive choice, they both suffer a moderate loss. But if one cooperates while the other competes, the competitor obtains a large reward and the cooperator suffers a large loss. It's really a perplexing situation. Cooperation is attractive because of its moderate reward. But if you cooperate and the other person doesn't, you end up with a large loss. And if both of you compete, you both lose.

By now, thousands of players have tried to figure out what to do in the prisoner's dilemma game and researchers have a pretty good understanding of how people behave in this mixed-motive dilemma. Often, they reciprocate. Tit-for-tat, cooperation is matched by cooperation in return, while competition provokes competitive reactions (Enzle et al., 1975). But cooperation and competitiveness

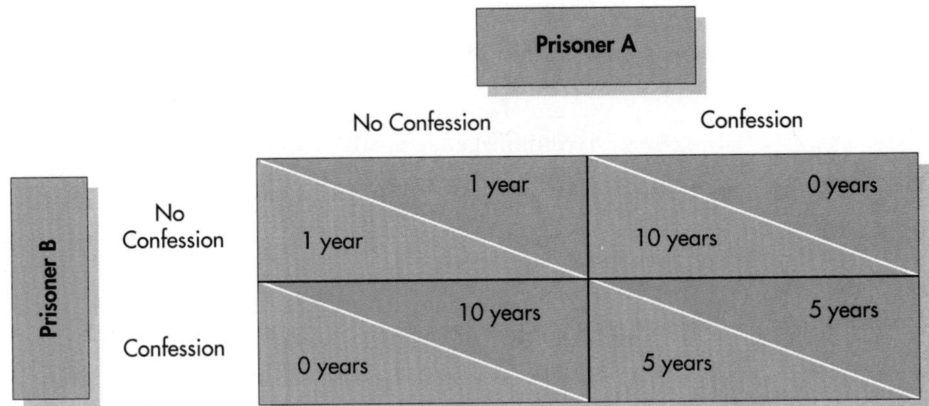

Figure 11.8 **The Prisoner's Dilemma.** In the original prisoner's dilemma, from which the game took its name, each of two criminals is offered immunity from prosecution in exchange for a confession. If both stay silent, both get off with a light sentence on a minor charge (upper left). If both confess, both receive a moderate sentence (lower right). But if one turns state's evidence while the other stays mum, the confessing criminal goes free and the silent one spends a long time in jail.

are not equally powerful. Competitiveness is a very strong determinant of reciprocity. Once one player makes a competitive move, the other player is highly likely to follow suit (Kelley & Stahelski, 1970). Cooperation is less constraining on the other person: People who are consistently and unconditionally cooperative can be exploited and taken advantage of (Komorita et al., 1993). When British Prime Minister Neville Chamberlain tried to prevent war by cooperating with Hitler, it gave Hitler the opportunity to become more aggressive.

Individual differences also influence whether behavior will be cooperative or competitive. Different people have different preferences for their own and another's outcomes (Van Lange, 1992). People with a *cooperative orientation* seek to maximize joint gains. Those with an *individualistic orientation* seek to maximize their own gain and are less cooperative, as are those with a *competitive orientation,* who seek to maximize their own gain relative to that of others.

Groups as well as individuals can play the prisoner's dilemma game. Typically, groups are less cooperative and more competitive than individuals. According to John Schopler and his colleagues (1993), the competitiveness of groups has its roots in fear and greed: the fear that the other group will exploit ours, and the greedy desire to maximize the outcomes achieved by our group at the other group's expense. Individuals, too, can be driven by fear and greed, but competition between groups intensifies such motives.

Social Dilemmas The prisoner's dilemma game sets up a trap for those who play it: Attempts to gain an advantage will backfire if the other party also makes the competitive choice. This notion that the pursuit of self-interest can sometimes be self-destructive forms the basis for what is called a **social dilemma.** In a social dilemma, what is good for one is bad for all. If everyone takes the most self-rewarding choice, everyone suffers the greatest loss. Social dilemmas come in the following two basic types:

social dilemma A situation in which a self-interested choice by everyone creates the worst outcome for everyone.

1. *Resource Dilemmas:* If people take as much as they want of a limited resource that does not replenish itself, nothing will be left for anyone. Garrett Hardin (1968) called this process the "tragedy of the commons." In former times, people would let their animals graze on the town's lush, grassy commons. But if all the animals grazed to their hearts' content, and to their owners' benefit, the commons would be stripped, the animals' food supply diminished, and the owners' welfare threatened. Today, the tragedy of the commons is a clear and present danger on a global scale. Deforestation, air pollution, ocean dumping, massive irrigation, overfishing, commercial development of wilderness areas, a rapidly increasing population in some developing countries, and an overconsuming population in the richest nations—all pit individual self-interest against the common good. Selfish responses to resource dilemmas are social sins of commission; people take too much.
2. *Public Goods Dilemmas:* In contrast, the failure of those who use public services—the blood supply, public broadcasting, schools, roads, parks, and so forth—to contribute to their support is a social sin of omission. If no one gives, the service can't continue (Olson, 1965). Again, private gain conflicts with the public good.

But when does individual desire prevail? Research comparing the two types of social dilemmas indicates that those who possess easy access to resources or plenty of potential contributions are more cooperative in resource dilemmas than in

A social dilemma is created by a conflict between private benefit and the public good. When individuals dump trash at their convenience, they spoil the environment for everyone.

public goods dilemmas (van Dijk & Wilke, 1995). Among those with little access or few contributions, however, cooperation is greater in public goods dilemmas than in resource dilemmas. In other words, the "have's" find it easier to stop taking than to give, while the "have not's" would rather give than stop taking.

Solving Social Dilemmas Resource and public goods dilemmas pose a serious threat to the quality of life and even to life itself. How can we solve them? Among the many possibilities that have been examined (Komorita & Parks, 1994), two major approaches stand out. One emphasizes psychological factors, and the other highlights structural arrangements (see Table 11.2).

The psychological factors that influence people's behavior in a social dilemma include a variety of personal characteristics. For instance, the effects of personal orientation in a resource dilemma are similar to those found in the prisoner's dilemma game. People with a cooperative orientation are less likely to behave in a competitive, resource-consuming fashion than are people with individualistic or competitive orientations (Parks, 1994). Mood, too, affects behavior when resources are scarce. People experiencing negative moods, such as anger and sadness, have difficulty delaying gratification and take what they want without sufficient regard for the long-term consequences (Knapp & Clark, 1991). In a highly competitive environment, a good mood increases efforts to preserve the common good (Hertel & Fiedler, 1994). Prior experience also has an impact. Individuals given a chance to manage their own, privately controlled resource are more socially responsible in using a collectively controlled resource than are those without this preliminary opportunity (Allison & Messick, 1985). And people who have had a successful experience in working cooperatively are more likely to contribute to a public good (Allison & Kerr, 1994).

Information about what others are doing is another important determinant of responses to a social dilemma. Imagine that you live in an area suffering from a water shortage, and you learn that others are making a serious effort to conserve.

Table 11.2 Solving Social Dilemmas

Psychological Factors

- Possessing certain personal characteristics
  - Having a cooperative personal orientation
  - Being in a good mood
  - Having hands-on experience with managing endangered resources
  - Having been successful in working cooperatively
- Learning about how others are behaving
  - Following the lead of unselfish models
  - Responding to the crisis created by selfish models
- Being in a small group
  - Having a sense of identification with other people facing the same dilemma
  - Believing that one's own efforts make a difference
  - Making a commitment to cooperate

Structural Arrangements

- Creating a payoff structure that rewards cooperative behavior and/or punishes selfish behavior
- Removing resources from the public domain and handing them over to private ownership
- Establishing an authority to control the resource

Behavior in a social dilemma is influenced by both psychological factors and structural arrangements. The characteristics listed here contribute to the solution of a social dilemma through direct effects on individuals or through deliberate modifications of social structures.

What's your reaction? On the one hand, the socially responsible behavior of others encourages you to cooperate as well (Orbell et al., 1988). On the other hand, since you know that others are trying to remedy the problem, you may be tempted to engage in social loafing and take a *free ride:* letting others sacrifice without giving up anything yourself (Shepperd, 1993a).

But what if you learn that others are making selfish choices? Every night on the TV news you see people watering their lawns and washing their cars. Are you prepared to give up showers and to drink bottled water? Here, too, there are counteracting tendencies. On the one hand, the socially irresponsible behavior of others encourages you to follow suit. When you see other people taking a free ride, you may feel you'd be a *sucker* to continue your own efforts to conserve (Kerr, 1983). On the other hand, you realize the resource is being rapidly depleted, and you feel the need for urgent action. Because selfish models evoke both selfish motives and societal concerns, people exposed to such models are slow to respond to a crisis (Messick et al., 1983). Interestingly, though, when a resource is endangered by purely environmental forces rather than aggravated by human actions, people are more likely to conserve (Rutte et al., 1987; Samuelson et al., 1984). The absence of selfish models allows cooperation to emerge.

The size of the group also affects responses to a social dilemma. Large groups are more likely to exploit scarce resources than are small ones (Allison et al., 1992). There are three major reasons for the influence of group size. First, it's harder to identify with the welfare of others when the group is large, and people are more socially responsible when they share a meaningful group membership with the other people affected by the dilemma (Kramer & Brewer, 1984). Second, people believe that their actions have more of an impact in a small group (Kerr, 1989), and the more they think that their contribution matters, the more likely they are to contribute to a public good (Kerr, 1992a; Shepperd, 1993a). Third, people are are more likely to make an explicit commitment to cooperate in a small group, and the more committed they are, the more they contribute (Kerr & Kaufman-Gilliland, 1994).

But many social dilemmas involve very large groups—a city, a state, a nation, the whole world. In these circumstances, the psychological factors we have described may be less effective. Various structural arrangements, such as those listed in Table 11.2, offer an alternative. Consider, for instance, making charitable contributions tax deductible. This structural tactic is designed to increase contributions by appealing to an individual's selfish interests. Unless we are willing to write every good act into the tax code, however, such egoistic solutions to social dilemmas are limited (Lynn & Oldenquist, 1986). Another option is to privatize what are now collectively owned resources. At least in the United States, when a resource belongs to only one person, it is depleted less rapidly than when it is shared among members of a group (Martichuski & Bell, 1991). But privatizing a resource means that what one gets, others lose. Who gets? Who decides who gets?

The most commonly employed structural solution to social dilemmas is to set up a controlling authority (Messick et al., 1983; Sato, 1987). The Environmental Protection Agency (EPA) was established by the federal government to protect the quality of the environment. But maintaining a regulating authority such as the EPA is not cost-free (Yamagishi, 1986). If regulatory agencies fail to work effectively, the society suffers a double loss—of the endangered resource and of the funds used to support the agency. To solve a social dilemma, people often have to decide where to place their trust: in their fellow citizens or in government authorities.

The Intergroup Public Goods Paradigm Usually, we think of resource and public goods dilemmas as *intra*group problems: Will the members of the group conserve or exploit resources? Will the members of the group give or withhold contributions? But sometimes more than one group is involved in the dilemma and *inter*group interactions affect its resolution. For example, Israel and Jordan recently agreed to cooperate on the management of one of the most precious resources in the Middle East—water. And when sports teams compete, the victory is a public good shared by all members of the winning team regardless of their individual contributions.

The intergroup public goods (IPG) paradigm combines intragroup and intergroup responses to a public goods dilemma (Rapoport et al., 1989). In this paradigm, two groups are eligible for a single reward. Within each group, every member makes an individual decision about whether to invest his or her own private resources in order to help the group obtain the reward. The groups themselves can compete or cooperate for the reward, which is a public good that must be shared by all members of the winning group or successful collaboration.

In the highly competitive structure of the IPG paradigm, cooperation and communication within a group *decrease* cooperation between groups (Bornstein, 1992; Bornstein et al., 1989; see also Thompson, 1993). Thus, within-group cooperation is the solution to social dilemmas involving only one group, but it damages the prospects for a solution to a multigroup dilemma. Furthermore, competition between groups *enhances* cooperation within each group (Bornstein & Ben-Yossef, 1994; Erev et al., 1993). Taken together, these two effects create a self-reinforcing feedback loop: Cooperation within a group intensifies conflict between groups, conflict between groups intensifies cooperation within each group, and so it goes. In the next section, we examine some other factors that contribute to the escalation of intergroup conflict.

Conflict Escalation

Violent conflicts between groups are probably no more common these days than in earlier times, perhaps even less so. But what has changed is our awareness of them. Previously, intergroup conflicts often erupted unobserved, hidden from view in far-off places. Today, we watch them on CNN—sometimes the fighting itself; more frequently, the agonizing aftermath of human suffering.

We see the city of Sarajevo become a shooting gallery where people are killed as they cross the street or stand in line for food. We gasp in horror at the piles of bodies in Rwanda. We shudder at the carnage created by suicide bombers in Israel. Bosnian Serbs versus Bosnian Muslims; Hutus versus Tutsis; Palestinians versus Israelis. Again and again, differences—religious, ethnic, racial, cultural, political—explode in hatred and bloodshed. What fans the flames of an escalating conflict? No doubt many factors are involved (Rubin et al., 1994). Here we concentrate on the effects of threats, resources, and perceptions.

Group conflict is hard to stop. After Israel and the Palestinian Liberation Organization signed initial peace accords, groups opposed to the peace process increased their violent attacks. In one of the worst incidents, two Palestinian suicide bombers killed twenty-one people at an Israeli army bus stop.

Threat Capacity It seems obvious that the ability to punish someone who engages in a prohibited behavior can act as a deterrent. You're less likely to mess with someone who can mess right back with you. If both parties hold their fire, a balance of terror can work. But as we will see, having the capacity to attack can present an irresistible temptation to do so.

A classic study conducted by Morton Deutsch and Robert Krauss (1960) makes the point. These investigators asked pairs of female subjects to imagine that each of them was in charge of a trucking company carrying merchandise over a road to a specific destination. For every completed trip, subjects would earn a flat rate minus operating expenses calculated at the rate of one cent per minute. Each subject was assigned a name for her trucking company, either Acme or Bolt, and was given the road map shown in Figure 11.9.

Subjects started from separate starting points and went to separate destinations. At one place, however, their paths crossed on a one-lane road. To avoid the one-lane road, subjects could take an alternative route, but the bypass took longer to travel and therefore increased operating expenses. At each end of the one-lane road was a gate. In the *bilateral-threat* condition, each player in the trucking game had control over one of the gates. In the *unilateral-threat* condition, only one of the players controlled a gate. In the *no-gates* condition, neither player controlled a gate and the road was wide open to all traffic.

Players who controlled a gate were allowed to close it—and they did. The consequence of being able to block the other person's progress was clear: Both players suffered. Overall, players earned more money in the no-gate condition than in

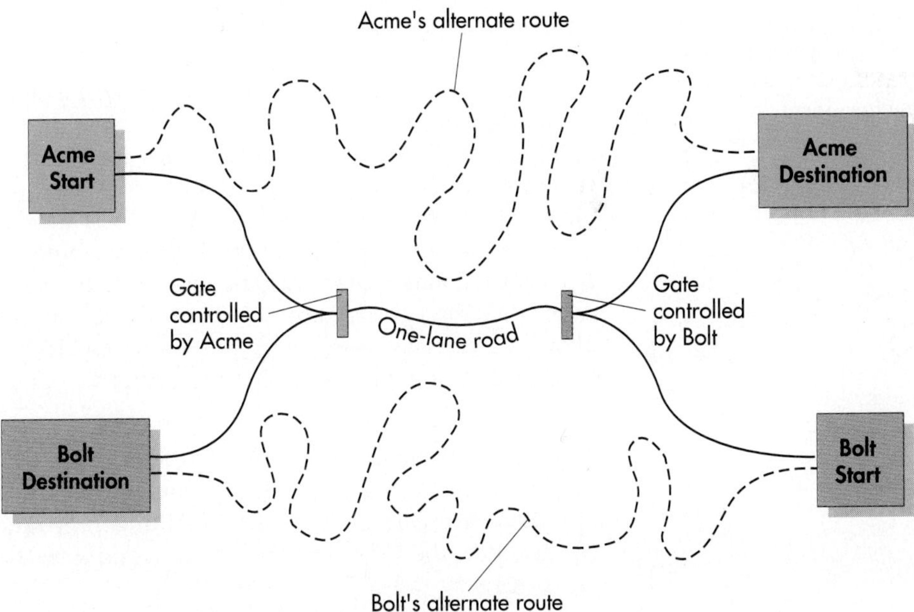

Figure 11.9 **The Road Map for the Acme and Bolt Trucking Game.** In the trucking game devised by Deutsch and Krauss, subjects were assigned to either the Acme or the Bolt Trucking Company and were instructed to deliver their merchandise as quickly as possible. The quickest route is over the one-lane road. Having control over a gate blocking use of this road reduced the players' ability to cooperate with each other. (Deutsch & Krauss, 1960.)

the unilateral condition, and those in the bilateral condition earned least of all. These results suggest that once coercive means are available, people use them even when doing so damages their own outcomes.

A similar process may affect the behavior of those charged with keeping the peace. In a study of English and Australian police, those officers who favored the use of arrest for dealing with a noncompliant citizen reported having experienced high levels of resistance from suspects during the actual performance of their patrol activities (Wilson & Gross, 1994). Those officers who favored the use of noncoercive tactics (such as exchanging information, and bargaining and compromising) reported lower levels of resistance while on duty. Though correlational, these findings are consistent with the notion that the power to punish can sometimes be more effective when it is *not* used than when it is too readily put into practice.

Resources Like all behaviors, conflict requires resources. The individual or group must devote time and energy to the effort to prevail. Significant financial costs are often involved, and the support of others can be highly valuable. All else being equal, people with adequate resources at their disposal are more likely to engage in overt conflict than are those without resources (Martin, 1986).

But what happens when the allocation of resources fails to achieve the desired outcome? Do people cut their losses? Remarkably often, the answer is no. Faced with a disastrous military campaign, a plunge in the stock market, an abusive marriage, or a budget overrun on a construction project, people often persist in making even larger investments. This process of throwing good money after bad is called **entrapment** (Brockner & Rubin, 1985). Entrapment occurs when commitments to a failing course of action are increased to justify investments already made.

entrapment The condition in which commitments to a failing course of action are increased to justify investments already made.

A number of factors promote entrapment, including the desire to reduce cognitive dissonance (see Chapter 10) by casting past decisions in the best possible light, the urge to save face, institutional inertia that makes it hard to change direction, and receiving negative information only after costly commitments have already been made (Bobocel & Meyer, 1994; Staw & Ross, 1989). Processes like group polarization and groupthink that promote extreme judgments and defective decision making may also increase entrapment. Indeed, entrapment has been called "a subset of groupthink" (Kameda & Sugimori, 1993). However it comes about, entrapment contributes to conflict escalation by motivating those on the losing side of a conflict to keep trying to come out on top.

Perceptions of the Other Stereotypes and prejudice play a major role in conflict escalation between groups. During conflict, the opposing group and its members are often perceived as "the other"—strange, foreign, alien. Held at a psychological distance, the other becomes a screen on which it is possible to project one's worst fears.

Here's what people see: First, there's a *mirror image:* What we see in our enemies is what our enemies see in us. As Urie Bronfenbrenner (1961) discovered when he visited the Soviet Union during the Cold War, the Soviets saw us as aggressive, exploitative, and untrustworthy—just like we saw them.

Second, there's a *double standard:* Whatever we do is good; whatever our enemies do is bad. When Stuart Oskamp (1965) asked American college students to

For some groups, their sense of "us" requires identifying another group as "them." Dehumanization is the ultimate "us" versus "them" distinction.

evaluate identical actions taken by the United States and the Soviet Union, he found that U.S. actions were evaluated more favorably than those taken by the Soviets. This double standard persisted through the 1980s among American students and, to a lesser extent, French-Canadian students (Tobin & Eagles, 1992).

Third, there are *conflict-maintaining attributions:* The most negative explanation is always preferred. Like the partners in an unhappy intimate relationship (see Chapter 6), opponents are inclined to believe the worst about each other and to discount more positive indications. For example, John Foster Dulles, U.S. Secretary of State during the 1950s, attributed declines in Soviet hostility to economic weakness, ulterior motives, policy failures, and internal problems (Holsti, 1962). The possibility of more peaceful intentions seems never to have been considered.

Taken to extremes, negative views of the other can result in *dehumanization,* the perception that people lack human qualities or are "subhuman." Based on malicious stereotypes about outgroups, dehumanization is both a consequence of hostility between groups and an incitement to intergroup conflict (Bandura, 1990; Struch & Schwartz, 1989). Indeed, fueled by dehumanization, the sporadic violence of rampaging mobs can escalate into systematic state-sanctioned genocide—as aggression against the outgroup is justified by dehumanization, which is used to excuse more aggression, which requires more dehumanization to justify, and so on (Bar-Tal, 1990).

Dehumanization is the ultimate version of "us" versus "them," removing all religious and ethical constraints against the taking of human life. As George Orwell discovered during the Spanish Civil War, the cure for dehumanization is to restore the human connection. Sighting an enemy soldier holding up his trousers with both hands while running beside a nearby trench, Orwell was unable to take the easy shot:

> I had come here to shoot at "Fascists"; but a man who is holding up his trousers isn't a "Fascist," he is visibly a fellow creature, similar to yourself, and you don't feel like shooting at him. (p. 254)

Table 11.3 Factors That Promote and Sustain the Escalation of Between-Group Conflict

- Pressures for conformity, such as group cohesiveness and groupthink, that make it difficult for individuals to oppose the group's increasingly aggressive position
- The group polarization process that increases the extremity of group members' attitudes and opinions
- Ingroup cooperation that increases the likelihood of between-group conflict, which in turn increases ingroup cooperation
- Premature use of threat capacity that triggers aggressive retaliation
- Possession of sufficient resources that make it possible to become involved in overt conflict
- Entrapment that seeks to justify past investments through the commitment of additional resources
- Negative perceptions of "the other" that promote acceptance of aggressive behavior and enhance cohesiveness of the ingroup "us" against the outgroup "them"

Reducing Conflict

With all the forces pressing it forward (see Table 11.3 for a summary), conflict escalation is hardly surprising. But the desire for peace is still strong and pervasive. Around the world, some long-standing, deeply ingrained conflicts between groups have begun to move in a more peaceful direction. Adopting majority rule, South Africa elected Nelson Mandela as its first black president. The Irish Republican Army and pro-British paramilitary groups declared a cease-fire in Northern Ireland. Israel and the Palestinian Liberation Organization signed peace accords, as did Israel and Jordan. And the former superpower antagonists, the United States and Russia, now work together on many economic programs, political issues, and scientific projects. All of these developments are still fragile and vulnerable to disruption. A lasting peace isn't guaranteed, but at least it has been given a chance. In this section, we examine the kind of sustained effort that peacemaking requires.

True GRIT Every once in a while, individual leaders try to break the gridlock of intergroup conflict by taking a unilateral step toward peace. John Kennedy banned atmospheric nuclear tests without a pledge from the Soviets to do likewise; Anwar Sadat flew to Jerusalem uncertain of the reception he would receive; Mikhail Gorbachev withdrew Soviet forces from Afghanistan before meeting with Ronald Reagan in Moscow. The notion that unilateral concessions can reverse an escalating conflict is central to a peacemaking strategy developed by Charles Osgood (1962): **graduated and reciprocated initiatives in tension-reduction (GRIT).**

graduated and reciprocated initiatives in tension-reduction (GRIT) A strategy for unilateral, persistent efforts to establish trust and cooperation between opposing parties.

To see how GRIT works, imagine yourself using its four basic components (Lindskold et al., 1986a, 1986b).

1. You issue a general statement of your intention to reduce conflict. You also clearly announce your peaceful intentions each time you take a tension-

Nelson Mandela and F.W. DeKlerk in a televised debate during their campaigns for the South African presidency. The cordial and dignified behavior of both candidates helped reduce tensions during the election. Mandela's historic victory marked the end of apartheid.

reducing initiative. Throughout, you invite the other party to reciprocate. By taking these steps, you hope to enlist public support and put pressure on the other party to respond cooperatively.

2. You carry out your tension-reducing initiatives as announced, even if there is no immediate reciprocation. These acts serve to establish your credibility. You enhance your credibility further by employing tension-reducing initiatives that can be verified by the other party or by neutral outside observers.
3. Once the other party makes a cooperative move, you quickly reciprocate. Your cooperative response risks at least as much as—and, if possible, more than—the other party's cooperative behavior.
4. You maintain a retaliatory capability in order to deter exploitation by the other party. If the other party attacks, you retaliate at precisely the same level. Once you have retaliated, you resume your unilateral tension-reducing efforts.

Reciprocal, tit-for-tat strategies like GRIT are maximally responsive: Cooperation is met with cooperation, attack with attack (Axelrod, 1984; Komorita et al., 1992). By giving the other party a greater sense of control over the interaction, the perceived risk of being cooperative is reduced (Friedland, 1990). GRIT also prevents exploitation by retaliating if necessary and avoids conflict escalation by keeping retaliatory actions within the level established by the other party. But GRIT is not simply reactive. It patiently, persistently, and proactively seeks peace.

In addition to obtaining immediate benefits for both parties, practice in GRIT can smooth the way for future bargaining efforts where GRIT is not explicitly employed. This added advantage was demonstrated in a study by Svenn Lindskold and Gyuseog Han (1988) in which male subjects participated in the prisoner's dilemma game described earlier in this chapter. Subjects believed they were playing PDG with another subject, but in actuality the other player's moves were programmed by the experimenters.

During the PDG, some subjects were given experience with GRIT. In this condition, the simulated player sent a note announcing, "I will be making [the cooperative choice] on the next trial." He then made that choice and continued to do so unless the subject chose the competitive response. If that happened, the simulated player retaliated by making the competitive response, but then went back to making cooperative choices. The simulated player's choice was communicated to the real subject prior to every trial. Subjects in the no-message control condition were presented with the same pattern of choices from the simulated player, but did not receive any prior communications about those choices.

After the PDG was over, subjects worked on a bargaining task involving the same (simulated) other player and were told to make as much money as they could. Those who had been the recipients of GRIT obtained the maximum joint profit more frequently and more quickly than did subjects who had not received any messages. Interestingly, when subjects were asked to evaluate the other person, those in the GRIT condition were *not* more positive in their evaluations than were those in the no-message control condition. These findings suggest that it is not necessary to like an opponent to cooperate on various ventures. Instead, the essential elements are establishing at least a minimal level of trust and recognizing that one's own interests will benefit.

Negotiating The sequence employed by Lindskold and Han in their study—first GRIT, then bargaining—parallels real-world interactions. Unilateral concessions are useful for beginning the peace process, but extended negotiations are usually required to reach a final agreement. Negotiations on complex issues such as nuclear arms control and international environmental protection, as well as efforts to make peace in volatile regions such as the Middle East, often go on for years or even decades.

But negotiations are not restricted to the international scene. Unions and management engage in collective bargaining to establish employee contracts. Divorcing couples negotiate the terms of their divorce, by themselves or through their lawyers. Indeed, negotiations occur whenever there is a conflict that the parties wish to resolve without getting into an open fight or relying on an imposed legal settlement. There is an immense amount of research on negotiation and bargaining (Pruitt & Carnevale, 1993; Sheppard et al., 1990). In this section, we focus on those findings most relevant to conflict reduction.

Flexibility is perhaps the single most important factor in successful negotiations (Rubin et al., 1990; Thompson, 1990b). The most effective strategy combines flexibility and strength (McGillicuddy et al., 1984). For example, compromising late in a bargaining session is often a more successful approach than compromising early or not at all (Nemeth & Brilmayer, 1987). A weak negotiator who compromises early invites exploitation; a rigid one who refuses to compromise at all sets the stage for the breakdown of negotiations.

integrative complexity Complex information processing involving the search for information, the prediction of outcomes, the weighing of options, and the consideration of potential strategies.

Flexible behavior at the negotiating table requires the kind of complex information processing that Peter Suedfeld (1992) and Philip Tetlock (1988) call **integrative complexity:** searching for information, predicting outcomes, weighing options, and considering various potential strategies. A study of the statements of fourteen Middle Eastern leaders during the Persian Gulf crisis found that the statements of some leaders supposedly involved in negotiations actually became less complex and more simplistic—suggesting that their minds were already made up (Suedfeld et al., 1993).

According to Dean Pruitt and Peter Carnevale (1993), there are a number of assumptions that can impair cognitive and behavioral flexibility during negotiations:

- *Reactive devaluation:* Assuming that whatever is good for the other party is bad for you, also called the "incompatibility perception" (Thompson, 1995).
- *Cognitive heuristics:* Relying too much on salient information and obvious characteristics (as described in Chapter 3).
- *Anchoring:* Giving too much weight to initial offers.
- *Loss framing:* Being so concerned about avoiding a loss that opportunities for agreement are missed.

The other key element in successful negotiations is to understand the point of view of the other person, even if you disagree with it. It is always difficult for participants in a dispute to listen carefully to each other and to reach some reasonable understanding of the other person's perspective. Communication difficulties are especially likely during negotiations between individuals and groups from different cultures (Berry et al., 1992). Table 11.4 lists some common assumptions made by negotiators from the United States and other western countries that are not always shared by representatives from other cultures (Kimmel, 1994). If negotiators are not aware of these kinds of cross-cultural differences, the inevitable misunderstandings may prevent them from achieving a successful outcome.

But what constitutes success in negotiations? Perhaps the most common successful outcome is a 50-50 compromise, or what Jeffrey Rubin (1994) calls "concession-convergence." Here the negotiators start at each extreme and gradually work toward a mutually acceptable midpoint. Rubin emphasizes that under some circumstances, this is an entirely appropriate approach and a perfectly acceptable result.

integrative agreement A negotiated resolution to a conflict in which all parties obtain outcomes that are superior to what they would have obtained from an equal division of the contested resources.

Some negotiators, however, achieve a higher level of success. When **integrative agreements** are reached, both parties obtain outcomes that are superior to a 50-50 split. Take, for instance, the tale of the orange and two sisters. One sister wanted the juice to drink; the other wanted the peel for a cake. So they sliced the orange in half and each one took her portion. These sisters suffered from an advanced case of the "fixed pie" syndrome. They assumed that whatever one of them won, the other lost. In fact, however, each of them could have had the whole thing: all of the juice for one, all of the peel for the other. An integrative agreement was well within their grasp, but they failed to see it. Indeed, the ability to achieve integrative agreements is an acquired skill: Experienced negotiators obtain them more often than do inexperienced ones (Thompson, 1990b).

During particularly difficult or significant negotiations, outside assistance may be sought. Some negotiations rely on an *arbitrator* who has the power to impose a settlement. But it is more common for conflicting parties to request the participation of a *mediator* who works with them to try to reach a voluntary agreement. Traditionally, mediators have been employed in labor-management negotiations and international conflicts (Carnevale, 1985). But, increasingly, they help resolve a wide range of other disputes, such as those involving tenants and landlords, divorcing couples, and feuding neighbors (Pruitt & Kressel, 1985). Trained in negotiation and conflict management, mediators can often increase the likelihood of reaching a cooperative solution (Cahn, 1992).

Table 11.4 Cultural Assumptions about Negotiating

Assumptions Made by Negotiators from the U.S. and other Western Countries	Alternatives
Negotiation is a business, not a social activity.	The first step in negotiating is to develop a trusting relationship between the individual negotiators.
Substantive issues are more important than social and emotional issues.	If you don't feel strongly about an issue, then it isn't important to you.
Communication is direct and verbal.	Some of the most important communications are nonverbal.
Written contracts are binding; oral commitments are not.	Written contracts are less meaningful than oral communications because the nonverbal context clarifies people's intentions.
Current information and ideas are more valid than historical or traditional opinions and information.	History and tradition are more valid than current information and ideas.
The representatives at the table have a great deal of latitude in reaching acceptable agreements for their sponsors.	Representatives have very little latitude.
Time is very important; punctuality is expected; deadlines should be set and adhered to.	Building a relationship takes time and is more important than punctuality; setting deadlines is an effort to humiliate the other party.

People from different cultures make different assumptions about the negotiation process. This table summarizes some assumptions commonly made by U.S. and other western negotiators. It also presents some alternative assumptions that may be held by negotiators from other cultures. As you can see, such different assumptions could make it very difficult to reach a successful agreement. (Based on Kimmel, 1994.)

Mediators, too, emphasize the importance of flexibility. In one study, questionnaires were completed by 255 professional mediators (Lim & Carnevale, 1990). Their responses indicated that no one tactic was seen as uniformly superior. Instead, these mediators believed that tactics should be adjusted to fit the specific situation. Flexibility alone, however, is not sufficient. Trust is also required. Mediators who are perceived as fair and unbiased are much more likely to be successful (Shapiro & Brett, 1993; Welton & Pruitt, 1987). And offering suggestions for possible 50-50 compromises appears to be particularly effective in establishing a mediator's evenhandedness (Conlon et al., 1994). Attempting to mediate conflicts between the United States and the leaders of first North Korea and then Haiti, former President Jimmy Carter made conciliatory statements that were widely criticized. Was Carter being "weak" and "soft-headed"? Or was he deliberately and shrewdly building up the trust necessary to secure a mutually beneficial agreement?

Finding Common Ground Ever since the human species first appeared on planet Earth, there have been countless conflicts between innumerable groups. Each of these conflicts is unique, as is every attempt at conflict resolution. Still, all efforts to find a constructive solution to conflict require some common ground to build upon. Recognition of a **superordinate identity** is one way that common ground can be established between groups in conflict. When group members perceive that they have a shared identity, a sense of belonging to something larger than and encompassing their own groups, the attractiveness of outgroup members increases (Gaertner et al., 1989) and interactions between the groups often become more peaceful (Coombs, 1987; Turner, 1981).

superordinate identity The perception by members of different groups that they all belong to a larger whole.

But how can groups engaged in violent conflict, bashing each other both verbally and physically, identify with each other? As described in Chapter 4, Muzafer Sherif and his colleagues (1961) faced this problem when the fierce intergroup competition and rivalry they had created between two groups of boys at summer camp resisted all initial efforts to restore the peace. Propaganda about how nice the other group was didn't work, nor did having the boys get together under pleasant circumstances. Only when the Rattlers and the Eagles had to cooperate to get what both groups wanted did negative perceptions and aggressive behaviors cease. *Superordinate goals* elicit cooperation by appealing to people's self-interest. Because everyone stands to benefit, no one has to be altruistic or compassionate to cooperate in the pursuit of a mutual goal.

Superordinate goals have another valuable characteristic: They can produce a superordinate identity. The experience of intergroup cooperation increases the sense of belonging to a single superordinate group (Gaertner et al., 1990). Even the mere expectation of a cooperative interaction increases empathy (Lanzetta & Englis, 1989), which plays a constructive role in human affairs—enhancing helpfulness and reducing aggression. Empathy can be narrowly focused, eliciting concern for only one individual instead of the group as a whole (Batson et al., 1995). But extensive empathic connections between various members of each group could lay the foundation for an inclusive, rather than exclusive, social identity.

Germans demonstrate against neo-Nazi groups and anti-Semitism. The sign, "I am a foreigner worldwide," proclaims that since we are all foreigners somewhere, there is no "them," only a superordinate human identity as "us."

On the road to peace, both kinds of common ground are needed. Cooperation on shared goals makes similarities more visible, and a sense of a shared identity makes cooperation more likely. Those who would make peace, not war, realize that it is in their own self-interest to do so and understand that the cloak of humanity is large enough to cover a multitude of lesser differences.

REVIEW

COLLECTIVE PROCESSES: THE PRESENCE OF OTHERS

- In collectives, people are engaged in common activities but have minimal direct interaction.

Social Facilitation: When Others Arouse Us

- In an early experiment, Triplett found that children performed faster when they worked side by side rather than alone.
- Social facilitation refers to two effects that occur when individual contributions are identifiable: The presence of others enhances performance on easy tasks but impairs performance on difficult tasks.
- The theories of mere presence, evaluation apprehension, and distraction-conflict give different answers to (1) whether social facilitation is necessarily social, and (2) whether the mere presence of others is sufficient to affect performance.

Social Loafing: When Others Relax Us

- In early research on easy tasks involving pooled contributions, Ringelmann found that individual output declined when people worked with others.
- But social loafing is reduced or eliminated when people value the task, their own contribution to it, or the group itself.
- A unified paradigm integrates social facilitation, social loafing, and what we've called "social security": when the presence of others enhances performance on difficult tasks involving pooled contributions.

Deindividuation: When People Lose Control

- Deindividuation diminishes a person's sense of individuality and reduces constraints against deviant behavior.
- Two types of environmental cues can increase deviant behavior: (1) accountability cues, such as anonymity, signal that individuals will not be held responsible for their actions, and (2) attentional cues, such as intense environmental stimulation, produce a deindividuated state in which the individual acts impulsively.
- Large crowds, which can both increase anonymity and decrease self-awareness, are especially violent when the number of victims is small.
- The effects of deindividuation depend on the characteristics of the group. In the context of an antagonistic social identity, antisocial behavior increases; in the context of a benevolent social identity, prosocial behavior increases.

GROUP PROCESSES: INTERACTING WITH OTHERS

Joining a Group

- People join a group for its own sake or to interact with its members.
- Those preparing to join are optimistic about the rewards of group membership.
- The socialization of newcomers into a group relies on the relationship they form with old-timers who act as models, trainers, and mentors.

Roles, Norms, and Cohesiveness

- Interacting groups have three major features: an expected set of behaviors for members (roles), rules of conduct for members (norms), and forces that push members together (cohesiveness).
- When men and women feel equally competent about task performance, they adopt similar roles.
- The pressures toward conformity in a cohesive group make it hard to blow the whistle on misconduct.

Group Polarization: Gaining Conviction

- When individuals who have similar, although not identical, opinions participate in a group discussion, their opinions become more extreme.
- Explanations for group polarization emphasize the persuasiveness of arguments heard, social comparison with a perceived group norm, and the influence of one's own ingroup.

Groupthink: Losing Perspective

- Groupthink refers to an excessive tendency to seek concurrence among group members.
- The symptoms of groupthink produce defective decision making, which can lead to a bad decision.
- Among the factors that are supposed to increase groupthink: The role of cohesiveness is uncertain; structural features, such as a highly directive leader, seem crucial; and situational stress may contribute but not be essential.

Group Performance

- Group performance is influenced by the type of task (additive, conjunctive, or disjunctive) and the quality of group process.
- Contrary to illusions about the effectiveness of brainstorming, groups in which members interact face-to-face produce fewer creative ideas than the same number of people working alone.
- Biased sampling refers to the tendency for groups to pay more attention to shared information than to unshared information.
- Communication networks may fail to work well because they are inefficient, overloaded, or disrupted by competition among the participants.

COOPERATION, COMPETITION, AND CONFLICT: RESPONDING TO DIFFERENCES

Mixed Motives and Difficult Dilemmas

- In mixed-motive situations, such as the prisoner's dilemma game (PDG), there are incentives for both competition and cooperation.
- Reciprocity, personal orientation, and being in a group influence behavior in the PDG.
- In a social dilemma, private benefit conflicts with the public good. Selfish responses to social dilemmas include excessive exploitation of resources and failure to contribute to public services.
- Behavior in a social dilemma is influenced by psychological factors and structural arrangements.
- Although within-group cooperation is the solution to social dilemmas involving only one group, it decreases cooperation between groups and therefore damages the prospects for a solution to a multigroup dilemma.

Conflict Escalation

- The premature use of the capacity to punish can elicit retaliation and escalate conflict.
- Having the resources to engage in conflict makes conflict more likely. Entrapment refers to the tendency to commit more resources to a failing endeavor in order to justify past investments.
- Perceptions of the other that contribute to conflict escalation include: unfavorable mirror images, a double standard, conflict-maintaining attributions, and dehumanization.

Reducing Conflict

- GRIT—an explicit strategy for the unilateral, persistent pursuit of trust and cooperation between opposing parties—is a useful strategy for beginning the peace process.
- Flexibility and understanding of the other party's perspective are the two key ingredients of a successful negotiation.
- Negotiating success can be defined in terms of a mutual compromise or an integrative agreement in which outcomes exceed a 50–50 split.
- Mediators can often be helpful in achieving success in negotiations.
- Superordinate goals and a superordinate identity increase the likelihood of a peaceful resolution of differences.

KEY TERMS

collectives, p. 413
social facilitation, p. 414
mere presence, p. 414
evaluation apprehension, p. 414
distraction-conflict theory, p. 415
social loafing, p. 416
deindividuation, p. 419
group polarization, p. 427
groupthink, p. 428
brainstorming, p. 431
social dilemma, p. 438
entrapment, p. 444
graduated and reciprocated initiatives in tension-reduction (GRIT), p. 446
integrative complexity, p. 448
integrative agreement, p. 449
superordinate identity, p. 451

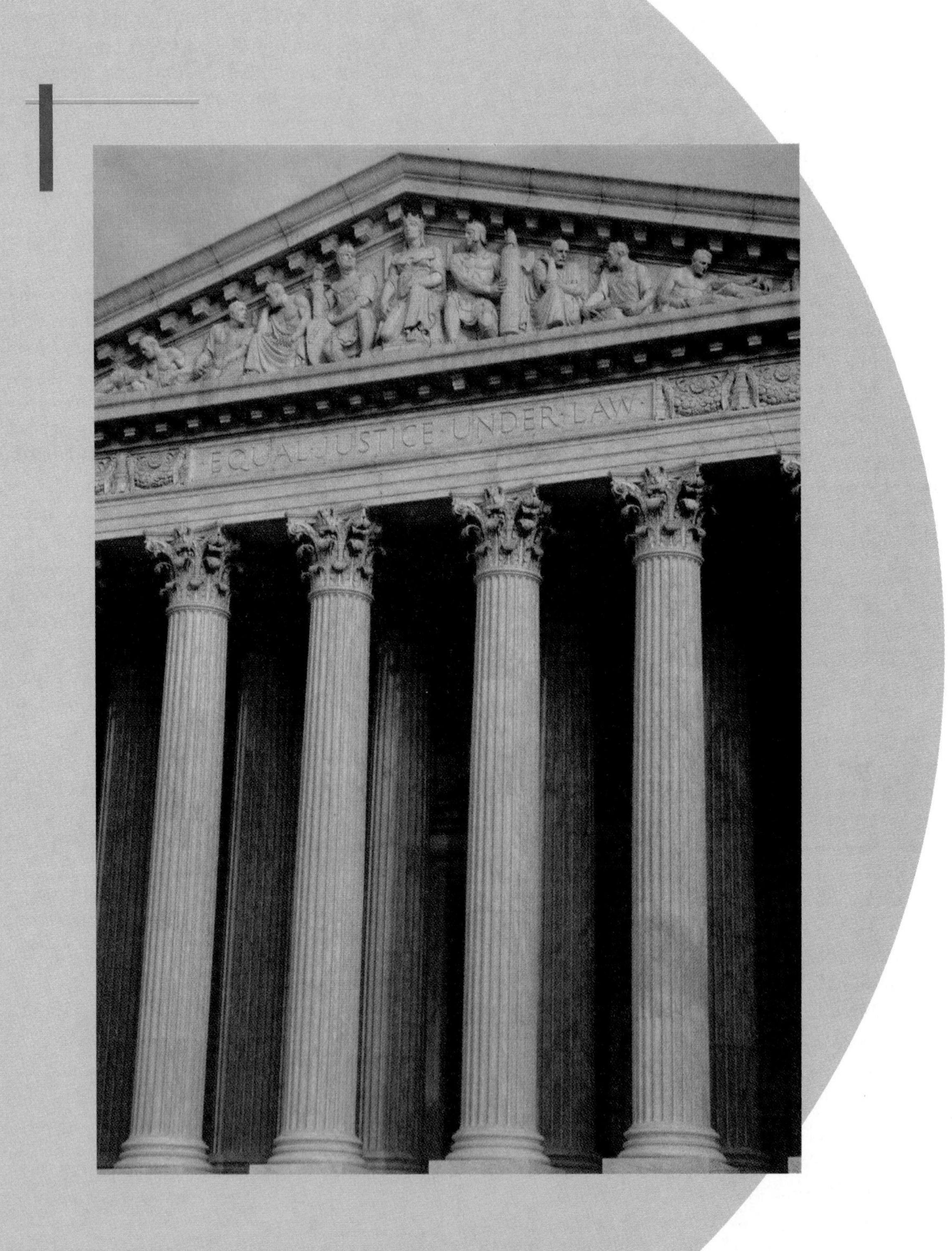
EQUAL JUSTICE UNDER LAW

Chapter 12

Law

OUTLINE

PREVIEW

This chapter examines applications of social psychology to the law. First, we consider three stages in the life of a jury trial: the *selection of jurors,* an often controversial process; *the courtroom drama* in which the evidence is presented; and the deliberations of *the jury as a group.* Next, we consider *posttrial factors* such as sentencing and the prison experience, a possible result of a guilty verdict. Finally, we discuss *perceptions of justice* inside and outside the courtroom.

It has been called "the trial of the century." From the moment O. J. Simpson was named a suspect in the murders of his ex-wife Nicole Brown and her friend Ronald Goldman, it was apparent that this case would attract worldwide attention. Simpson was, after all, a Hall of Fame football hero, sportscaster, and actor. Now everyone would watch as police cars and a helicopter trailed him in his white Ford Bronco on a Los Angeles freeway. Celebrity, sports, sex, money, racial tension, and violence. This trial would have it all, and the stage was set.

As in live theater, the trial was packed with drama. Outside the courthouse, hundreds of TV cameras and microphones lined the parking lot. In an area that became known as "Camp O. J.," street musicians performed, bystanders held up signs, and vendors sold T-shirts, buttons, and other souvenirs. The courtroom itself was filled with journalists from all over the world, cameras, easels, a computer, and a wall-mounted projection screen. Yet it was so quiet you could hear a pin drop. At center stage were Simpson and his "dream team" lawyers Robert Shapiro, F. Lee Bailey, and Johnnie Cochran; Marcia Clark and her team of Los Angeles prosecutors; and Judge Lance Ito. Also in attendance were the jury, court personnel, photographers, reporters, victims' families, and a select group of spectators. It was the toughest ticket in town.

The question for the jury to decide was simple: Did Simpson stab his wife and her friend to death? If so, was the act premeditated, or was it committed during a fit of rage? The prosecution presented pictures, witnesses, and the tape of a 911 phone call as evidence that Simpson had been physically abusive of his wife. In addition, blood-soaked socks and a glove were found in Simpson's house, stains were found in his car, and DNA tests linked the blood to the victims. In turn, the defense argued that Simpson was at home when the murders were committed, that he was physically unable to overpower the two victims, that the police had contaminated the crime scene and planted evidence to frame Simpson, and that the DNA tests were unreliable. All in all, the trial lasted for several months.

Regardless of how one feels about the O. J. Simpson trial, it serves to illustrate the profound importance of social psychology at work in the legal system. What kinds of people do lawyers select as jurors, and why? Can witnesses accurately recall the details of crimes and other events? How do juries reach unanimous de-

In the so-called trial of the century, the most prominent actors were O. J. Simpson and his "dream team" defense lawyers Johnnie Cochran and Robert Shapiro (left), prosecutor Marcia Clark (right), and Judge Lance Ito (center).

cisions, often after days of exhausting deliberation? What factors influence the severity of the sentence imposed by judges? In this chapter, we take social psychology into the courtroom to answer these questions. But first, let's place trials in a broader context.

In the American criminal justice system, trials are just the tip of an iceberg. Once a crime takes place, it must be detected and reported in order to draw attention. Through an investigation, the police must then find a suspect and decide whether to make an arrest. If they do, the suspect is held in custody or bail is set, and either a judge or a grand jury decides if there is sufficient evidence for a formal accusation. If there is, the prosecuting and defense attorneys begin a lengthy process of discovery during which they gather evidence. At this point, many defendants plead guilty as part of a deal negotiated by the lawyers. In cases that do go to trial, the ordeal does not end with a verdict. After conviction, the judge imposes a sentence, and the defendant decides whether to appeal to a higher court. For those in prison, decisions concerning their release are made by parole boards.

As Figure 12.1 illustrates, the criminal justice apparatus is complicated, and the actors behind the scenes are numerous. Yet through it all, the trial—a relatively infrequent event—is the heart and soul of the system. The threat of trial motivates parties to gather evidence and, later, to negotiate a deal. And when it's over, the trial forms the basis for later sentencing and appeals decisions. Social psychologists have a lot to say about trials—and about other aspects of the legal system as well (Kagehiro & Laufer, 1992). In the following pages, we divide this event into three stages: selection of jurors, presentation of evidence, and the jury's deliberations.

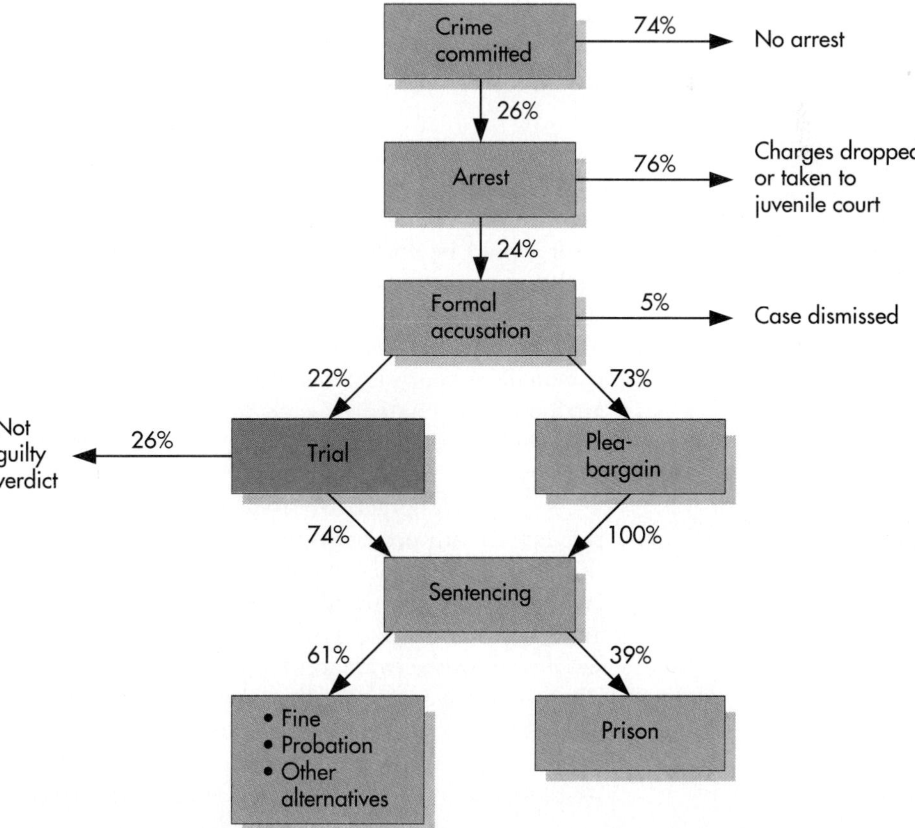

Figure 12.1 **Overview of the American Criminal Justice System.** This flow chart presents the movement of cases through different branches of the criminal justice system. Percentages indicate the proportion of cases that reach a particular stage. As this chart illustrates, the trial is just one aspect of the criminal justice system. (Based on Konecni & Ebbesen, 1982. As adapted from the President's Commission on Law Enforcement and Administration of Justice, 1967.)

SELECTION OF JURORS

The original jury that was picked to try O. J. Simpson consisted of four men and eight women. Two of the jurors were White, eight were Black, one was Hispanic, and one was American Indian. With millions of Los Angeles residents to choose from, how was this particular group selected, and why?

Jury selection is a three-stage process. First, a court compiles a master list of eligible citizens who live in the community. Second, so that a representative sample from this community can be obtained, a certain number of people from the list are randomly drawn and summoned for duty. If you've ever been called, you know what happens next. Before people who appear in court are selected for a jury, they are subjected to what is known as the **voir dire,** a pretrial interview in which the judge or the opposing lawyers question prospective jurors for signs of bias. If someone knows one of the parties, has an interest in the outcome of the case, or has already formed an opinion, the judge will excuse that person. In fact, if it can be demonstrated that an entire community is biased, perhaps due to pretrial publicity, the trial might be postponed or moved to another location.

voir dire The pretrial examination of prospective jurors by the judge or opposing lawyers to uncover signs of bias.

Although the procedure seems straightforward, there is more to the story. In addition to excluding individuals who are clearly biased, lawyers are permitted to make **peremptory challenges.** That is, they can reject a certain limited number of prospective jurors even if they seem fair and open-minded, and they can do so without having to state reasons or win the judge's approval. Why would a lawyer challenge someone who, at least on the surface, appears to be impartial? What guides the decision to accept some jurors and reject others? These questions make the voir dire very interesting to social psychologists (Hans & Vidmar, 1986; Kassin & Wrightsman, 1988).

peremptory challenges The means by which lawyers can exclude a limited number of prospective jurors without the judge's approval.

Trial Lawyers as Intuitive Psychologists

Before the O. J. Simpson trial began, lawyers speculated that the ideal defense juror would be someone who is older, black, male, and a football fan. Indeed, trial lawyers have been known to use such strategies to select juries. Under pressure to make choices quickly and without much information, lawyers rely on implicit personality theories and stereotypes. As described in Chapter 3, an implicit personality theory is a set of assumptions that people make about how certain attributes are related to each other and to behavior. When people believe that all members of a group share the same attributes, these theories are called stereotypes.

As far as trial practice is concerned, numerous how-to books claim that the astute lawyer can predict a juror's verdict by simple demographics (Fulero & Penrod, 1990). Take occupation, for example. It has been suggested that athletes lack sympathy for fragile and injured victims, that engineers are unemotional, and that cabinetmakers are so meticulous in their work that they are never fully satisfied with the evidence. Rumor has it that prosecutors exclude butchers from juries on the assumption that anyone who cuts up dead animals for a living will not easily be shocked by the details of a violent crime. Clarence Darrow, perhaps the most prominent trial attorney of the twentieth century, thought that jurors of southern European descent favored the defense whereas those of Scandinavian heritage favored the prosecution. Still other so-called jury experts offer advice based on clothing, handwriting, body language, and astrology. Perhaps the most interesting rule is also the simplest: "If you don't like a juror's face, chances are he doesn't like yours either!" (Wishman, 1986, pp. 72–73).

Pretrial Attitudes and Bias

If assumptions based on surface appearances were correct, it would be easy to predict how jurors would vote. But the folk wisdom of trial lawyers is not supported by research. Demographic factors such as sex, age, race, income, education, marital status, and occupation do not consistently predict juror decisions (Hastie et al., 1983). Personality factors are not consistently informative either (Kassin & Wrightsman, 1983)—although jurors who have an authoritarian personality are generally prone to convict (Narby et al., 1993). Sure, there are individual differences among jurors, but simple cookbook recipes such as "women are lenient" can prove hopelessly misleading. Sometimes, women are more lenient as jurors than men are; at other times it's the other way around. Whether a juror characteristic predicts verdicts depends on the specifics of each and every case. Hence the birth of a new service industry: scientific jury selection.

Scientific Jury Selection Rather than rely on hunches, successful financial investors, baseball managers, and gamblers play the odds whenever they can. Now, many trial lawyers do too. In recent years, the "art" of jury selection has been transformed into a "science."

It all began during the Vietnam War, when the federal government prosecuted a group of antiwar activists known as the Harrisburg Seven. The case against the defendants was strong, and the trial was to be held in Harrisburg, Pennsylvania. To help the defense select a jury, sociologist Jay Schulman and his colleagues (1973) surveyed the local community by interviewing 840 residents. Two kinds of information were taken from each resident: demographics (for example, sex, race, age, and education) and attitudes relevant to the trial (for example, attitudes toward the government, the war, and political dissent). By analyzing the correlations between demographics and attitudes, Schulman's team came up with a profile of the ideal juror for the defense: "a female Democrat with no religious preference and a white-collar job or a skilled blue-collar job" (p. 40). Guided by this result, the defense team went on to select its jury. The rest is history. Against all odds, the trial ended with a hung jury, split 10 to 2 in favor of acquittal.

scientific jury selection A method of selecting juries through surveys that yield correlations between demographics and trial-relevant attitudes.

Today, that technique—known as **scientific jury selection**—is used often, especially in civil trials involving large amounts of money. The procedure is simple. Because lawyers are often not allowed to ask jurors intrusive and personal questions, they try to determine jurors' attitudes from known information about their backgrounds. This information can be obtained through a communitywide survey, in which statistical relationships are sought between general demographic factors and attitudes relevant to a particular case. Then, during the voir dire, lawyers ask prospective jurors about their backgrounds and use peremptory challenges to exclude those whose profiles are associated with unfavorable attitudes.

As you might expect, scientific jury selection is a controversial enterprise. As long as the prospective jurors themselves are not approached, it is legal. But is it effective? Hard to say. Although lawyers who have used scientific jury selection boast an impressive winning percentage, it is impossible to know whether these victories are attributable to jury selection surveys. Social psychologists assume that attitudes can influence verdicts and that scientific jury selection can help lawyers identify these attitudes. As we'll see, such a linkage is found in cases involving rape and capital punishment.

Rape Myths In December 1991, Americans were riveted to their TV screens to watch the trial of William Kennedy Smith—live from Palm Beach, Florida. Then in February 1992, public attention shifted to Indianapolis, Indiana, where former heavyweight boxing champion Mike Tyson was being accused of rape by a contestant of the Miss Black America beauty pageant. In the first case, the woman had met Smith in a bar and then drove him at 2 A.M. to the Kennedy family's estate on the beach. In the second case, the woman had met Tyson at the pageant and joined him in his hotel room, also late at night. Tearfully, both women testified that they were physically overpowered and raped. In response, both defendants claimed that the women were consenting sexual partners. On the surface, these "he said, she said" trials seemed similar. In one important way, however, they were not: Smith's jury found him innocent; Tyson's found him guilty.

Few crimes test the criminal justice system as rape does. On the one hand, false accusations made by vindictive, regretful, or money-seeking lovers can put innocent men in prison. On the other hand, genuine rape victims are often humiliated by defense lawyers who try to justify a client's actions by impugning the victim's character and sexual lifestyle. Many states have thus enacted **rape shield laws** designed to limit the kinds of embarrassing and often irrelevant personal questions that are asked of victims who testify (Borgida, 1981). Still, if it comes down to one person's word against another's, the judge and jury confront the question of credibility: Who should be believed, the victim or the defendant?

rape shield laws Statutes that restrict the kinds of personal questions lawyers can ask rape victims who take the witness stand.

Eugene Borgida and Nancy Brekke (1985) found that perceptions of the victim and the defendant depend largely on one's beliefs and attitudes about rape. In a series of studies, hundreds of men and women from the twin cities of Minneapolis and St. Paul took part in mock juries. After filling out questionnaires,

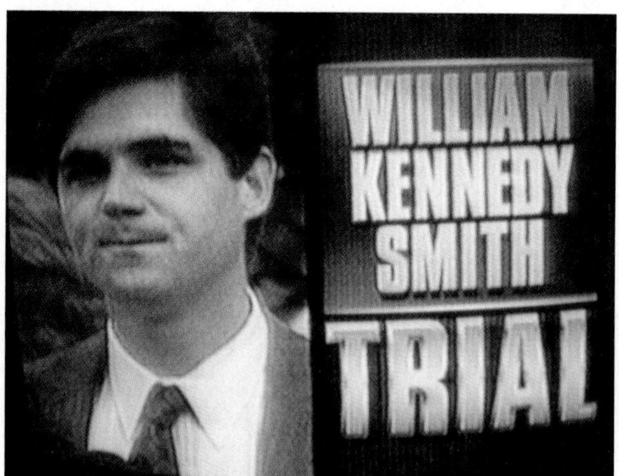

A few years ago, William Kennedy Smith (left) and Mike Tyson (right) were put on trial. In both cases, women testified that they were raped, and the men claimed that there was mutual consent. On the surface, these trials seemed similar. But were they? Smith was acquitted, while Tyson was convicted and sentenced to prison.

subjects watched a simulated trial in which a woman said she was forcibly raped but the man claimed she had freely consented to have sex. The results showed that subjects' decisions were unrelated to their personality or demographic backgrounds, including gender. What did make a difference, however, were their attitudes about women and rape. As measured by the Rape Myth Acceptance Scale, subjects who agreed that "women have an unconscious wish to be raped" or that "any healthy woman can successfully resist a rapist if she really wants to" were less likely to vote guilty than were those who disagreed with these statements. Other studies show that jurors who empathize with rape victims—perhaps because they personally knew someone who had once been raped—are more likely to trust the woman's side of the story than are those who do not (Wiener et al., 1989).

Death Qualification If you had to sentence someone to die, could you do it? Not everyone answers this question in the same way. Yet your answer could mean the difference between life and death for a defendant convicted of murder. Today, a vast majority of states in the United States permit capital punishment. Among those that do, it is often the jury that decides not only the verdict but the sentence as well: Should the convicted murderer be imprisoned for life or executed?

death qualification A jury-selection procedure used in capital cases that permits judges to exclude prospective jurors who say they would not vote for the death penalty.

In cases that involve crimes punishable by death, a special jury-selection practice known as **death qualification** is used. Through death qualification, judges may exclude all prospective jurors who say they would refuse to vote for the death penalty. These jurors are then excluded for the entire trial. To ensure that

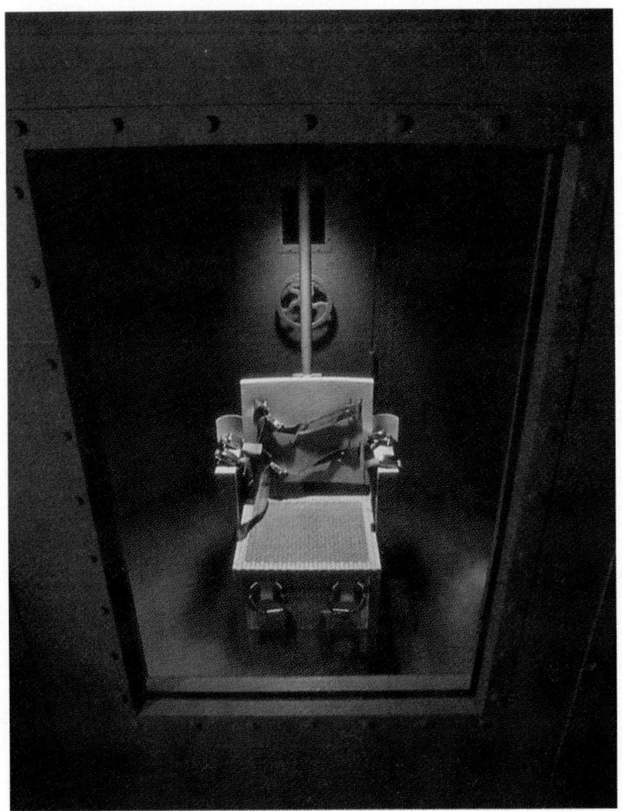

Juries must often decide whether to sentence a convicted murderer to death—in this case, in a gas chamber.

sentencing decisions are unbiased, it makes sense to exclude those who admit they are not open-minded. But does this selection practice tip the balance toward the prosecution when it comes to the *verdict?* Are death-qualified juries prone to convict?

Through a series of studies, Phoebe Ellsworth, Craig Haney, and their colleagues have examined this question. Their results show that compared to people who oppose the death penalty, those who support it are more prosecution-minded on a host of issues. For example, they are more concerned about crime, more trustful of police, more cynical about defense lawyers, and less tolerant of procedures that protect the accused (Fitzgerald & Ellsworth, 1984; Haney et al., 1994).

When it comes to verdicts, the difference between jurors who are death-qualified and those who are excluded can be substantial. In one study, 288 people watched a staged videotaped murder trial and then participated in mock juries. Subjects who said they were willing to impose the death penalty were more likely to vote guilty before deliberating than were those who would have been excluded for their refusal to impose a death sentence. This difference persisted even after subjects deliberated on juries (Cowan et al., 1984). Similar results have also been found in studies of real jurors (Moran & Comfort, 1986).

As the research evidence mounted, American courts had to face a sobering prospect. Had the hundreds of prisoners on "death row" been tried by juries that were biased against them? In *Lockhart* v. *McCree* (1986), the U.S. Supreme Court considered the issue. To inform the Court of recent research, the American Psychological Association submitted an exhaustive review of the literature (Bersoff & Ogden, 1987)—but to no avail. In an opinion that disappointed many

No doubt this prospective juror would survive the death qualification test.

"Are we to understand, then, that you would have no scruples about imposing the death penalty?"

social psychologists, the Court rejected the APA's claims and ruled that death qualification does not violate a defendant's right to a fair trial.

Should the Supreme Court have been persuaded by the evidence? Some say yes (Ellsworth, 1991), others say no (Elliott, 1991). Either way, it is now important to devise alternative, nonprejudicial methods that can be used to select future capital juries. It turns out, for example, that many people who are excluded because of their *general* opposition to capital punishment admit that they would impose the death penalty on *specific* defendants found guilty of committing atrocious acts of violence (Cox & Tanford, 1989). Clearly, this issue is one that continues to interest social psychologists (Costanzo & White, 1994).

Ethical Dilemmas Before concluding our review of jury selection, let's consider some of the delicate ethical issues that it raises. Is justice enhanced or impaired by scientific jury selection? Is the real goal for lawyers to eliminate jurors who are biased, or to create a jury slanted in their direction? These are difficult questions, and the answers frequently depend on whom you ask.

Proponents of scientific jury selection argue that picking juries according to survey results is simply a more refined version of what lawyers are permitted to do by intuition. The problem, they say, is not the *science* but the *law* that permits attorneys to use peremptory challenges to exclude jurors who are not obviously biased. However, critics argue that scientific jury selection may tip the scales of justice in favor of wealthy clients who can afford to pay for the service. The implications are disturbing. In rape trials, and in trials involving the death penalty, prosecution and defense lawyers can stack juries in their favor by conducting pretrial survey research. In other cases too, lawyers can sometimes use science to increase the chance of winning.

THE COURTROOM DRAMA

Once a jury is selected, the trial officially begins, and much of the evidence previously gathered comes to life. The trial itself is a well-orchestrated event. Lawyers for both sides make opening statements. Witnesses answer questions under oath. Lawyers make closing arguments. The judge instructs the jury. Yet there are many problems in this all-too-human enterprise: The evidence may not be accurate, jurors may be biased by extraneous factors, and judges' instructions may fall on deaf ears. In this section, we identify some of the problems and possible solutions.

The Defendant

Beginning with the news that he was a suspect, climaxing the night that his white Bronco was followed by the Los Angeles police, and continuing with his physical presence in the courtroom, all eyes were focused on O. J. Simpson. Few defendants command this extraordinary degree of attention. But when a defendant speaks, police officers, lawyers, judges, and juries all listen. Sometimes what they hear are pleas of innocence; at other times they hear confessions.

Police Confessions Years ago, police detectives used brute force and intimidation to get confessions. Today "third degree" tactics are more psychological in nature. In *Criminal Interrogation and Confessions,* a popular how-to manual written for the police, Fred Inbau and his colleagues (1986) present sixteen elaborate ploys that can be used to extract confessions. One approach is to minimize the offense by making excuses on behalf of the suspect. Lulled into a false sense of security and led to expect leniency, the suspect caves in. A second approach is to frighten the suspect into submission by exaggerating the charges or pretending to have damaging evidence. In this scenario, the suspect is led to think that it is futile to mount a defense. A third approach is to befriend the suspect and use the relationship to offer sympathy and friendly advice. These ploys may sound as though they come from a television script, but they are frequently used in real life (Gudjonsson, 1992; Wrightsman & Kassin, 1993).

Do people ever confess to crimes they did not commit? Occasionally, yes. As hard as it is to believe, there are some chilling cases on record. Sometimes innocent suspects confess under pressure as an act of *compliance,* merely to escape an aversive interrogation; in other instances, suspects actually come to believe that they are guilty of the crime, illustrating the process of *internalization.*

Is it really possible to convince people that they are guilty of an act they did not commit? In a study analyzing an interrogation ploy frequently used by the police, Kassin and Kiechel (in press) recruited pairs of college students to work on a fast- or slow-paced reaction time computer task. At one point, the computer crashed and subjects were accused of having caused the damage by pressing a key they were specifically instructed to avoid. All subjects were truly innocent and denied the charge. In half the sessions, however, the second student (who was really a confederate) said that she saw the subject hit the forbidden key. Demonstrating the process of compliance, many subjects confronted by this false witness signed a confession handwritten by the experimenter. And demonstrating the process of internalization, some of those subjects later "admitted" their guilt to a stranger (also a confederate) who had overheard the commotion and, when the two were alone, asked what happened. On both measures, confessions were most likely to be drawn from subjects who had worked on a fast-paced task, a situation that heightened uncertainty concerning their own actions (see Table 12.1). It seems that despite innocence, people who are vulnerable to suggestion can be induced to confess and internalize guilt by the presentation of false evidence—an interrogation tactic commonly used by the police.

This problem is evident in the story of Paul Ingram, a man recently charged with rape and a host of satanic cult crimes that included the slaughter of newborn babies. During six months of interrogations, Ingram was hypnotized, informed of graphic crime details, led to believe by a police psychologist that sex offenders typically repress their offenses, and urged by the minister of his church to confess. Eventually Ingram "recalled" crime scenes to specification, pleaded guilty, and was sentenced to prison. In fact, there was no physical evidence that the alleged events had ever occurred, and an expert who reviewed the case for the state concluded that Ingram had been brainwashed. At one point, this expert accused Ingram of a bogus crime. At first he denied the charge. But eventually Ingram confessed—and embellished the story in the process (Ofshe & Watters, 1994; Wright, 1994).

The Ingram case never went to trial, but it raises another key question: How does the legal system treat confessions brought out by various deceptive methods of interrogation? The procedure is straightforward. Whenever a suspect confesses but then retracts the statement and goes to trial, the judge must determine whether the statement was voluntary or coerced. If it was clearly coerced—as when a suspect is isolated for a long period of time, deprived of food or sleep,

Table 12.1 Factors That Promote False Confessions

	Control		False Witness	
	Slow	Fast	Slow	Fast
Compliance	35%	65%	89%	100%
Internalization	0%	12%	44%	65%

As subjects worked on a fast- or slow-paced task, the computer crashed and they were accused of causing the damage by pressing a key they were told to avoid. A confederate then said that she did or did not see the subject hit the forbidden key. As shown, many subjects signed a confession (compliance), and some even "admitted" their guilt in private to another confederate (internalization). Despite their innocence, many subjects confessed on both measures in the fast-false witness condition. (Kassin & Kiechel, in press.)

threatened, or abused—the confession is excluded. If not, it is admitted into evidence for the jury to evaluate.

Juries are then confronted with a classic attributional dilemma: A suspect's statement may indicate guilt (personal attribution), or it may simply be a way to avoid the aversive consequences of silence (situational attribution). According to attribution theory, jurors should reject all confessions made in response to external pressure. But wait. Research on the "fundamental attribution error" shows that observers overattribute behavior to persons and overlook the influence of situational forces (see Chapter 3). Is it possible that jurors view the suspect who confesses as guilty, despite the pressures of interrogation? It depends.

First, it depends on the methods used to elicit the confession. Consider your reaction to two common ploys: a *threat* of harm or punishment and a *promise* of leniency or immunity from prosecution. By law, both of these tactics are unacceptable. Psychologically, however, there's an important difference. When mock jurors hear that a defendant confessed after being threatened, they completely discount the confession—that is, they judge it to have been coerced and vote for acquittal. However, when a defendant is said to have confessed in response to an offer of favorable treatment, people do not completely disregard the confession. They concede that it was involuntary, but they vote guilty anyway. This pattern has been called the *positive coercion bias* (Kassin & Wrightsman, 1985).

The jury's interpretation of confession evidence also depends on how that evidence is presented. Today, many police departments videotape confessions for the record (Geller, 1993). But how are these events staged for the camera and shown in court? As described in Chapter 3, research shows that observers who watch two people having a conversation overemphasize the impact on that interaction of the person who is visually salient. On the basis of this finding, Daniel Lassiter and his colleagues (1992) taped a mock confession from three different camera angles: Either the suspect or the interrogator or both were visible. Even though all subjects heard the same exchange of words, those who watched the suspect considered the situation to be less coercive than did those who focused on the interrogator. The practical implications are striking. When the camera directs all eyes at the accused, jurors are likely to underestimate the amount of pressure exerted by the "hidden" interrogator. Yet that is precisely how confessions are normally taped.

polygraph A mechanical instrument that records physiological arousal from multiple channels; it is often used as a lie-detector test.

The Lie-Detector Test Sometimes people confess after being told that they have failed the **polygraph,** or lie-detector test (Lykken, 1981). A polygraph is an instrument that records multiple channels of physiological arousal. Rubber tubes are strapped around the suspect's torso to measure breathing; blood pressure cuffs are wrapped around the upper arm to measure pulse rate; and electrodes are placed on the fingertips to record perspiration. The instrument is used to detect deception on the assumption that when people lie, they become anxious in ways that can be measured. Here's how the test is used. After convincing a suspect that the polygraph is effective and establishing his or her baseline level of arousal, the examiner asks a series of yes-no questions and compares how the suspect reacts to emotionally arousing *crime-relevant questions* ("Did you stab your wife?") and *control questions* that are arousing but not relevant to the crime ("Did you hurt anybody when you were young?"). In theory, innocent suspects—whose denials are truthful—should be more aroused by the control questions, and guilty suspects—whose denials are false—should be more aroused by the crime-relevant questions (Podlesny & Raskin, 1977).

Does the lie-detector test really work? Although many people think it is foolproof, professional opinion is split. Some researchers report accuracy rates in the range of 80 to 90 percent (Horvath, 1984; Raskin, 1986). Others say that these claims are exaggerated and misleading (Lykken, 1981). One problem is that truthful persons too often fail the test. For example, a study of polygraph records obtained from police files revealed that although 98 percent of suspects later known to be guilty were correctly identified as such, 45 percent of those who were eventually found innocent were judged deceptive (Patrick & Iacono, 1991). A second problem is that the test can be faked. Studies show that you can beat the polygraph by using mental "countermeasures" such as distraction, or by tensing your muscles, biting your tongue, or squeezing your toes while answering the *control* questions. By artificially inflating the responses to "innocent" questions, one can mask the stress that is aroused by lying in reply to the crime-relevant questions (Honts et al., 1994).

What, then, are we to conclude? After carefully reviewing all the research, Leonard Saxe and his colleagues (1985) determined that there is no simple answer. Under certain conditions—for example, when the suspect is naive and the examiner is competent—it is possible for the polygraph to detect truth and deception at fairly high levels of accuracy. Still, the problems are hard to overcome—which is why many states refuse to allow polygraph test results into evidence. As an alternative, some researchers are now trying to develop a test that distinguishes between truth and deception through the measurement of involuntary electrical activity in the brain (Bashore & Rapp, 1993). At this point, it is too early to tell whether this type of test is any more accurate (Rosenfeld, 1995).

The Eyewitness

"I'll never forget that face!" When these words are uttered, police officers, judges, and juries all take notice. Sometimes, however, eyewitnesses make mistakes. Consider the sad story of William Jackson, identified by two crime victims, convicted, and sent to prison. Five years later, it was revealed that Jackson was

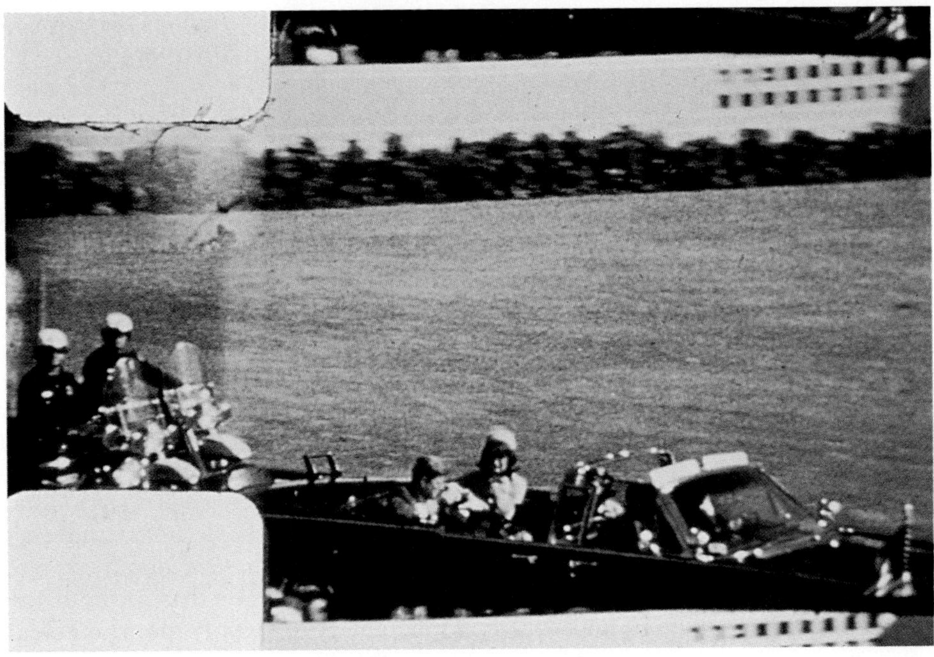

After the tragic assassination of President John F. Kennedy, dozens of eyewitnesses came forward to describe what they saw. Some reported one gunman in the sixth-floor window of a nearby building; others reported two or three gunmen in the building; and still others thought the shots were fired from the ground. Such are the pitfalls of eyewitness testimony.

innocent so he was released. But the damage was done. "They took away part of my life, part of my youth," he said ("We're Sorry," 1982).

An estimated 77,000 people a year are charged with crimes solely on the basis of eyewitness evidence (Goldstein et al., 1989). As eyewitnesses, people can be called on to remember just about anything: a face, an accident, a conversation, or—as in the trial of O. J. Simpson—the presence of a white Ford Bronco parked on the street. Over the years, hundreds of controlled studies have been conducted. From this research, three conclusions can be drawn: (1) eyewitnesses are not perfect, (2) certain factors systematically influence their performance, and (3) judges and juries are not well informed about these factors (Yarmey, 1979; Williams et al., 1992; Wells, 1993).

People tend to think that human memory is like a video camera: If you turn on the power and focus the lens, all observations will be recorded for subsequent playback. Unfortunately, it's not that simple. Researchers find it useful to view memory as a three-stage process involving *acquisition, storage,* and *retrieval.* The first of these stages, acquisition, refers to a witness's perceptions at the time of the event in question. Second, the witness stores the acquired information in memory to avoid forgetting. Third, when the information is needed, the witness retrieves it from storage. This model suggests that errors can occur at three different points.

Acquisition Some kinds of persons and events are more difficult to perceive than others. Common sense tells us that brief exposure time, poor lighting, distance, physical disguise, and distraction are all factors that can severely limit a witness's perceptions. Research has uncovered other less obvious factors as well.

Consider the effects of a witness's mental and emotional state. Often witnesses are asked to recall a bloody shooting, car wreck, or assault, emotional events that arouse high levels of stress. Arousal has a complex effect on memory. Realizing the importance of what they are seeing, highly aroused witnesses zoom in on the central features of an event—perhaps the culprit, the victim, or a weapon. As a direct result of this narrowed attention, however, arousal impairs a witness's memory for other details (Burke et al., 1992; Christianson, 1992). Alcohol, a drug often involved in crime, also causes problems. When subjects in one study witnessed a live staged crime, those who had earlier consumed fruit juice were more accurate in their recollections than were those who had been served an alcoholic beverage (Yuille & Tollestrup, 1990).

weapon-focus effect The tendency for weapons to draw attention and impair a witness's ability to identify the culprit.

The **weapon-focus effect** is also an important factor. Research shows that when a criminal pulls out a gun, a razor blade, or a knife, witnesses are less able to identify that culprit than if no weapon is present (Steblay, 1992). There are two reasons for this effect. First, people are agitated by the sight of a menacing stimulus—as when the subjects in one study were approached by an experimenter holding a syringe or threatening to administer an injection (Maass & Kohnken, 1989). Second, even in a harmless situation, a witness's eyes are fixed to the weapon like magnets—drawing attention away from the face. To demonstrate, Elizabeth Loftus and her colleagues (1987) showed subjects slides of a customer who walked up to a bank teller and pulled out either a gun or a checkbook. By recording eye movements, these researchers found that subjects spent more time looking at the gun than at the checkbook. The net result was an impairment in their ability to identify the criminal in a line-up.

cross-race identification bias The tendency for people to have difficulty identifying members of a race other than their own.

There is still another important consideration. By varying the racial make-up of subjects and target persons in laboratory and real-life interactions, researchers discovered that people find it relatively difficult to recognize members of a race other than their own—an effect known as the **cross-race identification bias** (Malpass & Kravitz, 1969; Brigham & Malpass, 1985; Bothwell et al., 1989). To demonstrate, eighty-six convenience store clerks in El Paso, Texas, were asked to identify three customers—one White, one Black, and one Mexican-American—all experimental confederates who had stopped in and made a purchase earlier that day. Figure 12.2 shows that the White, Black, and Mexican-American clerks were all most likely to make accurate identifications of customers belonging to their own racial or ethnic group (Platz & Hosch, 1988). To some extent, the problem that "they all look alike" stems from a lack of interracial contact. James Li and his colleagues (in press) thus found that the cross-race identification bias is *not* exhibited by white subjects who are avid basketball fans—a sport in which the majority of players are Black.

Storage In the fall of 1991, law professor Anita Hill accused Supreme Court justice Clarence Thomas of sexual harassment. She asserted that he had made certain statements ten years earlier—statements she said she could repeat word for word. That same year, TV star Roseanne said that she had vivid memories of being sexually abused as a baby by her mother. These stories have little in common, but both raise the same question: Can remembrances of the past be trusted?

As one would expect, memory for faces and events tends to decline with the passage of time. Longer intervals between an event and its retrieval are generally associated with increased forgetting (Shapiro & Penrod, 1986). But not all recollections fade, and time alone does not cause memory slippage. After witnessing an event, we often generate and receive new information about it. Consider the plight of those who witnessed the 1963 assassination of John F. Kennedy. When it was over, they undoubtedly talked to each other, described the experience to friends, read about the suspect, and answered questions from investigators, reporters, and others. If you were to interview these witnesses today, you would

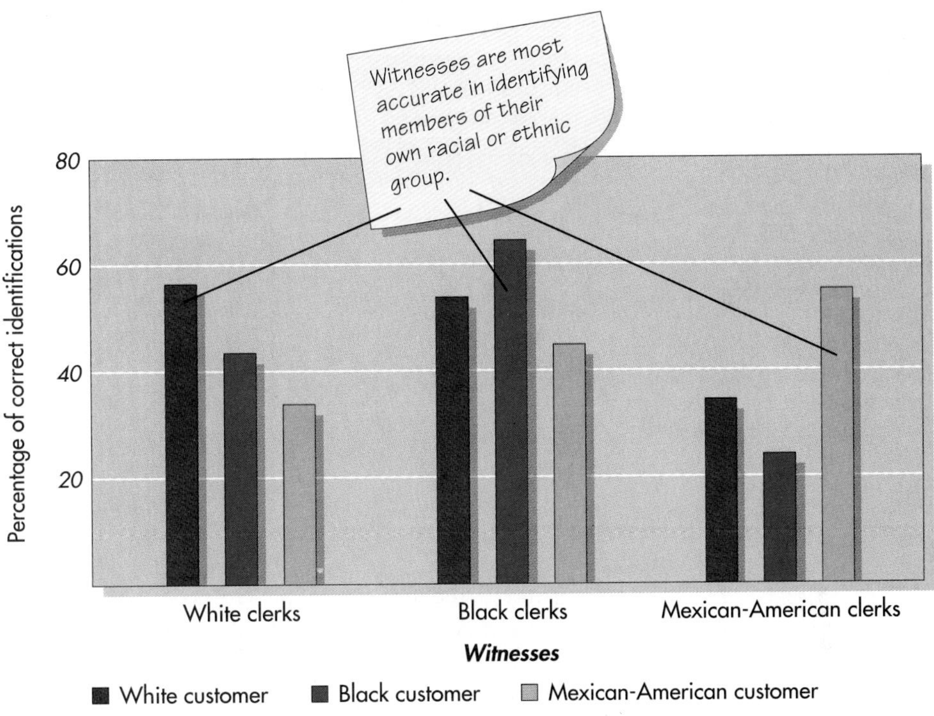

Figure 12.2 The Cross-Race Identification Bias. In this study, convenience store clerks tried to identify three customers—one White, one Black, and one Mexican-American—all of whom had stopped in during the day. As you can see, the clerks were more likely to correctly identify customers of their own racial or ethnic group. (Platz & Hosch, 1988.)

have to wonder: Are their original memories still "pure," uncontaminated by postevent information?

reconstructive memory The theoretical concept that eyewitness memory can be altered by exposure to postevent information.

According to Elizabeth Loftus (1979), the answer is probably no. Based on an extensive program of research, Loftus proposed a theory of **reconstructive memory.** After we observe something, she says, later information about the event—whether true or not—becomes integrated into the fabric of our memory. To illustrate, consider a classic experiment by Loftus and John Palmer (1974). Subjects viewed a film of a traffic accident and then answered questions, including the following: "About how fast were the cars going when they *hit* each other?" Other subjects received the same question, except that the verb *hit* was replaced by *smashed, collided, bumped,* or *contacted.* Even though all subjects saw the same accident, the wording of the question affected their reports. Figure 12.3 shows that subjects given the "smashed" question estimated the highest average speed and those responding to the "contacted" question estimated the lowest. But there's more. One week later, subjects were called back for additional probing. Had the wording of the questions caused subjects to reconstruct their memories of the accident? Yes. When asked whether they had seen broken glass at the accident site (none was actually present), 32 percent of the "smashed" subjects said they had. Consistent with Loftus's theory, what these subjects remembered of the accident was based on two sources: the event itself and postevent information.

Loftus's provocative theory has aroused much controversy. Does postevent information actually alter or impair a witness's real memory, never to be retrieved again (Loftus et al., 1989; Belli et al., 1992; Weingardt et al., 1995)? Or do subjects merely follow the experimenter's "suggestion," leaving their true memory intact for retrieval under the right conditions (Dodson & Reisberg, 1991;

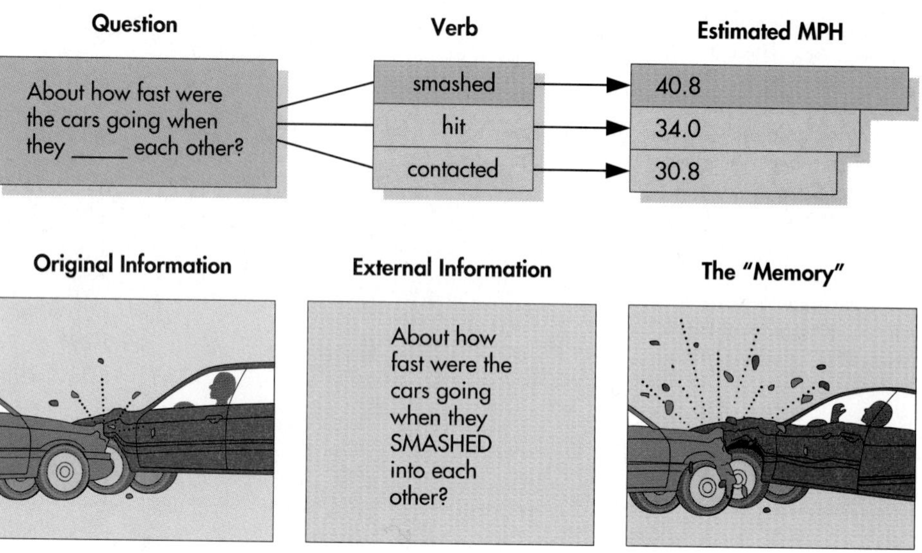

Figure 12.3 Biasing Eyewitness Reports with Loaded Questions. Subjects viewed a film of a traffic accident and then answered this question: "About how fast were the cars going when they (hit, smashed, or contacted) each other?" As shown, the wording of the question influenced speed estimates (top). One week later, it also caused subjects to reconstruct their memory of other aspects of the accident (bottom). (Loftus & Palmer, 1974.)

McCloskey & Zaragoza, 1985)? As this theoretical debate rages on, the all-important practical lesson remains: Whether memory is truly altered or not, eyewitness *reports* are hopelessly biased by postevent information.

This phenomenon raises an additional question. If adults can be misled by postevent information, what about children? In 1983, Judy Johnson complained to the police in Manhattan Beach, California, that her two-year-old son had been molested at the McMartin Pre-School by Raymond Buckey, a teacher. Before long, the police contacted other parents and charged that Ray and his mother, Peggy McMartin Buckey, had sexually abused hundreds of boys and girls. In interviews with a social worker, several children said they were forced to play "naked games." Some even told bizarre stories of satanic rituals in which they drank blood, dug up bodies at cemeteries, jumped out of airplanes, and sacrificed animals on a church altar.

Were the stories accurate? Were the children competent to testify in court? On the one hand, there were striking consistencies in the reports of different children. On the other hand, the social worker who conducted the interviews often prompted the children with suggestive questions, urging them to describe acts they had initially denied and scolding those who claimed ignorance. Based on the testimony of eleven children, the case went to trial. Then in 1990, after thirty-three months—the longest criminal trial in American history—the jury found the defendants not guilty. As one juror explained, "I believe that the children believed what they were saying, but I couldn't tell if they were repeating what they had been told. . . . I had a hard time picking fact from fiction" (Mydans, 1990, p. A18).

Can leading questions cause children to confuse appearance and reality? Since the McMartin case, thousands of child sex-abuse cases have inundated the courts. With each complaint, judges struggle to decide: Are preschoolers competent to take the witness stand, or are they too suggestible, too prone to confuse reality and fantasy? In the McMartin trial, the jury did not trust the young children's recollections. Yet in many cases, defendants are convicted solely on the basis of such testimony. To provide some guidance to the courts, researchers have been studying children's eyewitness memory (Ceci & Bruck, 1993; Perry & Wrightsman, 1991).

Nothing an eyewitness does has greater impact than a line-up identification. When the police make an arrest, they often call on witnesses to view a line-up that includes the suspect and other individuals. The line-up may take place within days of a crime or months later. Either way, this procedure often results in tragic cases of mistaken identity. Through the application of eyewitness research findings, as we'll see, this risk can be reduced (Wells, 1993).

Basically, four factors affect identification performance. The first is the line-up *construction*. A few years ago, comedian Richard Pryor performed in a skit on the TV show *Saturday Night Live* in which he appeared in a line-up alongside a nun, a refrigerator, and a duck. Lo and behold, the eyewitness—having already described a male criminal—picked Pryor. It obviously doesn't take a social psychologist to see the problem with this particular situation. To be fair, a line-up should include four or five innocent persons, called "foils," who match the witness's description of the culprit (Lüüs & Wells, 1991) or resemble the suspect in general appearance (Nosworthy & Lindsay, 1990). Indeed, anything that makes the suspect distinctive, compared to the others, increases his or her chance of being selected (Buckhout, 1974). This is what happened in the case of Steve Titus, a man mistakenly accused of rape when the police showed the victim his photograph along with pictures of five other men. Although the foils resembled Titus in appearance, his picture stood out like a sore thumb. It was smaller than all the others and was the only one without a border. Titus was also the only man in the group with a smile on his face (Loftus & Ketcham, 1991).

Second, line-up *instructions* to the witness are important. In a study by Roy Malpass and Patricia Devine (1981), students saw a staged act of vandalism, after which they attended a line-up. Half of the students received "biased" instructions: They were led to believe that the culprit was in the line-up. The others were told that he might or might not be present. Line-ups were then presented either with or without the culprit. When subjects received biased instructions, they felt compelled to identify *someone*. The result was that many subjects picked an innocent person (see Table 12.2). Again, the story of Steve Titus is a case in point. The police told the victim to pick her assailant from a group of six photographs. After studying the pictures for several minutes and shaking her head in

Table 12.2 Effects of Line-up and Instructions on False Identifications

	Percentage of False Identifications	
	Unbiased Instructions	Biased Instructions
Culprit Present	0	25
Culprit Absent	33	78

After witnessing a crime, subjects were told either that the culprit was in the line-up (biased instruction) or that he might or might not be present (unbiased instruction). Subjects then viewed a line-up in which the real culprit was present or absent. Notice the percentage of subjects in each group who identified an innocent person. Those who received the biased instruction were far more likely to make a false identification, picking an innocent person rather than no one at all—especially when the real culprit was not in the line-up. (Malpass & Devine, 1981.)

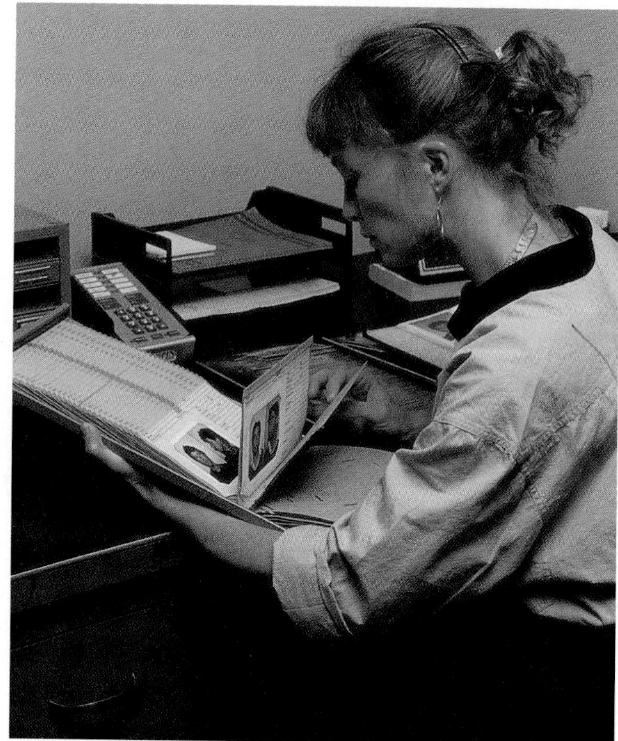

When eyewitnesses look at a spread of photographs all at once, they tend to make relative judgments by picking the one face that comes closest to the criminal. But when witnesses look through pictures one at a time, as shown here, they tend to make absolute judgments by comparing each face to their memory of the criminal. This procedure reduces the risk of a false identification.

confusion, she was urged to concentrate and make a choice. "This one is the closest," she said. "It has to be this one" (Loftus & Ketcham, 1991, p. 38).

Third, the *format* of a lineup also influences whether a witness feels compelled to make a selection. Specifically, research shows that when witnesses confront a spread of photographs, they tend to make relative, multiple choice–like judgments by picking the target who looks the most like the suspect—a strategy that sets witnesses up for a false identification. The solution? When the same photos are shown sequentially, one at a time, witnesses become more likely to make absolute judgments by comparing each target person to their memory of the criminal. In this situation, witnesses are less likely to make false identifications (Lindsay & Wells, 1985; Lindsay et al., 1991). Indeed, Richard Gonzalez and his colleagues (1993) have found that in a procedure known as a *showup*—in which the police bring the suspect in alone, without foils—witnesses become more cautious and make judgments that are absolute rather than relative.

The fourth factor is perhaps the most subtle, as it pertains to *mugshot-induced biases*. When witnesses view a line-up after having looked at mug shots, they are inclined to identify anyone whose photograph they have previously seen (Brigham & Cairns, 1988; Brown et al., 1977; Gorenstein & Ellsworth, 1980). Clearly, the person looks familiar—but from the crime scene or from the photos? All too often, witnesses remember a face but forget the circumstances in which they originally saw it.

Courtroom Testimony Eyewitnesses can be inaccurate, but that's only part of the problem. The other part is that their in-court testimony is persuasive and not easy to evaluate. To understand how juries view eyewitness testimony, Gary Wells, Rod Lindsay, and others conducted an impressive series of experiments in which they staged the theft of a calculator in front of unsuspecting research subjects who were cross-examined after trying to pick the culprit from a photo spread. Other subjects served as mock jurors, observed the questioning, and judged the witnesses. The result was sobering: Jurors overestimated eyewitness accuracy and could not distinguish between witnesses who made correct identifications and those who did not (Lindsay et al., 1981; Wells et al., 1979).

There appear to be two problems. First, the subject of human memory is not something we know about through common sense. Brian Cutler and his colleagues (1988), for example, found that mock jurors were not sensitive enough to the effects of line-up instructions, weapon focus, and other aspects of an eyewitnessing situation. Yet a witness's behavior may provide clues as to his or her accuracy. Recent research shows that it is possible to distinguish between accurate and inaccurate identifications simply by asking witnesses to describe the decision-making process. Specifically, David Dunning and Lisa Beth Stern (1994) staged a crime and found that witnesses who made a correct identification from photographs described the judgment as quick, effortless, and automatic ("His face just popped out at me"); those who were inaccurate described a more careful and deliberate process-of-elimination strategy ("I compared the photos to each other to narrow the choices"). It appears that the witness who recognizes the culprit's face does so instantly, without much thought (Sporer, 1993).

The second problem is that subjects in this study—and others as well—base their judgments on how *confident* the witness was, a factor that surprisingly does not predict accuracy (Bothwell et al., 1987; Wells & Murray, 1984). Why are eyewitness confidence and accuracy not related? The reason, according to Elizabeth Lüüs and Wells (1994), is that confidence levels can be altered by factors that do not have an impact on identification accuracy. To demonstrate, these investigators staged a theft in front of pairs of subjects and had each subject separately identify the culprit from a photographic line-up. After the subjects made an identification, the experimenter led them to believe that their partner, a co-witness, either had picked the same person, a similar-looking different person, or a dissimilar-looking different person; or had said that the thief was not in the line-up. Subjects were then questioned by a police officer about what they saw. The key question: On a scale from 1 to 10, how confident are you in your identification? As shown in Figure 12.5, subjects became more confident when told that a co-witness had picked the same person or a dissimilar alternative and less confident when told that the co-witness had selected a similar alternative or none at all. In other words, eyewitnesses can become more or less confident as a result of social factors that are unrelated to identification accuracy.

The Eyewitness Expert Having identified some of the problems with information obtained from defendants and eyewitnesses, psychologists can perhaps put their knowledge to use by educating juries so they can better evaluate the evidence. But is this a goal that can and should be achieved? More and more, psychologists are being asked to testify as expert witnesses on coerced confessions, the polygraph, the suggestibility of children in abuse cases, and the coping behavior of rape victims and battered wives (Frazier & Borgida, 1992; Schuller & Vidmar, 1992). Possibly the most controversial form of expert testimony is on the subject of eyewitness evidence. Like physicians who testify about a patient's medical condition, and like economists who testify on antitrust matters, eyewitness experts are often called by one party or the other to tell the jury about relevant theory and memory research. What, specifically, do they say to the jury? Which

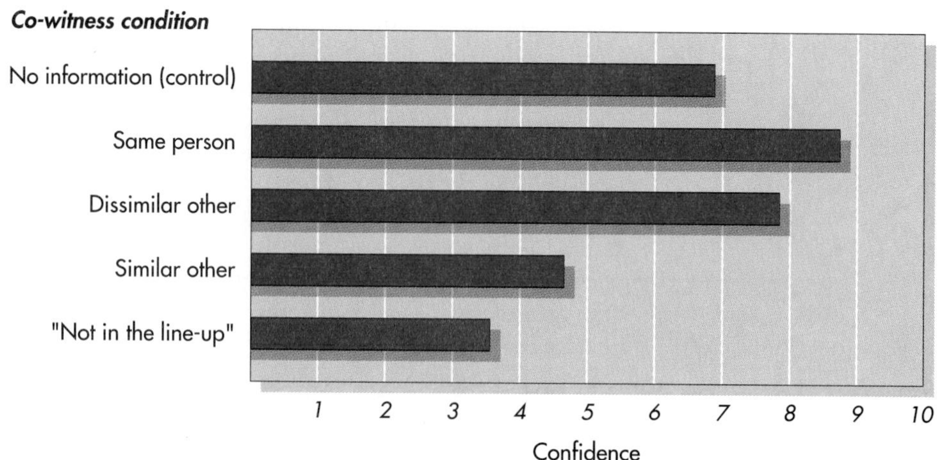

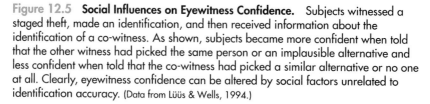

Figure 12.5 **Social Influences on Eyewitness Confidence.** Subjects witnessed a staged theft, made an identification, and then received information about the identification of a co-witness. As shown, subjects became more confident when told that the other witness had picked the same person or an implausible alternative and less confident when told that the co-witness had picked a similar alternative or no one at all. Clearly, eyewitness confidence can be altered by social factors unrelated to identification accuracy. (Data from Lüüs & Wells, 1994.)

research findings do the experts present in court? Based on a survey of sixty-three eyewitness experts (Kassin et al., 1989), Table 12.3 lists some of the phenomena believed to be most worthy of expert testimony—many of which are not known by the average person (Kassin & Barndollar, 1992).

Psychologists disagree over whether advice from experts helps or hinders the jury (Loftus, 1983; McCloskey & Egeth, 1983; Elliott, 1993; Kassin et al., 1994). So, who is right? Is the jury better off with or without help from experts? Although it's too early to draw firm conclusions, research suggests two ways in which experts can help jurors to become more competent judges of an eyewitness. First, it's clear that eyewitness experts lead people to scrutinize the evidence more carefully. Since people place too much faith in eyewitness testimony, a dose of skepticism is a healthy outcome. Second, it is possible, but not yet certain, that expert testimony can help jurors to distinguish between credible and noncredible eyewitnesses (Cutler et al., 1989; Wells, 1986).

Nonevidentiary Influences

Early in the O. J. Simpson trial, the defendant approached the jury box, lifted his pants, and displayed the scars on his knees. A few days later, Denise Brown, Nicole's sister, broke down and cried on the witness stand as gruesome crime photos triggered a gasp in the courtroom. Also during the trial, Simpson's story was released in a book, prosecutor Marcia Clark became embroiled in a child custody suit with her ex-husband, and defense lawyers were caught withholding key evidence. In this case, however, as in others, the jury was shielded from some of these events and told to disregard the rest. The question is, To what extent are jurors influenced by information that is not in evidence?

Table 12.3 What Eyewitness Experts Say in Court

Eyewitness Factor	Statement
Wording of questions	An eyewitness's testimony about an event can be affected by how the questions put to that witness are worded.
Line-up instructions	Police instructions can affect an eyewitness's willingness to make an identification and/or the likelihood that he or she will identify a particular person.
Postevent information	Eyewitness testimony about an event often reflects not only what the witness actually saw but also information obtained later on.
Accuracy-confidence	An eyewitness's confidence is not a good predictor of his or her identification accuracy.
Mug-shot biases	Eyewitnesses sometimes identify as a culprit someone they have seen in another situation or context.
Cross-race bias	Eyewitnesses are better at identifying others of the same race than they are at identifying members of another race.
Weapon focus	The presence of a weapon impairs an eyewitness's ability to accurately identify the perpetrator's face.

Presented with a list of eyewitness factors, sixty-three experts were asked what research findings were strong enough to present in court. These statements are ranked according to the amount of support they elicited from the experts. (Kassin et al., 1989.)

Pretrial Publicity Many cases find their way into the mass media long before they appear in court. Recent examples include the grisly multiple-murder trial of Jeffrey Dahmer, the case of the Los Angeles police officers who beat Rodney King, and the trials of William Kennedy Smith, Mike Tyson, Lorena Bobbitt, and the Menendez brothers. In each instance, the system struggled with this dilemma: Does exposure to pretrial news stories corrupt prospective jurors?

Public opinion surveys consistently show that the more people know about a case, the more likely they are to presume the defendant guilty, even when they claim to be impartial (Moran & Cutler, 1991). There is nothing particularly mysterious about this result. The information in news reports usually comes from the police or the district attorney's office, so it often reveals facts unfavorable to the defense. The real question is whether these reports have an impact on juries that go on to receive hard evidence in court and deliberate to a verdict.

To examine the effects of pretrial publicity, Geoffrey Kramer and his colleagues (1990) played a videotaped re-enactment of an armed robbery trial to hundreds of subjects participating in 108 mock juries. Before watching the tape, subjects were exposed to news clippings about the case. Some received material that was neutral. Others received information that was incriminating—revealing,

As a general rule, the more people know about a case, the more likely they are to presume the defendant guilty. In the O. J. Simpson trial, as in other high-profile cases, pretrial publicity can endanger the defendant's right to a fair trial.

for example, that the defendant had a prior record or implicating him in a hit-and-run accident in which a small child was killed. Even though subjects were instructed to base their decisions solely on the evidence, pretrial publicity had a marked effect. Among subjects exposed to neutral material, 33 percent voted guilty after deliberating in a jury. Among those exposed to the prejudicial material, that figure increased to 48 percent. What's worse, judges and defense lawyers could not identify in a simulated voir dire which jurors were biased by the publicity. As shown in Figure 12.6, 48 percent of those who were questioned and not challenged—jurors who said they were unaffected by the publicity—went on to

"My client has been convicted by the media, but I am confident that his conviction will be overturned on appeal by the three major networks and the 'Times.'"

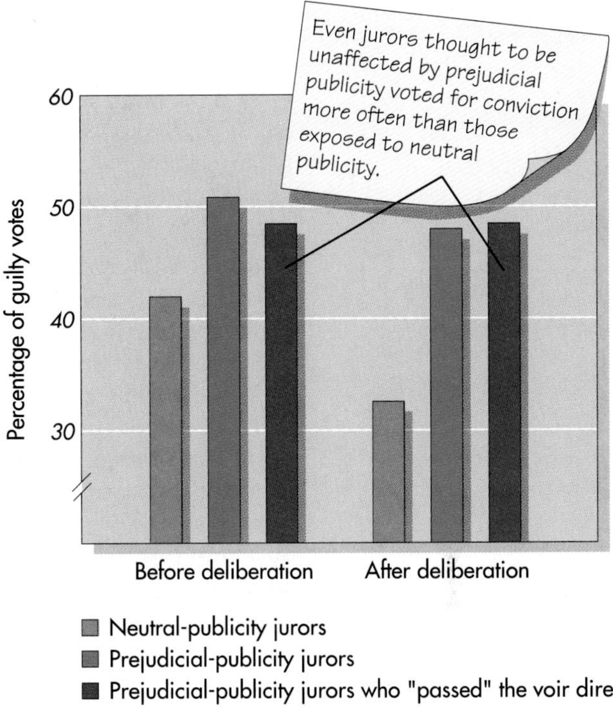

Figure 12.6 **Contaminating Effects of Pretrial Publicity.** In this study, subjects were exposed to prejudicial or neutral news reports about a defendant, watched a videotaped trial, and voted before and after participating in a mock jury deliberation. As shown, pretrial publicity increased the conviction rate slightly before deliberations (left). After deliberations, however, it more clearly increased the conviction rate—even among subjects perceived as impartial by judges and lawyers (right). (Data from Kerr et al., 1991.)

vote guilty (Kerr et al., 1991). The impact of pretrial publicity is even more powerful when the news is presented on television rather than in print (Ogloff & Vidmar, 1994).

Pretrial publicity is potentially dangerous in two respects. First, it often divulges information that, for one reason or another, is not allowed into the trial record. Second is the matter of timing. Because many news stories precede the actual trial, jurors learn about certain facts even before they enter the courtroom. From what we know about the power of first impressions, the implications are clear. If jurors receive prejudicial news information about a defendant *before* trial, that information will distort the way they interpret the rest of the case. So, is there a solution? Since this biasing effect persists despite jury-selection practices and cautionary instructions from the judge, justice may demand that highly publicized cases be postponed or moved to other, less informed communities.

Inadmissible Testimony Just as jurors are biased by news stories, they occasionally receive extralegal information from the trial itself. In his opening statement, for example, Simpson's lawyer—Johnnie Cochran—repeatedly referred to witnesses who would not later testify. With each passing reference, prosecutor Marcia Clark objected. Eventually, the judge issued a warning to Simpson's lawyer and ordered the jury to disregard the information. Then just a few weeks later, the judge had to warn the prosecutors—and again instruct the jury to disregard the information.

If something seems wrong with this series of events, you should know that it is a scene often replayed in the courtroom. But can people really strike information from their minds the way court reporters can strike it from the record? Can people resist the forbidden fruit of inadmissible testimony? Common sense suggests they cannot. So does the research. In one study, a group of mock jurors read about a murder case based on evidence so weak that not a single subject voted guilty. A second group read the same case, except that the prosecution introduced an illegally obtained tape recording of a phone call made by the defendant: "I finally got the money to pay you off. . . . When you read the papers tomorrow, you'll know what I mean." The defense argued that the illegal tape should not be admissible, but the judge disagreed. As a result, the conviction rate increased to 26 percent. In a third group, as in the second, the tape was introduced and the defense objected. This time, however, the judge sustained the objection and told jurors to disregard it. Still, 35 percent of them voted for conviction (Sue et al., 1973). Other studies as well have revealed that jurors are not deterred by "limiting instructions" (Greene & Dodge, 1995).

Similar results were found in a study of "dirty tricks." In that study, mock jurors read a transcript in which a lawyer implied in a cross-examination question that the opponent's expert witness had a tarnished reputation. Although no proof was offered, subjects who were exposed to the question lowered their estimates of this witness's credibility. In fact, the witness became "damaged goods" regardless of whether the question was met with an admission, a denial, or an objection sustained by the judge (Kassin et al., 1990). This use of presumptuous cross-examination questions was seen in the Simpson trial when defense lawyer F. Lee Bailey, without proof, asked police officer Mark Fuhrman, "Did you plant the bloody glove in Simpson's house?"

Why are people unable or unwilling to follow a judge's plea to disregard inadmissible evidence? Imagine yourself in the jury box, and three reasons become apparent. First, the added instruction draws attention to the information in controversy. It's like being told *not* to think about white bears. Try it, and you'll see the problem. When people try to suppress a particular thought, that thought intrudes upon consciousness with remarkable frequency (Wegner, 1989). A second reason is that instructions to disregard, like censorship, restrict a juror's decision-making freedom. Accordingly, they can backfire by arousing reactance. Thus, when a judge emphasizes the ruling by forbidding jurors from considering the information, they become even *more* likely to use it (Wolf & Montgomery, 1977). The third reason is the easiest to understand. Jurors want to reach the right decision. If they stumble onto relevant information, they want to use it—whether it satisfies the law's technical rules or not. Had you taken part in the experiment described earlier, wouldn't the incriminating phone call have led you to doubt the defendant's innocence? Apparently, it's hard to ignore information that seems relevant to a case (Wissler & Saks, 1985).

The Judge's Instructions

One of the most important rituals in any trial is the judge's instruction to the jury. Through these instructions, juries are educated about relevant legal concepts, informed of the verdict options, admonished to disregard extralegal factors, and advised on how to conduct their deliberations. To make verdicts adhere to the law, juries are supposed to comply with these instructions. The task seems simple enough, but there are problems.

To begin with, the jury's intellectual competence has been called into question. For years, the courts have doubted whether jurors understood their instructions. One skeptical judge put it bluntly when he said that "these words may as well be spoken in a foreign language" (Frank, 1949, p. 181). To some extent, he was right. When actual instructions are tested with mock jurors, the results reveal high levels of misunderstanding—a serious problem in light of the fact that jurors have many misconceptions about the law (Smith, 1991). Fortunately, there is hope. When conventional instructions (which are esoteric, poorly written, and filled with legal jargon) are rewritten in plain English, comprehension rates increase markedly (Elwork et al., 1982).

Comprehension is a necessary first step, but presentation factors are also important. Consider the following study (Kassin & Wrightsman, 1979). Subjects watched an auto-theft trial that included, for the defense, an all-important instruction stating that the defendant is presumed innocent and that the prosecutor must prove guilt beyond a reasonable doubt. The statement itself was easy to understand. The key, however, was its *timing*. Among subjects who never received the instruction, 63 percent voted guilty. When the instruction followed the evidence, as is the custom in most courts, the conviction rate remained high at 59 percent. Only when the instruction preceded the evidence did the rate drop sharply, to 37 percent. Why did the postevidence instructions have virtually no impact? The researchers asked half of the subjects for their opinions at various points during the trial and found that these mid-trial opinions were predictive of final verdicts. In other words, it was simply too late for a presumption-of-innocence instruction because many subjects had already made up their minds. Indeed, Lynne FosterLee and her colleagues (1993) found that pre-evidence instructions increased the decision-making competence of mock jurors in a complex civil case.

jury nullification The jury's power to disregard, or "nullify," the law when it conflicts with personal conceptions of justice.

Incomprehension and poor timing are two reasons why a judge's instructions have little impact. But there's a third reason: juries sometimes disagree with the law—thus raising the controversial issue of **jury nullification.** You may not realize it, but juries—because they deliberate in private—can choose to disregard, or "nullify," their judge's instructions. The pages of history are filled with poignant examples. Consider the case of someone tried for euthanasia, or "mercy killing." By law, it is murder. But to the defendant, it might be a noble act performed on behalf of a loved one. Faced with this kind of conflict, over which public opinion is divided (Sugarman, 1986), juries often evaluate the issue in human terms, disregard their judge's instructions, and vote for acquittal (Horowitz & Willging, 1991).

THE JURY AS A GROUP

Anyone who has seen *Twelve Angry Men* can appreciate how colorful and passionate a jury's deliberation can be. As we saw in Chapter 9, this film classic opens with a jury eager to convict a young man of murder—no ifs, ands, or buts. The group selects a foreman and takes a show-of-hands vote. The result is an 11-to-1 majority, with actor Henry Fonda the lone dissenter. After many tense moments, Fonda manages to convert his peers, and the jury votes unanimously for acquittal.

It is often said that the unique power of the jury stems from the fact that individuals come together privately as a *group*. Is this assumption justified? *Twelve Angry Men* is fiction, but does it realistically portray what transpires in the jury room? And in what ways does the legal system control the group dynamics?

Leaders, Participants, and Followers

In theory, all jurors are created equal. In practice, however, dominance hierarchies develop. As in other decision-making groups, a handful of individuals control the discussion; others participate at a much lower rate; and still others watch

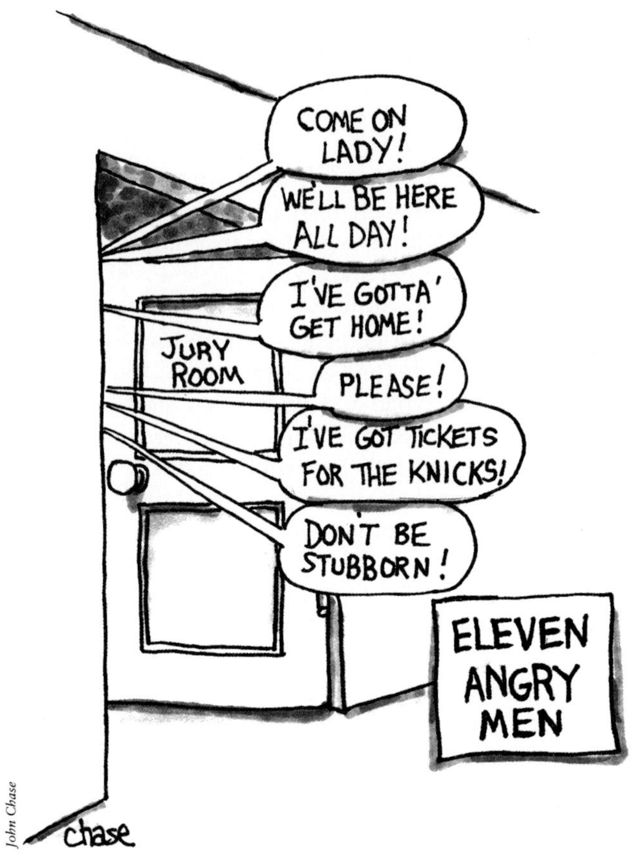

John Chase

from the sidelines, speaking only to cast their votes (Hastie et al., 1983; Saks, 1977). It's almost as if there's a jury within the jury. So, what kinds of people emerge as leaders?

It is natural to assume that the foreperson is the leader. The foreperson, after all, calls for votes, acts as a liaison between the judge and jury, and announces the verdict in court. It seems like a position of importance, yet the selection process is rather casual, as the jury picks a member within the first minute or so. It's interesting, that the outcomes follow a predictable pattern (Stasser et al., 1982). People of higher occupational status or with prior experience on a jury are frequently chosen. Sex differences are also common. Norbert Kerr and his colleagues (1982) examined the records of 179 trials held in San Diego and found that 50 percent of the jurors were female but 90 percent of the forepersons were male. Other patterns, too, are evident. The first person who speaks is often chosen as foreperson (Strodtbeck et al., 1957). And when jurors deliberate around a rectangular table, those who sit at the heads of the table are more likely to be chosen than are those seated in the middle (Bray et al., 1978; Strodtbeck & Hook, 1961). Adding to the complete picture is the fact that men are more likely than women to speak first and take the prominent seats (Nemeth et al., 1976).

If you find such inequalities bothersome, fear not: forepersons may act as nominal leaders, but they do *not* exert more than their fair share of influence over the group. In fact, although they spend more time than others talking about procedural matters, they spend less time expressing opinions on the verdict (Hastie et al., 1983). It may be most accurate to think of the foreperson not as the jury's leader but as its moderator. In *Twelve Angry Men,* actor Martin Balsam—not Henry Fonda—was the foreperson. He was also among the least influential members of the jury.

The Deliberation Process

If the walls of the jury room could talk, they would say that the decision-making process passes through three stages (Hastie et al., 1983; Stasser et al., 1982). Like other problem-solving groups, juries begin in a relaxed, open-ended *orientation* period during which they set an agenda, raise questions, and explore the facts. Then, as soon as differences of opinion are revealed—usually when the first vote is taken—factions develop and the group shifts abruptly into a period of *open conflict.* With the battle lines sharply drawn, discussion takes on a more focused, argumentative tone. Together, jurors scrutinize the evidence, construct stories to account for that evidence, and discuss the judge's instructions (Pennington & Hastie, 1992). If all jurors agree, they return a verdict. If not, the majority tries to achieve a consensus by converting the holdouts through information and social pressure. At that point, the group enters a period of *reconciliation,* during which it smooths over the conflicts and affirms its satisfaction with the outcome. If the holdouts continue to disagree, the jury declares itself hung. This process is diagrammed in Figure 12.7.

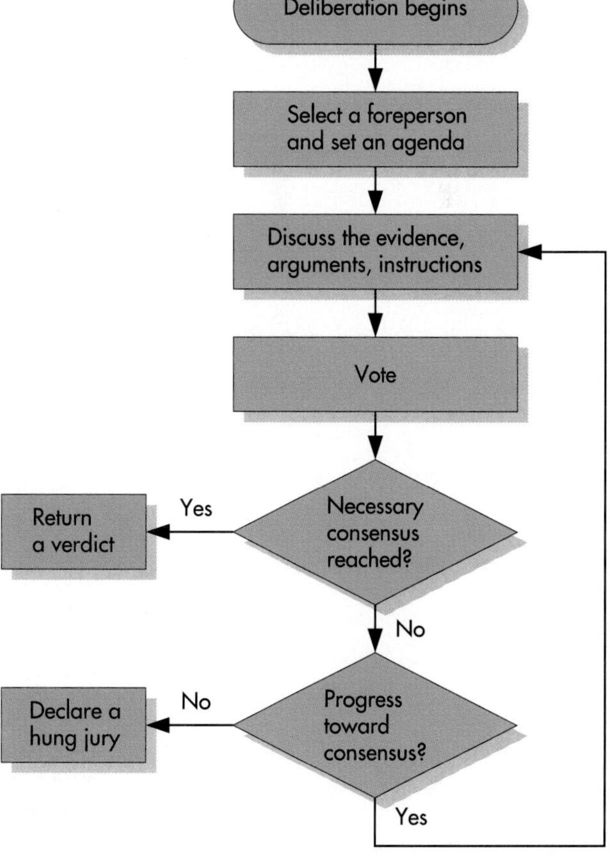

Figure 12.7 **Jury Deliberations: The Process.** Juries move through various tasks en route to a verdict. They begin by setting an agenda and reviewing the case. If all jurors agree, they return a verdict. If not, they continue to discuss the case until they reach a consensus. If the holdouts refuse to vote with the majority, the jury declares itself hung. (Based on Hastie et al., 1983.)

When it comes to decision-making *outcomes,* deliberations are not as important as might be assumed. This surprising result was first discovered by Harry Kalven and Hans Zeisel (1966). By interviewing the members of 225 criminal juries, they were able to reconstruct how these juries split on their very first vote. Out of 215 juries that opened with an initial majority, 209 reached a final verdict consistent with that vote. This result—and the result of mock-jury research (Kerr, 1981; Stasser & Davis, 1981; Tanford & Penrod, 1986; see Table 12.4)—led Kalven and Zeisel to conclude that "the deliberation process might well be likened to what the developer does for an exposed film; it brings out the picture, but the outcome is predetermined" (1966, p. 489). Henry Fonda's heroics notwithstanding, one can usually predict the final verdict by knowing what the individual jurors think as they enter the jury room.

leniency bias The tendency for jury deliberation to produce a tilt toward acquittal.

There is one reliable exception to this majority-wins rule. It is that deliberation tends to produce a **leniency bias** favoring the criminal defendant. All other factors being equal, individual jurors are more likely to vote guilty on their own than in a group; they are also more prone to convict before deliberations than after (MacCoun & Kerr, 1988). Look again at Table 12.4, and you'll see that juries that are equally divided in their initial vote are likely to return not-guilty verdicts. Apparently, it is easier to raise a reasonable doubt in other people's minds than to remove such a doubt. It is interesting to note that, in their classic study entitled *The American Jury* (1966), Kalven and Zeisel surveyed 555 judges who reported how they would have voted in some 3,500 jury trials. Judges and juries agreed 78 percent of the time. When they disagreed, it was usually because the jury acquitted a defendant thought to be guilty by the judge. Perhaps these disagreements are due, in part, to the fact that juries function as groups, and judges as individuals.

Table 12.4 The Road to Agreement: From Individual Votes to a Group Verdict

	Final Jury Verdicts (percent)		
Initial Votes (Guilty–Not Guilty)	Conviction	Acquittal	Hung
6–0	100	0	0
5–1	78	7	16
4–2	44	26	30
3–3	9	51	40
2–4	4	79	17
1–5	0	93	7
0–6	0	100	0

Research has shown that these verdicts are reached by mock juries that begin with different combinations of initial votes. You can see that the results support the majority-wins rule. But also note the evidence for a leniency bias: When the initial vote is split, juries gravitate toward acquittal. (Kerr, 1981, as cited in Stasser et al., 1982.)

Knowing that the majority tends to prevail doesn't tell us *how* juries manage to resolve disagreements en route to a verdict. From the conformity studies discussed in Chapter 9, we conclude that there are two possibilities. Sometimes, people conform because, through a process of *informational influence,* they are genuinely persuaded by what others say. At other times, people yield to the pressures of *normative influence* by changing their overt behavior in the majority's direction even though, privately, they disagree. When it comes to jury deliberations, justice demands that consensus be reached through a vigorous exchange of views and information, not by heavy-handed social pressure. But is it? Research shows that juries achieve unanimity not by one process or the other but by both (Kaplan & Schersching, 1981; Tanford & Penrod, 1986). The problem is that certain factors can upset the delicate balance between informational and normative influence. Social pressure is increased, for example, in juries that vote by a public roll call or show of hands (Davis et al., 1989) and in deadlocked juries that are called into the courtroom and urged by the judge to resolve their differences (Smith & Kassin, 1993).

Within the past twenty-five years, the U.S. Supreme Court has in two ways altered the decision-making dynamics of the jury. In the following pages, we look at these important changes and what they mean.

Jury Size: How Small Is Too Small?

In Boulder, Colorado, lawyer Melvin Tatsumi had a client who was charged with criminal mischief. Fearing the "mob mentality of 12 people," he requested a one-person jury ("It would be easy," 1985). Although the judge went along with the idea, the district attorney argued that "a jury of one is a contradiction of terms." An appeals court agreed.

How many people does it take to form a jury? In keeping with the British tradition, twelve used to be the magic number. Then, in the case of *Williams* v. *Florida* (1970), the defendant, Williams, was convicted of armed robbery by a six-person jury. He appealed the verdict to the U.S. Supreme Court but lost. As a result of this precedent, American courts are today permitted to cut their trial expenses by using six-person juries in cases that do not involve the death penalty. Juries consisting of fewer than six people are not permitted (*Ballew* v. *Georgia,* 1978).

What is the impact of a six-person jury? The Supreme Court approached the question as a social psychologist would. It sought to determine whether the change would affect the decision-making process. Unfortunately, the Court misinterpreted the available research so badly that Michael Saks concluded it "would not win a passing grade in a high school psychology class" (1974, p. 18). Consider whether a reduction in size affects the minority's ability to resist normative pressures. The Supreme Court didn't think it would. Citing Solomon Asch's (1956) conformity studies, the Court argued that a juror's resistance depends on the *proportional* size of the majority. But is that true? Is the lone dissenter caught in a 5-to-1 bind as well insulated from the group norm as the minority in a 10-to-2 split? To the Court, these 83-to-17 percent divisions are psychologically identical. Yet Asch's research showed the opposite—that the mere presence of a single ally enables dissenters to maintain their independence better than anything else. The size of a jury has another implication as well. The smaller the jury, the less likely it is to represent minority segments of the population, and the more likely it is to begin deliberating at or near unanimity. As a result, smaller juries spend less time deliberating (Saks, 1977).

Less-Than-Unanimous Verdicts

The jury's size is not all that has changed. In 1972, the Supreme Court considered whether states may accept jury verdicts that are not unanimous. In one case, two defendants had been convicted by non-unanimous juries—one by a vote of 11 to 1, the other by 10 to 2 (*Apodaca* v. *Oregon,* 1972). In a second case, the verdict was determined by a 9-to-3 margin (*Johnson* v. *Louisiana,* 1972). In both decisions, the Supreme Court upheld the verdicts.

The Court was divided in its view of these cases. Five justices argued that a non-unanimous decision rule would not adversely affect the jury; four justices believed that it would reduce the intensity of deliberations and undermine the potential for minority influence. Table 12.5 presents these alternative points of view. Which do you find more convincing? Imagine yourself on a jury that needs only a 9-to-3 majority to return a verdict. You begin by polling the group and find that you already have the nine votes needed. What next? According to one script, the group continues to argue vigorously and with open minds. According to the alternative scenario, the group begins to deliberate, but the dissenters are

Table 12.5 *Johnson* v. *Louisiana* (1972): Contrasting Views

Mr. Justice White, for the Majority:
We have no grounds for believing that majority jurors, aware of their responsibility and power over the liberty of the defendant, would simply refuse to listen to arguments presented to them in favor of acquittal, terminate discussion, and render a verdict. On the contrary, it is far more likely that a juror presenting reasoned argument in favor of acquittal could either have his arguments answered or would carry enough other jurors with him to prevent conviction. A majority will cease discussion and outvote a minority only after reasoned discussion has ceased to have persuasive effect or to serve any other purpose—when a minority, that is, continues to insist upon acquittal without having persuasive reasons in support of its position.

Mr. Justice Douglas, for the Minority:
Non-unanimous juries need not debate and deliberate as fully as most unanimous juries. As soon as the requisite majority is attained, further consideration is not required either by Oregon or by Louisiana even though the dissident jurors might, if given the chance, be able to convince the majority. . . . The collective effort to piece together the puzzle of historical truth . . . is cut short as soon as the requisite majority is reached in Oregon and Louisiana. . . . It is said that there is no evidence that majority jurors will refuse to listen to dissenters whose votes are unneeded for conviction. Yet human experience teaches us that polite and academic conversation is no substitute for the earnest and robust argument necessary to reach unanimity.

Notice the contrasting views in the U.S. Supreme Court's decision to permit non-unanimous jury verdicts. Justice White wrote the majority opinion, and Justice Douglas wrote the dissent. The decision was reached by a vote of 5 to 4.

quickly cast aside because their votes are not important. Again, which scenario seems more realistic?

To answer that question, Reid Hastie and his colleagues (1983) recruited more than eight hundred people from the Boston area to take part in sixty-nine mock juries. After watching a re-enactment of a murder trial, the groups were instructed to reach a verdict by a 12-to-0, a 10-to-2, or an 8-to-4 margin. The differences were striking. Compared to juries needing unanimous decisions, the others spent less time discussing the case and more time voting. After reaching the required number of votes, they often rejected the holdouts, terminated discussion, and returned a verdict. Afterward, subjects in the non-unanimous juries rated their peers as more closed-minded and themselves as less informed and less confident about their final decision. What's worse, Hastie's team saw in tapes of the deliberations that majority-rule juries adopted "a more forceful, bullying, persuasive style" (1983, p. 112).

Today, a few states permit less-than-unanimous verdicts in criminal trials. A substantial number do so for civil cases. Yet it is clear that this procedure weakens jurors who are in the voting minority, breeds closed-mindedness, inhibits discussion, and leaves many jurors uncertain about their decisions. Henry Fonda, step aside. The jury has reached its verdict.

POSTTRIAL: TO PRISON AND BEYOND

Before taking O. J. Simpson to trial, the Los Angeles district attorney had to make a decision: If Simpson were to be convicted of first-degree murder, would the state seek the death penalty or life imprisonment? Fearful that jurors would hesitate to vote guilty, the district attorney's office chose not to seek the death penalty.

The Sentencing Process

For those convicted of crimes, the jury's verdict is followed by a sentence. Sentencing decisions—usually made by judges, not juries—are often controversial. One reason for the controversy is that many people see judges as too lenient (Stalans & Diamond, 1990). Another reason is that people disagree on the goals served by imprisonment. People who think that the purpose is to punish, incapacitate, or deter offenders from committing future crimes prefer longer sentences. Those who say that prison should reform and rehabilitate convicted felons believe shorter terms make more sense (McFatter, 1978).

Judges also disagree about sentencing-related issues. In fact, a common complaint is that there is too much *sentencing disparity*—that punishments are inconsistent from one judge to the next. Anthony Partridge and William Eldridge (1974) compiled identical sets of files taken from twenty actual cases, sent them to fifty federal judges, and found major disparities in their sentencing decisions. In one case, for example, judges had read about a man who was convicted of extortion and tax evasion. One judge recommended a three-year prison sentence, while another recommended twenty years in prison and a fine of $65,000. It is hard to believe these two judges read the same case. But other research reveals similar differences. In Dade County, Florida, Judge Ellen Morphonios became known as "Maximum Morphonios" when she sentenced an offender to a prison term of 1,698 years and then reassured him that he would probably serve only half that time! In contrast, New York State judge Bruce Wright is nicknamed "Turn 'Em Loose Bruce" for his reputation for leniency (Wrightsman et al., 1994).

What seems to be the problem? Ebbe Ebbesen and Vladimir Konecni (1981) analyzed sentencing records in San Diego, California. As in previous research, they found a good deal of inconsistency, but not because the judges used idiosyncratic strategies or based decisions on extralegal factors. Rather, these judges tended to use the same strategy. They made decisions quickly and closely followed the pre-sentencing advice of their probation officers. Sentencing disparity is a problem, in part, because judges receive conflicting recommendations from those who advise them. And like the rest of us, those who advise them differ in their beliefs about the goals of imprisonment (Carroll et al., 1987).

The Prison Experience

It is no secret that many prisons are overcrowded and that prison life can be cruel, violent, and degrading. The setting is highly oppressive and regimented, many prison guards are abusive, and inmates often fall into a state of despair (Paulus, 1988). Thus, it is natural for social psychologists to wonder: Is there something in the situation that leads guards and prisoners to behave as they do? Would the rest of us react in the same way?

For ethical reasons, one obviously cannot place subjects inside a real prison. So a team of researchers from Stanford University did the next best thing. They constructed their own prison in the basement of their psychology department building (Haney et al., 1973; Zimbardo et al., 1973). Complete with iron-barred cells, a solitary-confinement closet, and a recreation area for guards, the facility housed twenty-one subjects—all healthy and stable men between the ages of seventeen and thirty who had answered a newspaper ad promising fifteen dollars a day for a two-week study of prison life. By the flip of a coin, half the subjects were designated as guards; the other half became prisoners. Neither group received specific instructions on how to fulfill its role.

On the first day, each of the subject prisoners was unexpectedly "arrested" at his home, booked, fingerprinted, and driven to the simulated prison by officers of the local police department. The prisoners were then stripped, searched, and dressed in loose-fitting smocks with an identification number, a nylon stocking to cover their hair, rubber sandals, and a chain bolted to the ankle. The guards were supplied with khaki uniforms, nightsticks, handcuffs, keys, reflector sunglasses, and whistles. The rules specified that prisoners were to be called by number, routinely lined up to be counted, fed three bland meals, and permitted three supervised toilet visits per day. The stage was set. Subjects were on their own. It remained to be seen just how seriously they would take their roles and react to one another in this novel setting.

The events of the next few days were startling. Filled with a sense of power and authority, three or four guards became progressively more abusive. They harassed the inmates, forced them into crowded cells, woke them during the night, and subjected them to hard labor and solitary confinement. These guards were particularly cruel when they thought they were alone with a prisoner. The prisoners themselves were rebellious at first, but their efforts were met with retaliation. Soon they all became passive and demoralized. After thirty-six hours, the experimenters had to release their first prisoner, who was suffering from acute depres-

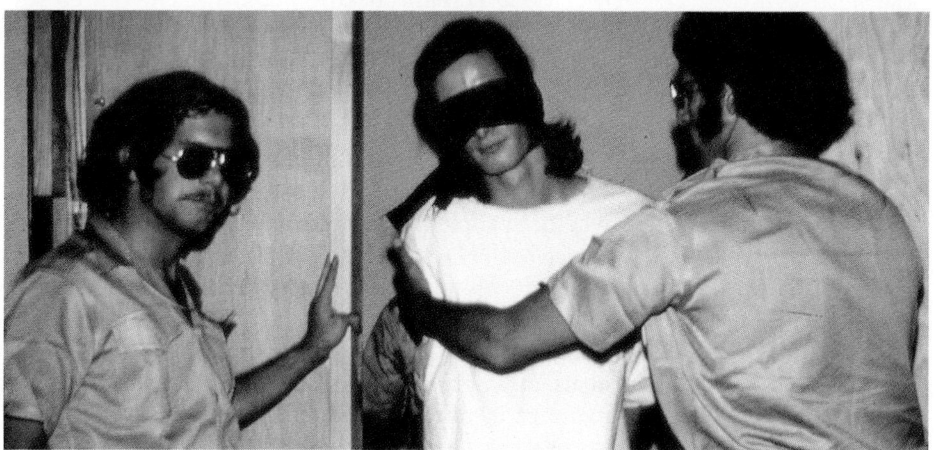

In this simulation study of prison behavior, subjects were arbitrarily assigned to be prisoners or guards. Local police officers arrested the prisoners, who were brought to a jail constructed at Stanford University. After several days, the guards took on cruel, authoritarian roles that demoralized the prisoners to such an extent that the experiment was terminated.

sion. On subsequent days, other prisoners had to be released. By the sixth day, the remaining prisoners were so shaken by the experience that the study was terminated. It is reassuring, if not remarkable, that after a series of debriefing sessions, subjects seemed to show no signs of lasting distress.

Although this study has been criticized on both methodological and ethical grounds (Banuazizi & Movahedi, 1975; Savin, 1973b), its results are impressive. Within a brief period of time, under relatively mild conditions, and with a group of men not prone to violence, the Stanford study recreated the behaviors actually found behind prison walls. Apparently, even "normal" people can become dehumanized by their institutional roles. At this point, however, research with real inmates in real prisons is needed for a more thorough examination of the effects of overcrowding and other aspects of prison life (Ruback & Innes, 1988).

JUSTICE: A MATTER OF PROCEDURE?

People tend to measure the success of a legal system by its ability to achieve fair and accurate results. But is that all there is to justice? Let's step back for a moment from the specifics and ask if it is possible to define justice in a way that is unrelated to outcomes.

In a book entitled *Procedural Justice* (1975), John Thibaut and Laurens Walker proposed that our satisfaction with the way disputes are resolved—legal or otherwise—depends not only on outcomes but also on the procedures used to achieve those outcomes. Two aspects of procedure are important: *decision control*—whether a procedure affords the involved parties the power to accept, reject, or otherwise influence the final decision; and *process control*—whether it offers the parties an opportunity to present their case to a third-party decision maker. In the courtroom, of course, the disputants are limited in their decision control. Thus, their satisfaction must depend on whether they feel that they had a chance to express their views.

There are two ways to look at the effects of process control on perceptions of justice. Originally, it was thought that people want an opportunity to express their opinions only because having a "voice" in the process improves their chances of achieving a favorable ruling. In this view, process control is satisfying because it increases decision control (Thibaut & Walker, 1978). Recent research, however, suggests that people value the chance to present their side of a story even when doing so does not influence the ultimate outcome. In other words, process control is more than just an instrumental means to an end. By making people feel that their voice is worth hearing, process control can be an end in itself (Lind et al., 1990; Lind & Tyler, 1988).

This aspect of the legal system is very important. It means, for example, that whether people agree or disagree with how a case turns out, they can at least find solace in the fact that both sides had their "day in court." Yet certain members of the legal community are openly critical of that so-called day in court. As law professor Alan Dershowitz put it, "Nobody really wants justice. Winning is the only thing to most participants in the criminal justice system, just as it is to professional athletes" (1982, p. xvi). Dershowitz's skepticism is centered on something that many of us take for granted: the **adversarial model** of justice. In the adversarial system—as practiced in North America, Great Britain, and a handful of other countries—the prosecution and defense oppose each other, each presenting one side of the story in an effort to win a favorable verdict. In contrast, most other countries use an **inquisitorial model,** in which a neutral investigator gathers the evidence from both sides and then presents the findings in court. With two such different methods of doing justice, social psychologists could not resist the temptation to make comparisons. Which system, they ask, do people prefer?

adversarial model A dispute-resolution system in which the prosecution and defense present opposing sides of the story.

inquisitorial model A dispute-resolution system in which a neutral investigator gathers evidence from both sides and presents the findings in court.

To make the comparison, Laurens Walker and his colleagues (1974) constructed a business simulation in which two companies competed for a cash prize. Assigned to the role of president of a company, subjects learned that someone on their staff was accused of spying on the competition. To resolve the dispute, a "trial" was held. In some cases, the trial followed an adversarial procedure in which the two sides were presented by law students who were chosen by subjects and whose payment was contingent on winning. Other cases followed an inquisitorial model in which a single law student—appointed by the experimenter and paid regardless of the outcome—presented both sides. Regardless of whether they had won or lost the verdict, subjects who took part in an adversarial trial were more satisfied than those involved in an inquisitorial trial. Even impartial observers preferred the adversarial proceedings.

Other researchers have reported similar results, not only with American and British subjects who are used to the adversary system but with French and West Germans as well (Lind et al., 1978). It seems that any method that offers participants a *voice* in the proceedings—including methods that are nonadversarial—is seen as fair and just (Folger & Greenberg, 1985; Sheppard, 1985). Even among Chinese subjects—whose culture emphasizes social harmony and who prefer to resolve disputes in ways that minimize conflict—process control is desirable (Leung, 1987). In matters of justice, people are motivated not only by a desire for personal gain but also by the need to be recognized, respected, and treated fairly by others (Tyler, 1994).

CLOSING STATEMENT

This chapter focuses on the trial process, the events that precede it, and the events that follow from it. Yet we've only scratched the surface. In recent years, more and more judges, lawyers, and policy makers have come to recognize that social psychology can make important contributions to the legal system. Thus, with increasing frequency, social psychologists are called on for expert advice in and out of court and are cited in judicial opinions. Indeed, as the trial of O. J. Simpson suggests and as research confirms, evidence—the human beings who provide it and those who evaluate it—is an imperfect human enterprise. Through an understanding of social psychology, we can clearly identify some of the problems—and perhaps even the solutions.

REVIEW

- Embedded in a large criminal justice system, relatively few cases come to trial.
- Yet the trial is the heart and soul of the system.

SELECTION OF JURORS

- Once called for service, prospective jurors are questioned by the judge or lawyers.
- Those who exhibit a clear bias are excluded. A limited number of others may also be rejected by lawyers.

Trial Lawyers as Intuitive Psychologists

- Pressured to make juror selections quickly, lawyers rely on implicit personality theories and stereotypes.

Pretrial Attitudes and Bias

- General demographic and personality factors do not reliably predict how jurors will vote.
- Lawyers sometimes hire psychologists to conduct surveys that identify correlations between demographics and trial-relevant attitudes.
- Research shows that beliefs about rape predict juror verdicts in rape cases.
- Jurors who favor the death penalty are more likely to find defendants guilty than are jurors who oppose the death penalty.
- Intuitive and scientific jury-selection methods raise ethical issues concerning their effects on justice.

THE COURTROOM DRAMA

- Once the jury is selected, evidence previously gathered is presented in court.

The Defendant

- The police elicit confessions by using various ploys. Under pressure, people sometimes confess to crimes they didn't commit.
- Judges and juries are supposed to reject coerced confessions, but sometimes they do not.
- By recording physiological arousal, the polygraph can be used as a lie-detector test.

- Polygraphers report high rates of accuracy, but truthful persons are too often judged guilty and the test can be faked.

The Eyewitness

- Eyewitness memory is a three-stage process involving acquisition, storage, and retrieval.
- During acquisition, witnesses who are highly aroused zoom in on the central features of an event but are impaired in their memory for peripheral details.
- The presence of a weapon hinders a witness's ability to identify the perpetrator.
- Witnesses have trouble recognizing members of a race other than their own.
- During storage, misleading postevent information influences eyewitness testimony.
- Research shows that young children are particularly suggestible in this regard.
- Line-ups are biased when a suspect is distinctive, when the police imply that the criminal is in the line-up, when witnesses make relative judgments, and when the suspect appeared in pre-line-up photographs.
- In court, jurors overestimate credibility, cannot distinguish between accurate and inaccurate witnesses, and are not aware of certain factors that influence performance.
- People are too readily persuaded by a witness's confidence—a factor that does not reliably predict identification accuracy.
- Psychologists are sometimes called to testify as experts on eyewitness evidence.
- Expert testimony leads people to scrutinize eyewitnesses more carefully.

Nonevidentiary Influences

- The more pretrial knowledge people have about a case, the more likely they are to presume the defendant guilty.
- Research shows that pretrial publicity can bias jury verdicts.
- Once inadmissible testimony leaks out in court, the jury is contaminated by it.
- A judge's cautionary instruction may worsen the situation by drawing attention to the forbidden testimony, arousing reactance, and leading jurors to see the information as relevant.

The Judge's Instructions

- The judge's instructions often have little impact, in part because jurors often do not comprehend them.
- The instructions are usually delivered subsequent to the evidence—after many jurors have formed an opinion.
- Jurors may not follow instructions that conflict with their personal conceptions of justice.

THE JURY AS A GROUP

Leaders, Participants, and Followers

- Dominance hierarchies develop in the jury room.
- Certain people are more likely than others to be elected foreperson, but they also tend to play the role of moderator rather than that of group leader.

The Deliberation Process

- Jury deliberations pass through three stages: orientation, open conflict, and reconciliation.
- After the voting, factions form and the period of open conflict is filled with informational and normative pressures.
- When it comes to outcomes, the initial majority typically wins, although deliberation tends to produce a bias toward leniency.

Jury Size: How Small Is Too Small?

- The U.S. Supreme Court ruled that the use of six-person juries is acceptable.
- But these smaller groups do not deliberate for as long as twelve-person juries and contain less minority representation.

Less-Than-Unanimous Verdicts

- In some states, juries are permitted to reach verdicts by a less-than-unanimous majority.
- But research shows that once the required majority is reached, these juries reject the holdouts, terminate discussion, and return a verdict.

POSTTRIAL: TO PRISON AND BEYOND

The Sentencing Process

- Many people believe that judges are too lenient, and punishments for the same offense are often inconsistent from one case to another.
- Part of the problem is that people have different views of the goals of sentencing.

The Prison Experience

- Stanford researchers built a simulated prison and recruited male adults to act as guards and prisoners.
- Some guards were abusive, prisoners became passive, and the study had to be terminated.

JUSTICE: A MATTER OF PROCEDURE?

- Satisfaction with justice depends not only on winning and losing but also on the procedures used to achieve the outcome.
- People of all cultures prefer models of justice that offer participants a voice in the proceedings.

KEY TERMS

voir dire, p. 458
peremptory challenges, p. 458
scientific jury selection, p. 459
rape shield laws, p. 460
death qualification, p. 461
polygraph, p. 466
weapon-focus effect, p. 468
cross-race identification bias, p. 468
reconstructive memory, p. 469
jury nullification, p. 481
leniency bias, p. 484
adversarial model, p. 490
inquisitorial model, p. 490

NYSE
NYSE

Chapter

13 Business

PREVIEW

This chapter examines the social side of business—specifically, the role of social factors in the workplace. First we look at social influences on *personnel selection and performance appraisals* made within organizations. Then we examine the roles of *leadership* and worker *motivation*. Finally, we explore stock market investing, a form of *economic risk-taking*.

OUTLINE

Whenever two adults meet for the first time, the opening line of their conversation is predictable: "So, what do you do?" "Oh, I'm a (social psychologist). And you?" For many people, work is an integral part of their personal identity. Sure, we would all rather spend a Monday morning lying on a warm and breezy beach, reading a novel, and sipping a tropical fruit drink, but most people spend more time working than playing. In large part, we work to make money. Yet jobs also provide us with activity, a sense of purpose, and a social community. Thus, people who lose their jobs are psychologically devastated—even when they are not to blame and even when they have enough money to carry them through the period of unemployment (Price, 1992). Think about it. If you suddenly won a state lottery or inherited a large fortune, would you still work? Several surveys reveal that three out of four Americans say yes (Myers, 1992). Accordingly, it is important to identify the social factors that influence this significant human experience.

industrial/organizational (I/O) psychology The study of human behavior in business and other organizational settings.

This chapter examines **industrial/organizational (I/O) psychology,** the study of human behavior in business and other organizations. I/O psychology is broad and includes in its ranks both social and nonsocial psychologists who conduct research, teach in business schools or universities, and work in private industry. Whatever the setting, I/O psychology raises important practical questions about job interviewing, evaluations and promotions, leadership, motivation, economic decision making, and other aspects of life in the workplace.

The impact of social psychological factors in the workplace was first recognized in 1924—thanks, oddly enough, to a study of industrial lighting. That year, a team of psychologists sought to examine the effects of lighting on workers at the Hawthorne plant of Western Electric near Chicago (Roethlisberger & Dickson, 1939). Proceeding logically, the researchers turned the lights up in a test room, kept the original lighting in a control room, and compared the effects. Much to their surprise, productivity rates increased in both rooms and then increased as well when the illumination was diminished to a level so low that workers could barely see what they were doing! Over the next five years, no matter what the researchers did—whether they varied the number of coffee breaks, the length of the workweek, location, incentive system, or method of payment—productivity always increased.

It seemed that the project had failed, as no single change in working conditions had a unique effect on productivity. Think for a moment about the results, however, and you will see why the Hawthorne studies are so important. With striking consistency, it was the presence of researchers in the factory and the special attention they gave to employees, not the specific changes in conditions, that made a difference. As soon as the workers realized they were being singled out for attention, they became more motivated and worked harder. Many researchers criticized the methods used in this study and the interpretation of the results (Adair, 1984; Parsons, 1974). Still, the phenomenon that has come to be known as the **Hawthorne effect** laid a foundation for I/O psychology and the study of social influences in the workplace.

Hawthorne effect The finding that workers who were observed increased their productivity regardless of what actual changes were made in the work setting.

The two of us who wrote this textbook work on college campuses, surrounded by students, professors, and administrators. We spend our time in classrooms, offices, laboratories, and libraries. For women and men in other occupations—store clerks, taxicab drivers, construction workers, doctors, secretaries, farmers, teachers, accountants, carpenters, musicians, firefighters, and airline pilots—the workplace is very different. Yet despite the diversity of roles and settings, certain common concerns arise: How are job applicants selected? How is performance on the job evaluated? What makes for an effective leader who can exert influence over others and mobilize their support? What motivates a person to work hard and feel satisfied with a job? And what factors influence the kinds of economic decisions that people make? Let's enter the workplace and address these important questions.

PERSONNEL SELECTION

For all kinds of organizations, the secret to success begins with the recruitment and development of a competent staff. For that reason, personnel selection is the first important step (Schuler et al., 1993).

Traditional Employment Interviews

Anyone who has ever applied for a desirable job knows that often you have to climb hurdles and jump through hoops to get hired. The routine is a familiar one: you submit a resumé, fill out an application, and perhaps bring in samples of your work or take a standardized test of your ability or personality. You may even be put on the "hot seat" in a live face-to-face interview (Schmidt et al., 1992).

In a traditional employment interview, a representative of the organization and an applicant meet in person to discuss the job. The interview provides a two-way opportunity for the applicant and employer to evaluate each other. What a social perception dilemma these opportunities present! As an applicant, you have only a half-hour or so to make a favorable impression. As an interviewer, you have the same brief period of time to penetrate the applicant's self-presentation and learn enough about the person to make a sound hiring decision.

Very few employers would consider hiring a complete stranger for a responsible position without an interview. Think about it, would you? Like most of us, you probably have faith in your ability to size people up. In the words of one professional head-hunter (a consultant who helps companies find qualified executives), "A good interviewer can probe the candidate's basic mental and emotional patterns and determine whether he will fit not only the job but also the company" (Bauman, 1982). But the question remains: Do interviews promote sound hiring, or do they produce decisions that are biased by various personal characteristics? Civil rights laws explicitly forbid employers to discriminate on the basis of sex, race, age, religion, national origin, or physical disability (Landy et al., 1994). Can anyone guarantee, however, that these factors do not influence the evaluation of job applicants? And does the interview process itself intensify or diminish those possible biases?

Research suggests that interviewing has mixed effects. On the positive side, live interviews may actually diminish the tendency to make stereotyped judgments. Studies on sex differences show that when prospective employers rate applicants from resumés and other written material, they tend to evaluate men more favorably than women (Powell, 1987)—at least for occupations that are not stereotypically feminine (Glick et al., 1988). As employers receive more in-

Robert Mankoff/The Cartoon Bank

"Let me see if I've got this straight—from '61 to '67 you plied your trade, from '67 to '73 you practiced your craft and since then you've tended your garden."

formation about an applicant's credentials, however, this bias is reduced (Tosi & Einbender, 1985). What happens in a live interview? Does gender become more salient, or do job-relevant attributes take over? To answer this question, Laura Graves and Gary Powell (1988) studied 483 interviewers who visited college campuses to recruit prospective graduates for entry-level corporate jobs. While on campus, each interviewer rated one student and answered this question: "What are the chances that this applicant will receive a job offer from your company?" Of the applicants sampled, 53 percent were male, 47 percent female. More to the point, there was no evidence of sex discrimination, as men and women were equally likely to get hired. Apparently, face-to-face interaction brings to life the applicant's speaking ability, interest in the company, and other relevant attributes that do not show up on paper.

The bad news is that although interviews sometimes result in the right selection of employees, they also lack a high level of predictive validity (Harris, 1989). What's worse, an employer's preconceptions about an applicant can distort the whole interview process. Thus, when white subjects questioned an applicant who was black rather than white, they sat farther away and held shorter interviews—a distant interpersonal style that causes interviewees to behave in a more nervous, awkward manner (Word et al., 1974). And when subjects in another study were led to believe that an applicant was not suitable for a particular job, they prepared interview questions that sought negative rather than positive information (Binning et al., 1988).

In a field study illustrating the problem, Amanda Phillips and Robert Dipboye (1989) surveyed 34 managers from different branch offices of a large corporation and 164 job applicants whom they had interviewed. They found that the managers' pre-interview expectations, which were based on written application materials, influenced the kinds of interviews they conducted as well as the outcomes: the higher their expectations, the more time they spent "recruiting" rather than evaluating and the more likely they were to make a favorable hiring decision. Similarly, Thomas Dougherty and his colleagues (1994) found that interviewers with positive rather than negative expectations sounded warmer, more outgoing, and more cheerful. They also gave more information and spent more time pro-

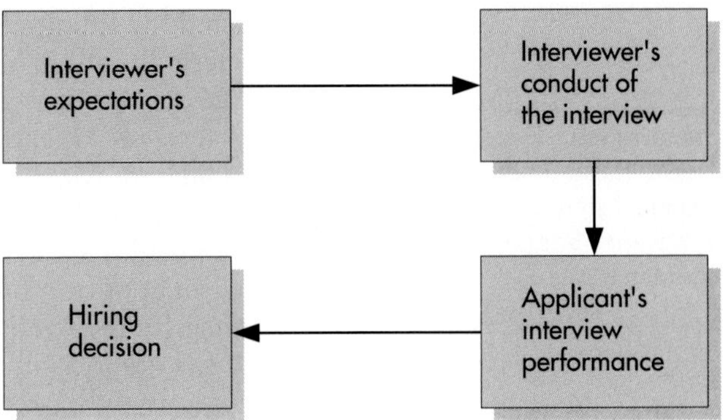

Figure 13.1 Job Interviews: A Self-Fulfilling Prophecy? One study indicates that interviewers' expectations influence the kinds of interviews conducted and applicants' performance. The higher the expectations, the more the interviewer tries to impress rather than evaluate the applicant and make a favorable hiring decision. Without realizing it, employers may use job interviews to create a reality that supports their prior beliefs. (Phillips & Dipboye, 1989.)

moting the company. It seems that job interviews can become part of a vicious cycle, or self-fulfilling prophecy. Without realizing it, employers use the opportunity to create realities that bolster their preexisting beliefs (see Figure 13.1).

"Scientific" Alternatives to the Traditional Interview

Live interviews bring to life both job-relevant and -irrelevant personal characteristics. Given that the process is so variable, should interviews be eliminated? Should they be "computerized," leaving applicants to interact with companies via a programmed sequence of questions and answers administered on a microcomputer (Martin & Nagao, 1989)? Chances are, not too many people would feel comfortable making important decisions in such an impersonal manner. Is it possible, then, to preserve the human touch of an interview, while eliminating bias and error?

To improve the prediction of job performance, organizations have sought more "scientific" methods of evaluation. It is estimated, for example, that thousands of firms in the United States and many more in Europe use *graphology,* or handwriting analysis, to predict job-relevant traits such as honesty, sales ability, and leadership potential (Rafaeli & Klimoski, 1983). Controlled research, however, does not support the claim that handwriting can be used in this way. In one study, for example, professional graphologists tried to predict various aspects of job performance by analyzing the handwriting contained in the autobiographical sketches of bank employees. From the information in those same materials, the researchers also made predictions about these same employees. A comparison of predicted and actual employee performance revealed that the graphologists were no more effective than the researchers. In fact, they were no more accurate than they would have been by flipping a coin (Ben-Shakhar et al., 1986).

Some organizations use the *polygraph,* or lie-detector test, as a screening device. As described in Chapter 12, the polygraph is an instrument that records physiological arousal in different parts of the body. Based on the assumption that lying creates stress, a polygraph examiner conducts an interview and then compares the subject's level of arousal in response to various kinds of questions. Those who administer lie-detector tests argue that it sharpens their ability to hire employees who are capable and honest. But opponents argue that the test invades an individual's privacy, that it is often misused, and that its results are not sufficiently accurate. Research shows that there are considerable problems with use of the polygraph (Saxe et al., 1985). For that reason, the U.S. government in

1988 passed the Employee Polygraph Protection Act, a bill limiting the use of lie-detector tests to jobs in law enforcement, national security, and public safety.

integrity tests Paper-and-pencil questionnaires designed to test a job applicant's honesty and character.

In place of the polygraph, many companies now require applicants to take an **integrity test**—a paper-and-pencil questionnaire designed to assess a person's honesty and character by asking questions concerning substance abuse, shoplifting, petty theft, and other transgressions. The responses are scored by computer. Narrative profiles are provided, and arbitrary cutoff scores are often used to determine if an applicant has "passed" or "failed" (Camara & Schneider, 1994).

Are integrity tests valid enough for use in personnel selection? Although there is reason for skepticism, the research thus far suggests that these instruments do predict various work-related behaviors (Goldberg et al., 1991; Sackett et al., 1989). In one experiment, Michael Cunningham and his colleagues (1994) found that actual job applicants score higher on integrity tests than do nonmotivated laboratory subjects—but that their scores match those obtained by subjects specifically instructed to portray themselves as honest. This result suggests that, in employment settings, people may fudge their responses in order to present themselves in a favorable light. So, does this self-presentation bias compromise the validity of integrity tests? Not necessarily. In a second experiment, the same investigators overpaid research subjects by $5 and found that those with high rather than low test scores were more likely to return the extra cash. Other research corroborates this point. In particular, Deniz Ones and his colleagues (1993) conducted a meta-analysis of tests administered to thousands of workers. The result: Test scores were predictive of job performance and counterproductive behaviors such as theft, absenteeism, lateness, and disciplinary problems.

structured interviews Interviews in which each job applicant is asked a standard set of questions and evaluated on the same criteria.

Another way to improve selection judgments without the aid of physiological recordings or integrity tests is through **structured interviews.** A structured interview is like a standardized test in that the same information is obtained in the same situation from all applicants who are then compared on a common, relevant set of dimensions (Campion et al., 1988). By asking a standard set of questions or using a standard set of tasks, employers can prevent themselves from unwittingly conducting biased interviews that merely confirm their preconceptions. So far, research has shown that structured interviews are successful—indeed, better than conventional interviews—in the selection of insurance agents, sales clerks, and other workers (Wiesner & Cronshaw, 1988).

A second possible improvement is the use of *assessment centers* in which a group of applicants takes part in a group of activities—written tests, role-playing exercises, and so on—that are monitored by a group of evaluators. Instead of one method (an interview) and one evaluator (an interviewer), multiple methods and multiple evaluators are used. Assessment centers are said to be more effective than traditional interviews at finding applicants who will succeed in a particular position (Gaugler et al., 1987; Thornton & Byham, 1982). To this point, however, researchers have been unable to identify the reasons for this success (Landy et al., 1994).

Affirmative Action

Affirmative action—the policy whereby preference in hiring and promotion is given to women and other underrepresented minority groups—is one of the most emotional and explosive social issues of our time. On one side of the debate, liberals argue that preferential treatment is necessary to overcome past inequities.

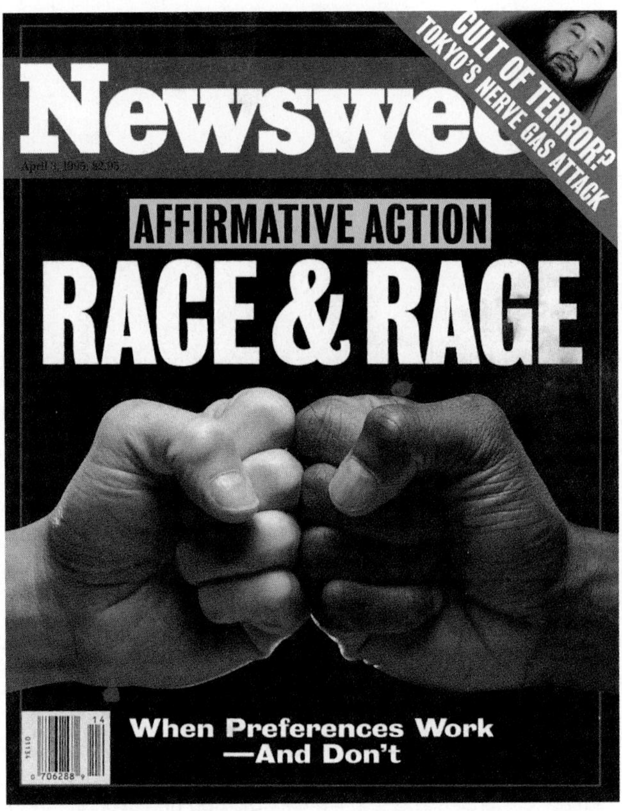

As shown in this 1995 *Newsweek* cover, affirmative action is one of the most explosive social issues of our time. The question researchers seek to answer is, What are the effects?

On the other side, conservatives claim that such policy results in reverse discrimination. Surveys show that Americans are sharply divided on the issue—with women more supportive than men, and Blacks more supportive than Whites (Kravitz & Platania, 1993).

As the political debate rages, questions have been raised about the impact of affirmative action on those whom the policy is designed to help. In a series of studies, Madeline Heilman and her colleagues selected male and female college students to serve as leaders of a two-person task. The students were then led to believe that they were chosen for the leadership role either by a preferential selection process that was based on gender or by a merit-selection process that was based on their credentials and qualifications. As depicted in Figure 13.2, the women (but not the men) who thought they were chosen because of their sex later devalued their own performance, even after receiving positive feedback (Heilman et al., 1987). They also sought simple rather than demanding work assignments (Heilman et al., 1991) and were later less likely to recommend female job applicants for an entry-level position (Heilman et al., 1993). This research helps to explain why female business managers who think they were hired through affirmative action are often unhappy with their work (Chacko, 1982). It may also help to explain the observation made by black law professor Stephen Carter, in his book *Reflections of an Affirmative Action Baby,* that minorities "resist being thought of as beneficiaries" (1991, p. 21).

There are three explanations as to why preferential selection practices can have such a range of negative effects. First, people perceive a procedure as unjust to the extent that it excludes those who are qualified simply because of their sex,

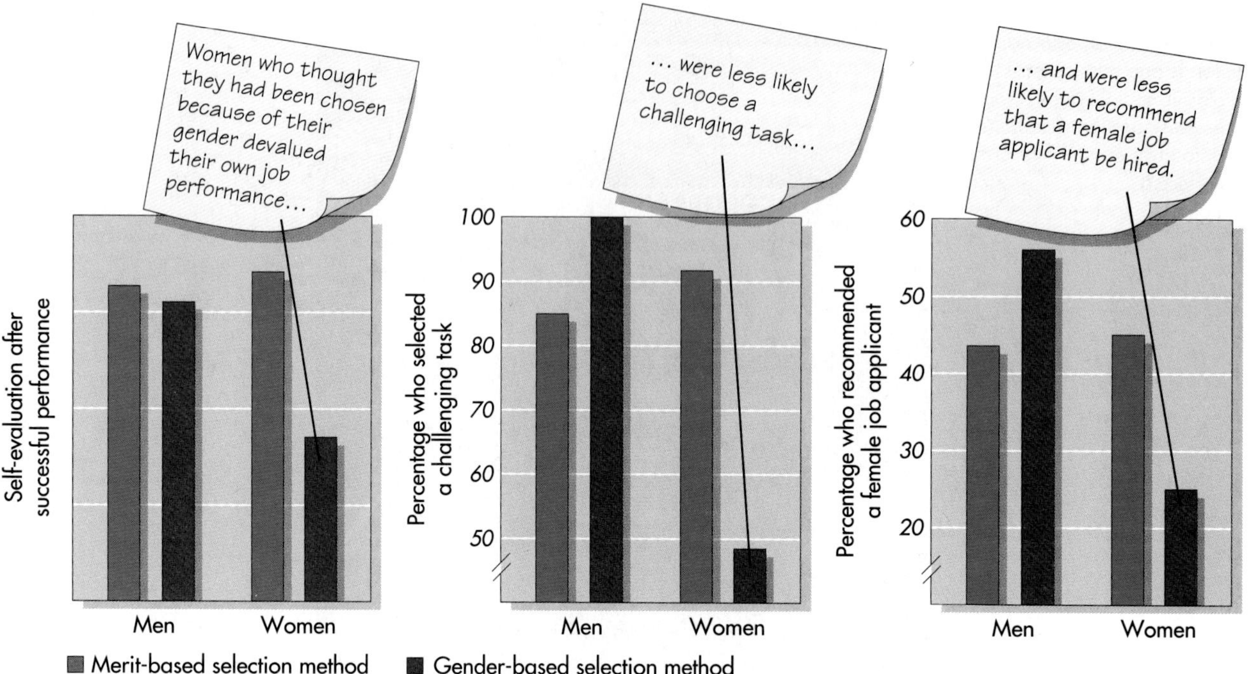

Figure 13.2 **Paradoxical Effects of Affirmative Action on Women.** College students assigned to act as task leaders were led to believe that they were selected on the basis of merit or gender. The selection method had no effect on the self- and other evaluations made by male leaders. However, women who thought they were selected because of gender later devalued their own job performance (left), sought simple rather than demanding work assignments (middle), and were less favorable toward a female job applicant (right). (Data from Heilman et al., 1987; Heilman et al., 1991; Heilman et al., 1993.)

skin color, or ethnic background (Barnes Nacoste, 1994). Second, recipients become less able to attribute job success to their own abilities and efforts, leading them—and co-workers, as well—to harbor doubts about their competence (Heilman et al., 1992; Major et al., 1994). Third, preferential selection is seen as a form of assistance, a situation that very often triggers a defensive reaction among recipients for whom receiving help threatens their self-esteem (Turner & Pratkanis, 1994).

So, are women, minorities, and other recipients of affirmative action doomed to feel stigmatized—like second-class citizens in the workplace? Not necessarily. The way that people react to a preferential selection procedure depends on how that procedure is structured and implemented. Specifically, a good deal of research now shows that people draw negative inferences about themselves and others when employment selections are made *solely* on the basis of sex, skin color, or ethnic background. But everyone's reactions to a preferential selection process are more favorable when it is clear that merit-based factors also play a role and that the person chosen is competent and qualified for the position (Nacoste, 1987; Arthur et al., 1992; Heilman et al., 1993; Major et al., 1994). Accordingly, Marlene Turner and Anthony Pratkanis (1994) offer guidelines on how to manage affirmative action programs in order to make them seem supportive rather than threatening to all concerned (see Table 13.1). In the meantime, the fiery political debate may have overshadowed a key point: that many

Table 13.1 Managing Affirmative Action

1. Set and communicate clear and explicit *qualifications* criteria (background, knowledge, skills, etc.) to be used in selection decisions.
2. Be certain that selection procedures are perceived as fair by targeted applicants and their co-workers.
3. Provide the target applicant and co-workers with specific feedback concerning the target's job qualifications.
4. Develop socialization strategies that keep target applicants from making negative self-attributions.
5. Emphasize the target applicant's unique contributions to the organization.
6. Point out that affirmative action does not imply hiring by quotas, since other job-relevant attributes are considered as well.
7. Recognize that affirmative action is not a panacea, and that it cannot be expected to solve all the problems faced by the targeted groups.

Preferential selection practices are often seen as unjust, and they often lead recipients to doubt their own competence and exhibit a lowered self-esteem. Turner and Pratkanis (1994) recommend that the above steps be taken to minimize these negative effects.

organizations (such as police departments, universities, small businesses, and corporations) benefit from having a diverse staff—and that hiring women and minorities is often "good for the bottom line" (Annin, 1995).

PERFORMANCE APPRAISALS

performance appraisal The process of evaluating an employee's work within the organization.

Even after a person is hired for a job, the evaluation process continues. Nobody enjoys being scrutinized by a boss, or by anyone else for that matter. Still, **performance appraisal**—the process of evaluating an employee's work and communicating the results to that person—is an inevitable fact of life in the workplace. Performance appraisals provide a basis for placement decisions, transfers, promotions, changes in salary, bonuses, and layoffs. They also give feedback to employees about their status within the organization. It's no wonder that I/O psychologists have studied this process in great detail.

It would be easy if a worker's performance could be measured by *objective*, quantifiable criteria—if typists could be evaluated by the number of lines they type, automobile dealers by the number of cars they sell, and doctors by the number of patients they treat. Quantitative measures like these are often not available, however; nor do they take into account the quality of work. By necessity, then, performance appraisals are usually based on *subjective* measures—perceptions of employees by their supervisors, co-workers, customers, clients, and sometimes even themselves (Landy & Farr, 1983).

Supervisor Ratings

Based on the assumption that supervisors are informed about the performance of their subordinates, they are most often called on to make evaluations. But are these ratings accurate? And is the process fair? The process has both benefits and drawbacks. On the one hand, research shows that supervisors are influenced more by a worker's job knowledge, ability, technical proficiency, and dependability than by less relevant factors such as friendliness (Borman et al., 1995). On the other hand, as we'll see, people predictably fall prey to the social perception biases described elsewhere in this book.

Over the years, several appraisal-related problems have been identified. One is the *halo effect,* a failure to discriminate among distinct aspects of a worker's performance (Cooper, 1981). In Chapter 3, we saw that people's impressions of one another are guided by implicit personality theories—that is, by preconceptions we have about the relationships among traits. Believing someone is warm, we assume that he or she is also generous and good-natured. In a similar manner, supervisors who believe that a worker is unproductive may also rate that same worker negatively on teamwork, loyalty, independence, creativity, and other distinct dimensions. Halo effects are most pronounced when evaluators rate someone they don't know well or when a time delay has caused their memory of performance to fade (Kozlowski et al., 1986; Murphy & Balzer, 1986). Lacking specific information, people fall back on implicit theories and assume that one aspect of performance implies other aspects as well. Note, however, that although this effect often leads people to make judgments that are in error, there are times when the halo we see over others is real (Murphy et al., 1993).

Second, it may be difficult for supervisors to make repeated evaluations of the same worker, each time through fresh eyes. In a series of experiments, subjects were asked to watch a teacher present three videotaped lectures and, then, to evaluate his or her speaking ability, organization, preparation, rapport, and so on (Murphy et al., 1985; Smither et al., 1988). For some subjects, the first two lectures were low in quality; for others, they were high in quality. On the third tape, all subjects watched the same average performance. The result? Even though subjects rated each lecture independently, their final evaluations showed signs of a *contrast effect:* Those who initially observed negative performances judged the average lecture more favorably than did those who had watched the positive performances. Practically speaking, this finding suggests that supervisors who conduct many performance appraisals may judge an employee's work in light of previous observations. One performance sets a standard for another. It's no wonder that entertainers worry about taking the stage right after a "tough act to follow."

A third problem is that evaluators are often indiscriminate in their numerical ratings of others. Because of what is known as the *restriction of range problem,* some people provide uniformly high, lenient ratings; others are inclined to give negative, low ratings; and still others gravitate toward the center of a numerical scale. In all cases, people who use a restricted range of ratings fail to make adequate distinctions. Sometimes, the differences between raters are considerable. For example, in a study of male and female business students—all of whom had supervisory experience—women were more generous than men in their ratings of others, regardless of the actual level of performance (Benedict & Levine, 1988).

Self-Evaluations

Although performance appraisals are usually made by supervisors, input is often sought from co-workers, clients, customers, and others whose opinions are relevant. You may not realize it, but by filling out course-evaluation surveys in college, you may have had an influence on tenure and promotion decisions involving your professors.

One particularly interesting source of information comes from self-evaluations. If you've ever had to describe yourself in a job application, you know that self-evaluations are not exactly a lesson in modesty. As discussed in Chapter 2, people generally perceive themselves in overly flattering terms, taking credit for success, denying the blame for failure, having an inflated sense of control, and exhibiting unrealistic optimism about the future. Add the fact that people like to present themselves favorably to others, and it comes as no surprise that self-evaluations in the workplace are consistently more positive than the ratings made by supervisors (Campbell & Lee, 1988)—and are less predictive of job success (Shore et al., 1992). For example, recent studies show that workers underestimate the number of times they are absent compared to co-workers (Harrison & Shaffer, 1994; Johns, 1994).

Another reason why self-evaluations should be taken with a grain of salt is that there are individual differences in the extent to which people present themselves in a positive light. For example, men are generally more boastful than women and are more likely to overestimate their performance (Beyer, 1990). Insofar as performance appraisals are based on self-evaluations, then, this gender difference puts female employees at a disadvantage.

New and Improved Methods of Appraisal

Performance appraisals cannot always be trusted. When objective measures of work are not available, however, organizations have no choice but to rely on the imperfect human judge. For researchers, the challenge is to find ways to boost the accuracy of the evaluations that are made.

One solution concerns the timing of evaluations in relation to the observation of performance. Evaluations are less prone to error when made right after performance than when there is a delay of days, weeks, or months. Once memory for the details begins to fade, evaluators fall back on stereotypes and other biases (Heneman & Wexley, 1983; Murphy & Balzer, 1986). A second solution is to increase the number of evaluators used. As in assessment centers, a multiple-rater system—in which a final evaluation represents the average of ratings made by independent sources—is better than a single rater (Sackett & Wilson, 1982). Whatever bias a single individual brings to bear on his or her performance ratings can thus be offset, to some extent, by the ratings of others. Third, it is possible to teach the skills necessary for accurate appraisals. Various training programs have been developed, and research suggests that accuracy can be boosted by alerting evaluators to the biases of social perception, focusing their attention on job-relevant behaviors, sharpening their memory skills, informing them of performance norms that serve as a frame of reference within the organization, and providing them with practice and feedback in the use of rating scales (Bernardin & Beatty, 1984; Hedge & Kavanagh, 1988; Day & Sulsky, 1995). No system will ever be perfect, but much improvement is possible—particularly when people are motivated to be accurate (Salvemini et al., 1993).

Due Process Considerations

Part of the problem with performance appraisals is that people exhibit social perception biases that often result in a loss of *accuracy.* In this all-too-human enterprise, however, there's also another problem: *fairness*. Appraisals of job performance—because they influence personnel decisions—are often biased, sometimes even deliberately distorted, by those motivated by political and self-serving agendas within the workplace. Office politics is an organizational fact of life (Longnecker et al., 1987).

To enhance fairness, Robert Folger and his colleagues (1992) have proposed a "due process" model of performance appraisal. In general, this model is designed to guard the rights of employees in the same way that the criminal justice system seeks to protect the accused. The model consists of three principles. The first is that there should be *adequate notice*—that is, clear performance standards that employees can understand and ask questions about. The second is that employees should receive a *fair hearing,* in which they are evaluated by supervisors who know their work, and in which they receive timely feedback as well as an opportunity to present their own case. The third principle is that appraisals should be based on *evidence* of job performance, not on prejudice, corruption, or other external considerations. As indicated by research on reactions to pay-raise decisions, procedural fairness can be just as important to workers as a favorable outcome (Folger & Konovsky, 1989).

LEADERSHIP

Regardless of where you're employed, the work experience depends in large part on the quality of leadership in the organization. A leader is someone who can move a group of people toward a common goal. The question is, What personal and situational factors make for effective leaders? There is no single formula. Some leaders succeed by winning supporters, others by mending fences, uniting rivals, negotiating deals, building coalitions, solving problems, or stirring emotions. Whatever the strategy, there is one common denominator: good leadership requires social influence (Bass, 1990; Hollander & Offermann, 1990; House & Podsakoff, 1994).

What personal and situational factors make for effective leaders? At the Center for Creative Leadership, located in Greensboro, North Carolina, consultants try to evaluate managers by observing work team interactions through a one-way mirror.

The Trait Approach

One approach is to identify traits that characterize "natural-born" leaders. According to the "great person theory" of history, exceptional individuals rise up to determine the course of human events. This approach has had some support over the years, since traits such as intelligence, ambition, a need for power, self-confidence, a high energy level, and an ability to adapt to change are characteristic of people who go on to become leaders (Kenny & Zaccaro, 1983; Winter, 1987; Hogan et al., 1994). Even physical height may play a role—a possibility suggested by research showing that male and female managers in a corporation were, on average, more than an inch taller than nonmanagement employees (Egolf & Corder, 1991). In this regard, it's interesting that between the years 1900 and 1992, the tallest candidate for U.S. president won an astonishing twenty-one out of twenty-three elections (1972 and 1976 being the only exceptions).

Think about some of the great leaders of the twentieth century, those who could transform the status quo by making supporters believe that anything is possible. Martin Luther King, Jr., was that kind of leader. For better or for worse, so were Vladimir Lenin, Adolf Hitler, Franklin D. Roosevelt, Mahatma Gandhi, John F. Kennedy, Fidel Castro, and Nelson Mandela. In the best seller *In Search of Excellence,* Thomas Peters and Robert Waterman (1982) studied sixty-two of America's best businesses and found that their success was due largely to the ability of the leaders to elicit extraordinary efforts from ordinary human beings.

transformational leaders Leaders who inspire followers to transcend their own needs in the interest of a common cause.

What's so special about these individuals? Based on the work of political scientist James MacGregor Burns (1978), Bernard Bass (1985) calls them **transformational leaders.** Transformational leaders motivate followers to transcend their personal needs in the interest of a common cause. Through a blend of consciousness raising and raw emotional inspiration, they articulate a vision for the future and mobilize others to join in that vision. Bass and his colleagues asked people who work for business managers, executives, army officers, school principals, government bureaucrats, fire chiefs, and store owners to describe the most out-

Shown at his famous "I have a dream" speech in Washington D. C., in August 1963, Martin Luther King, Jr. was a transformational leader who inspired massive change by making supporters believe that anything was possible.

Table 13.2 Characteristics of Transformational Leaders

Characteristic	Description
Charisma	Has a vision; gains respect, trust, and confidence; promotes a strong identification of followers. ("Has a sense of mission which he or she communicates to me")
Inspiration	Gives pep talks, increases optimism and enthusiasm, and arouses emotion in communications. ("Uses symbols and images to focus our efforts")
Intellectual Stimulation	Actively encourages a re-examination of existing values and assumptions; fosters creativity and the use of intelligence. ("Enables me to think about old problems in new ways")
Individualized Consideration	Gives personal attention to all members, acts as advisor, and gives feedback in ways that are easy to accept, understand, and use for personal development. ("Coaches me if I need it")

When people are asked to describe the best leaders they know, four characteristics are most often cited: charisma, an ability to inspire others, intellectual stimulation, and individualized consideration. These attributes are evident in the descriptions above.
(Bass & Avolio, 1990.)

standing leaders they know (Bass & Avolio, 1990; Hater & Bass, 1988). As shown in Table 13.2, the descriptions revealed four attributes: charisma, inspiration, intellectual stimulation, and individualized consideration of others.

Interactional Models

An alternative is to view leadership as an interaction between personal and situational factors. According to this approach, great leaders are, to some extent, a product of their time, place, and circumstance—and different situations call for different styles of leadership. For example, Bass (1985) argued that transformational leaders are most likely to emerge in times of growth, change, and crisis.

Illustrative of the interactional approach is the **contingency model of leadership,** developed by Fred Fiedler (1967), which takes both traits and situations into account. According to Fiedler, the key difference among leaders is whether they are more *task oriented* (single-mindedly focused on the job) or more *relations oriented* (concerned about the feelings of employees). According to Fiedler, the amount of control a leader has determines which type of leadership is more effective. Leaders enjoy *high situational control* when they have good relations with staff, a position of power, and a clearly structured task. In contrast, leaders exhibit *low situational control* when they have poor relations with their staff, limited power, and a task that is not clearly defined.

contingency model of leadership The theory that leadership effectiveness is determined both by the personal characteristics of leaders and by the control afforded by the situation.

Combining these personal and situational components, research on various work groups suggests that task-oriented leaders are the most effective in clear-cut situations that are either low or high in control and that relations-oriented leaders perform better in situations that afford a moderate degree of control. In low-control situations, groups need guidance, which task-oriented leaders provide by staying focused on the job. In high-control situations, when conditions are already favorable, the same leaders maintain a relaxed, low profile. Relations-oriented leaders are different. They offer too little guidance in low-control situations, and they meddle too much in high-control situations. In ambiguous situations, however, relations-oriented leaders—precisely because of their open, participative, social style—motivate workers to solve problems in creative ways. This pattern of results is illustrated in Figure 13.3.

Studies of military units, sports teams, schools, hospitals, and other organizations generally support Fiedler's contingency model (Peters et al., 1985; Strube & Garcia, 1981; Schriesheim et al., 1994). Although the results are far from perfect (Vecchio, 1983), the main point is well taken: Good leadership requires a "match" between personal style and the demands of a specific situation (Fiedler & Chemers, 1984). A mismatch—that is, the wrong type of person for the situation—can have negative consequences for both the leader and the organization. For example, Martin Chemers and his colleagues (1985) surveyed college administrators to determine both their leadership style and their situational control. The result: Mismatches were associated with increased job stress, stress-related illness, and absence from work—symptoms that diminish a leader's productivity and competence (Fiedler & Garcia, 1987; Fiedler et al., 1992).

Although Fiedler's model takes both persons and situations into account, Edwin Hollander (1985) criticizes its "top-down" view of leadership in which the workers are portrayed as inert, passive, and faceless creatures to be soothed or aroused at management's discretion. Instead, says Hollander, leadership is a two-way street in which there is a mutual influence between leader and followers. In Hollander's *transactional* model, an effective leader provides tangible rewards, listens to followers, and fulfills their needs in exchange for an expected level of job performance. Perhaps that is why people are more likely to support leaders who allow them to express their opinions (Tyler et al., 1985).

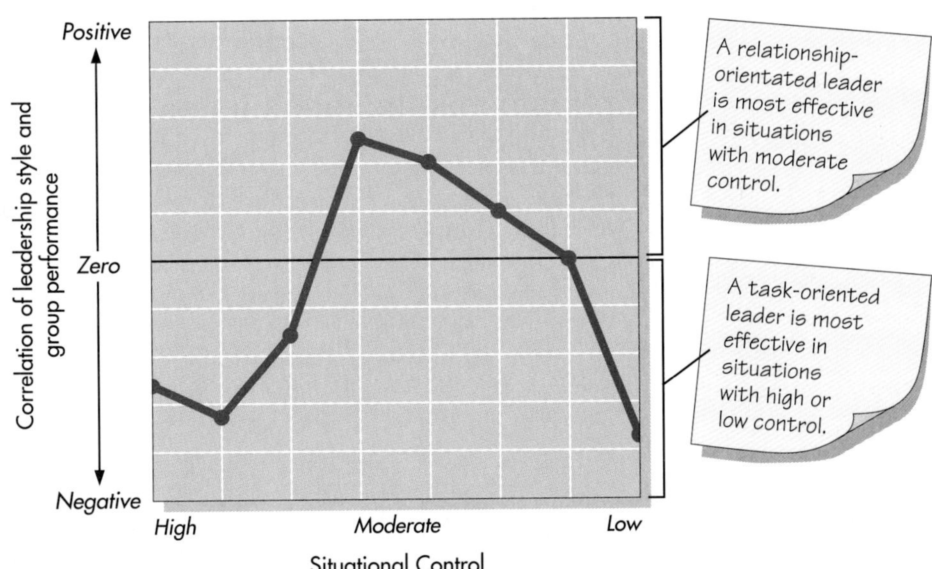

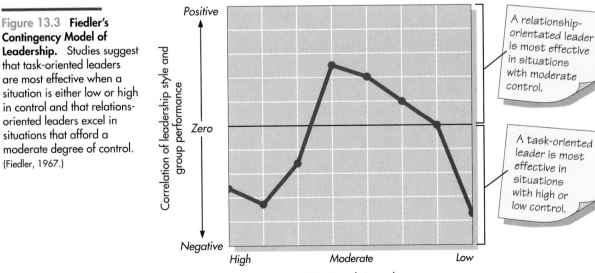

Figure 13.3 Fiedler's Contingency Model of Leadership. Studies suggest that task-oriented leaders are most effective when a situation is either low or high in control and that relations-oriented leaders excel in situations that afford a moderate degree of control. (Fiedler, 1967.)

Leadership Among Women and Minorities

Look at the leaders of America's Fortune 500 companies, and you'll find that only 3.6 percent of board-of-directors members are women—a percentage that is not much higher in the health-care industry, government, or educational institutions. Now look at the percentage of African Americans, Hispanics, and Asians in the top ranks of the same organizations, and you'll find that they fare even worse. Even today, you can count on one hand the number of U.S. senators who are female or the number of major-league baseball managers who are black. Despite the progress that has been made in entry- and middle-level positions, working women and minorities who seek positions of leadership still seem blocked by a "glass ceiling"—a barrier so subtle that it's transparent, yet so strong that it keeps them from reaching the top of the hierarchy (Morrison & Von Glinow, 1990). Women may also encounter "glass walls" that prevent them from moving laterally within an organization—from positions in public relations to those in core areas such as production, marketing, and sales (Lopez, 1992).

Clearly, women are qualified for positions of power. Research shows that male and female managers have similar aspirations, abilities, values, and job-related skills. Indeed, Alice Eagly and Blair Johnson (1990) meta-analyzed the results of 150 studies of sex differences in leadership and found that female leaders in the workplace are as task oriented as their male counterparts. Similarly, Eagly and her colleagues (1995) found that male and female leaders are equally effective. The only difference seems to be that men are more controlling and women more democratic in their approaches. As a result, men are more effective as leaders in positions that require a more directive style (for example, in the military), whereas women are more effective in managerial settings that require openness and cooperation.

This portrayal of women leaders is consistent with Judy Rosener's (1990) impression, as reported in the *Harvard Business Review,* that although female executives used to feel a need to prove they were tough, today's generation of leading women are drawing successfully on qualities traditionally viewed as feminine. It's also consistent with Sally Helgesen's (1990) observation that female managers interact more with subordinates, invite them to participate in the decision-making process, share information and power, and spin more extensive networks, or "webs of inclusion"—a leadership style she calls the "feminine advantage."

So what's wrong? If women are competent at leadership, why have so few managed to reach the top? For women, the path to power—from their entry into the labor market, to recruitment in an organization, and up the promotion ladder—is something of an "obstacle course" (Ragins & Sundstrom, 1989). One problem is that many women are deeply conflicted about having to juggle a career and family responsibilities (Crosby, 1991). But another problem is societal. Lingering stereotypes portray women as followers rather than as leaders, and many people are uneasy about women who assume leadership roles. In one study, men and women who were seated at the head of the table in all-male or all-female groups were automatically tagged as leaders. In mixed-sex groups, however, this head-of-the-table bias applied only to men who sat in that position (Porter et al., 1985). In another study, subjects were observed from behind a one-way mirror as they took part in a discussion group with male and female confederates who were trained to behave similarly. Regardless of their sex, all confederates who played an assertive role were quite reasonably perceived as leaders. Yet subjects smiled and nodded less often, and frowned more often, in response to the female leaders—a subtle but sure sign of disapproval (Butler &

Although women are underrepresented within positions of leadership, some do manage to break through the "glass ceiling." In 1992, Christine Todd Whitman was elected Governor of New Jersey. Now she is considered a national political leader for the Republican Party.

Geis, 1990). Combining the results of sixty-one studies, Eagly and her colleagues (1992) concluded that female leaders are devalued in comparison to equivalent males when they adopt a "masculine" style of leadership (directive and task focused) or occupy "masculine" positions (for example, as business manager or athletic coach).

Statistics show that minorities also fight an uphill battle for leadership positions in the workplace. In interviews, 84 percent of black MBA graduates from five prestigious business schools said they believed that race had a negative impact on their salaries, performance appraisals, and promotions (Jones, 1986). Research does not clearly suggest that employee evaluations are biased by race (Sackett & DuBois, 1991; Waldman & Avolio, 1991). Still, in light of what social psychologists know about the subtleties of modern racism, as described in Chapter 4, business leaders should beware of the indirect ways in which minorities may be handicapped in the pursuit of leadership. A study of Blacks in the banking industry, for example, revealed that they often feel excluded socially from informal work groups, are not "networked," and lack the sponsors, role models, and mentors that are so helpful for upward mobility within an organization (Irons & Moore, 1985).

MOTIVATION

A key question that I/O psychologists ask is, What motivates individuals to work hard, and to work well? What determines *your* on-the-job performance? Are you driven by strictly economic concerns, or do you have other personal needs to fulfill? There is no single answer. At work, as in the rest of life, our behavior often stems from the convergence of many different motives.

Economic Reward Models

Out of necessity, people work for money. In strictly economic terms, however, payment is more complicated than it may appear. To begin with, an employee's overall satisfaction with his or her compensation depends not only on salary (gross income, take-home pay) but also on raises (upward or downward changes in pay, how these changes are determined), the method of distribution (number of checks received, salary differences within the company), and benefits (vacation time, sick leave, insurance, pensions, and other services). Each of these factors is part of the formula for satisfaction (Heneman & Schwab, 1985; Judge & Welbourne, 1994). In fact, many rewards are not monetary but symbolic—such as titles, office size and location, carpeting, furnishings, windows, and the ability to regulate access by others (Becker, 1981; Sundstrom, 1986).

Perhaps the most popular theory of worker motivation is Victor Vroom's (1964) *expectancy theory.* According to Vroom, people are rational decision makers who analyze the benefits and costs of possible courses of action and exert effort when they believe it will produce a desired outcome, whether monetary or symbolic. Expectancy theory has been used successfully to predict various job-related behaviors and career choices such as which college to attend or which job offer to accept (Mitchell, 1974). And as an application of the theory, organizations have devised some new and innovative motivational programs. A survey of 1,600 companies revealed that many of them use (1) individual incentive programs that provide an opportunity to earn time off or extra pay; (2) small-group incentive plans, in which members of a work unit can win bonuses for reaching specified goals; (3) profit-sharing plans, in which workers earn money from company profits; (4) recognition programs that single out "employees of the month" for gifts or trophies; and (5) pay-for-knowledge plans that raise salaries for workers who are flexible and can perform different jobs within a work unit (Horn, 1987). People may strive for reward, but there's more to money than just economics and more to motivation than just the size of a paycheck. In short, social psychological factors must also be considered.

Leo Cullum/The Cartoon Bank.

Intrinsic Motivation

Under certain conditions, reward systems that increase *extrinsic motivation* may undermine *intrinsic motivation*. As discussed in Chapter 2, people are extrinsically motivated when they engage in an activity for money, recognition, or other tangible rewards, and they are intrinsically motivated when they perform for the sake of interest, challenge, or sheer enjoyment. Business leaders want employees to feel intrinsically motivated and committed to their work. So where do expectancy theory and incentive programs fit in? Is tangible reward the bottom line or not?

When people start getting paid for a task they already enjoy, they sometimes lose interest in it. In the first demonstration of this effect, Edward Deci (1971) recruited college students to work for three one-hour sessions on block-building puzzles they found interesting. During the first and third sessions, all subjects were treated in the same manner. In the second session, however, half of the subjects were paid one dollar for each puzzle they completed. To measure intrinsic motivation, Deci left subjects alone during a break in the first and third sessions and recorded the amount of time they spent on the puzzles rather than on other available activities. Compared to subjects in the unrewarded group, those who had been paid in the second session later showed less interest in the puzzles when the money was no longer available (see Figure 13.4).

This finding, that rewards undermine intrinsic motivation, has been established in numerous studies (Deci & Ryan, 1985; Lepper & Greene, 1978). By

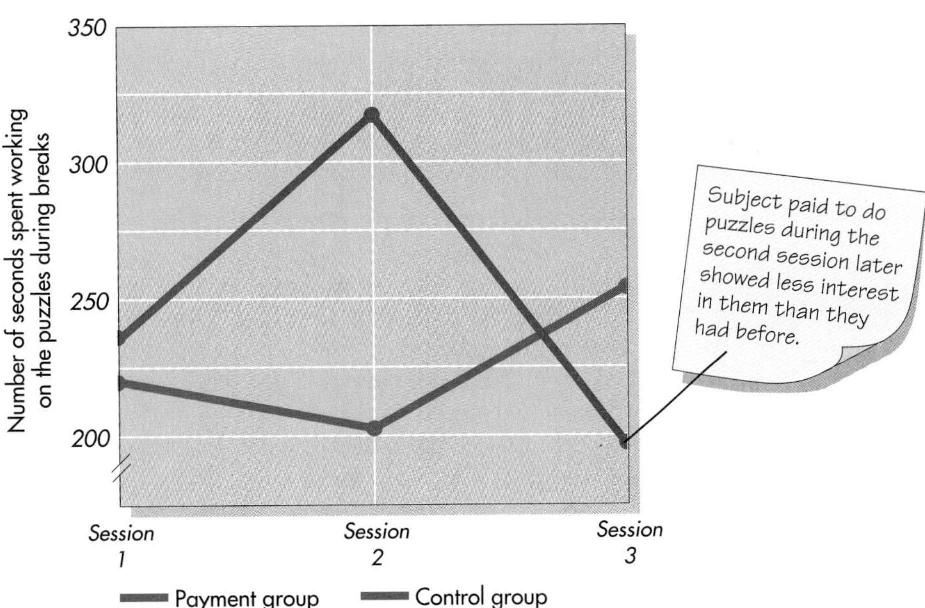

Figure 13.4 **The Effect of Payment on Intrinsic Motivation: Turning Play into Work.** In this study, subjects worked three times on puzzles they found interesting. After each session the amount of free time spent on the puzzles served as a record of intrinsic motivation. During the second session, half of the subjects were paid for puzzles they completed, and half were not. Those paid in the second session later showed less interest in the puzzles when the money was no longer available. (Deci, 1971.)

making people feel controlled rather than autonomous, various extrinsic factors commonly found in the workplace—punishment, close supervision, evaluation, deadlines, and competition—also have adverse effects on motivation and on performance. Thus, Teresa Amabile (1983b) found that people who were paid for artistic activities produced less creative work than those who were not paid, a finding that extends to creative problem-solving situations as well (McGraw & McCullers, 1979). To be maximally productive, people must feel internally driven, not compelled by outside forces.

If money undermines intrinsic motivation, how should employers use monetary incentives? To answer this question, we need to recognize that a reward can serve two different functions, depending on how it is presented. On the one hand, it can be perceived as *controlling* our behavior, a function that results in the detrimental effects just described (for example, a weekly salary or sales commission). On the other hand, reward can have *informational* value if it offers positive feedback about the quality of our performance (for example, earned bonuses and scholarships). Research shows that although controlling rewards adversely affects intrinsic motivation, informational reward has a positive effect (Harackiewicz, 1979; Ryan et al., 1983). In addition, reward appears to increase effort and stimulate creative thought—so long as it is not presented as the predominant reason for such activity (Eisenberger & Selbst, 1994). In a study of managers and their subordinates in an office-machine company, Deci and his colleagues (1989) found that the less controlling the managers were, the more satisfied the workers were with the company as a whole. Indeed, when Studs Terkel (1974) interviewed secretaries, stock brokers, baseball players, garbage collectors, and other workers, over and over again he heard two complaints: The employees were being too closely watched, or "spied on," and they were getting too little positive feedback—in other words, too much control and not enough strokes.

Equity Motivation

A second aspect of payment that influences motivation is the perception that it is *fair.* According to *equity theory,* presented in Chapter 6, people want rewards to be equitable. In other words, the ratio between inputs and outcomes should be the same for the self as for others. Relative to co-workers, then, the better your job performance is, the more money you should earn. If you feel overpaid or underpaid, however, you will experience distress—and try to relieve it by (1) restoring actual equity, say, by working less or getting a raise, or (2) convincing yourself that equity already exists (Greenberg, 1982).

Equity theory has some fascinating implications for behavior in the workplace. Consider, for example, Jerald Greenberg's (1988) study of employees in a large insurance firm. To allow for refurbishing, close to 200 workers had to be moved temporarily from one office to another. Randomly, the workers were assigned to offices that usually belonged to others who were higher, lower, or equal in rank. Predictably, the higher the rank, the more spacious the office, the fewer the number of occupants, and the larger the desk. Would the random assignments influence job performance? By keeping track of the number of insurance cases processed, and by rating the complexity of the cases and the quality of the decisions made, Greenberg was able to derive a measure of job performance for each worker before, during, and after the office switch. To restore equity, he reasoned, workers assigned to higher-status offices would feel overcompensated and improve their job performance, and those sent to lower-status offices would feel undercompensated and lower their performance. That is exactly what happened. Figure 13.5 shows that the results offered sound support for equity theory.

Satisfaction depends not only on equity outcomes but also on the belief that the *procedures* used to determine those outcomes were fair and clearly communicated (Brockner et al., 1990; Folger, 1986; Moorman, 1991). For example, Greenberg (1990) studied workers in three manufacturing plants owned by the same parent company. Business was slow, so the company reduced its payroll through temporary pay cuts. Would the cuts make workers feel underpaid? If so, how would the workers restore equity? Concerned that the policy might trigger employee theft, Greenberg randomly varied the conditions in the three plants. In one, the employees were told, without an explanation, that they would receive a 15 percent pay cut for ten weeks. In the second, the same pay cut was accompanied by an explanation and expressions of regret. In the third plant, salaries were not cut. By keeping track of inventories for the ten weeks before, during, and after the pay cuts, Greenberg was able to estimate the employee theft rate. The result: Workers whose pay was cut stole more from the company, presumably to restore equity—but only when not provided with an adequate explanation for their loss. In the laboratory as well, subjects who were underpaid for participation often restored equity by stealing—particularly when they were not given a valid explanation (Greenberg, 1993).

Equity in the workplace is important, perhaps more for men than for women. In studies of reward allocation, subjects are led to believe that they and a partner are working at a task for which they will be paid. They work separately, receive false feedback on their performance, and then are told that they must decide how to divide a joint reward. In this situation, women typically pay themselves less than men do and react less strongly when they are underpaid by others (Major & Deaux, 1982). Similarly, a study of male and female graduates of an Ivy League

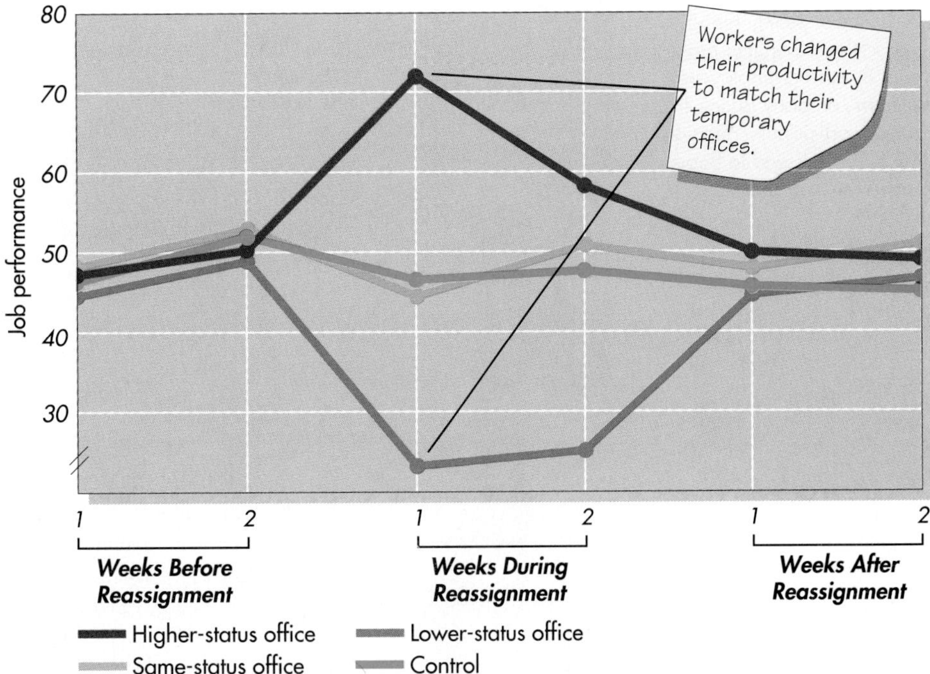

Figure 13.5 Equity in the Workplace. Insurance company workers were moved temporarily to offices that were higher, lower, or equal in status to their own rank. Supporting equity theory, those assigned to higher-status offices increased their job performance, and those sent to lower-status offices showed a decrease. When workers were reassigned to original offices, productivity levels returned to normal. (Greenberg, 1988.)

business school showed that the men were more likely to negotiate starting salaries that were higher than those initially offered (Gerhart & Rynes, 1991).

The gender wage gap has been narrowing in recent years, but at a snail's pace. In 1980, women earned 60 cents for every dollar that men were paid. By 1990, the figure was up only slightly, to 68 cents. That may be why, in a survey of career expectations among male and female college seniors, the women expected to earn $1,238 less than the men upon entering the job market and $18,659 less at the peak of their careers (Jackson et al., 1992).

There are several possible explanations for this difference. First, women expect lower pay than men do, even when they are just as qualified—an expectation that stems, perhaps, from a history of discrimination (Major & Konar, 1984). Second, women tend to care less about money and more about interpersonal relationships (Crosby, 1982). Third, women may be satisfied with less money because they tend to compare themselves to other women, not to the more highly paid men (Chesler & Goodman, 1976). Fourth, women tend to evaluate themselves less favorably than do men, so even when they work harder and perform better, they feel less entitled (Major et al., 1984). Whatever the explanation, these findings have to make you wonder. Will working women of the future be content to remain underpaid? Is the gender wage gap here to stay? Not necessarily. If the sex difference in reward expectations is rooted in experience, it should diminish as successive generations of women become more established in high-paying careers.

Quality Circles

In addition to intrinsic motivation and pay equity, job satisfaction is influenced by the extent to which people are included in important organizational decisions.

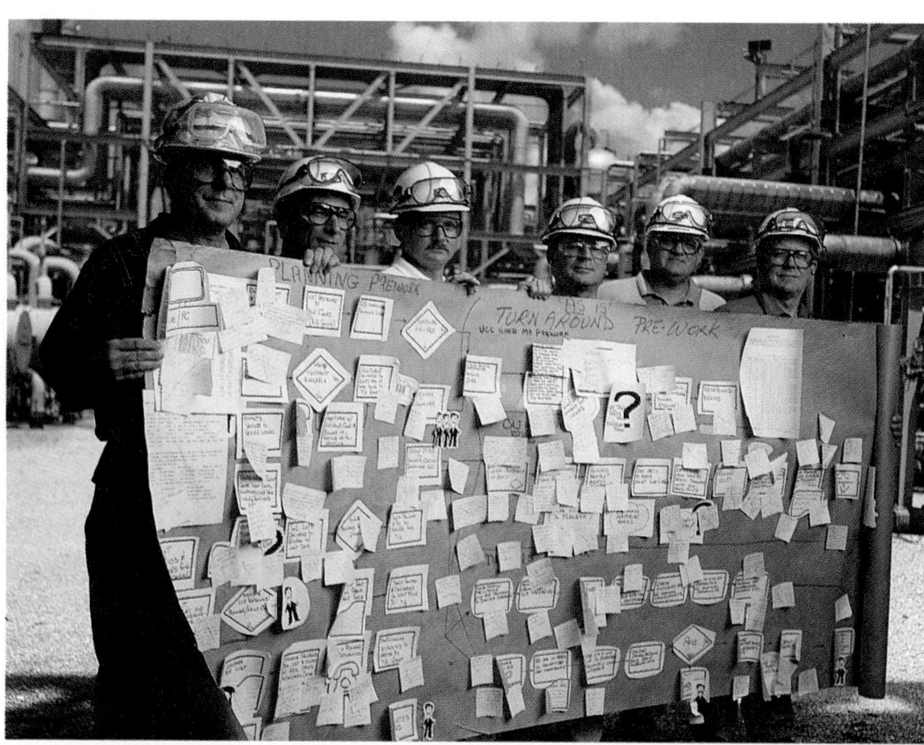

At Union Carbide, these workers completely reengineered their chemical process map. By giving employees a voice in company policy, this sort of participative decision making is believed to boost motivation and productivity.

In recent years, American companies have introduced *participative decision making (PDM)* by giving employees a voice in decisions that used to be made by management alone. According to its proponents, PDM boosts employee morale, increases motivation and productivity, and reduces turnover and absenteeism. Benefits such as these have been found especially in situations where employees want input (Vroom & Jago, 1988) and participate in decision making directly rather than indirectly, through elected representatives (Rubenowitz et al., 1983).

One form of PDM, imported from Japan in the 1980s, has generated some excitement in recent years. As Japanese industries soared to the top of the world market, business leaders in other countries tried to discover their secret to success. In doing so, they learned that Japanese workers exhibit high levels of commitment to their jobs, perhaps because they take part in *quality circles*. A quality circle is a small group of employees who do similar work and meet regularly to exchange ideas on how to improve their product, the production process, or the work environment. Based on the success of Japanese companies, many American corporations—including General Motors, Ford, Westinghouse, RCA, and General Electric—adopted the concept. Promising to boost productivity, quality circles are catching on.

Are quality circles all they're cracked up to be? To find out, Mitchell Marks and his colleagues (1986) assessed both job satisfaction and productivity among machine operators in an American corporation. Half of the operators took part in a quality circle; the other half did not. Before the program, questionnaire measures of satisfaction were administered as part of a companywide policy to monitor changes in the workplace. Twenty months after the quality circles had begun, the same questionnaires were readministered. Organizational records were also used to measure changes in productivity and attendance. As you can see in Figure 13.6, the results were impressive. Compared to employees who did not participate, those who took part in the quality circle felt more content. They liked having a voice in decision making and held more positive views of the company, their own achievements, and the opportunity for advancement. On measures of performance, they exhibited both an increase in productivity and a decrease in absenteeism.

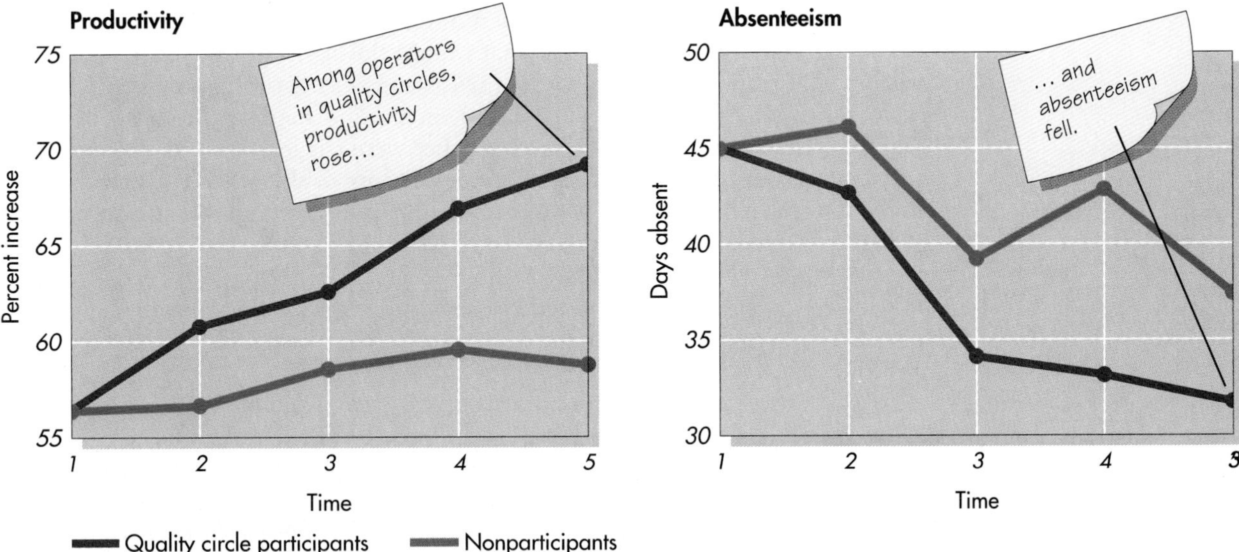

Figure 13.6 Benefits of the Quality Circle. For twenty months, machine operators who took part in quality circles were compared to those who did not. As shown, participants exhibited two improvements in their job performance: increased productivity (left) and decreased absenteeism (right). (Marks et al., 1986.)

ECONOMIC RISK-TAKING

October 19, 1987, was called Black Monday. On that day, the stock market dived even more deeply than it had during the famous crash of 1929, resulting in an estimated loss of $500 billion. Worst of all, no one really knew why. Was the economy on the verge of collapse, or were psychological factors to blame? Some analysts sought rational economic reasons, citing a rising American trade deficit, an increase in the prime rate, and political events at home and abroad. Others said the crash was triggered by false beliefs, fear-arousing rumors, conformity pressures, and other social influences—compounded by the speed with which brokers could buy and sell stocks through computers. Forget interest rates, trade deficits, and the gross national product, they said; if you want to predict the market, talk to investors.

The odds of making money are far better on the stock market than in gambling casinos—as a majority of investors come out ahead. In many ways, however, putting money into stocks is like gambling. In a book entitled *A Random Walk Down Wall Street,* economist Burton Malkiel (1981) reported that over the long haul, mutual fund portfolios compiled by experts perform no better than randomly selected groups of stocks! Indeed, when *Consumer Reports* evaluated the advice of professional brokers, it concluded that "a monkey throwing darts at the stock pages . . . could probably do as well in overall investment performance, perhaps even better" (Shefrin & Statman, 1986, p. 52).

Like most people, you may be puzzled by this cynical remark. Don't some professionals turn a greater profit than others? And if stock prices rise and fall in reaction to economic conditions, can't the astute investor take advantage of these relationships? The answer to both questions is "not necessarily." It's true that some brokers perform better than others for a period of time, perhaps even four or five years. But investors are no more likely to succeed after a string of wins than after a string of losses. Since many traders have access to the same information, and since prices can change at a moment's notice, movements in the market cannot be predicted with reliability. The only way to guarantee profit is to use confidential information—an illegal activity.

If stock market decisions are not made on strictly economic grounds, then what are they based on? Recent research suggests that predictions of the future on Wall Street are influenced by social psychological factors. Shortly after the October 1987 crash, economist Robert Shiller sent questionnaires to a group of active traders to try to determine what caused the crisis. For the nearly 1,000 investors who responded, the key event was the news concerning the market itself, including a sharp decline that occurred on the morning of the crash. In other words, price movements in the stock market were triggered not by objective economic information but by other price movements in the market. Does this phenomenon ring a bell? Research on social comparison (Chapter 2) and conformity (Chapter 9) has shown that when people feel they cannot clearly and concretely measure their own opinion, they turn to others for information. Perhaps that is why investors are more influenced by news and stock market tips during periods of rising or falling prices than during periods of relative stability (Schachter et al., 1985).

With respect to coin flips and other chance events, gamblers often assume that a hot streak is due to turn cold, and vice versa. Yet when it comes to games of skill such as basketball, people often make the opposite assumption—that hot streaks forecast continued success and that cold spells predict failure. Both assumptions are incorrect. One event does not imply another. But what about the

Robert Mankoff/The Cartoon Bank.

"Spurred by hopes for a continued revitalization of the American short story along with expectations that rock and roll will never die, the stock market staged a brisk rally today in moderately active trading."

ups and downs of the stock market? Do either of these beliefs influence the decisions made by investors? How would *you* play the money game?

To see what happens, Stanley Schachter and his colleagues (1987) presented college students with recent price histories of stocks that had increased, decreased, or remained stable over a three-week period. The conventional wisdom of Wall Street is that investors should "buy low and sell high." Yet, as Figure 13.7 shows, most subjects decided to buy stocks that were on the rise and sell those that were on the decline. In a follow-up study, similar decisions were made by a more sophisticated group of students attending the business school at Columbia University.

Do people always go with the flow of the marketplace, or do they sometimes conform to the buy low–sell high rule? Paul Andreasson (1987) argued that the

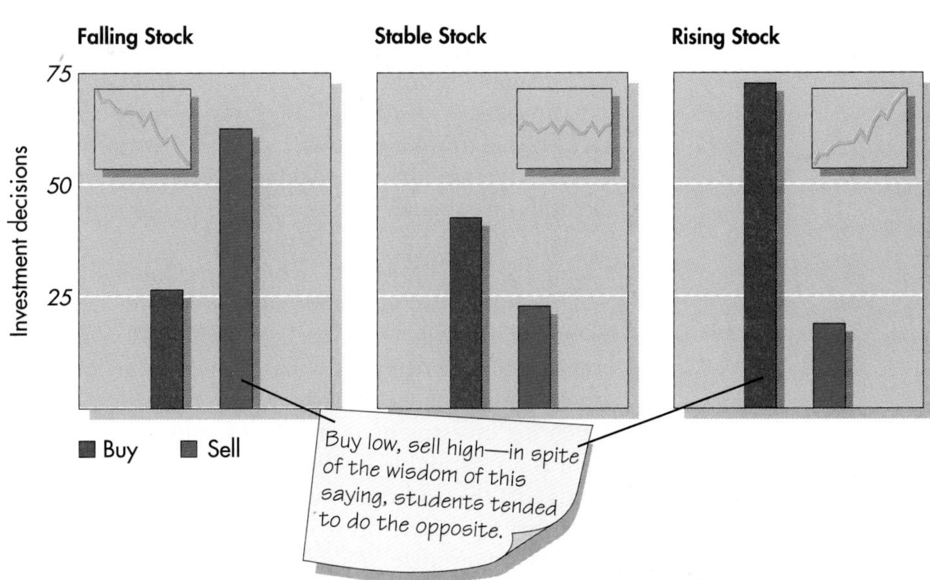

Figure 13.7 Simulated Stock Market: Using the Past to Predict the Future. In this study, subjects learned the recent trends of stocks that increased, decreased, or remained stable. As shown, most subjects chose to buy stocks that had risen (right) and to sell those that had fallen (left). (Schachter et al., 1987.)

answer depends on attributions. According to Andreasson, investors may well follow conventional wisdom. But what about price changes for which they have an explanation? What if a rise in stock prices is attributed to certain world events? As far as the market is concerned, attributions such as these can produce a self-fulfilling prophecy by leading investors to believe that the changes will persist—that rising prices will continue to climb and declining prices will continue to fall. To test his hypothesis, Andreasson simulated the market on a computer and found that without news stories to explain fluctuations, subjects assumed that prices would return to previous levels, so they bought stocks when the price was low and sold when the price was high. However, subjects who also received *Wall Street Journal* explanations for the changes pursued the strategy observed by Schachter and his colleagues (1987): they rode with stocks that were climbing and bailed out of those that were on the decline. It doesn't stretch the imagination to see how these findings relate to Black Monday. Faced with changes in the market, the financial news media often seize on current events for a quick explanation. Whether the resultant attributions are correct or incorrect is irrelevant. Either way, they can turn an initial dip in the market into a full-fledged crash.

Stock market behavior is complicated by another social factor. Hersh Shefrin and Meir Statman (1985) believe that many investors lack the self-control necessary for sound investment decisions. When people own shares of a stock that is climbing, they often sell too early so they can enjoy the quick pleasure of making a profit. This tendency is easy to understand. But when people own stock that is falling, they often wait too long before selling in the hope that they might avoid a financial loss. Why do people continue to hang on in a failing situation? When the handwriting is on the wall, why compound the problem by throwing good money after bad?

In *Too Much Invested to Quit,* Alan Teger (1980) described a dollar-auction game that illustrates part of the dilemma. Imagine yourself in the following situation. The auctioneer tells you and other participants that a one-dollar bill is about to be sold. As in a typical auction, the highest bidder will receive the dollar in exchange for the amount bid. Yet contrary to convention, the second highest bidder must also pay the amount bid—and will receive nothing in return. You and the other participants are asked not to communicate, and the minimum opening bid is set at five cents. Then before you know it, the bidding begins. In laboratory experiments, two subjects compete in the auction. They are supplied with a small amount of money that is theirs to keep, and they are free to quit the experiment at any time. What happens next can be startling. Some pairs reasonably choose to take the money and run without making a single bid. Other pairs, however, get involved in escalating bidding wars. According to Tegar, bidding for the dollar frequently climbs into the five-dollar range—more than the amount allocated for play by the experimenter. On one occasion, the auctioneer had to terminate the game after the two participants had bid $24.95 and $25.00.

The dollar auction helps us understand how people can become financially overcommitted in real life. In Chapter 11, we saw that individuals and groups often become *entrapped* by their own initial commitments as they try to justify or salvage investments already made. In business, the economic conditions under which an investment is made sometimes justify continued commitment. When there is a reasonable likelihood of success, and when potential earnings are high relative to the additional necessary costs, it pays to persist. In certain long-term investments, sizable up-front costs simply have to be endured before the delayed benefits materialize. As in the dollar auction, however, entrapment may also occur when economic conditions do not provide a basis for optimism. On these occasions, investors take a failing course of action to justify prior decisions, protect their self-esteem, and save face in front of others (Brockner & Rubin, 1985; Staw & Ross, 1987; Bobocel & Meyer, 1994). As a result, investors who are losing money on a failing stock too often try to "hang tough" and "weather the storm"—only to sink deeper and deeper.

On a more positive note, investors can be taught to use various "de-escalation strategies" designed to make them more responsive to available evidence and keep them from throwing good money after bad (Simonson & Staw, 1992). For example, Richard Larrick and his colleagues (1990) found that people often violate the *sunk cost principle* of economics, which states that only future costs and benefits, not past commitments, or "sunk costs," should be considered in making a decision. To appreciate the practical implications, imagine that you bought a fifteen-dollar ticket to a basketball game weeks in advance but then, on the day of the game, you don't feel well, it's snowing, and your favorite player is injured. Do you still go to the game to make sure you use the ticket? Not wanting to "waste" the money, many of us would go—even though the money is already sunk, and even though we would have to bear the added costs of getting sick, driving in bad weather, and sitting through a boring game. To see if there is a more "rational" economic choice, ask yourself this question: Would you go to the game if someone called that day and offered you a free ticket? If you said that you would go if you had paid for the ticket but not if it were free, then, like investors who don't know when to cut their losses, you fell into the sunk cost trap and should have stayed home.

In a study of University of Michigan professors, Larrick and his colleagues (1990) found that the economists were more likely than their counterparts in other disciplines to use the sunk cost principle—not only in hypothetical problems but in their own personal decisions. More important, they found that ordinary people can be taught to apply the rule as well. Indeed, a full month after one brief training session, college students were more likely to report using the rule in their own lives. Sometimes a little knowledge can go a long way.

REVIEW

- This chapter presents applications of social psychology to the workplace.
- In business, behavior is influenced not only by economic factors but by social psychology as well.
- The Hawthorne studies showed that worker productivity was increased by the attention paid to the workers.

PERSONNEL SELECTION

- Recruiting a competent staff is the first important step in the development of a successful organization.

Traditional Employment Interviews

- Employment interviews have mixed effects on hiring decisions.
- There seems to be less stereotype-based discrimination in decisions made with interviews than without.
- But interviews often give rise to poor selection decisions, in part because interviewer expectations bias the interview process and predetermine the outcome.

"Scientific" Alternatives to the Traditional Interview

- Many companies use graphology, lie-detector tests, integrity tests, and other "scientific" approaches.
- A more effective method is the structured interview in which applicants are evaluated in a standardized manner.

Affirmative Action

- Research shows that women and minorities devalue their own performance when they think they were preferentially selected.
- But reactions are more favorable when merit-based factors are also thought to play a role and when the person chosen is said to be qualified for the position.

PERFORMANCE APPRAISALS

- Performance appraisals entail the evaluation of an employee and communication of the results to that person.
- Sometimes objective measures of performance are available, but usually evaluations are based on subjective judgments.

Supervisor Ratings

- Research shows that supervisor ratings are based largely on job-relevant characteristics.
- They may also be biased by the halo effect, contrast effects, and the tendency to use a restricted range on a numerical scale.

Self-Evaluations

- Self-evaluations also figure into performance appraisals, but these tend to be self-serving and inflated.
- Self-evaluations are higher among men than women.

New and Improved Methods of Appraisal

- Performance appraisals can be improved.
- It helps to make ratings shortly after an observation, use multiple raters, and train raters in the necessary skills.

Due Process Considerations

- Due process is an important factor in procedural fairness.

LEADERSHIP

- Leadership requires social influence.
- There are two approaches to understanding the determinants of good leadership.

The Trait Approach

- One approach is to search for personal traits associated with effective leaders.
- Transformational leaders motivate followers through charisma, inspiration, intellectual stimulation, and personal concern for others.

Interactional Models

- A second approach assumes that leadership is determined by an interaction of personal and situational factors.
- In Fiedler's contingency model, task-oriented leaders excel in high- and low-control situations, and relations-oriented leaders are effective in moderate-control situations.

Leadership Among Women and Minorities

- Despite recent gains, working women and minorities are still underrepresented in positions of leadership.
- Many women are qualified, but they encounter obstacles such as gender stereotypes and uneasiness about women in leadership roles.
- Part of the problem for Blacks is that they feel excluded from social networks within the workplace.

MOTIVATION

- Both economic and social factors influence worker motivation.

Economic Reward Models

- On the economic side, Vroom's expectancy theory states that workers behave in ways designed to produce a desirable outcome.
- Various incentive programs are thus used to motivate by reward.

Intrinsic Motivation

- When people perceive a reward as controlling of their behavior, they lose interest in the work itself.
- When a reward represents positive information about the quality of the work, it can enhance intrinsic motivation.

Equity Motivation

- Equity theory says that a worker's perception of fairness is important to his or her motivation.
- People adjust their productivity levels upward when they feel overpaid and downward when they feel underpaid.

- For various reasons, women accept as equitable a lower level of pay than men.

Quality Circles

- Workers want to participate in organizational decision making.
- Quality circles appear to enhance worker satisfaction and productivity.

ECONOMIC RISK-TAKING

- Sharp changes in the stock market can be triggered by news of what other investors are doing.
- Investors are influenced by attributions for price movements in the news media—attributions that can set in motion a self-fulfilling prophecy.
- People get entrapped by their initial commitments, which lead them to stick to failing courses of action.
- People can be taught de-escalation strategies such as the rule that only future costs and benefits are relevant to economic decisions.

KEY TERMS

industrial organizational (I/O) psychology, p. 496
Hawthorne effect, p. 496
integrity tests, p. 500
structured interviews, p. 500
performance appraisal, p. 503
transformational leaders, p. 507
contingency model of leadership, p. 508

I PROMISE
NEVER
TO SMOKE
I PROMISE
NEVER
TO SMOKE
I PROMISE
NEVER
TO SMOKE
I PROMISE
NEVER
TO SMOKE

Chapter 14

Health

PREVIEW

This chapter explores the social psychology of psychological and physical health. We focus first on the process of *stress and coping*. Three aspects of this process are examined: *stressful events*, an individual's *appraisal* of these events and of possible ways to cope with them, and *coping* strategies aimed at reducing stress. Then in the closing section, we discuss some approaches to *treatment and prevention*.

OUTLINE

When Laurence Sterne, the eighteenth-century English novelist, weighed the value of good health, he concluded that it was "above all gold and treasure." Most would agree. Because health matters so much, health care is always near the top of every country's political agenda. The long and complex debate about health care in the United States, likely to continue in one form or another into the next century, provides a clear illustration of the intensity of people's beliefs and feelings about this issue. Everyone cares about health and its care—including social psychologists.

For over a decade, research on health has been one of the most rapidly expanding areas in social psychology (Snyder & Forsyth, 1991). Social psychologists focusing on health are employed in colleges and universities, schools of medicine and of public health, and government agencies. Their investigations examine both psychological and physical conditions.

social-clinical interface The study of social psychological factors involved in psychological health and distress.

health psychology The study of physical health and illness by psychologists from various areas of specialization.

The study of social psychological factors involved in psychological health is called the **social-clinical interface.** Here, social psychologists share similar interests with clinical and counseling psychologists, who specialize in the study and treatment of psychological disorders. The social-clinical interface is an active and challenging area of theory and research (Ruble et al., 1992). Social psychology also plays a vital role in **health psychology,** the study of physical health and illness by psychologists from various areas of specialization (Adler & Matthews, 1994). Health psychologists make an important contribution to the understanding, treatment, and prevention of disease and injury. This chapter draws on both the social-clinical interface and health psychology to address two major health concerns: the process of stress and coping, and approaches to treatment and prevention.

STRESS AND COPING

Here's a list of people who differ in many ways. But what do they have in common?

Students studying for a big exam
People who have lost their job
Soldiers on a battlefield
Children in the inner city
Refugees
Working mothers
Survivors of natural disasters

The answer is stress. All of these people are coping with stress brought on by life events that range from troublesome to life threatening. Stress is universal. At some time or another, everyone faces the need to cope with it. In their study of stress and coping, social psychologists emphasize psychological factors: thoughts, feelings, and behaviors prompted by life events, personality, and social relations. But such factors do not exist in a vacuum. The process of stress and coping is also influenced by genetic inheritance and physiology. Culture has its effects as well. For example, American college students appear to experience more stress than do Chinese students (Gerdes & Guo, 1994).

Because stress is multiply determined, there is wide variation in how people react to threatening, potentially stressful events (Folkman & Lazarus, 1985). Individuals differ: The exact same event that wreaks havoc on the health of some can be harmless for others. And each person varies, responding effectively in some situations but being overwhelmed on other occasions. The model of stress and coping developed by Richard Lazarus and Susan Folkman takes these kinds of variations into account (Lazarus, 1991; Lazarus & Folkman, 1984).

According to these researchers, the stress and coping process outlined in Figure 14.1 is an ongoing transaction between the environment and the person, unique for each individual at each point in time. **Stress** is an unpleasant state that arises when people perceive that the demands of an event seriously tax or exceed their ability to satisfy or alter those demands. Such perceptions, collectively called **appraisal,** determine whether stress will be experienced. Appraisal also affects the person's **coping** strategy: those thoughts, feelings, and behaviors by which the individual tries to reduce stress. Coping effectively with stress helps maintain good health; coping poorly can harm it. In the following pages, we examine each of these components of the stress and coping process: potentially stressful events, appraisal, and various coping responses.

stress An unpleasant state in which people perceive the demands of an event as taxing or exceeding their ability to satisfy or alter those demands.

appraisal Judgments about the demands made by a potentially stressful event and about one's ability to meet those demands.

coping Efforts to reduce stress.

STRESSFUL EVENTS

Researchers define and measure stressful occurrences in many ways (Cohen et al., 1995). But what events do *you* consider stressful? If you jot down a list of your prime candidates, you might find a few general categories emerging. Here, we divide potential stressors into three types: life events, microstressors, and major crises.

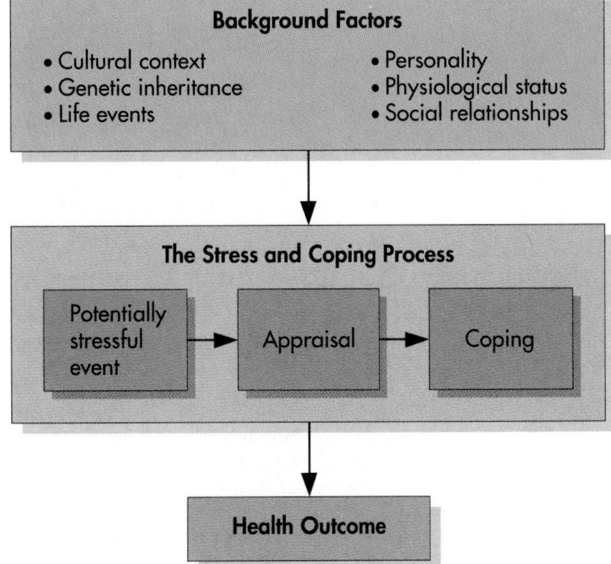

Figure 14.1 **The Stress and Coping Process.** This process involves a potentially stressful event, the appraisal of that event and of coping possibilities, and attempts to cope. Played out against a variety of background factors unique to each individual, the stress and coping process influences health outcomes.

Life Events: When Does Change Hurt?

In his pioneering work on stress, Thomas Holmes proposed that all change is stressful because it forces people to adapt to new, unfamiliar circumstances (Holmes & Rahe, 1967). Holmes acknowledged that some changes require more adjustment than do others. Nevertheless, he believed that the change produced by positive life events (such as getting married or receiving a promotion) as well as by negative ones (such as getting divorced or being fired) is stressful and can damage a person's health. This perspective generated a great deal of research—and a great deal of controversy. Are positive and negative events functionally equivalent because both produce changes in people's lives? Do they have similar effects on health?

Probably not. It now appears that positive and negative life events have different implications for stress and coping. One reason for this difference lies in the nature of emotional experience. With some exceptions (Green et al., 1993), most researchers believe that positive and negative emotions are distinct and relatively independent (Goldstein & Strube, 1994; Watson, 1988). Happiness is not the absence of distress, nor is distress the absence of happiness, and a person can have both feelings simultaneously (Carver & Scheier, 1990). Thus, the emotional consequences of positive and negative life events run on separate tracks.

So, it seems, do the health consequences (Taylor, 1991). Negative life events are often associated with physical illness and psychological distress (Sarason & Sarason, 1984). For the most part, however, the long-term effects on health of adjusting to positive life events are either beneficial or trivial (Stewart et al., 1986; Thoits, 1983).

In order to separate positive and negative life events, researchers ask subjects to indicate whether a given event had a positive or negative impact on their life. Some items from one widely used questionnaire, the Life Experiences Survey (Sarason et al., 1978), are reprinted in Table 14.1. Impact ratings on this scale are summed separately for positive and negative events. Then the relationship of each score to various health measures is examined.

But this approach, too, has its problems. For example, Darrin Lehman and his colleagues (1993) have some serious reservations about the meaning of positive life events reported by those who have undergone a severe trauma. In their study of the long-term adjustment of individuals who had lost a loved one in an automobile accident, self-reported positive life changes were *not* related to well-being. These researchers suggest that people who have suffered traumatic losses may sometimes create an illusion of positive change in order to convince others, and even themselves, that they are better off than they actually are.

negative affectivity A pervasive tendency to experience distress, dissatisfaction, and a wide variety of negative emotions.

Concerns have also been raised about reports of negative life events. Here, the critical ingredient is what is traditionally called neuroticism or, more recently, **negative affectivity**—a pervasive tendency to experience distress, dissatisfaction, and a wide variety of negative emotions (Watson & Clark, 1984). Individuals high in negative affectivity report more negative life events, physical symptoms, and psychological distress than do those low in negative affectivity (Clark & Watson, 1991; Magnus et al., 1993). Now, consider the association between self-reported negative life events and self-reported symptoms or distress. Do negative life events have any real association with health? Or are both types of self-reports simply a consequence of the personality trait of negative affectivity?

To find out, Sheldon Cohen and his colleagues (1993) investigated susceptibility to the common cold. After completing a series of questionnaires, 394 healthy volunteers were exposed to a virus and quarantined. The greater the number of

Table 14.1 The Life Experiences Survey: Instructions and Sample Items

Listed below are some events that sometimes bring about change in the lives of those who experience them and that necessitate social readjustment. Please check those events that you have experienced in the recent past, indicating whether you experienced them during the past six or twelve months. Also, for each item checked, please indicate the extent to which you viewed the event as having either a positive or a negative impact on your life at the time the event occurred. A rating of −3 would indicate an extremely negative impact. A rating of 0 suggests no impact either positive or negative. A rating of +3 would indicate an extremely positive impact.

	0 to 6 mo.	7 mo. to 1 yr.	extremely negative (−3)	moderately negative (−2)	somewhat negative (−1)	no impact (0)	slightly positive (+1)	moderately positive (+2)	extremely positive (+3)
1. Marriage									
2. Death of a close friend									
3. Ending of formal schooling									
4. Leaving home for the first time									

By asking subjects to indicate whether a specific event had a positive or negative impact on their lives, the Life Experiences Survey makes it possible to examine the effects of positive and negative life events separately. These two types of life events have different health consequences. (Based on Sarason et al., 1978.)

negative life events subjects had reported, the more likely they were to become ill. This result was independent of both perceived stress and negative affectivity. Thus, negative life events can have a distinct association with physical health that is not accounted for by negative affectivity. Similar conclusions have been reached in studies of psychological distress. Once negative affectivity has been taken into account, stressful life events are still associated with increased psychological distress, though the effect is small (Ormel & Wohlfarth, 1991).

Microstressors: The Hassles of Everyday Life

Research on stress and coping examines the enduring "microstressors" of ordinary life as well as the more abrupt shifts of life change. Strained relationships, deadlines, fighting traffic, running the rat race, and struggling to make ends meet are unfortunate but inevitable aspects of the daily routine. These kinds of everyday hassles can contribute to distress and illness (Kohn et al., 1991). Interpersonal conflicts appear to be the most upsetting of daily stressors, with a longer-lasting impact than most others (Bolger et al., 1989).

Some daily aggravations are architecturally induced. Take, for example, two common types of college dormitories: those with long corridors (as shown in Figure 14.2A) and those divided into suites (Figure 14.2B). When Andrew Baum

Figure 14.2 Stress in the Dorms. Research on stress in different types of dormitories indicated that corridor residence is more stressful than suite life. (Baum & Valins, 1977.)

A. Long-Corridor Residence

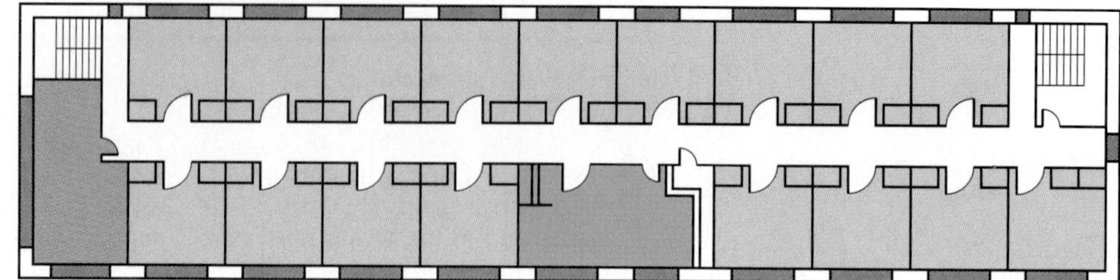

B. Suite Residence

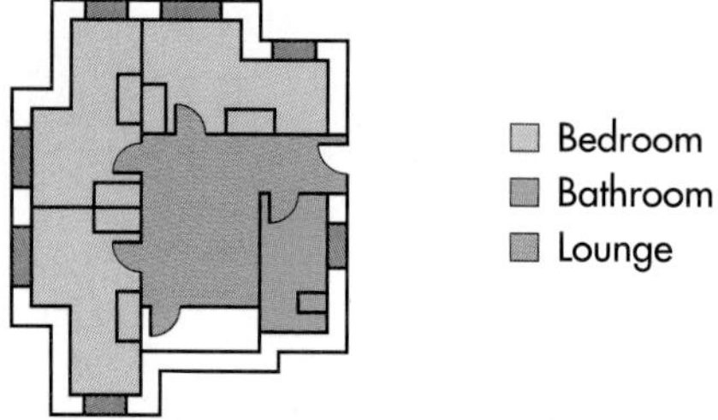

and Stuart Valins (1979) compared first-year college students living in these two types of dorms, they found that corridor residents experienced more stress than those in suites. But why? The answer lies in the way these spatial arrangements affect social control. Because corridor residents have to share more space with more people (such as in the bathroom and lounge areas), it is more difficult for them to avoid unwanted social contacts.

Research on prison crowding reveals a similar pattern. The number of inmates sharing a space has a greater effect on stress than does the amount of space available (Paulus, 1988). In college or in prison, unpredictable and uncontrollable social interaction is stressful. It may also be dangerous. Crowded prisons and massive dormitories are often plagued with vandalism and violence. At the University of Cincinnati, the problems in Sander Hall, a 26-story tower housing 1,300 students, proved insurmountable. On June 23, 1991, university administrators pulled the plug and blew it up!

Just as architectural arrangements organize the space we live in, so the roles we play impose a certain order on our daily lives. People can occupy a great many different roles—friend, lover, psychology major, tennis player, employee, party animal, family member, and so on—or just a few. Research on **self-complexity** indicates that individuals who view themselves as having many distinct roles or identities are less prone to psychological distress and stress-related illness than are those who have a less complex self-concept (Linville, 1987). Note, however, that the type of self-complexity may be crucial. Having many distinct *negative* identities is associated with greater depression (Woolfolk et al., 1995), while having many distinct *positive* identities is especially beneficial for individuals who have experienced traumatic events (Morgan & Janoff-Bulman, 1994).

self-complexity The number of distinct roles or identities people believe they have.

But what about external reality? Do those who actually enact multiple roles benefit from not having all their eggs in one basket, or do they suffer from overload? Concern about multiple roles has increased in the United States as large numbers of married women with children have entered the work force. Despite their employment obligations, however, these women take responsibility for

Greater positive self-complexity and involvement in multiple, satisfying social roles are both associated with increased well-being. Here, one individual is shown in her activities as an artist, a body-builder, and a mother.

much more of the housework and child care than their husbands do (Blair & Johnson, 1992; Peterson & Gerson, 1992). But not all partnerships are inequitable. For example, French-Canadian married couples are more likely to share household tasks than are English-Canadian couples (Brayfield, 1992), and gay and lesbian couples allocate housework more equally between partners than do heterosexual couples (Kurdek, 1993). Among employed wives, those whose husbands share less of the household labor are less satisfied with the support they receive, less satisfied with their marriage, and more depressed (Piña & Bengtson, 1993).

Nevertheless, having multiple roles is usually associated with increased well-being among women (Crosby & Jaskar, 1993). Employed women experience less psychological distress and better physical health than do unemployed women (Spitze, 1988; Verbrugge, 1987). For both men and women, however, the benefits of multiple roles depend on the quality of these roles. Among married women, employment is clearly beneficial only for those who have positive attitudes about their jobs (Repetti et al., 1989). Among married men, those who perceive their family relationships as rewarding suffer less distress from problems at work (Barnett et al., 1992). Based on their research on dual-earner couples, Rosalind Barnett and her colleagues (1993) see an emerging similarity in role patterns. For many men and women in our society today, their well-being depends on the quality of their experiences both at work and at home.

Major Crises: Catastrophe and War

As an alternative to examining the cumulative impact of multiple life events and daily hassles, some research focuses on a single crisis. Various major stressors have been studied, including divorce (Bloom et al., 1978), widowhood (Stroebe & Stroebe, 1983), the loss of a child (McIntosh et al., 1993), airplane crashes (Jacobs et al., 1990), adjusting to a new culture (Rogler et al., 1991; Williams & Berry, 1991), and wartime effects on civilians (Hobfoll et al., 1989). In this section, we concentrate on two major stressors that have received particular attention: environmental catastrophes and war.

Environmental disasters can be psychologically devastating. Anxiety, somatic complaints, alcohol consumption, and phobias increase in the wake of an environmental catastrophe (Rubonis & Bickman, 1991). The 1979 accident at the Three Mile Island nuclear plant illustrates the point. Near meltdown in the core of a nuclear reactor exposed residents of surrounding communities to radioactive gases and required the evacuation of over 100,000 people. Studies conducted after the accident revealed sharply increased stress among individuals living close to the plant, with mothers of young children suffering the highest levels of psychological distress (Hartsough & Savitsky, 1984). At least some residents still exhibited stress up to six years later, although stress reactions appear to have fully dissipated by the end of a decade (Baum & Fleming, 1993).

The Three Mile Island disaster was caused by human error. As frightening as such accidents are, naturally caused catastrophes can be even more upsetting (Rubonis & Bickman, 1991). Do you remember where you were on January 17, 1994? If you happened to be near Los Angeles, you'll probably never forget that day. Struck by an earthquake measuring 6.6 on the Richter scale, houses collapsed, highways buckled, water mains burst, and overpasses fell apart. Fifty-five people died. A few years earlier, the San Francisco Bay area had suffered a similar disaster. Fires raged out of control, thousands were left homeless, and the death toll reached sixty-two.

By coincidence, Susan Nolen-Hoeksema and Jannay Morrow (1991) had administered some trauma-relevant measures to a group of Stanford University students two weeks before the 1989 San Francisco earthquake. Follow-up assessments ten days after the quake and again six weeks later provided these investigators with that rarest of studies: a before-and-after examination of coping with a natural disaster. This research found that individuals who were more distressed before the quake and those who encountered more danger during the quake experienced greater psychological distress after the quake.

Of all the major stressors, war is one of the worst. Soldiers in combat believe they have to kill or be killed. They suffer terrible anxiety, see awful things, and

This photo shows some of the devastation produced by the 1994 earthquake near Los Angeles. Psychological adjustment in the aftermath of a natural disaster is influenced by people's personal characteristics before the disaster and their experiences during the disaster.

posttraumatic stress disorder The experience of enduring physical and psychological symptoms after an extremely stressful event.

sometimes commit horrible deeds. Given this level of stress, it's not surprising that when the war is over, some veterans suffer from **posttraumatic stress disorder (PTSD)**, enduring physical and psychological problems after an extremely stressful event. For example, a study of veterans who served overseas during Operation Desert Storm found that 16 to 19 percent of those surveyed reported PTSD symptoms (such as recurrent memories, nightmares, restricted emotions, sleep disturbances, and irritability) four to ten months after homecoming (Sutker et al., 1993).

For some individuals, PTSD can last much longer. According to research conducted by the Centers for Disease Control (1988), some 2 percent of the veterans of the Vietnam War still exhibited symptoms of posttraumatic stress disorder more than fifteen years after their military service was completed. Those with the most dangerous combat experiences were the most likely to develop the disorder (Goldberg et al., 1990). When a Vietnam vet, who in 1968 lost both legs and part of his hands to a booby trap in Danang Province, committed suicide in 1994, his widow suggested a fitting memorial: "To the list of names of victims of the Vietnam War, add the name of Lewis Puller. He suffered terrible wounds that never really healed."

As traumatic as wartime service can be, sometimes the wounds can heal. Among veterans of World War II and the Korean War, exposure to heavy combat was associated with more postwar stress, but also with becoming more resilient and less helpless over time (Elder & Clipp, 1989). No one knows exactly why some people recover from a crisis and others do not. Many researchers, however, believe that the appraisal process makes a crucial contribution to the outcome.

Lewis B. Puller Jr. was the son of the most decorated Marine in the history of the Corps, a Marine combat leader in Vietnam, a Pulitzer Prize winning author, and, according to his widow, a wartime fatality more than twenty-five years after his tour of duty was over.

APPRAISAL

Some 2,500 years ago, an anonymous author wrote an extraordinary poem about human suffering: the Book of Job. A pious and prosperous man as the poem begins, Job is soon beset by great calamities. He loses his property, his children, and his health. Job and his friends try to understand how these terrible things could happen. His friends argue that Job's plight must be a punishment sent by God and tell Job to repent. Because he believes that his sufferings far exceed any wrongdoing on his part, Job cannot accept this explanation. In despair, he doubts his capacity to withstand continued hardship and longs for death. But eventually Job finds strength and peace through trusting in God's will.

From the perspective of the model displayed in Figure 14.1, Job and his friends were engaged in the process of appraisal. They considered explanations for Job's suffering and formed expectations about his ability to cope with his situation. These same themes are found in research on stress and coping.

Explanations: Learned Helplessness and Depression

Depression is a psychological disorder characterized by negative moods (such as feelings of sadness or apathy), low self-esteem, pessimism, lack of initiative, and slowed thought processes. Other symptoms include disturbances in sleeping and eating patterns, and reduced sexual interest. Each year, around 3 percent of the U.S. population experiences a major depression (Coyne, 1994). Many more suffer from brief, relatively mild bouts with the "blues." Women are about twice as likely as men to suffer from depression (Nolen-Hoeksema & Girgus, 1994). Although there are numerous influences on depression (including social relations, physiological processes, and genetic inheritance), social psychologists have paid particular attention to the role of cognitive factors. Here, we examine a view of depression that highlights people's explanations for the bad things that happen to them.

learned helplessness The phenomenon in which experience with an uncontrollable event creates passive behavior toward a subsequent threat to well-being.

The original **learned helplessness** model of depression was based on observations of animals and humans exposed to uncontrollable, aversive stimulation. In one study, dogs that received a series of electric shocks over which they had no control later failed to escape from additional shocks by crossing a barrier into a shock-free compartment (Seligman & Maier, 1967). Those that had not received uncontrollable shocks quickly learned the escape routine. Similarly, human subjects exposed to inescapable bursts of noise failed to protect themselves in a later situation where the noise could be easily avoided (Hiroto, 1974).

According to Martin Seligman (1975), these findings demonstrated two important points. First, he proposed that organisms exposed to an uncontrollable event learn something—namely, that control is not possible. Faced with this knowledge, they stop trying to exert control, even in a different situation. Second, he noted that nondepressed human subjects exposed to uncontrollable events exhibit many of the characteristics of depressed individuals: feelings of discouragement, pessimism about solving problems, and lack of initiative. Thus, concluded Seligman, depression can be considered a form of learned helplessness.

Not everyone agreed with Seligman's reasoning and his theory soon became highly controversial (Buchwald et al., 1978; Wortman & Brehm, 1975). To address shortcomings in the original formulation, Lyn Abramson and her colleagues (1978) developed the *reformulated* model of learned helplessness. This model holds that perceiving a lack of control in one situation is *not* sufficient to produce helpless feelings and behaviors in a different situation. Instead, the person's attributions about what caused the initial lack of control must be considered. The reformulated model specifies three types of attributions for the cause of an uncontrollable event:

- *Stable versus unstable:* Is the cause seen as enduring (stable) or as temporary (unstable)?
- *Global versus specific:* Is the cause seen as extending across many events in the person's life (global) or as limited to a particular occasion (specific)?
- *Internal versus external:* Does the person attribute the cause to personal characteristics and behaviors (internal) or to environmental forces (external)?

According to the reformulated model, those individuals who make *stable* and *global* attributions for an uncontrollable event are more likely to expect future events to be uncontrollable. In turn, the expectation of a lack of control produces passive and helpless behavior in new situations. Those who make *internal* attributions are said to be more likely to develop low self-esteem. Taken together, these three attributions for an uncontrollable event elicit a depressive reaction (see Figure 14.3).

Attributions that are stable, global, and internal usually refer to enduring personal characteristics: For example, a student may blame a bad exam grade on a lack of intellectual ability. In this case, the person expects a relatively *fixed* aspect

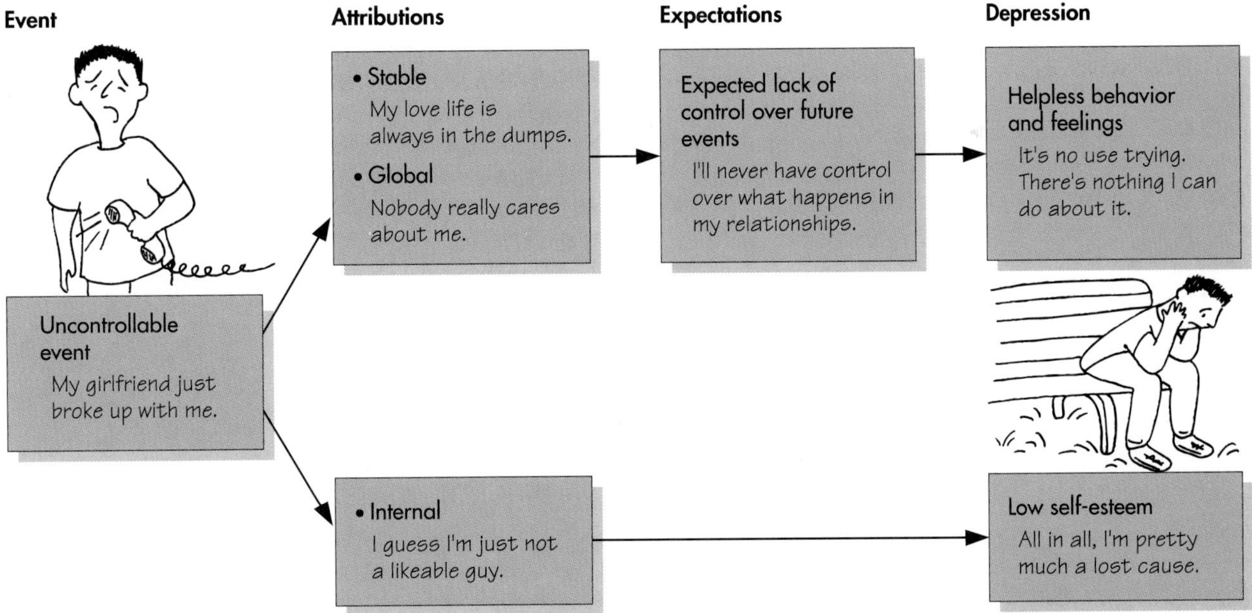

Figure 14.3 **The Reformulated Model of Learned Helplessness.** According to this model, stable and global attributions for an uncontrollable event create the expectation of a lack of control over future events. This expectation then produces depressed behavior and feelings. An internal attribution is said to lead to low self-esteem, which characterizes many depressed individuals.

of the *self* to produce poor outcomes on a *variety* of future intellectual tasks. Such an attributional "triple whammy" locks the person into the worst possible box: a bleak future caused by one's own unchangeable characteristics.

What would make someone close the attributional lock on such a depressing box? Sometimes the situation holds the key. When Vincent Foster, a close friend of President Bill Clinton, encountered harsh criticism about his performance as deputy White House counsel, he couldn't shake it off. Before coming to Washington, Foster had been a successful lawyer and, from all accounts, a happy, well-adjusted individual. But nothing in his past, it seems, had prepared him for the unrelenting pressures and personal attacks visited upon those at the center of political power. He should have walked away. Instead, he took it all to heart and took his own life.

Explanations are not always situationally induced. Sometimes they are a matter of personal style. Across a variety of situations, some people habitually use stable, global, and internal attributions to explain unpleasant outcomes. The reformulated model of learned helplessness maintains that individuals who have this **depressive explanatory style** are at greater risk for depression. People who tend to use unstable, specific, and external attributions to discount success and other positive life events may also be at greater risk. Table 14.2 displays an example from the Attributional Style Questionnaire, a frequently used measure of explanatory style.

depressive explanatory style A habitual tendency to attribute negative events to causes that are stable, global, and internal.

Three approaches have been taken to assessing the influence of the depressive explanatory style. First, style and depression can be measured at the same time. In their review of more than a hundred studies, Paul Sweeney and his colleagues (1986) found a clear association between the depressive explanatory style and being depressed. But concurrent correlations can be produced by many different causes. To explore the possibility of a specific causal relationship, prospective studies investigate the relationship between initial style and later adjustment. In one such study, the responses made by ninety-nine male college graduates in 1946 to an open-ended question about their wartime experiences were scored for depressive explanatory style (Peterson et al., 1988). When their physical health status was assessed at age forty-five and older, those men who had displayed a depressive explanatory style in their youth tended to have more health problems than did those whose youthful explanatory style was more optimistic.

But even prospective studies do not represent the best test of whether depressive explanatory style could cause depression. According to the reformulated model, depressive explanatory style is a vulnerability factor that has negative consequences *only* when the individual experiences stress. Thus, the best test of the model requires an initial measure of depressive explanatory style followed by the actual occurrence of a stressful event. The results of research that meets this best-test standard are mixed. In some studies, individuals with a pre-existing depressive explanatory style were more likely to become depressed after a stressful event (Metalsky et al., 1987; Riskind et al., 1987), but in others, explanatory style was not predictive (Follette & Jacobson, 1987; Ramírez et al., 1992).

Although the reformulated model of learned helplessness has fared better than its predecessor, it has not escaped criticism. Some researchers have proposed that the types of attributions in the model should be expanded (Anderson & Riger, 1991). Others have called for greater specificity in determining what kinds of stressful events will evoke the depressive explanatory style (Brewer, 1993). Perhaps most important, the causal impact of attributions is disputed. As we have seen, the results of best-test studies are inconsistent. And some research on trau-

Table 14.2 The Attributional Style Questionnaire: An Example

Try to vividly imagine yourself in the situation that follows. If such a situation happened to you, what would you feel had caused it? Events may have many causes, but we want you to pick only one—the *major* cause if this event happened to *you*. Please write this cause in the blank provided. Next we ask you some questions about this cause. Circle one number after each question.

Situation: You meet a friend who acts in a hostile manner toward you.

1. Write down the *one* major cause ______________________________
2. Is this cause due to something about you or to something about other people or circumstances?

Totally due to other people or circumstances	1 2 3 4 5 6 7	Totally due to me

3. In the future, will this cause again be present?

Will never again be present	1 2 3 4 5 6 7	Will always be present

4. Is the cause something that influences just this situation, or does it also influence other areas of your life?

Influences just this particular situation	1 2 3 4 5 6 7	Influences all situations in my life

The Attributional Style Questionnaire measures attributions about imagined events—both positive and negative. In this example, you are asked to imagine a specific negative event and then indicate your attributions for its cause. High ratings on questions 2 through 4 indicate internal, stable, and global attributions. (Based on Peterson & Seligman, 1987.)

matic events, such as the loss of a child from sudden infant death syndrome, indicates that attributions are more likely to be a symptom of distress rather than a cause (Downey et al., 1990). This uncertainty about causation is not surprising, nor is it unusual. Like many variables of interest to health researchers, the depressive explanatory style is a pre-existing personal characteristic that cannot be experimentally manipulated. Thus, research on it is necessarily correlational and cannot conclusively determine causal effects.

Expectations: Agency and Outcome

Attributions for why a distressing event has occurred were never the only element considered by theories within the learned helplessness tradition. Instead, as you can see in Figure 14.3, expectations about lack of control over future events were said to have the most direct influence on helpless behavior. Hopelessness theory, the most recent revision of learned helplessness, adds another expectation to the mix: that these future events will be unpleasant (Abramson et al., 1989). To be hopeless is to expect bad things that cannot be changed for the better.

A sense of hopelessness does appear to serve as a major link between negative life events and depression (Metalsky & Joiner, 1992; Whisman & Kwon, 1993).

Moreover, there is a large body of research on each of the two types of expectations involved: agency expectations for personal control over future events and outcome expectations about the quality of these events. Let's examine how these future forecasts relate to people's health.

Agency Expectations: Perceived Control, Hardiness, and Self-Efficacy Expecting to have control over what happens to you is usually associated with more effective coping in stressful situations. For instance, perceived control over physically stressful stimulation, such as unpleasant noise, reduces the negative aftereffects produced by such stressors (Glass & Singer, 1972). Perceptions of control may be especially meaningful for people whose lives are regulated to a large extent by others. Elderly residents of nursing homes who were given increased control over daily events became happier and more active (Langer & Rodin, 1976; Schulz, 1976). Follow-up studies of these senior citizens suggested that continuing expectations of control had positive effects on health and longevity, while abrupt loss of perceived control was damaging (Rodin & Langer, 1977; Schulz & Hanusa, 1978).

Health-related perceptions of control have also been studied as an individual difference (Lefcourt & Davidson-Katz, 1991). Among cancer patients, those with strong beliefs in their control over the course of their illness (G. Marks et al., 1986; Taylor et al., 1984) or over their emotions and physical symptoms (Thompson et al., 1993) were better adjusted than those with weaker control beliefs. Similarly, an increased sense of personal control over health-related events is associated with better psychological adjustment among cardiac (Helgeson, 1992) and AIDS patients (Reed et al., 1993).

Another individual difference in agency expectations is called "hardiness." It combines three components:

- *Control:* The belief that one's outcomes are controlled by one's own actions
- *Challenge:* The perception of change as a normal part of life
- *Commitment:* Having a sense of meaning and mastery in one's life

Management personnel in a large company who obtained high scores on hardiness reported less serious illnesses than did those who obtained low scores (Kobasa et al., 1982). However, the influence of hardiness on *actual* health, as opposed to self-reports, is not clear (Allred & Smith, 1989; Wiebe & Williams, 1992). It is also not clear whether the combination really works. Control and commitment appear to have much stronger associations with psychological health than does the challenge component (Florian et al., 1995).

self-efficacy A person's belief that he or she is capable of the specific behavior required to produce a desired outcome in a given situation.

Perceived control refers to expectations that we can control what happens to us. But, as Albert Bandura (1977a) has emphasized, people can exert control only by doing something. Bandura's concept of **self-efficacy** refers to a situation-specific, positive expectation that what needs to be done can be done. Consider, for example, two individuals with differing skills: one excels at athletics; the other is a superb musician. Put them both on a tennis court, and the athlete will have a greater sense of self-efficacy about performing well than will the musician. Put them both in a band, however, and the musician will have more self-efficacy. High levels of self-efficacy about managing pain are associated with greater pain tolerance (O'Leary, 1985). A greater sense of self-efficacy about coping with abortion-related events is associated with better post-abortion adjustment (Cozzarelli, 1993).

Outcome Expectations: Optimism Skipping over the issues of control and efficacy, outcome expectations go right to the bottom line. What's going to happen? A good time or a bad one? To be optimistic is to have positive outcome expectations. Optimism is associated with better adjustment among arthritis (Long & Sangster, 1993) and breast-cancer patients (Carver et al., 1993), as well as among individuals recovering from coronary by-pass surgery (Scheier et al., 1989).

Pollyanna's Health

Pollyanna is the name of the upbeat heroine created by American writer Eleanor Porter. Although Pollyanna used to get bad press for her boundless belief that even the most ominous cloud has a bright and shining silver lining, the research reviewed in this section indicates that Pollyanna should be an outstandingly healthy person. As we've seen, *not* having a depressive explanatory style, expecting control over outcomes, and anticipating desirable outcomes are associated with a healthy adjustment.

That's not all. As described in Chapter 2 on the Social Self, people seem to have a million ways to help them feel good about themselves. They take credit for success and distance themselves from failure, find excuses for shortcomings, discover favorable comparisons with others, and have unrealistic beliefs about their ability to control events and secure desirable outcomes. These self-enhancing inclinations, called "positive illusions," occur more frequently among well-adjusted individuals (Taylor & Brown, 1988). And there's more. Negative self-evaluations can inhibit immune responses (Strauman et al., 1993), whereas self-efficacy is associated with enhanced functioning of the immune system (Wiedenfeld et al., 1990). Enhanced immunological response plays a crucial role in resistance to tumors and infection. Thus, the message seems clear: Looking at life through rose-colored glasses is good for you.

But there are some serious problems with assuming that the positive thinking of a Pollyanna leads straight to good health. First, we need to be very careful about that word *leads*. As noted earlier, the causal relationship between attributions and health continues to be debated. Similar controversy exists about whether unrealistically positive beliefs about the self, one's control over events, and the likelihood of good outcomes are beneficial for mental health (Colvin & Block, 1994; Taylor & Brown, 1994).

As for immune functioning, the effects of self-relevant and stress-related factors are typically small and within the normal range (Andersen et al., 1994). The health implications of such normal variations are not well understood. In any event, no credible scientist believes that explanations and expectations are the *sole* determinants of a person's health status. Positive thinking cannot guarantee good health, and it would be a cruel mistake to blame victims of illness for a "bad attitude" (Krantz & Hedges, 1987).

Second, there are concerns about exactly what is assessed by measures of positive thinking. Earlier in this chapter, we described negative affectivity, the pervasive tendency to experience a wide range of negative emotions. Another broad personality dimension is traditionally called extraversion or, more recently, **positive affectivity**—the pervasive tendency to experience a variety of positive emotions and engage in a range of positive behaviors (Watson et al., 1992). The issue, much debated and still unresolved, is whether these two dimensions can subsume all the various measures of positive thinking described in this chapter.

positive affectivity The pervasive tendency to experience a variety of positive emotions and engage in a range of positive behaviors.

Consider, for example, the Life Orientation Test (LOT), a widely used measure of optimism (Scheier & Carver, 1987). Some researchers have claimed that the LOT actually measures the *absence* of negative affectivity (T. W. Smith et al., 1989). Others argue that at least some of the associations between the LOT and health-relevant factors are independent of negative affectivity (Scheier et al., 1994). And still others assert that the LOT measures both optimism and pessimism, which may reflect the presence of both positive and negative affectivity (Marshall et al., 1992). Trying to sort through all of this, researchers have begun to systematically assess the relationship between specific health-related personality variables such as optimism and more general dimensions of personality (Marshall et al., 1994). On the road from our explanations and expectations to health, are there a large number of small paths or only a few broad highways? We don't know yet, but the attempt to find out is moving into high gear.

Finally, we need to be aware of the drawbacks to positive illusions, especially extremely unrealistic ones. For example, excessively positive self-evaluations appear to be associated with negative interpersonal consequences (Colvin et al., 1995). Illusions of control can also be detrimental, as indicated by a study examining control beliefs and depression in patients suffering from a loss of kidney function (Christensen et al., 1991). Here, the perception of greater health controllability was associated with *less* depression among those who had not had a kidney transplant, but with *more* depression for those whose transplant had failed. Faced with some setbacks, a sense of control can help us bounce back (Helgeson, 1992). But persistent, unrealistic beliefs in control can do more harm than good when the actual loss of control is severe and unmistakable.

Which brings us back to Job. At the end of the Biblical account, Job recovers his health, property, and family prosperity. He does not, however, regain the sense of personal control and optimism he enjoyed prior to being struck by calamity. Instead, Job's hard-won serenity is based on his belief that life has meaning and purpose. Such beliefs may be particularly important for those confronted with extremely stressful experiences, such as the loss of a child (McIntosh et al., 1993). Pollyanna has her charm, but Job is a hero of the human condition.

At a funeral, survivors gather to pay their respects to the individual who has died, to console one another, and to find meaning in life despite a tragic loss.

COPING

When people cope, they attempt to reduce the stress produced by a threat that strains or exceeds their resources. Like Job, many individuals cope with misfortune by actively seeking meaning in their lives (Terry, 1994). There are, however, many other ways to cope, and researchers often examine general categories of coping that include many specific responses. Two types of coping are widely recognized (Folkman & Lazarus, 1985). **Problem-focused coping** consists of cognitive and behavioral efforts to alter a stressful situation. **Emotion-focused coping** consists of cognitive and behavioral efforts to reduce the distress produced by a stressful situation. Some investigators also emphasize a third type of coping: seeking social support (Ptacek et al., 1994). This section compares problem-focused and emotion-focused coping strategies, and then considers how the support we receive from other people can affect our health.

problem-focused coping Cognitive and behavioral efforts to alter a stressful situation.

emotion-focused coping Cognitive and behavioral efforts to reduce the distress produced by a stressful situation.

Problem-Focused Coping

Problem-focused coping seems a prime candidate for a starring role in the war against stress. Surely those active, direct, assertive efforts are associated with better health. Well, sometimes yes (Aspinwall & Taylor, 1992). But it has often turned out to be surprisingly difficult to demonstrate the benefits of this kind of coping (Carver & Scheier, 1994; Zeidner & Hammer, 1992). There are, no doubt, many reasons why problem-focused coping might not have positive consequences in a specific situation. Research on the effects of exerting control provides some insight into a more general explanation. Perhaps there can be too much of even a good thing.

Control: The Need for Flexibility We have seen that *beliefs* in personal control have a positive association with health. But what about the *actual use* of control? Is it always beneficial to confront a stressor head-on and try to control it? The answer is no. There are costs to imposing control, and at times these costs exceed the rewards (Burger, 1989). To exert control, an individual must remain vigilant, alert, and actively engaged. Such efforts are physiologically taxing (Light & Obrist, 1980). And with control comes responsibility. If people aren't sure that their efforts at control will be fully successful, the responsibility of having control can be a source of emotional turmoil (Burger et al., 1983; Rodin et al., 1980). The first exam, a new job, unfamiliar people to get to know—all of these circumstances can be highly stressful as individuals attempt to exert control without being confident of success.

Because of the costs of effort and responsibility, the benefits of exercising control will vary depending on the demands of the stressful situation and the resources of the individual (Matthews et al., 1980; Miller, 1981). Beneficial use of control involves selectivity and efficiency: selecting what can, in fact, be controlled and exercising only that level of control necessary for success (Aldwin & Revenson, 1987). Although indiscriminate efforts to maintain or regain control can create a momentarily comforting illusion of control, they may reduce actual control over relevant events and increase stress (Friedland et al., 1992). There are times to go it alone and times to ask for help; times to "bear down" and times to "mellow out." The trick is knowing when to do which.

Blame: Where to Place It? When we hear the word *control,* we usually think of active efforts to manage something: win that argument, stop that criticism, change those job requirements. But control comes in many guises. Knowledge, for instance, is a form of control. Knowing why something happened increases the likelihood of making sure it goes your way—if not now, then the next time. When we blame others for our own negative outcomes, we pit this potential gain in future control (maybe we can manage to avoid the harmful individual from here on out) against the immediate cost of admitting that, right now, we've lost control to the other person. In this contest, the need for current control usually comes out ahead: Across a variety of major life events, blaming others is associated with *poor* adjustment (Tennen & Affleck, 1990). There are, however, some exceptions. Blaming others for a technological disaster (for example, chemical contamination of one's neighborhood) appears beneficial for the victims (Solomon et al., 1989) as does blaming the abusing spouse for marital violence (Andrews, 1992). In these situations, holding others responsible for inflicting harm encourages behavioral responses (such as seeking financial compensation or police protection) that meet the victim's needs.

But what about self-blame? According to Ronnie Janoff-Bulman (1979), it's important to distinguish between blaming your behavior and blaming your enduring personal characteristics. Because behavior can be changed, behavioral self-blame is an *unstable,* internal attribution that opens the door to future control. By modifying our behavior, we might be able to reduce current stresses or avoid future ones. In contrast, enduring personal characteristics are hard to change. Similar to the depressive explanatory style described earlier in this chapter, characterological self-blame is a *stable,* internal attribution that puts us at the mercy of what we regard as undesirable aspects of the self. Thus, behavioral self-blame should be associated with good adjustment and characterological self-blame with poor adjustment.

The most extensive test of these predictions has come in a set of studies examining women's adjustment after having been raped. As would be expected, characterological self-blame is sometimes a stronger predictor of psychological distress than is behavioral self-blame (Hill & Zautra, 1989). But both types of self-blame are usually associated with distress (Frazier & Schauben, 1994; Meyer & Taylor, 1986). Contrary to the theoretical prediction, rape victims who blame their behavior for their victimization do *not* cope better than those who blame their character. However, behavioral self-blame may have some advantages for coping with less traumatic but still unpleasant experiences (Anderson et al., 1994).

Heartaches: Type A and Hostility We turn now to a type of person for whom control seems to be a way of life. In the 1950s, two cardiologists, Meyer Friedman and Ray Rosenman, began studying the relationship between cholesterol level and coronary heart disease (CHD). CHD was then, as it is now, the leading cause of death in the United States. Based on their research, Friedman and Rosenman developed the concept of the **Type A behavior pattern** (Friedman & Rosenman, 1959).

Type A behavior pattern A pattern of behavior characterized by extremes of competitive striving for achievement, a sense of time urgency, hostility, and aggression.

Individuals exhibiting this behavior pattern are characterized by extremes of competitive striving for achievement, a sense of time urgency, hostility, and aggression. Friedman and Rosenman classified subjects as Type A by means of a *structured interview* in which information is gathered about subjects' past experiences, and observations are made of nonverbal behaviors such as rapidity and explosiveness of speech, expressive gestures, and general restlessness. Among the more than three thousand men participating in the Western Collaborative Group Study, those initially classified as Type A later developed CHD at twice the rate of those not so classified (Rosenman et al., 1975).

By the early 1980s, the influence of Type A on CHD was widely accepted. A panel of distinguished scientists convened by the National Heart, Lung and

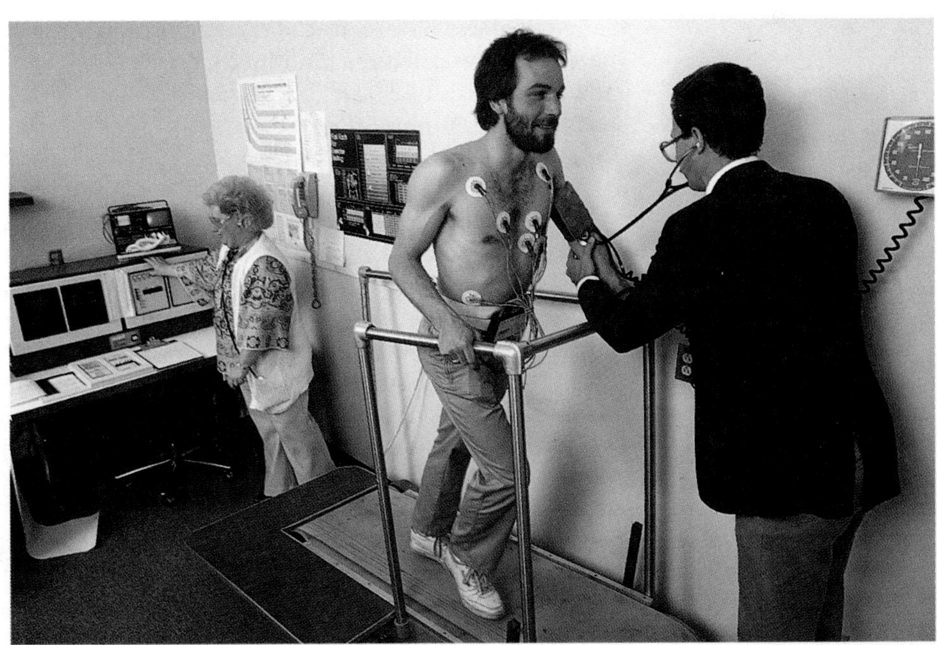

The treadmill test is a standard part of the diagnostic procedures used to examine people for the presence of coronary heart disease (CHD).

Blood Institute concluded that the Type A pattern was a risk factor for CHD, comparable to more traditional risks such as high blood pressure, smoking, high blood cholesterol, and obesity (Review Panel, 1981). But science, like time, moves on. Subsequent studies of the association between Type A and CHD obtained much weaker results than had the earlier ones (Matthews & Haynes, 1986). Moreover, this association varies depending on the way in which Type A is measured and the kind of population being studied (Matthews, 1988; Miller et al., 1991). Certainty about the bad effects of "hurry sickness" and "workaholism" began to crumble.

In its place, a new line of inquiry sprang up. Perhaps the problem with Type A as a predictor of CHD is that the behavior pattern is too broad, too all-encompassing. If so, could there be a specific component that is particularly damaging to health? Currently, hostility is the leading suspect for the dubious distinction of being the toxic element contained in the Type A behavior pattern (Siegman & Smith, 1994). Hostility can be assessed through the Type A structured interview (Dembroski & Costa, 1987), but most investigators rely on the self-report hostility scale known as Ho (Cook & Medley, 1954).

The story of Ho is a good example of some of the problems encountered by the long-term studies necessary to track people's health status. Ho began as a set of 250 items that discriminated between two groups of teachers who had previously been classified as having either good or bad rapport with their students. This initial set was then whittled down to the 50 items judged on content to best reflect hostility. As Richard Contrada and Lee Jussim (1992) indicate, Ho is not a good scale; exactly which and how many aspects of personality it measures cannot be determined. But Ho was available when decades ago subjects were enrolled in long-term research on health. The results of six such longitudinal studies have now been published. In three of them, early Ho predicted later CHD, all-cause mortality, or both (Smith, 1992).

Since Ho can sometimes predict health outcomes up to twenty-eight years after it was measured, researchers have tried to cope as best they can with its poor construction. Based on its correlations with other self-report measures, Ho seems to assess hostile attitudes, anger, suspiciousness, resentment, mistrust, and negative views of others (Smith & Christensen, 1992b). How might such feelings and beliefs affect CHD? The answer is similar to that proposed for the health effects of Type A: physiological reactivity (for example, increased heart rate and elevated blood pressure), which acts as a strain on the heart.

But reactivity is not identical for Type A's and hostile individuals. Type A is associated with increased reactivity across a variety of stressful or challenging situations (Lyness, 1993). Hostility, as measured by the Ho scale, is associated with increased reactivity *only* in stressful social situations. As Timothy Smith (1992) has suggested, hostile individuals may not only react more strongly to unpleasant interactions with others, they may also create more such interactions through their own angry, suspicious behavior. Physiological reactivity to interpersonal stress is viewed as a major contributor to hypertension and CHD (Ewart & Kolodner, 1994; Lassner et al., 1994), although we still have a great deal to learn about the complex relationships among stress, reactivity, and disease (Blascovich & Katkin, 1993; Tomaka et al., 1993).

The downsizing of Type A to hostility has been countered by an upsizing to more general dimensions of personality such as an agreeable-antagonistic continuum (Costa et al., 1989) and a "maladaptive personality" (Friedman & Booth-Kewley, 1987). Moreover, physiological reactivity is not the only possible mediator between personality and health. Perhaps, for instance, hostile individuals are more likely to live dangerously and to engage in poor health habits such as less exercise and more alcohol consumption (Leiker & Hailey, 1988). Whatever the outcome of this continuing debate, it serves to warn us against oversimplified notions about psychology and health. Enlarging our understanding of the connection between mind and body requires patient, careful research by investigators willing to re-examine their assumptions. It's not a job for the faint-hearted!

Emotion-Focused Coping

When people rely on emotion-focused coping in response to a stressful situation, they seek to manage their emotions rather than modify the threat. Emotion-focused coping comes in two kinds: approach versus avoidance. This section examines the health effects of each of these strategies. Then we consider the impact of self-focus on both types of emotion-focused coping.

Approach: When Expression Helps According to James Pennebaker (1990), it's no accident that religious rituals, psychotherapy, consciousness-raising sessions, and self-help groups place a premium on "opening up" through self-disclosure and spontaneous emotional expression. Confession, he says, is good for the body as well as the soul. But why? Pennebaker's **theory of inhibition and confrontation** offers two reasons. First, *not* confronting one's feelings and beliefs about a distressing event requires active inhibition, which is physiologically stressful. Second, the failure to translate the psychological consequences of a trauma into language makes it more difficult to understand the event and cope with it.

theory of inhibition and confrontation The theory that inhibiting one's reactions to a traumatic event is damaging to physical health, whereas expressing one's reactions is beneficial.

Confrontation reverses these harmful effects: Physiological stress is reduced and coping is facilitated. Although people often confront their feelings by talking to others, there are other possible modes of expression. In Pennebaker's own research, for instance, subjects talk into a tape recorder or write down their thoughts and feelings. Those who talk or write about upsetting events usually show improvement on various indicators of physical health. The benefits of confrontation may be especially strong when extremely traumatic events are being described (Greenberg & Stone, 1992) and when women rather than men are disclosing (Stanton et al., 1994).

As Pennebaker and his colleagues (1990) have discovered, however, confrontation is not without its drawbacks. Compared with first-semester college students who provided a written description of their day's activities, those who wrote down their "very deepest thoughts and feelings about coming to college" for twenty minutes on each of three consecutive days were less likely in subsequent months to go to the student health center for treatment of an illness. But those who confronted their thoughts and emotions about coming to college were also more homesick and more worried about college at the end of the semester. Under some circumstances at least, it appears that there is a psychological cost for the physical-health benefits of confronting personal conflicts and fears.

Avoidance: Can It Help? But what about avoiding and denying your feelings when you're upset? Is this, as Pennebaker contends, harmful to your health? Sometimes yes. Active suppression of physical pain can prolong its intensity (Cioffi & Holloway, 1993). Husbands and wives who more often resort to escape-avoidance coping in response to a stressful event report more psychological distress than do those who less often employ this type of coping (Giunta & Compas, 1993). Chronic long-term avoidance and denial may prevent a person from ever coming to terms with a stressful experience (Suls & Fletcher, 1985).

But denial and avoidance can sometimes be beneficial (Ward et al., 1988). A severe trauma with long-lasting consequences—such as the death of a loved one, a life-threatening illness, job loss, or divorce—calls into question basic assumptions about personal invulnerability, the meaningfulness of life, and self-worth (Janoff-Bulman & Timko, 1987). Individuals faced with such serious threats to their understanding of themselves and the world in which they live need psychological breathing space, time to incorporate the trauma without demolishing their psychological integrity. If unable to avoid or deny these threats early in the coping process, they may be overwhelmed.

Distraction, another form of avoidance coping, can also be beneficial in some circumstances. Consider what happens when terrorists or criminals take innocent victims hostage for political reasons or financial ransom. Police surround the airplane or building; negotiations begin. We all hold our breath, concerned about getting the hostages out alive and worried about their condition. Are certain ways of coping with this frightening situation particularly effective? To help answer this question, fifty-seven airline employees voluntarily participated in a training exercise conducted by the Special Operations and Research Staff from the FBI Academy (Strentz & Auerbach, 1988; see also Auerbach et al., 1994). Some of the volunteers were trained in problem-focused coping techniques that included helping each other, interacting with their captors, and gathering intelligence. Other volunteers were trained in emotion-focused coping techniques designed to decrease anxiety: distraction, deep breathing, and muscle relaxation. Volunteers in a control condition did not receive instruction in either type of coping.

After the training session, the volunteers were "abducted" by FBI agents acting as terrorists. Automatic weapons were fired (with blanks), and bloody injuries were simulated. The volunteers were "held captive" in one room and isolated by pillow cases placed over their heads. A few cooperative "hostages"

In a daring rescue, French commandos stormed an Air France jetliner, killed the four Algerian terrorists who had hijacked the plane and murdered two passengers, and freed 173 passengers and crew. Simulation research conducted by the FBI examined what techniques would help people cope effectively when they were held hostage.

were released. Four days later, other FBI agents "stormed" the building and "rescued" the hostages. The exercise was conducted in a very realistic manner, and the volunteers reported that it had been exceedingly stressful. Volunteers' self-reports as well as observations of their behavior revealed that subjects who had been instructed in anxiety-management techniques coped better than those given training in problem solving or no training at all. In this kind of situation where the individual had very little control over events, distraction and other emotion-focused techniques were more effective in reducing psychological distress than were problem-focused efforts to exert control. As we will see in the next section, however, the health consequences of distraction depend on the form it takes.

Self-Focus: Getting Trapped Versus Getting Out Self-focus might be called the Dennis Hopper of emotion-focused coping. Just as Hopper seems to show up in countless movies as the evil villain, so self-focus intensifies some of the most undesirable consequences of emotion-focused coping. Here's the script.

As described in Chapter 2, focusing on the self can be induced by various kinds of external situations such as mirrors, cameras, and audiences. Mood, too, can induce it. Research by Peter Salovey (1992) indicates that, compared with a neutral mood state, both positive and negative moods increase awareness of the self. Thus, when a stressful event occurs, the negative feelings that arise magnify self-focus. What happens next depends on a person's view of self. Individuals with a negative self-concept experience more negative moods when self-focused than do those with a positive self-concept (Sedikides, 1992). The end result is a self-perpetuating feedback loop: Negative mood increases self-focus, which among those with a negative self-concept increases negative mood even further (see Figure 14.4). This vicious circle forms the basis for a **self-focus model of depression** (Pyszczynski & Greenberg, 1992). Round and round it goes, digging the

self-focus model of depression The hypothesis that depressive mood and negative self-evaluations are intensified and maintained by a focus on the self.

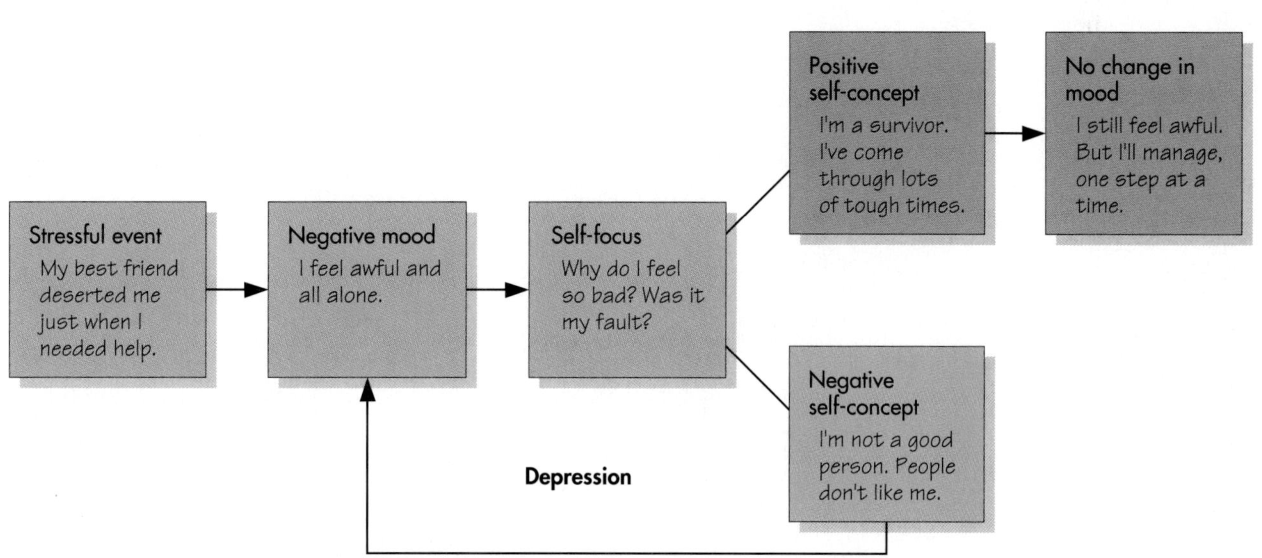

Figure 14.4 **Self-Focus and Depression.** Stressful events produce negative feelings, which intensify self-focus. However, self-focus increases negative mood only among people with a negative self-concept. As you can see, the combination of a negative mood, self-focus, and a negative self-concept creates a self-perpetuating vicious circle of increasing depression.

pit of depression deeper and deeper. In this case, coping with stress by focusing on your feelings only makes things worse.

Caught in such a trap, why don't people break out? One reason may be that depressed, self-focused individuals don't feel capable of engaging in distracting activities (Lyubomirsky & Nolen-Hoeksema, 1993). Unfortunately, even those who do escape often jump from the frying pan straight into the fire. Substance abuse of all kinds (alcohol, drugs, cigarettes, and overeating), promiscuous sexual behavior, chronic aggressive behavior, self-mutilation, and suicide may all be increased by people's attempts to avoid an uncomfortable state of self-awareness (Baumeister, 1990; Baumeister & Scher, 1988). These kinds of distraction have nothing to recommend them.

As it turns out, women and men differ in their likelihood of getting trapped in a self-focused approach to negative emotions versus trying to escape self-focus through self-destructive behaviors (Nolen-Hoeksema, 1993). Across a variety of ethnic backgrounds, women are more likely to experience depression and men are more likely to engage in antisocial behavior and substance abuse (Dohrenwend et al., 1992). Women brood; men act out. Both suffer.

Fortunately, there are some healthier alternatives. First, there is an important difference between passive and active approaches to emotions. Passive brooding about one's depressed condition, called a ruminative response style, maintains

Healthy distractions, like exercise, are a good way to break out of the trap of self-focused depression. Unhealthy distractions, like an alcohol binge, reduce self-focus at a self-destructive cost.

depression among both men and women (Katz & Bertelson, 1993; Nolen-Hoeksema et al., 1994). In contrast, an active effort to understand and express one's feelings ("take a real look at my feelings," "let my emotions go," "take time to express my emotions") is associated with reduced depression, but only for women (Stanton et al., 1994). Among men, adopting an active approach to emotional expression is associated with increased depression over time. It appears that the kind of active emotional confrontation recommended by Pennebaker may have greater psychological costs for men than for women.

Both men and women, however, can profit from constructive distraction. There are many healthy kinds of distraction: exercise, gardening, reading, helping others. Whatever the specific activity, it should be difficult, demanding, and fully engaging. Research by Ralph Erber and Abraham Tesser (1992) found that subjects in a negative mood felt better after performing a difficult task than did those who performed a simple task or no task at all. Difficult tasks, it appears, can "absorb" a bad mood. But this paper-towel effect is not limited to negative emotions; a good mood is also reduced by an absorbing task. The prescription is obvious. In a bad mood, throw yourself into (a healthy) something; in a good mood, stay focused.

Social Support: When Others Care

If the world is crashing down around you, what do you do? Do you try to stop it? Do you try to manage your emotions? Or do you try to get some help from others? So far, we have described the advantages and disadvantages of problem-focused and emotion-focused ways of coping. Now we consider the role of social support.

Models of Social Support In Chapter 7 on Helping Others, we examined various influences on people's willingness to provide help as well as recipients' reactions to the help they obtain. Research on social support examines how assistance from others is related to physical and mental health. Several different models of social support have been proposed.

Early studies often defined social support in terms of a person's *number of social contacts*. For example, one study of over six thousand residents of Alameda County, California, used a measure of social support that combined (1) marital status, (2) contact with close friends and relatives, (3) church membership, and (4) formal and informal group associations (Berkman & Syme, 1979). During a nine-year follow-up of mortality rates, it was found that those with more extensive social contacts lived longer. In general, social ties are a good predictor of better health and longer life (House et al., 1988), especially for men (Pilisuk et al., 1993; Rogers, 1995).

Despite its predictive utility, the social contact model has some crucial flaws. One of these flaws is the failure to distinguish between the positive effects of the presence of social support and the negative effects of its absence. For example, married individuals have better health than the unmarried. Why? Is marriage a benefit? Or is being unmarried associated with greater health risks? A comprehensive review of the relevant research concluded that unmarried costs—such as social isolation and single parenthood—have more impact than marital rewards (Burman & Margolin, 1992).

In addition, the social contact model ignores the fact that all relationships have costs. Even very good relationships can sometimes be a source of stress

(Coyne & Smith, 1991). After the Three Mile Island nuclear accident, men who lived nearby showed fewer indications of stress if they had good relationships with their wives (Solomon et al., 1987). However, women who had good marital relationships were *more* likely to experience stress. Because of their traditional responsibilities for taking care of others, women incur higher "costs of caring" than do men (Kessler et al., 1985). Indeed, according to Vicki Helgeson (1994), excessive attention to either one's own well-being or that of others increases health risks. A more balanced perspective is healthier.

The disadvantages of social contacts are even more apparent in stressful relationships: Those who have more of them are more distressed (Rook, 1984). Most relationships, however, are neither all-good nor all-bad, but have both good aspects and bad ones. Like positive and negative emotions, supportive and stressful interactions are distinct, relatively independent factors (Lakey et al., 1994). And, at least under some circumstances, the negative effects of negative interactions are greater than the positive effects of social support (Helgeson, 1993).

Another reason why a simple count of social contacts is not an adequate model of social support is that too many such contacts can actually reduce social support. Consider the plight of the urban poor in India, packed into overcrowded residences (up to eleven people per room) that are often without running water and indoor toilets. Like college students and prisoners who lack control over their social contacts, impoverished Indians living in overcrowded homes are more stressed than those living in less crowded circumstances. They also have *less* social support (Evans et al., 1989). But how could more crowding produce less social support? The key, it seems, is social withdrawal (Evans & Lepore, 1993). Faced with a lack of control over social contacts, people withdraw from social interactions, thereby losing social support and, over time, experiencing increased psychological distress.

A street scene in India illustrates the density of its population in some urban areas. Overcrowding is associated with *less* social support. Faced with a lack of control over social contracts in overcrowded situations, individuals withdraw from social interactions, lose social support, and experience greater psychological distress.

A second model of social support focuses on the *number of helpers* available to a person in need. This perspective defines social support in terms of the number of people from whom an individual has received support in the recent past (Barrera & Ainlay, 1983). Individuals with a greater number of providers should have better health. It seems reasonable. But, in fact, research has typically found that those with more providers experience *worse* health (Cohen & Hoberman, 1983). Such findings illustrate the interactive nature of social support. It isn't some inert substance we carry in our pocket to ensure protection against adversity. To obtain support from others, people must seek it out. Since they are more likely to seek social support when they need it, those who have more need usually have more supporters (Conn & Peterson, 1989).

A third model of social support emphasizes the quality of a person's relationships rather than their quantity. The *intimacy model* predicts that having a close, confiding relationship with a significant other will be associated with better health. And often it is. Women who have an intimate relationship with a spouse or boyfriend are less likely to become depressed than are those without such a relationship (Brown & Harris, 1978; Costello, 1982). Similarly, among gay and bisexual men infected with HIV, those with a history of close, confiding relationships have lower levels of suicidal intent (Schneider et al., 1991).

But tender loving care from others does not always improve an individual's health status. For example, overprotectiveness by family and friends can make it more difficult for an individual to engage in unpleasant behaviors (such as dietary control, exercise, and learning to manage pain without medications) necessary for recovery (Kaplan & Toshima, 1990). No doubt, overprotectiveness usually stems from good intentions. But it may sometimes cloak resentment and irritation. In a study of stroke patients, caretakers perceived by the patient as being overprotective were more likely to have negative attitudes toward the patient (Thompson & Sobolew-Shubin, 1993).

Consistent with the intimacy model of social support, women who have a close, confiding relationship with a husband or boyfriend are less likely to become depressed than those without such a relationship.

The fourth and final model of social support defines social support in terms of its *perceived availability* (Sarason et al., 1983). Compared with those who doubt the adequacy of their social resources, individuals who believe that ample support is available to them cope more effectively in many different situations: in school (Cutrona et al., 1994), after an abortion (Major & Cozzarelli, 1992), and after participating in a simulated chemical and biological warfare environment (Fullerton et al., 1992)—to give just a few examples. In almost any stressful or demanding situation that you can imagine, perceived support is associated with better adjustment.

The question is why. Perceived support does not simply reflect received support; the two are only weakly related (Lakey & Cassady, 1990). Instead, perceived support may be located more in the eye of the beholder than in the social environment. The person who perceives high levels of available social support is what Irwin Sarason and his colleagues (1994) call a "social optimist." Such individuals possess a strong sense of self-efficacy, positive evaluations of the self, low anxiety, and positive expectations about social interactions (Sarason et al., 1983). They have better social skills and are better liked by others (Sarason et al., 1985). And they see things differently: Persons who are high in perceived social support and believe support to be important interpret the exact same supportive behaviors as more helpful than do those who are low in perceived support and believe support to be relatively unimportant (Lakey et al., 1992).

There is, then, no one perfect model of social support. Each of the four we have examined has limitations, but each one also describes crucial aspects of a complex social transaction between those who provide support and those who receive it.

buffer effect The effect whereby a protective factor, such as social support, shields a person from the adverse effects of high stress.

Effects of Social Support There are a number of ways in which social support can affect health. At first, affectionate assistance from others was thought to provide a buffer against stress (Cassel, 1974; Cobb, 1976). In a **buffer effect,** stress and social support interact. When stress is low, social support doesn't matter. But when stress is high, social support protects the individual from harmful consequences. Thus, the combination of high stress *and* little social support produces the worst health.

Research by Judith Siegel (1990) illustrates that stress-buffering effects are not confined to social support from humans. In this study, over 1,000 individuals sixty-five years of age or older were asked whether they owned a pet and, if they did, what kind. The number of negative life events experienced in the previous six months was also assessed. Subjects then reported every two months over a one-year period on how many times they had contacted a physician. The results of this study indicated that having a pet acted as a buffer against negative life events (see Figure 14.5). Among subjects with few negative life events, there was no significant advantage in having a pet. However, among individuals with many negative events, those who had a pet reported fewer contacts with physicians than those who did not have one. More detailed analyses revealed that dogs served to buffer the stress of their owners, but cats or birds did not. Thanks, Fido!

Buffer effects can occur across social domains. Think for a moment about your entire social network. What happens when one part of it goes sour? Does it help to have support elsewhere? It seems so. In a study of college students, perceived support from a friend reduced psychological distress when there was con-

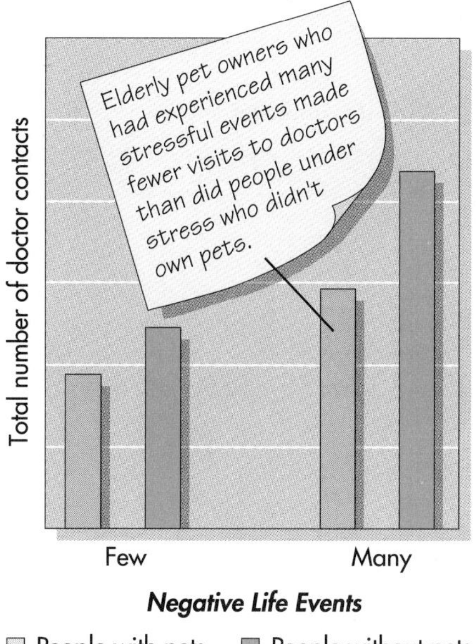

Figure 14.5 **Coping with Negative Life Events: Dogs Only.** Among elderly subjects who had experienced few negative life events in the past six months, pet ownership was not significantly correlated with the number of times they contacted a physician. However, for those who had experienced many negative events, pet owners had fewer doctor contacts. Animal-specific analyses indicated that only dogs buffered their owners from stress, not cats or birds. (Data from Siegel, 1990.)

flict with a roommate. Similarly, perceived support from a roommate reduced psychological distress when there was conflict with a friend (Lepore, 1992). Like multiple positive identities and satisfying social roles, multiple sources of social support promote well-being. More good baskets are better.

The exact mechanism by which buffer effects occur is not known. Probably there are various different pathways. Recently, however, physiological reactivity has been highlighted. Although the presence of a friend can increase reactivity under embarrassing conditions (Glass et al., 1970), having a friend nearby usually reduces reactivity to stress (Kamarck et al., 1990; Snydersmith & Cacioppo, 1992). From this perspective, social support is the opposite of hostility and conflict (Smith & Christensen, 1992a): social support reducing reactivity, hostility and conflict increasing it. Moreover, just as hostile individuals appear to act in ways that create the stressful interpersonal situations to which they react so strongly, the behavior of social optimists who perceive lots of available support creates the positive social environment that can reduce reactivity to stress. These relationships are diagrammed in Figure 14.6. Now add gender. There is some evidence that perceived social support reduces women's physiological reactivity more than men's, while hostility increases men's physiological reactivity more than women's (Linden et al., 1993).

But the effects of social support are not always confined to stressful situations. In the nine-year longitudinal study described earlier in this section, there was a *direct* relationship between social support and health (Berkman & Syme, 1979).

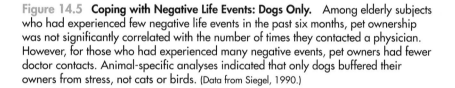

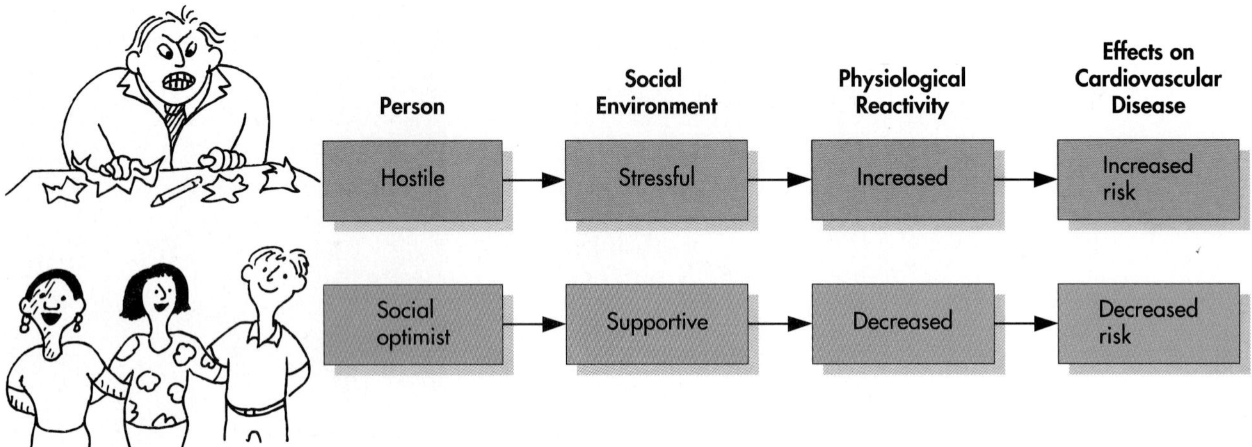

Figure 14.6 **Reactivity: Hostility Versus Social Support.** Increasingly, research on hostility and social support suggests that they are opposites in many respects. Hostile individuals appear to act in ways that create stressful interactions to which they react more vigorously than do nonhostile individuals. Social optimists who perceive high levels of available social support act in ways that create supportive interactions which reduce reactivity. Over time, these very different behavioral and physiological patterns could influence the likelihood of cardiovascular disease.

Residents of Alameda County who had more social contacts lived longer—regardless of the level of potential stressors such as poor health, poor health practices, and limited financial resources.

Direct effects of social support on health and mortality may, at least in part, be related to the immune system. A number of studies have found that low levels of social support are associated with decrements in immune functioning (Adler & Matthews, 1994; Theorell et al., 1995). In one study, the presence of secretory immunoglobulin A (S-IGA), a major antibody contained in bodily secretions, was measured in college students before, during, and after their final exams (Jemmott & Magloire, 1988). Those who reported more adequate social support had higher levels of S-IGA. This association between social support and S-IGA was not affected by the level of stress, which was highest during the exam period.

Despite their differences, we should not draw the line between buffer and direct effects of social support too sharply. The method of operation can change over time: Buffer effects in a new situation can turn into direct effects as people become familiar with their social surroundings (Lepore et al., 1991). Understanding what social support is and how it operates is an important endeavor because so many of life's difficulties occur in a social context and so much of how we cope with stress involves other people. As we will see in the next section, treatment and prevention are also influenced by our relations with others.

TREATMENT AND PREVENTION

Social psychology contributes in many different ways to the development of treatment interventions and prevention programs. Here, we focus first on how choice of treatment affects treatment effectiveness and then on ways to increase people's healthy behaviors.

Treatment: Choice and Effort

When you seek treatment for a psychological or physical problem, do you want to have a choice about the treatment you receive? Although the notion of patient-choice, as opposed to doctor-dictate, used to be regarded with considerable skepticism by the medical community, there is increasing evidence that choice is beneficial. Even relatively minor choices, such as allowing a patient to decide the order in which procedures will be performed, can reduce psychological distress (Miller & Mangan, 1983). And providing more significant choices, such as deciding on the type of treatment, has been shown to increase the effectiveness of treatments for alcoholism (Miller, 1985) and obesity (Mendonca & Brehm, 1983).

Choice of an *effortful* treatment may be particularly beneficial. The individual making such a choice is confronted with the need to justify having voluntarily taken on a difficult and perhaps unpleasant activity. As described in Chapter 10 on Attitudes, this predicament arouses cognitive dissonance. One way to reduce dissonance in this situation is to become more motivated to succeed: "Why have I chosen to do this? Because I really want to get better." Since highly motivated individuals should be more careful and conscientious about carrying out the prescribed treatment, they should improve more.

Danny Axsom (1989) tested this proposition in a study on snake phobia. Subjects, all highly snake-phobic, either were or were not given an explicit choice about undertaking a treatment that was described as either requiring "*extreme* exertion" or being "so easy." Among these four experimental conditions, subjects given an explicit choice about continuing an effortful treatment reported the greatest motivation to change their phobic behavior and came closest to the five-foot-long New Jersey corn snake used to measure approach behavior.

The emphasis on active problem-focused coping created by providing choices is highly appropriate for treatments, such as diet and exercise regimes, that require high levels of attention and involvement from the patient. But there are times when efforts to exert control over our thoughts and behaviors can backfire and produce the exact opposite of what we desire (Wegner, 1994). For example, individuals experiencing anxiety-based problems such as insomnia or sexual-performance difficulties can get caught in a vicious cycle of trying, failing, becoming more anxious, trying harder, failing again, and so forth (Tennen & Affleck, 1991). For these problems, *not* trying is often the best medicine. Distraction, too, can sometimes be useful, having beneficial effects in treatments ranging from dental procedures (Anderson et al., 1991) to chemotherapy for cancer patients (Carey & Burish, 1988).

As we saw earlier in this chapter, there is no magic answer about what kind of coping strategy is best. Nor is there any universally beneficial treatment approach. The art of treatment requires custom-tailoring: selecting the treatment best suited to the individual.

Prevention: Getting the Message Across

We live in what could aptly be described as the "era of prevention." So many serious threats to health are preventable. Just watch TV, read a newspaper, leaf through a magazine, or sit in on a health education class: There are programs for AIDS prevention, campaigns to persuade smokers to break their habit, and laws that mandate the wearing of seat belts. To a large extent, we know what to do and what not to do to promote good health and to avoid disease and injury. But how do we convince ourselves and others to translate that knowledge into action?

There are any number of ways to slice the prevention pie. We can concentrate on the three essential ingredients of information, motivation, and behavior (Fisher et al., 1994). We can try to reduce risks or increase protections; we can target high-risk populations or provide universal coverage (Coie et al., 1993). We can apply the cost-benefit analysis included in most major theories of prevention (Weinstein, 1993). Across a range of perspectives, however, several basic factors emerge (see Figure 14.7). Let's consider them one by one.

The first step toward good health depends on the relative pleasure to be derived from healthy versus unhealthy behaviors. If a healthy behavior is more enjoyable than an unhealthy one, then presumably all we would need to do is try it out and we'd be convinced. Usually, however, it's not this easy. Unhealthy habits may be enjoyable; healthy behaviors (at least initially) may require extra effort. So why switch? To do so, we have to recognize that, unless we change our ways, our health is threatened.

Perhaps because this is such an obvious first step, there may have been too much emphasis placed on it. As described in Chapter 10, graphic displays of frightening consequences ("fear appeals") were once a popular device: the gory lung-cancer operation to impress the smoker with the dangers of smoking, the bloody accident victim to persuade people to use seat belts. But fear appeals have some serious drawbacks. Instead of motivating the individual to engage in healthy behavior, they can produce helpless resignation, wishful fantasies about escape, and avoidance of thinking about the threat (Rippetoe & Rogers, 1987). Because of these possible negative consequences, fear appeals are seldom used in isolation and are more effective when combined with the other factors discussed in this section.

The role of our own perceptions of risk may also have been overestimated. Most models of prevention assume that perceived risk increases the likelihood of adopting healthy behaviors and avoiding risky ones. But *higher* perceived risk is usually associated with *more* risky behaviors (Goldman & Harlow, 1993). The solution to this apparent contradiction is timing. Since most research examines risk and behavior simultaneously, what we're getting is an accurate read-out of

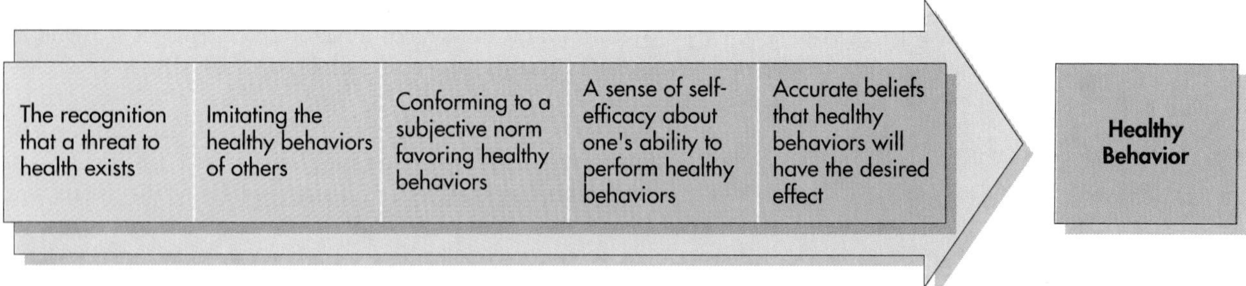

Figure 14.7 **Aiming for Good Health.** Several major factors help convince people to engage in healthy practices. Recognition that a threat to health exists is a necessary first step. Positive models and healthy subjective norms encourage people to adopt health-protective behaviors. A sense of self-efficacy about being able to carry out healthy behaviors and the belief that such behaviors will be effective increase the likelihood of active efforts.

current conditions (Weinstein & Nicolich, 1993). If you are engaging in more risky behaviors, you are, in fact, running a higher risk.

An adequate test of the effects of perceived risk requires prospective research, in which perceptions are measured first and behavior is assessed at a later time. These investigations indicate that perceived vulnerability is associated with preventive behaviors in some health areas, but not in others. For example, an individual's perception of the risk of getting AIDS appears to have little if any relationship with whether that person will adopt safe-sex practices (Gerrard et al., 1993). When it comes to sexual practices, people need to be aware of the risks involved, but such awareness is usually not sufficient to produce changes in their behavior (van der Pligt et al., 1993).

The next two steps toward good health rely on other people. When those around us act in healthy ways and indicate their support for healthy behaviors, they provide good models and help establish healthy norms. Direct modeling can be useful; for example, we are more likely to wear seat belts if we see others wearing theirs (Howell et al., 1990). But as a glance at the mass media quickly reveals, models of unhealthy behavior often take center stage. An examination of the most popular movies from 1977 to 1988 found that after a decline in the mid-1980s, depictions of risky habits (such as cigarette smoking, alcohol use, and illegal drug use) began to rise toward the end of the decade (Terre et al., 1991). The shifts over time for displays of smoking behavior are illustrated in Figure 14.8.

Besides eliciting direct imitation, models also contribute to the development of subjective norms, our beliefs about what others expect us to do. As described in Chapter 10, subjective norms provide an important context for the influence of attitudes on behavior. The theory of reasoned action, for instance, stipulates that both attitudes and norms affect our intentions to act (Ajzen & Fishbein, 1980; Fishbein & Ajzen, 1975). And they do. Both positive attitudes toward safe sex

These "Buckle Up Dummies" are trying to get our attention so that we will imitate their healthy behavior and buckle up too.

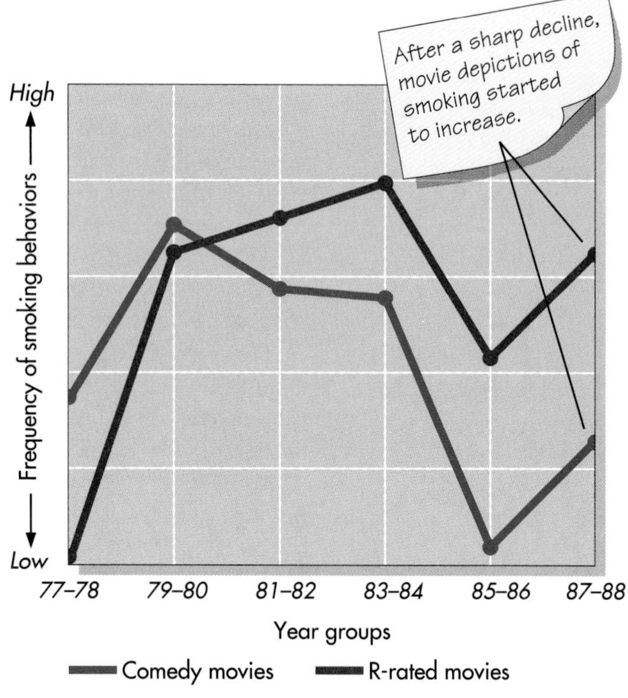

Figure 14.8 **Smoking in the Movies.** After eliminating science fiction and fantasy films as well as those set in the distant past or future, Lisa Terre and her colleagues examined the frequency of smoking behaviors in the remaining most popular movies from 1977 to 1988. As you can see from the trends in comedy and R-rated movies, such portrayals declined in the mid-1980s but then increased. Mass media depictions of risky health practices provide unhealthy models for people to imitate and establish subjective norms encouraging unhealthy behaviors. (Adapted from Terre et al., 1991.)

and perceived pressures from significant others to adopt safe-sex behaviors increase intentions to practice safe sex (Chan & Fishbein, 1993; Cochran et al., 1992). Intervention strategies that rely on social pressure appear to be effective. In an elaborate series of studies conducted by Jeffrey Kelly and his colleagues (1991, 1992), self-reports by gay men of high-risk sexual behavior decreased after opinion leaders in the gay community had been trained to advocate safe-sex practices to their peers. It is always possible, of course, that people's intentions and self-reports conform more to subjective norms than does their actual behavior (Galligan & Terry, 1993). Still, behavior change is a slippery slope and taking one step down the path increases the likelihood that others will follow.

Subjective norms aren't always enlisted in support of healthy practices. Unfortunately, they can also sustain unhealthy behaviors. It goes like this. First, in what is called the "false consensus effect" (discussed in Chapter 3), those who engage in unhealthy behaviors overestimate the prevalence of such behaviors among their peers (Chassin et al., 1990; Suls et al., 1988). Second, these overestimates serve as subjective norms encouraging individuals to continue their unhealthy practices. And, third, those who initially believe that more of their peers engage in unhealthy behaviors are themselves more heavily involved in such behaviors at a later time (Marks et al., 1992). Confronted by such a closed circle, the best way to cut through it is to provide accurate information about who does what. On one college campus, for example, self-reported heavy drinking declined after an intensive public information campaign stressing the actual facts about student drinking (DeAngelis, 1994).

The fourth step toward health emphasizes a person's confidence about performing healthy behaviors. Self-efficacy, knowing we can do what needs to be done, enhances both the adoption and maintenance of various healthy behaviors, including safe-sex practices, nonsmoking, and abstinence from alcohol (Goldman & Harlow, 1993; Maddux, 1991). Moreover, fear appeals work best when

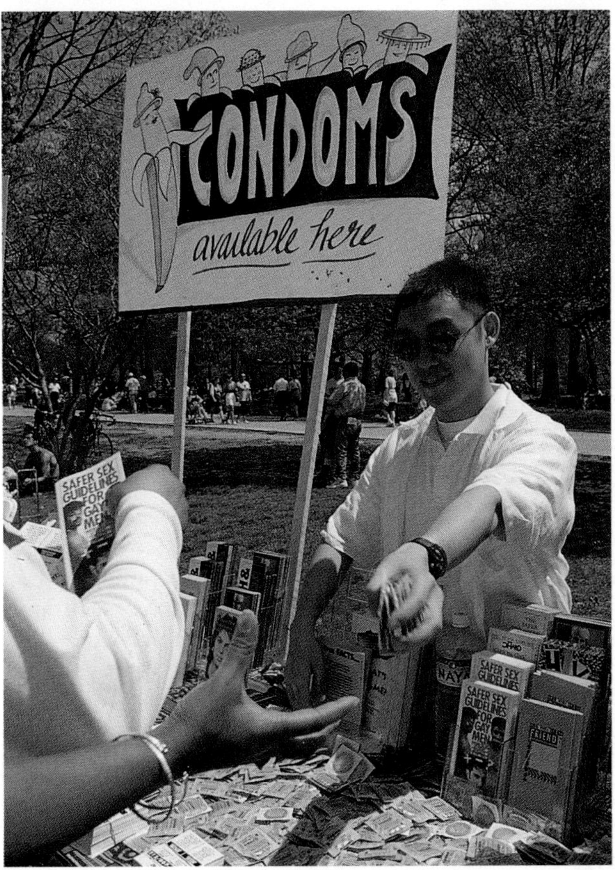

By handing out free condoms, this individual is sending the message that he expects others to practice safe-sex. This kind of social pressure, called a subjective norm, plays an important role in promoting healthy behaviors.

combined with information reassuring people that they can perform the desired health practice (Rogers, 1983). If people do not know how to perform the necessary behaviors, they should be taught. Smoking-prevention programs often teach young children specific techniques for resisting peer pressures and refusing the offer of a cigarette (Baum, 1984; Evans et al., 1984).

Finally, people need good, solid, accurate information about the effectiveness of the healthy behaviors they are being urged to adopt (Weinstein, 1989). When people believe that something works, they are more likely to develop positive attitudes about it and try it out. Beware, however, of being too easily convinced. In one study, subjects who had been reassured that a proposed prevention program was highly likely to be successful were quite positive in their evaluation of the program, regardless of the quality of the arguments that supported its probable success (Gleicher & Petty, 1992). Subjects provided with a weaker expectation of success were more discerning; they based their evaluations on the quality of the arguments presented. In the short run, people can be tricked by false promises. But in the long run, accuracy will usually prevail.

By now, the social nature of prevention should be abundantly clear. Information about health risks and preventive benefits comes from other people. What people do and what they say provide models and create norms. Even our own sense of self-efficacy may depend on others to teach us what we need to know. It also goes the other way around. Just as other people influence us, so we affect the health-related behaviors practiced by others. Prevention is very much a social phenomenon in which we are all involved.

REVIEW

STRESS AND COPING

- Stress is an unpleasant state that arises when people perceive that the demands of an event strain their ability to satisfy those demands.
- Appraisal determines whether stress will be experienced and influences how the person copes.
- Coping responses consist of the thoughts, feelings, and behaviors by which the person attempts to reduce stress.

STRESSFUL EVENTS

Life Events: When Does Change Hurt?

- Early research on life events maintained that change itself was damaging to health. More recent research indicates that, usually, only negative life events are harmful.
- Individuals high in negative affectivity report more stressful life events as well as more symptoms and distress. When this tendency is taken into account, negative life events are still associated with poor health, though the effect may be small.

Microstressors: The Hassles of Everyday Life

- Sharing living space decreases control over social interactions and is stressful.
- Having multiple positive self-identities and multiple high-quality social roles is associated with increased well-being.

Major Crises: Catastrophe and War

- Both pre-existing personal characteristics as well as experiences during a natural disaster influence distress afterward.
- In posttraumatic stress disorder, individuals suffer psychological and physical problems long after the event itself is over.
- Soldiers who are exposed to heavy combat are especially likely to experience posttraumatic stress disorder.

APPRAISAL

Explanations: Learned Helplessness and Depression

- In the original learned helplessness model of depression, experiencing an uncontrollable event was said to create depressive symptoms.
- In contrast, the reformulated model highlights causal attributions.
- The depressive explanatory style is a habitual tendency to make stable, global, and internal attributions for negative events. Research has obtained mixed results on whether this style can be a cause of depression.

Expectations: Agency and Outcome

- Hopelessness theory, a third-generation model of learned helplessness, emphasizes agency expectations about personal control over future events and outcome expectations about the quality of future events.
- Both agency expectations (such as perceived control, hardiness, and a sense of self-efficacy) and outcome expectations (such as optimism) are associated with better adjustment.

Pollyanna's Health

- Positive illusions about control and oneself are associated with good health, but the causal relationship is unclear.
- It is uncertain whether there are many dimensions of positive thinking or just a few.
- Extremely unrealistic positive illusions can have undesirable health consequences.
- Among those confronting extremely stressful events, a sense of meaning and purpose may be more beneficial than excessively positive explanations or expectations.

COPING

Problem-Focused Coping

- In problem-focused coping, the individual engages in thoughts and behaviors that attempt to alter a stressful situation.
- Because exerting control has physiological and psychological costs, control efforts can sometimes increase stress rather than reduce it.
- Blaming others is usually associated with poor adjustment.
- Most research indicates that both behavioral and characterological self-blame are associated with increased distress.

- Early research on the hard-driving, control-oriented Type A behavior pattern found it to be a strong predictor of coronary heart disease. Subsequent research, however, obtained much weaker results.
- Many investigators now believe that hostility is the toxic element contained in the Type A behavior pattern.
- Hostility (as measured by the Ho scale) predicted long-term health outcomes in half of the long-term studies now available.
- Both Type A and hostility increase physiological reactivity to stress, which can contribute to hypertension and CHD.

Emotion-Focused Coping

- In emotion-focused coping, the individual engages in thoughts and behaviors that attempt to reduce the distress produced by a stressful situation. There are two types of emotion-focused coping: approach and avoidance.
- Research on the theory of inhibition and confrontation indicates that confronting one's feelings about upsetting events is beneficial for physical health.
- In situations that the individual cannot control, distraction and anxiety-management can reduce psychological distress.
- Focusing on one's feelings is not always beneficial. Self-focus increases negative mood among individuals who have a negative self-concept.
- Distractions can be self-destructive.
- Women are more likely to experience depression and men are more likely to engage in self-destructive distractions. Both men and women can benefit from constructive distractions that are difficult and demanding.

Social Support: When Others Care

- Various models of social support have been proposed: the number of social contacts a person has; the number of helpers assisting a person in need; the presence of a close, confiding relationship; and the perceived availability of social support.
- In a buffer effect, social support has no effect in unstressful circumstances but does enhance well-being under stress. Buffer effects on health may occur, at least in part, through reductions in physiological reactivity.
- In a direct effect, social support enhances well-being regardless of the level of stress experienced. Direct effects on health may occur, at least in part, through enhanced functioning of the immune system.

TREATMENT AND PREVENTION

Treatment: Choice and Effort

- Giving patients some choice about the treatment they will receive reduces psychological distress and can increase treatment effectiveness.
- The voluntary choice of an effortful treatment appears to be particularly beneficial.
- Under some circumstances, avoidance strategies, such as being distracted and *not* trying to take charge, have positive effects on health.

Prevention: Getting the Message Across

- In order to adopt health practices that are not immediately enjoyable, individuals have to recognize that a threat to their health exists. However, while necessary for behavior change, perception of risk is not sufficient.
- The behaviors of others serve as models for healthy or unhealthy imitation.
- Subjective norms, beliefs about what others expect us to do, can encourage healthy or unhealthy behaviors.
- A sense of self-efficacy enhances the adoption and maintenance of healthy behaviors.
- Accurate beliefs that preventive actions are effective sustain commitment to healthy behaviors.

KEY TERMS

social-clinical interface, p. 526
health psychology, p. 526
stress, p. 527
appraisal, p. 527
coping, p. 527
negative affectivity, p. 528
self-complexity, p. 530
posttraumatic stress disorder, p. 533
learned helplessness, p. 534
depressive explanatory style, p. 536
self-efficacy, p. 538
positive affectivity, p. 540
problem-focused coping, p. 541
emotion-focused coping, p. 541
Type A behavior pattern, p. 543
theory of inhibition and confrontation, p. 545
self-focus model of depression, p. 547
buffer effect, p. 552

Glossary

Actor-observer effect The tendency to attribute our own behavior to situational causes and the behavior of others to personal factors. *(p. 100)*

Adversarial model A dispute-resolution system in which the prosecution and defense present opposing sides of the story. *(p. 490)*

Aggression Behavior intended to injure another person. *(p. 288)*

Altruistic Motivated by the desire to increase another's welfare. *(p. 252)*

Applied research Research whose goals are to enlarge the understanding of naturally occurring events and to find solutions to practical problems. *(p. 15)*

Appraisal Judgments about the demands made by a potentially stressful event and about one's ability to meet those demands. *(p. 527)*

Arousal-affect model The proposal that aggression is influenced by both the intensity of arousal and the type of emotion produced by a stimulus. *(p. 302)*

Arousal:cost-reward model The proposition that people react to emergency situations by acting in the most cost-effective way to reduce the arousal of shock and alarm. *(p. 276)*

Attachment style The way a person typically interacts with significant others. *(p. 214)*

Attitude A positive or negative reaction to a person, object, or idea. *(p. 370)*

Attribute ambiguity Circumstances in which the causes of behavior are unclear. *(p. 194)*

Attribution theory A group of theories that describe how people explain the causes of behavior. *(p. 91)*

Audience inhibition A person's reluctance to help for fear of making a bad impression on observers. *(p. 275)*

Balance theory The theory that people desire consistency in their thoughts, feelings, and social relationships. *(p. 165)*

Base-rate fallacy The finding that people are relatively insensitive to consensus information presented in the form of numerical base rates. *(p. 95)*

Basic research Research whose goal is to increase the understanding of human behavior, often by testing hypotheses based on a theory. *(p. 15)*

Basking in reflected glory (BIRGing) Increasing self-esteem by associating with others who are successful. *(p. 66)*

Belief in a just world The belief that individuals get what they deserve in life, an orientation that leads people to disparage victims. *(p. 101)*

Belief perseverance The tendency to maintain beliefs even after they have been discredited. *(p. 109)*

Brainstorming A technique that attempts to increase creative ideas by encouraging group members to speak freely without criticizing their own or others' contributions. *(p. 431)*

Buffer effect The effect whereby a protective factor, such as social support, shields a person from the adverse effects of high stress. *(p. 552)*

Bystander effect The effect whereby the presence of others inhibits helping. *(p. 270)*

Catharsis The reduction of the motive to aggress that is said to result from any imagined, observed, or actual act of aggression. *(p. 298)*

Central route to persuasion The process in which a person thinks carefully about a communication and is influenced by the strength of its arguments. *(p. 378)*

Central traits Traits that exert a powerful influence on overall impressions. *(p. 107)*

Cognitive dissonance An unpleasant psychological state often aroused when a person holds two conflicting cognitions. *(p. 399)*

Cognitive heuristics Information-processing shortcuts that enable us to make judgments that are quick but often in error. *(p. 94)*

Cognitive-neoassociation analysis The view that unpleasant experiences create negative affect, which in turn stimulates associations connected with anger and fear. Emotional and behavioral outcomes then depend, at least in part, on higher-order cognitive processing. *(p. 303)*

Collectives People engaged in common activities but with minimal direct interaction. *(p. 413)*

Collectivism A cultural orientation in which interdependence, cooperation, and social harmony take priority over personal goals. *(p. 342)*

Communal relationships Relationships in which the participants expect and desire mutual responsiveness to each other's needs. *(p. 212)*

Companionate love A secure, trusting, stable partnership. *(p. 213)*

Comparison level (CL) The average, general outcome an individual expects in a relationship. *(p. 204)*

Comparison level for alternatives (CL alt) The average, general outcome an individual expects from alternative relationships or lifestyles. *(p. 204)*

Compliance Changes in behavior that are elicited by direct requests. *(p. 346)*

Confirmation bias The tendency to seek, interpret, and create information that verifies existing beliefs. *(p. 108)*

Conformity The tendency to change our perceptions, opinions, or behavior in ways that are consistent with group norms. *(p. 333)*

Contact hypothesis The theory that direct contact between hostile groups will reduce prejudice under certain conditions. *(p. 155)*

Contingency model of leadership The theory that leadership effectiveness is determined both by the personal characteristics of leaders and by the control afforded by the situation. *(p. 508)*

Contrast effect A tendency to perceive stimuli that differ from expectations as being even more different than they really are. *(p. 124)*

Convenience sample A sample selected because the subjects are readily available to the researcher. *(p. 22)*

Coping Efforts to reduce stress. *(p. 527)*

Correlation An association between two variables. A correlation is positive when both variables increase or decrease together. It is negative when as one variable increases, the other decreases. *(p. 15)*

Correspondent inference theory The theory that we make inferences about a person when his or her actions are freely chosen, unexpected, and result in a small number of desirable effects. *(p. 91)*

Covariation principle A principle of attribution theory that people attribute behavior to factors that are present when a behavior occurs and absent when it does not. *(p. 92)*

Cross-race identification bias The tendency for people to have difficulty identifying members of a race other than their own. *(p. 468)*

Cultivation The process by which the mass media (particularly television) construct a version of social reality for the viewing public. *(p. 312)*

Cycle of family violence The transmission of violence across generations. *(p. 325)*

Death qualification A jury-selection procedure used in capital cases that permits judges to exclude prospective jurors who say they would not vote for the death penalty. *(p. 461)*

Debriefing A disclosure, made to subjects after research procedures are completed, in which the researcher explains the purpose of the research, attempts to resolve any negative feelings, and emphasizes the scientific contribution made by subjects' participation. *(p. 33)*

Deception Research methods that provide false information to subjects. *(p. 24)*

Deindividuation The loss of a person's sense of individuality and the reduction of normal constraints against deviant behavior. *(p. 419)*

Demand/withdraw interaction pattern When one partner is nagging, critical, and insistent about discussing relationship problems, while the other is withdrawn, silent, and defensive. *(p. 233)*

Dependent variables The factors measured in an experiment to see if they are affected by the independent variable. *(p. 19)*

Depressive explanatory style A habitual tendency to attribute negative events to causes that are stable, global, and internal. *(p. 536)*

Diffusion of responsibility The belief that others will or should take the responsibility for providing assistance to a person in need. *(p. 273)*

Discrimination Any behavior directed against persons because of their membership in a particular group. *(p. 121)*

Displacement Aggressing against a substitute target because aggressive acts against the source of the frustration are inhibited by fear or lack of access. *(p. 298)*

Distraction-conflict theory The theory that the presence of others will produce social facilitation effects only when those others distract from the task and create attentional conflict. *(p. 415)*

Door-in-the-face technique A two-step compliance technique in which an influencer prefaces the real request with a request so large that it is rejected. *(p. 351)*

Downward social comparison Defensive tendency to compare ourselves to others who are worse off than we are. *(p. 67)*

Egocentric bias Bias toward perceiving and recalling oneself as a central actor in past events. *(p. 52)*

Egoistic Motivated by the desire to increase one's own welfare. *(p. 252)*

Elaboration The process of thinking about and scrutinizing the arguments contained in a persuasive communication. *(p. 378)*

Emotional aggression Inflicting harm for its own sake. *(p. 289)*

Emotion-focused coping Cognitive and behavioral efforts to reduce the distress produced by a stressful situation. *(p. 541)*

Empathy-altruism hypothesis The proposition that empathic concern for a person in need produces an altruistic motive for helping. *(p. 253)*

Entrapment The condition in which commitments to a failing course of action are increased to justify investments already made. *(p. 444)*

Equity theory The theory that people are most satisfied with a relationship when the ratio between benefits and contributions is similar for both partners. *(p. 205)*

Evaluation apprehension The theory that the presence of others will produce social facilitation effects only when those others are seen as potential evaluators. *(p. 414)*

Exchange relationships Relationships in which the participants expect and desire strict reciprocity in their interactions. *(p. 212)*

Excitation transfer The process whereby arousal caused by one stimulus is added to arousal from a second stimulus and the combined arousal is attributed to the second stimulus. *(p. 217)*

Experiment A form of research that can demonstrate causal relationships because (1) the experimenter has control over the events that occur and (2) subjects are randomly assigned to conditions. *(p. 17)*

Experimental realism The degree to which experimental procedures are involving to subjects and lead them to behave naturally and spontaneously. *(p. 24)*

Experimenter expectancy effects The effects produced when an experimenter's expectations about the results of an experiment affect his or her behavior toward a subject and thereby influence the subject's responses. *(p. 21)*

External validity The degree to which one can be reasonably confident that the same results would be obtained for other people and in other situations. *(p. 22)*

Facial feedback hypothesis The hypothesis that changes in facial expression can lead to corresponding changes in emotion. *(p. 44)*

Facial electromyograph (EMG) An electronic instrument that records facial muscle activity associated with emotions and attitudes. *(p. 372)*

False-consensus effect The tendency to overestimate the consensus of our own opinions, attributes, and behaviors. *(p. 95)*

Foot-in-the-door technique A two-step compliance technique in which an influencer prefaces the real request by first getting a person to comply with a much smaller request. *(p. 349)*

Frustration-aggression hypothesis The idea that (1) frustration always elicits the motive to aggress and (2) all aggression is caused by frustration. *(p. 297)*

Fundamental attribution error The tendency to focus on the role of personal causes and underestimate the impact of situations on other people's behavior. *(p. 96)*

Good mood effect The effect whereby a good mood increases helping behavior. *(p. 248)*

Graduated and reciprocated initiatives in tension-reduction (GRIT) A strategy for unilateral, persistent efforts to establish trust and cooperation between opposing parties. *(p. 446)*

Group Two or more persons perceived as related because of their interactions, membership in the same social category, or common fate. *(p. 121)*

Group polarization The exaggeration through group discussion of initial tendencies in the thinking of group members. *(p. 427)*

Groupthink A group decision-making style characterized by an excessive tendency among group members to seek concurrence. *(p. 428)*

Guilt Feelings of discomfort or distress produced by people's belief that they have violated their own personal standards or by the fear that others will perceive such violations. *(p. 249)*

Habituation Adaptation to something familiar, so that both physiological and psychological responses are reduced. *(p. 311)*

Hard-to-get effect The tendency to prefer people who are highly selective in their social choices over those who are more readily available. *(p. 181)*

Hawthorne effect The finding that workers who were observed increased their productivity regardless of what actual changes were made in the work setting. *(p. 496)*

Health psychology The study of physical health and illness by psychologists from various areas of specialization. *(p. 526)*

Heuristic A rule of thumb used to evaluate a message superficially, without careful thinking about its content. *(p. 379)*

Hindsight bias The tendency, once an event has occurred, to overestimate one's ability to have foreseen the outcome. *(p. 53)*

Hypothesis A testable prediction about the conditions under which an event will occur. *(p. 13)*

Idiosyncrasy credits Interpersonal "credits" that a person earns by following group norms. *(p. 345)*

Illusory correlation An overestimate of the association between variables that are only slightly or not at all correlated. *(p. 125)*

Implicit personality theory A network of assumptions people make about the relationships among traits and behaviors. *(p. 106)*

Impression formation The process of integrating information about a person to form a coherent impression. *(p. 103)*

Independent variables The factors manipulated in an experiment to see if they affect the dependent variables. *(p. 19)*

Individualism A cultural orientation in which independence, autonomy, and self-reliance take priority over group allegiances. *(p. 342)*

Industrial/organizational (I/O) psychology The study of human behavior in business and other organizational settings. *(p. 496)*

Informational influence Influence that produces conformity when a person believes others are correct in their judgments. *(p. 336)*

Information integration theory The theory that impressions are based on (1) perceiver dispositions and (2) a weighted average of a target person's traits. *(p. 104)*

Informed consent An individual's deliberate, voluntary decision to participate in research, based on the researcher's description of what will be required during such participation. *(p. 32)*

Ingroup favoritism The tendency to discriminate in favor of ingroups over outgroups. *(p. 135)*

Inoculation hypothesis The idea that exposure to weak versions of a persuasive argument increases later resistance to that argument. *(p. 396)*

Inquisitorial model A dispute-resolution system in which a neutral investigator gathers evidence from both sides and presents the findings in court. *(p. 490)*

Instrumental aggression Inflicting harm in order to obtain something of value. *(p. 289)*

Insufficient deterrence A condition in which people refrain from engaging in a desirable activity, even though only mild punishment is threatened. *(p. 401)*

Insufficient justification A condition in which people freely perform an attitude-discrepant behavior without receiving a large reward. *(p. 400)*

Integrative agreement A negotiated resolution to a conflict in which all parties obtain outcomes that are superior to what they would have obtained from an equal division of the contested resources. *(p. 449)*

Integrative complexity Complex information processing involving the search for information, the prediction of outcomes, the weighing of options, and the consideration of potential strategies. *(p. 448)*

Integrity test Paper-and-pencil questionnaire designed to test a job applicant's honesty and character. *(p. 500)*

Interactionist perspective An emphasis on how both an individual's personality and environmental characteristics influence behavior. *(p. 9)*

Internal validity The degree to which there can be reasonable certainty that the independent variables in an experiment caused the effects obtained on the dependent variables. *(p. 21)*

Interrater reliability The degree to which different observers agree on their observations. *(p. 28)*

Intimate relationships Close relationships between two adults involving at least one of the following: emotional attachment, fulfillment of psychological needs, and interdependence. *(p. 201)*

Investment Resources put into a relationship that cannot be retrieved if that relationship ends. *(p. 204)*

Jealousy The reaction to a perceived threat to a relationship. *(p. 226)*

Jigsaw classroom A cooperative learning method used to reduce racial prejudice through interaction in group efforts. *(p. 158)*

Jury nullification The jury's power to disregard, or "nullify," the law when it conflicts with personal conceptions of justice. *(p. 481)*

Kinship selection Preferential helping of blood relatives, so that genes held in common will survive. *(p. 245)*

Learned helplessness The phenomenon in which experience with an uncontrollable event creates passive behavior toward a subsequent threat to well-being. *(p. 534)*

Leniency bias The tendency for jury deliberation to produce a tilt toward acquittal. *(p. 484)*

Loneliness A feeling of deprivation about existing social relations. *(p. 170)*

Low-balling A two-step compliance technique in which the influencer secures agreement with a request but then increases the size of that request by revealing hidden costs. *(p. 350)*

Matching hypothesis The proposition that people are attracted to and form relationships with those who are similar to them in particular characteristics, such as physical attractiveness. *(p. 186)*

Mere exposure The phenomenon whereby the more often people are exposed to a stimulus, the more positively they evaluate that stimulus. *(p. 192)*

Mere presence The theory that the mere presence of others is sufficient to produce social facilitation effects. *(p. 414)*

Misattribution An inaccurate explanation that shifts the cause for arousal from the true source to another one. *(p. 169)*

Mitigating information Information about a person's situation indicating that he or she should not be held fully responsible for aggressive actions. *(p. 306)*

Modern racism A form of prejudice that surfaces in subtle ways when it is safe, socially acceptable, and easy to rationalize. *(p. 148)*

Mundane realism The degree to which the experimental situation resembles places and events that exist in the real world. *(p. 23)*

Need for cognition (NC) A personality variable that distinguishes people on the basis of how much they enjoy effortful cognitive activities. *(p. 393)*

Negative affectivity A pervasive tendency to experience distress, dissatisfaction, and a wide variety of negative emotions. *(p. 528)*

Negative affect reciprocity A quid-pro-quo exchange of behaviors expressing negative feelings. *(p. 233)*

Negative state relief model The proposition that people help others in order to counteract their own feelings of sadness. *(p. 252)*

Nonverbal behavior Behavior that reveals a person's feelings without words—through facial expressions, body language, and vocal cues. *(p. 86)*

Normative influence Influence that produces conformity when a person fears the negative social consequences of appearing deviant. *(p. 336)*

Norm of justice A moral standard emphasizing that people should help those who deserve assistance. *(p. 265)*

Norm of social responsibility A moral standard emphasizing that people should help those who need assistance. *(p. 265)*

Obedience Behavior change produced by the commands of authority. *(p. 355)*

Outgroup homogeneity effect The tendency to assume that there is greater similarity among members of outgroups than of ingroups. *(p. 123)*

Overjustification The tendency for intrinsic motivation to diminish for activities that have become associated with reward or other extrinsic factors. *(p. 47)*

Passionate love Romantic love characterized by high arousal, intense attraction, and fear of rejection. *(p. 213)*

Peremptory challenges The means by which lawyers can exclude a limited number of prospective jurors without the judge's approval. *(p. 458)*

Performance appraisal The process of evaluating an employee's work within the organization. *(p. 503)*

Peripheral route to persuasion The process in which a person does not think carefully about a communication and is influenced instead by superficial cues. *(p. 378)*

Personal attribution Attribution to internal characteristics of an actor, such as ability, personality, mood, or effort. *(p. 91)*

Personal norms An individual's feelings of moral obligation to provide help to specific others in specific situations. *(p. 265)*

Personal space The physical distance people prefer to maintain between themselves and others. *(p. 191)*

Persuasion The process of changing attitudes. *(p. 377)*

Pluralistic ignorance The state in which people mistakenly believe that their own thoughts and feelings are different from those of others, even though everyone's behavior is the same. *(p. 272)*

Polygraph A mechanical instrument that records physiological arousal from multiple channels; it is often used as a lie-detector test. *(p. 466)*

Pornography Explicit sexual material. *(p. 313)*

Positive affectivity The pervasive tendency to experience a variety of positive emotions and engage in a range of positive behaviors. *(p. 540)*

Posttraumatic stress disorder The experience of enduring physical and psychological symptoms after an extremely stressful event. *(p. 533)*

Prejudice Negative feelings toward persons based on their membership in certain groups. *(p. 132)*

Primacy effect The tendency for information presented early in a sequence to have more impact on impressions than information presented later. *(p. 107)*

Priming The tendency for recently used words or ideas to come to mind easily and influence the interpretation of new information. *(p. 104)*

Private conformity The change of beliefs that occurs when a person privately accepts the position taken by others. *(p. 336)*

Private self-consciousness A personality characteristic of individuals who are introspective, often attending to their own inner states. *(p. 61)*

Problem-focused coping Cognitive and behavioral efforts to alter a stressful situation. *(p. 541)*

Psychological reactance The theory that people react against threats to specific behavioral freedoms by perceiving a threatened freedom as more attractive and trying to reestablish it. *(p. 195)*

Public conformity A superficial change in overt behavior, without a corresponding change of opinion, produced by real or imagined group pressure. *(p. 336)*

Public self-consciousness A personality characteristic of individuals who focus on themselves as social objects, as seen by others. *(p. 61)*

Rape shield laws Statutes that restrict the kinds of personal questions lawyers can ask rape victims who take the witness stand. *(p. 460)*

Realistic conflict theory The theory that hostility between groups is caused by direct competition for limited resources. *(p. 133)*

Reciprocity A quid-pro-quo mutual exchange—for example, liking those who like us. *(p. 165)*

Reconstructive memory The notion that eyewitness memory can be altered by exposure to postevent information. *(p. 469)*

Relative deprivation Feelings of discontent aroused by the belief that one fares poorly compared to others. *(p. 134)*

Representative sample A sample that reflects the characteristics of the population of interest. *(p. 22)*

Scientific jury selection A method of selecting juries through surveys that yield correlations between demographics and trial-relevant attitudes. *(p. 459)*

Self-awareness theory The theory that self-focused attention leads people to notice self-discrepancies, thereby motivating either an escape from self-awareness or a change in behavior. *(p. 58)*

Self-complexity The number of distinct roles or identities people believe they have. *(p. 530)*

Self-concept The sum total of an individual's beliefs about his or her own personal attributes. *(p. 41)*

Self-disclosure Revelations about the self that a person makes to other people. *(p. 207)*

Self-discrepancy theory The theory linking the perception of discrepancies between a person's self-concept and various self-guides to specific, negative emotional states. *(p. 57)*

Self-efficacy A person's belief that he or she is capable of the specific behavior required to produce a desired outcome in a given situation. *(p. 538)*

Self-esteem An affective component of the self, consisting of a person's positive and negative self-evaluations. *(p. 56)*

Self-focus model of depression The hypothesis that depressive mood and negative self-evaluations are intensified and maintained by a focus on the self. *(p. 547)*

Self-fulfilling prophecy The process by which one's expectations about a person eventually lead that person to behave in ways that confirm those expectations. *(p. 111)*

Self-handicapping Behaviors designed to sabotage one's own performance in order to provide a subsequent excuse for failure. *(p. 64)*

Self-monitoring The tendency to change behavior in response to the self-presentation concerns of the situation. *(p. 74)*

Self-perception theory The theory that when internal cues are difficult to interpret, people gain self-insight by observing their own behavior. *(p. 43)*

Self-persuasion The processes by which people change their attitudes in response to their own actions. *(p. 401)*

Self-presentation Strategies people use to shape what others think of them. *(p. 71)*

Self-reference effect The finding that information is recalled better when it is relevant to the self than when it is not. *(p. 52)*

Self-schemas Beliefs people hold about themselves that guide the processing of self-relevant information. *(p. 53)*

Sexism Discrimination based on a person's gender. *(p. 139)*

Sex ratio The number of men per 100 women in a given population. When men outnumber women, the sex ratio is high; when women outnumber men, the sex ratio is low. *(p. 229)*

Situational attribution Attribution to factors external to an actor, such as the task, other people, or luck. *(p. 91)*

Sleeper effect A delayed increase in the persuasive impact of a noncredible source. *(p. 385)*

Social anxiety A feeling of discomfort in the presence of others, often accompanied by the social awkwardness and inhibition characteristic of shyness. *(p. 168)*

Social categorization The classification of persons into groups on the basis of common attributes. *(p. 123)*

Social-clinical interface The study of social psychological factors involved in psychological health and distress. *(p. 526)*

Social cognition The study of how people perceive, remember, and interpret information about themselves and others. *(p. 12)*

Social comparison theory The theory that people evaluate their own abilities and opinions by comparing themselves to others. *(p. 49)*

Social dilemma A situation in which a self-interested choice by everyone creates the worst outcome for everyone. *(p. 438)*

Social exchange A perspective that views people as motivated to maximize benefits and minimize costs in their relationships with others. *(p. 203)*

Social facilitation The finding that the presence of others enhances performance on easy tasks but impairs performance on difficult tasks. *(p. 414)*

Social identity theory The theory that people favor ingroups over outgroups in order to enhance their self-esteem. *(p. 135)*

Social impact theory The theory that social influence depends on the strength, immediacy, and number of source persons relative to target persons. *(p. 364)*

Social learning theory The proposition that behavior is learned through the observation of others as well as through the direct experience of rewards and punishments. *(p. 295)*

Social loafing A group-produced reduction in individual output on easy tasks where contributions are pooled. *(p. 416)*

Social norms General rules of conduct reflecting standards of social approval and disapproval. *(p. 264)*

Social perception A general term for the processes by which people come to understand one another. *(p. 82)*

Social psychology The scientific study of the way individuals think, feel, desire, and act in social situations. *(p. 6)*

Social roles theory The theory that small gender differences are magnified in perception by the contrasting social roles occupied by men and women. *(p. 144)*

Sociobiology The application of the principles of evolutionary biology to the understanding of social behavior. *(p. 183)*

Stage theories Theories reflecting the view that relationships develop through a specific set of stages in a specific order. *(p. 202)*

Stereotypes Beliefs that associate groups of people with certain traits. *(p. 122)*

Stress An unpleasant state in which people perceive the demands of an event as taxing or exceeding their ability to satisfy or alter those demands. *(p. 527)*

Structured interviews Interviews in which each job applicant is asked a standard set of questions and evaluated on the same criteria. *(p. 500)*

Superordinate goals Shared goals that can be achieved only through cooperation. *(p. 133)*

Superordinate identity The perception by members of different groups that they all belong to a larger whole. *(p. 451)*

That's-not-all technique A two-step compliance technique in which the influencer begins with an inflated request, then decreases the apparent size of that request by offering a discount or bonus. *(p. 352)*

Theory An organized set of principles used to explain observed phenomena. *(p. 14)*

Theory of inhibition and confrontation The theory that inhibiting one's reactions to a traumatic event is damaging to physical health, whereas expressing one's reactions is beneficial. *(p. 545)*

Theory of planned behavior The theory that attitudes toward a specific behavior combine with subjective norms and perceived control to influence a person's action. *(p. 374)*

Theory of social penetration A theory about the development of close relationships that emphasizes the gradual increase in the breadth and depth of exchanges between partners. *(p. 208)*

Threat-to-self-esteem model The theory that reactions to receiving assistance depend on whether help is perceived as supportive or threatening. *(p. 276)*

Transformational leaders Leaders who inspire followers to transcend their own needs in the interest of a common cause. *(p. 507)*

Two-factor theory of emotion The theory that the experience of emotion is based on two factors: physiological arousal and a cognitive interpretation of that arousal. *(p. 50)*

Type A behavior pattern A pattern of behavior characterized by extremes of competitive striving for achievement, a sense of time urgency, hostility, and aggression. *(p. 543)*

Voir dire The pretrial examination of prospective jurors by the judge or opposing lawyers to uncover signs of bias. *(p. 458)*

Weapon-focus effect The tendency for weapons to draw attention and impair a witness's ability to identify the culprit. *(p. 468)*

Weapons effect The tendency of weapons to increase the likelihood of aggression by their mere presence. *(p. 304)*

What-is-beautiful-is-good stereotype The belief that physically attractive individuals also possess desirable personality characteristics. *(p. 176)*

References

Abbey, A. (1982). Sex differences in attributions for friendly behavior: Do males misperceive females' friendliness? *Journal of Personality and Social Psychology, 42,* 830–838.

Abeles, R. P. (1976). Relative deprivation, rising expectations and black militancy. *Journal of Social Issues, 32,* 119–137.

Abelson, R. P. (1981). Psychological status of the script concept. *American Psychologist, 36,* 715–729.

Abelson, R. P., Aronson, E., McGuire, W. J., Newcomb, T. M., Rosenberg, M. J., & Tannenbaum, P. H. (1968). *Theories of cognitive consistency: A sourcebook.* Chicago: Rand McNally.

Abramson, L. Y., Metalsky, G. I., & Alloy, L. B. (1989). Hopelessness depression: A theory-based subtype of depression. *Psychological Review, 96,* 358–372.

Abramson, L. Y., Seligman, M. E. P., & Teasdale, J. (1978). Learned helplessness in humans: Critique and reformulation. *Journal of Abnormal Psychology, 87,* 49–74.

Acker, M., & Davis, M. H. (1992). Intimacy, passion and commitment in adult romantic relationships: A test of the triangular theory of love. *Journal of Social and Personal Relationships, 9,* 21–50.

Adair, J. G. (1984). The Hawthorne effect: A reconsideration of the methodological artifact. *Journal of Applied Psychology, 69,* 334–345.

Adams, J. S. (1965). Inequity in social exchange. In L. Berkowitz (Ed.), *Advances in experimental social psychology* (Vol. 2, pp. 267–299). New York: Academic Press.

Aderman, D. (1972). Elation, depression, and helping behavior. *Journal of Personality and Social Psychology, 24,* 91–101.

Aderman, D., Brehm, S. S., & Katz, B. (1974). Empathic observation of an innocent victim: The just world revisited. *Journal of Personality and Social Psychology, 29,* 342–347.

Adler, N., & Matthews, K. (1994). Health psychology: Why do some people get sick and some stay well? *Annual Review of Psychology, 45,* 229–259.

Adorno, T., Frenkel-Brunswik, E., Levinson, D., & Sanford, R. N. (1950). *The authoritarian personality.* New York: Harper.

Affleck, G., Tennen, H., Urrows, S., & Higgins, P. (1994). Person and contextual features of daily stress reactivity: Individual differences in relation of undesirable daily events with mood disturbance and chronic pain intensity. *Journal of Personality and Social Psychology, 66,* 329–340.

Aguinis, H., Pierce, C. A., & Quigley, B. M. (1993). Conditions under which a bogus pipeline procedure enhances the validity of self-reported cigarette smoking: A meta-analytic review. *Journal of Applied Social Psychology, 23,* 352–373.

Ahuvia, A. C., & Adelman, M. B. (1992). Formal intermediaries in the marriage market: A typology and review. *Journal of Marriage and the Family, 54,* 452–463.

Aida, Y., & Falbo, T. (1991). Relationships between marital satisfaction, resources, and power strategies. *Sex Roles, 24,* 43–56.

Ainsworth, M., Blehar, M. C., Waters, E., & Wall, S. (1978). *Patterns of attachment: A psychological study of the strange situation.* Hillsdale, NJ: Erlbaum.

Ajzen, I. (1991). The theory of planned behavior. *Organizational Behavior and Human Decision Processes, 50,* 179–211.

Ajzen, I., & Fishbein, M. (1977). Attitude-behavior relations: A theoretical analysis and review of empirical research. *Psychological Bulletin, 84,* 888–918.

Ajzen, I., & Fishbein, M. (1980). *Understanding attitudes and predicting social behavior.* Englewood Cliffs, NJ: Prentice-Hall.

Ajzen, I., & Madden, T. J. (1986). Prediction of goal-directed behavior: Attitudes, intentions, and perceived behavioral control. *Journal of Experimental Social Psychology, 22,* 453–474.

Aldag, R. J., & Fuller, S. R. (1993). Beyond fiasco: A reappraisal of the groupthink phenomenon and a new model of group decision processes. *Psychological Bulletin, 113,* 533–552.

Aldwin, C. M., & Revenson, T. A. (1987). Does coping help? A reexamination of the relation between coping and mental health. *Journal of Personality and Social Psychology, 53,* 337–348.

Alicke, M. D., & Largo, E. (1995). The role of the self in the false consensus effect. *Journal of Experimental Social Psychology, 31,* 28–47.

Alicke, M. D., Smith, R. H., & Klotz, J. L. (1986). Judgments of physical attractiveness: The role of faces and bodies. *Personality and Social Psychology Bulletin, 12,* 381–389.

Allen, J. B., Kenrick, D. T., Linder, D. E., & McCall, M. A. (1989). Arousal and attribution: A response-facilitation alternative to misattribution and negative-reinforcement models. *Journal of Personality and Social Psychology, 57,* 261–270.

Allen, V. L. (1965). Situational factors in conformity. In L. Berkowitz (Ed.), *Advances in Experimental Social Psychology, 2,* 133–175.

Allen, V. L., & Levine, J. M. (1969). Consensus and conformity. *Journal of Experimental Social Psychology, 5,* 389–399.

Allen, V. L., & Levine, J. M. (1971). Social support and conformity: The role of independent assessment of reality. *Journal of Experimental Social Psychology, 7,* 48–58.

Alley, T. R. (1988). *Social and applied aspects of perceiving faces.* Hillsdale, NJ: Erlbaum.

Allison, S. T., & Kerr, N. L. (1994). Group correspondent biases and the provision of public goods. *Journal of Personality and Social Psychology, 66,* 688–698.

Allison, S. T., McQueen, L. R., & Schaerfl, L. M. (1992). Social decision making processes and the equal partitionment of shared resources. *Journal of Experimental Social Psychology, 28,* 23–42.

Allison, S. T., & Messick, D. M. (1985). Effects of experience on performance in a replenishable resource trap. *Journal of Personality and Social Psychology, 49,* 943–948.

Allport, F. H. (1924). *Social psychology.* Boston: Houghton Mifflin.

Allport, F. H., et al. (1953). The effects of segregation and the consequences of desegregation: A social science statement. *Minneapolis Law Review, 37,* 429–440.

Allport, G. W. (1954). *The nature of prejudice.* Reading, MA: Addison-Wesley.

Allport, G. W., & Postman, L. J. (1947). *The psychology of rumor.* New York: Holt.

Allred, K. D., & Smith, T. W. (1989). The hardy personality: Cognitive and physiological responses to evaluative threat. *Journal of Personality and Social Psychology, 56,* 257–266.

Aloise-Young, P. A. (1993). The development of self-presentation: Self-promotion in 6- to 10-year-old children. *Social Cognition, 11,* 201–222.

Altman, I. (1973). Reciprocity of interpersonal exchange. *Journal for Theory of Social Behavior, 3,* 249–261.

Altman, I., & Taylor, D. A. (1973). *Social penetration: The development of interpersonal relationships.* New York: Holt, Rinehart and Winston.

Amabile, T. M. (1983a). Brilliant but cruel: Perceptions of negative evaluators. *Journal of Experimental Social Psychology, 19,* 146–156.

Amabile, T. M. (1983b). *The social psychology of creativity.* New York: Springer-Verlag.

Amabile, T. M., Hill, K. G., Hennessey, B. A., & Tighe, E. M. (1994). The work preference inventory: Assessing intrinsic and extrinsic motivation orientations. *Journal of Personality and Social Psychology, 66,* 950–967.

Amato, P. R. (1983). Helping behavior in urban and rural environments: Field studies based on a taxonomic organization of helping episodes. *Journal of Personality and Social Psychology, 45,* 571–586.

Ambady, N., & Rosenthal, R. (1992). Thin slices of expressive behavior as predictors of interpersonal consequences: A meta-analysis. *Psychological Bulletin, 111,* 256–274.

Ambady, N., & Rosenthal, R. (1993). Half a minute: Predicting teacher evaluations from thin slices of nonverbal behavior and physical attractiveness. *Journal of Personality and Social Psychology, 64,* 431–441.

American Psychological Association (1992). Ethical principles of psychologists and code of conduct. *American Psychologist, 47,* 1597–1611.

Amir, Y. (1969). Contact hypothesis in ethnic relations. *Psychological Bulletin, 71,* 319–342.

Andersen, B. L., Kiecolt-Glaser, J. K., & Glaser, R. (1994). A biobehavioral model of cancer stress and disease course. *American Psychologist, 49,* 389–404.

Andersen, S. M., & Ross, L. (1984). Self-knowledge and social inference: I. The impact of cognitive/affective and behavioral data. *Journal of Personality and Social Psychology, 46,* 280–293.

Anderson, C. A. (1989). Temperature and aggression: Ubiquitous effects of heat on occurrence of human violence. *Psychological Bulletin, 106,* 74–96.

Anderson, C. A., & DeNeve, K. M. (1992). Temperature, aggression, and the negative affect escape model. *Psychological Bulletin, 111,* 347–351.

Anderson, C. A., Deuser, S. E., & DeNeve, K. M. (1995). Hot temperatures, hostile affect, hostile cognition, and arousal: Tests of a general model of affective aggression. *Personality and Social Psychology Bulletin, 21,* 434–448.

Anderson, C. A., & Harvey, R. J. (1988). Discriminating between problems in living: An examination of depression, loneliness, shyness, and social anxiety. *Journal of Social and Clinical Psychology, 6,* 482–491.

Anderson, C. A., Lepper, M. R., & Ross, L. (1980). Perseverance of social theories: The role of explanation in the persistence of discredited information. *Journal of Personality and Social Psychology, 39,* 1037–1049.

Anderson, C. A., Miller, R. S., Riger, A. L., Dill, J. C., & Sedikides, C. (1994). Behavioral and characterological attributional styles as predictors of depression and loneliness: Review, refinement, and test. *Journal of Personality and Social Psychology, 66,* 549–558.

Anderson, C. A., & Riger, A. L. (1991). A controllability attributional model of problems in living: Dimensional and situational interactions in the prediction of depression and loneliness. *Social Cognition, 9,* 149–181.

Anderson, C. A., & Sechler, E. S. (1986). Effects of explanation and counterexplanation on the development and use of social theories. *Journal of Personality and Social Psychology, 50,* 24–34.

Anderson, N. H. (1965). Averaging versus adding as a stimulus combination rule in impression formation. *Journal of Experimental Social Psychology, 70,* 394–400.

Anderson, N. H. (1968). Likableness ratings of 555 personality-trait words. *Journal of Personality and Social Psychology, 9,* 272–279.

Anderson, N. H. (1981). *Foundations of information integration theory.* New York: Academic Press.

Anderson, N. H., & Hubert, S. (1963). Effects of concomitant verbal recall on order effects in personality impression formation. *Journal of Verbal Learning and Verbal Behavior, 2,* 379–391.

Anderson, R. A., Baron, R. S., & Logan, H. (1991). Distraction, control, and dental stress. *Journal of Applied Social Psychology, 21,* 156–171.

Andreasson, P. B. (1987). On the social psychology of the stock market: Aggregate attributional effects and the regressiveness of prediction. *Journal of Personality and Social Psychology, 53,* 490–496.

Andrews, B. (1992). Attribution processes in victims of marital violence: Who do women blame and why? In J. H. Harvey, T. L. Orbuch, & A. L. Weber (Eds.), *Attributions, accounts, and close relationships* (pp. 176–193). New York: Springer-Verlag.

Annin, P. (1995, April 3). Battleground Chicago: Report from the front: How racial preferences really work—or don't. *Newsweek,* pp. 26–33.

Apodaca v. *Oregon,* 406 U.S. 404 (1972).

Apple, W., Streeter, L. A., & Krauss, R. M. (1979). Effects of pitch and speech rate on personal attributions. *Journal of Personality and Social Psychology, 37,* 715–727.

Archer, D., & Gartner, R. (1984). *Violence and crime in cross-national perspective.* New Haven, CT: Yale University Press.

Archer, D., Iritani, B., Kimes, D. D., & Barrios, M. (1983). Five studies of sex differences in facial prominence. *Journal of Personality and Social Psychology, 45,* 725–735.

Archibald, F. S., Bartholomew, K., & Marx, R. (1995). Loneliness in early adolescence: A test of the cognitive discrepancy model of loneliness. *Personality and Social Psychology Bulletin, 21,* 296–301.

Arendt, H. (1963). *Eichmann in Jerusalem: A report on the banality of evil.* New York: Viking.

Arkin, R. M. (1981). Self-presentation styles. In J. T. Tedeschi (Ed.), *Impression management theory and social psychological research* (pp. 311–333). New York: Academic Press.

Aron, A. (1988). The matching hypothesis reconsidered again: Comment on Kalick and Hamilton. *Journal of Personality and Social Psychology, 54,* 441–446.

Aron, A., Aron, E. N., & Smollan, D. (1992). Inclusion of Other in the Self Scale and the structure of interpersonal closeness. *Journal of Personality and Social Psychology, 63,* 596–612.

Aron, A., Aron, E. N., Tudor, M., & Nelson, G. (1991). Close relationships as including other in the self. *Journal of Personality and Social Psychology, 60,* 241–253.

Aronoff, J., Barclay, A. M., & Stevenson, L. A. (1988). The recognition of threatening facial stimuli. *Journal of Personality and Social Psychology, 54,* 647–655.

Aronoff, J., Woike, B. A., & Hyman, L. M. (1992). Which are the stimuli in facial displays of anger and happiness? *Journal of Personality and Social Psychology, 62,* 1050–1066.

Aronson, E. (1969). The theory of cognitive dissonance: A current perspective. In L. Berkowitz (Ed.), *Advances in experimental social psychology* (Vol. 4, pp. 1–34). New York: Academic Press.

Aronson, E. (1988). *The social animal.* San Francisco, CA: Freeman.

Aronson, E., Blaney, N., Stephan, C., Sikes, J., & Snapp, M. (1978). *The jigsaw classroom.* Beverly Hills, CA: Sage.

Aronson, E., Brewer, M., & Carlsmith, J. M. (1985). Experimentation in social psychology. In G. Lindzey & E. Aronson (Eds.), *Handbook of social psychology* (Vol. 1, 3rd ed., pp. 441–486). New York: Random House.

Aronson, E., & Carlsmith, J. M. (1963). Effect of severity of threat on the devaluation of forbidden behavior. *Journal of Abnormal and Social Psychology, 66,* 584–588.

Aronson, E., & Carlsmith, J. M. (1968). Experimentation in social psychology. In G. Lindzey & E. Aronson (Eds.), *Handbook of social psychology* (Vol. 2, 2nd ed., pp. 1–79). Reading, MA: Addison-Wesley.

Aronson, E., & Cope, V. (1968). My enemy's enemy is my friend. *Journal of Personality and Social Psychology, 8,* 8–12.

Aronson, E., & Linder, D. (1965). Gain and loss of esteem as determinants of interpersonal attractiveness. *Journal of Experimental Social Psychology, 1,* 156–172.

Aronson, E., & Mills, J. (1959). The effect of severity of initiation on liking for a group. *Journal of Abnormal and Social Psychology, 59,* 177–181.

Aronson, E., & Worchel, S. (1966). Similarity versus liking as determinants of interpersonal attractiveness. *Psychonomic Science, 5,* 157–158.

Arthur, W., Jr., Doverspike, D., & Fuentes, R. (1992). Recipients' affective responses to affirmative action interventions: A cross-cultural perspective. *Behavioral Sciences and the Law, 10,* 229–243.

Asch, S. E. (1946). Forming impressions of personality. *Journal of Abnormal and Social Psychology, 41,* 258–290.

Asch, S. E. (1951). Effects of group pressure upon the modification and distortion of judgments. In H. Guetzkow (Ed.), *Groups, leadership, and men.* Pittsburgh, PA: Carnegie Press.

Asch, S. E. (1955, November). Opinions and social pressure. *Scientific American,* pp. 31–35.

Asch, S. E. (1956). Studies of independence and conformity: A minority of one against a unanimous majority. *Psychological Monographs, 70,* 416.

Asch, S. E., & Zukier, H. (1984). Thinking about persons. *Journal of Personality and Social Psychology, 46,* 1230–1240.

Askenasy, H. (1978). *Are we all Nazis?* Secaucus, NJ: Lyle Stuart.

Aspinwall, L. G., & Taylor, S. E. (1992). Modeling cognitive adaptation: A longitudinal investigation of the impact of individual differences and coping on college adjustment and performance. *Journal of Personality and Social Psychology, 63,* 989–1003.

Aspinwall, L. G., & Taylor, S. E. (1993). The effects of social comparison direction, threat, and self-esteem on affect, self-evaluation, and expected success. *Journal of Personality and Social Psychology, 64,* 708–722.

Associated Press. (1988, October 10). Skirting the issue? *The National Law Journal,* p. 43.

Atkinson, M. P., & Glass, B. L. (1985). Marital age heterogamy and homogamy, 1900–1980. *Journal of Marriage and the Family, 47,* 685–691.

Attorney General's Commission on Pornography (1986, July). *Final report.* Washington, DC: U.S. Department of Justice.

Auerbach, S. M., Kiesler, D. J., Strentz, T., Schmidt, J. A., & Serio, C. D. (1994). Interpersonal impacts and adjunctment to the stress of simulated captivity: An empirical test of the Stockholm Syndrome. *Journal of Social and Clinical Psychology, 13,* 207–221.

Aukett, R., Richie, J., & Mill, K. (1988). Gender differences in friendship patterns. *Sex Roles, 19,* 57–66.

Averill, J. R. (1982). *Anger and aggression.* New York: Springer-Verlag.

Axelrod, R. (1984). *The evolution of cooperation.* New York: Basic Books.

Axsom, D. (1989). Cognitive dissonance and behavior change in psychotherapy. *Journal of Experimental Social Psychology, 25,* 234–252.

Axsom, D., & Cooper, J. (1985). Cognitive dissonance and psychotherapy: The role of effort justification in inducing weight loss. *Journal of Experimental Social Psychology, 21,* 149–160.

Axsom, D., Yates, S., & Chaiken, S. (1987). Audience response as a heuristic cue in persuasion. *Journal of Personality and Social Psychology, 53,* 30–40.

Axtell, R. E. (1993). *Do's and taboos around the world* (3rd ed.). New York: John Wiley.

Babad, E., & Katz, Y. (1991). Wishful thinking—against all odds. *Journal of Applied Social Psychology, 21,* 1921–1938.

Bailey, D. S., & Taylor, S. P. (1991). Effects of alcohol and aggressive disposition on human physical aggression. *Journal of Research in Personality, 25,* 334–342.

Bailey, J. M., Gaulin, S., Agyei, Y., & Gladue, B. A. (1994). Effects of gender and sexual orientation on evolutionarily relevant aspects of human mating psychology. *Journal of Personality and Social Psychology, 66,* 1081–1093.

Baldwin, M. W., & Holmes, J. G. (1987). Salient private audiences and awareness of the self. *Journal of Personality and Social Psychology, 52,* 1087–1098.

Bales, R. F. (1958). Task roles and social roles in problem-solving groups. In E. E. Maccoby, T. M. Newcomb, & E. L. Hartley (Eds.), *Readings in social psychology* (3rd ed., pp. 437–447). New York: Holt.

Ballew v. *Georgia,* 435 U.S. 223 (1978).

Banaji, M. R., Hardin, C., & Rothman, A. J. (1993). Implicit stereotyping in person judgment. *Journal of Personality and Social Psychology, 65,* 272–281.

Banaji, M. R., & Prentice, D. A. (1994). The self in social contexts. *Annual Review of Psychology, 45,* 297–332.

Banaji, M. R., & Steele, C. M. (1989). Alcohol and self-evaluation: Is a social cognition approach beneficial? *Social Cognition, 7,* 137–151.

Bandura, A. (1973). *Aggression: A social learning analysis.* Englewood Cliffs, NJ: Prentice-Hall.

Bandura, A. (1977a). Self-efficacy: Toward a unifying theory of behavioral change. *Psychological Review, 84,* 191–215.

Bandura, A. (1977b). *Social learning theory.* Englewood Cliffs, NJ: Prentice-Hall.

Bandura, A. (1983). Psychological mechanisms of aggression. In R. G. Geen & E. I. Donnerstein (Eds.), *Aggression: Theoretical and empirical reviews: Vol. l. Theoretical and methodological issues* (pp. 1–40). New York: Academic Press.

Bandura, A. (1990). Selective activation and disengagement of moral control. *Journal of Social Issues, 46,* 27–46.

Bandura, A., Ross, R., & Ross, S. (1961). Transmission of aggression through imitation of aggressive models. *Journal of Abnormal and Social Psychology, 63,* 575–582.

Banuazizi, A., & Movahedi, S. (1975). Interpersonal dynamics in a simulated prison: A methodological analysis. *American Psychologist, 30,* 152–160.

Bargal, D., Gold, M., & Lewin, M. (1992). Introduction: The heritage of Kurt Lewin. *Journal of Social Issues, 48*(2), 3–13.

Bargh, J. A. (1992). Does subliminality matter to social psychology? Awareness of the stimulus versus awareness of its interpretation. In R. F. Bornstein & T. S. Pittman (Eds.), *Perception without awareness: Cognitive, clinical and social perspectives* (pp. 236–255). New York: Guilford.

Bargh, J. A., Chaiken, S., Govender, R., & Pratto, F. (1992). The generality of the automatic attitude activation effect. *Journal of Personality and Social Psychology. 62,* 893–912.

Bargh, J. A., Lombardi, W. J., & Higgins, E. T. (1988). Automaticity of chronically accessible constructs in person x situation effects on person perception: It's just a matter of time. *Journal of Personality and Social Psychology, 55,* 599–605.

Bargh, J. A., & Pietromonaco, P. (1982). Automatic information processing and social perception: The influence of trait information presented outside of conscious awareness on impression formation. *Journal of Personality and Social Psychology, 43,* 437–449.

Barnes, R. D., Ickes, W., & Kidd, R. F. (1979). Effects of the perceived intentionality and stability of another's dependency on helping behavior. *Personality and Social Psychology Bulletin, 5,* 367–372.

Barnes Nacoste, R. (1994). If empowerment is the goal . . .: Affirmative action and social interaction. *Basic and Applied Social Psychology, 15,* 87–112.

Barnett, R. C., Marshall, N. L., & Pleck, J. H. (1992). Men's multiple roles and their relationship to men's psychological distress. *Journal of Marriage and the Family, 54,* 358–367.

Barnett, R. C., Marshall, N. L., Raudenbush, S. W., & Brennan, R. T. (1993). Gender and the relationship between job experience and psychological distress: A study of dual-earner couples. *Journal of Personality and Social Psychology, 64,* 794–806.

Baron, R. A. (1977). *Human aggression.* New York: Plenum.

Baron, R. A. (1983a). The control of human aggression: An optimistic perspective. *Journal of Social and Clinical Psychology, 1,* 97–119.

Baron, R. A. (1983b). The control of human aggression: A strategy based on incompatible responses. In R. G. Geen & E. I. Donnerstein (Eds.), *Aggression: Theoretical and empirical reviews: Vol. 2. Issues in research* (pp. 173–190). New York: Academic Press.

Baron, R. A., & Ball, R. L. (1974). The aggression-inhibiting influence of nonhostile behavior. *Journal of Experimental Social Psychology, 10,* 23–33.

Baron, R. A., & Kepner, C. R. (1970). Model's behavior and attraction toward the model as determinants of adult aggressive behavior. *Journal of Personality and Social Psychology, 14,* 335–344.

Baron, R., Logan, H., Lilly, J., Inman, M., & Brennan, M. (1994). Negative emotion and message processing. *Journal of Experimental Social Psychology, 30,* 181–201.

Baron, R. A., & Ransberger, V. M. (1978). Ambient temperature and the occurrence of collective violence: The "long, hot summer" revisited. *Journal of Personality and Social Psychology, 36,* 351–360.

Baron, R. A., & Richardson, D. R. (1994). *Human aggression* (2nd ed.). New York: Plenum.

Baron, R. M. (1988). An ecological framework for establishing a dual-mode theory of social knowing. In D. Bar-Tal & A. W. Kruglanski (Eds.), *The social psychology of knowledge* (pp. 48–82). New York: Cambridge University Press.

Baron, R. S. (1986). Distraction-conflict theory: Progress and problems. In L. Berkowitz (Ed.), *Advances in experimental social psychology* (Vol. 19, pp. 1–40). Orlando, FL: Academic Press.

Barrera, M., Jr., & Ainlay, S. L. (1983). The structure of social support: A conceptual and empirical analysis. *Journal of Community Psychology, 11,* 133–143.

Bar-Tal, D. (1990). Causes and consequences of delegitimization: Models of conflict and ethnocentrism. *Journal of Social Issues, 46,* 65–81.

Bar-Tal, D., & Saxe, L. (1976). Perceptions of similarly and dissimilarly attractive couples and individuals. *Journal of Personality and Social Psychology, 33,* 772–781.

Bashore, T. R., & Rapp, P. E. (1993). Are there alternatives to traditional polygraph procedures? *Psychological Bulletin, 113,* 3–22.

Bass, B. M. (1985). *Leadership and performance beyond expectations.* New York: Free Press.

Bass, B. M. (1990). *Bass & Stogdill's handbook of leadership: Theory, research, & managerial applications* (3rd ed.). New York: Free Press.

Bass, B. M., & Avolio, B. J. (1990). *Manual: The multifactor leadership questionnaire.* Palo Alto, CA: Consulting Psychologists Press.

Bassili, J. N., & Provencal, A. (1988). Perceiving minorities: A factor-analytic approach. *Personality and Social Psychology Bulletin, 14,* 5–15.

Bassili, J. N., & Racine, J. P. (1990). On the process relationship between person and situation judgments in attribution. *Journal of Personality and Social Psychology, 59,* 881–890.

Batson, C. D. (1991). *The altruism question.* Hillsdale, NJ: Erlbaum.

Batson, C. D. (1993). Communal and exchange relationships: What is the difference? *Personality and Social Psychology Bulletin, 19,* 677–683.

Batson, C. D., Batson, J. G., Griffitt, C. A., Barrientos, S., Brandt, J. R., Sprengelmeyer, P., & Bayly, M. J. (1989). Negative-state relief and the empathy-altruism hypothesis. *Journal of Personality and Social Psychology, 56,* 922–933.

Batson, C. D., Batson, J. G., Slingsby, J. K., Harrell, K. L., Peekna, H. M., & Todd, R. M. (1991). Empathic joy and the empathy-altruism hypothesis. *Journal of Personality and Social Psychology, 61,* 413–426.

Batson, C. D., Batson, J. G., Todd, R. M., Brummett, B. H., Shaw, L. L., & Aldeguer, C. M. R. (1995). Empathy and the collective good: Caring for one of the others in a social dilemma. *Journal of Personality and Social Psychology, 68,* 619–631.

Batson, C. D., Coke, J. S., Jasnoski, M. L., & Hanson, M. (1978). Buying kindness: Effect of an extrinsic incentive for helping on perceived altruism. *Personality and Social Psychology Bulletin, 4,* 86–91.

Batson, C. D., Duncan, B. D., Ackerman, P., Buckley, T., & Birch, K. (1981). Is empathic emotion a source of altruistic motivation? *Journal of Personality and Social Psychology, 40,* 290–302.

Batson, C. D., Dyck, J. L., Brandt, J. R., Batson, J. G., Powell, A. L., McMaster, M. R., & Griffitt, C. (1988). Five studies testing two new egoistic alternatives to the empathy-altruism hypothesis. *Journal of Personality and Social Psychology, 55,* 52–77.

Batson, C. D., Fultz, J., Schoenrade, P. A., & Paduano, A. (1987). Critical self-reflection and self-perceived altruism: When self-reward fails. *Journal of Personality and Social Psychology, 53,* 594–602.

Batson, C. D., Klein, T. R., Highberger, L., & Shaw, L.L. (1995). Immortality from empathy-induced altruism: When compassion and justice conflict. *Journal of Personality and Social Psychology, 68,* 1042–1054.

Batson, C. D., O'Quin, K., Fultz, J., Vanderplas, M., & Isen, A. M. (1983). Influence of self-reported distress and empathy on egoistic versus altruistic motivation to help. *Journal of Personality and Social Psychology, 45,* 706–718.

Baum, A. (Ed.). (1984). Social psychology and cigarette smoking [Special issue]. *Journal of Applied Social Psychology, 14*(3).

Baum, A., & Fleming, I. (1993). Implications of psychological research on stress and technological accidents. *American Psychologist, 48,* 665–672.

Baum, A., & Valins, S. (1977). *Architecture and social behavior: Psychological studies of social density.* Hillsdale, NJ: Erlbaum.

Baum, A., & Valins, S. (1979). Architectural mediation of residential density and control: Crowding and the regulation of social contact. In L. Berkowitz (Ed.), *Advances in experimental social psychology* (Vol. 12, pp. 131–175). New York: Academic Press.

Bauman, M. H. (1982, August 16). What you can and can't learn from interviews. *The Wall Street Journal.*

Baumeister, R. F. (1982). A self-presentational view of social phenomena. *Psychological Bulletin, 91,* 3–26.

Baumeister, R. F. (1990). Suicide as escape from self. *Psychological Review, 97,* 90–113.

Baumeister, R. F. (1991). *Escaping the self.* New York: Basic Books.

Baumeister, R. F., Chesner, S. P., Sanders, P. S., & Tice, D. M. (1988). Who's in charge here? Group leaders do lend help in emergencies. *Personality and Social Psychology Bulletin, 14,* 17–22.

Baumeister, R. F., & Newman, L. S. (1994). How stories make sense of personal experiences: Motives that shape autobiographical narratives. *Personality and Social Psychology Bulletin, 20,* 676–690.

Baumeister, R. F., & Scher, S. J. (1988). Self-defeating behavior patterns among normal individuals: Review and analysis of common self-destructive tendencies. *Psychological Bulletin, 104,* 3–22.

Baumeister, R. F., & Tice, D. M. (1984). Role of self-presentation and choice in cognitive dissonance under forced compliance: Necessary or sufficient causes? *Journal of Personality and Social Psychology, 46,* 5–13.

Baumeister, R. F., & Wotman, S. R. (1992). *Breaking hearts: The two sides of unrequited love.* New York: Guilford Press.

Baumeister, R., Stillwell, A. M., & Hetherington, T. F. (1994). Guilt: An interpersonal approach. *Psychological Bulletin, 115,* 243–267.

Baumrind, D. (1964). Some thoughts on ethics of research: After reading Milgram's "Behavioral Study of Obedience." *American Psychologist, 19,* 421–423.

Baumrind, D. (1985). Research using intentional deception: Ethical issues revisited. *American Psychologist, 40,* 165–174.

Baxter, L. A. (1987). Self-disclosure and disengagement. In V. J. Derleg & J. H. Berg (Eds.), *Self-disclosure: Theory, research, and therapy* (pp. 155–174). New York: Plenum.

Beach, S. R. H., & Tesser, A. (1993). Decision making power and marital satisfaction: A self-evaluation maintenance perspective. *Journal of Social and Clinical Psychology, 12,* 471–494.

Beaman, A. L., Cole, C. M., Preston, M., Klentz, B., & Steblay, N. M. (1983). Fifteen years of foot-in-the-door research: A meta-analysis. *Personality and Social Psychology Bulletin, 9,* 181–196.

Beaman, A. L., Klentz, B., Diener, E., & Svanum, S. (1979). Objective self-awareness and transgression in children: A field study. *Journal of Personality and Social Psychology, 37,* 1835–1846.

Beck, E. M., & Tolnay, S. E. (1990). The killing fields of the deep south: The market for cotton and the lynching of blacks, 1882–1930. *American Sociological Review, 55,* 526–539.

Becker, F. D. (1981). *Workspace.* New York: Praeger.

Bedau, A., & Radelet, M. (1987). Miscarriages of justice in potentially capital cases. *Stanford Law Review, 40,* 21–179.

Beggan, J. K. (1992). On the social nature of nonsocial perception: The mere ownership effect. *Journal of Personality and Social Psychology, 62,* 229–237.

Bell, P. A. (1992). In defense of the negative affect escape model of heat and aggression. *Psychological Bulletin, 111,* 342–346.

Bellezza, F. S. (1992). Recall of congruent information in the self-reference task. *Bulletin of the Psychonomic Society, 30,* 275–278.

Belli, R. F., Windschitl, P. D., McCarthy, T. T., & Winfrey, S. E. (1992). Detecting memory impairment with a modified test procedure: Manipulating retention interval with centrally presented event items. *Journal of Experimental Psychology: Learning, Memory, and Cognition, 18,* 356–367.

Belmore, S. M. (1987). Determinants of attention during impression formation. *Journal of Experimental Psychology: Learning, Memory, and Cognition, 13,* 480–489.

Belsky, J. (1993). Etiology of child maltreatment: A developmental-ecological analysis. *Psychological Bulletin, 114,* 413–434.

Bem, D. J. (1965). An experimental analysis of self-persuasion. *Journal of Experimental Social Psychology, 1,* 199–218.

Bem, D. J. (1967). Self-perception: An alternative interpretation of cognitive dissonance phenomena. *Psychological Review, 74,* 183–200.

Bem, D. J. (1972). Self-perception theory. In L. Berkowitz (Ed.), *Advances in experimental social psychology* (Vol. 6, pp. 1–62). New York: Academic Press.

Bem, S. L. (1981). Gender schema theory: A cognitive account of sex typing. *Psychological Review, 88,* 354–364.

Benassi, M. A. (1982). Effects of order of presentation, primacy, and physical attractiveness on attributions of ability. *Journal of Personality and Social Psychology, 43,* 48–58.

Benedict, M. E., & Levine, E. L. (1988). Delay and distortion: Tacit influences on performance appraisal effectiveness. *Journal of Applied Psychology, 73,* 507–514.

Benefit beat. (1991, June 10). *Time,* p. 15.

Ben-Shakhar, G., Bar-Hillel, M., Bilu, Y., Ben-Abba, E., & Flug, A. (1986). Can graphology predict occupational success? Two empirical studies and some methodological ruminations. *Journal of Applied Psychology, 71,* 645–653.

Benson, P. L., Karabenick, S. A., & Lerner, R. M. (1976). Pretty pleases: The effects of physical attractiveness, race, and sex on receiving help. *Journal of Experimental Social Psychology, 12,* 409–415.

Berg, J. H., & McQuinn, R. D. (1986). Attraction and exchange in continuing and noncontinuing dating relationships. *Journal of Personality and Social Psychology, 50,* 942–952.

Berglas, S., & Jones, E. E. (1978). Drug choice as a self-handicapping strategy in response to noncontingent success. *Journal of Personality and Social Psychology, 36,* 405–417.

Berkman, L., & Syme, S. L. (1979). Social networks, host resistance, and mortality: A nine-year follow-up study of Alameda County residents. *American Journal of Epidemiology, 109,* 186–204.

Berkowitz, L. (1962). *Aggression: A social psychological analysis.* New York: McGraw-Hill.

Berkowitz, L. (1965). Some aspects of observed aggression. *Journal of Personality and Social Psychology, 2,* 359–369.

Berkowitz, L. (1968). Impulse, aggression, and the gun. *Psychology Today,* 2(4), pp. 18–22.

Berkowitz, L. (1972). Social norms, feelings, and other factors affecting helping and altruism. In L. Berkowitz (Ed.), *Advances in experimental social psychology.* (Vol. 6, pp. 63–108). New York: Academic Press.

Berkowitz, L. (1987). Mood, self-awareness, and willingness to help. *Journal of Personality and Social Psychology, 52,* 721–729.

Berkowitz, L. (1989). Frustration-aggression hypothesis: Examination and reformulation. *Psychological Bulletin, 106,* 59–73.

Berkowitz, L. (1990). On the formulation and regulation of anger and aggression: A cognitive-neoassociationistic analysis. *American Psychologist, 45,* 494–503.

Berkowitz, L. (1993). *Aggression: Its causes, consequences, and control.* New York: McGraw-Hill.

Berkowitz, L., & Alioto, J. T. (1973). The meaning of an observed event as a determinant of its aggressive consequence. *Journal of Personality and Social Psychology, 28,* 206–217.

Berkowitz, L., & Donnerstein, E. (1982). External validity is more than skin deep: Some answers to criticisms of laboratory experiments. *American Psychologist, 37,* 245–257.

Berkowitz, L., & Heimer, K. (1989). On the construction of the anger experience: Aversive events and negative priming in the frustration of feelings. In L. Berkowitz (Ed.), *Advances in experimental social psychology* (Vol. 22, pp. 1–37). San Diego: Academic Press.

Berkowitz, L., & LePage, A. (1967). Weapons as aggression-eliciting stimuli. *Journal of Personality and Social Psychology, 7,* 202–207.

Berman, M., Gladue, B., & Taylor, S. (1993). The effects of hormones, Type A behavior pattern, and provocation on aggression in men. *Motivation and Emotion, 17,* 125–138.

Bernardin, H. J., & Beatty, R. W. (1984). *Performance appraisal: Assessing human behavior at work.* Boston: Kent.

Berndt, T. J. (1979). Developmental changes in conformity to peers and parents. *Developmental Psychology, 15,* 606–616.

Bernstein, W. M., Stephenson, B. O., Snyder, M. L., & Wicklund, R. A. (1983). Causal ambiguity and heterosexual affiliation. *Journal of Experimental Social Psychology, 19,* 78–92.

Berry, D. S. (1990). Taking people at face value: Evidence for the kernel of truth hypothesis. *Social Cognition, 8,* 343–361.

Berry, D. S., & Zebrowitz-McArthur, L. (1986). Perceiving character in faces: The impact of age-related craniofacial changes in social perception. *Psychological Bulletin, 100,* 3–18.

Berry, J. W. (1979). A cultural ecology of social behavior. *Advances in Experimental Social Psychology, 12,* 177–206.

Berry, J. W., Poortinga, Y. H., Segall, M. H., & Dasen, P. R. (1992). *Cross-cultural psychology: Research and application.* Cambridge, UK: Cambridge University Press.

Berscheid, E. (1966). Opinion change and communicator-communicatee similarity and dissimilarity. *Journal of Personality and Social Psychology, 4,* 670–680.

Berscheid, E. (1983). Emotion. In H. H. Kelley, E. Berscheid, A. Christenson, J. H. Harvey, T. L. Huston, G. Levinger, E. McClintock, L. A. Peplau, & D. R. Peterson, *Close relationships* (pp. 110–168). New York: Freeman.

Berscheid, E. (1992). A glance back at a quarter century of social psychology. *Journal of Personality and Social Psychology, 63,* 525–533.

Berscheid, E. (1994). Interpersonal relationships. *Annual Review of Psychology, 45,* 79–129.

Berscheid, E., Dion, K., Walster, E., & Walster, G. W. (1971). Physical attractiveness and dating choice: A test of the matching hypothesis. *Journal of Experimental Social Psychology, 7,* 173–189.

Berscheid, E., & Peplau, L. A. (1983). The emerging science of relationships. In H. H. Kelley, E. Berscheid, A. Christenson, J. H. Harvey, T. L. Huston, G. Levinger, E. McClintock, L. A. Peplan, & D. R. Peterson, *Close relationships* (pp. 1–19). New York: Freeman.

Berscheid, E., Snyder, M., & Omoto, A. M. (1989). The relationship closeness inventory: Assessing the closeness of interpersonal relationships. *Journal of Personality and Social Psychology, 57,* 792–807.

Berscheid, E., & Walster, E. (1974a). A little bit about love. In T. Huston (Ed.), *Foundations of interpersonal attraction* (pp. 355–381). New York: Academic Press.

Berscheid, E., & Walster, E. (1974b). Physical attractiveness. In L. Berkowitz (Ed.), *Advances in experimental social psychology* (Vol. 7, pp. 157–215). New York: Academic Press.

Berscheid, E., & Walster, E. (1978). *Interpersonal attraction* (2nd ed.). Reading, MA: Addison-Wesley.

Berscheid, E., Walster, E., & Campbell, R. (1972). *Grow old along with me.* Unpublished manuscript, Department of Psychology, University of Minnesota.

Bersoff, D. N., & Ogden, D. W. (1987). In the Supreme Court of the United States: *Lockhart* v. *McCree. American Psychologist, 42,* 59–68.

Betancourt, H., & Blair, I. (1992). A cognition (attribution)-emotion model of violence in conflict situations. *Personality and Social Psychology Bulletin, 18,* 343–350.

Bettencourt, B. A., Brewer, M. B., Croak, M. R., & Miller, N. (1992). Cooperation and the reduction of intergroup bias: The role of reward structure and social orientation. *Journal of Experimental Social Psychology, 28,* 301–319.

Betzig, L. (1989). Causes of conjugal dissolution: A cross-cultural study. *Current Anthropology, 30,* 654–676.

Beyer, S. (1990). Gender differences in the accuracy of self-evaluations of performance. *Journal of Personality and Social Psychology, 59,* 960–970.

Bickman, L. (1974). The social power of a uniform. *Journal of Applied Social Psychology, 4,* 47–61.

Biden, J. R., Jr. (1993). Violence against women: The congressional response. *American Psychologist, 48,* 1059–1061.

Bierbrauer, G. (1979). Why did he do it? Attributions of obedience and the phenomenon of dispositional bias. *European Journal of Social Psychology, 9,* 67–84.

Bierhoff, H. W., Klein, R., & Kramp, P. (1991). Evidence for the altruistic personality from data on accident research. *Journal of Personality, 59,* 263–280.

Bierly, M. M. (1985). Prejudice toward contemporary outgroups as a generalized attitude. *Journal of Applied Social Psychology, 15,* 189–199.

Biernat, M. (1991). Gender stereotypes and the relationship between masculinity and femininity: A developmental analysis. *Journal of Personality and Social Psychology, 61,* 351–365.

Binning, J. F., Goldstein, M. A., Garcia, M. F., & Scatteregia, J. H. (1988). Effects of preinterview impressions on questioning strategies in same- and opposite-sex employment interviews. *Journal of Applied Psychology, 73,* 30–37.

Bisanz, G. L., & Rule, B. G. (1989). Gender and the persuasion schema: A search for cognitive invariants. *Personality and Social Psychology Bulletin, 15,* 4–18.

Björkqvist, K., & Niemelä, P. (1992). New trends in the study of female aggression. In K. Björkqvist & P. Niemelä (Eds.), *Of mice and women: Aspects of female aggression* (pp. 3–16). San Diego: Academic Press.

Björkqvist, K., Österman, K., & Kaukiainen, A. (1992). The development of direct and indirect aggressive strategies in males and females. In K. Björkqvist & P. Niemelä (Eds.), *Of mice and women: Aspects of female aggression* (pp. 51–64). San Diego: Academic Press.

Blair, S. L., & Johnson, M. P. (1992). Wives' perceptions of the fairness of the division of household labor: The intersection of housework and ideology. *Journal of Marriage and the Family, 54,* 570–581.

Blake, R. R., & Mouton, J. S. (1984). *Solving costly organizational conflicts.* San Francisco: Jossey-Bass.

Blanchard, D. C., & Blanchard, R. J. (1984). Affect and aggression: An animal model applied to human behavior. In R. J. Blanchard & D. C. Blanchard (Eds.), *Advances in the study of aggression* (Vol. 1, pp. 1–62). New York: Academic Press.

Blanchard, F. A., Lilly, T., & Vaughn, L. A. (1991). Reducing the expression of racial prejudice. *Psychological Science, 2,* 101–105.

Blascovich, J. (1992). A biopsychosocial approach to arousal regulation. *Journal of Social and Clinical Psychology, 11,* 213–237.

Blascovich, J., & Katkin, E. S. (Eds.). (1993). *Cardiovascular reactivity to psychological stress and disease.* Washington, DC: American Psychological Association.

Blascovich, J., & Kelsey, R. M. (1990). Using electrodermal and cardiovascular measures of arousal in social psychological research. In C. Hendrick & M. S. Clark (Eds.), *Review of personality and social psychology: Vol. 11. Research methods in personality and social psychology* (pp. 45–73). Newbury Park, CA: Sage.

Blass, T. (1984). Social psychology and personality: Toward a convergence. *Journal of Personality and Social Psychology, 47,* 1013–1027.

Blass, T. (1991). Understanding behavior in the Milgram obedience experiment: The role of personality, situations, and their interactions. *Journal of Personality and Social Psychology, 60,* 398–413.

Blass, T. (1992). The social psychology of Stanley Milgram. *Advances in Experimental Social Psychology, 25,* 227–329.

Blass, T., & Krackow, A. (1991, June). *The Milgram obedience experiments: Students' views vs. scholarly perspectives and actual findings.* Paper presented at the annual meeting of the American Psychological Society, Washington, DC.

Blood, R. O., & Wolfe, D. M. (1960). *Husbands and wives: The dynamics of married living.* New York: Free Press.

Bloom, B., Asher, S. J., & White, S. W. (1978). Marital disruption as a stressor: A review and analysis. *Psychological Bulletin, 85,* 867–894.

Bobo, L. (1988). Attitudes toward the black political movement: Trends, meaning, and effects of racial policy preferences. *Social Psychology Quarterly, 51,* 287–302.

Bobocel, D. R., & Meyer, J. P. (1994). Escalating commitment to a failing course of action: Separating the roles of choice and justification. *Journal of Applied Psychology, 79,* 360–363.

Bochner, S. (1994). Cross-cultural differences in the self-concept: A test of Hofstede's individualism/collectivism distinction. *Journal of Cross Cultural Psychology, 25,* 273–283.

Bochner, S., & Insko, C. A. (1966). Communicator discrepancy, source credibility, and opinion change. *Journal of Personality and Social Psychology, 4,* 614–621.

Bodenhausen, G. V. (1990). Stereotypes as judgmental heuristics: Evidence of circadian variations in discrimination. *Psychological Science, 1,* 319–322.

Bolger, N., DeLongis, A., Kessler, R. C., & Schilling, E. A. (1989). Effects of daily stress and negative mood. *Journal of Personality and Social Psychology, 57,* 808–818.

Bonacich, P., & Schneider, S. (1992). Communication networks and collective action. In W. B. G. Liebrand, D. M. Messick, & H. A. M. Wilke (Eds.), *Social dilemmas: Theoretical issues and research findings* (pp. 225–245). Oxford: Pergamon Press.

Bond, C. F., Jr. (1982). Social facilitation: A self-presentational view. *Journal of Personality and Social Psychology, 42,* 1042–1050.

Bond, C. F., Jr., & Titus, L. T. (1983). Social facilitation: A meta-analysis of 241 studies. *Psychological Bulletin, 94,* 265–292.

Boninger, D. S., Brock, T. C., Cook, T. D., Gruder, C. L., & Romer, D. (1990). Discovery of reliable attitude change persistence resulting from a transmitter tuning set. *Psychological Science, 1,* 268–271.

Boninger, D. S., Krosnick, J. A., & Berent, M. K. (1995). Origins of attitude importance: Self-interest, social identification, and value relevance. *Journal of Personality and Social Psychology, 68,* 61–80.

Booth, A., & Johnson, D. (1988). Premarital cohabitation and marital success. *Journal of Family Issues, 9,* 255–272.

Booth-Kewley, S., & Friedman, H. S. (1987). Psychological predictors of heart disease: A quantitative review. *Psychological Bulletin, 101,* 343–362.

Borgida, E. (1981). Legal reform of rape laws: A psycholegal approach. In L. Bickman (Ed.), *Applied social psychology annual* (Vol. 2, pp. 211–241). Beverly Hills, CA: Sage.

Borgida, E., & Brekke, N. (1981). The base-rate fallacy in attribution and prediction. In J. H. Harvey, W. J. Ickes, & R. F. Kidd (Eds.), *New directions in attribution research* (Vol. 3, pp. 66–95). Hillsdale, NJ: Erlbaum.

Borgida, E., & Brekke, N. (1985). Psychological research on rape trials. In A. Burgess (Ed.), *Research handbook on rape and sexual assault* (pp. 313–324). New York: Garland.

Borgida, E., & Campbell, B. (1982). Belief relevance and attitude-behavior consistency: The moderating role of personal experience. *Journal of Personality and Social Psychology, 42,* 239–247.

Borman, W. C., White, L. A., & Dorsey, D. W. (1995). Effects of ratee task performance and interpersonal factors on supervisor and peer performance ratings. *Journal of Applied Psychology, 80,* 168–177.

Bornstein, G. (1992). The free-rider problem in intergroup conflicts over step-level and continuous public goods. *Journal of Personality and Social Psychology, 62,* 597–606.

Bornstein, G., & Ben-Yossef, M. (1994). Cooperation in intergroup and single-group social dilemmas. *Journal of Experimental Social Psychology, 30,* 52–67.

Bornstein, G., Rapoport, A., Kerpel, L., & Katz, T. (1989). Within- and between-group communication in intergroup competition for public goods. *Journal of Experimental Social Psychology, 25,* 422–436.

Bornstein, R. F. (1989). Exposure and affect: Overview and meta-analysis of research, 1968–1987. *Psychological Bulletin, 106,* 265–289.

Bornstein, R. F. (1994). Dependency as a social cue: A meta-analytic review of research on the dependency-helping relationship. *Journal of Research in Personality, 28,* 182–213.

Bornstein, R. F., & D'Agostino, P. R. (1992). Stimulus recognition and the mere exposure effect. *Journal of Personality and Social Psychology, 63,* 545–552.

Bornstein, R. F., Krukonis, A. B., Manning, K. A., Mastrosimone, C. C., & Rossner, S. C. (1993). Interpersonal dependency and health service utilization in a college student sample. *Journal of Social and Clinical Psychology, 12,* 262–279.

Bostwick, T. D., & DeLucia, J. L. (1992). Effects of gender and specific dating behavior on perceptions of sex willingness and date rape. *Journal of Social and Clinical Psychology, 11,* 14–25.

Bothwell, R. K., Brigham, J. C., & Malpass, R. S. (1989). Cross-racial identification. *Personality and Social Psychology Bulletin, 15,* 19–25.

Bothwell, R. K., Deffenbacher, K. A., & Brigham, J. C. (1987). Correlation of eyewitness accuracy and confidence: Optimality hypothesis revisited. *Journal of Applied Psychology, 72,* 691–695.

Bower, G. H. (1993). The fragmentation of psychology? *American Psychologist, 48,* 905–907.

Boyden, T., Carroll, J. S., & Maier, R. A. (1984). Similarity and attraction in homosexual males: The effects of age and masculinity-femininity. *Sex Roles, 10,* 939–948.

Bradbury, T. N., & Fincham, F. D. (1990). Attributions in marriage: Review and critique. *Psychological Bulletin 107,* 3–33.

Bradbury, T. N., & Fincham, F. D. (1992). Attributions and behavior in marital interaction. *Journal of Personality and Social Psychology, 63,* 613–628.

Branscombe, N. R., & Wann, D. L. (1994). Collective self-esteem consequences of outgroup derogation when a valued social identity is on trial. *European Journal of Social Psychology, 24,* 641–657.

Branscombe, N. R., Wann, D. L., Noel, J. G., & Coleman, J. (1993). In- group or out-group extremity: Importance of the threatened social identity. *Personality and Social Psychology Bulletin, 19,* 381–388.

Brauer, M., Judd, C. M., & Gliner, M. D. (1995). The effects of repeated expressions on attitude polarization during group discussions. *Journal of Personality and Social Psychology, 68,* 1014–1029.

Bray, R. M., Johnson, D., & Chilstrom, J. T., Jr. (1982). Social influence by group members with minority opinions: A comparison of Hollander & Moscovici. *Journal of Personality and Social Psychology, 43,* 78–88.

Bray, R. M., Struckman-Johnson, C., Osborne, M., McFarlane, J., & Scott, J. (1978). The effects of defendant status on decisions of student and community juries. *Social Psychology, 41,* 256–260.

Brayfield, A. A. (1992). Employment resources and housework in Canada. *Journal of Marriage and the Family, 54,* 19–30.

Brean, H. (1958, March 31). What hidden sell is all about. *Life,* pp. 104–114.

Breckler, S. J. (1984). Empirical validation of affect, behavior, and cognition as distinct components of attitude. *Journal of Personality and Social Psychology, 47,* 1191–1205.

Brehm, J. W. (1956). Post-decision changes in desirability of alternatives. *Journal of Abnormal and Social Psychology, 52,* 384–389.

Brehm, S. S. (1992). *Intimate relationships* (2nd ed.). New York: McGraw-Hill.

Brehm, S. S., & Brehm, J. W. (1981). *Psychological reactance: A theory of freedom and control.* New York: Academic Press.

Brehm, S. S., & Smith, T. W. (1986). Social psychological approaches to psychotherapy and behavior change. In S. L. Garfield & A. E. Bergin (Eds.), *Handbook of psychotherapy and behavior change* (3rd ed., pp. 69–115). New York: Wiley.

Brewer, B. W. (1993). Self-identity and specific vulnerability to depressed mood. *Journal of Personality, 61,* 343–364.

Brewer, M. B. (1988). A dual process model of impression formation. In T. K. Srull & R. S. Wyer, Jr. (Eds.), *Advances in social cognition* (Vol. 1, pp. 1–36). Hillsdale, NJ: Erlbaum.

Brewer, M. B. (1991). The social self: On being the same and different at the same time. *Personality and Social Psychology Bulletin, 17,* 475–482.

Brewer, M. B. (1993). Social identity, distinctiveness, and in-group homogeneity. *Social Cognition, 11,* 150–164.

Brewer, M. B., Dull, V., & Lui, L. (1981). Perceptions of the elderly: Stereotypes as prototypes. *Journal of Personality and Social Psychology, 41,* 656–670.

Brewer, M. B., & Miller, N. (1984). Beyond the contact hypothesis: Theoretical perspectives on desegregation. In N. Miller & M. B. Brewer (Eds.), *Groups in contact: The psychology of desegregation* (pp. 281–302). New York: Academic Press.

Briggs, S. R., & Cheek, J. M. (1988). On the nature of self-monitoring: Problems with assessment, problems with validity. *Journal of Personality and Social Psychology, 54,* 663–678.

Brigham, J. C., & Cairns, D. L. (1988). The effect of mugshot inspections on eyewitness identification accuracy. *Journal of Applied Social Psychology, 18,* 1394–1410.

Brigham, J. C., Maass, A., Snyder, L. S., & Spaulding, K. (1982). The accuracy of eyewitness identifications in a field setting. *Journal of Personality and Social Psychology, 42,* 673–681.

Brigham, J. C., & Malpass, R. S. (1985). The role of experience and contact in the recognition of faces of own- and other-race persons. *Journal of Social Issues, 41,* 139–155.

Brinthaupt, R. M., Moreland, R. L., & Levine, J. M. (1991). Sources of optimism among prospective group members. *Personality and Social Psychology Bulletin, 17,* 36–43.

Brockner, J. (1983). Low self-esteem and behavioral plasticity: Some implications. In L. Wheeler & P. Shaver (Eds.), *Review of personality and social psychology* (Vol. 4, pp. 237–271). Beverly Hills, CA: Sage.

Brockner, J., DeWitt, R. L., Grover, S., & Reed, T. (1990). When is it important to explain why? Factors affecting the relationship between managers' explanations of a layoff and survivors' reactions to the layoff. *Journal of Experimental Social Psychology, 26,* 389–407.

Brockner, J., & Rubin, J. Z. (1985). *Entrapment in escalating conflicts: A social psychological analysis.* New York: Springer-Verlag.

Brodkey, H. (1993, July 5). The central face. *The New Yorker,* p. 31.

Bronfenbrenner, U. (1961). The mirror-image in Soviet-American relations. *Journal of Social Issues, 17,* 45–56.

Brown, B. B., Clasen, D. R., & Eicher, S. A. (1986). Perceptions of peer pressure, peer conformity dispositions, and self-reported behavior among adolescents. *Developmental Psychology, 22,* 521–530.

Brown, C. E., Dovidio, J. F., & Ellyson, S. L. (1990). Reducing sex differences in visual displays of dominance: Knowledge is power. *Personality and Social Psychology Bulletin, 16,* 358–368.

Brown, E., Deffenbacher, K., & Sturgill, W. (1977). Memory for faces and the circumstances of encounter. *Journal of Applied Psychology, 62,* 311–318.

Brown, G. W., & Harris, T. (1978). *Social origins of depression: A study of psychiatric disorder in women.* New York: Free Press.

Brown, J. D. (1991). Staying fit and staying well: Physical fitness as a moderator of life stress. *Journal of Personality and Social Psychology, 60,* 555–561.

Brown, J. D., & Dutton, K. A. (1995). The thrill of victory, the complexity of defeat: Self-esteem and people's emotional reactions to success and failure. *Journal of Personality and Social Psychology, 68,* 712–722.

Brown, J. D., Novick, N. J., Lord, K. A., & Richards, J. M. (1992). When Gulliver travels: Social context, psychological closeness, and self-appraisals. *Journal of Personality and Social Psychology, 62,* 717–727.

Brown, J. D., & Smart, S. A. (1991). The self and social conduct: Linking self-representations to prosocial behavior. *Journal of Personality and Social Psychology, 60,* 368–375.

Brown, N. R., & Siegler, R. S. (1992). The role of availability in the estimation of national populations. *Memory and Cognition, 20,* 406–412.

Brown, R. (1965). *Social psychology.* New York: Free Press.

Brown, R. (1986). *Social psychology* (2nd ed.). New York: Free Press.

Brown, R., & Kulik, J. (1977). Flashbulb memories. *Cognition, 5,* 73–99.

Browne, A. (1993). Violence against women by male partners: prevalence, outcomes, and policy implications. *American Psychologist, 48,* 1077–1087.

Bruch, M. A., Gorsky, J. M., Collins, T. M., & Berger, P. A. (1989). Shyness and sociability examined: A multicomponent analysis. *Journal of Personality and Social Psychology, 57,* 904–915.

Bruck, M., Ceci, S. J., Francoeur, E., & Barr, R. (1995). "I hardly cried when I got my shot!" Influencing children's reports about a visit to their pediatrician. *Child Development, 66,* 193–208.

Bruner, J. S., & Potter, M. C. (1964). Interference in visual recognition. *Science, 144,* 424–425.

Bruner, J. S., & Tagiuri, R. (1954). Person perception. In G. Lindzey (Ed.), *Handbook of social psychology* (Vol. 2, pp. 634–654). Reading, MA: Addison-Wesley.

Bryan, J. H., & Test, M. A. (1967). Models and helping: Naturalistic studies in aiding behavior. *Journal of Personality and Social Psychology, 6,* 400–407.

Bryson, J. B. (1991). Modes of response to jealousy-evoking situations. In P. Salovey (Ed.), *The psychology of jealousy and envy* (pp. 178–207). New York: Guilford.

Buchwald, A. M., Coyne, J. C., & Cole, C. S. (1978). A critical evaluation of the learned helplessness model of depression. *Journal of Abnormal Psychology, 87,* 180–193.

Buckhout, R. (1974, December). Eyewitness testimony. *Scientific American,* pp. 23–31.

Buehler, R., & Griffin, D. (1994). Change-of-meaning effects in conformity and dissent: Observing construal processes over time. *Journal of Personality and Social Psychology, 67,* 984–996.

Bulcroft, R. A., & Bulcroft, K. A. (1993). Race differences in attitudinal and motivational factors in the decision to marry. *Journal of Marriage and the Family, 55,* 338–355.

Bull, R., & Rumsey, N. (1988). *The social psychology of facial appearance.* New York: Springer-Verlag.

Burger, J. M. (1986). Increasing compliance by improving the deal: The that's-not-all technique. *Journal of Personality and Social Psychology, 51,* 277–283.

Burger, J. M. (1989). Negative reactions to increases in perceived control. *Journal of Personality and Social Psychology, 56,* 246–256.

Burger, J. M. (1991). Changes in attributions over time: The ephemeral fundamental attribution error. *Social Cognition, 9,* 182–193.

Burger, J. M., Brown, R., & Allen, C. K. (1983). Negative reactions to personal control. *Journal of Social and Clinical Psychology, 1,* 322–342.

Burger, J. M., & Petty, R. E. (1981). The low-ball compliance technique: Task or person commitment? *Journal of Personality and Social Psychology, 40,* 492–500.

Burke, A., Heuer, F., & Reisberg, D. (1992). Remembering emotional events. *Memory and Cognition, 20,* 277–290.

Burman, B., & Margolin, G. (1992). An analysis of the association between marital relationships and health problems: An interactional perspective. *Psychological Bulletin, 112,* 39–63.

Burnkrant, R. E., & Howard, D. J. (1984). Effects of the use of introductory rhetorical questions versus statements on information processing. *Journal of Personality and Social Psychology, 47,* 1218–1230.

Burns, J. M. (1978). *Leadership.* New York: Harper & Row.

Burnstein, E., Crandall, C., & Kitayama, S. (1994). Some neo-Darwinian decision rules for altruism: Weighing cues for inclusive fitness as a function of the biological importance of the decision. *Journal of Personality and Social Psychology, 67,* 773–789.

Burnstein, E., & Schul, Y. (1982). The informational basis of social judgments: The operations in forming an impression of another person. *Journal of Experimental Social Psychology, 18,* 217–234.

Burson, N., Carling, R., & Kramlich, D. (1986). *Composites: Computer-generated portraits.* New York: Morrow.

Burt, M. C. (1980). Cultural myths and supports for rape. *Journal of Personality and Social Psychology, 38,* 217–230.

Bushman, B. J. (1984). Perceived symbols of authority and their influence on compliance. *Journal of Applied Social Psychology, 14,* 501–508.

Bushman, B. J. (1988). The effects of apparel on compliance: A field experiment with a female authority figure. *Personality and Social Psychology Bulletin, 14,* 459–467.

Bushman, B. J., & Cooper, H. M. (1990). Effects of alcohol on human aggression: An integrative research review. *Psychological Bulletin, 107,* 341–354.

Bushman, B. J., & Geen, R. J. (1990). Role of cognitive-emotional mediators and individual differences in the effects of media violence on aggression. *Journal of Personality and Social Psychology, 58,* 156–163.

Buss, A. H. (1980). *Self-consciousness and social anxiety.* San Francisco: Freeman.

Buss, A. H., & Perry, M. (1992). The aggression questionnaire. *Journal of Personality and Social Psychology, 63,* 452–459.

Buss, D. M. (1988). The evolution of human intrasexual competition: Tactics of mate attraction. *Journal of Personality and Social Psychology, 54,* 616–628.

Buss, D. M. (1989). Sex differences in human mate preferences: Evolutionary hypotheses tested in 37 cultures. *Behavioral and Brain Sciences, 12,* 1–14.

Buss, D. M. (1994). *The evolution of desire: Strategies of human mating.* New York: Basic Books.

Buss, D. M., Gomes, M., Higgins, D. S., & Lauterbach, K. (1987). Tactics of manipulation. *Journal of Personality and Social Psychology, 52,* 1219–1229.

Buss, D. M., Larsen, R. J., Westen, D., & Semmelroth, J. (1992). Sex differences in jealousy: Evolution, physiology, and psychology. *Psychological Science, 3,* 251–255.

Buss, D. M., & Schmitt, D. P. (1993). Sexual strategies theory: An evolutionary perspective on human mating. *Psychological Review, 100,* 204–232.

Butler, D., & Geis, F. L. (1990). Nonverbal affect responses to male and female leaders: Implications for leadership evaluations. *Journal of Personality and Social Psychology, 58,* 48–59.

Buunk, B. P. (1991). Jealousy in close relationships: An exchange-theoretical perspective. In P. Salovey (Ed.), *The psychology of jealousy and envy* (pp. 148–177). New York: Guilford.

Buunk, B., & Hupka, R. B. (1987). Cross-cultural differences in the elicitation of sexual jealousy. *Journal of Sex Research, 23,* 12–22.

Byrne, D. (1971). *The attraction paradigm.* New York: Academic Press.

Byrne, D., & Clore, G. L. (1970). A reinforcement model of evaluative processes. *Personality: An International Journal, 1,* 103–128.

Byrne, D., Clore, G. L., & Smeaton, G. (1986). The attraction hypothesis: Do similar attitudes affect anything? *Journal of Personality and Social Psychology, 51,* 1167–1170.

Cacioppo, J. T., Crites, S. L., Berntson, G. G., & Coles, M. G. H. (1993). If attitudes affect how stimuli are processed, should they not affect the event-related brain potential? *Psychological Science, 4,* 108–112.

Cacioppo, J. T., & Petty, R. E. (1981). Electromyograms as measures of extent and affectivity of information processing. *American Psychologist, 36,* 441–456.

Cacioppo, J. T., & Petty, R. E. (1982). The need for cognition. *Journal of Personality and Social Psychology, 42,* 116–131.

Cacioppo, J. T., & Petty, R. E. (1984). The need for cognition: Relationship to attitudinal processes. In R. P. McGlynn, J. E.

Maddux, C. D. Stoltenberg, & J. H. Harvey (Eds.), *Interfaces in psychology: Social perception in clinical and counseling psychology* (pp. 113–139). Lubbock, TX: Texas Tech Press.

Cacioppo, J. T., Petty, R. E., Losch, M. E., & Kim, H. S. (1986). Electromyographic activity over facial muscle regions can differentiate the valence and intensity of affective reactions. *Journal of Personality and Social Psychology, 50,* 260–268.

Cacioppo, J. T., Petty, R. E., & Morris, K. (1983). Effects of need for cognition on message evaluation, recall, and persuasion. *Journal of Personality and Social Psychology, 45,* 805–818.

Cacioppo, J. T., Rourke, P. A., Marshall-Goodell, B. S., Tassinary, L. G., & Baron, R. S. (1990). Rudimentary physiological effects of mere observations. *Psychophysiology, 27,* 177–186.

Cacioppo, J. T., & Tassinary, L. G. (1990). Inferring psychological significance from physiological signals. *American Psychologist, 45,* 16–28.

Cahn, D. D. (1992). *Conflict in intimate relationships.* New York: Guilford.

Caldwell, M. A., & Peplau, L. A. (1984). The balance of power in lesbian relationships. *Sex Roles, 10,* 587–599.

Callaway, M. R., Marriott, R. G., & Esser, J. K. (1985). Effects of dominance on group decision making: Toward a stress-reduction explanation of groupthink. *Journal of Personality and Social Psychology, 49,* 949–952.

Camacho, L. M., & Paulus, P. B. (1995). The role of social anxiousness in group brainstorming. *Journal of Personality and Social Psychology, 68,* 1071–1080.

Camara, W. J., & Schneider, D. L. (1994). Integrity tests: Facts and unresolved issues. *American Psychologist, 49,* 112–119.

Cameron, J., & Pierce, W. D. (1994). Reinforcement, reward, and intrinsic motivation: A meta-analysis. *Review of Educational Research, 64,* 363–423.

Campbell, D. J., & Lee, C. (1988). Self-appraisal in performance evaluation: Development versus evaluation. *Academy Management Review, 13,* 302–313.

Campbell, J. D., & Fairey, P. J. (1989). Informational and normative routes to conformity. *Journal of Personality and Social Psychology, 57,* 457–468.

Campion, M. A., Pursell, E. D., & Brown, B. K. (1988). Structured interviewing: Raising the psychometric properties of the employment interview. *Personnel Psychology, 41,* 25–42.

Carey, M. P., & Burish, T. G. (1988). Etiology and treatment of the psychological side effects associated with cancer chemotherapy: A critical review and discussion. *Psychological Bulletin, 104,* 307–325.

Carli, L. L. (1990). Gender, language, and influence. *Journal of Personality and Social Psychology, 59,* 941–951.

Carli, L. L., Ganley, R., & Pierce-Otay, A. (1991). Similarity and satisfaction in roommate relationships. *Personality and Social Psychology Bulletin, 17,* 419–426.

Carlsmith, J. M., & Anderson, C. A. (1979). Ambient temperature and the occurrence of collective violence: A new analysis. *Journal of Personality and Social Psychology, 37,* 337–344.

Carlson, M., Charlin, V., & Miller, N. (1988). Positive mood and helping behavior: A test of six hypotheses. *Journal of Personality and Social Psychology, 55,* 211–229.

Carlson, M., Marcus-Newhall, A., & Miller, N. (1990). Effects of situational aggressive cues: A quantitative review. *Journal of Personality and Social Psychology, 58,* 622–633.

Carlson, M., & Miller, N. (1987). Explanation of the relation between negative mood and helping. *Psychological Bulletin, 102,* 91–108.

Carlson, R. (1984). What's social about social psychology? Where's the person in personality research? *Journal of Personality and Social Psychology, 47,* 1304–1309.

Carnegie, D. (1936). *How to win friends and influence people.* New York: Pocket Books. (Reprinted in 1972)

Carnelley, K. B., Pietromonaco, P. R., & Jaffe, K. (1994). Depression, working models of others, and relationship functioning. *Journal of Personality and Social Psychology, 66,* 127–140.

Carnevale, P. J. (1985). Mediation of international conflict. *Applied Social Psychology Annual, 6,* 87–105.

Carpenter, S. (1993). Organization of in-group and out-group information: The influence of gender-role orientation. *Social Cognition, 11,* 70–91.

Carroll, J. S., Perkowitz, W. T., Lurigio, A. J., & Weaver, F. M. (1987). Sentencing goals, causal attributions, ideology, and personality. *Journal of Personality and Social Psychology, 52,* 107–118.

Carter, S. L. (1991). *Reflections of an affirmative action baby.* New York: Basic Books.

Carter, S. L. (1994, December 5). "Let us pray." *The New Yorker,* pp. 60–78.

Cartwright, D., & Zander, A. (1960). Group cohesiveness: Introduction. In D. Cartwright & A. Zander (Eds.), *Group dynamics: Research and theory* (2nd ed., pp. 69–94). Evanston, IL: Row, Peterson.

Carver, C. S. (1975). Physical aggression as a function of objective self-awareness and attitudes toward punishment. *Journal of Experimental Social Psychology, 11,* 510–519.

Carver, C. S., Pozo, C., Harris, S. D., Noriega, V., Scheier, M. F., Robinson, D. S., Ketcham, A. S., Moffet, Jr., F. L., & Clark, K. C. (1993). How coping mediates the effect of optimism on distress: A study of women with early stage breast cancer. *Journal of Personality and Social Psychology, 65,* 375–390.

Carver, C. S., & Scheier, M. F. (1981). *Attention and self-regulation: A control-theory approach to human behavior.* New York: Springer-Verlag.

Carver, C. S., & Scheier, M. F. (1990). Origins and functions of positive and negative affect: A control-process view. *Psychological Review, 97,* 19–35.

Carver, C. S., & Scheier, M. F. (1994). Situational coping and coping dispositions in a stressful transaction. *Journal of Personality and Social Psychology, 66,* 184–195.

Caspi, A., & Harbener, E. S. (1990). Continuity and change: Assortive marriage and the consistency of personality in adulthood. *Journal of Personality and Social Psychology, 58,* 250–258.

Cassel, J. (1974). Psychosocial processes and "stress": Theoretical formulation. *International Journal of Health Services, 6,* 471–482.

Cate, R. M., & Lloyd, S. A. (1988). Courtship. In S. Duck (Ed.), *Handbook of personal relationships: Theory, research, and interventions* (pp. 409–427). New York: Wiley.

Cate, R. M., & Lloyd, S. A. (1992). *Courtship.* Newbury Park, CA: Sage.

Cate, R. M., Lloyd, S. A., & Long, E. (1988). The role of rewards and fairness in developing premarital relationships. *Journal of Marriage and the Family, 50,* 443–452.

Ceci, S. J., & Bruck, M. (1993). Suggestibility of the child witness: A historical review and synthesis. *Psychological Bulletin, 113,* 403–439.

Ceci, S. J., Peters, D., & Plotkin, J. (1985). Human subjects review, personal values, and the regulation of social science research. *American Psychologist, 40,* 994–1002.

Ceci, S. J., Ross, D. F., & Toglia, M. P. (1987). Suggestibility of children's memory: Psycholegal implications. *Journal of Experimental Psychology, 116,* 38–49.

Centers for Disease Control Vietnam Experience Study. (1988). Health status of Vietnam veterans: I. Psychosocial characteristics. *Journal of the American Medical Association, 259,* 2701–2707.

Chacko, T. I. (1982). Women and equal employment opportunity: Some unintended effects. *Journal of Applied Psychology, 67,* 119–123.

Chaiken, S. (1979). Communicator physical attractiveness and persuasion. *Journal of Personality and Social Psychology, 37,* 1387–1397.

Chaiken, S. (1980). Heuristic versus systematic information processing and the use of source versus message cues in persuasion. *Journal of Personality and Social Psychology, 39,* 752–766.

Chaiken, S. (1987). The heuristic model of persuasion. In M. P. Zanna, J. M. Olson, & C. P. Herman (Eds.), *Social influence: The Ontario symposium* (Vol. 5, pp. 3–39). Hillsdale, NJ: Erlbaum.

Chaiken, S., & Baldwin, M. W. (1981). Affective-cognitive consistency and the effect of salient behavioral information on the self-perception of attitudes. *Journal of Personality and Social Psychology, 41,* 1–12.

Chaiken, S., Liberman, A., & Eagly, A. (1989). Heuristic and systematic information processing within and beyond the persuasion context. In J. Uleman and J. A. Bargh (Eds.), *Unintended thought* (pp. 212–252). New York: Guilford.

Chan, D. K., & Fishbein, M. (1993) Determinants of college women's intentions to tell their partners to use condoms. *Journal of Applied Social Psychology, 23,* 1455–1470.

Chapdelaine, A., Kenny, D. A., & LaFontana, K. M. (1994). Matchmaker, matchmaker, can you make me a match? Predicting liking between two unacquainted persons. *Journal of Personality and Social Psychology, 67,* 83–91.

Chapman, L. J. (1967). Illusory correlation in observational report. *Journal of Verbal Learning and Verbal Behavior, 6,* 151–155.

Chassin, L., Presson, C. C., & Sherman, S. J. (1990). Social psychological contributions to the understanding and prevention of adolescent cigarette smoking. *Personality and Social Psychology Bulletin, 16,* 133–151.

Check, J. V. P., & Guloien, T. H. (1989). Reported proclivity for coercive sex following repeated exposure to sexually violent pornography, nonviolent dehumanizing pornography, and erotica. In D. Zillmann & J. Bryant (Eds.), *Pornography: Research advances and policy considerations* (pp. 159–184). Hillsdale, NJ: Erlbaum.

Chemers, M. M., Hays, R. B., Rhodewalt, F., & Wysocki, J. (1985). A person-environment analysis of job stress: A contingency model explanation. *Journal of Personality and Social Psychology, 49,* 628–635.

Cheng, P. W., & Novick, L. R. (1990). A probabilistic contrast model of causal induction. *Journal of Personality and Social Psychology, 58,* 545–567.

Chesler, P., & Goodman, E. J. (1976). *Women, money, and power.* New York: Morrow.

Children's Defense Fund (1994). *State of America's Children.* Washington, DC: Children's Defense Fund.

Christensen, A., & Heavey, C. L. (1993). Gender differences in marital conflict: The demand/withdraw interaction pattern. In S. Oskamp & M. Costanzo (Eds.), *Gender issues in contemporary society* (pp. 113–141). Newbury Park, CA: Sage.

Christensen, A. J., Turner, C. W., Smith, T. W., Holman, J. M., Jr., & Gregory, M. C. (1991). Health locus of control and depression in end-stage renal disease. *Journal of Counseling and Clinical Psychology, 59,* 419–424.

Christensen, L. (1988). Deception in psychological research: When is its use justified? *Personality and Social Psychology Bulletin, 14,* 664–675.

Christianson, S. (1992). Emotional stress and eyewitness memory: A critical review. *Psychological Bulletin, 112,* 284–309.

Christopher, F. S., Owens, L. A., & Stecker, H. L. (1993a). An examination of single men's and women's sexual aggressiveness in dating relationships. *Journal of Social and Personal Relationships, 10,* 511–527.

Christopher, F. S., Owens, L. A., & Stecker, H. L. (1993b). Exploring the dark side of courtship: A test of a model of male premarital sexual aggressiveness. *Journal of Marriage and the Family, 55,* 469–479.

Cialdini, R. B. (1993). *Influence: Science and practice* (3rd ed.). Glenview, IL: Scott, Foresman.

Cialdini, R. B., & Ascani, K. (1976). Test of a concession procedure for inducing verbal, behavioral, and further compliance with a request to give blood. *Journal of Applied Psychology, 61,* 295–300.

Cialdini, R. B., Borden, R. J., Thorne, A., Walker, M. R., Freeman, S., & Sloan, L. R. (1976). Basking in reflected glory: Three (football) field studies. *Journal of Personality and Social Psychology, 34,* 366–375.

Cialdini, R. B., Cacioppo, J. T., Bassett, R., & Miller, J. A. (1978). Low-ball procedure for producing compliance: Commitment then cost. *Journal of Personality and Social Psychology, 36,* 463–476.

Cialdini, R. B., Darby, B. L., & Vincent, J. E. (1973). Transgressional altruism: A case for hedonism. *Journal of Personality and Social Psychology, 9,* 502–516.

Cialdini, R. B., & De Nicholas, M. E. (1989). Self-presentation by association. *Journal of Personality and Social Psychology, 57,* 626–631.

Cialdini, R. B., & Fultz, J. (1990). Interpreting the negative mood-helping literature via "mega" analysis: A contrary view. *Psychological Bulletin, 107,* 210–214.

Cialdini, R. B., Kallgren, C. A., & Reno, R. R. (1991). A focus theory of normative conduct: A theoretical refinement and reevaluation of the role of norms in human behavior. *Advances in Experimental Social Psychology, 24,* 201–234.

Cialdini, R. B., Reno, R. R., & Kallgren, C. A. (1990). A focus theory of normative conduct: Recycling the concept of norms to reduce littering in public places. *Journal of Personality and Social Psychology, 58,* 1015–1026.

Cialdini, R. B., Schaller, M., Houlihan, D., Arps, K., Fultz, J., & Beaman, A. L. (1987). Empathy-based helping: Is it selflessly or selfishly motivated? *Journal of Personality and Social Psychology, 52,* 749–758.

Cialdini, R. B., Vincent, J. E., Lewis, S. K., Catalan, J., Wheeler, D., & Darby, B. L. (1975). Reciprocal concessions procedure for inducing compliance: The door-in-the-face technique. *Journal of Personality and Social Psychology, 31,* 206–215.

Cini, M. A., Moreland, R. L., & Levine, J. M. (1993). Group staffing levels and responses to prospective and new group members. *Journal of Personality and Social Psychology, 65,* 723–734.

Cioffi, D., & Holloway, J. (1993). Delayed costs of suppressed pain. *Journal of Personality and Social Psychology, 64,* 274–282.

Darby, B. L. (1975). Reciprocal concessions procedure for inducing compliance: The door-in-the-face technique. *Journal of Personality and Social Psychology, 31,* 206–215.

Clark, L. A., & Watson, D. (1991). General affective dispositions in physical and psychological health. In C. R. Snyder & D. R. Forsyth (Eds.), *Handbook of social and clinical psychology: The health perspective* (pp. 221–245). New York: Pergamon Press.

Clark, M. S. (1983a). Reactions to aid in communal and exchange relationships. In J. D. Fisher, A. Nadler, & B. DePaulo (Eds.), *New directions in helping: Vol. 1. Recipient reactions to aid* (pp. 281–304). New York: Academic Press.

Clark, M. S. (1983b). Some implications of close social bonds for help-seeking. In B. M. DePaulo, A. Nadler, & J. D. Fisher (Eds.), *New directions in helping: Vol. 2. Help-seeking* (pp. 205–229). New York: Academic Press.

Clark, M. S. (1984). Record keeping in two types of relationships. *Journal of Personality and Social Psychology, 47,* 549–557.

Clark, M. S., & Mills, J. (1979). Interpersonal attraction in exchange and communal relationships. *Journal of Personality and Social Psychology, 37,* 12–24.

Clark, M. S., & Mills, J. (1993). The difference between communal and exchange relationships: What it is and is not. *Personality and Social Psychology Bulletin, 19,* 684–691.

Clark, M. S., Mills, J., & Powell, M. C. (1986). Keeping track of needs in communal and exchange relationships. *Journal of Personality and Social Psychology, 51,* 333–338.

Clark, M., Mills, J. R., & Corcoran, D. M. (1989). Keeping track of needs and inputs of friends and strangers. *Personality and Social Psychology Bulletin, 15,* 533–542.

Clark, M. S., Ouellette, R., Powell, M. C., & Milberg, S. (1987). Recipient's mood, relationship type, and helping. *Journal of Personality and Social Psychology, 53,* 94–103.

Clark, M. S., & Waddell, B. (1985). Perceptions of exploitation in communal and exchange relationships. *Journal of Social and Personal Relations, 2,* 403–418.

Clark, R. D., III, & Maass, A. (1990). The effects of majority size on minority influence: *European Journal of Psychology, 20,* 99–117.

Clark, R. D., III, & Maass, A. (1988). Social categorization in minority influence: The case of homosexuality. *European Journal of Social Psychology, 18,* 347–364.

Clark, R. D., III, & Word, L. E. (1972). Why don't bystanders help? Because of ambiguity? *Journal of Personality and Social Psychology, 24,* 392–400.

Clary, E. G., & Orenstein, L. (1991). The amount and effectiveness of help: The relationship of motives and abilities to helping behavior. *Personality and Social Psychology Bulletin, 17,* 58–64.

Clore, G. L., & Byrne, D. (1974). A reinforcement-affect model of attraction. In T. L. Huston (Ed.), *Foundations of interpersonal attraction* (pp. 143–170). New York: Academic Press.

Coates, D., Renzaglia, G. J., & Embree, M. C. (1983). When helping backfires: Help and helplessness. In J. D. Fisher, A. Nadler, & B. DePaulo (Eds.), *New directions in helping: Vol. 1. Recipient reactions to aid* (pp. 251–279). New York: Academic Press.

Cobb, S. (1976). Social support as a moderator of life stress. *Psychosomatic Medicine, 38,* 300–314.

Cochran, S. D., & Mays, V. M. (1989). Women and AIDS-related concerns: Roles for psychologists in helping the worried well. *American Psychologist, 44,* 529–535.

Cochran, S. D., Mays, V. M., Ciarletta, J., Caruso, C., & Mallon, D. (1992). Efficacy of the theory of reasoned action in predicting AIDS-related sexual risk reduction among gay men. *Journal of Applied Social Psychology, 22,* 1481–1501.

Cohen, E. G. (1984). The desegregated school: Problems in status power and interethnic climate. In N. Miller, & M. B. Brewer (Eds.), *Groups in contact: The psychology of desegregation* (pp. 77–96). New York: Academic Press.

Cohen, S., & Hoberman, H. M. (1983). Positive events and social supports as buffers of life change. *Journal of Applied Social Psychology, 13,* 99–125.

Cohen, S., Kessler, R. C., & Gordon, L. U. (1995). *Measuring stress: A guide for health and social scientists.* New York: Oxford University Press.

Cohen, S., Tyrrell, D. A. J., & Smith, A. P. (1993). Negative life events, perceived stress, negative affect, and susceptibility to the common cold. *Journal of Personality and Social Psychology, 64,* 131–140.

Coie, J. D., Watt, N. F., West, S. G., Hawkins, J. D., Asarnow, J. R., Markham, H. L., Ramey, S. L., Shure, M. B., & Long, B. (1993). The science of prevention: A conceptual framework and some direction for a national research program. *American Psychologist, 48,* 1013–1022.

Cole, W., Emery, M., & Horowitz, J. M. (1993, May 24). What should we teach our children about sex? *Time,* pp. 60–66.

Collins, N. L., & Miller, L. C. (1994). Self-disclosure and liking: a meta-analytic review. *Psychological Bulletin, 116,* 457–475.

Collins, N. L., & Read, S. J. (1990). Adult attachment, working models, and relationship quality in dating couples. *Journal of Personality and Social Psychology, 58,* 644–663.

Colman, A. M. (1991). Crowd psychology in South African murder trials. *American Psychologist, 46,* 1071–1079.

Colvin, C. R., & Block, J. (1994). Do positive illusions foster mental health? An examination of the Taylor and Brown formulation. *Psychological Bulletin, 116,* 3–20.

Colvin, C. R., Block, J., & Funder, D. C. (1995). Overly positive self-evaluations and personality: Negative implications for mental health. *Journal of Personality and Social Psychology, 68,* 1152–1162.

Colvin, C. R., & Funder, D. C. (1991). Predicting personality and behavior: A boundary on the acquaintanceship effect. *Journal of Personality and Social Psychology, 60,* 884–894.

Commission on Obscenity and Pornography. (1970). *Report of the commission on obscenity and pornography.* New York: Bantam Books.

Commission on Violence and Youth. (1993). *Violence and youth: Psychology's response* (Vol. I). Washington, DC: American Psychological Association.

Condon, J. W., & Crano, W. D. (1988). Inferred evaluation and the relation between attitude similarity and interpersonal attraction. *Journal of Personality and Social Psychology, 54,* 789–797.

Condry, J., & Condry, S. (1976). Sex differences: A study of the eye of the beholder. *Child Development, 47,* 812–819.

Conger, J. D., Conger, A. J., & Brehm, S. S. (1976). Fear level as a moderator of false feedback effects in snake phobics. *Journal of Consulting and Clinical Psychology, 44,* 135–141.

Conlon, D. E., Carnevale, P., & Ross, W. H. (1994). The influence of third-party power and suggestions on negotiation: The surface value of compromise. *Journal of Applied Social Psychology, 24,* 1084–1113.

Conn, M. K., & Peterson, C. (1989). Social support: Seek and ye shall find. *Journal of Social and Personal Relationships, 6,* 345–358.

Contrada, R. J., & Jussim, L. (1992). What does the Cook-Medley hostility scale measure? In search of an adequate measurement model. *Journal of Applied Social Psychology, 22,* 615–627.

Conway, M. A. (1990). *Autobiographical memory: An introduction.* Philadelphia: Open University Press.

Conway, M. A., & Dewhurst, S. A. (1995). The self and recollective experience. *Applied Cognitive Psychology, 9,* 1–19.

Cook, H. B. K. (1992). Matricality and female aggression in Margariteño society. In K. Björkqvist & P. Niemelä (Eds.), *Of mice and women: Aspects of female aggression* (pp. 149–162). San Diego: Academic Press.

Cook, S. W. (1975). A comment on the ethical issues involved in West, Gunn, and Chernicky's "Ubiquitous Watergate: An Attributional Analysis." *Journal of Personality and Social Psychology, 32,* 66–68.

Cook, S. W. (1984). The 1954 social science statement and school desegregation: A reply to Gerard. *American Psychologist, 39,* 819–832.

Cook, S. W. (1985). Experimenting on social issues: The case of school desegregation. *American Psychologist, 40,* 452–460.

Cook, S. W., & Pelfrey, M. (1985). Reactions to being helped in cooperating interracial groups: A context effect. *Journal of Personality and Social Psychology, 49,* 1231–1245.

Cook, T. D., & Campbell, D. T. (1979). *Quasi-experimentation: Design and analysis issues for field settings.* Chicago: Rand McNally.

Cook, T. D., Gruder, C. L., Hennigan, K. M., & Flay, B. R. (1979). History of the sleeper effect: Some logical pitfalls in accepting the null hypothesis. *Psychological Bulletin, 86,* 662–679.

Cook, T. D., Leviton, L. C., & Shadish, W. R., Jr. (1985). Program evaluation. In G. Lindzey & E. Aronson (Eds.), *Handbook of social psychology* (Vol. 1, 3rd ed., pp. 699–777). New York: Random House.

Cook, T. D., & Shadish, W. R. (1994). Social experiments: Some developments over the past fifteen years. *Annual Review of Psychology, 45,* 545–580.

Cook, W. W., & Medley, D. M. (1954). Proposed hostility and Pharisaic-virtue scales for the MMPI. *Journal of Applied Psychology, 38,* 414–418.

Cooley, C. H. (1902). *Human nature and the social order.* New York: Schocken Books. (Reprinted in 1964)

Coombs, C. H. (1987). The structure of conflict. *American Psychologist, 42,* 355–363.

Cooper, H., & Good, T. (1983). *Pygmalion grows up: Studies in the expectation communication process.* New York: Longman.

Cooper, J., & Fazio, R. H. (1984). A new look at dissonance theory. In L. Berkowitz (Ed.), *Advances in experimental social psychology* (Vol. 17, pp. 229–267). New York: Academic Press.

Cooper, J., Zanna, M. P., & Goethals, G. R. (1974). Mistreatment of an esteemed other as a consequence affecting dissonance reduction. *Journal of Experimental Social Psychology, 10,* 224–233.

Cooper, W. H. (1981). Ubiquitous halo. *Psychological Bulletin, 90,* 218–224.

Coopersmith, S. (1967). *The antecedents of self-esteem.* San Francisco: Freeman.

Coovert, M. D., & Reeder, G. D. (1990). Negativity effects in impression formation: The role of unit formation and schematic expectations. *Journal of Experimental Social Psychology, 26,* 49–62.

Copeland, J. T. (1994). Prophecies of power: Motivational implications of social power for behavioral confirmation. *Journal of Personality and Social Psychology, 67,* 264–277.

Cornell, L. L. (1989). Gender differences in remarriage and divorce in Japan and the United States. *Journal of Marriage and the Family, 51,* 457–463.

Cosmides, L., & Tooby, J. (1992). Cognitive adaptations for social exchange. In J. H. Barkow, L. Cosmides, & J. Tooby (Eds.), *The adapted mind: Evolutionary psychology and the generation of culture* (pp. 163–228). Oxford: Oxford University Press.

Costa, P. T., Jr., McCrae, R. P., & Dembroski, T. M. (1989). Agreeableness versus antagonism: Explication of a potential risk factor for CHD. In A. W. Siegman & T. M. Dembroski (Eds.), *In search of coronary-prone behavior: Beyond Type A* (pp. 41–63). Hillsdale, NJ: Erlbaum.

Costanzo, M., & White, L.T. (Eds.). (1994). The death penalty in the United States [Special issue]. *Journal of Social Issues, 50,* (2).

Costello, C. G. (1982). Social factors associated with depression: A retrospective community study. *Psychological Medicine, 12,* 329–339.

Cota, A. A., Evans, C. R., Dion, K. L., Kilik, L., & Longman, R. S. (1995). The structure of group cohesion. *Personality and Social Psychology Bulletin, 21,* 572–580.

Cotterell, N., Eisenberger, R., & Speicher, H. (1992). Inhibiting effects of reciprocation wariness on interpersonal relationships. *Journal of Personality and Social Psychology, 62,* 658–668.

Cottrell, N. B. (1968). Performance in the presence of other human beings: Mere presence, audience, and affiliation effects. In E. C. Simmel, R. A. Hoppe, & G. A. Milton (Eds.),

Social facilitation and imitative behavior (pp. 91–110). Boston: Allyn & Bacon.

Cottrell, N. B., Wack, D. L., Sekerak, G. J., & Rittle, R. H. (1968). Social facilitation of dominant responses by the presence of an audience and the mere presence of others. *Journal of Personality and Social Psychology, 9,* 245–250.

Cowan, C. L., Thompson, W. C., & Ellsworth, P. C. (1984). The effects of death qualification on jurors' predisposition to convict and on the quality of deliberation. *Law and Human Behavior, 8,* 53–80.

Cox, M., & Tanford, S. (1989). An alternative method of capital jury selection. *Law and Human Behavior, 13,* 167–183.

Coyne, J. C. (1994). Self-reported distress: Analog or ersatz depression? *Psychological Bulletin, 116,* 29–45.

Coyne, J. C., & Smith, D. A. F. (1991). Couples coping with a myocardial infarction: A contextual perspective on wives' distress. *Journal of Personality and Social Psychology, 61,* 404–412.

Cozby, P. C. (1973). Self-disclosure: A literature review. *Psychological Bulletin, 79,* 73–91.

Cozzarelli, C. (1993). Personality and self-efficacy as predictors of coping with abortion. *Journal of Personality and Social Psychology, 65,* 1224–1236.

Cramer, R. E., McMaster, M. R., Bartell, P. A., & Dragna, M. (1988). Subject competence and the minimization of the bystander effect. *Journal of Applied Social Psychology, 18,* 1133–1148.

Crick, N. R., & Dodge, K. A. (1994). A review and reformulation of social information-processing mechanisms in children's social adjustment. *Psychological Bulletin, 115,* 74–101.

Crites, S. L., Fabrigar, L. R., & Petty, R. E. (1994). Measuring the affective and cognitive properties of attitudes: Conceptual and methodological issues. *Personality and Social Psychology Bulletin, 20,* 619–634.

Crocker, J. C., & Major, B. (1989). Social stigma and self-esteem: The self-protective properties of stigma. *Psychological Review, 96,* 608–630.

Crocker, J., & Luhtanen, R. (1990). Collective self-esteem and ingroup bias. *Journal of Personality and Social Psychology, 58,* 60–67.

Crocker, J., Voelkl, K., Testa, M., & Major, B. (1991). Social stigma: The affective consequences of attributional ambiguity. *Journal of Personality and Social Psychology, 60,* 218–228.

Crohan, S. E. (1992). Marital happiness and spousal consensus on beliefs about marital conflict: A longitudinal investigation. *Journal of Social and Personal Relationships, 9,* 89–102.

Cronbach, L. J. (1955). Processes affecting scores on "understanding of others" and "assumed similarity." *Psychological Bulletin, 52,* 177–193.

Crosby, F. (1976). A model of egoistical relative deprivation. *Psychological Review, 83,* 85–113.

Crosby, F. (1982). *Relative deprivation and working women.* New York: Oxford University Press.

Crosby, F., Bromley, S., & Saxe, L. (1980). Recent unobtrusive studies of black and white discrimination and prejudice: A literature review. *Psychological Bulletin, 87,* 546–563.

Crosby, F. J. (1991). *Juggling.* New York: Free Press.

Crosby, F. J., & Jaskar, K. L. (1993). Women and men at home and at work: Realities and illusions. In S. Oskamp & M. Costanzo (Eds.), *Gender issues in contemporary society* (pp. 143–171). Newbury Park, CA: Sage.

Crowley, A. E., & Hoyer, W. D. (1994). An integrative framework for understanding two-sided persuasion. *Journal of Consumer Research, 20,* 561–574.

Croyle, R., & Cooper, J. (1983). Dissonance arousal: Physiological evidence. *Journal of Personality and Social Psychology, 45,* 782–791.

Crutchfield, R. S. (1955). Conformity and character. *American Psychologist, 10,* 195–198.

Csikszentmihalyi, M., & Figurski, T. J. (1982). Self-awareness and aversive experience in everyday life. *Journal of Personality, 50,* 15–28.

Cunningham, J. A., Strassberg, D. S., & Haan, B. (1986). Effects of intimacy and sex-role congruency on self-disclosure. *Journal of Social and Clinical Psychology, 4,* 393–401.

Cunningham, M. R. (1979). Weather, mood, and helping behavior: Quasi experiments with the sunshine Samaritan. *Journal of Personality and Social Psychology, 37,* 1947–1956.

Cunningham, M. R., Shaffer, D. R., Barbee, A. P., Wolff, P. L., & Kelley, D. J. (1990). Separate processes in the relation of elation and depression to helping: Social versus personal concerns. *Journal of Experimental Social Psychology, 26,* 13–33.

Cunningham, M. R., Steinberg, J., & Grev, R. (1980). Wanting to and having to help: Separate motivations for positive mood and guilt-induced helping. *Journal of Personality and Social Psychology, 38,* 181–192.

Cunningham, M. R., Wong, D. T., & Barbee, A. P. (1994). Self-presentation dynamics on overt integrity tests: Experimental studies of the Reid Report. *Journal of Applied Psychology, 79,* 643–658.

Cupach, W. R., & Comstock, J. (1990). Satisfaction with sexual communication in marriage: Links to sexual satisfaction and dyadic adjustment. *Journal of Social and Personal Relationships, 7,* 179–186.

Curtis, R. C., & Miller, K. (1986). Believing another likes or dislikes you: Behaviors making the beliefs come true. *Journal of Personality and Social Psychology, 51,* 284–290.

Cutler, B. L., Penrod, S. D., & Dexter, H. R. (1989). The eyewitness, the expert, and the jury. *Law and Human Behavior, 13,* 311–332.

Cutler, B. L., Penrod, S. D., & Stuve, T. E. (1988). Juror decision making in eyewitness identification cases. *Law and Human Behavior, 12,* 41–55.

Cutrona, C. (1982). Transition to college: Loneliness and the process of social adjustment. In L. A. Peplau & D. Perlman (Eds.), *Loneliness: A sourcebook of current theory, research, and therapy* (pp. 291–309). New York: Wiley.

Cutrona, E. C., Cole, V., Colangelo, N., Assouline, S. G., & Russell, D. W. (1994). Perceived parental social support and academic achievement: An attachment theory perspective. *Journal of Personality and Social Psychology, 66,* 369–378.

Dabbs, J. M., Jr., Frady, R. L., Carr, T. S., & Besch, N. F. (1987). Saliva testosterone and criminal violence in young adult prison inmates. *Psychosomatic Medicine, 49,* 174–181.

Dabbs, J. M., Jr., Hopper, C. H., & Jurkovic, G. J. (1990). Testosterone and personality among college students and military veterans. *Personality and Individual Differences, 11,* 1263–1269.

Dabbs, J. M., Jr., & Morris, R. (1990). Testosterone, social class, and antisocial behavior in a sample of 4,462 men. *Psychological Science, 1,* 209–211.

Dabbs, J. M., Jr., Ruback, R. B., Frady, R. L., Hopper, C. H., & Sgoutas, D. S. (1988). Saliva testosterone and criminal violence among women. *Personality and Individual Differences, 9,* 269–275.

Daly, M., & Wilson, M. (1988). *Homicide.* New York: Aldine de Gruyter.

Danheiser, P. R., & Graziano, W. G. (1982). Self-monitoring and cooperation as a self-presentational strategy. *Journal of Personality and Social Psychology, 42,* 497–505.

Darley, J. M., & Batson, C. D. (1973). From Jerusalem to Jericho: A study of situational and dispositional variables in helping behavior. *Journal of Personality and Social Psychology, 27,* 100–108.

Darley, J. M., & Fazio, R. (1980). Expectancy confirmation processes arising in the social interaction sequence. *American Psychologist, 35,* 867–881.

Darley, J. M., Fleming, J. H., Hilton, J. L., & Swann, W. B., Jr. (1988). Dispelling negative expectancies: The impact of interaction goals and target characteristics on the expectancy confirmation process. *Journal of Experimental Social Psychology, 24,* 19–36.

Darley, J. M., & Gross, P. H. (1983). A hypothesis-confirming bias in labeling effects. *Journal of Personality and Social Psychology, 44,* 20–33.

Darwin, C. (1872). *The expression of the emotions in man and animals.* London: John Murray.

Davidson, A. R., & Jaccard, J. J. (1979). Variables that moderate the attitude-behavior relation: Results of a longitudinal survey. *Journal of Personality and Social Psychology, 37,* 1364–1376.

Davidson, A. R., Yantis, S., Norwood, M., & Montano, D. E. (1985). Amount of information about the attitude object and attitude-behavior consistency. *Journal of Personality and Social Psychology, 49,* 1184–1198.

Davies, P. T., & Cummings, E. M. (1994). Marital conflict and child adjustment: An emotional security hypothesis. *Psychological Bulletin, 116,* 387–411.

Davis, J. H., Kameda, T., Parks, C., Stasson, M., & Zimmerman, S. (1989). Some social mechanics of group decision-making: The distribution of opinion, polling sequence, and implications for consensus. *Journal of Personality and Social Psychology, 57,* 1000–1012.

Davis, M. H. (1994). *Empathy: A social psychological approach.* Madison, WI: Browon & Benchmark.

Davis, M. H., Luce, C., & Kraus, S. J. (1994). The heritability of characteristics associated with dispositional empathy. *Journal of Personality, 62,* 369–391.

Davis, S. (1990). Men as success objects and women as sex objects: A study of personal advertisements. *Sex Roles, 23,* 43–50.

Dawes, R. M., & Smith, T. L. (1985). Attitude and opinion measurement. In G. Lindzey & E. Aronson (Eds.), *The handbook of social psychology* (Vol. 2, pp. 509–566). New York: Random House.

Dawkins, R. (1989). *The selfish gene* (2nd Ed.). Oxford: Oxford University Press.

Day, D. D., & Sulsky, L. M. (1995). Effects of frame-of-reference training and information configuration on memory organization and rating accuracy. *Journal of Applied Psychology, 80,* 158–167.

DeAngelis, T. (1993, August). *APA Monitor*, p. 16.

DeAngelis, T. (1994, December). Perceptions influence student drinking. *American Psychological Association Monitor,* p. 35.

Deaux, K., & Emswiller, T. (1974). Explanations for successful performance on sex-linked tasks: What is skill for the male is luck for the female. *Journal of Personality and Social Psychology, 29,* 80–85.

Deaux, K., & Hanna, R. (1984). Courtship in the personals column: The influence of gender and sexual orientation. *Sex Roles, 11,* 363–375.

Deaux, K., & Lewis, L. L. (1984). The structure of gender stereotypes: Interrelationships among components and gender label. *Journal of Personality and Social Psychology, 46,* 991–1004.

Deaux, K., & Major, B. (1987). Putting gender into context: An interactive model of gender-related behavior. *Psychological Review, 94,* 369–389.

DeBono, K. G. (1987). Investigating the social-adjustive and value-expressive functions of attitudes: Implications for persuasion processes. *Journal of Personality and Social Psychology, 52,* 279–287.

DeBono, K. G., & Packer, M. (1991). The effects of advertising appeal on perceptions of product quality. *Personality and Social Psychology Bulletin, 17,* 194–200.

Deci, E. L. (1971). Effects of externally mediated rewards on intrinsic motivation. *Journal of Personality and Social Psychology, 18,* 105–115.

Deci, E. L., Connell, J. P., & Ryan, R. M. (1989). Self-determination in a work organization. *Journal of Applied Psychology, 74,* 580–590.

Deci, E. L., & Ryan, R. M. (1985). *Intrinsic motivation and self-determination in human behavior.* New York: Plenum.

DeJong, W. (1979). An examination of self-perception mediation of the foot-in-the-door effect. *Journal of Personality and Social Psychology, 37,* 2221–2239.

DeKeseredy, W. S., Schwartz, M. D., & Tait, K. (1993). Sexual assault and stranger aggression on a Canadian university campus. *Sex Roles, 28,* 263–277.

Demaré, D., Lips, H. M., & Briere, J. (1993). Sexually violent pornography, anti-women attitudes, and sexual aggression: A structural equation model. *Journal of Research in Personality, 27,* 285–300.

DeMaris, A., & MacDonald, W. (1993). Premarital cohabitation and marital instability: A test of the unconventionality hypothesis. *Journal of Marriage and the Family, 55,* 399–407.

DeMaris, A., & Rao, K. V. (1992). Premarital cohabitation and subsequent marital stability in the United States: A reassessment. *Journal of Marriage and the Family, 54,* 178–190.

Dembroski, D. M., & Costa, Jr., P. T. (1987). Coronary prone behavior: Components of the Type A pattern and hostility. *Journal of Personality, 55,* 211–236.

Dengerink, H. A., Schnedler, R. W., & Covey, M. K. (1978). Role of avoidance in aggressive responses to attack and no attack. *Journal of Personality and Social Psychology, 36,* 1044–1053.

Dennis, A. R., & Valacich, J. S. (1993). Computer brainstorms: More heads are better than one. *Journal of Applied Psychology, 78,* 531–537.

DePalma, M. T., Koszewski, W. M., Case, J. G., Barile, R. J., DePalma, B. F., & Oliaro, S. M. (1993). Weight control practices of lightweight football players. *Medicine and Science in Sports and Exercise, 25,* 694–701.

DePaulo, B. M. (1992). Nonverbal behavior and self-representation. *Psychological Bulletin, 111,* 203–243.

DePaulo, B. M., Dull, W. R., Greenberg, J. M., & Swaim, G. W. (1989). Are shy people reluctant to help? *Journal of Personality and Social Psychology, 56,* 834–844.

DePaulo, B. M., Epstein, J. A., & LeMay, C. S. (1990). Responses of the socially anxious to the prospect of interpersonal evaluation. *Journal of Personality, 58,* 623–640.

DePaulo, B. M., Lassiter, G. D., & Stone, J. I. (1982). Attentional determinants of success at detecting deception and truth. *Personality and Social Psychology Bulletin, 8,* 273–279.

DePaulo, B. M., & Tang, J. (1994). Social anxiety and social judgment: The example of detecting deception. *Journal of Research in Personality, 28,* 142–153.

Dépret, E. F., & Fiske, S. T. (1993). Social cognition and power: Some cognitive consequences of social structure as a source of control deprivation. In G. Weary, F. Gleicher, & K. L. Marsh (Eds.), *Control motivation and social cognition* (pp. 176–202). New York: Springer-Verlag.

Derlega, V. J., Metts, S., Petronio, S., & Margulis, S. T. (1993). *Self-disclosure.* Newbury Park, CA: Sage.

Derlega, V. J., Wilson, M. & Chaikin, A. L. (1976). Friendship and disclosure reciprocity. *Journal of Personality and Social Psychology, 34,* 578–587.

Dershowitz, A. M. (1982). *The best defense.* New York: Vintage Books.

Desforges, D. M., Lord, C. G., Ramsey, S. L., Mason, J. A., Van Leeuwen, M. D., West, S. C., & Lepper, M. R. (1991). Effects of cooperative contact on changing negative attitudes toward stigmatized social groups. *Journal of Personality and Social Psychology, 60,* 531–544.

Deutsch, F. M. (1989). The false consensus effect: Is the self-justification hypothesis justified? *Basic and Applied Social Psychology, 10,* 83–99.

Deutsch, M., & Gerard, H. B. (1955). A study of normative and informational social influences upon individual judgment. *Journal of Abnormal and Social Psychology, 51,* 629–636.

Deutsch, M., & Krauss, R. M. (1960). The effect of threat upon interpersonal bargaining. *Journal of Abnormal and Social Psychology, 61,* 181–189.

Devine, P. G. (1989). Stereotypes and prejudice: Their automatic and controlled components. *Journal of Personality and Social Psychology, 56,* 5–18.

Devine, P. G., & Baker, S. M. (1991). Measurement of racial stereotype subtyping. *Personality and Social Psychology Bulletin, 17,* 44–50.

Devine, P. G., Monteith, M. J., Zuwerink, J. R., & Elliot, A. J. (1991). Prejudice with and without compunction. *Journal of Personality and Social Psychology, 60,* 817–830.

Diehl, M., & Stroebe, W. (1991). Productivity loss in idea-generating groups: Tracking down the blocking effect. *Journal of Personality and Social Psychology, 61,* 392–403.

Diener, E. (1979). Deindividuation, self-awareness, and disinhibition. *Journal of Personality and Social Psychology, 37,* 1160–1171.

Diener, E. (1980). Deindividuation: The absence of self-awareness and self-regulation in group members. In P. B. Paulus (Ed.), *Psychology of group influence* (pp. 209–242). Hillsdale, NJ: Erlbaum.

Diener, E., Fraser, S. C., Beaman, A. L., & Kelem, R. T. (1976). Effects of deindividuation variables on stealing among Halloween trick-or-treaters. *Journal of Personality and Social Psychology, 33,* 178–183.

Digman, J. M. (1990). Personality structure: Emergence of the five-factor model. *Annual Review of Psychology, 41,* 417–440.

Dillard, J. P. (1991). The current status of research on sequential -request compliance techniques. *Personality and Social Psychology Bulletin, 17,* 283–288.

Dindia, K., & Allen, M. (1992). Sex differences in self-disclosure: A meta-analysis. *Psychological Bulletin, 112,* 106–124.

Dion, K. K., Berscheid, E., & Walster, E. (1972). What is beautiful is good. *Journal of Personality and Social Psychology, 24,* 285–290.

Dion, K. L. (1987). What's in a title? The Ms. stereotype and images of women's title of address. *Psychology of Women Quarterly, 11,* 21–36.

Dion, K. L., & Cota, A. A. (1991). The Ms. stereotype: Its domain and the role of explicitness in title preference. *Psychology of Women Quarterly, 15,* 403–410.

Dion, K. L., & Dion, K. K. (1976). Love, liking and trust in heterosexual relationships. *Personality and Social Psychology Bulletin, 2,* 187–190.

Dion, K. L., & Dion, K. K. (1988). Romantic love: Individual and cultural perspectives. In R. J. Sternberg & M. L. Barnes (Eds.), *The psychology of love* (pp. 264–289). New Haven, CT: Yale University Press.

Dodd, D. K. (1985). Robbers in the classroom: A deindividuation exercise. *Teaching in Psychology, 12,* 89–91.

Dodson, C., & Reisberg, D. (1991). Indirect testing of eyewitness memory: The (non)effect of misinformation. *Bulletin of the Psychonomic Society, 29,* 333–336.

Dohrenwend, B. P., Levav, I., Shrout, P. E., Schwartz, S., Naveh, G., Link, B. G., Skodol, A. E., & Stueve, A. (1992). Socioeconomic status and psychiatric disorders: The causation-selection issue. *Science, 255,* 946–952.

Dollard, J., Doob, L. W., Miller, N. E., Mowrer, O. H., & Sears, R. R. (1939). *Frustration and aggression.* New Haven, CT: Yale University Press.

Donne, J. (1975). Meditation, 17. In A. Raspa (Ed.), *Devotions upon emergent occasions* (p. 87). Montreal: McGill-Queen's University Press. (Original work published 1624)

Donnerstein, E. (1984). Pornography: Its effects on violence against women. In N. M. Malamuth & E. Donnerstein (Eds.), *Pornography and sexual aggression* (pp. 53–81). New York: Academic Press.

Donnerstein, E., & Berkowitz, L. (1981). Victim reactions in aggressive erotic films as a factor in violence against women. *Journal of Personality and Social Psychology, 41,* 710–724.

Donnerstein, E., & Donnerstein, M. (1976). Research in the control of interracial aggression. In R. G. Geen and E. C.

O'Neal (Eds.), *Perspectives on aggression* (pp. 133–168). New York: Academic Press.

Donnerstein, E., & Hallam, J. (1978). Facilitating effects of erotica on aggression against women. *Journal of Personality and Social Psychology, 36,* 1270–1277.

Donnerstein, E., Linz, D., & Penrod, S. (1987). *The question of pornography.* New York: Free Press.

Dornbusch, S. M., Hastorf, A. H., Richardson, S. A., Muzzy, R. E., & Vreeland, R. S. (1965). The perceiver and the perceived: Their relative influence on categories of interpersonal perception. *Journal of Personality and Social Psychology, 1,* 434–440.

Dougherty, T. W., Turban, D. B., & Callender, J. C. (1994). Confirming first impressions in the employment interview: A field study of interviewer behavior. *Journal of Applied Psychology, 79,* 659–665.

Dovidio, J. F. (1984). Helping behavior and altruism: An empirical and conceptual overview. In L. Berkowitz (Ed.), *Advances in experimental social psychology* (Vol. 17, pp. 361–427). New York: Academic Press.

Dovidio, J. F., Allen, J. L., & Schroeder, D. A. (1990). Specificity of empathy-induced helping: Evidence for altruistic motivation. *Journal of Personality and Social Psychology, 59,* 249–260.

Dovidio, J. F., Brown, C. E., Heltman, K., Ellyson, S. L., & Keating, C. F. (1988a). Power displays between women and men in discussion of gender-linked tasks: A multichannel study. *Journal of Personality and Social Psychology, 55,* 580–587.

Dovidio, J. F., Ellyson, S. L., Keating, C. F., Heltman, K., & Brown, C. E. (1988b). The relationship of social power to visual displays of dominance between men and women. *Journal of Personality and Social Psychology, 54,* 233–242.

Dovidio, J. F., Evans, N., & Tyler, R. (1986). Racial stereotypes: The contents of their cognitive representations. *Journal of Experimental Social Psychology, 22,* 22–37.

Dovidio, J. F., & Gaertner, S. L. (1981). The effects of race, status, and ability on helping behavior. *Social Psychology Quarterly, 44,* 192–203.

Dovidio, J. F., & Gaertner, S. L. (1983). The effects of sex, status, and ability on helping behavior. *Journal of Applied Social Psychology, 13,* 191–205.

Dovidio, J. F., & Gaertner, S. L. (Eds.). (1986). *Prejudice, discrimination, and racism: Theory and research.* Orlando, FL: Academic Press.

Dovidio, J. F., Piliavin, J. A., Gaertner, S. L., Schroeder, D. A., & Clark, R. D., II. (1991). The arousal: cost-reward model and the process of intervention: A review of the evidence. In M. S. Clark (Ed.), *Review of personality and social psychology 12: Prosocial behavior* (pp. 86–118). Newbury Park, CA: Sage.

Downey, G., Silver, R. C., & Wortman, C. B. (1990). Reconsidering the attribution-adjustment relation following a major negative event: Coping with the loss of a child. *Journal of Personality and Social Psychology, 59,* 925–940.

Doyle, J. A. (1983). *The male experience.* Dubuque, IA: Brown.

Drigotas, S. M., & Rusbult, C. E. (1992). Shall I stay or should I go? A dependence model of breakups. *Journal of Personality and Social Psychology, 62,* 62–87.

Driscoll, R., Davis, K. W., & Lipetz, M. E. (1972). Parental interference and romantic love. *Journal of Personality and Social Psychology, 24,* 1–10.

D'Souza, D. (1991). *Illiberal education: The politics of race and sex on campus.* New York: Free Press.

Dubrovsky, V. J., Kiesler, S., & Sethna, B. N. (1991). The equalization phenomenon: Status effects in computer-mediated and face-to-face decision-making groups. *Human-Computer Interaction, 6,* 119–146.

Duck, S. (Ed.) (1988). *Handbook of personal relationships: Theory, research, and interventions.* New York: Wiley.

Duck, S., & Wright, P. H. (1993). Reexamining gender differences in same-gender friendships: A close look at two kinds of data. *Sex Roles, 28,* 709–727.

Duclos, S. E., Laird, J. D., Schneider, E., Sexter, M., Stern, L., & Van Lighten, O. (1989). Emotion-specific effects of facial expressions and postures on emotional experience. *Journal of Personality and Social Psychology, 57,* 100–108.

Dudycha, G. J., & Dudycha, M. M. (1941). Childhood memories: A review of the literature. *Psychological Bulletin, 38,* 668–682.

Duncan, B. L. (1976). Differential social perception and attribution of intergroup violence: Testing the lower limits of stereotyping of blacks. *Journal of Personality and Social Psychology, 34,* 590–598.

Dunn, D. S., & Wilson, T. D. (1990). When the stakes are high: A limit to the illusion-of-control effect. *Social Cognition, 8,* 305–323.

Dunning, D., Griffin, D. W., Milojkovic, J. D., & Ross, L. (1990). The overconfidence effect in social prediction. *Journal of Personality and Social Psychology, 58,* 568–581.

Dunning, D., Perie, M., & Story, A. L. (1991). Self-serving prototypes of social categories. *Journal of Personality and Social Psychology, 61,* 957–968.

Dunning, D., & Stern, L. B. (1994). Distinguishing accurate from inaccurate eyewitness identifications via inquiries about decision processes. *Journal of Personality and Social Psychology, 67,* 818–835.

Dutton, D. G., & Aron, A. P. (1974). Some evidence for heightened sexual attraction under conditions of high anxiety. *Journal of Personality and Social Psychology, 30,* 510–517.

Dutton, D. G., Saunder, K., Starzomski, A., & Bartholomew, K. (1994). Intimacy-anger and insecure attachment as precursors of abuse in intimate relationships. *Journal of Applied Social Psychology, 24,* 1367–1386.

Duval, S., & Wicklund, R. A. (1972). *A theory of objective self-awareness.* New York: Academic Press.

Duval, T. S., Duval, V. H., & Mulilis, J. P. (1992). Effects of self-focus, discrepancy between self and standard, and outcome expectancy favorability on the tendency to match self to standard or to withdraw. *Journal of Personality and Social Psychology, 62,* 340–348.

Eagly, A. H. (1987). *Sex differences in social behavior: A social-role interpretation.* Hillsdale, NJ: Erlbaum.

Eagly, A. H., Ashmore, R. D., Makhijani, M. G., & Longo, L. C. (1991). What is beautiful is good, but . . . : A meta-analytic review of research on the physical attractiveness stereotype. *Psychology Bulletin, 110,* 107–128.

Eagly, A. H., & Carli, L. L. (1981). Sex of researchers and sex-typed communications as determinants of sex differences in influenceability: A meta-analysis of social influence studies. *Psychological Bulletin, 90,* 1–20.

Eagly, A. H., & Chaiken, S. (1993). *The psychology of attitudes.* Fort Worth, TX: Harcourt, Brace Jovanovich.

Eagly, A. H., & Chravala, C. (1986). Sex differences in conformity: Status and gender-role interpretations. *Psychology of Women Quarterly, 10,* 203–220.

Eagly, A. H., & Crowley, M. (1986). Gender and helping behavior: A meta-analytic review of the social psychological literature. *Psychological Bulletin, 100,* 283–308.

Eagly, A. H., & Johnson, B. T. (1990). Gender and leadership style: A meta-analysis. *Psychological Bulletin, 108,* 233–256.

Eagly, A. H., Karau, S. J., & Makhijani, M. G. (1995). Gender and effectiveness of leaders: A meta-analysis. *Psychological Bulletin, 117,* 125–145.

Eagly, A. H., & Kite, M. E. (1987). Are stereotypes of nationalities applied to both women and men? *Journal of Personality and Social Psychology, 53,* 451–462.

Eagly, A. H., Makhijani, M. G., & Klonsky, B. G. (1992). Gender and evaluation of leaders: A meta-analysis. *Psychological Bulletin, 111,* 3–22.

Eagly, A. H., & Steffen, V. J. (1984). Gender stereotypes stem from the distribution of women and men into social roles. *Journal of Personality and Social Psychology, 46,* 735–754.

Eagly, A. H., & Steffen, V. J. (1986). Gender and aggressive behavior: A meta-analytic review of the social psychology literature. *Psychological Bulletin, 100,* 309–330.

Eagly, A. H., & Wood, W. (1982). Inferred sex differences in status as a determinant of gender stereotypes about social influence. *Journal of Personality and Social Psychology, 43,* 915–928.

Eagly, A. H., & Wood, W. (1991). Explaining sex differences in social behavior: A meta-analytic perspective. *Personality and Social Psychology Bulletin, 17,* 306–315.

Eagly, A. H., Wood, W., & Chaiken, S. (1978). Causal inferences about communicators and their effect on opinion change. *Journal of Personality and Social Psychology, 36,* 424–435.

Eagly, A. H., Wood, W., & Chaiken, S. (1981a). An attribution analysis of persuasion. In J. Harvey, W. Ickes, & R. Kidd (Eds.), *New directions in attribution research* (Vol. 3, pp. 37–62). Hillsdale, NJ: Erlbaum.

Eagly, A. H., Wood, W., & Fishbaugh, L. (1981b). Sex differences in conformity: Surveillance by the group as a determinant of male nonconformity. *Journal of Personality and Social Psychology, 40,* 384–394.

Ebbesen, E. B., Kjos, G. L., & Konecni, V. J. (1976). Spatial ecology: Its effects on the choice of friends and enemies. *Journal of Experimental Social Psychology, 12,* 505–518.

Ebbesen, E. B., & Konecni, V. J. (1981). The process of sentencing adult felons: A causal analysis of judicial decisions. In B. D. Sales (Ed.), *The trial process* (pp. 413–458). New York: Plenum.

Eckes, T. (1994). Explorations in gender cognition: Content and structure of female and male subtypes. *Social Cognition, 12,* 37–60.

Eden, D. (1990). Pygmalion without interpersonal contrast effects: Whole groups gain from raising manager expectations. *Journal of Applied Psychology, 75,* 394–398.

Edwards, K. (1990). The interplay of affect and cognition in attitude formation and change. *Journal of Personality and Social Psychology, 59,* 202–216.

Egolf, D. B., & Corder, L. E. (1991). Height differences between low and high job status female and male corporate employees. *Sex Roles, 24,* 365–373.

Ehrlichman, H., & Eichenstein, R. (1992). Private wishes: Gender similarities and differences. *Sex Roles, 26,* 399–422.

Eisenberg, N., Cialdini, R. B., McCreath, H., & Shell, R. (1987). Consistency-based compliance: When and why do children become vulnerable? *Journal of Personality and Social Psychology, 52,* 1174–1181.

Eisenberg, N., Fabes, R. A., Miller, P. A., Fultz, J., Shell, R., Mathy, R. M., & Reno, R. R. (1989). Relation of sympathy and personal distress to prosocial behavior: A multimethod study. *Journal of Personality and Social Psychology, 57,* 55–66.

Eisenberg, N., Fabes, R. A., Murphy, B., Karbon, M., Maszk, P., Smith, M., O'Boyle, C., & Suh, K. (1994). The relations of emotionality and regulation to dispositional and situational empathy-related responding. *Journal of Personality and Social Psychology, 66,* 776–797.

Eisenberg, N., & Miller, P. A. (1987). The relation of empathy to prosocial and related behaviors. *Psychological Bulletin, 101,* 91–119.

Eisenberger, R., Cotterell, N., & Marvel, J. (1987). Reciprocation ideology. *Journal of Personality and Social Psychology, 53,* 743–750.

Eisenberger, R., & Selbst, M. (1994). Does reward increase or decrease creativity? *Journal of Personality and Social Psychology, 66,* 1116–1127.

Eisenman, R. (1993). Belief that drug usage in the United States is increasing when it is really decreasing: An example of the availability heuristic. *Bulletin of the Psychonomic Society, 31,* 249–252.

Ekman, P., & Davidson, R. J. (1993). Voluntary smiling changes regional brain activity. *Psychological Science, 4,* 342–345.

Ekman, P., Davidson, R. J., & Friesen, W. V. (1990). The Duchenne smile: Emotional expression and brain physiology II. *Journal of Personality and Social Psychology, 58,* 342–353.

Ekman, P., Friesen, W. V., & Ellsworth, P. (1972). *Emotion in the human face.* Elmsford, NY: Pergamon Press.

Ekman, P., & Friesen, W. V. (1974). Detecting deception from the body or face. *Journal of Personality and Social Psychology, 29,* 288–298.

Ekman, P., Friesen, W. V., O'Sullivan, M., Chan, A., Diacoyanni-Tarlatzis, I., Heider, K., Krause, R., LeCompte, W. A., Pitcairn, T., Ricci-Bitti, P., Scherer, K., Tomita, M., & Tzavaras, A. (1987). Universals and cultural differences in the judgments of facial expressions of emotion. *Journal of Personality and Social Psychology, 53,* 712–717.

Ekman, P., & O'Sullivan, M. (1991). Who can catch a liar? *American Psychologist, 46,* 913–920.

Elder, G. H., Jr. (1969). Appearance of education in marriage mobility. *American Sociological Review, 34,* 519–533.

Elder, G. H., Jr., & Clipp, E. C. (1989). Combat experience and emotional health: Impairment and resilience in later life. *Journal of Personality, 57,* 311–341.

Elkin, R. A., & Leippe, M. R. (1986). Physiological arousal, dissonance, and attitude change: Evidence for a dissonance-arousal link and a "don't remind me" effect. *Journal of Personality and Social Psychology, 51,* 55–65.

Elliot, A. J., & Devine, P. G. (1994). On the motivational nature of cognitive dissonance: Dissonance as psychological discomfort. *Journal of Personality and Social Psychology, 67,* 382–394.

Elliot, A. J., & Harackiewicz, J. M. (1994). Goal setting, achievement orientation, and intrinsic motivation: A mediational analysis. *Journal of Personality and Social Psychology, 66,* 968–980.

Elliott, R. (1991). Social science data and the APA: The *Lockhart* brief as a case in point. *Law and Human Behavior, 15,* 59–76.

Elliott, R. (1993). Expert testimony about eyewitness identification. *Law and Human Behavior, 17,* 423–437.

Ellsworth, P. C. (1991). To tell what we know or wait for Godot? *Law and Human Behavior, 15,* 77–90.

Elmer-Dewitt, P. (1991, November 25). How safe is sex? *Time,* pp. 72–74.

Elms, A., & Milgram, S. (1966). Personality characteristics associated with obedience and defiance toward authoritative command. *Journal of Experimental Research in Personality, 1,* 282–289.

Elwork, A., Sales, B. D., & Alfini, J. J. (1982). *Making jury instructions understandable.* Charlottesville, VA: Miche.

Emery, R. E. (1989). Family violence. *American Psychologist, 44,* 321–328.

Enzle, M. E., & Anderson, S. C. (1993). Surveillant intentions and intrinsic motivation. *Journal of Personality and Social Psychology, 64,* 257–266.

Enzle, M. E., Hansen, R. D., & Lowe, C. A. (1975). Causal attribution in the mixed-motive game: Effects of facilitory and inhibitory environmental forces. *Journal of Personality and Social Psychology, 31,* 50–54.

Epstein, J. L. (1985). After the bus arrives: Resegregation in desegregated schools. *Journal of Social Issues, 41,* 23–43.

Epstein, S. (1983). A research paradigm for the study of personality and emotions. In M. M. Page (Ed.), *Nebraska Symposium on Motivation: 1982* (pp. 91–154). Lincoln: University of Nebraska Press.

Erber, R. & Tesser, A. (1992). Task effort and the regulation of mood: The absorption hypothesis. *Journal of Experimental Social Psychology, 28,* 339–359.

Erev, I., Bornstein, G., & Galili, R. (1993). Constructive intergroup competition as a solution to the free rider problem: A field experiment. *Journal of Experimental Social Psychology, 29,* 463–478.

Eron, L. D. (1986). Interventions to mitigate the psychological effects of media violence on aggressive behavior. In L. R. Huesmann & N. M. Malamuth (Eds.), *Journal of Social Issues: Media Violence and Antisocial Behavior, 42*(3), 155–169.

Eron, L. D. (1987). The development of aggressive behavior from the perspective of a developing behaviorism. *American Psychologist, 42,* 435–442.

Eron, L. D., Gentry, J. H., & Schlegel, P. (1994). *Reason to hope: A psychosocial perspective on violence and youth.* Washington, DC: American Psychological Association.

Eron, L. D., & Huesmann, L. R. (1984). The control of aggressive behavior by changes in attitudes, values, and the conditions of learning. In R. J. Blanchard & D. C. Blanchard (Eds.), *Advances in the study of aggression* (Vol. 1, pp. 139–171). New York: Academic Press.

Eron, L. D., Huesmann, L. R., Lefkowitz, M. M., & Walder, L. O. (1972). Does television cause aggression? *American Psychologist, 27,* 253–263.

Evans, G. W., & Lepore, S. J. (1993). Household crowding and social support: A quasiexperimental analysis. *Journal of Personality and Social Psychology, 65,* 308–316.

Evans, G. W., Palsane, M. N., Lepore, S. J., & Martin, J. (1989). Residential density and psychological health: The mediating effects of social support. *Journal of Personality and Social Psychology, 57,* 994–999.

Evans, R. I., Smith, C. K., & Raines, B. E. (1984). Deterring cigarette smoking in adolescents: A psychosocial-behavioral analysis of an intervention strategy. In A. Baum, S. E. Taylor, & J. E. Singer (Eds.), *Handbook of psychology and health: Vol. 4. Social psychological aspects of health* (pp. 301–318). Hillsdale, NJ: Erlbaum.

Ewart, C. K., & Kolodner, K. B. (1994). Negative affect, gender, and repressive style predict elevated ambulatory blood pressure in adolescents. *Journal of Personality and Social Psychology, 66,* 596–605.

Fabes, R. A., Fultz, J., Eisenberg, N., May-Plumlee, T., & Christopher, F. S. (1989). Effects of rewards on children's prosocial motivation: A socialization study. *Developmental Psychology, 25,* 509–515.

Farr, R. M. (1991). The long past and the short history of social psychology. *European Journal of Social Psychology, 21,* 371–380.

Fazio, R. H. (1987). Self-perception theory: A current perspective. In M. P. Zanna, J. M. Olson, & C. P. Herman (Eds.), *Social influence: The Ontario Symposium* (Vol. 5, pp. 129–150). Hillsdale, NJ: Erlbaum.

Fazio, R. H. (1990a). Multiple processes by which attitudes guide behavior: The MODE model as an integrative framework. In M. P. Zanna (Ed.), *Advances in experimental social psychology* (Vol. 23, pp. 75–109). New York: Academic Press.

Fazio, R. H. (1990b). A practical guide to the use of response latency in social psychological research. In C. Hendrick & M. S. Clark (Eds.), *Review of personality and social psychology: Vol. 11. Research methods in personality and social psychology* (pp. 74–97). Newbury Park, CA: Sage.

Fazio, R. H., Effrein, E. A., & Falender, V. J. (1981). Self-perceptions following social interactions. *Journal of Personality and Social Psychology, 41,* 232–242.

Fazio, R. H., & Zanna, M. P. (1981). Direct experience and attitude-behavior consistency. In L. Berkowitz (Ed.), *Advances in experimental social psychology* (Vol. 14, pp. 162–202). New York: Academic Press.

Fazio, R. H., Zanna, M. P., & Cooper, J. (1977). Dissonance and self perception: An integrative view of each theory's proper domain of application. *Journal of Experimental Social Psychology, 13,* 464–479.

Feeney, J. A., & Noller, P. (1990). Attachment style as a predictor of adult romantic relationships. *Journal of Personality and Social Psychology, 58,* 281–291.

Feeney, J. A., Noller, P., & Callan, V. J. (1994). Attachment style, communication and satisfaction in the early years of marriage. In K. Bartholomew & D. Perlman (Eds.), *Advances in personal relationships* (Vol. 5, pp. 269–308). London: Jessica Kingsley Publishers.

Feeney, J. A., Peterson, C., & Noller, P. (1994). Equity and marital satisfaction over the family life cycle. *Personal Relationships, 1,* 83–99.

Fehr, B. (1993). How do I love thee? Let me consult my prototype. In S. Duck (Ed.), *Individuals in relationships* (pp. 87–120). Newbury Park, CA: Sage.

Fehr, B., & Russell, J. A. (1991). The concept of love viewed from a prototype perspective. *Journal of Personality and Social Psychology, 60,* 425–438.

Fein, S. (1991). The suspicious mind. Doctoral dissertation, University of Michigan.

Fein, S., Hilton, J. L., & Miller, D. T. (1990). Suspicion of ulterior motivation and the correspondence bias. *Journal of Personality and Social Psychology, 58,* 753–764.

Fein, S., & Spencer, S. J. (1993). Self-esteem and stereotype-based downward social comparison. Paper presented at the annual Meeting of the American Psychological Society, Toronto, August 1993.

Feindler, E. L., & Becker, J. V. (1994). Interventions in family violence involving children and adolescents. In L. D. Eron, J. H. Gentry, & P. Schegel (eds.), *Reason to hope: A psychosocial perspective on violence and youth* (pp. 405–430). Washington, DC: American Psychological Association.

Feingold, A. (1988). Matching for attractiveness in romantic partners and same-sex friends: A meta-analysis and theoretical critique. *Psychological Bulletin, 104,* 226–235.

Feingold, A. (1990). Gender differences in effects of physical attractiveness on romantic attraction: A comparison across five research paradigms. *Journal of Personality and Social Psychology, 59,* 981–993.

Feingold, A. (1991). Sex differences in the effects of similarity and physical attractiveness on opposite-sex attraction. *Basic and Applied Social Psychology, 12,* 357–367.

Feingold, A. (1992a). Gender differences in mate selection preferences: A test of the parental investment model. *Psychological Bulletin, 112,* 125–139.

Feingold, A. (1992b). Good-looking people are not what we think. *Psychological Bulletin, 111,* 304–341.

Feingold, A. (1994). Gender differences in personality: a meta-analysis. *Psychological Bulletin, 116,* 429–456.

Fellner, C. H. & Marshall, J. R. (1981). Kidney donors revisited. In J. P. Rushton & R. M. Sorrentino (Eds.), *Altruism and helping behavior* (pp. 351–365). Hillsdale, NJ: Erlbaum.

Felmlee, D. H. (1994). Who's on top? Power in romantic relationships. *Sex Roles, 31,* 275–295.

Felson, R. B. (1989). Parents and the reflected appraisal process: A longitudinal analysis. *Journal of Personality and Social Psychology, 56,* 965–971.

Fenigstein, A., & Abrams, D. (1993). Self-attention and the egocentric assumption of shared perspectives. *Journal of Experimental Social Psychology, 29,* 287–303.

Fenigstein, A., Scheier, M. F., & Buss, A. H. (1975). Public and private self-consciousness: Assessment and theory. *Journal of Consulting and Clinical Psychology, 43,* 522–527.

Ferguson, T. J., & Rule, B. G. (1983). An attributional perspective on anger and aggression. In R. G. Geen & E. I. Donnerstein (Eds.), *Aggression: Theoretical and empirical reviews: Vol. l. Theoretical and methodological issues* (pp. 41–74). New York: Academic Press.

Festinger, L. (1950). Informal social communication. *Psychological Review, 57,* 271–282.

Festinger, L. (1951). Architecture and group membership. *Journal of Social Issues, 7,* 152–163.

Festinger, L. (1954). A theory of social comparison processes. *Human Relations, 7,* 117–140.

Festinger, L. (1957). *A theory of cognitive dissonance.* Stanford, CA: Stanford University Press.

Festinger, L., & Carlsmith, J. M. (1959). Cognitive consequences of forced compliance. *Journal of Abnormal and Social Psychology, 58,* 203–210.

Festinger, L., Pepitone, A., & Newcomb, T. (1952). Some consequences of de-individuation in a group. *Journal of Abnormal and Social Psychology, 47,* 382–389.

Festinger, L., Schachter, S., & Back, K. W. (1950). *Social pressures in informal groups: A study of human factors in housing.* New York: Harper.

Fiedler, F. E. (1967). *A theory of leadership effectiveness.* New York: McGraw-Hill.

Fiedler, F. E., & Chemers, M. M. (1984). *Improving leadership effectiveness: The leader match concept* (2nd ed.). New York: Wiley.

Fiedler, F. E., & Garcia, J. E. (1987). *Leadership: Cognitive resources and performance.* New York: Wiley.

Fiedler, F. E., Murphy, S. E., & Gibson, F. W. (1992). Inaccurate reporting and inappropriate variables: A reply to Vecchio's (1990) examination of cognitive resource theory. *Journal of Applied Psychology, 77,* 372–374.

Filsinger, E. E., & Thoma, S. J. (1988). Behavioral antecedents of relationship stability and adjustment: A five-year longitudinal study. *Journal of Marriage and the Family, 50,* 785–795.

Fincham, F. D., & Bradbury, T. N. (1989). Perceived responsibility for marital events: Egocentric or partner-centric bias? *Journal of Marriage and the Family, 51,* 27–35.

Fincham, F. D., & Bradbury, T. N. (1993). Marital satisfaction, depression, and attributions: A longitudinal analysis. *Journal of Personality and Social Psychology, 64,* 442–452.

Finkelhor, D., & Dziuba-Leatherman, J. (1994). Victimization of children. *American Psychologist, 49,* 173–183.

Fischer, C. S. (1976). *The urban experience.* New York: Harcourt Brace Jovanovich.

Fischhoff, B. (1975). Hindsight ≠ foresight: The effect of outcome knowledge on judgment under uncertainty. *Journal of Experimental Psychology: Human Perception and Performance, 1,* 288–299.

Fishbein, M. (1980). A theory of reasoned action: Some applications and implications. In H. E. Howe & M. M. Page (Eds.), *Nebraska Symposium on Motivation* (Vol. 27, pp. 65–116). Lincoln: University of Nebraska Press.

Fishbein, M., & Ajzen, I. (1972). Attitudes and opinions. In P. H. Mussen & M. R. Rosenzweig (Eds.), *Annual Review of Psychology, 23,* 487–544.

Fishbein, M., & Ajzen, I. (1975). *Beliefs, attitudes, intention, and behavior: An introduction to theory and research.* Reading, MA: Addison-Wesley.

Fishbein, M., & Stasson, M. (1990). The role of desires, self-predictions, and perceived control in the prediction of training session attendance. *Journal of Applied Social Psychology, 20,* 173–198.

Fisher, C. B., & Fyrberg, D. (1994). Participant partners: College students weigh the costs and benefits of deceptive research. *American Psychologist, 49,* 417–427.

Fisher, J. D., Bell, P. A., & Baum, A. (1984). *Environmental psychology* (2nd ed.). New York: Holt, Rinehart and Winston.

Fisher, J. D., Fisher, W. A., Williams, S. S., & Malloy, T. E. (1994). Empirical tests of an information-motivation-behavioral skills model of AIDS-preventive behavior with gay men and heterosexual university students. *Health Psychology, 13,* 238–250.

Fisher, J. D., Nadler, A., & Whitcher-Alagna, S. (1982). Recipient reactions to aid. *Psychological Bulletin, 91,* 27–54.

Fiske, A. P. (1991). The cultural relativity of selfish individualism: Anthropological evidence that humans are inherently sociable. In M. S. Clark (Ed.), *Review of personality and social psychology: Vol. 12. Prosocial behavior* (pp. 176–214). Newbury Park, CA: Sage.

Fiske, A. P. (1992). The four elementary forms of sociality: Framework for a unified theory of social relations. *Psychological Review, 99,* 689–723.

Fiske, S. T. (1993). Social cognition and social perception. *Annual Review of Psychology, 44,* 155–194.

Fiske, S. T., Bersoff, D. N., Borgida, E., Deaux, K., & Heilman, M. E. (1991). Social science research on trial: Use of sex stereotyping research in *Price Waterhouse v. Hopkins. American Psychologist, 46,* 1049–1060.

Fiske, S. T., & Neuberg, S. L. (1990). A continuum of impression formation from category-based to individuating processes: Influences of information and motivation on attention and interpretation. In M. P. Zanna (Ed.), *Advances in experimental social psychology* (Vol. 23, pp. 1–74). New York: Academic Press.

Fitzgerald, F. S. (1925). *The Great Gatsby.* New York: Scribner.

Fitzgerald, J. M. (1988). Vivid memories and the reminiscence phenomenon: The role of self-narrative. *Human Development, 31,* 261–273.

Fitzgerald, R., & Ellsworth, P. C. (1984). Due process vs. crime control: Death qualification and jury attitudes. *Law and Human Behavior, 8,* 31–52.

Fitzpatrick, M. A. (1988). *Between husbands and wives: Communication in marriage.* Newbury Park, CA: Sage.

Fleming, J. H. (1994). Multiple audience problems, tactical communication, and social interaction: A relational-regulation perspective. *Advances in Experimental Social Psychology, 26,* 215–292.

Fleming, J. H., & Darley, J. M. (1991). Mixed messages: The multiple audience problem and strategic communication. *Social Cognition, 9,* 25–46.

Fleming, J. H., & Scott, B. A. (1991). The costs of confession: The Persian Gulf War POW tapes in historical and theoretical perspective. *Contemporary Social Psychology, 15,* 127–138.

Fleming, J. S., & Courtney, B. E. (1984). The dimensionality of self-esteem: II. Hierarchical facet model for revised measurement scales. *Journal of Personality and Social Psychology, 46,* 404–421.

Fletcher, G. J. O., Danilovics, P., Fernandez, G., Peterson, D., & Reeder, G. D. (1986). Attributional complexity: An individual differences measure. *Journal of Personality and Social Psychology, 51,* 875–884.

Fletcher, G. J. O., Rosanowski, J., & Fitness, J. (1994). Automatic processing in intimate contexts: The role of close-relationship beliefs. *Journal of Personality and Social Psychology, 67,* 888–897.

Florian, V., Mikulincer, M., & Taubman, O. (1995). Does hardiness contribute to mental health during a stressful real-life situation? The roles of appraisal and coping. *Journal of Personality and Social Psychology, 68,* 687–695.

Flowers, M. L. (1977). A laboratory test of some implications of Janis's groupthink hypothesis. *Journal of Personality and Social Psychology, 35,* 888–896.

Foa, E. B., & Foa, U. G. (1980). Resource theory: Interpersonal behavior as exchange. In K. J. Gergen, M. S. Greenberg, & R. H. Willis (Eds.), *Social exchange: Advances in theory and research* (pp. 77–101). New York: Plenum.

Folger, R. (1986). Rethinking equity theory: A referent cognitions model. In H. W. Bierhoff, R. L. Cohen, & J. Greenberg (Eds.), *Justice in social relations* (pp. 145–162). New York: Plenum.

Folger, R., & Greenberg, J. (1985). Procedural justice: An interpretive analysis of personnel systems. In K. Rowland & G. Ferris (Eds.), *Research in personnel and human resource management* (Vol. 3, pp. 141–183). Greenwich, CT: JAI Press.

Folger, R., & Konovsky, M. A. (1989). Effects of procedural and distributive justice on reactions to pay raise decisions. *Academy of Management Journal, 32,* 115–130.

Folger, R., Konovsky, M. A., & Cropanzano, R. (1992). A due process metaphor for performance appraisal. *Research in Organizational Behavior, 14,* 129–177.

Folkes, V. S. (1982). Forming relationships and the matching hypothesis. *Personality and Social Psychology Bulletin, 8,* 631–636.

Folkman, S., & Lazarus, R. S. (1988). Coping as a mediator of emotion. *Journal of Personality and Social Psychology, 54,* 466–475.

Folkman, S., & Lazarus, R. S. (1985). If it changes it must be a process: Study of emotion and coping during three stages of a college examination. *Journal of Personality and Social Psychology, 48,* 150–170.

Follette, V. M., & Jacobson, N. S. (1987). Importance of attributions as a predictor of how people cope with failure. *Journal of Personality and Social Psychology, 52,* 1205–1211.

Fontaine, G. (1990). Cultural diversity in intimate intercultural relationships. In D. D. Cahn (Ed.), *Intimates in conflict: A communication perspective* (pp. 209–224). Hillsdale, NJ: Erlbaum.

Forgas, J. P. (1995). Mood and judgment: The Affect Infusion Model (AIM). *Psychological Bulletin, 117,* 39–66.

Forgas, J. P. (1992). Mood and the perception of atypical people: Affect and prototypicality in person memory and impressions. *Journal of Personality and Social Psychology, 62,* 863–875.

Forgas, J. P. (1993). On making sense of odd couples: Mood effects on the perception of mismatched relationships. *Personality and Social Psychology Bulletin, 19,* 59–70.

Forgas, J. P., & Bower, G. H. (1987). Mood effects on person-perception judgments. *Journal of Personality and Social Psychology, 53,* 53–60.

Forsyth, D. R. (1990). *Group dynamics* (2nd ed.). Pacific Grove, CA: Brooks/Cole.

Forsythe, S. M. (1990). Effects of applicant's clothing on interviewer's decision to hire. *Journal of Applied Social Psychology, 20,* 1579–1595.

Fossett, M. A., & Kiecolt, K. J. (1993). Mate availability and family structure among African Americans in U.S. metropolitan areas. *Journal of Marriage and the Family, 55,* 288–302.

FosterLee, L., Horowitz, I. A., & Bourgeois, M.J. (1993). Juror competence in civil trials: Effects of preinstruction and evidence technicality. *Journal of Applied Psychology, 78,* 14–21.

Fosterling, F. (1989). Models of covariation and attribution: How do they relate to the analogy of analysis of variance? *Journal of Personality and Social Psychology, 57,* 615–625.

Fosterling, F. (1992). The Kelley model as an analysis of variance analogy: How far can it be taken? *Journal of Experimental Social Psychology, 28,* 475–490.

Fowler, F. J., Jr. (1993). *Survey research methods* (2nd ed.). Newbury Park, CA: Sage.

Frable, D. E. S. (1989). Sex typing and gender ideology: Two facets of the individual's gender psychology that go together. *Journal of Personality and Social Psychology, 56,* 95–108.

Frable, D. E. S., & Bem, S. L. (1985). If you're gender-schematic, all members of the opposite sex look alike. *Journal of Personality and Social Psychology, 49,* 459–468.

Franck, K. A. (1980). Friends and strangers: The social experience of living in urban and non-urban settings. *Journal of Social Issues, 36*(3), 52–71.

Frank, J. (1949). *Courts on trial.* Princeton, NJ: Princeton University Press.

Frank, M. G., Ekman, P., & Friesen, W. V. (1993). Behavioral markers and recognizability of the smile of enjoyment. *Journal of Personality and Social Psychology, 64,* 83–93.

Frazier, P., & Schauben, L. (1994). Causal attributions and recovery from rape and other stressful events. *Journal of Social and Clinical Psychology, 13,* 1–14.

Frazier, P. A., & Borgida, E. (1992). Rape trauma syndrome: A review of case law and psychological research. *Law and Human Behavior, 16,* 293–311.

Freedman, J. L. (1988a). Keeping pornography in perspective. *Contemporary Psychology, 33,* 858–860.

Freedman, J. L. (1988b). Television violence and aggression: What the evidence shows. *Applied Social Psychology Annual, 8,* 144–162.

Freedman, J. L., & Fraser, S. C. (1966). Compliance without pressure: The foot-in-the-door technique. *Journal of Personality and Social Psychology, 4,* 195–202.

Freedman, J. L., & Sears, D. O. (1965). Warning, distraction, and resistance to influence. *Journal of Personality and Social Psychology, 1,* 262–266.

French, J. P. R., Jr., & Raven, B. H. (1959). The bases of social power. In D. Cartwright (Ed.), *Studies in social power* (pp. 150–167). Ann Arbor: University of Michigan Press.

Freud, S. (1905). Fragments of an analysis of a case of hysteria. *Collected papers* (Vol. 3). New York: Basic Books. (Reprinted in 1959)

Freud, S. (1920). *Beyond the pleasure principle: A study of the death instinct in human aggression* (J. Strachey, Trans.). New York: Bantam Books. (Reprinted in 1959)

Freud, S. (1922). *Group psychology and the analysis of the ego.* New York: Liverright. (Reprinted in 1951)

Freud, S. (1928). Dostoevsky and parricide. In J. Strachey (Ed.), *Freud: The collected papers.* New York: Basic Books. (Reprinted in 1959)

Frey, D. L., & Gaertner, S. L. (1986). Helping and the avoidance of inappropriate interracial behavior: A strategy that perpetuates a nonprejudiced self-image. *Journal of Personality and Social Psychology, 50,* 1083–1090.

Friedland, N. (1990). Attribution of control as a determinant of cooperation in exchange interactions. *Journal of Applied Social Psychology, 20,* 303–320.

Friedland, N., Keinan, G., & Regev, Y. (1992). Controlling the uncontrollable: Effects of stress on illusory perceptions of controllability. *Journal of Personality and Social Psychology, 63,* 923–931.

Friedman, H. S., & Booth-Kewley, S. (1987). The "disease-prone personality": A meta-analytic view of the construct. *American Psychologist, 42,* 539–555.

Friedman, M., & Rosenman, R. H. (1959). Association of specific overt behavior pattern with blood and cardiovascular findings: Blood cholesterol level, blood clotting time, incidence of arcus senilis and clinical coronary artery disease. *Journal of the American Medical Association, 169,* 1286–1296.

Friedman, W. J. (1993). Memory for the time of past events. *Psychological Bulletin, 113,* 44–66.

Friend, R., Rafferty, Y., & Bramel, D. (1990). A puzzling misinterpretation of the Asch "conformity" study. *European Journal of Social Psychology, 20,* 29–44.

Friman, P. C., Allen, K. D., Kerwin, M. L. E., & Larzelere, R. (1993). Changes in modern psychology: A citation analysis of the Kuhnian displacement thesis. *American Psychologist, 48,* 658–664.

Frost, D. E., & Stahelski, A. J. (1988). The systematic measurement of French and Raven's bases of social power in workgroups. *Journal of Applied Social Psychology, 18,* 375–389.

Fulero, S., & Penrod, S. D. (1990). Attorney jury selection folklore: What do they think and how can psychology help? *Forensic Reports, 3,* 223–259.

Fullerton, C. S., Ursano, R. J., Kaq, T., & Bhartiya, V. R. (1992). The chemical and biological warfare environment: Psychological responses and social supports in a high-stress environment. *Journal of Applied Social Psychology, 22,* 1608–1624.

Fultz, J., Batson, C. D., Fortenbach, V. A., McCarthy, P. M., & Varney, L. L. (1986). Social evaluation and the empathy-altruism hypothesis. *Journal of Personality and Social Psychology, 50,* 761–769.

Fultz, J., & Nielsen, M. E. (1993). Anticipated vicarious affect and willingness to be exposed to another's suffering. *Basic and Applied Social Psychology, 14,* 273–283.

Funder, D. C. (1982). On the accuracy of dispositional vs. situational attributions. *Social Cognition, 1,* 205–222.

Funder, D. C. (1987). Errors and mistakes: Evaluating the accuracy of social judgment. *Psychological Bulletin, 101,* 75–90.

Furnham, A. (1993). Just world beliefs in twelve societies. *Journal of Social Psychology, 133,* 317–329.

Furnham, A., & Bitar, N. (1993). The stereotyped portrayal of men and women in British television advertisements. *Sex Roles, 29,* 297–310.

Gaertner, S. L., & Dovidio, J. F. (1986). The aversive form of racism. In J. F. Dovidio & S. L. Gaertner (Eds.), *Prejudice, discrimination, and racism: Theory and research* (pp. 61–89). Orlando, FL: Academic Press.

Gaertner, S. L., Mann, J. A., Dovidio, J. F., Murrell, A. J., & Pomare, M. (1990). How does cooperation reduce intergroup bias? *Journal of Personality and Social Psychology, 59,* 692–704.

Gaertner, S. L., Mann, J. A., Murrell, A. J., & Dovidio, J. F. (1989). Reducing intergroup bias: The benefits of recategorization. *Journal of Personality and Social Psychology, 57,* 239–249.

Gaertner, S. L., & McLaughlin, J. P. (1983). Racial stereotypes: Associations and ascriptions of positive and negative characteristics. *Social Psychology Quarterly, 46,* 23–30.

Galligan, R. F., & Terry, D. J. (1993). Romantic ideals, fear of negative implications, and the practice of safe sex. (1993). *Journal of Applied Social Psychology, 23,* 1685–1711.

Gallup, G. G., Jr. (1977). Self-recognition in primates: A comparative approach to the bidirectional properties of consciousness. *American Psychologist, 32,* 329–337.

Gallupe, R. B., Bastianutti, L. M., & Cooper, W. H. (1991). Unblocking brainstorms. *Journal of Applied Psychology, 76,* 137–142.

Gamson, W. A., Fireman, B., & Rytina, S. (1982). *Encounters with unjust authority.* Homewood, IL: Dorsey.

Gangestad, S., & Snyder, M. (1991). Taxonomic analysis redux: Some statistical considerations for testing a latent class model. *Journal of Personality and Social Psychology, 61,* 141–146.

Ganong, L., & Coleman, M. (1994). *Remarried family relationships.* Newbury Park, CA: Sage.

Garcia, S., Stinson, L., Ickes, W., Bissonnette, V., & Briggs, S. R. (1991). Shyness and physical attractiveness in mixed-sex dyads. *Journal of Personality and Social Psychology, 61,* 35–49.

Gardner, W., & Wilcox, B. L. (1993). Political intervention in scientific peer review: Research on adolescent sexual behavior. *American Psychologist, 48,* 972–983.

Gaugler, B. B., Rosenthal, D. B., Thornton, G. C., III, & Bentson, C. (1987). Meta-analysis of assessment center validity. *Journal of Applied Psychology, 72,* 493–511.

Gavin, L., & Furman, W. (1989). Age difference in adolescents' perceptions of their peer groups. *Developmental Psychology, 25,* 827–834.

Geen, R. G. (1981). Behavioral and physiological reactions to observed violence: Effects of prior exposure to aggressive stimuli. *Journal of Personality and Social Psychology, 40,* 868–875.

Geen, R. G., & McCown, E. J. (1984). Effects of noise and attack on aggression and physiological arousal. *Motivation and Emotion, 8,* 231–241.

Geen, R. G., & Thomas, S. L. (1986). The immediate effects of media violence on behavior. In L. R. Huesmann & N. M. Malamuth (Eds.), *Journal of Social Issues, 42*(3), 7–27.

Geis, F. L. (1993). Self-fulfilling prophecies: A social psychological view of gender. In A. E. Beal & R. J. Sternberg (Eds.), *The psychology of gender* (pp. 9–54). New York: Guilford.

Geis, F. L., Brown, V., Jennings (Walstedt), J., & Porter, N. (1984). TV commercials as achievement scripts for women. *Sex Roles, 10,* 513–525.

Geiselman, R. E., Haight, N. A., & Kimata, L. G. (1984). Context effects in the perceived physical attractiveness of faces. *Journal of Experimental Social Psychology, 20,* 409–424.

Geller, W. A. (1993). *Videotaping interrogations and confessions.* Washington, DC: National Institute of Justice.

Gelles, R. J., & Cornell, C. P. (1990). *Intimate violence in families* (2nd ed.). Newbury Park, CA: Sage.

Gelles, R. J., & Straus, M. A. (1988). *Intimate violence.* New York: Simon & Schuster.

George, J. M., & Brief, A. P. (1992). Feeling good–doing good: A conceptual analysis of the mood at work—organizational spontaneity relationship. *Psychological Bulletin, 112,* 310–329.

Gerard, H. B. (1983). School desegregation: The social science role. *American Psychologist, 38,* 869–877.

Gerard, H. B., Whilhelmy, R. A., & Connolley, R. S. (1968). Conformity and group size. *Journal of Personality and Social Psychology, 8,* 79–82.

Gerbner, G., Gross, L., Morgan, M., & Signorielli, N. (1980). The "mainstreaming" of American violence: Profile no. 11. *Journal of Communications, 30*(3), 10–29.

Gerbner, G., Gross, L., Morgan, M., & Signorielli, N. (1986). Living with television: The dynamics of the cultivation process. In J. Bryant & D. Zillmann (Eds.), *Perspectives on media effects* (pp. 17–40). Hillsdale, NJ: Erlbaum.

Gerdes, E. P., & Guo P. (1994). Coping differences between college women and men in China and the United States. *Genetic, Social, and General Psychology Monographs, 120,* 169–198.

Gergen, K. J. (1973). Social psychology as history. *Journal of Personality and Social Psychology, 26,* 309–320.

Gergen, K. J. (1994). Exploring the postmodern: Perils or potentials? *American Psychologist, 49,* 412–416.

Gerhart, B., & Rynes, S. (1991). Determinants and consequences of salary negotiations by male and female MBA graduates. *Journal of Applied Psychology, 76,* 256–262.

Gerrard, M., Gibbons, F. X., Warner, T. D., & Smith, G. E. (1993). Perceived vulnerability to HIV infection and AIDS-preventive behavior: A critical review of the evidence. In J. B. Pryor & G. D. Reeder (Eds.), *The social psychology of HIV infection* (pp. 59–84). Hillsdale, NJ: Erlbaum.

Gettelman, T. E., & Thompson, J. K. (1993). Actual differences and stereotypical perceptions in body image and eating disturbance: A comparison of male and female heterosexual and homosexual samples. *Sex Roles, 29,* 545–562.

Gibbons, A. (1993). Evolutionists take the long view on sex and violence. *Science, 261,* 987–988.

Gibbons, F. X. (1978). Sexual standards and reactions to pornography: Enhancing behavioral consistency through self-focused attention. *Journal of Personality and Social Psychology, 36,* 976–987.

Gibbons, F. X. (1990). Self-attention and behavior: A review and theoretical update. In M. P. Zanna (Ed.), *Advances in experimental social psychology* (Vol. 23, pp. 249–303). New York: Academic Press.

Gibbons, F. X., & McCoy, S. B. (1991). Self-esteem, similarity, and reactions to active versus passive downward comparison. *Journal of Personality and Social Psychology, 60,* 414–424.

Gibbons, F. X., & Wicklund, R. A. (1982). Self-focused attention and helping behavior. *Journal of Personality and Social Psychology, 43,* 462–474.

Gibbs, N. (1993, January 18). "'Til death do us part." *Time,* pp. 36–45.

Gigone, D., & Hastie, R. (1993). The common knowledge effect: Information sharing and group judgment. *Journal of Personality and Social Psychology, 65,* 959–974.

Gilbert, D. T., & Hixon, J. G. (1991). The trouble of thinking: Activation and application of stereotypic beliefs. *Journal of Personality and Social Psychology, 60,* 509–517.

Gilbert, D. T., & Jones, E. E. (1986). Perceiver-induced constraint: Interpretations of self-generated reality. *Journal of Personality and Social Psychology, 50,* 269–280.

Gilbert, D. T., & Krull, D. S. (1988). Seeing less and knowing more: The benefits of perceptual ignorance. *Journal of Personality and Social Psychology, 54,* 193–202.

Gilbert, D. T., Krull, D. S., & Malone, P. S. (1990). Unbelieving the unbelievable: Some problems in the rejection of false information. *Journal of Personality and Social Psychology, 59,* 601–613.

Gilbert, D. T., & Malone, P. S. (1995). The correspondence bias. *Psychological Bulletin, 117,* 21–38.

Gilbert, D. T., McNulty, S. E., Giuliano, T. A., & Benson, J. E. (1992). Blurry words and fuzzy deeds: The attribution of obscure behavior. *Journal of Personality and Social Psychology, 62,* 18–25.

Gilbert, D. T., & Osborne, R. E. (1989). Thinking backward: Some curable and incurable consequences of cognitive busyness. *Journal of Personality and Social Psychology, 57,* 940–949.

Gilbert, D. T., Pelham, B. W., & Krull, D. S. (1988). On cognitive busyness: When person perceivers meet persons perceived. *Journal of Personality and Social Psychology, 54,* 733–740.

Gilbert, S. J. (1981). Another look at the Milgram obedience studies: The role of the gradated series of shocks. *Personality and Social Psychology Bulletin, 7,* 690–695.

Gillig, P. M., & Greenwald, A. G. (1974). Is it time to lay the sleeper effect to rest? *Journal of Personality and Social Psychology, 29,* 132–139.

Gilligan, C. (1982). *In a different voice: Psychological theory and women's development.* Cambridge, MA: Harvard University Press.

Gilovich, T. (1991). *How we know what isn't so: The fallibility of human reason in everyday life.* New York: Free Press.

Giunta, C. T., & Compas, B. E. (1993). Coping in marital dyads: Patterns and associations with psychological symptoms. *Journal of Marriage and the Family, 55,* 1011–1017.

Gladue, B. A. (1991). Aggressive behavioral characteristics, hormones, and sexual orientation in men and women. *Aggressive Behavior, 17,* 313–326.

Gladue, B. A., & Delaney, H. J. (1990). Gender differences in perception of attractiveness of men and women in bars. *Personality and Social Psychology Bulletin, 16,* 378–391.

Glass, D. C., Gordon, A., & Henchy, T. (1970). The effects of social stimuli on psychophysiological reactivity to an aversive film. *Psychonomic Science, 20,* 255–256.

Glass, D. C., & Singer, J. E. (1972). *Urban stress.* New York: Academic Press.

Gleicher, F., & Petty, R. E. (1992). Expectations of reassurance influence the nature of fear-stimulated attitude change. *Journal of Experimental Social Psychology, 28,* 86–100.

Glenn, N. D. (1989). Intersocietal variation in the mate preferences of males and females. *Behavioral and Brain Science, 12,* 21–23.

Glick, P. (1991). Trait-based and sex-based discrimination in occupational prestige, occupational salary, and hiring. *Sex Roles, 25,* 351–378.

Glick, P., Zion, C., & Nelson, C. (1988). What mediates sex discrimination in hiring decisions? *Journal of Personality and Social Psychology, 55,* 178–186.

Godfrey, D. K., Jones, E. E., & Lord, C. G. (1986). Self-promotion is not ingratiating. *Journal of Personality and Social Psychology, 50,* 106–115.

Goethals, G. R., Cooper, J., & Naficy, A. (1979). Role of foreseen, foreseeable, and unforeseeable behavioral consequences in the arousal of cognitive dissonance. *Journal of Personality and Social Psychology, 37,* 1179–1185.

Goethals, G. R., & Darley, J. (1977). Social comparison theory: An attributional approach. In J. M. Suls & R. L. Miller (Eds.), *Social comparison processes: Theoretical and empirical perspectives* (pp. 259–278). Washington, DC: Hemisphere.

Goethals, G. R., & Reckman, R. (1973). The perception of consistency in attitudes. *Journal of Experimental Social Psychology, 9,* 491–501.

Goffman, E. (1955). On face-work: An analysis of ritual elements in social interaction. *Psychiatry, 18,* 213–231.

Goffman, E. (1959). *The presentation of self in everyday life.* Garden City: Doubleday.

Goldberg, J., True, W. R., Eisen, S. A., & Henderson, W. G. (1990). A twin study of the effects of the Vietnam War on posttraumatic stress disorder. *Journal of the American Medical Association, 263,* 1227–1232.

Goldberg, L. R. (1978). Differential attribution of trait-descriptive terms to oneself as compared to well-liked, neutral, and disliked others: A psychometric analysis. *Journal of Personality and Social Psychology, 36,* 1012–1028.

Goldberg, L. R. (1993). The structure of phenotypic personality. *American Psychologist, 48,* 26–34.

Goldberg, L. R., Grenier, J. R., Guion, R., Sechrest, L. B., & Wing, H. (1991). *Questionnaires used in the prediction of trustworthiness in pre-employment selection decisions: An A.P.A. task force report.* Washington, DC: American Psychological Association.

Goldberg, P. (1968). Are women prejudiced against women? *Transaction, 5,* 28–30.

Goldman, J. A., & Harlow, L. L. (1993). Self-perception variables that mediate AIDS-preventive behavior in college students. *Health Psychology, 12,* 489–498.

Goldman, M. (1986). Compliance employing a combined foot-in-the-door and door-in-the-face procedure. *Journal of Social Psychology, 126,* 111–116.

Goldstein, A. G., Chance, J. E., & Schneller, G. R. (1989). Frequency of eyewitness identification in criminal cases: A survey of prosecutors. *Bulletin of the Psychonomic Society, 27,* 71–74.

Goldstein, M. D., & Strube, M. J. (1994). Independence revisited: The relation between positive and negative affect in a naturalistic setting. *Personality and Social Psychology Bulletin, 20,* 57–64.

Gonzales, M. H., & Meyers, S. A. (1993). "Your mother would like me": Self-presentation in the personals ads of heterosexual and homosexual men and women. *Personality and Social Psychology Bulletin, 19,* 131–142.

Gonzalez, R., Ellsworth, P. C., & Pembroke, M. (1993). Response biases in lineups and showups. *Journal of Personality and Social Psychology, 64,* 525–537.

Goodman, G. S., Hirschman, J., Hepps, D., & Rudy, L. (1991). Children's memory for stressful events. *Merrill-Palmer Quarterly, 37,* 109–158.

Gorenstein, G. W., & Ellsworth, P. C. (1980). Effect of choosing an incorrect photograph on a later identification by an eyewitness. *Journal of Applied Psychology, 65,* 616–622.

Gorman, C. (1994, September 19). Let's not be too hasty. *Time,* p. 71.

Gosselin, P., Kirouac, G., & Dore, F. Y. (1995). Components and recognition of facial expression in the communication of emotion by actors. *Journal of Personality and Social Psychology, 68,* 83–96.

Gottlieb, J., & Carver, C. S. (1980). Anticipation of future interaction and the bystander effect. *Journal of Experimental Social Psychology, 16,* 253–260.

Gottman, J. M. (1994). *What predicts divorce?* Hillsdale, NJ: Erlbaum.

Gottman, J. M., & Levenson, R. L. (1988). The social psychophysiology of marriage. In P. Noller & M. A. Fitzpatrick (Eds.), *Perspectives on marital interaction* (pp. 182–200). Clevedon, England: Multilingual Matters.

Gottman, J. M., & Levenson, R. W. (1992). Marital processes predictive of later dissolution: Behavior, physiology, and health. *Journal of Personality and Social Psychology, 63,* 221–233.

Gould, S. J. (1992, November 19). The confusion over evolution. *New York Review of Books,* pp. 47–54.

Gould, S. J. (1994, October 20). So near and yet so far. *New York Review of Books,* pp. 24–28.

Gouldner, A. W. (1960). The norm of reciprocity: A preliminary statement. *American Sociological Review, 25,* 161–178.

Graham, S. (1992). "Most of the subjects were white and middle class": Trends in published research on African Americans in selected APA journals, 1970–1989. *American Psychologist, 47,* 629–639.

Granberg, D., & Brent, E. (1983). When prophecy bends: The preference-expectation link in U.S. presidential elections. *Journal of Personality and Social Psychology, 45,* 477–491.

Graves, L. M., & Powell, G. N. (1988). An investigation of sex discrimination in recruiters' evaluations of actual applicants. *Journal of Applied Psychology, 73,* 20–29.

Gray-Little, B., & Burks, N. (1983). Power and satisfaction in marriage: A review and critique. *Psychological Bulletin, 93,* 513–538.

Graziano, W. G., Jensen-Campbell, L. A., Shebilske, L. J., & Lundgren, S. R. (1993). Social influence, sex differences, and judgments of beauty: Putting the *interpersonal* back in interpersonal attraction. *Journal of Personality and Social Psychology, 65,* 522–531.

Graziano, W. G., Leone, C., Musser, L. M., & Lautenschlager, G. J. (1987). Self-monitoring in children: A differential approach to social development. *Developmental Psychology, 23,* 571–576.

Green, D. P., Goldman, S. L., & Salovey, P. (1993). Measurement error masks bipolarity in affect ratings. *Journal of Personality and Social Psychology, 64,* 1029–1041.

Greenberg, J. (1982). Approaching equity and avoiding inequity in groups and organizations. In J. Greenberg & R. L. Cohen (Eds.), *Equity and justice in social behavior* (pp. 389–435). New York: Academic Press.

Greenberg, J. (1988). Equity and workplace status: A field experiment. *Journal of Applied Psychology, 73,* 606–613.

Greenberg, J. (1990). Employee theft as a reaction to underpayment inequity: The hidden costs of pay cuts. *Journal of Applied Psychology, 75,* 561–568.

Greenberg, J. (1993). Stealing in the name of justice: Informational and interpersonal moderators of theft reactions to underpayment equity. *Organizational Behavior and Human Decision Processes, 54,* 81–103.

Greenberg, J., & Folger, R. (1988). *Controversial issues in social research methods.* New York: Springer-Verlag.

Greenberg, J., & Pyszczynski, T. (1985). The effects of an overheard ethnic slur on evaluations of the target: How to spread a social disease. *Journal of Experimental Social Psychology, 21,* 61–72.

Greenberg, J., Solomon, S., Pyszczynski, T., Rosenblatt, A., Burling, J., Lyon, D., Simon, L., & Pinel, E. (1992). Why do people need self-esteem? Converging evidence that self-esteem serves an anxiety-buffering function. *Journal of Personality and Social Psychology, 63,* 913–922.

Greenberg, M. A., & Stone, A. A. (1992). Emotional disclosure about traumas and its relation to health: Effects of previous disclosure and trauma severity. *Journal of Personality and Social Psychology, 63,* 75–84.

Greenberg, M. S., & Westcott, D. R. (1983). Indebtedness as a mediator of reactions to aid. In J. D. Fisher, A. Nadler, & B. M. DePaulo (Eds.), *New directions in helping: Vol. 1. Recipient reactions to aid* (pp. 85–112). New York: Academic Press.

Greene, E., & Dodge, M. (1995). The influence of prior record evidence on juror decision-making. *Law and Human Behavior, 19,* 67–78.

Greenwald, A. G. (1968). Cognitive learning, cognitive responses to persuasion, and attitude change. In A. Greenwald, T. Brock, & T. Ostrom (Eds.), *Psychological foundations of attitudes* (pp. 147–170). New York: Academic Press.

Greenwald, A. G. (1980). The totalitarian ego: Fabrication and revision of personal history. *American Psychologist, 35,* 603–618.

Greenwald, A. G., & Banaji, M. R. (1989). The self as a memory system: Powerful but ordinary. *Journal of Personality and Social Psychology, 57,* 41–54.

Greenwald, A. G., & Banaji, M. R. (1995). Implicit social cognition: Attitudes, self-esteem, and stereotypes. *Psychological Review, 102,* 4–27.

Greenwald, A. G., & Pratkanis, A. R. (1984). The self. In R. S. Wyer & T. K. Srull (Eds.), *Handbook of social cognition* (Vol. 3, pp. 129–178). Hillsdale, NJ: Erlbaum.

Greenwald, A. G., Pratkanis, A. R., Leippe, M. R., & Baumgardner, M. H. (1986). Under what conditions does theory obstruct research progress? *Psychological Review, 93,* 216–229.

Greenwald, A. G., Spangenberg, E. R., Pratkanis, A. R., & Eskenazi, J. (1991). Double-blind tests of subliminal self-help audiotapes. *Psychological Science, 2,* 119–122.

Griffin, D., & Bartholomew, K. (1994). Models of the self and other: Fundamental dimensions underlying measures of adult attachment. *Journal of Personality and Social Psychology, 67,* 430–445.

Gross, A. E., & Latané, J. G. (1974). Receiving help, reciprocation, and interpersonal attraction. *Journal of Applied Social Psychology, 4,* 210–223.

Grossman, M., & Wood, W. (1993). Sex differences in intensity of emotional experience: A social role interpretation. *Journal of Personality and Social Psychology, 65,* 1010–1020.

Grote, N. K., & Frieze, I. H. (1994). The measurement of friendship-based love in intimate relationships. *Personal Relationships, 1,* 275–300.

Gruber, K. J., & White, J. W. (1986). Gender differences in the perceptions of self's and others' use of power strategies. *Sex Roles, 15,* 109–118.

Gruder, C. L., Cook, T. D., Hennigan, K. M., Flay, B. R., Alessis, C., & Halamaj, J. (1978). Empirical tests of the absolute sleeper effect predicted from the discounting cue hypothesis. *Journal of Personality and Social Psychology, 36,* 1061–1074.

Gudjonsson, G. (1992). *The psychology of interrogations, confessions, and testimony.* Chichester: John Wiley.

Guerin, B. (1986). Mere presence effects in humans: A review. *Journal of Experimental Social Psychology, 22,* 38–77.

Guerrero, L. K., & Andersen, P. A. (1991). The waxing and waning of relational intimacy: Touch as a function of relational stage, gender and touch avoidance. *Journal of Social and Personal Relationships, 8,* 147–165.

Guimond, S., & Dubé-Simard, L. (1983). Relative deprivation theory and the Quebec nationalist movement: The cognition-emotion distinction and the personal-group deprivation issue. *Journal of Personality and Social Psychology, 44,* 526–535.

Guttentag, M., & Secord, P. F. (1983). *Too many women? The sex ratio question.* Beverly Hills, CA: Sage.

Gwaltney, L. (1986). *The dissenters.* New York: Random House.

Hakmiller, K. L. (1966). Threat as a determinant of downward comparison. *Journal of Experimental Social Psychology* (Suppl. 1), 32–39.

Halford, W. K., Hahlweg, K., & Dunne, M. (1990). The cross-cultural consistency of marital communication associated with marital distress. *Journal of Marriage and the Family, 52,* 487–500.

Hall, D. R., & Zhao, J. Z. (1995). Cohabitation and divorce in Canada: Testing the selectivity hypothesis. *Journal of Marriage and the Family, 57,* 421–427.

Hall, E. T. (1966). *The hidden dimension.* Garden City, NY: Doubleday.

Hall, J. A., & Veccia, E. M. (1990). More "touching" observations: New insights on men, women, and interpersonal touch. *Journal of Personality and Social Psychology, 59,* 1155–1162.

Hamilton, D. L., & Gifford, R. K. (1976). Illusory correlation in interpersonal perception: A cognitive basis of stereotypic judgments. *Journal of Experimental Social Psychology, 12,* 392–407.

Hamilton, D. L., & Rose, T. L. (1980). Illusory correlation and the maintenance of stereotypic beliefs. *Journal of Personality and Social Psychology, 39,* 832–845.

Hamilton, W. D. (1964). The genetical evolution of social behavior: I and II. *Journal of Theoretical Biology, 7,* 1–52.

Hammersla, J. F., & Frease-McMahan, L. (1990). University students' priorities: Life goals vs. relationships. *Sex Roles, 23,* 1–14.

Hammond, W. R., & Yung, B. (1993). Psychology's role in the public health response to assaultive violence among young African-American men. *American Psychologist, 48,* 142–154.

Hampton, R. L., Gelles, R. J., & Harrop, J. W. (1989). Is violence in black families increasing? A comparison of 1975 and 1985 national survey rates. *Journal of Marriage and the Family, 51,* 969–980.

Han, S., & Shavitt, S. (1994). Persuasion and culture: Advertising appeals in individualistic and collectivistic societies. *Journal of Experimental Social Psychology, 30,* 326–350.

Haney, C., Banks, C., & Zimbardo, P. (1973). Interpersonal dynamics in a simulated prison. *International Journal of Criminology and Penology, 1,* 69–97.

Haney, C., Hurtado, A., & Vega, L. (1994). "Modern" death qualification: New data on its biasing effects. *Law and Human Behavior, 18,* 619–633.

Hans, V. P., & Vidmar, N. (1986). *Judging the jury.* New York: Plenum.

Hansen, C. H. (1989). Priming sex-role stereotypic event schemas with rock music videos: Effects on impression favorability, trait inferences, and recall of a subsequent male-female interaction. *Basic and Applied Social Psychology, 10,* 371–391.

Hansen, C. H., & Hansen, R. D. (1988). Finding the face in the crowd: An anger superiority effect. *Journal of Personality and Social Psychology, 54,* 917–924.

Hansen, J. E., & Schuldt, W. J. (1984). Marital self-disclosure and marital satisfaction. *Journal of Marriage and the Family, 46,* 923–926.

Hansson, R. O., Stroebe, M. W., & Stroebe, W. (1988). Bereavement and widowhood. *Journal of Social Issues, 44,* 37–52.

Harackiewicz, J. M. (1979). The effects of reward contingency and performance feedback on intrinsic motivation. *Journal of Personality and Social Psychology, 37,* 1352–1363.

Harackiewicz, J. M., & Elliot, A. J. (1993). Achievement goals and intrinsic motivation. *Journal of Personality and Social Psychology, 65,* 904–915.

Hardin, G. (1968). The tragedy of the commons. *Science, 162,* 1243–1248.

Haritos-Fatouros, M. (1988). The official torturer: A learning model for obedience to the authority of violence. *Journal of Applied Social Psychology, 18,* 1107–1120.

Harkins, S. G., & Petty, R. E. (1981). Effects of source magnification of cognitive effort on attitudes: An information processing view. *Journal of Personality and Social Psychology, 40,* 401–413.

Harkins, S. G., & Petty, R. E. (1987). Information utility and the multiple source effect. *Journal of Personality and Social Psychology, 52,* 260–268.

Harkins, S. G., & Szymanski, K. (1987). Social loafing and social facilitation: New wine in old bottles. In C. Hendrick (Ed.), *Review of personality and social psychology: Group processes and intergroup relations* (Vol. 9, pp. 167–188). Beverly Hills, CA: Sage.

Harris, L. (1987). *Inside America.* New York: Vintage Books.

Harris, M. J., Milich, R., Corbitt, E. M., Hoover, D. W., & Brady, M. (1992). Self-fulfilling effects of stigmatizing information on childrens social interactions. *Journal of Personality and Social Psychology, 63,* 41–50.

Harris, M. J., Moniz, A. J., Sowards, B. A., & Krane, K. (1994). Mediation of interpersonal expectancy effects: Expectancies about the elderly. *Social Psychology Quarterly, 57,* 36–48.

Harris, M. J., & Rosenthal, R. (1985). Mediation of interpersonal expectancy effects. *Psychological Bulletin, 97,* 363–386.

Harris, M. M. (1989). Reconsidering the employment interview: A review of recent literature and suggestions for future research. *Personnel Psychology, 42,* 691–726.

Harrison, D. A., & Shaffer, M. A. (1994). Comparative examinations of self-reports and perceived absenteeism norms: Wading through Lake Wobegon. *Journal of Applied Psychology, 79,* 240–251.

Hartley, E. L. (1946). *Problems in prejudice.* New York: King's Crown Press.

Hartsough, D. M., & Savitsky, J. C. (1984). Three Mile Island: Psychology and environmental policy at a crossroads. *American Psychologist, 39,* 1113–1122.

Harvey, J. H., Orbuch, T. L., & Weber, A. L. (Eds.). (1992). *Attributions, accounts, and close relationships.* New York: Springer-Verlag.

Harvey, J. H., Town, J. P., & Yarkin, K. L. (1981). How fundamental is the "fundamental attribution error"? *Journal of Personality and Social Psychology, 43,* 345–346.

Haslam, N., & Fiske, A. P. (1992). Implicit relationship prototypes: Investigating five theories of the cognitive organization of social relationships. *Journal of Experimental Social Psychology, 28,* 441–474.

Hass, R. G. (1981). Effects of source characteristics on the cognitive processing of persuasive messages and attitude change. In R. Petty, T. Ostrom, & T. Brock (Eds.), *Cognitive responses in persuasion* (pp. 141–172). Hillsdale, NJ: Erlbaum.

Hass, R. G. (1984). Perspective taking and self-awareness: Drawing an E on your forehead. *Journal of Personality and Social Psychology, 46,* 788–798.

Hass, R. G., & Eisenstadt, D. (1990). The effects of self-focused attention on perspective-taking and anxiety. *Anxiety Research, 2,* 165–176.

Hass, R. G., & Grady, K. (1975). Temporal delay, type of forewarning, and resistance to influence. *Journal of Experimental Social Psychology, 11,* 459–469.

Hass, R. G., Katz, I., Rizzo, N., Bailey, J., & Moore, L. (1992). When racial ambivalence evokes negative affect, using a disguised measure of mood. *Personality and Social Psychology Bulletin, 18,* 786–797.

Hastie, R. (1984). Causes and effects of causal attribution. *Journal of Personality and Social Psychology, 46,* 44–56.

Hastie, R., Penrod, S. D., & Pennington, N. (1983). *Inside the jury.* Cambridge, MA: Harvard University Press.

Hatch, O. G. (1982). Psychology, society, and politics. *American Psychologist, 37,* 1031–1037.

Hater, J. J., & Bass, B. M. (1988). Superiors' evaluations and subordinates' perceptions of transformational and transactional leadership. *Journal of Applied Psychology, 73,* 695–702.

Hatfield, E. (1988). Passionate and companionate love. In R. J. Sternberg & M. L. Barnes (Ed.), *The psychology of love* (pp. 191–217). New Haven, CT: Yale University Press.

Hatfield, E., Greenberger, E., Traupmann, J., & Lambert, P. (1982). Equity and sexual satisfaction in recently married couples. *Journal of Sex Research, 18,* 18–32.

Hatfield, E., & Rapson, R. L. (1987). Passionate love: New directions in research. In W. H. Jones & D. Perlman (Eds.), *Advances in personal relationships* (Vol. 1, pp. 109–139). Greenwich, CT: JAI Press.

Hatfield, E., & Rapson, R. L. (1993). *Love, sex, and intimacy: Their psychology, biology, and history.* New York: HarperCollins.

Hatfield, E., & Sprecher, S. (1986). *Mirror, mirror. . . . The importance of looks in everyday life.* Albany, NY: State University of New York Press.

Haverkamp, B. E. (1993). Confirmatory bias in hypothesis testing for client-identified and counselor self-generated hypotheses. *Journal of Counseling Psychology, 40,* 303–315.

Hawkins, J. W., & Aber, C. S. (1993). Women in advertisements in medical journals. *Sex Roles, 28,* 233–242.

Hawkins, S. A., & Hastie, R. (1990). Hindsight: Biased judgments of past events after the outcomes are known. *Psychological Bulletin, 107,* 311–327.

Hayduk, L. A. (1983). Personal space: Where we now stand. *Psychological Bulletin, 94,* 293–335.

Hays, R. B. (1985). A longitudinal study of friendship development. *Journal of Personality and Social Psychology, 48,* 909–924.

Hays, R. B. (1988). Friendship. In S. Duck (Ed.), *Handbook of personal relationships: Theory, research, and interventions* (pp. 391–408). New York: Wiley.

Hazan, C., Hutt, M. J., & Markus, H. (1991). Continuity and change in inner working models of attachment. Unpublished manuscript, Department of Human Development, Cornell University.

Hazan, C., & Shaver, P. (1987). Romantic love conceptualized as an attachment process. *Journal of Personality and Social Psychology, 52,* 511–524.

Hearold, S. (1986). A synthesis of 1043 effects of television on social behavior. In G. Comstock (Ed.), *Public communication and behavior* (Vol. 1, pp. 65–133). Orlando, FL: Academic Press.

Heatherton, T. F., & Polivy, J. (1991). Development and validation of a scale for measuring state self-esteem. *Journal of Personality and Social Psychology, 60,* 895–910.

Hedge, J. W., & Kavanagh, M. J. (1988). Improving the accuracy of performance evaluations: Comparison of three methods of performance appraiser training. *Journal of Applied Psychology, 73,* 68–73.

Heesacker, M., Petty, R. E., & Cacioppo, J. T. (1983). Field dependence and attitude change: Source credibility can alter persuasion by affecting message-relevant thinking. *Journal of Personality, 51,* 653–666.

Heider, F. (1958). *The psychology of interpersonal relations.* New York: Wiley.

Heilman, M. E., Block, C. J., & Lucas, J. A. (1992). Presumed incompetent? Stigmatization and affirmative action efforts. *Journal of Applied Psychology, 77,* 536–544.

Heilman, M. E., Kaplow, S. R., Amato, M. A., & Stathatos, P. (1993). When similarity is a liability: Effects of sex-based preferential selection on reactions to like-sex and different-sex others. *Journal of Applied Psychology, 78,* 917–927.

Heilman, M. E., Rivero, J. C., & Brett, J. F. (1991). Skirting the competence issue: Effects of sex-based preferential selection on task choices of women and men. *Journal of Applied Psychology, 76,* 99–105.

Heilman, M. E., Simon, M. C., & Repper, D. P. (1987). Intentionally favored, unintentionally harmed? Impact of sex-based preferential selection on self-perceptions and self-evaluations. *Journal of Applied Psychology, 72,* 62–68.

Helgesen, S. (1990). *The female advantage: Women's ways of leadership.* New York: Doubleday Currency.

Helgeson, V. S. (1992). Moderators of the relation between perceived control and adjustment to chronic illness. *Journal of Personality and Social Psychology, 63,* 652–666.

Helgeson, V. S. (1993). Two important distinctions in social support: Kind of support and perceived versus received. *Journal of Applied Social Psychology, 23,* 825–845.

Helgeson, V. S. (1994). Relation of agency and communion to well-being: Evidence and potential explanations. *Psychological Bulletin, 116,* 412–428.

Heller, J. F., Pallak, M. S., & Picek, J. M. (1973). The interactive effects of intent and threat on boomerang attitude change. *Journal of Personality and Social Psychology, 26,* 273–279.

Henchy, T., & Glass, D. C. (1968). Evaluation apprehension and the social facilitation of dominant and subordinate responses. *Journal of Personality and Social Psychology, 10,* 446–454.

Henderson-King, D. H., & Veroff, J. (1994). Sexual satisfaction and marital well-being in the first years of marriage. *Journal of Social and Personal Relationships, 11,* 509–534.

Hendrick, C., & Hendrick, S. (1989). Research on love: Does it measure up? *Journal of Personality and Social Psychology, 56,* 784–794.

Hendrick, S. S., & Hendrick, C. (1992a). *Liking, loving, and relating* (2nd ed.). Pacific Grove, CA: Brooks/Cole.

Hendrick, S. S., & Hendrick, C. (1992b). *Romantic love.* Newbury Park, CA: Sage.

Hendrick, S. S., & Hendrick, C. (1993). Lovers as friends. *Journal of Social and Personal Relationships, 10,* 459–466.

Hendrick, S. S., & Hendrick, C. (1995). Gender differences and similarities in sex and love. *Personal Relationships, 2,* 55–65.

Heneman, H. G., & Schwab, D. P. (1985). Pay satisfaction: Its multidimensional nature and measurement. *International Journal of Psychology, 20,* 129–141.

Heneman, R. L., & Wexley, K. N. (1983). The effects of time delay in rating and amount of information observed on performance rating accuracy. *Academy of Management Journal,* 677–686.

Henley, N. M. (1977). *Body politics: Power, sex, and nonverbal communication.* Englewood Cliffs, NJ: Prentice-Hall.

Hensley, T. R., & Griffin, G. W. (1986). Victims of groupthink. *Journal of Conflict Resolution, 30,* 497–531.

Hepworth, J. T., & West, S. G. (1988). Lynchings and the economy: A time-series reanalysis of Hovland and Sears (1940). *Journal of Personality and Social Psychology, 55,* 239–247.

Herman, C. P., Zanna, M. P., & Higgins, E. T. (1986). *Physical appearance, stigma, and social behavior: The Ontario Symposium* (Vol. 3). Hillsdale, NJ: Erlbaum.

Hersh, S. M. (1986). *"The target is destroyed": What really happened to flight 007 and what America knew about it.* New York: Random House.

Hertel, G., & Fiedler, K. (1994). Affective and cognitive influences in a social dilemma game. *European Journal of Social Psychology, 24,* 131–145.

Hewstone, M., & Brown, R. (1986). Contact is not enough: An intergroup perspective on the "contact hypothesis." In M. Hewstone & R. Brown (Eds.), *Contact and conflict in intergroup encounters* (pp. 1–44). Oxford, England: Basil Blackwell.

Hewstone, M., & Jaspars, J. (1987). Covariation and causal attribution: A logical model of the intuitive analysis of variance. *Journal of Personality and Social Psychology, 53,* 663–672.

Higgins, E. T. (1989). Self-discrepancy theory: What patterns of self-beliefs cause people to suffer? In L. Berkowitz (Ed.), *Advances in experimental social psychology* (Vol. 22, pp. 93–136). New York: Academic Press.

Higgins, E. T., Bond, R. N., Klein, R., & Strauman, T. (1986). Self-discrepancies and emotional vulnerability: How magnitude, accessibility, and type of discrepancy influence affect. *Journal of Personality and Social Psychology, 51,* 5–15.

Higgins, E. T., King, G. A., & Mavin, G. H. (1982). Individual construct accessibility and subjective impressions and recall. *Journal of Personality and Social Psychology, 43,* 35–47.

Higgins, E. T., Rholes, C. R., & Jones, C. R. (1977). Category accessibility and impression formation. *Journal of Experimental Social Psychology, 13,* 141–154.

Higgins, E. T., & Rholes, W. S. (1978). "Saying is believing": Effects of message modification on memory and liking for the person described. *Journal of Experimental Social Psychology, 14,* 363–378.

Higgins, R. L., & Harris, R. N. (1988). Strategic "alcohol" use: Drinking to self-handicap. *Journal of Social and Clinical Psychology, 6,* 191–202.

Higgins, R. L., Synder, C. R., & Berglas, S. (1990). *Self-handicapping: The paradox that isn't.* New York: Plenum.

Hill, C. T., & Stul, D. E. (1987). Gender and self-disclosure. In V. J. Derlega & J. H. Berg (Eds.), *Self-disclosure: Theory, research, and therapy* (pp. 81–100). New York: Plenum.

Hill, J. L., & Zautra, A. J. (1989). Self-blame attributions and unique vulnerability as predictors of post-rape demoralization. *Journal of Social and Clinical Psychology, 8,* 368–375.

Hilton, J. L., & Darley, J. M. (1985). Constructing other persons: A limit on the effect. *Journal of Experimental Social Psychology, 21,* 1–18.

Hilton, J. L., & Darley, J. M. (1991). The effects of interaction goals on person perception. *Advances in Experimental Social Psychology, 24,* 235–267.

Hilton, J. L., & Fein, S. (1989). The role of typical diagnosticity in stereotype-based judgments. *Journal of Personality and Social Psychology, 57,* 201–211.

Hilton, J. L., Fein, S., & Miller, D. T. (1993). Suspicion and dispositional inference. *Personality and Social Psychology Bulletin, 19,* 501–512.

Hindy, C. G., Schwarz, J. C., & Brodsky, A. (1989). *If this is love, why do I feel so insecure?* New York: Atlantic Monthly Press.

Hines, N. J., & Fry, D. P. (1994). Indirect modes of aggression among women of Buenos Aires, Argentina. *Sex Roles, 30,* 213–236.

Hinsz, V. B. (1989). Facial resemblance in engaged and married couples. *Journal of Social and Personal Relationships, 6,* 223–229.

Hinsz, V. B., Tindale, R. S., Nagao, D. H., Davis, J. H., & Robertson, B. A. (1988). The influence of the accuracy of individuating information on the use of base rate information in probability judgment. *Journal of Experimental Social Psychology, 24,* 127–145.

Hiroto, D. S. (1974). Locus of control and learned helplessness. *Journal of Experimental Psychology, 102,* 187–193.

Hirt, E. R., Deppe, R. K., & Gordon, L. J. (1991). Self-reported versus behavioral self-handicapping: Empirical evidence for a theoretical distinction. *Journal of Personality and Social Psychology, 61,* 981–991.

Hirt, E. R., Zillman, D., Erickson, G. A., & Kennedy, C. (1992). Costs and benefits of allegiance: Changes in fans' self-ascribed competencies after team victory versus defeat. *Journal of Personality and Social Psychology, 63,* 724–738.

Hitler, A. (1933). *Mein Kampf* (E. T. S. Dugdale, Trans.). Cambridge, MA: Riverside.

Hixon, J. G., & Swann, W. B., Jr. (1993). When does introspection bear fruit? Self-reflection, self-insight, and interpersonal choices. *Journal of Personality and Social Psychology, 64,* 35–43.

Hobfoll, S. E., Lomranz, J., Eyal, N., Bridges, A., & Tzemach, M. (1989). Pulse of a nation: Depressive mood reactions of Israelis to the Israel-Lebanon War. *Journal of Personality and Social Psychology, 56,* 1002–1012.

Hoffman, K. L., Demo, D. H., & Edwards, J. N. (1994). Physical wife abuse in a non-Western society: An integrated theoretical approach. *Journal of Marriage and the Family, 56,* 131–146.

Hofling, C. K., Brotzman, E., Dalrymple, S., Graves, N., & Pierce, C. (1966). An experimental study of nurse-physician relations. *Journal of Nervous and Mental Disease, 143,* 171–180.

Hofstede, G. (1980). *Culture's consequences.* Beverly Hills, CA: Sage.

Hogan, R., Curphy, G. J., & Hogan, J. (1994). What we know about leadership: Effectiveness and personality. *American Psychologist, 49,* 493–504.

Hogg, M. A., & Abrams, D. (1990). Social motivation, self-esteem and social identity. In D. Abrams & M. Hogg (Eds.), *Social identity theory: Constructive and critical advances* (pp. 28–47). New York: Springer-Verlag.

Hogg, M. A., Cooper-Shaw, L., & Holzworth, D. W. (1993). Group prototypicality and depersonalized attraction in small interactive groups. *Personality and Social Psychology Bulletin, 19,* 452–465.

Hogg, M. A., Turner, J. C., & Davidson, B. (1990). Polarized norms and social frames of reference: A test of the self-categorization theory of group polarization. *Basic and Applied Social Psychology, 11,* 77–100.

Hollander, E. P. (1958). Conformity, status, and idiosyncrasy credit. *Psychological Review, 65,* 117–127.

Hollander, E. P. (1985). Leadership and power. In G. Lindzey & E. Aronson (Eds.), *Handbook of social psychology* (3rd ed., Vol. 2, pp. 485–537). New York: Random House.

Hollander, E. P., & Offermann, L. R. (1990). Power and leadership in organizations. *American Psychologist, 45,* 179–189.

Holloway, M. (1994). Trends in women's health: A global view. *Scientific American, 271* (2), 76–83.

Holmes, D. S. (1976a). Debriefing after psychological experiments I. Effectiveness of postdeception dehoaxing. *American Psychologist, 31,* 858–867.

Holmes, D. S. (1976b). Debriefing after psychological experiments II. Effectiveness of postexperimental desensitizing. *American Psychologist, 31,* 868–875.

Holmes, T. H., & Rahe, R. H. (1967). The Social Readjustment Rating Scale. *Journal of Psychosomatic Research, 11,* 213–218.

Holsti, O. R. (1962). The belief system and national images: A case study. *Journal of Conflict Resolution, 6,* 244–252.

Holtgraves, T., & Bailey, C. (1991). Premise acceptability and message effectiveness. *Basic and Applied Social Psychology, 12,* 157–176.

Holtgraves, T., & Yang, J. N. (1992). Interpersonal underpinnings of request strategies: General principles and differences due to culture and gender. *Journal of Personality and Social Psychology, 62,* 246–256.

Holtzworth-Munroe, A., & Jacobson, N. S. (1987). An attributional approach to marital dysfunction and therapy. In J. E. Maddux, C. D. Stoltenberg, & R. Rosenwein (Eds.), *Social processes in clinical and counseling psychology* (pp. 153–170). New York: Springer-Verlag.

Holtzworth-Munroe, A., & Stuart, G. L. (1994). Typologies of male batterers: Three subtypes and the differences among them. *Psychological Bulletin, 116,* 476–497.

Homans, G. C. (1961). *Social behavior.* New York: Harcourt, Brace & World.

Honeycutt, J. M., Woods, B. L., & Fontenot, K. (1993). The endorsement of communication conflict rules as a function of engagement, marriage and marital ideology. *Journal of Social and Personal Relationships, 10,* 285–304.

Honts, C. R., Raskin, D. C., & Kircher, J.C. (1994). Mental and physical countermeasures reduce the accuracy of polygraph tests. *Journal of Applied Psychology, 79,* 252–259.

Hoorens, V., & Nuttin, J. M. (1993). Overvaluation of own attributes: Mere ownership or subjective frequency? *Social Cognition, 11,* 177–200.

Horn, J. C. (1987, July). Bigger pay for better work. *Psychology Today,* pp. 54–57.

Horney, K. (1939). *New ways in psychoanalysis.* New York: Norton.

Horowitz, I. A., & Willging, T. E. (1991). Changing views of jury power: The nullification debate, 1787–1988. *Law and Human Behavior, 15,* 165–182.

Horvath, F. (1984). Detecting deception in eyewitness cases: Problems and prospects in use of the polygraph. In G. Wells & E. Loftus (Eds.), *Eyewitness testimony: Psychological perspectives* (pp. 214–255). New York: Cambridge University Press.

House, J. S., Landis, K. R., & Umberson, D. (1988). Social relationships and health. *Science, 241,* 540–545.

House, R. J., & Podsakoff, P. M. (1994). Leadership effectiveness: Past perspectives and future directions for research. In J. Greenberg (Ed.), *Organizational behavior: The state of the science* (pp. 45–82). Hillsdale, NJ: Erlbaum.

Houston, D. A. (1990). Empathy and the self: Cognitive and emotional influences on the evaluation of negative affect in others. *Journal of Personality and Social Psychology, 59,* 859–868.

Houts, A. C., Cook, T. D., & Shadish, W. R., Jr. (1986). The person-situation debate: A critical multiplist perspective. *Journal of Personality, 54,* 52–105.

Hovland, C. I., Janis, I. L., & Kelley, H. H. (1953). *Communication and persuasion: Psychological studies of opinion change.* New Haven, CT: Yale University Press.

Hovland, C. I., Lumsdaine, A. A., & Sheffield, F. D. (1949). *Experiments on mass communication.* Princeton, NJ: Princeton University Press.

Hovland, C. I., & Sears, R. R. (1940). Minor studies in aggression: VI. Correlation of lynchings with economic indices. *Journal of Psychology, 9,* 301–310.

Hovland, C. I., & Weiss, W. (1951). The influence of source credibility on communication effectiveness. *Public Opinion Quarterly, 15,* 635–650.

Howard, D. J. (1990a). The influence of verbal responses to common greetings on compliance behavior: The foot-in-the-mouth effect. *Journal of Applied Social Psychology, 20,* 1185–1196.

Howard, D. J. (1990b). Rhetorical question effects on message processing and persuasion: The role of information availability and the elicitation of judgment. *Journal of Experimental Social Psychology, 26,* 217–239.

Howell, R. H., Owen, P. D., & Nocks, E. C. (1990). Increasing safety belt use: Effects of modeling and trip length. *Journal of Applied Social Psychology, 20,* 254–263.

Huesmann, L. R., & Eron, L. D. (Eds.). (1986). *Television and the aggressive child: A cross-national comparison.* Hillsdale, NJ: Erlbaum.

Huesmann, L. R., Eron, L. D., Klein, R., Brice, P., & Fischer, P. (1983). Mitigating the imitation of aggressive behaviors by changing children's attitudes about media violence. *Journal of Personality and Social Psychology, 44,* 899–910.

Hull, J. G., & Mendolia, M. (1991). Modeling the relation of attributional style, expectancies, and depression. *Journal of Personality and Social Psychology, 61,* 85–97.

Hull, J. G., & Young, R. D. (1983). Self-consciousness, self-esteem, and success-failure as determinants of alcohol consumption in male social drinkers. *Journal of Personality and Social Psychology, 44,* 1097–1109.

Hull, J. G., Young, R. D., & Jouriles, E. (1986). Applications of the self-awareness model of alcohol consumption: Predicting patterns of use and abuse. *Journal of Personality and Social Psychology, 51,* 790–796.

Humphreys, K., & Rappaport, J. (1993). From the community mental health movement to the war on drugs: A study in the definition of social problems. *American Psychologist, 48,* 892–901.

Huston, A., Donnerstein, E., Fairchild, H., Feshbach, N. D., Katz, P. A., Murray, J. P., Rubinstein, E. A., Wilcox, B. L., & Zuckerman, D. (1992). *Big world, small screen: The role of television in American society.* Lincoln: University of Nebraska Press.

Huston, T. L. (1983). Power. In H. H. Kelley, E. Berscheid, A. Christenson, J. H. Harvey, T. L. Huston, G. Levinger, E. McClintock, L. A. Peplau, & D. R. Peterson, *Close relationships* (pp. 169–219). New York: Freeman.

Huston, T. L., & Geis, G. (1993). In what ways do gender-related attributes and beliefs affect marriage? *Journal of Social Issues, 49,* 87–106.

Huston, T. L., & Vangelisti, A. L. (1991). Socioemotional behavior and satisfaction in marital relationships: A longitudinal study. *Journal of Personality and Social Psychology, 61,* 721–733.

Ickes, W., Bissonnette, V., Garcia, S., & Stinson, L. L. (1990). Implementing and using the Dyadic Interaction Paradigm. In C. Hendrick & M. S. Clark (Eds.), *Review of personality and social psychology: Vol. 11. Research methods in personality and social psychology* (pp. 16–44). Newbury Park, CA: Sage.

Ickovics, J. R., & Rodin, J. (1992). Women and AIDS in the United States: Epidemiology, natural history, and mediating mechanisms. *Health Psychology, 11,* 1–16.

Inbau, F. E., & Reid, J. E. (1986). *Criminal interrogation and confessions* (3rd ed.). Baltimore: Williams & Wilkins.

Ingram, R. E., (1990). Self-focused attention in clinical disorders: Review and a conceptual model. *Psychological Bulletin, 107,* 156–176.

Insko, C. A., Drenan, S., Solomon, M. R., Smith, R., & Wade, T. J. (1983). Conformity as a function of the consistency of positive self-evaluation with being liked and being right. *Journal of Experimental Social Psychology, 19,* 341–358.

Insko, C. A., Sedlak, A. J., & Lipsitz, A. (1982). A two-valued logic or two-valued balance resolution of the challenge of agreement and attraction effects in p-o-x triads, and a theoretical perspective on conformity and hedonism. *European Journal of Social Psychology, 12,* 143–167.

Intons-Peterson, M. J., Roskos-Ewoldsen, B., Thomas, L., Shirley, M., & Blut, D. (1989). Will educational materials reduce negative effects of exposure to sexual violence? *Journal of Social and Clinical Psychology, 8,* 256–275.

Irons, E. D., & Moore, G. W. (1985). *Black managers: The case of the banking industry.* New York: Praeger.

Isen, A. M. (1970). Success, failure, attention, and reaction to others: The warm glow of success. *Journal of Personality and Social Psychology, 15,* 294–301.

Isen, A. M. (1984). Toward understanding the role of affect in cognition. In R. S. Wyer & T. K. Srull (Eds.), *Handbook of social cognition* (Vol. 3, pp. 179–236). Hillsdale, NJ: Erlbaum.

Isen, A. M., Clark, M., & Schwartz, M. H. (1976). Duration of the effect of good mood on helping: "Footprints in the sands of time." *Journal of Personality and Social Psychology, 34,* 385–393.

Isen, A. M., & Levin, P. A. (1972). Effect of feeling good on helping: Cookies and kindness. *Journal of Personality and Social Psychology, 21,* 384–388.

Isen, A. M., Shalker, T. E., Clark, M., & Karp, L. (1978). Affect, accessibility of material in memory, and behavior: A cognitive loop? *Journal of Personality and Social Psychology, 36,* 1–12.

It would be easy to poll this jury. (1985). *National Law Journal.*

Izard, C. E. (1990). Facial expressions and the regulation of emotions. *Journal of Personality and Social Psychology, 58,* 487–498.

Jackson, J. M. (1986). In defense of social impact theory: Comment on Mullin. *Journal of Personality and Social Psychology, 50,* 511–513.

Jackson, J. M., & Williams, K. D. (1985). Social loafing on difficult tasks: Working collectively can improve performance. *Journal of Personality and Social Psychology, 49,* 937–942.

Jackson, L. A., Gardner, P. D., & Sullivan, L. A. (1992). Explaining gender differences in self-pay expectations: Social comparison standards and perceptions of fair pay. *Journal of Applied Psychology, 77,* 651–663.

Jacobs, G. A., Quevillon, R. P., & Stricherz, M. (1990). Lessons from the aftermath of Flight 232: Practical considerations for the mental health professional's response to air disasters. *American Psychologist, 45,* 1329–1335.

James, W. (1890). *Psychology.* New York: Holt.

Janis, I. L. (1968). Attitude change via role playing. In R. Abelson, E. Aronson, W. McGuire, T. Newcomb, M. Rosenberg, & P. Tennenbaum (Eds.), *Theories of cognitive consistency: A sourcebook* (pp. 810–818). Chicago: Rand McNally.

Janis, I. L. (1982). *Groupthink* (2nd ed.). Boston: Houghton Mifflin.

Janis, I. L., & Feshbach, S. (1953). Effects of fear arousing communications. *Journal of Abnormal and Social Psychology, 48,* 78–92.

Janis, I. L., Kaye, D., & Kirschner, P. (1965). Facilitating effects of "eating while reading" on responsiveness to persuasive communications. *Journal of Personality and Social Psychology, 1,* 181–186.

Janis, I. L., & King, B. T. (1954). The influence of role playing on opinion change. *Journal of Abnormal and Social Psychology, 49,* 211–218.

Jankowiak, W. R., & Fischer, E. F. (1992). A cross-cultural perspective on romantic love. *Ethnology, 31,* 149–155.

Jankowiak, W. R., Hill, E. M., & Donovan, J. M. (1992). The effects of sex and sexual orientation on attractiveness judgments: An evolutionary interpretation. *Ethology and Sociobiology, 13,* 73–85.

Janoff-Bulman, R. (1979). Characterological versus behavioral self-blame: Inquiries into depression and rape. *Journal of Personality and Social Psychology, 37,* 1798–1809.

Janoff-Bulman, R., & Timko, C. (1987). Coping with traumatic life events: The role of denial in light of people's assumptive worlds. In C. R. Snyder & C. E. Ford (Eds.), *Coping with negative life events: Clinical and social psychological perspectives* (pp. 135–159). New York: Plenum.

Jemmott, J. B., III, & Magloire, K. (1988). Academic stress, social support, and secretory immunoglobulin A. *Journal of Personality and Social Psychology, 55,* 803–810.

Jemmott, J. B., III, Ashby, K. L., & Lindenfeld, K. (1989). Romantic commitment and the perceived availability of opposite-sex persons: On loving the one you're with. *Journal of Applied Social Psychology, 19,* 1198–1211.

Jencks, C. (1994, April 21). The homeless. *New York Review of Books,* pp. 20–28.

Jenkins-Hall, K., & Sacco, W. P. (1991). Effects of client race and depression on evaluations by white therapists. *Journal of Social and Clinical Psychology, 10,* 322–333.

Jennings (Walstedt), J., Geis, F. L., & Brown, V. (1980). Influence of television commercials on women's self-confidence and independent judgment. *Journal of Personality and Social Psychology, 38,* 203–210.

Jensen-Campbell, L. A., Graziano, W. G., & West, S. G. (1995). Dominance, prosocial orientation, and female preferences: Do nice guys really finish last? *Journal of Personality and Social Psychology, 68,* 427–440.

Jepson, C., & Chaiken, S. (1990). Chronic issue-specific fear inhibits systematic processing of persuasive communications. *Journal of Social Behavior and Personality, 5,* 61–84.

Johansson, G., von Hofsten, C., & Jansson, G. (1980). Event perception. *Annual Review of Psychology, 31,* 27–53.

Johns, G. (1994). Absenteeism estimates by employees and managers: Divergent perspectives and self-serving perceptions. *Journal of Applied Psychology, 79,* 229–239.

Johnson v. *Louisiana,* 406 U.S. 356 (1972).

Johnson, B. T. (1994). Effects of outcome-relevant involvement and prior information on persuasion. *Journal of Experimental Social Psychology, 30,* 556–579.

Johnson, B. T., & Eagly, A. H. (1989). Effects of involvement on persuasion: A meta-analysis. *Psychological Bulletin, 106,* 290–314.

Johnson, D. (1993). Psychology in Washington: The politics of violence research. *Psychological Science, 4,* 131–133.

Johnson, D. J., & Rusbult, C. E. (1989). Resisting temptation: Devaluation of alternative partners as a means of maintaining commitment in close relationships. *Journal of Personality and Social Psychology, 57,* 967–980.

Johnson, R. D., & Downing, L. L. (1979). Deindividuation and valance of cues: Effects on prosocial and antisocial behavior. *Journal of Personality and Social Psychology, 37,* 1532–1538.

Johnson, W. O. (1991, August 5). How far have we come? *Sports Illustrated,* pp. 39–47.

Johnston, L. C., & Hewstone, M. (1992). Cognitive models of stereotype change 3: Subtyping and the perceived typicality of disconfirming group members. *Journal of Experimental Social Psychology, 28,* 360–386.

Johnston, L. C., & Macrae, C. N. (1994). Changing social stereotypes: The case of the information seeker. *European Journal of Social Psychology, 24,* 581–592.

Jones, E. E. (1964). *Ingratiation: A social psychological analysis.* New York: Appleton-Century-Crofts.

Jones, E. E. (1990). *Interpersonal perception.* New York: Freeman.

Jones, E. E., & Davis, K. E. (1965). A theory of correspondent inferences: From acts to dispositions. In L. Berkowitz (Ed.), *Advances in experimental social psychology* (Vol. 2, pp. 219–266). New York: Academic Press.

Jones, E. E., Davis, K. E., & Gergen, K. (1961). Role playing variations and their informational value for person perception. *Journal of Abnormal and Social Psychology, 63,* 302–310.

Jones, E. E., & Harris, V. A. (1967). The attribution of attitudes. *Journal of Experimental Social Psychology, 3,* 1–24.

Jones, E. E., & Nisbett, R. E. (1972). The actor and the observer: Divergent perceptions of causality. In E. E. Jones, D. E. Kanouse, H. H. Kelley, R. E. Nisbett, S. Valins, & B. Weiner (Eds.), *Attribution: Perceiving the causes of behavior* (pp. 79–94). Morristown, NJ: General Learning Press.

Jones, E. E., & Pittman, T. S. (1982). Toward a general theory of strategic self presentation. In J. Suls (Ed.), *Psychological perspectives on the self.* Hillsdale, NJ: Erlbaum.

Jones, E. E., Rhodewalt, F., Berglas, S., & Skelton, J. A. (1981). Effects of strategic self-presentation on subsequent self-esteem. *Journal of Personality and Social Psychology, 41,* 407–421.

Jones, E. E., Rock, L., Shaver, K. G., Goethals, G. R., & Ward, L. M. (1968). Pattern of performance and ability attribution: An unexpected primary effect. *Journal of Personality and Social Psychology, 10,* 317–340.

Jones, E. E., & Sigall, H. (1971). The bogus pipeline: A new paradigm for measuring affect and attitude. *Psychological Bulletin, 76,* 349–364.

Jones, E. W. (1986). Black managers: The dream deferred. *Harvard Business Review, 64,* 84–93.

Jones, W. H., & Carpenter, B. N. (1986). Shyness, social behavior, and relationships. In W. H. Jones, J. M. Cheek, & S. R. Briggs (Eds.), *Shyness: Perspectives on research and treatment* (pp. 227–238). New York: Plenum.

Jones, W. H., Hobbs, S. A., & Hackenbury, D. (1982). Loneliness and social skills deficits. *Journal of Experimental Social Psychology, 42,* 682–689.

Josephs, R. A., Markus, H. R., & Tafarodi, R. W. (1992). Gender and self-esteem. *Journal of Personality and Social Psychology, 63,* 391–402.

Judd, C. M., Drake, R. A., Downing, J. W., & Krosnick, J. A. (1991a). Some dynamic properties of attitude structures: Context-induced response facilitation and polarization. *Journal of Personality and Social Psychology, 60,* 193–202.

Judd, C. M., & Park, B. (1993). Definition and assessment of accuracy in social stereotypes. *Psychological Review, 100,* 109–128.

Judd, C. M., Ryan, C. S., & Park, B. (1991b). Accuracy in the judgment of in-group and out-group variability. *Journal of Personality and Social Psychology, 61,* 366–379.

Judge, T. A., & Welbourne, T. M. (1994). A confirmatory investigation of the dimensionality of the Pay Satisfaction Questionnaire. *Journal of Applied Psychology, 79,* 461–466.

Jussim, L. (1989). Teacher expectations: Self-fulfilling prophecies, perceptual biases, and accuracy. *Journal of Personality and Social Psychology, 57,* 469–480.

Jussim, L. (1991). Social perception and social reality: A reflection-construction model. *Psychological Review, 98,* 54–73.

Kagehiro, D. K., & Laufer, W. S. (Eds.). (1992). *Handbook of psychology and law.* New York: Springer-Verlag.

Kahle, L. R., & Homer, P. M. (1985). Physical attractiveness of the celebrity endorser: A social adaptation perspective. *Journal of Consumer Research, 11,* 954–961.

Kahneman, D., Slovic, P., & Tversky, A. (Eds.). (1982). *Judgment under uncertainty: Heuristics and biases.* New York: Cambridge University Press.

Kahneman, D., & Tversky, A. (1973). On the psychology of prediction. *Psychological Review, 80,* 237–251.

Kalick, S. M., & Hamilton, T. E., III. (1986). The matching hypothesis revisited. *Journal of Personality and Social Psychology, 51,* 673–682.

Kalick, S. M., & Hamilton, T. E., III. (1988). Closer look at a matching simulation: Reply to Aron. *Journal of Personality and Social Psychology, 54,* 447–451.

Kallgren, C. A., & Wood, W. (1986). Access to attitude-relevant information in memory as a determinant of attitude-behavior consistency. *Journal of Experimental Social Psychology, 22,* 328–338.

Kalven, H., & Zeisel, H. (1966). *The American jury.* Boston: Little, Brown.

Kamarck, T. W., Manuck, S. B., & Jennings, J. R. (1990). Social support reduces cardiovascular reactivity to psychological challenge: A laboratory model. *Psychosomatic Medicine, 52,* 42–58.

Kameda, T., & Sugimori, S. (1993). Psychological entrapment in group decision making: An assigned decision rule and a groupthink phenomenon. *Journal of Personality and Social Psychology, 65,* 282–292.

Kaplan, M. F. (1987). The influencing process in group decision making. In C. Hendrick (Ed.), *Review of personality and social psychology: Group processes* (Vol. 8, pp. 189–212). Beverly Hills, CA: Sage.

Kaplan, M. F., & Schersching, C. (1981). Juror deliberation: An information integration analysis. In B. Sales (Ed.), *The trial process* (pp. 235–262). New York: Plenum.

Kaplan, R. M., & Toshima, M. T. (1990). The functional effects of social relationships on chronic illness and disability. In B. R. Sarason, I. G. Sarason, & G. R. Pierce (Eds.), *Social support: An interactional view* (pp. 427–453). New York: Wiley.

Karau, S. J., & Williams, K. D. (1993). Social loafing: A meta-analytic review and theoretical integration. *Journal of Personality and Social Psychology, 65,* 681–706.

Kashima, Y., & Kerekes, A. R. Z. (1994). A distributed memory model of averaging phenomena in person impression formation. *Journal of Experimental Social Psychology, 30,* 407–455.

Kassin, S. M. (1979). Consensus information, prediction, and causal attribution: A review of the literature and issues. *Journal of Personality and Social Psychology, 37,* 1966–1981.

Kassin, S. M., & Barndollar, K. A. (1992). On the psychology of eyewitness testimony: A comparison of experts and prospective jurors. *Journal of Applied Social Psychology, 22,* 1241–1249.

Kassin, S. M., Ellsworth, P. C., & Smith, V. L. (1989). The "general acceptance" of psychological research on eyewitness testimony: A survey of the experts. *American Psychologist, 44,* 1089–1098.

Kassin, S. M., Ellsworth, P. C., & Smith, V. L. (1994). *Deja vu* all over again: Elliott's critique of eyewitness experts. *Law and Human Behavior, 18,* 203–210.

Kassin, S. M., & Kiechel, K. L. (in press). The social psychology of false confessions: Compliance, internalization, and confabulation. *Psychological Science.*

Kassin, S. M., Rigby, S., & Castillo, S. R. (1991). The accuracy-confidence correlation in eyewitness testimony: Limits and extensions of the retrospective self-awareness effect. *Journal of Personality and Social Psychology, 61,* 698–707.

Kassin, S. M., Williams, L. N., & Saunders, C. L. (1990). Dirty tricks of cross-examination: The influence of conjectural evidence on the jury. *Law and Human Behavior, 14,* 373–384.

Kassin, S. M., & Wrightsman, L. S. (1979). On the requirements of proof: The timing of judicial instruction and mock juror verdicts. *Journal of Personality and Social Psychology, 37,* 1877–1887.

Kassin, S. M., & Wrightsman, L. S. (1983). The construction and validation of a Juror Bias Scale. *Journal of Research in Personality, 17,* 423–442.

Kassin, S. M., & Wrightsman, L. S. (1985). Confession evidence. In S. M. Kassin & L. S. Wrightsman (Eds.), *The psychology of evidence and trial procedure* (pp. 67–94). Beverly Hills, CA: Sage.

Kassin, S. M., & Wrightsman, L. S. (1988). *The American jury on trial: Psychological perspectives.* Washington, DC: Hemisphere.

Katz, D., & Braly, K. W. (1933). Racial stereotypes of 100 college students. *Journal of Abnormal and Social Psychology, 28,* 280–290.

Katz, E. J., & Bertelson, A. D. (1993). The effects of gender and response style on depressed mood. *Sex Roles, 29,* 509–514.

Katz, I., Wackenhut, J., & Hass, G. (1986). Racial ambivalence, value duality, and behavior. In J. F. Dovidio & S. L. Gaertner, (Eds.), *Prejudice, discrimination, and racism: Theory and research* (pp. 35–60). Orlando, FL: Academic Press.

Katzev, A. R., Warner, R. L., & Acock, A. C. (1994). Girls or boys? Relationship of child gender to marital instability. *Journal of Marriage and the Family, 56,* 89–100.

Keelan, J. P. R., Dion, K. L., & Dion, K. K. (1994). Attachment style and heterosexual relationships among young adults: A short-term panel study. *Journal of Social and Personal Relationships, 11,* 201–214.

Kelley, H. H. (1950). The warm-cold variable in first impressions of persons. *Journal of Personality, 18,* 431–439.

Kelley, H. H. (1967). Attribution theory in social psychology. In D. Levine (Ed.), *Nebraska Symposium on Motivation* (Vol. 15, pp. 192–241). Lincoln: University of Nebraska Press.

Kelley, H. H. (1983). Love and commitment. In H. H. Kelley, E. Berscheid, A. Christenson, J. H. Harvey, T. L. Huston, G. Levinger, E. McClintock, L. A. Peplau, & D. R. Peterson, *Close relationships* (pp. 265–314). New York: Freeman.

Kelley, H. H., & Stahelski, A. J. (1970). Social interaction basis of cooperators' and competitors' beliefs about others. *Journal of Personality and Social Psychology, 16,* 66–91.

Kelly, J. A., St. Lawrence, J. S., Diaz, Y. E., Stevenson, L. Y., Hauth, A. C., Brasfield, T. L., Kalichman, S. C., Smith, J. E., & Andrew, M. E. (1991). HIV risk behavior reduction following intervention with key opinion leaders of a population: An experimental community-level analysis. *American Journal of Public Health, 81,* 168–171.

Kelly, J. A., St. Lawrence, J. S., Stevenson, L. Y., Hauth, A. C., Kalichman, S. C., Diaz, Y. E., Brasfield, T. L., Koob, J. J., & Morgan, M. G. (1992). Community AIDS/HIV risk reduction: The effects of endorsements by popular people in three cities. *American Journal of Public Health, 82,* 1483–1489.

Kelman, H. C. (1961). Processes of opinion change. *Public Opinion Quarterly, 25,* 57–78.

Kelman, H. C. (1967). Human use of human subjects: The problem of deception in social psychology experiments. *Psychological Bulletin, 67,* 1–11.

Kelman, H. C., & Hamilton, V. L. (1989). *Crimes of obedience: Toward a social psychology of authority and responsibility.* New Haven, CT: Yale University Press.

Kelman, H. C., & Hovland, C. I. (1953). "Reinstatement" of the communicator in delayed measurement of opinion change. *Journal of Abnormal and Social Psychology, 48,* 327–335.

Keneally, T. (1993). *Schindler's list.* New York: Simon & Schuster. (Original 1982 edition published by Hemisphere Publishers).

Kenny, D. A. (1994). *Interpersonal perception: A social relations analysis.* New York: Guilford.

Kenny, D. A., Albright, L., Malloy, T. E., & Kashy, D. A. (1994). Consensus in interpersonal perception: Acquaintance and the Big Five. *Psychological Bulletin, 116,* 245–258.

Kenny, D. A., & DePaulo, B. M. (1993). Do people know how others view them? An empirical and theoretical account. *Psychological Bulletin, 114,* 145–161.

Kenny, D. A., Horner, C., Kashy, D. A., & Chu, L. (1992). Consensus at zero acquaintance: Replication, behavioral cues, and stability. *Journal of Personality and Social Psychology, 62,* 88–97.

Kenny, D. A., & Zaccaro, S. J. (1983). An estimate of variance due to traits in leadership. *Journal of Applied Psychology, 68,* 678–685.

Kenrick, D. T. (1986). How strong is the case against contemporary social and personality psychology? A response to Carlson. *Journal of Personality and Social Psychology, 50,* 839–844.

Kenrick, D. T. (1994). Evolutionary social psychology: From sexual selection to social cognition. In M. P. Zanna (Ed.), *Advances in experimental social psychology* (Vol. 26, pp. 75–121). San Diego: Academic Press

Kenrick, D. T., Groth, G. E., Trost, M. R., & Sadalla, E. K. (1993). Integrating evolutionary and social exchange perspectives on relationships: Effects of gender, self-appraisal, and involvement level on mate selection criteria. *Journal of Personality and Social Psychology, 64,* 951–969.

Kenrick, D. T., & Keefe, R. C. (1992). Age preferences in mates reflect sex differences in human reproductive strategies. *Behavioral and Brain Sciences, 15,* 75–133

Kenrick, D. T., Montello, D. R., Gutierres, S. E., & Trost, M. R. (1993). Effects of physical attractiveness on affect and perceptual judgments: When social comparison overrides social reinforcement. *Personality and Social Psychology Bulletin, 19,* 195–199.

Kernis, M. H., & Waschull, S. B. (1995). The interactive roles of stability and level of self-esteem: Research and theory. *Advances in Experimental Social Psychology, 27,* 93–141.

Kerr, N. L. (1981). Social transition schemes: Charting the group's road to agreement. *Journal of Personality and Social Psychology, 41,* 684–702.

Kerr, N. L. (1983). Motivation losses in small groups: A social dilemma. *Journal of Personality and Social Psychology, 45,* 819–828.

Kerr, N. L. (1989). Illusions of efficacy: The effects of group size on perceived efficacy in social dilemmas. *Journal of Experimental Social Psychology, 25,* 287–313.

Kerr, N. L. (1992a). Efficacy as a causal and moderating variable in social dilemmas. In W. B. G. Liebrand, D. M. Messick, & H. A. M. Wilke (Eds.), *Social dilemmas: Theoretical issues and research findings* (pp. 59–80). Oxford: Pergamon Press.

Kerr, N. L. (1992b). Issue importance and group decision making. In S. Worchel, W. Wood, & J. A. Simpson (Eds.), *Group process and productivity* (pp. 68–88). Newbury Park, CA: Sage.

Kerr, N. L., Harmon, D. L., & Graves, J. K. (1982). Independence of multiple verdicts by jurors and juries. *Journal of Applied Social Psychology, 12,* 12–29.

Kerr, N. L., & Kaufman-Gilliland, C. M. (1994). Communication, commitment, and cooperation in social dilemmas. *Journal of Personality and Social Psychology, 66,* 513–529

Kerr, N. L., Kramer, G. P., Carroll, J. S., & Alfini, J. J. (1991). On the effectiveness of voir dire in criminal cases with prejudicial pretrial publicity: An empirical study. *American University Law Review, 40,* 665–701.

Kerr, N. L., & MacCoun, R. J. (1985). The effects of jury size and polling method on the process and product of jury deliberation. *Journal of Personality and Social Psychology, 48,* 349–363.

Kessler, R. C., McLeod, J. D., & Wethington, E. (1985). The costs of caring: A perspective on the relationship between sex and psychological distress. In I. G. Sarason & B. R. Sarason (Eds.), *Social support: Theory, research and applications* (pp. 491–506). Dordrecht, The Netherlands: Martinus Nijhoff.

Kiesler, C. A. (1971). *The psychology of commitment.* New York: Academic Press.

Kiesler, C. A., & Kiesler, S. B. (1969). *Conformity.* Reading, MA: Addison-Wesley.

Kihlstrom, J. F. (1987). Introduction to the special issue: Integrating personality and social psychology. *Journal of Personality and Social Psychology, 53,* 989–992.

Kihlstrom, J. F., & Cantor, N. (1984). Mental representations of the self. In L. Berkowitz (Ed.), *Advances in experimental social psychology* (Vol. 17, pp. 1–47). New York: Academic Press.

Kilham, W., & Mann, L. (1974). Level of destructive obedience as a function of transmitter and executant roles in the Milgram obedience paradigm. *Journal of Personality and Social Psychology, 29,* 696–702.

Kilpatrick, D. G., Edmunds, C. N., & Seymour, A. (1992). *Rape in America.* Arlington, VA: National Victim Center.

Kimble, G. A. (1994). A frame of reference for psychology. *American Psychologist, 49,* 510–519.

Kimmel, P. R. (1994). Cultural perspectives on international negotiations. *Journal of Social Issues, 50,* 179–196.

Kinder, D. R., & Sears, D. O. (1981). Prejudice and politics: Symbolic racism versus racial threats to the good life. *Journal of Personality and Social Psychology, 40,* 414–431.

Kipnis, D. (1994). Accounting for the use of behavior technologies in social psychology. *American Psychologist, 49,* 165–172.

Kirkpatrick, L. A., & Davis, K. E. (1994). Attachment style, gender, and relationship stability: A longitudinal analysis. *Journal of Personality and Social Psychology, 66,* 502–512.

Kirkpatrick, L. A., & Hazan, C. (1994). Attachment styles and close relationships: A four-year prospective study. *Personal Relationships, 1,* 123–142.

Kite, M. E. (1992). Age and the spontaneous self-concept. *Journal of Applied Social Psychology, 22,* 1828–1837.

Kitson, G. C., & Morgan, L. A. (1990). The multiple consequences of divorce: A decade review. *Journal of Marriage and the Family, 52,* 913–924.

Klein, J. G. (1991). Negativity effects in impression formation: A test in the political arena. *Personality and Social Psychology Bulletin, 17,* 412–418.

Klein, S. B., & Loftus, J. (1988). The nature of self-referent encoding: The contributions of elaborative and organizational processes. *Journal of Personality and Social Psychology, 55,* 5–11.

Klein, W. M., & Kunda, Z. (1992). Motivated person perception: Constructing justifications for desired beliefs. *Journal of Experimental Social Psychology, 28,* 145–168.

Klein, W. M., & Kunda, Z. (1993). Maintaining self-serving social comparisons: Biased reconstruction of one's past behaviors. *Personality and Social Psychology Bulletin, 19,* 732–739.

Kleinke, C. L. (1986). Gaze and eye contact: A research review. *Psychological Bulletin, 100,* 78–100.

Kluegel, J. R. (1990). Trends in whites' explanations of the black-white gap in socioeconomic status, 1977–1989. *American Sociological Review, 55,* 512–525.

Knapp, A., & Clark, M. S. (1991). Some detrimental effects of negative mood on individuals' ability to solve resource dilemmas. *Personality and Social Psychology Bulletin, 17,* 678–688.

Knight, G. P., Johnson, L. G., Carlo, G., & Eisenberg, N. (1994). A multiplicative model of the dispositional antecedents of a prosocial behavior: Predicting more of the people more of the time. *Journal of Personality and Social Psychology, 66,* 178–183.

Knowles, E. S. (1980). An affiliative-conflict theory of personal and group spatial behavior. In P. B. Paulus (Ed.), *Psychology of group influence* (pp. 133–188). Hillsdale, NJ: Erlbaum.

Knowles, E. S. (1983). Social physics and the effects of others: Tests of the effects of audience size and distance on social judgments and behavior. *Journal of Personality and Social Psychology, 45,* 1263–1279.

Knox, R. E., & Inskter, J. A. (1968). Postdecision dissonance at post-time. *Journal of Personality and Social Psychology, 8,* 319–323.

Kobasa, S. C., Maddi, S. R., & Kahn, S. (1982). Hardiness and health: A prospective study. *Journal of Personality and Social Psychology, 42,* 168–177.

Koch, S. (1993). "Psychology" or "The Psychological Studies"? *American Psychologist, 48,* 902–904.

Koestner, R., Franz, C., & Weinberger, J. (1990). The family origins of empathic concern: A 26-year longitudinal study. *Journal of Personality and Social Psychology, 58,* 709–717.

Kohlberg, L. (1981). *The philosophy of moral development: Moral stages and the idea of justice: Vol. 1. Essays on moral development.* New York: Harper & Row.

Kohn, P. M., Lafreniere, K., & Gurevich, M. (1991). Hassles, health, and personality. *Journal of Personality and Social Psychology, 61,* 478–482.

Kojetin, B. S. (1993). *Adult attachment styles with romantic partners, friends, and parents.* Ph.D. thesis, University of Minnesota, Minneapolis.

Kolditz, T. A., & Arkin, R. M. (1982). An impression management interpretation of the self-handicapping strategy. *Journal of Personality and Social Psychology, 43,* 492–502.

Kollock, P., Blumstein, P., & Schwartz, P. (1985). Sex and power in interaction: Conversational privileges and duties. *American Sociological Review, 50,* 34–46.

Komorita, S. S., Chan, D. K-S., & Parks, C. (1993). The effects of reward structure and reciprocity in social dilemmas. *Journal of Experimental Social Psychology, 29,* 252–267.

Komorita, S. S., & Parks, C. D. (1994). *Social dilemmas.* Madison, WI: Brown & Benchmark.

Komorita, S. S., Parks, C. D., & Hulbert, L. G. (1992). Reciprocity and the induction of cooperation in social dilemmas. *Journal of Personality and Social Psychology, 62,* 607–617.

Konecni, V. J., & Ebbesen, E. B. (1982). *The criminal justice system: A social-psychological analysis.* San Francisco: Freeman.

Korte, C. (1980). Urban-nonurban differences in social behavior and social psychological models of urban impact. *Journal of Social Issues, 36* (3), 29–51.

Koss, M. P., Gidycz, C. A., & Wisniewski, N. (1987). The scope of rape: Incidence and prevalence of sexual aggression and victimization in a national sample of higher education students. *Journal of Consulting and Clinical Psychology, 55,* 162–170.

Koss, M. P., Goodman, L. A., Browne, A., Fitzgerald, L. F., Keita, G. P., & Russo, N. F. (1994). *No safe haven.* Washington, DC: American Psychological Association.

Kowalski, R. M. (1992). Nonverbal behaviors and perceptions of sexual intentions: Effects of sexual connotativeness, verbal response, and rape outcome. *Basic and Applied Social Psychology, 13,* 427–445.

Kowalski, R. M. (1993a). Inferring sexual interest from behavioral cues: Effects of gender and sexually relevant attitudes. *Sex Roles, 29,* 13–36.

Kowalski, R. M. (1993b). Interpreting behaviors in mixed-gender encounters: Effects of social anxiety and gender. *Journal of Social and Clinical Psychology, 12,* 239–247.

Kowalski, R. M., & Wolfe, R. (1994). Collective identity orientation, patriotism, and reactions to national outcomes. *Personality and Social Psychology Bulletin, 20,* 533–540.

Kozlowski, S. W., Kirsch, M. P., & Chao, G. T. (1986). Job knowledge, ratee familiarity, conceptual similarity, and halo error: An exploration. *Journal of Applied Psychology, 71,* 45–49.

Kramer, G. P., Kerr, N. L., & Carroll, J. S. (1990). Pretrial publicity, judicial remedies, and jury bias. *Law and Human Behavior, 14,* 409–438.

Kramer, R. M., & Brewer, M. B. (1984). Effects of group identity on resource use in a simulated commons dilemma. *Journal of Personality and Social Psychology, 46,* 1044–1057.

Krantz, D. S., & Hedges, S. M. (1987). Some cautions for research on personality and health. *Journal of Personality, 55,* 351–357.

Kraus, S. J. (1995). Attitudes and the prediction of behavior: A meta-analysis of the empirical literature. *Personality and Social Psychology Bulletin, 21,* 58–75.

Kraut, R. E. (1973). Effects of social labeling on giving to charity. *Journal of Experimental Social Psychology, 9,* 551–562.

Kravitz, D. A., & Martin, B. (1986). Ringelmann rediscovered: The original article. *Journal of Personality and Social Psychology, 50,* 936–941.

Kravitz, D. A., & Platania, J. (1993). Attitudes and beliefs about affirmative action: Effects of target and of respondent sex and ethnicity. *Journal of Applied Psychology, 78,* 928–938.

Krebs, D. (1987). The challenge of altruism in biology and psychology. In C. Crawford, M. Smith, & D. Krebs (Eds.), *Sociobiology and psychology: Ideas, issues, and applications* (pp. 81–118). Hillsdale, NJ: Erlbaum.

Krueger, J., & Clement, R. W. (1994). The truly false consensus effect: An ineradicable and egocentric bias in social perception. *Journal of Personality and Social Psychology, 67,* 596–610.

Kruglanski, A. W. (1989). The psychology of being "right": The problem of accuracy in social perception and cognition. *Psychological Bulletin, 106,* 395–409.

Kruglanski, A. W., & Freund, T. (1983). The freezing and unfreezing of lay-inferences: Effects of impressional primacy, ethnic stereotyping, and numerical anchoring. *Journal of Experimental Social Psychology, 19,* 448–468.

Kruglanski, A. W., & Mayseless, O. (1988). Contextual effects in hypothesis testing: The role of competing alternatives and epistemic motivations. *Social Cognition, 6,* 1–20.

Kruglanski, A. W., & Webster, D. M. (1991). Group members' reactions to opinion deviates and conformists at varying degrees of proximity to decision deadline and of environmental noise. *Journal of Personality and Social Psychology, 61,* 212–225.

Kulik, J. A., Mahler, H. I. M., & Earnest, A. (1994). Social comparison and affiliation under threat: Going beyond the affiliate-choice paradigm. *Journal of Personality and Social Psychology, 66,* 301–309.

Kunda, Z. (1987). Motivated inference: Self-serving generation and evaluation of causal theories. *Journal of Personality and Social Psychology, 53,* 636–647.

Kunda, Z. (1990). The case of motivated reasoning. *Psychological Bulletin, 108,* 480–498.

Kurdek, L. A. (1991a). Correlates of relationship satisfaction in cohabiting gay and lesbian couples: Interpretation of contextual, investment, and problem-solving models. *Journal of Personality and Social Psychology, 61,* 910–922.

Kurdek, L. A. (1991b). The dissolution of gay and lesbian couples. *Journal of Social and Personal Relationships, 8,* 265–278.

Kurdek, L. A. (1991c). Sexuality in homosexual and heterosexual couples. In K. McKinney & S. Sprecher (Eds.), *Sexuality in close relationships* (pp. 177–191). Hillsdale, NJ: Erlbaum.

Kurdek, L. A. (1992). Relationship stability and relationship satisfaction in cohabiting gay and lesbian couples: A prospective longitudinal test of the contextual and interdependence models. *Journal of Social and Personal Relationships, 9,* 125–142.

Kurdek, L. A. (1993). The allocation of household labor in gay, lesbian, and heterosexual married couples. *Journal of Social Issues, 49,* 127–139.

Kurdek, L. A. (1994). Areas of conflict for gay, lesbian, and heterosexual couples: What couples agree about influences relationship satisfaction. *Journal of Marriage and the Family, 56,* 923–934.

Kurland, N. B. (1995). Ethical intentions and theories of reasoned action and planned behavior. *Journal of Applied Social Psychology, 25,* 297–313.

Lacayo, R. (1991, April 1). Law and disorder. *Time,* pp. 18–21.

Lacayo, R. (1992, May 11). Anatomy of an acquittal. *Time,* pp. 30–32.

Lacayo, R. (1993, November 1). A slap for a broken head. *Time,* pp. 46–47.

Lacayo, R. (1994, November 14). Stranger in the shadows. *Time,* pp. 46–47.

LaFrance, M. (1992). Gender and interruptions: Individual infraction or violation of the social order? *Psychology of Women Quarterly, 16,* 497–512.

Laird, J. D. (1974). Self-attribution of emotion: The effects of expressive behavior on the quality of emotional experience. *Journal of Personality and Social Psychology, 29,* 475–486.

Lakey, B., & Cassady, P. B. (1990). Cognitive processes in perceived social support. *Journal of Personality and Social Psychology, 59,* 337–343.

Lakey, B., Moineau, S., & Drew, J. B. (1992). Perceived social support and individual differences in the interpretation and recall of supportive behaviors. *Journal of Social and Clinical Psychology, 11,* 336–348.

Lakey, B., Tardiff, T. A., & Drew, J. B. (1994). Negative social interactions: Assessment and relations to social support, cognition, and psychological distress. *Journal of Social and Clinical Psychology, 13,* 42–62.

Lamb, C. S., Jackson, L. A., Cassiday, P. B., & Priest, D. J. (1993). Body figure preferences of men and women: A comparison of two generations. *Sex Roles, 28,* 345–358.

Lamm, H., & Myers, D. G. (1978). Group-induced polarization of attitudes and behavior. In L. Berkowitz (Ed.), *Advances in experimental social psychology* (Vol. 11, pp. 145–195). New York: Academic Press.

Landy, F. J., & Farr, J. L. (1983). *The measurement of work performance: Methods, theory, and applications.* New York: Academic Press.

Landy, F. J., Shankster, L. J., & Kohler, S. S. (1994). Personnel selection and placement. *Annual Review of Psychology, 45,* 261–296.

Langer, E. J. (1989). *Mindfulness.* Reading, MA: Addison-Wesley.

Langer, E. J., Blank, A., & Chanowitz, B. (1978). The mindlessness of ostensibly thoughtful action. *Journal of Personality and Social Psychology, 36,* 635–642.

Langer, E. J., & Rodin, J. (1976). The effects of choice and enhanced personal responsibility for the aged: A field experiment in an institutional setting. *Journal of Personality and Social Psychology, 34,* 191–198.

Langlois, J. H. (1986). From the eye of the beholder to behavioral reality: Development of social behaviors and social relations as a function of physical attractiveness. In C. P. Herman, M. P. Zanna, & E. T. Higgins (Eds.), *The Ontario Symposium: Vol. 3. Physical appearance, stigma, and social behavior* (pp. 23–51). Hillsdale, NJ: Erlbaum.

Langlois, J. H., Ritter, J. M., Casey, R. J., & Sawin, D. B. (1995). Infant attractiveness predicts maternal behaviors and attitudes. *Developmental Psychology, 31,* 464–472.

Langlois, J. H., & Roggman, L. A. (1990). Attractive faces are only average. *Psychological Science, 1,* 115–121.

Langlois, J. H., Roggman, L. A., & Musselman, L. (1994). What is average and what is not average about attractive faces? *Psychological Science, 5,* 214–220.

Lanzetta, J. T. (1955). Group behavior under stress. *Human Relations, 8,* 29–52.

Lanzetta, J. T., & Englis, B. G. (1989). Expectations of cooperation and competition and their effects on observers' vicarious emotional responses. *Journal of Personality and Social Psychology, 56,* 543–554.

LaPiere, R. T. (1934). Attitudes vs. action. *Social Forces, 13,* 230–237.

Laplace, A. C., Chermack, S. T., & Taylor, S. P. (1994). Effects of alcohol and drinking experience on human physical aggression. *Personality and Social Psychology Bulletin, 20,* 439–444.

Larrick, R. P., Morgan, J. N., & Nisbett, R. E. (1990). Teaching the use of cost-benefit reasoning in everyday life. *Psychological Science, 1,* 362–370.

Larsen, K. S. (1990). The Asch conformity experiment: Replication and transhistorical comparisons. *Journal of Social Behavior and Personality, 5,* 163–168.

Larsen, R., & Csikszentmihalyi, M. (1983). The Experience Sampling Method. In H. T. Reis (Ed.), *New directions for naturalistic methods in the behavioral sciences* (pp. 41–56). San Francisco: Jossey-Bass.

Larson, J. R., Jr. (1986). Supervisors' performance feedback to subordinates: The impact of subordinate performance valence and outcome dependence. *Organizational Behavior and Decision Processes, 37,* 391–408.

Larson, J. R., Jr., Foster-Fishman, P. G., & Keys, C. B. (1994). Discussion of shared and unshared information in decision-making groups. *Journal of Personality and Social Psychology, 67,* 446–461.

Lassiter, G. D. (1988). Behavior perception, affect, and memory. *Social Cognition, 6,* 150–176.

Lassiter, G. D., Slaw, R. D., Briggs, M. A., & Scanlan, C. R. (1992). The potential for bias in videotaped confessions. *Journal of Applied Social Psychology,* 22, 1838–1851.

Lassiter, G. D., Stone, J. I., & Rogers, S. L. (1988). Memorial consequences of variation in behavior perception. *Journal of Experimental Social Psychology, 24,* 222–239.

Lassner, J. B., Matthews, K. A., & Stoney, C. M. (1994). Are cardiovascular reactors to asocial stress also reactors to social stress? *Journal of Personality and Social Psychology, 66,* 69–77.

Latané, B. (1981). The psychology of social impact. *American Psychologist, 36,* 343–356.

Latané, B., & Darley, J. M. (1970). *The unresponsive bystander: Why doesn't he help?* New York: Appleton-Century-Crofts.

Latané, B., & Nida, S. (1981). Ten years of research on group size and helping. *Psychological Bulletin, 89,* 308–324.

Latané, B., Williams, K., & Harkins, S. (1979). Many hands make light the work: The causes and consequences of social loafing. *Journal of Personality and Social Psychology, 37,* 822–832.

Latané, B., & Wolf, S. (1981). The social impact of majorities and minorities. *Psychological Review, 88,* 438–453.

Lau, R. R. (1985). Two explanations for negativity effects in political behavior. *American Journal of Political Science, 29,* 119–138.

Lau, S., & Gruen, G. E. (1992). The social stigma of loneliness: Effect of target person's and perceiver's sex. *Personality and Social Psychology Bulletin, 18,* 182–189.

Laumann, E. O., Gagnon, J. H., Michael, R. T., & Michaels, S. (1994). *The social organization of sexuality.* Chicago: University of Chicago Press.

Laupa, M., & Turiel, E. (1993). Children's concepts of authority and social contexts. *Journal of Educational Psychology, 85,* 191–197.

Lawrence, V. W. (1991). Effect of socially ambiguous information on white and black children's behavioral and trait perceptions. *Merrill-Palmer Quarterly, 37,* 619–630.

Lazarus, R. S. (1984). On the primacy of cognition. *American Psychologist, 39,* 124–129.

Lazarus, R. S. (1991). *Emotion and adaptation.* New York: Oxford University Press.

Lazarus, R. S., & Folkman, S. (1984). *Stress, appraisal, and coping.* New York: Springer.

Leana, C. R. (1985). A partial test of Janis' groupthink model: Effects of group cohesiveness and leader behavior on defective decision making. *Journal of Management, 11,* 5–17.

Leary, M. R. (1983). *Understanding social anxiety: Social, personality, and clinical perspectives.* Beverly Hills, CA: Sage.

Leary, M. R. (1987). A self-presentation model for the treatment of social anxieties. In J. E. Maddux, C. D. Stoltenberg, & R. Rosenwein (Eds.), *Social processes in clinical and counseling psychology* (pp. 126–138). New York: Springer.

Leary, M. R., & Kowalski, R. M. (1990). Impression management: A literature review and two-component model. *Psychological Bulletin, 107,* 34–47.

Leary, M. R., Tchividjian, L. R., & Kraxberger, B. E. (1994). Self-presentation can be hazardous to your health: Impression management and health risk. *Health Psychology, 13,* 461–470.

Leavitt, H. J. (1951). Some effects of certain communication patterns on group performance. *Journal of Abnormal and Social Psychology, 46,* 38–50.

Le Bon, G. (1895). *Psychologie des foules.* Paris: Félix Alcan.

Lee, J. A. (1977). A typology of styles of loving. *Personality and Social Psychology Bulletin, 3,* 173–182.

Lee, J. A. (1988). Love-styles. In R. J. Sternberg & M. L. Barnes (Ed.), *The psychology of love* (pp. 38–67). New Haven, CT: Yale University Press.

Lefcourt, H. M., & Davidson-Katz, K. (1991). Locus of control and health. In C. R. Snyder & D. R. Forsyth (Eds.), *Handbook of social and clinical psychology: The health perspective* (pp. 246–266). New York: Pergamon Press.

Lefkowitz, M. M., Eron, L. D., Walder, L. O., & Huesmann, L. R. (1977). *Growing up to be violent.* New York: Pergamon Press.

Lehman, D. R., Davis, C. G., DeLongis, A., Wortman, C. B., Bluck, S., Mandel, D. R., & Ellard, J. H. (1993). Positive and negative life changes following bereavement and their relations to adjustment. *Journal of Social and Clinical Psychology, 12,* 90–112.

Lehman, D. R., Lempert, R. O., & Nisbett, R. E. (1988). The effects of graduate training on reasoning: Formal discipline and thinking about everyday-life events. *American Psychologist, 43,* 431–442.

Leigh, B. C., & Stacy, A. W. (1993). Alcohol outcome expectancies: Scale construction and predictive utility in higher-order confirmatory models. *Psychological Assessment, 5,* 216–229.

Leigh, G. K., Homan, T. B., & Burr, W. R. (1987). Some confusions and exclusions of the SVR theory of dyadic pairing: A response to Murstein. *Journal of Marriage and the Family, 49,* 933–937.

Leiker, M., & Hailey, B. J. (1988). A link between hostility and disease: Poor health habits? *Behavioral Medicine, 14,* 129–133.

Leinbach, M. D., & Fagot, B. I. (1993). Categorical habituation to male and female faces: Gender schematic processing in infancy. *Infant Behavior and Development, 16,* 317–332.

Leippe, M. R., & Eisenstadt, D. (1994). Generalization of dissonance reduction: Decreasing prejudice through induced compliance. *Journal of Personality and Social Psychology, 67,* 395–413.

Lennox, R. D. (1988). The problem with self-monitoring: A two-sided scale and a one-sided theory. *Journal of Personality Assessment, 52,* 58–73.

Leonard, K. E. (1989). The impact of explicit aggressive and implicit nonaggressive cues on aggression in intoxicated and sober roles. *Personality and Social Psychology Bulletin, 15,* 390–400.

Lepore, S. J. (1992). Social conflict, social support, and psychological distress: Evidence of cross-domain buffering effects. *Journal of Personality and Social Psychology, 63,* 857–867.

Lepore, S. J., Evans, G. W., & Schneider, M. L. (1991). Dynamic role of social support in the link between chronic stress and psychological distress. *Journal of Personality and Social Psychology, 61,* 899–909.

Lepowsky, M. (1994). Women, men, and aggression in an egalitarian society. *Sex Roles, 30,* 199–211.

Lepper, M. R., & Greene, D. (Eds.). (1978). *The hidden costs of reward.* Hillsdale, NJ: Erlbaum.

Lepper, M. R., Greene, D., & Nisbett, R. E. (1973). Undermining children's intrinsic interest with extrinsic reward: A test of the "overjustification" hypothesis. *Journal of Personality and Social Psychology, 28,* 129–137.

Lerner, M. J. (1980). *The belief in a just world: A fundamental delusion.* New York: Plenum.

Lerner, M. J., & Meindl, J. R. (1981). Justice and altruism. In J. P. Rushton & R. M. Sorrentino (Eds.), *Altruism and helping behavior: Social, personality, and developmental perspectives* (pp. 213–232). Hillsdale, NJ: Erlbaum.

Lerner, M. J., & Simmons, C. H. (1966). Observers' reaction to the "innocent victim": Compassion or rejection? *Journal of Personality and Social Psychology, 4,* 203–210.

Leung, K. (1987). Some determinants of reactions to procedural models for conflict resolution: A cross-national study. *Journal of Personality and Social Psychology, 53,* 898–908.

Levenson, R. W., & Gottman, J. M. (1985). Physiological and affective predictors of change in relationship satisfaction. *Journal of Personality and Social Psychology, 49,* 85–94.

Leventhal, H. (1970). Findings and theory in the study of fear communications. In L. Berkowitz (Ed.), *Advances in experimental social psychology* (Vol. 5, pp. 119–186). New York: Academic Press.

Leventhal, H., Watts, J. C., & Pagano, F. (1967). Effects of fear and instructions on how to cope with danger. *Journal of Personality and Social Psychology, 6,* 313–321.

Levin, I. P., Schnittjer, S. K., & Thee, S. L. (1988). Information framing effects in social and personal decisions. *Journal of Experimental Social Psychology, 24,* 520–529.

Levine, J. M. (1989). Reaction to opinion deviance in small groups. In P. B. Paulus (Ed.), *Psychology of group influence* (2nd ed., pp. 187–231). Hillsdale, NJ: Erlbaum.

Levine, J. M., & Moreland, R. L. (1990). Progress in small group research. *Annual Review of Psychology, 41,* 585–634.

Levine, R. A., & Campbell, D. T. (1972). *Ethnocentrism: Theories of conflict, ethnic attitudes, and group behavior.* New York: Wiley.

Levine, R. V., Martinez, T. S., Brase, G., & Sorenson, K. (1994). Helping in 36 U.S. cities. *Journal of Personality and Social Psychology, 67* (1), 69–82.

Levy, M. B., & Davis, K. E. (1988). Love styles and attachment styles compared: Their relation to each other and to various relationship characteristics. *Journal of Social and Personal Relationships, 5*, 429–471.

Lewin, K. (1935). *A dynamic theory of personality.* New York: McGraw-Hill.

Lewin, K. (1947). Group decision and social change. In T. M. Newcomb & E. L. Hartley (Eds.), *Readings in social psychology* (pp. 330–344). New York: Holt.

Lewin, K. (1951). Problems of research in social psychology. In D. Cartwright (Ed.), *Field theory in social science* (pp. 155–169). New York: Harper & Row.

Lewis, M., & Brooks-Gunn, J. (1979). *Social cognition and the acquisition of self.* New York: Plenum.

Lewontin, R. C. (1995, June 8). Reply. *The New York Review of Books*, p. 69.

Lewontin, R. C., Rose, S., & Kamin, L. J. (1984). *Not in our genes.* New York: Pantheon Books.

Li, J. C., Dunning, D., & Malpass, R. S. (in press). Cross-racial identification among European Americans: Basketball fandom and the contact hypothesis.

Liebert, R. M., & Sprafkin, J. (1988). *The early window* (3rd ed.). New York: Pergamon Press.

Lifton, R. J. (1986). *The Nazi doctors: Medical killing and the psychology of genocide.* New York: Basic Books.

Light, K. C., & Obrist, P. A. (1980). Cardiovascular response to stress: Effects of opportunity to avoid shock experience, and performance feedback. *Psychophysiology, 17*, 243–252.

Lightdale, J. R., & Prentice, D. A. (1994). Rethinking sex differences in aggression: Aggressive behavior in the absence of social roles. *Personality and Social Psychology Bulletin, 20*, 34–44.

Likert, R. (1932). A technique for the measurement of attitudes. *Archives of Psychology, 140*, 1–55.

Lim, R. G., & Carnevale, P. J. D. (1990). Contingencies in the mediation of disputes. *Journal of Personality and Social Psychology, 58*, 259–272.

Lind, E. A., Erickson, B. E., Friedland, N., & Dickenberger, M. (1978). Reactions to procedural models for adjudicative conflict resolution: A cross national study. *Journal of Conflict Resolution, 22*, 318–341.

Lind, E. A., Kanfer, R., & Farley, P. C. (1990). Voice, control, and procedural justice: Instrumental and noninstrumental concerns in fairness judgments. *Journal of Personality and Social Psychology, 59*, 952–959.

Lind, E. A., & Tyler, T. R. (1988). *The social psychology of procedural justice.* New York: Plenum.

Linden, W., Chambers, L., Maurice, J., & Lenz, J. W. (1993). Sex differences in social support, self-deception, hostility, and ambulatory cardiovascular activity. *Health Psychology, 12*, 376–380.

Linder, D. E., Cooper, J., & Jones, E. E. (1967). Decision freedom as a determinant of the role of incentive magnitude in attitude change. *Journal of Personality and Social Psychology, 6*, 245–254.

Lindsay, R. C. L., Lea, J. A., & Fulford, J. A. (1991). Sequential lineup presentation: Technique matters. *Journal of Applied Psychology, 76*, 741–745.

Lindsay, R. C. L., & Wells, G. L. (1985). Improving eyewitness identifications from lineups: Simultaneous versus sequential lineup presentations. *Journal of Applied Psychology, 70*, 556–564.

Lindsay, R. C. L., Wells, G. L., & Rumpel, C. M. (1981). Can people detect eyewitness-identification accuracy within and across situations? *Journal of Applied Psychology, 66*, 79–89.

Lindskold, S., & Han, G. (1988). GRIT as a foundation for integrative bargaining. *Personality and Social Psychology Bulletin, 14*, 335–345.

Lindskold, S., Han, G., & Betz, B. (1986a). The essential elements of communication in the GRIT strategy. *Personality and Social Psychology Bulletin, 12*, 179–186.

Lindskold, S., Han, G., & Betz, B. (1986b). Repeated persuasion in interpersonal conflict. *Journal of Personality and Social Psychology, 51*, 1183–1188.

Linville, P. W. (1987). Self-complexity as a cognitive buffer against stress-related illness and depression. *Journal of Personality and Social Psychology, 52*, 663–676.

Linville, P. W., Fischer, G. W., & Salovey, P. (1989). Perceived distributions of the characteristics of in-group and out-group members: Empirical evidence and a computer simulation. *Journal of Personality and Social Psychology, 57*, 165–188.

Linville, P. W., & Jones, E. E. (1980). Polarized appraisals of out-group members. *Journal of Personality and Social Psychology, 38*, 689–703.

Linz, D., & Donnerstein, E. (1992, September 30). Research can help us explain violence and pornography. *Chronicle of Higher Education*, pp. B3–B4.

Linz, D., Donnerstein, E., & Penrod, S. (1987). The findings and recommendations of the Attorney General's Commission on Pornography: Do the psychological "facts" fit the political fury? *American Psychologist, 42*, 946–953.

Linz, D., Wilson, B. J., & Donnerstein, E. (1992). Sexual violence in the mass media: Legal solutions, warnings, and mitigation through education. *Journal of Social Issues, 48*, 145–171.

Lloyd, S. A., Cate, R. M., & Henton, J. M. (1984). Predicting premarital relationship stability: A methodological refinement. *Journal of Marriage and the Family, 46*, 71–76.

Locher, P., Unger, R., Sociedade, P., & Wahl, J. (1993). At first glance: Accessibility of the physical attractiveness stereotype. *Sex Roles, 28*, 729–743.

Lockard, J. S., & Paulhus, D. L. (1988). *Self-deception: An adaptive mechanism?* Englewood Cliffs, NJ: Prentice-Hall.

Locke, K. D., & Horowitz, L. M. (1990). Satisfaction in interpersonal interactions as a function of similarity in level of dysphoria. *Journal of Personality and Social Psychology, 58*, 823–831.

Lockhart v. *McCree*, 54 U.S.L.W. 4449 (1986).

Locksley, A., Borgida, E., Brekke, N., & Hepburn, C. (1980). Sex stereotypes and social judgment. *Journal of Personality and Social Psychology, 39*, 821–831.

Loftus, E. F. (1979). *Eyewitness testimony.* Cambridge, MA: Harvard University Press.

Loftus, E. F. (1983). Silence is not golden. *American Psychologist, 38*, 564–572.

Loftus, E. F. (1993). Desperately seeking memories of the first few years of childhood: The reality of early memories. *Journal of Experimental Psychology: General, 122*, 274–277.

Loftus, E. F., Donders, K., Hoffman, H. G., & Schooler, J. W. (1989). Creating new memories that are quickly accessed and confidently held. *Memory and Cognition, 17,* 607–616.

Loftus, E. F., & Ketcham, K. (1991). *Witness for the defense: The accused, the eyewitness, and the expert who puts memory on trial.* New York: St. Martin's Press.

Loftus, E. F., Loftus, G. R., & Messo, J. (1987). Some facts about "weapon focus." *Law and Human Behavior, 11,* 55–62.

Loftus, E. F., & Palmer, J. C. (1974). Reconstruction of automobile destruction: An example of the interaction between language and memory. *Journal of Verbal Learning and Verbal Behavior, 13,* 585–589.

Loftus, G. R., & Loftus, E. F. (1976). *Human memory: The processing of information.* Hillsdale, NJ: Erlbaum.

London, P. (1970). The rescuers: Motivational hypotheses about Christians who saved Jews from the Nazis. In J. R. Macaulay & L. Berkowitz (Eds.), *Altruism and helping behavior* (pp. 241–250). New York: Academic Press.

Long, B. C., & Sangster, J. I. (1993). Dispositional optimism/pessimism and coping strategies: Predictors of psychosocial adjustment of rheumatoid and osteoarthritis patients. *Journal of Applied Social Psychology, 23,* 1069–1091.

Long, E. C. J., & Andrews, D. W. (1990). Perspective taking as a predictor of marital adjustment. *Journal of Personality and Social Psychology, 59,* 126–131.

Longley, J., & Pruitt, D. G. (1980). Groupthink: A critique of Janis's theory. In L. Wheeler (Ed.), *Review of personality and social psychology* (Vol. 1, pp. 74–93). Beverly Hills, CA: Sage.

Longnecker, C. O., Gioia, D. A., & Sims, H. P. (1987). Behind the mask: The politics of employee appraisal. *Academy of Management Executive, 1,* 183–193.

Lopez, J. A. (1992, March 3). Study says women face glass walls as well as ceilings. *Wall Street Journal,* pp. B1, B8.

Lord, C. G., & Saenz, D. S. (1985). Memory deficits and memory surfeits: Differential cognitive consequences of tokenism for tokens and observers. *Journal of Personality and Social Psychology, 49,* 918–926.

Lore, R. K., & Schultz, L. A. (1993). Control of human aggression: A comparative perspective. *American Psychologist, 48,* 16–25.

Lorenz, K. (1966). *On aggression.* New York: Harcourt, Brace & World.

Lortie-Lussier, M. (1987). Minority influence and idiosyncrasy credit: A new comparison of the Moscovici and Hollander theories of innovation. *European Journal of Social Psychology, 17,* 431–446.

Losch, M. E., & Cacioppo, J. T. (1990). Cognitive dissonance may enhance sympathetic tonus, but attitudes are changed to reduce negative affect rather than arousal. *Journal of Experimental Social Psychology, 26,* 289–304.

Lott, A. J., & Lott, B. E. (1974). The role of reward in the formation of positive interpersonal attitudes. In T. L. Huston (Ed.), *Foundations of interpersonal attraction* (pp. 171–189). New York: Academic Press.

Lott, B. (1985). The devaluation of women's competence. *Journal of Social Issues, 41,* 43–60.

Lovdal, L. T. (1989). Sex role messages in television commercials: An update. *Sex Roles, 21,* 715–724.

Luks, A. (1988, October). Helper's high. *Psychology Today,* pp. 39–40.

Lundberg-Love, P., & Geffner, R. (1989). Date rape: Prevalence, risk factors, and a proposed model. In M. A. Pirog-Good & J. E. Stets (Eds.), *Violence in dating relationships: Emerging social issues* (pp. 169–184). New York: Praeger.

Lupfer, M. B., Clark, L. F., Hutcherson, H. W. (1990). Impact of context on spontaneous trait and situational attributions. *Journal of Personality and Social Psychology, 58,* 239–249.

Lüüs, C. A. E., & Wells, G. L. (1991). Eyewitness identification and the selection of distractors for lineups. *Law and Human Behavior, 15,* 43–58.

Lüüs, C. A. E., & Wells, G. L. (1994). The malleability of eyewitness confidence: Co-witness and perseverance effects. *Journal of Applied Psychology, 79,* 714–723.

Lykken, D. T. (1981). *A tremor in the blood: Uses and abuses of the lie detector.* New York: McGraw-Hill.

Lykken, D. T., & Tellegen, A. (1993). Is human mating adventitious or the result of lawful choice? A twin study of mate selection. *Journal of Personality and Social Psychology, 65,* 56–68.

Lyness, S. A. (1993). Predictors of difference between Type A and B individuals in heart rate and blood pressure reactivity. *Psychological Bulletin, 114,* 266–295.

Lynn, M., & Mynier, K. (1993). Effect of server posture on restaurant tipping. *Journal of Applied Social Psychology, 23,* 678–685.

Lynn, M., & Oldenquist, A. (1986). Egoistic and nonegoistic motives in social dilemmas. *American Psychologist, 41,* 529–534.

Lynn, S. J., & Bates, K. (1985). The reaction of others to enacted depression: The effects of attitude and topic valence. *Journal of Social and Clinical Psychology, 3,* 268–282.

Lyubomirsky, S., & Nolen-Hoeksema, S. (1993). Self-perpetuating properties of dysphoric rumination. *Journal of Personality and Social Psychology, 65,* 339–349.

Maass, A., & Clark, R. D., III. (1984). Hidden impact of minorities: Fifteen years of minority influence research. *Psychological Bulletin, 95,* 428–450.

Maass, A., & Kohnken, G. (1989). Eyewitness identification: Simulating the "weapon effect." *Law and Human Behavior, 13,* 397–408.

Maass, A., Milesi, A., Zabbini, S., & Stahlberg, D. (1995). Linguistic intergroup bias: Differential expectancies or in-group protection? *Journal of Personality and Social Psychology, 68,* 116–126.

Macaulay, J. R. (1970). A shill for charity. In J. Macaulay & L. Berkowitz (Eds.), *Altruism and helping behavior* (pp. 43–59). New York: Academic Press.

Maccoby, E. E., & Jacklin, C. N. (1974). *The psychology of sex differences.* Stanford, CA: Stanford University Press.

MacCoun, R. J., & Kerr, N. L. (1988). Asymmetric influence in mock jury deliberation: Jurors' bias for leniency. *Journal of Personality and Social Psychology, 54,* 21–33.

Mackie, D. M. (1986). Social identification effects in group polarization. *Journal of Personality and Social Psychology, 50,* 720–728.

Mackie, D. M., Asuncion, A. G., & Rosselli, F. (1992). Impact of positive affect on persuasion processes. *Review of Personality and Social Psychology, 14,* 247–270.

Mackie, D. M., & Cooper, J. (1984). Attitude polarization: Effects of group membership. *Journal of Personality and Social Psychology, 46,* 575–585.

Mackie, D. M., & Worth, L. T. (1989). Processing deficits and the mediation of positive affect in persuasion. *Journal of Personality and Social Psychology, 57,* 27–40.

Mackie, D. M., Worth, L. T., & Asuncion, A.G. (1990). Processing of persuasive in-group messages. *Journal of Personality and Social Psychology, 58,* 812–822.

MacLeod, C., & Campbell, L. (1992). Memory accessibility and probability judgments: An experimental evaluation of the availability heuristic. *Journal of Personality and Social Psychology, 63,* 890–902.

Macrae, C. N., Bodenhausen, G. V., Milne, A. B., & Jetten, J. (1994). Out of mind but back in sight: Stereotypes on the rebound. *Journal of Personality and Social Psychology, 67,* 808–817.

Macrae, C. N., Milne, A. B., & Bodenhausen, G. V. (1994). Stereotypes as energy-saving devices: A peek inside the cognitive toolbox. *Journal of Personality and Social Psychology, 66,* 37–47.

Madden, T. J., Ellen, P. S., & Ajzen, I. (1992). A comparison of the theory of planned behavior and the theory of reasoned action. *Personality and Social Psychology Bulletin, 18,* 3–9.

Maddux, J. E. (1991). Self-efficacy. In C. R. Snyder & D. R. Forsyth (Eds.), *Handbook of social and clinical psychology: The health perspective* (pp. 57–78). New York: Pergamon Press.

Maddux, J. E., Norton, L. W., & Leary, M. R. (1988). Cognitive components of social anxiety: An investigation of the integration of self-presentation theory and self-efficacy theory. *Journal of Social and Clinical Psychology, 6,* 180–190.

Maddux, J. E., & Rogers, R. W. (1980). Effects of source expertness, physical attractiveness, and supporting arguments on persuasion: A case of brains over beauty. *Journal of Personality and Social Psychology, 39,* 235–244.

Magnus, K., Diener, E., Fujita F., & Pavot, W. (1993). Extraversion and neuroticism as predictors of objective life events: A longitudinal analysis. *Journal of Personality and Social Psychology, 65,* 1046–1053.

Major, B., Carrington, P. I., & Carnevale, P. J. D. (1984). Physical attractiveness and self-esteem: Attributions for praise from an other-sex evaluator. *Personality and Social Psychology Bulletin, 10,* 43–50.

Major, B., & Cozzarelli, C. (1992). Psychosocial predictors of adjustment to abortion. *Journal of Social Issues, 48,* 121–142.

Major, B., & Deaux, K. (1982). Individual differences in justice behavior. In J. Greenberg & R. L. Cohen (Eds.), *Equity and justice in social behavior* (pp. 13–76). New York: Academic Press.

Major, B., Feinstein, J., & Crocker, J. (1994). Attributional ambiguity of affirmative action. *Basic and Applied Social Psychology, 15,* 113–142.

Major, B., & Konar, E. (1984). An investigation of sex differences in pay expectations and their possible causes. *Academy of Management Journal, 27,* 777–792.

Major, B., McFarlin, D. B., & Gagnon, D. (1984). Overworked and underpaid: On the nature of gender differences in personal entitlement. *Journal of Personality and Social Psychology, 47,* 1399–1412.

Major, B., Schmidlin, A. M., & Williams, L. (1990). Gender patterns in social touch: The impact of setting and age. *Journal of Personality and Social Psychology, 58,* 634–643.

Makepeace, J. (1989). Dating, living together, and courtship violence. In M. A. Pirog-Good & J. E. Stets (Eds.), *Violence in dating relationships: Emerging social issues* (pp. 94–107). New York: Praeger.

Malamuth, N. M. (1983). Factors associated with rape as predictors of laboratory aggression against women. *Journal of Personality and Social Psychology, 45,* 432–442.

Malamuth, N. M. (1984). Aggression against women: Cultural and individual causes. In N. M. Malamuth & E. I. Donnerstein (Eds.), *Pornography and sexual aggression* (pp. 19–52). New York: Academic Press.

Malamuth, N. M. (1986). Predictors of naturalistic sexual aggression. *Journal of Personality and Social Psychology, 50,* 953–962.

Malamuth, N. M., & Billings, V. (1986). The function and effects of pornography: Sexual communications versus the feminist model in light of research findings. In J. Bryant & D. Zillmann (Eds.), *Perspectives on media effects* (pp. 83–108). Hillsdale, NJ: Erlbaum.

Malamuth, N. M., & Brown, L. M. (1994). Sexually aggressive men's perceptions of women's communications: Testing three explanations. *Journal of Personality and Social Psychology, 67,* 699–712.

Malamuth, N. M., & Check, J. V. P. (1981). The effects of mass media exposure on acceptance of violence against women: A field experiment. *Journal of Research in Personality, 15,* 436–446.

Malamuth, N. M., Check, J. V. P., & Briere, J. (1986). Sexual arousal in response to aggression: Ideological, aggressive, and sexual correlates. *Journal of Personality and Social Psychology, 50,* 330–340.

Malamuth, N. M., & Donnerstein, E. I. (1982). The effects of aggressive-pornographic mass media stimuli. In L. Berkowitz (Ed.), *Advances in experimental social psychology* (Vol. 15, pp. 103–136). New York: Academic Press.

Malinosky-Rummell, R., & Hansen, D. J. (1993). Long-term consequences of childhood physical abuse. *Psychological Bulletin, 114,* 68–79.

Malkiel, B. (1981). *A random walk down Wall Street* (2nd ed.). New York: Norton.

Malloy, T. E., & Albright, L. (1990). Interpersonal perception in a social context. *Journal of Personality and Social Psychology, 58,* 419–428.

Malpass, R. S., & Devine, P. G. (1981). Eyewitness identification: Lineup instructions and the absence of the offender. *Journal of Applied Psychology, 66,* 482–489.

Malpass, R. S., & Kravitz, J. (1969). Recognition for faces of own and other race. *Journal of Personality and Social Psychology, 13,* 330–334.

Manis, M., Nelson, T. E., & Shedler, J. (1988). Stereotypes and social judgment: Extremity, assimilation, and contrast. *Journal of Personality and Social Psychology, 55,* 28–36.

Mann, T. (1994). Informed consent for psychological research: Do subjects comprehend consent forms and understand their legal rights? *Psychological Science, 5,* 140–143.

Manucia, G. K., Baumann, D. J., & Cialdini, R. B. (1984). Mood influences on helping: Direct effects or side effects? *Journal of Personality and Social Psychology, 46,* 357–364.

Manz, C. C., & Sims, H. P., Jr. (1982). The potential for "groupthink" in autonomous work groups. *Human Relations, 35,* 773–784.

Marco, C. A., & Suls, J. (1993). Daily stress and the trajectory of mood: Spillover, response assimilation, contrast, and chronic negative affectivity. *Journal of Personality and Social Psychology, 64,* 1053–1063.

Margolin, G., & Wampold, B. E. (1981). A sequential analysis of conflict and accord in distressed and nondistressed marital partners. *Journal of Consulting and Clinical Psychology, 49,* 554–567.

Margolin, L., & White, L. (1987). The continuing role of physical attractiveness in marriage. *Journal of Marriage and the Family, 49,* 21–28.

Marks, G., Graham, J. W., & Hansen, W. B. (1992). Social projection and social conformity in adolescent alcohol use: A longitudinal analysis. *Personality and Social Psychology Bulletin, 18,* 96–101.

Marks, G., & Miller, N. (1982). Target attractiveness as a mediator of assumed attitude similarity. *Personality and Social Psychology Bulletin, 8,* 728–735.

Marks, G., & Miller, N. (1987). Ten years of research on the false-consensus effect: An empirical and theoretical review. *Psychological Bulletin, 102,* 72–90.

Marks, G., Richardson, J. L., Graham, J. W., & Levine, A. (1986). Role of health locus of control beliefs and expectations of treatment efficacy in adjustment to cancer. *Journal of Personality and Social Psychology, 51,* 243–250.

Marks, M. L., Mirvis, P. H., Hackett, E. J., & Grady, J. F., Jr. (1986). Employee participation in a quality circle program: Impact on quality of work life, productivity, and absenteeism. *Journal of Applied Psychology, 71,* 61–69.

Markus, H. (1977). Self-schemata and processing information about the self. *Journal of Personality and Social Psychology, 35,* 63–78.

Markus, H., Hamill, R., & Sentis, K. P. (1987). Thinking fat: Self-schemas for body weight and the processing of weight-relevant information. *Journal of Applied Social Psychology, 17,* 50–71.

Markus, H., & Nurius, P. (1986). Possible selves. *American Psychologist, 41,* 954–969.

Markus, H. R., & Kitayama, S. (1991). Culture and the self: Implications for cognition, emotion, and motivation. *Psychological Review, 98,* 224–253.

Marlowe, D., & Gergen, K. (1969). Personality and social interaction. In G. Lindzey & E. Aronson (Eds.), *The handbook of social psychology* (2nd ed., pp. 590–665). Reading, MA: Addison-Wesley.

Marques, J. M. (1990). The black sheep effect: Outgroup homogeneity in social comparison settings. In D. Abrams & M. Hogg (Eds.), *Social identity theory: Constructive and critical advances* (pp. 131–151). New York: Springer-Verlag.

Marsh, H. W., & Parker, J. W. (1984). Determinants of student self-concept: Is it better to be a relatively large fish in a small pond even if you don't learn to swim as well? *Journal of Personality and Social Psychology, 47,* 213–231.

Marshall, G. N., Wortman, C. B., Kusulas, J. W., Hervig, L. K., & Vickers, R. R., Jr. (1992). Distinguishing optimism from pessimism: Relations to fundamental dimensions of mood and personality. *Journal of Personality and Social Psychology, 62,* 1067–1074.

Marshall, G. N., Wortman, C. B., Vickers, R. R., Jr., Kusulas, J. W., & Hervig, L. K. (1994). The five-factor model of personality as a framework for personality-health research. *Journal of Personality and Social Psychology, 67,* 278–286.

Marshall, W. L. (1989). Pornography and sex offenders. In D. Zillmann & J. Bryant (Eds.), *Pornography: Research advances and policy considerations* (pp. 185–214). Hillsdale, NJ: Erlbaum.

Martichuski, D. K., & Bell, P. A. (1991). Reward, punishment, privatization, and moral suasion in a commons dilemma. *Journal of Applied Social Psychology, 21,* 1356–1369.

Martin, C. L. (1987). A ratio measure of sex stereotyping. *Journal of Personality and Social Psychology, 52,* 489–499.

Martin, C. L., & Nagao, D. H. (1989). Some effects of computerized interviewing on job applicant responses. *Journal of Applied Psychology, 74,* 72–80.

Martin, C. L., & Parker, S. (1995). Folk theories about sex and race differences. *Personality and Social Psychology Bulletin, 21,* 45–57.

Martin, C. L., Wood, C. H., & Little, J. K. (1990). The development of gender stereotype components. *Child Development, 61,* 1891–1904.

Martin, J. (1986). The tolerance of injustice. In J. M. Olson, C. P. Herman, & M. P. Zanna (Eds.), *Relative deprivation and social comparison: The Ontario Symposium* (Vol. 4, pp. 217–242). Hillsdale, NJ: Erlbaum.

Martin, L. L., Seta, J. J., & Crelia, R. (1990). Assimilation and contrast as a function of people's willingness and ability to expend effort in forming an impression. *Journal of Personality and Social Psychology, 59,* 27–37.

Masciuch, S., & Kienapple, K. (1993). The emergence of jealousy in children 4 months to 7 years of age. *Journal of Social and Personal Relationships, 10,* 421–435.

Maslach, C. (1979). Negative emotional biasing of unexplained arousal. *Journal of Personality and Social Psychology, 37,* 953–969.

Masters, W. H., & Johnson, V. E. (1979). *Homosexuality in perspective.* Boston: Little, Brown.

Mathes, E. W. (1992). *Jealousy: The psychological data.* Lanhan, MD: University Press of America.

Mathur, M., & Chattopadhyay, A. (1991). The impact of moods generated by TV programs on responses to advertising. *Psychology and Marketing, 8,* 59–77.

Matthews, K. A. (1988). Coronary heart disease and Type A behaviors: Update on and alternative to the Booth-Kewley and Friedman (1987) quantitative review. *Psychological Bulletin, 104,* 373–380.

Matthews, K. A., Batson, C. D., Horn, J., & Rosenman, R. H. (1981). "Principles in his nature which interest him in the fortunes of others . . . ": The heritability of empathic concern for others. *Journal of Personality, 49,* 237–247.

Matthews, K. A., & Haynes, S. G. (1986). Type A behavior pattern and coronary disease risk: Update and critical evaluation. *American Journal of Epidemiology, 123,* 923–958.

Matthews, K. A., Scheier, M. F., Brunson, B. I., & Carducci, B. (1980). Attention, unpredictability, and reports of physical symptoms: Eliminating the benefits of predictability. *Journal of Personality and Social Psychology, 38,* 525–537.

Mauro, R. (1992). Affective dynamics: Opponent processes and excitation transfer. In M. S. Clark (Ed.), *Review of Personality and Social Psychology: Emotion* (Vol. 13, pp. 150–174). Newbury Park, CA: Sage.

McAdams, D. P. (1982). Intimacy motivation. In A. J. Stewart (Ed.), *Motivation and society* (pp. 133–171). San Francisco: Jossey-Bass.

McAdams, D. P. (1988). Personal needs and personal relationships. In S. Duck (Ed.), *Handbook of personal relationships: Theory, research, and interventions* (pp. 7–22). New York: Wiley.

McAdams, D. P., & Bryant, F. B. (1987). Intimacy motivation and subjective mental health in a nationwide sample. *Journal of Personality, 55,* 395–414.

McAdams, D. P., Healy, S., & Krause, S. (1984). Social motives and friendship patterns. *Journal of Personality and Social Psychology, 47,* 828–838.

McAdams, D. P., & Vaillant, G. E. (1982). Intimacy motivation and psychosocial adjustment: A longitudinal study. *Journal of Personality Assessment, 46,* 586–593.

McArthur, L. A. (1972). The how and what of why: Some determinants and consequences of causal attribution. *Journal of Personality and Social Psychology, 22,* 171–193.

McCarthy, C. R. (1981). The development of federal regulations for social science research. In A. J. Kimmel (Ed.), *New directions for methodology of social and behavioral science (No. 10): Ethics of human subject research* (pp. 31–39). San Francisco: Jossey-Bass.

McCaul, K. D., Ployhart, R. E., Hinsz, V. B., & McCaul, H. S. (1995). Appraisals of a consistent versus a similar politician: Voter preferences and intuitive judgments. *Journal of Personality and Social Psychology, 68,* 292–299.

McCauley, C. (1989). The nature of social influence in groupthink: Compliance and internalization. *Journal of Personality and Social Psychology, 57,* 250–260.

McClelland, D. C. (1951). *Personality.* New York: Holt, Rinehart and Winston.

McClelland, D. C. (1985). How motives, skills, and values determine what people do. *American Psychologist, 40,* 812–825.

McCloskey, L. A., & Coleman, L. M. (1992). Difference without dominance: Children's talk in mixed- and same-sex dyads. *Sex Roles, 27,* 241–257.

McCloskey, M., & Egeth, H. (1983). Eyewitness identification: What can a psychologist tell a jury? *American Psychologist, 38,* 550–563.

McCloskey, M., Wible, C. G., & Cohen, N. J. (1988). Is there a special flashbulb memory mechanism? *Journal of Experimental Psychology: General, 117,* 171–181.

McCloskey, M., & Zaragoza, M. (1985). Misleading postevent information and memory for events: Arguments and evidence against memory impairment hypotheses. *Journal of Experimental Psychology, 114,* 3–18.

McConahay, J. B. (1986). Modern racism, ambivalence, and the modern racism scale. In J. F. Dovidio & S. L. Gaertner (Eds.), *Prejudice, discrimination, and racism: Theory and research* (pp. 91–125). Orlando, FL: Academic Press.

McConnell, A. R., Sherman, S. J., & Hamilton, D. L. (1994). Illusory correlation in the perception of groups: An extension of the distinctiveness-based account. *Journal of Personality and Social Psychology, 67,* 414–429.

McCrae, R. R., & John, O. P. (1992). An introduction to the five-factor model and its applications. *Journal of Personality, 60,* 175–216.

McDougall, W. (1908). *An introduction to social psychology.* London: Methuen.

McFatter, R. M. (1978). Sentencing strategies and justice: Effects of punishment philosophy on sentencing decisions. *Journal of Personality and Social Psychology, 36,* 1490–1500.

McGillicuddy, N. B., Pruitt, D. G., & Syna, H. (1984). Perceptions of fairness and strength of negotiation. *Personality and Social Psychology Bulletin, 10,* 402–409.

McGinniss, J. (1983). *Fatal vision.* New York: Signet.

McGonagle, K. A., Kessler, R. C., & Gotlib, I. H. (1993). The effects of marital disagreement style, frequency, and outcome on marital disruption. *Journal of Social and Personal Relationships, 10,* 385–404.

McGovern, T. V., Furumoto, L., Halpern, D. F., Kimble, G. A., & McKeachie, W. J. (1991). Liberal education, study in depth, and the arts and sciences major—psychology. *American Psychologist, 46,* 598–605.

McGrath, J. E., & Hollingshead, A. B. (1994). *Groups interacting with technology.* Thousand Oaks, CA: Sage.

McGraw, K. O., & McCullers, J. C. (1979). Evidence of a detrimental effect of extrinsic incentives on breaking a mental set. *Journal of Experimental Social Psychology, 15,* 285–294.

McGuire, W. J. (1964). Inducing resistance to persuasion. In L. Berkowitz (Ed.), *Advances in experimental social psychology* (Vol. 1, pp. 192–229). New York: Academic Press.

McGuire, W. J. (1967). Some impending reorientations in social psychology: Some thoughts provoked by Kenneth Ring. *Journal of Experimental Social Psychology, 3,* 124–139.

McGuire, W. J. (1968). Personality and susceptibility to social influence. In E. F. Borgatta & W. W. Lambert (Eds.), *Handbook of personality theory and research* (pp. 1130–1187). Chicago: Rand McNally.

McGuire, W. J. (1969). The nature of attitudes and attitude change. In G. Lindzey & E. Aronson (Eds.), *Handbook of social psychology* (2nd ed., Vol. 3, pp. 136–314). Reading, MA: Addison-Wesley.

McGuire, W. J., & McGuire, C. V. (1988). Content and process in the experience of self. In L. Berkowitz (Ed.), *Advances in experimental social psychology* (Vol. 20, pp. 97–144). New York: Academic Press.

McGuire, W. J., McGuire, C. V., & Winton, W. (1979). Effects of household sex composition on the salience of one's gender in the spontaneous self-concept. *Journal of Experimental Social Psychology, 15,* 77–90.

McIntosh, D. N., Silver, R. C., & Wortman, C. B. (1993). Religion's role in adjustment to a negative life event: Coping with the loss of a child. *Journal of Personality and Social Psychology, 65,* 812–821.

McLeod, J. D., & Eckberg, D. A. (1993). Concordance for depressive disorders and marital quality. *Journal of Marriage and the Family, 55,* 733–746.

McMullen, P. A., & Gross, A. E. (1983). Sex differences, sex roles, and health-related help-seeking. In B. M. DePaulo, A. Nadler, & J. D. Fisher (Eds.), *New directions in helping: Vol. 2. Help-Seeking* (pp. 233–263). New York: Academic Press.

McNulty, S. E., & Swann, W. B., Jr. (1994). Identity negotiation in roommate relationships: The self as architect and consequence of social reality. *Journal of Personality and Social Psychology, 67,* 1012–1023.

Mead, G. H. (1934). *Mind, self, and society.* Chicago: University of Chicago Press.

Mearns, J. (1991). Coping with a breakup: Negative mood regulation expectancies and depression following the end of a romantic relationship. *Journal of Personality and Social Psychology, 60,* 327–334.

Mednick, S. A., Gabrielli, W. F., Jr., & Hutchings, B. (1987). Genetic factors in the etiology of criminal behavior. In S. A. Mednick, T. E. Moffitt, & S. A. Stack (Eds.), *The causes of crime: New biological approaches* (pp. 74–91). Cambridge, UK: Cambridge University Press.

Mednick, S. A., & Kandel, E. S. (1988). Congenital determinants of violence. *Bulletin of the American Academy of Psychiatry and the Law, 16,* 101–109.

Meeus, W. H. J., & Raaijmakers, Q. A. W. (1986). Administrative obedience: Carrying out orders to use psychological-administrative violence. *European Journal of Social Psychology, 16,* 311–324.

Meindl, J. R., & Lerner, M. J. (1983). The heroic motive: Some experimental demonstrations. *Journal of Experimental Social Psychology, 19,* 1–20.

Melamed, T. (1991). Individual differences in romantic jealousy: The moderating effect of relationship characteristics. *European Journal of Social Psychology, 21,* 455–461.

Meleshko, K. G. A., & Alden, L. E. (1993). Anxiety and self-disclosure: Toward a motivational model. *Journal of Personality and Social Psychology, 64,* 1000–1009.

Melton, G. (1992). Children as partners for justice: Next steps for developmentalists. *Monographs of the Society for Research in Child Development, 57*(5) (Serial No. 229).

Melton, G. B., Levine, R. J., Koocher, G. P., Rosenthal, R., & Thompson, W. C. (1988). Community consultation in socially sensitive research. *American Psychologist, 43,* 573–581.

Mendonca, P. J., & Brehm, S. S. (1983). Effects of choice on behavioral treatment of overweight children. *Journal of Social and Clinical Psychology, 1,* 343–358.

Merikle, P., & Skanes, H. E. (1992). Subliminal self-help audiotapes: A search for placebo effects. *Journal of Applied Psychology, 77,* 772–776.

Merton, R. (1948). The self-fulfilling prophecy. *Antioch Review, 8,* 193–210.

Messick, D. M., & Cook, K. S. (Eds.). (1983). *Equity theory: Psychological and sociological perspectives.* New York: Praeger.

Messick, D. M., & Mackie, D. M. (1989). Intergroup relations. *Annual Review of Psychology, 40,* 51–81.

Messick, D. M., Wilke, H., Brewer, M. B., Kramer, R. M., Zemke, P. E., & Lui, L. (1983). Individual adaptation and structural change as solutions to social dilemmas. *Journal of Personality and Social Psychology, 44,* 294–309.

Metalsky, G. I., Halberstadt, L. J., & Abramson, L. Y. (1987). Vulnerability to depressive mood reactions: Toward a more powerful test of the diathesis-stress and causal mediation components of the reformulated theory of depression. *Journal of Personality and Social Psychology, 52,* 386–393.

Metalsky, G. I., & Joiner, Jr., T. E. (1992). Vulnerability to depressive symptomatology: A prospective test of the diathesis-stress and causal mediation components of the hopelessness theory of depression. *Journal of Personality and Social Psychology, 63,* 667–675.

Meyer, C. B., & Taylor, S. E. (1986). Adjustment to rape. *Journal of Personality and Social Psychology, 50,* 1226–1234.

Miceli, M. P., Dozier, J. B., & Near, J. P. (1991). Blowing the whistle on data fudging: A controlled field experiment. *Journal of Applied Social Psychology, 21,* 271–295.

Michaels, J. W., Edwards, J. N., & Acock, A. C. (1984). Satisfaction in intimate relationships as a function of inequality, inequity, and outcomes. *Social Psychology Quarterly, 47,* 347–357.

Mikulincer, M., Florian, V., & Weller, A. (1993). Attachment styles, coping strategies, and posttraumatic psychological distress: The impact of the Gulf War in Israel. *Journal of Personality and Social Psychology, 64,* 817–826.

Milavsky, J. R., Kessler, R. C., Stipp, H. H., & Rubens, W. S. (1982). *Television and aggression: A panel study.* New York: Academic Press.

Milgram, S. (1963). Behavioral study of obedience. *Journal of Abnormal and Social Psychology, 67,* 371–378.

Milgram, S. (1964). Issues in the study of obedience: A reply to Baumrind. *American Psychologist, 19,* 848–852.

Milgram, S. (1970). The experience of living in cities. *Science, 167,* 1461–1468.

Milgram, S. (1974). *Obedience to authority: An experimental view.* New York: Harper & Row.

Milgram, S., Bickman, L., & Berkowitz, L. (1969). Note on the drawing power of crowds of different size. *Journal of Personality and Social Psychology, 13,* 79–82.

Milgram, S., & Sabini, J. (1978). On maintaining urban norms: A field experiment in the subway. In A. Baum, J. E. Singer, & S. Valins (Eds.), *Advances in environmental psychology* (Vol. 1). Hillsdale, NJ: Erlbaum.

Millar, M. G., & Millar, K. U. (1990). Attitude change as a function of attitude type and argument type. *Journal of Personality and Social Psychology, 59,* 217–228.

Millar, M. G., & Tesser, A. (1989). The effects of affective-cognitive consistency and thought on the attitude-behavior relation. *Journal of Experimental Social Psychology, 25,* 189–202.

Miller, A. G. (1986). *The obedience experiments: A case study of controversy in social science.* New York: Praeger.

Miller, A. G., Jones, E. E., & Hinkle, S. (1981). A robust attribution error in the personality domain. *Journal of Experimental Social Psychology, 17,* 587–600.

Miller, B. C. (1993). Families, science, and values: Alternative view of parenting effects and adolescent pregnancy. *Journal of Marriage and the Family, 55,* 7–21.

Miller, C. T. (1984). Self-schemas, gender, and social comparison: A clarification of the related attributes hypothesis. *Journal of Personality and Social Psychology, 46,* 1222–1229.

Miller, D. T. (1977). Altruism and threat to a belief in a just world. *Journal of Experimental Social Psychology, 13,* 113–124.

Miller, D. T., & McFarland, C. (1987). Pluralistic ignorance: When similarity is interpreted as dissimilarity. *Journal of Personality and Social Psychology, 53,* 298–305.

Miller, D. T., & McFarland, C. (1991). When social comparison goes awry: The case of pluralistic ignorance. In J. Suls

& T. Wills (Eds.), *Social comparison: Contemporary theory and research* (pp. 287–313). Hillsdale, NJ: Erlbaum.

Miller, D. T., & Prentice, D. A. (1994). Collective errors and errors about the collective. *Personality and Social Psychology Bulletin, 20,* 541–550.

Miller, D. T., Turnbull, W., & McFarland, C. (1990). Counterfactual thinking and social perception: Thinking about what might have been. *Advances in Experimental Social Psychology, 23,* 305–331.

Miller, J. G. (1984). Culture and the development of everyday social explanation. *Journal of Personality and Social Psychology, 46,* 961–978.

Miller, J. G., & Bersoff, D. M. (1994). Cultural influences on the moral status of reciprocity and the discounting of endogenous motivation. *Personality and Social Psychology Bulletin, 20,* 592–602.

Miller, J. G., Bersoff, D. M., & Harwood, R. L. (1990). Perceptions of social responsibility in India and in the United States: Moral imperatives or personal decisions? *Journal of Personality and Social Psychology, 58,* 33–47.

Miller, M. L., & Thayer, J. F. (1989). On the existence of discrete classes in personality: Is self-monitoring the correct joint to carve? *Journal of Personality and Social Psychology, 57,* 143–155.

Miller, N., & Brewer, M. B. (Eds.) (1984). *Groups in contact: The psychology of desegregation.* New York: Academic Press.

Miller, N., & Campbell, D. T. (1959). Recency and primacy in persuasion as a function of the timing of speeches and measurements. *Journal of Abnormal and Social Psychology, 59,* 1–9.

Miller, N., & Carlson, M. (1990). Valid theory-testing meta-analyses further question the negative state relief model of helping. *Psychological Bulletin, 107,* 215–225.

Miller, N., & Cooper, H. (Eds.). (1991). Meta-analysis in personality and social psychology [Special issue]. *Personality and Social Psychology Bulletin, 17*(3).

Miller, N. E. (1941). The frustration-aggression hypothesis. *Psychological Review, 48,* 337–342.

Miller, P. A., & Eisenberg, N. (1988). The relation of empathy to aggressive and externalizing/antisocial behavior. *Psychological Bulletin, 103,* 324–344.

Miller, S. M. (1981). Predictability and human stress: Toward a clarification of evidence and theory. In L. Berkowitz (Ed.), *Advances in experimental social psychology* (Vol. 14, pp. 203–256). New York: Academic Press.

Miller, S. M., & Mangan, C. E. (1983). Interacting effects of information and coping style in adapting to gynecologic stress: Should the doctor tell all? *Journal of Personality and Social Psychology, 45,* 223–236.

Miller, T. Q., Heath, L., Molcan, J. R., & Dugoni, B. L. (1991a). Imitative violence in the real world: A reanalysis of homicide rates following championship prize fights. *Aggressive Behavior, 17,* 121–134.

Miller, T. Q., Turner, C. W., Tindale, R. S., Posavac, E. J., & Dugon, B. L. (1991b). Reasons for the trend toward null findings in research on Type A behavior. *Psychological Bulletin, 110,* 469–485.

Miller, W. R. (1985). Motivation for treatment: A review with special emphasis on alcoholism. *Psychological Bulletin, 98,* 84–107.

Mills, J. (1976). A procedure for explaining experiments involving deception. *Personality and Social Psychology Bulletin, 2,* 3–13.

Mitchell, T. R. (1974). Expectancy models of job satisfaction, occupational preference, and effort: A theoretical, methodological, and empirical appraisal. *Psychological Bulletin, 81,* 1096–1112.

Moghaddam, F. M., Taylor, D. M., & Wright, S. C. (1993). *Social psychology in cross-cultural perspective,* New York: W. H. Freeman and Co.

Monteith, M. J., Devine, P. G., & Zuwerink, J. R. (1993). Self-directed versus other-directed affect as a consequence of prejudice-related discrepancies. *Journal of Personality and Social Psychology, 64,* 198–210.

Montepare, J. M., & McArthur, L. Z. (1988). Impressions of people created by age-related qualities of their gaits. *Journal of Personality and Social Psychology, 55,* 547–556.

Montgomery, R. L., & Haemmerlie, F. M. (1986). Self-perception theory and the reduction of heterosexual anxiety. *Journal of Social and Clinical Psychology, 4,* 503–512.

Montgomery, R. L., & Haemmerlie, F. M. (1987). Self-perception theory and heterosocial anxiety. In J. E. Maddux, C. D. Stoltenberg, & R. Rosenwein (Eds.), *Social processes in clinical and counseling psychology* (pp. 139–152). New York: Springer-Verlag.

Mooney, K. M., Cohn, E. S., & Swift, M. B. (1992). Physical distance and AIDS: Too close for comfort? *Journal of Applied Social Psychology, 22,* 1442–1452.

Moore, B. S., Underwood, B., & Rosenhan, D. L. (1973). Affect and altruism. *Developmental Psychology, 8,* 99–104.

Moore, K. A., Snyder, N. A., & Daly, M. (1992). *Facts at a glance.* Washington, DC: Child Trends.

Moore, T. E. (1982). Subliminal advertising: What you see is what you get. *Journal of Marketing, 46,* 38–47.

Moorhead, G., & Montanari, J. R. (1986). An empirical investigation of the groupthink phenomenon. *Human Relations, 39,* 399–410.

Moorman, R. H. (1991). Relationship between organizational justice and organizational citizenship behaviors: Do fairness perceptions influence employee citizenship? *Journal of Applied Psychology, 76,* 845–855.

Moran, G., & Comfort, C. (1986). Neither "tentative" nor "fragmentary": Verdict preference of impaneled felony jurors as a function of attitude toward capital punishment. *Journal of Applied Psychology, 71,* 146–155.

Moran, G., & Cutler, B. L. (1991). The prejudicial impact of pretrial publicity. *Journal of Applied Social Psychology, 21,* 345–367.

Moray, N. (1959). Attention in dichotic listening: Affective cues and the influence of instructions. *Quarterly Journal of Experimental Psychology, 11,* 56–60.

Moreland, R. L., & Beach, S. R. (1992). Exposure effects in the classroom: The development of affinity among students. *Journal of Experimental Social Psychology, 28,* 255–276.

Moreland, R. L., Hogg, M. A., & Hains, S. C. (1994). Back to the future: Social psychological research on groups. *Journal of Experimental Social Psychology 30,* 527–555.

Moreland, R. L., & Levine, J. M. (1989). Newcomers and oldtimers in social groups. In P. B. Paulus (Ed.), *Psychology of group influence* (2nd ed., pp. 143–186). Hillsdale, NJ: Erlbaum.

Morgan, H. J., & Janoff-Bulman, R. (1994). Positive and negative self-complexity: Patterns of adjustment following traumatic versus non-traumatic life experiences. *Journal of Social and Clinical Psychology, 13,* 63–85.

Mori, D., Chaiken, S., & Pliner, P. (1987). Eating lightly and the self-presentation of femininity. *Journal of Personality and Social Psychology, 53,* 693–702.

Morris, M. W., & Peng, K. (1994). Culture and cause: American and Chinese attributions for social and physical events. *Journal of Personality and Social Psychology, 67,* 949–971.

Morrison, A. M., & Von Glinow, M. A. (1990). Women and minorities in management. *American Psychologist, 45,* 200–208.

Moschandreas, K. (1993, Dec. 20). Letter to the editor. *The New Yorker,* pp. 12–13.

Moscovici, S. (1980). Toward a theory of conversion behavior. In L. Berkowitz (Ed.), *Advances in Experimental Social Psychology, 6,* 149–202.

Moscovici, S. (1985). Social influence and conformity. In G. Lindzey & E. Aronson (Eds.), *The handbook of social psychology* (3rd ed., pp. 347–412). New York: Random House.

Moscovici, S., Lage, E., & Naffrechoux, M. (1969). Influence of a consistent minority on the responses of a majority in a color perception task. *Sociometry, 32,* 365–380.

Moscovici, S., & Personnaz, B. (1991). Studies in social influence VI: Is Lenin orange or red? Imagery and social influence. *European Journal of Social Psychology, 21,* 101–118.

Moscovici, S., & Zavalloni, M. (1969). The group as a polarizer of attitudes. *Journal of Personality and Social Psychology, 12,* 125–135.

Moskowitz, G. B. (1993). Individual differences in social categorization: The influence of personal need for structure on spontaneous trait inferences. *Journal of Personality and Social Psychology, 65,* 132–142.

Mouton, J., Blake, R., & Olmstead, J. (1956). The relationship between frequency of yielding and the disclosure of personal identity. *Journal of Personality, 24,* 339–347.

Muehlenhard, C. L. (1988). Misinterpreted dating behaviors and the risk of date rape. *Journal of Social and Clinical Psychology, 6,* 20–37.

Muehlenhard, C. L., Goggins, M. F., Jones, J. M., & Satterfield, A. T. (1991). Sexual violence and coercion in close relationships. In K. McKinney & S. Sprecher (Eds.), *Sexuality in close relationships* (pp. 155–175). Hillsdale, NJ: Erlbaum.

Mueller, J. H. (1982). Self-awareness and access to material rated as self-descriptive and nondescriptive. *Bulletin of the Psychonomic Society, 19,* 323–326.

Mugny, G. (1982). *The power of minorities.* London: Academic Press.

Mugny, G., & Perez, J. A. (1991). *Social psychology of minority influence.* Cambridge: Cambridge University Press.

Mullen, B. (1983). Operationalizing the effect of the group on the individual: A self-attention perspective. *Journal of Experimental Social Psychology, 19,* 295–322.

Mullen, B. (1985). Strength and immediacy of sources: A meta-analytic evaluation of the forgotten elements of social impact theory. *Journal of Personality and Social Psychology, 48,* 1458–1466.

Mullen, B. (1986). Atrocity as a function of lynch mob composition: A self-attention perspective. *Personality and Social Psychology Bulletin, 12,* 187–197.

Mullen, B., & Copper, C. (1994). The relation between group cohesiveness and performance: An integration. *Psychological Bulletin, 115,* 210–227.

Mullen, B., Dovidio, J. F., Johnson, C., & Copper, C. (1992). In-group and out-group differences in social projection. *Journal of Experimental Social Psychology, 28,* 422–440.

Mullen, B., Johnson, C., & Salas, E. (1991). Productivity loss in brainstorming groups: A meta-analytic integration. *Basic and Applied Social Psychology, 12,* 3–23.

Murphy, K. R., & Balzer, W. K. (1986). Systematic distortions in memory-based behavior ratings and performance evaluation: Consequences for rating accuracy. *Journal of Applied Psychology, 71,* 39–44.

Murphy, K. R., Balzer, W. K., Lockhart, M. C., & Eisenman, E. J. (1985). Effects of previous performance on evaluations of present performance. *Journal of Applied Psychology, 70,* 72–84.

Murphy, K. R., Jako, R. A., & Anhalt, R. L. (1993). Nature and consequences of halo error: A critical analysis. *Journal of Applied Psychology, 78,* 218–225.

Murray, H. A. (1938). *Explorations in personality.* New York: Oxford University Press.

Murstein, B. I. (1972). Physical attractiveness and marital choice. *Journal of Personality and Social Psychology, 22,* 8–12.

Murstein, B. I. (1986). *Paths to marriage.* Beverly Hills, CA: Sage.

Murstein, B. I. (1987). A clarification and extension of the SVR theory of dyadic pairing. *Journal of Marriage and the Family, 49,* 929–933.

Murstein, B. I., Merighi, J. R., & Vyse, S. A. (1991). Love styles in the United States and France: A cross-cultural comparison. *Journal of Social and Clinical Psychology, 10,* 37–46.

Mydans, S. (1990, January 19). For jurors, facts could not be sifted from fantasies. *New York Times,* p. A18.

Myers, D. G. (1992). *The pursuit of happiness.* New York: Avon Books.

Myers, D. G., & Bishop, G. D. (1970). Discussion effects on racial attitudes. *Science, 169,* 778–779.

Myers, D. G., & Lamm, H. (1976). The group polarization phenomenon. *Psychological Bulletin, 83,* 602–627.

Nacoste, R. W. (1987). But do they care about fairness? The dynamics of preferential treatment and minority interest. *Basic and Applied Social Psychology, 8,* 177–191.

Nadler, A. (1986). Helpseeking as a cultural phenomenon: Differences between city and kibbutz dwellers. *Journal of Personality and Social Psychology, 51,* 976–982.

Nadler, A., & Fisher, J. D. (1986). The role of threat to self-esteem and perceived control in recipient reactions to help: Theory development and empirical validation. In L. Berkowitz (Ed.), *Advances in experimental social psychology* (Vol. 19, pp. 81–122). New York: Academic Press.

Narby, D. J., Cutler, B. L., & Moran, G. (1993). A meta-analysis of the association between authoritarianism and jurors' perceptions of defendant culpability. *Journal of Applied Psychology, 78,* 34–42.

Nardi, P. M., & Sherrod, D. (1994). Friendship in the lives of gay men and lesbians. *Journal of Social and Personal Relationships, 11,* 185–199.

National Center on Child Abuse and Neglect. (1988). *Study findings: Study of national incidence and prevalence of child abuse and neglect: 1988.* Washington, DC: U.S. Department of Health and Human Services.

National Law Journal (1990). Rock group not liable for deaths (September 10), p. 33.

Neisser, U. (1981). John Dean's memory: A case study. *Cognition, 9,* 1–22.

Nemeth, C. (1986). Differential contributions of majority and minority influence. *Psychological Review, 93,* 23–32.

Nemeth, C., & Brilmayer, A. G. (1987). Negotiation versus influence. *European Journal of Social Psychology, 17,* 45–56.

Nemeth, C., & Chiles, C. (1988). Modelling courage: The role of dissent in fostering independence. *European Journal of Social Psychology, 18,* 275–280.

Nemeth, C., Endicott, J., & Wachtler, J. (1976). From the '50s to the '70s: Women in jury deliberations. *Sociometry, 39,* 38–56.

Nemeth, C., & Kwan, J. (1987). Minority influence, divergent thinking, and detection of correct solutions. *Journal of Applied Social Psychology, 17,* 788–799.

Nemeth, C., Mayseless, O., Sherman, J., & Brown, Y. (1990). Exposure to dissent and recall of information. *Journal of Personality and Social Psychology, 58,* 429–437.

Neuberg, S. L. (1989). The goal of forming accurate impressions during social interactions: Attenuating the impact of negative expectancies. *Journal of Personality and Social Psychology, 56,* 374–386.

Neuberg, S. L., & Fiske, S. T. (1987). Motivational influences on impression formation: Outcome dependency, accuracy-driven attention, and individuating processes. *Journal of Personality and Social Psychology, 53,* 431–444.

Neuberg, S. L., Judice, T. N., Virdin, L. M., & Carrillo, M. A. (1993). Perceiver self-presentational goals as moderators of expectancy influences: Ingratiation and the disconfirmation of negative expectancies. *Journal of Personality and Social Psychology, 64,* 409–420.

Newcomb, T. M. (1961). *The acquaintance process.* New York: Holt, Rinehart and Winston.

Newman, L. S. (1993). How individualists interpret behavior: Idiocentrism and spontaneous trait inference. *Social Cognition, 11,* 243–269.

Newman, L. S., & Uleman, J. S. (1989). Spontaneous trait inference. In J. S. Uleman & J. A. Bargh (Eds.), *Unintended thought* (pp. 155–188). New York: Guilford.

Newtson, D. (1974). Dispositional inference from effects of actions: Effects chosen and effects foregone. *Journal of Experimental Social Psychology, 10,* 487–496.

Newtson, D., Hairfield, J., Bloomingdale, J., & Cutino, S. (1987). The structure of action and interaction. *Social Cognition, 5,* 191–237.

Nezlek, J. B. (1993). The stability of social interaction. *Journal of Personality and Social Psychology, 65,* 930–941.

Nezlek, J. B., & Pilkington, C. J. (1994). Perception of risk in intimacy and social participation. *Personal Relationships, 1,* 45–62.

Nieva, V. F., & Gutek, B. A. (1981). *Women and work: A psychological perspective.* New York: Praeger.

Nisbett, R. E. (1993). Violence and U.S. regional culture. *American Psychologist, 48,* 441–449.

Nisbett, R. E., Fong, G. T., Lehman, D. R., & Cheng, P. W. (1987). Teaching reasoning. *Science, 238,* 625–631.

Nisbett, R. E., & Ross, L. (1980). *Human inference: Strategies and shortcomings of social judgment.* Englewood Cliffs, NJ: Prentice-Hall.

Nisbett, R. E., & Schachter, S. (1966). Cognitive manipulation of pain. *Journal of Experimental Social Psychology, 2,* 227–236.

Nisbett, R. E., & Wilson, T. D. (1977). Telling more than we can know: Verbal reports on mental processes. *Psychological Review, 84,* 231–259.

Noel, J. G., Wann, D. L., & Branscombe, N. R. (1995). Peripheral ingroup membership status and public negativity toward outgroups. *Journal of Personality and Social Psychology, 68,* 127–137.

Nolen-Hoeksema, S. (1993). Sex differences in control of depression. In D. M. Wegner & J. W. Pennebaker (Eds.), *Handbook of mental control* (pp. 306–324). Englewood Cliffs, NJ: Prentice-Hall.

Nolen-Hoeksema, S., & Girgus, J. S. (1994). The emergence of gender differences in depression during adolescence. *Psychological Bulletin, 115,* 424–443.

Nolen-Hoeksema, S., & Morrow, J. (1991). A prospective study of depression and posttraumatic stress symptoms after a natural disaster: The 1989 Loma Prieta earthquake. *Journal of Personality and Social Psychology, 61,* 115–121.

Nolen-Hoeksema, S., Parker, L. E., & Larson, J. (1994). Ruminative coping with depressed mood following loss. *Journal of Personality and Social Psychology, 67,* 92–104.

Noller, P., Feeney, J. A., Bonnell, D., & Callan, V. J. (1994). A longitudinal study of conflict in early marriage. *Journal of Social and Personal Relationships, 11,* 233–252.

Noller, P., & Fitzpatrick, M. A. (1990). Marital communication in the eighties. *Journal of Marriage and the Family, 52,* 832–843.

Nosworthy, G. J., & Lindsay, R. C. L. (1990). Does nominal lineup size matter? *Journal of Applied Psychology, 75,* 358–361.

Ofshe, R., & Watters, E. (1994). *Making monsters: False memories, psychotherapy, and sexual hysteria.* New York: Charles Scribner's Sons.

Oggins, J., Veroff, J., & Leber, D. (1993). Perceptions of marital interaction among black and white newlyweds. *Journal of Personality and Social Psychology, 65,* 494–511.

Ogilvy, D. (1985). *Ogilvy on advertising.* New York: Vintage Books.

Ogloff, J. R. P., & Vidmar, N. (1994). The impact of pretrial publicity on jurors: A study to compare the relative effects of television and print media in a child sex abuse case. *Law and Human Behavior, 18,* 507–525.

Ohbuchi, K., & Kambara, T. (1985). Attacker's intent and awareness of outcome, impression management, and retaliation. *Journal of Experimental Social Psychology, 21,* 321–330.

Ohbuchi, K., Kameda, M., & Agarie, N. (1989). Apology as aggression control: Its role in mediating appraisal of and response to harm. *Journal of Personality and Social Psychology, 56,* 219–227

O'Leary, A. (1985). Self-efficacy and health. *Behaviour Research and Therapy, 23,* 437–451.

O'Leary, K. D., Barling, J., Arias, I., Rosenbaum, A., Malone, J., & Tyree, A. (1989). Prevalence and stability of physical aggression between spouses: A longitudinal analysis. *Journal of Consulting and Clinical Psychology, 57,* 263–268.

O'Leary, K. D., & Smith, D. A. (1991). Marital interaction. *Annual Review of Psychology, 42,* 191–212.

Oliner, S. P., & Oliner, P. M. (1988). *The altruistic personality: Rescuers of Jews in Nazi Europe.* New York: Free Press.

Oliver, M. G., & Hyde, J. S. (1993). Gender differences in sexuality: A meta-analysis. *Psychological Bulletin, 114,* 29–51.

Olson, J. M. (1988). Misattribution, preparatory information, and speech anxiety. *Journal of Personality and Social Psychology, 54,* 758–767.

Olson, J. M., Herman, C. P., & Zanna, M. P. (Eds.). (1986). *Relative deprivation and social comparison: The Ontario Symposium* (Vol. 4). Hillsdale, NJ: Erlbaum.

Olson, J. M., & Ross, M. (1988). False feedback about placebo effectiveness: Consequences for the misattribution of speech anxiety. *Journal of Experimental Social Psychology, 24,* 275–281.

Olson, M. (1965). *The logic of collective action.* Cambridge, MA: Harvard University Press.

Olzak, S., & Nagel, J. (1986). *Competitive ethnic relations.* New York: Academic Press.

Omoto, A. M., & Snyder, M. (1995). Sustained helping without obligation: Motivation, longevity of service, and perceived attitude change among AIDS volunteers. *Journal of Personality and Social Psychology, 68,* 671–686.

Ones, D. S., Viswesvaran, C., & Schmidt, F. L. (1993). Comprehensive meta-analysis of integrity test validities: Findings and implications for personnel selection and theories of job performance. *Journal of Applied Psychology, 78,* 679–703.

Orbell, J. M., Dragt, van de A. J. C., & Dawes, R. M. (1988). Explaining discussion-induced cooperation. *Journal of Personality and Social Psychology, 54,* 811–819.

Ormel, J., & Wohlfarth, T. (1991). How neuroticism, long-term difficulties, and life situation change influence psychological distress: A longitudinal model. *Journal of Personality and Social Psychology, 60,* 744–755.

Orne, M. T. (1962). On the social psychology of the psychological experiment: With particular reference to demand characteristics and their implications. *American Psychologist, 17,* 776–783.

O'Rourke, D. F., Houston, B. K., Harris, J. K., & Snyder, C. R. (1988). The Type A behavior pattern: Summary, conclusions, and implications. In B. K. Houston & C. R. Snyder (Eds.), *Type A behavior pattern: Research, theory, and intervention* (pp. 312–334). New York: Wiley.

Orwell, G. (1942). Looking back on the Spanish War. In S. Orwell & I. Angus (Eds.), *The collected essays, journalism and letters of George Orwell: Vol. 2. My country right or left, 1940–1943* (pp. 249–267). New York: Harcourt, Brace & World. (Reprinted in 1968)

Osborn, A. F. (1953). *Applied imagination.* New York: Scribner.

Osgood, C. E. (1962). *An alternative to war or surrender.* Urbana: University of Illinois Press.

Oskamp, S. (1965). Attitudes toward U.S. and Russian actions: A double standard. *Psychological Reports, 16,* 43–46.

Oskamp, S. (Ed.). (1988). *Television as a social issue: Applied social psychology annual* (Vol. 8). Newbury Park, CA: Sage.

Ostrom, T. M., & Sedikides, C. (1992). Out-group homogeneity effects in natural and minimal groups. *Psychological Bulletin, 112,* 536–552.

Ottati, V. C., Riggle, E. J., Wyer, R. S., Schwarz, N., & Kuklin-ski, J. (1989). Cognitive and affective bases of opinion survey responses. *Journal of Personality and Social Psychology, 57,* 404–415.

Otten, C. A., Penner, L. A., & Altabe, M. N. (1991). An examination of therapists' and college students' willingness to help a psychologically distressed person. *Journal of Social and Clinical Psychology, 10,* 102–120.

Overbye, D. (1993, April 26). Who's afraid of the big bad bang? *Time,* p. 74.

Oyserman, D. (1993). The lens of personhood: Viewing the self and others in a multicultural society. *Journal of Personality and Social Psychology, 65,* 993–1009.

Packard, V. (1957). *The hidden persuaders.* New York: Pocket Books.

Paik, H., & Comstock, G. (1994). The effects of television violence on antisocial behavior: A meta-analysis. *Communication Research, 21,* 516–546.

Pallak, S. R. (1983). Salience of a communicator's physical attractiveness and persuasion: A heuristic versus systematic processing interpretation. *Social Cognition, 2,* 158–170.

Palys, T. S. (1986). Testing the common wisdom: The social content of video pornography. *Canadian Psychology, 27,* 22–35.

Park, B. (1986). A method for studying the development of impressions of real people. *Journal of Personality and Social Psychology, 51,* 907–917.

Park, B., & Judd, C. M. (1990). Measures and models of perceived group variability. *Journal of Personality and Social Psychology, 59,* 173–191.

Parkinson, S. (1994). Scientific or ethical quality? *Psychological Science, 5,* 137–138.

Parks, C. D. (1994). The predictive ability of social values in resource dilemmas and public goods games. *Personality and Social Psychology Bulletin, 20,* 431–438.

Parrott, W. G., & Smith, R. H. (1993). Distinguishing the experiences of envy and jealousy. *Journal of Personality and Social Psychology, 64,* 906–920.

Parsons, H. M. (1974). What happened at Hawthorne? *Science, 183,* 922–932.

Partridge, A., & Eldridge, W. B. (1974). *The second circuit sentencing study: A report to the judges of the second circuit.* Washington, DC: Federal Judicial Center.

Patrick, C. J., & Iacono, W. G. (1991). Validity of the control question polygraph test: The problem of sampling bias. *Journal of Applied Psychology, 76,* 229–238.

Patterson, G. R. (1984). Siblings: Fellow travelers in coercive family processes. In R. J. Blanchard & D. C. Blanchard (Eds.), *Advances in the study of aggression* (Vol. 1, pp. 173–215). New York: Academic Press.

Patterson, G. R. (1986). Performance models for antisocial boys. *American Psychologist, 41,* 432–444.

Patterson, M. L. (1983). *Nonverbal behavior: A functional perspective.* New York: Springer-Verlag.

Paulhus, D., Graf, P., & Van Selst, M. (1989). Attentional load increases the positivity of self-presentation. *Social Cognition, 7,* 389–400.

Paulus, P. B. (1988). *Prison crowding: A psychological perspective.* New York: Springer-Verlag.

Paulus, P. B., & Dzindolet, M. T. (1993). Social influence processes in group brainstorming. *Journal of Personality and Social Psychology, 64,* 575–586.

Paulus, P. B., Dzindolet, M. T., Poletes, G., & Camacho, L. M. (1993). Perception of performance in group brainstorming: The illusion of group productivity. *Personality and Social Psychology Bulletin, 19,* 78–89.

Paulus, P. B., Larey, T. S., & Ortega, A. H. (1995). Performance and perceptions of brainstormers in an organizational setting. *Basic and Applied Social Psychology, 17,* 249–265.

Paunonen, S. V. (1989). Consensus in personality judgments: Moderating effects of target-rater acquaintanceship and behavior observability. *Journal of Personality and Social Psychology, 56,* 823–833.

Paykel, E. S. (1982). *Handbook of affective disorders.* New York: Guilford.

Pedersen, F. A. (1991). Secular trends in human sex ratios: Their influence on individual and family behavior. *Human Nature, 2,* 271–291.

Peek, C. W., Fischer, J. L., & Kidwell, J. S. (1985). Teenage violence toward parents: A neglected dimension of family violence. *Journal of Marriage and the Family, 47,* 1051–1058.

Peirce, K. (1993). Socialization of teenage girls through teen-magazine fiction: The making of a new woman or an old lady? *Sex Roles, 29,* 59–68.

Pelham, B. W., & Swann, W. B., Jr. (1989). From self-conceptions to self-worth: The sources and structure of self-esteem. *Journal of Personality and Social Psychology, 57,* 672–680.

Pendry, L. F., & Macrae, C. N. (1994). Stereotypes and mental life: The case of the motivated but thwarted tactician. *Journal of Experimental Social Psychology, 30,* 303–325.

Pennebaker, J. W. (1989). Confession, inhibition, and disease. In L. Berkowitz (Ed.), *Advances in experimental social psychology* (Vol. 22, pp. 211–244). San Diego: Academic Press.

Pennebaker, J. W. (1990). *Opening up.* New York: Morrow.

Pennebaker, J. W., Colder, M., & Sharp, L. K. (1990). Accelerating the coping process. *Journal of Personality and Social Psychology, 58,* 528–537.

Pennebaker, J. W., Dyer, M. A., Caulkins, R. J., Litowitz, D. L., Ackreman, P. L., Anderson, D. B., & McGraw, K. M. (1979). Don't the girls get prettier at closing time: A country and western application to psychology. *Personality and Social Psychology Bulletin, 5,* 122–125.

Penner, L. A., Dertke, M. C., & Achenbach, C. J. (1973). The "flash" system: A field study of altruism. *Journal of Applied Social Psychology, 3,* 362–370.

Penner, L. A., & Fritzsche, B. A. (1993). Magic Johnson and reactions to people with AIDS: A natural experiment. *Journal of Applied Social Psychology, 23,* 1035–1050.

Pennington, N., & Hastie, R. (1992). Explaining the evidence: Tests of the story model for juror decision making. *Journal of Personality and Social Psychology, 62,* 189–206.

Peplau, L. A., Bikson, T. K., Rook, K. S., & Goodchilds, J. D. (1982). Being old and living alone. In L. A. Peplau & D. Perlman (Eds.), *Loneliness: A sourcebook of current theory, research, and therapy* (pp. 327–347). New York: Wiley.

Peplau, L. A., Russell, D., & Heim, M. (1979). The experience of loneliness. In I. Frieze, D. Bar-Tal, & J. Carroll (Eds.), *New approaches to social problems: Applications of attribution theory* (pp. 53–78). San Francisco: Jossey-Bass.

Perdue, C. W., Dovidio, J. F., Gurtman, M. B., & Tyler, R. B. (1990). Us and them: Social categorization and the process of intergroup bias. *Journal of Personality and Social Psychology, 59,* 475–486.

Perdue, C. W., & Gurtman, M. B. (1990). Evidence for the automaticity of ageism. *Journal of Experimental Social Psychology, 26,* 199–216.

Perlman, D., & Oskamp, S. (1971). The effects of picture context and exposure frequency on evaluations of negroes and whites. *Journal of Experimental and Social Psychology, 7,* 503–514.

Perlman, D., & Peplau, L. A. (1981). Toward a social psychology of loneliness. In S. Duck & R. Gilmour (Eds.), *Personal relationships, 3: Personal relationships in disorder* (pp. 31–56). New York: Academic Press.

Perrett, D. I., May, K. A., & Yoshikawa, S. (1994). Facial shape and judgments of female attractiveness. *Nature, 368,* 239–242.

Perry, N. W., & Wrightsman, L. S. (1991). *The child witness: Legal issues and dilemmas.* Newbury Park, CA: Sage.

Peters, L. H., Hartke, D. D., & Pohlmann, J. T. (1985). Fiedler's contingency theory of leadership: An application of the meta-analytic procedures of Schmidt and Hunter. *Psychological Bulletin, 97,* 274–285.

Peters, T. J., & Waterman, R. H. (1982). *In search of excellence: Lessons from America's best-run companies.* New York: Warner.

Peterson, C., & Seligman, M. E. P. (1987). Explanatory style and illness. *Journal of Personality, 55,* 237–265.

Peterson, C., Seligman, M. E. P., & Vaillant, G. E. (1988). Pessimistic explanatory style is a risk factor for physical illness: A thirty-five-year longitudinal study. *Journal of Personality and Social Psychology, 55,* 23–27.

Peterson, R. R., & Gerson, K. (1992). Determinants of responsibility for child care arrangements among dual-earner couples. *Journal of Marriage and the Family, 54,* 527–536.

Pettigrew, T. F. (1969). Racially separate or together? *Journal of Social Issues, 25,* 43–69.

Pettigrew, T. F., & Martin, J. (1987). Shaping the organizational context for black American inclusion. *Journal of Social Issues, 43,* 41–78.

Petty, R. E., & Cacioppo, J. T. (1983). The role of bodily responses in attitude measurement and change. In J. Cacioppo & R. Petty (Eds.), *Social psychophysiology: A sourcebook* (pp. 51–101). New York: Guilford.

Petty, R. E., & Cacioppo, J. T. (1984). The effects of involvement on response to argument quantity and quality: Central and peripheral routes to persuasion. *Journal of Personality and Social Psychology, 46,* 69–81.

Petty, R. E., & Cacioppo, J. T. (1986). *Communication and persuasion: Central and peripheral routes to attitude change.* New York: Springer-Verlag.

Petty, R. E., & Cacioppo, J. T. (1990). Involvement and persuasion: Tradition versus integration. *Psychological Bulletin, 107,* 367–374.

Petty, R. E., Cacioppo, J. T., & Goldman, R. (1981a). Personal involvement as a determinant of argument-based persuasion. *Journal of Personality and Social Psychology, 41,* 847–855.

Petty, R. E., Cacioppo, J. T., & Heesacker, M. (1981b). Effects of rhetorical questions on persuasion: A cognitive response analysis. *Journal of Personality and Social Psychology, 40,* 432–440.

Petty, R. E., & Krosnick, J. A. (Eds.) (1993). *Attitude strength: Antecedents and consequences.* Hillsdale, NJ: Erlbaum.

Petty, R. E., Schumann, D. W., Richman, S. A., & Strathman, A. J. (1993). Positive mood and persuasion: Different roles for affect under high- and low-elaboration conditions. *Journal of Personality and Social Psychology, 64,* 5–20.

Pfau, M., & Burgoon, M. (1988). Inoculation in political campaign communication. *Human Communication Research, 15,* 91–111.

Pfau, M., Kenski, H. C., Nitz, M., & Sorenson, J. (1990). Efficacy of inoculation strategies in promoting resistance to political attack messages: Application to direct mail. *Communication Monographs, 57,* 25–43.

Phillips, A. P., & Dipboye, R. L. (1989). Correlational tests of predictions from a process model of the interview. *Journal of Applied Psychology, 74,* 41–52.

Phillips, D. P. (1983). The impact of mass media violence on U.S. homicides. *American Sociological Review, 48,* 560–568.

Phillips, D. P. (1986). Natural experiments on the effects of mass media violence on fatal aggression: Strength and weaknesses of a new approach. In L. Berkowitz (Ed.), *Advances in experimental social psychology* (Vol. 19, pp. 207–250). New York: Academic Press.

Phillips, R. (1988). *Putting asunder: A history of divorce in Western society.* Cambridge, England: Cambridge University Press.

Pietromonaco, P. R., & Rook, K. S. (1987). Decision style in depression: The contribution of perceived risk versus benefits. *Journal of Personality and Social Psychology, 52,* 399–408.

Pietromonaco, P. R., Rook, K. S., & Lewis, M. A. (1992). Accuracy in perceptions of interpersonal interaction: Effects of dysphoria, friendship, and similarity. *Journal of Personality and Social Psychology, 63,* 247–259.

Piliavin, J. A., Dovidio, J. F., Gaertner, S. S., & Clark, R. D., III. (1981). *Emergency intervention.* New York: Academic Press.

Pilisuk, M., Montgomery, M. B., Parks, S. H., & Acredolo, C. (1993). Loss of control, life stress, and social networks: Gender differences in health status of the elderly. *Sex Roles, 28,* 147–166.

Piña, D. L., & Bengtson, V. L. (1993). The division of household labor and wives' happiness: Ideology, employment and perceptions of support. *Journal of Marriage and the Family, 55,* 901–912.

Pines, A., & Aronson, E. (1983). Antecedents, correlates, and consequences of sexual jealousy. *Journal of Personality, 51,* 108–136.

Pittman, T. S. (1975). Attribution of arousal as a mediator of dissonance reduction. *Journal of Experimental Social Psychology, 11,* 53–63.

Pittman, T. S., & Heller, J. F. (1987). Social motivation. *Annual Review of Psychology, 38,* 461–489.

Planalp, S., & Benson, A. (1992). Friends' and acquaintances' conversations I: Perceived differences. *Journal of Social and Personal Relationships, 9,* 483–506.

Platz, S. J., & Hosch, H. M. (1988). Cross-racial/ethnic eyewitness identification: A field study. *Journal of Applied Social Psychology, 18,* 972–984.

Pliner, P., & Chaiken, S. (1990). Eating, social motives, and self-presentation in women and men. *Journal of Experimental Social Psychology, 26,* 240–254.

Pliner, P., Chaiken, S., & Flett, G. L. (1990). Gender differences in concern with body weight and physical appearance over the life span. *Personality and Social Psychology Bulletin, 16,* 263–273.

Plomin, R., & Fulker, D. W. (1987). Behavioral genetics and development in early adolescence. In R. M. Lerner & T. T. Foch (Eds.), *Biological-psychosocial interactions in early adolescence* (pp. 63–94). Hillsdale, NJ: Erlbaum.

Plomin, R., Nitz, K., & Rowe, D. C. (1990). In M. Lewis & S. Miller (Eds.), *Handbook of developmental psychopathology* (pp. 199–133). New York: Plenum Press.

Plous, S. (1989). Thinking the unthinkable: The effects of anchoring on likelihood estimates of nuclear war. *Journal of Applied Social Psychology, 19,* 67–91.

Plous, S. (1991). Biases in the assimilation of technological breakdowns: Do accidents make us safer? *Journal of Applied Social Psychology, 21,* 1058–1082.

Podlesny, J. A., & Raskin, D. C. (1977). Physiological measures and the detection of deception. *Psychological Bulletin, 84,* 782–799.

Polivy, J., Garner, D. M., & Garfinkel, P. E. (1986). Causes and consequences of the current preference for thin female physiques. In C. P. Herman, M. P. Zanna, & E. T. Higgins (Eds.), *The Ontario Symposium: Vol. 3. Physical appearance, stigma, and social behavior* (pp. 89–112). Hillsdale, NJ: Erlbaum.

Poole, D. A., & White, L. T. (1991). Effects of question repetition on the eyewitness testimony of children and adults. *Developmental Psychology, 27,* 975–986.

Poppen, P. J., & Segal, N. J. (1988). The influence of sex and sex role orientation on sexual coercion. *Sex Roles, 19,* 689–701.

Porter, N., Geis, F. L., Cooper, E., & Newman, E. (1985). Androgyny and leadership in mixed-sex groups. *Journal of Personality and Social Psychology, 49,* 808–823.

Povinelli, D. J., Rulf, A. B., & Bierschwale, D. T. (1994). Absence of knowledge attribution and self-recognition in young chimpanzees. *Journal of Comparative Psychology, 108,* 74–80.

Powell, G. N. (1987). The effects of sex and gender on recruitment. *Academy of Management Review, 12,* 731–743.

Powell, M. C., & Fazio, R. M. (1984). Attitude accessibility as a function of repeated attitudinal expression. *Personality and Social Psychology Bulletin, 10,* 139–148.

Pozo, C., Carver, C. S., Wellens, A. R., & Scheier, M. F. (1991). Social anxiety and social perception: Construing others' reactions to the self. *Personality and Social Psychology Bulletin, 17,* 355–362.

Pratap, A. (1990, August 13). "Romance and a little rape." *Time,* p. 69.

Pratkanis, A., & Aronson, E. (1992). *Age of propaganda: The everyday use and abuse of persuasion.* San Francisco: Freeman.

Pratkanis, A. R. (1989). The cognitive representation of attitudes. In A. R. Pratkanis, S. J. Breckler, & A. G. Greenwald (Eds.) *Attitude structure and function* (pp. 71–93). Hillsdale, NJ: Erlbaum.

Pratkanis, A. R. (1992). The cargo-cult science of subliminal persuasion. *Skeptical Inquirer, 16,* 260–272.

Pratkanis, A. R., Eskenazi, J., & Greenwald, A. G. (1994). What you expect is what you believe (but not necessarily what you get): A test of the effectiveness of subliminal self-help audiotapes. *Basic and Applied Social Psychology, 15,* 251–276.

Pratkanis, A. R., Greenwald, A. G., Leippe, M. R., & Baumgardner, M. H. (1988). In search of reliable persuasion effects: III. The sleeper effect is dead. Long live the sleeper effect. *Journal of Personality and Social Psychology, 54,* 203–218.

Pratkanis, A. R., & Turner, M. E. (1994). Nine principles of successful affirmative action: Mr. Branch Rickey, Mr. Jackie Robinson, and the integration of baseball. *Nine: A Journal of Baseball History and Social Policy Perspectives, 3,* 36–65.

Pratto, F., & Bargh, J. A. (1991). Stereotyping based on apparently individuating information: Trait and global components of sex stereotypes under attention overload. *Journal of Experimental Social Psychology, 27,* 26–47.

Pratto, F., & John, O. P. (1991). Automatic vigilance: The attention-grabbing power of negative social information. *Journal of Personality and Social Psychology, 61,* 380–391.

Prentice, D. A. (1990). Familiarity and differences in self- and other-representations. *Journal of Personality and Social Psychology, 59,* 369–383.

Prentice, D. A., & Miller, D. T. (1993). Pluralistic ignorance and alcohol use on campus: Some consequences of misperceiving the social norm. *Journal of Personality and Social Psychology, 64,* 243–256.

Prentice, D. A., Miller, D. T., & Lightdale, J. R. (1994). Asymmetries in attachments to groups and to their members: Distinguishing between common-identity and common-bond groups. *Personality and Social Psychology Bulletin, 20,* 484–493.

Prentice-Dunn, S., & Rogers, R. W. (1980). Effects of deindividuating situational cues and aggressive models on subjective deindividuation and aggression. *Journal of Personality and Social Psychology, 39,* 104–113.

Prentice-Dunn, S., & Rogers, R. W. (1982). Effects of public and private self-awareness on deindividuation and aggression. *Journal of Personality and Social Psychology, 43,* 503–513.

Prentice-Dunn, S., & Rogers, R. W. (1983). Deindividuation in aggression. In R. G. Geen & E. I. Donnerstein (Eds.), *Aggression: Theoretical and empirical reviews: Vol. 2. Issues in research* (pp. 155–171). New York: Academic Press.

President's Commission on Law Enforcement and Administration of Justice (1967). *The challenge of crime in a free society.* Washington, DC: U.S. Government Printing Office.

Price, R. H. (1992). Psychosocial impact of job loss on individuals and families. *Current Directions in Psychological Science, 1,* 9–11.

Prins, K. S., Buunk, B. P., & VanYperen, N. W. (1993). Equity, normative disapproval, and extramarital relationships. *Journal of Social and Personal Relationships, 10,* 39–53.

Proctor, R. C., & Eckerd, W. M. (1976). *"Toot-Toot"* or spectator sports. Psychological and therapeutic implications. *American Journal of Sports Medicine, 4,* 78–83.

Prud'Homme, A. (1991, March 25). Police brutality! *Time,* pp. 16–18.

Pruitt, D. G. (1981). *Negotiation behavior.* New York: Academic Press.

Pruitt, D. G., & Carnevale, P. J. (1993). *Negotiation in social conflict.* Pacific Grove, CA: Brooks/Cole.

Pruitt, D. G., & Kressel, K. (1985). The mediation of social conflict: An introduction. *Journal of Social Issues, 41*(2), 1–10.

Pryor, J. B., & Merluzzi, T. V. (1985). The role of expertise in processing social interaction scripts. *Journal of Experimental Social Psychology, 21,* 362–379.

Psychological Inquiry. (1995), *6,* #1.

Ptacek, J. T., Smith, R. E., & Dodge, K. L. (1994). Gender differences in coping with stress: When stressor and appraisals do not differ. *Personality and Social Psychology Bulletin, 20,* 421–430.

Purcell, P., & Stewart, L. (1990). Dick and Jane in 1989. *Sex Roles, 22,* 177–185.

Pyszczynski, T., & Greenberg, J. (1992). *Hanging on and letting go.* New York: Springer-Verlag.

Qualter, T. H. (1962). *Propaganda and psychological warfare.* New York: Random House.

Quattrone, G. A. (1986). On the perception of a group's variability. In S. Worchel & W. G. Austin (Eds.), *Psychology of intergroup relations* (2nd ed.). Chicago: Nelson Hall.

Quattrone, G. A., & Jones, E. E. (1980). The perception of variability within ingroups and outgroups: Implications for the law of small numbers. *Journal of Personality and Social Psychology, 38,* 141–152.

Radecki-Bush, C., Farrell, A. D., & Bush, J. P. (1993). Predicting jealous responses: The influence of adult attachment and depression on threat appraisal. *Journal of Social and Personal Relationships, 10,* 569–588.

Rafaeli, A., & Klimoski, R. J. (1983). Predicting sales success through handwriting analysis: An evaluation of the effects of training and handwriting sample context. *Journal of Applied Psychology, 68,* 212–217.

Ragins, B. R., & Sundstrom, E. (1989). Gender and power in organizations: A longitudinal perspective. *Psychological Bulletin, 105,* 51–88.

Rainville, R. E., & Gallagher, J. G. (1990). Vulnerability and heterosexual attraction. *Sex Roles, 23,* 25–31.

Rajecki, D. W. (1982). *Attitudes.* Sunderland, MA: Sinauer.

Ramírez, E., Maldonado, A., & Martos, R. (1992). Attributions modulate immunization against learned helplessness in humans. *Journal of Personality and Social Psychology, 62,* 139–146.

Rapoport, A., Bornstein, G., & Erev, I. (1989). Intergroup competition for public goods: Effects of unequal resources and relative group size. *Journal of Social and Personality Psychology, 56,* 748–756.

Raskin, D. C. (1986). The polygraph in 1986: Scientific, professional, and legal issues surrounding application and acceptance of polygraph evidence. *Utah Law Review,* 29–74.

Read, S. J. (1987). Constructing causal scenarios: A knowledge structure approach to causal reasoning. *Journal of Personality and Social Psychology, 52,* 288–302.

Redmond, M. R., Mumford, M. D., & Teach, R. (1993). Putting creativity to work: Effects of leader behavior on subordinate creativity. *Organizational Behavior and Human Decision Processes, 55,* 120–151.

Reed, G. M., Taylor, S. E., & Kemeny, M. E. (1993). Perceived control and psychological adjustment in gay men with AIDS. *Journal of Applied Social Psychology, 23,* 791–824.

Reeder, G. D. (1993). Trait-behavior relations and dispositional inference. *Personality and Social Psychology Bulletin, 19,* 586–593.

Reeder, G. D. & Brewer, M. B. (1979). A schematic model of dispositional attribution in interpersonal perception. *Psychological Review, 86,* 61–79.

Regan, D. T. (1971). Effects of a favor and liking on compliance. *Journal of Experimental Social Psychology, 7,* 627–639.

Regan, D. T., & Kilduff, M. (1988). Optimism about elections: Dissonance reduction at the ballot box. *Political Psychology, 9,* 101–107.

Reicher, S. D. (1984). The St. Pauls' riot: An explanation of the limits of crowd action in terms of a social identity model. *European Journal of Social Psychology, 14,* 1–21.

Reicher, S., & Levine, M. (1994). On the consequences of deindividuation manipulations for the strategic communication of self: Identifiability and the presentation of social identity. *European Journal of Social Psychology, 24,* 511–524.

Reifman, A., Klein, J. G., & Murphy, S. T. (1989). Self-monitoring and age. *Psychology and Aging, 4,* 245–246.

Reik, T. (1944). A psychologist looks at love. In T. Reik (Ed.), *Of love and lust* (pp. 1–194). New York: Farrar, Straus and Cudahy. (Reprinted in 1957)

Reis, H. T., & Wheeler, L. (1991). Studying social interaction with the Rochester Interaction Record. In M. P. Zanna (Ed.), *Advances in experimental social psychology* (Vol. 24, pp. 269–318). San Diego: Academic Press.

Reis, H. T., Wilson, I. M., Monestere, C., Bernstein, S., Clark, K., Seidl, E., Franco, M., Gioioso, E., Freeman, L., & Radoane, K. (1990). What is smiling is beautiful and good. *European Journal of Social Psychology, 20,* 259–267.

Reisenzein, R. (1983). The Schachter theory of emotion: Two decades later. *Psychological Bulletin, 94,* 239–264.

Remley, A. (1988, October). The great parental value shift: From obedience to independence. *Psychology Today, 56–59.*

Remondet, J. H., Hansson, R. O., Rule, B., & Winfrey, G. (1987). Rehearsal for widowhood. *Journal of Social and Clinical Psychology, 5,* 285–297.

Reno, R. R., Cialdini, R. B., & Kallgren, C. A. (1993). The trans-situational influence of norms. *Journal of Personality and Social Psychology, 64,* 104–112.

Repetti, R. L., Matthews, K. A., & Waldron, I. (1989). Employment and women's health: Effects of paid employment on women's mental and physical health. *American Psychologist, 44,* 1394–1401.

Report of the Presidential Commission on the Space Shuttle Challenger Accident. (1986, June 6). Washington, D.C., U.S. Government Printing Office.

Review Panel on Coronary-Prone Behavior and Coronary Heart Disease (1981). Coronary-prone behavior and coronary heart disease: A critical review. *Circulation, 63,* 1199–1215.

Rhodes, N., & Wood, W. (1992). Self-esteem and intelligence affect influenceability: The mediating role of message reception. *Psychological Bulletin, 111,* 156–171.

Rhodewalt, F. (1990). Self-handicappers: Individual differences in the preference for anticipatory, self-protective acts. In R. L. Higgins, C. R. Synder, & S. Berglas (Eds.), *Self-handicapping: The paradox that isn't,* pp. 69–106. New York: Plenum.

Rhodewalt, F., & Agustsdottir, S. (1986). Effects of self-presentation on the phenomenal self. *Journal of Personality and Social Psychology, 50,* 47–55.

Rhodewalt, F., Morf, C., Hazlett, S., & Fairfield, M. (1991). Self-handicapping: The role of discounting and augmentation in the preservation of self-esteem. *Journal of Personality and Social Psychology, 61,* 122–131.

Rice, M. E., & Grusec, J. E. (1975). Saying and doing: Effects on observer performance. *Journal of Personality and Social Psychology, 32,* 584–593.

Rich, M. K., & Cash, T. F. (1993). The American image of beauty: Media representations of hair color for four decades. *Sex Roles, 29,* 113–124.

Richardson, D. R., & Hammock, G. S. (1991). Alcohol and acquaintance rape. In A. Parrot & L. Bechofer (Eds.), *Acquaintance rape: The hidden crime* (pp. 83–95). New York: Wiley.

Ringelmann, M. (1913). Recherches sur les moteurs animés: Travail de l'homme. *Annales de l'Institut National Agronomique, 2e série, tom XII,* 1–40.

Rippetoe, P. A., & Rogers, R. W. (1987). Effects of components of protection-motivation theory on adaptive and maladaptive coping with a health threat. *Journal of Personality and Social Psychology, 52,* 596–604.

Riskind, J. H., Rholes, W. S., Brannon, A. M., & Burdick, C. A. (1987). Attributions and expectations: A confluence of vulnerabilities in mild depression in a college student population. *Journal of Personality and Social Psychology, 52,* 349–354.

Robinson, I., Ziss, K., Ganza, B., Katz, S, & Robinson, E. (1991). Twenty years of the sexual revolution, 1965–1985: An update. *Journal of Marriage and the Family, 53,* 216–220.

Rodin, J. (1985). The application of social psychology. In G. Lindzey & E. Aronson (Eds.), *Handbook of social psychology* (Vol. 2, 3rd ed., pp. 805–881). New York: Random House.

Rodin, J., & Langer, E. J. (1977). Long-term effects of a control-relevant intervention with the institutionalized aged. *Journal of Personality and Social Psychology, 35,* 897–902.

Rodin, J., Rennert, K., & Solomon, S. L. (1980). Intrinsic motivation for control: Fact or fiction. In A. Baum & J. E. Singer (Eds.), *Advances in environmental psychology: Vol. 2. Applications of personal control* (pp. 131–148). Hillsdale, NJ: Erlbaum.

Rodin, M. J., Price, J. M., Bryson, J. B., & Sanchez, F. J. (1990). Asymmetry in prejudice attribution. *Journal of Experimental Social Psychology, 26,* 481–504.

Roese, N. J., & Jamieson, D. W. (1993). Twenty years of bogus pipeline research: A critical review and meta-analysis. *Psychological Bulletin, 114,* 363–375.

Roese, N. J., & Olson, J. M. (1994). Attitude importance as a function of repeated attitude expression. *Journal of Experimental Social Psychology, 30,* 39–51.

Roethlisberger, F. J., & Dickson, W. J. (1939). *Management and the worker.* Cambridge, MA: Harvard University Press.

Rofé, Y. (1984). Stress and affiliation: A utility theory. *Psychological Review, 91,* 235–250.

Rogers, M., Miller, N., Mayer, F. S., & Duval, S. (1982). Personal responsibility and salience of the request for help: Determinants of the relation between negative affect and helping behavior. *Journal of Personality and Social Psychology, 43,* 956–970.

Rogers, R. G. (1995). Marriage, sex, and mortality. *Journal of Marriage and the Family, 57,* 515–526.

Rogers, R. W. (1983). Cognitive and psychological processes in fear appeals and attitude change: A revised theory of protection motivation. In J. Cacioppo & R. Petty (Eds.), *Social psychophysiology: A sourcebook* (pp. 153–176). New York: Guilford.

Rogers, R. W., & Mewborn, R. C. (1976). Fear appeals and attitude change: Effects of a threat's noxiousness, probability of occurrence, and the efficacy of coping responses. *Journal of Personality and Social Psychology, 34,* 54–61.

Rogers, R. W., & Prentice-Dunn, S. (1981). Deindividuation and anger-mediated interracial aggression: Unmasking regressive racism. *Journal of Personality and Social Psychology, 41,* 63–73.

Rogers, T. B., Kuiper, N. A., & Kirker, W. S. (1977). Self-reference and the encoding of personal information. *Journal of Personality and Social Psychology, 35,* 677–688.

Rogler, L. H., Cortes, D. E., & Malgady, R. G. (1991). Acculturation and mental health status among Hispanics: Convergence and new directions for research. *American Psychologist, 46,* 585–597.

Rohrer, J. H., Baron, S. H., Hoffman, E. L., & Swander, D. V. (1954). The stability of autokinetic judgments. *Journal of Abnormal and Social Psychology, 49,* 595–597.

Romzek, B. S., & Dubnick, M. J. (1987). Accountability in the public sector: Lessons from the Challenger tragedy. *Public Administration Review, 47,* 227–238.

Rook, K. S. (1984). The negative side of social interaction: Impact on psychological well-being. *Journal of Personality and Social Psychology, 46,* 1097–1108.

Rook, K. S. (1987). Reciprocity of social exchange and social satisfaction among older women. *Journal of Personality and Social Psychology, 52,* 145–154.

Rook, K. S., Pietromonaco, P. R., & Lewis, M. A. (1994). When are dysphoric individuals distressing to others and vice versa? Effects of friendship, similarity, and interaction task. *Journal of Personality and Social Psychology, 67,* 548–559.

Rose, S., & Frieze, I. H. (1993). Young singles' contemporary dating scripts. *Sex Roles, 28,* 499–509.

Rosen, S. (1983). Perceived inadequacy and help-seeking. In B. M. DePaulo, A. Nadler, & J. D. Fisher (Eds.), *New directions in helping: Vol. 2. Help-Seeking* (pp. 73–107). New York: Academic Press.

Rosen, S., Tomarelli, M. M., Kidda, M. L., Jr., & Medvin, N. (1986). Effects of motive for helping, recipient's inability to reciprocate, and sex on devaluation of the recipient's competence. *Journal of Personality and Social Psychology, 50,* 729–736.

Rosenbaum, M. E. (1986). The repulsion hypothesis: On the nondevelopment of relationships. *Journal of Personality and Social Psychology, 51,* 1156–1166.

Rosenberg, M. (1965). *Society and the adolescent self-image.* Princeton, NJ: Princeton University Press.

Rosener, J. B. (1990). Ways women lead. *Harvard Business Review, 68,* 119–125.

Rosenfeld, J. P. (1995). Alternative views of Bashore and Rapp's (1993) alternatives to traditional polygraphy: A critique. *Psychological Bulletin, 117,* 159–166.

Rosenfield, D., Folger, R., & Adelman, H. F. (1980). When rewards reflect competence: A qualification of the overjustification effect. *Journal of Personality and Social Psychology, 39,* 368–376.

Rosenhan, D. L. (1970). The natural socialization of altruistic autonomy. In J. R. Macaulay & L. Berkowitz (Eds.), *Altruism and helping behavior* (pp. 251–268). New York: Academic Press.

Rosenhan, D. L., Salovey, P., & Hargis, K. (1981). The joys of helping: Focus of attention mediates the impact of positive affect on altruism. *Journal of Personality and Social Psychology, 40,* 899–905.

Rosenman, R. H., Brand, R. J., Jenkins, C. D., Friedman, M., Strau, R., & Wurm, M. (1975). Coronary heart disease in the Western Collaborative Group Study: Final follow-up experience of 8 1/2 years. *Journal of the American Medical Association, 233,* 872–877.

Rosenthal, R. (1966). *Experimenter effects in behavioral research.* New York: Appleton-Century-Crofts.

Rosenthal, R. (1976). *Experimenter effects in behavioral research.* New York: Irvington.

Rosenthal, R. (1985). From unconscious experimenter bias to teacher expectancy effects. In J. B. Dusek, V. C. Hall, & W. J. Meyer (Eds.), *Teacher expectancies* (pp. 37–65). Hillsdale, NJ: Erlbaum.

Rosenthal, R. (1991). *Meta-analytic procedures for social research* (2nd ed.). Newbury Park, CA: Sage.

Rosenthal, R. (1994). Science and ethics in conducting, analyzing, and reporting psychological research. *Psychological Science, 5,* 127–134.

Rosenthal, R., & Jacobson, L. (1968). *Pygmalion in the classroom: Teacher expectation and pupils' intellectual development.* New York: Holt, Rinehart and Winston.

Rosnow, R. L., Rotheram-Borus, M. J., Ceci, S. J., Blanck, P. D., & Koocher, G. P. (1993). The institutional review board as a mirror of scientific and ethical standards. *American Psychologist, 48,* 821–826.

Ross, E. A. (1908). *Social psychology: An outline and source book.* New York: Macmillan.

Ross, L. (1977). The intuitive psychologist and his shortcomings: Distortions in the attribution process. In L. Berkowitz (Ed.), *Advances in experimental social psychology* (Vol. 10, pp. 174–221). New York: Academic Press.

Ross, L., Amabile, T. M., & Steinmetz, J. L. (1977a). Social roles, social control, and biases in social-perception processes. *Journal of Personality and Social Psychology, 35,* 485–494.

Ross, L., Bierbrauer, G., & Hoffman, S. (1976). The role of attribution processes in conformity and dissent. *American Psychologist, 31,* 148–157.

Ross, L., Greene, D., & House, P. (1977b). The false consensus phenomenon: An attributional bias in self-perception and social-perception processes. *Journal of Experimental Social Psychology, 13,* 279–301.

Ross, L., Lepper, M. R., & Hubbard, M. (1975). Perseverance in self-perception and social perception: Biased attributional processes in the debriefing paradigm. *Journal of Personality and Social Psychology, 32,* 880–892.

Ross, M. (1989). The relation of implicit theories to the construction of personal histories. *Psychological Review, 96,* 341–357.

Ross, M., McFarland, C., & Fletcher, G. J. O. (1981). The effect of attitude on the recall of personal histories. *Journal of Personality and Social Psychology, 40,* 627–634.

Ross, M., & Sicoly, F. (1979). Egocentric biases in availability and attribution. *Journal of Personality and Social Psychology, 37,* 322–336.

Rossi, P. H. (1990). The old homeless and the new homelessness in historical perspective. *American Psychologist, 45,* 954–959.

Rotenberg, K. J., & Kmill, J. (1992). Perception of lonely and nonlonely persons as a function of individual differences in loneliness. *Journal of Social and Personal Relationships, 9,* 325–330.

Rothbart, M., & Lewis, S. (1988). Inferring category attributes from exemplary attributes: Geometric shapes and social categories. *Journal of Personality and Social Psychology, 55,* 861–872.

Rotton, J., & Frey, J. (1985). Air pollution, weather, and violent crimes: Concomitant time-series analysis of archival data. *Journal of Personality and Social Psychology, 49,* 1207–1220.

Ruback, R. B., & Innes, C. A. (1988). The relevance and irrelevance of psychological research: The example of prison crowding. *American Psychologist, 43,* 683–693.

Ruback, R. B., & Weiner, N. A. (Eds.). (1995). *Interpersonal violent behaviors: Social and cultural aspects.* New York: Springer Publishing.

Rubenowitz, S., Norrgren, F., & Tannenbaum, A. S. (1983). Some social psychological effects of direct and indirect participation in ten Swedish companies. *Organization Studies, 4,* 243–259.

Rubenstein, C. M., & Shaver, P. (1982). *In search of intimacy.* New York: Delacorte.

Rubin, D. C. (Ed.). (1986). *Autobiographical memory.* New York: Cambridge University Press.

Rubin, J. Z. (1994). Models of conflict management. *Journal of Social Issues, 50,* 33–45.

Rubin, J. Z., Kim, S. H., & Peretz, N. M. (1990). Expectancy effects and negotiation. *Journal of Social Issues, 46,* 125–139.

Rubin, J. Z., Provenzano, F. J., & Luria, Z. (1974). The eye of the beholder: Parents' views on sex of newborns. *American Journal of Orthopsychiatry, 44,* 512–519.

Rubin, J. Z., Pruitt, D. G., & Kim, S. H. (1994). *Social conflict: Escalation, stalemate, and settlement.* New York: McGraw-Hill.

Rubin, Z. (1973). *Liking and loving.* New York: Holt, Rinehart and Winston.

Rubin, Z., Hill, C. T., Peplau, L. A., & Dunkel-Schetter, C. (1980). Self-disclosure in dating couples: Sex roles and the ethic of openness. *Journal of Marriage and the Family, 42,* 305–317.

Rubin, Z., & Peplau, L. A. (1975). Who believes in a just world? *Journal of Social Issues, 31*(3), 65–89.

Ruble, D. N., Costanzo, P. R., & Oliveri, M. E. (Eds.). (1992). *The social psychology of mental health: Basic mechanisms and applications.* New York: Guilford.

Rubonis, A. V., & Bickman, L. (1991). Psychological impairment in the wake of disaster: The disaster-psychopathology relationship. *Psychological Bulletin, 109,* 384–399.

Runciman, W. C. (1966). *Relative deprivation and social justice: A study of attitudes to social inequality in twentieth century England.* Berkeley: University of California Press.

Rusbult, C. E. (1983). A longitudinal test of the investment model: The development (and deterioration) of satisfaction and commitment in heterosexual involvement. *Journal of Personality and Social Psychology, 45,* 101–117.

Rusbult, C. E., & Buunk, B. P. (1993). Commitment processes in close relationships: An interdependence analysis. *Journal of Social and Personal Relationships, 10,* 175–204.

Rusbult, C. E., & Martz, J. M. (1995). Remaining in an abusive relationship: An investment model analysis of nonvoluntary dependence. *Personality and Social Psychology Bulletin, 21,* 558–571.

Rusbult, C. E., Verette, J., Whitney, G. A., Stovik, L. K., & Lipkus, I. (1991). Accommodation processes in close relationships: Theory and preliminary empirical evidence. *Journal of Personality and Social Psychology, 60,* 53–78.

Ruscher, J. B., & Fiske, S. T. (1990). Interpersonal competition can cause individuating processes. *Journal of Personality and Social Psychology, 58,* 832–843.

Ruscher, J. B., Fiske, S. T., Miki, H., & Van Manen, S. (1991). Individuating processes in competition: Interpersonal versus intergroup. *Personality and Social Psychology Bulletin, 17,* 595–605.

Rushton, J. P. (1981). The altruistic personality. In J. P. Rushton & R. M. Sorrentino (Eds.), *Altruism and helping behavior: Social, personality, and developmental perspectives* (pp. 251–266). Hillsdale, NJ: Erlbaum.

Rushton, J. P., Fulker, D. W., Neale, M. C., Nias, D. K. B., & Eysenck, H. J. (1986). Altruism and aggression: The heritability of individual differences. *Journal of Personality and Social Psychology, 50,* 1192–1198.

Rushton, J. P., Russell, R. J. H., & Wells, P. A. (1984). Genetic similarity theory: Beyond kin selection. *Behavior Genetics, 14,* 179–193.

Russell, D. E. H. (1984). *Sexual exploitation.* Beverly Hills, CA: Sage.

Russell, J. A. (1994). Is there universal recognition of emotion from facial expression? A review of cross-cultural studies. *Psychological Bulletin, 115,* 102–141.

Russell, D., Cutrona, C. E., Rose, J., & Yurko, K. (1984). Social and emotional loneliness: An examination of Weiss's typology of loneliness. *Journal of Personality and Social Psychology, 46,* 1313–1321.

Russell, J. A., & Fehr, B. (1994). Fuzzy concepts in a fuzzy hierarchy: Varieties of anger. *Journal of Personality and Social Psychology, 67,* 186–205.

Rutkowski, G. K., Gruder, C. L., & Romer, D. (1983). Group cohesiveness, social norms, and bystander intervention. *Journal of Personality and Social Psychology, 44,* 545–552.

Rutte, C. G., Wilke, H. A. M., & Messick, D. M. (1987). Scarcity or abundance caused by people or the environment as determinants of behavior in the resource dilemma. *Journal of Experimental Social Psychology, 23,* 208–216.

Ruvolo, A., & Markus, H. (1992). Possible selves and performance: The power of self-relevant imagery. *Social Cognition, 9,* 95–124.

Ryan, R. M., Mims, V., & Koestner, R. (1983). Relation of reward contingency and interpersonal context to intrinsic motivation: A review and test using cognitive evaluation theory. *Journal of Personality and Social Psychology, 45,* 736–750.

Sackett, P. R., Burris, L. R., & Callahan, C. (1989). Integrity testing for personnel selection: An update. *Personnel Psychology, 42,* 491–525.

Sackett, P. R., & DuBois, C. L. Z. (1991). Rater-ratee race effects on performance evaluation: Challenging meta-analytic conclusions. *Journal of Applied Psychology, 76,* 873–877.

Sackett, P. R., & Wilson, M. A. (1982). Factors affecting the consensus judgment process in managerial assessment centers. *Journal of Applied Psychology, 67,* 10–17.

Sacks, O. (1985). *The man who mistook his wife for a hat.* New York: Summit.

Sadalla, E. K., Kenrick, D. T., & Bershure, B. (1987). Dominance and heterosexual attraction. *Journal of Personality and Social Psychology, 52,* 730–738.

Saenz, D. S. (1994). Token status and problem-solving deficits: Detrimental effects of distinctiveness and performance monitoring. *Social Cognition, 12,* 61–74.

Safer, M. (1980). Attributing evil to the subject, not the situation: Student reactions to Milgram's film on obedience. *Personality and Social Psychology Bulletin, 6,* 205–209.

Sagar, H. A., & Schofield, J. W. (1980). Racial and behavioral cues in black and white children's perceptions of ambiguously aggressive acts. *Journal of Personality and Social Psychology, 39,* 590–598.

Saks, M. J. (1974). Ignorance of science is no excuse. *Trial, 10,* 18–20.

Saks, M. J. (1977). *Jury verdicts.* Lexington, MA: Lexington Books.

Salovey, P. (1992). Mood-induced focus of attention. *Journal of Personality and Social Psychology, 62,* 699–707.

Salovey, P., & Rodin, J. (1984). Some antecedents and consequences of social-comparison jealousy. *Journal of Personality and Social Psychology, 47,* 780–792.

Salovey, P., & Rodin, J. (1988). Coping with envy and jealousy. *Journal of Social and Clinical Psychology, 7,* 15–33.

Salvemini, N. J., Reilly, R. R., & Smither, J. W. (1993). The influence of rater motivation on assimilation effects and accuracy in performance ratings. *Organizational Behavior and Human Decision Processes, 55,* 41–60.

Samuelson, C. D., Messick, D. M., Rutte, C. G., & Wilke, H. (1984). Individual and structural solutions to resource dilemmas in two cultures. *Journal of Personality and Social Psychology, 47,* 94–104.

Sanders, G. S., & Baron, R. S. (1977). Is social comparison irrelevant for producing choice shifts? *Journal of Experimental Social Psychology, 13,* 303–314.

Sanford, R. N. (1950). *The authoritarian personality.* New York: Harper.

Sanna, L. J. (1992). Self-efficacy theory: Implications for social facilitation and social loafing. *Journal of Personality and Social Psychology, 62,* 774–786.

Sanoff, A. P., & Leight, K. (1994). Altruism is in style. *U.S. News and World Report* (*America's Best Colleges: 1994 College Guide*), pp. 25–28.

Santee, R. T., & Maslach, C. (1982). To agree or not to agree: Personal dissent amid social pressure to conform. *Journal of Personality and Social Psychology, 42,* 690–700.

Santos, M. D., Leve, C., & Pratkanis, A. R. (1994). Hey buddy, can you spare seventeen cents? Mindful persuasion and the pique technique. *Journal of Applied Social Psychology, 24,* 755–764.

Sapolsky, B. S. (1984). Arousal, affect, and the aggression-moderating effect of erotica. In N. M. Malamuth & E. I. Donnerstein (Eds.), *Pornography and sexual aggression* (pp. 85–113). New York: Academic Press.

Sarason, B. R., Sarason, I. G., Hacker, T. A., & Basham, R. B. (1985). Concomitants of social support: Social skills, physical attractiveness and gender. *Journal of Personality and Social Psychology, 49,* 469–480.

Sarason, I. G., Johnson, J. H., & Siegel, J. M. (1978). Assessing the impact of life changes: Development of the Life Experiences Survey. *Journal of Consulting and Clinical Psychology, 46,* 932–946.

Sarason, I. G., Levine, H. M., Basham, R. B., & Sarason, B. R. (1983). Assessing social support: The social support questionnaire. *Journal of Personality and Social Psychology, 44,* 127–139.

Sarason, I. G., & Sarason, B. R. (1984). Life changes, moderators of stress, and health. In A. Baum, S. E. Taylor, & J. E. Singer (Eds.), *Handbook of psychology and health: Vol. 4. Social psychological aspects of health* (pp. 279–299). Hillsdale, NJ: Erlbaum.

Sarason, I. G., Sarason, B. R., & Pierce, G. R. (1994). Social support: Global and relationship-based levels of analysis. *Journal of Social and Personal Relationships, 11,* 295–312.

Sarason, I. G., Sarason, B. R., Pierce, G. R., Shearin, E. N., & Sayers, M. H. (1991). A social learning approach to increasing blood donations. *Journal of Applied Social Psychology, 21,* 896–918.

Sarnoff, I., & Zimbardo, P. (1961). Anxiety, fear, and social affiliation. *Journal of Abnormal and Social Psychology, 62,* 356–363.

Sarwer, D. B., Kalichman, S. C., Johnson, J. R., Early, J., & Ali, S. K. (1993). Sexual aggression and love styles: An exploratory study. *Archives of Sexual Behavior, 22,* 265–275.

Sato, K. (1987). Distribution of the cost of maintaining common resources. *Journal of Experimental Social Psychology, 23,* 19–31.

Saulnier, K., & Perlman, D. (1981). The actor-observer bias is alive and well in prison: A sequel to Wells. *Personality and Social Psychology Bulletin, 7,* 559–564.

Savin, H. B. (1973a). Ethics for gods and men. *Cognition, 2,* 257.

Savin, H. B. (1973b). Professors and psychological researchers: Conflicting values in conflicting roles. *Cognition, 2,* 147–149.

Saxe, L., Dougherty, D., & Cross, T. (1985). The validity of polygraph testing: Scientific analysis and public controversy. *American Psychologist, 38,* 355–366.

Scarr, S. (1988). Race and gender as psychological variables: Social and ethical issues. *American Psychologist, 43,* 56–59.

Schachter, S. (1951). Deviation, rejection, and communication. *Journal of Abnormal and Social Psychology, 46,* 190–207.

Schachter, S. (1959). *The psychology of affiliation: Experimental studies of the sources of gregariousness.* Stanford, CA: Stanford University Press.

Schachter, S. (1964). The interaction of cognitive and physiological determinants of emotional state. In L. Berkowitz

(Ed.), *Advances in experimental social psychology* (Vol. 1, pp. 49–80). New York: Academic Press.

Schachter, S., Hood, D., Gerin, W., Andreasson, P. B., & Rennert, M. (1985). Some causes and consequences of dependence and independence in the stock market. *Journal of Economic Behavior and Organization, 6,* 339–357.

Schachter, S., Ouellette, R., Whittle, B., & Gerin, W. (1987). Effects of trends and of profit or loss on the tendency to sell stock. *Basic and Applied Social Psychology, 8,* 259–271.

Schachter, S., & Singer, J. (1962). Cognitive, social, and physiological determinants of the emotional state. *Psychological Review, 69,* 379–399.

Schachter, S., & Singer, J. (1979). Comments on the Maslach and Marshall-Zimbardo experiments. *Journal of Personality and Social Psychology, 37,* 989–995.

Schafer, R. B., & Keith, P. M. (1980). Equity and depression among married couples. *Social Psychology Quarterly, 43,* 430–435.

Schaller, M. (1991). Social categorization and the formation of social stereotypes: Further evidence for biased information processing in the perception of group-behavior correlations. *European Journal of Social Psychology, 21,* 25–35.

Schaller, M., & Cialdini, R. B. (1988). The economics of empathic helping: Support for a mood management motive. *Journal of Experimental Social Psychology, 24,* 163–181.

Scharfe, E., & Bartholomew, K. (1994). Reliability and stability of adult attachment patterns. *Personal Relationships, 1,* 23–43.

Scheier, M. F., & Carver, C. S. (1983). Two sides of the self: One for you and one for me. In J. Suls and A. G. Greenwald (Eds.), *Psychological perspectives on the self* (Vol. 2, pp. 123–157). Hillsdale, NJ: Erlbaum.

Scheier, M. F., & Carver, C. S. (1987). Dispositional optimism and physical well-being: The influence of generalized outcome expectancies on health. *Journal of Personality, 55,* 169–210.

Scheier, M. F., Carver, C. S., & Bridges, M. W. (1994). Distinguishing optimism from neuroticism (and trait anxiety, self-mastery, and self-esteem): A reevaluation of the Life Orientation Test. *Journal of Personality and Social Psychology, 67,* 1063–1078.

Scheier, M. F., Carver, C. S., & Gibbons, F. X. (1979). Self-directed attention, awareness of bodily states, and suggestibility. *Journal of Personality and Social Psychology, 37,* 1576–1588.

Scheier, M. F., Fenigstein, A., & Buss, A. H. (1974). Self-awareness and physical aggression. *Journal of Experimental Social Psychology, 10,* 264–273.

Scheier, M. F., Matthews, K. A., Owens, J. F., Magovern, G. J., Sr., Lefebrvre, R. C., Abbott, R. A., & Carver, C. S. (1989). Dispositional optimism and recovery from coronary-artery bypass surgery: The beneficial effects on physical and psychological well-being. *Journal of Personality and Social Psychology, 57,* 1024–1040.

Scher, S. J., & Cooper, J. (1989). Motivational basis of dissonance: The singular role of behavioral consequences. *Journal of Personality and Social Psychology, 56,* 899–906.

Schlenker, B. R. (1982). Translating actions into attitudes: An identity-analytic approach to the explanation of social conduct. In L. Berkowitz (Ed.), *Advances in experimental social psychology* (Vol. 15, pp. 193–247). New York: Academic Press.

Schlenker, B. R., & Leary, M. R. (1982). Social anxiety and self-presentation: A conceptualization and model. *Psychological Bulletin, 92,* 641–669.

Schlenker, B. R., & Trudeau, J. V. (1990). The impact of self-presentations on private self-beliefs: Effects of prior self-beliefs and misattribution. *Journal of Personality and Social Psychology, 58,* 22–32.

Schlenker, B. R., & Weigold, M. F. (1992) Interpersonal processes involving impression regulation and management. *Annual Review of Psychology, 43,* 133–168.

Schlenker, B. R., Weigold, M. F., & Hallam, J. R. (1990). self-serving attributions in social context: Effects of self-esteem and social pressure. *Journal of Personality and Social Psychology, 58,* 855–863.

Schmidt, F. L. (1992). What do data really mean? Research findings, meta-analysis, and cumulative knowledge in psychology. *American Psychologist, 47,* 1173–1181.

Schmidt, F. L., Ones, D. S., & Hunter, J. E. (1992). Personnel selection. *Annual Review of Psychology, 43,* 627–670.

Schmidt, G., & Weiner, B. (1988). An attribution-affect-action theory of behavior: Replications of judgments of help-giving. *Personality and Social Psychology Bulletin, 14,* 610–621.

Schneider, D. J. (1973). Implicit personality theory: A review. *Psychological Bulletin, 79,* 294–309.

Schneider, S. G., Taylor, S. E., Hammen, C., Kemeny, M. E., & Dudley, J. (1991). Factors influencing suicide intent in gay and bisexual suicide ideators: Differing models for men with and without human immunodeficiency virus. *Journal of Personality and Social Psychology, 61,* 776–778.

Schoen, R. (1992). First unions and the stability of first marriages. *Journal of Marriage and the Family, 54,* 281–284.

Schoeneman, T. J., & Rubanowitz, D. E. (1985). Attributions in the advice columns: Actors and observers, causes and reasons. *Personality and Social Psychology Bulletin, 11,* 315–325.

Schoenrade, P. A., Batson, C. D., Brandt, J. R., & Loud, R. E., Jr. (1986). Attachment, accountability, and motivation to benefit another not in distress. *Journal of Personality and Social Psychology, 51,* 557–563.

Schofield, J. W. (1982). *Black and white in school: Trust, tension, or tolerance?* New York: Praeger.

Schofield, J. W. (1986). Causes and consequences of the colorblind perspective. In J. F. Dovidio & S. L. Gaertner (Eds.), *Prejudice, discrimination, and racism: Theory and research* (pp. 231–253). Orlando, FL: Academic Press.

Schopler, J. (1970). An attribution analysis of some determinants of reciprocating a benefit. In J. R. Macaulay & L. Berkowitz (Eds.), *Altruism and helping behavior* (pp. 231–238). New York: Academic Press.

Schopler, J., Insko, C. A., Graetz, K. A., Drigotas, S., Smith, V. A., & Dahl, K. (1993). Individual-group discontinuity: Further evidence for mediation by fear and greed. *Personality and Social Psychology Bulletin, 19,* 419–431.

Schriesheim, C. A., Tepper, B. J., & Tetrault, L. A. (1994). Least preferred co-worker score, situational control, and leadership effectiveness: A meta-analysis of contingency model performance predictions. *Journal of Applied Psychology, 79,* 561–573.

Schroeder, D. A., Dovidio, J. F., Sibicky, M. E., Matthews, L. L., & Allen, J. L. (1988). Empathy concern and helping behavior: Egoism or altruism? *Journal of Experimental Social Psychology, 24,* 333–353.

Schroeder, D. A., Penner, L. A., Dovidio, J. F., & Piliavin, J. A. (1995). *The psychology of helping and altruism: Problems and puzzles.* New York: McGraw-Hill.

Schuler, H., Farr, J. L., & Smith, M. (Eds.). (1993). *Personnel selection and assessment: Industrial and organizational perspectives.* Hillsdale, NJ: Erlbaum.

Schuller, R. A., & Vidmar, N. (1992). Battered woman syndrome evidence in the courtroom: A review of the literature. *Law and Human Behavior, 16,* 273–291.

Schulman, J., Shaver, P., Colman, R., Emrick, B., & Christie, R. (1973, May). Recipe for a jury. *Psychology Today*, pp. 37–44, 77, 79–84.

Schultz, N. R., Jr., & Moore, D. (1984). Loneliness: Correlates, attributions, and coping among older adults. *Personality and Social Psychology Bulletin, 10,* 67–77.

Schulz, R. (1976). Effects of control and predictability on the physical and psychological well-being of the institutionalized aged. *Journal of Personality and Social Psychology, 33,* 563–573.

Schulz, R., & Hanusa, B. H. (1978). Long-term effects of control and predictability-enhancing interventions: Findings and ethical issues. *Journal of Personality and Social Psychology, 36,* 1194–1201.

Schuman, H., & Johnson, M. P. (1976). Attitudes and behavior. *Annual Review of Sociology, 2,* 161–207.

Schuman, H., Steeh, C., & Bobo, L. (1985). *Racial attitudes in America.* Cambridge, MA: Harvard University Press.

Schwartz, S. H. (1977). Normative influences on altruism. In L. Berkowitz (Ed.), *Advances in experimental social psychology* (Vol. 10, pp. 221–279). New York: Academic Press.

Schwartz, S. H., & Gottlieb, A. (1980). Bystander anonymity and reaction to emergencies. *Journal of Personality and Social Psychology, 39,* 418–430.

Schwartz, S. H., & Howard, J. A. (1982). Helping and cooperation: A self-based motivational model. In V. J. Derlega & J. Grzelak (Eds.), *Cooperation and helping behavior: Theories and research* (pp. 327–353). New York: Academic Press.

Schwarz, N., Bless, H., & Bohner, G. (1991a). Mood and persuasion: Affective states influence the processing of persuasive communications. In M. P. Zanna (Ed.), *Advances in experimental social psychology* (Vol. 24, pp. 161–199). New York: Academic Press.

Schwarz, N., Hippler, H. J., Deutsch, B., & Strack, F. (1985). Response scales: Effects of category range on reported behavior and comparative judgments. *Public Opinion Quarterly, 49,* 388–395.

Schwarz, N., & Kurz, E. (1989). What's in a picture? The impact of face-ism on trait attribution. *European Journal of Social Psychology, 19,* 311–316.

Schwarz, N., Strack, F., Hilton, D., & Naderer, G. (1991b). Base rates, representativeness, and the logic of conversation: The contextual relevance of "irrelevant" information. *Social Cognition, 9,* 67–84.

Schwarzwald, J., Raz, M., & Zvibel, M. (1979). The applicability of the door-in-the-face technique when established behavioral customs exist. *Journal of Applied Social Psychology, 9,* 576–586.

Scott, L., & O'Hara, M. W. (1993). Self-discrepancies in clinically anxious and depressed university students. *Journal of Abnormal Psychology, 102,* 282–287.

Searcy, E., & Eisenberg, N. (1992). Defensiveness in response to aid from a sibling. *Journal of Personality and Social Psychology, 62,* 422–433.

Sears, D. O. (1986). College sophomores in the laboratory: Influences of a narrow data base on social psychology's view of human nature. *Journal of Personality and Social Psychology, 51,* 515–530.

Sears, D. O. (1994). On separating church and state. *Psychological Science, 5,* 237–239.

Sears, D. O., & Allen, H. M., Jr. (1984). The trajectory of local desegregation controversies and whites' opposition to busing. In N. Miller & M. B. Brewer (Eds.), *Groups in contact: The psychology of desegregation* (pp. 123–151). New York: Academic Press.

Sears, D. O., & Kinder, D. R. (1985). Whites' opposition to busing: On conceptualizing and operationalizing group conflict. *Journal of Personality and Social Psychology, 48,* 1141–1147.

Secord, P. F. (1983). Imbalanced sex ratios: The social consequences. *Personality and Social Psychology Bulletin, 9,* 525–543.

Sedikides, C. (1990). Effects of fortuitously activated constructs versus activated communication goals on person impressions. *Journal of Personality and Social Psychology, 58,* 397–408.

Sedikides, C. (1992). Attentional effects on mood are moderated by chronic self-conception valence. *Personality and Social Psychology Bulletin, 18,* 580–584.

Sedikides, C. (1993). Assessment, enhancement, and verification determinants of the self-evaluation process. *Journal of Personality and Social Psychology, 65,* 317–338.

Sedikides, C., & Anderson, C. A. (1994). Causal perceptions of intertrait relations: The glue that holds person types together. *Personality and Social Psychology Bulletin, 20,* 294–302.

Sedikides, C., & Jackson, J. M. (1990). Social impact theory: A field test of source strength, source immediacy and number of targets. *Basic and Applied Social Psychology, 11,* 273–281.

Segal, N. L. (1993). Twin, sibling, and adoption methods: Tests of evolutionary hypotheses. *American Psychologist, 48,* 943–956.

Segrin, C., & Dillard, J. P. (1992). The interactional theory of depression: A meta-analysis of the research literature. *Journal of Social and Clinical Psychology, 11,* 43–70.

Seligman, C., Bush, M., & Kirsch, K. (1976). Relationship between compliance in the foot-in-the-door paradigm and size of first request. *Journal of Personality and Social Psychology, 33,* 517–520.

Seligman, M. E. P. (1975). *On depression, development, and death.* San Francisco: Freeman.

Seligman, M. E. P., & Maier, S. F. (1967). Failure to escape traumatic shock. *Journal of Experimental Psychology, 74,* 1–9.

"Series killers." (1993, October 25). *Time,* p. 20.

Shaffer, D. R., Smith, J. E., & Tomarelli, M. (1982). Self-monitoring as a determinant of self-disclosure reciprocity during the acquaintance process. *Journal of Personality and Social Psychology, 43,* 163–175.

Shanab, M. E., & Yahya, K. A. (1977). A behavioral study of obedience in children. *Journal of Personality and Social Psychology, 35,* 530–536.

Shanab, M. E., & Yahya, K. A. (1978). A cross cultural study of obedience. *Bulletin of the Psychonomic Society, 11,* 267–269.

Shapiro, D. L., & Brett, J. M. (1993). Comparing three processes underlying judgments of procedural justice: A field study of mediation and arbitration. *Journal of Personality and Social Psychology, 65,* 1167–1177.

Shapiro, P. N., & Penrod, S. (1986). Meta-analysis of facial identification studies. *Psychological Bulletin, 100,* 139–156.

Sharpe, D., Adair, J. G., & Roese, N. J. (1992). Twenty years of deception research: A decline in subjects' trust? *Personality and Social Psychology Bulletin, 18,* 585–590.

Sharpsteen, D. J. (1993). Romantic jealousy as an emotional concept: A prototype analysis. *Journal of Social and Personal Relationships, 10,* 69–82.

Shaver, K. G. (1970). Defensive attribution: Effects of severity and relevance on the responsibility assigned for an accident. *Journal of Personality and Social Psychology, 14,* 101–113.

Shaver, P., & Brennan, K. A. (1992). Attachment styles and the "Big Five" personality traits: Their connections with each other and with romantic relationship outcomes. *Personality and Social Psychology Bulletin, 18,* 536–545.

Shaver, P., Hazan, C., & Bradshaw, D. (1988). Love as attachment: The integration of three behavioral systems. In R. J. Sternberg & M. L. Barnes (Eds.), *The psychology of love* (pp. 68–99). New Haven, CT: Yale University Press.

Shaver, P., & Rubenstein, E. (1980). Childhood attachment experience and adult loneliness. In L. Wheeler (Ed.), *Review of personality and social psychology* (Vol. 1, pp. 42–73). Beverly Hills, CA: Sage.

Shaver, P. R., & Hazan, C. (1993). Adult romantic attachment: Theory and evidence. In D. Perlman & W. H. Jones (Eds.), *Advances in personal relationships* (Vol. 4, pp. 29–70). London: Kingsley.

Shaver, P. R., Wu, S., & Schwartz, J. C. (1992). Cross-cultural similarities and differences in emotion and its representation: A prototype approach. In M. S. Clark (Ed.), *Review of Personality and Social Psychology: Vol. 13. Emotion* (pp. 175–212). Newbury Park, CA: Sage.

Shaw, L. L., Batson, C. D., & Todd, R. M. (1994). Empathy avoidance: Forestalling feeling for another in order to escape the motivational consequences. *Journal of Personality and Social Psychology, 67,* 879–887.

Shaw, M. E. (1954). Some effects of unequal distribution of information upon group performance in various communication nets. *Journal of Abnormal and Social Psychology, 49,* 547–553.

Shefrin, H. M., & Statman, M. (1985). The disposition to sell winners too early and ride losers too long: Theory and evidence. *Journal of Finance, 40,* 777–790.

Shefrin, H. M., & Statman, M. (1986, February). How not to make money in the stock market. *Psychology Today,* pp. 52–57.

Sheldon, W. H. (1954). *Atlas of man: A guide for somatotyping the adult male of all ages.* New York: Harper & Row.

Shell, R. M., & Eisenberg, N. (1992). A developmental model of recipients' reactions to aid. *Psychological Bulletin, 111,* 413–433.

Sheppard, B. H. (1985). Justice is no simple matter: Case for elaborating our model of procedural fairness. *Journal of Personality and Social Psychology, 49,* 953–962.

Sheppard, B. H., Bazerman, M. H., & Lewicki, R. J. (Eds.). (1990). *Research on negotiation in organizations* (Vol. 2). Greenwich, CT: JAI Press.

Sheppard, B. H., Hartwick, J., & Warshaw, P. R. (1988). The theory of reasoned action: A meta-analysis of past research with recommendations for modifications and future research. *Journal of Consumer Research, 15,* 325–343.

Shepperd, J. A. (1993a). Productivity loss in performance groups: A motivation analysis. *Psychological Bulletin, 113,* 67–81.

Shepperd, J. A. (1993b). Student derogation of the Scholastic Aptitude Test: Biases in perceptions and presentations of college board scores. *Basic and Applied Social Psychology, 14,* 455–473.

Shepperd, J. A., & Arkin, R. M. (1991). Behavioral other-enhancement: Strategically obscuring the link between performance and evaluation. *Journal of Personality and Social Psychology, 60,* 79–88.

Sherif, M. (1936). *The psychology of social norms.* New York: Harper.

Sherif, M. (1966). *In common predicament: Social psychology of intergroup conflict and cooperation.* Boston: Houghton Mifflin.

Sherif, M., Harvey, L. J., White, B. J., Hood, W. R., & Sherif, C. W. (1961). *The Robbers Cave experiment: Intergroup conflict and cooperation.* Middletown, CT: Wesleyan University Press. (Reprinted in 1988)

Sherman, L. W. (1992). The influence of criminology on criminal law: Evaluating arrests for misdemeanor domestic violence. *Journal of Criminal Law and Criminology, 83,* 1–145.

Sherman, S. J., Presson, C., & Chassin, L. (1984). Mechanisms underlying the false consensus effect: The special role of threats to the self. *Personality and Social Psychology Bulletin, 10,* 127–138.

Sherrod, D. (1989). The influence of gender on same-sex friendships. In C. Hendrick (Ed.), *Review of personality and social psychology: Vol. 10. Close relationships* (pp. 164–186). Newbury Park, CA: Sage.

Shore, T. H., Shore, L. M., & Thornton, G. C., III. (1992). Construct validity of self- and peer evaluations of performance dimensions in an assessment center. *Journal of Applied Psychology, 77,* 42–54.

Shotland, R. L. (1989). A model of the causes of date rape in developing and close relationships. In C. Hendrick (Ed.), *Review of personality and social psychology: Vol. 10. Close relationships* (pp. 247–270). Newbury Park, CA: Sage.

Shotland, R. L., & Heinold, W. D. (1985). Bystander response to arterial bleeding: Helping skills, the decision-making process, and differentiating the helping response. *Journal of Personality and Social Psychology, 49,* 347–356.

Shotland, R. L., & Straw, M. K. (1976). Bystander response to an assault: When a man attacks a woman. *Journal of Personality and Social Psychology, 34,* 990–999.

Shrauger, J. S., & Schoeneman, T. (1979). Symbolic interactionist view of the self-concept: Through the looking-glass darkly. *Psychological Bulletin, 86,* 549–573.

Shukla, A., & Kapoor, M. (1990). Sex role identity, marital power, and marital satisfaction among middle-class couples in India. *Sex Roles, 22,* 693–706.

Shure, G. H., Meeker, R. J., & Hansford, E. A. (1965). The effectiveness of pacifist strategies in bargaining games. *Journal of Conflict Resolution, 9,* 106–117.

Sieber, J. E., & Stanley, B. (1988). Ethical and professional dimensions of socially sensitive research. *American Psychologist, 43,* 49–55.

Siegel, J. M. (1990). Stressful life events and use of physician services among the elderly: The moderating role of pet ownership. *Journal of Personality and Social Psychology, 58,* 1081–1086.

Siegman, A. W., & Boyle, S. (1993). Voices of fear and anxiety and sadness and depression: The effects of speech rate and loudness on fear and anxiety and sadness and depression. *Journal of Abnormal Psychology, 102,* 430–437.

Siegman, A. W., & Smith, T. W. (1994). *Anger, hostility, and the heart.* Hillsdale, NJ: Erlbaum.

Sigall, H., & Landy, D. (1973). Radiating beauty: The effects of having a physically attractive partner on person perception. *Journal of Personality and Social Psychology, 28,* 218–224.

Sigall, H., & Page, R. (1971). Current stereotypes: A little fading, a little faking. *Journal of Personality and Social Psychology, 18,* 247–255.

Sigelman, L., & Welch, S. (1991). *Black Americans' views of racial inequality: The dream deferred.* New York: Cambridge University Press.

Silka, L. (1989). *Intuitive judgments of change.* New York: Springer-Verlag.

Silverstein, B., Perdue, L., Peterson, B., & Kelly, E. (1986a). The role of the mass media in promoting a thin standard of bodily attractiveness for women. *Sex Roles, 14,* 519–532.

Silverstein, B., Perdue, L., Peterson, B., Vogel, L., & Fantini, D. A. (1986b). Possible causes of the thin standard of bodily attractiveness for women. *The International Journal of Eating Disorders, 5,* 907–916.

Simmons, C. J., Bickart, B. A., & Lynch, J. G. (1993). Capturing and creating public opinion in survey research. *Journal of Consumer Research, 20,* 316–329.

Simons, R. L., Johnson, C., Beaman, J., & Conger, R. D. (1993). Explaining women's double jeopardy: Factors that mediate the association between harsh treatment as a child and violence by a husband. *Journal of Marriage and the Family, 55,* 713–723.

Simonson, I., & Staw, B. W. (1992). Deescalation strategies: A comparison of techniques for reducing commitment to losing courses of action. *Journal of Applied Psychology, 77,* 419–426.

Simpson, J. A. (1987). The dissolution of romantic relationships: Factors involved in relationship stability and emotional distress. *Journal of Personality and Social Psychology, 53,* 683–692.

Simpson, J. A. (1990). Influence of attachment styles on romantic relationships. *Journal of Personality and Social Psychology, 59,* 971–980.

Simpson, J. A., & Gangestad, S. W. (1991). Individual differences in sociosexuality: Evidence for convergent and discriminant validity. *Journal of Personality and Social Psychology, 60,* 870–883.

Simpson, J. A., & Gangestad, S. W. (1992). Sociosexuality and romantic partner choice. *Journal of Personality, 60,* pp. 31–51.

Simpson, J. A., Gangestad, S. W., & Lerma, M. (1990). Perception of physical attractiveness: Mechanisms involved in the maintenance of romantic relationships. *Journal of Personality and Social Psychology, 59,* 1192–1201.

Sinclair, R. C., Hoffman, C., Mark, M. M., Martin, L. M., & Pickering, T. L. (1994). Construct accessibility and the misattribution of arousal: Schachter and Singer revisited. *Psychological Science, 5,* 15–19.

Singelis, T. M. (1994). The measurement of independent and interdependent self-construals. *Personality and Social Psychology Bulletin, 20,* 580–591.

Singer, J. L., & Singer, D. G. (1983). Psychologists look at television: Cognitive, developmental, personality, and social policy implications. *American Psychologist, 38,* 826–834.

Singh, D. (1993). Adaptive significance of female physical attractiveness: Role of waist-to-hip ratio. *Journal of Personality and Social Psychology, 65,* 293–307.

Sistrunk, F., & McDavid, J. W. (1971). Sex variable in conforming behavior. *Journal of Personality and Social Psychology, 17,* 200–207.

Skinner, B. F. (1953). *Science and human behavior.* New York: Macmillan.

Skitka, L. J., & Tetlock, P. E. (1993). Providing public assistance: Cognitive and motivational processes underlying liberal and conservative policy preferences. *Journal of Personality and Social Psychology, 65,* 1205–1223.

Skov, R. B., & Sherman, S. J. (1986). Information-gathering processes: Diagnosticity, hypothesis confirmatory strategies, and perceived hypothesis confirmation. *Journal of Experimental Social Psychology, 22,* 93–121.

Skowronski, J. J., & Carlston, D. E. (1989). Negativity and extremity biases in impression formation: A review of explanations. *Psychology Bulletin, 105,* 131–142.

Slamecka, N. J., & Graff, P. (1978). The generation effect: Delineation of a phenomenon. *Journal of Experimental Psychology: Human Learning and Memory, 4,* 592–604.

Slovic, P., Fischhoff, B., & Lichtenstein, S. (1982). Facts versus fears: Understanding perceived risk. In D. Kahneman, P. Slovic, & A. Tversky (Eds.), *Judgment under uncertainty: Heuristics and biases* (pp. 463–489). New York: Cambridge University Press.

Smeaton, G., Byrne, D., & Murnen, S. K. (1989). The repulsion hypothesis revisited: Similarity irrelevance or dissimilarity bias? *Journal of Personality and Social Psychology, 56,* 54–59.

Smith, C. A. (1991). The self, appraisal, and coping. In C. R. Snyder & D. R. Forsyth (Eds.), *Handbook of social and clinical psychology: The health perspective* (pp. 116–137). New York: Pergamon Press.

Smith, E. R., Becker, M. A., Byrne, D., & Przbyla, D. P. J. (1993). Sexual attitudes of males and females as predictors of interpersonal attraction and marital compatibility. *Journal of Applied Social Psychology, 23,* 1011–1034.

Smith, H. S., & Cohen, L. H. (1993). Self-complexity and reactions to a relationship breakup. *Journal of Social and Clinical Psychology, 12,* 367–384.

Smith, K. D., Keating, J. P., & Stotland, E. (1989). Altruism reconsidered: The effect of denying feedback on a victim's status to empathic witnesses. *Journal of Personality and Social Psychology, 57,* 641–650.

Smith, P. B., & Bond, M. H. (1993). *Social psychology across cultures: Analysis and perspective.* New York: Harvester/Wheatsheaf.

Smith, R., Kim, S. H., & Parrott, W. G. (1988). Envy and jealousy: Semantic problems and experiential distinctions. *Personality and Social Psychology Bulletin, 14,* 401–409.

Smith, S. S., & Richardson, D. (1983). Amelioration of deception and harm in psychological research: The important role of debriefing. *Journal of Personality and Social Psychology, 44,* 1075–1082.

Smith, T. W. (1992). Hostility and health: Current status of a psychosomatic hypothesis. *Health Psychology, 11,* 139–150.

Smith, T. W., & Christensen, A. J. (1992a). Cardiovascular reactivity and interpersonal relations: Psychosomatic processes in social context. *Journal of Social and Clinical Psychology, 11,* 279–301.

Smith, T. W., & Christensen, A. J. (1992b). Hostility, health, and social contexts. In H. S. Friedman (Ed.), *Hostility, coping, and health* (pp. 33–48). Washington, DC: American Psychological Association.

Smith, T. W., Pope, M. K., Rhodewalt, F., & Poulton, J. L. (1989). Optimism, neuroticism, coping, and symptom reports: An alternative interpretation of the Life Orientation Test. *Journal of Personality and Social Psychology, 56,* 640–648.

Smith, T. W., Snyder, C. R., & Perkins, S. C. (1983). The self-serving function of hypochondriacal complaints: Physical symptoms as self-handicapping strategies. *Journal of Personality and Social Psychology, 44,* 787–797.

Smith, V. L. (1991). Prototypes in the courtroom: Lay representations of legal concepts. *Journal of Personality and Social Psychology, 61,* 857–872.

Smith, V. L., & Kassin, S. M. (1993). Effects of the dynamite charge on the deliberations of deadlocked mock juries. *Law and Human Behavior, 17,* 625–643.

Smither, J. W., Reilly, R. R., & Buda, R. (1988). Effect of prior performance information on ratings of present performance: Contrast versus assimilation revisited. *Journal of Applied Psychology, 73,* 487–496.

Smolowe, J. (1993, Fall Special Issue). "Intermarried . . . with children." *Time,* pp. 64–65.

Smolowe, J. (1994, February 7). ". . . And throw away the key." *Time.* pp. 54–59.

Snyder, C. R., & Forsyth, D. R. (Eds.). (1991). *Handbook of social and clinical psychology: The health perspective.* New York: Pergamon Press.

Snyder, C. R., & Higgins, R. L. (1988). Excuses: Their effective role in the negotiation of reality. *Psychological Bulletin, 104,* 23–35.

Snyder, C. R., Higgins, R. L. & Stucky, R. J. (1983). *Excuses: Masquerades in search of grace.* New York: Wiley.

Snyder, C. R., Lassegard, M. A., & Ford, C. E. (1986). Distancing after group success and failure: Basking in reflected glory and cutting off reflected failure. *Journal of Personality and Social Psychology, 51,* 382–388.

Snyder, M. (1974). The self-monitoring of expressive behavior. *Journal of Personality and Social Psychology, 30,* 526–537.

Snyder, M. (1987). *Public appearances private/realities: The psychology of self-monitoring.* New York: Freeman.

Snyder, M. (1992). Motivational foundations of behavioral confirmation. *Advances in Experimental Social Psychology, 25,* 67–114.

Snyder, M. (1993). Basic research and practical problems: The promise of a "functional" personality and social psychology. *Personality and Social Psychology Bulletin, 19,* 251–264.

Snyder, M., & DeBono, K. (1985). Appeals to image and claims about quality: Understanding the psychology of advertising. *Journal of Personality and Social Psychology, 49,* 586–597.

Snyder, M., & Gangestad, S. (1986). On the nature of self-monitoring: Matters of assessment, matters of validity. *Journal of Personality and Social Psychology, 51,* 125–139.

Snyder, M., & Haugen, J. A. (1994). Why does behavioral confirmation occur? A functional perspective on the role of the perceiver. *Journal of Experimental Social Psychology, 30,* 218–246.

Snyder, M., & Ickes, W. (1985). Personality and social behavior. In G. Lindzey & E. Aronson (Eds.), *Handbook of social psychology* (Vol. 2, 3rd ed., pp. 883–947). New York: Random House.

Snyder, M., & Monson, T. C. (1975). Persons, situations, and the control of social behavior. *Journal of Personality and Social Psychology, 32,* 637–644.

Snyder, M., & Swann, W. B., Jr. (1978). Behavioral confirmation in social interaction: From social perception to social reality. *Journal of Personality and Social Psychology, 36,* 1202–1212.

Snyder, M., Tanke, E. D., & Berscheid, E. (1977). Social perception and interpersonal behavior: On the self-fulfilling nature of social stereotypes. *Journal of Personality and Social Psychology, 35,* 656–666.

Snyder, M. L., & Wicklund, R. A. (1981). Attribute ambiguity. In J. H. Harvey, W. Ickes, & R. F. Kidd (Eds.), *New directions in attribution research* (Vol. 3, pp. 197–221). Hillsdale, NJ: Erlbaum.

Snydersmith, M. A., & Cacioppo, J. T. (1992). Parsing complex social factors to determine component effects: I. Autonomic activity and reactivity as a function of human association. *Journal of Social and Clinical Psychology, 11,* 263–278.

Solano, C. H., & Koester, N. H. (1989). Loneliness and communication problems: Subject anxiety or objective skills? *Personality and Social Psychology Bulletin, 15,* 126–133.

Solomon, S., Greenberg, J., & Pyszczynski, T. (1991). A terror-management theory of social behavior: The psychological functions of self-esteem and cultural worldviews. *Advances in Experimental Social Psychology, 24,* 93–159.

Solomon, S. D., Regier, D. A., & Burke, J. D. (1989). Role of perceived control in coping with disaster. *Journal of Social and Clinical Psychology, 8,* 376–392.

Solomon, S. D., Smith, E. M., Robins, L. N., & Fischbach, R. L. (1987). Social involvement as a mediator of disaster-induced stress. *Journal of Applied Social Psychology, 17,* 1092–1112.

Sommers, S. (1984). Reported emotions and conventions of emotionality among college students. *Journal of Personality and Social Psychology, 46,* 207–215.

South, S. J. (1993). Racial and ethnic differences in the desire to marry. *Journal of Marriage and the Family, 55,* 357–370.

Spanier, G. B. (1992). Divorce: A comment about the future. In T. L. Orbuch (Ed.), *Close relationship loss: Theoretical approaches* (pp. 207–212). New York: Springer-Verlag.

Special report: A crime as American as a Colt .45. (1995, August 15). *Newsweek,* 22–23, 45.

Spence, J. T., Deaux, K., & Helmreich, R. L. (1985). Sex roles in contemporary American society. In G. Lindzey & E. Aronson (Eds.), *Handbook of social psychology* (Vol. 2, 3rd ed., pp. 149–178). New York: Random House.

Spitze, G. (1988). Women's employment and family relations: A review. *Journal of Marriage and the Family, 50,* 595–618.

Spivey, C. B., & Prentice-Dunn, S. (1990). Assessing the directionality of deindividuated behavior: Effects of deindividuation, modeling, and private self-consciousness on aggressive and prosocial responses. *Basic and Applied Social Psychology, 11,* 387–403.

Sporer, S. L. (1993). Eyewitness identification accuracy, confidence, and decision times in simultaneous and sequential lineups. *Journal of Applied Psychology, 78,* 22–33.

Sprecher, S. (1985). Sex differences in bases of power in dating relationships. *Sex Roles, 12,* 449–462.

Sprecher, S. (1994). Two sides to the breakup of dating relationships. *Personal Relationships, 1,* 199–222.

Sprecher, S., Aron, A., Hatfield, E., Cortese, A., Potapova, E., & Levitskaya, A. (1994). Love: American style, Russian style, and Japanese style. *Personal Relationships, 1,* 349–369.

Sprecher, S., & Felmlee, D. (1992). The influence of parents and friends on the quality and stability of romantic relationships: A three-wave longitudinal investigation. *Journal of Marriage and the Family, 54,* 888–900.

Sprecher, S., & Hatfield, E. (1982). Self-esteem and romantic attraction. *Recherches de Psychologie Sociale, 4,* 61–81.

Sprecher, S., & McKinney, K. (1993). *Sexuality.* Newbury Park, CA: Sage.

Sprecher, S. Sullivan, Q., & Hatfield, E. (1994). Mate selection preferences: Gender differences examined in a national sample. *Journal of Personality and Social Psychology, 66,* 1074–1080.

Stalans, L. J., & Diamond, S. S. (1990). Formation and change in lay evaluations of criminal sentencing: Misperception and discontent. *Law and Human Behavior, 14,* 199–214.

Stangor, C., & Lange, J. E. (1994). Mental representations of social groups: Advances in understanding stereotypes and stereotyping. *Advances in Experimental Social Psychology, 26,* 357–416.

Stangor, C., Lynch, L., Changming, D., & Glass, B. (1992). Categorization of individuals on the basis of multiple social features. *Journal of Personality and Social Psychology, 62,* 207–218.

Stangor, C., Sullivan, L. A., & Ford, T. E. (1991). Affective and cognitive determinants of prejudice. *Social Cognition, 9,* 359–380.

Stanley, S. M., & Markman, H. J. (1992). Assessing commitment in personal relationships. *Journal of Marriage and the Family, 54,* 595–608.

Stanton, A. L., Danoff-Burg, S., Cameron, C. L., & Ellis, A. P. (1994). Coping through emotional approach: Problems of conceptualization and confounding. *Journal of Personality and Social Psychology, 66,* 350–362.

Stasser, G. (1992). Pooling of unshared information during group discussions. In S. Worchel, W. Wood, & J. A. Simpson (Eds.), *Group process and productivity* (pp. 48–67). Newbury Park, CA: Sage.

Stasser, G., & Davis, J. H. (1981). Group decision making and social influence: A social interaction sequence model. *Psychological Review, 88,* 523–551.

Stasser, G., Kerr, N. L., & Bray, R. M. (1982). The social psychology of jury deliberations: Structure, process, and product. In N. Kerr & R. Bray (Eds.), *The psychology of the courtroom* (pp. 221–256). New York: Academic Press.

Stasser, G., & Stewart, D. (1992). Discovery of hidden profiles by decision-making groups: Solving a problem versus making a judgment. *Journal of Personality and Social Psychology, 63,* 426–434.

Stasser, G., & Titus, W. (1985). Pooling of unshared information in group decision making: Biased information sampling during discussion. *Journal of Personality and Social Psychology, 48,* 1467–1478.

Staw, B. M., & Ross, J. (1987). Behavior in escalation situations: Antecedents, prototypes, and solutions. In L. L. Cummings and B. M. Staw (Eds.), *Research in organizational behavior* (Vol. 9). Greenwich, CT: JAI Press.

Staw, B. M., & Ross, J. (1989). Understanding behavior in escalation situations. *Science, 246,* 216–220.

Steblay, N. M. (1987). Helping behavior in rural and urban environments: A meta-analysis. *Psychological Bulletin, 102,* 346–356.

Steblay, N. M. (1992). A meta-analytic review of the weapon-focus effect. *Law and Human Behavior, 16,* 413–424.

Steele, C. M. (1988). The psychology of self-affirmation: Sustaining the integrity of the self. In L. Berkowitz (Ed.), *Advances in experimental social psychology* (Vol. 21, pp. 261–302). New York: Academic Press.

Steele, C. M., & Josephs, R. A. (1990). Alcohol myopia: Its prized and dangerous effects. *American Psychologist, 45,* 921–933.

Steele, C. M., Spencer, S. J., & Lynch, M. (1993). Self-image resilience and dissonance: The role of affirmational resources. *Journal of Personality and Social Psychology, 64,* 885–896.

Steil, J. M., & Weltman, K. (1992). Influence strategies at home and at work: A study of sixty dual-career couples. *Journal of Social and Personal Relationships, 9,* 65–88.

Steiner, I. D. (1972). *Group process and productivity.* New York: Academic Press.

Stephan, W. G. (1985). Intergroup relations. In G. Lindzey & E. Aronson (Eds.), *Handbook of social psychology* (Vol. 2, pp. 599–658). New York: Random House.

Stephan, W. G. (1986). The effects of school desegregation: An evaluation 30 years after Brown. In M. J. Saks & L. Saxe (Eds.), *Advances in applied social psychology* (Vol. 3, pp. 181–206). Hillsdale, NJ: Erlbaum.

Stephan, W. G., Ageyev, V., Coates-Shrider, L., Stephan, C. W., & Abalakina, M. (1994). On the relationship between stereotypes and prejudice: An international study. *Personality and Social Psychology Bulletin, 20,* 277–284.

Stephen, T. (1987). Taking communication seriously: A reply to Murstein. *Journal of Marriage and the Family, 49,* 937–938.

Stepper, S., & Strack, F. (1993). Proprioceptive determinants of emotional and nonemotional feelings. *Journal of Personality and Social Psychology, 64,* 211–220.

Sternberg, R. J. (1986). A triangular theory of love. *Psychological Review, 93,* 119–135.

Sternberg, R. J. (1987). Liking versus loving: A comparative evaluation of theories. *Psychological Bulletin, 102,* 331–345.

Stets, J. E. (1991). Cohabiting and marital aggression: The role of social isolation. *Journal of Marriage and the Family, 53,* 669–680.

Stets, J. E. (1993). Control in dating relationships. *Journal of Marriage and the Family, 55,* 673–685.

Stets, J. E., & Straus, M. A. (1989). The marriage license as a hitting license: A comparison of assaults in dating, cohabiting, and married couples. *Journal of Family Violence, 41,* 33–52.

Stets, J. E., & Straus, M. A. (1990). Gender differences in reporting marital violence and its medical and psychological consequences. In M. A. Straus & R. J. Gelles (Eds.), *Physical violence in American families: Risk factors and adaptations to violence in 8,145 families* (pp. 151–165). New Brunswick, NJ: Transaction Publishers.

Stewart, A. J., Sokol, M., Healy, J. M., Jr., & Chester, N. L. (1986). Longitudinal studies of psychological consequences of life changes in children and adults. *Journal of Personality and Social Psychology, 50,* 143–151.

Stice, E., & Shaw, H. E. (1994). Adverse effects of the media-portrayed thin-ideal on women and linkages to bulimic symptomatology. *Journal of Social and Clinical Psychology, 13,* 288–308.

Stone, W. F., Lederer, G., & Christie, R. (Eds.) (1993). *Strength and weakness: The authoritarian personality today.* New York: Springer-Verlag.

Storms, M. D. (1973). Videotape and the attribution process: Reversing actors' and observers' points of view. *Journal of Personality and Social Psychology, 27,* 165–175.

Storms, M. D., & Thomas, G. (1977). Reactions to physical closeness. *Journal of Personality and Social Psychology, 35,* 412–418.

Strauman, T. J. (1992). Self-guides, autobiographical memory, and anxiety and dysphoria: Toward a cognitive model of vulnerability to emotional distress. *Journal of Abnormal Psychology, 101,* 87–95.

Strauman, T. J., Lemieux, A. M., & Coe, C. L. (1993). Self-discrepancy and natural killer cell activity: Immunological consequences of negative self-evaluation. *Journal of Personality and Social Psychology, 64,* 1042–1052.

Straus, M. A., & Gelles, R. J. (1986). Societal change and change in family violence from 1975 to 1985 as revealed by two national surveys. *Journal of Marriage and the Family, 48,* 465–479.

Straus, M. A., Gelles, R. J., & Steinmetz, S. K. (1980). *Behind closed doors.* Garden City, NY: Anchor Books.

Straus, M. A., & Sweet, S. (1992). Verbal/symbolic aggression in couples: Incidence rates and relationships to personal characteristics. *Journal of Marriage and the Family, 54,* 346–357.

Strenta, A., & DeJong, W. (1981). The effect of a prosocial label on helping behavior. *Social Psychology Quarterly, 44,* 142–147.

Strentz, T., & Auerbach, S. M. (1988). Adjustment to the stress of simulated captivity: Effects of emotion-focused versus problem-focused preparation on hostages differing in locus of control. *Journal of Personality and Social Psychology, 55,* 652–660.

Striegel-Moore, R. H., Silberstein, L. R., & Rodin, J. (1986). Toward an understanding of risk factors for bulimia. *American Psychologist, 41,* 246–263.

Strodtbeck, F. L., & Hook, L. (1961). The social dimensions of a twelve-man jury table. *Sociometry, 24,* 397–415.

Strodtbeck, F. L., James, R., & Hawkins, C. (1957). Social status in jury deliberations. *American Sociological Review, 22,* 713–719.

Stroebe, W., & Diehl, M. (1991). You can't beat good experiments with correlational evidence: Mullen, Johnson, and Sala's meta-analytic misinterpretations. *Journal of Basic and Applied Social Psychology, 12,* 25–32.

Stroebe, W., Diehl, M., & Abakoumkin, G. (1992). The illusion of group effectivity. *Personality and Social Psychology Bulletin, 18,* 643–650.

Stroebe, W., Lenkert, A., & Jonas, K. (1988). Familiarity may breed contempt: The impact of student exchange on national stereotypes and attitudes. In W. Stroebe, A. W. Kruglanski, D. Bar-Tal, & M. Hewstone (Eds.), *The social psychology of intergroup conflict* (pp. 167–187). New York: Springer-Verlag.

Stroebe, M. S., & Stroebe, W. (1983). Who suffers more? Sex differences in health risks of the widowed. *Psychological Bulletin, 93,* 279–301.

Stroebe, W., & Stroebe, M. S. (1986). Beyond marriage: The impact of partner loss on health. In R. Gilmour & S. Duck (Eds.), *The emerging field of personal relationships* (pp. 203–224). Hillsdale, NJ: Erlbaum.

Strube, M. J., & Garcia, J. E. (1981). A meta-analytical investigation of Fiedler's contingency model of leadership effectiveness. *Psychological Bulletin, 90,* 307–321.

Struch, N., & Schwartz, S. H. (1989). Intergroup aggression: Its predictors and distinctness from in-group bias. *Journal of Personality and Social Psychology, 56,* 364–373.

Struckman-Johnson, C. J., Gilliland, R. G., Struckman-Johnson, D. L., & North, T. C. (1990). The effects of fear of AIDS and gender on responses to fear-arousing condom advertisements. *Journal of Applied Social Psychology, 20,* 1396–1410.

Struckman-Johnson, C., & Struckman-Johnson, D. (1994). Men pressured and forced into sexual experience. *Archives of Sexual Behavior, 23,* 93–114.

Sue, S., Smith, R. E., & Caldwell, C. (1973). Effects of inadmissible evidence on the decisions of simulated jurors: A moral dilemma. *Journal of Applied Social Psychology, 3,* 345–353.

Suedfeld, P. (1992). Bilateral relations between countries and the complexity of newspaper editorials. *Political Psychology, 13,* 601–611.

Suedfeld, P., Wallace, M. D., & Thachuk, K. L. (1993). Changes in integrative complexity among Middle East leaders during the Persian Gulf crisis. *Journal of Social Issues, 49,* 183–199.

Sugarman, D. B. (1986). Active versus passive euthanasia: An attributional analysis. *Journal of Applied Social Psychology, 16,* 60–76.

Sugarman, D. B., & Hotaling, G. T. (1989). Dating violence: Prevalence, context, and risk markers. In M. A. Pirog-Good & J. E. Stets (Eds.), *Violence in dating relationships: Emerging social issues* (pp. 3–32). New York: Praeger.

Sullivan, H. S. (1947). *Conceptions of modern psychiatry.* Washington, DC: William Allan White Psychiatric Foundation.

Suls, J., & Fletcher, B. (1985). The relative efficacy of avoidant and nonavoidant coping strategies: A meta-analysis. *Health Psychology, 4,* 249–288.

Suls, J., Wan, C. K., & Sanders, G. S. (1988). False consensus and false uniqueness in estimating the prevalence of health-protective behaviors. *Journal of Applied Social Psychology, 18,* 66–79.

Suls, J., & Wills, T. A. (Eds.). (1991). *Social comparison: Contemporary theory and research.* Hillsdale, NJ: Erlbaum.

Sundstrom, E. (1986). *Work places.* New York: Cambridge University Press.

Surgeon General's Scientific Advisory Committee on Television and Social Behavior. (1972). *Television and growing up: The impact of televised violence.* Washington, DC: U.S. Government Printing Office.

Surra, C. A., & Huston, T. L. (1987). Mate selection as a social transition. In D. Perlman & S. Duck (eds.), *Intimate relationships: Development, dynamics, and deterioration* (pp. 88–120). Newbury Park, CA: Sage.

Sutker, P. B., Uddo, M., Brailey, K., & Allain, A. N., Jr., (1993). War-zone trauma and stress-related symptoms in Operation Desert Shield/Storm (ODS) returnees. *Journal of Social Issues, 49,* 33–49.

Swallow, S. R., & Kuiper, N. A. (1993). Social comparison in dysphoria and nondysphoria: Differences in target similarity and specificity. *Cognitive Therapy and Research, 17,* 103–122.

Swann, W. B., Jr. (1984). Quest for accuracy in person perception: A matter of pragmatics. *Psychological Review, 91,* 457–477.

Swann, W. B., Jr. (1987). Identity negotiation: Where two roads meet. *Journal of Personality and Social Psychology, 53,* 1038–1051.

Swann, W. B., Jr., De La Ronde, C., & Hixon, J. G. (1994). Authenticity and positivity strivings in marriage and courtship. *Journal of Personality and Social Psychology, 66,* 857–869.

Swann, W. B., Jr., & Ely, R. J. (1984). A battle of wills: Self-verification versus behavioral confirmation. *Journal of Personality and Social Psychology, 46,* 1287–1302.

Swann, W. B., Jr., & Hill, C. A. (1982). When our identities are mistaken: Reaffirming self-conceptions through social interaction. *Journal of Personality and Social Psychology, 43,* 59–66.

Swann, W. B., Jr., Hixon, J. G., & De La Ronde, C. (1992a). Embracing the bitter "truth": Negative self-concepts and marital commitment. *Psychological Science, 3,* 118–121.

Swann, W. B., Jr., Stein-Seroussi, A., & Giesler, B. J. (1992b). Why people self-verify. *Journal of Personality and Social Psychology, 62,* 392–401.

Swann, W. B., Jr., Stein-Seroussi, A., & McNulty, S. E. (1992c). Outcasts in a white-lie society: The enigmatic worlds of people with negative self-concepts. *Journal of Personality and Social Psychology, 62,* 618–624.

Sweeney, P. D., Anderson, K., & Bailey, S. (1986). Attributional style in depression: A meta-analytic review. *Journal of Personality and Social Psychology, 50,* 974–991.

Sweet, J. A., & Bumpass, L. L. (1992). Disruption of marital and cohabitation relationships: A social demographic perspective. In T. L. Orbuch (Ed.), *Close relationship loss: Theoretical approaches* (pp. 67–89). New York: Springer-Verlag.

Swim, J., Borgida, E., Maruyama, G., & Myers, D. G. (1989). Joan McKay versus John McKay: Do gender stereotypes bias evaluations? *Psychological Bulletin, 105,* 409–429.

Swim, J. K. (1994). Perceived versus meta-analytic effect sizes: An assessment of the accuracy of gender stereotypes. *Journal of Personality and Social Psychology, 66,* 21–36.

Szymanski, L. A., Devlin, A. S., Chrisler, J. C., & Vyse, S. A. (1993). Gender role and attitudes toward rape in male and female college students. *Sex Roles, 29,* 37–57.

Tajfel, H. (Ed.). (1982). *Social identity and intergroup relations.* London: Cambridge University Press.

Tajfel, H., Billig, M. G., Bundy, R. P., & Flament, C. (1971). Social categorization and intergroup behavior. *European Journal of Social Psychology, 1,* 149–178.

Tambs, K., & Moum, T. (1992). No large convergence during marriage for health, lifestyle, and personality in a large sample of Norweigen spouses. *Journal of Marriage and the Family, 59,* 957–971.

Tanford, S., & Penrod, S. (1984). Social influence model: A formal integration of research on majority and minority influence processes. *Psychological Bulletin, 95,* 189–225.

Tanford, S., & Penrod, S. (1986). Jury deliberations: Discussion content and influence processes in jury decision-making. *Journal of Applied Social Psychology, 16,* 322–347.

Tannen, D. (1990). *You just don't understand: Women and men in conversation.* New York: Morrow.

Tarde, G. (1890). *Les lois de l'imitation. Étude sociologique.* Paris: Félix Alcan.

Tassinary, L. G., & Cacioppo, J. T. (1992). Unobservable facial actions and emotion. *Psychological Science, 3,* 28–33.

Tavris, C. (1992). *The mismeasure of woman.* New York: Simon & Schuster.

Taylor, D. M., & Moghaddam, F. M. (1994). *Theories of intergroup relations* (2nd ed.). Westport, CT: Praeger.

Taylor, S. E., (1989). *Positive illusions: Creative self-deceptions and the healthy mind.* New York: Basic Books.

Taylor, S. E. (1991). Asymmetrical effects of positive and negative events: The mobilization-minimization hypothesis. *Psychological Bulletin, 110,* 67–85.

Taylor, S. E., & Brown, J. D. (1988). Illusion and well-being: A social psychological perspective on mental health. *Psychological Bulletin, 103,* 193–210.

Taylor, S. E., & Brown, J. D. (1994). Positive illusions and well-being revisited: Separating fact from fiction. *Psychological Bulletin, 116,* 21–27.

Taylor, S. E., Falke, R. L., Shoptaw, S. J., & Lichtman, R. R. (1986). Social support, support groups, and the cancer patient. *Journal of Consulting and Clinical Psychology, 54,* 608–615.

Taylor, S. E., & Fiske, S. T. (1975). Point of view and perceptions of causality. *Journal of Personality and Social Psychology, 32,* 439–445.

Taylor, S. E., Lichtman, R. R., & Wood, J. V. (1984). Attributions, beliefs about control, and adjustment to breast cancer. *Journal of Personality and Social Psychology, 46,* 489–502.

Taylor, S. E., & Lobel, M. (1989). Social comparison activity under threat: Downward evaluation and upward contacts. *Psychological Review, 96,* 569–575.

Taylor, S. L., O'Neal, E. C., Langley, T., & Butcher, A. H. (1991). Anger arousal, deindividuation, and aggression. *Aggressive Behavior, 17,* 193–206.

Taylor, S. P., & Leonard, K. E. (1983). Alcohol and human physical aggression. In R. G. Geen & E. I. Donnerstein (Eds.), *Aggression: Theoretical and empirical reviews* (Vol. 2, pp. 77–101). New York: Academic Press.

Tedeschi, J. T. (Ed.). (1981). *Impression management theory and social psychological research.* New York: Academic Press.

Tedeschi, J. T., Schlenker, B. R., & Bonoma, T. V. (1971). Cognitive dissonance: Private ratiocination or public spectacle? *American Psychologist, 26,* 685–695.

Teger, A. (1980). *Too much invested to quit.* New York: Pergamon Press.

Tennen, H., & Affleck, G. (1990). Blaming others for threatening events. *Psychological Bulletin, 108,* 209–232.

Tennen, H., & Affleck, G. (1991). Paradox-based treatments. In C. R. Snyder & D. R. Forsyth (Eds.), *Handbook of social and clinical psychology: The health perspective* (pp. 624–643). New York: Pergamon Press.

Terkel, S. (1974). *Working.* New York: Pantheon Books.

Terkel, S. (1992). *Race: How blacks and whites think and feel about the American obsession.* New York: New Press.

Terre, L., Drabman, R. S., & Speer, P. (1991). Health-relevant behaviors in media. *Journal of Applied Social Psychology, 21,* 1303–1319.

Terry, D. J. (1994). Determinants of coping: The role of stable and situational factors. *Journal of Personality and Social Psychology, 66,* 895–910.

Tesser, A. (1978). Self-generated attitude change. In L. Berkowitz (Ed.), *Advances in experimental social psychology* (Vol. 11, pp. 288–338). New York: Academic Press.

Tesser, A. (1980). Self-esteem maintenance in family dynamics. *Journal of Personality and Social Psychology, 39,* 77–91.

Tesser, A. (1988). Toward a self-evaluation maintenance model of social behavior. In L. Berkowitz (Ed.), *Advances in experimental social psychology* (Vol. 21, pp. 181–227). New York: Academic Press.

Tesser, A. (1993). The importance of heritability in psychological research: The case of attitudes. *Psychological Review, 100,* 129–142.

Tesser, A., & Collins, J. E. (1988). Emotion in social reflection and comparison situations: Intuitive, systematic, and exploratory approaches. *Journal of Personality and Social Psychology, 55,* 695–709.

Tesser, A., Pilkington, C. J., & McIntosh, W. D. (1989). Self-evaluation maintenance and the mediational role of emotion: The perception of friends and strangers. *Journal of Personality and Social Psychology, 57,* 442–456.

Tesser, A., & Smith, J. (1980). Some effects of task relevance and friendship on helping: You don't always help the one you like. *Journal of Experimental Social Psychology, 16,* 582–590.

Tetlock, P. E. (1988). Monitoring the integrative complexity of American and Soviet foreign policy rhetoric: What can be learned? *Journal of Social Issues, 44,* 101–131.

Tetlock, P. E., Armor, D., & Peterson, R. S. (1994). The slavery debate in antebellum America: Cognitive style, value conflict, and the limits of compromise. *Journal of Personality and Social Psychology, 66,* 115–126.

Tetlock, P. E., Peterson, R. S., McQuire, C., Chang, S., & Feld, P. (1992). Assessing political group dynamics: A test of the groupthink model. *Journal of Personality and Social Psychology, 63,* 403–425.

Theorell, T., Blomkvist, V., Jonsson, H., Schulman, S., Berntorp, E., & Stigendal, L. (1995). Social support and the development of immune function in human immunodeficiency virus infection. *Psychosomatic Medicine, 57,* 32–36.

Thibaut, J. W., & Kelley, H. H. (1959). *The social psychology of groups.* New York: Wiley.

Thibaut, J., & Walker, L. (1975). *Procedural justice: A psychological analysis.* Hillsdale, NJ: Erlbaum.

Thibaut, J., & Walker, L. (1978). A theory of procedure. *California Law Review, 66,* 541–566.

Thibodeau, R., & Aronson, E. (1992). Taking a closer look: Reasserting the role of the self-concept in dissonance theory. *Personality and Social Psychology Bulletin, 18,* 591–602.

Thoits, P. A. (1983). Dimensions of life events that influence psychological distress: An evaluation and synthesis of the literature. In H. B. Kaplan (Ed.), *Psychosocial stress: Trends in theory and research* (pp. 33–103). New York: Academic Press.

Thomas, M. H. (1982). Physiological arousal, exposure to a relatively lengthy aggressive film, and aggressive behavior. *Journal of Research in Personality, 16,* 72–81.

Thompson, E. P., Roman, R. J., Moskowitz, G. B., Chaiken, S., & Bargh, J. A. (1994). Accuracy motivation attenuates covert priming: The systematic *re*processing of social information. *Journal of Personality and Social Psychology, 66,* 474–489.

Thompson, L. (1990a). An examination of naive and experienced negotiators. *Journal of Personality and Social Psychology, 59,* 82–90.

Thompson, L. (1990b). Negotiation behavior and outcomes: Empirical evidence and theoretical issues. *Psychological Bulletin, 108,* 515–532.

Thompson, L. (1993). The impact of negotiation on intergroup relations. *Journal of Experimental Social Psychology, 29,* 304–325.

Thompson, L. (1995). "They saw a negotiation": Partisanship and involvement. *Journal of Personality and Social Psychology, 68,* 839–853.

Thompson, S. C., & Sobolew-Shubin, A. (1993). Overprotective relationships: A nonsupportive side of social networks. *Basic and Applied Social Psychology, 14,* 363–383.

Thompson, S. C., Sobolew-Shubin, A., Galbraith, M. E., Schwankovsky, L., & Cruzen, D. (1993). Maintaining perceptions of control: Finding perceived control in low-control circumstances. *Journal of Personality and Social Psychology, 64,* 293–304.

Thompson, W. M., Dabbs, J. M., Jr., & Frady, R. L. (1990). Changes in saliva testosterone levels during a 90-day shock incarceration program. *Criminal Justice and Behavior, 17,* 246–252.

Thomson, E., & Colella, U. (1992). Cohabitation and marital stability: Quality or commitment? *Journal of Marriage and the Family, 54,* 259–267.

Thornton, B. (1992). Repression and its mediating influence on the defensive attribution of responsibility. *Journal of Research in Personality, 26,* 44–57.

Thornton, B., Hogate, L., Moirs, K., Pinette, M., & Presby, W. (1986). Physiological evidence for an arousal-based motivational bias in the defensive attribution of responsibility. *Journal of Experimental Social Psychology, 22,* 148–162.

Thornton, B., & Moore, S. (1993). Physical attractiveness contrast effect: Implications for self-esteem and evaluation of the social self. *Personality and Social Psychology Bulletin, 19,* 474–480.

Thornton, G. C., III, & Byham, W. C. (1982). *Assessment centers and managerial performance.* New York: Academic Press.

Thurstone, L. L. (1928). Attitudes can be measured. *American Journal of Sociology, 33,* 529–544.

Tice, D. M. (1991). Esteem protection or enhancement? Self-handicapping motives and attributions differ by trait self-esteem. *Journal of Personality and Social Psychology, 60,* 711–725.

Tilker, H. A. (1970). Socially responsible behavior as a function of observer responsibility and victim feedback. *Journal of Personality and Social Psychology, 14,* 95–100.

Time, (1994, June 27). p. 26.

Tobin, R. J., & Eagles, M. (1992). U.S. and Canadian attitudes toward international interactions: A cross-national test of the double-standard hypothesis. *Basic and Applied Social Psychology, 13,* 447–459.

Tolstedt, B. E., & Stokes, J. P. (1984). Self-disclosure, intimacy, and the depenetration process. *Journal of Personality and Social Psychology, 46,* 84–90.

Tomaka, J., Blascovich, J., Kelsey, R. M., & Leitten, C. L. (1993). Subjective, physiological, and behavioral effects of threat and challenge appraisal. *Journal of Personality and Social Psychology, 65,* 248–260.

Top, T. J. (1991). Sex bias in the evaluation of performance in the scientific, artistic, and literary professions: A review. *Sex Roles, 24,* 73–106.

Tornstam, L. (1992). Loneliness in marriage. *Journal of Social and Personal Relationships, 9,* 197–217.

Tosi, H. L., & Einbender, S. W. (1985). The effects of the type and amount of information in sex discrimination research: A meta-analysis. *Academy of Management Journal, 28,* 712–723.

Toufexis, A. (1993, April 19). Seeking the roots of violence. *Time,* pp. 52–53.

Tourangeau, R., Rasinksi, K. A., & D'Andrade, R. (1991). Attitude structure and belief accessibility. *Journal of Experimental Social Psychology, 27,* 48–75.

Trafimow, D., Triandis, H. C., & Goto, S. G. (1991). Some tests of the distinction between the private and collective self. *Journal of Personality and Social Psychology, 60,* 649–655.

Triandis, H. C. (1989). The self and social behavior in differing cultural contexts. *Psychological Review, 96,* 506–520.

Triandis, H. C. (1994). *Culture and social behavior.* New York: McGraw-Hill.

Triandis, H. C., Bontempo, R., Villareal, M. J., Asai, M., & Lucca, N. (1988). Individualism and collectivism: Cross-cultural perspectives on self-ingroup relationships. *Journal of Personality and Social Psychology, 54,* 323–338.

Tripathi, R. C., & Srivastava, R. (1981). Relative deprivation and intergroup attitudes. *European Journal of Social Psychology, 11,* 313–318.

Triplett, N. (1897-1898). The dynamogenic factors in pacemaking and competition. *American Journal of Psychology, 9,* 507–533.

Tripp, C., Jensen, T. D., & Carlson, L. (1994). The effects of multiple product endorsements by celebrities on consumers' attitudes and intentions. *Journal of Consumer Research, 20,* 535–547.

Trivers, R. L. (1972). Parental investment and sexual selection. In B. Campbell (Ed.), *Sexual selection and the descent of man* (pp. 136–179). Chicago: Aldine-Atherton.

Trope, Y. (1986). Identification and inferential processes in dispositional attribution. *Psychological Review, 93,* 239-257.

Trope, Y., Bassock, M., & Alon, E. (1984). The questions lay interviewers ask. *Journal of Personality, 52,* 90-106.

Trost, M. R., Maass, A., & Kenrick, D. T. (1992). Minority influence: Personal relevance biases cognitive processes and reverses private acceptance. *Journal of Experimental Social Psychology, 28,* 234-254.

Tucker, P., & Aron, A. (1993). Passionate love and marital satisfaction at key transition points in the family life cycle. *Journal of Social and Clinical Psychology, 12,* 135-147.

Turner, J. C. (1981). The experimental social psychology of intergroup behavior. In J. C. Turner & H. Giles (Eds.), *Intergroup behavior* (pp. 66-101). Oxford, England: Basil Blackwell.

Turner, J. C. (1987). *Rediscovering the social group: A self-categorization theory.* Oxford, England: Basil Blackwell.

Turner, J. C. (1991). *Social influence.* Pacific Grove, CA: Brooks/Cole.

Turner, J. C., & Oakes, P. J. (1989). Self-categorization theory and social influence. In P. B. Paulus (Ed.), *Psychology of group influence* (2nd ed., pp. 233-275). Hillsdale, NJ: Erlbaum.

Turner, J. C., Oakes, P. J., Haslam, S. A., & McGarty, C. (1994). Self and collective: Cognition and social context. *Personality and Social Psychology Bulletin, 20,* 454-463.

Turner, M. E., & Pratkanis, A. R. (1994). Affirmative action as help: A review of recipient reactions to preferential selection and affirmative action. *Basic and Applied Social Psychology, 15,* 43–70.

Turner, M. E., Pratkanis, A. R., Probasco, P., & Leve, C. (1992). Threat, cohesion, and group effectiveness: Testing a social identity maintenance perspective on groupthink. *Journal of Personality and Social Psychology, 63,* 781-796.

Tversky, A., & Kahneman, D. (1973). Availability: A heuristic for judging frequency and probability. *Cognitive Psychology, 5,* 207–232.

Tversky, A., & Kahneman, D. (1974). Judgment under certainty: Heuristics and biases. *Science, 185,* 1124–1131.

Tversky, B., & Tuchin, M. (1989). A reconciliation of the evidence on eyewitness testimony: Comments on McCloskey and Zaragoza. *Journal of Experimental Psychology, 118,* 86–91.

Tyler, T. R. (1994). Psychological models of the justice motive: Antecedents of distributive and procedural justice. *Journal of Personality and Social Psychology, 67,* 850–863.

Tyler, T. R., Rasinski, K. A., & Spodick, N. (1985). Influences of voice on satisfaction with leaders: Exploring the meaning of process control. *Journal of Personality and Social Psychology, 48,* 72–81.

United Nations. (1989). Special topic: International migration studies. In *United Nations demographic year book.* New York: Author.

U.S. Bureau of the Census (1994). *Statistical Abstract of the United States: 1994.* Washington, DC: The Reference Press.

U.S. Department of Health, Education, and Welfare. (1974, May 30). Protection of human subjects. *Federal Register, 39*(105): 18914–20 (45CFR, part 46).

Usher, J. A., & Neisser, U. (1993). Childhood amnesia and the beginnings of memory for four early life events. *Journal of Experimental Psychology: General, 122,* 155–165.

Vaillant, C. O., & Vaillant, G. E. (1993). Is the U-curve of marital satisfaction an illusion? A 40-year study of marriage. *Journal of Marriage and the Family, 55,* 230–239.

Vaillant, G. E. (1977). *Adaptation to life.* Boston: Little, Brown.

Vallone, R. P., Griffin, D. W., Lin, S., & Ross, L. (1990). Overconfident prediction of future actions and outcomes by self and others. *Journal of Personality and Social Psychology, 58,* 582–592.

van der Pligt, J., Otten, W., Richard, R., & van der Velde, F. (1993). Perceived risk of AIDS: Unrealistic optimism and self-protective action. In J. B. Pryor & G. D. Reeder (Eds.), *The social psychology of HIV infection* (pp. 39–58). Hillsdale, NJ: Erlbaum.

van Dijk, E., & Wilke, H. (1995). Coordination rules in asymmetric social dilemmas: A comparison between public good dilemmas and resource dilemmas. *Journal of Experimental Social Psychology, 31,* 1–27.

Van Lange, P. A. M. (1992). Rationality and morality in social dilemmas: The influence of social value orientations. In W. B. G. Liebrand, D. M. Messick, & H. A. M. Wilke (Eds.), *Social dilemmas: Theoretical issues and research findings* (pp. 133–146). Oxford: Pergamon Press.

VanYperen, N. W., & Buunk, B. P. (1990). A longitudinal study of equity and satisfaction in intimate relationships. *European Journal of Social Psychology, 20,* 287–309.

Vaux, A. (1988a). Social and emotional loneliness: The role of social and personal characteristics. *Personality and Social Psychology Bulletin, 14,* 722–734.

Vaux, A. (1988b). Social and personal factors in loneliness. *Journal of Social and Clinical Psychology, 6,* 462–471.

Vecchio, R. P. (1983). Assessing the validity of Fiedler's contingency model of leadership effectiveness: A closer look at Strube and Garcia. *Psychological Bulletin, 93,* 404–408.

Verbrugge, L. M. (1987). Role responsibilities, role burdens, and physical health. In F. Crosby (Ed.), *Spouse, parent, worker: On gender and multiple roles* (pp. 154–166). New Haven, CT: Yale University Press.

Vinokur, A., & Burnstein, E. (1974). Effects of partially shared persuasive arguments on group-induced shifts: A group-problem-solving approach. *Journal of Personality and Social Psychology, 29,* 305–315.

von Hippel, W., Sekaquaptewa, D., & Vargas, P. (1995). On the role of encoding processes in stereotype maintenance. *Advances in Experimental Social Psychology, 27,* 177–254.

Von Lang, J., & Sibyll, C. (Eds.). (1983). *Eichmann interrogated* (R. Manheim, Trans.). New York: Farrar, Straus & Giroux.

Vroom, V. H. (1964). *Work and motivation.* New York: Wiley.

Vroom, V. H., & Jago, A. G. (1988). *Managing participation in organizations.* Englewood Cliffs, NJ: Prentice-Hall.

Wagner, U., Wicklund, R. A., & Shaigan, S. (1990). Open devaluation and rejection of a fellow student: The impact of threat to self-definition. *Basic and Applied Social Psychology, 11,* 61–76.

Waldman, D. A., & Avolio, B. J. (1991). Race effects in performance evaluations: Controlling for ability, education, and experience. *Journal of Applied Psychology, 76,* 897–901.

Walker, L., LaTour, S., Lind, E. A., & Thibaut, J. (1974). Reactions of participants and observers to modes of adjudication. *Journal of Applied Social Psychology, 4,* 295–310.

Waller, N. G., & Shaver, P. R. (1994). The importance of nongenetic influences on romantic love styles: A twin-family study. *Psychological Science, 5,* 268–274.

Waller, R. J. (1992). *The bridges of Madison County.* New York: Warner Books.

Waller, W. W., & Hill, R. (1951). *The family, a dynamic interpretation.* New York: Dryden Press.

Walster, E. (1965). The effect of self-esteem on romantic liking. *Journal of Experimental Social Psychology, 1,* 184–197.

Walster, E. (1966). Assignment of responsibility for important events. *Journal of Personality and Social Psychology, 3,* 73–79.

Walster, E. (1971). Passionate love. In B. Murstein (Ed.), *Theories of attraction and love* (pp. 85–99). New York: Springer.

Walster, E., Aronson, V., Abrahams, D., & Rottman, L. (1966). The importance of physical attractiveness in dating behavior. *Journal of Personality and Social Psychology, 4,* 508–516.

Walster, E., & Festinger, L. (1962). The effectiveness of "overheard" persuasive communications. *Journal of Abnormal and Social Psychology, 65,* 395–402.

Walster, E., Walster, G. W., & Berscheid, E. (1978a). *Equity: Theory and research.* Boston: Allyn & Bacon.

Walster, E., Walster, G. W., Piliavin, J., & Schmidt, L. (1973). "Playing hard-to-get": Understanding an elusive phenomenon. *Journal of Personality and Social Psychology, 26,* 113–121.

Walster, E., Walster, G. W., & Traupmann, J. (1978b). Equity and premarital sex. *Journal of Personality,* 36, 82–92.

Ward, S. E., Leventhal, H., & Love, R. (1988). Repression revisited: Tactics used in coping with a severe health threat. *Personality and Social Psychology Bulletin, 14,* 735–746.

Warren, B. L. (1966). A multiple variable approach to the assortive mating phenomenon. *Eugenics Quarterly, 13,* 285–298.

Warshaw, R. (1988). *I never called it rape.* New York: Harper & Row.

Watson, D. (1982). The actor and the observer: How are their perceptions of causality divergent? *Psychological Bulletin, 92,* 682–700.

Watson, D. (1988). The vicissitudes of mood measurement: Effects of varying descriptors, time frames, and response formats on measures of positive and negative affect. *Journal of Personality and Social Psychology, 55,* 128–141.

Watson, D., & Clark, L. A. (1984). Negative affectivity: The disposition to experience aversive emotional states. *Psychological Bulletin, 96,* 465–490.

Watson, D., Clark, L. A., McIntyre, C., & Hamaker, S. (1992). Affect, personality, and social activity. *Journal of Personality and Social Psychology, 63,* 1011–1025.

Weary, G., & Edwards, J. A. (1994). Individual differences in causal uncertainty. *Journal of Personality and Social Psychology, 67,* 308–318.

Weaver, C. A. (1993). Do you need a "flash" to form a flashbulb memory? *Journal of Experimental Psychology: General, 122,* 39–46.

Webb, E. J., Campbell, D. T., Schwartz, R. D., Sechrest, L., & Grove, J. B. (1981). *Nonreactive measures in the social sciences* (2nd ed.). Boston: Houghton Mifflin.

Weber, J. G. (1994). The nature of ethnocentric attribution bias: Ingroup protection or enhancement? *Journal of Experimental Social Psychology, 30,* 482–504.

Weber, R., & Crocker, J. C. (1983). Cognitive processes in the revision of stereotypic beliefs. *Journal of Personality and Social Psychology, 45,* 961–967.

Webster, D. M. (1993). Motivated augmentation and reduction of the overattribution bias. *Journal of Personality and Social Psychology, 65,* 261–271.

Webster, D. M., & Kruglanski, A. W. (1994). Individual differences in the need for cognitive closure. *Journal of Personality and Social Psychology, 67,* 1049–1062.

Wedell, D. H., Parducci, A., & Geiselman, R. E. (1987). A formal analysis of ratings of physical attractiveness: Successive contrast and simultaneous association. *Journal of Experimental Social Psychology, 23,* 230–249.

Wegener, D. T., & Petty, R. E. (1994). Mood management across affective states: The hedonic contingency hypothesis. *Journal of Personality and Social Psychology, 66,* 1034–1048.

Wegner, D. M. (1980). The self in prosocial action. In D. M. Wegner & R. R. Vallacher (Eds.), *The self in social psychology* (pp. 131–157). New York: Oxford University Press.

Wegner, D. M. (1989). *White bears and other unwanted thoughts: Suppression, obsession, and the psychology of mental control.* New York: Viking.

Wegner, D. M. (1994). Ironic processes of mental control. *Psychological Review, 101,* 34–52.

Wegner, D. M., & Schaefer, D. (1978). The concentration of responsibility: An objective self-awareness analysis of group size effects in helping situations. *Journal of Personality and Social Psychology, 36,* 147–155.

Weick, K. E. (1985). Systematic observational methods. In G. Lindzey & E. Aronson (Eds.), *Handbook of social psychology* (Vol. 1, 3rd ed., pp. 567–634). New York: Random House.

Weigel, R. H., & Howes, P. W. (1985). Conceptions of racial prejudice: Symbolic racism reconsidered. *Journal of Social Issues, 41,* 117–138.

Weiner, B. (1985). "Spontaneous" causal thinking. *Psychological Bulletin, 97,* 74–84.

Weiner, B. (1993). On sin versus sickness: A theory of perceived responsibility and social motivation. *American Psychologist, 48,* 957–965.

Weingardt, K. R., Loftus, E. F., & Lindsay, D. S. (1995). Misinformation revisited: New evidence on the suggestibility of memory. *Memory and Cognition, 23,* 72–82.

Weinstein, N. D. (1980). Unrealistic optimism about future life events. *Journal of Personality and Social Psychology, 39,* 806–820.

Weinstein, N. D. (1989). Effects of personal experience on self-protective behavior. *Psychological Bulletin, 105,* 31–50.

Weinstein, N. D. (1993). Testing four competing theories of health-protective behavior. *Health Psychology, 12,* 324–333.

Weinstein, N. D., & Nicolich, M. (1993). Correct and incorrect interpretations of correlations between risk perceptions and risk behaviors. *Health Psychology, 12,* 235–245.

Weiss, B., Dodge, K. A., Bates, J. E., & Petit, G. S. (1992). Some consequences of early harsh discipline: Child aggression and a maladaptive social information processing style. *Child Development, 63,* 1321–1335.

Weiss, H. M., & Knight, P. A. (1980). The utility of humility: Self-esteem, information search, and problem-solving efficiency. *Organizational Behavior and Human Performance, 25,* 216–223.

Weiss, R. S. (1969). The fund of sociability. *Transaction, 7,* 36–43.

Weiss, R. S. (1973). *Loneliness.* Cambridge, MA: MIT Press.

Weldon, E., & Gargano, G. M. (1988). Cognitive loading: The effects of accountability and shared responsibility on cognitive effort. *Personality and Social Psychology Bulletin, 14,* 159–171.

Wells, G. L. (1986). Expert psychological testimony: Empirical and conceptual analyses of effects. *Law and Human Behavior, 10,* 83–95.

Wells, G. L. (1993). What do we know about eyewitness identification? *American Psychologist, 48,* 553–571.

Wells, G. L., Lindsay, R. C. L., & Ferguson, T. J. (1979). Accuracy, confidence, and juror perceptions in eyewitness identification. *Journal of Applied Psychology, 64,* 440–448.

Wells, G. L., & Loftus, E. F. (Eds.). (1984). *Eyewitness testimony: Psychological perspectives.* New York: Cambridge University Press.

Wells, G. L., & Murray, D. M. (1984). Eyewitness confidence. In G. Wells & E. Loftus (Eds.), *Eyewitness testimony: Psychological perspectives* (pp. 155–170). New York: Cambridge University Press.

Wells, G. L., & Petty, R. E. (1980). The effects of overt head-movements on persuasion: Compatibility and incompatibility of responses. *Basic and Applied Social Psychology, 1,* 219–230.

Welton, G. L., & Pruitt, D. G. (1987). The mediation process: The effects of mediator bias and disputed power. *Personality and Social Psychology Bulletin, 13,* 123–133.

We're sorry: A case of mistaken identity. (1982, October 4). *Time,* p. 45.

West, C., & Zimmerman, D. H. (1983). Small insults: A study of interruptions in cross-sex conversations between unacquainted persons. In B. Thorne, C. Dramarge, & N. Henley (Eds.), *Language, gender and society* (pp. 102–117). Rowley, MA: Newbury House.

West, S. G., Gunn, S. P., & Chernicky, P. (1975). Ubiquitous Watergate: An attributional analysis. *Journal of Personality and Social Psychology, 32,* 55–65.

Wetzel, C. G., & Insko, C. A. (1982). The similarity-attraction relationship: Is there an ideal one? *Journal of Experimental Social Psychology, 18,* 253–276.

Wheeler, L., Koestner, R., & Driver, R. E. (1982). Related attributes in the choice of comparison others. *Journal of Experimental Social Psychology, 18,* 489–500.

Wheeler, L., & Miyake, K. (1992). Social comparison in everyday life. *Journal of Personality and Social Psychology, 62,* 760–773.

Wheeler, L., Reis, H. T., & Bond, M. H. (1989). Collectivism-individualism in everyday social life: The middle kingdom and the melting pot. *Journal of Personality and Social Psychology, 57,* 79–86.

Whisman, M. A., & Kwon, P. (1993). Life stress and dysphoria: The role of self-esteem and hopelessness. *Journal of Personality and Social Psychology, 65,* 1054–1060.

Whitbeck, L. B., & Hoyt, D. R. (1994). Social prestige and assortive mating: A comparison of students from 1956 and 1988. *Journal of Social and Personal Relationships, 11,* 137–145.

White, G. L. (1980). Physical attractiveness and courtship progress. *Journal of Personality and Social Psychology, 39,* 660–668.

White, G. L. (1981a). A model of romantic jealousy. *Motivation and Emotion, 5,* 295–310.

White, G. L. (1981b). Some correlates of romantic jealousy. *Journal of Personality, 49,* 129–147.

White, G. L., Fishbein, S., & Rutstein, J. (1981). Passionate love: The misattribution of arousal. *Journal of Personality and Social Psychology, 41,* 56–62.

White, G. L., & Kight, T. D. (1984). Misattribution of arousal and attraction: Effects of salience of explanation of arousal. *Journal of Experimental Social Psychology, 20,* 55–64.

White, G. L., & Mullen, P. E. (1989). *Jealousy: Theory, research, and clinical strategies.* New York: Guilford.

White, J. W. (1983). Sex and gender issues in aggression research. In R. G. Geen & E. I. Donnerstein (Eds.), *Aggression: Theoretical and empirical reviews: Vol. 2. Issues in research* (pp. 1–26). New York: Academic Press.

White, P. A., & Younger, D. P. (1988). Differences in the ascription of transient internal states to self and other. *Journal of Experimental Social Psychology, 24,* 292–309.

White, P. H., & Harkins, S. G. (1994). Rate of source effects in the elaboration likelihood model. *Journal of Personality and Social Psychology, 67,* 790–807.

Whitley, B. E., Jr., (1993). Reliability and aspects of the construct validity of Sternberg's triangular love scale. *Journal of Social and Personal Relationships, 10,* 475–480.

Whittaker, J. O., & Meade, R. D. (1967). Social pressure in the modification and distortion of judgment: A cross-cultural study. *International Journal of Psychology, 2,* 109–113.

Wicker, A. W. (1969). Attitudes versus actions: The relationship between verbal and overt behavioral responses to attitude objects. *Journal of Social Issues, 25*(4), 41–78.

Wicklund, R. A. (1975). Objective self-awareness. In L. Berkowitz (Ed.), *Advances in experimental social psychology* (Vol. 8, pp. 233–275). New York: Academic Press.

Wicklund, R. A., & Frey, D. (1980). Self-awareness theory: When the self makes a difference. In D. M. Wegner & R. R. Vallacher (Eds.), *The self in social psychology* (pp. 31–54). New York: Oxford University Press.

Widmeyer, W. N., & Loy, J. W. (1988). When you're hot, you're hot! Warm-cold effects in first impressions of persons and teaching effectiveness. *Journal of Educational Psychology, 80,* 118–121.

Widom, C. S. (1989). Does violence beget violence? A critical examination of the literature. *Psychological Bulletin, 106,* 3–28.

Widom, C. S. (1991). A tail on an untold tale: Response to "Biological and genetic contributions to violence—Widom's untold tale." *Psychological Bulletin, 109,* 130–132.

Wiebe, D. J., & Williams, P. G. (1992). Hardiness and health: A social psychophysiological perspective on stress and adaptation. *Journal of Social and Clinical Psychology, 11,* 238–262.

Wiedenfeld, S. A., O'Leary, A., Bandura, A., Brown, S., Levine, S., & Raska, K. (1990). Impact of perceived self-efficacy in coping with stressors on components of the immune system. *Journal of Personality and Social Psychology, 59,* 1082–1094.

Wiederman, M. W., & Allgeier, E. R. (1992). Gender differences in mate selection criteria: Sociobiological or socioeconomic explanation? *Ethology and Sociobiology, 13,* 115–124.

Wiener, R. L., Weiner, A. T. F., & Grisso, T. (1989). Empathy and biased assimilation of testimonies in cases of alleged rape. *Law and Human Behavior, 13,* 343–355.

Wiesner, W. H., & Cronshaw, S. F. (1988). A meta-analytic investigation of the impact of interview format and degree of structure on the validity of the employment interview. *Journal of Occupational Psychology, 61,* 275–290.

Wilder, D. A. (1977). Perception of groups, size of opposition, and social influence. *Journal of Experimental Social Psychology, 13,* 253–268.

Wilder, D. A. (1986). Social categorization: Implications for creation and reduction of intergroup bias. In L. Berkowitz (Ed.), *Advances in experimental social psychology* (Vol. 19, pp. 291–355). New York: Academic Press.

Wilder, D. A., & Shapiro, P. (1991). Facilitation of outgroup stereotypes by enhanced ingroup identity. *Journal of Experimental Social Psychology, 27,* 431–452.

Williams v. *Florida,* 399 U.S. 78 (1970).

Williams, C. L., & Berry, J. W. (1991). Primary prevention of acculturative stress among refugees: Application of psychological theory and practice. *American Psychologist, 46,* 632–641.

Williams, J. E., & Best, D. L. (1982). *Measuring sex stereotypes: A thirty nation study.* Beverly Hills, CA: Sage.

Williams, K. D., Loftus, E. F., & Deffenbacher, K. A. (1992). Eyewitness evidence and testimony. In D. K. Kagehiro & W. S. Laufer (Eds.), *Handbook of psychology and law* (pp. 139–166). New York: Springer-Verlag.

Williams, K. R. (1992). Social sources of marital violence and deterrence: Testing an integrated theory of assaults between partners. *Journal of Marriage and the Family, 54,* 620–629.

Williamson, G. M., & Clark, M. S. (1989). Providing help and desired relationship type as determinants of changes in moods and self-evaluations. *Journal of Personality and Social Psychology, 56,* 722–734.

Williamson, G. M., & Clark, M. S. (1992). Impact of desired relationship type on affective reactions to choosing and being required to help. *Personality and Social Psychology Bulletin, 18,* 10–18.

Willis, F. N., & Carlson, R. A. (1993). Singles ads: Gender, social class, and time. *Sex Roles, 29,* 387–404.

Wills, T. A. (1981). Downward comparison principles in social psychology. *Psychological Bulletin, 90,* 245–271.

Wills, T. A. (1992). The helping process in the context of personal relationships. In S. Spacapan & S. Oskamp (Eds.), *Helping and being helped: Naturalistic studies* (pp. 17–48). Newbury Park, CA: Sage.

Wills, T. A., & DePaulo, B. M. (1991). Interpersonal analysis of the help-seeking process. In C. R. Snyder & D. R. Forsyth (Eds.), *Handbook of social and clinical psychology: The health perspective* (pp. 350–375). New York: Pergamon Press.

Willwerth, J. (1994). Madness in fine print. *Time,* pp. 62–63.

Wilson, C., & Gross, P. (1994). Police-public interactions: The impact of conflict resolution tactics. *Journal of Applied Social Psychology, 24,* 159–175.

Wilson, D. S., & Sober, E. (1994). Reintroducing group selection to the human behavioral sciences. *Behavioral and Brain Sciences, 17,* 585–654.

Wilson, D. W. (1981). Is helping a laughing matter? *Psychology, 18,* 6–9.

Wilson, T. D. (1985). Strangers to ourselves: The origins and accuracy of beliefs about one's own mental states. In J. H. Harvey & G. Weary (Eds.), *Attribution: Basic issues and applications* (pp. 9–36). New York: Academic Press.

Wilson, T. D., DePaulo, B. M., Mok, D. G., & Klaaren, K. J. (1993). Scientists' evaluations of research: The biasing effects of the importance of the topic. *Psychological Science, 4,* 322–325.

Wilson, T. D., & LaFleur, S. J. (1995). Knowing what you'll do: Effects of analyzing reasons on self-prediction. *Journal of Personality and Social Psychology, 68,* 21–35.

Wilson, T. D., & Schooler, J. W. (1991). Thinking too much: Introspection can reduce the quality of preferences and decisions. *Journal of Personality and Social Psychology, 60,* 181–192.

Winter, D. G. (1987). Leader appeal, leader performance, and the motive profiles of leaders and followers: A study of American presidents and elections. *Journal of Personality and Social Psychology, 52,* 41–46.

Wishman, S. (1986). *Anatomy of a jury: The system on trial.* New York: Times Books.

Wissler, R. L., & Saks, M. J. (1985). On the inefficacy of limiting instructions: When jurors use prior conviction evidence to decide on guilt. *Law and Human Behavior, 9,* 37–48.

Witte, K. (1992). Putting the fear back into fear appeals: The extended parallel process model. *Communication Monographs, 59,* 329–349.

Witteman, P. A. (1990, April 30). Vietnam: 15 years later. *Time,* pp. 19–21.

Wittenberg, M. T., & Reis, H. T. (1986). Loneliness, social skills, and social perception. *Personality and Social Psychology Bulletin, 12,* 121–130.

Wolf, S., & Montgomery, D. A. (1977). Effects of inadmissible evidence and level of judicial admonishment to disregard on the judgments of mock jurors. *Journal of Applied Social Psychology, 7,* 205–219.

Wolfe, D. A. (1985). Child-abusive parents: An empirical review and analysis. *Psychological Bulletin, 97,* 462–482.

Wood, G. (1978). The knew-it-all-along effect. *Journal of Experimental Psychology: Human Perception and Performance, 4,* 345–353.

Wood, J. (1989). Theory and research concerning social comparisons of personal attributes. *Psychological Bulletin, 106,* 231–248.

Wood, J. V., Giordano-Beech, M., Taylor, K. L., Michela, J. L., & Gaus, V. (1994). Strategies of social comparison among people with low self-esteem: Self-protection and self-enhancement. *Journal of Personality and Social Psychology, 67,* 713–731.

Wood, J. V., Taylor, S. E., & Lichtman, R. R. (1985). Social comparison in adjustment to breast cancer. *Journal of Personality and Social Psychology, 49,* 1169–1183.

Wood, N., & Cowan, N. (1995). The cocktail party phenomenon revisited: How frequent are attention shifts to one's name in an irrelevant auditory channel? *Journal of Experimental Psychology: Learning, Memory, and Cognition, 21,* 255–260.

Wood, W. (1987). Meta-analytic review of sex differences in group performance. *Psychological Bulletin, 102,* 53–71.

Wood, W., Kallgren, C. A., & Preisler, R. M. (1985a). Access to attitude-relevant information in memory as a determinant of persuasion: The role of message attributes. *Journal of Experimental Social Psychology, 21,* 73–85.

Wood, W., & Karten, S. J. (1986). Sex differences in interaction style as product of perceived sex differences in competence. *Journal of Personality and Social Psychology, 50,* 341–347.

Wood, W., Lundgren, S., Ouellette, J. A., Busceme, S., & Blackstone, T. (1994). Minority influence: A meta-analytic review of social influence processes. *Psychological Bulletin, 115,* 323–345.

Wood, W., Polek, D., & Aiken, C. (1985b). Sex differences in group task performance. *Journal of Personality and Social Psychology, 48,* 63–71.

Wood, W., Wong, F. Y., & Chachere, J. G. (1991). Effects of media violence on viewers' aggression in unconstrained social interaction. *Psychological Bulletin, 109,* 371–383.

Woolfolk, R. L., Novalany, J., Gara, M. A., Allen, L. A., & Polino, M. (1995). Self-complexity, self-evaluation, and depression: An examination of form and content within the self-schema. *Journal of Personality and Social Psychology, 68,* 1108–1120.

Worchel, S. (1974). The effect of three types of arbitrary thwarting on the instigation to aggression. *Journal of Personality, 42,* 300–318.

Worchel, S. (1992). Beyond a commodity theory analysis of censorship: When abundance and personalism enhance scarcity effects. *Basic and Applied Social Psychology, 13,* 79–92.

Word, C. O., Zanna, M. P., & Cooper, J. (1974). The nonverbal mediation of self-fulfilling prophecies in interracial interaction. *Journal of Experimental Social Psychology, 10,* 109–120.

Worth, L. T., & Mackie, D. M. (1987). Cognitive mediation of positive affect in persuasion. *Social Cognition, 5,* 76–94.

Wortman, C. B., & Brehm, J. W. (1975). Responses to uncontrollable outcomes: An integration of reactance theory and the learned helplessness model. In L. Berkowitz (Ed.), *Ad-*

vances in experimental social psychology (Vol. 8, pp. 277–336). New York: Academic Press.

Wright, J. C., Giammarino, M., & Parad, H. W. (1986). Social status in small groups: Individual-group similarity and the social "misfit." *Journal of Personality and Social Psychology, 50,* 523–536.

Wright, L. (1994). *Remembering Satan.* New York: Alfred A. Knopf.

Wright, M. H., Zautra, A. J., & Braver, S. L. (1985). Distortion in control attributions for real life events. *Journal of Research in Personality, 19,* 54–71.

Wright, P. H. (1982). Men's friendships, women's friendships and the alleged inferiority of the latter. *Sex Roles, 8,* 1–20.

Wright, P. H. (1988). Interpreting research on gender differences in friendship: A case for moderation and a plea for caution. *Journal of Social and Personal Relationships, 5,* 367–373.

Wright, P. H., & Keple, T. W. (1981). Friends and parents of a sample of high school juniors: An exploratory study of relationship intensity and interpersonal rewards. *Journal of Marriage and the Family, 43,* 559–570.

Wright, R. A., & Contrada, R. J. (1986). Dating selectivity and interpersonal attraction: Toward a better understanding of the "elusive phenomenon." *Journal of Social and Personal Relationships, 3,* 131–148.

Wright, R. A., Wadley, V. G., Danner, M., & Phillips, P. N. (1992). Persuasion, reactance, and judgments of interpersonal appeal. *European Journal of Social Psychology, 22,* 85–91.

Wrightsman, L. S., & Kassin, S. M. (1993). *Confessions in the courtroom.* Newbury Park, CA: Sage.

Wrightsman, L. S., Nietzel, M. T., & Fortune, W. H. (1994). *Psychology and the legal system* (3rd ed.). Pacific Grove, CA: Brooks/Cole.

Wu, C., & Shaffer, D. R. (1987). Susceptibility to persuasive appeals as a function of source credibility and prior experience with the attitude object. *Journal of Personality and Social Psychology, 52,* 677–688.

Wuthnow, R. (1991). *Acts of compassion.* Princeton, NJ: Princeton University Press.

Yamagishi, T. (1986). The provision of a sanctioning system as a public good. *Journal of Personality and Social Psychology, 51,* 110–116.

Yarmey, A. D. (1979). *The psychology of eyewitness testimony.* New York: Free Press.

Yoshikawa, H. (1994). Prevention as cumulative protection: Effects of early family support and education on chronic delinquency and its risks. *Psychological Bulletin, 115,* 28–54.

Young, R. K., Kennedy, A. H., Newhouse, A., Browne, P., & Thiessen, D. (1993). The effects of names on perceptions of intelligence, popularity, and competence. *Journal of Applied Social Psychology, 23,* 1770–1788.

Yuille, J. C., & Tollestrup, P. A. (1990). Some effects of alcohol on eyewitness memory. *Journal of Applied Psychology, 75,* 268–273.

Zaccaro, S. J., & McCoy, M. C. (1988). The effects of task and interpersonal cohesiveness on performance of a disjunctive group task. *Journal of Applied Social Psychology, 18,* 837–851.

Zajonc, R. B. (1965). Social facilitation. *Science, 149,* 269–274.

Zajonc, R. B. (1968). Attitudinal effects of mere exposure. *Journal of Personality and Social Psychology Monograph Supplement, 9*(2), 1–27.

Zajonc, R. B. (1980). Compresence. In P. B. Paulus (Ed.), *Psychology of group influence* (pp. 35–60). Hillsdale, NJ: Erlbaum.

Zajonc, R. B. (1984). On the primacy of affect. *American Psychologist, 39,* 117–123.

Zajonc, R. B. (1993). Brain temperature and subjective emotional experience. In M. Lewis & J. M. Haviland (Eds.), *Handbook of emotions* (pp. 209–220). New York: Guilford.

Zajonc, R. B., Adelmann, P. K., Murphy, S. T., & Niedenthal, P. M. (1987). Convergence in physical appearance of spouses. *Motivation and Emotion, 11,* 335–346.

Zajonc, R. B., Heingartner, A., & Herman, E. M. (1969). Social enhancement and impairment of performance in the cockroach. *Journal of Personality and Social Psychology, 13,* 82–92.

Zajonc, R. B., Murphy, S. T., & Inglehart, M. (1989). Feeling and facial efference: Implications of the vascular theory of emotion. *Psychological Review, 96,* 395–416.

Zajonc, R. B., Shaver, P., Tavris, C., & Kreveld, D. V. (1972). Exposure, satiation, and stimulus discriminability. *Journal of Personality and Social Psychology, 21,* 270–280.

Zanna, M. P., & Cooper, J. (1974). Dissonance and the pill: An attribution approach to studying the arousal properties of dissonance. *Journal of Personality and Social Psychology, 29,* 703–709.

Zanna, M. P., & Rempel, J. K. (1988). Attitudes: A new look at an old concept. In D. Bar-Tal & A. Kruglanski (Eds.), *The social psychology of knowledge* (pp. 315–334). New York: Cambridge University Press.

Zarate, M. A., & Smith, E. R. (1990). Person categorization and stereotyping. *Social Cognition, 8,* 161–185.

Zebrowitz, L. A., & McDonald, S. M. (1991). The impact of litigants' babyfacedness and attractiveness on adjudications in small claims courts. *Law and Human Behavior, 15,* 603–624.

Zebrowitz, L. A., Tenenbaum, D. R., & Goldstein, L. H. (1991). The impact of job applicants' facial maturity, gender, and academic achievement on hiring recommendations. *Journal of Applied Social Psychology, 21,* 525–548.

Zeidner, M., & Hammer, A. L. (1992). Coping with missile attack: Resources, strategies, and outcomes. *Journal of Personality, 60,* 710–746.

Zigler, E., Rubin, N., & Kaufman, J. (1988, May). Do abused children become abusive parents? *Parents,* pp. 100–104, 106.

Zillmann, D. (1978). Attribution and misattribution of excitatory reactions. In J. H. Harvey, W. Ickes, & R. F. Kidd (Eds.), *New directions in attribution research* (Vol. 2, pp. 335–368). Hillsdale, NJ: Erlbaum.

Zillmann, D. (1979). *Hostility and aggression.* Hillsdale, NJ: Erlbaum.

Zillmann, D. (1983). Arousal and aggression. In R. G. Geen & E. I. Donnerstein (Eds.), *Aggression: Theoretical and empirical reviews: Vol. I. Theoretical and methodological issues* (pp. 75–101). New York: Academic Press.

Zillmann, D. (1984). *Connections between sex and aggression.* Hillsdale, NJ: Erlbaum.

Zillmann, D., Baron, R., & Tamborini, R. (1981). Social costs of smoking: Effects of tobacco smoke on hostile behavior. *Journal of Applied Social Psychology, 11,* 548–561.

Zillmann, D., & Bryant, J. (1984). Effects of massive exposure to pornography. In N. M. Malamuth & E. I. Donnerstein (Eds.), *Pornography and sexual aggression* (pp. 115–138). New York: Academic Press.

Zillmann, D., Bryant, J., Cantor, J. R., & Day, K. D. (1975). Irrelevance of mitigating circumstances in retaliatory behavior at high levels of excitation. *Journal of Research in Personality, 9,* 282–293.

Zillmann, D., & Cantor, J. R. (1976). Effect of timing of information about mitigating circumstances on emotional responses to provocation and retaliatory behavior. *Journal of Experimental Social Psychology, 12,* 38–55.

Zillmann, D., Johnson, R. C., & Day, K. D. (1974). Attribution of apparent arousal and proficiency of recovery from sympathetic activation affecting excitation transfer to aggressive behavior. *Journal of Experimental Social Psychology, 10,* 503–515.

Zillmann, D., Katcher, A. H., & Milavsky, B. (1972). Excitation transfer from physical exercise to subsequent aggressive behavior. *Journal of Experimental Social Psychology, 8,* 247–259.

Zillmann, D., & Weaver, J. B. (1989). Pornography and men's sexual callousness toward women. In D. Zillmann & J. Bryant (Eds.), *Pornography: Research advances and policy considerations* (pp. 95–125). Hillsdale: Erlbaum.

Zimbardo, P. G. (1970). The human choice: Individuation, reason, and order versus deindividuation, impulse, and chaos. In W. J. Arnold & D. Levine (Eds.), *Nebraska Symposium on Motivation: 1969* (Vol. 17, pp. 237–307). Lincoln: University of Nebraska Press.

Zimbardo, P. G. (1973). On the ethics of intervention in human psychological research: With special reference to the Stanford prison experiment. *Cognition, 2,* 243–256.

Zimbardo, P. G. (1977). *Shyness.* New York: Jove.

Zimbardo, P. G. (1985, June). Laugh where we must, be candid where we can. *Psychology Today,* pp. 43–47.

Zimbardo, P. G., Banks, W. C., Haney, C., & Jaffe, D. (1973, April 8). The mind is a formidable jailer: A Pirandellian prison. *New York Times Magazine,* pp. 38–60.

Zimbardo, P. G., LaBerge, S., & Butler, L. D. (1993). Psychophysiological consequences of unexplained arousal: A posthypnotic suggestion paradigm. *Journal of Abnormal Psychology, 102,* 466–473.

Zuckerman, M., DePaulo, B. M., & Rosenthal, R. (1981). Verbal and nonverbal communication of deception. In L. Berkowitz (Ed.), *Advances in experimental social psychology* (Vol. 14, pp. 1–59). New York: Academic Press.

Zuckerman, M., & Kieffer, S. C. (1994). Race differences in faceism: Does facial prominence imply dominance? *Journal of Personality and Social Psychology, 66,* 86–92.

Zuckerman, M., Knee, C. R., Hodgins, H. S., & Miyake, K. (1995). Hypothesis confirmation: The joint effect of positive test strategy and acquiescence response set. *Journal of Personality and Social Psychology, 68,* 52–60.

Zuckerman, M., Lazzaro, M. M., & Waldgeir, D. (1979). Undermining effects of the foot-in-the-door technique with extrinsic rewards. *Journal of Applied Social Psychology, 9,* 292–296.

Credits

(Credits continued from copyright page)

Chapter 1: p. 2 *(Opener):* © Paul Chesley/Tony Stone Images. **p. 5:** © Suzanne & Nick Geary/Tony Stone Images. **p. 7:** *Figure 1.1* From Garth J. O. Fletcher, Janette Rosanowski and Julie Fitness, "Automatic Processing in Intimate Contexts: The Role of Close-Relationship Beliefs," *Journal of Personality and Social Psychology,* 67:5 (1994): 888–897 (Figure on page 893). Copyright © 1994 by the American Psychological Association. Reprinted by permission. **p. 9:** © Steve Ball/Black Star. **p. 10** *(left):* © Rick Friedman/Black Star. **p. 10** *(right):* © Alan L. Detrick/Photo Researchers. **p. 13:** © Alain Evrard/Photo Researchers. **p. 14:** *Table 1.2* From Gregory A. Kimble, "A Frame of Reference for Psychology," *American Psychologist,* 49:6 (1994): 510–519. Copyright © 1994 by the American Psychological Association, Inc. Reprinted by permission. **p. 16:** © Anthony Edgeworth/The Stock Market. **p. 20:** *Figure 1.4* From K. E. Leonard, "The impact of explicit aggressive and implicit nonaggressive cues on aggression in intoxicated and sober roles," *Personality and Social Psychology Bulletin, 15* (1989): 390–400. Copyright © 1989 by Sage Publications, Inc. Reprinted by permission of Sage Publications, Inc. **p. 22:** © Tim Davis/Photo Researchers. **p. 25** *(left):* © Coco McCoy/Rainbow. **p. 25** *(right):* © Dan McCoy/Rainbow. **p. 26:** *Table 1.4* Rosenberg, Morris: *Society and the Adolescent Self-Image.* Copyright © 1965 by Princeton University Press. Reprinted by permission of Princeton University Press. **p. 27:** Table 1.5 From N. Schwarz, H. J. Hippler, B. Deutsch and F. Strack, "Response scales: effects of category range on reported behavior and comparative judgments," *Public Opinion Quarterly, 49* (1985): 388–395. Copyright © 1985 by University of Chicago Press. Reprinted by permission of the University of Chicago Press. **p. 28:** © Brian Smith/Stock Boston. **p. 29:** © Dan McCoy/Rainbow.

Chapter 2: p. 38 *(Opener):* © Marie Brimberg/Woodfin Camp & Associates. **p. 41:** © Ursula Markus/Photo Researchers. **p. 45:** *Figure 2.1* From R. B. Zajonc, S. T. Murphy and M. Ingelhart, "Feeling and Facial Efference: Implications of the Vascular Theory of Emotion," *Psychological Review, 96* (1989): 406. Copyright © 1989 by the American Psychological Association. Reprinted by permission. **p. 46:** Everett Collection. **p. 48:** *Figure 2.2* From M. R. Lepper, D. Greene and K. E. Nisbett, "Undermining children's intrinsic interest with extrinsic reward: A test of the 'overjustification' hypothesis", *Journal of Personality and Social Psychology, 28* (1973): 129–137. Copyright © 1973 by the American Psychological Association. Reprinted by permission. **p. 51** *(both):* Visual/Gamma-Liaison. **p. 54** *(left):* © J. P. Laffont/Sygma. **p. 54** *(right):* © Jeffrey Cadge/The Image Bank. **p. 55:** *Figure 2.3* From H. R. Markus and S. Kitayama, "Culture and the self: Implications for cognition, emotion, and motivation", *Psychological Review, 98* (1991): 226. Copyright © 1991 by the American Psychological Association. Reprinted by permission. **p. 62:** *Figure 2.7* From Snyder, C. R., Higgins, R. L., and Stucky, R. J., *Excuses: Masquerades In Search Of Grace* (New York: Wiley, 1983) 39. **p. 62:** *Table 2.1* From A. Fenigstein, M. F. Scheier, and A. H. Buss, "Public and private self-consciousness: Assessment and theory," *Journal of Consulting and Clinical Psychology 43* (1975): 522–527. Copyright © 1975 by the American Psychological Association. Reprinted by permission. **p. 63:** © Bachmann/Photo Researchers. **p. 66:** Focus on Sports. **p. 68:** © J. L. Atlan/Sygma. **p. 69:** Phyllis L. Méras. **p. 72:** © Loren Santow/Tony Stone Images. **p. 74:** *Figure 2.9* From W. B. Swann, Jr., A. Stein-Sercussi, and B. J. Giesler, *Journal of Personality and Social Psychology 62* (1992): 392–401. Copyright © 1992 by the American Psychological Association. Reprinted by permission. **p. 75:** *Table 2.2* From M. Snyder and S. Gangestad, "On the nature of self-monitoring: Matters of assessment, matters of validity," *Journal of Personality and Social Psychology 51* (1986): 125–139. Copyright © 1986 by the American Psychological Association. Reprinted by permission.

Chapter 3: p. 80 *(Opener):* © Bob Daemmrich/The Image Works. **p. 83** *(left):* © P. F. Bentley/Black Star. **p. 83** *(right):* © Stephane Cardinale/Sygma. **p. 84:** © Jay Mather. **p. 85:** © Larry Mangino/The Image Works. **p. 87** *(top):* 6 emotion set, copyright Paul Ekman, 1975. *(bottom far left):* **p. 87** *(Figure 3.1)* From J. Aronoff, A. M. Barclay & L. A. Stevenson. "The recognition of threatening facial stimuli." *Journal of Personality and Social Psychology, 54* (1988): 651. Copyright © 1988 by the American Psychological Association. Reprinted by permission. **p. 87** *(bottom left):* © Harry Scull/Allsport. **p. 87** *(bottom center):* © Gary A. Conner/PhotoEdit. **p. 87** *(bottom right):* © Bushnell/ Soifer/Tony Stone Images. **p. 89:** *Table 3.1* From P. Ekman and M. O'Sullivan, "Who can catch a liar?" *American Psychologist 46* (1991): 913–920. Copyright © 1991 by the American Psychological Association. Reprinted by permission. **p. 92:** *Figure 3.2* From E. E. Jones and V. A. Harris, "The attribution of attitudes," *Journal of Experimental and Social Psychology, 3* (1967): 1–24. Copyright © 1967 by Academic Press. Reprinted by permission. **p. 95:** *Table 3.3* From J. Krueger and R. W. Clement, "The truly false consensus effect: An ineradicable and egocentric bias in social perception." *Journal of Personality and Social Psychology 67* (1994): 600. Copyright © 1994 by the American Psychological Association. Reprinted with permission. **p. 96:** © Bill Swersey/Gamma-Liaison. **p. 97:** courtesy of NBC. **p. 98:** *Figure 3.4* From L. Ross, T. M. Amabile, and J. L. Steinmetz, "Social roles, social control, and biases in social perception processes," *Journal of Personality and Social Psychology 35* (1977): 485–494. Copyright © 1977 by the American Psychological Association. Reprinted by permission. **p. 100:** *Figure 3.6* From J. G. Miller, "Culture and the Development of Everyday Social Explanation," *Journal of Personality and Social Psychology, 46* (1984): 961–978. Copyright © 1984 by the American Psychological Association. Reprinted by permission. **p. 103:** © Bob Daemmrich/The Image Works. **p. 106:** © Tony Savino/The Image Works. **p. 113:** *Figure 3.9* From J. T.

Copeland, "Prophecies of power: Motivational implications of social power for behavioral confirmation," *Journal of Personality and Social Psychology, 67* (1994): 273. Copyright © 1994 by the American Psychological Association. Reprinted by permission.

Chapter 4: p. 118 *(Opener):* © Macduff Everton/The Image Works. **p. 120:** © Terry Ashe/Gamma-Liaison. **p. 121:** © 1991 by George Holliday. **p. 126:** *Figure 4.2* From D. L. Hamilton and R. D. Gifford, "Illusory correlation in interpersonal perception: A cognitive basis of stereotypic judgments," *Journal of Experimental Social Psychology, 19* (1976): 78–92. **p. 123:** © Harvey Hutter & Company. **p. 134:** © Okoniewski/The Image Works. **p. 135:** © Will Hart. **p. 137:** *Figure 4.5* From S. Fein & S. J. Spencer, "Self-esteem and stereotype-based downward social comparison," Paper presented at the Meeting of the American Psychological Association, Toronto, August 1993. Reprinted by permission. **p. 139:** © Owen Stayner/Black Star. **p. 141:** © Pool/Gamma-Liaison. **p. 147:** Wide World Photos. **p. 148:** © Mike Bonner/Spartanburg Herald Tribune Journal/Sygma. **p. 149:** © Edward E. Pieratt/Comstock. **p. 151:** *Figure 4.8* From R. W. Rogers and S. Prentice-Dunn, "Deindividuation and anger mediated interracial aggression: Unmasking regressing racism," *Journal of Personality and Social Psychology, 41* (1981): 63–73. Copyright © 1981 by the American Psychological Association. Reprinted by permission. **p. 155:** © Mark Heckman. **p. 158:** Wide World Photos.

Chapter 5: p. 162 *(Opener):* © Tom McCarthy/PhotoEdit. **p. 165:** © David Young-Wolff/PhotoEdit. **p. 167** *(left):* © Elaine Rebman/PhotoResearchers. **p. 167** *(right)* © Joseph Nettis/Photo Researchers. **p. 171:** © Billy E. Barnes/Stock Boston. **p. 172:** *Figure 5.2* From P. Shaver and C. Rubenstein, "Childhood attachment experience and adult loneliness" *Review of Personality and Social Psychology 1* (1980): 42–73. Reprinted by permission of the authors. **p. 174:** *Figure 5.3:* 4 computer-generated composite sets, from Langlois, J. H., & Roggmann, L. A. (1990). Attractive faces are only average. *Psychological Science*, 1, 115–121. **p. 175** *(top left):* © L. Villota/The Stock Market. **p. 175** *(top right):* © Bachmann/Photo Researchers. **p. 175** *(bottom left):* © Art Wolfe/Tony Stone Images. **p. 175** *(bottom right):* © John Callahan/Tony Stone Images. **p. 176:** © 1982 Nancy Burson with Richard Carling & David Kramlich. **p. 178:** *Figure 5.4* From B. Major, P. I. Carrington and P. J. D. Carnevale, "Physical attractiveness and self-esteem: Attributions for praise for an other-sex evaluator," *Personality and Social Psychology Bulletin 10* (1984): 43–50. Copyright © 1984 by Sage Publications, Inc. Reprinted by permission of Sage Publications, Inc. and the authors. **p. 179** *(left)* © Ralph Dominguez/Globe Photos. **p. 179** *(center):* © D. Fineman/Sygma. **p. 179** *(right):* © Eric Robert/Sygma. **p. 183:** © James Smeal/Galella. **p. 186:** © Roy Morsch/The Stock Market. **p. 187:** © Fama Puljic/Sygma. **p. 191:** © Harry Benson.

Chapter 6: p. 198 *(Opener):* © Michael Dwyer/Stock Boston. **p. 200** *(left):* © Douglas Kirkland/Sygma. **p. 200** *(right):* © Tim Graham/Sygma. **p. 202:** *Figure 6.2* From Bernard I. Murstein, "Feedback: A clarification and extension of the SVR theory of dyadic pairing," *Journal of Marriage and the Family* 49:4 (1987): 929-933. Copyrighted © 1987/1979 by the National Council on Family Relations, 3989 Central Ave., N.E., Suite #550, Minneapolis, MN 55421. Reprinted by permission. **p. 207:** *Figure 6.4* Adapted from K. S. Prins, B. P. Buunk and N. W. VanYperen, "Normative disapproval and extramarital relationships," *Journal of Social and Personal Relationships 10* (1993): 39–53. Copyright © 1993 by Sage Publications Ltd. Reprinted by permission. **p. 208:** *Figure 6.5* Based on I. Altman and D. A. Taylor, *Social penetration: The Development of Interpersonal Relationships* (New York: Holt, Rinehart and Winston, 1973). Adapted by permission of the authors. **p. 210** *(left):* © David Joel/Tony Stone Images. **p. 210** *(right):* © Bob Daemmrich/Tony Stone Images. **p. 211:** *Table 6.2* Adapted table from *Liking and Loving. An Invitation to Social Psychology* by Zick Rubin, copyright © 1973 by Zick Rubin, reproduced by permission of the author. **p. 214:** *Table 6.4* From E. Hatfield and R. L. Rapson, "Passionate love: New directions in research" in W. H. Jones and D. Perlman (Eds.), *Advances in Personal Relationships 1* (1987): 109–139. Copyright © 1987 by JAI Press, Inc. Reprinted by permission. **p. 217:** *Table 6.6* From J. A. Lee, "A typology of styles of loving," *Journal of Personality and Social Psychology 3* (1977): 173–182. Copyright © 1977 by the American Psychological Association. Reprinted by permission. **p. 220:** © Bachmann/The Image Works. **p. 221:** *Figure 6.6* From Brent C. Miller, "Families, science, and values: Alternative views of parenting effects and adolescent pregnancy," *Journal of Marriage and the Family, 55:1* (1993): 14. Copyrighted © 1993 by the National Council on Family Relations, 3989 Central Ave., NE, Suite 550, Minneapolis, MN 55421. Reprinted by permission. **p. 223:** *Table 6.7* From J. A. Simpson and S. W. Gangestad, "Individual differences in sociosexuality: Evidence for convergent and discriminant validity." *Journal of Personality and Social Psychology 60* (1991): 872–883. Copyright © 1991 by the American Psychological Association. Reprinted by permission. **p. 225:** *Figure 6.8* From A. Aron, E. Aron and D. Smollan, "Inclusion of the Other in the Self Scale and the structure of interpersonal closeness," *Journal of Personality and Social Psychology, 63* (1992): 596–612. Copyright © 1992 by the American Psychological Association. Reprinted by permission. **p. 226:** © Vanessa Vick/Photo Researchers. **p. 233:** © Bob Daemmrich/The Image Works.

Chapter 7: p. 242 *(Opener):* photo by Rich Shveyda, The Signal newspaper, Santa Clarita, CA. **p. 244:** Leopold Page Collection/Gamma-Liaison. **p. 246:** © Mark Burnett/Photo Researchers. **p. 247:** © Jerry Irwin/Photo Researchers. **p. 249:** © Mugshots/The Stock Market. **p. 253:** © Michelle Bridwell/PhotoEdit. **p. 254:** (bottom): Newport News Daily Press. **p. 255:** *Figure 7.4* From C. D. Batson, B. D. Duncan, P. Ackerman, T. Buckley, and K. Birch, "Is empathetic emotion a source of altruistic motivation?" *Journal of Personality and Social Psychology 40* (1981): 290–302. Copyright © 1981 by the American Psychological Association. Reprinted by permission. **p. 257:** *Figure 7.5* From K. D. Smith, J. P. Keating, and E. Stotland, "Altruism reconsidered: the effect of denying feedback on a victim's status to empathic witnesses," *Journal of Personality and Social Psychology 57* (1989): 641–650. Copyright © 1989 by the American Psychology Association. Reprinted by permission. **p. 259:** *(right):* Wide World Photos. **p. 261:** *Figure 7.7* From A. Tesser and J. Smith, "Some effects of task relevance and friendship on helping: You don't always help the one you like," *Journal of Experimental Social Psychology 16* (1980): 582–590. Copyright © 1980 by Academic Press. Reprinted by permission. **p. 262:** © Kevin Carter/Sygma. **p. 263:** *Figure 7.8* From D. T. Miller, "Altruism and threat to a belief in a just world," *Journal of Experimental Social Psychology, 13* (1977): 113–124. Copyright © 1977 by Academic Press. Reprinted by permission. **p. 264:** Charles C. Wall, Ph.D., Professor of Management, Bakersfield College, Bakersfield, CA 93305. **p. 269:** *Table 7.1* From "Helpfulness index: How US Cities rank," *The Boston Globe*, July 7, 1994. Reprinted courtesy of The Boston Globe. **p. 271:** © Jan Lukas/Photo Researchers. **p. 273:** © Mathieu Polak/Sygma. **p. 274:** © John Barr/Gamma-Liaison. **p. 275:** Charles H. Porter IV/Sygma. **p. 278:** © David Joel/Tony Stone Images. **p. 279:** *Figure 7.12* From A. Nadler and J. D. Fisher, "The role of threat to self-esteem and perceived control in recipient reactions to help: Theory development and empirical validation," *Advances in Experimental Social Psychology, 19* (1986): 81–122. Copyright © 1986 by Academic Press. **p. 280:** © Peter Blakely/SABA.

Chapter 8: p. 284 *(Opener):* © Crandall/The Image Works. **p. 286:** © Olivier Laude/Gamma-Liaison. **p. 289:** Wide World Photos. **p. 293:** © Robert Yager/Tony Stone Images. **p. 294:** © Dennis MacDonald/PhotoEdit. **p. 295:** © Eduardo Citrinblum/Onyx. **p. 296** *(top):* © Esaias Baitel/Gamma-Liaison. **p. 296** *(bottom):* UPI/Bettmann. **p. 300:** *Figure 8.3A* From R. A. Baron and B. M. Ransberger, "Ambient temperature and the occurrence of collective violence: "The 'Long, Hot Summer' revisited," *Journal of Personality and Social Psychology, 36* (1978): 351–360. Copyright © 1978 by the American Psychological Association. Reprinted by permission; *Figure 8.3B* From J. M. Carlsmith and C. A. Anderson, "Ambient temperature and the occurrence of collective violence: A new analysis," *Journal of Personality and Social Psychology, 37* (1979): 377–344. Copyright © 1979 by the American Psychological Association. Reprinted by permission. **p. 305** *(top): Figure 8.9* Adapted from Edward Donnerstein, Daniel Linz, and Steven Penrod, *The Question of Pornography: Research Findings and Policy Implications* (New York: The Free Press, 1987). Data from E. Donnerstein and L. Berkowitz, "Victim reactions in aggressive erotic films as a factor in violence against women," *Journal of Personality and Social Psychology, 41* (1981): 710–724. Copyright © 1981 by the American Psychological Association. Adapted by permission. *(bottom)* © Alon Reininger/Contact Press Images. **p. 307:** © Jim Tynan/Impact Visuals. **p. 308:** courtesy of Acclaim Entertainment, Inc. **p. 309:** *Table 8.1* From TIME, 25 Oct. 1993: 20. Copyright © 1993 by TIME, Inc. Reprinted by permission. **p. 310:** © Comstock, Inc. **p. 314:** Wide World Photos. **p. 315:** *Figure 8.8* From E. Donnerstein and J. Hallam, "Facilitating effects of erotica on aggression against women," *Journal of Personality and Social Psychology, 36* (1978): 1270–1277. Copyright © 1978 by the American Psychological Association. Reprinted by permission. **p. 318:** *Table 8.2* From M. C. Burt, "Cultural myths and supports for rape," *Journal of Personality and Social Psychology, 38* (1980): 217–230. Copyright © 1980 by the American Psychological Association. Reprinted by permission; *Figure 8.10* From N. M. Malamuth and J. V. P. Check, "The effects of mass media exposure on acceptance of violence against women. A field experiment.," *Journal of Research in Personality, 15* (1981): 436–446. Copyright © 1981 by Academic Press. Reprinted with permission of Academic Press and the authors. **p. 323:** Reuters/Bettmann. **p. 325:** © 1994 Capital Cities/ABC, Inc.

Chapter 9: p. 330: © Scott Robinson/Tony Stone Images. **p. 332** *(top):* © David R. Frazier/Photo Researchers. **p. 332** *(bottom):* © Bob Glasheen. **p. 335:** © William Vandivert. **p. 339:** *Figure 9.4* From R. R. Reno, R. B. Cialdini, and C. A. Kallgren, "The transituational influence of norms," *Journal of Personality and Social Psychology, 64* (1993): 104–112. Copyright © 1993 by the American Psychological Association. Reprinted by permission. **p. 341:** © Joe Sohm/The Image Works. **p. 341:** *Figure 9.5* From T. J. Berndt, "Developmental changes in conformity to peers and parents," *Developmental Psychology, 15* (1979): 606–616. Copyright © 1979 by the American Psychological Association. Reprinted by permission. **p. 343** *(top):* © 1994D Peter Ginter/Peter Menzel/*Material World*. **p. 343** *(bottom):* © Peter Menzel/*Material World*. **p. 348:** © Andy Levin/Photo Researchers. **p. 355:** Image Works. **p. 356:** © 1965 by Stanley Milgram. From the film *Obedience* distributed by Pennsylvania State University, Audio Visual Services. **p. 363:** © Alexandra Avakian/Contact Press Images. **p. 364:** © Bob Krist/Black Star. **p. 365:** *Figure 9.7* From B. Latane', "The psychology of social impact," *American Psychologist, 36* (1981): 344. Copyright © 1981 by the American Psychological Association. Reprinted by permission.

Chapter 10: p. 368 *(Opener):* © Mark Richards/PhotoEdit. **p. 371:** © Joe Sohm/The Image Works. **p. 373:** *Figure 10.1* From J. T. Cacioppo and R. E. Petty, "Electromyograms as measures of extent and affectivity of information processing," *American Psychologist, 36* (1981): 441–456. Copyright © 1981 by the American Psychological Association. Reprinted by permission. **p. 376:** © T. K. Wanstal/The Image Works. **p. 379** *(left):* © Dennis Brack/Black Star. **p. 379** *(right):* Wide World Photos. **p. 384:** © 1992 Revlon, Inc. **p. 385:** *Figure 10.4* From R. E. Petty, J. T. Cacioppo, and R. Goldman, "Personal involvement as a determinant of argument-based persuasion," *Journal of Personality and Social Psychology, 41* (1981): 847–855. Copyright © 1981 by the American Psychological Association. Reprinted by permission. **p. 389:** *Figure 10.7* From S. Bochner and C. A. Insko, "Communicator discrepancy, source credibility, and opinion change," *Journal of Personality and Social Psychology, 4* (1966): 614–621. Copyright © 1966 by the American Psychological Association. Reprinted by permission. **p. 390:** Courtesy of Centers for Disease Control, National AIDS Information and Education Program. **p. 393:** *Table 10.1* From J. T. Cacioppo and R. E. Petty, "The need for cognition," *Journal of Personality and Social Psychology, 42* (1982): 116–131. Copyright © 1982 by the American Psychological Association. Reprinted by permission. **p. 394:** *Figure 10.8* From M. Snyder and K. G. DeBono, "Appeals to image and claims about quality: Understanding the psychology of advertising," *Journal of Personality and Social Psychology, 49* (1985): 586–597. Copyright © 1985 by the American Psychological Association. Reprinted by permission. **p. 398:** © Richard Pasley/Stock Boston. **p. 402:** © Bob Krist/Black Star. **p. 407:** *Figure 10.11* From C. M. Steele, S. J. Spencer, and M. Lynch, "Self-image resilience and dissonance:

The role of affirmational resources," *Journal of Personality and Social Psychology*, 64 (1993): 885–896. Copyright © 1993 by the American Psychological Association. Reprinted by permission.

Chapter 11: **p. 410** *(Opener):* © Tom Sanders/Aerial Focus. **p. 412** *(left):* © Joan Marcus. **p. 412** *(right):* Reuter/Bettmann. **p. 416:** *Figure 11.2* From B. Latane, K. Williams, and S. Harking, "Many hands make light the work: The causes and consequences of social loafing," *Journal of Personality and Social Psychology, 37* (1979): 822–832. Copyright © 1979 by the American Psychological Association. Reprinted by permission. **p. 417:** © Tom Sobolik/Black Star. **p. 419:** © Paula Bronstein/Impact Visuals. **p. 422:** © Agostini/Gamma-Liaison. **p. 424:** © Zigy Kaluzny/Tony Stone Images. **p. 426:** © Ann States/SABA. **p. 429:** *Figure 11.6* Based on I. L. Janis, *Groupthink*, Second Edition (Boston: Houghton Mifflin Company, 1982). Used by permission. **p. 431** *(left):* Channel 9 Australia/Gamma-Liaison. **p. 431** *(right):* Wide World Photos. **p. 432:** © Stephen Feld/The Stock Solution. **p. 435** *(left)* © David Welcher/Sygma. **p. 435** *(right):* The Image Works. **p. 439:** © Louis Psihoyos/Time Magazine. **p. 442:** Wide World Photos. **p. 447:** Reuters/Bettmann. **p. 451:** Reuters/Bettmann.

Chapter 12: **p. 454** *(Opener):* © Superstock. **p. 456** *(left and right):* Wide World Photos. **p. 456** *(center):* © David Butow/Black Star. **p. 457:** *Figure 12.1* Konecni, V. J. and Ebbeson, E. B., *The Criminal Justice System: A Social Psychological Analysis*, p. 12. Copyright © 1982 by W. H. Freeman & Company Publishers. Reprinted by permission. **p. 460** *(left):* © Jesse Nemerofsky. **p. 460** *(right):* Wide World Photos. **p. 461:** © Taylor/Fabricuius/Gamma-Liaison. **p. 462:** The cartoon by Lee Lorenz is reproduced from *Disorderly Conduct,* Verbatim Excerpts from Actual Court Cases, selected by Rodney R. Jones, Charles M. Sevilla, and Gerald F. Uelman, by permission of W. W. Norton and Company, Inc. Illustrations copyright © Lee Lorenz. **p. 467:** "Zapruder Frame"; copyright 1992, 1967, 1963 LMH Company c/o James Lorin Silverberg, Esq., Washington, D.C., (202)332-7978. All Rights Reserved. **p. 469:** *Figure 12.2* S. J. Platz and Hosch, H. M., "Cross-racial ethnic eyewitness justification: A field study," *Journal of Applied Social Psychology, 18* (1988): 972–984. **p. 470:** *Figure 12.3* From E. F. Loftus and J. C. Palmer, "Reconstruction of automobile destruction: An example of the interaction between language and memory," *Journal of Verbal Learning and Verbal Behavior, 13* (1974): 585–589. **p. 473:** *Table 12.2* From "Eyewitness identification: Lineup instructions and the absence of the offender," *Journal of Applied Psychology,* 66 (1981): 482–489. Copyright © 1981 by the American Psychological Association. Reprinted by permission. **p. 474:** © David E. Dempster. **p. 477:** *Table 12.3* From S. M. Kassin, P. C. Ellsworth and B. L. Smith, "The 'general acceptance' of psychological research on eyewitness testimony: A survey of the experts," *American Psychologist, 44* (1989): 1089–1098. Copyright © 1989 by the American Psychological Association. **p. 478:** © E. Agostini/Gamma-Liaison. **p. 483:** *Figure 12.7* From R. Hastie, S. D. Penrod & N. Pennington, *Inside the Jury*. (Cambridge, MA: Harvard University Press, 1983). **p. 484:** *Table 12.4* From G. Stasser, N. Kerr and R. Bray (Eds.), "The social psychology of jury deliberations: Structure, process, and product." In *The Psychology of the Courtroom.* Copyright © 1982 by the Academic Press. Reprinted by permission of the Academic Press and the authors **p. 489:** P. G. Zimbardo, Inc., Stanford, CA 94305.

Chapter 13: **p. 494** *(Opener):* © Owen Franken/Stock Boston. **p. 499:** *Figure 13.1* From R. L. Dipboye and T. M. Macan "A Process View of the Selection - Recruitment Interview" appearing in *Readings in Personnel in Human Resource Management.* Reprinted by permission of West Publishing. **p. 501:** © Newsweek. **p. 506:** © Jay Dickman. **p. 507:** © Topham/The Image Works. **p. 508:** *Table 13.2* Modified and reproduced by special permission of the Publisher, Consulting Psychologists Press, Inc., Palo Alto, CA 94303, from *Transformational Leadership Development: Manual for the Multifactor Leadership Questionnaire*, by Bernard M. Bass, Ph.D., and Bruce J. Avolio, Ph.D. Copyright © 1990 by Consulting Psychologists Press, Inc. All rights reserved. Further reproduction is prohibited without the Publisher's written consent. **p. 509:** *Figure 13.3* From F. E. Fielder, *A Theory of Leadership Effectiveness.* Copyright © 1967 by Fred E. Fielder. Reprinted by permission. **p. 511:** © Donna Binder/Impact Visuals. **p. 513:** *Figure 13.4* From E. L. Deci, "Effects of externally mediated rewards on intrinsic motivation," *Journal of Psychology and Social Psychology, 18* (1971) 105–115. Copyright © 1971 by the American Psychological Association. Reprinted by permission. **p. 515:** *Figure 13.5* From J. Greenberg, "Equity and workplace status: A field experiment," *Journal of Applied Psychology, 73* (1988): 606–613. Copyright © 1988 by the American Psychological Association. Reprinted by permission. **p. 516:** © John Chiasson/Gamma-Liaison. **p. 517:** *Figure 13.6* From M. L. Marks, P. H. Mirvis, E. J. Hackett, and J. F. Grady, Jr., "Employee participation in a quality of work life, productivity, and absenteeism," *Journal of Applied Psychology, 71* (1986): 61–69. Copyright © 1986 by the American Psychological Association. Reprinted by permission.

Chapter 14: **p. 524** *(Opener):* © Brad Markel/Gamma-Liaison. p. 531 *(all):* © David Young-Wolff/PhotoEdit. **p. 529:** *Table 14.1* From I. G. Sarason, J. H. Johnson and J. M. Siegel, "Assessing the impact of life changes: Development of the life experiences survey," *Journal of Consulting and Clinical Psychology,* 46 (1978): 932–946. Copyright © 1978 by the American Psychological Association. Reprinted by permission. **p. 532:** © D. Kennerly/Gamma-Liaison. **p. 533:** © Dana Fineman/Sygma. **p. 537:** *Table 14.2* From *Journal of Psychology, 55* (1987): 2. Copyright © 1987 by Duke University Press. Reprinted with permission. **p. 541:** © Mark Reinstein/The Image Works. **p. 543:** © Stacy Pick/Stock Boston. **p. 546:** © Serge Pagano/Sipa. **p. 548** *(left):* © Jon Feingersh/The Stock Market. **p. 548** *(right):* © Bob Daemmrich/Stock Boston. **p. 550:** © Porterfield/Chickering /Photo Researchers. **p. 553:** © Myrleen Ferguson Cate/PhotoEdit. **p. 557:** © Terry Farmer/Tony Stone Images. **p. 558:** *Figure 14.8* From L. Terre, R. S. Drabman, and P. Speer, "Health-related behaviors in media," *Journal of Applied Social Psychology, 21*, 1303–1319. Adapted by permission **p. 559:** © Vanessa Vick/Photo Researchers.

Name Index

Subject Index